THE MACMILLAN GUIDE TO CORRESPONDENCE STUDY

Sixth Edition

Compiled and Edited by
Modoc Press, Inc.

MACMILLAN LIBRARY REFERENCE USA
Simon & Schuster Macmillan
NEW YORK

Prentice Hall International
LONDON / MEXICO CITY / NEW DELHI / SINGAPORE / SYDNEY / TORONTO

Acknowledgments

The compilers of this *Guide* extend their sincerest appreciation to the institutions listed herein for their prompt and comprehensive responses to the questionnaires and other inquiries. Gratitude is also due the American Council on Education and the Distance Education and Training Council.

Macmillan Library Reference USA
Simon & Schuster Macmillan
1633 Broadway
New York, NY 10019

Printed in the United States of America

printing number
1 2 3 4 5 6 7 8 9 10

ISSN 1068–2481

Contents

Introduction

Each year approximately three million students pursue their education without leaving their homes. Correspondence study makes it possible for these individuals to accomplish educational goals they might otherwise never have been able to attain. Students can enroll at any time of the year and study at their own pace during times convenient to their schedule. Correspondence study is often less expensive than conventional classroom education, and it is becoming recognized by more and more educational authorities as a valid, successful, and effective method to accomplish an educational objective. While one individual may complete the necessary requirements for a degree program through correspondence, another can learn a new vocation; still another can be introduced to a new worthwhile avocation. Many individuals find correspondence study an excellent method for reviewing a subject taken many years before or for getting an update on changes and improvements in their field of specialization.

Correspondence study, also known as home study or independent study, is offered by an educational institution that provides lesson materials by mail, prepared in a sequential and logical order. Upon the completion of a lesson, the student sends the assigned work to the school for correction, grading, comments, and subject guidance by qualified instructors. In some courses, audio cassettes are used for both instruction and lesson fulfillment. Some institutions are now using video cassettes to present coursework. The use of a personal computer is also becoming more prevalent in conjunction with correspondence study. An indication of those courses requiring access to special equipments (audio, VHS recorder, or a specified personal computer) is given in the course description.

Correspondence courses and programs vary greatly in subject matter, level, and length. Some courses require only a few weeks to complete, while others, particularly those programs leading to a degree, may require three or four years of study.

The pursuit of an educational goal by means of correspondence requires personal discipline and initiative. Lesson assignments must be completed on a regular schedule and within the time limits set by the institution. The great variety of correspondence courses available from institutions in the United States makes it possible for the prospective student to choose from a multitude of subject areas at every level from elementary to graduate.

The *Guide* has been designed to present the subject areas available from accredited schools, describe the courses offered, give details about admission requirements and procedures, and indicate to the prospective student the tuition and fees involved.

Organization

There are three main parts to the *Guide*. Section 1 includes those colleges and universities offering correspondence courses for which credits earned can be transferred to a formal degree program, noncredit courses that are professional in nature, and courses that have been developed for career enrichment. Section 2 includes proprietary home study schools that are privately owned and operated and that offer vocational correspondence programs as well as courses at the high school, college, and professional levels. Section 3 includes those correspondence schools that are operated by private foundations, nonprofit organizations, federal agencies, and the U.S. military establishment. The comprehensive Subject Index includes all subject categories used to identify the courses listed in all sections of the *Guide*. For suggestions on the use of the Subject Index, see "How to use this *Guide*" (p. x).

Data Collection

Entries in the *Guide* were compiled from questionnaires that were mailed to and returned by the schools identified as offering correspondence courses. Descriptions of the courses were obtained from the catalogs and brochures prepared by the institutions. Entries that do not display course descriptions, particularly state-affiliated colleges, are members of consortia, and courses available from them handled by a central office. A reference will direct the prospective student to that central agency.

School Catalogs

The *Guide* is a compilation of information necessary for prospective students to choose a correspondence course and the appropriate school. When prospective students find a correspondence course of interest in the *Guide*, we strongly recommend that they contact the school for its current catalog. The catalog contains not only an application form but also important information about the school, required textbooks, necessary equipment, and other facts that students would need to know in order to pursue a course of study successfully.

It is sometimes necessary for a school to discontinue a course due to unavailability of course materials, textbooks, or faculty. Also, tuition costs and other fees may change without notice. All schools reserve the right to make any changes in course materials or prices as necessary.

Prerequisites

Many courses listed in the *Guide* have prerequisites. The nature of certain subjects, particularly foreign languages, the various sciences, and mathematics, requires that a student has taken the prerequisite course. In many subjects, each course beyond the very basic makes fundamental use of the lessons of previous courses. The prospective student can be sure of any prerequisites requirement by consulting the school catalog.

Accreditation

Institutions listed in Sections 1 and 2 in the *Guide* are fully accredited. The accreditation has been granted by one of the following: the Distance Education and Training Council, one of the six academic Regional Accrediting Commissions, or a nationally recognized accrediting association, such as the American Association of Bible Colleges. All of these accrediting agencies are recognized by the U.S. Department of Education.

Institutions included in Section 3 are those schools that do not fall within the specific category of a college/university or a proprietary school. The schools are sponsored by private foundations (e.g., John Tracy Clinic), government agencies (e.g., Graduate School, USDA), and the military establishment (e.g., Marine Corps Institute). These schools have accreditation and/or professional affiliations which are so noted under Accreditation with each entry.

The Accrediting Process

Accreditation is a unique feature of American education practice. The accrediting process involves self-study by the educational institutions and evaluation by appointed commissions comprising members from other schools. This process operates through the nationally recognized accrediting agencies and associations and certain state bodies. These agencies have adopted criteria reflecting the qualities of a sound educational program and they have developed procedures for evaluating institutions or programs to determine whether they are operating at levels of required quality. The agencies also seek to stimulate continued educational improvement to help assure that accreditation status may serve as an authentic index of educational quality.

The Regional Accrediting Commissions accredit institutions with liberal arts, science, and general programs. Regional accreditation applies to the entire institution and signifies that each of the component parts of an institution is contributing to the achievement of the institution's objectives. Correspondence courses offered by the colleges and universities are accredited because of their sponsorship by a Department of Continuing Education, a Department of Independent Study, a Department of Extended Studies, or a similar functional entity within the institution. The Regional Agencies that have accredited the individual schools in Section 1, Colleges and Universities, are:

> Middle States Association of Colleges and Schools
> New England Association of Schools and Colleges
> North Central Association of Colleges and Schools
> Northwest Association of Schools and Colleges
> Southern Association of Colleges and Schools
> Western Association of Schools and Colleges

All of the schools listed in Section 2 and most of those in Section 3 have been accredited by the Accrediting Commission of the Distance Education and Training Council (DETC). In each case, the DETC's Accrediting Commission has determined that the school offers quality instruction and meets the standards established by the Commission. The standards require that a school: state its educational objectives clearly; offer sufficiently comprehensive, accurate, up-to-date, educationally sound instructional materials and methods to meet these announced objectives; provide adequate examination services, encouragement to students, and attention to individual differences; have a qualified faculty; enroll only students who can be expected to benefit from the instruction; maintain adequate student services; show satisfactory student progress and success; be honest in its advertising and promotional materials; carefully select, train, and supervise its field representatives; show financial resources adequate to carry out all obligations to students; use a satisfactory tuition refund policy; maintain student records properly; and demonstrate a satisfactory period of ethical operation. The accrediting process must be repeated at intervals of not more than five years. The Accrediting Commission of DETC is recognized as an official accrediting agency by the U.S. Department of Education.

Many of the colleges and universities listed in the Guide are members of the National University Continuing Education Association (NUCEA). This association has developed criteria and standards that are followed by member institutions. An institution's membership is indicated in the individual entries under Accreditation.

Credit

Most colleges and universities will allow some credit for courses taken by correspondence to be applied toward undergraduate degree programs. Similarly, those colleges and universities featuring nontraditional education may grant correspondence credit toward Continuing Education Units (CEUs), External Degree programs, and Certificate programs. Each college/university has its own policy, and oftentimes colleges and departments within one university will have differing criteria. Students wishing to transfer correspondence credit are strongly advised to consult their college or university for the current policy, not only for the number of credits allowed but also for the transferability of specific courses. Credits are usually characterized by quarter hours or semester hours, depending upon the school's practice. Generally, one quarter hour equals two-thirds of a semester hour. High school credits are usually based on the Carnegie Unit of one-half unit per high school semester per subject. Occasionally, colleges offering high school courses will grant diplomas; usually, however, they grant units that are transferable toward diplomas to be awarded by high schools.

Proprietary correspondence schools listed in Section 2 generally grant diplomas or certificates upon completion of their programs. Several of these schools grant Associate Degrees, academic credit for college-level courses, and high school diplomas.

Those private schools listed in Section 3 grant certificates and academic credit. The military sponsored schools offer courses for academic credit to qualified personnel. In some cases, courses have been evaluated by the Office on Education Credit and Credentials. Program on Noncollegiate Sponsored Instruction, of the American Council on Education. Recommendations for college credit for many of the courses, particularly for the Graduate School, USDA, can be found in *The National Guide to Educational Credit for Training Programs* published jointly by the American Council on Education and Oryx Press.

Military Personnel

To provide opportunities for military personnel to achieve educational, vocational, and career goals, each military service has established a voluntary education program. While many service members can take advantage of local civilian education centers with traditional, formal classroom educational programs, circumstances of many others often prevent access to these programs. Correspondence study courses offer these individuals the opportunity to pursue an educational objective.

The Defensive Activity for Non-Traditional Education Support (DANTES) is an educational service organization providing support to the voluntary education programs of the military services. DANTES is based on the fundamental philosophy of a partnership between the military and civilian education communities to make maximum use of what is available from civilian schools and colleges through correspondence study. It also makes possible educational opportunities of the greatest quality, effectiveness, and range available. Military service members should consult with their local Education Officer for details regarding enrollment in courses listed in this *Guide*.

In Section 3, Private, Nonprofit, and Governmental Institutions, four military organizations are listed that offer programs accredited by the National Home Study Council: Army Institute for Professional Development, United States Coast Guard Institute, Extension Course Institute (USAF), and Marine Corps Institute. Because these organizations restrict enrollment in their courses to active/reserve military personnel and civilian employees of the military establishment, their courses have not been listed. Individuals interested in these organizations should contact their base Education Officer for further details.

How to Use This Guide

The use of abbreviations has been eliminated throughout this *Guide* so that the user need not refer to any list for interpretation. The entries for institutions in all sections of the *Guide* have been arranged in similar format and in alphabetical order (letter by letter) in each Section. Following the name, address, telephone number, and description of the institution, there are listed various headings that are self-explanatory. Preceding the course listings and descriptions, a heading indicates the academic level of the courses to follow. These levels appear in the following order: College, High School, Noncredit (Career enrichment and continuing education courses), Professional, Elementary, Vocational, and Graduate. Within each level, the subject areas are listed in alphabetical order. Under the subject area heading, the courses are listed beginning with the most basic course and ending with the most advanced. This arrangement is similar to that found in the institution's catalog. For those courses with similar titles, a course number has been inserted at the beginning of the description. This similarity in course title occurs most often when a course is continued into a second or third term. Prospective students are advised to note the subject area and course title and refer to the school catalog for the appropriate course numbers, which are always requested on institutions' enrollment applications.

A List of Institutions and the page number for each institution's entry can be found on page xi of the *Guide*. Should prospective students have a particular institution in mind, they can go directly to the entry for that institution and peruse the course listings. It is recommended that the Subject Index be used as the entry point to this *Guide*. The Subject Index lists subject area (Accounting, Animal Science, Astronomy, etc.) along with the names of the institutions offering courses in that subject. Page number references are cited following the name of the institution.

LIST OF INSTITUTIONS

Section 1
Colleges and Universities

Adams State College

Division of Extended Studies
208 Edgemont
Alamosa, Colorado 81102   (719) 589-7671

Description:

Adams State College opened in 1921 offering a four-year program leading to a baccalaureate degree and a life certificate to teach in Colorado public schools. Although teacher education ranks foremost and was the original purpose of the college, the program has been broadened to include the liberal arts, preprofessional and vocational programs. Adams State College participates in the Colorado Consortium for Independent Study which is composed of the independent study offices of six institutions of higher education in Colorado: Adams State College, Colorado State University, University of Colorado, University of Northern Colorado, University of Southern Colorado, and Metropolitan State College of Denver. The consortium strives to provide quality independent study opportunities and to avoid duplication of courses offered by consortium members. The correspondence student should consult the listings in this *Guide* of all member schools of the consortium for a complete offering of subject matter.

Faculty:

Alberta Coolbaugh, Assistant Director of Extended Studies; Liz Martinez, Registrar. There is a faculty of 19 members.

Academic Levels:

College
Graduate

Admission Requirements:

Open enrollment. Some courses require prerequisites.

Tuition:

$70 per semester hour. Rate subject to change without notice. Refund allowed within forty days minus an administration fee.

Enrollment Period:

The maximum time allowed to complete a course is 1 year; minimum time is 2 weeks per semester hour. A 12-month extension may be granted upon payment of an extension fee of $20 per semester hour.

Equipment Requirements:

Textbooks and supplies must be purchased by the student and can be ordered from the Bookstore-College Center, Adams State College, Alamosa, CO 81102 (telephone 719-589-7911)

Credit and Grading:

Grading system is A, B, C, D, F with plus and minus recorded and averaged. Minimum passing grade is D. Credit is awarded in semester hours.

Accreditations:

North Central Association of Colleges and Schools. Member of: National University Continuing Education Association.

BUSINESS

Personal Finance

An introductory course designed to expose students to practical means of making decisions on a host of financial dilemmas: banking, budgeting, consumer protection laws, credit, housing, insurance, interest, investments, and retirement. (3 semester hours)

Business Computer Applications

Use of word processing, electronic spreadsheet and data base systems software in typical business applications. Format, enter, exit, and print documents. Prepare spreadsheets, graphs. Create, sort, edit, list, program, and report on data bases. Students must have access to an IBM compatible personal computer, WordPerfect, Quattro Pro, and Dbase software. (3 semester hours)

Business Law

This basic business law course presents those areas most crucial to understanding the legal environment of business. It covers topics encountered in everyday businesses such as law concerning contracts, property, product liability, sales and commercial paper (Uniform Commercial Code), legal concerns for employers and principal-agents, as well as business organization forms. (3 semester hours)

Business Communications

Practice in writing and analyzing various types of business and personal business letters and reports. Communication techniques for educational administrators as well as business managers. (3 semester hours)

Business Statistics

Provides a basic understanding of the fundamental principles with emphasis on the application of statistical techniques to the analysis and solution of real business problems. (3 semester hours)

Fundamentals of Income Tax

Study of federal income tax on individual and property transactions. Objectives of taxation given major emphasis. The Internal Revenue Code is discussed in addition to the text in order to acquaint the student with the ultimate sources of tax law. (3 semester hours)

Governmental and Institutional Accounting

Study of accounting procedures related to governmental units and nonprofit institutions. (3 semester hours)]

Principles of Management

Explores theory and practice of managing an organization and its personnel with emphasis on planning, designing, and controlling to meet the needs of modern public or private organizations. Includes emerging trends and international issues. (3 semester hours)

Auditing

Study of ethical standards, auditing standards, audit procedures, and evolution of internal control to learn how financial statements are examined and audit reports are prepared. (3 semester hours)

Personnel Management

Recruiting, testing, interviewing, training, and evaluating workers; planning for personnel needs; establishing personnel functions; employment laws; establishing pay plans. (3 semester hours)

Organizational Behavior

Behavior of individuals and small groups in organizational settings. Managerial style, social system analysis, motivation and communication. (3 semester hours)

Industrial Relations

Federal and state legislation and execution and executive orders governing the employer-employee relationship; legal rights of organizations and collective bargaining. (3 semester hours)

Total Quality Management

Concepts and techniques of quality improvement processes. Defining quality in customer satisfaction terms and improving quality of products and service through modern techniques. (3 semester hours)

ECONOMICS

Managerial Economics

Application and integration of microeconomic theory and the tools of decision science to managerial decision making. Particular emphasis placed on estimating demand and cost functions as well as the effects of time and uncertainty. (3 semester hours)

ENGLISH

Communication Arts

Course ENG 101. A course designed to provide students with the grammar and composition skills needed to write effective expository essays. (3 semester hours)

Course ENG 102. This course is designed to introduce the student to the basics of writing a college research paper. The student will write a major research paper, following a series of outlines provided by the instructor. (3 semester hours)

Development of Vocabulary

The course is designed to increase the student's vocabulary through a systematic word-building approach. The emphasis is on learning word families through the study of bases, prefixes, and suffixes derived from the Greek and Latin languages. (2 semester hours)

ENVIRONMENTAL STUDIES

Toxic Chemicals: Sources and Effects

Introduction to sources and health effects of chemicals of environmental importance on man and other organisms. Regulations and laws governing permissible exposure limits are also studied. (3 semester hours)

Environmental Control

The study of water and wastewater pollution and its control, solid and hazardous waste disposal problems and potential solutions. Pollution control laws are also covered. (2 semester hours)

HISTORY

History of the Southwest

This course concentrates on a comparative analysis of the Mexican-American settlement, the Native Americans, and the influx of Anglo settlers into the Southwest region. The diversity of social structure, technology, and ideology will be investigated. (3 semester hours)

Mexico

A survey of political-historical developments in Mexico which include the colonial period, the struggles for Independence and the Revolution of 1910. Major focus will be the effects of these historical events on the development of the modern state. (3 semester hours)

MATHEMATICS

Arithmetic

A course for students needing a review of the basics of arithmetic: numeration, operations on whole numbers, factoring, prime numbers, operations on numbers of arithmetic, decimal numerals, percent, measures, ratio and proportion, averages, and an introduction to algebra. Course is graded on a pass/fail basis only. (3 semester hours)

Algebra Skills

A beginning course in algebra. Course includes a review of arithmetic, equations, polynomials, factoring, systems of equations and graphs, inequalities, fractional equations, and the quadratic equation. Course is graded on a pass/fail basis only. (3 semester hours)

Mathematics in the Elementary School

159. Designed for those planning to teach K–8. Includes content material and methodology for the following: problem solving, sets, whole numbers and integers, real numbers, numeration systems, ratio and percents, and elementary number theory. (3 semester hours)

259. A continuation of the course above. Includes content material and methodology for the following: geometry, measurement and the metric system, introduction to algebra, introduction to probability and statistics. (3 semester hours)

Differential Equations

A course in elementary differential equations emphasizing techniques rather than theory. Topics covered include equations of order one, linear equations, systems and power series methods. (3 semester hours)

PHYSICAL EDUCATION

Basic Foundation of Sports Conditioning

This course is designed to provide information relative to the basic foundations of sport conditioning, including primary training principles, strength development, plyometric concepts and applications. (2 semester hours)

PSYCHOLOGY

Success Psychology: Becoming A Master Student

The purpose of the course is to provide an opportunity for students to learn and adopt methods that promote success in school and in life. Topics to be explored include time management, memory, reading skills, note taking, disarming tests, creativity, relationships, health, money, management, resources, and attitudes, affirmations, and visualizations. (3 semester hours)

Human Development: From Conception through Middle Childhood

The course examines the challenge of human development, genetic influence across the life span, prenatal development and birth, physical and cognitive development in infancy and toddlerhood, the development of language and communication skills, physical and cognitive development in early childhood, social and personality development in early childhood, physical and cognitive development in middle childhood, and social and personality development in middle childhood. (3 semester hours)

Human Development: Adolescence through Old Age, Death and Dying

The course examines physical and cognitive development in adolescence, new perspectives in adulthood, physical and cognitive development in early adulthood, social and personality development in early adulthood, physical development in later adulthood, cognitive development in later adulthood, social and personality development in later adulthood, and dying, death, and coping with loss. (3 semester hours)

Psychological Testing

This course examines functions and origins of psychological testing, nature and use of psychological tests, social and ethical considerations in testing, norms and interpretation, reliability, validity, item analysis, individual tests, tests for special populations, group testing, psychological issues in intelligence testing, multiple aptitudes; educational, occupational and clinical testing; self-report inventories; measuring interests, values, and attitudes; projective techniques and other assessment techniques. (3 semester hours)

SOCIOLOGY

The Formation and Strengthening of the Self-Concept

This course deals with three issues related to self-concept. First, it outlines how the self-concept is formed with special emphasis on weak versus strong. Second, it examines the ramifications of weak and strong self-concepts for life adjustments and inner-personal-relationships. Third, it gives some strategies that may be helpful in strengthening weak self-concepts. The technique utilized to help the student understand these concepts is presentation of material followed by questions designed to bring out aspects of the student's life which pertain to his or her self-concept formation. (2 semester hours)

Improving Communication Within the Family

This is an applied course whose participants implement an effective and non-threatening program designed to increase meaningful communication within their own families or others of their choosing. The program consists of guidelines to good family communication, directions on how to implement them, and many activities to illustrate each guideline and stimulate family communication. (2 semester hours)

GRADUATE COURSES

SCIENCE

Contemporary Topics in the Physical Sciences

The goal of this course is to familiarize teachers with some of the more important developments and issues in chemistry, physics, geology, and engineering from the mid-20th century to the present time. Example topics may include new materials (polymers, ceramics), superconductivity, miniaturization of electronics, instrumentation (lasers, MRI, CAT), environmental issues, catalysts, new medicines, seismic monitoring, and others. The course will utilize readings (from both technical and popular journals) and videotapes. Evaluation will be based on four exams and a research paper discussing in more detail the impact of one of these developments/issues on modern society. Students must submit evidence of possessing a baccalaureate degree to take this graduate-level course. (2 semester hours)

Contemporary Topics in Biology

Introduction to the biology of current topics such as drug and alcohol addiction, AIDS, organ transplantation, cancer, and genetic engineering. Course goals will include achieving an understanding of both the science and ethical implications that will allow classroom presentation of these same topics at the secondary level. Course materials will include assigned readings, videos, and instructor-prepared summaries. Two exams and one paper will be required. Students must submit evidence of possessing a baccalaureate degree to take this graduate-level course. (2 semester hours)

Alabama, University of

Independent Study Division
College of Continuing Studies
345 Martha Parham West, Box 870388
Tuscaloosa, Alabama 35487-0388
(205) 348-7642

Description:

The University of Alabama opened on April 12, 1831 in response to the State Legislature's declaration to "establish a seminary of learning." On April 4, 1865, Federal troops burned all but four buildings, and the campus lay dormant until 1871 when determined alumni revived the institution and set its future course. Today the University of Alabama is a thriving 645-acre campus that is a pleasing blend of historic nostalgia and contemporary exuberance.

Since 1920, the University of Alabama Independent Study Program has established a tradition of providing quality education in nontraditional settings. Undergraduate credit courses in many academic areas of the university are available as well as many high school courses. Enrollees may earn credit toward baccalaureate degrees, high school diplomas, licensure requirements and certification as well as an upgrade of job skills. Students who enroll in Independent Study join an academic community of the University of Alabama which is known for the excellence and diversity of its programs.

Faculty:

John C. Burgeson, Director, Independent Study Division. There is a faculty of 50 members.

Academic Levels:
College
High School

Degree/Certificate Programs:

Up to twenty-five percent of the credits required for a baccalaureate degree may be earned through independent study; however, at the University of Alabama, degrees are not awarded based on correspondence credit only.

Admission Requirements:

Students may enroll in independent study at any time; however, when they are in residence at **any** college or university, it is necessary to have written permission of the academic dean before application for independent study will be accepted. High school students who plan to apply independent study credits for graduation requirements must have written approval of their principals. Students under suspension from any institution of higher education will not be allowed to enroll in independent study courses until they are eligible to return to the institution which has initiated the suspension. Enrollment in independent study does not require, nor does it constitute, formal admission to the University of Alabama. Any person who has the proper prerequisites for a specific course may be enrolled.

Tuition:

$55 per semester hour plus $35 registration fee. All fees are payable in advance. The university reserves the right to discontinue or revise courses, change instructors, and adjust fees without advance notice as circumstances require. A refund of 100 percent if withdrawal within 72 hours of receipt of materials; 75 percent of tuition may be granted if withdrawal is made within thirty days of enrollment. No refund of course fees will be made after thirty days from date of enrollment. Registration and supply fees and postal charges are not refundable. If lessons have been submitted, there will be a charge deducted from the refund. Students are responsible for postage on lessons sent to the Independent Study Division. The Division will pay for postage on

5

materials, return of lessons, and any other communications sent to the student. The use of airmail is recommended for all students overseas with costs to be assumed by the student. Fees for high school level courses are $65 per one-half unit course and are payable in advance with the application for enrollment. Fees for high school courses are not refundable after enrollment has been accepted. If enrollment is declined, remittance will be returned.

Enrollment Period:

Minimum time for completion of a course is six consecutive weeks from date of enrollment, plus three weeks for processing examination. Maximum time for completion of a course is one year from date of enrollment, including final examination. A six-month course extension may be obtained if the student has submitted at least one-half of the lessons required for course completion and a written request for an extension. The Independent Study office must receive the request and the extension fee of $40 prior to the course enrollment expiration date. Extensions apply to college courses only. Credits are awarded in semester hour units.

Equipment Requirements:

Textbooks are supplied by the student and may be ordered from the University Supply Store. For more information, contact Book Department, Box 0291, Tuscaloosa, AL 35487-0291, telephone (205) 348-6126.

Credit and Grading:

A, B, C, D, F. Minimum passing grade is D (60 percent). Upon completion of a course, including final examination, a report card will be mailed to the student by the Independent Study Office. Notice of completion and grade will also be filed in the University Office of Records which will issue an official transcript upon written request. When a course grade is conditioned, with the grade designation "I," a second examination to remove the condition is allowed within a one-month period from date of first examination. A fee is assessed for the second examination. If a conditional grade is not removed, the grade automatically becomes an "F" after the one-month grace period.

Library Services:

The resources of the University of Alabama libraries are available to students enrolled in independent study course upon presentation of current receipts for fees. Library privileges are valid for three months and are renewable.

Accreditations:

Southern Association of Colleges and Schools. Member of: National University Continuing Education Association.

COLLEGE COURSES

ASTRONOMY

Introduction to Astronomy

History of astronomy, the solar system, stars, galaxies, and the universe. Recent discoveries about pulsars, black holes, and quasars will be discussed. (3 semester hours)

BIOLOGY

Medical Etymology

A study of the derivation, meaning, and usage of terms associated with the vocabulary of medicine and medically related fields. Cassette tapes are used in conjunction with the text in this course. (2 semester hours)

Human Anatomy and Physiology without Laboratory

BSC 213c. A survey of human anatomy and physiology which includes: cellular aspects; tissues and skin; the skeletal, muscular, nervous, and endocrine systems; and the special senses of sight, hearing, taste, and smell. The anatomy and physiology of each subject area are presented in an integrated manner with an emphasis on physiology and health-related aspects of a system. This course has a video component. (4 semester hours)

BSC 214c. A survey of human anatomy and physiology which includes: the respiratory, circulatory, digestive, urinary, and reproductive systems; and human development and heredity. The anatomy and physiology of each subject area are presented in an integrated manner with an emphasis on physiology and health-related aspects of a system. This course has a video component. (4 semester hours)

CHEMICAL ENGINEERING

Process Calculations

Quantitative study of physical and chemical processes and chemical reactions. Calculations for gases, vapors, humidity, and process material balances. (3 semester hours)

Thermodynamics Calculations

Calculation of thermal effects of chemical and physical processes. First law of thermodynamics, industrial heat balances, and simultaneous energy and material balances. (3 semester hours)

CLASSICAL STUDIES

Greek and Roman Mythology

An introduction to classical mythology itself and the principal Greek and Roman myths. (3 semester hours)

CONSUMER SCIENCES

Individual and Family Resource Management

Management in terms of values and goals sought by individuals and families. The importance of decision making to obtain satisfaction. (3 semester hours)

Introduction to Personal Financial Planning

What is an IRA? How can you obtain credit and use it wisely? How can a money market fund help consumers reach their financial goals? What type of insurance do you need? This course presents a systems approach to individual financial planning. The various facets of an effective financial plan are examined and opportunities in the financial planning profession are discussed. (3 semester hours)

Household Equipment

Principles of selection, use, care, and energy usage of household equipment. It is a consumer-oriented course which emphasizes how to make wise purchasing decisions. (3 semester hours)

Consumer Protection

Laws and agencies affecting the consumer's well-being, sources of consumer information, discussion of current consumer issues. (3 semester hours)

Concepts and Techniques as Related to Family Financial Investments

Concepts and methods of family financial management. Conventional topics such as credit, insurance, housing, taxes, savings institutions, the stock market, mutual funds, and estate planning are presented with observations as to both risks and rewards. (3 semester hours)

COUNSELOR EDUCATION

Guidance for Teachers

The sociological, psychological, and philosophical bases for guidance in schools. Appropriate for both elementary and secondary teachers. (3 semester hours)

CRIMINAL JUSTICE

Introduction to Criminal Justice

An overview of the criminal justice system with an emphasis on the roles and problems of the law enforcement, courts, and correctional components. (3 semester hours)

Introduction to Law Enforcement

Development of law enforcement: organization and jurisdiction of local, state, and federal law enforcement agencies; functions of police officers. (3 semester hours)

Introduction to Private Security

This course is designed to introduce the student to the organization and management of the security function in industry, business, and government. This will involve the exploration of the protection of personnel, facilities, and other assets from the perspective of loss prevention and control, and risk management. (3 semester hours)

Introduction to Corrections

General overview of U.S. corrections; jails and prisons; institutional procedures; recent innovations; and the future of corrections. (3 semester hours)

Criminal Investigation

Fundamentals of criminal investigation from crime scene search to follow-up investigations and case operations. (3 semester hours)

Organization and Management Concepts in Criminal Justice

Formal organization theory and personnel administration with emphasis on law enforcement agencies. (3 semester hours)

Crime Prevention and Control

This course will explore the "prophylactic" model of crime control in addition to the contemporary "remedial" model. (3 semester hours)

ECONOMICS

Principles of Microeconomics

An introduction to economic analyses concentrating on consumer and producer behavior, competitive and imperfect markets, public policy and regulation, and income distribution. (3 semester hours)

Principles of Macroeconomics

An introduction to economic analysis concentrating on national income, price levels, employment, monetary and fiscal policies, and growth theory. (3 semester hours)

History of Economic Concepts

A study of the development of economic theory from Adam Smith to the present day. (3 semester hours)

ENGLISH

English Composition I

College-level expository writing, critical reading, and library research. (3 semester hours)

English Composition II

Analysis of literature and expository writing about literature. (3 semester hours)

Introduction to Creative Writing

Study and practice in the writing of poetry and fiction. (3 semester hours)

English Literature I

A survey of English literature from its beginnings to 1800. (3 semester hours)

English Literature II

A survey of English literature from 1800 to the present. (3 semester hours)

American Literature I

A survey of American literature from Colonial America to 1865. (3 semester hours)

American Literature II

A survey of American literature from 1865 to the present. (3 semester hours)

Fiction Writing

An introductory workshop in fiction writing. (3 semester hours)

Poetry Writing

An introductory workshop in poetry writing. (3 semester hours)

Major American Writers I

A critical examination of major American writers from Colonial times to the Civil War. (3 semester hours)

Southern Literature

A survey of the development of Southern literature from its beginnings to the present. The course is designed to help students acquire a better understanding of the South today: its culture, its problems, and its prospects. (3 semester hours)

Shakespeare

An introduction to Shakespeare's plays. Various aspects of Elizabethan life and customs, philosophy, and politics; history and psychology will also be examined as they relate to the dramas. (3 semester hours)

Major Romantic Authors

Survey of English Romanticism, concentrating on the major poetry of Blake, Wordsworth, Coleridge, Byron, Shelley, and Keats. (3 semester hours)

The English Novel

A critical evaluation of important British novels from the eighteenth century to the present. (3 semester hours)

Images of Women in Literature

Examination of images of women drawn from English and American literature of the nineteenth and twentieth centuries. Particular attention will be directed toward the question of women's aesthetics. (3 semester hours)

FINANCE

Money and Banking

An overview of the financial system in which business operates with emphasis on financial institutions, instruments, and markets. (3 semester hours)

Business Finance

A study of the financial objectives of business enterprise, sources of capital, the financial management of business assets. Emphasis is on establishing a framework for making financing, investing, and dividend decisions. (3 semester hours)

Principles of Real Estate

A survey of various aspects of real estate business and economics, including marketing, finance, development, law, appraising, etc. (3 semester hours)

Personal Insurance Planning

The role of insurance in serving individuals and families exposed to economic loss. (3 semester hours)

Transportation

A survey of American transportation agencies, the services they render to American business, and the system of state and federal regulations under which they operate. (3 semester hours)

Money and Capital Markets

An overall view of the financing process and the role of financial markets. Areas covered will be characteristics of instruments traded in money and capital markets, determinants and the relationships between different asset prices, and international aspects of financial markets. (3 semester hours)

Investments

A study of the various investment media, together with analysis models of investment management. Emphasis is on investment decision making and portfolio analysis. (3 semester hours)

Public Finance

A study of the principles of taxation, government expenditures, borrowing and fiscal administration. (3 semester hours)

International Finance

An examination of international financial economics and the international financial system, with emphasis on the theories, techniques, and practices relevant to international financial management. (3 semester hours)

Real Estate Appraisal

A study of the sources of real estate value, the techniques for estimating property value, and the effective use of appraisal information. (3 semester hours)

Real Estate Finance

A study of the institutions of real estate finance, factors affecting the flow of funds, investment analysis, and procedures involved in real estate financing. (3 semester hours)

Business Risk Management

The role of insurance in serving business firms and governmental bodies exposed to economic loss. (3 semester hours)

GEOGRAPHY

Survey of Geography

A general study of geography, designed for elementary education majors or others who need some knowledge of basic geographic concepts. (3 semester hours)

World Regional Geography

Study of the physical and cultural features, economy, and populations of the world's geographic regions. (3 semester hours)

Principles of Human Geography

A general study of the principles of human geography including heritage and culture, patterns of economic development and change, demographic trends, natural resource systems, industrialism and agriculture, political space, and human impact on the global environment. (3 semester hours)

Geography of the U.S. and Canada

An analysis of the physical and cultural framework of the United States and Canada. (3 semester hours)

Geography of Europe

Review of the regional geography of Western Europe with a country-by-country analysis of economic and cultural patterns. (3 semester hours)

Industrial Development and Planning

An understanding of industrial development and planning and the complexities of the industrial space economy forms the basis for this course. (3 semester hours)

GERMAN

Elementary German

101C. An introduction. (4 semester hours)

102C. A continuation of the above course. (4 semester hours)

Intermediate German

201C. (3 semester hours)

202C. A continuation of the above course. (3 semester hours)

German Unification and Contemporary Europe

German culture and history is approached through the lens of German unification and the European Revolution of 1989-90. Societal institutions in Germany are surveyed and discussed. Germany's political role is discussed in European context. (3 semester hours)

HISTORY

Western Civilization to 1648

A history of Western civilization from its origins in Greece and Rome, through the Middle Ages, the Renaissance and Reformation, the age of discovery and expansion during the emergence of modern Europe. (3 semester hours)

United States History since 1877

Society, politics, and foreign policy from Reconstruction to the present. Highlights include industrialism, reform, Spanish-American War, World War I, Depression, New Deal, World War II, Cold War, McCarthyism, Watergate. (3 semester hours)

Comparative World Civilization

Examines various civilizations in the world prior to 1500 A.D. and compares their governments, societies, economies, religions, science, learning and technology. (3 semester hours)

American Civilization I: Colonial Period

Colonization of the American continent, with concentration on English settlements, their development and emergence as a new nation during the War of Independence; the confederation period and the early government under the Constitution. (3 semester hours)

American Civilization II: The Nineteenth Century

Explores the century that began with the presidency of Thomas Jefferson and ended with Theodore Roosevelt's empire-making charge up San Juan Hill in Cuba during the Spanish-American War. (3 semester hours)

Colonial Latin America

Formation of the largely Spanish-speaking world from the shock of Conquest to the trials of freedom that spawned the modern nations of Latin America. (3 semester hours)

Modern Latin America since 1808

Survey of political, economic, and social life in the nineteenth and twentieth centuries, with emphasis on the larger countries—Brazil, Mexico, and Argentina. (3 semester hours)

England to 1688

A history of Western civilization in one country, from Anglo-Saxon times to the growth of absolutism and resistance. (3 semester hours)

England since 1688

From the Glorious Revolution to post World War II, covering nearly three centuries; emphasis on social and cultural topics as well as foreign affairs. (3 semester hours)

HUMAN DEVELOPMENT AND FAMILY STUDIES

Human Development

Overview of human development from conception through adulthood to death. Continuity is stressed. (3 semester hours)

Marriage and the Family

A study of modern marriage and family relations from a combination of sociological and psychological perspectives. (3 semester hours)

Child Development - School Age

Growth and development from five through twelve years. Characteristics, behavior expectancies, and guidance techniques. Includes some observation and experience with children. (3 semester hours)

Child Development - Adolescence

Introduction to theory and research on adolescent development. Special attention is focused on major transitions that occur in cognitive, social, and moral domains. Psychological effects of physical maturation, influences of family, schools, and peer relations on adolescent development are also considered. (3 semester hours)

JOURNALISM

Feature Writing

Theories, techniques, and practices of writing newspaper and magazine feature articles. (3 semester hours)

LIBRARY SCIENCE

Library Research

An introduction to library research through the directed use of a local library. The libraries used for this course must be no smaller than that of a junior college. Libraries smaller than a junior college level will not have adequate resources to complete this course. (2 semester hours)

MANAGEMENT

Organizational Theory and Behavior

A course designed to integrate organizational theory and other behavioral science concepts into effective managerial tools for use in work organizations. (3 semester hours)

MASS COMMUNICATIONS

Introduction to Mass Communication

Introduction to the fields of communication, including theory, law and regulation, social implications, mass media operations. (3 semester hours)

Mass Communication Law and Regulation

Study of laws and regulations affecting the mass media and the fields of mass communication. (3 semester hours)

MATHEMATICS

High School Algebra

Offered for students with an entrance deficiency of high school credit in algebra. (1 unit entrance credit only) *Tuition:* $200.

College Algebra

Intermediate level algebra course including work on functions, graphs, linear equations and inequalities, quadratic equations, systems of equations, operations with exponents and radicals. The solving of verbal problems is stressed. (3 semester hours)

Precalculus I

An algebra course with emphasis on functions: polynomial functions, rational functions, and the exponential and logarithmic functions. Graphs are stressed. Equations, inequalities, and systems of equations are also included. (3 semester hours)

Precalculus Algebra II

A continuation of the above course. It includes the study of the trigonometric and inverse trigonometric functions with emphasis on the analytic properties and also advanced topics in algebra such as properties of complex numbers, zeros of polynomials, and conic sections. (3 semester hours)

Introduction to Mathematical Reasoning

The inherent nature of mathematics, accessible problems in various fields, and the historical and contemporary roles of mathematics in human intellectual achievement. Students are led through numerous puzzles, constructions, and illuminating exercises to the development of mathematical ideas. Topics include the mathematical way of thinking, number sequences, functions, large numbers and logarithms, polygons, mathematical curves, counting and the mathematics of change, topology, and the concept of infinity. (3 semester hours)

Introduction to Mathematical Reasoning II

A continuation of the above course with an emphasis on applications and problem-solving techniques. Topics include ways to represent information, the uses and misuses of statistics, applications of graph theory to management problems, and applications of game theory. (3 semester hours)

Introduction to College Mathematics

Topics include linear and quadratic functions, matrices, systems of equations, inequalities and linear programming, exponential and logarithmic functions, sequences, elementary mathematics of finance, and limits. Applications involving business and economics are an important part of this course. (3 semester hours)

Introduction to Calculus

A brief overview of calculus. It includes differentiation and integration of algebraic, exponential, and logarithmic functions and some work on partial derivatives, maximum and minimum of functions of two variables, and Lagrange multipliers. Only business-related applications are covered. (3 semester hours)

Analytic Geometry and Calculus

The first course in the three-part basic calculus sequence. Topics include the limit of a function; the derivative of algebraic, trigonometric, exponential, and logarithmic functions; and the definite integral. Applications of the derivative are covered in detail, including related rates, approximations of error using differentials, maxima and minima problems, and curve sketching using calculus. There is also a view of selected topics from algebra at the beginning of the course. (4 semester hours)

Calculus and Analytic Geometry

The second course in the three-part basic calculus sequence. Topics include vectors in the plane and space, lines and planes in space, applications of integration (such as area, volume, arc length, work, and average value of a function), a further study of trigonometric functions and the hyperbolic function (including inverses), techniques of integration, polar coordinates, and parametric equations. (4 semester hours)

Calculus

The last course in the three-part basic calculus sequence. This course covers the last third of the basic calculus sequence. Topics include indeterminate forms, improper integrals, Taylor polynomials, infinite series, vector functions, functions of two or more variables and their partial derivatives, applications of partial differentiation (including Lagrangian multipliers), quadric and cylindrical surfaces, and multiple integration (including Jacobian). (4 semester hours)

MUSIC APPRECIATION

Introduction to Listening

Presupposes no musical training on the student's part. Emphasis is upon what to listen for in music. (3 semester hours)

NUTRITION

Introduction to Human Nutrition

Introduction to principles of the science of nutrition with implications for and applications to food selection for individuals of all ages. (3 semester hours)

Child Nutrition

Basic principles of nutrition with application to the child. This course is intended for teachers, students, parents, Head Start personnel, health professionals, and preschool professionals. (3 semester hours)

PHILOSOPHY

Introduction to Philosophy

A comprehensive survey of the main topics of philosophy. God, mind, nature, free will, duty, rights, justice, reason, truth, knowledge. The purpose of the course will be to introduce the student to historically significant ways of thinking about these topics. (3 semester hours)

Ethics

An introduction to competing views of how one ought to live, designed to promote the development of a reasoned view of one's own. Includes such topics as the nature of justice and of rights, the relationship of law and morality. (3 semester hours)

PHYSICS

Descriptive Physics for Non-Science Majors I

A study of the chief topics of classical and modern physics. Designed for non-science majors who wish an introductory course with no mathematical prerequisites. (3 semester hours)

POLITICAL SCIENCE

Introduction to American Politics

A survey of the principles, political institutions, and practices of American national, state, and local politics. (3 semester hours)

Introduction to Public Policy

A survey of problems encountered by American governmental units in fields such as foreign affairs, agriculture, welfare, education, health, and business regulations. (3 semester hours)

Public Administration

A study of the administrative principles and practices in the areas of organization, personnel management, budgeting, government regulation, and democratic controls. (3 semester hours)

State and Local Government

A study of the institutions and functions of American state and local government and their relationship to the political process. (3 semester hours)

Political Parties and Elections

Activities of pressure groups and parties in American politics. Attention is given to the social composition, organization, finance, and nominating process of parties. (3 semester hours)

PSYCHOLOGY

Introduction to Psychology

Basic principles of psychology. (3 semester hours)

Psychology of Adjustment

Basic principles of mental health and an understanding of the individual models of behavior. (3 semester hours)

Elementary Statistical Methods

Methods are presented which make possible inferences about a population from a knowledge of small samples. (3 semester hours)

Applied Psychology

An examination of current uses of psychology. (3 semester hours)

RELIGIOUS STUDIES

Introduction to Religious Studies

Various methodological approaches to the academic study of religion with examples of religious life and though drawn from a variety of Eastern and Western traditions. (3 semester hours)

SOCIOLOGY

Introduction to Sociology

An introduction to the systematic study of human social behavior. (3 semester hours)

Analysis of Social Problems

A study of contemporary social problems, including definition, description, and analysis. Special emphasis on rapid social change, cultural complexity, and intensified mobility. (3 semester hours)

The Family

A sociological analysis of traditional and alternative forms of family; theories and research emphasizing structure, process, and functions. (3 semester hours)

Criminology

Theories of criminality, types of delinquent and criminal behavior, causation, criminal and chancery laws, crime control by police, and criminal courts. (3 semester hours)

SPANISH

Intermediate Spanish

201C. A basic grammar review and introduction to reading. (3 semester hours)

202C. A basic grammar review and introduction to reading. (3 semester hours)

Advanced Grammar and Composition

Review of Spanish grammar with emphasis on written expression in Spanish. (3 semester hours)

Survey of Spanish Literature I

Spanish literature from the Middle Ages to the present. Readings from important authors, lectures, and reports. (3 semester hours)

Survey of Spanish Literature II

Spanish literature from the nineteenth century to the present. Readings from important authors, lectures, and reports. (3 semester hours)

STATISTICS

Statistical Methods I

Interpreting graphs, descriptive statistics, simple regression and correlation, designing experiments, probability. (3 semester hours)

Statistical Methods II

Hypothesis testing, analysis of variance, chi-square test, simple and multiple regression and correlation, time series. (3 semester hours)

TELECOMMUNICATIONS

Introduction to Telecommunication

The impact of the public, government, advertising, and the media industry on the formation and current operation of all aspects of telecommunication and film in the United States. (3 semester hours)

THEATRE

History of the Theater I

Beginnings to the Restoration. (3 semester hours)

History of the Theater II

Restoration to the twentieth century. (3 semester hours)

Playwriting I

An introduction to the process and mechanics of dramatic writing. (3 semester hours)

Dramatic Theory and Criticism

A survey including Aristotelian theory with later concentration on current trends. Also focuses on reviewing for the stage and film. (3 semester hours)

HIGH SCHOOL COURSES

BUSINESS EDUCATION

Basic Business Procedures

9A. The first semester covers a study of entry-level skills needed for office work. Units of study include business letters, business and financial reports, oral communications, telecommunications, filing, and records management. Typing skill is not required to complete this course, but it will help the student complete the work more quickly. This course is not a prerequisite for the course below. (½ unit)

9B. The second semester covers a study of entry-level skills needed for office work. Units of study include mailing and shipping, processing data, reprographics, purchasing and receiving, inventories, sales, recordkeeping, and applying for employment. Typing skill is not required to complete this course, but it will help the student complete the work much more quickly. (½ unit)

General Business

10a. A study of the business and economic environment in daily life, concerned with four aspects of economics: personal management economics, consumer economics, social economics, occupational or career economics. (½ unit)

10B. A continuation of the above course. A study of all business activities which provides a perspective for specialized business courses. Units of study include business and consumer use of credit, insurance, investments, and taxes. It also provides an opportunity to evaluate and choose a career. (½ unit)

COMPUTER EDUCATION

Computer Education

A one semester course designed to acquaint the student with the fundamentals of data processing and electronic information technology. The course examines the nature of computer information, the history and development of computer technology, how computers are being used in a variety of situations, and careers associated with computer use. The activities and assignments for this course may be completed without access to a computer. Exercises are included for those who do have access to a computer. (½ unit)

ENGLISH

Ninth-Grade English

9A. This course directs the student in the practical use of grammar skills. The student will use these skills in original writing as they are coordinated with literature assignments. This course includes the study of the novel, the short story, and the essay. (½ unit)

9B. This course is a continuation of the above course. The course begins with a review of basic grammar usage and paragraph development. Composition assignments are assigned throughout the course. The second part of this course focuses on the study of poetry, drama, and biography. (½ unit)

Tenth-Grade English

10A. This course challenges the student to use the tools of grammar usage in written expressions. Additional work is given in word forms and sentence structure. A deeper understanding of the types of literature is gained through the reading of short stories, plays, poems, essays, and novels. (½ unit)

10B. A continuation of the above course. Grammar skills are incorporated in the writing assignments. The literature unit covers lessons on drama, poetry, and biography. The student will explore the literary devices used by different authors in their works. (½ unit)

Eleventh-Grade English

11A. This course introduces the student to an appreciation of American literature. The student learns to make a critical analysis of the works of the different periods of literature. Writing skills and self-expression are developed as the student coordinates literature study and correct usage. (½ unit)

11B. A continuation of the above course. The student learns to read for depth and for critical analysis. A coordination of language skills with literature models is continued. (½ unit)

Twelfth-Grade English

12A. This course is an introduction to historical insight into the language and includes readings in English literature from the Anglo-Saxon period through the Romantic Age. The student is required to develop and perfect language skills through extensive writing practice. (½ unit)

12B. This course is a continuation of the above course and includes a study of English literature from the Romantic Age through the Modern Age. The student is also required to gain proficiency in more advanced writing. (½ unit)

Basic Grammar Review

This course is a general review of the basic elements of English grammar, including word study (spelling and vocabulary), mechanics (punctuation and capitalization), and sentence structure. Each lesson contains exercises designed to help the student gain an understanding of the rules and practices of standard English. (½ unit)

ETIQUETTE

Etiquette

An elective course in the standard rules of good manners and proper social behavior. (½ unit)

HEALTH EDUCATION

Health Education

Education for the health of the individual, family, and community. The course will improve the health-related knowledge, attitudes, and behaviors. Focuses on the importance, nature, and extent of the following areas: first aid, CPR, safety, disease, nutrition, tobacco, alcohol, drugs, mental health, heredity, physical fitness, the human body, personal health, environmental health, and health services. (½ unit)

MATHEMATICS

Algebra I

9A. The basics of beginning algebra are presented. Topics included are: symbols and sets, properties of operations, signed numbers, operations with polynomials, solutions of first-degree equations and inequalities in one variable, and solutions of verbal problems using equations and inequalities. Special emphasis is placed on procedures, use of the number line for graphical purposes, and methods for solving verbal problems. (½ unit)

9B. A continuation of the above course with emphasis on extending the range of problems which can be solved by the study of inequalities, functions and relations, graphs in the coordinate plane, systems of open sentences, irrational numbers, and quadratic functions and equations. (½ unit)

Unified Geometry

10A. This course combines the study of plane, solid, space, and coordinate geometry. The basic theorems, postulates, and definitions related to angles, parallel lines, triangles, and polygons will be taught. Also, a large amount of time will be spent on the concept of direct and indirect proofs. (½ unit)

10B. A continuation of the above course in which areas of study will include the Pythagorean Theorem, special right triangles, constructions, circles and their angles and segments, the areas of all regular polygons and circles, volume of regular right solids, and locus. (½ unit)

Algebra II

11A. Topics presented include a review and extension of topics previously studied, fundamental operations, signed numbers, special products and factors, fractions, simple and fractional equations, algebraic, geometrical, and matrix solutions of systems of equations of the first degree, and exponents. A special effort is made to use verbal problems to illustrate methods of personal problem-solving. (½ unit)

11B. In this second semester course, the topics presented include the solution of quadratic equations, exponents, radicals, and logarithms; complex numbers; algebraic and graphical solution of simultaneous second-degree equations in two unknowns; equations of higher degree; theory of equations; sequences and series; binomial theorem; and verbal problems. (½ unit)

Trigonometry

This course is based on a modern textbook which maintains a proper balance between the analytical and numerical aspects of the subject. Topics presented are the trigonometry of the right triangle; operations applied to related algebraic and trigonometric expressions; trigonometric functions; complex numbers; quadratic equations; trigonometric relationships; identities and conditional equations; graphs of trigonometric functions; applications of the fundamental laws of oblique triangles; and solutions of oblique triangles. (½ unit)

General Mathematics

13A. This course is designed for students who have not mastered the basic skills of arithmetic involving whole numbers, fractions, and decimals. Students will spend a large amount of time on basic math principles and operations with whole numbers, fractions and decimals. Students will spend part of their time applying their knowledge of mathematics to everyday problem situations. (½ unit)

13B. This course is designed for students who have mastered some of the basic skills of arithmetic involving whole numbers, fractions, and decimals. Students will quickly review basic skills and then study percents and conversion of measurements. The emphasis of the course is the use of mathematical skills to solve consumer-related problems. (½ unit)

Consumer Mathematics

This course provides students with a comprehensive study of the types of consumer decisions most adults make. It is designed to provide the practical mathematics required to make these decisions. Students who take this course should already be familiar with computations involving whole numbers, fractions, decimals, and percents. Some areas of study include budgets, commissions, discounts, taxes, checking and saving accounts, buying on credit, wages, deductions, car purchases, insurance, utility bills, Consumer Price Index, and scale drawings. (½ unit)

SCIENCE

Physical Science

9A. A survey of physical science which includes the study of composition and transformation of matter and the principles of measurement. The course is designed to introduce fundamental chemistry concepts including the atomic theory, different classes of chemical reactions, and the use of chemical equations. (½ unit)

9B. A survey of physical science which separates physics into classical topics of mechanics, heat, sound, light, electricity, and magnetism. The course is designed to integrate physical laws and phenomena with concrete, everyday objects, situations, and events for environmental and practical applications. (½ unit)

Biology

11a. A study of living things that covers what life is, the structural basis of life, and how life changes with time, and the processes of living things. (½ unit)

11b. A continuation of the above course. The unit covers the world of plants and animals and the biosphere. (½ unit)

SOCIAL STUDIES

Alabama History

This course traces the development of Alabama history, with an overview of its political, social and economic resources. (½ unit)

World Geography

This course encompasses the study of the major geographical regions of the world. It focuses on the topographical features of a region, its political geography, its climates, and cultural factors relating to geography such as ethnic groups, customs, and lifestyles. Environmental problems due to pollution and the use and abuse of natural resources, and current world problems and challenges are also explored. (½ unit)

World History

10A. This first semester covers earliest civilization through the Renaissance. It is the purpose of this course to point out and trace the social, economic, and political developments which gave rise to succeeding world conditions. Special attention is given to developing the student's powers of observation and inference. (½ unit)

10B. The second semester of the above course covers the Renaissance through modern times. This course also traces the social, economic, and political developments which gave rise to succeeding world conditions. Special attention is given to developing the student's powers of observation and inference. (½ unit)

U.S. History

11A. A comprehensive study from the Colonial Period to about 1900. Social, political, economic, and cultural institutions are considered, with a special emphasis on constitutional history. (½ unit)

11B. The second semester of the above course begins with imperialism in the late 1890s and continues through modern times. Social, political, economic, and cultural institutions are examined. (½ unit)

Economics

A study of basic theoretical economic principles and concepts. While some emphasis is placed upon consumerism and the comparison of economic systems in other countries, particularly the Soviet Union, the intent of the course is to help the student understand and analyze economic systems through the use of economic concepts, principles, and theories. (½ unit)

U.S. Government

This course involves a study of the institutions and functions of the U.S. federal, state, and local governments and their relationship to the political process. The student should acquire a working knowledge of the structure of government and be better able to understand political behavior and make intelligent political decisions. The basic purpose of the course is to develop competent citizens who are politically aware and are able to be contributing members of a democratic society. (½ unit)

Sociology

The study of human and social behavior. This course emphasizes socialization, social interaction, social organization, social institutions, cultural and social change, and social problems. (½ unit)

SPANISH

First Year Spanish

1A. This course is designed to help the student attain an acceptable degree of proficiency in the skills of listening, speaking, reading, and writing. Emphasis is placed on a practical vocabulary and grammatical study of the language. Geographical and cultural points are also introduced. (½ unit)

1B. A continuation of the above course. It reinforces the student's skills in writing and further develops his reading and comprehension skills through the addition of selected readings in Spanish. (½ unit)

Second Year Spanish

2A. Designed to help the student attain an acceptable degree of proficiency in the skills of listening, speaking, reading, and writing.

Emphasis is placed on a practical vocabulary and a grammatical study of the language. (½ unit)

2B. This continuation of the above course reinforces the student's skills in writing and further develops reading and comprehension skills through the addition of selected readings in Spanish. (½ unit)

Alaska, University of - Fairbanks
Center for Distance Education and
Independent Learning
130 Harper Building
Box 756700
Fairbanks, Alaska 99775-6700 (907) 474-5353

Description:

The University of Alaska dates from May 4, 1915 when the Honorable James Wickersham, delegate to Congress from Alaska, laid the cornerstone on land set aside by Congress on March 4 for support of a land-grant college. Today the University's statewide system includes major urban centers at Fairbanks, Anchorage, Juneau, and community colleges at Anchorage, Bethel, Fairbanks, Juneau, Kenai, Ketchikan, Kodiak, Kotzebue, Nome, Palmer, Sitka, and Valdez.

The Center for Distance Education and Independent Learning was begun in 1959. It currently enrolls more that 2,100 students annually.

Faculty:

James Stricks, Director. There is a faculty of 50.

Academic Levels:

College

Degree/Certificate Programs:

The University of Alaska Fairbanks will accept 32 semester credit hours of correspondence study toward a baccalaureate degree, and 15 hours toward an associate degree.

Admission Requirements:

Formal admission to the University of Alaska Fairbanks is not required. High school graduates or adults who have passed the age of high school graduation may enroll in any correspondence course for which they meet the prerequisite. Students may enroll at anytime during the year.

Tuition:

$67 per semester hour credit, due upon enrollment. An additional $20 postage and handling per course. Tuition assistance available only to Alaskan students. A student may withdraw from a correspondence study course if a Course Withdrawal Form and a UAF Drop/Add Form is submitted within sixty days of the original enrollment date. If eligible, a student will receive a refund of fifty percent of tuition and eighty percent of the books/materials costs if the items are returned unmarked and in good condition (and are still being used for the course). No refunds will be processed after the sixty day time period.

Enrollment Period:

The maximum time allowed to complete a course is one year; minimum time is three months. One six-month extension is allowed for a $50 fee.

Equipment Requirements:

Textbooks are not covered by tuition, and may be purchased through the Center for Distance Education on the Fairbanks campus. Students who have access to books through other sources may utilize them provided they can obtain the proper edition of the text. Several courses require cassette players and access to a videotape player.

Credit and Grading:

Examinations must be proctored. Grading system is A, B, C, D, F. Minimum passing grade varies by course. Credit is awarded in semester hour credits.

Library Services:

Books and materials are on reserve at the UA Fairbanks Rasmussen Library. For students in Alaska but outside the Fairbanks area, a toll free number (1-800-478-5348) is available for interlibrary loan of materials.

Accreditations:

Northwest Association of Schools and Colleges. Member of: National University Continuing Education Association.

COLLEGE COURSES

ACCOUNTING

Elementary Accounting I

An introduction course in accounting concepts and procedures for service businesses and for merchandising businesses owned by a single proprietor. (3 semester hours)

Elementary Accounting II

A continuation of introductory accounting concepts and procedures emphasizing the problems of businesses organized as partnerships or corporations and performing manufacturing operations. (3 semester hours)

ADVERTISING

Principles of Advertising

Advertising including strategy, media use, creation and production of advertisements, and measurement of advertising effectiveness. (3 semester hours)

ALASKA NATIVE STUDIES

Alaska Native Claims Settlement Act

A general survey of the Alaska Native Settlement Act. It will include a brief historical overview of land claims of various tribes in the Lower 48 and in Alaska leading to the Settlement Act of 1971. The current status of various Native corporations, including regional, village, and nonprofit corporations. Special attention to the discussion of future issues related to implementation of ANCSA. (3 semester hours)

The Alaska Native Land Settlement

Native corporation goals and methods as they implement the Alaska Native Claims Settlement Act and establish themselves within the larger political economy. (3 semester hours)

ANTHROPOLOGY

Introduction to Anthropology

Introduction to the study of human societies and cultures based on the findings of the four subfields of the discipline: archaeological, biological, cultural, and linguistic. (3 semester hours)

Oral Tradition: Folklore and Oral History

Study and collection of folklore and oral history and importance in communication; advantages, disadvantages of their recording and study. Sociological anthropology and anthropological linguistics related to oral traditions. Methods of folklorists and historians. Field project. (3 semester hours)

Native Cultures of Alaska

An introduction to the traditional Aleut, Eskimo, and Indian (Athabaskan and Tlingit) cultures of Alaska. Comparative information on Eskimo and Indian cultures in Canada is also presented. Includes a discussion of linguistic groupings as well as the cultural groups; presentation of population changes through time; subsistence patterns, social organization and religion in terms of local ecology. Precontact interaction between native groups of Alaska is also explored. A general introductory course presenting an overall view of the cultures of Native Alaskans. (3 semester hours)

AVIATION TECHNOLOGY

Private Pilot Ground School

Study of aircraft and engine operation and limitations, aircraft flight instruments, navigation computers, national weather information and dissemination service. Federal Aviation Regulations, flight information publications, radio communications, and radio navigation in preparation for FAA Private Pilot written exam. (4 semester hours)

BIOLOGY

Natural History of Alaska

Aspects of the physical environment peculiar to the north and important in determining the biological setting; major ecosystems concepts to develop an appreciation for land use and wildlife management problems in both terrestrial and aquatic situations. (3 semester hours)

Introduction to Marine Biology

A general survey of marine organisms, evolution of marine life, habitats and communities of ocean zones, productivity, and marine resources. (3 semester hours)

BUSINESS

Introduction to Business

Business organization, nature of major business functions such as management, finance, accounting, marketing, personal administration. Opportunities and requirements for professional business careers. (3 semester hours)

Basics of Investing

This course covers personal financial planning, goal setting, and investing. Also, a study will be made of stocks, bonds, trusts, securities, options, real estate, and other investment vehicles. The topics of inflation, taxes, interest rates, retirement, and selecting financial planners are covered. (3 semester hours)

Real Estate Law

A practical course surveying the various kinds of deeds and conveyances, mortgages, liens, rentals, appraisals, and other transactions in the field of real estate and the law. (3 semester hours)

Applied Business Law I

A survey of the legal aspects of business problems including basic principles, institutions and administration of law in contracts, agency, employment and personal sales and property ownership. (3 semester hours)

Applied Business Law II

A survey of legal aspects of business problems including basic principles, institutions, and administration of law in insurance, suretyship (negotiable instruments), partnerships, corporations, trusts, wills, bankruptcy, torts, and business crimes. (3 semester hours)

COMPUTER SCIENCE

Introduction to Computer Programming

Concepts of structured programming and algorithm design within the syntax of the PASCAL programming language. (3 semester hours)

ECONOMICS

Principles of Economics

Goals, incentives, and outcomes of economic behavior with applications and illustrations from current issues: operation of markets for goods, services, and factors of production; the behavior of firms and industries in different types of competition; and income distribution. The functioning and current problems of aggregate economy, determination and analysis of aspects of international exchange. (4 semester hours)

EDUCATION

Literature for Children

Criteria for evaluating children's books and application of criteria to books selected by student, study of outstanding authors, illustrators and content of specific categories of literature, book selection aids, and effective use of literature to promote learning. (3 semester hours)

Diagnosis and Evaluation of Learning

Detailed information about the teaching/learning process in the classroom emphasizing making teaching decisions. The student will learn the strengths and weaknesses of various forms of diagnosis and evaluation of learning, with particular emphasis on problems encountered in cross-cultural settings. Attention will be given to informal, formal, process, and product assessment. (3 semester hours)

The Exceptional Learner

Foundation for understanding, identifying, and serving the exceptional learner in rural and urban settings. A special emphasis is placed on working with exceptional learners in the regular classroom. The unique needs of exceptional students in rural settings from bilingual/multicultural backgrounds are covered. (3 semester hours)

Building a Practical Philosophy of Education

A study of philosophy as a distinct discipline with its own terminology, concepts, and processes and how it functions in the field of education. Special emphasis is given to an application of philosophy of education to cross-cultural situations in Alaskan classrooms. (3 semester hours)

Electronic Mail and Online Services

Introduction to telecommunications using a personal computer and modem. Learn to use the services available through the University of Alaska Network including electronic mail. SLED library services, Alaskanet, and Legislative Information Office system. Requires access to a computer and modem. (1 semester hour)

Introduction to Internet I

Accessing Internet services include USENET, a global electronic bulletin board; TELNET to log on to other computer systems; and the GOPHER and Worldwide Web menu systems. (1 semester hour)

Introduction to the Internet II

Additional Internet resources including ARCHIE file searches, FTP file transfers, binary file uploads/downloads, and listservers. (1 semester hour)

Using the Internet

Accessing Internet services including USENET; a global electronic bulletin board; TELNET to log on to other computer systems; GOPHER and Worldwide Web menu systems; ARCHIE file searches; FTP file transfers; binary uploads/downloads; and listservers. (1 semester hour)

Applying Telecommunications

Design and implementation of an approved project using telecommunications in the classroom or workplace, or an in-depth research paper. (1 semester hour)

Problems in Educational Practice

Identify, analyze, and treat a problem related to own professional practice, discussing relevant literature. Must include practical remedial suggestions and be responsible for own library resources; access to copying machine. Full-time teachers or school administrators only. (1 semester hour)

Education and Cultural Processes

Advanced study of the function of education as a cultural process and its relation to other aspects of a cultural system. Students will prepare a study examining some aspect of education in a particular cultural context. (3 semester hours)

Education and Socio-Economic Change

Examination of social change processes, particularly related to the deliberate development of new institutions and resulting forms of new consciousness. Emphasis on role of education and schooling in this development dynamic. (3 semester hours)

Educational Administration in Cultural Perspective

Examines issues related to the social organization and sociopolitical context of schools, administrative and institutional change processes and the changing role of administrators in education, using a crosscultural framework for analysis. (3 semester hours)

ENGLISH

Preparatory College English

Instruction in writing to improve students' fluency and accuracy and communication skills. (3 semester hours)

Methods of Written Communication

Instruction in writing expository prose, including generating topics as part of the writing process. Practice in developing, organizing, revising, and editing essays. (3 semester hours)

Intermediate Exposition with Modes of Literature

Instruction in writing through close analysis of literature. Research paper required. (3 semester hours)

Introduction to Creative Writing: Poetry

A study of the forms and techniques of poetry for beginning students; discussion of students' work. (3 semester hours)

Literature of Alaska and Yukon Territory

Study of representative works of fiction, verse, and nonfiction which deal with Alaska and the Yukon Territory. (3 semester hours)

GEOGRAPHY

Introductory Geography

World regions, an analysis of environment, with emphasis on major culture realms. (3 semester hours)

Elements of Physical Geography

Analysis of the processes that form the physical environment and the resulting physical patterns. Study of landforms, climate, soils, water resources, vegetation, and their world and regional patterns. (3 semester hours)

Geography of Alaska

Regional, physical, and economic geography of Alaska. Special consideration of the state's renewable and nonrenewable resources, and of plans for their wise use. Frequent study of representative maps and visual materials. (3 semester hours)

GEOLOGY

Principles of Geology

Provides an understanding of earth processes (both on the earth's surface and at depth) and the origin and classification of major rock types. Other topics include factors that have shaped the Earth, geologic events and processes occurring today, and ideas of future occurrences. (3 semester hours)

HEALTH

Science of Nutrition

This is an introductory course in which the principles of nutrition and how they relate to the life cycle are studied. The effect this course has upon the student's thinking relative to nutrition and upon the student's dietary habits is an important outcome. An objective is improvement, if needed, in the student's nutritional status. (3 semester hours)

HISTORY

Western Civilization I

The origins and major political, economic, social, and intellectual developments of western civilization to 1500. (3 semester hours)

Alaska, Land and Its People

A survey of Alaska from earliest days to present, its peoples, problems, and prospects. (3 semester hours)

History of the United States I

The discovery of Americas to 1865; colonial period, revolution, formation of the constitution, western expansion, Civil War. (3 semester hours)

History of the United States II

History of the U.S. from the Reconstruction to the present. (3 semester hours)

History of Alaska

Alaska from prehistoric times to the present, including major themes such as Native Alaska, colonial Alaska, military Alaska, statehood, Alaska Native Claims Settlement Act of 1971, and the Alaska National Interest Lands Act of 1980. (3 semester hours)

Polar Exploration and Its Literature

A survey of polar exploration efforts of all Western nations from 870 A.D. to the present and a consideration of the historical sources of this effort. (3 semester hours)

JOURNALISM

Introduction to Mass Communications

History and principles of mass communications and the role of the information media in American society. Introduction to professional aspects of mass communications, including both print and broadcast. (3 semester hours)

Introduction to Broadcasting

Principles of broadcasting as they relate to the people of the United States, including history, government involvement, and social effects. (3 semester hours)

History of the Cinema

History and development of the medium of film in the United States and abroad during the last 100 years. (3 semester hours)

Film and TV Criticism

Theoretical approaches to viewing, analyzing, and evaluating film and television program content. (3 semester hours)

Magazine Article Writing

Writing articles for publication. (3 semester hours)

Mass Media Law and Regulation

Common law, statutory law, and administrative law that affects the mass media, including libel, copyright, access to the media, constitutional problems, privacy, shield laws, and broadcast regulations. (3 semester hours)

Publishing, Production, and Theory

Writing, editing, and production techniques for high school publications including short courses on desktop publishing, basic and electronic photography, advertising, management, and legal liabilities. (3 semester hours)

LINGUISTICS

Nature of Language

The study of language: systematic analysis of human language and description of its grammatical structure, distribution, and diversity. (3 semester hours)

MARKETING

Principles of Marketing

Managing of a firm's marketing effort focusing on products, distribution, pricing, and promotion to targeted consumers. Practices appropriate to domestic or international, small or large, goods or services, and for-profit or non-profit organizations included. (3 semester hours)

MATHEMATICS

Basic College Mathematics

Operations with whole numbers, fractions, decimals and signed numbers. Percents and ratios. Evaluating algebraic expressions. Introduction to geometric figures. Metric system. (3 semester hours)

Elementary Algebra

First year high school algebra. Evaluating and simplifying algebraic expressions, solving first degree equations and inequalities, integral exponents, polynomials, factoring, rational expressions. (3 semester hours)

Review of Elementary Algebra

This course is designed to assist students in reviewing material covered in the course above. (1 semester hour)

Intermediate Algebra

Second year high school algebra. Operations with rational functions, radicals, rational exponents, complex numbers, quadratic equations, and inequalities. Cartesian coordinate system and graphing, systems of equations, determinants and logarithms. (3 semester hours)

Review of Elementary Algebra

Reviews material covered in the above course. (1 semester hour)

Review of Basic Geometry

High school geometry without formal proofs. Definitions, measurements, parallel lines, triangles, polygons, circles, area, solid figures and volume. (1 semester hour)

Elementary Functions

A study of algebraic, logarithmic, and exponential functions, together with selected topics from algebra. (3 semester hours)

Trigonometry

A study of trigonometric functions. (3 semester hours)

Concepts and Contemporary Applications of Mathematics

Applications of math in modern life, including uses of graph theory in management science; probability and statistics in industry, government, and science; geometry in engineering and astronomy. Problem solving emphasized. (3 semester hours)

Concepts of Math

Mathematical though and history for students with a limited math background. Mathematical reasoning rather than formal manipulation. May include number theory, topology, set theory, geometry, algebra, and analysis. (3 semester hours)

Calculus I

Techniques and application of differential and integral calculus, vector analysis, partial derivatives, multiple integrals, and infinite series. (4 semester hours)

Calculus II

Techniques and application of differential and integral calculus, vector analysis, partial derivatives, multiple integrals, and infinite series. (4 semester hours)

Calculus III

Techniques and application of differential and integral calculus, vector analysis, partial derivatives, multiple integrals, and infinite series. (4 semester hours)

Mathematics for Elementary School Teachers I

Elementary set theory, numeration systems, and algorithms of arithmetic, devisors, multiples, integers, introduction to rational numbers. (3 semester hours)

Mathematics for Elementary School Teachers II

A continuation of the above course. Real numbers systems and subsystems, logic, informal geometry, metric system, probability, and statistics. (3 semester hours)

MINERALOGY

Minerals, Man, and the Environment

A general survey of the impact of the mineral industries on man's economic, political, environmental systems. (3 semester hours)

Mineral Exploration Techniques

This course covers the modern, scientific exploration and prospecting techniques utilized in Alaska since the 1970s. Exploration design, ore deposit models, exploration geochemistry, geophysics, drilling sampling and geostatistics will be studies. (3 semester hours)

MUSIC

Music Fundamentals

An introductory study of the language of music. Includes basic notation, melodic and rhythmic writing, scales, bass and treble clefs, and basic harmony. (3 semester hours)

PETROLEUM TECHNOLOGY

Survey of Energy Industries

Overview of global energy supply and demand, alternate energy options, and petroleum production technology. (1 semester hour)

Fundamentals of Petroleum

This course is designed to give an overall view of the petroleum industry in terms that are understandable by the layperson as well as the professional. Included are lessons on petroleum geology, prospecting, leasing, drilling, production, pipelines, refining, processing, and marketing. (3 semester hours)

POLITICAL SCIENCE

Introduction to Government and Politics

Principles, institutions, and practices of American national government; the Constitution, federalism, interest groups, parties, public opinion, and elections. (3 semester hours)

PSYCHOLOGY

Introduction to Psychology

Fundamentals and basic principles of general psychology emphasizing both the natural science orientation and the social science orientation including the environment, heredity, and psychological basis for integrated behavior; visual perception and its sensory basis; audition and the other senses; motivation and emotion; basic processes in learning, problem solving, and thinking; personality; psychological disorders; and the prevention, treatment, and therapeutic strategies. (3 semester hours)

Developmental Psychology in Crosscultural Perspective

The development of persons is examined from both a psychological and crosscultural perspective. Key topics will be the development of cognition, personality, and social behavior with attention to relevant research on those cultures found in Alaska. (3 semester hours)

Drugs and Drug Dependence

Multidisciplinary approach to the study of drugs and drug abuse emphasizing acute and chronic alcoholism, commonly abused drugs, law enforcement and legal aspects of drug abuse, medical uses of drugs, physiological aspects of drug abuse, medical uses of drugs, physiological aspects of drug abuse, psychological and sociological causes and manifestations of drug abuse, recommended drug education alternatives and plans, and the treatment and rehabilitation of acute and chronic drug users. (3 semester hours)

Child Development

Study of development from prenatal through middle childhood including the cognitive, emotional, social, and physical aspects of the young child. Course includes child observations. Emphasis is on the roles of heredity and environment in the growth process. (3 semester hours)

Personality

Psychological and social/cultural determinants of personality formation including appropriate theories. (3 semester hours)

Abnormal Psychology

A study of abnormal behavior, its causes, treatment, and social impact. The major classification of disorder. (3 semester hours)

Biological Psychology

All behavior, thought, and feelings are the result of complex patterns of brain activity. Brain structure, major functions of the brain and the mechanisms responsible for them. The work of neuroscientists in studying the brain. Brain diseases and disorders and how they are treated. (3 semester hours)

SOCIOLOGY

Individual, Society, and Culture

An examination of the complex social arrangements guiding individual behavior and common human concerns in contrasting cultural contexts. (3 semester hours)

Introduction to Sociology

An introduction to the science of man as a social being, emphasizing the interactional, structural, and normative aspects of social behavior. An attempt is made to construct a cross-cultural framework in understanding and predicting human behavior. (3 semester hours)

Social Institutions

A continuation of the above course. Application of the concepts learned by developing and carrying out short surveys of sociological phenomena. Institutions of society, such as family, political and economic order, are examined, including their operation in the Alaska rural and cross-cultural milieu. (3 semester hours)

The Family: A Crosscultural Perspective

The study of comparative patterns of marriage and family relationships. Various approaches such as the developmental, systems, and social psychological are used to analyze these relationships. The family is followed through the stages of the family life cycle, such as mate selection, marriage, early marital interaction, parenthood, the middle and late years, and possible dissolution. Attention is given to crosscultural differences in Alaska as well as in other parts of the world. (3 semester hours)

STATISTICS

Elementary Probability and Statistics

Descriptive statistics, frequency distributions, sampling distributions, elementary probability, estimation of population parameters, hypothesis testing (one and two sample problems), correlation, simple linear regression, and one-way analysis of variance. Parametric and nonparametric methods. (3 semester hours)

TOURISM

Tourism Principles and Practices

Forces which influence the international and domestic hospitality, leisure, travel, and recreation industries. Socioeconomic models and measure of regional impact, demand, supply. (3 semester hours)

American College
270 Bryn Mawr Avenue
Bryn Mawr, Pennsylvania 19010
(215) 896-4500

Description:

The American College is the nation's oldest and largest distance-education, accredited institution for professional studies in the financial services. It is a private, nonprofit, degree-granting college whose programs, created by a resident faculty located on its campus in Bryn Mawr, Pennsylvania, are undertaken by over 45,000 students located throughout the United States and in more than 20 foreign countries. The college was established in 1927 to serve the professional education and certification needs of persons primarily involved in life insurance sales and management. This mission was carried out through a collegiate-level course of study leading to the Chartered Life Underwriter (CLU) professional designation.

In recent years The American College has broadened its offerings to reflect the rapidly changing financial services marketplace. Courses that cover personal insurance, financial planning, estate planning, pension studies, employee benefits, tax planning, and a full array of management subjects are designed not only for insurance-related students but also for men and women in other financial services careers. Programs now include the CLU with a choice of life insurance or personal insurance specialization, the Chartered Financial Consultant (ChFC) professional designation for financial planning specialists, and a graduate degree, the Master of Science in Financial Services.

The Solomon S. Huebner School, named for the founder of the College, administers the two certification programs, the CLU and the ChFC. The School of Advanced Career Studies offers Advanced Graduate courses and specialty certificates, workshops, and seminars that provide in-depth knowledge in areas such as advanced estate planning, advanced pension planning, business tax planning, employee benefit planning. Special company training and incentive programs known as Premier Schools are also sponsored by SACS in conjunction with the Davis W. Gregg Educational Conference Center. The Graduate School of Financial Services administers the curriculum leading to the Master of Science in Financial Services degree.

Faculty:
Dr. Samuel H. Weese, President.

Academic Levels:
Professional
Graduate

Degree/Certificate Programs:
Professional Certification; Master of Science in Financial Services. A maximum of 9 credits toward the MSFS may be transferred from other accredited educational institutions and must have been earned in courses essentially similar to

those of the College and they must have been earned within 7 years of application for admission to a degree program.

Admission Requirements:

The basic requirement for admission to the Huebner School is a high school education or its equivalent. Candidates for admission to the MSFS program are evaluated individually based on educational and professional background. While most candidates have a bachelor's degree from an accredited college or university, consideration is given to persons with a combination of college and professional education.

Tuition:

$145 per credit. Rates subject to change without notice. Contact the school for current fees.

Enrollment Period:

Huebner School courses are self-paced. Candidates for the Master of Science in Financial Services degree must complete all requirements within seven years of formal admission to the program. A two-week residency session is required.

Equipment Requirements:

The tuition fee for the Huebner courses does not include the recommended study materials. Study guides and text and readings books are available from Professional Book Distributors, Columbus, Ohio.

Credit and Grading:

Huebner students have the choice of a traditional paper and pencil examination or a computer-administered test. Paper and pencil tests are given in January and June in a nationwide network of examination centers. Computer examinations are offered year-round in testing centers in many cities. To be awarded the CLU and ChFC designations, candidates must pass the ten required courses for the designation, meet specified experience requirements, and agree to comply with The American College Code of Ethics and Procedures. The MSFS degree requires 36 credits earned for both required and elective courses. Examinations for three-credit courses are two hours in length and combine objective and short essay questions and, in some instances, case problems. Examinations for one-credit modules are one hour long and are composed of either objective or short essay questions.

Library Services:

The Vane B. Lucas Memorial Library serves the research needs of the campus faculty and staff and is open to the public as well. The library offers facilities for study and research as well as services such as interlibrary loan and computer-database-produced bibliographies.

Accreditations:

Middle States Association of College and Schools.

PROFESSIONAL COURSES

FINANCIAL SERVICES

Personal Risk Management and Insurance

This course focuses on an understanding of the personal loss exposures facing families and individuals and how these exposures can be treated with insurance and other financial products and services. This course includes coverage of automobile insurance, homeowners insurance, and other property and liability policies relevant to individuals. Health insurance and social insurance are also discussed. In addition to assignments on the nature and use of specific types of insurance products, the course material is integrated through the use of case studies. (Noncredit)

Fundamentals of Financial Planning

This course deals with the basics of financial planning. Topics include the financial planning process; measuring client risk propensities; communication skills; gathering client information; using time-value analysis in financial planning; basics of income, estate, and gift tax planning; basics of insurance, investment, and retirement planning; computerizing a financial planning practice; the regulatory and ethical environment; and a sample financial planning case. Option computer exercises are included. (Noncredit)

Income Taxation

The federal income tax system with particular reference to the taxation of life insurance and annuities. The income taxation of individuals, sole proprietorships, partnerships, and corporations is also covered. (Noncredit)

The Financial System in the Economy

This survey course provides an overview of the financial services business. Included is an examination of the financial markets in the U.S. economic system, the principal institutions operating in these markets, the economic functions they perform, and the products and services they provide to clients. A highly significant aspect of this course is its examination of the rapidly changing regulatory and competitive environment within which financial services institutions and professionals work and the major currently unresolved issues whose resolution will shape the future environment. Optional computer exercises are included. (Noncredit)

Individual Life and Health Insurance

This course includes coverage of social insurance, individual insurance products, insurance operations, and insurance regulation. Most of the course is devoted to the insurance policies available for the personal needs of individuals, such as individual life, annuities, disability income, medical, and long-term care insurance. The taxation and use of these policies in the financial planning process are also discussed, as well as a description of the benefits provided under social security and other social insurance plans. The remainder of the course is concerned with insurance company organization, operations, reserves, and regulation. The coverage of regulation explains some of the constraints applicable to insurers in carrying on daily operations and on setting and investing reserves. Optional computer exercises are included. (Noncredit)

Life Insurance Law

Topics discussed in this course include legal aspects of contract formation, policy provisions, assignments, ownership rights, creditor rights, beneficiary designations, disposition of life insurance proceeds, life insurance agency, and medical insurance provisions. Also included are discussions of the legal environment and the issues of insurance advertising and privacy. This course emphasizes the judicial constraints and influences on life insurance companies. (Noncredit)

Group Benefits

This course contains an analysis of group insurance benefits, including the regulatory environment, contract provisions, marketing, underwriting, rate making, plan design, and alternative funding methods. (Noncredit)

Planning for Retirement Needs

This course focuses on retirement planning for the business, the business owner, and the individual. It consists of two major parts. The first nine assignments cover qualified plans, nonqualified plans, and IRAs; the remaining four assignments cover retirement needs for individual clients. This course emphasizes the practical knowledge needed for choosing the best retirement plan and designing a plan that will meet a client's needs from a tax and retirement standpoint. Personal retirement planning and retirement distribution planning are also discussed. (Noncredit)

Investments

Various aspects of investment principles and their application to personal finance are covered. Topics include risks, yields, securities markets, understanding of financial statements, limited income securities, valuation of common stock, real estate, mutual funds, options, futures, tax-advantaged investments, and principles of portfolio management. Optional computer exercises are included. (Noncredit)

Wealth Accumulation Planning

The course focuses on the principles of personal taxation and tax-advantaged investments, including risk and return; the acquisition, ownership, and disposition of property; principles of depreciation; capital gains and losses; installment sales; exchanges; passive-activity-loss rules; and forms of real estate ownership. An overview of tax-leveraged and tax-incentive investments, with an emphasis on the major tax, investment, and organizational characteristics of real estate, and the basics of oil and gas, agricultural, and equipment-leasing limited partnerships is provided. Life-cycle planning for the living estate—a framework for accumulation and retirement planning, including methods for preserving wealth, tax planning, time-value and budgeting concepts, and special tools and strategies such as IRAs, Keoghs, tax-saving portfolio management techniques, and income-shifting strategies—is also discussed. Optional computer exercises are included. (Noncredit)

Fundamentals of Estate Planning I

Various aspects of estate and gift tax planning, including the nature, valuation, transfer, administration, and taxation of property, are discussed. Particular emphasis is given to a basic understanding of the unified estate and gift tax system. This course covers gratuitous transfers of property outright of using trusts, wills, power of appointment, federal estate and gift taxation, the marital deduction, and other estate planning devices. Also covered is the estate planning process, which includes the client interview, fact-finding, and the development of appropriate personal estate plans using various estate planning devices. Optional computer exercises are included. (Noncredit)

Planning for Business Owners and Professionals

This course focuses on the tax and legal aspects of organizing a business; compensation planning for the business owner; problems in continuing a business after an owners' death and the insured buy-sell agreement; retirement of a business owner, including estate planning and estate-freezing techniques; methods for transferring a family business; lifetime disposition of a business interest—taxable and tax-free dispositions and the use of the installment sale and other methods; business uses of life and health insurance for the benefit of business owners; disability buy-sell agreements; key employee life and health

insurance plans; and business uses of property and liability insurance. This course also covers special problems of professional corporations. (Noncredit)

Financial Planning Applications

This case course is aimed at integrating the various techniques, tools, and products covered in the ChFC program with the financial planning process outlined in *Fundamentals of Financial Planning*. Students receive practical experience in analyzing and solving realistic financial problems of individuals and businesses. Cases range from simple fact patterns and basic documents to complex situations involving not only personal financial problems but also financial problems associated with businesses and business ownership. Clients used in the cases vary by age, income, family status, occupation, objectives, and related financial problems. (Noncredit)

Fundamentals of Estate Planning II

The estate and gift tax principles with emphasis placed on life insurance planning applications are covered. Topics include the construction of the gross estate for federal estate tax purposes; valuation principles used in the estate planning process; the use of the charitable contribution as an estate planning technique; planning opportunities stemming from the marital relationship; the taxation of trusts; estate planning implications of the employer-employee relationship; estate planning considerations involving oil and gas interests; estate planning considerations involving a principal residence; and a case study reflecting procedural aspects of the estate planning process. (Noncredit)

Financial Decision Making at Retirement

This course focuses on the financial decisions that clients face as they approach, reach, and pass retirement age and on the tools and techniques financial advisers may employ to assist their clients with these decisions. Topics include estimating retirement income and capital needs; retiree medical coverage, long-term care, life care communities, and other housing arrangements; home equity conversion; social security benefits; qualified and nonqualified plans, SEPs, and IRAs; retirement plan distribution options including annuity options, rollovers, lump-sum distributions, forward averaging, minimum required distribution rules, and the 15 percent excise tax; investment planning and asset allocation; succession planning for business owners; and various related estate planning issues. A practical computer applications supplement is included. The programs are related to the minimum-distribution rules, the 15 percent excise tax, lump-sum distribution, early social security benefits, and other planning areas. (Noncredit)

Business Taxation and Planning

This course is intended to help students understand the nature of tax problems and possible solutions that arise in the operations of today's businesses. The focus of the course is the major federal tax attributes of various business entities and the implications of common transactions affecting the financial services professional, including methods of tax accounting and tax laws governing the information and operation of regular corporations, S corporations, and partnerships. Special topics cover the alternative minimum tax as it relates to corporate tax planning and the use of business life insurance in general and also as it pertains to business valuation considerations and buy-sell arrangements. (Noncredit)

GRADUATE COURSES

FINANCIAL SERVICES

Financial Institutions

This course examines the various financial institutions, considers how they interact and compete to provide essential services, and considers how they are affected by government regulation, technology, and the increasingly global marketplace. (3 credits)

Business Valuation

This course covers the process and principles of establishing current and potential business and asset valuation for estate planning purposes, buy-sell agreements, equitable distribution, key person insurance, and numerous other business decisions. (3 credits)

Advanced Pension and Retirement Planning I

The first of three advanced pension and retirement planning courses introduces the design of qualified retirement plans and their tax treatment, with detailed coverage, using case studies, of defined-contribution plans, IRAs, and tax-deferred annuity plans. This course emphasizes applications to closely held businesses and their owners. (3 credits)

Advanced Estate Planning I

Comprehensive and in-depth coverage of the Internal Revenue Code with a section-by-section approach for study purposes is provided. This course stresses advanced knowledge of the estate, gift, and income tax laws essential to estate planning. (3 credits) liquidity needs. (3 credits)

Advanced Estate Planning II

This course begins with a review of wills, intestacy, community property, and probate laws. Individual state laws are recognized. Special attention is given to interpersonal relationships between the estate planning team and the client. Also covered are the estate planning needs of business owners, executives, divorced and/or remarried persons, and those persons considering charitable donations. Many case studies are included. (3 credits)

Personal Tax Planning

Current tax laws, new cases, revenue rulings, and regulations for income tax planning are introduced. Strategies and techniques for tax reductions are presented, including law for income allocation, tax shelters, income shifting, and deduction recognition and timing. (3 credits)

Professionals and Organizational Behavior

This course presents a comprehensive view of behavior in organizations. Designed around a performance-oriented framework, this course follows three levels of analysis that include the individual, the group, and the organization. Motivation, leadership, interpersonal influence, decision making, and communication are emphasized, and case studies are included. (3 credits)

Human Resource Management

The financial services manager's role in recruiting, selecting, developing, utilizing, rewarding, and maximizing human resource potential is examined. This course covers routine operational situations as well as the macroenvironment impact on the human resources of the organization and includes case study applications. (3 credits)

Marketing Management of Services

This course explores marketing management principles, particularly as they relate to analysis of various marketing environments, evaluation of marketing opportunities, and development and implementation of strategic and short-range marketing programs. Corporate and marketing strategies for service businesses are emphasized. (3 credits)

Decision Making in Financial Services

Managerial decision making, including interdisciplinary aspects as well as psychological, sociological, political, and quantitative decision-making techniques, is focused on. This course emphasizes practical and theoretical managerial decision making applied to financial services professionals and uses case studies when appropriate. (3 credits)

Professional Self-Management

This course covers the combination of disciplines essential for individuals to improve their own ability to manage successfully and includes segments on leadership, time management, and listening. (3 credits)

Executive Compensation

Designing executive compensation plans with an emphasis on owner-employees of closely held businesses is explained. This course covers cash and bonus compensation, stock options, and other forms of compensation with restricted property, life insurance, and other death benefits; nonqualified deferred compensation; health and disability plans; and various fringe benefits. It stresses plan installation, administration, ERISA, tax, and other law compliance. (3 credits)

Advanced Pension and Retirement Planning I

This course focuses on qualified defined-benefit plans and their unique uses in retirement planning for professionals and closely held business owners. It covers design, tax, and funding aspects with detailed case studies and features optional use of computer work sheet software for plan design. (3 credits)

Advanced Pension and Retirement Planning III

This course, the capstone of the three advanced pension and retirement planning courses, emphasizes gathering information about client needs and developing optimum plan design integrating all advanced planning techniques. Case studies stress application to professionals and closely held businesses. (3 credits)

Business Tax Planning

An advanced-level tax law and planning course oriented toward the business enterprise, this course considers sole proprietorships, corporations, and partnerships for tax planning purposes. A broad range of tax and nontax topics is covered that spans the spectrum from inception to dissolution of a business. (3 credits)

Appalachian State University
Boone, North Carolina 28608 (704) 262-2000

Description:

The Appalachian State University is part of the system of public higher education of the State of North Carolina. It evolved from the Appalachian Training School, created in 1903, which was founded to prepare teachers for public school education. ASU is a participant in a consortium of eight institutions within the University of North Carolina System offering college-level correspondence courses and other opportunities for individualized study at a distance from the university campuses. In the consortium arrangement, each institution originating a course provides instruction and awards academic credit, while responsibility for administration of the program lies with the office of Independent Studies at the University of North Carolina at Chapel Hill. SEE **North Carolina, University of - Chapel Hill.**

Faculty:

J. Pat Knight, Member of UNC Independent Studies Advisory Committee.

Accreditations:

Southern Association of Colleges and Schools.

Arizona, University of

Correspondence Study Department
Division of Extended University
1955 East 6th Street
Tucson, Arizona 85719   (602) 621-1896

Description:

The University of Arizona was organized in accordance with the Morrill Act of July 2, 1962, creating the "Land-Grant Colleges." It now has a campus enrollment in excess of 30,000 students, conducts programs throughout the year both on campus and off campus, and offers studies and educational tours in countries around the world. The Colleges of the University are Agriculture, Architecture, Arts & Sciences, Business & Public Administration, Education, Engineering, Law, Medicine, Mines, Nursing, Pharmacy, and Graduate.

Each correspondence course offered by the University of Arizona is designed to parallel, as nearly as possible, the same course offered on campus. Textbooks, assignments, and examinations are prepared accordingly. Group study is encouraged whenever possible.

Over 275 credit courses and a variety of noncredit courses are available to students anywhere in the world. Over 10,000 students from all over the world are served each year.

Faculty:

Leslie Dykstra, Senior Program Coordinator. There is a faculty of 120 members.

Academic Levels:

College
High School
Noncredit

Degree/Certificate Programs:

Credits are applicable toward the high school diploma, associate degree, baccalaureate degree. At the college level, correspondence study provides opportunities so that students who are unable to attend campus classes can continue their education; those who have had college work can add to their academic record; those who have never attended college can embark upon a program which may eventually lead to a degree. At the high school level, independent study courses may be used to satisfy requirements for a diploma or to remove a deficiency for the college-bound student. Up to 60 semester-hour credits may be accepted for a baccalaureate degree at the University of Arizona.

Admission Requirements:

Open enrollment. Students may register at any time. Students are advised to register for no more than one course at a time. Correspondence students are not required to make application for admission to The University of Arizona.

Military personnel should process DANTES applications through their base Education Office. Upon receipt of a DANTES application, Independent Study will send the course Study Guide to the applicant.

Veterans should contact their local or regional Veterans Administration Office for eligibility and registration information. Tucson area veterans should contact the Veterans Affairs Office at the University of Arizona.

High school students must have registration form signed by their counselor or principal. If applicant is attending The University of Arizona, the registration form must be signed by the student's Dean or advisor.

Tuition:

$93 per semester hour for college courses. $75 per high school course (½ unit). Tuition and fees are payable in advance. MasterCard and VISA acceptable. Textbooks are not included and may be ordered from the University bookstore. Prices are subject to change without notice. A student must withdraw from a course within 30 days of registration to be eligible for refund. A partial refund will be granted provided no lessons have been submitted and the course study guide is returned in satisfactory condition. A fee will be charged if the study guide is not returned or cannot be used by another student. The same policy applies to a change of course except that a processing fee will also be charged.

Enrollment Period:

Students have nine months from date of registration to complete a course. Because prompt completion of courses is desirable, time extensions are not encouraged. However, a three-month extension may be granted if circumstances justify. Only one extension will be permitted and a time-extension processing fee is charged ($25 for college courses; $20 for high school courses). The minimum period before a final examination will be permitted is 60 days for a 3-credit college course or 6 weeks for a high school course. All lessons must have been corrected and returned to the student before the final exam may be taken.

Credit and Grading:

Credit earned by correspondence study is not considered residence credit at the University of Arizona. Thus, such credit will count toward an undergraduate degree, but the grade received will not be averaged into the cumulative grade point average of the student. Graduate credit is not available for any correspondence course. Letter grades are used. The minimum passing grade is D. The transfer of credit from one institution to another is always optional with the institution to which the credit is being transferred. A student who plans to transfer credit should determine whether this can be done before enrollment in correspondence courses.

Method of examination: Tucson area students take examinations at the Correspondence Office Testing facility on the University of Arizona campus. Students residing outside the Tucson area take examinations in their local communities under the auspices of a proctor arranged by the student and approved by the Extended University Correspondence Department office.

Credit for college courses is granted in semester hours; high school courses in ½ units.

Library Services:

Students are authorized to use the University Library by showing their registration receipt or they may obtain books from the University's interlibrary loan Service.

Accreditations:

North Central Association of Colleges and Schools. Member of: National University Continuing Education Association.

COLLEGE COURSES

ACCOUNTING

Introduction to Financial Accounting

Concepts involved in accounting for assets, liabilities and owner's equity, financial statements. (3 semester hours)

Introduction to Managerial Accounting

Concepts involved in uses of accounting data in the managerial process. (3 semester hours)

AFRICAN AMERICAN STUDIES

Introduction to Black Studies

Introductory survey of the literature, history, culture, and social issues affecting black Americans. (3 semester hours)

AMERICAN INDIAN STUDIES

Introduction to American Indian Studies

Examines diversity of American Indian tribes, successive colonization waves, conflict between Native Americans and colonizing nations. (3 semester hours)

Prehistoric Peoples of the Southwest

Nontechnical discussion of the lifeways of the ancient people of the Southwest. (3 semester hours)

Native Peoples of the Southwest

Nontechnical discussion of Southwestern Indian cultures from historic times to the present. (3 semester hours)

ANATOMY

Human Reproductive Biology

Structure and function of the human reproductive system with emphasis on physiological mechanisms which regulate fertilization, pregnancy, birth, puberty, reproductive control and reproductive senescence. (2 semester hours)

ANIMAL SCIENCE

Feeds and Feeding

Selection, evaluation, and use of feeds for specific purposes; balancing rations for livestock and poultry. (3 semester hours)

ANTHROPOLOGY

Introduction to Physical Anthropology and Archaeology

Basic concepts and methods used by physical anthropologists and archaeologists. (3 semester hours)

Introduction to Cultural Anthropology and Linguistic Anthropology

Basic concepts and methods used by cultural and linguistic anthropologists. (3 semester hours)

Cultural Anthropology

Contemporary theories and methods in use among cultural anthropologists. (3 semester hours)

Prehistoric Peoples of the Southwest

Nontechnical discussion of the lifeways of the ancient people of the Southwest. (3 semester hours)

Native Peoples of the Southwest

Nontechnical discussion of Southwestern Indian cultures from historic times to the present. (3 semester hours)

The Nature of Language

An introduction to the basic concepts of linguistic anthropology and their implications for the study of culture and society. (3 semester hours.

Human Evolution

Neontological and paleontological approaches to human evolution and variation, nonhuman primate studies, biomolecular and anatomical variation, biocultural responses to environmental stress. (3 semester hours)

ASTRONOMY

Essentials of Astronomy

A survey of astronomy, with attention to its interdisciplinary aspects and its relationships to other sciences. (3 semester hours)

ATMOSPHERIC SCIENCE

Introduction to Meteorology and Climatology

An introduction to weather processes and climate, including fronts and cyclones, precipitation processes, the wind systems of the world, severe storms, and weather modification. (3 semester hours)

BOTANY

Introductory Botany

Structure, function, development, and economic importance of flowering plants; brief overview of plant diversity. (3 semester hours)

Plants Useful to Man

Course for teachers and others wishing information on the uses of plants, foods, and food plants, medicinal plants, plants and industry, plants in textiles and other manufacturers. (2 semester hours)

CHINESE STUDIES

Chinese Humanities

Major trends and traditions in the arts, literatures and languages, religions and philosophies of China. (3 semester hours)

History of China

Historical development of China, 750–1900 A.D. (3 semester hours)

Modern Chinese History

Historical survey of the period since 1911 which examines the revolutionary developments shaping contemporary China. (3 semester hours)

EAST ASIAN STUDIES

Asian Religions

Religions of India and the Far East. (3 semester hours)

Modern East Asia: A History

Historical survey of China and Japan during the 19th and 20th centuries, along with the factors that have influenced East Asian countries. (3 semester hours)

ECONOMICS

Principles of Economics

Course 201a. Nature of economics, price theory for the product market, factor prices, international economics. (3 semester hours)

Course 201b. Introduction to the theory of national income and employment, money and banking, economic growth and stabilization. (3 semester hours)

Survey of Economic Thought

Introduction to current economic theory. (3 semester hours)

ENGINEERING

Computer Methods for Engineering

Application of numerical methods and computer programming techniques to the solution of numerical problems of engineering systems. (3 semester hours)

Introduction to Engineering Probability and Statistics

Axioms of probability, discrete and continuous distributions, sampling distributions. Engineering applications of statistical estimation, hypothesis testing, confidence intervals. (3 semester hours)

ENGLISH

Modern Literature

Readings in modern fiction, drama, and poetry. (3 semester hours)

Major American Writers

Intensive study of selected works by major American writers. (3 semester hours)

ENTOMOLOGY

Insects and Society

Introduction to the biology, ecology, and management of insects affecting man and his interests. (3 semester hours)

FAMILY STUDIES

Dynamics of Family Relations

The modern family and its relationships, with emphasis on marriage and interpersonal relationships. (3 semester hours)

Life Span Family Relations

Behavioral science approach to family development through the life span. (3 semester hours)

Family and Consumer Resources

Section 1. Self and the World of Work. The goal of this course is to focus on self-awareness, which is one of the most important steps of career planning. You will learn how to use identity inventories which are designed to sharpen your perceptions of self and the world of work. You will learn how to discover the *real you* by exploring your interests; aptitudes and skills; personal work values; lifestyle prefer-ences; feelings toward work and personality traits. As a result, you will create an ''Identify Snapshot'' of your interests, skills, and values, matched with occupational career choices. (1 semester hour)

Section 2. Realistic Decisions and Career Related Experiences. The importance of decisions, developing career goals, risks and uncertainty; the value of volunteering and interning; graduate school or work; planning for long-term career success; exploring the world of work in the '90s. (1 semester hour)

FRENCH

Elementary French I

Listening, speaking, reading and writing; an introduction to the basic structures and vocabulary of French. This course is divided into two syllabi of two credits each. (4 semester hours)

Elementary French II

Listening, speaking, reading and writing; an introduction to the basic structures of French, continuation. This course is divided into two syllabi of two credits each. (4 semester hours)

Intermediate French I

Continued skill development; reinforcement of basic language skills. This course is divided into two syllabi of two credits each. (4 semester hours)

Intermediate French II

Continued skill development; reinforcement of basic language skills. This course is divided into two syllabi of two credits each. (4 semester hours)

The French Novel and Society

French literature in translation. (3 semester hours)

Existentialism and the Absurd: The French Foundations

French literature in translation. (3 semester hours)

GEOGRAPHY

World Regional Geography

Geographic concepts and information organized by conventional region and nation. (3 semester hours)

GEOLOGY

Introduction to Physical Geology

Earth's materials; surface and internal geologic processes; development of plate tectonics model. (3 semester hours)

Introduction to Geology II

Geologic history of the earth with emphasis on North America; modern concepts on the origin of life and evolution. (3 semester hours)

GERMAN

Elementary German I

This course is divided into two syllabi of two credits each. (4 semester hours)

Elementary German II

This course is divided into two syllabi of two credits each. (4 semester hours)

Intermediate German I

Speaking, understanding, writing, and reading German. This course is divided into two syllabi of two credits each. (4 semester hours)

Intermediate German II

Speaking, understanding, writing, and reading German. This course is divided into two syllabi of two credits each. (4 semester hours)

HEALTH EDUCATION

Personal Health and Wellness

Introduces and analyzes basic personal and community health problems, with emphasis on current scientific information essential to health promotion and maintenance of individual health. (3 semester hours)

School Health Education

Emphasis upon health science information applicable to health education classes; for students preparing to teach in the public schools. (3 semester hours)

International Health Problems

Interprets the major health problems of not only the developed and emerging nations but also the situations in underdeveloped countries; includes assistance programs by international health groups. (3 semester hours)

Safety Education and Accident Prevention

Analysis of accident prevention programs in schools, colleges, communities, and in industry. Emphasis will be placed upon specific protective measures pertaining to athletics, physical education, recreation, highway safety, and vocational training. (3 semester hours)

HISTORY

History of Western Civilization: Backgrounds and Formation to 1648

The western heritage of ideas, values, and artistic expression in interaction with economic, social, and political processes and experiences. (3 semester hours)

History of Western Civilization: Emergence of the Modern World—Since 1648

The western heritage of ideas, values, and artistic expression in interaction with economic, social, and political processes and experiences. (3 semester hours)

History of the United States from 1607 to 1877

Political, economic, and social history of the American people from the founding of colonial Jamestown in 1607 to 1877. (3 semester hours)

History of the United States from 1877 to the Present

Political, economic, and social history of the American people from the end of Reconstruction to the present. (3 semester hours)

History of England to 1603

Survey of English history from pre-history to 1603, with emphasis on legal and constitutional history. (3 semester hours)

History of England from 1603 to the Present

Survey of English history from 1603 to the present, with emphasis on political and social history. (3 semester hours)

The French Revolution and Napoleon

The origins and progress of the Revolution in France. (3 semester hours)

United States: 1945 to Present

American society and the role of the United States in world affairs from the Yalta Conference to the present. (3 semester hours)

History of American Foreign Relations to 1914

Examines the rise of America from a struggling colony to a world class power, including its relations with Europe, Latin America, and Asia. (3 semester hours)

History of American Foreign Relations Since 1914

Examines the pivotal role played by the United States in world affairs since World War I, focusing on America's struggle with revolutionary movements in Europe, Asia, and Latin America. (3 semester hours)

Modern Chinese History

Historical survey of the period since 1911 which examines the revolutionary developments shaping contemporary China. (3 semester hours)

MARKETING

Introduction to Marketing

Role of marketing in the economy and in business and nonprofit organizations; environmental factors affecting marketing; nature of marketing management decisions. (3 semester hours)

Retailing Management

Management of the retail store, its environment, personnel, buying, merchandising, pricing, advertising, promotion, selling, expense control, and customer service. (3 semester hours)

MATHEMATICS

Survey of Mathematical Thought

A study of the nature of mathematics and its role in civilization, utilizing historical approaches and computational examples. (3 semester hours)

Introduction of College Algebra

Basic concepts of algebra, linear equations and inequalities, relations and functions, quadratic equations, system of equations. (3 semester hours)

College Algebra

Brief review and continuation of the above course; functions, mathematical models, systems of equations and inequalities, exponential and logarithmic functions, polynomial and rational functions, sequences and series. (3 semester hours)

Plane Trigonometry

Not applicable to math major or minor. (2 semester hours)

Finite Mathematics

Elements of set theory and counting techniques, probability theory, linear systems of equations, matrix algebra; linear programming with simplex method, Markov chains. (3 semester hours)

Elements of Calculus

Introductory topics in differential and integral calculus. (3 semester hours)

Calculus

Course 125a. Differentiation and integration of elementary functions. Applications to graphing, maximization, areas and volumes, physical problems. (3 semester hours)

Course 125b. A continuation of *Calculus 125a.* (3 semester hours)

Introduction to Ordinary Differential Equations

Solution methods for ordinary differential equations, qualitative techniques; includes matrix methods approach to systems of linear equations and series solutions. (3 semester hours)

Mathematics in Modern Society

The course will examine topics such as voting schemes, apportionment problems, network problems critical paths, Fibonacci numbers, population models, symmetry, fractals data analysis, probability, and statistics. (3 semester hours)

MUSIC

Basic Musicianship

Introduction to the rudiments of musical notation, harmony, rhythm, and melody. (3 semester hours)

Survey of Music I

Introductory course which concentrates on developing perceptual skills through a study of many types of music, with emphasis on Western art music of the 18th, 19th, and 20th centuries, as well as popular and ethnic musics. (3 semester hours)

Survey of Music II

A continuation of the above course, with emphasis on Western art music, particularly that of the Medieval through the Baroque eras, and the music of other cultures. (3 semester hours)

Music in World Cultures

Overview of nonwestern music in selected world cultures. Introduction to music of India, the Arab world, China, Japan, Indonesia, Oceania, Native Americans, Africa, and Latin America. (3 semester hours)

NEAR EAST STUDIES

Middle Eastern Humanities

Major trends and traditions in the arts, literatures and languages, religions and philosophies of the Middle East. (3 semester hours)

Islamic Thought

Traditional ideological systems of Islamic countries and their evolutionary transformations. (3 semester hours)

Indian Civilizations

Survey of traditional and contemporary social, political, and thought patterns of India. (3 semester hours)

PHYSICS

Introductory Physics

Course 102a. Designed for the liberal arts and life science majors with no calculus background. Survey of the basic fields of physics, with emphasis on applications to other fields and historical development. (3 semester hours)

Course 102b. A continuation of the above course. (3 semester hours)

PLANT PATHOLOGY

General Plant Pathology

Detailed study of representative plant diseases, with emphasis on basic concepts of diagnosis, cause, epidemiology, and control. (3 semester hours)

POLITICAL SCIENCE

American National Government

General study of the constitutional bases, organization, and functioning of the American national government; recent and current trends. (3 semester hours)

Introduction to International Relations

Study of the international system, its actors and their capabilities; ends and means of foreign policy; international tension, conflict, and cooperation. (3 semester hours)

American State and Local Government

General study of state and local government; recent and current trends. (3 semester hours)

Arizona Government

Constitution, historical background, theory, structure, powers, interrelationships, and functions of the system of state and local government based upon the Arizona Constitution. Meets the Arizona Constitution requirement for teacher certification. (1 semester unit)

Soviet Foreign Policy

Ends and means of Soviet foreign policy; the decision-making process; Soviet relations with the West and developing nations. (3 semester hours)

Minority Groups and American Politics

Political problems of the poor; analysis of systematic poverty in the U.S. and theories of causation; selected policy problems: education, housing, job training, enforcement of antidiscrimination statutes; future of "power" movements. (3 semester hours)

RECORDS MANAGEMENT

Records/Information Management

Systems of information management; creation, distribution, storage, transfer and disposition of office records; management aspect of establishing information systems and evaluating their efficiency. (3 semester hours)

RENEWABLE NATURAL RESOURCES

Conservation of Natural Resources

Conservation and multiple use of renewable natural resources including forest, watershed, range, wildlife, and recreation; history of forest and range use and its present status. (3 semester hours)

RUSSIAN

Elementary Russian

Course 101a. This course is divided into two syllabi of two credits each. (4 semester hours)

Course 101b. This course is divided into two syllabi of two credits each. (4 semester hours)

SOCIOLOGY

Introduction to Sociology

Sociological concepts and principles with special reference to contemporary society. (3 semester hours)

Sociology of Women

Sociological approach to women's roles in American society, with emphasis on trends and problems relating to sex-role identification and socialization. (3 semester hours)

Minority Relations and Urban Society

Analysis of minority relations and mass movements in urban society; trends in the modern world with special reference to present-day race problems and social conflict. (3 semester hours)

World Population

Basic concepts of population studies; analysis of social trends, problems and solutions in relation to environmental factors with reference to both advanced and developing nations. (3 semester hours)

Sociology of Religion

Religion as a social institution with special reference to industrial societies. (3 semester hours)

American Social Problems

An examination of current theoretical perspectives and research on social problems. (3 semester hours)

Collective Behavior and Social Movements

Study of riots, panics, crazes reform, and revolutionary movements; their origins, social bases, careers, and consequences. (3 semester hours)

Sociology of the Family

Analysis of the modern family and its characteristics in a social and historical setting. (3 semester hours)

Juvenile Delinquency

Nature, causes, and consequences of delinquent behavior. (3 semester hours)

Criminology

Study of the social origins of criminal law, criminal behavior, and reactions to crime. (3 semester hours)

SPANISH

First Semester Spanish

This course is divided into two syllabi of two credits each. (4 semester hours)

Second Semester Spanish

This course is divided into two syllabi of two credits each. (4 semester hours)

Second Year Spanish

Course 201. This course is divided into two syllabi of two credits each. (4 semester hours)

Course 202. This course is divided into two syllabi of two credits each. (4 semester hours)

STATISTICS

Introduction to Statistics

Descriptive statistics. Basic probability concepts and probability distributions, elementary sampling theory and techniques of estimation, hypothesis testing, regression, and correlation. Some analysis of variance and nonparametric tests if time permits. (3 semester hours)

Statistical Methods in Biological Sciences

Organization and summarization of data, concepts of probability, probability distributions of discrete and continuous random variables, point and interval estimation, elements of hypothesis testing, regression and correlation analysis, chi-square distribution and analysis of frequencies, introduction to analysis of variance as well as nonparametric statistics, with special emphasis on analysis of biological and clinical data. (3 semester hours) (3 semester hours)

HIGH SCHOOL COURSES

ACCOUNTING

Elementary Accounting

Course 11a. The total bookkeeping process - terms, recordkeeping, and business transactions. Preparing worksheets and financial statements. (½ unit)

Course 11b. The second half of Course 11a. (½ unit)

BLACK STUDIES

Black Studies

A view of the history and culture of black people in America beginning with a brief glimpse of the great empires of the Sudan and Nile Valley in Africa, and continuing through to the protest generation of Martin Luther King, Jr. The course will cover the growth of slavery as cotton agriculture became the dominant source of Southern wealth, and the racism which developed out of it into a full-blown American ideology. (½ unit)

COMPUTER SCIENCE

Basic Computer Awareness

This one semester course develops an awareness of computer uses in our society and related career opportunities. It introduces students to the operation of a microcomputer and computer programming, and develops understanding of application software. This course provides opportunities for those with or without an available computer. (½ unit)

ENGLISH

English 9a

In the first semester of the freshman year, students read and critique John Steinbeck's *The Pearl* and *The Red Pony.* In writing about the novel and in completing grammar workbook assignments, students develop and reinforce their use of grammar, spelling, vocabulary and punctuation. (½ unit)

English 9b

Students examine selected short stories as improved reading and comprehension techniques are developed. A review of grammar, language structures, sentence patterns, and the modification of the sentence is included in this course. Students will also study *Romeo and Juliet.* (½ unit)

Basic English Skills 9–10

Course 9-10A. Students work to master the concepts of grammar and composition needed to communicate effectively with others. In addition to reading four novels, students will work on grammatical language arts and writing concepts. Comprehensive tests will be turned in with the completed lessons. (½ unit)

Course 9-10 B. This course is a continuation of Basic English Skills 9-10A. Students will read four novels, study sentence structure, capitalization, punctuation, word structure, and vocabulary, and apply these concepts to various composition models. (½ unit)

English 10a

The sophomore year provides students with the opportunity to read and analyze Sir Arthur Conan Doyle's classic of English literature, *The Hound of the Baskervilles,* as well as Mary Shelley's *Frankenstein.* Students continue to improve language skills through in-depth grammar study. (½ unit)

English 10b

This course emphasizes the study of the short story as students examine various elements of the genre, read widely, and discuss their reading through written assignments. Composition studies include the examination of the paragraph and the short essay, with attention to grammar, spelling, punctuation and language usage. (½ unit)

Basic English Skills 11–12

Course 11-12A. The student will study and master the concepts of grammar and composition needed to communicate effectively with others. In addition to reading four short novels, the student will work on grammatical language arts and writing concepts. This will be followed by comprehensive tests which will be turned in with the completed assignments. (½ unit)

Course 11-12B. This course is a continuation of Basic English Skills 11-12A. In addition to reading four novels, the student will study and master sentence structure, capitalization, punctuation, word structure, and vocabulary, and will apply these concepts to various composition models. (½ unit)

English 11a

The first semester of the junior year focuses on the study of the American short story as students further develop their ability to analyze in prose. Students are instructed in writing of clear, concise compositions. Additionally, grammar skills are reinforced through ongoing workbook assignments. (½ unit)

English 11b

This course focuses on the study of the American novel as students read and critique Ernest Hemingway's popular *The Old Man and the Sea.* Students receive practice in writing the expository essay and complete workbook assignments in grammar, punctuation and language usage. (½ unit)

English 11-12 (Vocabulary Study)

A course designed to expand the vocabulary including proper usage, correct methods of adding prefixes and suffixes to root words, and increase confidence in the spelling of difficult words and their derivatives. (½ unit)

English 12a

The senior year provides students with an opportunity for continued development of reading and writing skills through the study of Erich Maria Remarque's *All Quiet on the Western Front,* a novel drawn from German literature. Also included in the course studies is a comprehensive review of grammar and language structures. (½ unit)

English 12b

Language skills are continually developed and refined in this course through the critique of short stories drawn from world literature. Students read widely and write compositions based on their reading. Additionally, a set of workbook assignments will be completed in a comprehensive review of grammar and language structures. (½ unit)

ESL 1A/ESL 1B

This two semester course for the beginning English-as-a-Second Language student will stress vocabulary development using the basic language skills. Each lesson is designed around a thematic unit and will reinforce listening, reading, writing, and speaking skills. (1 unit)

Creative Writing

This course is designed for students who are interested in writing fiction and poetry, and who have attained some degree of proficiency in expository writing. (½ unit)

FAMILY STUDIES

Child Development

Course A. Designed for the junior or senior high school student, or for an adult who wants to learn the steps in the physical, emotional and social, and intellectual development of children through age six. Topics of general interest relating to children, such as prevention of child abuse, choosing a daycare center, effects of a divorce, step-parenting, and helping a child develop self-esteem are also surveyed. Conception through year one is covered in this course. (½ unit)

Course B. A continuation of the above course. Covers years two through year six. (½ unit)

Skills for Living

Preparing a budget; maintaining checking and savings accounts; interest charges; installment loans; purchasing new and used cars; financing; renting apartments; FHA and VA mortgages; life insurance; how to write a resume, complete a job application, dress and prepare for a job interview; getting along on the job; and what an employer looks for in an employee. (½ unit)

GEOGRAPHY

World Geography

Course 10a. World climate, land forms, and vegetation. Special attention to the Northern Hemisphere. Equivalent to the first semester of high school geography. (½ unit)

Course 10b. Relationships between the physical environment and what man does and can do within that physical framework. Special attention to the Southern Hemisphere. Equivalent to the second semester of high school geography. (½ unit)

GOVERNMENT

American Political Process

The American political process. Appraising the system and learning to evaluate how well the system meets the needs of our society. A senior year course. (½ unit)

Arizona Government

Major emphasis begins with the creation of Arizona as a state and proceeds to an examination of the principles and organization of the government. Issues facing the people and political processes in the future. (½ unit)

United States Government

An investigation of the functions and responsibilities of our national government. Special emphasis on the executive, legislative, and judicial branches. (½ unit)

American/Arizona Political Process

It is the intent of this course to provide the student with knowledge of, and encourage participation in the American political process. (½ unit)

United States/Arizona Government

First Semester. Covers the history and development of both the federal and various state constitutions, civil rights legislation according to both federal and state constitutions, and the composition and duties of both the federal congress and the state legislatures. Information particular to the state of Arizona from the Constitution of the State of Arizona supplements the textbook lessons. (½ unit)

Second Semester. Examines the national and state executive and judicial departments. Particular attention is focused on the responsibilities of the President of the United States and his co-members of the Executive Department. Information particular to the state of Arizona from the Constitution of the State of Arizona, Articles V-XXVII, supplements the textbook lessons. (½ unit)

HEALTH

Introduction to Health Science

Introduces and analyzes basic personal and community health problems, with emphasis on current scientific information essential to health promotion and maintenance of individual health. (½ unit)

HISTORY

Arizona History

Arizona from the early Spanish explorations to the future potential of the state. Focus on explorations, geography, politics, and people responsible for the growth of Arizona as a state. The creation of the territory and the quest for statehood. (½ unit)

United States History to 1865

A breakdown survey of the nation's early beginnings from the founding of Jamestown through the era of Reconstruction. (½ unit)

United States History from 1865

A continuation of United States History to 1865, beginning with the early industrialization period to present day America. (½ unit)

World History

Course 11A. Prehistoric culture through Renaissance (1450). (½ unit)

Course 11B. A continuation of the above course. The Age of Exploration beginning in 1450, through the present. (½ unit)

U.S. Arizona History

Course 11C/11D. (1 unit)

World History/Geography

First Semester. Emphasizes how geography influenced history, beginning with selected prehistoric societies, and continuing up to the year 1450. (½ unit)

Second Semester. Covers 1450 through the present. (½ unit)

LATIN

Latin A-1

First year, first semester Latin. (½ unit)

Latin B-1

First year, second semester Latin. (½ unit)

Latin A-2

Second year, first semester Latin. (½ unit)

Latin B-2

Second year, second semester Latin. (½ unit)

MATHEMATICS

General Math

Course 9A. Review of topics covered in arithmetic that are prerequisite for an algebra course. (½ unit)

Course 9B. Continued review of basic arithmetic leading to the study of algebra. (½ unit)

Elementary Algebra

Course 9C. The first semester of high school algebra. Basic work in simple equations, fractions, and factoring. A freshman-level course. (½ unit)

Course 9D. The second semester of high school algebra. For the freshman level of high school. (½ unit)

Plane Geometry

Course 10A. A beginning course in geometry. The study of lines, angles, rectangles, circles, and related figures. Provides an introduction to logical reasoning and precise definitions. (½ unit)

Course 10B. The second semester of beginning geometry. (½ unit)

Plane Trigonometry

The standard material of plane trigonometry as taught at the junior level of high school. (½ unit)

Consumer Mathematics

The bulk of mathematics used in this course is from the foundational field of arithmetic. The student is expected to master any of these skills he or she does not already have at his or her command. In addition, some limited concepts of algebra and geometry will be employed as they relate to the normal consumer activities of life and as they are used in some careers that affect our everyday life. (½ unit)

MUSIC

Music Appreciation I

An introductory music course which concentrates on developing listening skills through the study of musical elements. (½ unit)

Music Appreciation II

This course traces musical history from antiquity to modern times through study and listening to examples. (½ unit)

SCIENCES

Biology

Course 9A. Observation and experiment; measurement; characteristics and organization of life; structure and function of cells; classification of living things. (½ unit)

Course 9B. The second semester of Biology. Structure and function of the human body; genetics; ecology; biomes; humans and the environment. (½ unit)

Basic Earth Science

Course 10A. Study of the earth's matter, oceans and atmosphere, landforms, and changes within the earth. (½ unit)

Course 10B. The second semester of Basic Earth Science. (½ unit)

SOCIAL STUDIES

Free Enterprise

Supply and demand; buying on credit; single proprietorship, partnership, and corporations; job hunting; unions and collective bargaining; taxes and governmental spending; banks and economic growth; foreign trade; types of economic systems. This course satisfies the Arizona requirement of one semester of Free Enterprise for graduation from high school. (½ unit)

Elementary Psychology

Basic concepts of psychology. The study of man and his behavior. (½ unit)

Elementary Sociology

The basic concept of sociology. Principles of human society including the family, groups, and the controls society places upon itself. (½ unit)

Cultures Around the World A

In addition to studying the cultural and political aspects of various regions, the following study skills will be incorporated: map reading, making inferences, constructing a time line, detecting bias, and others. Family life, religion, and art will be covered. Also covered will be Africa, China, Japan, and India. (½ unit)

Cultures Around the World B

A continuation of the above course focusing on Latin America, the Middle East, the Soviet Union, and Western Europe. (½ unit)

SPANISH

Spanish

Course 1A. First year, first semester. (½ unit)

Course 1B. First year, second semester. (½ unit)

Course 2A. Second year, first semester. (½ unit)

Course 2B. Second year, second semester. (½ unit)

VOCATIONAL EDUCATION

Introduction to Auto Body Repair and Painting

Acquaints the student with some of the fundamentals of automotive body repair. Covers all phases of body work and includes everything from painting and refinishing to tips on how to approach your own work of restoration projects. (½ unit)

Introduction to Auto Repair and Service I & II

This is a two-part study of the design, construction, and operation of automotive systems. These courses explore virtually every part of a car and are designed for budding professionals as well as do-it-yourselfers. (1 unit)

Vocational/Technical/Career Math

Provides the student with a handbook of basic math for various occupations. Using actual math examples, eight different occupational categories (covering a total of 150 different occupations) are considered. (½ unit)

NONCREDIT COURSES

ART

Art Basics

The elements of art will be explored—line, texture, color, shape, value, and space. These elements are continuously explored when artwork is being produced. Most activities will be executed on paper using a variety of art materials. Some techniques will be introduced. Though some drawing is involved, this is not a drawing course, but an introduction to the essentials of artwork. (Noncredit) *Tuition:* $65; no textbook required.

AUTOMOBILE REPAIR

Everything You Ever Wanted to Know About Car Repair, But Were Afraid to Ask

Learn how you can save money on routine car maintenance and repairs, and feel more secure driving on Arizona's highways. This course provides new and experienced drivers with step-by-step instructions and clear illustrations covering the most common areas of maintenance and repair, including tires, underhood, general and preventative maintenance, emergency tips, tools to carry along, and detailing. (Noncredit) *Tuition:* $65; no textbook required.

Ford Mustang 1964½—1973: A Survey of Ford's Original Ponycar

This introductory course is designed for enthusiasts of all ages and for those wishing to learn more about the Mustang hobby. Material to be covered includes the history, recognition, and proper use for Ford's first generation Mustang, and buying and maintenance tips. Also included will be a current bluebook value guide. (Noncredit) *Tuition:* $65 plus textbook.

CALLIGRAPHY

Learning Calligraphy

Learn the ancient art of calligraphy (beautiful writing) in this specially created correspondence course. Beginners receive clear, concise instruction in italic-style lower and uppercase letterforms, with stroke sequence techniques of each letter given in detail. (Noncredit) *Tuition:* $60; no textbook required.

HORTICULTURE

Plants and Microorganisms

Ambiotic relationships established by higher plants with other plant species, with fungi, with bacteria, and with several other microorga-nisms, are the subject of this course. Among the important plant associations between their roots, leaves, or seeds are mycorrhizal fungi, nitrogen-fixing bacteria, and several other forms of microscopic flora and fauna. Students will examine some of these associations and their utility in human affairs. (Noncredit) *Tuition:* $60; reference books can be obtained at public libraries.

MUSEUM STUDIES

Introduction to Museum Work

This fundamental course in museum studies deals with museology: the theory, philosophy, organization, and functioning of museums. (Noncredit) *Tuition:* $60 plus textbook.

Focus on Museums' Collections

This essential course in museum studies is concerned with the most fundamental activities of museums: the collecting, preserving, and recording of carefully selected objects, and related matters. It also examines carefully the position and work of the registrar, the person directly in charge of the collections. (Noncredit) *Tuition:* $60; textbook required.

MUSIC

Great Composers

Comparison and contrast of great composers of various periods: Baroque—Bach and Handel; Classical—Mozart and Beethoven; Romantic—Wagner and Brahms; 20th century—Stravinsky and Schoenberg. (Noncredit) *Tuition:* $65; four audiotapes included.

Rock and Roll to Heavy Metal: A History

Explore the elements and sources of rock as well as how to listen to it. Numerous styles and types of rock will be studied, beginning with pre-Bill Haley, and including Elvis Presley, the Beatles, folk-rock, country-rock, jazz-rock, funk, disco, heavy metal, punk, new wave, and sounds of the 1980s. (Noncredit) *Tuition:* $60 plus textbook.

Introduction to the Recording Arts

This is a course designed to expose you to some of the language and devices used to record most everything in the audio realm. You will explore capturing sound onto tape, and some of the knowledge required of a recording engineer. (Noncredit) *Tuition:* $50 plus textbook.

PERSONAL DEVELOPMENT

Weight Control

Learn to eat sparingly, properly, and only at mealtimes with the help of hypnosis. This is a very positive program—no scare tactics or aversion techniques. These tapes deal with confidence, self-image, motivation for exercise, diminishing your appetite, and your appestate. With proper application of these tapes, you will learn how to control your appetite so that you can lose weight easily, effortlessly, and permanently. (Noncredit) *Tuition:* $35; no textbook required.

How to Prepare and Deliver a Dynamite Presentation

Develop your presentation skills in the privacy of your own home or office through an audio cassette seminar featuring interviews with six top professional speakers. This course is presented in ten thirty minute modules. You will have the opportunity to put the lessons into practice by recording your own presentation and having it critiqued by the instructor. (Noncredit) *Tuition:* $99; no textbook required.

Getting a Job in Today's Changing Market

Topics include: what makes you employable; preparation for the interview; resumes/cover letters; finding the job you want; job search strategies; interviewing tips before, during, and after. (Noncredit) *Tuition:* $65; no textbook required.

Color Yourself

Take the guesswork out of looking your best. You will discover what colors are best suited for your skin tone, hair, and eye color. Gain practical advice on putting these colors to use in your day-to-day wardrobe, as well as on how to buy clothes that complement your body type. (Noncredit) *Tuition:* $45; includes course guide; an optional 45-color swatch is available for and additional $20.

REAL ESTATE

Risk Management

Analysis of a logical and systematic approach to uncertainty regarding real estate loss; the identification, analysis, and evaluation of risk and the selection of the most advantageous method of treating it. (Noncredit) *Tuition:* $65 plus textbook.

SPANISH

Beginning Conversational Spanish

Learn to purchase travel tickets, go through customs, take a taxi, register in a hotel, bargain in a marketplace, etc. *Tuition:* $99; no textbook required.

STUDY SKILLS

Improving Study Techniques

Positive hypnotic reinforcement can teach you to relax and clear your mind in order to memorize material more effectively and efficiently. This program of three tapes allows a more solid comprehension of materials studied and can enable the mind to retain information and recall it when necessary. (Noncredit) *Tuition:* $40; no textbook required.

WRITING

Creative Writing

This course is designed for those who are interested in writing fiction and poetry. You will write character sketches, plot situations, and complete short stories, in addition to narratives, poetry, and one-act plays. Utilizing a series of structured and non-structured situations, you will learn to cultivate an individual writing style which will allow you to develop your writing talents to a higher degree. (Noncredit) *Tuition:* $60 plus textbook.

Arizona State University
College of Extended Education
Independent Study by Correspondence
404 Farmer Education Building
Tempe, Arizona 85287-1811   (800) 533-4806

Description:
The Territorial Normal School of Arizona opened its doors in February 1886 in a four-room building and with an enrollment of 33 students. In the intervening years the school has experienced successive changes in scope, name, and governance. In 1958, the present name was adopted.

College credit correspondence courses are specifically designed for the student unable to attend classes in person, and are offered for those seeking to fulfill degree objectives as well as for those who wish to increase their professional and intellectual skills.

Faculty:
Shari I. Westbrook, Administrative Associate, Independent Study by Correspondence. There is a faculty of 40.

Academic Levels:
College

Degree/Certificate Programs:
Up to 30 correspondence credits may be applied toward the Bachelor degree.

Admission Requirements:
High school diploma or GED.

Tuition:
$77 per credit hour. Prices subject to change without notice and usually on an annual basis. Refund within 60 days if student withdraws minus a $25 processing fee and a per lesson charge of $4 for each lesson submitted and graded.

Enrollment Period:
The maximum time to complete a course is one year. A six-month extension may be permitted with payment of a $25 extension fee.

Equipment Requirements:
Textbooks are not included in tuition and must be purchased by the student; they are available from the university bookstore. Some courses require the use of audio tapes.

Credit and Grading:
Letter grades are used with "A" being the highest and "E" being failure; minimum passing grade is "D." Examinations must be proctored. Credit is awarded in semester hour units.

Accreditations:
North Central Association of Colleges and Schools. Member of: National University Continuing Education Association.

COLLEGE COURSES

BUSINESS ADMINISTRATION

Business Communications

Written and oral reporting. Organization, analysis, and presentation of business information, using electronic and other media. (3 semester hours)

Fundamentals of Management Communication

Intrapersonal, interpersonal, and administrative communication within management contexts. (3 semester hours)

Business Report Writing

Organization and preparation of reports incorporating electronic databases, word processing, and graphics. (3 semester hours)

Business Law

Legal and ethical aspects of agency, partnerships, corporations, bankruptcy, antitrust, securities, and other regulations of business. (3 semester hours)

Management and Organizational Behavior

Administrative, organizational, and behavioral theories and functions of management, contributing to the effective and efficient accomplishment of organizational objectives. (3 semester hours)

COMMUNICATIONS

Elements of Intercultural Communication

Basic concepts, principles, and skills for improving communication between people from different minority, racial, ethnic, and cultural backgrounds. (3 semester hours)

Gender and Communication

Introduction to gender-related communication. Verbal, nonverbal, and paralinguistic differences and similarities are examined within social, psychological, and historic perspectives. (3 semester hours)

Intercultural Communication Theory and Research

Survey and analysis of major theories and research dealing with communication between people of different cultural backgrounds, primarily in international settings. (3 semester hours)

Crisis Communication

Role of communication in crisis development and intervention. (3 semester hours) and provide various coping strategies. (3 semester hours)

Communication and Aging

Critical study of changes in human communicative patterns through the later adult years, with attention on intergenerational relationships and self-concept functions. (3 semester hours)

Medical Communication

The role of communication in the medical field; doctor-patient, doctor-staff, and staff-patient relationships; technical communication problems in the medical field. (3 semester hours)

CRIMINAL JUSTICE

The Justice System

Overview of the criminal justice system. Roles of law enforcement personnel, the courts, and correctional agencies. Philosophical and theoretical views on historical perspective. (3 semester hours)

Concepts and Issues of Justice

Issues relating to justice policies, perspectives, techniques, roles, institutional arrangements, management, uses of research, and innovative patterns. (3 semester hours)

American Indian Justice

This course explores critical and controversial issues related to American Indian experiences with white American justice. It also addresses topics such as cultural survival, tribal sovereignty, and law. (3 semester hours)

Research in Justice Studies

Focus is on developing and evaluating research designs, data collection, and the relationship between validity and reliability. Methods for conducting research are also stressed. (3 semester hours)

The Police Function

Alternative objectives, strategies, programs, institutional arrangements, roles, perspectives, and interagency relationships of the police. (3 semester hours)

The Adjudication Function

History and development of courts, trial by jury, and other dispute resolution mechanisms; selection and removal of judges and juries; organization, structure, and jurisdiction of courts; trial and nontrial processes of the judiciary. (3 semester hours)

Prevention of Delinquent and Criminal Behavior

Theories of prevention, individual, group and community approaches; intervention at appropriate stages; contemporary law enforcement and corrections practices. (3 semester hours)

Community Relations in the Justice System

Focus on developing an informed plan and policy for incorporating research findings about the surrounding community within various justice services and agencies. Topics include social stratification, minority groups, and victimology. (3 semester hours)

Substantive Criminal Law

Criminal liability. Crimes against person, property, and society. Governmental sanctions of individual conduct as formulated by legislatures and the courts. (3 semester hours)

Procedural Criminal Law

The criminal process. Constitutional and legal problems associated with arrest, search and seizure, and due process of law. (3 semester hours)

EDUCATION

Successful Recareering

Vocational changes available through recareering. Based on case studies, the course is geared to those contemplating a career change or directors, trainers or paraprofessionals who work with adults seeking career change. (3 semester hours)

Understanding Educational Administration

Examination of the legal, professional, and organizational bases of schools to gain an understanding of the role of the administrator in the teaching process. Intended for lay persons interested in education, such as school board and task force members. (3 semester hours)

Elementary School Organization and Management

Overall program of the elementary school. Practical approaches to discipline and to planning, organizing, and managing the classroom. (3 semester hours)

Home-School Relations

Develops students' personal philosophies regarding the role of school personnel, especially the teacher, in home-school relationships. Methods of working effectively with parents. (3 semester hours)

FAMILY RELATIONS

Marriage and Family Relationships

Issues, challenges, and opportunities relating to present-day family living. Factors influencing interrelations within the family. (3 semester hours)

FINE ARTS

Art of the Western World I

History of Western art from the Paleolithic period through the Middle Ages. (3 semester hours)

Art of the Western World II

History of Western art from the Renaissance to the present. (3 semester hours)

Western American Art

A critical study of themes in western American art from 1800 to 1940. (3 semester hours)

FRENCH

Elementary French

FRE 101. Basic structure and vocabulary of French through reading and writing the language. (4 semester hours)

FRE 102. A continuation of the above course. (4 semester hours)

Intermediate Grammar Review

A thorough review of French grammar, including full attention to literary usage. (4 semester hours)

Intermediate Reading

Extensive reading in 19th and 20th century literary and cultural texts. Designed to increase the student's vocabulary and to teach prompt recognition of stylistic usages and grammatical structures. (4 semester hours)

French Literature

FRE 321. Representative masterpieces and significant movements of French literature of the middle ages through the 18th century. (3 semester hours)

FRE 322. Literature of the 19th and 20th centuries. (3 semester hours)

GERMAN

Elementary German

GER 101. Basic introduction to German. Covers the grammatical cases of nouns and pronouns, essential word order in main and subordinate clauses, usage of prepositions, and formation of the imperative and present and present perfect tenses of verbs. (4 semester hours)

GER 102. Completes the introduction to German begun in the above course and deals with modal auxiliary verbs, the past and past perfect tenses of verbs, the passive voice and subjunctive usage of verbs; adjective endings, relative pronouns, da- and wo- compounds, and time expressions. (4 semester hours)

Intermediate German

GER 201. An intensive review of grammar practices in reading and translating modern German prose. (4 semester hours)

GER 202. Concludes the second year sequence with a continuation of the grammar review and further practice in the reading and translating of modern German prose. (4 semester hours)

HISTORY

The United States

HIS 103. American history from colonial times through the Civil War period. (3 semester hours)

HIS 104. Growth of the Republic from the Civil War period to the present day. (3 semester hours)

Introduction to Japan

Historical survey of the people, culture, politics, and economy of Japan. (3 semester hours)

Asian Civilizations

The civilizations of China, Japan, and India as well as Southeast Asia. (3 semester hours)

Contemporary America

The United States from 1945 to the present. (3 semester hours)

The United States and Japan

Cultural, political and economic relations in the 19th and 20th centuries, with emphasis on the post-World War II period. (3 semester hours)

Japan

HIS 477. Political, economic, social, and cultural history of the Japanese people. Course covers from early times to the 19th century. (3 semester hours)

HIS 478. Political, economic, social, and cultural history of the Japanese people. Covers the 19th century to the present. (3 semester hours)

ITALIAN

Elementary Italian

ITA 101. Basic grammar supplemented by simple prose readings. (4 semester hours)

ITA 102. A continuation of the above course. (4 semester hours)

Intermediate Italian

ITA 201. Intensive review of the fundamentals of Italian grammatical structure to increase the student's ability in composition, translation, and idiomatic expression. (4 semester hours)

ITA 202. A continuation of the above course. (4 semester hours)

MATHEMATICS

Intermediate Algebra

Topics from basic algebra such as linear equations, polynomials, factoring, exponents, roots, and radicals. (3 semester hours)

College Algebra

Linear and quadratic functions, systems of linear equations, logarithmic and exponential functions, sequences, series, and combinatorics. (3 semester hours)

Finite Mathematics

Topics from linear algebra, linear programming, combinatorics, probability, and mathematics of finance. (3 semester hours)

Precalculus

Intensive preparation for calculus. Topics include functions (including trigonometric), matrices, polar coordinates, vectors, complex numbers and mathematical induction. (3 semester hours)

Brief Calculus

Differential and integral calculus of elementary functions with applications. (3 semester hours)

POLITICAL SCIENCE

Public Policy Development

Relationships between policy development and administrative processes as affected by the various roles of legislative bodies, executive, and administrative agencies. (3 semester hours)

American National Government

Powers, functions, and agents of American political institutions. Meets the federal government requirement for teacher certification. (3 semester hours)

Arizona Constitution and Government

Constitution and government of the State of Arizona. Meets Arizona government requirement for teacher certification. (2 semester hours)

PSYCHOLOGY

Introduction to Psychology

Major areas of theory and research in psychology. (3 semester hours)

Personality Theory and Research

Definition and description of personality in terms of theoretical and methodological approaches. (3 semester hours)

Abnormal Psychology

Historical and current definitions, theory, and research concerning abnormal behavior. Major categories of psychopathology including related treatment approaches. (3 semester hours)

SOCIOLOGY

Introduction to Sociology

Fundamentals of sociology, organization of human groups and society, processes of interaction and social change. (3 semester hours)

Courtship and Marriage

An overview of courtship, marriage, and related processes, focusing on problematical aspects of these institutions from the sociological perspective. (3 semester hours)

Sociology of Work

Social and cultural analysis of industry. Occupational roles, status, and social participation of workers. (3 semester hours)

Sociology of Deviant Behavior

A sociological analysis of stigmatized behaviors and conditions, including the causes, effects, and management of stigma. (3 semester hours)

Women's Roles

Sociological analysis of the development, nature, and consequences of traditional and alternative roles of women in contemporary society. (3 semester hours)

SPANISH

Elementary Spanish

SPA 101. Basic fundamentals of the language. (4 semester hours)

SPA 102. A continuation of the above course. (4 semester hours)

Intermediate Spanish

SPA 201. Intensive review of fundamentals plus composition and reading. (4 semester hours)

SPA 202. A continuation of the above course. (4 semester hours)

SPEECH AND HEARING SCIENCE

Introduction to Speech and Hearing Science

The normative and disordered process of human communication. (3 semester hours)

Introduction to Phonetics

An introduction to English phonetics with emphasis on phonetic transcription, articulation, phonology, and disorders of speech. (3 semester hours)

Sketching Skills for Speech Clinicians

Simple sketching skills for preparing more effective visual materials both before and during therapy sessions. Ideas are presented to help incorporate sketching skills as part of the therapy process. (1 semester hour)

Nature of Fluency Disorders

History and nature of fluency disorders. (2 semester hours)

Arkansas, University of
Department of Independent Study
Division for Continuing Education
2 University Center
Fayetteville, Arkansas 72701   (800) 638-1217

Description:

The University of Arkansas is a state-controlled coeducational university. It was established as a land-grant institution in 1871 to provide the finest educational opportunities to all students, regardless of race, color, or creed.

Faculty:

Gary McHenry, Director, Department of Independent Study.

Academic Levels:

College
High School

Degree/Certificate Programs:

The University of Arkansas does not offer a degree entirely by correspondence. Under normal circumstances, a student may apply no more than 30 semester hours of correspondence credit toward a degree at the University.

Admission Requirements:

There are no specific entrance requirements. Formal admission to the University of Arkansas is not required of a student who takes course by correspondence and acceptance for correspondence study does constitute admission to the University. A student may enroll at any time.

Tuition:

For residents of Arkansas, tuition is $45 per semester hour for college courses and $50 per half unit for high school courses. For non-resident students, tuition is $50 per semester hour for college courses and $55 per half unit for high school courses. An additional postage fee of $5 per course is charged which covers the cost of all returned lessons, books, and materials. Postage charges are nonrefundable. Students must pay postage on all lessons and materials that he/she mails to the Department of Independent Study. Students living outside the United States should use airmail only. A refund of 75 percent of the tuition on credit courses will be made if the student withdraws from a course and requests the refund in writing within 30 days of his/her official enrollment date. If any lessons have been submitted during the 30 day period, a deduction of $5 per lesson will be charged against the 75 percent refund amount. There are no refunds for noncredit courses. Additional course materials charges and workbook charges are added to the cost of the course. Some courses have added charges for audiocassettes. For information on fees for noncredit courses for which CEUs are awarded, contact the Independent Study Office.

Enrollment Period:

The enrollment period for each course is 6 months from the date of enrollment. If a minimum of one third of lesson assignments has not been turned in by the end of a 60 day period after the date of enrollment, the student may be dropped from the course without any refund of fees. The minimum time in which a course can be completed depends on the amount of credit and the number of assignments involved. As a general rule, assignments in college courses may be submitted at a rate no greater than 3 lessons per course per week (a week is any 7-day period). A 6-month extension of course time may be granted and if approved, a charge of $40 per college course or $25 per high school course will be assessed plus an additional book rental fee on each textbook.

Equipment Requirements:

Textbooks used in most of the courses offered by the Department of Independent Study may be rented directly from the Department. Rental charges for each course are based on the number and replacement costs of the textbooks. Textbooks are rented for 6-month periods only. Some courses will require the use of a cassette player to be supplied by the student.

Credit and Grading:

It is the responsibility of students to know before enrollment whether courses taken through the Department of Independent Study will be accepted for credit by their own institutions or certifying agency. Instructors may use letter grades, number grades, or S (satisfactory) and U (unsatisfactory) to indicate the quality of work. The mark INC means that a lesson is either incomplete or for some reason unacceptable and that it must be appropriately modified and re-submitted before a grade will be assigned. In most courses, credit is based wholly on the grade made on the supervised examinations. If a student makes a grade of F on the final examination, the student will not be awarded credit for the course. All Arkansas residents must take examinations at one of the official exam centers. Nonresidents must arrange to have the examination supervised by an appropriate official (dean, registrar, director of testing, or director of continuing education) at any college or university. High school course examinations will be supervised by the principal or counselor of the school being attended. Credit is awarded in semester hour units for college level courses and one-half units for high school level courses. Students who take noncredit courses may earn continuing education units (CEUs) if the courses are successfully completed. One CEU is defined as the equivalent of 10 contact hours of participation in a continuing education course.

Accreditations:

North Central Association of Colleges and Schools. Member of: National University Continuing Education Association.

COLLEGE COURSES

ACCOUNTING
Principles of Accounting I
Fundamentals of data collection, classification, and interpretation. Includes preparation and analysis of financial statements. (3 semester hours)
Principles of Accounting II
Fundamentals of data collection, classification, and interpretation. Includes preparation and analysis of financial statements and uses of data for resources allocation and production decisions within the firm. (3 semester hours)

AGRICULTURE
Principles of Agricultural Economics
Deals with the principles of economics as applied to the business of farming. (3 semester hours)
Principles of Genetics
Gives the student a nontechnical introduction to the study of heredity in animals. (3 semester hours)

ANTHROPOLOGY
Introduction to Cultural Anthropology
An introduction to the nature of culture and its influence on human behavior and personality. (3 semester hours)
Indians of North America
A survey of the Indians of North America, including Mexico and Yucatan. (3 semester hours)

BOTANY
General Botany
An elementary treatment of the fundamental principles and concepts of botany. (3 semester hours)
Plant Geography
The geographical distribution of plants and their relation to ecology and to commercial botany. (3 semester hours)

BUSINESS
Legal Environment of Business
Introduction to the legal environment of business. Topics covered in this survey course include: foundations of the American legal system, including business ethics and corporate social responsibility; the regulatory and competitive environment of business, including labor and employment law; and private law affecting business, including contracts, agency, and the law of business organizations. (3 semester hours)

COMMUNICATIONS
Basic Course in the Arts: Film Lecture
Introduction to film as entertainment and art. How to look at film through a study of composition, lighting, editing, sound, acting. (3 semester hours)
Parliamentary Procedure
The basic principles and rules of parliamentary procedure. (1 semester hour)
Television Writing
Comprehensive analysis of the techniques and styles for television

commercials, PSAs, and investigative documentaries. (3 semester hours)

CRIMINAL JUSTICE

Introduction to Criminal Justice I

A survey of the field of law enforcement. Local, state, and federal systems, police organizations, problems, and functions. (3 semester hours)

Introduction to Criminal Justice II

A survey of the field of correction, from conviction and sentencing through confinement to release into the community. (3 semester hours)

DRAMA

Introduction to Dramatic Art

An introduction to the drama, history, theory, and practice of the theatre, from ancient to modern times. (3 semester hours)

History of the Theatre III

An exploration of the dominant theatrical modes which flourished from 1850 to the present. Emphasis on the key playwrights, directors, and producers who shaped the period. Representative plays included. (3 semester hours)

ECONOMICS

Economic Development of the United States

Development of American economic institutions from Colonial times to the present. Survey of present-day economic institutions and problems. (3 semester hours)

Principles of Macroeconomics

Macroeconomic analysis including aggregate employment, income, fiscal and monetary policy, growth, and business cycle. (3 semester hours)

Principles of Microeconomics

Microeconomic analysis including market structures, supply and demand, production costs, price and output, international economics. (3 semester hours)

ELEMENTARY EDUCATION

Children's Literature

Required reading and study of books for children, together with a study of authors and illustrations of children's books and the carrying on of various activities in connection with the sharing of books read. (3 semester hours)

Teaching Science

Purposes, curriculum, and techniques of teaching science. A course designed to provide optimal curriculum and instructional strategies for teaching science to children in the elementary school. An inquiry hands-on approach utilizing the processes of science with ordinary easy to get materials that provide everyday examples of science concepts and principles will be emphasized. (3 semester hours)

Teaching Mathematics

Professional course in arithmetic for elementary school teachers. (3 semester hours)

Teaching Reading: Primary to Emergent and Developmental Literature

This course focuses on teaching readiness and developmental reading in pre-kindergarten, kindergarten, and grades one through three including diagnostic teaching. (3 semester hours)

ENGINEERING

Engineering Statistics

Fundamentals of probability and distribution theory with applications to various branches of engineering; experimental procedures and sample size; statistical decision theory including significance testing and estimation. (3 semester hours)

ENGLISH

Composition

1013. A study of the general principles and practices of composition and the application of these through the experiences of reading and writing. (3 semester hours)

1023. A continuation of the above course. A larger number of original compositions required. (3 semester hours)

Vocabulary Building

A developmental course designed to increase the student's vocabulary and thereby improve his/her reading comprehension and writing. Some attention is given to pronunciation and spelling. (3 semester hours)

Essay Writing

For the nontechnical student who wishes to improve his/her written English but who is not particularly interested in the art of creative writing. (3 semester hours)

English Literature from the Beginning to 1798

(3 semester hours)

English Literature from 1798 to the Present

(3 semester hours)

Intermediate Composition

(3 semester hours)

ENVIRONMENTAL SCIENCE

Environmental Science

Series of discussions and readings introducing the topic of environmental science including factors related to water, soil, and air quality. (3 semester hours)

FRENCH

Elementary French

1003. A beginning course in the essentials of French grammar and introduction to the reading of simple narrative style. (3 semester hours)

1013. A continuation of the study of essential French grammar and introduction to the reading of simple narrative style. (3 semester hours)

Intermediate French

2003. Completes the introduction of basic French grammar and develops reading and writing skills. (3 semester hours)

2013. Further develops the student's ability to read and write French through the study of several modern French literary works. (3 semester hours)

Ph.D. Reading Requirement

A rapid course in the fundamentals of French for advanced students who do not desire to follow the usual curriculum but who need to acquire a practical reading knowledge of French in the shortest possible time. (3 semester hours)

Advanced Grammar and Composition

Strengthens the student's knowledge of French grammar and develops capability for written expression. (3 semester hours)

French Civilization

A study of France's behavioral pattern as seen in its present lifestyle and in its social, political, economical, judicial, and educational institutions. (3 semester hours)

GEOGRAPHY

Physical Geography

The physical or natural factors in man's environment with emphasis on landforms and climate. (3 semester hours)

Human Geography

A basic course dealing with the field and function of geography. (3 semester hours)

Emerging Nations

Survey of problems, development potential, and physical and human resources of the developing world. Aerial coverage includes Latin America, Africa, Middle East, and Monsoon Asia. (3 semester hours)

Developed Nations

Survey of the human and physical resources and the problems of the developed world. Aerial coverage includes Europe, Anglo-America, the former USSR, Japan, and Australia. (3 semester hours)

Conservation of Natural Resources

A study of the theory and growth of conservation and the wise use of the major natural resources of the United States. (3 semester hours)

Geography of the U.S. and Canada

The geography of the United States and its northern neighbor, Canada. (3 semester hours)

GERMAN

Elementary German

1003. 1st semester. An introduction to the basic elements of German grammar with emphasis on the skills of reading and writing the language. The practical vocabulary, dialogues, and reading passages will also impart insights into German culture and into cultural differences between German-speaking countries and the United States. (3 semester hours)

1013. 2nd semester. A continuation of Course 1003. (3 semester hours)

Intermediate German

2003. 3rd semester. A thorough review of the fundamentals of German grammar with an expanded vocabulary and more advanced reading. The practical exercises and the cultural reader will better enable the student to understand life in the German-speaking countries today. (3 semester hours)

2013. 4th semester. A continuation of Course 2003. (3 semester hours)

Ph.D. Reading Requirement

A rapid course in the fundamentals of German for advanced students who do not desire to follow the usual curriculum but who need to acquire a practical reading knowledge of German in the shortest possible time. (3 semester hours)

German Civilization

From pre-historic times to the present. (3 semester hours)

HEALTH EDUCATION

Personal Health and Safety

A study of personal health problems with emphasis on protection and promotion of individual health and safety. (3 semester hours)

Introduction to Human Sexuality

An examination of human sexuality with a critical analysis of male and female attitudes and values affecting self-understanding and gender identity. (3 semester hours)

Teaching Drug Education

Designed specifically for educators, provides an overview of drugs of use, misuse, and abuse in society. This course also assists the educator in developing a sequential drug education program in public, private, or community educational settings. This course challenges educators to consider the complex nature of prevention and implement comprehensive education/prevention programs in various community educational settings. The course emphasizes planning and teaching activities for practical application. (3 semester hours)

HISTORY

History of the American People to 1877

(3 semester hours)

History of the American People 1877 to Present

(3 semester hours)

History of the American Indian

Survey of American Indian history from European contact to present. Emphasis will be upon tribal reaction to white society and U.S. governmental policy. (3 semester hours)

African American History

Blacks in the United States from the rise of the slave trade and the plantation system through emancipation and up to the present, with emphasis, in recent decades on the rise of the ghetto, ideologies, institutional developments, and the protest movements. (3 semester hours)

Arkansas and the Southwest

Political, economic, social, and cultural development of Arkansas from the coming of the Indian to the twentieth century, with special emphasis on Arkansas as a national and regional component. (3 semester hours)

Colonial America to 1763

Political, economic, and social history of Anglo-America from the founding of Jamestown to the end of the American Revolution. (3 semester hours)

HOME ECONOMICS

Nutrition in Health

A study of the functions of food, body processes, optimum diets, in relation to health and physical fitness. (3 semester hours)

JOURNALISM

Introduction to Mass Communications

A survey of mass media (newspapers, radio, TV, magazine, advertising, public relations, photography, etc.) which stresses the importance of communication agencies in today's society and introduces the student to the various areas of professional work in journalism. (3 semester hours)

Journalistic Style and Usage

A course designed to introduce basic journalistic writing styles and techniques, to reinforce standard grammar rules and to acquaint students with Associated Press style (conventions of punctuation, spelling, etc. used in many mass media enterprises). (3 semester hours)

LATIN

Introduction to Latin Poetry

Rome's greatest epic poem is studied in terms of translation, poetic style, and literary importance. The student will translate from Latin into English selections from the first six books. In addition, the student will read the entire poem in English, learn to scan the poetic meter (dactylic hexameter) and develop an appreciation for the *Aeneid*'s contribution to the people of ancient Rome as well as to people of all ages. (3 semester hours)

MANAGEMENT

Introduction to Business

A survey of the organization, principles, and practices of the business world. Provides a general view of the field as a whole and serves as a foundation for specialized courses. (3 semester hours)

Business Communications

Emphasis on applying and understanding principles of writing and oral communication as applied to the management process. (3 semester hours)

MATHEMATICS

Math Patterns

Terminal course in mathematics for nonscience students. Deals in a general way with some of the major themes of modern mathematics without emphasis on manipulation techniques. (3 semester hours)

College Algebra

(3 semester hours)

Plane Trigonometry

(3 semester hours)

Finite Mathematics

Selected topics in probability, vectors and matrices, linear programming. (3 semester hours)

Calculus I

(5 semester hours)

Calculus II

(5 semester hours)

Calculus III

(3 semester hours)

MICROBIOLOGY

Microorganisms in Human Affairs

Basic concepts of microbiology are presented and particular emphasis is made on microorganisms that are pathogenic for mankind. (3 semester hours)

PHILOSOPHY

Introduction to Philosophy

A definition of basic philosophical concepts and a consideration of their relation to science, art, and religion. (3 semester hours)

Introduction to Ethics

Basic concepts of moral philosophy; historical perspective and logical thinking on the theory of the good, principles of rights and obligations, including both theoretical and practical issues. (3 semester hours)

Logic

Traditional and modern methods of deductive and inductive inference. (3 semester hours)

PHYSICAL EDUCATION

Methods and Materials in Physical Education for Elementary Schools

Program planning and techniques of teaching physical education activities on the elementary school level. (3 semester hours)

Organization and Administration of Physical Education

Plans of organization, administrative policies, budget and finance, legal aspects, staff, physical plant, publicity and public relations, time schedules, student leaders, and programs. (3 semester hours)

Measurement Concepts in Kinesiology

The theory of measurement in physical education, the selection and administration of appropriate tests, and the interpretation of their results by fundamental statistical procedures. (3 semester hours)

POLITICAL SCIENCE

American National Government

A survey of the basic ideas, structures, and political processes of the national government of the United States. (3 semester hours)

State and Local Government

Organization and function of the state and local governments in the United States, intergovernmental relations, administration, adjudication, and the organization and function of political parties on state and local levels. (3 semester hours)

PSYCHOLOGY

General Psychology

A comprehensive introduction to the psychological behavior of humans. (3 semester hours)

Social Psychology

Introduction to the problems, theories, and experiments of social psychology. (3 semester hours)

Abnormal Psychology

An analysis of the factors that interfere with the development of normal personality traits. (3 semester hours)

Infancy and Early Childhood

Psychological factors influencing development from the prenatal period through five years of age. Emphasizes interaction of heredity and environmental influences on personality, perception, learning, motivation, cognition, and socialization. Focuses on infant and pre-school age child. (3 semester hours)

Psychology of Business and Industry

Application of psychological principles to the problems of business and industry with emphasis upon employee morale and attitudes, labor turnover, industrial relations, safety, fatigue, etc. (3 semester hours)

Childhood and Adolescence

Psychological factors influencing development from six years through adolescence. Emphasizes the interaction of heredity and environment particularly as they influence cognition, motivation, perception, learning, emotion, and personality of the school age child and adolescent. (3 semester hours)

Exceptional Children

The psychological problems of children whose behavior deviates from that of normal children. (3 semester hours)

Adulthood and Aging

Psychological factors occurring from young adulthood through old age. Emphasis on cognitive, personality, physical, and psychological characteristics. (3 semester hours)

Educational Psychology

Psychological theories and concepts applied to the educational process. Investigates the learner and instructional variables in a wide range of educational settings. (3 semester hours)

Psychological Tests

The nature and theory of the individual and group tests of intelligence, personality, interests, and attitudes. (3 semester hours)

SECONDARY EDUCATION

Middle School Principles and Methods

Principles and methods of teaching in the middle grades. (3 semester hours)

Teaching of Mathematics

Methods and materials used in teaching high school mathematics. (3 semester hours)

SOCIOLOGY

General Sociology

Culture, society, personality, social processes, and social structures are the main topics. (3 semester hours)

Social Problems

Social disorganization, social strains, and deviant behavior, including consideration of war, poverty, ethnic relations, delinquency, crime, drug addiction, mental illness, and population problems. (3 semester hours)

Marriage and the Family

A sociological analysis of courtship, marriage, and parenthood patterns with emphasis on the contemporary American family. (3 semester hours)

Population Problems

Gives the student an understanding of the size, composition, and characteristics of populations, particularly the American population. (3 semester hours)

Criminology

A study of the criminal and crime, the causes of crime, processes of criminal justice, penal and correctional institutions and methods, and the prevention and treatment of crime. (3 semester hours)

Urban Sociology

The processes of urbanization, the nature or urban social organization, the impact of urban culture on non-urban society and the implications for policy and planning. Includes study of foreign as well as American communities. (3 semester hours)

Deviant Behavior

Analysis of the nature and origins of morally condemned conduct; examines the various theoretical approaches to the study of deviance; considers empirical data concerning types of deviance; and explores why we have deviance and what can be done about it. (3 semester hours)

Black Ghetto

The original, continuity, problems, and personalities of the American black community and its contributions to national and international life. (3 semester hours)

SPANISH

Elementary Spanish

1003. 1st semester. Stress, correct pronunciation and oral comprehension—leads to active mastery of basic grammar and limited reading ability. (3 semester hours)

1013. 2nd semester. A continuation of the above course. (3 semester hours)

Intermediate Spanish

2003. 3rd semester. Leads to greater facility in spoken Spanish and to more advanced reading skills. (3 semester hours)

2013. 4th semester. A continuation of the above course. (3 semester hours)

Intensive Spanish Reading

A rapid course in the fundamentals of Spanish for advanced students who do not desire to follow the usual curriculum but who need to acquire a practical reading knowledge of Spanish in the shortest possible time. (3 semester hours)

Advanced Grammar

For majors and advanced students covering the problematic areas of Spanish syntax and usage. (3 semester hours)

Latin American Civilization

(3 semester hours)

WESTERN CIVILIZATION

Institutions and Ideas of Western Civilization

1003. A study of civilization from ancient times through 1715. (3 semester hours)

1013. A continuation of the above course. (3 semester hours)

WORLD LITERATURE

Introduction to Literature

Selected works from the Greek epic down to the masterpieces of Renaissance literature. (3 semester hours)

Masterpieces from World Literature

A study of literary masterpieces from the seventeenth century to the present. (3 semester hours)

ZOOLOGY

Conservation of Natural Resources

Conservation of soils, minerals, water, power resources, forests, and wildlife in the United States. (3 semester hours)

HIGH SCHOOL COURSES

COMPUTER LITERACY

Computer Literacy I

An introductory course in computer concepts; the development of computers, applications of computers in various professional areas, and the social implications of computer technology. (½ unit)

Computer Literacy II

A study of how computers work; programming languages and software design; the specific applications of word processing, desktop publishing, electronic spreadsheets, database management, telecommunications, and BASIC programming. (½ unit)

ENGLISH

English 9a

The first six lessons include the grammatical structure of sentences and some work in writing. The last eight lessons are devoted to world literature. (½ unit)

English 9b

A continuation of English 9a with the same division of subject matter. Provides the equivalent of work done in the second semester of the regular freshman class. (½ unit)

English 9 Grammar

A course for students entering their first year of high school. This course will help students develop a better understanding and use of the English language. The lessons cover the eight parts of speech, basic sentence parts and patterns, phrases, clauses, English usage, capitalization, abbreviations, punctuation, spelling, and letter writing. (½ unit)

English 9 Literature

A course for students in their freshman year of high school. This course introduces students to both classic and contemporary literature that will encourage growth in the reading, thinking, and writing processes. The selections to be read include short stories, poetry, nonfiction stories, Shakespearean and modern drama. (½ unit)

English 10a

The first eight lessons contain activities and drills in structural English. The remaining eight lessons are devoted to the reading and to the discussion of materials especially adapted to teenage experiences. (½ unit)

English 10b

A continuation of English 10a and planned in much the same manner. (½ unit)

English 10 Grammar

A course for students in their second year of high school. Students will find that there is no area of study more relevant than communication. This course should help students develop better communication by improving their writing and speaking skills. The lessons cover the eight parts of speech, sentence parts and patterns, phrases, clauses, English usage, capitalization, abbreviation, and punctuation. (½ unit)

English 10 Literature

A course designed to introduce sophomores to fine literature from a variety of literary works. The lessons cover short stories, nonfiction works, poetry, the legends of King Arthur, a modern drama, and a Shakespearean drama. It is hoped that enjoyment, knowledge, appreciation, and a life-long habit of reading might be achieved as a result of this course. (½ unit)

English 11a

Grammar and literature. Begins with a review of freshman and sophomore English. The literature is selected from American writers of both yesterday and today. (½ unit)

English 11b

Grammar and literature. A continuation of English 11a. (½ unit)

English 11 - Grammar

Covers the basic materials in the language arts for the junior year in high school English. It consists of twelve lessons in the study of grammar, spelling, punctuation, and vocabulary with some attention to the arts of reading and observing. Combines the grammar work of both semesters of junior English with the exclusion of the literature study. (½ unit)

English 11 - Literature

Covers the study of literature for the junior year in high school English. It consists of sixteen lessons in the study of the historical background of American literature, the study of the biographies of American authors, and the reading of selections from American literature. Combines the study of literature for both semesters of junior English with the exclusion of the study of grammar. (½ unit)

English 12a

Grammar and literature. This course is the first semester of senior English. The selections in literature are from English writers. Emphasis on better communication. (½ unit)

English 12b

Grammar and literature. A continuation of English 12a. The work is divided between composition and literature in much the same manner. Emphasis on better communication. (½ unit)

English 12 Grammar

Covers the basic materials in the language arts for the senior year in high school. It consists of twenty-four lessons in the study of grammar, spelling, punctuation, and vocabulary with some attention to the arts of reading and observing. Combines the grammar work of both semesters of senior English with the exclusion of the study of literature. Emphasis on better communication. (½ unit)

English 12 Literature

Covers the study of literature for the senior year in high school English. It consists of twenty-four lessons in the study of the historical background of English literature, the study of the biographies of English authors, and the reading of selections from English literature. Combines the study of literature for both semesters of senior English with the exclusion of the study of grammar. (½ unit)

World Literature

Course WLIT I. 1st semester. Acquaints the student with major authors and works of the Eastern world, Greek and Roman literature, and literature of the Middle Ages. (½ unit)

Course WLIT II. 2nd semester. A continuation of the above course, designed to familiarize the student with major authors and literary works of the Western world from the Renaissance to the present. (½ unit)

Vocabulary Improvement

For average and above-average students in grades ten, eleven, and twelve to enrich their active vocabulary and improve understanding of passive vocabulary through context. (½ unit)

Dynamics of Study Skills

A course for high school students designed to help students improve reading and comprehension of text materials and including related areas such as note taking, critical thinking, and text taking. (½ unit)

Introduction to Mythology

Covers Greek, Roman, Norse, African, and Native American myths and heroic tales. (½ unit)

Language Arts I

A study of the most elementary principles of language usage. The vocabulary and verbal illustrations are chosen to meet the needs of the slow learner and the needs of the able student who completely lacks background in this subject. (½ unit)

Language Arts II

A continuation of the above course. Consists of a study of fundamental structures and usages that are more advanced than those studied in the above course and are dependent upon an understanding of the material covered in that course. (½ unit)

Business Communications

Covers principles of grammar, punctuation, and usage; principles and techniques of writing various types of business letters, memos, and informal reports; and the practice of oral communication, as well as practical suggestions for improving reading and listening. (½ unit)

FRENCH

French Ia

Primary objective is acquiring communication skills in French. Assignments include current conversational vocabulary in everyday situations: getting acquainted, getting information, and hearing, sharing, and making plans. Grammar is learned through its function in real communication exercises, not as isolated items. Other subjects covered include recreation, sports, travel, health. (½ unit)

French 1b

A continuation of French Ia. (½ unit)

HOME ECONOMICS

Home Economics I

Nutrition, food and health. Covers the general practice of good nutrition; the various nutrients and their relationship to good health; personal nutrition and wright control; and buying, storing, and preparing food. (½ unit)

Home Economics II

Etiquette for daily use. A short study and review of currently acceptable good manners and common courtesy according to recognized arbiters. One aim is to increase poise, self-confidence, and tact. (½ unit)

INDUSTRIAL ARTS

Basic Drafting

12a. Helpful to those who plan to pursue a college educational program, or work in technical, architectural, educational, and engineering fields. (½ unit)

12b. A continuation of the above course. (½ unit)

LATIN

Latin Ia

A thorough treatment of Latin grammar, exclusive of the subjunctive mood and its uses. The primary objective is the comprehension of Latin grammar. It seeks, also, to enlarge the student's English vocabulary with a study of Latin derivatives, to arouse interest in the civilization and culture of Rome, and to provide insight into English grammar. (½ unit).

Latin Ib

A continuation of Latin Ia. (½ unit)

MATHEMATICS

Pre-Algebra I

Includes whole numbers, decimals, fractions, equations, an introduction to algebra, and will cover the basic skills required for the first semester of Math II. (½ unit)

Pre-Algebra II

Includes an introduction to algebra, ratio and proportions, integers, percentages, geometry and measurements, and will cover the basic skills required for the second semester of Math II (½ unit)

Algebra

9a. Corresponds to the work of the first half year of algebra in high school. (½ unit)

9b. A continuation of the above course. (½ unit)

Geometry

10a. This course will contain topics that are usually taught in a high school geometry course. (½ unit)

10b. A continuation of the above course. (½ unit)

Algebra 11a

This course is especially designed to prepare students for college courses in mathematics. (½ unit)

Algebra 11b

A continuation of the above course. (½ unit)

Calculus 12a

For students who wish to get an overview of calculus by covering limits, the derivative and applications of the derivative. (½ unit)

Calculus 12b

A continuation of Calculus 12a. The concepts of integration and functions (logarithmic, exponential, and trigonometric) are covered. (½ unit)

Applied Mathematics Ia

Designed toward application and practice of mathematics concepts and skills in practical, world-of-work problem-solving activities and labs using calculators. (½ unit)

Applied Mathematics Ib

A continuation of the above course. (½ unit)

SCIENCE

Biology

10a. A study of life, both plant and animal. (½ unit)

10b. A continuation of the above course. (½ unit)

Physiology and Hygiene

11a. The chief emphasis in this course is on the general principle of healthful living. (½ unit)

11b. A continuation of the above course. (½ unit)

General Science

11a (1st semester). A course designed to help students understand how scientific principles and techniques apply to their health, possible careers, hobbies, and home life. (½ unit)

11b (2nd semester). A continuation of the above course. (½ unit)

SOCIAL STUDIES

Civics

9a. This the first half of a ninth grade course in civics. An effort has been made to present the text materials in such a manner as to help in the development of those skills and ideals which are essential to the understanding and assuming of his/her responsibilities as a citizen of his community, state, and nation. (½ unit)

9b. A continuation of the above course. (½ unit)

World History

10a. Represents the first half of tenth grade world history which covers the period from early Egyptian and Greek civilization to the monarchs of the seventeenth and eighteenth centuries. (½ unit)

10b. Represents the second half of tenth grade world history which begins with the monarchs of the seventeenth and eighteenth centuries and continues through World War II. (½ unit)

World Geography

Ia (1st semester). A course presented as a general geography of the entire world with emphasis on factual information. (½ unit)

Ib (2nd semester). A continuation of the above course. (½ unit)

United States History

11a (1st semester). Represents the first half of eleventh grade American history. Course begins with the exploration period, covers the Civil War, and ends with the beginning of the machine age in America. (½ unit)

11b (2nd semester). Represents the second half of eleventh grade American history. Course begins with the period following the Civil War and progresses through World War II. (½ unit)

Global Studies

GLOB I (1st semester). The purpose of this course is to provide the framework for understanding the events happening in the world. (½ unit)

GLOB II (2nd semester). A continuation of the above course. (½ unit)

American Government

GOVT A. (1st semester). This course is the first half of the twelfth grade American Government and is concerned with the organization and function of the national government. (½ unit)

GOVT B. (2nd semester). A continuation of the above course. Concerned with the organization and function of state and local government, including that of the state of Arkansas. (½ unit)

Economics

This course is a survey of the basic aspects of the economy. The aims of the course include: economic literacy, improved decision making, and enhanced background for further economic study. (½ unit) (½ unit)

Sociology

A basic introduction to the study of sociology designed to provide a better understanding of how people function in a society. Covers such topics as the family, population problems, the environment, race, crime, the aged, and American cities. (½ unit)

SPANISH

Spanish Ia

This corresponds with the first half year of work in Spanish in high school. (½ unit)

Spanish Ib

A continuation of Spanish Ia. (½ unit)

Arkansas State University
Independent Study Programs
Center For Off-Campus Programs
P.O. Box 2260
State University, Arkansas 72467
(501) 972-3052

Description:
Arkansas State University developed one of the four state agricultural schools established in 1909 by an act of the Arkansas General Assembly. The institution has undergone many changes and extensive growth during the intervening years, and now offers a wide variety of programs culminating in associate, bachelor, master, and specialist degrees. The Center for Continuing Education is maintained to provide opportunities for off-campus study, and supports the University in also offering a wide variety of programs.

Independent study courses are offered as a service to persons desiring individual study at home. The independent-study-by-correspondence offerings are the same quality and content as the class offerings on the campus.

Faculty:
Dr. J. Larry Williams, Associate Vice President for Off-Campus Programs and Continuing Education; Verlene Ringgenberg, Coordinator of Credit Programs.

Academic Levels:
College

Degree/Certificate Programs:
A candidate for a degree at Arkansas State University must complete at least 32 semester hours in residence, and may apply up to 31 semester hours of correspondence study toward a degree. Correspondence credits may apply toward associate or baccalaureate degrees.

Admission Requirements:
Any person enrolling in correspondence study at ASU must have met the regular entrance requirements. Individuals who wish to pursue courses of special interest without submitting academic credentials may accumulate up to 18 semester hours of undergraduate nondegree credit. Thereafter, nondegree students must comply with university admission requirements or obtain a written waiver from the Director of Admissions and Records.

Tuition:
$63 per credit hour plus $4 per credit hour for mailing materials and returning lessons. All tuition and fees must be paid at the time of enrollment. No refund will be made unless claimed at the time of withdrawal. The periods of student enrollment and refund are as follows: two weeks or less, 80%; third and fourth weeks, 60%; fifth week, 40%; after five weeks, none.

Enrollment Period:
The maximum period to complete a course is six months. A three-month extension from end of expiration date may be granted upon payment of a $15 fee. The minimum time permitted to complete a course is five weeks.

Equipment Requirements:
Textbook costs are not included in the tuition. They may be purchased separately by the student or rented from ASU. Workbooks are required on some courses and must be purchased by the student.

Credit and Grading:
The grading system is A, B, C, D, F; the minimum passing grade is D. Examinations must be monitored by a University-approved proctor, or may be taken at ASU or

one of the colleges/universities designated by ASU. Credit is awarded in semester hour units.

Accreditations:

North Central Association of Colleges and Schools. Member of: National University Continuing Education Association.

COLLEGE COURSES

ACCOUNTING

Principles of Accounting I

The accounting cycle for merchandising and service oriented business organizations. Primary emphasis is on accounting principles applicable to measuring assets, liabilities, owners' equity, and income. (3 semester hours)

Principles of Accounting II

Special measurement problems for partnerships and corporations. The course also covers rudimentary accounting and reporting for manufacturing companies. A part of the course is devoted to special reports, and managerial uses of accounting data for the decision-making functions. (3 semester hours)

ADMINISTRATIVE SERVICES

Elementary Shorthand

Gregg shorthand, including brief forms, vocabulary building, reading, dictation, and practice in the application of fundamental principles. (3 semester hours)

Office Management and Control

The "capstone" course that gives the student the opportunity to apply in a simulated office situation the theories, concepts, processes, and decision-making elements of administration learned in the previous business fields. (3 semester hours)

BIOLOGY

Genetics

The study of heredity and variation with application to plants and animals. (3 semester hours)

BUSINESS ADMINISTRATION

Introduction to Business

A survey course to acquaint beginning students with major institutions and practices in the business world, to provide the elementary concepts of business, and to serve as an orientation course for the selection of a specific major. (3 semester hours)

COMPUTER INFORMATION SYSTEMS

Introduction to Computer Information Systems

An overview of computers and their role in providing accurate and timely management information. Stresses computer organization, storage media and devices, file processing techniques, programming languages and software, computer systems and configurations, computer-based information systems, and computer terminology. Provides fundamental understanding of the capabilities and limitations of computers in management decision making. (3 semester hours)

CRIMINAL JUSTICE

Introduction to Criminal Justice

The introductory survey course in criminology dealing with the main components of the criminal justice system including the police, courts, and corrections, as well as issues and procedures pertinent to the operation of the components. (3 semester hours)

DRAMA

Introduction to Theater

Basic principles of theatrical traditions and terminology. (3 semester hours).

History of the Theater I

A survey of the history of the theater from the Greek Period to the Renaissance Period. (3 semester hours)

History of the Theater II

A survey of the history of the theater from the Renaissance Period to the Modern Period.(3 semester hours)

ECONOMICS

Principles of Macroeconomics

A study of how economic systems operate, with much stress placed on money, banking, and national income. Designed to increase awareness of economic problems and encourage the student to analyze alternative solutions. (3 semester hours)

Principles of Microeconomics

Emphasis is placed on value, prices, distribution, international economics and current problems. (3 semester hours)

ENGLISH

Freshman English I

Study and practice of fundamentals of written communication including principles of grammar, punctuation, spelling, organization, and careful analytical reading. (3 semester hours)

Freshman English II

Continues the practice of the above course to develop further the skills learned in that course. Based on reading and discussion of various types of writing, the students' essays will provide practice in different kinds of rhetorical development including research and documentation. (3 semester hours)

Introduction to Literature of the Western World I

An introduction to the analysis and interpretation of literary works from several historical periods ranging from early civilization through the Renaissance. (3 semester hours)

Introduction to Literature of the Western World II

An introduction to the analysis and interpretation of literary works from several historical periods ranging from the Renaissance to the present. (3 semester hours).

GEOGRAPHY

World Regional Geography

A general survey of geographic regions of the world, emphasizing the different ways of living and thinking by man in these different regions. (3 semester hours)

HEALTH

Principles of Personal Health

Principles, problems, and practices in prevention health care and the development of positive health behavior. (3 semester hours)

Human Sexuality

Emphasis given to human reproduction, courtship, marriage, parenthood premarital/extramarital sex, and deviate sexual behavior. (3 semester hours)

Drug Use and Abuse

An exploration of the physical, mental, emotional, and social aspects of drug use and abuse. Special attention will be focused on proper use of drugs within contemporary society. (3 semester hours)

HEALTH SERVICES ADMINISTRATION

Medical Terminology

Basic language related to medical science and the health professions: word analysis, construction spelling, definition. (3 semester hours)

HISTORY

World Civilization to 1660

A survey of the great civilizations, with emphasis on the main historical currents influencing modern society. (3 semester hours)

World Civilization Since 1660

A survey of major developments in Europe during the past three centuries. (3 semester hours)

The United States to 1876

A survey of social, economic, and political developments from Columbus to the end of Reconstruction. (3 semester hours)

The United States Since 1876

A survey of the social, economic, and political developments from Reconstruction to the present. (3 semester hours)

History of Arkansas

A study of social, economic, and political developments from the coming of the white man to the present. (3 semester hours)

JOURNALISM

Principles of Public Relations

Nature and theoretical foundation of public relations; its role in society; practitioners and dynamics of the process. (3 semester hours)

MATHEMATICS

College Algebra

Quadratics, polynomials, exponential and logarithmic functions, equations, and models; linear system, matrices and determinants; mathematical induction. (3 semester hours)

NURSING

Basic Human Nutrition

Basic concepts of nutrition including factors that impact nutritional practices. Special attention to age-related nutritional needs. (3 semester hours)

Clinical Pharmacology in Nursing I

Concepts essential to safe, effective administration of basic pharmacological agents in well-defined clinical situations. (3 semester hours)

POLITICAL SCIENCE

United States Government

Study of the Constitution, government, and politics of the United States. (3 semester hours)

PSYCHOLOGY

Introduction to Psychology

A study of the important scientific principles of human behavior, with emphasis on their application to personal and social problems. (3 semester hours)

History of Psychology

An overview of the history of psychology and recent systematic development. (3 semester hours)

Introduction to Social Psychology

An analysis of the situational factors which influence various behaviors including agression, altruism, and interpersonal attraction. (3 semester hours)

Child Psychology

A study of the principles and patterns of mental, social, emotional, and physical development. (3 semester hours)

Psychology of Adolescent Development

Factors influencing development during adolescence and aging as they influence cognition, motivation, perception learning, emotion, and personality. (3 semester hours)

Educational Psychology

A survey of psychological principles as they apply to education. (3 semester hours)

PUBLIC RELATIONS

Principles of Public Relations

Nature and theoretical foundation of public relations; its role in society; practitioners and dynamics of the process. (3 semester hours)

SOCIOLOGY

Principles of Sociology

Human and social behavior. (3 semester hours)

Social Problems

Application of sociological concepts and methods of the analysis of current social problems in the United States, including family and community disorganization, delinquency and crime, mental illness, and intergroup relations. (3 semester hours)

Auburn University
Distance Learning and Outreach Technology
204 Mell Hall
Auburn, Alabama 36849-5611 (334) 844-5103

Description:

Chartered in 1856, Auburn University traces its beginning to the East Alabama Male College, a private liberal arts institution whose doors opened in 1859. From 1861 to 1866, the college was closed because of the Civil War. The college had begun an affiliation with the Methodist Church before the war. Due to financial straits, the church transferred legal control of the institution to the State in 1872, making it the first land-grant college in the South to be established separate from the state university. It thus became the Agricultural and Mechanical College of Alabama. Women were admitted in 1892 and in 1899 the name changed again, to the Alabama Polytechnic Institute. In 1960, the school became known as Auburn University. The 1,871-acre campus includes ten Undergraduate Schools and a Graduate School.

As a land-grant university, Auburn is dedicated to service to Alabama and the nation through its three divisions: instruction, research, and extension. Independent Study offers college-level courses that are equivalent to courses taught on campus. Credit earned through completion of Independent Study courses is usually transferable to other institutions. Noncredit courses are also offered and the same standards of quality apply as in credit courses.

Faculty:

Richard A. Alekna, Director, Independent Study; Ernestine Morris, Coordinator. There are 18 faculty members and 2 counselors.

Academic Levels:
   College
   Noncredit
   Professional

Degree/Certificate Programs:

Independent Study courses may count toward twenty-five percent of the credit hours needed for a baccalaureate degree at Auburn University.

Admission Requirements:

Open enrollment to anyone who may profit from college-level courses. Exceptional high school students may enroll with the permission of their principals. Overseas enrollments accepted.

Tuition:

$37 per quarter hour, plus a $15 registration fee per course. Noncredit fee information by request. Refund policy: credit courses, no refunds made after one month from date of registration. The amount of the fee less the registration fee will be refunded upon written request if received within one month after the registration date, provided no work has been submitted. For noncredit courses, no refunds granted after enrollment. Textbook costs not included in fees; see Equipment Requirements below. Credit courses are approved for Veterans and other eligible persons under the provisions of the GI Bill.

Enrollment Period:

The student may enroll at any time of the year and study at his/her own pace, at home or any other convenient location. The maximum time for completion of a course is one year; the minimum time is one month. If time beyond the maximum is necessary, a three-month extension may be granted upon the payment of a $20 extension fee; should a second extension of three months be requested, a fee of $25 will be charged.

Equipment Requirements:

All courses require textbooks; some require typewriter, cassette, or other special equipment. These are all supplied by the student. Textbooks may be purchased locally or ordered (separately from tuition payments) from Independent Study.

Credit and Grading:

Grading formulas and minimum passing grades are determined by the instructors. All assignments must be submitted and graded before the final examination will be administered. Because of the nature of correspondence study, the examination grade is given a weight of 100 percent in the final course grade. Independent Study does not evaluate transcripts from other institutions nor offer an external degree into which credits may be transferred. All homework is done on the honor system. Examinations must be monitored by an approved proctor. Credit is awarded in quarter hour units.

Accreditations:

Southern Association of Colleges and Schools. Member of: National University Continuing Education Association.

COLLEGE COURSES

BIOLOGY

Perspectives in Biology

Principles of biology with emphasis upon the relationship between man and modern biological science. Specific subject areas include cellular structure, biologically important organic molecules, photosynthesis, cellular respiration, inheritance, evolution, and ecology. These topics are all developed with a view toward understanding how the human organism exists as both an individual biological entity and as an important interacting member of the natural world. Laboratory work is primarily in the areas of cell biology and inheritance. (5 quarter hours)

Criminal Justice

This course focuses on the three major components of the American criminal justice system: the police, courts, and jails or prisons. Information concerning the legal process is also presented. In particular, the rights of individuals who come in contact with the criminal justice system are examined. (3 quarter hours)

Survey of Law Enforcement

Introduction to the philosophical and historical backgrounds; agencies and processes; purposes and functions; administration and technical problems; career orientation. More specifically, this course provides the opportunity for a student to become informed about the wide areas of activity which today's law enforcement official encounters as a public servant. (5 quarter hours)

ECONOMICS

Economics

I. Economic principles with emphasis upon the macroeconomic aspects of the national economy. (5 quarter hours)

II. A continuation of economic principles with emphasis upon the microeconomic aspects of the economy. (5 quarter hours)

GEOGRAPHY

World Geography

An examination of the socioeconomic patterns of development in Europe, the Pacific World, Latin America, North Africa and the Middle East, and Asia. (5 quarter hours)

Introduction to Human Geography

An introduction to the various subfields of human/cultural geography, including population, agricultural geography, linguistic geography, the geography of religion, ethnic geography, and economic and urban geography. (5 quarter hours)

HEALTH EDUCATION

Health Science

Basic understanding concerning sound health practices and protection. Physical, mental, and social aspects of personal and community health are considered. (2 quarter hours)

HISTORY

History of the United States since 1865

A survey of the political, social, and economic development of the United States from 1865 to the present. (5 quarter hours)

History of Alabama

A brief history of Alabama. (5 quarter hours)

MATHEMATICS

College Algebra

The primary goal is to teach basic mathematical skills. Topics include algebraic techniques, coordinate geometry, functions and their graphs, logarithms and exponential functions. A hand-held calculator is required. (5 quarter hours)

PHYSICAL EDUCATION

History and Principles of Physical Education

A brief overview of significant ideas and events in the development of health education, physical education, and recreation. (3 quarter hours)

PSYCHOLOGY

Psychology

An introduction to the scientific study and interpretation of human behavior. Consideration of such topics as learning, motivation, emotion, intelligence, perception, personality, and interpersonal relationships is included in the reading and related exercises. (5 quarter hours)

Adult Development

Psychological development from adolescence through adulthood. (5 quarter hours)

Special Topics: Maturity and Aging

Development psychology relating to changes in and problems of human maturity from early adulthood to old age. (5 quarter hours)

VOCATIONAL EDUCATION

Development of Vocational Education

Historical perspective of the development of vocational education, with an overview of its nature and purpose relative to the technological society. (5 quarter hours)

Learning Resources in Vocational Education

A study of the selection, preparation, and use of instructional materials related to the specialization areas of vocational and adult education. (5 quarter hours)

Ball State University
Independent Study By Correspondence
School of Continuing Education and Public Service
Carmichael Hall, Room 200
Muncie, Indiana 47306-0130   (800) 872-0369

Description:
Ball State University, derived from the Indiana State Normal School, Eastern Division, was founded in 1918. In 1929 it became known as Ball State Teachers College. It 1965 it was renamed Ball State University in recognition of its growth in enrollment, in physical facilities, and in the variety and quality of its educational programs and services. Members of the regular Ball State faculty plan, develop, and teach courses in the Independent Study Program. Approximately 1,000 students are enrolled in the correspondence program.

Faculty:
Judith B. Roepke, Dean, School of Continuing Education and Public Service; Thomas A. Ray, Director, Correspondence Program; Diane K. Buck, Correspondence Program Coordinator. There is a faculty of 54 members.

Academic Levels:
College

Degree/Certificate Programs:
Only 30 semester hours of Independent Study (correspondence) credit will count toward a B.S. degree at Ball State; only 9 semester hours will apply toward a major or minor; not more than 6 semester hours may apply toward professional courses for teachers.

Admission Requirements:
Independent Study By Correspondence at Ball State University is open to all interested persons. Correspondence courses could interest and benefit students who are in a degree program and wish to accelerate their progress at Ball State; professional, business, or industrial personnel who wish to supplement their academic training; teachers who need additional undergraduate credits for their certification; members of the Armed Forces or others not close to an educational institution who wish to work toward a degree; high school graduates who are interested in further education though not currently enrolled at the university; and persons who do not wish to work toward a degree, but who want to read and study the courses for their cultural value.

Prospective students should contact the School of Continuing Education, Independent Study By Correspondence for a registration card. Upon submission of the registration card, applicants should allow approximately two weeks for the registration to be processed.

With the approval of the high school principal or counselor, high school juniors and seniors may enroll for some university-level courses for credit. Information and application forms are available from the Director, Correspondence Program. Ball State's Independent Study By

Correspondence Program does not encourage overseas enrollment due to the time delays and excessive postage.

The transfer value of credits earned through the Ball State Independent Study Program rests with the institution to which the student hopes to transfer credit.

Tuition:

The registration fee for undergraduate Independent Study courses is $93 per semester hour and must be paid in full when student begins the course. At the time the *Study Guide* is received, the student will also receive a number of large envelopes for use in mailing lessons to the university. All postage is the responsibility of the student. For persons sixty years of age or older, the registration is half the regular fee. Indicate on the registration form if you are sixty or older. Fees do not cover the cost of texts and other learning materials required. Refund policy: no lesson or one lesson submitted, 80 percent refund; two lessons submitted, 60 percent refund; three lessons submitted, 40 percent refund. No refunds after two months from enrollment date.

Enrollment Period:

A maximum of nine months and a minimum of one month are allowed to complete a course. Under certain circumstances, there may be a three-month extension upon payment of a $25 fee per course.

Equipment Requirements:

Textbooks are furnished by the student. They may be purchased locally or ordered through the Ball State Bookstore. A $3.50 postage fee and 5 percent sales tax (Indiana residents) should be added to the cost of the book(s).

Credit and Grading:

Proctored examinations are required for most courses. Assistance is given in finding a qualified proctor in student's home community. The minimum passing grade is D. Each instructor has his/her own grading system. Credit is awarded in semester hour units. A student enrolled in the Independent Study Program is identified as a "special student" of the university.

Library Services:

Books may be borrowed from the General Collections Unit at the Ball State Library, either in person or by mail. Course study guides provide information for this service. The only cost involved is postage.

Accreditations:

North Central Association of Colleges and Schools. Member of: National University Continuing Education Association.

COLLEGE COURSES

ACCOUNTING

Principles of Accounting 1

An introduction to accounting with emphasis on the basic principles underlying the accounting cycle. Includes the preparation of reports to management and external users of financial statements. (3 semester hours)

Principles of Accounting 2

A continuing of Principles of Accounting 1 with emphasis on financial statement analysis and managerial and cost accounting concepts. (3 semester hours)

ANTHROPOLOGY

Anthropology of a Changing World

Anthropological survey of selected peoples of the world representing a variety of human lifeways. Focuses on global social change and issues related to contemporary human problems. (3 semester hours)

ASTRONOMY

Mysteries of the Sky

A nontechnical and nonmathematical multimedia excursion into the vast reaches of the sky, including information about the sun, the moon, shooting stars, comets, super-novae, white dwarfs, pulsars, black holes, and life on other planets. (3 semester hours)

BUSINESS COMMUNICATIONS

Principles of Business Correspondence

Principles and basic elements of effective letter writing with emphasis on the psychological approach, reader point of view, positive tone, and appropriate format for personal and business letters and job applications. (3 semester hours)

Records Administration

Administration and supervision of office records systems; knowledge, techniques, and skills involved in planning, controlling, organizing, selecting, and retaining records in business and industry. Some hands-on laboratory experience with dBase III+ software for records processing and database management. office automation software for records processing and database management. All students must have departmental approval to enroll by correspondence. (3 semester hours)

CRIMINAL JUSTICE

Introduction to the American Criminal Justice System

An overview of the criminal justice system and a summary of vocational opportunities. Students must have access to a typewriter or computer. (3 semester hours)

Data and Theories of Crime and Delinquency

Examines the legal definitions of criminal and delinquent behavior, typologies of crime and criminals; the trends in reported distribution of crime and delinquency within the population; and current theoretical explanations. (3 semester hours)

Processing Adult and Juvenile Offenders

Emphasizes the juvenile and adult justice systems, their components, recent changes, and future developments. (3 semester hours)

Research Methods in Criminal Justice

Introduction to research methods used in criminology and criminal justice. Emphasizes the design, implementation, interpretation, and evaluation of qualitative and quantitative research. (3 semester hours)

Policing in American Society

Examination and analysis of the development of the police in America in the past, present, and future. Emphasizes institutional context of police activity, bureaucratization of the police, professionalization, the role of the police, and the police and community change. (3 semester hours)

Criminal Law

Emphasis on the practical aspects of the application of Indiana

Criminal law for present and prospective criminal justice practitioners; purposes and functions of the substantive criminal law; historical foundations; the limits of the criminal law. (3 semester hours)

Criminal Evidence

Rules of evidence as they apply in criminal investigation and criminal court are examined with discussion of relevant ethical issues. (3 semester hours)

Crisis Intervention in Criminal Justice

Study of theoretical and practical bases for accurately assessing and responding to crises that are unique to the criminal justice profession. (3 semester hours)

Police Systems and Organizations

Examination of issues and developing trends confronting the management and administration of police in the United States. Emphasizes development in the provision of law enforcement and social services by police at the local, state, and federal levels. (3 semester hours)

Institutional Corrections

An in-depth inquiry into the function, structure, and operations of American adult and juvenile correctional institutions. (3 semester hours)

Community Corrections

The organization and operation of community-based correctional programs throughout the United States. Topics include probation, parole, halfway houses, group homes, diversion, restitution, and community service programs, with an emphasis on the most popular programs and practices. (3 semester hours)

ECONOMICS

Survey of Economic Ideas

The important conclusions of modern economics are surveyed and applied to topics chosen by the instructor. Especially valuable to students with no high school background in economics. (3 semester hours)

Elementary Microeconomics

A study of why people specialize as producers and exchange what they produce with others. Includes analysis of how market structure affects prices. Discusses the issue of whether self-interested economic behavior promotes or hinders society. (3 semester hours)

Elementary Macroeconomics

A survey of the major explanations for fluctuations in general business conditions. The focus is how the private sector's economic behavior is affected by various governmental policies and institutions. (3 semester hours)

ENGLISH

English Composition 1

Introduction to composition with an emphasis on writing short essays. Includes assigned readings. Specific competencies are measured by the English department at the beginning and end of the semester. All students must have departmental permission to enroll by correspondence. (3 semester hours)

English Composition 2

Further instruction in composition with emphasis on writing longer essays. Assigned readings. Introduction to basic research methods. Specific competencies will be identified at the beginning of the semester and measured at the end of the semester. All students must have departmental permission to enroll by correspondence. (3 semester hours)

World Literature

Introduction to selected pieces of world, British, and American literature for class and individual oral and written interpretation and evaluation for those who are not English majors or minors. All students must have departmental permission to enroll by correspondence. (3 semester hours)

FINANCE

Personal Finance

The fundamental principles of general business and related economic concepts are considered from the viewpoint of the consumer. Some of the topics studied are consumer buying and the use of credit, banking, insurance, investment, budgeting, and taxation. (3 semester hours)

GEOGRAPHY

Earth, Sea, and Sky: A Geographic View

Selected aspects of the physical environment and their relationship to human occupancy of the earth. All students must have departmental permission to enroll by correspondence. (3 semester hours)

Physical Geography and Earth Science Concepts for Teachers

Earth-sun relationships, weather and climate, geologic processes (including earth structure and sculpturing of the earth's surface); conservation principles as they pertain directly to the material taught. Designed primarily for students in elementary education programs. All students must have departmental permission to enroll by correspondence. (3 semester hours)

Global Geography

A basic survey course emphasizing geographic facts and interdependencies between the developed and developing world. Emphasizes physical and social environmental interdependencies. All students must have departmental permission to enroll by correspondence. (3 semester hours)

Weather 1

How and why the weather changes, the characteristics of weather, and an examination of weather instruments. All students must have departmental permission to enroll by correspondence. (3 semester hours)

Climate

Introduction to climate, with emphasis on regional distribution. How and why climates differ across the earth. All students must have departmental permission to enroll by correspondence. (3 semester hours)

Geography of Indiana

A geographic examination of the physical, cultural, and economic diversity of the state. Field experiences supplement classroom activities. All students must have departmental permission to enroll by correspondence. (3 semester hours)

GEOLOGY

People and the Geological Environment

An introductory study of the materials, structure, and surface features of the earth; the processes responsible for their development; and the application of geologic knowledge to mankind's environmental and resource problems. (3 semester hours)

Historical Geology

An introduction to the physical history of the earth in relation to the development of life throughout geologic time. (3 semester hours)

Geomorphology
Study of landforms and their evolution. (3 semester hours)

HEALTH

Fundamentals of Human Health
Emphasizes life-style behaviors contributing to health promotion and disease prevention. General areas affecting health status are identified and suggestions made as to how health-related behaviors, self-care, and individual decisions contribute to wellness and influence dimensions of health. (3 semester hours)

Community Health Problems
Organization of official and unofficial health agencies at international, national, state, and local levels. Exploration of causative community conditions and diagnoses of disease and programs to combat these conditions. Focuses on selected communicable, noncommunicable, and behavior problems including traffic safety. (3 semester hours)

Alcohol Problems
A study of alcohol as a mood modifier, its use, non-use, and abuse in drinking societies. Critical and controversial issues relevant to alcohol ingestion will be explored for medical, economic, legal, educational, historical, physiological, and public health implications. (3 semester hours)

Drug Dependence and Abuse
Analyzes the medical, psychological, sociological, and legal dimensions of drug use in the United States. Examines the incidence and prevalence of drug abuse together with the roles played by school and community in dealing with this health problem. (3 semester hours)

Health Quackery
Health services and consumer protection organizations. An analysis of fraudulent health practices and nostrums, available health care systems and health products. (3 semester hours)

Death and Dying
Analyzes the relationship between death and health with emphasis upon the physiological, medical, psychological, legal, and consumer aspects of dying in contemporary America. Investigates problems that relate to the meaning of death, care for the dying, death ritual, bereavement, and death education. (3 semester hours)

HISTORY

Introduction to the History of Business in the United States
Surveys the function of business in the United States from colonial times to the modern day. Focuses on the role of individual business people as decision makers and innovators with primary emphasis on the twentieth century. (3 semester hours)

Western Civilization
A survey of the major themes and developments in the evolution of Western civilization from its origins to the present with emphasis on key problems, critical turning points, recurring issues, and cultural growth and heritage. Special stress on the character of and crises confronting the Western world in the nineteenth and twentieth centuries. (3 semester hours)

World Civilization 1
A survey of the development of world civilization from the dawn of civilization in Southwestern Asia and North Africa to the early modern world. (3 semester hours)

World Civilization 2
A survey of the development of world civilization from the early modern world to the present. (3 semester hours)

American History, 1492–1876
Survey of the political, diplomatic, economic, cultural, and sociological forces and adjustments that have affected the history of the United States to 1876. (3 semester hours)

American History, 1877–Present
Survey of the political, diplomatic, economic, cultural, and sociological forces and adjustments that have affected the history of the United States since 1877. (3 semester hours)

Introduction to Sport in American Life
A thorough examination of historical, sociological, and psychological aspects of sport in our society. Not sport-appreciation oriented; an examination of what happens to both competitors and spectators as they become involved with a sport activity. (3 semester hours)

Introduction to Public History
An overview of opportunities for non-teaching history-related careers in preservation, archival work, records management, museology, historical editing, living history and public parks programs, corporate history, and others. Students make a concentrated study of at least one field of public history and have contact with working professionals. (3 semester hours)

The United States and the Vietnam War
Historical analysis of American involvement in Vietnam from 1945 to 1975, with discussions of the military, political, diplomatic, and social effects of the war. Includes background information on Vietnamese history as well as its continuing legacy. (3 semester hours)

The Spanish Borderlands
The Anglo-American/Spanish-American frontier, 1550–1850, from Florida to Texas, New Mexico, and California. (3 semester hours)

Recent United States History: 1945 to the Present
A study of the United States in the modern world and an examination of the efforts of America to preserve a society that is prosperous and humane while adjusting to technological change and continuing social and intellectual ferment. (3 semester hours)

History of Indiana
Exploration, colonization, and development of the state from the earliest time to the present. (3 semester hours)

INSURANCE

Principles of Insurance
A survey of the major areas of insurance, such as fire, transportation, casualty, health, life insurance, and fidelity and surety bonds. (3 semester hours)

JOURNALISM

Mass Media in Society
Study of mass media in their historical and societal contexts with emphasis on practitioner issues including ethics, state of the art, and future. (3 semester hours)

Introduction to Advertising
A survey of advertising communication process. Focuses on communication research, creative strategy, campaign planning, function of mass media as carriers of advertising, and evaluation of advertising effectiveness. (3 semester hours)

MANAGEMENT

Management Principles
Introduction to the basic concepts and principles of management.

Focuses on structures within companies and processes within firms to bring principles to bear on the practical problems of managing organizations. (3 semester hours)

PHILOSOPHY

Introduction to Philosophy

An introduction to important philosophical problems: the existence of God, whether ethical values are subjective, the extent of our freedom. These topics and others may be approached by examining the ideas of great philosophers or current thinkers. (3 semester hours)

Ethics

A discussion of some of the central problems in ethics, such as the justification of ethical beliefs, theories of right and wrong, the conditions of moral responsibility and a discussion of current moral issues. (3 semester hours)

PHYSICAL EDUCATION

Introduction to Sports Medicine

Introduction to athletic training and sports medicine. Various responsibilities and occupational opportunities in these fields will be discussed. (1 semester hour)

Prevention and Care of Athletic Injuries

Introduction to the prevention, recognition, evaluation, treatment, and rehabilitation of common athletic injuries. Other essential information concerning athletic health care is also presented. (3 semester hours)

PHYSICS

Introduction to Energy and Space Sciences

Nonmathematical study of the basic forms of energy with emphasis on nuclear energy generation. Survey of some of the means of transmitting energy forms such as sound, heat, radio, and light. Introduction to astronomy, gravity, and the mechanics of space travel. (3 semester hours)

POLITICAL SCIENCE

American National Government

The organization and operation of national government as it relates to current issues such as civil rights, welfare, ecology, consumer protection, and international relations. (3 semester hours)

State and Local Politics

Practices, politics, and structures of state and local governments in the United States with an emphasis on Indiana. (3 semester hours)

Urban Government in the United States

Structure, functions, problems, and trends in city, urban, and metropolitan governments. (3 semester hours)

Public Administration

Organization, personnel, and functions of the various agencies of administration—national, state, and local. (3 semester hours)

Public Opinion and Political Behavior

The nature of public opinion, instruments, techniques, and institutions involved in formation of public opinion; and the political uses and implications at home and abroad of public opinion and propaganda. (3 semester hours)

Metropolitan Problems

An analysis of cities and metropolitan communities; examines the nature, characteristics, functions, governmental structure, intergovernmental relations, social make-up and problems, economic base, decision-making structure, and other related aspects; considers the present and future role of planning and citizen participation. (3 semester hours)

PSYCHOLOGY

General Psychology

Introduction to various areas of psychology and the contributions of each to an understanding of the behavior of people as they interact with their environment. (3 semester hours)

Elementary Statistics

Descriptive statistics and statistics of inference. The computation, application, and interpretation of various elementary statistics. (3 semester hours)

RELIGIOUS STUDIES

Religions in American Culture

Traditional religious groups in the United States with attention to developments, institutions, and distinctive practices and beliefs. The groups and the subjects treated will be adjusted to the interests of the students. (3 semester hours)

Religions of the World

An introductory survey of the major religions of the world (Hinduism, Buddhism, Judaism, Islam, Christianity, and others), emphasizing how people live out their faiths in their daily lives. (3 semester hours)

SOCIOLOGY

Principles of Sociology

An introduction to sociology including basic concepts used in sociological analysis. Attention is given to the world as a single society, the nature of society, culture, interpersonal and intergroup relations, and social institutions, world population, and worldwide economic and political arrangements. (3 semester hours)

Sociology of Deviant Behavior

An overview of theory and research on deviant behavior. Reviews three essential forms: deviance arising from disability in social and physical functioning, deviance arising from violation of social norms, and deviance arising from membership in groups observing radical social ideologies. (3 semester hours)

Social Problems

A survey of the nature and range of social problems, the conditions that give rise to them, and the methods by which our society attempts to cope with them. (3 semester hours)

Society and the Individual

Analysis of processes involved in the interaction between person and group, including the dynamics of group influence on personal behavior and the effect of personal variables on the functioning of primary and secondary groups in contemporary society. (3 semester hours)

Sociological Research Design

A basic course in principles and techniques for organizing, conducting, and analyzing sociological research; research strategies; and selection of appropriate techniques for a variety of research problems. (3 semester hours)

Social Statistics

The calculation, application, and interpretation of statistics used in social and behavioral sciences. (3 semester hours)

Leisure and Popular Culture

Discussion of issues related to the uses and distribution of nonwork time and activities. Trends in recreation, folk arts, and the growing leisure industries. The effect of leisure activities on the natural environment and other quality-of-life issues. (3 semester hours)

The Family

The role of the family in contemporary society, factors influencing trends in family structure, functions, roles, stability, and their implications for both the community and individuals at varying stages of the family life cycle. (3 semester hours)

Social Gerontology

Social aspects of aging in contemporary American society and elsewhere, with emphasis on special needs and emerging community and national programs for meeting them. (3 semester hours)

THEATRE

Introduction to Theatre

An overview of the field of theatre with special reference to the origin of drama. (3 semester hours)

Baptist Bible College
Correspondence School
628 East Kearney
Springfield, Missouri 65803   (417) 869-9811

Description:

The Baptist Bible College Correspondence School was instituted in 1973 under the leadership of Dr. G.B. Vick, former president of the college, and Kenneth Gillming, academic dean. Miss Lillia Walbridge was installed as director of the school and she organized, planned, and laid a firm foundation upon which the school could build a sound educational program.

The Correspondence School was designed to be an instrument to aid those who have an interest in increasing their knowledge of the Bible, but find themselves unable to proceed with their studies as a resident student. Many missionaries find the materials to be greatly beneficial in training their national pastors. Courses are written by various professors of Baptist Bible College are offered in Bible, Theology, and Christian Teaching. The preparation of the courses and grading of lessons are done under the guidance of the director of the Correspondence School with the assistance of the Correspondence Department personnel.

Faculty:

Dr. Joseph K. Gleason, Director of Correspondence Study.

Academic Levels:

College

Degree/Certificate Programs:

A maximum of 8 credit hours are applicable as elective courses toward a degree at Baptist Bible College if a student decides to attend on a resident basis at a later time. For each course that the student successfully completes, he/she will receive a certificate of completion. If a student successfully completes all correspondence courses that are available, he/she will receive a "Correspondence Achievement Certificate" for the entire course of study.

Admission Requirements:

Correspondence courses may be started at anytime during the year.

Tuition:

Tuition is listed below following each course description. However, contact the college for current price information. An additional postage fee of $3 should be added to the course fee.

Enrollment Period:

The course enrollment begins with the date of the enrollment and will expire precisely at the end of 12 months. All students may proceed with their courses as rapidly as they wish, as long as they diligently and thoroughly study the material that the course requires. Each student will be allowed a 1-year extension if unable to complete the course in the first year period. Thereafter, a fee of $5 will be requested for reinstatement.

Equipment Requirements:

Students are responsible for purchasing the textbook and syllabus required for a course.

Credit and Grading:

Each course completed will be individually and carefully graded with comments and corrections to aid the student. Grades will be indicated by the following grading scale: A (100-94 percent), B (93-87 percent), C (86-79 percent, D (78-70 percent), F (below 70 percent). Minimum passing grade is 70 percent. The Administration and Division Directors of Baptist Bible College, upon review of the correspondence courses, have stated that no college credit will be awarded for the courses listed below until they have been revised at some future date. Contact the Director of Correspondence Study for current information.

Accreditations:

American Association of Bible Colleges.

COLLEGE COURSES

BIBLE

History of the Christian Church

This is a survey of the growth and development of the Christian church, beginning with the apostolic days and ending with the movement of the Baptist Bible Fellowship. (Noncredit) *Tuition:* $25.

Exposition of Genesis

This study of the "book of beginnings" in detail is to establish a spiritual foundation for understanding the entire Bible. Every major doctrine will be found in Genesis that is recognized in the New Testament. The study of Genesis is a prerequisite toward mastery of the Scripture. (Noncredit) *Tuition:* $25.

Exposition of Exodus

Detailed and careful exposition of the book of Exodus is here combined with practical application to the believer's life today. In this second book in the canon, the major theme is that of redemption, and the story it unfolds is vitally important today. (Noncredit) *Tuition:* $25.

Old Testament Survey

The study of this course includes a section-by-section, book-by-book study of the Old Testament, with general information as to authorship, time of writing, and classification. (Noncredit) *Tuition:* $30.

Life of Christ

A study of the four gospel narratives: Matthew, Mark, Luke, and John. The miracles and parables, as well as discourses are analyzed in detail. (Noncredit) *Tuition:* $25.

Life of Paul

A study of the life and epistles of the Apostle Paul with emphasis on the book of Acts as a biographical work. (Noncredit) *Tuition:* $25.

New Testament Survey

Each book of the new Testament is studied in its relationship to the rest of the New Testament. A simple outline of each book is given, with a more detailed analysis of its content. Information as to authorship, date, purpose and recipients of each book is included. (Noncredit) *Tuition:* $35.

Revelation

A study of the book of Revelation in depth, with emphasis on correlation of prophecy with the events of the present day. (Noncredit) *Tuition:* $25.

Fundamental Baptists Versus the Cults

The scriptural beliefs of fundamental Baptists are covered. (Noncredit) *Tuition:* $25.

ENGLISH

English Grammar

The goal of this course is to assist the student in becoming a writer with assurance. It will be a study of grammar, sentence structure, capitalization, and punctuation. Frequently, the student will be asked to compose sentences pertaining to a certain area of study. This self-programmed study furnishes many easy-to-understand illustrations. (Noncredit) *Tuition:* $30.

MUSIC

The Music Ministry

The purpose of this course is to help those in Christian service and those preparing for Christian leadership have a better understanding of the possibilities and benefits of a vital music program in the local church. This course includes a study of the entire scope of the music program in the local church, including a look at the historical development of sacred music. (Noncredit) *Tuition:* $25.

RELIGIOUS EDUCATION

Biblical Christian Counseling

This course is offered for the purpose of aiding the pastor (or Christian counselor) in his counseling. Among the sixty subjects covered in the course materials are: marriage/divorce, drugs, alcoholism, depression, guilt, and family problems. (Noncredit) *Tuition:* $25.

Child Growth and Development

This course includes a study of the home, the importance of children and why we should reach them early in life. Other areas of study include characteristics of children and youth at each age level, with special emphasis given in the areas of physical, mental, social, and spiritual development. (Noncredit) *Tuition:* $25.

ETTA Preliminary

This course is designed for the local church and community leadership preparation classes. It leads to successful teaching for Sunday School teachers and officers. Six subjects are covered—three cover different

aspects of the Bible, and three cover areas of Christian Education. (Noncredit) *Tuition:* $45.

ETTA Advanced

The advanced program gives a deep understanding of God's Word and an insight into different fields of Christian service. A prerequisite of this course is the completion of the preliminary program described above. (Noncredit) *Tuition:* $45.

Toward Teaching Improvement

An in-depth study of techniques, methods, and aids in Sunday School teaching. The materials provide many new ideas for both old and new teachers. (Noncredit) *Tuition:* $25.

VBS in the Local Church

The main objectives of this course are to enable the student to: (1) recognize the supreme importance of effective Bible teaching; (2) organize and prepare developmental, Bible-centered, behavioral curriculum for the church; (3) plan curricula and write Bible lessons for a variety of age groups of the Daily Vacation Bible School. (Noncredit) *Tuition:* $25.

Love: Foundation for Marriage

The purpose of this course is to lead the student into a detailed study of the home. Areas of study include: effective marriage communication, the pattern for God's kind of family, developing a good family altar, and many more. (Noncredit) *Tuition:* $25.

THEOLOGY

Doctrine and Administration of the Local Church

A study in the organization and administration of the local church according to the New Testament. (Noncredit) *Tuition:* $25.

Pastoral Theology

The study of various problems of the pastorate and the methods of dealing with them effectively. Also, various suggestions are proposed concerning the strengthening of promotional and public relation qualities of the pastor. (Noncredit) *Tuition:* $25.

Premillenialism

This course is a detailed outline of the subject of Premillenialism, discussing the three fields of Prophecy: Amillenialism, Postmillenialism, and Premillenialism. (Noncredit) *Tuition:* $25.

Systematic Theology

This course gives detailed instruction in the great doctrines of the Bible: Jesus Christ, the Holy Spirit, Man, Salvation, the Church, the Scriptures, Angels, Satan, and the Last Things. (Noncredit) *Tuition:* $25.

Bemidji State University
Center for Extended Learning
External Studies Program
1500 Birchmont Drive N.E.
Bemidji, Minnesota 56601   (218) 755-3924

Description:

The External Studies Program at Bemidji State University is a part of the Center for Extended Learning. The program can be traced back to 1972 when Chancellor G. Theodore Mitau issued a press release in Alexandria mentioning the possibilities of an External Degree in the State University System. A committee was soon formed to plan a curriculum procedure to fit an adult, off-campus population. The External Degree was approved by the Faculty Senate in 1973 and the first students were admitted in November of that year.

Faculty:
Lorraine F. Cecil, Coordinator, External Studies. There is a faculty of 32.

Academic Levels:
College

Degree/Certificate Programs:
Associate, Bachelor.

Admission Requirements:
High school diploma or GED equivalent. Official transcripts of previous academic work must be submitted to the Coordinator. International students are not accepted except for U.S. citizens residing abroad.

Tuition:
In-state tuition $51.45 per credit; out-of-state $99.20 per credit. All fees subject to change. Contact the Center for External Learning for current rates. External Degree students are eligible for financial aid just as if they were on campus. Interested students should write to the Financial Aid Office for details. The External Degree student may be eligible for Veterans Benefits and should check with the Registrar's Office for eligibility. A student may withdraw from an External Studies class by notifying the External Studies Office in writing any time previous to ten days of the ending date of the class. Refund policy: 100 percent refund granted if notification is given within one week of the beginning date of the class; 75 percent refund granted if notification is given within two weeks of the class; 50 percent refund granted if notification is given within three weeks of the beginning date of the class; 25 percent refund granted if notification is given within four weeks of the beginning date of the class. No refund is granted if notification is given after four weeks of the beginning date of the class.

Enrollment Period:
Students may enroll at any time. All courses grant residence credit. Any course may be taken for noncredit. A student should finish his/her class in a twelve-week period and by the ending date specified. If not completed within the twelve weeks the student will be given an Incomplete. The student will have one year to clear the Incomplete and receive a grade for the class. Any Incomplete not cleared after one year will be changed to E.

Equipment Requirements:
Students must purchase or borrow textbooks. The rental of audio and/or video cassettes may be required for some courses.

Credit and Grading:
There is no limit on the number of credits earned by correspondence which may be applied toward a degree at Bemidji. Correspondence credits from other accredited institutions are acceptable. Examinations must be proctored by a test administrator to whom the exams are sent. Tests are not automatically sent—they have to be requested from the Coordinator. Letter grades are used. The minimum passing grade is D. Credit is awarded in quarter hour units.

Library Services:
Students may use interlibrary loan service or use the Bemidji University Library just as if the student were on campus. He/she may write or call; by giving one's student number the student will be able to check out books.

Accreditations:
North Central Association of Colleges and Schools.

COLLEGE COURSES

ANTHROPOLOGY

Becoming Human: Tracing Our Origins

Humans as biological and cultural organisms. The physical origin of humans and the primates; the interplay of biological and cultural factors in our evolution; physical variations among modern human populations. (4 quarter hours)

Cultural Anthropology

Comparative study of a variety of modern human groups serves to illustrate the methodology of the course. Analyses of technologies, family forms, social organizations, religions, and cultural change. (4 quarter hours)

Native North Americans

Examination of the variety of native North American cultures (north of Mexico). Survey of linguistic and archaeological background; emphasis on social and ecological adjustments. (4 quarter hours)

Religions of Preliterate Societies

Functions of religion in preliterate societies. A comparative analysis of the role of religion on a scale of increasing societal complexity. (4 quarter hours)

North American Prehistory

Origins and development of the prehistory cultural traditions of North America. Culture areas will be studies from an ecological perspective. (4 quarter hours)

Archaeology and Ethnography of Minnesota

Peoples and cultures of Minnesota from the earliest prehistoric occupations to historic settlement. Indian occupation of Minnesota. Indian groups and lifeways at the time of Euro-American contact. (4 quarter hours)

Methods in Archaeology

Archaeological methodology with an emphasis on methods and techniques of excavation. (4 quarter hours)

BIOLOGY

Human Physiology

Functions of the organ systems of the human body, with emphasis on the physiology of exercise. (3 quarter hours)

CRIMINAL JUSTICE

Criminal Justice and Society

A general introduction to the philosophies, principles, and social aspects which underlie the formulation of law and the administration of justice in the United States. Provides an overview of the institutions and relationships of those agencies composing the criminal justice system. (4 quarter hours)

Judicial Process

Examines the criminal justice judicial process. Covers judicial involvement from pre-arrest warrant issuance to appellate court review. Focuses on the role, function, and behavior of prosecutors, defense attorneys, and judges. (4 quarter hours)

Correctional Processes

Provides the student with an understanding of corrections as a major part of the criminal justice system. Focuses on principles, assumptions, and processes pertaining to achieving correctional goals and objectives beginning with sentencing by the court through discharge from jurisdiction. (4 quarter hours)

Police Behavior

Examines the relationship between the police and the community at both the organizational and individual level. Focuses on the vital role and responsibility of the community for crime and criminal justice processes, and the implications of these interactions for the individual officer at both a professional and personal level. (4 quarter hours)

Methods of Crime Prevention Planning

A systemic overview of crime prevention presented within a framework of a planned, proactive response to crime by all components of the criminal justice system. Examines principles of planning, research, and evaluation as applied to crime prevention. (4 quarter hours)

Applied Minnesota Statutory Law

Utilizes the case method. Studies Minnesota statutes as they apply to crimes against persons, crimes against property, crimes against the administration of criminal justice, and violations of traffic and game laws. (4 quarter hours)

Criminal Investigation

Designed to acquaint the student with the problems and techniques involved in the investigation of a crime. Emphasizes concepts and principles related to criminal investigations. Also included are the relevant rules of evidence for the criminal investigator. (4 quarter hours)

Criminal Procedures

This course focuses on the rights of the criminally accused, primarily those involved in the pre-trial stages of the criminal process. The Bill of Rights including the 4th, 5th, 6th, and 14th Amendments pertaining to search and seizure, eye-witness identification, confessions, and interrogations as well as other due process issues will be examined. (4 quarter hours)

Community Corrections

In-depth examination of community corrections programs including: program planning, implementation and evaluation, physical plant designs, client's rights, intake, contracting, release, use of community resources, and use of various treatment modalities. The functions of social work in correctional settings will be examined from a historical and contemporary view. (4 quarter hours)

Seminar in Criminal Justice

Course entails advanced study in the theories, philosophies, and practices in criminal justice. Requires extensive review of writings with emphasis on recent developments in the practice of criminal justice. (4 quarter hours)

ECONOMICS

Consumer Economics

The principles and techniques of economic analysis dealing with households. Theories of household behavior. Development and analysis of economic problems encountered by households. (4 quarter hours)

Business and Government

A study of business firms and their tactics of market control, the development of antitrust law and policy, the judicial interpretation of law, the effects of government regulation over business firms, and government regulation of public utility rates and services. (4 quarter hours)

ENGLISH

Freshman English

26-121. Emphasis is on improving skills and effectiveness in written communication based on critical reading, other means of observation, and extensive writing. (4 quarter hours)

26-123. Reading and analysis of the major types of imaginative literature as sources for critical writing. (4 quarter hours)

Understanding Fiction

A study of representative novels and short stories from a variety of types and backgrounds. (3 quarter hours)

The Bible as Literature

A study of selected Old and New Testament books and their literary significance. (4 quarter hours)

The Short Story

A study of the history, development, structure, and technique of the short story as a literary genre. (3 quarter hours)

The Novel

Study of the novel as a literary form, with analysis of representative works illustrative of major literary movements. (4 quarter hours)

History of the English Language

A chronological study of all major aspects of linguistic changes in the history of English from the Anglo-Saxon age to the present, culminating in modern American dialectical differences. (4 quarter hours)

GEOGRAPHY

World Regional Geography

A survey of physical, cultural, and economic aspects of world regions. An introduction to how constituent parts of the world differ from one another in their associated resources, cultures, and economics. Attention is given to the interrelationships, interdependencies, and associations that bind together the diverse communities of the world. (4 quarter hours)

Introduction to Human Geography

Emphasizes the study of geographical relationships and interactions of cultural, social, economic, and political phenomena. Topical approach to investigate the regional patterns of population, religions, languages, urban and rural settlements, and other attributes of the cultural landscape. (4 quarter hours)

HEALTH

Nutrition

Fundamentals of diet and food utilization, including discussion of health problems related to diet; current trends in food consumption and practice in evaluation of diets. (3 quarter hours)

Community Health

An introduction to public and community health with an analysis of current health problems as they affect groups of people; study of epidemiological method; environmental health concerns. (3 quarter hours)

Safety Education

Problems and projects relative to accident facts, safety problems of home, school, highway, and playground. A study of liability, insurance, and legal responsibilities of teachers. Development of a school safety program. (3 quarter hours)

Health and Drug Education

Study of health-related issues in modern society as they relate to personal and community health. Particular emphasis on chemical abuse, chronic and degenerative disease, mental health, environmental health, family life, and safety. Basic principles of health, nutrition, and personal health. (4 quarter hours)

HISTORY

United States History and Life 1890–1929

A survey of American civilization form 1890–1929. (4 quarter hours)

United States History and Life 1929–1945

The Depression, the FDR Era and World War II. (4 quarter hours)

United States History and Life 1945–Present

A survey of American history since World War II. (4 quarter hours)

Western Civilization

I. The ancient empires, Greece, Rome, the rise of Christianity, Medieval Europe. (4 quarter hours)

II. The Renaissance, the Reformation, the expansion of Europe, the French Revolution, and Napoleon. (4 quarter hours)

III. The Industrial Revolution, Karl Marx and Marxism, Imperialism, World War I, World War II, the world since 1945. (4 quarter hours)

The Great War: 1914–1918

Background and origins of the war; major diplomatic and military aspects of the war; historical consequences of the war. (4 quarter hours)

Vietnam War Era 1945–1975

Indigenous Vietnamese culture, French colonial regime, Vietnamese nationalism and Marxism, United States military involvement, American decision-making process, impact of the war in the U.S. politically, economically, and socially. (4 quarter hours)

17th–18th Century America

Evolution of colonial life, the achievement of independence, the formation of the union and the early years of the republic. (4 quarter hours)

19th Century United States

Territorial expansion, sectional conflict, and the evolution of urban and industrial America, 1815 to 1901. (4 quarter hours)

20th Century United States

The Progressive Movement, two World Wars, normalcy, the New Deal, and global politics. United States growth since 1900. (4 quarter hours)

Minnesota History to 1900

Growth of Minnesota from the age of the fur trade to the modern state. (4 quarter hours)

Medieval England

Anglo-Saxon monarchy; Norman conquest; feudalism and common law; "Freedom of the Church," evolution of parliament. (4 quarter hours)

Tudor and Revolutionary England 1485–1714

Tudor royal administration; Church of England; Parliament and Tudor absolutism; 17th century revolution; England as a great power. (4 quarter hours)

20th Century China

The political, social, and economic history of Communist China. (4 quarter hours)

India, Pakistan, and Bangladesh

Pre-Hindu civilization, Hindu India, the Muslim conquest, British India, independence, the problems of contemporary India, Pakistan, and Bangladesh. (4 quarter hours)

The Study of History

Definitions of history; introduction to U.S. and European historiography; introduction to historical research. (4 quarter hours)

American Revolution and New Nation

The American Revolution and the new nation, 1763 to 1800. Structure of colonial society, British imperial policy, military and diplomatic phases, the social consequences, period of the Confederation. (4 quarter hours)

The Franklin D. Roosevelt Era, United States, 1930–1945

The New Deal reform and recovery programs, effects of the depression and World War II on U.S. society and economy. Problems of foreign policy. United States in World War II. (4 quarter hours)

United States History Since 1945

The Age of Affluence and Anxiety, developments in recent times in the social, economic, constitutional, political, military, and diplomatic areas. (4 quarter hours)

Greece and Rome

The beginnings and development of the Greek and Roman worlds; political, economics, and cultural life. (4 quarter hours)

Medieval Europe

Medieval church and papacy, feudal and manorial institutions; towns and commerce; the beginnings of national monarchies. (4 quarter hours)

The Renaissance and The Later Middle Ages

The rise of modern political and economic institutions in Europe and the intellectual and cultural transformation of Italy and northern Europe as a result of the humanist revolution. (4 quarter hours)

Luther, Calvin, and The Reformation

The religious revolutions of the 16th century and the rise of modern religious ideas and churches; growing commerce and secular power politics; the beginning of modern liberalism. (4 quarter hours)

The French Revolution and Napoleon

Causes of the revolution; the outburst of liberty, nationalism, and radicalism and the transformation of French society from 1789 to 1799; nationalism and dictatorship in France and Europe under Napoleon. (4 quarter hours)

Japan and Korea

A social, cultural, and political survey. (4 quarter hours)

INDUSTRIAL EDUCATION

Orientation to Industrial, Technical, and Vocational Education

An introduction to program planning, employment trends, technical developments, license requirements and future trends in the various programs. (1 quarter hour)

Impact of Technology on Man and Society

A survey of technological trends, production techniques, and manpower needs. A study of the social implications of automation and cybernetics on modern society. (3 quarter hours)

MUSIC

Introduction to Music

A course in music appreciation with an emphasis on the various styles and types of art music in western civilization. Presentations include: biographical information about composers, study and listening to representative compositions, and the relations of music to all art and history. (3 quarter hours)

PHILOSOPHY

Introduction to Philosophy

Selected works and/or views of well-known philosophers. Selection and approach vary with instructor. (4 quarter hours)

Problems of Philosophy

Some of the main problems of philosophy such as knowledge, truth, mind, God, perception, freedom. (4 quarter hours)

Ethics

Theories of right and wrong, good and bad, duty, conscience, moral judgement. (4 quarter hours)

Death and Survival

An examination of the nature of death and the possibility of survival. (4 quarter hours)

PHYSICAL EDUCATION

Foundations of Physical Education

Fundamental concepts and basic philosophy underlying physical education. Survey of trends in the field of physical education. History, present philosophy, and objectives analyzed and examined. (4 quarter hours)

Techniques of Neuromuscular Relaxation

Introduction to and practice in Jacobson's neuromuscular relaxation and other relaxation techniques to improve the student's awareness of muscular tension. (1 quarter hour)

Jogging and Conditioning

Attainment of optimum physical efficiency through selected programs of exercise. (1 quarter hour)

Organization and Administration of Physical Education

Discussion and lectures on administrative policies and activities, curriculum development, intramural athletics, staff, intercollegiate athletics, financing, care of equipment, and publicity. (4 quarter hours)

Understanding Physical Impairments

A study of the types of physical impairments encountered in development/adapted physical education and how these impairments generally and specifically affect physical learning ability. Designed to provide a medically oriented background for developmental/adapted physical education teachers and others who need this type of background for teaching. (3 quarter hours)

POLITICAL SCIENCE

American Government

A study of theory and practice of democratic government. Foundation for intelligent action as a citizen. (3 quarter hours)

Introduction to Political Science

An introduction to concepts, principles, institutions, processes, functions, policies, and problems of modern government. Behaviorism will be emphasized. (4 quarter hours)

Introduction to Public Administration

The study of administration, formulation, and execution of public policy at the local, state, and national levels. Administrative organization, personnel management, finance, intergovernmental relationships. (3 quarter hours)

State and Local Government

A study of the politics, organization, and function of state and local governments. Special emphasis upon decision making and programs. (4 quarter hours)

Political Parties and Elections

The study of the organization and function of American political parties and their influence upon political campaigns and elections with emphasis upon increasing relationship between media and politics. (4 quarter hours)

Governments and Politics of Western Europe and the USSR

An analysis of political structures of Britain, France, Germany, and the USSR. Political developments, parties, ideologies, and foreign policies will be discussed. (4 quarter hours)

PSYCHOLOGY

General Psychology

I. Introduction to the study of behavior and general survey of psychological principles. (3 quarter hours)

II. A continuation of the above course. (3 quarter hours)

Introduction to Applied Psychology

Introduction to the field of applied psychology, exploration of human services treatment modalities, survey of agencies and services. Volunteer service is required of the student. (3 quarter hours)

Psychology of Adjustment

A survey course dealing with healthy personality development; ways in which we behave, why we behave that way, and ways we can attempt to gain insight into ourselves to reach our full potential. (3 quarter hours)

Human Sexuality

A survey of the physiological aspects of human sexual behavior with an emphasis on health sexual adjustment within the total context of human interaction. (4 quarter hours)

Investigation of Behavior

Basic research and statistical concepts underlying the study of behavior. (4 quarter hours)

Human Response to Death

A psychological approach to death as a major event in human life. (3 quarter hours)

Learning and Cognition

Survey of research, theories, and applications in the areas of classical and operant conditioning and cognition. (4 quarter hours)

Abnormal Psychology

Mental disorders and behavioral deviations: causes, manifestations, and treatment. (4 quarter hours)

Social Psychology

Survey of contemporary research in affiliation, interpersonal perception and attraction, aggression and altruism, group dynamics, conformity, compliance and attitude formation, and change. (4 quarter hours)

Industrial and Organizational Psychology

The application of psychological theories, methods and principles of people in work settings. Personal selection, evaluation, and training. Work motivation and job satisfaction. Leadership. Organizational factors and working conditions. Human factors engineering. (4 quarter hours)

Child and Adolescent Psychology

Review of theories and research on the psychological, physiological, and environmental factors influencing child and adolescent development. Individual differences and adolescent problems of adjustment. Methods and skills in assessment, recording, and observation. (4 quarter hours)

Psychology of Adulthood and Aging

Psychological and physiological characteristics of mature individuals and the elderly, with emphasis on cognitive, affective, and behavioral change. (4 quarter hours)

Family Systems

An introduction to family systems theories and interview techniques. (4 quarter hours)

Personality Theory

A survey of theories of personality development. (4 quarter hours)

Pre-Internship Seminar

Selection of internship site and preparation for internship responsibilities. (1 quarter hour)

RECREATION

Recreation Leadership

Discussion of present trends in recreation, recreation's relation to physical education activities, methods of organizing activities for groups, materials available, and problems of leadership. (2 quarter hours)

Introduction to Community Recreation

The scope of community recreation and the basic social values of recreation in relation to other social institutions. Consideration of program content of community recreation programs. (3 quarter hours)

Recreation Field Work

The field word should differ in type and intensity as the student progresses in the program. The total experience should be gained from at least two different types of agencies conducting recreation programs and possessing accepted standards of staff facilities and program. Field work experience includes: observation, leadership, committee work, management of unit operations, participating in group experiences. (3 quarter hours)

SOCIAL WORK

Social Work in Health Care Systems

Focuses on the application of social work in a variety of health care settings. Designed to develop beginning knowledge of: medical terminology, physiology, health care systems and insurance issues, the effect of illness and disease on the patient and family members, the importance of considering patients' rights and the intersection of cultural, gender age, affectionate preference, socioeconomic class on the interactions between the patient and the health care system and professionals, and working as member of an interdisciplinary health care team. (3 quarter hours)

Social Work with the Elderly

This course is designed to enable the student to understand and apply knowledge of social work with the elderly in society. Emphasizes the historical background of aging, use of the systems/generalist framework for practice with the elderly, assessment and intervention strategies, and the role of policy including the impact of prejudice and discrimination on the elderly. (4 quarter hours)

SOCIOLOGY

Introduction to Sociology

Basic concepts and theories of society. Culture, social institutions, socialization, race relations, social class and collective behavior as they relate to an understanding of modern society. (4 quarter hours)

Family Violence

A study of current theory and research related to the problem of family violence and responses to this problem including: premarital violence, spousal violence, and violence in parent-child relationships including sexual abuse. (4 quarter hours)

Social Statistics

Designed especially for students majoring in sociology and social work. Emphasis on both the understanding of statistical techniques and the application of such techniques. Subjects covered will include measures of central tendency, variability, and association. Probability, sampling, and hypotheses testing will also be considered. (4 quarter hours)

Boise State University
1910 University Drive
Boise, Idaho 83725   (208) 385-3486

Description:
Established in 1932 as a community college, Boise State University progressed to a four-year university with the first graduation in 1967. The university became part of the state system in 1969. Credit for correspondence study is available from Boise State University but all courses are administered by the Correspondence Study in Idaho office at the University of Idaho campus in Moscow, Idaho. SEE **Idaho, University of.**

Accreditations:
Northwest Association of Schools and Colleges.

Brigham Young University
Department of Independent Study
206 Harman Continuing Education Building
P.O. Box 21514
Provo, Utah 84602-1514   (801) 378-2868

Brigham Young University

Description:

Brigham Young University began as an academy of the Church of Jesus Christ of Latter-day Saints in 1875 and became a university in 1903. It is now the nation's largest privately-sponsored institution of higher learning. In 1921 it established the Department of Independent Study as an element of the Division of Continuing Education. BYU's Independent Study program is currently one of the largest university-affiliated correspondence programs in America.

The Department of Independent Study features college-level courses, high school courses, and non-credit "personal enrichment" courses. There are currently over 27,000 enrollments in the Independent Study program. Brigham Young University has developed new ways of providing independent study, such as computer-assisted instruction, video courses, and satellite transmission.

Faculty:

R. Dwight Laws, Director, Department of Independent Study. All college-level courses are taught by Brigham Young University faculty members. High school instructors are either teachers in nearby high schools or university personnel experienced in teaching high school students. Special noncredit courses are taught by university professors, high school teachers, and other specialists. There is a total Independent Study faculty of 350 members and 7 instructional designers.

Academic Levels:

College
High School
Noncredit

Degree/Certificate Programs:

Certificate, Associate, Diploma. The Bachelor of Independent Studies Degree involves study of a broad range of basic and relevant subjects from the fine arts, social sciences, physical sciences, and religion, all under the direction of university faculty and advisers. This degree program, designed especially for the adult student, is a directed program of home study with no specific major or minor. The bachelor's program is open to anyone twenty-one years of age or older who has been approved by the Department of Degrees by Independent Study.

An Associate of Arts in English can be earned entirely through Independent Study. Those students who have already earned a baccalaureate or higher degree are not eligible for BYU associate degrees. Up to 36 semester hours of Independent Study credit may be applied toward a baccalaureate degree and up to 18 hours of credit toward an associate degree from Brigham Young University. All college-level BYU Independent Study courses are fully accredited and may be transferred to any university that accepts transfer credits from BYU. Any credit course offered by the Department of Independent Study may also be taken on a noncredit basis. Many Independent Study courses fulfill requirements for a teaching certificate or for certificate renewal.

Admission Requirements:

There are no admission requirements to take an Independent Study course. However, enrollment in Independent Study courses does not constitute admission to the University. In order for a student to be admitted to the University as a full-time student, he/she must make formal application and be accepted before enrolling. Some courses have prerequisites. Student must have a working knowledge of the English language.

Tuition:

College courses, $72 per semester hour. High school courses, $65 per ½ unit. Courses taken for noncredit have the same fee as if taken for credit. Fees for personal enrichment courses vary. Postage prepaid in the U.S. If located outside the U.S., the student must include an additional fee for airmail postage. Refund policy: A processing fee of $15 per course plus $9 per lesson assignment submitted and $10 for each exam taken is assessed on all college course tuition refunds. For a maximum tuition refund, the signed request must be submitted within thirty days of enrollment. Calculation of a refund is based upon the date the signed request and course materials are received at the Independent Study office. A limited number of tuition scholarship and grants are available (contact the Independent Study Office for information).

Enrollment Period:

Required completion time per course is one year from date of enrollment. The minimum time is one week per credit. A three-month extension may be granted upon payment of a $15 fee.

Equipment Requirements:

Textbooks required for courses are listed in the Independent Study Catalog. Books are paid for by the student and may be purchased locally or through BYU. Some courses require materials in addition to the textbook)s) and study guide. These materials must be purchased through BYU Independent Study.

Credit and Grading:

Credit is awarded in semester hours. Most courses require one or more midcourse examinations and a final examination. For some courses book reports, special projects, and/or term papers may be required. Students living in Utah County must take their examinations at the Independent Study Office. Others must have an approved supervisor in their presence while taking an examination. Honor system prevails for lesson completion. Although grades received on lessons are duly considered, a student must pass the supervised final examination to receive a grade for the course. Grading system: Letter grades A through E are used with the minimum passing grade of D.

Library Services:

Students in the local area can receive, upon request and approval, a limited access library card to the University Library.

Accreditations:

Northwest Association of Schools and Colleges. Member of: National University Continuing Education Association.

COLLEGE COURSES

ACCOUNTING

Principles of Accounting

Financial and managerial accounting principles. Basic accounting statements, processes, and management applications. (3 semester hours)

Principles of Financial Accounting

First course in the concepts and methods underlying financial statements. (3 semester hours)

Principles of Managerial Accounting

Second course in the elementary series covering managerial problems and the control of business operations. (3 semester hours)

AMERICAN HERITAGE

American Heritage

Synthesis of American constitutional and economic principles, and patterns of historical development. (3 semester hours)

ANIMAL SCIENCE

Applied Animal Nutrition

Principles of formulating feeds. (3 semester hours)

Pet and Laboratory Animal Nutrition

Nutrition and feeding principles of dogs, cats, horses, and laboratory animals. (2 semester hours)

ANTHROPOLOGY

Social/Cultural Anthropology

Aspects of society and culture: kinship, beliefs, economy, and political order among peoples worldwide. Methods and perspectives used in social/cultural anthropology. (3 semester hours)

Introduction to Archaeology

Review of great archaeological discoveries about the ancient world. Overview of world prehistory. (3 semester hours)

ART

Introduction to Calligraphy

Basic skills in handlettering. (2 semester hours)

ART HISTORY

Survey of Western Art 1

Art and architecture of the Western world, covering periods from primitve to Renaissance. (3 semester hours)

Survey of Western Art 2

Art and architecture of the Western world, covering periods from Renaissance to contemporary. (3 semester hours)

Nineteenth-Century European Art

History and appreciation of nineteenth-century art in Europe. (3 semester hours)

Modern Art

Modern European art and theory. (3 semester hours)

BIOLOGY

Principles of Biology

Introductory course for general education students. (3 semester hours)

Heredity and Reproduction

Principles of inheritance. (3 semester hours)

BOTANY

Plants Through the Ages

Comparative and evolutionary investigation of the origin and development of plants. (3 semester hours)

BUSINESS MANAGEMENT

Personal Finance

Practical course in money management and utilizing savings. (2 semester hours)

Financial Management

Financial management from the viewpoint of the business manager, emphasizing profitability, liquidity, and long-range financial planning. (3 semester hours)

Marketing Management

Market segmentation, product service, promotion, channel, pricing strategies. Marketing principles in consumer and industrial markets, profit and nonprofit organizations, domestic and international companies, and small and large firms. (3 semester hours)

CHEMISTRY

Elementary College Chemistry

Structure of matter and the chemical consequences of that structure. For nonscience majors. (3 semester hours)

CIVIL ENGINEERING

Engineering Mechanics - Statics

Concepts of mechanics: force systems in equilibrium, resultants, friction, centroids, utilization of vector algebra. (2 semester hours)

Engineering Mechanics - Mechanics of Materials

Fundamental concepts of elastic stress and strain relations; cylinders and spheres; torsion; beam theory, including bending stresses; deflections; and two-dimensional elastic theory. (3 semester hours)

Engineering Mechanics - Dynamics

Concepts of dynamics applied to particles, systems of particles, rigid bodies, vibrations systems, and nonrigid particles of systems. (3 semester hours)

Hydraulics and Fluid Flow Theory

Fluid properties, fluid statics and dynamics, viscous flow, boundary layer concepts of pipe and open-channel flow. (3 semester hours)

CLOTHING AND TEXTILES

Textiles

Natural and synthetic textile fibers, yarns, fabric construction, dyes, and finishes; application to use and performance of textile fabrics. (3 semester hours)

COMMUNICATIONS

Mass Communications and Society

Historical roles of mass media in society emphasizing media effects on individuals and institutions. (3 semester hours)

Public Speaking

Principles and methods of public speaking; speaking experiences. Access to tape recorder needed. (3 semester hours)

Theory of Communication and Persuasion

History, development, and criticism of communication theory. Principles and ethics of persuasion. (2 semester hours)

Rhetorical Methods

Speech composition and oral/audiovisual presentation for public and professional use. (3 semester hours)

Writing for Mass Audiences

Analysis of audience, purpose and context; selection and use of appropriate voice, structure, and techniques for effective written communication. (3 semester hours)

Debate and Argumentation Strategies

Reasoning, logic, issues, strategies, and audiences in formal and informal argumentation and debate. (4 semester hours)

Magazine Writing

Analysis of nonfiction magazine markets and criticism of articles written in the course. (3 semester hours)

COMPUTER SCIENCE

Elementary Computer Applications

Computer organization, problem solving, and information systems, emphasizing use of the computer for problem solving rather than developing programming skills. Requires access to IBM PC or compatible with at least 256K of memory, two 5.25 inch floppy drives or one floppy and one hard drive, DOS 2.1 or above, and a standard Pascal compiler; a monochrome monitor with a graphics card may be used, but a color monitor with a graphics card that supports CGA is recommended. (2 semester hours)

DANCE

Aerobic Dance

Dance and other rigorous activities performed to music to attain cardiovascular fitness. You must engage in this program for at least thirteen weeks to receive credit for this course. (½ semester hour)

Social Dance, Beginning

Traditional and popular ballroom dance; also social skills. (½ semester hour)

ECONOMICS

Economic Principles and Problems

Strengths and weaknesses of the markets and governments for solving basic problems of social organization or conflict, including policy response to inflation, unemployment, pollution, poverty, growth, etc. (3 semester hours)

EDUCATIONAL LEADERSHIP

The Professional Teacher

The teacher and the school: employment, control, professional relations, the law, finance, and professional affiliation. (1 semester hour)

EDUCATIONAL PSYCHOLOGY

Fieldwork in Special Education for Elementary Education Majors

Field lab experience for teachers working with students who have special learning needs. (1 semester hour)

Education of Exceptional Children

Required for all elementary education and special education majors. (2 semester hours)

Test and Measurement Theory

Basic test and measurement theories. Types of tests. Reliability and validity. Standardization and test construction. (3 semester hours)

Special Topics in Education

Course E PSY 515R. Independent Study offers these courses as professional and practical assistance to inservice teachers:

Section 2. Changing Undesired Emotions Through Rational Self-Counseling. Rational self-control of undesired emotions. How one produces one's own emotions, how to rid one's self of undesirable ones, and how to produce more desirable ones. Applicable to ages twelve and up. (1 semester hour)

Section 3. How to Teach Concepts. A practical approach to teaching concepts effectively. (2 semester hours)

Section 4. You Can't Build a Fire with Snowballs: How to Motivate Students. Effective ways to help students become more responsible, self-controlled, self-motivated individuals. (1 semester hour)

Section 5. Resolving Student Hostility. A practical course. Topics and skills include creating safe and trusting conditions, breaking the cycle of hostility, placing responsibility properly, exploring consequences, and the commitment process. (2 semester hours)

Section 6. Introduction to the Education of Children with Visual Handicaps. Major issues in the education of those with visual handicaps, their characteristics and needs, and research gaps needing attention. (2 semester hours)

Section 7. Psychosocial Implications of Visual Handicaps. Assumptions underlying procedures for assisting those with vision loss; dealing with motivation; emotions, attitudes; the notion of a psychology and a sociology of vision loss. (3 semester hours)

Section 10. Developing Capable People. Seven essential characteristics basic to young people for becoming capable, caring, and responsible people; developing self-discipline, good interpersonal skills, responsibility, judgment, and problem-solving skills. (2 semester hours)

Section 43. Classroom Management: Obtaining Student Cooperation. A practical approach to effective classroom management. Reinforcement principles and motivational techniques applicable to all age levels. (1 semester hour)

Section 50. Applied Behavior Analysis for Teachers and Parents. Practical course to help teachers change behavior of exceptional students. (2 semester hours)

Section 51. Implementing Public Law 94-142, "Education of All Handicapped Children Act." For regular and special classroom teachers, counselors, school administrators, and parents. How to design and implement sound educational programs for handicapped children, consistent with Public Law 94-142. Rights of handicapped children and their parents under the law. (1 semester hour)

Education of the Gifted and Talented

Various approaches to educating the gifted and talented. This course is designed as an introduction to the terminology, key principles, and current methodology in education of the gifted and talented student. (2 semester hours)

Educating Students with Severe and Profound Disabilities

Educational implications in identifying and classifying individuals with severe and profound disabilities. (3 semester hours)

Introduction to Counseling and Guidance Services

Introduction to the counseling profession: history, philosophy, issues, trends, and current status. Role of counselor in school and community agency settings. (3 semester hours)

ELECTRICITY

Basic Electricity

Theory of electricity and electronics; magnetism, DC/AC circuits, semiconductors, and introduction to digital processes for automated systems. Technical reports of lab activities. (3 semester hours)

ELEMENTARY EDUCATION

Children's Literature

Trends and titles in children's and adolescent literature. Reading and critiquing as well as practical uses of children's literature in both school and home, emphasizing nonfiction titles to teach effective lessons and curriculum content. (3 semester hours)

Special Topics in Education

Course EL ED 515R. Independent Study offers these courses as professional and practical assistance to inservice teachers:

Section 1. Nonfiction Children's Literature. Creative yet practical ways of identifying nonfiction books for children to enjoy. Worthwhile nonfiction books are studies and current bibliographies provided. (1 semester hour)

Section 2. Teaching Language Arts in the Elementary School. Theory and Evaluation of language arts, including language acquisition, oral language development, listening, writing, handwriting, spelling, grammar, and developmental reading. (2 semester hours)

Section 3. How to Teach Concepts. A practical approach to teaching concepts effectively. Required: classroom or neighborhood children to teach for one lesson. (2 semester hours)

Section 5. Legitimate Legibility: Italic Handwriting. Italic letter forms; the eight joins that make print into logical, beautiful cursive italic handwriting. (1 semester hour)

Section 9. Early Childhood Learning Experiences. Organizing and preparing meaningful learning experiences for preschool children throughout the year. A systematic approach to important concepts a young child can learn in a fun and creative manner. Required: six or more children to teach. (2 semester hours)

Section 10. Developing Capable People. Seven essential characteristics basic to young people for becoming capable, caring, and responsible people; developing self-discipline, good interpersonal skills, responsibility, judgment, and problem-solving skills. (2 semester hours)

Section 11. The Role of Decoding in Learning to Read. A proven, research-based approach to teaching sight word, phonics, and structural analysis skills. (1 semester hour)

Section 12. Reading: Developing Comprehension. A proven, research-based approach to teaching comprehension: developing the reader's background and vocabulary. Improving comprehension processes and skills, comprehension and different types of discourse, and teaching comprehension in the content areas. (2 semester hours)

Section 13. Reflective Teaching. Improving professional and personal decision-making ability in teaching through reflection. Theory of reflection and using your reflective journal entries to write Description, Interpretation, Evaluation, and Plan (DIEP) summaries. Required: access to a classroom for at least five weeks. (1 semester hour)

Section 14. Elementary School Mathematics: Curriculum Standards, Grades K−4. Translating mathematical theory into applied instruction for grades K−4 guided by the National Council for Teachers of Mathematics. (1 semester hour)

Section 15. Elementary School Mathematics: Curriculum Standards, Grades 5-8. Translating mathematical theory into applied instruction for grades 5−8 guided by the National Council of Teachers of Mathematics. (1 semester hour)

Section 16. Elementary School Mathematics Assessment. Assessment standards, practices, process, and products identified by the National Council of Teachers of Mathematics to teach grades K−4 and/or 5−8 through thinking skills and performance. (1 semester hour)

Section 34. Improving Discipline in the Schools: Eight Discipline Models. Principles and strategies to enhance teacher-student rapport, help the teacher understand and change student behavior, and help students make long-term behavioral improvements. (1 semester hour)

Section 60. Teaching Reading in the Content Areas. A flexible, practical course in teaching reading in the content areas. (2 semester hours)

Section 63. Teaching Reading in the Content Areas. Three-credit version of the above course. (3 semester hours)

Section 64. Teaching Reading in the Content Areas. For students who need one additional hour of credit. (1 semester hour)

ENGLISH

College Writing and Reading

Basic principles of critical reading and expository writing—purpose, structure, logic, and language. (3 semester hours)

Writing for Children and Adolescents

Theory and practice of writing prose and verse for youth readership. Special attention to requirements of the realistic adolescent novel. (3 semester hours)

Creative Writing

Individual sections may deal with poetry, personal essays, fiction, science fiction, or combinations of these. (3 semester hours)

Writing Personal History

(3 semester hours)

Introduction to the English Language

Overview of English from linguistic point of view, emphasizing structure of English and social, biological, and psychological aspects of language. (3 semester hours)

Vocabulary Building

Developing an effective vocabulary through study of prefixes, suffixes, and roots. (2 semester hours)

Introduction to Literature: Fiction, Drama, Poetry

Introduction to various literary themes, forms, and authors. (3 semester hours)

Masterpieces of American Literature

Selected readings from Puritan times to the present. (3 semester hours)

Fundamentals of Literary Interpretation and Criticism

Introduction to concepts and practice of literary analysis, emphasizing formal elements of fiction, poetry, and drama. (3 semester hours)

Critical Writing and Research

Literature-based expository and research writing. (3 semester hours)

Perspectives in English Literature 1

Applying fundamentals of literary analysis to representative British authors and works to 1800; emphasis on intrinsic values and historical-cultural contexts. (3 semester hours)

Perspectives in English Literature 2

Critical study of representative British authors and works since 1800; emphasis on intrinsic values and historical-cultural contexts. (3 semester hours)

Perspectives in American Literature

Critical study of representative American authors and works; emphasis on intrinsic values and historical-cultural contexts. (3 semester hours)

Argumentative and Critical Writing

Expository and persuasive writing focusing on practical reasons for evaluating audiences, generating and structuring an argument, and making stylistic decisions. (3 semester hours)

Exposition Writing for Elementary Education Majors

Improving writing proficiency by focusing on the writing process, collaborative writing, and techniques for teaching writing. (3 semester hours)

Writing in the Social Sciences

Writing characteristic of disciplines inquiring into human behavior and institutions; focuses on correspondence, proposals, library paper, critiques, and arguments. (3 semester hours)

Technical Writing

Writing scientific and technical proposals, articles, reports, and memoranda. (3 semester hours)

Writing of Fiction

Creation of style and technique in prose fiction; discipline and practice of the writer. (3 semester hours)

Writing of Poetry

Creation of style and technique in poetry; discipline and practice of the poet. (3 semester hours)

Modern American Usage

Current conventions and effective use of American English. (3 semester hours)

Grammar and Usage

Study of grammar and usage in various applications. (3 semester hours)

The English Novel

Great novels of the past three centuries selected from the writings of Defoe, Fielding, Scott, Austen, Thackeray, Brontë, Dickens, Eliot, Hardy, Conrad, and other major novelists. (3 semester hours)

The American Novel

Great novels of the American tradition selected from Cooper, Hawthorne, Melville, Twain, James, Dreiser, Cather, Hemingway, Faulkner, Steinbeck, Fitzgerald, Bellow, Malamud, and other major novelists. (3 semester hours)

The Bible as Literature

Literary artistry, human values, and cultural significance of the Bible. (3 semester hours)

The Short Story

Critical study of American, English, and European short stories, emphasizing those of the twentieth century. (3 semester hours)

American Literature Since 1914

Significant trends in American literature from World War I to the present. (3 semester hours)

Modern Poetry

Major twentieth-century English and American poets. (3 semester hours)

English Literature from 1780 to 1832: The Romantic Period

Includes writings of Blake, Wordsworth, Coleridge, Byron, Shelley, Keats, and their contemporaries. (3 semester hours)

English Literature from 1832 to 1890: The Victorian Period

Includes writings of Carlyle, Tennyson, Browning, Arnold, Dickens, the Rossettis, Swinburne, Meredith, Hopkins, and their contemporaries. (3 semester hours)

Shakespeare

Intensive reading and discussion of at least eight representative plays. (3 semester hours)

English Literature 1603–1660: The Late Renaissance Period

English drama, poetry, and prose of the Stuart period. (3 semester hours)

Eminent Authors and Themes in Literature

Section 1. Christian Fantasy. Selected readings in the fiction of J.R.R. Tolkien and C.S. Lewis to introduce the profundities of literature through some of the finest and most readable writings of the genre. (3 semester hours)

Literature for Adolescents

Intended especially for English-teaching majors and minors. (3 semester hours)

FAMILY SCIENCES

Human Development

Growth and development of the child from conception through adolescence; influences of family, peers, and schools. (3 semester hours)

Special Topics in Family Sciences

Section 1. Early Childhood Learning Experiences. Organizing and preparing meaningful learning experiences for preschool children throughout the year. A systematic approach to important concepts a young child can learn in a fun and creative manner. Required: six or more children to teach. (2 semester hours)

Supervision of Marriage and Family Therapy

Designed to fulfill the American Association for Marriage and Family Therapy Approved Supervisor designation requirements for directed study of the literature related to the theory and practice of marriage and family therapy supervision. (2 semester hours)

FOOD SCIENCE AND NUTRITION

Essentials of Nutrition

Food-oriented study of nutrition facts and principles as a basis for dietary choices; consequences of choices; scientifically examining controversial topics. (3 semester hours)

Special Problems in Food Science and Nutrition

Individual study for qualified students. (1 to 3 semester hours)

GEOGRAPHY

Introduction to Geography

The physical environment. Distributions and interrelationships of climates, landforms, soils, and natural resources, and their significance to man. (3 semester hours)

Geography and World Affairs

Survey of the world, stressing geography of major political regions. (3 semester hours)

Introduction to Cultural Geography

Culture distributions and their relationship to existing geographic phenomena. (3 semester hours)

Tour Operation

Broad overview of tour operations; travel counseling. (3 semester hours)

Tourism: A Conceptual Framework

Introduction to tourism as a field of study; four elements of tourism: dynamic, service, functional, and consequential. (3 semester hours)

Tourism: Patterns and Analysis

Patterns of domestic and international tourism; interrelationships between geography and tourism in understanding the patterns and their impact. (3 semester hours)

United States and Canada

Analysis of the natural environment, historical development, cultural patterns, economic systems, and the political structures of geographic regions. (3 semester hours)

GEOLOGY

Introduction to Geology

Cultural focus on physical and environmental geology for nonscience majors; rocks and minerals. (3 semester hours)

Life of the Past

Cultural focus on historical geology for nonscience majors; fossils. (3 semester hours)

GERMAN

Grammar and Composition 1

Perfecting grammar, reading, writing, listening, and speaking skills using current news items from German-speaking countries as a basis. (3 semester hours)

Grammar and Composition 2

A continuation of the above course. (3 semester hours)

German Literary Periods and Movements

In-depth study of one of the following: medieval, Renaissance and baroque, eighteenth century and Romanticism, realism, *fin-de-siècle* Vienna, naturalism, 1890–1945, 1945–present. (3 semester hours)

Special Studies in German

Section 1. German For Family Historians and Genealogists. German grammar, handwriting, printing, and translation found in parish and civil registries. (3 semester hours)

HEALTH

First Aid and Safety Instruction

Emergency procedures for sudden illness and traumatic injuries. Leads to first aid and CPR certifications. (2 semester hours)

Health and Life-Style Management

Course HLTH 129. Self-responsibility approach to health and wellness. (1 semester hours)

Course HLTH 130. Comprehensive focus on knowledge and skills needed for health and wellness. (2 semester hours)

History, Philosophy, and Foundations of Health

Principles of the discipline and preparation for professional service. Theoretical models of health, professional and ethical issues, and future trends. Introductory course. (2 semester hours)

First Aid and Emergency Care

In-depth coverage of first aid procedures for injuries and sudden illness. Leads to first aid and CPR certifications. (3 semester hours)

Safety Education

Magnitude of the accident problem, risk taking, principles of accident prevention and control, and safety instruction. (2 semester hours)

School Health for Elementary Teachers

Health for the elementary teacher, emphasizing his or her role as a health educator, and an appraisal of health problems of the elementary student. (3 semester hours)

School Health for Secondary Teachers

Certification course. Fundamental principles; adolescent health problems. (2 semester hours)

Consumer Health

Current consumer health issues; selecting proper health products, services, and information; sources of consumer health protection. (2 semester hours)

Organization and Administration of Driver and Traffic Safety Education

Organization, administration, and supervision of high school driver education programs. (2 semester hours)

Community Health

Individual, school, and community involvement in preventing disease, improving human efficiency, and prolonging life. (2 semester hours)

Health Crisis Intervention

Intervention techniques applied to health crises such as death and dying, suicide, grief and mourning, euthanasia, child abuse, abortion, and sexual assault. (2 semester hours)

Driver and Safety Education Workshop

Section 1. Individual Curriculum Projects. Completion of a curriculum project initiated by the enrollee: the classroom phase, behind-the-wheel phase, simulator, driving range, driver improvement or defensive driving aspects of driver education. (1 to 7 semester hours)

Health and the Aging Process

Theories of aging as a normal process, as a pathological process; health promotion and extension of life. (2 semester hours)

HEBREW

First-Year Biblical Hebrew

Course HEB 131. Old Testament Hebrew. Provides foundation in grammar and vocabulary; reading Hebrew prose texts in Bible. (4 semester hours)

Course HEB 132. A continuation of *Course HEB 131.* (4 semester hours)

HISTORY

History of the United States Through 1877

Discovery, colonization, American Revolution, establishment of the Constitution, foreign affairs, westward expansion, sectionalism, Civil War, and reconstruction. (3 semester hours)

History of the United States Since 1877

Industrialization, urbanization, imperialism, progressivism, world wars, New Deal, and current problems. (3 semester hours)

World Civilization to 1500

Word civilization from Greek antiquity to Renaissance; explores fundamental questions in the human experience, examines formative events in history, and seeks to teach value of important texts. (3 semester hours)

World Civilization from 1500

World civilization from Renaissance to present; explores fundamental questions in the human experience, examines formative events in history, and seeks to teach value of important texts. (3 semester hours)

The Family in Europe

Nature and development of marriage and family life and structure from the ancient to modern era. (3 semester hours)

The Family and the Law in American History

The interaction of families with law and government as illustrated in original American sources; individual family histories reconstructed in the broader perspective of history. (3 semester hours)

Soviet and Post-Soviet Russia

Modern Russia, emphasizing the rise of communism and the development of the USSR. (3 semester hours)

English History to 1689

Political, social, and cultural developments from prehistoric times to the Glorious Revolution. Medieval, Tudor, and Stuart periods. (3 semester hours)

English History Since 1689

Emergence of Britain as a great colonial and industrial power, as well as more recent decline of Britain's influence. Emphasis also on cultural developments. (3 semester hours)

Modern Latin America

National period (1810 to present); independence, institutional development, culture, and inter-American relations. (3 semester hours)

Utah

Contributions of Native Americans, explorers, mountain men, Mormons, and Gentiles to nineteenth century. Politics, economics, and social and cultural development in twentieth century. (3 semester hours)

Writing Family Histories

Selecting themes and sources and determining issues to be dealt with. (3 semester hours)

American Family History

Early settlement to the present. (3 semester hours)

Paleography

Interpreting and reading English language handwriting in documents and a study of social structure including heraldry, 1500–1900. (3 semester hours)

North American Family History

In-depth examination of the sources and problem solving in North America:

Section 1. Northeastern United States and Canada. Methods and sources for Canada East, Canada West, Connecticut, Delaware, Maine, Massachusetts, New Hampshire, New Jersey, New York, Pennsylvania, Rhode Island, and Vermont. (3 semester hours)

Section 2. Southern United States. Methods and sources for Alabama, Florida, Georgia, Kentucky, Louisiana, Maryland, Mississippi, North Carolina, Tennessee, Virginia, and West Virginia. (3 semester hours)

Section 3. Midwestern States. Methods and sources for Arkansas, Illinois, Indiana, Iowa, Kansas, Missouri, Ohio, Oklahoma, Michigan, Nebraska, Texas, and Wisconsin. (3 semester hours)

British Family History

In-depth examination of the sources and problem solving in Britain:

Section 1. England and Wales from 1700. Research methods and sources peculiar to early Britain and modern England and Wales: civil registration, parish registers, census, probates, and military and nonconformist records. (3 semester hours)

Section 3. Scotland and Ireland. Sources and genealogical techniques peculiar to Scotland and Ireland, including civil registration, parish registers, census, probates, and military and related records. (3 semester hours)

Germanic/Slavic Family History

Section 1. Germanic Sources: An Introduction. Overview of German alphabet, script, and printing; other primary registers; census, birth, tax, land, probate, and other primary sources; secondary sources; migration records; naming patterns. (3 semester hours)

Oral History Interviewing and Processing

Oral methods of research and writing history; focus on family histories. Techniques of interviewing; transcribing and processing interviews. Creating historical documents. (3 semester hours)

Seminar and Special Problems

Section 1. Practicum. Solving personal genealogical problems in preparation for accreditation. (2 semester hours)

Section 2. Seminar. Attendance at approved family history seminar(s). (2 semester hours)

HUMANITIES

Introduction to the Humanities

Study of the arts emphasizing forms and relationships, the development of critical skills, and an awareness of traditional humanistic values. (3 semester hours)

Arts in Western Culture 2

Western civilization from Renaissance to the present from the perspective of traditional humanistic values reflected in its arts and ideas; examines fundamental questions about human experience, formative events in history, and the value of important literary and artistic texts. (3 semester hours)

INSTRUCTIONAL SCIENCE

Microcomputers in the Schools

Applying computer technology in public schools; evaluating educational software programs, using computer tools, computer programming in LogoWriter. Requires access to a microcomputer (Apple IIe or Apple IIGS preferred), a printer, and Appleworks or some other word processing program. (1 semester hour)

Special Topics in Instructional Science

Section 1. Use the Bible to Teach Reading. A practical, research-proven approach in how to use the Bible to teach children between five and twelve years of age to read. (1 semester hour)

Section 6. Instructional Technology in Teaching. Organizing

Organizing, creating, presenting, and evaluating instruction, emphasizing both the process and the product(s). (2 semester hours)

Section 18. An Alternative to Ability Grouping for Reading Instruction

That Works. How to conduct whole-group instruction in reading; theoretical rationale behind Companion Reading Programs. (1 semester hour)

Section 19. Companion Reading Programs: Practicum. Previous or concurrent use of the Companion Reading Programs. (2 semester hours)

Section 22. Applying the Structured Tutoring Model in Reading. Teaching children to sound out words and teaching them sight words (i.e., words that cannot be read phonetically) using procedures based on empirical research. (2 semester hours)

Section 24. Applying the Structured Tutoring Model to Advanced Reading Skills. Teaching phonetic rules, common word segments,] prefixes, suffixes; reading polysyllabic words, additional sight words, comprehension; and rate. (2 semester hours)

Section 25. Applying the Structured Tutoring Model to Basic Mathematics. Teaching the mathematical concepts, computational skills, etc., required between kindergarten and third grade. (2 semester hours)

Section 30. Microcomputers in the Schools. Applying computer technology in public schools; evaluating educational software programs, using computer tools, computer programming in LogoWriter. (1 semester hour)

LATIN

Latin for Genealogists

Development of a reading knowledge of simple Latin prose found in parish, notarial, and other records of interest to genealogists, family historians, and archivists. Introduction to the organization, structure, content of such records. (3 semester hours)

MANAGEMENT COMMUNICATIONS

Written Business Communication

Including case analysis and problem solving. (3 semester hours)

MANAGERIAL ECONOMICS

Economics of Market Systems

Models of decision making, business strategy, and price information in the contemporary market system. (3 semester hours)

Macroeconomics For Business Decisions

Models of aggregate economic fluctuations, economic growth, inflation, and interest rates. (3 semester hours)

MATHEMATICS

College Algebra

Functions, polynomials, theory of equations, exponential and logarithmic functions, matrices, determinants, systems of linear equations, permutations, combinations, binomial theorem. (3 semester hours)

Trigonometry

Circular functions, triangle relationships, identities, inverse trig functions, trigonometric equations, vectors, complex numbers, DeMoivre's theorem. (2 semester hours)

Calculus 1

Plane analytic geometry; one-dimensional differential and integral calculus, with applications. (4 semester hours)

Calculus 2

Plane analytic geometry: one-dimensional differential and integral calculus, with applications. (4 semester hours)

Introduction to Calculus

Introduction to plane analytic geometry and one-dimensional calculus. (4 semester hours)

History of Mathematics

Development of mathematics, emphasizing the underlying principles and motivations. (3 semester hours)

Finite Math for Teachers

Sets, logic, combinatorics, and probability. Required of prospective secondary mathematics teachers. (3 semester hours)

Survey of Geometry

Euclidean, non-Euclidean, and finite geometries. (3 semester hours)

Basic Concepts of Mathematics

Logic and number theory, number and numeration systems, informal geometry, and probability. (4 semester hours)

Concepts of Mathematics

Modular arithmetic, real numbers, complex numbers, relations and functions, informal geometry, and consumer math. (3 semester hours)

Advanced Engineering Mathematics

Math 312. Ordinary differential equations, linear algebra, vector calculus; an introduction to partial differential equations. (3 semester hours)

Math 313. A continuation of the above course. (3 semester hours)

Elementary Linear Algebra

Linear systems, matrices, vectors and vector spaces, linear transformations, determinants, inner product spaces, eigenvalues, and eigenvectors. (3 semester hours)

MICROBIOLOGY

General Microbiology

Microbial world, emphasizing communicable diseases, their cause and control. (3 semester hours)

MUSIC

Introduction to Music

Designed to aid nonmusic majors in developing skills needed for listening to music creatively. Emphasis on masterworks of Western music from major style periods. (3 semester hours)

Basic Piano Skills

Instruction in piano for nonmajors. (2 semester hours)

Piano Techniques and Literature

A continuation of the above course. (2 semester hours)

Cooperative Education

The following sections present progressively difficult level of organ performance skills related to hymns, organ repertoire, music theory, and accompanimental skills to prepare an organist for competent church service playing. Sample hymns, compositions, and other requirements are listed for each level as a guide to the level's respective difficulty at the beginning of the level:

Section 1. Organ Performance, Level 1. For those with no formal organ study. (2 semester hours)

Section 2. Organ Performance, Level 2. Basic pedal and manual technique; ability to play #1 from Marcel Dupre's 79 chorales and LDS Hymn #125. (2 semester hours)

Section 3. Organ Performance, Level 3. More difficult organ techniques exercises; ability to play #4 or #52 from Marcel Dupre's 79 chorales and LDS Hymns #116 and #67; advancing theory and registrational concepts. (3 semester hours)

Section 4. Organ Performance, Level 4. Increasingly difficult organ technique; ability to play Bach's Prelude and Fugue in C (from 8 short) and LDS hymns #188 and #172; progressively difficult theory and registration studies; accompaniments; sight-reading and simple transposition. (3 semester hours)

Section 5. Organ Performance, Level 5. More advanced technical studies; ability to play Bach's Christ lag in Todesbanden (Orgelbuchlein), Brahms' Eleven Chorale Preludes #2, and LDS hymns #175, #50, and #40; more advanced studies in theory, registration, choral accompaniment, sight-reading, and transposition. (4 semester hours)

Section 6. Organ Performance, Level 6. Continuing technical studies; ability to play Bach's Toccata and Fugue in D Minor, Mendelssohn's Sonata #2, and LDS Hymns #83, #69, and #134; advancing studies in theory, registration, choral accompaniment, sight-reading, and transposition. (5 semester hours)

NURSING

Nursing and Medical Technology

Nursing and medical terminology for prenursing and beginning nursing students or those interested in health occupations. (2 semester hours)

ORGANIZATIONAL BEHAVIOR

Fundamentals of Organizational Behavior

Organizational behavior at three levels: individual, group, and organizational. Motivation, communication, rewards, leadership, conflict, decision making, organizational structure, performance evaluation, and organizational change. (3 semester hours)

PHILOSOPHY

Introduction to Philosophy

Articulating, assessing, and defending fundamental positions on topics such as reason, knowledge, science, education, ethics and politics, and religion. (3 semester hours)

Introduction to Logic

Formal logic, its history, and its use in analyzing and evaluating arguments. (3 semester hours)

PHYSICAL EDUCATION

Bowling, Beginning

Beginning bowling. (½ semester hour)

Fitness for Living

Correct concepts for cardiovascular endurance, strength, flexibility, and weight control. (½ semester hour)

Jogging

Students enhance physical fitness through jogging or running 140 miles or completing 750 Cooper's points. (½ semester hour)

Swimming, Intermediate

Students must engage in an exercise program for at least eight weeks. (½ semester hour)

Tennis, Beginning

(½ semester hour)

Administration of Athletic and Intramural Programs

Management styles and techniques for interschool athletic and in-tramural program; policies concerning eligibility, contest management, safety, facilities, and legal aspects. (3 semester hours)

PHYSICAL SCIENCE

Physical Science Fundamentals

Interdisciplinary course administered by the Physics and Astronomy Department. (3 semester hours)

PHYSICS

Introductory Applied Physics

Course PHSCS 105. Applied physics course not requiring calculus. Topics include mechanics, heat, wave motion, and sound. (3 semester hours)

Course PHSCS 106. A continuation of the above course. Topics include electricity and magnetism, atomic and nuclear physics, and optics. (3 semester hours)

Descriptive Astronomy

Nonmathematical presentation of our knowledge of the content and history of the cosmos. (3 semester hours)

POLITICAL SCIENCE

American Government and Politics

Origin and development of federal Constitution; national, state, and local governments and politics. (3 semester hours)

Western Political Heritage 1

Western civilization from Greek antiquity to Renaissance, primarily from perspective of political philosophy and scriptures; exploring fundamental questions in human experience; examining formative events in human experience; understanding value of important texts. (3 semester hours)

Western Political Heritage 2

Western civilization from Renaissance to present, primarily from perspective of political philosophy; exploring fundamental questions in human experience; examining formative events in history; understanding value of important texts. (3 semester hours)

PSYCHOLOGY

General Psychology

Basic course in modern scientific psychology. (3 semester hours)

Understanding and Improving Your Memory

Principles of human learning and memory; study skills and methods for improving memory. (1 semester hour)

Personal and Social Adjustment

Concepts of adjustment and application of psychological principles for coping with stress and interpersonal, emotional, and psychosexual difficulties. (3 semester hours)

Psychological Statistics

Descriptive analysis and hypothesis testing applied to psychological research data. (3 semester hours)

Parenting

Theories and skills related to quality parent-child relationships. (3 semester hours)

Sex Roles in the Family and Society

Biological and social contributions to sex role development, sexual self-concept, and complementarity of sex roles. (3 semester hours)

Developmental Psychology: Childhood

Physical, mental, emotional, and social development of the child. (3 semester hours)

Developmental Psychology: Adolescence

Development and maturation during adolescence; research methodology. (3 semester hours)

Developmental Psychology: Adulthood

Stability, and change in psychological, physiological, and interpersonal processes through early, middle, and late adulthood. (3 semester hours)

Organizational Psychology

Personal, interactional, and structural aspects of organizations, motivation, decision making, problem-solving communication, leadership, organizational structure, change. (3 semester hours)

Sport Psychology

Application of psychological principles to sporting activities. (3 semester hours)

Personality

Individual patterns of behavior, thought, and emotion from perspective of diverse personality theories and their associated strategies of research, assessments, and personality change. (3 semester hours)

Abnormal Psychology

Dynamics of maladjustment; major psychological disorders and therapeutic procedures. (3 semester hours)

Exceptional Children

Exceptionalities and their psychological significance; gifted, mentally retarded, and physically and emotionally handicapped children. (3 semester hours)

Introduction to Social Psychology

Conformity and obedience; socialization, norms and roles; attitudes, leadership, group processes. (3 semester hours)

Interpersonal Growth and Group Processes

Effective interpersonal relationships and group functioning. (3 semester hours)

Leadership Development

Principles and practices of successful leadership: decision making, communications, planning, team building, motivation, and interpersonal skills. (3 semester hours)

Environmental Psychology

Interaction between people and their physical context. (3 semester hours)

RECREATION MANAGEMENT

Introduction to Therapeutic Recreation

Agencies, services, programs, and practices related to therapeutic recreation. (3 semester hours)

Assessment in Therapeutic Recreation

Patient assessment, treatment plan development, and counseling procedures. (3 semester hours)

Aging and Leisure

Understanding recreation and leisure services for the aging and aged in both community and institutional settings. (2 semester hours)

RELIGIOUS EDUCATION

Introduction to the Book of Mormon

Course REL A 121. Origin and teachings of the Book of Mormon. Covers 1 Nephi through Alma 29. (2 semester hours)

Course REL A 122. A continuation of the above course. Origins and teachings of the Book of Mormon. Covers Alma 30 through Moroni 10. (2 semester hours)

The New Testament

Course REL A 211. The Gospels. (2 semester hours)

Course REL A 212. A continuation of the above course. The Book of Acts, the Epistles, and the Apocalypse (Revelation). (2 semester hours)

Doctrines of the Gospel

Doctrines of The Church of Jesus Christ of Latter-day Saints as taught in the scriptures and by latter-day prophets. (2 semester hours)

Introduction to LDS Family History (Genealogy)

Introduction to family history program of the Church; emphasizes temple ordinances for ancestors in first generations and use of Church resources to simplify temple and family history activities. (2 semester hours)

The Old Testament

Course REL A 301. Introduction to the structure and teachings of the Old Testament from Genesis through 2 Samuel. (2 semester hours)

Course REL A 302. A continuation of the above course. Covers 1 Kings through Malachi. (2 semester hours)

Writings of Isaiah

Historical, prophetic, doctrinal, and literary values of Isaiah, emphasizing latter-day interpretation and application. (2 semester hours)

The Doctrine and Covenants

Course REL C 324. Origin and content, and teachings of the Doctrine and Covenants. Discusses Sections 1 through 70. (2 semester hours)

Course REL C 325. A continuation of above course. Considers Sections 71 through 138. (2 semester hours)

The Pearl of Great Price

Origin and content of the Pearl of Great Price. (2 semester hours)

Teachings of the Living Prophets

Calling and function of the living prophets, emphasizing their teachings through recent conference reports. (2 semester hours)

Latter-day Saint History From 1805 to 1844

Church history and doctrine, from the birth of Joseph Smith to his martyrdom. (2 semester hours)

Latter-day Saint Church History From 1844 to the Present

Church history and doctrine, from the martyrdom to the present. (2 semester hours)

Special Studies in Religion; Ancient Scripture

Section 1. The Writings of John. Literary and doctrinal study of the Gospel of John, the three epistles, and Revelation of John. (1 semester hour)

Sharing the Gospel

Focuses upon the purpose, skills, and doctrines of missionary work and prepares prospective missionaries for a more meaningful MTC and mission experience. (2 semester hours)

Special Studies in Religion: Church History and Doctrine

Section 2. Presidents of the Church. The lives and contributions of the presidents of the LDS Church. (1 semester hour).

Section 6. Latter-day Saint Temples. The nature of temples, how temple service has unfolded over time, and the purpose and scope of temple responsibilities and opportunities. (1 semester hour)

Introduction to the Book of Mormon

Course REL A 421. Origin and teachings of the Book of Mormon (for returned missionaries and mature students). Covers 1 Nephi through Alma 29. (2 semester hours)

Course REL A 422. A continuation of the preceding course (for returned missionaries and mature students). Covers Alma 30 through Moroni 10. (2 semester hours)

Special Topics in Church History and Doctrine

Section 1. Introduction to Military Ministry. Preparation of new military chaplains who find themselves in a religiously pluralistic and predominantly Protestant context, to be immediately effective in leading worship, in preaching, and in guiding the teaching ministry within a chapel. Emphasis is on practical ministry within a theological and spiritual context. (3 semester hours)

Section 2. Introduction to Military Ministry, Part 2. A continuation of the above course. (3 semester hours)

SECONDARY EDUCATION

Theory and Methods of Secondary Teaching

Course SC ED 376R. This course number is used to accommodate BYU's preservice teachers. Some of these courses are also listed under Course SC ED 515R (Special Topics in Education) to accommodate inservice teachers who need graduate-level course numbers. Transcript titles may be different under the different course numbers.

Section 11. Creativity in the Classroom. How to use the creative process in designing and using student-centered activities. Emphasizes student rather than teacher creativity. (1 semester hour)

Section 13. Reflective Teaching. Improving professional and personal decision-making ability in teaching through reflection. Theory of reflection and using your reflective journal entries to write Description, Interpretation, Evaluation, and Plan (DIEP) summaries. Required: access to a classroom for at least five weeks. (1 semester hour)

Section 34. Improving Discipline in the Schools: Eight Discipline Models. Principles and strategies to enhance teacher-student rapport, help the teacher understand and change student behavior, and help students make long-term behavioral improvements. (1 semester hour)

Section 35. Evaluating Student Learning. Introduction to evaluation, designing an instrument, interpreting student test performance, affective multiple-talent, and creative evaluation. (1 semester hour)

Section 36. Simulation and Games. Practical experience in applying simulations and games to the classroom. (1 semester hour)

Section 45. Formulating Useful Instructional Objectives. How to write significant objectives in the cognitive and psychomotor areas, adapt existing objectives, and apply these in the classroom. (1 semester hour)

Section 46. Questioning That Turns Students On Rather Than Off. Effective questioning techniques. (1 semester hour)

Section 60. Teaching Reading in the Content Areas. Flexible, practical course in teaching reading in content courses. Assignments assigned according to one's teaching subject(s) and grade level(s). (1 semester hour)

Section 61. Teaching Reading in the Content Areas. For students who need one additional hour of credit. (1 semester hour)

Section 62. Teaching Reading in the Content Areas. For students who need two additional hours of credit. (2 semester hours)

Special Topics in Education

Course SC ED 515R. Independent Study offers these courses as professional and practical assistance to inservice teachers:

Section 3. How to Teach Concepts. A practical approach to teaching concepts effectively. Required: classroom or neighborhood children to teach for one lesson. (2 semester hours)

Section 5. Legitimate Legibility: Italic Handwriting. Italic letter forms; the eight joins that make print into logical beautiful cursive italic handwriting. (1 semester hour)

Section 10. Developing Capable People. Seven essential characteristics basic to young people for becoming capable, caring, and responsible people; developing self-discipline, good interpersonal skills, responsibility, judgment, and problem-solving skills. (2 semester hours)

Section 11. Creativity in the Classroom. How to use the creative process in designing and using student-centered activities. Emphasizes student rather than teacher creativity. (1 semester hour)

Section 12. Reading: Developing Comprehension Skills. A proven, research-based approach to teaching comprehension; developing the reader's background and vocabulary, improving comprehension processes and skills, comprehension and different types of discourse, and teaching comprehension in the content areas. (2 semester hours)

Section 13. Reflective Teaching. Improving professional and personal decision-making ability in teaching through reflection. Theory of reflection and using your reflective journal entries to write Description, Interpretation, Evaluation, and Plan (DIEP) summaries. Required: access to a classroom for at least five weeks. (1 semester hour)

Section 34. Improving Discipline in the Schools: Eight Discipline Models. Principles and strategies to enhance teacher-student rapport, help the teacher understand and change student behavior, and help students make long-term behavioral improvements. (1 semester hour)

Section 35. Evaluating Student Learning. Introduction to evaluation, designing an instrument, interpreting student test performance, affective multiple-talent, and creative evaluation. (1 semester hour)

Section 36. Simulation and Games. Practical experience in applying simulations and games to the classroom. (1 semester hour)

Section 37. Creativity in the Classroom. How to use the creative process in designing and using student-centered activities. Emphasizes student rather than teacher creativity. Using brainstorming and seeing beyond the obvious, forging ideas to convert to lessons, and applying these ideas to specific products or performance in the classroom and in daily life. (1 semester hour)

Section 45. Formulating Useful Instructional Objectives. How to write significant objectives in the cognitive and psychomotor areas, adapt existing objectives, and apply these in the classroom. (1 semester hour)

Section 46. Questioning That Turns Students On Rather Than Off. Effective questioning techniques. (1 semester hour)

Section 60. Teaching Reading in the Content Areas. A flexible, practical course in teaching reading in content areas. (1 semester hour)

Section 63. Teaching Reading in the Content Areas. A three-credit version of the above course. (3 semester hours)

Section 64. Teaching Reading in the Content Areas. For students who need one additional hour of credit. (3 semester hours)

SOCIAL WORK

Family Interaction

The family system through life cycle stages; intrafamily processes;

stresses and challenges; individual and family well-being; family interaction with societal systems. (3 semester hours)

Introduction to Social Work Research Methods

Qualitative and quantitative designs. Problem formulation, data collection, statistical analysis, writing, and presenting results. (3 to 5 semester hours)

Introduction to the Field of Social Work

Social welfare as a social institution; social work as a profession. (3 semester hours)

Social Welfare Programs and Services

The Social Security Act, federal block grants, federal transfer programs, and the private social welfare sector. (2 semester hours)

SOCIOLOGY

Introductory Sociology

Social group influence, social interaction, processes, organization, and change; family, religion, government, population, culture, race relations. (3 semester hours)

Current Social Problems

Individual deviance (violence, insanity, drugs, sex, crime, etc.) and social disorganization (poverty, race and sex discrimination, divorce, overpopulation, etc.). Conditions, causes, solutions. (3 semester hours)

Applied Social Statistics

Introductory descriptive and inferential statistics; graphing, central tendency, variation, hypothesis testing and parameter estimation, measures of association, correlation, and regression. (3 semester hours)

Family Interaction

The family system through the life cycle stages; intrafamily processes; stresses and challenges; individual and family well-being; family interaction with societal systems. (3 semester hours)

Methods of Research in Sociology

Tools of social research; survey, experimentation, content analysis, secondary analysis, data processing and analysis, and report writing. (3 semester hours)

Sociology of Education

Social origins of goals and curricula; theories of change and control; the nature of achievement in education. (3 semester hours)

Introduction to Social Psychology

Conformity and obedience, socialization, norms and role attitudes, leadership, and group processes. (3 semester hours)

Interpersonal Growth and Group Processes

Effective interpersonal relationships and group functioning. (3 semester hours)

Sociology of Aging

Demographic and societal factors affecting aging, agencies serving older citizens, and the role of the community in solving problems of the aged. (2 semester hours)

SPANISH

Second-Year Spanish

Review of grammar, reading, writing, conversation. (4 semester hours)

Introduction to Spanish Literature

Readings in modern Hispanic literatures, focusing on formal literary analysis. (3 semester hours)

Survey of Spanish Literature

Literary masterpieces of Spain. (3 semester hours)

STATISTICS

Principles of Statistics 1

Stemplots, boxplots, histograms, scatterplots; central tendency, variability; confidence intervals and hypothesis testing involving one and two means and proportions; contingency tables, regression; computer package. (3 semester hours)

Elements of Mathematical Statistics

Probability, random variables, frequency distributions, estimation and tests of hypothesis from a theoretical standpoint. (3 semester hours)

STUDY SKILLS

Effective Study and Learning

Learning to learn: motivation, time management, reading, listening, notetaking, test preparation, and memorizing; cognitive and ethical development in a learning environment. (2 semester hours)

Life Planning and Decision Making

Individual development in life planning and decision making, emphasizing self-awareness as a basis for valuing, goal setting, and decision making in areas of common interest to college-age adults. (2 semester hours)

Special Topics in Student Development

Section 1. Analytical Reading. Development of an advanced reading skill that includes a sophisticated, concept-related vocabulary and a clear differentiation of main topic and supporting details, and a reasoning attitude that identifies time and space, cause and effect, reason and consequence, and premise and conclusion. Course content is general in nature so that skills can be transferred to any specific discipline. (1 semester hour)

THEATRE

Introduction to the Theatre

Appreciation of theatre through lectures viewing productions, reading, writing, demonstrations, and productions. (3 semester hours)

Playwriting

Theory and technique of writing the one-act and full-length play. (3 semester hours)

HIGH SCHOOL COURSES

ART

General Art, Part 1

Creative thinking, experiments with art media, ''studio'' experiences with drawing, collage and design; art appreciation, criticism, and history to the Renaissance. (½ unit)

General Art, Part 2

Using art in daily living such as advertising, interior design, and wearable art; op-art printing; art history and appreciation, early eighteenth century to the present, and some ethnic art. (½ unit)

Drawing

Development of drawing skills. Proportions, pattern, depth and light; incorporating imagination and creativity into drawings. (½ unit)

Calligraphy

A simple B-pen alphabet as well as Celtic, Gothic, and Italic styles. How to use and decorate each style. (½ unit)

Legitimate Legibility: Italic Handwriting

Italic letter forms; the eight joins that make print into a logical, legible, beautiful cursive italic handwriting. (½ unit)

General Photography

Gaining a working knowledge of basic photographic principles. (½ unit)

BUSINESS

Work Study

For those who have jobs or who wish to find a job and earn credit for their work experience. Meets Utah requirements for work experience credit. (½ unit)

On-the-Job Work Experience

For students who already have jobs; have previously completed the above course; and desire to earn credit for on-the-job experience. Meets Alpine School District requirements for work experience credit. (½ unit)

Entrepreneurship: Starting Your Own Business

What organization is and does; forms of ownership—corporation, individual, partners, franchises; financial control; the organization of personnel; and the role the government plays in marketing. (½ unit)

Accounting (Bookkeeping), Part 1

Setting up a bookkeeping system and keeping the records of special sales and cash receipts, journals, and ledgers. (½ unit)

Accounting (Bookkeeping), Part 2

Payroll records, taxes, debts, and accounts receivable; solving problems dealing with depreciation and fixed assets; and using a cash register correctly. (½ unit)

Beginning Keyboarding, Part 1

Typing announcements, personal notes, postal cards, letters, tabulations, tables, outlines, and manuscripts. Speed objective: thirty to forty words per minute. (½ unit)

Beginning Keyboarding, Part 2

Increasing speed to the forty to sixty words per minute range; improving accuracy and production skills; and typing business letters, manuscripts, and reports correctly. Identifying and correcting tabulation problems. (½ unit)

Business Law, Part 2 (BUS 09)

Math skills essential to buying a car, home, and insurance; budgeting; investing; traveling; and other practical applications. (½ unit)

Business Law, Part 2 (BUS 10)

A continuation of the above course. Math skills essential to shopping; using credit; reading graphs and statistical and financial reports; making measurements; running a business; other practical applications. (½ unit)

Understanding Taxes

Practical course in preparing income tax returns. Topics include role of taxes in society and voluntary compliance; preparing Form 1040A, Form 1040, and Schedule A; and progressing from the simplest form to more complicated tax situations. (½ unit)

Business Communications

Using the parts of speech and punctuation in correct business form; writing effective sentences and paragraphs; using style, tone, and simplicity for message power; and using words correctly to help obtain a job. (½ unit)

Business Law, Part 1

Rights and obligations concerning contracts, bailments, buyer and seller relations, debtors, and creditors. (½ unit)

Business Law, Part 2

Rights and obligations concerning negotiable instruments, employer and employee relations, insurance, property, and the laws of rentals and wills. (½ unit)

Speed Writing

Rapid recording of notes in a proven notetaking system. Speedwriting improves note-taking skills for school and work. (½ unit)

Basic Marketing, Part 1

Basic working knowledge of marketing and distribution, including marketing careers, marketing functions, market segmentation, and channels of distribution. (½ unit)

Basic Marketing, Part 2

Continuation of the above course. Advertising, personal selling, sales promotion, public relations, and marketing trends. (½ unit)

Advertising

Planning a major advertising campaign for a consumer; using appropriate copy, layout, design, media promotion, goals, and mailing. (½ unit)

Psychology and Human Relations in Marketing

Employer-employee relationships, human relations in the formal and informal organization, personal attributes an employer expects, and the role in improving human relations played by management and employee. (½ unit)

Fashion Merchandising

Preparations for careers in the marketing of clothing and clothing-related articles for personal wear and adornment. Gaining employment in retail department or specialty stores. (½ unit)

Real Estate

Preparation for careers as residential real estate sales specialists. Marketing residential real estate and such related activities as obtaining listings, qualifying buyers, showing properties, explaining financing, handling offers and counter offers, maintaining professionalism, and planning career advancement. (½ unit)

CHINESE

Beginning Chinese (Mandarin)

Pronunciation, fundamentals of grammar, and recognition of basic Chinese characters. (½ unit)

COMPUTER SCIENCE

Understanding Computers and Information Processing

Hardware functions and software applications; impact of computers on knowledge, communications, graphics, technical design, and careers in society. (½ unit)

Elementary Computer Applications, Part 1

Computer organization, problem solving, and information systems; emphasizing use of the computer for problem solving and developing programming skills. (½ unit)

Elementary Computer Applications, Part 2

Continuation of the above course. (½ unit)

Word Processing Computer Skills

Introduction to and application of word processing. (½ unit)

DRIVER EDUCATION

Driver Education

The driving task, interaction with traffic, driving in different environments and conditions, and the responsibilities of a driver. Meets the thirty hours of instruction required for student licensing by most states. It is usually also necessary to take six hours of actual driving instruction from a private instructor or a school driver education instructor. Students must be at least 15½ years old. (½ unit)

ENGLISH

Ninth-Grade English, Part 1

Reading enhancement through learning literary terms while reading exciting short stories, poems, plays, and novels; improving writing skills through essays, journal entries, and grammatical exercises. (½ unit)

Ninth-Grade English, Part 2

Appreciating the wide gamut of literature from William Shakespeare's *Romeo and Juliet* to science fiction and even the macabre to a novel about Indian culture; developing thinking and writing skills. (½ unit)

Tenth-Grade English, Part 1

Interpreting literature (emphasis on short stories), improving writing skills, some journal and essay writing, and preparing a job application. (½ unit)

Tenth-Grade English, Part 2

Literature (more short stories and drama), introduction to poetry, writing personal narrative, and more journal and essay writing. (½ unit)

Eleventh-Grade English, Part 1

Reading and analyzing various American literature selections (1600–1900); understanding their historical and cultural context; applying literary terms; developing vocabulary; improving writing skills. (½ unit)

Eleventh-Grade English, Part 2

Continuing skills developed in the above course by reading American literature selections from 1900 to present; three writing assignments; descriptive, expository, creative. (½ unit)

Twelfth-Grade English, Part 1

Exploration of ideas, life, and language through reading and writing about world literature. Writing will focus on ideas, voice, organization, word choice, sentence fluency, and usage. (½ unit)

Twelfth-Grade English, Part 2

Exploring more world literature on the human experience with more opportunity to write rich descriptions using ideas, voice, organization, word choice, sentence fluency, and usage. (½ unit)

Business English

Using the parts of speech and punctuation in correct business form; writing effective sentences and paragraphs; using style, tone, and simplicity for message power; and using words correctly to help obtain a job. (½ unit)

Understanding Literature

Reading, analyzing, and interpreting short stories, poetry, novels, and plays at the surface, subtle, symbolic, and personal levels. (½ unit)

Self-Esteem: A Search for Dignity and Worth

Building self-esteem based on the experiences of others through literature. Analyzing the effects of goal choice, relative effort, and the ability to accept results; applying the learned concepts to the problems of real people. (½ unit)

The Year 2100

The future through speculative literature; looking at the best and worst future possibilities if present trends in society and present human traits continue—as seen by writers. (½ unit)

Practical English: Review of Fundamentals

Review of English Fundamentals: sentence structure; parts of speech; punctuation and capitalization; and writing phrases, clauses, and paragraphs. (½ unit)

Spelling

A remedial course. Patterns for spelling most words; how to master words that don't follow patterns; using meaning to choose between commonly confused similar words. (½ unit)

Analytical Reading

A logical, reasoning approach to reading. Understanding main ideas and facts, verbal descriptions of sequence, cause and effect, and classification of ideas. Attention to vocabulary related to understanding the text. (½ unit)

The Bible as Literature

Nonsectarian introduction to the King James Version of the Bible as a great classic of English literature. (½ unit)

Reading Comprehension

Understanding the main idea; isolating details and recalling specific facts; retaining concepts and organizing facts; using meaning clues; and using recall patterns. (½ unit)

Remedial Reading

A course to help individuals strengthen their reading skills by recognizing roots, affixes, and other structural aspects of words and by using the dictionary and other reading materials. (½ unit)

Developmental Reading with Short Stories

Reading with comprehension; recognizing clues that increase understanding of both ideas and words; recognizing roots, affixes, and other structural aspects of words; and reading both fiction and biography. (½ unit)

Developmental Reading with Short Stories

Emphasizes the joys of reading that appeal specifically to the concerns and interests of young people. All books have significant literary merit as well as relevant and universal human themes. (½ unit)

Expository Writing: Explaining Your Ideas

The most common type of writing: reports, directions, opinions, explanations, analyses. (½ unit)

Narrative and Descriptive Writing: The Art of Storytelling

How to write a good story—a series of happenings (description, conversation, commentary, but mostly actions). (½ unit)

Creative Writing

Improving creative writing skills by strengthening powers of observation. How to reveal character; how to develop scenes, point of view, plot, conflict, tone, and theme. (½ unit)

HEALTH

General Health

Making independent, informed decisions concerning physical, mental, and social well-being. Discovering capability and responsibility for developing attitudes and patterns of behavior that will promote a full and satisfying life, regardless of age. (½ unit)

Brigham Young University

HOME ECONOMICS

Basic Clothing Construction, Part 1

Clothing impressions, selecting flattering styles, choosing fabrics and patterns, and understanding patterns and fitting them to you. (½ unit)

Basic Clothing Construction, Part 2

Pressing techniques, and sewing projects: tote bag, shorts, skirt or pants, and a tailored shirt. (½ unit)

Clothing: Fashion Fundamentals

The messages clothes send, how clothes reflect the future, deciding what to wear and why, how to buy clothes, the garment industry, and sewing basics. (½ unit)

Foods, Part 1

Food-oriented study of nutrition, technological advancements, and methods of preparation that help in making dietary choices. (½ unit)

Foods, Part 2

A study of cooking principles, regional American foods, foreign culture and foods, and careers in the food industry. (½ unit)

Interior Design and Decoration

How to develop and organize interior environments to enjoy comforts and aesthetic pleasures of "good taste," regardless of budget and circumstances. (½ unit)

Child Development, Part 1

Prenatal development, birth, behavioral development in infancy, and trends in child care. (½ unit)

Child Development, Part 2

Developmental principles and approaches concerning the toddler, the preschool child, the middle years of childhood, and adolescence. (½ unit)

Preparing for Responsible Parenthood

Practical preparation for parenthood: dating and marriage, adjustment to married life, building the marriage relationship, managing money, inviting children into the marriage, raising children, and coping with problems and pressures. Emphasis on forming values and setting goals to help in the future marriage relationship. (½ unit)

Consumer Economics

Necessary consumer information and skills to live productive lives in today's marketplace: checking accounts, interest, savings accounts, consumer protection, credit, budgeting, shelter, buying a car, insurance, and the job market. (½ unit)

INDUSTRIAL EDUCATION

Leathercraft

A practical approach. Preparation of leather for carving, major tanning processes, finishing and caring for leather, and proper steps in carving leather into a good design. (½ unit)

House Wiring

Electrical principles and procedures for wiring a home, basement, or room. Circuits, grounding systems, conductors, rewiring projects, code requirements, and safety. (½ unit)

Auto Body Repair

Basic principles and "how-to" steps for auto body reconstruction and repair. Fundamentals of auto body work and projects for easy individual applications. (½ unit)

Small Engine Repair

Fundamentals of small engine repair and servicing. Access to a small engine (e.g., lawnmower) required. (½ unit)

Automotive Fundamentals, Part 1

Engine parts, ignition systems, cooling systems, lubrication systems, fuel systems, kinds of engines, and engine measurements. Application principles not required, but the course provides for easy individual application as desired. (½ unit)

Automotive Fundamentals, Part 2

Continuation of the above course. Engine clutches, transmissions, drive lines, rear axle assemblies, frames, bodies, suspension systems, wheels and tires, front wheel alignment and steering systems, brakes, and electrical system fundamentals. (½ unit)

MASS MEDIA

Man and Mass Media

Analyze, critique, and discover, in ways that are fun as well as informative, our fast-lane, mass-media world that tries to inform us, entertain us, or persuade us to believe, buy, or do things that we would not otherwise do. Become a more effective, intelligent mass media consumer. (½ unit)

MATHEMATICS

Remedial Arithmetic, Part 1

Adding, subtracting, multiplying, and dividing whole numbers up to seven numerals; reducing to lowest terms; applying the fundamental operations to proper and mixed fractions of up to five digits; writing correct notation for a set and identifying the null set; intersection, union, and complement of sets. Ninth-grade level. (½ unit)

Remedial Arithmetic, Part 2

Defining and identifying the additive, multiplicative, commutative, associative, and distributive properties in step-by-step solutions to problems; squaring and obtaining square roots and solving percentage and decimal problems. (½ unit)

Fundamental Mathematical Skills with a Calculator, Part 1

Practical experiences in basic mathematics leading to mathematical literacy and self-confidence with word problems and formulas. Use of a hand-held calculator for solving math problems. (½ unit)

Applied Math, Part 1

Using mathematics to solve problems on the job. Learning to use your calculator; estimating; measuring; graphs, charts, and tables; working with data; and lines and angles. (½ unit)

Applied Math, Part 2

Two- and three-dimensional shapes; ratios and proportions; scale drawings; signed numbers and vectors; scientific notation; precision, accuracy and tolerance; powers and roots. (½ unit)

Business and Consumer Mathematics, Part 1

Math skills essential to buying a car, home, and insurance; budgeting; investing; traveling; and other practical applications. (½ unit)

Business and Consumer Mathematics, Part 2

Continuation of the above course. Math skills essential to shopping; using credit; reading graphs and statistical and financial reports; making measurements; running a business; other practical applications. (½ unit)

Pre-Algebra, Part 1

Using fundamental mathematical functions with integers, fractions, and decimals; using order of operations to evaluate variable expressions; solving variable equations using transformations; translating word sentences into mathematical equations; and solving word problems. (½ unit)

Pre-Algebra, Part 2

Using ratios, rates, and proportions to solve problems; changing fractions, percents, and decimals; solving problems involving percentages, discounts, mark-ups, commissions, profit, simple and compound interest, etc. (½ unit)

Beginning Algebra, Part 1

Properties of decimal numbers; operations involving union, intersection, and complements of sets; using the language of algebra to state fundamental properties of real numbers; and operations using additive and multiplicative inverses and absolute values. (½ unit)

Beginning Algebra, Part 2

Solving graph equations and linear inequalities for one and two variables, factoring polynomials, simplifying elementary expressions involving exponents and radicals, solving quadratic exponents and radicals, and solving quadratic equations by the basic quadratic formula. (½ unit)

Second Course in Algebra, Part 1

Solving equations and problems involving variables, factoring quadratic equations, manipulating fractions with variables, using common formulas, squaring and cubing numbers, multiplying and dividing radicals, and solving irrational equations. (½ unit)

Second Course in Algebra, Part 2

Drawing graphs of figures and equations; graphing linear functions; simplifying expressions involving exponents; using logarithms; using basic trigonometric ratios; determining the midpoint, slope, and distance between two points in coordinate geometry; and solving quadratic inequalities graphically. (½ unit)

Plane Geometry, Part 1

Principles of plane geometry—deductive reasoning, hypotheses, postulates, corollaries, conclusions, assumptions, and formal proofing; writing the converse, inverse, and contrapositive of a theorem; and constructing geometric figures using the basic tools of geometry. (½ unit)

Plane Geometry, Part 2

Proving the Pythogorean theorem with a formal demonstration; finding the area of any triangle using Hero's formula; applying principles relating to circles, angles, and arcs to problems; identifying the first, second, third, and fourth term of a proportion; and constructing geometric figures using theorems and corollaries. (½ unit)

Trigonometry, Part 1

Deriving and graphically representing trigonometric relationships and functions, and using trigonometric functions in a variety of problem situations. (½ unit)

Trigonometry, Part 2

Solving problems dealing with identities, trigonometric equations, functions of complex numbers, and inverses. (½ unit)

Analytic Geometry

Algebra, trigonometry. Analytic geometry needed in calculus, including the line, the circle, the parabola, the ellipse, the hyperbola, polar coordinates, three-dimensional rectangular coordinates. (½ unit)

Calculus 1, Part 1

Mechanics of calculus applicable to the sciences and engineering, including limits and continuity, the derivative, applications of the derivative, the definite integral, applications of the definite integral, transcendental functions. (½ unit)

Calculus 1, Part 2

The definite integral, application of the definite integral, and transcendental functions. (½ unit)

Calculus 2, Part 1

Methods of integration, trigonometric substitutions and partial fractions, and geometric integrals. (½ unit)

Calculus 2, Part 2

Intermediate forms and improper integrals, infinite series, alternating and power series. (½ unit)

Pre-Algebra, Part 1

Using fundamental mathematical functions with integers, fractions, and decimals; using order of operations to evaluate variable expressions; solving variable equations using transformations, translating word sentences into mathematical equations, and solving word problems. (½ unit)

Pre-Algebra, Part 2

Using ratios, rates, and proportions to solve problems; changing fractions, percents, and decimals; solving problems involving percentages, discounts, mark-ups, commissions, profit, simple and compound interest, etc. (½ unit)

MUSIC

Beginning Guitar, Part 1

Uses tapes and extensive step-by-step instruction to teach forty-four folk and contemporary songs. Logical progression in chords and technique. Skills, theory, elementary transposition, and arrangements. (½ unit)

Beginning Guitar, Part 2

Continuation of the above course. (½ unit)

PHYSICAL EDUCATION

Fitness for Living

Medical clearance or physical exam required. An individualized, programmed approach to physical fitness—cardiovascular endurance, strength, flexibility. (½ unit)

Tennis

The serve, volley, and other skills necessary to play tennis; written and unwritten rules of the game; and singles and doubles strategy. Access to appropriate equipment is required. (½ unit)

Bowling

Correct approach, delivery, and scoring. Access to appropriate equipment for twenty-three games is required. (½ unit)

Aerobic Dance

Aerobic dance performed to music to attain cardiovascular fitness. The student must engage in this program for at least thirteen weeks to receive credit for this course. (½ unit)

Jogging

Medical clearance or physical exam required. Guidance in becoming more physically fit and in setting up a long-term program to maintain fitness. The student must engage in this course for at least eight weeks and jog a minimum of sixty miles. (½ unit)

Golf

Grip, stance, backswing, downswing, follow through, short game, putting, problem shots, proper club for fairway dis-

Brigham Young University

tance/rough/greens/sandtraps; golf terminology, rules, etiquette, traditions, etc. Requires 54 holes of golf over three to four months. (½ unit)

SCIENCE

Biology, Part 1

Introduction to the themes important in the study of biology; what life is; the structural basis of life; how life maintains continuity; how life may change with time; the structure and function of the human body systems. (½ unit)

Biology, Part 2

Comparisons of the world of plants and the world of animals, leading to the basic principles of ecology. Tissue and organ functioning in plants and animals. (½ unit)

Ecology

Life as it naturally exists in the soil, lakes, ponds, bogs, flowing water, tidal marshes, seashore, grasslands, tundra, shrub lands, and forest; the ecosystem and its interrelationships; environmental influences; and succession. Studies supplemented with field trips. (½ unit)

Human Physiology/Anatomy

Structure and function of all body systems; aspects of cellular biology, biochemistry, and genetics as they relate to the human body. Technology that extends and improves the quality of life: transplants, implants, genetic engineering. (½ unit)

The Drug Scene

A study of the psychological and physiological dangers associated with drug abuse. How to say NO! Prevention and treatment for drug abuse. (½ unit)

Taxidermy

Beginning course in taxidermy. Techniques and procedures for mounting birds, mammals, and fish. (½ unit)

General Astronomy

Nonmathematical look at astronomy designed for both science and nonscience students; study of galaxies, stars, planets, moons, and other features of the universe; instruments and methods used by astronomers. (½ unit)

Earth Science, Part 1

Study of the earth and earth processes designed for science and nonscience students; study of matter, minerals, rocks, resources, oceans, maps, tectonics, volcanoes, and earthquakes. (½ unit)

Earth Science, Part 2

A continuation of the above course. Study of weathering, erosion, water, soils, glaciers, weather, climate, fossils, and dinosaurs. (½ unit)

General Chemistry

A nonmathematical treatment of basic chemistry for the nonscience students: atoms, molecules, compounds, solids, liquids, and gases and their chemical interaction in our daily life. All laboratory experiments can be completed in the kitchen at home. (½ unit)

Chemistry, Part 1

Principles of dimensional/unit analysis, naming chemicals, moles and molecular weight, equations, stoichiometry, gaseous state, densities, acids, and bases. (½ unit)

Chemistry, Part 2

Principles of atomic structure, electron configuration, electron dot, covalent bonding, molecular structure, periodic table, thermochemistry, solutions and water, redox reactions, electrochemistry, and nuclear chemistry. (½ unit)

Physics, Part 1

Nonmathematical treatment of motion and inertia, Newton's second and third laws, momentum and energy, circular motion, and center of gravity, rotation and gravitation, gravitational interactions and satellites, etc. (½ unit)

Physics, Part 2

Nonmathematical treatment of change of state, thermodynamics, wave and sound, light and color, lenses, electrical charges and fields, current and circuits satellites, magnetism, nuclear reaction, etc. (½ unit)

SELF-GUIDANCE

Personal Freedom: How to Gain Control of Your Life

A practical course that considers freedom and interaction with others, freedom from conflict, and freedom within the family. (½ unit)

Preparation for Responsible Adulthood

Practical course in laying a foundation for successful, responsible adulthood; effective use of time, setting attainable goals, working effectively with others, and applying effective attitudes and perspectives. (½ unit)

Dating—Romance and Reason

Identifying the kind of person one wants to date, developing a set of criteria to determine when one is falling in love, and analyzing the pros and cons of going steady. (½ unit)

Education and Career Planning

Evaluation of self-interests and values, researching occupations that are of interest, and drawing conclusions about self and the world of work in order to evaluate directions that might be inviting for career preparation and planning. (½ unit)

How to Find Your Roots

How to discover who your ancestors were and something about their lives, including how to survey what relatives (some distantly related, whom you don't know) and other researchers have found and how to begin original research. (½ unit)

Practical Decision Making

Applying creative thinking, personal values, life goals, and decision-making skills to important decisions. Emphasizes academic and vocational areas but is easily applied to decisions in other areas. (½ unit)

Preparing for Life

Important skills, such as getting a job, finding a place to live, managing money, handling a checking account, understanding loan procedures, and participating in civic responsibilities. (½ unit)

Studying in High School

Improving and developing study skills in preparation for college and/or success in high school studies. Emphasis on note-taking, listening, time management, reading, preparing for exams, etc. (½ unit)

Understanding and Improving Your Memory

What memory is, how it works, general principles, and specific techniques for improving memory in a wide range of situations. (½ unit)

Project Self-Discovery

Increasing one's knowledge of what people are like and improving one's powers of self-understanding and self-expression. Gaining self-confidence, self-acceptance, and a more meaningful life. (½ unit)

Peer Counseling

The course gives you and a friend the opportunity to see how you feel about many issues; developing and practicing new communication skills. (½ unit)

SOCIAL SCIENCE

U.S. History: Liberty and Social Change

The development of liberty and the causes of social change in the U.S., the state of our freedoms today, and how to maintain liberty and meet change in the future. (½ unit)

U.S. History: The Economy/The American Character

American history as a reflection of the character of the men and women who shaped the U.S., the development of the economic system, and the impact of both character and the economy today. (½ unit)

U.S. History: The Constitution/Democratic Governance

United States Constitution, emphasizing its historical development, the three branches of government, and the rights and responsibilities of citizens. Meets the Utah democratic governance requirement. (½ unit)

U.S. History: Foreign Policy

Exploration of the ideas and personalities that have shaped U.S. foreign policy and shifts that have occurred in that policy. (¼ unit)

U.S. History: Government

Government of the United States as an extension of one's personal liberty. Important ideas relating to individual responsibility in our system of government. (¼ unit)

World History: The Modern Era

Major events of the nineteenth and twentieth centuries, beginning with the industrialization of Europe and America. Causes and consequences of regional and global conflicts during this period. (¼ unit)

World History: Eastern Hemisphere (Asia, the Middle East, and Africa)

Overview of the major events, personalities, and cultures of the Eastern Hemisphere. (½ unit)

World History: Western Hemisphere (North and South America)

Overview of the history and cultures of North and South America. (½ unit)

World History: Europe and Russia

Overview of the major events, personalities, and cultures of Europe and Russia. (½ unit)

World History: Ancient Civilizations

Emphasis on river valley civilizations in Asia and Europe, as well as Latin America. (½ unit)

American Government, Part 1

The American system of government, including its origins, development, citizen rights, voting, public opinion, Congress, the law-making process, and fiscal policy. (½ unit)

American Government, Part 2

American government, including such topics as the presidency, foreign policy, the bureaucracy, the court system, state government, local governments, and future government. (½ unit)

Consumer Economics

Necessary consumer information and skills to live productive lives in today's marketplace: checking accounts, interest, savings accounts, consumer protection, credit, budgeting, shelter, buying a car, insurance, and the job market. (½ unit)

Economics/American Free Enterprise

The worker's role, the functions of a business firm, and the problem of economy; types of economies; managing personal affairs; and the worker's relationship to governmental and international economic activity. (½ unit)

Sociology, Part 1

Social organizations and their effect upon human behavior. (½ unit)

Sociology, Part 2

A continuation of the above course. (½ unit)

World Geography: The Western Hemisphere

Geography, its effects and its five themes applied to the U.S., Canada, all of Latin America, and the Caribbean. (½ unit)

World Geography: The Eastern Hemisphere

Geography, its effects and its five themes applied to Britain, Nordic nations, Central and Eastern Europe, Asia, Africa, and the Mediterranean region. (½ unit)

Introduction to Psychology

Basic theories and principles of psychology. Guides the student to a better understanding of self. The student will also study consciousness and adolescent development, as well as traditional topics such as behaviorism, personality, learning, and social psychology. (½ unit)

SPEECH

Introduction to Public Speaking

Speech communication process; planning and preparing a speech; using the body and voice to communicate; wording, arranging, and outlining. Beginning and ending a speech effectively. Access to cassette tape recorder needed. (½ unit)

NONCREDIT COURSES

BUSINESS

Understanding Taxes

Practical course in preparing income tax returns. Topics include role of taxes in society and voluntary compliance. (Noncredit) *Tuition:* $33.

COMPUTER SCIENCE

Understanding Computers and Information Processing

Identify hardware functions and software applications as computers impact knowledge, communications, graphics, technical design, and careers in society. (Noncredit) *Tuition:* $64.

Word Processing Skills

Introduction to and application of word processing. (Noncredit) *Tuition:* $64.

ENGLISH

Expository Writing: Explaining Your Ideas

The most common types of writing: reports, directions, opinion, explanations, analyses, etc. This writing "sets forth" or "exposes" a writer's ideas directly and explicitly. (Noncredit) *Tuition:* $64.

Narrative and Descriptive Writing: The Art of Storytelling

How to write a good story—a series of happenings (description, conversation, commentary but mostly actions. (Noncredit) *Tuition:* $64.

Building Your Vocabulary

Vocabulary building through the study of Greek and Latin roots and prefixes, words of description, and vigorous verbs. (Noncredit) *Tuition:* $30.

Reading for Speed and Comprehension

Building reading skills to increase reading speed and comprehension. (Noncredit) *Tuition:* $64.

English at Home, Part 1

Introduction to the English language. Specifically for speakers of Spanish. Simple vocabulary and grammar using written and oral activities. (Noncredit) *Tuition:* $64.

English at Home, Part 2

A continuation of the preceding course. Specifically for speakers of Spanish. (Noncredit) *Tuition:* $64.

English at Home, Part 3

A continuation of the preceding course for any non-English speaker. Assumes some knowledge of English. All instructions are given in English. (Noncredit) *Tuition:* $64.

FAMILY EDUCATION

Preparing Your Child To Succeed In School

A practical, research-proven approach for parents who wish to provide their children with cognitive skill training before they start school. (Noncredit) *Tuition:* $25.

Early Childhood Learning Experiences for the Home

Organizing and preparing learning experiences throughout the year for the preschool child. (Noncredit) *Tuition:* $64.

Tutoring Your Children: Reading Skills 1

Teaching children to sound out words and teaching them sight words (words that cannot be read phonetically) using procedures that have been scientifically proven. Required: Access to a tape recorder and to one person who is a nonreader or who has reading difficulties. (Noncredit) *Tuition:* $25.

Tutoring Your Children: Reading Skills 2

Teaching phonetic rules, common word segments, prefixes, and suffixes; the reading of polysyllabic words and additional sight words; and the improvement of comprehension and rate. Required: access to a tape recorder and to one person who needs help with the above reading skills. (Noncredit) *Tuition:* $25.

Raising Children in Truth and Light: Schools, Parents, Educational Principles

Correct principles of education; the parent/teacher; the child/student; the environment; the materials. (Noncredit) *Tuition:* $64.

Use the Book of Mormon to Teach Reading

A practical, research-proven approach in how to use the Bible to teach children between five and twelve years of age to read. (Noncredit) *Tuition:* $64.

Use the Bible to Teach Reading

A practical, research-proven approach in how to use the Bible to teach children between five and twelve years of age to read. (Noncredit) *Tuition:* $64.

FAMILY HISTORY

Eight Convenient Steps to Finding Your Roots

An introductory course. How and where to begin, obtaining new information, how to organize and use a filing system, major libraries and archives, using more specialized records and sources, and evaluating progress and setting new genealogical goals. (Noncredit) *Tuition:* $64.

North American Research

Section 1. Northeastern States and Canada. Methods and sources for Canada east, Canada west, Connecticut, Delaware, Main, Massachusetts, New Hampshire, New Jersey, New York, Pennsylvania, Rhode Island, and Vermont. (Noncredit) *Tuition:* $64.

Section 2. Southern States. Methods and sources for Alabama, Florida, Georgia, Kentucky, Louisiana, Maryland, Mississippi, North Carolina, Tennessee, Virginia, and West Virginia. (Noncredit) *Tuition:* $64.

Section 3. Midwestern States. Methods and sources for Arkansas, Illinois, Indiana, Iowa, Kansas, Missouri, Ohio, Oklahoma, Michigan, Nebraska, Texas, and Wisconsin. (Noncredit) *Tuition:* $64.

British Research 1

Section 1. Introduction to British Research. Overview of British research; organizing and notekeeping, gaining access to the records; procedures in searching the records; determining what is already known; tracking LDS pioneer lines to England; geographical and historical considerations. (Noncredit) *Tuition:* $64.

Section 2. England and Wales Since 1700, Part 1. Civil registration, census records, parish registers, bishops' transcripts and nonconformist records; and marriage, probate, and cemetery records. (Noncredit) *Tuition:* $64.

Section 3. England and Wales Since 1700, Part 2. Poorlaw and court records; military, naval, and merchant marine records; occupational and tax records; other genealogical sources; and solving some difficult problems. (Noncredit) *Tuition:* $64.

Section 7. Scotland. Bibliographic research tools, civil registration, census records, parish registration, kirk session records, and nonconformist registers. (Noncredit) *Tuition:* $64.

Section 8. Ireland. Bibliographic research tools, civil registration, census records and substitutes, parish registers, and Catholic, Presbyterian, and other church records. (Noncredit) *Tuition:* $64.

Writing Family Histories

Selecting themes and sources and determining issues to be dealt with. (Noncredit) *Tuition:* $64.

FINE ARTS

Drawing

For the beginning or advanced artist. Techniques of drawing accuracy not covered in traditional art courses, including technical skills of perspective, methods of analyzing one's work (e.g., positive-negative shape analysis, vertical-horizontal analysis), and a developmental sequence of drawing. (Noncredit) *Tuition:* $64.

Calligraphy

Basic skills in handlettering. (Noncredit) *Tuition:* $66.

A Better Way - Italic Handwriting

The student learns to print the italic letter forms then moves into learning the eight joints that will make one's print into a logical, legible, beautiful cursive italic handwriting. (Noncredit) *Tuition:* $64.

Flat Pattern Designing

Previous experience in clothing construction. Dress design and pattern making from a basic sloper. (Noncredit) *Tuition:* $64.

Guitar for Everyone, Part 1

A beginning course in guitar using tapes and extensive step-by-step instruction in folk and contemporary music. Logical progression in chords and technique. Skills, theory, elementary transposition, and arrangement are covered as the student learns to play forty-four songs. (Noncredit) *Tuition:* $64.

Guitar for Everyone, Part 2

A continuation of the preceding course. (Noncredit) *Tuition:* $64.

HEALTH

Hooked on Aerobics

Dance and other rigorous activities performed to music to attain cardiovascular fitness. (Noncredit) *Tuition:* $64.

MATHEMATICS

Beginning Algebra

Arithmetic, beginning algebra, and geometry, emphasizing application. (Noncredit) *Tuition:* $144.

Intermediate Algebra

Elementary logic, real number system, equations and inequalities (linear, polynomial, rational, and radical expressions), graphing, function notation, inverse functions, exponential functions, systems of equations, variations. (Noncredit) *Tuition:* $144.

MUSIC

Organ Certification Program

The sections described below present progressively difficult level of organ performance skills related to hymns, organ repertoire, music theory, and accompanimental skills to prepare an organist for competent church service playing. Students provide their own organ teacher if needed. Sample hymns, compositions, and other requirements are listed for each level as a guide to the level's respective difficulty at the beginning of the level. Full specification of skills and competencies provided upon enrollment.

Organ 71 Certification Level 1. For those with no formal organ study. (Noncredit) *Tuition:* $64.

Organ 72 Certification Level 2. Basic pedal and manual technique; ability to play #1 from Marcel Dupre's 79 chorales and LDS hymn #125; beginning theory and registration concepts. (Noncredit) *Tuition:* $64.

Organ 73 Certification Level 3. More difficult organ technique exercises; ability to play #4 or #52 from Marcel Dupre's 79 chorales and LDS hymns #116 and #67; advancing theory and registrational concepts. (Noncredit) *Tuition:* $94.

Organ 74 Certification Level 4. Increasingly difficult organ technique; ability to play Bach's Prelude and Fugue in C (from 8 short), and LDS hymns #172 and #188; progressively difficult theory and registration studies; accompaniments; sight-reading and simple transposition. (Noncredit) *Tuition:* $94.

Organ 75 Certification Level 5. More advanced technical studies; ability to play Bach's Christ lag in Todesbanden (Orgelbuchlein), Brahms' Eleven Chorale Preludes #2, and LDS hymns #175, #50, and #40; more advanced studies in theory, registration, choral accompaniment, sight-reading, and transposition. (Noncredit) *Tuition:* $119.

Organ 76 Certification Level 6. Continuing technical studies; ability to play Bach's Toccata and Fugue in D Minor, Mendelssohn's Sonata #2, and LDS hymns #83, #69, and #134; advancing studies in theory, registration, choral accompaniment, sight-reading, and transposition. (Noncredit) *Tuition:* $149.

Service Playing Certification

Certification is determined through a playing and a written evaluation covering organ techniques, registration, repertoire, hymn playing, theory, and sight-reading. (Noncredit) *Tuition:* $25.

PERSONAL DEVELOPMENT

Understanding and Improving Relationships

Key principles governing successful relationships. Emphasizes wide application of these principles in such situations as overcoming depression and obesity. (Noncredit) *Tuition:* $64.

Changing Undesired Emotions Through Rational Self-Counseling

Rational self-control of undesired emotions. How you produce your own emotions, how to rid yourself of undesirable ones, and how to produce more desirable ones. (Noncredit) *Tuition:* $64.

Dealing with Loneliness: Toward Successful Coping

A sensitive exploration of loneliness, and a practical process for coping with it. (Noncredit) *Tuition:* $64.

Resolving Student Hostility

A practical course in human relationships, emphasizing application to all aspects of life. Topics and skills include creating safe and trusting conditions, accepting and liking self, developing equal relationships with others, breaking the cycle of hostility, placing responsibility properly, exploring consequences, and understanding the commitment process. (Noncredit) *Tuition:* $64.

TAXIDERMY

Taxidermy

Beginning course in taxidermy. Techniques and procedures for mounting birds, mammals, and fish. (Noncredit) *Tuition:* $64.

California, University of
Center for Media and Independent Learning
University of California Extension
2000 Center Street
Suite 400
Berkeley, California 94704   (510) 642-4124

Description:

The University of California Extension program is associated with the various campuses of the university system and brings class offerings to local residents. The Independent Study at the University of California has expanded its horizons by a merger with the university's Extension Media Center. The new department is called the Center for Media and Independent Learning. Courses by correspondence are offered to individuals who do not find it convenient to attend classes. The program offers over 200 college-level and continuing education courses. The majority of the 6,000 students enrolled in the program live in the western United States, but Armed Forces or corporate personnel living abroad temporarily also participate. Although students may not earn a degree through this program, credit earned through University of California Extension may be applied toward undergraduate degrees at the discretion of the degree-granting institution or toward continuing education requirements. For information about high school correspondence courses contact the Center for Media and Independent Learning.

California, University of

Faculty:

Mary Beth Almeda, Director, Center for Media and Independent Learning. There are 130 instructors from business and professional fields.

Academic Levels:
College
High School
Noncredit

Degree/Certificate Programs:

Undergraduate credit earned by correspondence Study is accepted at the University of California toward the unit requirements for the baccalaureate degree. The Center for Media and Independent Learning does not offer degree programs. Matriculated students attending the University who wish to apply correspondence credit toward a degree must secure written approval from the dean of their school or college prior to enrolling for credit in a course. High school courses are available and are designed primarily for students in regular attendance at a high school but may be taken by anyone. The courses may be applied (1) for credit toward high school graduation (upon approval of the student's high school principal), and (2) in fulfillment of requirements for entrance to a university or college. High school courses listed below are equivalent of a high school term or semester course with attendance one hour each day, five days a week. Students interested in high school courses should write to University Extension for information.

Three certificate programs offered by University Extension can be completed entirely through Independent Learning: Certificate in Business, Award in General Business Studies, and Award in Accounting. Studies. Those interested in these programs should contact the Independent Learning office.

Admission Requirements:

Open enrollment. Enrollment in University Extension does not constitute admission to the University of California. Members of the U.S. Armed Forces may enroll through DANTES and should contact their Education Officers for information.

Tuition:

Course fees are listed below following the course description and are valid to 1995; an increase in fees can be expected on an annual basis. Fees are payable at registration and payment must be in U.S. funds. Registration by telephone is possible if using MasterCard or Visa. Variable postage fees outside of the continental U.S. Refunds possible up to 60 days from enrollment. Requests for a refund must be made in writing.

Enrollment Period:

The maximum time allowed to complete a course is twelve months from the date of enrollment. One extension of six months may be allowed for upon payment of a fee for each course. The minimum time allowed to complete a course is four months.

Equipment Requirements:

The cost of textbooks and materials is not included in the course fee. Textbooks may be ordered locally or from the Berkeley Book Store.

Credit and Grading:

Most courses require supervised final examinations; a few require mid-course examinations as well. Final examinations generally weigh heavily in the determination of final course grades. The proctor must be approved by the Independent Study office. The grading system is A, Excellent; B, Good; C, Fair; D, Barely Passed; F, Not Passed. A grade of F may be raised only by retaking the course. Most Independent Learning credit courses may be taken on a Not-for-Credit basis and this must be specified at time of enrollment. Credit is awarded in either semester hour or quarter hour units; see parenthetical indication at the end of the course descriptions below.

Accreditations:

Western Association of Schools and Colleges. Member of: National University Continuing Education Association.

COLLEGE COURSES

ACCOUNTING

Administrative Accounting

Covers accounting and its uses in analyzing, planning, and controlling the operations of organizations of all types. (3 semester units) *Tuition:* $355.

Introduction to Accounting

Introduces the identification, measurement, and reporting of the financial effects of economic events on enterprises. Covers basic accounting data, records and statements including control accounts, journals, ledgers, income determination, interest, taxes, dividends, merchandising, adjusting entries, work sheets, financial statements, closing entries, cash flow and consolidated statements. (3 semester units) *Tuition:* $355.

Managerial Accounting

The uses of accounting systems and their effects on the process of managing an enterprise are discussed in this course. Topics include classification of costs and revenue on several bases for various uses; budgeting and standard costs accounting; analyses of relevant costs and other data for decision making. (3 semester units) *Tuition:* $355.

Accounting: Intermediate I

This continued study of accounting theory and practice reviews the accounting cycle and preparation of accounting statements. Topics include the environment and conceptual framework of financial accounting, statement of income and retained earnings, balance sheet and statement of cash flows, the time value of money, cash and receivables, valuation of inventories, acquisition and disposition of property, depreciation and depletion, and current liabilities and contingencies. (3 semester units) *Tuition:* $355.

Accounting: Intermediate II

A continuation of the above course. Topics include long-term liabilities; stockholders' equity; dilutive securities; earnings per share calculations; investments; revenue recognition; accounting for income taxes, pensions, and leases; error analysis; statement analysis; and full disclosure in reporting. (3 semester units) *Tuition:* $355.

Accounting: Advanced I

Applies accounting theory to a broad selection of topics of current accounting practice with emphasis on consolidated statements. Discusses merger negotiations and covers aspects of preparing (3 semester units) *Tuition:* $355.

Accounting: Advanced II

A continuation of the above course. Topics include accounting for partnerships (partnership formation and operation, legal dissolution, and liquidation; fiduciary and institutional accounting); bankruptcy accounting, accounting for estates and trusts, governmental accounting, and accounting for installment sales and consignments; and accounting for international operations, including foreign currency translations. (3 semester units) *Tuition:* $355.

Cost Accounting

An intensive study covering basic cost accumulation systems and refinements used to determine costs of products or activities in various types of enterprises. Emphasis on managerial cost analysis and management decision planning. (3 semester units) *Tuition:* $355.

Auditing

Examines the concepts and problems in professional verification of financial and related information, including ethical, legal, and other professional issues, historical developments, and current concerns. (4 semester units) *Tuition:* $355.

Electronic Data Processing and Operational Auditing

Examines the concepts and techniques used to ensure internal control in an electronic data processing environment; shows how to evaluate the efficiency, economy, and effectiveness of an organization through operational auditing. Topics include audit objectives, physical security, data integrity, program security and reliability, and detection and prevention of computer crime. The course is designed for external and internal auditors as well as those planning to enter the accounting profession. (3 semester units) *Tuition:* $355.

Governmental Accounting

Focus is on the preparation of financial statements, the principles of procedures of accounting, financial reporting, and budgeting and auditing for governmental entities. Discusses various specific types of funds and accounting for investments. Stresses uniform compilation of financial data acceptable to all types of governmental units; includes up-to-date coverage of Governmental Accounting Standards Board rulings as well as AICPA pronouncements and auditing requirements. (4 semester units) *Tuition:* $355.

Federal Income Tax for Individuals

A review of the federal income tax law as it relates to individuals. Problems are assigned to provide the student with practice in application of tax principles to specific situations. (3 semester units) *Tuition:* $355.

Federal Income Tax for Partnerships, Corporations, and Related Areas

Covers the federal income tax law as it relates to partnerships and corporations. Topics include estates and trusts, social security taxes, federal estate tax, federal gift tax, problems in filing returns and obtaining refunds, and installment and deferred payment sales. (3 semester units) *Tuition:* $355.

ADULT EDUCATION

Adult Education Methods and Materials

Examines several effective methods of developing curriculum units for adult learners and of applying them in the classroom. Provides students with an opportunity to critique their own teaching styles and to consider other methods. (2 semester units) *Tuition:* $320.

Adult Education Principles

Looks at the scope, history, and financing of adult education; explores adult learning theory and process, and future directions for adult education. (2 semester units) *Tuition:* $320.

ANTHROPOLOGY

Introduction to Physical Anthropology

Human evolution and primate social behavior are examined from] historically. Topics include our prehuman fossil ancestors, evolutionary processes, our place in the animal kingdom, principles of genetics, and biosocial evolution in human beings, as well as the uses and misuses of anthropology. (4 semester units) *Tuition:* $355.

Introduction to Social and Cultural Anthropology

Focuses on the structure and dynamics of human culture and social institutions, including social structure, kinship, marriage, gender, culture contact, and cultural change. Uses a broad range of ethnographic videos and texts to illuminate the history of anthropology as a field, review the transformation of traditional cultures through time and colonial expansion, and examine the nature and future of contemporary global society with its problems of nationalism, ethnic strife, and modernization. Requires access to a VCR. (4 semester units) *Tuition:* $355.

Exploring Contemporary Culture through Film

Culture, identity, and modernity, three fundamental concepts of anthropology, are explored using a variety of ethnographic videos and texts. Reviews contemporary debates on the nature of cultural change, including topics such as migration, urban growth, tourism, transnational economic and cultural exchange, resistance, and cultural continuity. Issues of visual anthropology are discussed. (3 semester units) *Tuition:* $355.

ART

Beginning Drawing

Introduces drawing as a means of developing perception and insight. By using a variety of media, techniques, and approaches the student is encouraged to arrive at an individual approach as an extension of a unique self. (2 semester units) *Tuition:* $315.

Introduction to Modern Painting

Covers some of the most influential modern artists, including Picasso, Matisse, Duchamp, and Klee. Emphasis is on major movements in Western art (cubism, surrealism, dada, expressionism, and others) as they relate to such significant developments as World War I, psychoanalysis, fascism, the atom bomb, and space exploration. (1 semester unit) *Tuition:* $295.

Acrylic Painting

Explores techniques for using acrylics, obtaining both watercolor and oil effects. Your creative, individual search for image and style is encouraged. (2 semester units) *Tuition:* $315.

Italic Lettering and Handwriting

Teaches the skill of graceful writing, with emphasis on the development of traditional forms emanating from the Renaissance. (2 semester units) *Tuition:* $315.

Individual Study in Art

Provides the opportunity for you to pursue your own art study project under professional guidance. Select any area of study—from prehistoric art to the latest art movements. Research art education and the ways that art has been or could be taught. Make your own art in the style and medium of your choice—original examples, written reports, slides, audiotapes, or a combination of media. (2 semester units)

ART HISTORY

Ancient Art: Egypt

Examines the architecture, sculpture, and painting of ancient Egypt from the prehistoric period (ca. 4000 B.C.) to the Roman occupation (ca. A.D. 325). Presents background on Old, Middle, and New Kingdoms, including the reign of Tutankhamen; origins and development of the Egyptian way of life, religious beliefs, and beliefs about life after death, correlating the evolution of Egyptian society with the artistic and political history of ancient Egypt and the Near East. (4 quarter units) *Tuition:* $335.

ASTRONOMY

Introduction to General Astronomy

An essentially nonmathematical description of modern astronomy with emphasis on the structure and evolution of stars, galaxies, and the universe. The course includes discussion of studies of pulsars, quasars, and black holes; the solar system; and space exploration of the planets. (4 semester units) *Tuition:* $355.

BIOCHEMISTRY

Introductory Biochemistry

An introduction to the basic chemistry and overall structure of the most important biological macromolecules. Topics include the study of enzyme catalysis, cellular architecture, and intermediary metabolism (carbohydrates, amino acids, lipids, nucleotides), including special processes such as photosynthesis, biological oxidation, and energy production. Biochemical genetics, the mechanism of protein synthesis, and ways in which biological systems react to their environment and regulate their own internal activities are considered. (3 semester units) *Tuition:* $335.

BIOLOGICAL SCIENCE

Modern Biology

Covers structures and activities fundamental to all forms of life. Examines the organization and function in the human as a representative vertebrate; reproduction and development; principles of heredity; evolutionary processes; kinds of living things; adaptations of organisms; and relationships of plants and animals, including humans, to each other and to their physical environment. (3 semester units) *Tuition:* $335.

The Biology of Cancer

This course examines the fundamental clinical and pathologic aspects of the many diseases called cancer from the patient's and health care professional's point of view. Topics include the biology of uncontrolled cellular growth, the origins and causes of cancer, issues surrounding its clinical diagnosis, modes of treatment, social and psychological effects of cancer, and cancer prevention. The roles of the patient, surgeon, pathologist, radiation oncologist, and medical oncologist are considered. The AIDS epidemic and its relationship to cancer are briefly examined. Designed for anyone with a personal or professional interest in learning about cancer. (3 semester units) *Tuition:* $335.

Principles and Techniques of Molecular Cell Biology

Explains how cells function and how research in cell and molecular biology is making its way out of the laboratory and into everyday life. Topics include gene regulation and expression, cell regulation, genetic engineering and cloning, the Human Genome Project, the genetic basis

of cancer, diseases of the immune system including AIDS, and the use of DNA technology in forensics. (3 semester units) *Tuition:* $335.

Introduction to Human Physiology

A comprehensive course focusing on basic internal and external environments underlying human life processes, including cells and membranes; nervous and muscle function; cardiovascular, respiratory, renal, and gastrointestinal physiology; metabolism, endocrinology, and reproduction. (3 semester units) *Tuition:* $335.

Survey of General Genetics

An introduction to the fundamentals of genetics at the molecular, organismal, and population levels. Topics include the molecular basis of gene function and mutation, Mendelian genetics, transmission transmission systems, regulation of cellular processes, developmental genetics, cytoplasmic inheritance, population genetics, and multifactoral inheritance. (3 semester units) *Tuition:* $335.

BOTANY

Plants and Civilization

Examines the biology, selection, and use of plants for human purposes, and the interrelation between the evolution of domesticated plants and human cultural evolution. (3 semester units) *Tuition:* $335.

Plant Life in California

Focuses on the vegetation, plant communities, and life zones of California; examines influences on patterns of vegetation; origins of California flora; plant distribution throughout the state, and basic ecological concepts. (3 semester units) *Tuition:* $335.

BUSINESS LAW

Introduction to Business Law

Acquaints you with the ethics and sources of law, including law of contracts (offer and acceptance, consideration, capacity of parties, and illegality) and agency law (liability of principal and agent, duties of principal and agent to each other, liability for torts, liability of third parties). Also covers the formation, operation, partnerships and corporations and corporate mergers and consolidations. (3 semester units) *Tuition:* $355.

CHEMISTRY

Introductory Chemistry

Covers general chemistry, atomic theory, chemical bonding, states of matter, kinetic molecular theory, solutions, periodic law, electrochemistry, reaction rates, chemical equilibrium and a brief introduction to organic chemistry. (3 quarter units) *Tuition:* $315.

Organic Chemistry

Designed for nonchemistry majors who want to gain an understanding of the theories as well as some applications of organic chemistry. The course begins with bonding and isomerism, then moves into a detailed discussion of the molecular structures and properties of various classes of organic compounds. Following a brief discussion of spectroscopy and structure determination methods, the course concludes by examining the role of organic compounds in our everyday living and in nature. Topics in this area include synthetic polymers, lipids and detergents, carbohydrates, amino acids, peptides, and proteins. (3 semester units) *Tuition:* $335.

Surface Phenomena in Physical and Biological Systems

An introduction to surface chemistry stressing basic concepts and practical applications. Topics include surface tension and adsorption, sufactants, emulsions and dispersions, double layer, biological membrane transport, characterization of solid particles, catalysis, chromatography, and biological macromolecules. Mathematics is kept to a minimum. (3 semester units) *Tuition:* $335.

CHINESE

Elementary Chinese: Course I

Teaches the foundations of vocabulary and grammar for Modern Standard Chinese (Mandarin), emphasizing reading and writing. You gain speech practice through listening and responding to the five audiocassette tapes provided with the course materials. (5 semester units) *Tuition:* $395.

Elementary Chinese: Course II

Guides your developing reading and writing skills in Modern Standard Chinese (Mandarin) and your continuing study of vocabulary. You gain additional speech practice through listening and responding to the seven audiocassette tapes provided with the course materials. (5 semester units) *Tuition:* $405.

COMPUTER SCIENCE

Concepts of Data Processing

A general introduction to computer information systems. Topics include computer history, computer applications and their social impact, career opportunities, hardware, input/output, problem definition, and computer languages. (3 semester units) *Tuition:* $335.

Using the UNIX Operating System

A comprehensive introduction to the UNIX operating system, designed for computer system programmers and users who wish to add an understanding of UNIX to their skills. Topics include logging in, the visual editor, file management, text processing, electronic mail, the directory structure, UNIX handling of files and processes, basic shell utilities, and writing shell scripts. (3 semester units) *Tuition:* $355.

Introduction to Programming with BASIC

Explains how to use the BASIC system commands and program statements and examines BASIC programming applications. Topics include system descriptions, entry of BASIC instructions, input and output, branching, looping, mathematical functions, subroutines and strings, arrays, file processing, and matrix commands. (3 semester units) *Tuition:* $355.

C Language Programming

Teaches you how to modify existing C language programs and develop auxiliary one and discusses the essential structure and functions of programs in C. The concepts studied include functions, control structures, pointers, strings, arrays, and dynamic allocation principles. (2 semester hours) *Tuition:* $335.

Introductory Pascal

A hands-on course using Pascal version 7. Teaches systems commands and program statements and how to use them to carry out a variety of operations. (3 semester units) *Tuition:* Contact the CMIL office for cost information.

Introduction to Computer Programming: FORTRAN

Thorough study of FORTRAN, the programming language most commonly used in the solution of engineering and scientific problems; includes digital computer problem-solving techniques. (3 semester units) *Tuition:* $355.

Systems Analysis and Design: An Overview

This foundation course examines information analysis and logical specification of the system development process in an organization. It emphasizes the use of analysis and design to meet business objectives. The course covers gathering, manipulating, storing, summarizing, and reporting management and operational information. It also provides an overview of modern information systems development tools, a survey of the steps in the development process, and an opportunity to acquire basic analytical and design skills. (3 semester units) *Tuition:* $355.

Concepts of Database Management Systems

An in-depth study of techniques for creating and using database applications, this course is organized around the database life cycle. Main topics include: requirements analysis and specification; logical database design; normalization; implementing the databases; recovery, concurrency, integrity and security concerns; and using the database. The course is oriented toward the relational data model and SQL, but there is some discussion on other models. Course notes include practical advice on implementing databases, self-study exercises to improve skills, and useful references to books and journal articles for future reading. (3 semester units) *Tuition:* $355.

Information Resource Management

An investigation of real-world information system development and implementation, using well-known organizations for case studies. Looks at key issues of the 90s such as strategic use of leading-edge information systems for competitive advantage. (2 semester units) *Tuition:* $335.

Fundamentals of Data Communications and Networks

Provides practical and current information on data communications concepts and equipment, including modems, DSUs/CSUs, installation procedures, and troubleshooting; focuses on how equipment and protocols are incorporated into small and large systems; and addresses protocols and standards issues in the United States and worldwide. Topics include learning the basic building blocks of communicating, analog vs. digital technologies, selecting and using PC hardware and communications software, distinguishing among different physical media used for transmission, and understanding local area network alternatives and gateways to other systems. *Tuition:* Contact the CMIL office for cost information.

C++ Language Programming

Provides an introduction to object-oriented programming using C++; teaches hands-on programming skills. (3 semester units) *Tuition:* Contact the CMIL office for cost information.

ECONOMICS

Introduction to Microeconomics

An introduction to basic economic analysis of prices and markets, consumer behavior, production and costs, competition, monopoly, government regulation, distribution and labor markets, and related social issues of concern. (3 semester units) *Tuition:* $335.

Introduction to Macroeconomics

An introduction to economic analysis and policy; course covers the market economy, government and the economy, the determinants of national income and the level of employment, money and banking, economic fluctuations and growth. (3 semester units) *Tuition:* $335.

Economic Principles and Problems

Covers principles of economic analysis, economic institutions, and issues of economic policy. Topics include the allocation of resources and distribution of income through the price system, as well as aggregate economics, including money and banking, national income, and international trade. (3 semester units) *Tuition:* $330.

Introduction to Statistical Methods

Introduces elements of statistical analysis; presentation and interpretation of data; descriptive statistics; theory of probability and basic sampling distributions; statistical inference and hypothesis testing;

introduction to correlation and regression. (4 quarter units) *Tuition:* $335.

EDUCATION

The Reading Program

Designed for elementary and secondary teachers and future teachers who wish to make their reading instruction more effective or improve their school's reading program. Topics include new research in early literacy, vocabulary development, writing, reading in the content areas, the role of oral language in the reading process, and teaching children with special needs. There are two sections, elementary-level and secondary-level. (3 semester units) *Tuition:* $360.

Literature for Children

Considers strategies for evaluating and selecting literature for children from preschool through adolescence and presents approaches to improving children's responses to literature. Explores ways to use literature in school reading programs and in specific subject areas; helps you discover what children want to read and familiarizes you with children's authors, illustrators, and current publications. (3 semester units) *Tuition:* $335.

ENGINEERING

Surveying Engineering Measurements

Covers the standards, units, equipment, and methods used in surveying engineering. Topics include tape, optical, and electronic measurements of distances; angular measurements; differential, profile, and trigonometric leveling; simple horizontal and vertical curves; traverse and area computations; transit and level adjustments; and treatment of errors. (2 semester units) *Tuition:* $315.

Introduction to Electrical Engineering

This introduction to the principles of electronic circuits and systems examines circuit fundamentals, passive and active electronic devices, amplifying circuits and building blocks of electronic systems. Other topics include a full coverage of operational amplifier circuits and digital circuits, including CMOS gates. (3 semester units) *Tuition:* $335.

Mathematics for Electronics

Designed to provide engineers, engineering students, and electronic technicians with mathematical tools useful for solving electrical circuit problems; may also be of interest to physics majors. Topics include engineering notation, applications of Kirchoff's Laws, Thevenin's Theorem, Norton's Theorem, the impedance triangle and other techniques of circuit analysis. There is also material on phasors and complex numbers, analyzing alternating-current circuits, logarithms, and Bode diagrams, time constants and transient circuit response, computer number systems, a little Boolean algebra, and the use of quadratic equations for describing electronic circuits. (2 semester units) *Tuition:* $315.

Introduction to Microprocessors

The basic elements of a microcomputer system are covered, as well as microprocessor architecture (organization and function); hardware (CPU, I/O, building blocks); and elementary microprocessor assembly and machine language programming. The course surveys available microprocessors and includes an introduction to 16-bit microprocessors and a comparison of Intel's 8086 and Motorola's 68000 chips. (2 semester units) *Tuition:* $315.

Digital Integrated Circuits in Logic Design

Covers the application of digital integrated circuits in digital system design. You develop a functional understanding of how digital circuits work and learn to design various basic digital circuits. Basic digital tools, combinational and sequential circuits, and major logic families are discussed. (3 semester units) *Tuition:* $335.

ENGLISH

Grammar and Composition for Students of English as a Second Language

Helps students who are learning English as a second or foreign language develop the grammar and writing skills in English that are required for university-level study. Teaches how to analyze, construct, and edit effective sentences and how to use organizational strategies and skills to produce successful essays. (3 semester units) *Tuition:* $335.

Freshman Composition and Literature

Course X2A. Teaches you to write college-level essays by acquainting you with each step in the writing process and providing practice in writing descriptive, narrative, and various forms of expository writing (comparison/contrast, argument, etc.). You will read and write about a variety of essays and Freud's *Civilization and Its Discontents.* (3 semester units) *Tuition:* $335.

Course X2B. Teaches you how to write about literature through the analysis, evaluation, and enjoyment of representative short stories, poems, plays, and a novel. Covers a variety of English and American writers as well as works in translation. (3 semester units) *Tuition:* $335.

Advanced English Composition

Expository writing (paragraphs and short essays) based on reading in five literary genres: short story, essay, poem, novel, and play. Instruction and practice in the techniques of developing ideas that emerge from reading and consideration of specific texts. (3 semester units) *Tuition:* $335.

Multicultural Literature

This course highlights the rich diversity of American culture in general and of American literature in particular. Using literary texts and related resources such as recommended films, you consider issues of race, ethnicity, class, and gender as they are viewed from a variety of cultural and personal perspectives. (3 semester units) *Tuition:* Contact the CMIL office for cost information.

The English Language

This course covers the structure and history of the English language; examines the evolving grammatical and semantic structure of the language in particular, with attention to the nature and function of languages in general. Traces the development of English from its Indo-European and Germanic roots to its modern forms around the world, to illuminate the connections between language and other elements of culture. Topics include the origin and derivation of words; historical changes in sounds, forms, and meaning; literary and philosophical influences on the language; and contributions from other languages and cultures. (4 semester units) *Tuition:* $355.

Mystery Fiction

A study of classic selections from the literature of detection. Topics include the disappearance of the Great Detective and the emergence of the hardboiled detective; the origins of the traditional sleuth in the works of Charles Dickens, Edgar Allan Poe, and Arthur Conan Doyle; and twentieth-century works representing the several emerging traditions. The course package includes material prepared by the course author, the late Dr. Elliot L. Gilbert, professor of English, UC Davis; an anthology of mystery fiction, a study guide, and an audiocassette tape of an interview with Ellery Queen and his biographer. (3 semester units) *Tuition:* $360.

Shakespeare

Covers all Shakespeare's sonnets and a choice of twelve of the following fifteen major plays: *A Midsummer Night's Dream, Romeo and Juliet, Richard II, Henry V, Much Ado about Nothing, Twelfth Night, Julius Caesar, Hamlet, Measure for Measure, Othello, King Lear, Macbeth, Coriolanus, The Winter's Tale.* (4 semester units) *Tuition:* $355.

The English Novel

Course XB125A. Surveys the English novel from its beginning to Scott and Austen. Acquaints you with individual authors, the development of the form, and permanent characteristics of the novel. (4 semester units) *Tuition:* $355.

Course XB125B. Focuses on the English novel of the Victorian period. Examines the history of the literary form with emphasis on how moral, social, psychological, political, and philosophical problems and values are portrayed. (4 semester units) *Tuition:* $355.

American Fiction

Course X135A. Surveys the major American novelists and short story writers of the nineteenth century, discussing major literary movements: romanticism, realism, and naturalism. An audiocassette tape containing supplemental lecture material is included in the course package. (3 semester units) *Tuition:* $335.

Course X158B. A survey of major American authors from the turn of the century to the present. Explores how we shape ourselves against social, economic, historical, and psychological pressures and how we relate as individuals to American history and culture. Considers the literary techniques of naturalism, realism, and modernism in both novels and short stories across the century. (4 quarter units) *Tuition:* $335.

ENVIRONMENTAL STUDIES

Environmental Issues

Studies the relationship between human society and the natural environment and examines cases of ecosystem maintenance and disruption. Issues discussed include economic development, population, energy, resources, technology, and alternative systems. Identifies our principal environmental problems, analyzes the social and physical concepts that connect them, and uses these concepts to identify possible solutions. (4 semester units) *Tuition:* $355.

FILM

The Art of the Film

Explores the techniques of evaluating and appreciating films. Selecting films for viewing from a range of classic and modern works, you learn to recognize what makes a well-crafted motion picture, discover how motion pictures are made, and investigate current film theories. Topics include the handling of space and time in motion pictures, the history and uses of sound, editing, performance, directing, narrative style, screenwriting, and film theory. Requires access to a VCR and video rental facilities. (3 semester units) *Tuition:* $335.

FINANCE

Mathematics of Finance

Covers simple and compound interest and discount; annuities; present value, discounted cash flow, internal rates of return; applications in investment, capital budgeting, bonds and amortization; life annuities and insurance. (3 semester units) *Tuition:* $355.

Investment Management

A comprehensive course for the novice investor as well as the experienced investor who would like a thorough review. Covers the investment environment and investment analysis, including the operation of U.S. securities markets and investment alternatives, such as common stocks, fixed income securities, convertible securities, and specialized investments. Principles of portfolio management and concepts of financial planning also are discussed. (2 semester units) *Tuition:* $335.

FRENCH

French: Elementary Course I

This beginner's course concentrates on grammar, readings, and writing. Speech practice is provided through listening and responding to tapes. (3 semester units) *Tuition:* $375.

French: Elementary Course II

Emphasizes sentence structure and composition with extensive speech practice provided by tapes. (3 semester units) *Tuition:* $390.

GEOLOGY

Introduction to Physical Geology

Acquaints you with the principles and concepts of physical geology, covering the origins of crustal materials, especially rocks, volcanos, earthquakes, plate tectonics, and the erosional processes and their role in landscape development. Important areas of geological interest especially those in the western United States, are emphasized in examples. (3 semester units) *Tuition:* $335.

Geology of California

Examines the geological framework of California and the history and origin of rocks and landscapes, with attention to each geological province: the Sierra Nevada; the Basin-Ranges; the Mojave and Colorado Deserts; the Transverse and Peninsular Ranges of southern California, including the Los Angeles and Ventura Basins; the Coast Ranges; the Great Valley; the Klamath Mountains; the Cascade Range; and the Modoc Lava Plateau. Discusses the rocks and structure of each province, the fault patterns and their structural and earthquake history, and natural areas of great human interest such as the Yosemite Valley, Death Valley, San Francisco Bay, Lassen National Park, and the Mother Lode. (4 quarter units) *Tuition:* $335.

GERMAN

German: Elementary Course I

Develops the basic language skills of reading, writing, understanding, and speaking. The informative text compares German and American geography and cultural institutions. (3 semester units) *Tuition:* $395.

German: Elementary Course II

Continues teaching the basic skills of reading, writing, understanding, and speaking. The text contrasts north, middle, and south Germany and its former East and West political divisions and describes the lives of Germany's greatest writers, Goethe and Schiller. (3 semester units) *Tuition:* $350.

German: Elementary Course III

Focuses on refining basic language skills. The textbook surveys the history of Germany and its social structure, characterizes the writers, Heinrich Heine and Thomas Mann, and briefly describes the other German-speaking countries, Austria and Switzerland. Three cassette tapes are provided with the course materials. (3 semester units)

GRAPHIC DESIGN

Publication Design

Teaches the effective ordering of image and text to achieve visual communication in a printed form. Helps you produce your own professional-looking publications. Intended for those seeking jobs whose responsibilities include publication (for example, the production of an organizational newsletter, brochures, or flyers). (2 semester units) *Tuition:* Contact the CMIL office for cost information.

Fundamentals of Graphic Design

Topics include principles of visual design; using graphic arts tools; proportioning and scaling art; combining art with type; layout guidelines; ordering photostats and typeset type; advertising methods; creative problem solving; and career opportunities in graphic design. You select a design project such as a brochure, poster, book jacket, letterhead, record album cover, or editorial spread, to begin or expand you design portfolio. (3 semester units) *Tuition:* $345.

HAZARDOUS MATERIALS

Principles of Hazardous Materials Management

A survey of the scientific, regulatory, and sociopolitical aspects of hazardous materials management. The course discusses hazard definitions; California and federal regulations; management of risks during production, storage (including underground), and transportation; management of hazardous wastes; toxicology; personal protection and safety; emergency planning; mitigation, response, and recovery—site-specific and community-wide; water and air impacts; government-industry-community relations; and mass-media relations. (2 semester units) *Tuition:* $380.

HISTORY

Western Civilization

This course explores the growth of Western civilization from late antiquity to the Renaissance. Topics include the revival of agriculture in medieval times, the building of urban civilizations, formulation of philosophical and political ideas in the Middle East and Greece, and the rise of Europe during the Middle Ages. (3 semester units) *Tuition:* $335.

The Development of World Civilization

Course X19. The Neolithic Age to the Renaissance. A comparative study of world civilizations from prehistoric times to the time of the European Renaissance, focusing on spiritual, political, intellectual, and artistic developments. Covers the ancient civilizations of Sumer, Egypt, Persia, and Greece; the beliefs and social organizations of India, China, and Japan; the rise and fall of Imperial Rome and China; Pre-Columbian America and early African cultures; the Mongol conquest of Eurasia; medieval culture and tension between East and West; and the shift toward modernity in the Renaissance. Since videos relating to significant people and events are suggested for viewing in each assignment, access to a VCR and video rental facilities is recommended. (3 semester units) *Tuition:* $335.

Course X24. 1500 to the Present. A comparative introduction to the major cultures of the world since 1500, focusing on social, political, intellectual, and artistic developments and responses to the dynamics of modernity. Covers the civilizations of the Western Hemisphere, Africa, and the Middle East; the beliefs and social organization of India, China, and Japan; European political and intellectual revolutions; the world wars and the cold war; anticolonialist movements; and today's political, economic, and environmental configurations across many regions. Since videos relating to significant people and events are suggested for viewing in each assignment, access to a VCR and video rental facilities is recommended. (3 semester units) *Tuition:* $335.

History of the United States

Course XD17A. Examines United States history from the age of European exploration of the Americas until 1877. Topics include exploration, settlement, colonial culture, the winning of independence, the Constitution, the new democracy, early American technology, expansionism, sectional conflict, the Civil War, and Reconstruction. (4 quarter units) *Tuition:* $335.

Course XD17B. United States history from the 1870s to the 1980s. Topics include settlement of the West, industrial growth, progressivism, the emergence of a consumer culture, the various wars, affluence and scarcity since World War II, the cultural revolution of the 1960s, Watergate, and the resurgence of conservatism. (4 quarter units) *Tuition:* $335.

The American West

This course examines America moving westward from the seventeenth century to the present. Focus is on the colonial frontiers of the Spanish, French, English, and Anglo-Americans and on the trans-Appalachian West and trans-Mississippi West. Topics include exploration and exploration and discovery, fur trade, agriculture, land speculation, transportation, mining, cattle raising, cultural clashes, international conflict, problems of water, and urbanization. Also discusses the relation of the frontier experience to American institutions and character in the twentieth century. (3 semester units) *Tuition:* $335.

HUMAN RESOURCES

Effective Personnel Administration

A practical guide to becoming an effective personnel administrator capable of influencing the direction, performance, and motivation of employees. Emphasizes the roles and functions of the personnel administrator at three levels: as a key player in an organization's overall planning, design, and development; as an administrator involved in selecting, training, motivating, and developing personnel; and as a manager of systems for job evaluation, compensation, benefits, and safety. (3 semester units) *Tuition:* $355.

Management of Human Resources

A close look at the broad field of management of human resources and labor relations in organizations. Focuses on the full range of human resource functions: developing job requirements, recruiting and selecting personnel, developing training programs, planning career development, motivating, facilitating communication, and creating a productive work environment. Also covers labor relations, including union recognition, collective bargaining, disciplinary actions, and appeal procedures, as well as employee compensation and security, benefits, safety, and health. (3 semester units) *Tuition:* $355.

Labor Relations and Collective Bargaining

Covers the development and growth of the American labor movement; the legal framework for collective bargaining; environment and issues of collective bargaining; management and union goals and strategies; negotiation processes, impasses, and strikes as well as dispute resolution; and administration of the management and labor contract. (3 semester units) *Tuition:* $355.

Achieving Effective Supervision

A problem-centered, active approach to supervision designed to strengthen your skills as a leader and motivator of employees. Special exercises and active field assignments develop key supervisory techniques and leadership styles that provide workable, pragmatic solutions to common problems. Topics include leadership, self-management, delegation, setting goals, standards, and controls. Emphasis is on supervisor-employee relationships; training, counseling, motivating, communicating, and evaluating performance in "real work" situations. The course is intended for supervisors, managers, and others who want to realize their full potential as effective organizational leaders. (3 semester units) *Tuition:* $355.

INTERNATIONAL BUSINESS

Introduction to International Business

Examines theories of competitive and comparative advantage; economic and political considerations related to multinational enterprises; practical procedures in international trade, foreign exchange, and international finance markets; cultural and national interest environments; and trading with third world, Pacific Rim, and former Communist Bloc countries. Also considers how decision-making methods employed in domestic business are applicable in international affairs. Real-life business situations are cited to illustrate the concepts presented. (3 semester units) *Tuition:* $355.

ITALIAN

Elementary Italian I

Teaches the fundamentals of Italian grammar, reading, and writing, and introduces elements of Italian culture. You gain speaking practice through listening and responding to the seven audiocassette tapes provided with the course material. (3 semester units) *Tuition:* $370.

Elementary Italian II

In this course you continue building your Italian language skills. You practice speaking and learn more about Italian culture with the aid of six audiocassette tapes provided with the course materials. (3 semester units) *Tuition:* $365.

MANAGEMENT

Introduction to Business Organization and Management

Principles and practices in the operation of both large and small businesses. Topics include introduction to management; the management environment; planning and strategy; organization, staffing, and change; leadership and motivation; and operation and control. (3 semester units) *Tuition:* $355.

Small Business Management

An overview of the opportunities and problems of small and new businesses. Coursework is structured around case studies that deal with development related to new services or products, financing, purchasing, and expansion. Emphasis is on initial assessment of risks, rather than on subsequent aspects of enterprise management. You examine characteristics of product, market, competition, and human factors; financial aspects including capital requirements, sales forecasts, costs and margins, investment returns, sources and nature of funds; and objectives and incentives. (3 semester units) *Tuition:* $355.

Managing Production and Operations

Expands and applies knowledge based on the unifying themes of classical management—planning, organizing, and controlling—to production and operations management. Covers issues confronting practicing production and operations managers: strategies to gain competitive advantage; forecasting; designing products, services, and processes; planning layouts; designing jobs; standards; work measurement; scheduling; inventory control; planning materials requirements; and managing for quality with emphasis on the contributions of Japanese manufacturers. (3 semester units) *Tuition:* $355.

Top Quality Management

Working with case studies and real-world applications, this course also examines the principles, techniques, background, and future of Total Quality Management (TQM). *Tuition:* Contact the CMIL office for cost information.

MARKETING

Principles of Marketing

Covers marketing's role in business decision making, marketing methods, marketing segmentation, consumer buying behavior, and marketing's effects on company profitability and image. Explores the complex interrelationships among product, price, promotion, distribution, customer service, packaging, and market research. (3 semester units) *Tuition:* $355.

MATHEMATICS

Intermediate Algebra

Covers real numbers, linear equations, factoring, graphs, radicals and exponents, quadratic equations. (2 semester units) *Tuition:* $315.

Plane Trigonometry

This course covers circular functions and their graphs, identities, inverses, trigonometric functions and equations, and solutions of triangles. (2 semester units) *Tuition:* $315.

Precalculus

Topics include algebra review (fractions, negative numbers, factoring, and linear and quadratic equations); functions; graphing; exponents, exponentials, and logarithms; word problems; and trigonometry. (2 semester units) *Tuition:* $400.

First Year Analytic Geometry and Calculus

Course X1.1. An introduction to differential and integral calculus, including elements of analytic geometry. Topics include inequalities and functions, limits and derivatives of trigometric functions, maxima and minima, antiderivatives, area, and the definite integral. Applications are also examined. (3 semester units) *Tuition:* $335.

Course X1.2. A continuation of the above course. Topics include arc length; surface area; differentiation and integration involving logarithmic, exponential, and inverse trigonometric functions; methods of integration; center of mass; improper integrals; infinite series, general second-degree equations; coordinate transformations; and polar coordinates. (3 semester units) *Tuition:* $335.

Course X1.3. A continuation of the above course. Topics include analytic geometry in three dimensions; vector calculus in the plane and in space; indeterminate forms; infinite series; functions of two and three variables; differential and integral calculus in two and three variables, including multiple integrals and applications. (3 semester units) *Tuition:* $335.

NUTRITION

Nutrition

Discusses essential nutrients and their functions in the human body; examines the effects of nutrients on tissues, nutrient requirements in various stages of human development, and nutrient content of foods. (3 semester units) *Tuition:* $335.

Clinical Nutrition

Covers biochemical and physiological bases for therapeutic diets, as well as the problems in planning diets for normal and pathological conditions. Topics include the patient, diets, metabolic stresses, diabetes, and diseases of the heart, kidney, gastrointestinal tract, liver, and blood. (3 semester units) *Tuition:* $335.

The New Nutrition

Explores the frontiers of nutritional science, with the goal of demystifying healthy eating; provides current information about diet and nutrition in terms of individual lifestyles, inherited health risks, tastes, and needs at all stages of life. Topics include obesity and weight control, fitness, heart disease and hypertension, cancer, diabetes, pregnancy and infant feeding, and nutritional information on fast food. (2 semester units) *Tuition:* $340.

PERSONAL DEVELOPMENT

Managing Stress and Conflict in the Workplace

This course offers practical ideas for recognizing, understanding, coping with, resolving, and preventing conflict and stress. Emphasizes ideas and techniques for addressing problems in the workplace yet is applicable to individuals' lives and relationships. (2 semester units) *Tuition:* $275.

Time Management

Topics include time assessment, facts and habits that influence one's use of time, how to set priorities for goals and activities, how to eliminate low-payoff tasks, and how to integrate effective time management methods into your daily life. (2 semester units) *Tuition:* $275.

PEST MANAGEMENT

Pest Control, Branch 1: Fumigation

Covers Branch 1 license area: Fumigation. (3 semester units) *Tuition:* $365.

Pest Control, Branch 2: General Pest

Covers Branch 2 license area: General Pest. (3 semester units) *Tuition:* $365.

Pest Control, Branch 3: Wood-Destroying Pests and Organisms - Prevention, Control, Corrections, and Repairs

Covers Branch 3 license area: Wood-Destroying Organisms—Prevention, Control, Corrections and Repairs. (3 semester units) *Tuition:* $365.

PHILOSOPHY

History of Western Philosophy from the Pre-Socratic Period to the End of the Middle Ages

Introduces major philosophical concerns and concepts in Western thought, beginning with early texts in which philosophy first becomes distinguishable from myth and concluding with the philosophical debates of medieval Christianity. Explores philosophical questions relating to politics, metaphysics, natural science, logic, ethics, and aesthetics. The philosophers covered include Plato, Aristotle, St. Augustine, and St. Thomas Aquinas. (3 semester units) *Tuition:* $335.

History of Buddhist Philosophy

Surveys the 2500 years of Buddhism, beginning in India with the teachings of the historical Buddha, progressing through the development of Mahayana thought and the philosophies of the Chinese and Japanese schools of Buddhism. (3 semester units) *Tuition:* $335.

PHYSICS

Concepts of Physics

A survey of important concepts in physics for the nonscience major. Covers historical and philosophical issues as well as introducing principles of physics: forces and motion, conservation laws, heat, vibrations and waves, and electricity and magnetism. In the second part of the course, students may study either topics in modern physics (relativity, quantum mechanics, and nuclear and elementary particle physics) or topics stressing physics in everyday life (properties of matter, sound, and light and practical uses of electricity). (4 quarter units) *Tuition:* $335.

POLITICAL SCIENCE

American Institutions

This course examines the basic workings of the Constitution and the institutions of the federal government (Congress, the presidency, the bureaucracy, and the judiciary), the American system of electoral politics (including parties, interest groups, social movements, public opinion, and participation), and several areas of public policy (defense, foreign policy, civil liberties, civil rights, the rights of minorities, social spending, welfare reform, and the political aspects of the economic system). Discussions are organized around theoretical questions of democracy and justice. (3 semester units) *Tuition:* $335.

PSYCHOLOGY

Critical Thinking

Teaches strategies for learning how to learn and for critical and creative thinking, including complex problem-solving; examines from a psychological standpoint why people think the way they do. Helps you identify the strengths and weaknesses in your thinking, avoid common errors in thinking, and develop higher-order thinking skills for your personal and professional development. (3 semester units) *Tuition:* $335.

Abnormal Psychology

Designed for anyone interested in the way we perceive and respond to our experiences, and especially for people considering careers in psychology. Covers the dynamics and prevention of abnormal behavior, including neuroses, psychoses, character disorders, psychosomatic reactions, schizophrenia, and other abnormal personality patterns. (4 quarter units) *Tuition:* $335.

General Psychology

An introduction to the principal areas, problems, and concepts of psychology. Topics include development, learning, perception, emotion, personality, and pathology. (3 semester units) *Tuition:* $335.

Adolescence

Designed for parents, teachers, social services personnel, and others who deal with adolescents. Considers adolescents' physical, mental, emotional, social, and personality characteristics. Discusses research findings from growth studies in this and other cultures and identifies the roles American adolescents play in home, school, social groups, and community. (3 semester units) *Tuition:* $335.

Psychology of Communication

Focuses on why people communicate the way they do and how they can communicate better; considers the practical applications of theory and research to personal and professional communication. Topics include the role of information in modern life, the importance of communication in building and maintaining relationships, special problems of communicating within groups and organizations, the uses and effects of television and mass media, and communication and the future of society. (3 semester units) *Tuition:* $335.

Developmental Psychology

An overview of child development, including prenatal development; birth and the newborn; physical, cognitive, language, emotional, and social development during infancy; preschool years; and middle childhood. (4 quarter units) *Tuition:* $335.

Social Psychology

Examines how an individual's behavior, feelings, and thoughts may be influenced by others. Topics include interpersonal attraction, prosocial and antisocial behavior, nonverbal communication, social influence, attitude change, environment and behavior, sex roles and sexual behavior, and research methods. (3 semester units) *Tuition:* $335.

Abnormal Psychology

Covers the dynamics and prevention of abnormal behavior, including neuroses, psychoses, character disorders, psychosomatic reactions, schizophrenia, and other abnormal personality patterns. (4 quarter units) *Tuition:* $335.

PUBLIC HEALTH

Sound Mind, Sound Society: Psychological and Social Health

This course provides perspectives for understanding social and psychological aspects of behavior, taking an interdisciplinary approach to normalcy and abnormality, crime and violence, sex and love, drug abuse including alcohol and tobacco, and suicide. Also covered are the treatment and prevention of social and health problems, and coping with personal and ethical difficulties. (2 semester units) *Tuition:* $315.

Alcohol, the Individual, and Society

Introduces the student to the wide variety of individual and social influences that contribute to alcohol-related problems. You learn to recognize ways alcohol has been regarded in society and identify factors that may contribute to current concepts about adverse consequences of alcohol use. The history of alcohol use, cultural influences, and theories about addictions and other alcohol problems are covered, as are prevention, formal recovery programs, and mutual self-help groups. (3 semester units)

Social Consequences of Alcohol and Other Drug Problems

Examines contemporary patterns of legal and illegal consumption of alcohol and other drugs in the United States. You identify and study the health, economic, and criminal justice consequences of drug use, using selected drugs as models. Society's options in responding to drug use, prevention strategies, and public policy issues are discussed. (2 semester units) *Tuition:* $315.

Community Responses to Alcohol and Other Drug Problems

Studies the broad range of community responses to alcohol and other drug problems, considering the prevention policies and activities of government, business, labor, health institutions, and citizen groups. (2 semester units) *Tuition:* $315.

PURCHASING

Purchasing: Basic Principles and Cases

Examines the functions and fundamentals of purchasing and materials management in organizations as diverse as manufacturing enterprises, government agencies, and schools, hospitals, and research organizations. Explains the place of purchasing in the modern business organization and how the right quality, price, and quantity are determined. Other topics include value analysis, vendor analysis, automation in purchasing, traffic, surplus materials, appraisal, control, and basic policies and procedures of purchasing practice. (3 semester units) *Tuition:* $355.

REAL ESTATE

Principles of Real Estate

This course covers the basic laws and principles of California real estate and teaches how to apply those principles to current real estate conditions and opportunities in your own community. The course provides the understanding, background, and terminology necessary for specialized courses. California law is stressed but many aspects are applicable to real estate interests in other states. (3 semester units) *Tuition:* Contact the CMIL office for cost information.

Real Estate Practice

Focus is on the practical aspects of marketing real estate. The economic framework and administration of the brokerage office; real estate contracts, pricing, and financing of transactions; investment opportunities, creative selling, tax aspects, and problems of subdividing and construction; and responsibilities of brokers and salespeople in influencing decisions of clients and governmental bodies. (3 semester units) *Tuition:* $355.

Real Estate Finance

This course presents a comprehensive analysis of real estate finance for the borrower, lender, investor, and adviser. Topics include legal aspects of property, the mortgage lending market, lending institutions, private lenders, conventional loans, government loan programs, property appraisal and valuation, processing of loans, construction financing, investment analysis, and nontraditional financing. (3 semester units) *Tuition:* $355.

Escrows and Land Titles

Presents a practical study of land titles in California and of related legal principles and problems, many of which are also applicable to the field in any state. Topics include history and background of titles to land in California, the nature and scope of title insurance, recording and constructive notice, the nature of property and estates or interests in land, methods of ownership of land, acquisition and transfer, voluntary liens and encumbrances, involuntary liens and their method of enforcement, how land is described, subdivision of land, easements and servitudes affecting ownership, taxes and assessments, court proceedings and their effect on title, and escrow procedures. (3 semester units) *Tuition:* $355.

RELIGIOUS STUDIES

Views of the Absolute in World Religions

Explores a variety of world religions, focusing on their definitions of the Absolute (e.g., God, Tao, the Void) and how the individual relates to it. Covers Islam, Judaism, Christianity, Hinduism, Taoism, Buddhism, and Native American traditions. (3 semester units) *Tuition:* $335.

SPANISH

Spanish: Elementary Course I

This beginner's course provides a foundation of vocabulary and grammar. Through written and aural/oral exercises you build a knowledge of the language. (3 semester units) *Tuition:* $365.

Spanish: Elementary Course II

Provides a continued study of Spanish vocabulary and grammar, in combination with written and listening/speaking exercises. (3 semester units) *Tuition:* $365.

Spanish: Elementary Course III

Further develops your knowledge of vocabulary and grammar and includes a thorough review of Spanish by written and aural/oral means. (3 semester units) *Tuition:* $355.

Spanish: Intermediate Course I

Reviews vocabulary, grammar, and sentence structure and provides further study in pronunciation and composition. (3 semester units) *Tuition:* $355.

Spanish for the Professions: Course I

Enables you to quickly attain a working knowledge of the Spanish language and build the vocabulary most suited to your needs. The study options are: Spanish for teachers and Spanish for medical personnel. The course is also suitable for those who wish to brush up on the language or prepare for graduate or proficiency examinations. (2 semester units) *Tuition:* $335.

Spanish for the Professions: Course II

Continues to build Spanish language skills applicable to the professional needs of teacher or medical personnel. You can improve communication skills for the workplace or use the course to review and practice for language proficiency examinations. (2 semester units) *Tuition:* $275.

STATISTICS

Introduction to Statistics

Examines population and variables and standard measures of location spread, and association. Also includes coverage of normal approximation, regression, probability and sampling, binomial distribution, interval estimation, and some standard significance tests. (4 semester units) *Tuition:* $355.

WRITING

Technical Writing

Develops your ability to organize information into manuals, journal articles, reports, and other technical publications. After reviewing the fundamentals of planning, research, and writing, you prepare short technical documents related to your own areas of interest. The course also covers document design and production principles, computerized "interactive" documentation, the use of desktop publishing, and taking your publication to press. (3 semester units) *Tuition:* $345.

Editorial Workshop

Teaches the fundamentals of copyediting and explains the copyeditor's role in the publishing cycle; develops your skill in copyediting books, magazines, newspapers, reports, manuals, newsletters, and other nonfiction. Covers both mechanical and substantive editing, with attention to various stylistic conventions and typical usage problems. The course is designed for beginning editors, more experienced editors needing structured review, and publications managers, newsletter writers, desktop publishers, word processors, and proofreaders who want to acquire editorial skills. (3 semester units) *Tuition:* $345.

Nonfiction Writing Workshop

A course to help you improve your personal and professional nonfiction writing through setting writing goals, gathering and organizing ideas and evidence, slanting your writing, planning and implementing the writing project, and revising your manuscripts. Early assignments present exercises in writing letters, reports, interviews, and short essays, and provide guidance on form, organization, and expression. In later assignments you select one writing area: business writing, personal journal, essays, writing for the social sciences, travel writing, or other nonfiction specialties. (3 semester units) *Tuition:* $345.

Magazine Article Writing

This course provides professional guidance in finding and summarizing article ideas and presents techniques for organizing and expanding those ideas into the types of articles that magazines buy. These types include informative, how-to-do-it, practical solution, art of living, controversial, profile, personal experience, nostalgic, and humor. (3 semester units) *Tuition:* $345.

Advanced Article Writing

This course offers professional guidance on four different articles you write. For each article you write an idea summary, a slant and worksheet, a query to the editor, and a completed manuscript. You may choose new articles, ones you have already written or both. (3 semester units) *Tuition:* $275.

Writing the Category Short Story

This course teaches professional techniques essential to writing a category short story (romance, confession, suspense, murder mystery, science fiction, or fantasy) for the popular market. You choose a short story category and develop a story from idea through slant, characterization, plot, and scene to the final draft. At each stage the instructor provides a professional critique. (3 semester hours) *Tuition:* $345.

Writing and Revising the Short Story

Based on the assumption that a writer learns by writing, the course covers the fundamental techniques of short story writing. It teaches how to reach readers through their senses and how to create conflict, character, point of view, plot, and voice. You write a complete draft of your short story and revise it to the point of being ready for submission to a literary magazine. (3 semester units) *Tuition:* $335.

Writing Novels for Children

This course teaches the skills needed for writing novels for young readers, from the beginning reader to the young adult. You learn to create character, setting, dialogue, and scene; to plot a story; and to revise for clarity and conciseness. You also learn to focus on the reader you wish to reach and to tap your own childhood experiences in finding stories to tell. In the final assignments you write and revise up to three chapters of a novel. (3 semester units) *Tuition:* $345.

Marketing and Publishing Fiction

Teaches the essential steps in marketing and publishing fiction: market research, planning, revising for specific markets, creating an effective manuscript packet, and making good use of editorial feedback. (2 semester units) *Tuition:* Contact the CMIL office for cost information.

HIGH SCHOOL COURSES

ENGLISH

Ninth Grade English: First Semester

This course covers the mechanics of the English language, and its structure and usage. The focus is on grammar and composition; the parts of speech, punctuation, vocabulary, spelling, and sentence structure. Students read selected short stories, essays, poems, biographies, and plays and write short original compositions and a book report. *Tuition:* $225.

Ninth Grade English: Second Semester

This further study of writing skills includes punctuation, the mechanics of structure, vocabulary development, and composition. Students read selected poems, plays, short stories, and essays and write short original compositions and a book report. *Tuition:* $225.

Tenth Grade English: First Semester

This continuation of language study emphasizes writing. Literature study focuses on the short story and the novel; these forms are used as models for short compositions. *Tuition:* $225.

Tenth Grade English: Second Semester

Focus on poetry and drama. Emphasis is on student writing with the essay and biography used as models for short compositions. *Tuition:* $225.

Eleventh Grade English: First Semester

The historical development of American literature is presented from the colonial period through the 19th century. *Tuition:* $225.

Eleventh Grade English: Second Semester

Students explore twentieth-century American literature through representative essays, short stories, poems, plays, novels, and biographies. *Tuition:* $225.

Twelfth Grade English: First Semester

Traces the development of English literature through readings of Shakespeare's *Macbeth*, selections from *Beowulf, The Canterbury Tales, Paradise Lost*, and other important literary works. Focus is on developing good written communication and the thoughtful evaluation of literature. *Tuition:* $225.

Twelfth Grade English: Second Semester

Continues surveying the historical development of English literature through readings of selected works by major authors of the Romantic age, the Victorian era, and the twentieth century. *Tuition:* $225.

MATHEMATICS

Elementary Algebra: First Semester

Topics include the formula, integers, fundamental operations, functions, equations in one and two variables, verbal problems, simultaneous equations, graphs of equations, and exponents. *Tuition:* $225.

Elementary Algebra: Second Semester

This course covers polynomials, factoring, algebraic fractions, square roots, quadratic and fractional equations, the number system, and inequalities. *Tuition:* $225.

Geometry: First Semester

This course develops a step-by-step understanding of basic geometrical assumptions before introducing more complex concepts. Topics include congruence of triangles, deductive and indirect proofs, similarities, parallelism, and inequalities. *Tuition:* $225.

Geometry: Second Semester

Major topics include right triangles, circles, constructions and loci, area and volume, coordinate geometry, and transformations. *Tuition:* $225.

Second Year Algebra: First Semester

Reviews algebraic essentials and offers study in advanced areas: linear functions and relations, systems of linear equations or inequalities, graphs in space, determinants, polynomial and rational expressions, sequences and series. *Tuition:* $225.

Second Year Algebra: Second Semester

A continuation of the above course covering radicals and irrational numbers, complex numbers and polynomial functions, quadratic relations and systems, conic sections, exponents and logarithms, permutations and combinations including the binomial expansion. *Tuition:* $225.

Trigonometry

Covers the following topics: functions of acute angles; solution of right triangles, exponents, logarithms; the general angle solution of oblique triangles; trigonometric equations; and graphs of the functions. Other topics include scientific notation, the radian and circular measure, and inverse trigonometric functions. *Tuition:* $225.

SCIENCE

Biology: First Semester (with Laboratory)

Discusses the different processes necessary for life, followed by analysis of these processes in representative organisms. Students examine the characteristics of living organisms and the scientific method; classification; basic chemistry; cellular organization; biochemistry; and energy production and release in living systems. Laboratory experiments are required in this course. *Tuition:* $225.

Biology: Second Semester (with Laboratory)

A continuation of the above course. Includes a study of the animal kingdom; biological nomenclature and classification; the fossil record; physiological processes of multicellular animals; ecosystems; and problems related to human ecology. Laboratory experiments are required. *Tuition:* Contact the CMIL office for cost information.

Health Science

Introduces health principles and practices that promote physical, mental, and social well-being. Topics include mental health, nutrition and physical fitness, human development and reproduction, and substance abuse. *Tuition:* $225.

Physics with Laboratory: First Semester

Introduces basic concepts in physics and their basic mathematical representations. Includes hands-on investigations that can be performed at home in fulfillment of laboratory requirements. Teaches problem-solving strategies and develops an appreciation for the presence of physics in everyday life. Topics include motion, forces, planetary motion, gravity, conservation of energy, heat, and kinetic theory. *Tuition:* $225.

Physics with Laboratory: Second Semester

A continuation of the above course. Covers mechanical waves, light, lenses, electrical forces and fields, electric current, electromagnetism, electromagnetic waves, atomic structure, and modern physics. Laboratory experiments provide observation of physical phenomena illustrating these concepts. *Tuition:* Contact the CMIL office for cost information.

SOCIAL STUDIES

Civics

Examines the nature and basic structure of national, state, and local government, reviews the origins of our democracy; and analyzes representative democracy and the individual's place in it. *Tuition:* $225.

American History: First Semester

United States history from the European background to settlement through the Civil War. Readings stress important themes and events and include excerpts from primary sources of each period. *Tuition:* $225.

American History: Second Semester

A continuation of the above course covering the major historical developments in United States history from 1865 to the present. *Tuition:* $225.

NONCREDIT COURSES

CAREER PLANNING

Career Counseling: Matching Yourself to a Career

The program consists of a complete series of counseling sessions (assignments), carefully developed questionnaires, and action-exercises, which are assessed by your instructor. (Noncredit) *Tuition:* $375.

COMMUNICATIONS

English Review for the Business Community

A refresher course emphasizing usage and writing skills and offering an intensive study of the sentence and its parts, the roles of words in sentences, punctuation, capitalization, and the use of abbreviations and numbers. You learn how to write effective sentences through illustrations and practice in applying principles studied. Provides preparation for more advanced writing and communications courses. (Noncredit) *Tuition:* $335.

ENGINEERING

Engineering Fundamentals

Designed to help those preparing for the fundamentals portions of the various state engineering examinations as well as for those reviewing for their work or for advanced study. Topics are ones ordinarily covered in the undergraduate engineering curriculum: Materials and problems in mathematics—differential and integral calculus. Mechanics—statics, dynamics, and friction. Fluid mechanics—hydrostatics, hydrodynamics, and frictional head loss in pipe lines. Thermodynamics—processes, cycles, work functions, and heat transfer. Mechanics of materials: beam stresses, shear and moment diagrams, rivet problems and torsion problems. Electricity and electronics—Ohm's law, alternating current circuitry, and three phase power. Chemistry—weights of reaction and combustion problems. Economics and investment theory—compound interest, depreciation, and recovery cost. (Noncredit) *Tuition:* $420.

RADIOLOGIC TECHNOLOGY

Principles of Radiologic Technology—Limited Permit: Core Area 800A

The focus is on protection of self and patients from excessive radiation, setting controls on the x-ray unit, handling and processing of x-ray film, fundamental patient positions for taking x-rays, evaluation of radiographs, basic concepts in physics and anatomy. (Noncredit) *Tuition:* $420.

Principles of Radiologic Technology—Limited Permit: Specialized Area 800C, Chest

This course explores special techniques for taking x-rays of the chest area, including the lungs, pleura, diaphragm, esophagus, trachea, bronchi, thorax, and vertebral column. (Noncredit) *Tuition:* $315.

Principles of Radiologic Technology—Limited Permit: Specialized Area 800E, Extremities

This course explores special techniques for taking x-rays of the upper- and lower-body extremities, including hand, wrist, forearm, elbow, humerus, shoulder, clavicle, scapula, foot, ankle, leg, knee, and hip. (Noncredit) *Tuition:* $315.

Principles of Radiologic Technology—Limited Permit: Specialized Area 800T, Torso-Skeletal

This course covers those specific skills related to anatomy and positioning needed for taking radiographs of the torso-skeletal system, including bone, join and muscle classification and movement, the thorax and shoulder girdle, and the spine and pelvic girdle. (Noncredit) *Tuition:* $315.

Principles of Radiologic Technology—Limited Permit: Laboratory 800R

Radiation protection and general radiography laboratory, covering methods of reducing radiation exposure for patients and personnel, radiographic contrast and detail, control of scatter, and quality control. (Noncredit) *Tuition:* $295.

WRITING

Writing Fundamentals

Helps you master the basics of writing clear, grammatically correct sentences. You review basic grammar, parts of speech, and punctuation rules. You learn how to introduce variety into your writing by using different types of sentences and how to combine sentences to improve your writing style. At the conclusion of the course you are introduced to writing effective paragraphs. (Noncredit) *Tuition:* $310.

Poetry Writing

A course in the elements of writing traditional verse. Through assigned exercises, you learn how to get started, and then you begin to master areas such as verse rhythms, line lengths, stanza patterns, and techniques of description. You learn how to choose the right word, avoid monotonous rhythm, find rhymes, and get sound effects. Some attention is also paid to writing free verse. (Noncredit) *Tuition:* $310.

Perfecting Your Poem: A Guide to Revision

This short course helps you revise your poems for communication, as well as for diction, rhythm and rhyme, sound, form, and imagery. It is based on a unique guide that lists over 60 aspects of a poem to explore as you revise, helping you determine what areas of your poems may need extra attention. (Noncredit) *Tuition:* $275.

Poetry of Self: The Writer Within

Not a course in writing poetry, the course is designed to help you to explore your own ideas and experiences and to find the writer in yourself. Each assignment consists of a self-exploratory writing experience using improvisation, associative methods, fantasy, detailed observation, and inquiry for personal myth. (Noncredit) *Tuition:* $310.

California State University, Dominguez Hills
Division of Extended Education
Humanities External Degree Program
1000 East Victoria Street
Carson, California 90747   (213) 516-3743

Description:

The Dominguez Hills campus of California State University was founded in 1960, and admitted its first students in 1965. It is today housed on a 346-acre site in southwest Los Angeles. The Division of Extended Education is a self-supporting branch of the University. Courses are offered for the continuing education of professionals, development for personal and professional goals, and general self-improvement. Many certificate programs offer a series of specially designed courses, indicating that the student has exposure to a significant amount of detailed study of the subject. In addition, the Division offers off-campus degrees. In the Humanities, the master's degree is offered through independent study correspondence courses. The student is given an interdisciplinary exposure (history, art, literature, music, philosophy) and may specialize in a particular discipline in culturally thematic cross-disciplinary areas. There are no residency requirements.

Faculty:

Margaret Gordon, Dean, Division of Extended Education; Arthur L. Harshman, Professor of Art and Academic Coordinator of the Humanities External Degree Program; Loretta Edwards, Program Secretary. There is a faculty of 20 for this program.

Academic Levels:
Graduate

Degree/Certificate Programs:

The Master of Arts in the Humanities offers a broad interdisciplinary exposure to all of the areas of the Humanities—history, literature, philosophy, music, and art—and the establishment of an integrative perspective among them, with emphasis on their interrelating effects and influences. The student is provided with the opportunity to specialize in a particular discipline of the Humanities, or in specific cultural thematic areas which could be traced across all of the humanistic disciplines. Since programs are individually designed for the student, course offerings and sequences vary; the student should check with the program office for detailed information about available and required courses. Graduation requires a minimum of 30 semester units, at least 15 of which must be graduate-level courses; not less than 21 semester units completed in the program; overall GPA of 3.0 or better; passing of Humanities Master of Arts "Advancement to Candidacy" examination.

Admission Requirements:

Bachelor of Arts or Science degree from a regionally-accredited college or university. The degree does not have to be in the Humanities. A 2.5 GPA in last 60 semester (90 quarter) transferable units. Successful completion of the GRE is not required for admission to the program nor necessary to achieve classified standing. Citizens of foreign countries are required to take special examination.

Tuition:

$120 per semester unit; $55 application fee. Fees subject to change without notice. Contact the school for current rates. Refund policy: 100 percent if withdrawal prior to the end of the first week; 65 percent of fees if withdrawal after the first week of the course has elapsed. After three weeks of the course time has elapsed, no refund will be made.

Enrollment Period:

A student may choose to remain on inactive status for two consecutive semesters; after that period, re-application is required. The maximum time to complete the requirements is 5 years; the minimum time is 1½ to 2 years.

Equipment Requirements:

Books and supplies must be purchased by the student.

Credit and Grading:

Letter grade system: A–F; minimum passing grade is D; Incomplete or Withdrawal not counted in grade average. Students whose GPA falls below 3.0 in any given semester will be placed on academic probation and will be expected to show improvement in the next semester so that the GPA will equal or exceed 3.0. A maximum of nine semester units of graduate work may be transferred-in. Credit is awarded in semester hour units.

Library Services:

Through interlibrary loan arrangements, the resources of the Southern California members of The California State University are accessible to External Degree program students.

Accreditations:

Western Association of Schools and Colleges.

GRADUATE COURSES

HUMANITIES

Defining the Humanities: History

Advanced study of the nature of history through examination of the Bolshevik Revolution. (2 semester hours)

Defining the Humanities: Literature

Advanced study of the nature of literature by examination of images of self in selected poems and novels. (2 semester hours)

Defining the Humanities: Music

Advanced study of music, focusing on concepts of meaning and form in music at a philosophical rather than theoretical level. The ability to read music not required. (2 semester hours)

Defining the Humanities: Art

Advanced study of key concepts in art by focusing on aesthetics and art theory. (2 semester hours)

Defining the Humanities: Philosophy

Advanced study of key concepts of philosophy by focusing on contemporary issues and conflicts and their analogues in traditional philosophical readings. (2 semester hours)

Humanities Encounter: Art

Visitation to three local museums to examine their architecture and collections. Open to non-local students by special arrangement. (2 or 3 semester hours)

Humanities Encounter: The Living Theatre

How to recognize, appreciate and evaluate a variety of dramatic experiences. (2 or 3 semester hours)

Humanities Encounter: Concert Music

Attendance and analysis of several concerts representing the general categories of symphonic, vocal, and chamber music. Open to non-local students by special arrangement. (2 or 3 semester hours)

Humanities Encounter: History

Exploring the historical roots of one's own community. Open to non-local students by special arrangement. (2 or 3 semester hours)

Humanities Encounter: Film

Watching and analyzing several movies with special focus on the techniques and content of the medium. (2 or 3 semester hours)

Evolution of Human Culture

An examination of the nature of change and cultural unfolding, using the development of the city as a key concept, and looking into three representative types of cities: ancient, medieval, and modern. (3 semester hours)

The Rational Perspective

The meaning of rationality from the perspectives of philosophy, history, literature, music, and art. Special emphasis on the possible differences between scientific and humanistic rationality. (3 semester hours)

The Para-Rational Perspective

Interdisciplinary exploration of non-rational alternatives in modern culture, focusing on the non-logical, the visionary, and the religious/mystical. (3 semester hours)

The Autonomous Individual

Interdisciplinary study of the nature of the creative act, including the following: the artist's vision of self; the defenses of personalism;

notions of aesthetics; and abstract of symbolic thought. (3 semester hours)

The Individual and Society

Exploration of the position of the individual in the classic and modern models of social and political organization; conservatism, liberalism, socialism, anarchism; study of the Utopian tradition; and study of aesthetic theories that connect the artist with society. (3 semester hours)

The Non-Western World

Interdisciplinary examinations of the non-western world by focusing on cultural characteristics of Japan. (3 semester hours)

Alienation, Estrangement, and Subcultures

Survey of the elements and historical implications of alienation and examination of subcultures as they exist in America. Readings from social philosophy as well as from Chicano and Afro-American studies. (3 semester hours)

World Religious Perspectives

Survey of ancient and modern religious systems, focusing upon an exploration of the general characteristics of religious beliefs. (3 semester hours)

Values and Morality in Twentieth-Century Thought

Examination of values and morality in modern culture against a backdrop of seemingly amoral scientific and technological progress. (3 semester hours)

Key Individuals, Art: Frank Lloyd Wright

Intensive study of the major buildings and architectural influence of Frank Lloyd Wright. (3 semester hours)

Key Individuals, Music: Beethoven

An examination of the life and music of Ludwig Van Beethoven; the ability to read music not required. (3 semester hours)

Key Individuals, Philosophy: Rousseau

An examination of the life, thought, and influence of Rousseau, focusing on several recurrent themes: self-other, rational-nonrational, classic-romantic, dependence-independence, democracy-totalitarianism. (3 semester hours)

Key Individuals, Literature: Hemingway and Faulkner

An examination of the major works and influence of two modern American authors, Ernest Hemingway and William Faulkner. (3 semester hours)

Key Individuals, History: Carnegie, Rockefeller, and Ford

Rise of American industrial capitalism, viewed through the activities of three business giants, and the course of American economic history to the present, with special emphasis on World War I and the Great Depression. (3 semester hours)

Nobel Laureates: Studies in Modern World Literature

Examination of representative major works by recent Noble Laureates whose art epitomizes diverse cultural, literary, and social viewpoints. Authors include Mann, Pirandello, Camus, Kawabata, Solzhenitsyn, Neruda, and Bellow. (3 semester hours)

Key Periods and Movements, Art: Contemporary Art

Exploration of the complex cultural development known as modern art by investigation of six major artistic movements: Cubism, Expressionism, Dada/Surrealism, Pop Art, Conceptual Art, and Technological Art. (3 semester hours)

Key Periods and Movements, Music: Baroque

Examination of Baroque music and the period in Western Europe (1600-1750) during which it evolved. The ability to read music not required. (3 semester hours)

Key Periods and Movements, Philosophy: The Biblical Movement

Examination of modern scholarship on the Bible and its impact on Christianity; analysis of three types of Bible interpretation: fundamentalism, liberalism, and humanism. (3 semester hours)

Key Periods and Movements, Literature: Archetypal Criticism

Exploration of a twentieth-century movement in literature, archetypal criticism, which focuses on recurrent patterns in literature and their analogues in folktale, dream, ritual, and myth. (3 semester hours)

Key Periods and Movements, History: The Age of Revolution

A study of the dynamics of economic change and political revolution with a comparison between the period 1776-1815 in Europe and North America and the period since World War II in Latin America. (3 semester hours)

Independent Study

Individually designed, faculty-guided study of a topic in literature, history, philosophy, music, art, and interdisciplinary topics. (3 semester hours)

Final Project

An individually planned project based on coursework taken in the program and involving basic research in a single discipline or on an interdisciplinary topic. (4 to 6 semester hours)

California State University, Sacramento
Office of Water Programs
6000 J Street
Sacramento, California 95819-6025
(916) 278-6142

Description:

California State University at Sacramento was founded in 1947. The Office of Water Programs develops training materials for the operators of drinking water and wastewater treatment systems. The materials were developed for the United States Environmental Protection Agency and the courses have been offered since 1972. The courses emphasize how to operate and maintain water and wastewater facilities and also pretreatment facility inspection. Over 13,000 persons enroll in the courses and over 50,000 training manuals are sold annually throughout the world.

Faculty:

Kenneth D. Kerri, Director, Office of Water Programs.

Academic Levels:

College
Noncredit
Vocational
Professional

Degree/Certificate Programs:

Up to six semester units of lower division extension credit can be earned for each course, with the exceptions of Small Water Systems, Water Distribution Systems, and

Metal Wastestreams, which are worth three semester units. When a student has completed a course, a CSUS registration packet can be requested. Upon notification from the University that the registration fee of $40 per semester unit (this fee is in addition to the course fee paid upon enrollment) has been paid, the course grade will be forwarded to the proper office. These lower division units often can be applied towards an A.A., A.S., B.A., or B.S. degree at a two- or four-year college or university.

If enrolled on a noncredit, vocational, or professional basis, nine continuing education units (CEUs) are earned upon successful completion of each course with the exception of the three courses listed above which are worth 4.5 CEUs. These CEUs can be used to meet educational requirements or work experience when applying for licensing examinations, maintaining a license, employment and/or promotion.

Admission Requirements:
Open enrollment.

Tuition:
$30 per course plus an additional $40 per unit fee for six semester units of university credit. Prices are subject to change without notice.

Enrollment Period:
Students may begin courses at any time and proceed at a convenient pace. Most students require from 50 to 150 hours of study to complete each course.

Equipment Requirements:
Cost of course manuals vary from $10 to $30 (see course listings below). California residents must add appropriate state tax to the cost of the manuals. Return of manuals must be approved before they are shipped to the Office of Water Programs. Returns will only be accepted up to six months from the date of purchase. All books returned must be in resaleable condition. A service fee will be deducted from the refund to cover the costs of handling returns and processing refunds. The total refund will depend on the condition of the returned manuals and the return/handling fee.

Credit and Grading:
Examinations on the honor system. Grading system: A, 90 to 100 percent; B, 80 to 90 percent; C, 70 to 80 percent; D, 60 to 70 percent; F, below 60 percent. The minimum passing grade is 70%.

Accreditations:
Western Association of Schools and Colleges.

COLLEGE COURSES

WASTEWATER TREATMENT
Operation of Wastewater Treatment Plants I

This course is designed to train operators in the safe and effective operation and maintenance of wastewater treatment plants. *Tuition:* $30; manual $20.

Operation of Wastewater Treatment Plants II

A continuation of Operation of Wastewater Treatment Plants I. Topics covered include: Activated Sludge (Conventional Activated Sludge Plants); Sludge Digestion and Solids Handling; Effluent Disposal; Plant Safety and Good Housekeeping; Maintenance; Laboratory Procedures and Chemistry; Applications of Computers for Plant O & M; Analysis and Presentation of Data; Records and Report Writing. *Tuition:* $30; manual $25.

Advanced Waste Treatment

This course is designed to train operators in the safe and effective operation of advanced wastewater treatment plants. Topics covered include: Odor Control; Activated Sludge (pure Oxygen and Operational Control Alternatives); Solids Handling and Disposal; Solids Removal from Secondary Effluents; Phosphorus Removal; Nitrogen Removal; Wastewater Reclamation; Instrumentation. *Tuition:* $30; manual $20.

Industrial Waste Treatment I

This course is designed to train operators in the safe and effective operation of industrial waste treatment plants. Topics covered include: The Industrial Plant Operator; Safety; Regulatory Requirements; Preventing and Minimizing Wastes at the Source; Industrial Wastewaters; Flow Measurement; Preliminary Treatment; Physical-Chemical Treatment Processes; Filtration; Physical Treatment Processes; Treatment of Metal Wastestreams; Instrumentation. *Tuition:* $30; manual $20.

Industrial Waste Treatment II

This course is designed to train operators in the safe and effective operation of industrial wastewater treatment plants. Topics covered include: The Industrial Plant Operator; Fixed Growth Processes (Trickling Filters and RBCs); Suspended Growth Processes (Activated Sludge); Sequencing Batch Reactors; Enhanced Biological (Nutrient) Control; Anaerobic Treatment; Residual Solids Management; Maintenance. *Tuition:* $30; manual $20.

Operation and Maintenance of Wastewater Collection Systems I

This course is designed to train personnel in the safe and effective operation and maintenance of wastewater collection systems. Topics covered include: The Wastewater Collection System Operator; Why Collection System Operations and Maintenance?; Wastewater Collection Systems; Safe Procedures; Inspecting and Testing Collection Systems; Pipeline Cleaning and Maintenance Methods; Underground Repair. *Tuition:* $30; manual $20.

Operation and Maintenance of Wastewater Collection Systems II

A continuation of Operation and Maintenance of Wastewater Collection Systems I. Topics covered include: Lift Stations; Equipment Maintenance; Sewer Rehabilitation; Safety; Administration; Organization for System Operation and Maintenance. *Tuition:* $30; manual $20.

Pretreatment Facility Inspection

This course is designed to train inspectors in the safe and efficient procedures for inspecting industrial pretreatment facilities. Topics covered include: The Pretreatment Facility Inspector; Development and Application of Regulations; Inspection of a Typical Industry; Safety in Pretreatment Inspection Work; Sampling Procedures for Wastewater; Wastewater Flow Monitoring; Industrial Wastewaters; Pretreatment Technology (Source Control); Industrial Inspection Procedures; Emergency Response; Pretreatment Program Administration. *Tuition:* $30; manual $30.

Treatment of Metal Wastestreams

This course is designed to train personnel in the safe and effective operation and maintenance of wastewater treatment facilities for electroplating, metal finishing, and printed circuit board manufacturing. Topics covered include: Need for Treatment; Sources for Wastewater; Material Safety Data Sheets (MSDS); Employee Right-To-Know Laws; Methods of Treatment; Sludge Treatment and Disposal; Operation, Maintenance and Troubleshooting. *Tuition:* $10; manual $10.

WATER TREATMENT

Small Water System Operation and Maintenance

This course is designed to train operators in the safe and effective operation and maintenance of small drinking water systems and treatment plants. Topics covered include: The Small Water System Operator; Water Sources and Treatment; Wells; Small Water Treatment Plants; Disinfection; Safety; Laboratory Procedures; Setting Water Rates for Small Water Utilities. *Tuition:* $30; manual $20.

Water Distribution System Operation and Maintenance

This course is designed to train operators in the safe and effective operation and maintenance of water distribution systems. Topics covered include: The Water Distribution System Operator; Storage Facilities; Distribution System Facilities; Water Quality Considerations in Distribution Systems; Distribution System Operation and Maintenance; Disinfection; Safety. *Tuition:* $30; manual $20.

Water Treatment Plant Operation I

This course is designed to train operators in the safe and effective operation and maintenance of drinking water treatment plants. Topics covered include: The Water Treatment Plant Operator; Water Resources and Treatment; Reservoir Management and Intake Structures; Coagulation and Flocculation; Sedimentation; Filtration; Disinfection; Corrosion Control; Taste and Odor Control; Plant Operation; Laboratory Procedures. *Tuition:* $30; manual $30.

Water Treatment Plant Operation II

A continuation of the Water Treatment Plant Operation I. Topics covered include: Iron and Manganese Control; Fluoridation; Softening; Trihalomethanes; Demineralization; Handling and Disposal of Process Wastes; Maintenance; Instrumentation; Safety; Advanced Laboratory Procedures; Drinking Water Regulations; Administration. *Tuition:* $30; manual $30.

Central Arkansas, University of
Continuing Education
201 Donaghey Avenue
Conway, Arkansas 72035   (501) 450-5268

Description:

The correspondence program at the University of Central Arkansas was begun in 1927 at what was then called the Arkansas Normal School. Instruction at the Normal School began in 1908 with 107 students. Enrollment at the University is currently 9,500 students. In 1975 the current name was adopted.

The purpose of the correspondence program is to bring a practical education within reach of all eligible persons interested in an enrichment program. By means of independent study, a thorough course of training at the lowest possible cost is offered to those who are unable to take work on campus. Average annual enrollment in correspondence courses is 1,500.

Faculty:

Dr. Clyde Reese, Dean, Continuing Education; Anthony Sitz, Registrar. There is a faculty of 56 members.

Academic Levels:

College

Degree/Certificate Programs:

Completion of courses provides credits toward the associate and baccalaureate degrees.One-fourth of total degree requirements may be earned through correspondence courses; no more than six of the last 30 hours may be from correspondence study.

Admission Requirements:

Students need not be admitted to University of Central Arkansas for enrolling in correspondence courses. High school graduation or GED required.

Tuition:

Contact the school for current tuition and fees. If withdrawal from a course within 30 days after enrollment, refund is 65% of fee paid; 50% refund during next 30 days; no refund after 60 days of enrollment.

Enrollment Period:

The maximum time to complete a course is 1 year; the minimum time is 8 weeks. An extension of 1 year may be granted upon payment of a $20 fee.

Equipment Requirements:

$10 textbook rental or purchased by the student; some courses require workbooks, maps, and other aids which are sold separately at cost.

Credit and Grading:

Grading system may vary with instructor; usually 90–100 (A); 80–89 (B), 70–79 (C), 60–69 (D); below 60 is failure. Credit is awarded in semester hours.

Accreditations:

North Central Association of Colleges and Schools.

COLLEGE COURSES

ASTRONOMY

Descriptive Astronomy

An introductory study of stars, star systems, and galaxies. The subjects of stellar evolution and cosmological models will also be included in the course. (3 semester hours)

ECONOMICS

Principles of Economics I

A introduction to the American economy, with emphasis on the factors which determine employment and income levels in the United States. (3 semester hours)

Principles of Economics II

A continuation of the above course with emphasis on composition and problems of national output, distribution of income and international trade. (3 semester hours)

EDUCATION

The American School System

The history, organization, and purposes of the American school system at the elementary level. (3 semester hours)

ENGLISH

English Literature I

A survey of English literature from the beginning through the eighteenth century, with emphasis on ideas and forms that have contributed to our culture pattern. (3 semester hours)

English Literature II

A survey of English literature from the eighteenth century to the present, with emphasis upon ideas and form that have contributed to our culture pattern. (3 semester hours)

English, Rhetoric, and Composition

Theories and applications of the principles of rhetoric and style as they relate to writing. (3 semester hours)

Children's Literature

Planning of reading lists for various ages. Reading study of many children's books. (3 semester hours)

Modern Grammars

Several systems of English grammar including the traditional, structural, and transformational-generative approaches. Introduction to the terminology of the modern science of linguistics and some particular problems related to the teaching of English grammar in public schools. (3 semester hours)

American Literature I

From the beginning to the Civil War. (3 semester hours)

American Literature II

From the Civil War to the present. (3 semester hours)

GEOGRAPHY

Introduction to Physical Geography

A study of the elements of the natural environment including landforms, weather, climate, soils and water, and their significance in terms of the human occupation of the earth. (3 semester hours)

Introduction to Human Geography

Man's spatial behavior in relation to the environment. Emphasis will be placed on distributions in the contemporary world. Topics include population, settlement, religion, economic and political activities, and the cultural landscape. (3 semester hours)

Conservation and Land Use

A study of the problems involved in the efficient, nonwasteful use of natural resources. Particular attention is given to the United States. (3 semester hours)

GERMAN

Reading German

An introductory course for beginners who wish to concentrate on developing reading skills. Each lesson offers readings from a variety of areas as well as short explanations of structural aspects of the language essential to the understanding of texts in German. (3 semester hours)

HEALTH EDUCATION

Health and Safety

Safety education, personal and community hygiene. (2 semester hours)

Human Sexuality

A course dealing with the biological, psychological, and social factors involved in human sexual behavior. (2 semester hours)

Administration of the School Health Program

A program of health for the elementary and secondary schools, health services, healthful living, health instruction, public relations and evaluations. (3 semester hours)

HISTORY

World History I

Analyzes the major contributions to the advancement of global civilizations from ancient times to the early modern period (*circa* 1600). (3 semester hours)

World History II

Traces the advancement of modern industrial and urban society from its European bases in the 17th century to its worldwide impact in the 20th century. (3 semester hours)

American Nation I

The development of the American people from the era of exploration to the close of the Civil War. (3 semester hours)

American Nation II

Survey of the United States from the Civil War to the present. (3 semester hours)

Europe, 1914–1939

Background and history of World War I; problems of peacemaking and international organization; the rise of Fascism, National Socialism and Japanese Imperialism; breaking of the peace. (3 semester hours)

HOME ECONOMICS

Nutrition in the Life Cycle

Principles and application of nutrition information to everyday living. (3 semester hours)

INDUSTRIAL EDUCATION

Introduction to Technical Drafting

The use of drawing instruments, lettering, types of projections, dimensions and notes, sections, and conventional practices in drafting. (3 semester hours)

MANAGEMENT

Introduction to Business

Survey of the American business system and individual business operation. Includes highlights of marketing, management, finance, accounting, economics, and business law, plus other related topics. (3 semester hours)

MATHEMATICS

Intermediate Algebra

Fundamental processes, linear equations, and graphs. (3 semester hours)

Mathematics for General Education

Designed as a terminal course to meet the general education aims of the college. (3 semester hours)

College Algebra

(3 semester hours)

Plane Trigonometry

(3 semester hours)

Numbers Systems for Elementary Teachers

A study of the structure of the real number system. (3 semester hours)

PHILOSOPHY

Effective Thinking

Designed to improve a person's ability to reason clearly and correctly and to make rational decisions based on understanding decision strategies, knowing how to use information, and being able to avoid erroneous thinking. (3 semester hours)

Introduction to Logic

Formal and informal reasoning including classical inductive and deductive systems, as well as elementary symbolic logic. (3 semester hours)

Origins of Hebrew Thought

An introduction to the historical background and major themes of Old Testament literature. (3 semester hours)

PHYSICAL EDUCATION

Principles of Physical Education

A study of the aims, objectives, and philosophies of physical education; the physical, social, and psychological contribution to modern life. (3 semester hours)

Recreation Administration

Problems connected with the choice, selection, and leadership of suitable recreation activities for different age levels. (3 semester hours)

Coaching Basketball

Coaching techniques of various offenses and defenses, philosophy and psychology of coaching methods, drills and fundamentals of different offenses and defenses in basketball, training methods, and proper eating habits. (2 semester hours)

Kinesiology

A study of the principles of human motion. Anatomical and mechanical analysis of everyday activities and physical education skills emphasized for the purpose of promoting normal physical development, improvement of posture, and increased efficiency in the use of the body. (3 semester hours)

PHYSICS

Physical Science for General Education

A study of the elementary principles of astronomy, chemistry, geology, meteorology, and physics. (4 semester hours)

POLITICAL SCIENCE

United States Government and Politics

Origin and adoption of the Constitution, basic principles of the American constitutional system, the machinery of popular control, and the structure of the national government. (3 semester hours)

International Relations

The methods and techniques used in the conduct of relations between nation-states with special study of the causes of international crises. (3 semester hours)

PSYCHOLOGY

General Psychology

An introduction to psychology as a behavioral science. Topics covered include sensation and psychological tests and measurement. (3 semester hours)

Educational Psychology

Designed to provide an introduction to the developmental foundations of human beings, the major theories of learning, applications of learning, application of learning theories and factors affecting human learning in diverse human populations. (3 semester hours)

Child Growth and Development

A general study of the physical, mental, emotional, and social development of children. (3 semester hours)

Adolescent Growth and Development

The objective of this course is to give the student a balanced and comprehensive picture of physical, emotional, social, moral, and intellectual growth of the adolescent. (3 semester hours)

SOCIOLOGY

Principles of Sociology

The study of sociology principles and concepts. Topics include social origins, cultural and personality basis of human change. (3 semester hours)

The Family

The design of this course includes a history of the dating, engagement, and marriage customs of the world. Both the physical and psychological aspects of marriage from the honeymoon through child rearing to old age are included. The statistical and emotional factors in broken marriages are also considered. (3 semester hours)

Juvenile Delinquency

A survey of the causes of juvenile delinquency, the juvenile court, detention and treatment facilities, and treatment and preventive programs. (3 semester hours)

SPECIAL EDUCATION

Introduction to Special Education

An introduction to all types of exceptional children with consideration of social and psychological aspects specific to such children. (3 semester hours)

Language Development of Exceptional Children

This course is intended to give a foundation for understanding language development and language problems in children. It will deal with incidence and types of language disorders and the teacher's role in working with these disorders in the classroom. (3 semester hours)

Nature and Needs of the Mentally Retarded

Descriptions of types and nature of mental retardation and implications for adjustment and education. (3 semester hours)

Education and Psychology of Exceptional Children

A survey of the characteristics and educational needs of impaired and gifted children. (3 semester hours)

Materials and Methods of Teaching the Mentally Retarded

This course considers instructional material, activities, and methods of teaching children who are mentally retarded. (3 semester hours)

Nature and Needs of the Physically Handicapped

Descriptions of types and nature of physically handicapped conditions and implications for adjustment and education. (3 semester hours)

Nature and Needs of the Cerebral Palsied Individual

Descriptions of types and nature of cerebral palsy and implications for adjustment and education. (3 semester hours)

Nature and Needs of Emotionally Disturbed Children

An introduction of concepts, practices, and trends in education for emotionally disturbed children and orientation to the dynamic provided. (3 semester hours)

Techniques in Work-Study Skills for Career Education for Exceptional Youth

A course designed to prepare special education majors in the various phases of prevocational and work-study programs at the junior and senior high school level. (3 semester hours)

Characteristics of the Mildly Handicapped

This course deals with the distinguishing characteristics and etiology of mildly handicapping conditions. (3 semester hours)

Classroom Management of Exceptional Children

Designed to provide students with competencies required to manage learning and classroom behaviors of exceptional children. Students will be exposed to accepted theoretical and functional principles of behavior management used and observed in the classroom. (3 semester hours)

Reading for Exceptional Children

Designed to provide an overview of the diagnosis and remediation of reading disabilities. (3 semester hours)

Methods and Materials for Secondary Level Mildly Handicapped

Designed to provide educational intervention strategies for teaching the secondary level mildly handicapped student. (3 semester hours)

Tests and Measurements for the Exceptional Student

Provides an overview of the basic concepts of assessment, types of tests used in special education, and the application of test results. (3 semester hours)

SPEECH

History of the Theatre I

Historical survey of the theatre arts from 1660 to the present. (3 semester hours)

History of the Theatre II

A continuation of the above course. (3 semester hours)

Evolution of Rhetorical Theory

A survey of the development of the principal rhetorical theories from ancient to modern times and the application of these theories to the analysis of outstanding speakers throughout history. (3 semester hours)

Central Baptist College
Correspondence Department
Conway, Arkansas 72032   (501) 329-6872

Description:

Central Baptist College is designed especially for the preparation of men and women for Christian Service. The college is the result of a move made by the Arkansas Missionary Baptist Association at its organizational meeting in Little Rock, Arkansas in 1950. At that meeting, a committee consisting of fifteen members was selected and authorized to make arrangements for the founding of a school.

The Correspondence Department provides directed study at the collegiate level for Christian workers and others whose vocational and other responsibilities prohibit their being enrolled for regular classes on the college campus. The department also helps develop individual study which will continue to be a source of enrichment for the student.

Faculty:
Gene Mitchell, Director.

Academic Levels:
College

Degree/Certificate Programs:
No student can obtain a degree unless he has been in actual residence a minimum of nine months or two semesters immediately preceding graduation.

Admission Requirements:
High school graduation or the equivalent; non-high school graduates with a minimum of fifteen units and a recommendation of the high school principal or superintendent may be admitted.

Tuition:
Contact the school for current tuition and fees.

Enrollment Period:
Students may enroll at any time.

Credit and Grading:
Letter grades are used: A, B, C, D, F. The minimum passing grade is D.

Equipment Requirements:
Students must purchase textbooks required for the courses. The College will buy textbooks back for one-half their original price.

Credit and Grading:
Credit is awarded in semester hour units.

Accreditations:
American Association of Bible Colleges.

COLLEGE COURSES

BIBLE

Survey of the Old Testament

Introduction to the Bible: its supernatural origin, literary structure, and composition. Old Testament history from the creation to the Post-Exilic Era, with stress on the divine mission of the Messianic race. (3 semester hours)

Inter-Biblical Period

Political and religious events during the four hundred years between the Testaments. Required of all correspondence students before the study of the New Testament. (2 semester hours)

Survey of the New Testament

A continuation of the above course, providing a brief review of the Inter-Biblical period and a survey of Christianity during the first century. Special emphasis is placed on the divine origin of the church, the ministry of the Holy Spirit, and the authority of the New Testament in the work of the churches. (3 semester hours)

Life of Christ

A study of the life of Christ as revealed in the four gospels. Special attention is given to His person and character, His travels, His teaching and miracles, and His methods of dealing with people. (3 semester hours)

Biblical Hermeneutics

Survey and evaluation of the various methods of interpreting the Scriptures. Required of all ministerial students. (3 semester hours)

The Pentateuch

The first five books of the Bible. The creation, fall, and redemption of man, the relation of Jesus and the church to the law. Students need to have access to a library for this course. (3 semester hours)

Hebrews and General Epistles

Hebrews to Jude. (3 semester hours)

Minor Prophets

A survey of the twelve minor prophets, Hosea to Malachi. (3 semester hours)

Isaiah

An in-depth analysis of the prophecy of Isaiah. Special attention to the historical setting, the prophecies of immediate and extended future of the covenant people, and the Christological content of the Messianic prophecies. (3 semester hours)

Revelation

Detailed analysis of the entire book with prophetic application of the various symbols employed in its imagery. (3 semester hours)

ENGLISH

English Literature II

British literature from the eighteenth century to the present era. Focus is given to literary themes, authors, and circumstantial events that shape the literature. (3 semester hours)

World Literature

I. An introduction to western literature from classical Greece through the Renaissance. Particular attention is given to the understanding of thematic trends, cultural developments, and comparative analysis of the major authors. (3 semester hours)

II. An introduction to western literature from the Enlightenment through Modernist period. Particular attention is given to the understanding of thematic trends, cultural developments, and comparative analysis of the major authors. (3 semester hours)

GREEK

New Testament Greek Grammar

Part I of a basic language course designed to familiarize the student with the elements of Koine Greek. The course stresses vocabulary, conjugation, declension, pronunciation, and translation. (3 semester hours)

HISTORY

U.S. History to 1865

A survey of social, economic, and political forces that have shaped the American nation. (3 semester hours)

U.S. History since 1865

A survey of social, economic, and political forces that have shaped the American nation. (3 semester hours)

History of Christianity

From the New Testament beginnings to the present. The course considers the major movements, personalities, denominational origins, and secular influences of almost 2,000 years of Christianity and Christianity's impact on the various cultures and nations of the past two centuries. (3 semester hours)

History of Baptists

Baptist distinctives from New Testament times to the present. (3 semester hours)

PASTORAL STUDIES

Sermon Preparation and Delivery

Preaching as an art, the selection of a text, the theme, the collection of material, the outlining of a sermon. (3 semester hours)

SOCIOLOGY

Introductory Sociology

The origin and development of society and the forms, institutions, and functions of human groups. (3 semester hours)

THEOLOGY

Christian Doctrine

Major, fundamental doctrines of the Bible. What Christians believe and why they believe it. (3 semester hours)

Central Bible College
Correspondence Division
3000 North Grant Avenue
Springfield, Missouri 65803   (417) 833-2551

Description:
 Central Bible College was established in 1922 and is owned and controlled by the General Council of the Assemblies of God, Springfield. It is a four-year college offering majors in Music, Bible, Christian Education, and Missions. Correspondence study was begun in 1961. The student in correspondence study has the opportunity to develop his/her initiative of thought and expression.

Faculty:
 Maurice Lednicky, President; Linda White, Correspondence Secretary; Eunice Bruegman, Registrar. There is a faculty of 12 members.

Academic Levels:
 College

Degree/Certificate Programs:
 Up to 12 semester units of correspondence study may be applied toward a Bachelor of Arts degree.

Admission Requirements:
 Any adult qualified to the work required is eligible to register for correspondence study. The student's capacity to study and the judgment of the college faculty as to the

suitability of the particular course are the determining factors.

Tuition:

Contact the college for current tuition and fees. Tuition must be paid in advance. No refunds are made.

Enrollment Period:

All courses must be completed within 8 months in order to receive academic credit. If unusual circumstances delay the completion of a correspondence course, permission for an extension of 2 months may be requested. If approved there will be a $15.00 charge. There are no refunds or exchanges permitted. Credit is awarded in semester hour credits.

Equipment Requirements:

Textbooks must be purchased by the student.

Credit and Grading:

Examinations must be proctored. Grading system: A, B, C, D, F. Minimum passing grade is D.

Accreditations:

American Association of Bible Colleges.

COLLEGE COURSES

BIBLE

Old Testament History and Literature

A survey of the Old Testament in the context of the history, geography, and culture of Old Testament times. The chief events, characters, and teachings of each book are studied in relation to their place in the ongoing revelation of God's plan. (3 semester hours)

Pentateuch

Each of the five books is studied in relation to Old Testament history and the divine plan. Factual content is stressed and detailed study is given to selected portions. (3 semester hours)

New Testament Survey

This course seeks to integrate the message of the various New Testament books, doctrines, and personalities. (3 semester hours)

Ezekiel and Daniel

Ezekiel, the prophet of Israel's apostasy, is studied to show the student God's great plan for the salvation of His people. The prophecies of Daniel, his visions, and foretelling of the "times of the Gentiles" are studied in this course. (3 semester hours)

The Gospel of John

The purpose of this study is to engage the student in a creative, teaching dialogue with the Biblical text and with the textbook. (2 semester hours)

Revelation

A thorough study of Revelation in which students are exposed to all the existing views on Revelation, but with a study in depth in accordance with futuristic interpretation principles. Special emphasis on the letters to the churches from the prophetic standpoint, the eschatology of the book, and the eternal state. (3 semester hours)

Romans and Galatians

A detailed study of Romans and Galatians, giving special attention to the background of each book, instruction and doctrinal teaching. (3 semester hours)

Hebrews

A detailed study of the book of Hebrews, emphasizing the supremacy of Jesus Christ and the perfect fulfillment of God's total plan revealed to mankind. (2 semester hours)

BIOLOGY

Biological Science

An integrated approach to understanding the living world; scientific principles as evidenced by life; introduction to the various fields of biology. (3 semester hours)

GREEK

Greek I

This course seeks to integrate the message of the various New Testament books, doctrines, and personalities. (3 semester hours)

HISTORY

Church History

First semester studies include growth of the church from the post-apostolic times to thirteenth-century mystics. Emphasis is on selected church fathers, founding the Roman church, its blight on medieval times. (3 semester hours)

U.S. History I

A general course in United States history, dealing with the social, economic, and political development of the United States to the Civil War. (3 semester hours)

U.S. History II

A general course in United States history, dealing with the social, economic, and political development of the United States from the Civil War to the present. (3 semester hours)

PASTORAL MINISTRIES

Homiletics

A careful study is given to the technical side of the sermon and its preparation. A survey is made of the various kinds of sermon outlines. Emphasis is given to the analysis of student-prepared outlines. (2 semester hours)

Church Administration

This course is designed to provide an opportunity for a study of the role of the minister as an administrator in church affairs. It includes an emphasis on such areas as the church staff, finance, architecture, and public relations. The course focuses special attention on foundation principles for church administrative procedures as they appear in Scripture and modern group dynamics. (3 semester hours)

PHYSICAL SCIENCE

Physical Science

Basic facts and laws of the physical world and their relationship to life and society; introduction to scientific method and practice by studying the development of some of the great theories of physical science. (3 semester hours)

PSYCHOLOGY

Introduction to Psychology

This course is designed to introduce the student to the field of psychology as it relates to human behavior. The textbook and the study guide have been written to help the student apply these principles to everyday experiences. (3 semester hours)

Educational Psychology

This course is a basic course in educational psychology focusing on learning theories and their application to the educational process. (3 semester hours)

SOCIOLOGY

Introduction to Sociology

A course on basic concepts of collective behavior and social institutions for the Christian worker. Includes investigations on religion, family, politics, and sports. (3 semester hours)

THEOLOGY

Systematic Theology I (God and Angelology)

The course is a study of God's existence, qualities of His Being, His nature, decrees, providence, and preservation. Special attention is given to the Trinity of God. Angelology includes a study of holy and unholy angels in light of Scripture. The study of angels is designed to teach the need for knowing how angels affect the lives of people. (2 semester hours)

Systematic Theology II (Christology, Soteriology, Anthropology, and Harmartiology)

Christology is a study of the Person of Christ. Special attention will be given to His deity, pre-existence, incarnation, works, death, atonement, resurrection, ascension, and His present-day work in His creation. Soteriology presents salvation through faith in Christ: regeneration, justification, sanctification, and the conditional security of the believer. Anthropology and harmartiology begin with the fall of Adam and Eve and show the consequences of the fall. The course deals with the present status of people and their destiny. Special attention will be given to various crucial issues that people face in this generation resulting from the fall. (3 semester hours)

Systematic Theology III (Pneumatology and Divine Healing)

This is a study of the Scripture as to the person, office, gifts, administration, and ministry of the Holy spirit; a scriptural presentation and defense of the distinctive doctrines held by the Assemblies of God; a practical study of the work of the Spirit in sanctification and in the Spirit-filled life. The course also includes a study of the work of Christ in Divine Healing. It views principles and examples of divine healing from both the Old and New Testaments as well as in church history with emphasis on prayer for the sick in the life of the minister. (3 semester hours)

Systematic Theology IV (Ecclesiology and Eschatology)

A thorough study of the doctrine of the church universal; its origin, organization and scope. An examination of the course and climax of the dispensations and covenants found in the Bible. The consummation of God's program in the end of this age; the final state of the righteous and wicked. (2 semester hours)

Central Florida, University of
4000 Central Florida Boulevard
Orlando, Florida 32816   (305) 275-2000

Description:
Correspondence courses are offered through the Department of Independent Study and Distance Education of the University of Florida in Gainesville. For courses available, SEE **Florida, University of.**

Accreditations:
Southern Association of Colleges and Schools.

Central Michigan University
Undergraduate Programs and Independent Learning
Rowe Hall 126
Mount Pleasant, Michigan 48859
                              (517) 774-3719

Description:
Founded in 1892, Central Michigan University achieved university status in 1959. Located near the center of the state's lower peninsula, the University is a comprehensive state institution offering undergraduate, graduate, preprofessional, and professional programs. University courses are offered by correspondence through Continuing Education and Community Services. Correspondence students are located throughout Michigan, in numerous other states, and in several foreign nations. Correspondence courses are offered on a year-around schedule and conform to the same standards of instruction that control those courses when they are taught on the University campus. Courses are available in most academic areas of study offered in the University. They may be applied to a wide variety of undergraduate degree programs.

Learning Package Courses are also available. Each learning package course is competency-based and criterion-referenced and has specific learning objectives outlined which guide the student to mastering the course content. The learning packages are generally print-oriented, but some have supplemental materials such as audiocassettes, videocassettes, or computer-assisted instruction to facilitate independent learning. The Learning Package Course is term-based (fall, spring, summer) and is indicated as such where appropriate below.

Faculty:
Judy Flaugher, Coordinator, Undergraduate Programs and Independent Learning.

Academic Levels:
College

Degree/Certificate Programs:
A maximum of 15 semester hours of correspondence credit may be applied toward a baccalaureate degree. Correspondence courses are not available for graduate credit and will apply only toward undergraduate credit.

Admission Requirements:
All students must be admitted to Central Michigan University. If the student has never registered for any courses at CMU, it will be necessary to apply for official admission and pay the one-time admission fee of $40 before enrolling in an independent study course. Payment of tuition/fees may be accomplished using Discover, Visa, or MasterCard.

Tuition:

$150 per semester credit hour. A correspondence course may be dropped and tuition refunded if a written request is received at the Office of Independent Study within 40 days of the initial registration and no lessons/exams have been sent in for evaluation. The tuition fee, less an administrative processing fee of $25, will be refunded. Instructional materials fees and postage/handling fees are not refundable.

Enrollment Period:

Home study through correspondence courses may be started at any time. Students are allowed 9 months from the date of enrollment to complete a course. If the work has not been completed in that length of time, an extension of 3 months can be requested, provided that 25 percent of the lesson assignments have been completed. A $10 fee must a accompany a written request for an extension. Students may proceed through their course at a rate that is mutually satisfactory to them and their instructor. Ideally, after the first lesson is submitted, another is not sent until the preceding one has been evaluated by the instructor and returned.

Equipment Requirements:

Textbooks must be purchased by the student and may be order directly from the University Center Bookstore. Course study guides will be sent from the Office of Independent Study as soon as admission and enrollment processing is completed. Audiocassettes are required for some courses and must be rented for a fee.

Credit and Grading:

All correspondence study courses require a final examination, under supervision, for their completion. The student must make his/her own arrangements for a proctor (local public school official) and two weeks before the student desires to write the examination, he must send the name, position, and address of the examining supervisor to Continuing Education and Community Services. The examination will be sent only to the person serving as the examiner. Letter grades are used. Credit is awarded in semester hour units.

Library Services:

As an independent study student, you may use the library facilities at CMU if you visit the campus, or you may call a toll-free library program number to receive assistance. withheld when the course is completed.

Accreditations:

North Central Association of Colleges and Schools. Member of: National University Continuing Education Association.

COLLEGE COURSES

ACCOUNTING

Principles of Accounting I

A Learning Package Course. Introduction to the accounting process; measurement and reporting principles for assets; liabilities, owners' equity, revenues, and expenses (3 semester credits)

Principles of Accounting II

A Learning Package Course. A continuation of study of financial accounting topics and analysis of data for management control and decision making. (3 semester credits)

BIOLOGY

Nature Study

Identification of local flora and fauna and their relationships to the environment. Materials important for teachers and for outdoor and recreational directors. (3 semester credits)

COMPUTER SCIENCE

Survey of Computer Science

Computer organization, low- and high-level computer languages, computer applications. (3 semester credits)

ECONOMICS

Principles of Economics I

Provides basic understanding of scarcity, the price system, role of government, money and banking, monetary policy, economic growth, international trade. (3 semester credits)

Principles of Economics II

Introduction to competitive and monopolistic economic behavior. Issues discussed include income distribution, agriculture, urban problems, poverty, unions, national defense, economic development, comparative economic systems. (3 semester credits)

ENGLISH

English Literature

Beginning to Romantic Period. (3 semester credits)

American Literature: Colonial Through the Romantic Period

Emphasis on major writers and trends. (3 semester credits)

American Literature: Realistic Period to the Present

Emphasis on major writers and trends. (3 semester credits)

Technical and Professional Report Writing

A Learning Package Course. Conducting research, organizing data, and writing technical and professional reports. (3 semester credits)

Shakespeare

A Learning Package Course. Study of 8−12 major comedies, histories, and tragedies, with consideration of their Elizabethan and Jacobean background. (3 semester credits)

FINANCE

Managerial Finance

A Learning Package Course. Basic principles and techniques of the acquisition, management, and distribution of financial resources. (3 semester credits)

GEOGRAPHY

Environment and Man

Introduction to the human use of the earth's surface and inquiry into selected environmental problems resulting from man's use of the physical landscape. (3 semester credits)

Cultures of the World

Population, political, economic, and other cultural phenomena and their world distribution patterns are presented upon a nontechnical background of physical geography. Also available as a Learning Package Course. (3 semester credits)

HEALTH EDUCATION

Community Health

A Learning Package Course. Introduction to public health services provided to citizens and educators by official and voluntary health agencies. (3 semester hours)

Health Services Administration

A Learning Package Course. Analysis of organizational patterns, planning procedures, fiscal management, personnel management, and other administrative concerns. (3 semester hours)

Personal Health

Individual and group health. Designed to assist students to live more effective and healthier lives through scientific knowledge, favorable attitudes and desirable health habits. (3 semester credits)

HISTORY

The Development of Western Civilization

Hist 101. Selected political, economic, social religious, intellectual and aesthetic elements in the background of present-day western civilization from the beginning of historic times to today. From ancient times to 1700 A.D. (3 semester credits)

Hist 102. A continuation of the above course. From 1700 to the present. (3 semester credits)

Westward Movement in America

The impact of territorial expansion in the United States upon economy, culture, and politics. (3 semester credits)

United States to 1865

A broad and interpretative study of the United States before the Civil War. (3 semester credits)

United States, 1865–Present

A broad and interpretative study of the United States since the Civil War. (3 semester credits)

JOURNALISM

Public Relations Principles and Practices

A Learning Package Course. Concepts and theories of public relations as a management function as practiced by corporations, nonprofit groups, and other organizations. Role of the practitioner stressed. (3 semester credits)

LIBRARY SCIENCE

Introduction to the Library

Practical skills to locate information in books, periodicals, newspapers, and documents in university and college libraries. (1 semester credit)

LINGUISTICS

Comparative Linguistics

Linguistics principles and their application to learning and teaching a second language. Explanations of native language interference. (3 semester credits)

MANAGEMENT

Fundamentals of Management

A Learning Package Course. Introduction to the concepts, techniques, and processes of management as they pertain to business and other organizations. (3 semester credits)

Personnel Management

A Learning Package Course. Procuring, developing, maintaining, and effectively using the work force in industrial management. (3 semester credits)

Production Management

A Learning Package Course. Relates sound management to manufacturing operations and to the operation of business as a whole. (3 semester credits)

Dynamics of Organizations Behavior

A Learning Package Course. Integrative theory of organizational behavior. Human motivation influenced by leadership, the organization itself and its social environment. (3 semester credits)

Communications and Management

A Learning Package Course. Appraises communications programs of organizations. Individual and group behavior examined along with interpersonal relationships which hinder or enhance the communications process. (3 semester credits)

Women in Management

A Learning Package Course. Opportunities, challenges, and problems of women in pursuing a career in management. Considers changing roles, legal aspects, differences and effect on male-female relationships. (3 semester credits)

MARKETING

Introduction to Marketing

A Learning Package Course. A basic introduction to the marketing environment and the marketing mix; marketing management and the place of marketing in world society. (3 semester credits)

MATHEMATICS

Plane Trigonometry

Solutions of triangles, trigonometric equations, and identities. (3 semester credits)

College Algebra

Complex numbers, introduction to functions, zeros, graphing, linear functions, quadratic functions, intersections of graphs, interpreting graphs, inequalities, polynomial and rational functions, algebra of functions. (3 semester credits)

MUSIC

Musical Man

Introduction to man's self-expression through the art of music. An intercultural and interdisciplinary exploration of the elements of music. (3 semester credits)

PHYSICS

Physics for Poets

Nonmathematical exploration of physical concepts; social and philosophical implications; utility and limitations of physics for solution of problems in the modern world. (3 semester credits)

POLITICAL SCIENCE

Introduction to American Government and Politics

Constitutional principles, the structure and operation of national, state, and local governments. (3 semester credits)

World Politics

Introductory conceptual analysis of international politics: East-West relations; the Communist camp; major areas of tension in Latin America, Africa, Middle East, and Asia. (3 semester credits)

PSYCHOLOGY

Social Psychology

A Learning Package Course. Empirical approach to understanding individual social behavior. Deals with the person and the social environment with a focus on attitudes, interpersonal behavior, and group processes. (3 semester credits)

Industrial/Organizational Psychology

The psychology of work and organizations. Introduction to the use and application of psychology in the workplace. (3 semester credits)

PUBLIC COMMUNICATION

Foundations of Communication Theory

Basic theories pertaining to spoken symbolic interaction, focusing mainly on the psychological and sociological aspects of interpersonal communication and public address. (3 semester credits)

Persuasion

Application of theories and principles underlying attitude change. (3 semester credits)

RECREATION

Administration of Recreation and Parks

The organization and administration of the recreation and parks program. Problems of surveys, finance, publicity, program planning, leadership, liability, and park facility planning and maintenance. (3 semester credits)

Community Recreation Programs

Programming leisure services for various populations including the handicapped, elderly, young, and social groups, and in a variety of settings (3 semester credits)

SOCIOLOGY

Social Psychology

Significance and impact of social interaction on the development of human nature. (3 semester credits)

Introduction to Human Sexuality

Processes of psychosexual development. Dimensions of sexual behavior and beliefs with reference to contemporary American society. (3 semester credits)

Racism and Inequality

Relations among various dominant and subordinate groups focusing on racism as structural inequality. (3 semester credits)

The Family

The family as a social institution, with emphasis upon the sociocultural factors which influence the family. Conditions which affect family stability. (3 semester credits)

SPANISH

Elementary Spanish I

Designed for students who have had no Spanish. Basic language skills. Introduction to the culture of the Spanish-speaking countries. (4 semester credits)

Elementary Spanish II

Basic language skills. (4 semester credits)

STATISTICS

Introduction to Statistics

Descriptive statistics, probability, sampling distributions, statistical inference, regression. (3 semester credits)

Chadron State College
Directed Independent Study Program
1000 Main Street
Chadron, Nebraska 69337   (308) 432-6211

Description:
Chadron State College is one of four colleges in the Nebraska State College System. Originally founded as a teacher training institution, the college now offers a wide variety of programs. The correspondence program was begun to accommodate teachers working toward degrees while they were employed as teachers during the school year.

Faculty:
Dr. Dowell Smith, Director, Regional Programs; Dale Williamson, Director of Admissions and Records. There is correspondence study faculty of 26 members.

Academic Levels:
College

Degree/Certificate Programs:
With certain limitations, undergraduate coursework offered by correspondence will be given equal status and will also share the same restrictions as credit earned in the classroom before the last thirty credit hours. Twelve of the last thirty credits required for a baccalaureate degree may be earned in correspondence study.

Admission Requirements:
High school graduation.

Tuition:
Undergraduate/Nebraska resident $50 per credit hour plus $4.50 fee per credit hour; graduate/Nebraska resident $62.75 per credit hour plus $4.50 fee per credit hour; undergraduate/nonresident $90 per credit hour plus $4.50 fee per credit hour; graduate/nonresident $112.50 per credit hour plus $4.50 fee per credit hour. Refund policy: 100 percent refund if requested within thirty days of enrollment. No refund is granted after thirty days. Administrative fees are nonrefundable.

Enrollment Period:
Study may commence at any time. It is recommended that a student enroll for no more than one course at any one time. However, with the permission of the Director, the individual may register for as many as six hours. Registration for a course is valid for one year. Maximum time to complete a course is one year; minimum time is seven days per credit hour.

Equipment Requirements:

Students may purchase texts from publishers or any source they desire. However, the Eagle Book Store, College Campus Center, Chadron, Nebraska 69337 conducts a mail service on all correspondence texts.

Credit and Grading:

Grading system is determined by the course instructor. The minimum passing grade is D. Examinations must be proctored and may be supervised by the instructor of the course, a county or city superintendent, or a high school principal. Credit is awarded in semester hour units.

Accreditations:

North Central Association of Colleges and Schools; National Council for Accreditation of Teacher Education.

COLLEGE COURSES

ACCOUNTING

Auditing

Duties and responsibilities of auditors, how to conduct an audit, preparation of audit reports and special auditing problems. (3 semester hours)

BUSINESS

Business Law I

Phases of law important to business people including contracts, negotiable instruments, agency and property laws. (3 semester hours)

Business Law II

Rules of law for sales, personal and real property, bailments, partnerships and corporations. (3 semester hours)

Intermediate Keyboarding

A second semester course in touch keyboarding with an emphasis on speed building, business letters, legal forms, and tabulation. (3 semester hours)

Records Management

Filing procedure and rules, various methods of filing, retention policies, micrographics and different filing equipment. (2 semester hours)

EARTH SCIENCE

Earth Science

This course introduces students to the general principles, concepts, ideas, and terminology of geology, oceanography, meteorology, and astronomy. (3 semester hours)

Physical Geology

this course provides students with an introduction to the physical nature of Earth, its landforms, and the ways in which geologic features are thought to originate and evolve. (3 semester hours)

ECONOMICS

Survey of Economics

Basic microeconomic and macroeconomic theories and concepts. The course is oriented towards the study of households, firms and governments within markets for goods, services, and resources. Macroeconomic concepts studied are gross national product, inflation, unemployment, government expenditures and revenues, monetary and fiscal policies, international trade, and interest rates. (3 semester hours)

Macroeconomics

A study of the economy as a whole including gross national product, inflation, unemployment, components of aggregate demand (total consumption, investment, etc.), aggregate supply, monetary and fiscal policy, and other current issues related to the U.S. economy. (3 semester hours)

Microeconomics

This course looks at the underlying causes of the supply and demand and what causes firms to supply and consumers to demand. Utility analysis helps explain the demand side while the market structure will explain the supply side. (3 semester hours)

EDUCATION

Introduction to Teaching

Surveys the work of a teacher and the public school system. (3 semester hours)

Play, Art, and Music for Young Children

Plan and carry out activities as well as develop coordinated programs in play, art, and music for preschool children. Utilize play, art, and music as media for preschool growth, development, and learning. Art and music are used as forms of play to teach developmental skills in the area of math, social science, and language arts, as well as in developing skills in coordination, movement, rhythm, creative expressions, etc. (3 semester hours)

The Middle School

Develops an understanding and insight into the philosophy, implementation, and improvement of the middle school from a theoretical and practical basis. Emphasis is placed upon the development, behavior, and special problems of middle school students; overall school program; methods of instruction; and the evaluation process. (3 semester hours)

ENGLISH

Composition I

Emphasizes the writing of well-organized, informal essays and the necessary critical thinking that precedes such writing. (3 semester hours)

Composition II

A continuation of the above course with increased emphasis on clarity of thought and expression in informal and formal, expository essays. (3 semester hours)

HEALTH

Personal Health and Wellness

Knowledge and practice in making decisions which affect the quality of life. Developing positive attitudes toward emotional and physical fitness. An emphasis on personal health assessment, awareness, and individual program planning. (3 semester hours)

Current Health Problems

(2 semester hours)

HUMAN ECOLOGY

Child Growth and Development

Human development from conception through adolescence. Covers social, emotional, intellectual, and physical development in children and includes the development of supportive attitudes in adults who work with children. Includes observations of children in laboratory and other settings. (3 semester hours)

Parent Involvement

The principles, methods, and techniques involving parents of children in early childhood programs. The course analyzes an optimal working relationship between home, school, and community with emphasis on positive child-rearing practices and experiences. (3 semester hours)

Management of Child Care Programs

The basic skills for planning and developing preschool programs including working effectively with other personnel, orientation and inservice training, policies and procedures, management and facilities necessary for administering a preschool program. The students will determine desirable attitudes and examine job responsibilities for workers with preschool children and apply this knowledge to personal job performance. (3 semester hours)

MANAGEMENT

Principles of Management

Management principles and the functions of management. Course proceeds from historical developments of modern management to application of principles of today. (3 semester hours)

MARKETING

Principles of Marketing

The marketing mix in a dynamic social, economic, and political environment. Focus is on the satisfaction of the needs of consumer and individual buyers and the social and ethical consequences of marketing. (3 semester hours)

Buyer Behavior

The contributions of psychology, sociology, anthropology, and other behavioral sciences to marketing including theoretical concepts of buyer behavior, the focus is the application of the conceptual material to marketing strategies and decision making. (3 semester hours)

MATHEMATICS

Introduction to Mathematics

The purpose of this course is to give the student an understanding of mathematics as it applies in the liberal arts context and that mathematics is a global language. The objective of this course will be to acquire the skill of fundamental processes of problem solving through an exposure to key concepts of the structure of mathematics, acquire knowledge of mathematics as the science of pattern, including the expression of pattern by using an algebraic function, and acquire knowledge of experimental and theoretical probability and simulations as well as learning the fundamentals of data collection and analysis. The history of mathematics will be integrated throughout each unit of this course. (3 semester hours)

Intermediate Algebra

Properties of real numbers, algebraic operations, expansion and factoring, fractions, integer exponents, rational exponents and radicals, linear and quadratic equations with applications. (4 semester hours)

PHYSICAL EDUCATION

Foundations of Physical Education

A study of the entire field of physical education primarily to acquaint the student with the abilities required in the field, the problems involved, and the status of the future of the profession. (2 semester hours)

History of Physical Education

The aims of the student of physical education studying history parallel those of students in other areas of history. In either case, the student is exploring history to gain a deeper appreciation of the heritage and to examine the successes and failures of the past in order to profit from these experiences of others. (2 semester hours)

Theory and Readings in Elementary Physical Education

To expose the future physical educator and elementary educator to the role of physical education toward augmenting the total development of the elementary school age child in the modern curriculum. (3 semester hours)

Adapted Physical Education

Designed to assist in learning to work with mainstreamed students. Emphasis on all forms of exercise for disease, impairment, and neuromuscular re-education. (2 semester hours)

POLITICAL SCIENCE

American National Government

The fundamentals of the federal system of government in the United States, including background, organization, processes, functions, political thought, public opinion in relation to politics and politico-economic relations. (3 semester hours)

PSYCHOLOGY

Child Psychology

Principles of psychology as applied to maturation, motivation, learning, emotions, and personal and social adjustment. (3 semester hours)

Developmental Psychology

Human development from conception to death. Objectives include discovering what changes take place, when they occur, their influence on behavior, their universality vs. individuality, and their predictability. Varied domains of human existence will be explored. (3 semester hours)

Adolescent Psychology

Philosophic, psychological, social, physical facts and issues that impact adolescents will be covered. (3 semester hours)

Psychopharmacology

Psychological and pharmacological aspects of alcohol and other drug abuse will be covered. Drug effects, understanding tolerance, and classification of drugs will be examined. (3 semester hours)

SAFETY

Safety Education

Accident prevention as related to school, home, farm, recreational, traffic, and industrial safety. (3 semester hours)

SOCIOLOGY

Introduction to Sociology

An introduction survey of the field of sociology, including its development, contemporary methods, major theories, and recent studies. (3 semester hours)

Cincinnati, University of
Open Learning Fire Service Program
College of Applied Science
2220 Victory Parkway
Cincinnati, Ohio 45206   (513) 556-6583

Cincinnati, University of

Description:

The University of Cincinnati was established and incorporated as Cincinnati College and Medical College of Ohio in 1819. The present name was adopted in 1870.

Open Learning for the Fire Service (OLFS) is an independent study program for fire service personnel throughout the country. The student is provided with the option of taking an individual fire course or pursuing a planned degree route. If qualified, a Bachelor of Science degree can be earned. Classroom attendance is not required. Funded and sponsored by the Federal Emergency Management Agency/National Fire Academy, OLFS is a consortium of seven colleges and universities that offer the program. The University of Cincinnati serves OLFS students in Indiana, Michigan, Minnesota, North Dakota, Ohio, South Dakota, Wisconsin, Florida, Louisiana, and Georgia.

Faculty:

Barbara Barkley, Director, OLFS, College of Applied Science.

Academic Levels:

College

Degree/Certificate Programs:

To earn a Bachelor of Science degree a student must be classified as a degree student. For those students who wish to pursue a particular subject, individual courses may be taken for credit. National Fire Academy certificates are awarded for successful completion of six courses.

Admission Requirements:

Open Learning courses are junior-senior level. Credits may be transferred in for approval and application to the baccalaureate degree.

Tuition:

Contact the university for current Open Learning tuition costs.

Equipment Requirements:

Textbooks must be purchased by the student.

Credit and Grading:

A–F. Examinations must be proctored. Credit is awarded in quarter hour units.

Accreditations:

North Central Association of Colleges and Schools.

COLLEGE COURSES

FIRE SERVICE

Fire Dynamics

Study of fluid mechanics and thermodynamic principles of fire propagation. Variables in pre- and post-flashover fire development. Study of geometric, material, gaseous, fluid flow, and thermodynamic parameters. Compartment and building fire models.

Political and Legal Foundations of Fire Protection

An analysis of the legal, political, and social variables of the government's role in public safety. Includes legal limitations and responsibility, liability of fire prevention organization and personnel.

The Community and the Fire Threat

The sociological, economic, and political characteristics of communities and their impact on the fire problem. Includes a study of community profiles and structures with consideration of the economic, geographic, and sociological variables of the fire threat. Examination of functional basis of the community, the diverse social roles of community agencies, and study of the fire service as a complex organization within the community.

Applications of Fire Research

Understanding of fire research, its application, and the transfer and implications of available research results for fire prevention and protection programs. National and international studies. Maintaining awareness of research developments.

Incendiary Fire Analysis and Investigation

Examination and procedures and techniques for collection, comparison and analysis of the physical evidence relative to the area of fire origin. Principles of evidence or ignition phenomena, and propagation variables. Legislative, economic, psychological and sociological variables of incendiary fire. Role of insurance and government programs. Data analysis and prediction techniques, including pattern analysis.

Fire Protection Structure and Systems Design

Design principles involved in structural fire protection with empirical or analytical tests and prediction procedures. Includes control detection and suppression design practices. Fundamentals of the hydraulic design of sprinkler and water spray systems with recent innovations.

Fire Related Human Behavior

Human behavior in fire incidents related to fire protection variables. Includes practices, programs, codes and ordinances, concepts of role, personal invulnerability, risk and group dynamic related to design aspects of buildings and the mitigation effects of fire in the modern society.

Fire Prevention Organization and Management

An overview of the techniques, procedures, programs, and agencies involved in fire prevention. Topics include public and private fire prevention functions, licenses, permits, zoning, legal aspects, inspection, investigation, planning, arson and incendiary diary analysis.

Analytic Approaches to Public Fire Protection

Systems analysis and its use and limitations in fire protection and other problem areas. Illustrated with case studies and models using the system approach to fire suppression and prevention.

Personnel Management for the Fire Service

Personnel management procedures and problems in the fire service. Includes manpower planning, labor relations, recruitment, selection, testing, performance appraisals, classification, motivation, politics, and management.

Advanced Fire Administration

An overview of organization and management techniques in the fire service. Topics include management of equipment and personnel, fire department functions, planning, resource development, labor relations, communication, financial management, and community relations.

Disaster and Fire Defense Planning

The concepts and principles of community fire risk assessment, as related to group fires and natural disasters. Includes regional and cooperative procedures and plans, the relationship of structural, climatic, and topographical variables to group fires, conflagrations, and natural disaster.

Cincinnati Bible College
Correspondence Department
2700 Glenway Avenue
P.O. Box 04320
Cincinnati, Ohio 45204-3200   (513) 244-8160

Description:
The Cincinnati Bible College is a four-year Bible college with a graduate school (Cincinnati Christian Seminary) whose corporate name is The Cincinnati Bible Seminary, founded in 1924. Correspondence study was first offered in 1978.

Faculty:
Priscilla Berry, Correspondence Coordinator. There is a faculty of 3 members.

Academic Levels:
College

Degree/Certificate Programs:
25 percent of the total requirements for a degree may be correspondence study credits (14 credits toward an associate degree; 33 credits toward a bachelor degree). All courses must be taken for credit. They cannot be taken for audit or graduate credit.

Admission Requirements:
High school graduation is required for college credit.

Tuition:
$159 per credit hour. Students will need a Bible to complete most correspondence courses. Refund policy: before one-third of the allotted time, one-half tuition is refunded; before one-half of allotted time, one-third of tuition is refunded.

Enrollment Period:
Students have three months to complete a semester hour course; six months to complete a two-hour course. This time is calculated from the date of shipment of materials. A student may request an extension if the course cannot be completed in the allotted time. Permission must be granted by the professor to do so. An extension form and $25 must be filed with the correspondence coordinator.

Equipment Requirements:
Student buys his/her own textbooks and materials. A film-strip projector is required for the Vacation Bible School Class. Also needed is a Bible. Several translations are acceptable; however, students are requested not to use ''The Living Bible.''

Credit and Grading:
Acceptability of correspondence credits transferred-in from other institutions is determined by the Dean for each individual instance. Examinations must be proctored. Grading system is similar to resident courses: A, B, C, D, E, F.

Minimum passing grade is D. Credit is awarded in semester hour units.

Accreditations:
American Association of Bible Colleges.

COLLEGE COURSES

BIBLE

Acts of Apostles
Part I. A practical study of the beginning and spread of Christianity during its first thirty years. Emphasis is placed on the message and methodology of evangelism, the organization of the church, the work of the Holy Spirit, and the Christian graces. (2 semester hours)
Part II. A continuation of the above course. (2 semester hours)

I Corinthians
Part I. A guided study through Paul's first letter to the Corinthian church. The instructor's analysis of the student's written answers to questions will give opportunity to determine whether the principles regarding dealing with the various church problems are grasped. (2 semester hours)
Part II. A continuation of the above course. (2 semester hours)

Ecclesiastes/Song of Songs
An exegetical study with special emphasis upon preaching values and practical application. (2 semester hours)

Epistles of James and John
A careful study of the problems of introduction and the exegesis of this epistle with a practical turn. (2 semester hours)

I, II Thessalonians
A guided study through Paul's first letters, I and II Thessalonians. The instructor's analysis of the student's written answers to questions will give opportunity to determine whether the context of the passage has been understood. (2 semester hours)

Foundations for Morals
An in-depth study of the Ten Commandments as seen in the light of the Sermon on the Mount. Students will apply Bible teachings to the many ethical and moral problems facing the world today. (2 semester hours)

City University
Distance Learning Program
16661 Northrup Way
Bellevue, Washington 98008   (800) 426-5596

Description:
City University is a private, independent, decentralized, nonprofit institution established in 1973. It provides instruction in communities throughout the state of Washington, as well as sites in Oregon, California, British Columbia, and Switzerland.

The independent study program known as Distance Learning offers courses to people around the world who are interested in taking one class or earning an entire degree. This program is for students who are not able to attend class in person because of location, or find it more convenient to complete courses independent of the classroom.

City University

Faculty:
Michael A. Pastore, President.

Academic Levels:
College
Graduate

Degree/Certificate Programs:
Associate of Science, Bachelor of Science, and various Master programs. Up to 65 lower division credits from approved sources may be transferred and applied to the Associate of Science in General Studies degree, and up to 90 lower division and 45 upper division credits may be transferred and applied to the baccalaureate degree programs if such credits are approved and applicable.

Admission Requirements:
High school graduation or equivalent.

Tuition:
Contact the university for individual course tuition. Rates subject to change without notice. VISA, Discover, American Express, and MasterCard accepted.

Enrollment Period:
Distance Learning courses begin on the first day of each month throughout the year and are 10 weeks in duration unless you are stationed outside of North America or an incarcerated student, in which case they are 20 weeks in duration.

Equipment Requirements:
Textbooks and additional materials must be purchased by the student.

Credit and Grading:
Credit is awarded in quarter hour units.

Accreditations:
Northwest Association of Schools and Colleges.

COLLEGE COURSES

ECONOMICS

Principles of Microeconomics

An introduction to microeconomic theory with real world applications. Students will learn how households, firms, and governments make decisions of what goods and services to produce, how to produce them and for whom to produce them. This course will help you apply the tools and skills learned from theory to current world events. (5 quarter hours)

Principles of Macroeconomics

An introduction to macroeconomic theory with real world applications. Students will learn how to apply the tools and skills acquired from theory to current real world topics such as inflation, unemployment, poverty, taxes, deficits, interest rates, gross national product, recession, and international trade. (5 quarter hours)

ENGLISH

English Composition

A writing course designed to teach students the arts of style, organization, and thoughtful content. Students are encouraged to think critically so that their writing style will reflect their ability to isolate crucial issues, reason logically, analyze problems effectively, and make sound decision. A series of supplemental videotapes illustrate how practical writing methods should be applied. (5 quarter hours)

FINE ARTS

Art of the Western World

A survey of major painting, sculptures, and works of architecture of the Western world. Each masterpiece will be examined in terms of artistic technique and value as well as the historical trends reflected in these works. Supplemental video instruction exposes students to great works of art located throughout the Western world. (5 quarter hours)

HUMANITIES

History and Culture of the African Continent

An example of the complexities of the African continent. Special attention will be devoted to the impact of nineteenth-century colonialism, the slave trade, twentieth-century political instability and the role of Africa as an international economic political power. A series of supplemental video lectures filmed on location in sixteen African countries expose the student to African geography and culture. (5 quarter hours)

Great American Poets

This course utilizes the videotape series "Voices and Visions" and text materials to provide a lively overview of thirteen major American poets and their poetry. Through the work of these poets the student is introduced to basic elements of poetry, such as voice, rhythm, structure, and sound. The student is also introduced to the unique factors which have combined to produce this diverse, distinctive body of original American poetry. (5 quarter hours)

MATHEMATICS

College Algebra

An examination of definitions and concepts of algebra including linear and quadratic equations and inequalities, systems of equations, functions, logarithms, matrices, determinates, sequences and series, and probability. Every concept includes practical, everyday applications which focus on reducing math anxiety. This course is designed for those students who determine that review or additional study in algebra is useful before participation in upper division mathematics and statistical courses. (5 quarter hours)

NATURAL SCIENCE

The Human Body

A theory course designed to update existing knowledge and expand understanding of the functioning of the human body. Emphasis is placed on ways in which this information can be applied to the processes of daily living, both in the students' own lives and in the workplace. (5 quarter hours)

An introduction to Geoscience: The Planet Earth

A survey of earth science. Topics emphasized are recent developments in atmospheric chemistry, geology, and astrophysics. The course will also explore the impact humans will continue to have on the fate of the earth. Supplemental video lectures narrated by world famous atmospheric chemists, geologist, and astrophysicists expose the students to recent discoveries in the field of earth science. (5 quarter hours)

An introduction to Neuroscience: Brain, Mind, and Behavior

A course designed to expose students to the latest neuroscientific understanding of the brain and its relation to behavior. Emphasis will be placed on the theme that all the normal functions of the brain and the disorders of the diseased brain, no matter how complex, will ultimately be explained in terms of basic components of the brain and the ways they interact. A supplemental series of videotapes narrated by world famous brain scientists expose the students to the brain's operating principles. (5 quarter hours)

Environmental Science

A course which explores environmental change on a global scale, emphasizing the fundamental concepts of matter, energy, and ecology as applied to contemporary concerns. Environmental issues impacting twenty-nine countries are illustrated in an accompanying video series in order to develop an international perspective on the environmental challenges facing the planet. (5 quarter hours)

PHILOSOPHY

Introduction to Ethics

An overview of classical, ethical theories, and moral responsibility; includes sources of morality, free will versus determinism, and debates centering on truth, knowledge, and justice. (5 quarter hours)

SOCIAL SCIENCE

Discovering Psychology

This course will broadly explore the field of psychology defined as "the scientific study of behavioral and mental processes." The treatment of mental disorders, the promotion of well being, and the application of psychology to social issues will also be discussed. (5 quarter hours)

The Seasons of Life: Understanding Human Development

This course investigates the biological, social, and psychological forces which shape our lives at various stages: prenatal development and birth; infancy and childhood; adolescent years; early, middle, and late adulthood; and death and dying. Patterns of difference due to factors such as gender, culture, disability, and socioeconomic status will also be addressed. (5 quarter hours)

History of Western Tradition I

An analysis of the ideas, events, and institutions that shaped life in the Western world from prehistory to the Renaissance. A series of video lectures expose the student to works illustrating the development of Western civilization exhibited at the Metropolitan Museum of Art in New York City. (5 quarter hours)

History of Western Tradition II

An analysis of the ideas, events, and institutions that shaped life in the Western world from the Reformation to the present day. A series of supplemental video lectures exposes the student to works illustrating the development of Western civilization exhibited at the Metropolitan Museum of Art in New York City. (5 quarter hours)

The Nuclear Age: World War II to the Present

An examination of nuclear strategy in the context of international and domestic politics since the development of atomic and hydrogen weapons. A series of videotapes details the development of contemporary nuclear politics. The impact of the collapse of the Soviet Union and formation of a Russian confederation will also be explored in the course. (5 quarter hours)

Interpreting the American Constitution

An examination of the evolution of the Constitution with an emphasis upon contemporary constitutional issues such as executive privilege, executive war powers and covert action, the death penalty, freedom of the press, the right to live and the right to die, and debates surrounding affirmative action and reverse discrimination. Supplemental video-

tapes expose the student to the opinions of Gerald Ford, Gloria Steinem, Bill Moyers, Archibald Cox, among others. (5 quarter hours)

STATISTICS

Statistics for Starters

This course is an introduction to statistics for anyone who has difficulty with the way statistics is usually presented, or who is simply intimidated by the subject. It presumes no statistical background and uses applications to explain statistical concepts without using mathematical symbols and equations. The applications range from sports, advertising, politics to medicine and psychology. This course will not teach you how to produce statistics but it will teach you how to understand them. (5 quarter hours)

Cogswell Polytechnical College
Open Learning for the Fire Service Program
10420 Bubb Road
Cupertino, California 95014   (408) 252-5550

Description:

Cogswell Polytechnical College is a private, independent, nonprofit institution. It was established as Cogswell Polytechnical School in 1887 and adopted its present name in 1930.

Open Learning for the Fire Service (OLFS) is an independent study program for fire service personnel throughout the country. If qualified, anyone may take the college courses and earn a Bachelor of Science degree. Classroom attendance is not required. Funded and sponsored by the Federal Emergency Management Agency/National Fire Academy, OLFS is a consortium of seven colleges and universities that offer the program. Cogswell serves OLFS students in Arizona, California, and Nevada.

Faculty:

Linda Fladger, Director, OLFS.

Academic Levels:

College

Degree/Certificate Programs:

To earn a Bachelor of Science degree through Cogswell OLFS program, a student must be classified as a degree student. Individual courses may be taken as a visitor.

Admission Requirements:

Associate degree in Fire Science is required; if the student does not have an associate degree, courses in the lower division must be completed before applying to the program. A student who does not have an associate degree and the required courses may still register for the upper division fire science courses to receive a certificate.

Tuition:

$275 per course (3 credits). $30 nonrefundable processing fee. Rates subject to change. Contact the college for current rates.

Enrollment Period:

Each of Cogswell's three semesters is approximately fifteen weeks in length. During those fifteen weeks, the student submits to the instructor three major written assignments, spaced approximately four weeks apart.

Equipment Requirements:

Textbooks must be purchased by the student.

Credit and Grading:

A–F. Examinations must be proctored. Credit is awarded in semester hour units.

Accreditations:

Western Association of Schools and Colleges.

COLLEGE COURSES

FIRE SERVICE

Fire Dynamics

Study of fire propagation phenomenon in both fuel and air regulated phases. Variables in pre- and post-flashover fire development. Study of geometric, material, gaseous, fluid flow, and thermodynamic parameters. Compartment and building fire models. (3 semester hours)

Political and Legal Foundations of Fire Protection

An analysis of the legal, political, and social variables of the government's role in public safety. Includes legal limitations and responsibility, liability of fire prevention organization and personnel. Review of judicial decisions. (3 semester hours)

The Community and the Fire Threat

Understanding the sociological, economic, and political characteristics of communities and their impact on the fire problem. Includes a study of community profiles and structures with consideration of the economic, geographic, and sociological variables of the fire threat. Examination of functional basis of the community, the diverse social roles of community agencies, and study of the fire service as a complex organization within the community. (3 semester hours)

Applications of Fire Research

Understanding of fire research, its application, and the transfer and implications of available research results for fire prevention and protection programs. National and international studies. Maintaining awareness of research developments. (3 semester hours)

Incendiary Fire Analysis and Investigation

Examination and procedures and techniques for collection, comparison and analysis of the physical evidence relative to the area of fire origin. Principles of evidence or ignition phenomena, and propagation variables. Legislative, economic, psychological and sociological variables of incendiary fire. Role of insurance and government programs. Data analysis and prediction techniques, including pattern analysis. (3 semester hours)

Fire Protection Structure and Systems Design

Design principles involved in structural fire protection with empirical or analytical tests and prediction procedures. Includes control detection and suppression design practices. Fundamentals of the hydraulic design of sprinkler and water spray systems with recent innovations. (3 semester hours)

Fire Related Human Behavior

Human behavior in fire incidents related to fire protection variables. Includes practices, programs, codes and ordinances, concepts of role, personal invulnerability, risk and group dynamic related to design aspects of buildings and the mitigation effects of fire in the modern society. (3 semester hours)

Fire Prevention Organization and Management

An overview of the techniques, procedures, programs, and agencies involved in fire prevention. Topics include public and private fire prevention functions, licenses, permits, zoning, legal aspects, inspection, investigation, planning, arson and incendiary diary analysis. (3 semester hours)

Analytic Approaches to Public Fire Protection

Systems analysis and its use and limitations in fire protection and other problem areas. Illustrated with case studies and models using the system approach to fire suppression and prevention. (3 semester hours)

Personnel Management for the Fire Service

Personnel management procedures and problems in the fire service. Includes manpower planning, labor relations, recruitment, selection, testing, performance appraisals, classification, motivation, politics, and management. (3 semester hours)

Advanced Fire Administration

An overview of organization and management techniques in the fire service. Topics include management of equipment and personnel, fire department functions, planning, resource development, labor relations, communication, financial management, and community relations. (3 semester hours)

Disaster and Fire Defense Planning

The concepts and principles of community fire risk assessment, as related to group fires and natural disasters. Includes regional and cooperative procedures and plans, the relationship of structural, climatic, and topographical variables to group fires, conflagrations, and natural disaster. (3 semester hours)

Colorado, University of
Independent Study Programs
Division of Continuing Education
1221 University Avenue
Boulder, Colorado 80309-0178 (800) 331-2801

Description:

Early in 1911, a High School Conference Committee determined that randomly-offered extension classes in Denver (under University of Colorado auspices) should be formalized. Subcommittees developed guidelines for departments wishing to offer extension classes and rules for credit to be allowed. On May 8, 1911, the Regents of the University of Colorado approved a Department of Correspondence and Extension. From that date, the department evolved through a series of changes to its present structure. Numbers of students in correspondence courses have increased from a few dozen in 1912 to approximately 4,000 students in 1995.

The university participates in the Colorado Consortium for Independent Study via Correspondence which is composed of the Independent Study offices of six institutions of higher education in Colorado: Adams State College, Colorado State University, University of Colorado, University of Northern Colorado, University of Southern Colorado, and Metropolitan State College of Denver. The consortium strives to provide quality independent study opportunities and to avoid duplication of courses offered by consortium members. The correspondence student should consult the listings in this *Guide* for all member schools of the Consortium for a complete offering of subjects.

Faculty:

Dr. John R. Dunn, Program Manager. There is a faculty of 35 plus 1 counselor.

Academic Levels:

College

Degree/Certificate Programs:

Correspondence credits may be applied toward certificate, diploma, and baccalaureate degree programs. Depending upon the department, up to thirty semester hours from correspondence courses may be allowed toward University of Colorado degree programs. Many courses are accepted by New York State's Regents External Degree Program.

Admission Requirements:

Open enrollment. Required: ability to read, write, and understand the English language. Students are advised to register in courses suitable to previous background and/or training.

Tuition:

College courses $70 per semester hour. Rates subject to change without notice. Some courses require rental of media packages. Deferred payment available; credit cards accepted. Courses eligible for VA benefits. Refund policy: must be requested within forty days of registration date; an administration fee may be withheld plus a charge for each lesson that has been graded.

Enrollment Period:

Maximum time to compete a course is 12 months; minimum time is 2 weeks per semester hour. A 12-month extension may be granted for a fee of $20 per semester hour.

Equipment Requirements:

Primarily textbooks, which must be supplied by the student, either purchased locally or ordered through the University book store. Some courses require a cassette player; typewritten work is preferred but not mandatory; some courses utilize calculators, straight edges; some require viewing plays and movies. All of these must be furnished by the student.

Credit and Grading:

Examinations must be proctored. Grading system is A, B, C, D, F with plus and minus recorded and averaged. The minimum passing grade D-. Credit is awarded in semester hour units. The Admissions Office determines the transferability of previously-completed correspondence courses from other institutions. University of Colorado correspondence courses are equivalent to those offered on campus.

Library Services:

Students may use local libraries to request that they order through Interlibrary Loan those materials not available locally. Receipt of tuition payment allows access to the University of Colorado Library.

Accreditations:

North Central Association of Colleges and Schools. Member of: National University Continuing Education Association.

COLLEGE COURSES

ANTHROPOLOGY

Principles of Anthropology 1

Evolution of humanity and culture from beginnings through early metal ages. Covers human evolution, race, prehistory, and the rise of early civilization. (3 semester hours)

Principles of Anthropology 2

Survey of the world's major culture areas; culture and its major components, such as subsistence, social organization, religion, and language. (3 semester hours)

Introduction to Physical Anthropology 1

Detailed consideration of human biology, humans' place in the animal kingdom, fossil evidence for human evolution. (3 semester hours)

Introduction to Physical Anthropology 2

Continuation of the above course. Quantitative analysis, genetics, and race are emphasized. (3 semester hours)

Introduction to Archaeology

Discusses history, basic concepts, techniques, and theoretical construction of archaeological field and laboratory investigations. (3 semester hours)

BUSINESS

Introduction to Financial Accounting

Preparation and interpretation of principal financial statements of the business enterprise, with emphasis on asset and liability valuation problems and determination of net income. (3 semester hours)

Managerial Cost Accounting 1

Measurement and reporting of product manufacturing and service costs. Identifies and analyzes the role of product costs in income determination. Includes computer processing of cost data. (3 semester hours)

Managerial Cost Accounting 2

Cost analysis for purposes of control and decision making. Analysis of cost behavior, role of accounting in planning and control, and managerial uses of cost accounting data. Includes use of computer-assisted decision models. (3 semester hours)

Introduction to Business

Explores the nature of business enterprise, the role of business in society, and the problems confronting business management. Discusses career opportunities in business. (3 semester hours)

Ethical Issues and the Legal Environment of Business

The examination of issues addressing ethical, legal, social, and environmental responsibilities of business toward government, customers, employees, and the general public. (3 semester hours)

COMMUNICATIONS

Communication and Society

This course seeks to increase students' awareness of the ways in which gender, dialect (ethnic, regional, and social class), and cultural background influence communication behavior and its consequences. (3 semester hours)

COMPUTER SCIENCE

Special Topics: Social, Ethical, and Professional Issues in Computer Science

An introduction to the larger social context in which the discipline of computing exists, with an emphasis on how the discipline interacts with and serves the interests of society. Social and ethical responsibilities of the computing professional are emphasized. Includes a survey of the kinds of risks that can accompany a computing application. Discussion of losses and questions of liability. Identification of the main forms of intellectual property, protection, and penalties for violation. (1 semester hour)

ECONOMICS

Principles of Microeconomics

Examines basic concepts of microeconomics, or the behavior and interactions of individuals, firms, and government. Topics include determining economic problems, how consumers and businesses make decisions, how markets work and how they fail, and how government actions affect markets. (4 semester hours)

Principles of Macroeconomics

An overview of the economy, examining the flows of resources and outputs and the factors determining the levels of income and prices. Policy problems of inflation, unemployment, and economic growth are explored. (4 semester hours)

EDUCATION

Children's Literature

Reading and evaluation of books, children's interests, authors and illustrators, folk literature, multicultural literature, modern fanciful tales and trends. (3 semester hours)

Literature for Adolescents

Reading and evaluation of books for junior and senior high school pupils. Emphasizes modern literature. (3 semester hours)

Special Topics: Understanding Child Abuse

Designed to acquaint the student with current information on child abuse. Includes history of abuse, abuse legislation, identification of types of abuse, recognition of abuse victims, the abusive family structure, and an examination of community agency roles. Specifically for school employees, this course is also appropriate for community agency personnel and interested community volunteers. Based primarily on Colorado law and reporting requirements, the course also provides guidance for those who are located in other states. (3 semester hours)

ENGLISH

Introduction to Creative Writing

Introduction to techniques of fiction and poetry. (3 semester hours)

Introduction to Fiction

Reading and analysis of short stories and novels. (3 semester hours)

Introduction to Women's Literature

An introduction to the study of literature by women in England and America. Covers both poetry and fiction and varying historical periods. Acquaints students with the contribution of women writers to the English literary tradition and investigates the nature of this contribution. (3 semester hours)

Masterpieces of American Literature

Enhances student understanding of the American literary and artistic heritage through an intensive study of a few centrally significant texts, emphasizing works written before the twentieth century. (3 semester hours)

Introduction to Poetry Workshop

An introductory course in poetry writing. (3 semester hours)

Shakespeare for Nonmajors

Introduces students to Shakespeare's major works: the histories, comedies and tragedies and may include the nondramatic poetry as well. (3 semester hours)

Intermediate Fiction Workshop

Intermediate course in fiction writing. (3 semester hours)

Modern and Contemporary Literature

Close study of significant twentieth-century poetry, drama, and prose works. (3 semester hours)

Report Writing

Instruction and practice in various forms of reports, papers, and articles. Style and editing are emphasized. (3 semester hours)

Chaucer: The Canterbury Tales

Short introduction to Middle English precedes study of the poetry. (3 semester hours)

Shakespeare 1

Shakespeare's works through 1600. Eleven early major comedies and histories are covered, plus general background of the Elizabethan period. Required viewing of a live production, a television presentation, or a film. (3 semester hours)

Shakespeare 2

Shakespeare's works after 1600. Seven major plays are covered, plus general background of the customs of the Elizabethans. Required viewing of a live production, a television presentation, or a film. (3 semester hours)

Survey of American Literature 1

Chronological survey of the literature from Bradford to Whitman. (3 semester hours)

Survey of American Literature 2

Chronological survey of the literature from Whitman to Faulkner. (3 semester hours)

The English Language

Outlines history of the language including a brief survey of sound changes affecting modern English, of history of grammatical forms, and of the vocabulary. Elementary knowledge of English grammar is assumed. (3 semester hours)

FINE ARTS

Basic Drawing

Introductory course, including pictorial design, life drawing, still life, and landscape, using varied drawing techniques and media. (3 semester hours)

Introduction to Asian Art (Multimdedia)

Designed for those having no previous experience in the study of

Asian art. Traces development of sculpture, painting, architecture, and other visual arts of South Asia, the Far East, and Southeast Asia, especially as they are connected by the religious themes of Hinduism and Buddhism. (3 semester hours)

Art for Elementary Teachers (Multimedia)

For persons planning to teach at the elementary level. Theoretical and practical elementary art methods for the non-art major are covered. (3 semester hours)

Women Artists from the Middle Ages to the Present

Surveys women's art of the west, emphasizing painting and sculpture. (3 semester hours)

GEOGRAPHY

Environmental Systems: Climate and Vegetation

Introduces the atmospheric environment of the Earth: elements and controls of climate and their implications for hydrology, vegetation, and soils. Emphasizes distribution of physical features across the earth's surface and interactions between humans and their environment, especially those leading to global change in the decade to century time scale. (4 semester hours)

Environmental Systems: Landforms and Soils

Introduces two essential aspects of the natural environment: landforms and soils. Emphasizes the genesis, distribution and utility of surface features in a variety of learning situations. (4 semester hours)

GEOLOGY

Introduction to Geology 1

Introductory geology for majors and nonmajors. Studies the Earth, its materials, its characteristics, its dynamic processes, and how it relates to people. (3 semester hours)

Introduction to Geology 2

Introductory geology for majors and nonmajors. Studies evolutionary history of the Earth and life. (3 semester hours)

HISTORY

History of Western Civilization 1

Survey course on the development of western civilization from its beginnings in the ancient Near East through the Reformation of the sixteenth century. (3 semester hours)

History of Western Civilization 2

Survey course dealing with political, economic, social, and intellectual development in European history from the sixteenth century to the present. Similarities and contrasts between European states are underscored, as is Europe's changing role in world history. (3 semester hours)

History of the United States to 1865

Survey of American history from first settlement until the end of the Civil War. (3 semester hours)

History of the United States Since 1865

Survey of social, economical, political, and cultural development of the United States from the close of the American Civil War to the present. (3 semester hours)

History of Colorado

Emphasizes historical variety and ethnic diversity of Colorado. Along with traditional themes in Colorado history such as the Gold Rush, attention is given to Indian and Hispanic activity and culture. (3 semester hours)

The Early American Frontier

Examines the westward movement from the Colonial period through 1850 in the region east of the Mississippi, with major stress on unique problems of societies on the successive frontiers and their relationship to the determination of national policies. (3 semester hours)

The Later American Frontier

Deals primarily with the Trans-Mississippi west during the nineteenth century, the westward advance of various frontiers and their influence upon national development. Emphasizes economic factors and the associated cultural and social growth of the region. (3 semester hours)

History of Russia Through the Seventeenth Century

Establishment and expansion of the Russian state and the development of the political, economic, and social machinery necessary to administer it, from ancient times to the reign of Peter the Great and the proclamation of a Russian empire. (3 semester hours)

Imperial Russia

Survey of major cultural, social, and economic changes from the reign of Peter the Great through the first Russian Revolution of 1905. (3 semester hours)

The Russian Revolution and the Soviet Regime

Covers in detail the significant social, economic, and political events of Soviet Russia from the February Revolution of 1917 to the present. (3 semester hours)

MATHEMATICS

College Algebra

Simplifying algebraic expressions, factoring, linear and quadratic equations, inequalities, exponentials, logarithms, functions and graphs, complex numbers, binomial theorem. (3 semester hours)

College Trigonometry

Development of the trigonometric functions of acute angles, any angles, and real numbers. Importance of the radian as a unit of measure. Includes solution of triangles, identities, formulas, law of sines and cosines, trigonometric functions, complex numbers, and logarithms. Emphasis is on analytical aspects in preparation for later work. (2 semester hours)

Mathematics for Social Science and Business

Systems of linear equations; an introduction to matrices, linear programming, and probability. (3 semester hours)

Calculus for Social Science and Business

Differential and integral calculus of algebraic, logarithmic, and exponential functions. (3 semester hours)

Analytic Geometry and Calculus 1

Topics include limits, derivatives of algebraic and trigonometric functions, applications of the derivative, integration, and applications of the definite integral. (5 semester hours)

Analytic Geometry and Calculus 2

Topics include transcendental functions, methods of integration, polar coordinates, conic sections, improper integrals, and infinite series. (5 semester hours)

MUSIC

Basic Music Theory

Introduction to tools used in notating, performing, creating, and listening to music. For nonmusic majors only who have little or no previous schooling in the subject. (3 semester hours)

NUTRITION

Nutrition, Health, and Performance

The basic principles of nutrition and their relationship to health. (3 semester hours)

NURSING

School Nurse Achievement Program (SNAP)

Advanced course in school nursing related to the clinical care of students with disabilities, special health needs, and chronic health conditions. Areas covered include screening procedures, medical technology procedures, practice standards, nursing process, supervision of paraprofessionals, team development, the health component of the Individualized Educational Plan (IEP) and Individualized Family Service Plan (IFSP), Individuals with Disabilities Education Act (IDEA), and its amendments. Clinical practicum highly recommended but not required for this course. Faculty assistance available in making arrangements for the practicum. (3 semester hours)

PHILOSOPHY

Introduction to Philosophy

Introduces fundamental questions of philosophy. (3 semester hours)

Ethics

Introductory study of major philosophies on the nature of the good for man, principles of evaluation, and moral choice. (3 semester hours)

Philosophy and Religion

Philosophical introduction to some of the central concepts and beliefs of religious tradition, focusing partially on the question of the existence of God and on the relation between religious beliefs and moral beliefs. (3 semester hours)

Twentieth-Century Philosophy

Study of three major philosophies in the twentieth century—existential, analytic, and Continental philosophy. (3 semester hours)

POLITICAL SCIENCE

The American Political System

Emphasizes interrelations among levels and branches of government, formal and informal institutions, processes, and behavior. (3 semester hours)

Introduction to International Relations

Introductory conceptual approaches, the actors, national and international dynamics of the international environment, problems, and issues. (3 semester hours)

PSYCHOLOGY

Introduction to Psychology

Surveys major topics in psychology: perception, development, personality, learning and memory and the biological bases of behavior. (3 semester hours)

Biological Psychology 1

Broad survey of biological bases of learning, motivation, emotion, sensory processes and perception, movement, comparative animal behavior, sex and reproductive activity, instinctual behavior, neurobiology of language and thought, and neuroanatomy in relation to behavior. (3 semester hours)

Biological Psychology 2

Integrates knowledge and facts presented in the above course into current topics in biopsychology. (3 semester hours)

Statistics and Research Methods in Psychology

Introduces descriptive and inferential statistics and their roles in psychological research. Topics include correlation, regression, t-test, analysis of variance, and selected nonparametric statistics. (4 semester hours)

Psychology of Adjustment

Surveys concepts bearing upon the processes of normal psychological adjustment, with emphasis upon using the concepts to understand common human problems in personal growth and relationships with others. (3 semester hours)

Child and Adolescent Psychology

Principles of development in childhood and adolescence. (3 semester hours)

Abnormal Psychology

Examines borderline disorders as extreme variations of the normal personality. Focuses on major functional and organic disorders, theories of mental disorders, and methods of psychotherapy. (3 semester hours)

Social Psychology

General psychological principles and underlying social behavior. Overview and analysis of major social psychological theories, methods, and topics including attitudes, conformity, aggression, attraction, social perception, helping behavior and group relations. (3 semester hours)

Psychology of Personality

Psychological study of structure, organization, and development of the person as a whole. Analysis of major theories, methods and research, including topics such as emotion, motivation, temperament, inner experience, identity and the self, personality change and the influence of sociocultural context. (3 semester hours)

History of Psychology

Includes outline of development of psychological theories since the Greek philosophers, the story of experimental psychology and its problems, and schools of psychological thinking. Students read original sources in English and English translations. (3 semester hours)

Developmental Psychology

Overview of major theories concerning the development of knowledge in children. Emphasis is on the contrast between empiricist, nativist, and constructivist viewpoints, as applied to the same content areas e.g., perception, cognition, social development. (3 semester hours)

SOCIOLOGY

Analyzing Society

An exploration of the U.S. society in global context, using basic sociological ideas, focusing on the nature of group life, social and moral order, social institutions, social disorganization, social problems, and social change. (3 semester hours)

Deviance in U.S. Society

Examination of deviant groups in the United States, emphasizing existing theory and research about such issues as deviant careers, deviant lifestyles and behavior, and processes of social control. (3 semester hours)

Social Conflict and Social Values

An exploration focusing on the origin, escalation, and resolution of social conflict theories, human values and social action, and use of simulation and negotiating exercises for learning conflict management skills. (3 semester hours)

Sex, Gender and Society 1

Examination of status and power differences between the sexes at individual and societal levels. Emphasizes historical cross-cultural context of gender roles and status, and reviews major theories of gender stratification. (3 semester hours)

Criminology

Scientifically studies criminal behavior with special attention given to development of criminal law and its use to define crime, the causes of law violation, and methods used to control criminal behavior. (3 semester hours)

Technology and Modernization

Analysis of social structures and social relationships that change in response to technological innovation. Emphasis also given to the role of technology in the development of countries other than the U.S. (3 semester hours)

Colorado State University
Correspondence Study
Division of Continuing Education
Spruce Hall
Fort Collins, Colorado 80523 (303) 491-5288

Description:

The mission of the Division of Continuing Education at Colorado State University is to serve the educational needs of citizens all across the nation. The goal is to provide lifelong learning opportunities to adults of all ages. By incorporating dedication to service, quality, action, integrity, leadership, and innovation into every course offering, the Division is prepared to meet its outreach mission as one of 68 land grant institutions in America. The independent study courses described below provide one alternative for those who prefer to learn in a primarily self-directed mode.

Continuing Education began in 1972 by providing adults of all ages the opportunity to continue learning. Whether adults are entering the workforce, training for new careers, seeking career advancement, striving to keep up with current professional information, or are interested in learning for personal enjoyment and satisfaction, the Division makes every effort to provide high quality instruction for each individual student.

Colorado State University is a member of the Colorado Consortium for Independent Study composed of the independent study offices of six institutions of higher education in Colorado: Adams State College, Colorado State University, University of Colorado, University of Northern Colorado, University of Southern Colorado, and Metropolitan State College of Denver. The consortium strives to provide quality independent study opportunities and to avoid duplication of courses offered by consortium members. The correspondence student should consult the listings in this *Guide* of all member schools of the Consortium for a complete offering of subjects.

Faculty:
Distance Learning Staff.

Academic Levels:
College

Degree/Certificate Programs:
There are no degree programs through correspondence study at Colorado State. However, the on-campus departments do accept correspondence courses for their programs. Student is advised to check with the department granting the degree as to the total number of semester hours earned by correspondence that will be accepted toward a degree. Correspondence transfer hours from other institutions must be evaluated by the appropriate department heads.

Admission Requirements:
Open enrollment. Some courses require prerequisites.

Tuition:
For academic credit courses, $70 per credit unit plus a $20 course fee (fee may vary). Tuition for noncredit courses vary. Additional fees for some courses. Visa and MasterCard accepted. Fees are subject to change without notice. Refund policy: if student withdraws within 30 calendar days and returns all course materials in proper order, he/she will receive all tuition minus an administration fee of $20. If syllabus has been used, an additional fee will be assessed.

Enrollment Period:
The maximum time allowed for completion of a course is generally 1 year; some courses 6 months. The minimum time to complete a course is 8 weeks. A 3-month or 6-month extension may be permitted upon payment of a fee of $20.

Equipment Requirements:
Textbooks and supplies must be purchased by the student, either locally or through the Colorado State University Bookstore. Each course syllabus gives details. Some courses require equipment to utilize audio tapes and slides. The tapes and slides are furnished in a "media packet," available for an additional fee.

Credit and Grading:
Examinations must be proctored. Grading system is A, B, C, D, F with plus and minus recorded and averaged. The minimum passing grade is D. Students should select a local school official as an examination proctor. Credit is awarded in semester hour units.

Library Services:
With a receipt, a correspondence student may use the CSU Library. Students are encouraged to use interlibrary loans.

Accreditations:
North Central Association of Colleges and Schools. Member of: National University Continuing Education Association.

Colorado State University

AGRICULTURE

Pesticide Management

The purpose of this course is to develop an ability on the part of the student to know and understand the reasons for using pesticides and how to apply them safely and correctly. The objectives of this course are to: gain an appreciation of what pesticides are and why they are used in today's environment; develop skills in handling pesticides safely and protecting oneself and the environment in a variety of pesticide use situations; understand the scope of the pest problems and to learn about the wide range of pesticides and formulations available for use; and gain the ability to understand and select the appropriate equipment and calibration techniques for proper pesticide application. (3 semester hours)

Management of On-Farm Stored Grain

This course is designed for students to gain an appreciation of the basic principles of grain storage, to understand grain storage problems and what to do about them, to know how to sample grain properly, to develop skill in devising management strategies, to learn about chemical controls and how to use pesticides safely, and to understand and be able to apply general gin safety principles. (1 semester hour)

Management and Control of Wood-Destroying Pests (Wood Preservation)

A study of trees and wood production: properties of wood, moisture content, and building uses; wood destroying agents; wood preservative chemicals; wood preservative treatment; industry regulations, standards and quality control, labels safety and environmental concerns. (2 semester hours)

Management and Control of Turfgrass Pests

This course covers turfgrass types and differentiating properties, classification of pests, pest management and control, environmental concerns and industry regulations, safety and skill development in pesticides application. (3 semester hours)

ANIMAL SCIENCE

Poultry Science and Production

A study of the application of science to the business of poultry food production in supplying low cost, high quality animal protein for human consumption. This course covers the commercial poultry industry, classification and nomenclature, avian anatomy and physiology, genetics, breeding, nutrition, disease control, egg and meat products, and management of a poultry enterprise. (2 semester hours)

Basic Nutrition for Pets

Nutrition and feeding of birds, mammals, fish, household and exotic pets. (2 semester hours)

Commercial Poultry Industry

Interrelated, unique aspects of modern poultry industry comparing specific commercial poultry production operations. (3 semester hours)

COMPUTER-ASSISTED DESIGN

AutoCAD

Important Note on Equipment Needs for AutoCAD. In order to participate in this instructional program, the student must have access to the following: AutoCAD 11, 10, 9, 2.6x, or 2.5x, a microcomputer capable of running AutoCAD, a mouse or digitizer (digitizer is required only for the advanced courses), and output device (pen plotter or printer). Additional fee of $60 per course.

AutoCAD Fundamentals: AutoCAD 9, 2.6x and 2.5x

This course is intended for the student with limited or no experience with AutoCAD. The course is designed to provide a clear understanding of the commands, features, and limitations associated with the basic operation of AutoCAD: mode settings, drawing setup, layering, associative dimensioning, polylines, and blocks. Hands-on exercises form the foundation of the course. The course is written for all disciplines which require methods of drafting, design, and engineering. (3 semester hours)

Advanced AutoCAD: AutoCAD9, 2.6x and 2.5x

This course is designed for students who already have a sound understanding of basic AutoCAD features and commands. The course covers advanced techniques including the use of symbol libraries, bills of materials, 3D, isometrics, screen, icon, and tablet menu development, digitizing, AutoLISP, and other advanced applications of AutoCAD. Challenging thought-provoking, hands-on exercises form the foundation of the course. (2 semester hours)

AutoCAD Fundamentals: AutoCAD 10

This course is designed to provide a clear understanding of the commands, features, and limitations associated with the basic operation of AutoCAD: mode settings, drawing setup, layering, associate dimensioning, polylines, and blocks. Hands-on exercises form the foundation of the course. The course is written for all disciplines which require methods of drafting, design, and engineering. (3 semester hours)

Advanced AutoCAD: AutoCAD 10

This course is designed for students who already have a sound understanding of basic AutoCAD features and commands. The course covers advanced techniques including the use of symbol libraries, bills of materials, 3D, isometrics, screen, icon, and table menu development, digitizing, AutoLISP, and other advanced applications of AutoCAD. (4 semester hours)

AutoCAD Fundamentals: AutoCAD 11

The purpose of this course is to provide a clear understanding of the commands, features, and limitations associated with the basic operation of AutoCAD Release 11. Each student will gain valuable hands-on experience using well-structured exercises and programmed study. The course presents a logical and well tested, step-by-step introduction to the AutoCAD commands, mode settings, drawing aids, shortcuts, and other characteristics of AutoCAD. (3 semester hours)

Advanced AutoCAD: AutoCAD 11

The purpose of this course is to provide a clear understanding of the commands, features, and limitations associated with the advanced operation and application of AutoCAD Release 11. Each student will gain valuable hands-on experience using well-structured exercises and programmed study. The course presents a logical and well-tested step-by-step approach to the advanced commands and characteristics of AutoCAD. The course features the use of isometrics, advanced 3D wireframe and solid modeling, external references, viewports in paper space, multiple view plotting, screen, tablet and icon menu development, AutoLISP, digitizing, slide shows, and other advanced operations. (3 semester hours)

AutoCAD Fundamentals: AutoCAD 12

The course presents a logical step-by-step introduction to the AutoCAD commands, mode settings, drawing aids, shortcuts, and other valuable characteristics of AutoCAD. (3 semester hours)

Advanced AutoCAD: AutoCAD 12

The purpose of this course is to provide a clear understanding of the commands, features, and limitations associated with the basic operation of AutoCAD Release 12. Each student will gain valuable hands-on experience using well-structured exercises and programmed study. The course presents a logical and well tested, step-by-step approach to the advanced commands and characteristics of AutoCAD. The course features the use of isometric drawing, advanced 3D wireframe and surface modeling, external references, viewports in paper space, multiple view plotting, screen, table, and icon menu development, AutoLISP, digitizing, slide shows, and other advanced operations. (3 semester hours)

ECONOMICS

Intermediate Macroeconomics

Develops the Keynesian model of national income determination and contrasts it with alternate perspectives, such as monetarism, supply-side economics, and rational expectations. Financial product and labor markets are analyzed and integrated into a comprehensive explanation of economic growth and decline. Careful attention is paid to policy issues such as inflation, unemployment, debt, and international trade. (3 semester hours)

EDUCATION

Educational Psychology

Psychological conditions of classroom learning and teaching including understanding needs of exceptional children in the classroom. (3 semester hours)

FISHERY AND WILDLIFE BIOLOGY

Hunter Education for Instructors

Designed to provide as well as to encourage hunter education instructors in providing high quality learning experiences by demonstrating knowledge of the learning processes; effective teaching behaviors; and knowledge, skills, and ethics associated with hunting. (2 semester hours)

Leopold's Ethic for Wilderness and Land

Philosophy, art, history, and science of wildlife and land management from writings of Aldo Leopold. (3 semester hours)

Wildlife Habitat on the Great Plains

Provides an overview of wildlife and habitat management on the Great Plains. Management of crops and grazing land in ecologically sound ways can encourage wildlife resources as a part of agricultural plans. Wildlife-based recreation is in demand by Great Plains landowners, wildlife and agricultural managers, and community leaders. (3 semester hours)

GRANTSMANSHIP

Grantsmanship and Proposal Writing

The purpose of this course is to teach not only the mechanics of proposal writing, but to give the student a feel for the "atmosphere" which is a part of the intangibles of the grantseekers art. More specifically the objectives of this course are: to develop the knowledge and skills required to be an effective proposal writer; become more knowledgeable about the sponsored projects funding process; to provide resource and reference tools that will allow the student to identify a broader range of funding possibilities and to do so in a highly efficient manner; and to improve the students' ratio between proposals submitted and proposals funded. (3 semester hours)

HISTORY

Afro-American History, 1619–1865

Survey of African background and slavery in the American South to abolition. (3 semester hours)

Imperial Russia

Tsarist Russia from its beginnings to the Revolution of 1905 with emphasis on the modern period. (3 semester hours)

HUMAN DEVELOPMENT AND FAMILY STUDIES

Decision Making: Personal and Family

Integration of management functions in the family for realizing values and goals. (3 semester hours)

Individual and Family Development

Basic principles and sequences in human development; family structure and functions as they support human development. (3 semester hours)

Creative Experiences for Preschool Children

Students in this course will acquire a foundation in theories of play and creativity. Examines the role of art, music, and literature in development. (3 semester hours)

Studying Young Children

Development of observation skills while participating in an early childhood center. (3 semester hours)

Children's Programming/Curriculum Development

Principles of designing and evaluating developmentally appropriate programs for children. (3 semester hours)

Play Behavior

Role of play in human development, designing developmental play environments, and guiding development through play. (3 semester hours)

Administration of Child Care Centers

Center administration related to program development and operations, budgeting, state regulations and licensing, and personnel issues. (3 semester hours)

NUTRITION

Nutrition and the Preschool Child

Principles of nutrition with emphasis on application to preschool children. (3 semester hours)

PHILOSOPHY

Practical Thinking

Students teach themselves to analyze and judge passages of argument; to note tacit assumptions; to recognize necessary/sufficient conditions. A computer with MS-DOS capability is required to complete assignments. (3 semester hours)

PSYCHOLOGY

Environmental Psychology

Environmental psychology is the study of the interrelationships of human behavior and the natural and developed environment. The course will address the theories of environment-behavior relationships including the topics of environmental perception, assessment, and cognition. Application of these concepts will occur through the exploration of current environmental issues: environmental hazards, pollution, crowding, the design of cities, and educational and recreational settings. The structure of the course will allow each student to apply the theories and concepts of environmental psychology to their particular setting, i.e., school, home, work psychology. (3 semester hours)

RECREATION AND NATURAL RESOURCES

Foundations of National Forest Lands

Discusses the history of national land policy, the policies and trends of the National Forest System Lands Program, the nature of the lands program at work, and the integration of the lands program into all National Forest management. (1 semester hour) *Tuition:* $90 plus $30 fee.

Special Uses Management

Presents the authorities, policies, and coordination required in special uses management along with how to process and administer special use authorizations. Special uses such as agricultural, aviation, communications, community, cultural, industrial, and water uses are discussed. (4 semester hours) *Tuition:* $360 plus $30 fee.

Linear Uses and FERC Licenses

Discusses authorizations, policies, background, procedures, and coordination for linear special uses such as roads, communications, and transmission and distribution systems; and for Federal Energy Regulatory Commission licenses. (3 semester hours) *Tuition:* $270 plus $30 fee.

Valuation and Landownership Adjustment

Examines the laws, regulations, policies, procedures, planning and coordination for valuation, title, exchange, purchase and donations, interchange, transfers, sales, negotiations, and condemnation. (5 semester hours) *Tuition:* $450 plus $30 fee.

Right-of-Way Acquisition

Describes the authorities, regulations, policy, philosophy, definitions, interrelationships, coordination, delegations, alternatives, planning, and management for rights-of-way acquisitions; and cooperative road construction and use (cost share) programs. (3 semester hours) *Tuition:* $270 plus $30 fee.

Foundations of Forest Recreation

History, philosophy, role, and sources of information of the Forest Service and national Forest Service. (1 semester hour) *Tuition:* $90 plus $30 fee.

Meeting the Needs of Recreation Users

Visitor behavior, communications and conflicts, working with volunteers, programs, partnerships, quality service, and role of interpretive services. (4 semester hours) *Tuition:* $360 plus $30 fee.

Recreation Special Uses and Appeals

Discusses recreation concessions and special uses pertaining to private commercial operations on National Forest System lands. The appeals process is also reviewed. (3 semester hours) *Tuition:* $270 plus $30 fee.

Trails, Facility Design, Operation and Maintenance

Trail planning, development, maintenance; recreation site planning, design operation, maintenance; visitor and resource protection. (3 semester hours) *Tuition:* $270 plus $30 fee.

Recreation, Visual and Cultural Resource Management

Economic analysis, recreation opportunity spectrum, visual and cultural resource management. (2 semester hours) *Tuition:* $210 plus $30 fee.

Off-Road Vehicle, River, and Winter Recreation

History, authorities, planning, management, and coordination of off-road, river, and winter recreation. (2 semester hours) *Tuition:* $210 plus $30 fee.

Wilderness Philosophy and Ethic Development

Discusses the philosophical origin of the wilderness concept and the themes and values wilderness provides. It also looks at the history of wilderness and at the conservation movement in America as well as wilderness in the international context. Managing wilderness as a distinct resource and the nonrecreational benefits of wilderness are also discussed. (3 semester hours) *Tuition:* $300 plus $30 fee.

National Wilderness Preservation System

A look at the early and key components of the Wilderness Act, wilderness legislation since 1964, related natural systems, and the similarities and differences in agency mandates and policies are studied. (3 semester hours) *Tuition:* $300 plus $30.

Management of the Wilderness Resource

Ecosystem characteristics and basic principles of wilderness management are studied. Separate teaching units discuss management of specific wilderness resources such as fire, wildlife, cultural, etc.; managing nonconforming uses such as range, minerals and motorized/mechanical uses; and Geographical Information Systems. (4 semester hours) *Tuition:* $400 plus $30 fee.

Management of Recreation Resources

How to manage for quality visitor experiences; common problems and solutions. Managing to minimize recreational impacts. Wilderness education and information techniques and how to deal with emergencies and law enforcement actions. (3 semester hours) *Tuition:* $300 plus $30 fee.

Wilderness Management Planning

Differences in planning among the four agencies. Basic planning concepts, a format for writing a "good" plan, and how to implement a plan. Limits of Acceptable Change planning system. (3 semester hours) *Tuition:* $300 plus $30 fee.

Wilderness Management Skills and Projections

The use of primitive means to achieve management objectives, use of "minimum tool," and no-trace camping methods. How to recruit, supervise, train and effectively use volunteers to enhance your wilderness program. Answers to: What does the future hold: How can I become a better wilderness management professional? (3 semester hours) *Tuition:* $300 plus $30 fee.

TEXTILES

Selection and Use of Textiles

Selection, use, and maintenance of apparel and interior textiles for the consumer, entrepreneur, merchandiser, designer, and/or interior designer. (3 semester hours)

ZOOLOGY

Biology of Aging

Aging as a basic phenomenon of animal life. (3 semester hours)

Columbia International University
Columbia Extension
7435 Monticello Road
P.O. Box 3122
Columbia, South Carolina 29230-3122
(803) 754-4100

Description:

Columbia International University (CIU) was founded in 1923 to prepare men and women for Christian ministry in the U.S. and overseas. Columbia Extension manages the distribution of approximately 50 independent learning courses offered by CIU's two postsecondary schools: Columbia Bible College (offering certificate, associate, and bachelor degree programs) and Columbia Biblical Seminary and Graduate School of Missions (offering certificate, master, and doctoral degree programs). Columbia Extension was begun in 1980 and currently serves 500 students located in 50 countries.

Faculty:

James A. Roche, Jr., Associate Dean for Extension Education; Michael J. Brown, Assistant Director of Admissions for Extension. There is a faculty of 19 members and 6 faculty assistants.

Academic Levels:
College
Graduate
Noncredit

Degree/Certificate Programs:
Bachelor, Graduate, Diploma, Certificate.

Admission Requirements:

High school graduation or GED, English fluency, testimony of Christian conversion experience and commitment to the Christian faith and lifestyle. Enrollment in a a course does not constitute enrollment in a degree program. The student must follow normal admission procedures. For either provisional or full admission, students must sign a statement indicating their agreement with the doctrinal and life standards of Columbia International University. Up 30 semester hours earned through correspondence/independent study may be applied toward an undergraduate degree; up to 18 semester hours toward a graduate degree; up to 15 semester hours for an associate degree.

Tuition:

$90 per semester hour for undergraduate courses; $150 per semester hour for graduate courses. Husband/wife discount for spouse enrolled for any course of equal or fewer credit hours. Inmate discount also available as well as for Christian workers. Veterans benefits accepted. Refund policy: If cancellation within fifteen days of enrollment and all materials returned unopened and undamaged, a full refund will be granted. If cancellation before second evaluation in course outline and within thirty days of enrollment, 50 percent of tuition fees will be refunded.

Enrollment Period:

Time limits for each course can be calculated at two months per credit hour with a minimum of six months. When special extenuating circumstances prohibit the completion of a course by the due date, a student may apply for a one-time extension of six months to be added to the course due date. This request must be made in writing and received at least one month before the course due date.

There is a $10 fee due and payable at the time of the request. There are no other extensions after this point.

Equipment Requirements:

Students must supply cassette player when required and purchase study guides and textbooks.

Credit and Grading:

All grading is done by a numerical system (0–100). The minimum passing grade for undergraduate courses is 70; for graduate courses, 65. All examinations for a course must be taken in the presence of a proctor (a pastor, chaplain, church leader, school faculty member, administrator, or other non-relative). The name of the proctor must be registered with the independent study office before acceptance of the completed examination. Proctor Arrangement forms are in the course study guide. Transfer credits must have been awarded by accredited institutions. Credit is awarded in semester hour units.

Library Services:

Students may request the loan of books in writing to the CIU library on the main campus.

Accreditations:

American Association of Bible Colleges; Association of Theological Schools in the United States and Canada; Southern Association of Colleges and Schools.

COLLEGE COURSES

APOLOGETICS

Christian Evidences

A survey of the science of apologetics, examining the reasonableness of the evidence for Christian faith, with emphasis on the major approaches taken in apologetics and the basic considerations of each. (2 semester hours)

BIBLE

Old Testament Survey: Genesis—Poetical Books

An introduction to the scope and content of the historical and poetical books of the Old Testament and to the importance of the main people and events of the period. (3 semester hours)

New Testament Survey: Gospels/Life of Christ

A chronological, synthetic study of the four Gospel records, emphasizing the time, place, circumstances, and persons involved in the events of our Lord's ministry, with a view to a fuller understanding of the significance of His words and works. (3 semester hours)

New Testament Survey: Acts—Revelation

Acts is used as an historical framework for study of the earlier New Testament letters as well as an introduction to its later letters and to the culmination in the apocalypse. Sustained application of the New Testament teachings to our individual and corporate lives as believers is integrated into the course. (3 semester hours)

Galatians

A detailed study of one of Paul's greatest and most influential letters set in the context of the life and times of the Apostle and the early church. Emphasis is on Paul's vindication of his apostleship and message, to call early Christians back from legalism to grace. (1 semester hours)

Old Testament Survey: Prophetic Books

A survey of the Old Testament prophetic books in their chronological order; historical background, theme, and plan of each book; enough study of detailed content to make the message of each book applicable to personal life. (3 semester hours)

Living your Faith: Studies in Amos

A thorough study of God's Word in the book of Amos through lectures and independent study. The course presents methods for discovering and teaching biblical principles so that students are challenged to live the Christian faith they profess. (1 semester hour)

Gospel of Mark: The Cross in our Lives

A study on the Gospel of Mark with emphasis on analyzing the content and purposes of the book, inductive Bible study methods, and applying and teaching biblical truths. (1 semester hour)

Ephesians

A verse-by-verse exposition of Ephesians against the background of the life and times of Paul and the Ephesian church. Emphasis is on the interaction of believers within the body of Christ and their relation to the lost world. (1 semester hour)

Philippians: How to Study and Teach a Bible Book

A ''how-to'' course demonstrating biblical learning and teaching techniques through a study of Philippians. Teachers and their students are encouraged to actively explore the pressures, problems, and principles that contemporary Christians share with the Philippian church. (1 semester hour)

Colossians/Philemon

A study in the New Testament letters of Colossians and Philemon using the English Bible and with particular emphasis on applied sanctification. (1 semester hour)

Principles of Bible Interpretation

The purpose of this course is to assist the student in gaining the knowledge and skill necessary to determine the meaning of any passage of Scripture and to apply it appropriately. The student will be able to use all the guidelines which have been studied, identify the meaning of any passage of Scripture, and exegete confidently. Access to reference material is needed for some assignments. (3 semester hours)

MISSIONS

Historical Perspective on Church and Mission

This course aims to help students become World Christians by providing a biblical basis for the involvement of all Christians in world evangelism, by reviewing the challenge from our heritage in missions, by investigating the spiritual needs of our contemporary world, and by highlighting current strategies for identifying and reaching the lost. (3 semester hours)

PASTORAL COUNSELING

Biblical Counseling by Encouragement

This course is based on the concept and belief that caring, mature Christians in local churches can and should learn to develop an encouragement/counseling ministry through the use of a well-timed word to stimulate one another to love and good deeds. Counseling by encouragement is the most basic form of counseling. This course is designed to help one understand the importance and techniques of this ministry in the local church. (1 semester hour)

THEOLOGY

Ethics and Sanctification

In pursuit of the ultimate goal of knowing God, the course will provide opportunity to explore two subjects commonly called ethics and sanctification. As an introduction to biblical ethics you will study God's character as a model for your own thinking and behavior; as an introduction to the biblical doctrine of holiness (sanctification) you will study God's provision for successful Christian living and our own responsibility for appropriating that provision. (3 semester hours)

Bibliology: Inerrancy and Authority of the Scriptures

A historical and biblical study of the nature of the Bible with special reference to the twentieth century debate over the inerrancy of the Scriptures. The evangelical position is presented regarding revelation, inspiration, the relationship of inspiration to theology, etc., and arguments against the evangelical position are stated and answered. (2 semester hours)

GRADUATE COURSES

ANTHROPOLOGY

Social Anthropology for Missionaries

An introduction to missionary anthropology. Application of anthropological principles is made to case studies, seeking to understand similarities and differences in human behavior patterns with a view to contextualizing the Christian message. The student also undertakes an ethnographical study. (3 semester hours)

BIBLE

Old Testament Survey: Genesis—Poetical Books

An introduction to the scope and content of the historical and poetical books of the Old Testament and to the importance of the main people and events of the period. (3 semester hours)

Old Testament Survey: Prophetic Books

A survey of the Old Testament prophetic books in their chronological order; historical background, theme, and plan of each book; enough study of detailed content to make the message of each book applicable to personal life. (3 semester hours)

New Testament Survey: Gospels/Life of Christ

A chronological study of the four Gospels, emphasizing the time, place, circumstances and persons involved in our Lord's ministry; with a view to a fuller understanding of the significance of His words and works. (3 semester hours)

New Testament Survey: Acts—Revelation

Acts is used as an historical framework for study of the earlier New Testament letters as well as an introduction to its later letters, and to the culmination in the apocalypse. Application of the New Testament teachings to our lives as believers is integrated into the course. (3 semester hours)

Conquest and Settlement

A study of the conquest and settlement period in Israel's history from the standpoint of archaeology, theological truths, and history. The books included in the study are Joshua, Judges, and Ruth. Special consideration is given to Late Bronze Age materials from Palestine which provide the cultural background for this era. (3 semester hours)

Basic Biblical Hermeneutics

The purpose of this course is to assist the student in gaining the knowledge and skill necessary to determine the meaning of any passage of Scripture and to apply it appropriately. The student will be able to use all the guidelines which have been studied, identify the meaning of any passage of Scripture, and exegete confidently. Access to reference materials is needed for some assignments. (3 semester hours)

Psalms

An introduction to the book of Psalms with emphasis on the principles involved in the exegesis of the hymnic literature and the application of these principles in select portions. Special attention is given to the various forms of the Psalms and their setting within the historical experience of Israel. (2 semester hours)

The Upper Room Discourse

An in-depth study of Jesus' last recorded teaching of his disciples in John 13–17. The passage is viewed in the light of its historical context and as the foundation for truth revealed in the epistles to the church. Emphasis is on a thorough knowledge of the facts, the significance of the content, and the interpretive problems. (1 semester hour)

Acts in Historical, Theological, and Missiological Perspective

This course is a study of the historical sequence of events in Acts, in light of Luke's theological themes. It helps one to develop the ability to soundly draw out timeless principles from the Acts narrative and then use them to develop and evaluate modern missions strategy. (3 semester hours)

The Christian and Old Testament Theology

A study of the foundational theology applied by the Old Testament for the New Testament Church. This study identifies the doctrinal focal point of both the Old and New Testaments. It also deals with the question of continuity and discontinuity between the Old and New Testament. Included are the topics of faith, the people of God, the doctrine of atonement, relationship between the law and wisdom theology, kingdom of God, the Messiah, the place of the Gentiles, the theology of the Holy Spirit, and the preparation for the New Covenant. (3 semester hours)

Romans

A rigorous study of the book of Romans which seeks to understand its message in the light of the original first century situation. Consideration is also given to the significance of the epistle's message for today. Special emphasis is placed on the development of exegetical skills. (3 semester hours)

Messianic Prophecy

A study of Old Testament Messianic themes and how they are fulfilled in Jesus Christ. This course emphasizes how to correctly interpret Bible prophecy, identifies Old Testament Messianic themes, and covers Old Testament passages which teach these themes. (2 semester hours)

CHRISTIAN EDUCATION

Leadership and Administration

A study designed to develop leadership potential in students and to give them a familiarity with various elements of the administrative process, including: goal setting and achieving, organization, delegation, human relations, group dynamics, supervision, and the training of other leaders. Though the principles are universal, the focus of the course is the Christian organization, particularly the Church. (3 semester hours)

CHURCH HISTORY

The Early and Medieval Church: 30 A.D.–1517

From catholic to Catholic. A survey of church development and expansion from the New Testament era to the beginning of the Protestant Reformation. The study chronicles the evolution of the early church from Jewish sect to state church and introduces the student to Medieval Synthesis—the church's complete control of western culture and society in later Middle Ages. Attention is given to theological developments, church expansion, leaders, movements, and cultural impact during the two periods. (3 semester hours)

The Reformation and the Modern Church: 1517–Present

A study of the five major phases of the Protestant Reformation—Lutheran, Reformed, Radical, Anglican, and Catholic—sets the stage for an evaluation of the church in the modern period. The course examines Reformation impact on the contemporary church, recent theological innovations, the emergence of the modern denomination, the lingering impact of revivalism on the church and the charismatic leaders that have shaped the church in the 20th century. (3 semester hours)

American Christianity

An introductory study of American Christianity from its beginnings to the present. From an examination of the uniqueness of American Christianity to the complex church of the 20th century, the course traces the dramatic journey of the church in this country through almost four centuries of development. Emphasis is placed on leaders, movements, issues, and theological trends that have shaped the American church. (3 semester hours)

MISSIONS

Introduction to Missions

An introduction to the biblical-theological foundation, the historical development, cross-cultural dimension and anthropological perspective of contemporary world missions. Attention is given to recent developments in church-mission strategy and to future projections. Designed as a foundation for other missions courses and to prepare the student to teach missions in a local church. (3 semester hours)

Principles of Community Development

This study includes approaches to development and change, the biblical basis for community development, mobilizing people to change, promoting grassroots participation, the literature of community development, and integrates lessons from field experience. (1 semester hour)

History of Missions

A survey of Christianity through the ages with emphasis on a cultural and structural analysis of its growth. The influence of personalities, political developments, cultural factors, and methods and strategies will be highlighted. Attention is given to the post-Reformation era emphasizing the causative factors that led to the present development of world missions. (3 semester hours)

Biblical Theology of Missions

A study of God's redemptive purpose and activity revealed through Israel's responsibility to the nations in the Old Testament and the mandates entrusted to the church in the New Testament. (3 semester hours)

Folk Religion

This course describes the basic features of animistic societies. Witchcraft, rituals magic, and ancestor worship are considered in relationship to the planting of indigenous churches. The danger of syncretistic belief systems is discussed, and Christian approaches to the spirit world are presented. (3 semester hours)

Contextualization of Theology

A study of the concept and practice of contextualization: historical roots, biblical and modern examples, relation of indigenization and the history of salvation and problems. Explored also are its implications and applications for evangelism, translation, theology, and third world theologies, theological education and Christianity in its relation to world religions. (3 semester hours)

Theologies of Liberation

A survey of liberation theologies with particular attention to their historical development and thematic elaboration in the social and religious context of Latin America. (3 semester hours)

Urban Missions and Ministry

A course that focuses on Christian mission and ministry in the world's growing cities. The biblical basis for urban ministry is presented and case studies of effective urban strategies worldwide are examined. Attention is given to urban issues such as ministry to the poor and homeless, pastoring and raising a family in the city, and planting urban churches. (3 semester hours)

THEOLOGY

Doctrine: Church

A study of the biblical doctrine of the Church including its purposes, structure and life, leadership, founding, functions, and its significance in the world today. Special emphasis will be given to the understanding, discovery, and development of spiritual gifts. (2 semester hours)

Principles of the Christian Life

In pursuit of the ultimate goal of knowing God, the course will provide opportunity to explore two subjects commonly called ethics and sanctification. As an introduction to biblical ethics you will study God's character as a model for your own thinking and behavior; as an introduction to the biblical doctrine of holiness (sanctification) you will study God's provision for successful Christian living and our own responsibility for appropriating that provision. (3 semester hours)

The Theology of Jonathan Edwards

This course examines the theology of Jonathan Edwards in detail. Taking a topical approach, the course covers Edwards' teachings regarding all the major points of systematic theology with particular emphasis on Edwards' unique theological contributions. (3 semester hours)

Columbia Union College
External Degree Program
7600 Flower Avenue
Takoma Park, Maryland 20912-7796
(800) 835-4212

Description:
Columbia Union College was established in 1904 as a coeducational Seventh-day Adventist institution. It offers degree programs in the arts, sciences, religion, health, and other professional fields.

Columbia Union College's External Degree Program and Home Study International's Collegiate Studies Program pool their resources and strengths in offering college-level courses and degree programs that may be completed by correspondence and individualized study. Columbia Union College provides the overall academic supervision and issues transcripts and degrees. Home Study International provides all student services—including enrollment ser-

vices, billing, furnishing of course materials, and processing of lessons and examinations. For a description of courses available, SEE **Home Study International** in Section 3 - Private, Nonprofit, and Governmental Institutions.

Accreditations:
Middle States Association of Colleges and Schools.

Concordia University
College of Continuing Education
Correspondence Study
7400 Augusta Street
River Forest, Illinois 60305-1499
(708) 209-3024

Description:
Concordia University was founded in 1864 and is a Christian liberal arts college offering both baccalaureate and master degrees. Concordia historically has prepared men and women for teaching in the parish schools of the Lutheran Church—Missouri Synod. Its enrollment still reflects a heavy emphasis on teacher education. However, Concordia also attracts those interested in preparing for public education and nursing as well as many other professions represented in its liberal arts program. Through its Correspondence Study Program, Concordia offers undergraduate college instruction for credit in keeping with approved standards for such work. The courses parallel or are identical with courses of the same titles offered on the Concordia campus. The same general standards apply, both as to course content and as to the quality of work expected from the student. The courses are prepared and conducted by members of the faculty.

The college is coeducational and has a student body that comes from all walks of life, representing varied racial and ethnic backgrounds. Over 35 states and several foreign countries are represented in the student body. The college is also the location of an English Language School with students coming from all parts of the world.

Faculty:
Carol Smid, Director of Correspondence Study. The Correspondence Study faculty has 22 members.

Academic Levels:
College

Degree/Certificate Programs:
A maximum of 48 quarter hours may be applied toward the Bachelor degree at Concordia. No independent study courses are offered for graduate credit.

Admission Requirements:
Application for independent study may be made at any time of the year. Required: a high school diploma or equivalent. High school seniors, in their last semester of school, may enroll in some core curricular courses offered through independent study on a noncredit basis. Their status will be changed to earning college credit in any of the

enrolled independent study courses after successful completion of their high school program. Overseas applicants accepted.

Tuition:

$98 per quarter hour ($392 for a 4 quarter hour course; $442 for 4½ quarter hour course). Rates are subject to change; contact the university for current rates. If a course is cancelled within 30 calendar days from date of registration and no assignments have been completed, 80 percent of the tuition is refunded. If a course is cancelled within 60 calendar days of registration and no more than one-half of the course has been completed, 60 percent of the tuition is refunded.

Enrollment Period:

All course requirements are to be completed within six months from the date of registration. Six-month extensions may be granted upon payment of an extension fee ($13 for the first extension, $19 each for second and third extensions).

Equipment Requirements:

Textbooks are paid for by the student and may be ordered through the Concordia Book Store. Additional postage fee is charged for overseas students.

Credit and Grading:

The unit of credit is the quarter hour. The quarter hour is equivalent to two-thirds of a semester hour. To obtain credit in most courses, the student will be required to complete mid-term and final examinations successfully. Examinations are proctored either on the Concordia campus, or by a recognized proctor. Grading system: A, Excellent; B, Good; C, Fair; D, Poor, but passing; F, Failure. Correspondence credit from other institutions may be transferred toward programs if the coursework is appropriate and the credit earned is from an accredited institution.

Accreditations:

North Central Association of Colleges and Schools; National Council for Accreditation of Teacher Education.

COLLEGE COURSES

ANTHROPOLOGY

Introduction to Cultural Anthropology

Theoretical perspectives and methods of cultural anthropology, emphasizing the comparative analysis of social systems in non-Western societies. (4 quarter hours)

ECONOMICS

Introduction to Economics

Basic principles of economics. The problems of businesses, governments, labor unions and nations as viewed from the perspective of economics. (4 quarter hours)

EDUCATION

Perspectives of the Teaching Profession

Orientation to the dynamics of the teaching profession through a variety of educational experiences, with special emphasis placed on observation and involvement at the school, parish, and community levels. (4 quarter hours)

Foundations of Education

Education as a field of study with special emphasis on historical and philosophical development of public and church-related schools. The nature and conditions of learning. Direct classroom observation supplements course work. (3 quarter hours)

Ethics of the Christian Teacher

Study of the status of Lutheran schools and teachers as well as the ethics of the Christian teacher in the ministry of Christian education in the parish. (1 quarter hour)

Educational Psychology

Cognitive, social, moral, and physical development of individuals as these interact in personality development and in the process of teaching and learning. Major theories are examined in terms of application to pedagogical practice in early childhood, elementary, middle, and secondary schools and in light of Christianity. (4 quarter hours)

Teaching of Reading

The reading process, the commercial reading programs available, the needs and interests of children, the methods and procedures for instruction, and the organization patterns for effective reading motivation. (4 quarter hours)

Tests and Measurements

Criteria for tests and test construction. Methods of evaluation. Planned programs for varied settings. (4 quarter hours)

Psychology and Methods of Teaching the Exceptional Child

Identification of characteristics; rules and regulations; performance limitations; informal assessment and recordkeeping procedures; differentiated instructional approaches; attitudes and methods to facilitate learning. (4 quarter hours)

Introduction to the Counseling Profession

Examination of the field of counseling. Historical perspectives and future trends. Role and functions of counselors in various settings. Goals of professional organizations, codes of ethics, legal issues, certification, and licensure. (4 quarter hours)

Reading in Middle and Secondary Schools

Reading for secondary education students. Emphasis on developing an understanding of the reading process; general appraisal of the readability of classroom materials, abilities, techniques, and additional resources for helping reluctant and retarded readers. (4 quarter hours)

Organization and Administration of Youth Ministry

Basic principles underlying youth work in a Christian congregation, with emphasis on the Gospel orientation. The person and role of the Christian youth counselor. Youth program materials and resources. (4 quarter hours)

Children's Literature

General survey of children's literature; criteria for evaluation; book selection. (4 quarter hours)

Classroom Management

Basic classroom management and student discipline; instructional planning and student progress. (4 quarter hours)

Foundations of Early Childhood

Historical, philosophical, sociological, and theological foundations of current thought and practice. Critical examination of a variety of current models. Issues of mainstreaming and cultural pluralism as they relate to the education of children from birth to Grade 3. (4 quarter hours)

ENGLISH

Shakespeare

Major plays in the development of Shakespeare. The more significant problems in Shakespeare criticism and interpretation. (4 quarter hours)

HISTORY

History of the American People

Social, economic, diplomatic, political, and cultural developments from exploration to contemporary times. Problems, concepts, movements, and interpretation. (4 quarter hours)

Reformation Era

Protestant Reformation, Roman Catholic Reformation, and the religious wars of the sixteenth and seventeenth centuries. Religious upheaval and its impact on society, politics, economics, and culture. (4 quarter hours)

MATHEMATICS

College Algebra

A review of topics from intermediate algebra, sets, functions, graphing quadratics, inequalities, and systems of equations; an introduction to mathematical induction, the theory of equations, matrices and determinants, and binomial theorem and complex numbers. (4 quarter hours)

College Trigonometry

Basic trigonometric ratios, functions, graphs and identities. Applications in a variety of fields. (4 quarter hours)

POLITICAL SCIENCE

American Government

Powers, structure, and operation of government at national, state, and local levels. The United States and Illinois constitutions. (4 quarter hours)

PSYCHOLOGY

General Psychology

Principles of human behavior. Scientific approach to psychology, individual differences, personality development, adjustment, emotions, sensory functions and perception. Child growth and development, the learning process, and techniques of evaluation in education. (4 quarter hours)

Educational Psychology

Cognitive, social, moral, and physical development of individuals as these interact in personality development and in the process of teaching and learning. Major theories are examined in terms of application to pedagogical practice in early childhood, elementary, middle, and secondary schools and in light of Christianity. (4 quarter hours)

Introduction to Counseling

Current counseling theories and issues; conditions for effective counseling in varied settings; multicultural concerns. (4 quarter hours)

Psychology and Methods for Teaching the Exceptional Child

Identification of characteristics; rules and regulations; performance limitations; informal assessment and recordkeeping procedures; differentiated instructional approaches; attitudes and methods to facilitate learning. (4 quarter hours)

Introduction to the Counseling Profession

Examination of the field of counseling. Historical perspectives and future trends. Role and functions of counselors in various settings. Goals of professional organizations, codes of ethics, legal issues, certification and licensure. (4 quarter hours)

Tests and Measurements

Criteria for tests and test construction. Methods of evaluation. Planned programs for varied settings. (4 quarter hours)

SOCIOLOGY

Introduction to Sociology

Basic sociological principles, the general societal structure and fundamental institutions, and our present forms of social interaction. (4 quarter hours)

Introduction to Cultural Anthropology

Theoretical perspectives and methods of cultural anthropology, emphasizing the comparative analysis of social systems in non-Western societies. (4 quarter hours)

Marriage and the Family

Investigation of American family functions and structures through cross-cultural, historical, and institutional analysis. Sociological theory and current research used to explore mate selection, marital adjustment, child rearing, post-parental years, and problems related to American marriage. (4 quarter hours)

THEOLOGY

History and Literature of the Old Testament

The Old Testament in the light of the ancient Near East and New Testament fulfillment. A brief treatment of canon and versions. Biblical geography and archaeology. Attention to the methods of interpreting the Old Testament. (4 quarter hours)

History and Literature of the New Testament

Origin, form, content, and purpose of the New Testament writings, with an emphasis on the problems and principles of interpretation. (4 quarter hours)

Faith of the Christian Church

The faith of the Christian Church as proclaimed in Holy Scriptures and confessed in the Book of Concord of 1580. Based on Martin Luther's two catechisms. Major topics: the Law and the Gospel, the Apostles Creed, Holy Baptism, The Lord's Supper. (4 quarter hours)

Christian Life

Perspectives of the Christian life on the basis of the Law/Gospel dialectic. Emphasis on the sinner-saint tension in relation to church, worship, ministry, and society. (4 quarter hours)

The Church in America

History and doctrines of Protestant and Roman Catholic denominations in America. Emphasis on Lutheranism and The Lutheran Church—Missouri Synod. (4 quarter hours)

Deaconess Work I

Role of the deaconess past and present within the context of church and ministry. Understanding of the history and structure of the LCMS, particularly in relationship to the deaconess. Familiarity with guiding ethical principles. (4 quarter hours)

The Reformation Era

Protestant Reformation, Roman Catholic Reformation, and the religious wars of the sixteenth and seventeenth centuries. Religious upheaval and its impact on society, politics, economics, and culture. (4 quarter hours)

Interpretation of Galatians and Ephesians

Careful study based on the best available translations. The Biblical theology of the epistles. Emphasis on the study of the books as letters rather than on verse-by-verse interpretation. (4 quarter hours)

Creighton University
Independent Study Program
2500 California Plaza
Omaha, Nebraska 68178   (800) 637-4279

Description:

Creighton University is a private, independent, nonprofit institution incorporated in 1879. The Independent Study Program offers students the opportunity for access to undergraduate general education courses developed by Creighton faculty members. The program maintains the same high degree of instructional quality that is maintained in on-campus courses at Creighton.

Faculty:

Dean Wolfe, Director, Independent Study Program, University College.

Academic Levels:

College

Degree/Certificate Programs:

Students must earn at least 48 hours in residence to qualify for a degree.

Admission Requirements:

High school graduation or equivalent. Students may register for a course any time during the year.

Tuition:

$400 per three semester-hour course.

Enrollment Period:

The minimum course completion time is twelve weeks, and the maximum is one year from the date of enrollment. A six-month extension may be granted upon approval by the program director and the payment of a $45 extension fee.

Equipment Requirements:

Textbook and supplementary materials must be purchased by the student.

Credit and Grading:

A–F. Examinations must be proctored. Credit is awarded in semester hour units.

Accreditations:

North Central Association of Colleges and Schools.

COLLEGE COURSES

ANTHROPOLOGY

Human Variation

Focus on the basic concepts of anthropology. Covers the basics of the subareas of physical, cultural, and archaeological anthropology. Includes a look at human and cultural variation in terms of evolutionary adaptation. (3 semester hours)

ENGLISH

Introduction to Literature II: Fiction

This introductory course examines short essays which discuss the short story as a literary form, its origin and development, and a wide sampling of stories, from early and traditional stories by Herman Melville, Nathaniel Hawthorne, Edgar Allan Poe all the way to more modern works by contemporary writers such as Walker, Updike, and Beattie. In addition, this course examines some elements of the novel and shows how the elements of fiction are handled in one representative modern novel, John Steinbeck's *The Grapes of Wrath*. Students will be primarily interested in how the various writers studied handle the elements of fiction: *theme; character development; plot; structure; context; point of view;* and *narrative and dramatic mix*. (3 semester hours)

Writers, Artists, and the Human Response to the Land

Examination of literature and art which express ideas and emotions generated by the human interaction with the natural environment. Its objective is twofold: to deepen the student's awareness of that environment, and to analyze the way gifted creative people have produced works of literary and visual art which convey both individual and universal human feelings evoked by nature and the landscape. The reading material includes two novels, a biography, some poetry, and nonfiction works, some of them from past times, some of them quite contemporary. (3 semester hours)

MATHEMATICS

Basic Algebra

Strongly recommended for the individual who has not had algebra for one or more years or who has had only one year or less of high school algebra. Reviews properties of arithmetic, signed numbers, linear equations and inequalities, polynomials, factoring, algebraic fractions, and roots and radicals. (3 semester hours)

Intermediate Algebra

Includes a review of roots and radicals, quadratic equations, relations and functions, systems of equations and exponential and logarithmic functions. (3 semester hours)

College Algebra

The emphasis in this course will be in two areas: (1) learning and using the fundamental properties of algebra and algebraic manipulation, and (2) problem solving using word problems. (3 semester hours)

Trigonometry

Continuation of topics from College Algebra which leads to the study of trigonometry. The traditional right-triangle approach to trigonometry as well as the analytic or circular function approach is studied. This course is designed to provide a firm basis for further study in calculus. (3 semester hours)

METEOROLOGY

Synoptic Meteorology I

Course of study will include a review of the basic laws of atmospheric thermodynamics, radiation, and hydrodynamics. Synoptic analysis of cyclones (extra tropical and tropical), fronts and their associated weather patterns, with an emphasis on developing diagnostic and forecasting techniques. Practical applications of air mass and frontal analysis are related to weather forecasting. Not an introductory course. Requires some knowledge of calculus and vector mathematics. (3 semester hours)

NUTRITION

Nutrition

This course familiarizes the student with the basic concepts of nutrition, to understand and appreciate the role of nutrition in promoting optimal health and prevention of disease and to relate nutrition to the changing needs of individuals throughout the life cycle. (3 semester hours)

PHILOSOPHY

Critical and Historical Introduction to Philosophy

An introductory course in philosophy which focuses on philosophical problems concerning the human person. The approach of the course is a combination of historical and problems. The historical part includes reading several philosophical classics. The problems part covers the following: the relationship of man to the state, social justice, the mind-body problem, life after death, and the existence of God. (3 semester hours)

PHYSICS

Sound and Music

This course was developed to acquaint the student with the ideas and the perspectives used in the physical sciences. The focus is on the topic of sound (the study of acoustics) to show the development of these ideas and perspectives. (3 semester hours)

Albert Einstein: The Man and the Myth

This course was developed for the student who wishes to learn about scientific ideas and scientific thought. The student will see that science is a "way of thinking," not a "collection of facts." The role Albert Einstein's ideas played in the evolution of science will be studied. Einstein will be seen as not only a great scientist but also as a socially concerned individual. (3 semester hours)

PSYCHOLOGY

Introductory Psychology

Introduction to the methodologies and basic concepts in the study of behavior. Course is intended to give the nonmajor an overview of the science of psychology while serving as a foundation for further study in psychology. (3 semester hours)

Child Psychology

The psychology of the child from prenatal development to middle childhood. Covers the norms of physical and psychological development as well as the range of individual differences. Focus is on normal developmental issues, both theoretical and practical, rather than on abnormal child psychology. Course attempts to present new and current information, integrate this information with prior knowledge of the student, and encourage better observation of and interaction with children. (3 semester hours)

Developmental Psychology

An overview of psychological, emotional, social, and physical patterns of behavior related to the following stages: prenatal, infancy, and early childhood; late childhood; adolescence; early adult years; middle adult years; and late adulthood. (3 semester hours)

Marriage and Family Values

Values clarification approach in exploring numerous value judgments that are made within the context of marriage and family living, e.g., decisions about dating practices, marriage partners, work allotment, leisure, child rearing. (3 semester hours)

SOCIOLOGY

Self and Society

The general objective of this introductory-level course is to familiarize the student with the social scientific approach to the analysis of social systems through the use of the methods of controlled observation and interpretation. As a means of developing familiarity with the central concepts, major points of view, and the leading sociologists, materials are used describing actual individuals, families, and communities in the United States. These "case studies" provide vivid real-life opportunities for discovering the applications and utility of a sociological point of view as a supplement to other points of view. (3 semester hours)

THEOLOGY

Introduction to Protestant Theology

The origin and development of Protestantism. The principal varieties of Protestant tradition. The contemporary status of Protestant thought. (3 semester hours)

Understanding the Life of Jesus: The Synoptic Gospels

Introduction to understanding the Gospels of Matthew, Mark, and Luke in the way they were understood by their first audiences. Course seeks to develop methods in applications that would facilitate and test such critical and historical understanding of the Gospels. The basic question in the course is "What did the authors say and mean to say to their contemporaries, and how do we know it?" (3 semester hours)

East Carolina University
East Fifth Street
Greenville, North Carolina 27834
(919) 757-6640

Description:

East Carolina University began in 1907 as a two-year teacher training institution. By 1920 it offered a four-year teacher education curriculum. By 1960 the college had become the state's third largest institution of higher learning. The General Assembly of North Carolina voted to elevate the college to the status of University in 1967. ECU is a participant in a consortium of eight institutions within the University of North Carolina System offering college-level correspondence courses and other opportunities for individualized study at a distance from the university campuses. In the consortium arrangement, each institution originating a course provides instruction and awards academic credit, while the responsibility for administration of the program lies with the office of Independent Studies at the University of North Carolina at Chapel Hill. SEE **North Carolina, University of - Chapel Hill.**

Faculty:

Diana Henshaw, Member of UNC Independent Studies Advisory Committee.

Accreditations:
Southern Association of Colleges and Schools.

East Texas State University
Division of Continuing Education
East Texas Station
Commerce, Texas 75428   (903) 886-5014

Description:
East Texas State University at Commerce began as East Texas Normal College in 1889 when founder William Leonidas Mayo opened the doors to a one-building campus in Cooper, Texas. In 1894, the college was named Mayo College and moved to Commerce. The name was changed to East Texas State University in 1965.

Faculty:
Ron Huffstutler, Dean, Division of Continuing Education and Institutional Research; Linda Sue Ebert, Supervisor of Correspondence. Faculty members number 21.

Academic Levels:
College

Degree/Certificate Programs:
The university will accept only 6 courses (18 semester hours) of correspondence credit toward a baccalaureate degree.

Admission Requirements:
The conditions for admission to correspondence work differ from those required for courses conducted in residence. However, in order to receive credit toward graduation for work done by correspondence, the student must have met the same prerequisites required of resident students. Students who are in residence at other colleges or universities must secure the advance approval of their deans for correspondence courses or assume the risk of failing to secure credit. Application for admission must be completed and an official copy of transcript should be provided. Undergraduates: transcript from college last attended. Graduates: transcript from institution from which the baccalaureate degree was obtained. High school students may not enroll in correspondence courses.

Tuition:
$120 per 3 semester-hour course. Rates subject to change; contact the university for current rates. If a student who has registered for a course notifies the Supervisor of Correspondence within fifteen days of registration that he desires to drop the course, eighty percent of the fee will be refunded; after fifteen days, no part of the fee will be returned.

Enrollment Period:
Maximum time for completion of course 1 year; minimum 45 days. A six-month extension may be granted upon request and payment of an extension fee. If the course is not completed at the end of the six-month extension period, the course will be terminated automatically.

Equipment Requirements:
Texts are supplied by the student. These can be ordered directly from the publisher or ordered from the University Bookstore, ETSU, Commerce, Texas 75428.

Credit and Grading:
Final or midterm examinations must be taken at a junior or senior college or university under the supervision of the Director of Testing, Counseling, Correspondence, or some similar administrator. The final examination should be taken within a month from the date of the completion of the lessons. Letter grades are awarded: A, B, C, D, F. Credit is awarded in semester hours.

Accreditations:
Southern Association of Colleges and Schools.

COLLEGE COURSES

BUSINESS

Business Organizations and Legal Transactions

A course in commercial law, including a study of partnerships, corporations, real estate, wills, trusts, and negotiable instruments law. (3 semester hours)

Communication Strategies in Business

The emphasis in this course is on interpersonal communication, letter writing, and small group communication. (3 semester hours)

Legal Environment of Business

A study of the legal environment and aspects of commerce, including administrative law, trade restraints, price discrimination, labor and employment law, common and statutory liability and regulation of professionals, as well as an analysis of basic principles of contract and negotiable instruments law and foreign and international aspects of business and commerce. (3 semester hours)

Records Management: Integrated Information Systems

A systems approach to managing paper, image, and digital records. Focus on developing a records center and the efficient management of the center. (3 semester hours)

ENGLISH

Black American Literature

The contribution of the American Black to literature is considered from a historical standpoint. Major emphasis is on the twentieth century, with interpretation and analysis of four genres: poetry, drama, short story, and novel. (3 semester hours)

Development of the English Language

This course is organized to provide perspective and sound historical criteria for understanding structure and usage in modern English. (3 semester hours)

Introduction to Literature

An introduction to the three major genres of literature: poetry, drama, and fiction. The course is designed to develop discriminating reading habits, and the student may be required to make analyses and value judgments based on critical thought. (3 semester hours)

Multi-Ethnic American Literature

A continuation of Introduction to Literature emphasizing literature to be read for enjoyment and interpretation of life, for literature's relative significance and perfection as one of the humanities. (3 semester hours)

HEALTH

Safety

a study in principles of accident prevention with emphasis on traffic, home, community, work, school, and general safety. A study of accident facts and statistics is included. (3 semester hours)

HISTORY

American Heritage

HIST 121. A course in American history to 1877 is focused on systematic efforts to solve major problems. The methods combine a background survey with critical examination of certain decisive events in our past in terms of their impact upon (1) the development of the historic ideals of American democracy and (2) the growth of social, economic, and political institutions. (3 semester hours)

HIST 122. A continuation of the preceding course, covering the years 1877 to the present. (3 semester hours)

History of Texas

This course covers the history of Texas beginning with the Spanish and Anglo-American settlements and carrying through with studies of the Texas Revolution, the period of the Republic of Texas, and the era of statehood with the development of its natural resources, agriculture, and industry. (3 semester hours)

World Civilization to 1660

A study of world civilizations from the earliest records to the beginnings of the modern era in the seventeenth century. The development of western civilization from Graeco-Roman times to the emergence of the new monarchies will be stressed. Non-Western societies in Africa and Asia will be studied not only for their own importance but for the influence of western civilization on world civilization. (3 semester hours)

World Civilization Since 1660

A study of the rise of modern Europe, the world, and the changes in western and eastern culture resulting from expansion and conflict. Stress will be placed on the changing political, social, cultural scene in Europe and the non-Western world. (3 semester hours)

MATHEMATICS

Elementary Algebra

The arithmetic and algebra of integers, rational numbers, exponents, linear equations and inequalities, problem solving, polynomials, quadratic equations. (3 semester hours)

Intermediate Algebra

Review of properties of real numbers, linear equations and inequalities, systems of linear equations and inequalities, polynomials, factoring, rational expressions, exponents and radicals, quadratic equations. (3 semester hours)

College Algebra

Quadratic equations; solutions of equations in several unknowns; ratio and proportion; variation; arithmetic and geometric progressions; the binomial theorem; permutations and combinations; elementary theory of equations. (3 semester hours)

Trigonometry

Trigonometric function; logarithms, radians, solutions of triangles; functions of composite angles; identities, trigonometric equations. (3 semester hours)

Mathematics for Business Applications

MATH 175. Review of elementary algebra; linear equations; quadratic equations; functions; inequalities; simple and compound interest; present value; annuities; amortization; systems of linear equations; linear programming. (3 semester hours)

MATH 176. Matrices; determinants, systems of linear equations; permutations and combinations; elementary probability; the derivative with applications to economics; optimization analysis; logarithmic and exponential functions. (3 semester hours)

Calculus I

Lines, circles, functions, limits, continuity, derivatives, curve sketching, and applications of the derivative. (3 semester hours)

Geometry for Elementary Teachers

Topics chosen from informal plane and solid geometry including properties of parallels, perpendiculars, triangles, and circles along with discoveries of many formulas for area of plane regions and volumes of solids. (3 semester hours)

PHYSICAL EDUCATION

Sports Management

An integrated study of traditional and contemporary sport management systems. Philosophies and principles of sport management will be applied to various sport program areas including personnel policies, leadership, facilities, equipment, recordkeeping, finance, legal implications, and program promotion. (3 semester hours)

PSYCHOLOGY

Introduction to Psychology

The aim of this course is to give a general understanding of the basic principles of psychology. (3 semester hours)

Psychology of Sexual Behavior

A study of the physiological and psychological factors involved in normal and abnormal human sexual behavior with emphasis upon marital adjustment. (3 semester hours)

Educational Psychology

Emphasis is given to the study and application of those aspects of psychology which influence the effectiveness of the teaching and learning process. (3 semester hours)

Child Growth and Development

How children grow and develop, the stages in the process, and the factors which influence growth and development are considered. (3 semester hours)

Psychology of Adolescence

The course considers the patterns of "teen-age" growth and development and the factors which influence them. (3 semester hours)

Understanding Human Development

This course follows the development of the individual through the public school years (primarily for students pursuing all-level certification program). (3 semester hours)

RECREATION

School and Community Recreation

This course offers a study of the recent trends in recreation and leisure-time pursuits, the organization and content of programs for school and community recreation programs. (3 semester hours)

SOCIOLOGY

Introduction to Sociology

Overview of major concepts and principles of sociology, including socialization, social control, social order, social stratification, ethnicity, social deviance, and social change. (3 semester hours)

Social Problems

An examination of traditional and persistent social problems such as inequality, social deviance, and mental illness. Consideration of the relationship between social structure and social problems. Special emphasis is placed upon understanding the process by which societal conditions come to be defined as problems. (3 semester hours)

Social Psychology

The study of the importance of others; influence on one's attitudes, perceptions, motivations, and behavior, the dynamic fragility and power of group participation, and the extent to which human potential is enhanced or severely limited in the context of group life. (3 semester hours)

The Family

This course is a general survey course on marriage and family patterns in the United States. Topics covered include family organization, the sociocultural environment surrounding the family, dating and courtship, interpersonal communication, role conflict, dual-career marriages, marital adjustment, family planning, human sexuality, pregnancy, pregnancy and childbirth, money management, divorce, remarriage and alternate family structure. (3 semester hours)

Eastern Kentucky University
Division of Extended Programs
Coats Box 27-A
Richmond, Kentucky 40475-3101
(606) 622-2001

Description:
Eastern Kentucky University is a regional coeducational public institution of higher education offering general and liberal arts programs, preprofessional and professional training in education and various other fields at both the undergraduate and graduate levels. Located in Richmond, Madison County, Kentucky, Eastern has a distinguished record of more than seven decades of educational service to the Commonwealth.

Continuing education had its beginning in 1921 and has developed to include independent study instruction through correspondence courses. Through the Division of Extended Programs a number of regular college and high school correspondence courses are offered as a means of study open to anyone who desires to continue his/her education in this manner. Correspondence courses cover essentially the same material as the same or similar courses offered on campus. Any correspondence course may be taken on a noncredit basis.

Faculty:
Marion Ogden, Director, Division of Extended Programs. Regular University faculty members serve as faculty for the correspondence program.

Academic Levels:
College
High School

Degree/Certificate Programs:
Up to 32 semester hours earned by correspondence may be applied toward the bachelor degree; up to 16 semester hours toward an associate degree.

Admission Requirements:
Open enrollment. The beginning date for a correspondence course coincides with the date of enrollment. A student may enroll for a course at any time during the calendar year.

Tuition:
College courses, $75 per semester hour; contact the university for the current tuition for high school courses. A student may request that a course be cancelled at any time, but no refund will be made on any course after five weeks from date of enrollment. After a course is once begun, no fees or any part of them will be refunded. Within five weeks from the date of enrollment, a student may request to withdraw from a course in which no assignments have been received by the university. A refund of 75 percent of the total instruction will be refunded provided that all assignments and materials have been returned in good condition and the withdrawal has been approved by the Director of Extended Programs.

Enrollment Period:
A course must be completed one year from the date of enrollment. No extension of time will be granted. The minimum time in which a course may be completed is five weeks. No extension time allowed; student may re-enroll for full tuition and have all previous work count toward completion of second enrollment.

Equipment Requirements:
Students may purchase books from their local dealer, from the publisher, or from the Eastern Kentucky University Book Store.

Credit and Grading:
All credits to be transferred-in are evaluated at the time of transfer. Examinations must be proctored. Grades are indicated by letters, to each of which is given a certain value in grade points per semester hour: A, Excellent, 4 grade points; B, Good, 3 grade points; C, Average, 2 grade points; D, Poor, 1 grade point; F, Failure, 0 grade points. A student enrolling in a correspondence course may choose the Pass-Fail option for certain courses providing he has written approval of the Dean of his College. Credit is awarded in semester hour units.

Library Services:
Students must have library identification card or student ID to use the University library facilities.

Accreditations:
Southern Association of Colleges and Schools.

COLLEGE COURSES

BIOLOGY

Economic Plants

Economic consideration of plants as sources of food, medicine, and other byproducts; the origin, domestication, general anatomy, and culture of plants; aspects of aesthetics and effects on society and world events. (3 semester hours)

BUSINESS

Introduction to Business

A survey of the functional areas of business administration. (3 semester hours)

Business Communication

Principles and practices of modern business communication; various types of business letters and reports are studied; emphasis on writing letters and reports. (3 semester hours)

Business and Office Calculations

Development of competency in business computations such as bank and sales records, discounts, commissions, markups, credit charges, payroll, taxes, depreciation, insurance, stocks, bonds, interest, and present value. (3 semester hours)

Legal Environment of Business

Law and the legal system; social forces that make the law; business response to the social and legal environment. Focus on government regulation and federal regulatory agencies which impact business decision making. (3 semester hours)

COMPUTER SCIENCE

Computer Literacy

Nontechnical survey of computer history and hardware; implications of use and misuse of computers; programming in the computer language BASIC; input/output, decision, looping, arrays. Use of an electronic computer with a printout capacity is necessary to complete many of the assignments in this course. (3 semester hours)

Introduction to Computer Information Systems

Introduction to computer hardware, software, and systems; management information systems and the role of the computer in business; spreadsheet, word processing, database, and programming concepts. (3 semester hours)

ECONOMICS

Principles of Economics I

Microeconomics, principles, and their application to the firm. Concepts of demand, supply, pricing, and resource allocation under various competitive conditions. (3 semester hours)

Principles of Economics II

Macroeconomics principles, such as national income; production; employment; the money and banking system; the modern theory of national income; economic growth; inflation; and the problems of economic stabilization. (3 semester hours)

Money and Banking

Functions of money; monetary systems; history of banking; functions of the commercial bank; bank assets and reserves; loans and discounts; bank supervision; the federal reserve system; central banking policies; monetary and fiscal policies (3 semester hours)

ENGLISH

English Composition I

A writing course reviewing sentence basics and methods of paragraph development and emphasizing rhetoric for essays; style, organization, coherence, persuasion in written discourse; extensive practice in composition for different purposes and audiences; study and practice to improve reading and speaking. (3 semester hours)

English Composition II

A writing course reviewing components of English Composition I and refining general composition skills; emphasis on expository and argumentative writing, including researched, documented papers and reports; study of research sources and methods and emphasis on analytical reading. (3 semester hours)

Survey of World Literature I

Selected readings from masterpieces of world literature from ancient times through the Renaissance. (3 semester hours)

Survey of World Literature II

Selected readings from masterpieces of world literature from the seventeenth century to the present. (3 semester hours)

ENVIRONMENTAL HEALTH SCIENCE

Introduction to Environmental Health Sciences

Elements of environmental health, including water and waste treatment, air pollution, food sanitation, vector control, solid waste disposal, and general sanitation problems. (3 semester hours)

Industrial Hygiene

Importance of protecting the work environment. Emphasizes the methods and techniques of maintaining health and safety in industry and agriculture. (3 semester hours)

Environmental and Industrial Toxicology

A study of the extent and significance of toxic agents in man's environment, and the physical, chemical, and biological processes which determine their behavior, fate, and effects on human health. (3 semester hours)

FINANCE

Business Finance

Financial principles and functions with applications to business organizations, including time-value of money, investment, dividend decision, capital structure, models and tools used for financial analysis. (3 semester hours)

GEOGRAPHY

Introduction to Geography

Study of the principles and concepts of sociology, including culture, personality, social structure, group, social processes, and social change. (3 semester hours)

Conservation, Technology, and Environmental Problems

Examination of environmental problems, their relationship to technology and the application of principles of conservation. (3 semester hours)

Economic Geography

Description and analysis of the world primary, secondary, and tertiary economic systems and functions. (3 semester hours)

HEALTH EDUCATION

Safety and First Aid

Accident problems in the home, school, recreation, at work, and on the highways. Lecture and practical instruction in meeting emergencies of all types with emphasis on methods of rescue, breathing, bleeding, poisons, burns, and shock. (2 semester hours)

Personal and Community Health

Study of factors enabling intelligent health decisions as they relate to the physical, mental, and social health of self, family, and community at present as well as the years beyond the college days. (2 semester hours)

HISTORY

American Civilization to 1877

Transition from colonial to independent republic; social, cultural and economic institutions derived from agrarian conditions; the influence of European foundations. (3 semester hours)

American Civilization since 1877

Conflicts between demands of an industrial society and agrarian values; interrelationships between world expressions and American experience. (3 semester hours)

Kentucky History

Social, economic, and political survey; Kentucky's role in national development. (3 semester hours)

INSURANCE

Principles of Risk and Insurance

Theory and practice of insurance and its economic and social significance; basic life, health, and property-liability insurance for businesses and families; review of the major lines of insurance. (3 semester hours)

LAW ENFORCEMENT

Criminal Justice in a Democracy

A general overview of the criminal justice system including a description of the major agencies; police, prosecution, courts, and correction and an analysis of their interdependence in the criminal justice process. (3 semester hours)

Introduction to Corrections

An introduction to the processes, procedures, and issues in modern corrections. Evolution of the various elements of the juvenile and adult corrections systems. (3 semester hours)

Delinquency and the Juvenile Justice System

Examines the meaning and causes of delinquency; focuses on the juvenile justice system with special emphasis on juvenile corrections. (3 semester hours)

MANAGEMENT

Introduction to Management

Introduces management concepts, theories, systems, and functions related to the performance of businesses and other organizations on dynamic environments. (3 semester hours)

Principles of Management

Management principles with emphasis on organization theory, human relations, interpersonal communications, production, business ethics, development of management thought, and managing in the international arena. (3 semester hours)

MARKETING

Introduction to Marketing

Introduces marketing concepts, techniques, and practices related to businesses and other organizations. (3 semester hours)

Marketing

An introduction to the marketing of goods and services in advanced market economics; study of the marketing mix, pricing, distribution, selling, promotional activities, consumer behavior, and marketing research. (3 semester hours)

Advertising

How advertising is organized; economic and social aspects; advertising research; basic media strategy; consumer behavior; using media the effectively; legal and other restraints; careers in advertising. (3 semester hours)

Consumer Behavior in Marketing

Role of consumer decision making as it affects the marketing firm; basic concepts of consumer behavior and interrelationships that exist between marketing and the behavioral sciences. (3 semester hours)

MATHEMATICS

College Algebra

Polynomial, exponential and logarithmic equations, functions and their graphs, roots of polynomial functions, sequences and series, mathematical induction. (3 semester hours)

Trigonometry

Radians and degrees, properties of trigonometric functions, multiple angle expressions, triangle solutions, inverse functions, complex numbers. (3 semester hours)

Mathematical Concepts for Middle and Elementary Teachers I

Concepts stressed over manipulation. Sets and fractions, whole numbers, integers, numeration, elementary number theory, introduction to use of microcomputers. (3 semester hours)

MUSIC

Enjoyment of Music

Provides the general college student with a cultural background in music. Masterpieces of music, composers, and techniques presented through listening materials and concert attendance. (3 semester hours)

PHILOSOPHY

Beginning Philosophy

Basic introductory course in philosophy. Consideration of perennial questions of the human experience, especially questions about reality, knowledge, self, values, and religious belief. (3 semester hours)

POLITICAL SCIENCE

Introduction to American Government

Principles, functions, and basic political institutions of the American system of government at the national level. (3 semester hours)

Kentucky Government and Politics

An overview of the Kentucky political system: major institutions, processes and political leaders, with emphasis on recent events and developments. (3 semester hours)

American State and Local Government

Study of the institutions and processes of government of the fifty states and of cities and counties. (3 semester hours)

PSYCHOLOGY

Psychology as a Social Science

Introduction to concepts in areas of psychology related to the social sciences, such as human development, learning, individual differences, personality development, adjustment, abnormal behavior, psychotherapy, social psychology, and applied psychology. (3 semester hours)

Life Span Developmental Psychology

A survey of theory and research in developmental psychology across the entire life span. (3 semester hours)

Abnormal Psychology

Descriptive study of the nature, course, classification, and prevalence of abnormal behavior, with attention to intellectual, personality, cognitive, sensory and motor functions. (3 semester hours)

REAL ESTATE

Real Estate Principles

Procedures involved in the ownership and transfer of real property; laws governing real estate transactions. (3 semester hours)

Real Estate Law

Businessman's point of view of real estate instruments, property rights and liabilities, estates, and interest and liens. (3 semester hours)

Real Estate Finance

Sources of funds for financing real estate transactions and financial instruments that are used and problems encountered in financing real property. (3 semester hours)

Real Estate Marketing

Factors in marketing residential, business, industrial, and farm property, such as listing, prospecting, advertising, showing, determining the needs of the client, qualifying clients, and closing the sale. (3 semester hours)

RELIGIOUS STUDIES

World Religions

Study of the basic notions found in the world's great religions. Attention is given to the historical context of the development of these religions and to the doctrines, rituals, and literature produced by them. (3 semester hours)

SCIENCE

History of Science

The development of scientific concepts through the ages; contribution of science to civilization; philosophy of science; biographical sketches. (3 semester hours)

SECURITY/SAFETY TECHNOLOGY

Introduction to Security

The role of security, its applications, and the security individual in modern society including an overview of the administrative, personnel, and physical aspects of the security field. (3 hours)

Legal Aspects of Fire Loss Prevention Services

A study and examination of criminal and civil law as applied to private security functions and practices. Emphasizes the legal responsibilities, liabilities, and authority of private security personnel. (3 semester hours)

Alcohol and Other Drugs—Traffic Crashes and Enforcement

An extensive investigation into traffic-related areas of alcohol and other drugs, their origin, development, use and misuse, and the many complexities that have developed as a direct or indirect result of their abuse in our society. (3 semester hours)

Current Developments in Driver and Traffic Safety

Current problems, issues, trends, and developments in traffic safety are reviewed, analyzed, and evaluated. (3 semester hours)

SOCIAL SCIENCE

Preindustrial World Civilizations

Analyzes the culture pattern of agrarian civilizations by examining societies in India, China, the Middle East, and Europe. Explores why industrialism developed first in Europe. (3 semester hours)

Industrialism in World Civilization

Investigates the Industrial Revolution and its spread in the nineteenth century. Analyzes the pattern of industrialism in the 20th century and the emerging global crisis. (3 semester hours)

SOCIOLOGY

Introductory Sociology

Basic principles and concepts of sociology, including culture, personality, social structure, group, social processes, and social change. (3 semester hours)

Sociology of the Family

Family as an institution in society; its relation to cultural transmission and personality development; its relation to wider institutional structure of society. (3 semester hours)

HIGH SCHOOL COURSES

CIVICS

Civics

This course is designed to help students learn basic knowledge and skills needed to become competent citizens. (½ unit)

ECONOMICS

Economics

This course explores the economic world with emphasis on application of principles to the solution of practical problems. Personal, national, and international aspects of economics will be studied. (½ unit)

ENGLISH

English Grammar

ENG 11. This course consists of twenty assignments in grammar and usage; parts of speech, syntax, sentence recognition and analysis, punctuation skills, and word building; spelling, using the dictionary; practicing in outlining, writing thesis sentences and developing paragraphs and short themes, with emphasis upon organization, content, and application of rules and grammar. (½ unit)

ENG 12. This course consists of twenty assignments in grammar and usage; review of parts of speech, syntax, sentence structure, and punctuation skills; word study and spelling; using the dictionary; practice in outlining, writing thesis sentences, and in developing long themes, with emphasis on organization, content, and careful proofreading. (½ unit)

American Literature

ENG 11A. This course consists of twenty assignments based on the growth of American literature—seventeenth through nineteenth centuries. (½ unit)

ENG 11B. A continuation of the above course. (½ unit)

British Literature

ENG 12A. This course consists if twenty assignments based on the Anglo-Saxon period, the Medieval Period, the Elizabethan Age, the seventeenth- and eighteenth-century literature. (½ unit)

ENG 12B. A continuation of the above course. Consists of twenty assignments based on a study of the Romantic Age, the Victorian Age, and the Modern Age of literature. (½ unit)

GEOGRAPHY

World Geography

10A. World problems treated geographically; geography in the modern world; the air age; relationship to earth and man, man and climate; man and the surface of the lands; man and natural resources. (½ unit)

10B. Life processes of civilization; manufacture and trade; transportation and communication; the geography of nations; nature of nations; British Empire; nations of the European Peninsula; the Soviet Union; nations of the Far East; and South American Republics; the United States and its neighbors. (½ unit)

GOVERNMENT

Government

The origin and development of the federal system of government; the organization and functions of the various departments; political rights and practice; relation of federal to state and local government; the organization and functions of state and local government; relation of state and local government of society through democracy. (½ unit)

HEALTH

Personal and Community Health Education

This course is designed to promote intelligent self-direction through interpretation of scientific information affecting health habits, attitudes, and knowledge. Emphasis is placed on personal and community health education. (½ unit)

HISTORY

World History

10A. This course explores the history of the world from its prehistoric origins through the development of Western European expansion and colonization in the early modern period. (½ unit)

10B. This course continues the study of world history with emphasis on the major political, economic, social, and technological developments in the era from the early eighteenth century to the modern world crisis. (½ unit)

American History

11A. This course traces the history of the United States from its colonial origins through the Civil War and Reconstruction with emphasis on major social, economic, and political changes. (½ unit)

11B. The course continues the study of American history, tracing the development of the United States as a world power through the late twentieth century. (½ unit)

SOCIOLOGY

Sociology

The social world—its nature, its processes, its part in making our personality; the principles, institutions and laws of the social world; its problems and maladjustments; prospects for intelligent reform for directing change toward progress. (½ unit)

Eastern Michigan University
Independent Study Office
Division of Continuing Education
327 Goodison Hall
Ypsilanti, Michigan 48197   (313) 487-1081

Description:
Eastern Michigan University is a multipurpose university whose roots date back to 1849 when the Michigan State Legislature designated it as its first institution to educate teachers to serve the public schools. It achieved university status in 1959.

Correspondence courses for university credit are available through the Division of Continuing Education. This distance learning program enables students to acquire knowledge and earn college credit at their own pace. Courses are not tied to semesters; students may enroll any time.

Faculty:
Michael J. McPhillips, Director, Independent Study.

Academic Levels:
College
Noncredit

Degree/Certificate Programs:
Up to 15 semester hours of credit earned through correspondence may be applied toward an undergraduate degree and 4 hours toward a graduate degree.

Admission Requirements:
Students must be officially admitted to Eastern Michigan University before enrolling for Independent Study coursework. Students should plan for one or more meetings on campus with the assigned instructor. Enrollment on a noncredit basis for any course is accepted.

Tuition:
$215 per course, payable in full at the time of enrollment. If a course is taken on a noncredit basis, 25 percent discount and the student is not required to sit for exam. Fee includes tuition, coursepacks, and University postage. If a student withdraws from a course within 3 days, 100 percent of tuition is refunded; if withdrawal is made 3 to 45 days after registration, 30 percent of tuition shall be refunded.

Enrollment Period:
Courses should be completed within 6 months from the date of enrollment; the minimum time to complete a course is 6 weeks. A six-month extension may be granted upon payment of a $10 fee.

Credit and Grading:
Credit is awarded in semester hour units. Examinations must be proctored.

Accreditations:
North Central Association of Colleges and Schools. Member of: National University Continuing Education Association.

COLLEGE COURSES

ENGLISH

Expository Writing

This course concentrates upon the writing of various types of essays with emphasis on improvement of style. (3 semester hours)

Modern English Grammar

An introduction to the syntax of modern English. Students will review traditional grammar and study descriptive and transformational grammar. (3 semester hours)

The History of the English Language

A study of the development of the language from its earliest stages to the present with attention to social influences as well as matters of sound, word formation, and sentence structure. (3 semester hours)

HISTORY

United States History to 1877

A study of United States history from the period of exploration through the Reconstruction of the South following the Civil War. (3 semester hours)

United History 1877-Present

A study of United States history from the end of Reconstruction to the present. (3 semester hours)

LITERATURE

The Reading of Literature

An introduction to the techniques of critical reading with equal emphasis on prose fiction, poetry, and drama. Development of a fundamental understanding and enjoyment of reading. (3 semester hours)

Introduction to Children's Literature

A concentrated reading course designed to impart the knowledge necessary for an appreciation and understanding of children's literature and its use in the schools. In addition to reading the classics and the critically acclaimed works of both fiction and nonfiction by modern writers, students will study poetry, folklore and mythology and examine the relationship between illustration and text. (3 semester hours)

MANAGEMENT

Basic Supervision

A study of basic supervision and practical techniques of leadership for those aspiring to management positions or recently appointed to first-line management. Includes theory plus case studies which will assist supervisors in human relations problems. (3 semester hours)

Business Communication

Study of principles, elements and practices underlying administrative communication. Particular attention is given to the thinking and creative processes involved in problem solving. Emphasis on the psychology, planning, and transmittal of business information. (3 semester hours)

MATHEMATICS

Intermediate Algebra

This course is a review of elementary algebra and a continuation into the study of functions, graphs, and quadratic equations. (3 semester hours)

REAL ESTATE

Real Estate Principles and Practices

A survey of real estate law, finance, appraising, brokerage and investments, including ownership interests, contracts, and open housing laws. (3 semester hours)

SOCIOLOGY

Introductory Sociology

Basic sociological concepts are used to analyze aspects of American society in intergroup relations, rural and urban communities, social classes and in family, educational, religious, governmental, and economic institutions. (3 semester hours)

TECHNOLOGY

Understanding Technology

A course to develop basic technological literacy by providing an introduction to technological concepts and problems, and to the technology of literature. Students will become familiar with several concrete technological systems and their dynamics, particularly as they relate to society. (3 semester hours)

Eastern Oregon State College
Continuing Education
8th and K Avenue
LaGrande, Oregon 97850 (503) 963-1381

Description:
Correspondence courses offered by Eastern Oregon State College are administered by the Office of Independent Study of the Oregon State System of Higher Education in Portland, Oregon. For courses available, SEE **Oregon State System of Higher Education.**

Faculty:
Dixie Lund, Director.

Accreditations:
Northwest Association of Schools and Colleges.

Eastern Washington University
Office of Continuing Education
Mail Stop 162
526 5th Street
Cheney, Washington 99004-431

(509) 359-2268

Description:
From a single schoolhouse in a pioneer town to 50 major buildings on a 350-acre campus, Eastern Washington University had grown to complete 113 years of service to the region in 1995. As educational needs changed, Eastern Washington University changed - from Cheney Academy to Cheney Normal (specializing in training teachers) to College of Education (four-year degree programs) to State College (diversified undergraduate degrees) to University (full-services, including extended programs and graduate

degree programs). EWU's courses are prepared and taught by regular members of the staff who are in charge of similar courses in residence. Instruction by correspondence is continuous throughout the year and students may begin at any time.

Faculty:

Richard E. Christenson, Assistant Director of Continuing Education; Jody L. Tait, Coordinator. The teaching staff numbers 17.

Academic Levels:

College

Degree/Certificate Programs:

A total of 45 credits earned in extension and/or correspondence courses may be counted toward the baccalaureate degree at EWU. A total of 5 correspondence credits may be counted toward the fifth year of teacher training. Correspondence credits may not be applied toward a master's degree.

Admission Requirements:

A high school graduate or any person over 18 years of age who is not currently attending high school may register for a correspondence course at any time. A student in residence at EWU must receive permission from his/her academic counselor before enrolling in a correspondence course. Teachers planning on using correspondence courses for pay increments or fifth year advancements should first check with their school districts to make sure correspondence courses are accepted in that particular district.

Tuition:

$70 per quarter hour credit. Fee must accompany the application. VISA or MasterCard acceptable. Withdrawal from a course within two weeks of enrollment will be refunded in full minus a $10 fee. Withdrawal within four weeks, one-half the tuition, minus a $10 fee. No withdrawals or refunds will be granted after four weeks from date of enrollment.

Enrollment Period:

Minimum time to complete a course is one month; maximum time is one year. A six-month extension may be granted at the discretion of the Director for a fee of $25. Only one extension is allowed.

Equipment Requirements:

Students are responsible for securing textbooks; books may be purchased locally or through the EWU Bookstore. Typewritten lessons preferred.

Credit and Grading:

Grading is by numeric system which is figured into the student's grade point average. Minimum passing grade is 1.3–0.7 (D). Examinations must be proctored by a University approved principal or superintendent. Some courses have no exams. Credit is awarded in quarter hour units.

Library Services:

Correspondence students may use the campus library by arrangement.

Accreditations:

Northwest Association of Schools and Colleges.

COLLEGE COURSES

ART

Basic Design

The exploration of analytical design problems, investigating elements in two dimensional space. (5 quarter hours)

Beginning Drawing

An introduction to fundamentals of drawing and figure construction. Students use a variety of media. (5 quarter hours)

AFRICAN AMERICAN STUDIES

Introduction to Black Culture

An interdisciplinary survey of black culture beginning with ancient African history and traditions through contemporary issues in the African American experience. Attention given to basic principles of history, sociology, political science, economics, and the arts in the study of the dynamics of black culture. (5 quarter hours)

BUSINESS

Accounting Principles I

This course is designed to introduce students to the concepts embodied and the techniques utilized in accumulating, classifying, and summarizing financial information in business firms for the purpose of reporting such information to interested users. (5 quarter hours)

Accounting Principles II

This course is designed to introduce students to the underlying principles of managerial accounting, the application of such data to managerial decisions and accounting problems associated with differing forms of business organization. (5 quarter hours)

EDUCATION

Puppets (Design and Production)

Students will research all types of hand-made puppets and will then design and produce several types of puppets that will be used for teaching and learning enrichment activities in their classroom. (3 quarter hours)

Production of Instructional Games

Students will evaluate handmade games and design and produce instructional games and learning activity materials that will be used in their teaching areas and grade levels for teaching/learning enrichment programs. (3 quarter hours)

Production of Three Dimensional Instructional Materials

The student will evaluate numerous three-dimensional teaching and learning materials such as: models, mock-ups, dioramas, relief maps, globes, mobiles, puppets, study kits, learning centers, displays, games, etc. The student will then design and produce selected 3-D materials that will be utilized as techniques to enrich the teaching-learning environment in their classroom. (3 quarter hours)

Writing Learning Activity Packets

The student develops a comprehensive learning activity package which is a self-teaching system for a selected subject area and grade level. (3 quarter hours)

Lettering Techniques and Basic Calligraphy

The content of this course is designed for instructors in all fields of work and for librarians and teachers in all grade levels who desire to produce lettered instructional materials and messages that are readable and that look professional. Over thirty varied lettering techniques are introduced and practiced. This course also presents an introduction to basic calligraphy: techniques, styles, patterns and practice exercises. (3 quarter hours)

Learning Centers (Design and Production)

Students will evaluate numerous learning centers. They will then design and construct learning centers for use in their teaching areas and grade levels for teaching/learning enrichment programs. They will also write plans for the materials they produce for use in their learning centers. The materials produced should be based upon school curriculum, strategies, objectives and the needs of their students. (3 quarter hours)

Bulletin Boards

This course is designed for instructors in all fields of work and for teachers in all grade levels who desire to produce professional-looking display materials and creative display and presentation boards for instruction. (3 quarter hours)

ENGLISH

Introduction to Literature

An examination of the human experience—people thinking, feeling, acting—as revealed and interpreted in literature, including short fiction, poetry, and drama. Attention will be given to the elements that make up literature, with principal emphasis on ideas, attitudes, problems, and values. (5 quarter hours)

Creative Writing

Designed to introduce students to the techniques and forms of imaginative writing. (5 quarter hours)

Literature of the Bible

The cultural and historical background of the Bible and the Christian movement and a study of selected books of the Old and New Testament as literature. (5 quarter hours)

American Literature to Whitman

The literature of America from colonial times to the Civil War. (5 quarter hours)

American Literature: Twain to Dreiser

The literature of America from the Civil War to the present time. (5 quarter hours)

Twentieth Century American Literature

Chief figures, works and trends in the literature of the United States since World War I. (5 quarter hours)

GOVERNMENT

Modern Government in American Context

A general introduction to the concepts, methods, and concerns involved in the study of government. The course discusses fundamental ideas such as power, ideology, and constitutionalism; the citizen in democratic politics; the structure and processes of major governmental institutions; and selected areas of policy-making. Emphasis on the comparison of the American political system with that of other, chiefly democratic, systems. (5 quarter hours)

HISTORY

The American Experience: A Survey

A broad survey of unique features of American experience, this course examines the origins and development of the American social, economic, and political heritage on the domestic and international scenes. (5 quarter credits)

History and Government of the Pacific Northwest

This course is designed to acquaint the student with the history of the Pacific Northwest and will cover three main themes: (1) the nature of Northwest regionalism, (2) the settlement of the Northwest as part of the larger westward movement, and (3) the history of the Northwest as a case study in American history. (5 quarter hours)

HUMANITIES

Great World Views

An analysis of selected writings from the viewpoint of what is said about human nature, the scheme of things, and man's place in that scheme. (5 quarter hours)

MARKETING EDUCATION

Methods of Teaching Marketing Education or Diversified Occupations

Prepares prospective teacher-coordinators for effective classroom teaching. The course includes creative projects and effective problem-solving. (4 quarter hours)

MATHEMATICS

Finite Mathematics

An introduction to the mathematical systems encountered in the study of the behavioral sciences. A study of matrices, linear systems, linear programming, set theory, and probability. (5 quarter hours)

PHYSICAL EDUCATION

Sport Psychology (American Coaching Effectiveness Program—Level II)

Presents information on motivation, communication, stress management, the use of mental imagery, and other topics for enhancing coaching-athlete relationships and for stimulating improved sport performances. (3 quarter hours)

Time Management (American Coaching Effectiveness Program (Level II)

Students will learn how to fight the battle of balancing a coaching schedule with a personal life and a full-time job. Causes of disorganized programs are analyzed and valuable solutions are offered. (3 quarter hours)

PSYCHOLOGY

General Psychology

A general introduction to psychology as the scientific study of behavior and thought: an overview of the areas of psychology and their development; methods in psychology; biological, sensory, and developmental influences on behavior; physiological and cognitive components of behavior; theories of learning; a survey of theories of normal and abnormal behavior; principles of psychotherapy; personality theory and testing; and social influences. (5 quarter hours)

Abnormal Psychology

This course explores and evaluates research and theoretical concepts relating to deviant and abnormal behavior. (5 quarter hours)

Social Psychology

Individual behavior as socially determined: interpersonal attraction, aggressiveness, attitude formation, group dynamics, conformity, and leadership. (5 quarter hours)

VOCATIONAL EDUCATION

Organization and Administration of Cooperative Programs

Operational procedures for conducting cooperative programs; includes the development of directed-work training, state requirements, and program organization and administration. (3 quarter hours)

Occupational Analysis

This course involves a study of using various analysis techniques in securing, analyzing, and converting the data into curriculum content for a program or course. The past development and the present status of analysis techniques are studied with particular emphasis on task analysis. Identification, inventory, classification, and validation of the analysis are discussed. (4 quarter hours)

Philosophy of Vocational Education

Relationship of vocational, career, and occupational education to general education and philosophy; concept of work, effect of Industrial Revolution; man's quest for dignity and work in a democratic and technological society. (4 quarter hours)

WOMEN'S STUDIES

Women in American History

Brings to life and surveys the accomplishments of the "lost women" of the past from colonial times to the present. Society's definition of the nature of women and their proper roles will be examined, as well as the actual life conditions of women and the social and economic functions they performed. (4 quarter hours)

Elizabeth City State University
Parkview Drive
Elizabeth City, North Carolina 27909
(919) 335-3305

Description:

Elizabeth City State University was established in 1891 as a normal school and became a four-year institution in 1937. It is a participant in a consortium of eight institutions within the University of North Carolina System offering college-level correspondence courses and other opportunities for individualized study at a distance from the university campuses. In the consortium arrangement, each institution originating a course provides instruction and awards academic credit, while responsibility for administration of the program lies with the office of Independent Studies at the University of North Carolina at Chapel Hill. SEE **North Carolina, University of - Chapel Hill.**

Faculty:

Dan Pearce, Member of UNC Independent Studies Advisory Committee.

Accreditations:

Southern Association of Colleges and Schools.

Embry-Riddle Aeronautical University
Department of Independent Studies
College of Continuing Education
600 South Clyde Morris Boulevard
Daytona Beach, Florida 32114 (904) 239-6397

Description:

Embry-Riddle Aeronautical University is the world's largest and oldest totally aviation-oriented, accredited university. A private, independent, coeducational institution founded in 1926, Embry-Riddle has an enrollment of about 13,000 full-time and part-time students. In addition to its traditional residential campuses in Daytona Beach, Florida, and Prescott, Arizona, Embry-Riddle serves the continuing education needs of the aviation industry through an extensive network of off-campus centers in the U.S. and Europe.

The Department of Independent Studies was inaugurated in 1980 and provides aviation professionals the opportunity to receive college credit in recognition of their aviation training and experience and complete an accredited aviation-oriented bachelor of science degree through independent study in the privacy of their own homes. On-campus classroom time is not required. Over 1,600 aviation professionals are currently pursuing degree requirements through the program. Over 500 students have completed degree requirements and graduated since 1983.

Faculty:

Thomas W. Pettit, Director, Department of Independent Studies. There is a faculty of 20 members plus 20 subject specialists and 5 counselors.

Academic Levels:
College

Degree/Certificate Programs:

Associate of Science in Professional Aeronautics; Bachelor of Science in Professional Aeronautics; Bachelor of Science in Aviation Business Administration.

Admission Requirements:

Applicants for the Associate or Bachelor of Science in Professional Aeronautics must have previous training and experience in an approved aviation specialty. College credits are granted for prior learning from previous aviation experience and training. Applicants for the Bachelor of Science in Aviation Business Administration are only required to meet the University's general admission requirements. Applicants may have credits from other educational institutions evaluated for transfer toward their Embry-Riddle curriculum requirements.

Tuition:

$140 per semester credit hour; shipping costs $6 (U.S.), $15 (Canada), $55 (overseas civilian address). Application fee $15. Guaranteed Student Loans (GSL) and Pell Grants are available for eligible independent study students. Full tuition refund if student withdraws from course during the first week of established term. No refund for withdrawal after the first week. Application fee is nonrefundable.

Degree-seeking students enrolled through the Department of Independent Studies who are eligible for Veterans Administration educational benefits may apply for such benefits. Active duty military personnel, National Guard, and Active Reserve personnel may apply for financial assistance through DANTES.

Enrollment Period:

Students have up to fifteen weeks to complete a course and final examination. Upon successful completion of the final examination, the student may immediately enroll in the next course. If the course cannot be completed within the specified fifteen-weeks, a five-week extension for a fee of $25 may be requested in writing no later than two weeks prior to the established term ending date. There is no limit to the number of correspondence credits, transfer credit, or advanced standing credit applied to a degree. All associate degree students must complete 15 semester hours of Embry-Riddle coursework. Bachelor degree students must complete 30 semester hours of coursework through Embry-Riddle.

Equipment Requirements:

The tuition fee includes course study guides and audiocassette tapes. Videotapes may be rented for $20 per course for those courses incorporating videotapes. Textbook charges vary depending upon the course.

Credit and Grading:

Letter grades are used. If the student does not complete a course within the prescribed term dates and has not requested and received an approved incomplete period, a grade of ''F'' will be issued one week after the term ending date. If the student has requested and received an approved extension, a grade of ''I'' (Incomplete) will be assigned. Credit is awarded in semester hours.

Accreditations:

Southern Association of Colleges and Schools. Member of: National University Continuing Education Association.

COLLEGE COURSES

AERONAUTICS

Professional Aeronautics

The following courses of the professional aeronautics curriculum are currently available. Because new courses are added and other changes may occur, contact the University for current availability.

History and Regulation of Aviation. (3 semester hours)

Basic Aerodynamics. (3 semester hours)

Airport Development and Operations. (3 semester hours)

Aviation Law. (3 semester hours)

Introduction to Computers in Aviation. (3 semester hours)

Microeconomics. (3 semester hours)

Macroeconomics. (3 semester hours)

English Composition and Literature I. (3 semester hours)

Technical Report Writing. (3 semester hours)

Introduction to Logic. (3 semester hours)

College Mathematics for Aviation I. (3 semester hours)

Statistics with Aviation Applications. (3 semester hours)

Accounting I. (3 semester hours)

Principles of Management. (3 semester hours)

Business Information Systems. (3 semester hours)

Aviation Insurance. (3 semester hours)

Analysis Methods for Management. (3 semester hours)

Management Planning and Control. (3 semester hours)

Explorations in Physics. (3 semester hours)

Emmaus Bible College
Emmaus Correspondence School
2570 Asbury Road
Dubuque, Iowa 52001-3009   (319) 588-8000

Description:

Emmaus Bible College and the Emmaus Correspondence School were founded in 1941–42 in Toronto, Ontario, Canada. For more than 40 years they have distributed self-study Bible courses throughout the world. Courses are printed in 101 languages and are presently being distributed in over 100 countries, allowing Emmaus to speak the language of 80 percent of the world's population. Presently, there is a growing penal ministry in institutions of North America and there is also a domestic ministry. An average of more than 1,400 courses distributed to students every day, or one course per minute, makes Emmaus one of the largest correspondence schools in the world.

Faculty:

Charles Fizer, Director; Darlene Fizer, Registrar.

Academic Levels:

College
Noncredit
Elementary

Degree/Certificate Programs:

Credit Certificates are issued for each course the student completes with an average grade of 70 percent or higher. Multiple Credit Certificates are awarded in successive 12 credit increments up to the 72-credit level of achievement. Children's Series Certificates are awarded upon completion of all of the children's courses.

Admission Requirements:

Anyone interested may order courses directly from Emmaus. There are no requirements for admission other than receiving and sending the first examination. Students outside the United States should contact a Regional Director of Emmaus Bible College in their respective countries.

Tuition:

None, other than grading fee for college-level courses. Other course cost varies, depending upon course. Contact the Emmaus Correspondence School for current information.

Enrollment Period:
A maximum of one year is allowed to complete a course.

Equipment Requirements:
Cassette lectures are currently available for some courses and can be ordered at the option of the student. Cassette players must be supplied by the student. Students must purchase

Credit and Grading:
All grades are in percentages. 70 percent and above is passing; 90 percent and above is ''With Honor''; 95 percent and above is ''With Distinction''. Minimum passing grade is 70 percent. Credits are awarded in credit hours. Correspondence course credits indicate the relative difficulty of each course in the Emmaus curriculum and are not intended to indicate equivalency of college-level instruction or transferability of credit to the resident programs of Emmaus Bible School or any other school. Students desiring to transfer Emmaus credits should contact the school to which they seek transfer and determine the eligibility/acceptance of Emmaus credits. Emmaus does not award degrees by correspondence study.

Library Services:
Various booklets and tracts plus other informational pieces are sent to the student.

Accreditations:
American Association of Bible Colleges.

COLLEGE COURSES

BIBLE

The Woman Who Pleases God

An advanced course emphasizing the importance of practical Christian living for women in and outside the home. (5 credits)

Faith on Trial

This course provides an in-depth study of the book of James. (5 credits)

NONCREDIT COURSES

BIBLE

Bible Prophecy Study

Bible Prophecy. This introductory study helps in understanding the order of future events. By showing the distinctive positions held by Israel, the Church, and the nations, God's prophetic plan is made clear. (1 certificate credit)

Messianic Psalms. The psalms that speak of the Lord Jesus Christ as Messiah, are among the most precious to the believer because they were used by Him to reveal His inner-most thoughts at the time of His passion. (1 certificate credit)

Minor Prophets. The minor prophets are little known and understood. These men of God spoke out about the issues of their day and at the same time gave prophecies that will be fulfilled in the Millenial Kingdom. This course will give you an excellent overview of these prophecies. (2 certificate credits)

Christian Life Study

Lessons for Christian Living. The most commonly asked questions by young believers are answered in this simple introductory study. Includes practical instruction on baptism, church membership, and guidance. (1 certificate credit)

Guide to Christian Growth. This simple course covers such topics as worship, scripture memorization, good works, the quiet time, and the fruit of the Spirit. (1 certificate credit)

I'll Take the High Road. This course is designed to mark out some of the early milestones along the Christian life. (1 certificate credit)

Plant My Feet on Higher Ground. A practical study on living a victorius Christian life. The student is taught the vital issues relevant to Biblical Christianity. (2 certificate credits)

Summary of the Bible. The contents of each book and its historical background are studied. (1 certificate credit)

Personal Evangelism. Young believers are taught basic principles in the important matter of winning others for the Lord Jesus Christ. (1 certificate credit)

God's Blueprint for Your Marriage. This course deals with the biblical foundation of marriage, roles of husband and wife, training of children, and other issues of practical help. (2 certificate credits)

The Woman Who Pleases God. Believers will want to study this course for its important and practical emphasis on Christian living for women in the home, the church, the secular world, and the mission field. (1 certificate credit)

Children's Study

Golden Keys. Lessons on the Bible giving a clear picture of salvation. Ages 8–11. (½ certificate credit)

Tell Me the Story of Jesus. A study of the life of the Lord Jesus in narrative style. Ages 8–11. (½ certificate credit)

Things Jesus Said and Did. Some of the miracles and parables of Jesus. Ages 10–11. (½ certificate credit)

Remember Thy Creator. A brief survey of the first book in the Bible. Ages 9-11. (½ certificate credit)

The Bible Tells Me So. A question and answer approach to Bible study. Teaches many key salvation verses. Ages 11–12. (½ certificate credit)

A Journey Through the Bible. A study of God's ways with men from the very beginning of time. Ages 12 and up. (½ certificate credit)

Doctrinal Study

Perfect Person Perfect Work. This comprehensive study of Christ's person and work covers His deity and humanity in detail. It takes you from His pre-incarnation to His exalted place as Lord of all in a coming day. (2 certificate credits)

Basic Bible Doctrines. This course guides the student through a topical study of the major teachings or ''doctrines'' of the scripture. (2 certificate credits)

Holy Spirit at Work. This study expounds the Person and Work of the Spirit of God in the world, the Church, and the individual believer. (1 certificate credit)

Rightly Dividing the Word is Truth. How many judgments does the Bible describe? What is the difference between the Jew, the Gentile, and the Church of God? What are the two natures of the believer? These and other practical questions are answered in this course which embodies Dr. Scofield's book of the same title adapting it to correspondence study. (1 certificate credit)

Thy Word is Truth. The basis of all belief for the child of God is the great fact of the verbal inspiration of the Bible. This important doctrine is defended in this course with clarity and warmth. (1 certificate credit)

Buried by Baptism. Every New Testament reference to baptism is studied. Includes topics such as baptismal regeneration, infant baptism, and baptism of the Holy Spirit in addition to the main theme of believer's baptism. (½ certificate credit)

The Lord's Supper. This course teaches the student obedience to the Lord's command "This do in remembrance of Me." (½ certificate credit)

Christ Loved the Church. The major themes of the New Testament Church are presented in a simple and concise manner. The Universal Church is considered in addition to "The Local Church." (1 certificate credit)

New Testament Book Study

Gospel of Matthew. Matthew gathers together those facts in the life and ministry of Jesus Christ which emphasize that He is both King and Messiah of Israel. (1 certificate credit)

Gospel of Mark. Mark emphasizes "Christ came not to be served, but to serve and to give His life a ransom for many." (1 certificate credit)

Gospel of Luke. Luke portrays the humanity of Christ. Content rather than chronology seems to be important to him. (1 certificate credit)

Gospel of John. This verse-by-verse exposition of John's Gospel is ideal for those who are seeking the way of salvation or for young Christians. (2 certificate credits)

Book of Acts. This simple course shows the amazing spread of the gospel and the dynamic witness of first century Christians. (1 certificate credit)

Epistle to the Romans. Deals with issues of sin and personal growth. (1 certificate credit)

First Corinthians. A verse-by-verse exposition subtitled "The Church and Its Charter," dealing with instruction for the local church and individual believers. (1 certificate credit)

Second Corinthians. This course, in a verse-by-verse exposition, affords a close look at "The Servant and His Service." A description of Paul's ministry and an account of his own defense of his apostleship. (1 certificate credit)

Galatians. The Epistle to the Galatians is Paul's strong rebuke of the spiritually deadening error of legalism. (1 certificate credit)

Ephesians. The wonderful place of the body of Christ, the Church, in God's counsels is given in this epistle more than in any other. (1 certificate credit)

Philippians, Colossians, and Philemon. A meaningful exposition of three of Paul's epistles from prison—Philippians, his letter of warmth, Colossians, his letter of glory, and Philemon, his letter of forgiveness. (1 certificate credit)

Thessalonian Epistles. A timely course for a day when the truth of Christ's coming again is openly denied. (2 certificate credits)

Timothy and Titus. Paul is writing in these letters to Timothy and Titus on the subject of the shepherd care of individuals and local churches. (1 certificate credit)

Epistle of James. James argues that faith must be seen, as he proceeds to unmask cheap imitation and to highlight the genuine. (1 certificate credit)

Epistles of John. The believer's responsibilities and privileges in the heavenly family are set forth uncompromisingly in these epistles. (½ certificate credit)

Revelation. Subtitled "Visions of Judgment and Glory," this is an introductory study of the "things which are and the things which shall be." (1 certificate credit)

Salvation Study

Born to Win. This twelve lesson salvation course has been specifically developed for North American prisoners in their own "language." (1 certificate credit)

Doing Time with Jesus. Designed as a follow-up to the above study, this course helps new converts face the problems unique to living the Christian life in prison. (1 certificate credit)

God is There. God is a personal being interested in every human being. He is not an impersonal influence or power. He loves all men and wants them to have a right relationship with Himself. (1 certificate credit)

Men Who Met The Master. This study deals with six men who had contact with the Lord Jesus in the events connected with His death and shows their reactions when they meet the Master. (½ certificate credit)

One God, One Way. A clear presentation of God's only way of salvation as found in Jesus Christ. With brief studies of the prophets Noah, Abraham, Moses, and David, the course leads up to a presentation of Jesus Christ fulfilling prophecy in His death for our sins. Especially designed for Muslims. (1 certificate credit)

The Greatest Man Alive. This course is designed to help you discover who He is, what He did, and how you can meet Him. (½ certificate credit)

What the Bible Teaches. While the primary purpose of this course is the simple presentation of the gospel, it also presents a valuable systematic outline on such subjects as the Bible, God, Man, Sin, Christ, Salvation, Heaven and Hell. (1 certificate credit)

The Word of God. Twelve simple lessons on the Gospel of John. Can be readily adaptable for use with children. (½ certificate credit)

The Servant of God. Twelve simple lessons on the Gospel of Mark. Readily adaptable for use with children. (½ certificate credit)

Teacher Training Study

How to Understand People. These lessons trace the child's development from infancy through the various stages of childhood and adolescence to maturity. (1 certificate credit)

How to Teach. This course is for anyone involved in teaching the Word of God in Sunday School, Bible Class, Daily Vacation Bible School, etc. (3 certificate credits)

Essential English. A good grasp of English opens doors of opportunity in every field—in high school and college, in business, and, most importantly, in telling others what the Lord Jesus can do for them. (3 certificate credits)

Intermediate Study

Old Testament Survey—Law and History. Learn how the Old Testament fits together. Trace Bible history from the earth's earliest ages to the end of the Babylonian captivity. (2 certificate credits)

Old Testament Survey—Poetry and Prophecy. Learn the principles which govern the poetic books; Job through Song of Solomon. Grasp the significance of Bible prophecy, its relation to times past, present, and future. (2 certificate credits)

New Testament Survey. Learn backgrounds, message and significance of New Testament books. Get a vital preview of the Gospels, Acts, Epistles, and Revelation. (2 certificate credits)

Preach the Word. This course will help you master the techniques of opening up a passage of Scripture. You will learn the basic principles of Bible interpretation. You will study ways of gathering message material, putting it together in a logical manner and presenting it with conviction and power. (3 certificate credits)

Exploring Song of Solomon. A course on the little-studied poetical book from the Old Testament. A typological approach guiding the student to fresh insights on the Person and Work of Christ. (2 certificate credits)

Empire State College
Center for Distance Learning
State University of New York
One Union Avenue
Saratoga Springs, New York 12866-4390
(518) 587-2100

Description:

Empire State College was founded as part of the State University of New York in 1971 as a nontraditional college to award associate and baccalaureate degrees to students who are prohibited by employment or personal restrictions on their time from attending a traditional "classroom" college. Thus, Empire State College serves primarily working adults. The college has no campus in the traditional sense. Its Center for Distance Learning, established in February 1979, offers adults a college program which requires no classroom attendance. Degrees from the Center are fully accredited by the State University of New York. Students may also enroll as a nonmatriculated student for a single course or for several courses.

The areas of concentration offered are Business, Community and Human Services, Fire Service Administration, Interdisciplinary Studies, and Liberal Studies. The Bachelor degree in Fire Service Administration is available to residents of New York, Rhode Island, Pennsylvania, Connecticut, Maine, and eastern Canada.

The Center for Distance Learning has three 15-week terms beginning in January, May, and September. Students may earn up to 16 credits per term. In addition to the regularly scheduled terms, a number of courses are available throughout the year. They are called Open Learning Courses and begin on the first of the month. The courses described below are representative of those offered. It is essential that prospective students contact the college for information regarding courses scheduled for a particular term or year.

Faculty:

Dr. Daniel Granger, Director, Center for Distance Learning; Margaret Craft, Assistant Director.

Academic Levels:
College

Degree/Certificate Programs:
Bachelor, Associate.

Admission Requirements:
High school diploma or equivalent, or proven ability to do college-level work.

Tuition:
Rates are subject to change; contact the college for current rate information. $107.35 per credit for nonmatriculated students. For students matriculating in a degree program, a one-time assessment fee is $200 payable at time of first enrollment. Depending upon the student's program of study, some equipment may be supplied by the student, others by the college. Payment required at time of registration. Financial aid is available to qualified students. A pro rata refund program is available up to 28 days after beginning the course.

Enrollment Period:

All courses are available on a 16-week semester basis only, except for Open Learning Courses. Classroom attendance is not required; local group study is available but not mandatory. Open Learning Courses commence at the beginning of any month. Courses are offered on a 4-term cycle except for Business, which rotates on a 2-term cycle. Courses vary from year to year.

Equipment Requirements:

Course materials may average $15 to $25 per credit in addition to tuition.

Credit and Grading:

Credit is awarded in semester hour units; a complete degree can be completed through the Center for Distance Learning. Transfer-in credits with C grade or higher are normally acceptable. The method of examination varies, dependent upon the academic program and the limitations of the student's time (and place). Grading is done by in-depth evaluation (contract evaluation), prepared by the individually-assigned faculty member. Letter grades are provided upon request when they are needed.

Accreditations:

Middle States Association of Colleges and Schools; New York State Board of Regents.

COLLEGE COURSES

BUSINESS

Accounting for Decision Making

The goal of this course is to instruct the student how to record, classify, summarize, and interpret financial data in preparation for decision-making processes in a single proprietorship. The rules prescribed by the Financial Accounting Standards Board provide the basis for all of the tasks required throughout the course. Current practices and procedures are integrated as they occur. (4–6 semester hours)

Accounting I

Covers the same areas as Accounting for Decision Making. (4 semester hours)

Accounting II

This course pursues further intensive study of the terms, concepts, and principles of accounting as they apply to a partnership and to a corporation. (4 semester hours)

Business Law I

The basic premise of this course is that it is essential for students to understand the development and current status of commercial law if they are to understand the relationship between commercial law and management functions. The course focuses on the nature and source of law and on the relationship of law to business. Major topics include: history of law and the judicial system, torts, contracts, sales, commercial paper, bailments, agency, and the Uniform Commercial Code. (4 semester hours)

Business Law II

This course is designed to help students better understand the application of legal machinery to the demands of modern business, as well as the importance of law in the management decision making process. Major topics include: partnerships, corporations, debtor and creditor relations, regulation of business, property, insurance, trusts, and wills. (4 semester hours)

Business Mathematics

The course's primary objective is to develop a student's proficiency in quantitative skills that relate to a wide range of business procedures including accounting, finance, insurance, and marketing. Each of the topics is designed to give the student an understanding of the uses of mathematics as a tool for making decisions in the business process. (4 semester hours)

Intermediate Accounting I

The major thrust of this course is a discussion of financial accounting functions and their relationship to issues of basic theory. The course offers intensive study of accounting principles that relate to cash, marketable securities, receivables, inventory, plant and equipment, intangible assets, and long-term investments. (4 semester hours)

Intermediate Accounting II

The course relates accounting principles to stockholders' equity, dilutive securities and investment, issues related to income measurement, and the preparation and analysis of financial statements. Long-term investments, capital stock, share earnings, securities and funds investments, revenue recognition, leases, pension funds, financial reporting, and basic financial statement analysis are all covered as prescribed by the American Institute of Certified Public Accountants. (4 semester hours)

Advanced Accounting

A wide variety of concepts are covered in this course, including: the statements of financial accounting concepts, distribution and liquidation, and the consolidation process with worksheets for consolidated balance sheets. The course also deals with consolidated income and retained earnings statements, followed by both the equity and cost methods, and acquisition of subsidiary companies, indirect and mutual holdings, fiduciaries, statements of affairs, insolvency, general and estate procedures, governmental units and General Fund Unites. (4 semester hours)

Statistics

This course covers the fundamental concepts and methods of descriptive and inferential statistics. Students should gain an understanding of the use of statistics and statistical methods in summarizing and interpreting information, particularly as these relate to management and making decisions. Problems and examples covering a wide variety of management-related situations are drawn from the public and private sectors. Major topics include: arranging data, tables and graphs, frequency distributions, measures of dispersion, probability, sampling, hypothesis testing, variances, regression, correlation, and multiple regression and modeling. (4 semester hours)

Economics - Macro

The course focuses primarily on inflation, unemployment, and economic growth from a perspective based in economics and history. It is designed to provide students with an understanding of the broad and general aspects of the economy as a whole. An understanding of basic economic theories, principles, and issues should help students to develop the criteria for applying their learning to specific situations. A basic knowledge of algebra and geometry is essential, though not required for the understanding of economic relationships (functions, identities, schedules, equations) as depicted in graphs. Topics include: evaluation of the market system, great economists, an overview of the economy, trends, economic tools, GNP, growth, production, saving and investment, demand, and money. (4 semester hours)

Economics - Micro

This is a foundation course. Its goal is to develop the student's understanding of microeconomics—the study of components of larger aggregates (e.g., prices of a given product)—by investigating a wide range of problems from prices to monopolies and from urban decay to industrial pollution. Prior knowledge of algebra and geometry is essential. Topics include: microeconomics, the anatomy of the market system, prices and allocation of resources, the market, competition and the firm, big business, market imperfections, income distribution, trade, the underdeveloped world, and economic planning. (4 semester hours)

Management Principles

This course introduces the student to the concepts through which a modern business organization can be studied as a system. The functions of management are discussed with an emphasis which encourages the student to find a practical application of the concept in his/her current work environment, or one which is familiar to the student. (4 semester hours)

Marketing Principles

This course treats marketing as a complete system of action in the complex field of business and socioeconomic systems. It is based on current situations: economic growth and birth rates, energy availability and costs, inflation, scarcity, competition, and value changes. The practical applications of marketing theory are employed throughout the course. Topics covered include: modern marketing, the market, the marketing mix, the product, the price system, the distribution structure, promotional activities, marketing in special fields, planning and evaluating the marketing effort, and marketing arithmetic. (4 semester hours)

Human Resources Management and Development

This course focuses on behavior foundations and human needs within a structure. Topics considered from a managerial standpoint include: the nature and process of decision making, the communication network within the organization (and that network's effectiveness), theoretical and practical leadership qualities, setting goals and the effectiveness of discipline. Other connected topics include: union influences, conflict and stress, the organizational structure and the effect of change on behavior and needs. (4 semester hours)

Corporate Finance

This course is for students who need a formal study of financial management and decision making. Major topics include: the financial environment, financial concepts, techniques of financial analysis and planning, the management of working capital, fixed assets and capital budgeting, cost of capital, capital structure, dividends, sources of long-term financing. (4 semester hours)

Advanced Quantitative Methods in Management

The course focuses on quantitative methods and techniques for decision-support in a management environment, including applications of the computer in this important area. Major topics include: formal project management tools and techniques, such as GANTT Charts and PERT/CPM Charts, use of Time Series Analysis for forecasting;

applications of Regression Analysis in management; and aspects of Decision Theory and simple modeling. (4 semester hours)

Money and Banking

This course provides a strong conceptual framework for the study, understanding, and application of the theories of money and banking, especially as they concern the changing aspects of modern society. The major topics include: intermediaries and banks, central banking, analysis of financial markets and interest rates. International finance, and monetary theory. (4 semester hours)

Organizational Behavior

Topics include: a background to organizational behavior; a microperspective of organizational behavior; cognitive processes and personality, motivation and learning; dynamics of organizational behavior; management process and organizational theory; management applications and personal organizational development. (4 semester hours)

Business Ethics

This course examines ethics through an in-depth study of a number of important social issues related to the conduct of business in modern society. These issues will be selected from a spectrum of topics which range from business and the environment to interpersonal relations. Specific topics may include: ethical theory and its application to business, theories of economic justice, corporate social responsibility, self-regulation and government, conflicts of interest and obligation, investment and production, and advertising issues. (4 semester hours)

Business Policy

This course focuses on state-of-the art business policy and strategic management, as well as the current conceptual framework for policy information and strategic planning, and the development of organizational policy as it relates to marketing, production, personnel, and financial areas. Major topics include: objectives and strategic management, strategic analysis and diagnosis, choice of strategy and strategic management, and implementation and evaluation of strategic management. (4 semester hours)

Marketing Management

This course examines the development and implementation of marketing programs in the major areas of product, product line development, marketing channels, pricing, sales force management, and advertising. (4 semester hours)

Marketing Research

This course examines concepts, skills, and techniques used in marketing research. It treats marketing as a total system of action within the business field and socioeconomic system. Topics include: marketing decision making, planning research, historical research, sampling, marketing experimentation, measurement concepts, data collection, marketing field work, analysis, preparing a report, and marketing information systems. (4 semester hours)

COMMUNITY AND HUMAN SERVICES

Human Development I: An Introduction

The course introduces students to an integrated and interdisciplinary view of human development and covers development over the entire life span. It emphasizes such issues as nature and nurture, continuity and discontinuity, stability and change. The course is more concerned with social and cultural influences on development than with physical development. Particular attention is given to the processes and institutions of socialization through early life, adolescence, the various stages of adulthood, and during old age. (4 semester hours)

Human Development II: Theoretical Perspectives

This course focuses on several major theoretical perspectives that are concerned with the growth and development of the person and further addresses the question, ''what kind of people do we want?'' There is more emphasis on social and cultural influences on development than on physiological factors. (4 semester hours)

Understanding Cultural and Group Differences

This course is an introduction to the dynamics of group identification and to some of the distinguishing characteristics associated with various social class and ethnic, cultural, and subcultural groups. Its approach is neither anthropological nor cross-cultural. (4 or 6 semester hours)

Introduction to Human Services

This is the basic course for all those interested in exploring the field of Community and Human Services. The course focuses on the organized system through which aid and assistance are given and on understanding the human factors involved in meeting human needs. (4 semester hours)

Introduction to Criminal Justice

This course provides information about the theories of crime and criminals, as well as society's understanding of the concepts and treatment of the criminals. The material is presented in three sections: (1) the nature of the crime; (2) problems in the assessment of crime; and (3) the administration of the segments of the criminal justice system. (4 semester hours)

Human Services Management

This course seeks to acquaint students with management and evaluation policies and procedures in the field of human services. Topics include: general management methods, relationships with clients and with other agencies, ways of controlling the effectiveness and efficiency of staff, methods of determining community needs and agency responses, the preparation of evaluations, and professional standards in the human services. (4 or 6 semester hours)

Normality and Treatment

The principle aim of this course is to promote a fundamental understanding of the ideas of normality and abnormality. These ideas are examined within historical and contemporary contexts. A consideration of the implications these conceptions pose for treatment is central to the course. The topics covered include: a consideration of what constitutes ''normal'' behavior, contemporary approaches to the ''abnormal,'' normality and abnormality in historical perspective, implications of treatment ''models'' (e.g., the medical model, the custodial model), and the role of culture in defining ''normal'' and ''abnormal.'' (8 semester hours)

Issues in Human Services

After basic consideration of various perspectives on the issues of public ''help'' for individuals, students examine the ''equal opportunity'' debate, contemporary question about the role of the state in providing assistance. Though the focus in that debate is usually on public schools, the issue of ''equality'' is at the heart of the discussion and has significant implications for the human services. Some of the ethical questions that arise for human service workers are considered and some practical issues are addressed. (4 or 6 semester hours)

Counseling Theory and Practicum

The purpose of these courses is to acquaint students with the major theories of counseling and to provide an overview of models and methodologies. The Carkhuff model, one widely-used system for the improvement of helping skills, is emphasized. The model is studied intensively to provide students an opportunity to learn how to approach and attempt to facilitate their own growth in a helping role. (4 semester credits; 8 semester credits with Practicum)

Human Services and Public Policy

This course provides students an opportunity to examine the explicit and implicit social policies that undergird some of the major programs encountered by workers in the field of Community and Human Services. The course reviews the major social service programs that have been put into place in the U.S. since the 1930s and pays particular attention to the programs of the last two decades. Students also explore both the debate between ''liberals'' and ''conservatives'' over human service programs and the philosophical assumptions on which these positions are based. (4 or 6 semester hours)

Human Services and Social Change

This course will lead students to a consideration of a number of issues that should be of concern to all within the field of Human Services— and indeed, to all citizens. (4 semester hours)

FIRE SERVICE ADMINISTRATION

Advanced Fire Administration

The course begins with a review of the history of the fire service and moves to a discussion of the fire service in the twentieth century. A major concern is the evolution of management theory and the application of theories to practical problems. Students are presented a wide range of topics, including: personnel administration; how to set goals; how to control, coordinate, direct, and organize a fire department; and how to match people with machines. Other significant topics include value engineering for apparatus, innovative water delivery, management by objectives, quality circles, prevention vs. suppression, emergency medical service, data collection, reports, records, computer fire insurance, budgeting, and productivity. (4 semester hours)

Fire Prevention Organization and Management

Using historical and contemporary contexts, this course provides an in-depth review of the agencies, procedures, programs, and techniques involved with fire prevention. The course is designed to prepare individuals who manage and perform prevention functions to operate efficiently and effectively. There are two primary goals: to help students develop an understanding of how the philosophy and practice of fire prevention evolved; and to help students related their jobs to fire prevention efforts at the local, state, and federal levels. (4 semester hours)

Personnel Management for the Fire Service

This course begins with a detailed review of basic personnel management concepts and their legal foundations. It then examines the role of the personnel administration and the processes of procuring, developing, allocating, and coordinating human resources. The course emphasizes the public agency aspect of the fire service. Specific topics include: personnel planning techniques; staffing procedures (recruitment, selection, orientation, and promotion); supervision and discipline; labor relations, affirmative action, and equal employment opportunity; employee motivation, productivity, compensation, and performance evaluations. (4 semester hours)

Analytic Approaches to Public Fire Protection

This course has its foundations in systems analysis, exploring both fire prevention and suppression systems. Because fire department deployment analysis is the subject of much of the course, there is significant exposure to mathematics for the fire service, including formulas for resolving issues of response time and other critical concerns. The course emphasizes data collection, analysis, presenta-tion and interpretation, simulation, resource allocation, planning, evaluation, and preparation of written objectives. (4 semester hours)

Fire Related Human Behavior

This course emphasizes the interaction of traditional fire service concerns with a range of social sciences, relating theory to practice. It focuses on the dynamics of human behavior in fire incidents and explores how these are related to fire prevention practices, programs, codes, and ordinances. The psychological effects of communication during emergencies and the conduct of post-fire interviews with victims and fire fighters are studied in depth. (4 semester hours)

Disaster and Fire Defense Planning

The goal of this course is to help students develop an understanding of ''disaster,'' the control of its consequences, the modes of preparation and planning for disaster contingencies, and the institutional context of disaster/fire defense planning. Specific topics include the background of disaster and fire defense planning; coordination of agencies in disasters; examination of community and industrial disaster organizations; Civil Defense emergency and fire department operations, preparations, and procedures; incident command; and preparation and planning for natural and hazardous material disasters. Methods of evaluating fire defense and disaster preparedness programs and the psychological dimensions of disaster related behavior are also included. (4 semester hours)

Fire Protection Structures and Systems Design

This course stresses the need for extensive theoretical knowledge of the impact of building construction and materials at the scene of a fire. It presents a detailed discussion of measurements of fire loads, fire test standards, fire endurance ratings, behavior of inorganic materials in fire, the design of fire protection for steel columns, surface flammability measurements, corridor flame spread, smoke test methods, and fire gases. Study also includes detection systems, smoke control systems, hydraulic analysis, pump design, sprinkler systems and design, and a comparison of various extinguishing systems (including potassium-based dry chemicals and aqueous film-forming forms). (4 semester hours)

Political and Legal Foundations of Fire Protection

A major purpose of this course is to provide students an understanding of the implications and relationships among the fire service, politics, and law. It is a study of the legal basis for the police power of government as it relates to public safety, legal limitations and responsibility, and liability of fire prevention organizations and personnel. The course seeks to integrate an awareness and knowledge of political and legal concepts with experience. It includes a review of the judicial system. Topics include civil and criminal law, progenitor laws, individual and department liability, personnel procedures and requirements (including test validity and equal employment opportunity), product liability, political actions and member rights, fire prevention and building codes, legal procedures, and legislation (historical and current) related to topics such as worker's compensation and landlord responsibilities. (4 semester hours)

Community and Fire Threat

This course examines the fire department as part of the complex organization of the community. It discusses how departments interact with their communities, reviews community profiles and structures, and considers the many variables within particular types of communities. Students will learn to summarize the social and psychocultural approaches to community study and give examples of adaptation to changing communities. The course covers community relationships between fire departments and citizens and between fire departments and local, state, and federal representatives. It looks at the backgrounds of communities and fire departments and the sociological, economic, and political characteristics of communities, including how these characteristics influence the fire problem. (4 semester hours)

Incendiary Fire Analysis

The complex problem of arson is analyzed through a comprehensive, sophisticated theoretical and practical study of the psychological and sociological factors by which identifying profiles of arsonists, pyromaniacs, and firesetters are developed. Topics include fire propagation and development, incendiary fire susceptibility, motivation, detection, and constitutional issues affecting fire investigation. The roles of insurance, legislative initiative, data analysis, and protection techniques are also covered. (4 semester hours)

Fire Dynamics

This course compares and contrasts the historical concepts and theories of combustion with current theories. It is concentrated theoretical study drawn from several areas of science, with an emphasis on the chemistry of diffusion flame combustion, oxidizers, reducing agents, temperature criteria, and molecular chain reactions. Topics include heat transfer, fuel configuration and geometry, thermal columns, ventilation, theoretical considerations of flashover, research concerning fire spread, computer models and molding as a means to understand fire phenomena (including the mechanics and limitation of models). (4 semester hours)

Application of Fire Research

Basic principles of research and the methodology of analyzing research reports are the foundations of this course. It examines the scientific methods, decision analysis, research hypothesis, validity, descriptive and intervention statistics, and the limitations of research application. The following topics are covered in detail: fire test development, development of fire safety standards, laboratory methods for testing flame spread, fire toxicology, fire modeling (probabilistic, modular, and field), fire resistance and structural research, methodologies for evaluation of extinguishing agents, computer simulation of occupant evacuation of buildings, convergence cluster behavior, technical improvements and procedural changes in transportation systems as a result of research, and thermal characteristics of various fabric materials. (4 semester hours)

INTERDISCIPLINARY STUDIES

Understanding the Visible World

Students engage in a series of activities which enable them to develop their ability to make accurate, detailed, and meaningful observations of their everyday environment and of a broad range of major works of art from a variety of historical periods. (4 semester hours)

Modern China

Students will become acquainted with the culture and society of pre-modern China; study the evolution of China's relationship with the outside world; be made aware of the efforts China has made over the last 150 years to become a modern industrialized society; and investigate the ways Chinese political civilization has organized itself during the last century and explore contemporary controversies within China regarding ideas like democracy and human rights. Students will develop a keen appreciation of the rise of modern China and its growing importance to the world community. (4 semester hours)

Brazil

Students will explore Brazil's history and geography to gain an appreciation for the interaction of the people with the land and how the colonial institutions shaped present-day Brazil. Students will study Brazil's efforts to join the ranks of industrialized nations as well as consider the plight of urban poor who have not benefited from Brazil's

economic development. Additionally, students will become familiar with the geographic, ethnic, and racial diversity of the country. (4 semester hours)

Introduction to the Humanities

This foundation course uses an interdisciplinary approach which combines literature, history, philosophy, art, and music to consider people in a cultural context formed by literary, philosophical, and artistic production. It offers a general overview of selected human accomplishments within specific disciplines in the humanities and provides methods for exploring each of these disciplines. Case studies are used throughout the course to show how these methods can be applied. (8 semester hours)

Principles and Strategies for Composition

This is an introductory course designed to cultivate skills identified by CDL tutors as essential to independent student writers. It is aimed at developing students' ability to produce the basic tools of communication in higher education—the essay and the research paper. Students engage primarily in the study of models of good writing. (4 semester hours)

The Western Tradition

This two-part video course (of the Annenberg/CPB Collection) weaves together history, art, literature, religion, geography, government, and economics. It will help students recognize the trends of history, identify parallels in the modern world and gain a sense of their own place in the evolution of human institutions. The first part addressed influential pre-Western civilizations and continues through the Middle Ages to the Renaissance. This second part begins with the Wars of Religion and continues through industrial modernization to the present. (4 semester hours)

Exploring Language

The sixteen units in this course introduce students to the variety of ways language is used in our society. The units offer, in effect, an introduction to sociolinguistics—the study of language in our society and how different categories of language affect our lives. (6 semester hours)

War and American Society

This course draws material from selected disciplines within the humanities to explore how and why America has gone to war and to examine how war has shaped the homefront and had a lasting effect on peacetime society. One aim is to develop and sharpen the student's analytical and research skills in the humanities, particularly through the use of primary sources. (6 semester hours)

Communications for Professionals

The course affords students the opportunity to deepen their awareness of writing and speaking processes, to practice skills, and to generate documents that originate in and are connected to their work environment. It focuses on actual rather than simulated exercises. (4 semester hours)

Literature of the Americas

This course presents three important literary traditions of North and South America: Spanish-American, Afro-American, and Canadian fiction. Students first study each group of works separately to get a sense of the uniqueness of each culture; they later compare the groups of works to get a sense of the universality of great literature. The opening and closing units of the Course Guide are designed to help students develop a critical methodology which can be used to analyze fiction in general and these fictions in particular. (6 semester hours)

The Religious Quest

This advanced level course has been adapted from a British Open

University offering created by an interdisciplinary course team from the humanities and social sciences. The focus is on the central aspects of any attempt to offer an interpretation of the meaning and purposes of human existence. The chief topics include: Hinduism, Buddhism, the religions of China and Japan, Judaism, Christianity, Islam, and African tribal religions. Related topics consider the search for meaning in life, the academic study of religions, varieties of religious beliefs and expression, and secular alternatives to religion. There are three basic questions: From what does the religion take its starting point? Towards what does it declare that human beings should be advancing? By what means does it say that persons are able to make this progress? (8 semester hours)

Ancient Greece

This course uses an interdisciplinary approach which includes history, sociology, philosophy, the history of art and architecture, and drama and literature to help students understand the particular qualities of this high civilization. By working through fourteen units of study, each carefully designed to support independent learning, students arrive at a substantial comprehension of this important historical era. (8 semester hours)

The Enlightenment

The course explores eighteenth century culture at its height (roughly, during the middle decades of the century). It does so through a close study of certain leading figures of the time and a number of major works of literature, philosophy, history, painting, and music. The course materials reveal the leading intellectual, social, and moral preoccupations of the period and illustrate both the cosmopolitans of eighteenth century values and the particular national emphases in the thought and art of England, France, and Colonial America. Among the figures studied are Pope, Hogarth, Gibbon, Diderot, Frederick the Great, Voltaire, Mozart, and Franklin. (8 semester hours)

LIBERAL STUDIES

Algebra

This introductory college-level course should provide or enhance facility in basic algebra concepts and problem-solving techniques. It can serve as a solid basis for further study in mathematics, statistics, finance, science, and other quantitative areas. (4 semester hours)

Topics in Biology

This course uses a topical approach to introduce students to three important areas of study within the field of biology: genetics, evolution, and ecology. (4 semester hours)

Introduction to Computers and BASIC Programming

This course is for students who have little or no experience with computers or programming. A general introduction to computers is included, but the major portion of the course is devoted to programming in BASIC, the most common high-level language for personal computers. A systematic and disciplined approach to problem solving is emphasized; examples and problems from a variety of application areas are used in the text, exercises, and assignments. Topics include: fundamental statements and commands; expressions and functions; interactive I/O; decision structures, branching, and control loops; string variables and character manipulation; subroutines; and an introduction to arrays and to files. NOTE: Students must have access to a computer which supports the BASIC language. (4 semester hours)

Computer Information Systems

This is NOT a computer programming course. It is designed to provide a solid introduction to the fundamental concepts of computer structure and function and to the wide range of applications in data and information processing. (4 semester hours)

Human Nutrition

This course provides a systematic study of micro- and macro-nutrients necessary for human health. It includes discussion of the digestion, absorption, metabolism, and dietary sources of these nutrients. It also explores the social, psychological, and economic forces which affect nutrition and food choice. Students will develop some ability to analyze the dietary adequacy of foods and diets critically. They will also critically discuss some current issues and topics in nutrition. (4 semester hours)

Environmental Health, Risks, and Policies

This upper-level course covers three major aspects of environmental concern: adverse health effects of environmental pollutants, the concepts of risk perception and risk assessment, and risk management. It also focuses on the uncertainty of risk by perception in the development of environmental policy and regulation. Topics include: a general introduction to the problems of air, water, and soil pollution; how pollutants enter the body and their target organs; the physiological effects associated with various pollutants; cultural and scientific bases of risk perception and assessment; the development of a specific risk factor with respect to environmental health (such as water quality criteria set by the Environmental Protection Agency); what data are used to determine risk and how are these values generated; where and how these risk figures are used in establishing standards, regulations, and policies. (4 semester hours)

Societies in Transition

The course explores societies that have been profoundly altered by the Industrial Revolution. It provides historical and cultural perspectives about the transformation of England, the United States, and the Third World. (4 semester hours)

Hispanic America

This course focuses on Spanish-speaking minorities in the United States: Puerto Ricans, Mexicans, Cubans, and other Hispanics. These groups will be studied in relation to push/pull factors (immigration, patterns of settlement, forces of assimilation); their entry into the political area will also be covered. The course draws upon perspectives from history and literature as well as upon recent perspectives in the social sciences on the phenomena of immigration and assimilation. (4 semester hours)

Competition and Cooperation: Cultural Anthropology

This course uses a comparative approach to examine assumptions about the bases of human competitiveness. It also examines why differences in competitive and cooperative behavior exist and delves into theories concerning the origins of human competitiveness. (4 semester hours)

The Adult Years

This is a foundation course. It has been developed by an interinstitutional course team for the International University Consortium, of which ESC is a member. Topics include: the meaning of being an adult, "the fountain of youth," adult romance and sexuality, multigenerational families and relationships, mid-life transitions, and images of adulthood in literature, friendships and marriage, continuity and change in the self, and the adult as learner. (6 semester hours)

Social Psychology

This course has been adapted from a British Open University course with the same title. A variety of theoretical perspectives are considered as frameworks to enable students to compare and contrast different attempts to integrate and explain the attitudes, beliefs, and behaviors of humans as interacting individuals. The object of the course is to help students understand social behavior and experience. (8 semester hours)

People and Organizations

This course considers the processes at work in complex organizations; it pays particular attention to the mechanisms of formal and informal social control. Topics include: the classification of organizations into types, power, roles, and making decisions. The relationship between "red tape," selection interviews, "good" management, management-worker conflicts, and the meaning(s) of job "enrichment" are also considered. (8 semester hours)

Perspectives in Sociology

This course explores a range of concepts, terms, and theoretical perspectives related to some key aspects of social behavior. It aims not only to convey an appreciation of the nature of sociology, its theories, and their applications in understanding social phenomena but to introduce students to some of the principal ways theoretical perspectives differ in their assumptions and methods. (8 semester hours)

Perspectives in Psychology

This course is an introduction to the meaning of theory in the social sciences. It pays particular attention to three perspectives in psychology: psychodynamic theory, behaviorism, and humanistic psychology. Two themes are encountered throughout the course: paradigms and human science. The course materials offer students an opportunity to explore a range of psychological concepts, methods, theoretical positions, and applications of theory. The course is also designed to develop skills in critical thinking and writing, as well as critical analysis from a social scientific perspective. (8 semester hours)

Introduction to American Government

This course explores the major features of American national government—the presidency, courts, judicial and legislative processes, and democratic theory. The course is based on a traditional framework, starting with the philosophy and background of the Constitution in order to establish the system's larger premises and examine the major branches of government. (4 or 8 semester hours)

State and Citizen

This course deals with the modern state. It examines government on the national level, but it is also concerned with smaller jurisdictions (towns, cities, and counties) as well as the Federal system of the United States. The course focuses on the character of modern citizenship and on those relationships between citizens and governments that we tend to call politics and which have to do with society and community. (4 or 8 semester hours)

Thinking About Education

This course focuses on the learning process. It offers students an opportunity to begin to develop the intellectual skills of analysis, synthesis, evaluation, and application. However, the course is intended not only to develop these skills, but also to lead students to an examination of what a college degree "should" be, from both general and personal perspectives. (4 or 6 semester hours)

Systems Organization

This course is an integrated introduction to systems analysis, that approach which separates the parts of a problem, defines each in relationship to the whole, and provides a method for understanding how their interaction produces a particular outcome. (8 semester hours)

Exploring the Future

This course does NOT enable students to predict the future. It is an upper-level interdisciplinary course designed to introduce students to various underlying assumptions about the major issues in the emerging field of "future studies." The focus is on the forces operating in society today that will shape our future as citizens of the U.S. and the world. Topics include: food and population, natural resources, science and technology, economic and political systems, telecommunications, and cultural values. After exploring the effects of social and technical change, students consider the implications of those types of change for society and for their own lives. The course concludes with a discussion of some alternative futures and their implications for those of us who will live them. (8 semester hours)

Modes of Inquiry I

This is an upper-level course that focuses on the thinking/learning process. It seeks to develop further the skills of analysis, synthesis, and evaluation and application. The emphasis is on the ways in which scholars in the natural and physical sciences ask and answer questions. Students consider the ways in which knowledge has been organized historically and how the scientific method has evolved. (4 semester hours)

Modes of Inquiry II

This course explores some of the questions students encountered as they examined the assumptions and methods of physical and biological sciences in Modes of Inquiry I. Students examine "inquiries" into the Civil War in Spain by historians, poets, and artists; consider the relationships between art, and other media, and historical (and contemporary) events; explore the meanings of interpreting "present history;" examine some of the potential conflicts between the work of the scholar and the requirements of national security; explore some of the methodological problems encountered by the social scientist and how his mode of inquiry can be seen as lying between the approach of the natural/biological scientist and the scholar in the humanities; examine the role of ideology in inquiry; and consider some of the limitations of inquiry in attempting to resolve some issues with "practical"—even ethical—implications. (4 semester hours)

Complexity, Management, and Change: Applying a Systems Approach

The principal objective of this course is to enable students to use the methods of systems analysis to understand complicated situations, to consider the consequences of various possible solutions to problems, and to formulate both short- and long-term strategies for innovation and change. (8 semester hours)

PERSONAL DEVELOPMENT

Educational Planning

This course helps students define and clarify their academic and career goals, needs, and options. It is intended to give students the opportunity to develop and design their own individualized program of studies and to identify the specific skills needed for their degree program, vocation, and life-long learning.

The course is open to matriculated students in the Center for Distance Learning only and is tutored by the student's assigned advisor.

Emporia State University
Division of Continuing Education
Emporia, Kansas 66801   (316) 343-1200

Description:

Correspondence courses offered by Emporia State University are administered by Independent Study at the University of Kansas, Lawrence, Kansas. For courses available, SEE **Kansas, University of.**

Eugene Bible College

Faculty:
Dr. Edward A. McGlone, Dean of Continuing Education.

Accreditations:
North Central Association of Colleges and Schools.

Eugene Bible College
External Studies Program
2155 Bailey Hill Road
Eugene, Oregon 97405   (503) 485-1780

Description:
Eugene Bible College is the official national college of Open Bible Standard Churches, Inc. The Department of External Studies was established to increase the availability of avocational education and offers a program of correspondence study to supplement on-campus classroom instruction. Correspondence courses are offered at the college level as well as courses for personal enrichment. A Christian Service Program is offered on a noncredit basis (contact the Department of External Studies for details).

Faculty:
Jeffrey E. Farmer, President.

Academic Levels:
College
Noncredit

Degree/Certificate Programs:
A maximum of 48 term hours may be transferred to a degree program through the External Studies Department. A one-year Bible Certificate is offered.

Admission Requirements:
Open enrollment policy. Acceptance as an external studies student does not imply acceptance as a residential student. External study students desiring to enroll in a residential program must meet all requirements for admission as stated in the college catalog and make formal application through the Director of Admissions.

Tuition:
$140 per college course; $70 per course for noncredit (audit). $10 registration fee. All courses are 4 credit hours in length. Tuition and fees subject to change without notice; contact the college for current rate information.

Enrollment Period:
A student has one year in which to complete any course. An extension of up to six months may be granted upon payment of a $30 time extension fee. Only two time extensions will be granted to a student for a course. The minimum completion time for a course is six weeks.

Equipment Requirements:
Textbooks must be purchased by the student.

Credit and Grading:
The grading system is A, B, C, D for passing work; F for failure. To receive credit toward a degree program, the student must earn a grade of C or better. Credit is awarded in quarter hour units.

Library Services:
The Open Bible College Resource Center houses the library on its upper floor; it is available to students in the vicinity of the college.

Accreditations:
American Association of Bible Colleges.

COLLEGE COURSES

BIBLE

Old Testament Survey

The work of God in relation to man begins in the Old Testament. All the events from man's creation up to the point of his redemption occur in this larger portion of the Bible. Along with the study of the progression of the nation of Israel, individuals who made significant contributions to this progress are thoroughly discussed. (4 quarter hours)

Genesis

In an interpretive study of Genesis, the origins of the universe, man, and evil are discussed along with other difficult questions. God's plan of redemption is traced from Eden to the formation of God's chosen people through whom mankind's redemption would be realized. Spiritual types and practical applications are included in this study. (4 quarter hours)

Pentateuch

In this study of Genesis through Deuteronomy, the origin of both the earth and mankind in general are covered, as well as the development of the nation of Israel until the nation's entrance into the promised land. Special studies on creation theories, the flood, and the concept of holiness in the book of Leviticus are also included. (4 quarter hours)

Old Testament Historical Books

This is an interpretive survey of historical books of the Old Testament, from Joshua through Esther. Special emphasis is given to Israel's messianic mission in the world as was first described in God's covenant with Abraham. The background, structure, and content of each book is examined, which helps provide understanding of the times and God's purpose to redeem the world through Jesus Christ. (4 quarter hours)

Major Prophets

A study of the lives of Isaiah, Jeremiah, and Ezekiel and of the divine message God asked each to proclaim. The course stresses the importance1 and meaning of each message and burden for the church today. (4 quarter hours)

Minor Prophets

A study of the minor prophets in the light of their times and ours, the doctrines they preached, and the meanings and fulfillments of their prophecies. This course covers 12 books of the Old Testament that are probably the most neglected in preaching, training, and devotional study. (4 quarter hours)

New Testament Survey

Knowledge, change, action: these terms reflect the objectives for New Testament Survey. A panoramic view unifies the messages of the various doctrines, personalities, and problems. You will be inspired to excel in your personal maturation as you practice the scriptural principles in your relationship with God, with others, and with yourself. (4 quarter hours)

The Gospel of John

The Gospel of John examines the life, character, and ministry of Jesus Christ not only in their historical context, but also from the divine perspective presented by John the Evangelist. The study of this course will greatly increase your understanding of John's Gospel and aid you in its interpretation. (4 quarter hours)

Acts

This study of Acts deals with the ministry of the Holy Spirit in the establishment of the New Testament Church. By analyzing the church in Acts, questions pertaining to growth of the contemporary church will be answered. The apparent defeats and setbacks described in the book of Acts, which became victories and advances for the gospel, form the basis for practical solutions to similar problems you may encounter today. (4 quarter hours)

Corinthians

An in-depth study of the Corinthian letters is intended to help you relate the Bible to contemporary church life. The exegetical method of Bible study is taught to help you understand the problems faced by these early Corinthian believers. As you study each major problem Paul faced, a possible solution or interpretation is presented which can be applied to the twentieth-century church. (4 quarter hours)

Galatians and Romans

An interpretive study of Paul's letters to the Galatians and Romans includes many details concerning the life and ministry of the apostle. The study guide helps answer questions in areas such as the relationship between Law and grace, salvation by faith, predestination, and the difference between Old and New Testament plans of salvation. (4 quarter hours)

Hebrews

Both an analytical and topical study are used to bring out the rich Christological truths in the Epistle to the Hebrews. You will be able to identify with the early Christians in their spiritual crises and feel the impact of the warnings and exhortations in the epistle by studying the background information. Insight is also given into the understanding of Old Testament forms of worship and their prophetic aspect. You will be led to a new appreciation of Christ as the fulfillment of the Old Covenant, and will be helped to appropriate by faith all the blessings that he offers. (4 quarter hours)

CHRISTIAN EDUCATION

Introduction to Christian Education

This course presents an overview of the function and place of Christian education in the local church today. It summarizes the biblical, theological, historical, and philosophical foundations, as well as the basic objectives of Christian education. It examines materials and methods for Christian teaching and leads the student to initiate or help improve the program of Christian education in his local church. (4 quarter hours)

MISSIONS

Introduction to Missions

More and more lay people are becoming involved in missions. They are working alongside the professional missionary in bigger projects than have ever before been undertaken. (4 quarter hours)

PASTORAL MINISTRIES

Apologetics

Faith and knowing are the two consistent themes of this course which examines and explains the relationship between them. The course will help you persuade others that there is no better way to follow than faith in and obedience to the God of the Christian Scriptures. (4 quarter hours)

A Strategy for Church Growth

This course is designed to acquaint students with the importance of the Great Commission in relation to world evangelism and church planting. By studying this course students will lean to identify the principles that underlie the growth of the church and to make a diagnostic study of a local church. They will also learn to identify reasons for growth or lack of growth. (4 quarter hours)

Principles of Preaching

This course stresses the purpose of preaching. It introduces the student to spiritual and practical techniques of sermon preparation and delivery. Attention is given to definition and discussion of types of sermons, and of structural parts within a sermon. Spiritual exhortation and practical exercises are found throughout each lesson. (4 quarter hours)

Pastoral Ministries

A study of the minister, his preparation, his relationships, and his primary ministerial responsibilities. The course guides the student in developing a biblical model of the ministry. (4 quarter hours)

Church Business

This is an introductory study of many of the principles, procedures, and techniques used in today's business world as they apply to the local church and its leadership. The student is taught organizing and staffing functions of the church which enable it to operate effectively, along with ideas on better management of the church's money, facilities, and equipment. (4 quarter hours)

Teaching in the Church

This course will develop the skills needed to understand the problems and possibilities associated with instructing others to teach creatively. It starts with a look at various views of revelation and the Bible, and arrives at an exciting biblical conclusion showing how God speaks to people through His Word. (4 quarter hours)

World Religions

This course furnishes a survey of eight of the nine major nonbiblical religions of the world. The final unit presents a survey of Judaism and Christianity and concludes with a comparison of all world religions. (4 quarter hours)

Educational Psychology

The course deals with the application of psychological principles to the design and guidance of educational experiences in educational psychology. It provides the student with the tools necessary to make the teaching-learning process a more effective and rewarding part of his ministry. The course maintains a Christian perspective and emphasizes the role of the Holy Spirit in its teaching. (4 quarter hours)

Principles of Counseling

An application of general counseling principles to pastoral counseling. The course emphasizes characteristics of people counseled, techniques of counseling, and the various forms of counseling. A strong biblical emphasis underlies the study. (4 quarter hours)

Evangelism Today

This course gives you a look at the basic theology and spiritual dynamics of evangelism. Several different methods of effective evangelization are discussed from both the New Testament era and the contemporary scene. (4 quarter hours)

Worship: A Biblical Survey

This course is a biblical survey of worship based on the theme

"Worship in Spirit and Truth." The study searches the biblical text from Genesis to Revelation, reviewing and interpreting those scriptures which provide insights for worship in Spirit. (4 quarter hours)

Cross-Cultural Communications

This course is dedicated to the special task of helping a person who would become a "sent one" to present Christ and His kingdom in an environment other than his own familiar culture. To do this we address: the relationship of communication and culture, how to reach people where they are, how different people think and express ideas across cultures and subcultures within a culture, and how the though and expression of people affect their behavior. (4 quarter hours)

THEOLOGY

The Holy Spirit

The person, work, gifts, and ministry of the Holy Spirit are examined in this biblical study. Among questions discussed from both the Old Testament and the New Testament are: Who is the Holy Spirit? What is the baptism in the Holy Spirit? How do I live a Spirit-filled life? You will be encouraged to apply these and other biblical teachings to your own personal teaching and preaching ministry. (4 quarter hours)

Christology

This course will introduce you to Old Testament prophecies concerning His present and future work. This study presents controversial historical and contemporary views of Jesus and relates them to the Word of God. With this course you will discover what the Scriptures really say about Jesus Christ. (4 quarter hours)

The Biblical Doctrines of Salvation

This course is a study of the doctrines of salvation—the work of Christ in bringing lost man into fellowship with God. This study includes the doctrines of repentance, faith, conversion, regeneration, justification, adoption, sanctification, and prayer in the life of a Christian. The twelve lessons stress applying salvation truths personally and sharing them with our contemporaries. (4 quarter hours)

Eschatology

This course is a study in the doctrine of eschatology or the area of biblical teaching dealing with the final outcome of the present order. In today's world there is an abundance of teaching concerning the "end times," some true and some false. The second coming of Christ, tribulation, and the value of predictive prophecy are among the topics discussed. As part of this course of study, you will also read about and analyze various current ideas in eschatology. (4 quarter hours)

Old Testament Biblical Theology

In the course the development of major Old Testament doctrines are traced. It deals with the Old Testament teaching about God, creation, man, sin, the Messiah, revelation, inspiration, angels, and Satan, just to name a few. It provides a wealth of material for preaching and teaching from the Old Testament. This advanced course of study should be preceded by courses in systematic theology and Old Testament. (4 quarter hours)

Theology and Angelology

A systematic study of the biblical doctrines of God and angels. Two main themes are covered: personal divine involvement and personal angelic involvement in the human activity. (4 quarter hours)

The Doctrines of Man and Sin

A study of the teachings of Scripture concerning man and sin. The course corrects some of the false ideas about the origin of man and his nature. Personal application of truth to the lives of students and persons too whom they will minister is a specific focus of the study. (4 quarter hours)

Florida, University of
Department of Independent Study By
Correspondence and Distance Education
2209 NW 13th Street, Suite D
Gainesville, Florida 32609-3498

(904) 392-1711

Description:

The University of Florida enrolled its first correspondence student in 1919 and since that time has enrolled over 250,000 people in university, high school, and noncredit courses. Over 5,000 students are enrolled each year. The university courses are offered in conjunction with the resident programs of all nine universities in Florida's State University System. All college course completions are shown on University of Florida transcripts, though faculty and courses are also drawn from Florida State University and the University of South Florida. A degree by correspondence is not offered; similarly, the high school courses complement resident programs but do not lead to a diploma through the university. The central office for administration and testing is at Gainesville; there are faculty offices at the various campuses of the University of Florida, Florida International University, Florida State University, and the University of South Florida. A current toll-free outside Florida telephone number for information is 1-800-327-4218.

Faculty:

Dr. Joanne M. East, Director; Tamara Maxwell, Program Assistant, Student Services.

Academic Levels:
College
High School
Noncredit
Vocational

Degree/Certificate Programs:

Correspondence credits toward the following programs will be accepted by the University of Florida: bachelor degree, associate degree, and certificate. A certificate is granted for noncredit courses. Individual colleges or departments may place restriction on courses to be used or maximum credit to be applied toward a degree. The university accepts correspondence transfer credits, after review, from accredited institutions only.

Admission Requirements:

Open enrollment for those not in school. Otherwise, approval of the student's dean, counselor, or high school principal is strongly recommended.

Tuition:

Florida resident $113.66 per 2-semester hour course, $170.49 per 3-semester hour course, $227.32 per 4-semester hour course; non-Florida resident $440.48 per 2-semester hour course, $660.72 per 3-semester hour course, $880.96 per 4-semester hour course. Continuing Professional Education Courses (noncredit): see course listings below. High

School Courses: $75 per course. A processing and handling fee is assessed for each course: $30 U.S. and Canada; $65 outside U.S. and Canada. Florida residents are subject to a sales tax on all materials (study guides, textbooks, tapes, etc.) purchased from Independent Study by Correspondence. Prices subject to change each fall semester. Full tuition must accompany application at time of enrollment. VISA and MasterCard accepted. The cost of noncredit courses varies with length of course. Refunds are allowed if requested in writing within two months of the time of enrollment. A charge of $5 per written assignment completed plus a $10 per course processing fee will be withheld.

Enrollment Period:

Maximum period to complete a course is one year; minimum is one month. Extension time varies; however, there are no extensions granted for university courses. An extension fee of $25 applies in most noncredit and high school courses.

Equipment Requirements:

Textbooks for each course must be furnished by the student. The textbooks may be purchased from the Independent Study Bookstore at the Gainesville address. Some courses require audio/videocassette tapes or special kits. Typewriter and cassette player required for some courses and are supplied by the student.

Credit and Grading:

Examinations must be proctored; they may be taken at Gainesville, Florida or will be sent to any educational institution. Letter grades of A, B, C, D, and E (failure) are used for university and high school courses. Assignments and examinations are combined for grading. Most noncredit courses award: O (Outstanding), S (Satisfactory), and U (Unsatisfactory). University credit is awarded in semester hour units; high school credit in ½ units.

Accreditations:

Southern Association of Colleges and Schools. Numerous professional credentialing organizations have recognized courses for continuing professional education. State agencies that license professionals in many states also have approved certain courses.

COLLEGE COURSES

ADVERTISING

Elements of Advertising

The role of advertising in a free economy and its place in mass communications media. A study of advertising appeals, product and market research, selection of media, testing of advertising effectiveness, and organization of the advertising profession. (3 semester hours)

AGRONOMY

Agronomy

Introduction to the principles and practices of field crop production. (3 semester hours)

ANTHROPOLOGY

Cultural Anthropology

The nature of culture. The content of cultures; languages, subsistence, economic structures, art and religion in human societies. The integration of culture. (3 semester hours)

Biological Anthropology: Human Evolution and Adaptation, Primate Behavior

Human evolution and the formation of races. Human relationship to other primates; human genetics; anthropoletry; formation of races; racial differences, distribution, and history. (3 semester hours)

ASTRONOMY

Discovering the Universe

An elementary, largely nonmathematical survey of our universe of stars, planets, and galaxies. Acquaints students with the development of astronomy as a human activity—with how we know as well as what we know. Primarily for those not majoring in physical science or mathematics. (3 semester hours)

BRAILLE

Braille Reading and Writing

Designed for transcribing and sight-reading standard English Braille. Methods of teaching literary Braille and diacritical marking. Provides information on communication systems for visually handicapped. Student should purchase or assure availability of a Brailler through a cooperating school or agency. (3 semester hours)

CHEMISTRY

Chemistry for Liberal Studies

A study of chemical principles. Intended to provide the nonscience major with an introduction to the study of the principles of chemistry without an extensive use of mathematics. Major topics include elementary atomic theory, gas laws, states of matter. (3 semester hours)

CHILD DEVELOPMENT

Child Growth and Development: The Foundation Years

The scientific study of the child from birth through middle childhood. (3 semester hours)

CRIMINAL JUSTICE

Introduction to Criminal Justice

Designed to provide freshman and sophomore students with knowledge of terminology, classification systems, trends, and theories of criminal justice. (3 semester hours)

Criminology

An examination of the field of criminology, including its theories, basic assumptions, and definitions. (3 semester hours)

Law Enforcement

An advanced survey of law enforcement concentrating on the police, with emphasis on functions (law enforcement, order maintenance, public service) and responsibilities (e.g., preservation of constitutional rights, community relations), including organizational and management aspects. (3 semester hours)

The Courts

Jurisdiction, policies, and procedures of courts in the administration of criminal justice. (3 semester hours)

ECONOMICS

Principles of Macroeconomics

The nature of economics, economic concepts, and institutions; emphasis on the accounting, analytical, and policy aspects of national income and product, as well as public finance, money and banking, and international trade. (3 semester hours)

Principles of Microeconomics

Theories of production, determination of prices, and distribution of income in regulated and unregulated industries. Attention is also given to the problems of industrial relations, to monopolies, and to comparative economic systems. (3 semester hours)

EDUCATION

Educational Psychology

An introduction to the application of psychology to the problems of education in a variety of settings. This course examines the theoretical and applied aspects of learning, motivation, human development, personality, and measurement and evaluation. (3 semester hours)

Social Foundations of Education

This course examines the current educational system in the United States. The analysis draws on the disciplines of philosophy, sociology, history, anthropology, political science, and psychology in order to foster critical thinking about prevailing practices and beliefs. The aim of the course is to deepen awareness of the role schools do and can play in a democratic society. (3 semester hours)

Measurement and Evaluation in Education

The basic principles and methods of measurement, evaluation, and test construction. (3 semester hours)

ENGLISH

American Fiction: 1900 to World War II

Includes works by Crane, Dreiser, Hemingway, Fitzgerald, Faulkner, Steinbeck, and Wright. (3 semester hours)

Beginning Fiction Writing

A beginning course designed to acquaint the student with the craft of fiction writing. Original works of fiction will be written and critiqued. (3 semester hours)

Expository and Argumentative Writing

A course offering instruction in critical reading and writing of expository and argumentative essays. (3 semester hours)

Writing About Literature

Writing about novels, short stories, drama, and poetry, primarily by American and British authors. Six papers are required. (3 semester hours)

Professional Communication

A professional communication course relevant in business, industry, government, and other institutional settings. Covers major elements of organizational communication with emphasis on composition of letters and memos, reports, proposals, manuals, and presentations. (3 semester hours)

Advanced Exposition

An advanced composition course in the methods of exposition: the writing of definition, classification, comparison and contrast, analysis, illustration, identification. (3 semester hours)

British Authors: Beginnings to 1790

Survey of English masterworks intended for students in liberal studies and those exploring a literature major. Includes authors such as Chaucer, Marlowe, Shakespeare, Jonson, Milton, Dryden, Congreve, Swift, Pope, Johnson, and Boswell. (3 semester hours)

British Authors: Early Romantics to the Present

Survey of English masterworks. Intended for students in liberal studies and those exploring a literature major. Includes authors such as Blake, Coleridge, Wordsworth, Mill, Browning, Wilde, Shaw, Conrad, Woolf, and Eliot. (3 semester hours)

English Novel: 19th Century

Includes works by Austen, Brontë, Dickens, Trollope, Hardy, Wells, and Conrad. (3 semester hours)

English Novel: 20th Century

Includes works by Conrad, Ford, Lawrence, Joyce, Forster, Woolf, Murdoch, Amis, and Fowles. (3 semester hours)

Language: Humanities Perspective

The nature of human language, its origins, and its relationship to thinking. (3 semester hours)

English Grammar

The basics of traditional English grammar. Designed to complement the composition and creative writing courses, as a review for those students who will take preprofessional exams and as a basic course for students interested in improving their knowledge of English. (2 semester hours)

FOOD SCIENCE

Man's Food

Discussion of current nutrition and food science topics concerning nutritional quality and safety of foods as they relate to one's health. (3 semester hours)

Fundamentals of Human Nutrition

The properties, functions, requirements, interrelationships and metabolism of nutrients. (3 semester hours

GEOGRAPHY

The Face of Florida

A study of the physical landscape of Florida; includes location, physiology, shorelines, soils, vegetation, climate, water problems, and environmental degradation. (3 semester hours)

Physical Landscapes

A study of physical landscapes with emphasis on the physical landscapes of the U.S. Considers the materials composing landscapes, processes fashioning landscapes, resources, and influences of physical landscapes on society. (3 semester hours)

Conservation of Resources

A survey of natural resources followed by study of wise and wasteful practices of utilization of these resources. (3 semester hours)

GEOLOGY

Exploring the Geological Sciences

Selected topics in the geological sciences for those not majoring in science. (3 semester hours)

Physical Geology

The earth's materials, structures and surface features and the processes that produced them. Supplementary lab exercises provide practical experience in rock and mineral identification, map interpretation and environment problems. (3 semester hours)

GERMAN

Beginning German 1

This first semester course aims to develop the student's skills in reading, writing, understanding, and speaking German. (4 semester hours)

Beginning German 2

A continuation of *Beginning German 1*. (3 semester hours)

Beginning German 3

A continuation of *Beginning German 2*. (3 semester hours)

HEALTH EDUCATION

Contemporary Health Science

A comprehensive approach to health concerns and problems in contemporary society, including methods of assessing individual health needs. (3 semester hours)

Medical Terminology for the Health-Related Professions

A study of the prefixes, suffixes, and word roots which are combined to constitute the language used in medicine and the health-related professions. Terms related to disease states, diagnostic procedures, and equipment are emphasized. (3 semester hours)

HISTORY

American Civilization

A broad survey covering the scope of American history from its early colonial beginnings to the present. The emphasis is upon placing the American experience in a broad setting. As such, movements and interpretations are stressed. (3 semester hours)

United States to 1877

Survey of the development of the United States from its colonial origins to the end of Reconstruction. (3 semester hours)

United States Since 1877

Survey of the emergence of modern America as an industrial and world power: the Progressive Era, Word War I, Great Depression, New Deal, World War II, the Cold War Era. (3 semester hours)

Economic History of the United States

Survey of American economic history from early colonial beginnings to the present. Analyzes the role of economic issues and events in American history. Proceeds chronologically through twelve time periods, with emphasis on the twentieth century. (3 semester hours)

United States Business History

This historical survey of American business from colonial times to the present includes manufacturing, industrial development, agribusiness, organized labor, finance, management approaches, and the evolution of business ethics. (3 semester hours)

Florida to 1845

Exploration and settlement, colonial history of Spanish and British Florida, U.S. territorial days to statehood. (3 semester hours)

Florida Since 1845

Statehood and secession; Civil War; Reconstruction; reform and reaction; Progressive Era; boom and bust; and diversification and growth since World War II. (3 semester hours)

Ancient and Medieval Civilizations

Provides a survey of Western traditions from the beginnings through the end of the Middle Ages. Emphasis is on patterns of thinking and on those institutions most distinctive of the Western tradition. (3 semester hours)

Nineteenth-Century Europe: A Survey

European history from the close of the Napoleonic Wars to the turn of the century, a period in which Europe was at the height of its wealth and power. Particular attention will be paid to the major powers. (3 semester hours)

Twentieth-Century Europe: A Survey

European history from the turn of the century through the two world wars. Particular attention will be paid to the major powers in this period when Europe declined from its preeminent position. (3 semester hours)

History of Russia, 1825 to Present

Examination of the social, economic, cultural, and political development of Russia from the reign of Tsar Nicholas I to the present day. Although internal history is stressed, appropriate attention will be paid to Russia's role in international relations. (3 semester hours)

Hitler's Third Reich

Deals with the background and nature of the Nazi regime, the character of Hitler's dictatorship, and the origins and course of World War II in its European context. It will also treat National Socialism's impact on German institutions as well as its racial consequences. (3 semester hours)

The Modern World to 1815

The origins and development of political, economic, social, and intellectual antecedents of the modern world from the end of the Middle Ages to 1815. (3 semester hours)

The Modern World Since 1815

The origins and development of political, economic, social, and intellectual developments in the modern world since 1815. (3 semester hours)

World War II

Avoiding the common Eurocentric approach, this course deals with World War II on a global basis. It analyzes the character of the Pacific theater as well as the European War, presenting both insights and contrasts between the various belligerents. (3 semester hours)

INSURANCE

Risk Management and Insurance

An introduction to the principles of risk management and insurance and their application to personal and business pure risk problems. (3 semester hours)

INTERDISCIPLINARY STUDIES

Law and Society

Explores the language of the law, legal issues, and the citizen's rights and obligations under the law. Students will learn to prepare simple legal instruments. They will also learn to look for and how to use available legal remedies for offenses against them. (3 semester hours)

JOURNALISM

Magazine and Feature Writing

Preparation of features and articles for publication in newspapers and magazines coordinated with study of magazine editing problems. Supervised marketing of pieces produced in the course. (3 semester hours)

MANAGEMENT

Introduction to Business

An introduction to the business world, including functions of business and management. Examination of the free enterprise system, forms of business ownership, and the role of business in society. (3 semester hours)

Concepts of Management

Introduction to the nature and process of management, with emphasis upon management of physical and human resources. (3 semester hours)

Personnel/Human Resource Management

Attention is focused on the theory and practice of modern personnel management and its relation to other management functions. Topics include: selection, training, job and performance evaluation, and incentive programs. Special attention is given to human resource management and development at various organizational levels. (3 semester hours)

Management of Labor and Industrial Relations

A managerial perspective of labor and manpower concepts and issues in industrial and post-industrial society and work organizations. (3 semester hours)

MARKETING

Basic Marketing Concepts

Gives the student an understanding of the decision areas and the ability to utilize marketing concepts to make business decisions. (3 semester hours)

MASS MEDIA

Survey of Mass Communication

Introduction to the various mass communication media, with special emphasis on the roles and responsibilities to society and the public. (2 semester hours)

Writing for Mass Communication

A preprofessional course designed to provide fundamental instruction and practice in writing as a basis for upper division courses in advertising, broadcasting, journalism, and public relations. Stresses the basic similarities in writing for all mass media. (3 semester hours)

MATHEMATICS

Basic College Algebra

Covers techniques of algebra; linear, polynomial, exponential and logarithmic functions, equations, and graphs; systems of equations and inequalities; counting; and applications. (3 semester hours)

Precalculus: Algebra and Trigonometry

College algebra, functions, coordinate geometry, exponential and logarithmic functions, and trigonometry. (4 semester hours)

Analytic Geometry and Calculus 1

Assumes a sound foundation in algebra and trigonometry. Self-test to measure student's preparation available on request. Introduction to analytic geometry, limits, continuity, differentiation of algebraic and trigonometric functions, differentials, introduction to integration and the fundamental theorem of calculus. (4 semester hours)

Analytic Geometry and Calculus 2

Techniques of integration; applications of integration; differentiation and integration of inverse trigonometric, exponential, and logarithmic functions; sequences and series. (4 semester hours)

MEDICAL TERMINOLOGY

Medical Terminology for the Health-Related Professions

A study of the prefixes, suffixes, and word roots which are combined to constitute the language used in medicine and the health-related professions. Terms related to disease states, diagnostic procedures, and equipment are emphasized. (3 semester hours)

NUTRITION

Fundamentals of Human Nutrition

A study of nutritional requirements, as well as the properties, functions, interrelationships, and metabolism of nutrients. (3 semester hours)

PHILOSOPHY

Introduction to Philosophy

Systematic introduction to the range of problems philosophy deals with and the variety of methods and styles with which they can be approached. (3 semester hours)

POLITICAL SCIENCE

International Relations

The nature of international relations: nationalism, imperialism, armaments; history of international relations, foreign policies, functions and problems of democracy; international organization; the United Nations. (3 semester hours)

American Federal Government

Basic principles of the federal constitution; civil rights; political parties and the electoral process. The structure and machinery of the federal government, including Congress, the President, and the judiciary. (3 semester hours)

American State and Local Government

State constitutions, political parties, and politics, legislatures, courts and chief executives. Functions of state, city, and county governments are discussed. (3 semester hours)

PSYCHOLOGY

Developmental Psychology

The effects of genetic, psychological, maturational, and social factors on behavior throughout the life cycle. (3 semester hours)

Industrial Psychology

Applications of psychological principles to industry. Topics include: selection, training, motivation, job satisfaction, supervision, decision making. (3 semester hours)

Personality

Methods and findings of personality theories and an evaluation of constitutional, biosocial, and psychological determinants of personality. (3 semester hours)

General Psychology

Introductory survey of the basic principles, theories, and methods of contemporary psychology. (3 semester hours)

Social Psychology

Survey of methods, empirical findings, and theoretical interpretations in the study of an individual's behavior as it is affected by others. (3 semester hours)

PUBLIC ADMINISTRATION

Public Administration in American Society

A general introductory course in public administration. Management of large-scale government bureaucracies, including organization, career systems, and financing. The role of bureaucracies in modern society in the formulation and implementation of public policy. (3 semester hours)

PUBLIC RELATIONS

Introduction to Public Relations

The nature and role of public relations, activities of public relations professionals, major influences which affect organizational behavior, the ethics and professional development of public relations professionals. (3 semester hours)

RELIGION

Religion in America

Examination of the scope and nature of religious movements and institutions in America. (3 semester hours)

Introduction to the Old Testament

History, religious thought and social institutions of ancient Israel as reflected primarily in its literature. (3 semester hours)

SOCIOLOGY

Principles of Sociology

Introduction to sociology as a social science. Analysis of American society: culture, socialization, deviance, bureaucracy, population, urbanization, social stratification and minorities. (3 semester hours)

Marriage and the Family

Development of masculine and feminine roles. Recent changes in premarital interaction: dating, sexual involvement, coed dorm living, and living together. Mutual adjustment and parenthood. Alternative life styles, including group marriage, communal living, and open marriage. (3 semester hours)

STATISTICS

Quantitative Methods for Business Decisions

An introductory course in undergraduate statistics. Designed specifically for business majors. Covers topics such as statistical description, probability, random variables and their distributions, and sampling distributions. (3 semester hours)

Introduction to Applied Statistics

Data collection, sample variation, basic probability, confidence intervals, hypothesis testing, analysis of variance, contingency tables, correlation, regression. (4 semester hours)

TEXTILES

Basic Textiles

Introduction to fibers, fabric structures, and finishes related to selection and care. Interrelationship between textile characteristics, properties, and end use. (3 semester hours)

HIGH SCHOOL COURSES

ACCOUNTING

Accounting I

This course teaches the fundamentals of double-entry bookkeeping for a service business. Topics include starting an accounting system; changes caused by business transactions; analyzing transactions into debit and credit parts; journalizing transactions and posting to a general ledger, work sheet, income statement, and balance sheet; adjusting and closing entries; checking accounts; journalizing, posting, and adjusting and closing entries for a merchandising business; and

using work sheet and financial statements of a merchandising partnership. (½ unit)

ART

Comprehensive Art I

This course is organized around a series of projects—most of which are individualized—involving the study of selected topics and forms of expression in two-dimensional art. It includes elements and principles of art, the influence of art on quality of life, techniques and skills, and art forms and styles. (½ unit)

Comprehensive Art II

A continuation of *Comprehensive Art I* in which the student pursues additional topics on the basis of individual interest and ability. The elements of color, value, line, space, form, and texture are organized to create two-dimensional art. The principles of emphasis, balance, rhythm, unity, repetition, contrast, and proportion are stressed. (½ unit)

ENGLISH

English I

Course ENG 9-A. This first semester of ninth-grade English is a course in basic composition, speech and literature. Composition study includes vocabulary building, the sentence, the paragraph, and the total written composition. Spelling and mechanics, as well as grammar and usage, are included. The speech component includes practice in preparing and delivering talks; students will tape-record these assignments and submit for grading. The study of literature is focused on reading and analyzing a novel. (½ unit)

Course ENG 9-B. In the second semester of ninth-grade English, students study the parts of speech, classification of sentences, capitalization, punctuation and spelling, and all the components of English grammar. The course stresses grade-level and content-area vocabulary, and knowledge of grammar, usage, spelling, and mechanics. Attention to study skills is included. (½ unit)

English II

Course ENG 10-A. This course involves the study of language and composition, giving attention to reading comprehension skills, reference skills, vocabulary, grammar, usage, spelling, mechanics, and the impact of the mass media. (½ unit)

Course ENG 10-B. The critical exploration of literary forms—short stories, poetry, plays, etc.—is the subject of this course, with Shakespearean drama as a major topic. Attention is given to reading comprehension skills, vocabulary, grammar, usage, spelling, and mechanics. Students will write short compositions on specific themes. (½ unit)

English III

Course ENG 11-A. This course includes frequent practice in writing essays of various types, with particular attention given to the writing of documented papers. Reference and summarizing skills are stressed. Listening, speaking, and writing assignments are related, when appropriate, to the study of American literature. Literature study includes the analysis of American literary works in various genres. Vocabulary study focuses upon verbal analogies and other patterns commonly found on standardized tests. (½ unit)

Course ENG 11-B. This course is a continuation of *ENG 11-A.* (½ unit)

English IV

Course ENG 12-A. This course is a survey of English literature from the Middle Ages through the Romantic period. It is designed to help improve the student's reading and writing skills. (½ unit)

Course ENG 12-B. This course is a survey of English literature from the Victorian Age through the twentieth century. It is designed to help improve the student's reading and writing skills. (½ unit)

HEALTH

Personal, Social, and Family Relationships

This course is designed to develop advanced knowledge and skills that promote positive social and emotional interactions and relationships. (½ unit)

Health I - Life Management Skills

This course is designed to help students understand their environment in terms of physical, mental, and social health. Topics include emotional development, coping with stress, planning and deciding, interpersonal relationships, nutrition principles, personal health planning, substance abuse, consumer skills, and locating help. Special requirement: The student must complete a half-day of Red Cross or American Heart Association training in emergency aid through CPR and obstructed airway clearance. (½ unit)

HUMANITIES

Humanities to 1500

This course includes the following topics: the history of art and literature in classical Greece and Rome, Judeo-Christian roots in Medieval Europe, the art and literature of the Middle Ages and the Renaissance through 1500, and African art and literature prior to the 16th century. Emphasis is on critical thinking about art and different cultures, as well as on factual knowledge. (½ unit)

MATHEMATICS

Explorations in Mathematics

Course MAT 9-A. The purpose of this course is to provide students with experience in mathematical problem-solving, communication, reasoning, and connections through the use of real-world problems and examples. (½ unit)

Course MAT 9-B. This course continues the student's exploration into mathematical problem-solving and reasoning. (½ unit)

Pre-Algebra

Course MAT 9-C. This is the first semester of Pre-Algebra. This course explores integers and rational numbers, ratios and proportions, percents and basic descriptive statistics, inequalities and graphing linear equations, number theory in factoring, and the properties of rational numbers. (½ unit)

Course MAT 9-D. This is the second semester of Pre-Algebra, including the following topics: linear equations and equalities, integer exponents, evaluating formulas, algebraic expressions. Pythagorean theorem, and polynomials. (½ unit)

Algebra I

Course MAT 10-A. This is the first semester of Algebra I, including the following topics: sets, variables, structure and properties of the real number system, first degree equations/inequalities, relations and functions, graphs, systems of linear equations/inequalities, integral exponents, polynomials, and factoring. (½ unit)

Course MAT 10-B. This is the second semester of Algebra I, including the following topics: rational algebraic expressions, irrational numbers, radical expressions, quadratic equations, and the use of linear equations to solve verbal problems. (½ unit)

Algebra II

Course MAT 11-A. This is the first semester of Algebra II, including the following topics: review and extension of the structure and properties of the real number system, linear relations and functions,

graphs in space, determinants, polynomial functions, polynomial and rational expressions, sequences and series, and solving verbal problems. (½ unit)

Course MAT 11-B. The second semester of Algebra II, including the following topics: review and extension of relations, functions, and graphs; graphs of quadratic equations and inequalities; rational and irrational exponents; quadratic systems; logarithms; complex numbers; and the use of systems of equations to solve verbal problems. (½ unit)

Business Mathematics I

Course MAT 11-C. This is the first semester of Business Mathematics and includes following topics: checkbook records, salary and wages, piece rate and overtime pay, net pay and fringe benefits, percent, commission, the metric system, budgeting and buying, elapsed time and due date, installment loans and credit cards, savings and insurance, real estate and education, home ownership expenses, and using money wisely. (½ unit)

Course MAT 11-D. This is the second semester of Business Mathematics and includes the following topics: transportation, taxes, the small business, the retailer, the wholesaler, the manufacturer, and special business and farm problems. (½ unit)

Informal Geometry

Course MAT 11-E. This is the first semester of Informal Geometry, including the following topics: geometric concepts, angles, triangles, polygons, parallelograms, trapezoids, congruence, ratios, proportions, and mean radicals. (½ unit)

Course MAT 11-F. This is the second semester of Informal Geometry, designed for studying geometry on an informal basis. It allows the student to further explore geometry without the rigid curriculum of a formal proof and is an excellent forerunner to regular geometry. Topics include polygons, congruence, right triangles, circles, volume, area, and basic constructions. (½ unit)

PEER COUNSELING

Peer Counseling I: Knowing Myself and Helping Others

This course will help the student to understand and communicate with other people. Topics include: learning about myself, communicating with myself, communicating with others both verbally and indirectly, active listening and problem solving, group dynamics and peer pressure, standing up for my beliefs, stress management, self-concept, and coping with interpersonal crisis. (½ unit)

Peer Counseling II: Project Self-Discovery

This course examines interpersonal relationships and teaches students the importance of setting goals. Topics explored under interpersonal relationships include identifying the characteristics of healthy relationships, and identifying the effects of being socially dysfunctional. Students also define positive and negative aspects of peer pressure and learn how peer pressure affects behavior. Goal setting includes the need for short- and long-term life and career goals and skills in decision making and problem solving. Topics include: "looking at myself," "talking with peers," "thinking and studying," "growing and peer pressure," "gaining self-confidence," and "looking at the future." (½ unit)

SCIENCE

Physical Science

Course SCI 9-A. This is the first semester of Physical Science. This course should give the student the basic knowledge of what is happening in the physical world. The two major fields of physical science that will concern the student in this course are chemistry and physics. Topics include scientific tools, motion and force, work, power, what are things made of, and the law of conservation of mass. (½ unit)

Course SCI 9-B. This is the second semester of Physical Science. Topics include the behavior of light, electricity, magnetism, acids, bases, and salts, and nuclear energy. (½ unit)

Fundamentals of Environmental Science

Course SCI 10-A. This is the first semester of Fundamentals of Environmental Science. Topics include ecosystems, evolution, water and waste management, and populations. (½ unit)

Course SCI 10-B. This is the second semester of Fundamentals of Environmental Science. Topics include soil and the soil ecosystem, water and air pollution, acid precipitation and factors affecting the climate, and economic risks. (½ unit)

SOCIAL STUDIES

World Geography

Course SST 9-A. This is the first semester of World Geography which is designed to give students an understanding of the interrelationships between people and their environment. Appropriate skills and concepts from both cultural and physical geography are used. Specific content includes, but is not limited to, an understanding of the relationship between physical geography and the economic, political, social, cultural, and historical aspects of human activity. (½ unit)

Course SST 9-B. This is the second semester of World Geography. The material is applied to the study of Western Europe, Eastern Europe, the Soviet Union, Latin America, North Africa, the Middle East, sub-Saharan Africa, southern and eastern Asia, the United States, and Canada. (½ unit)

World History

Course SST 10-A. This first semester of World History, organized both chronologically and topically, covers precivilization to the European Renaissance. Special areas of study are India, China, and Africa. (½ unit)

Course SST 10-B. This second semester of World History chronologically covers the period from the Reformation to post-World War II. Special attention is given to the emergence of democracy and communism as forms of government. (½ unit)

American History

Course SST 11-A. This first course provides an understanding of the chronological development of the American people. It covers American history from before Columbus to the late nineteenth century, including colonial society, national identity and growth, sectionalism, the Civil War, Reconstruction, economic and social development, and religion in a developing nation. It develops the ability to relate American society to past societies by placing current and historical events in context. Changes in historical patterns, and their causes and effects, are examined. (½ unit)

Course SST 11-B. The second semester course addresses American history from the late nineteenth century to the present, including economic expansion, international and domestic politics, the Depression, and political and social change. Critical thinking skills are stressed. It continues the themes of relating American society to past societies and the context of events and historical periods. National leadership, cultural diversity, changes in historical development, and the interaction of science, technology, and American society are examined. Vocabulary building is included. (½ unit)

American Government

This course is a study of the American system of government. It explores local, state, and national government; liberties; rights; voting;

running for office; pressure groups; and public opinion; as well as how American citizens can make an impact on their government. (½ unit)

Economics

This course is designed to introduce students to the basic principles of economics and the fundamental operations of the American system of free enterprise. This course helps students realize they are a part of our economic system and prepares them to play an intelligent, informed, participatory role in it. (½ unit)

NONCREDIT COURSES

CONDOMINIUMS

The Condominium Act for the Layperson

Designed to help one understand the Florida Condominium Act, Chapter 718, Florida Statutes. Each lesson focuses on specific sections of the law, which apply to the condominium association from turnover forward. The duties and responsibilities of a developer in terms of the development phase of a condominium are not covered unless they are relevant to the understanding of another statutory section of the law. The Division of Florida Land Sales, Condominiums and Mobile Homes Rules that clarify F.S. 718 are reviewed. (4 CEUs) *Tuition:* $80.

Special "Mini" Condominium Courses

The following topics are all included in CONDO 1. If you have already taken CONDO 1 you may not wish to enroll in these courses described below.

Introduction to Condominium Association Management. Topics include a history of condominiums, declaration of a condominium, mandatory documents, legal requirements for condominium associations, and the Condominium Act. (1.5 CEUs) *Tuition:* $40.

Developer and Unit-Owner-Controlled Condominium Associations. Designed to prepare unit owners, directors, officers, and managers to manage different types of condominium associations. (1.5 CEUs) *Tuition:* $40.

Records, Meetings, and Insurance Management for Community Associations. This course highlights the statutory requirements for recordkeeping, the conduct of membership and board meetings, and guidelines for insurance coverage. (1.5 CEUs) *Tuition:* $40.

Maintenance, Finance, and Enforcement Management for Community Associations. Outlines statutory requirements regarding finance and management and furnishes various forms and guidelines useful to the association. (1.2 CEUs) *Tuition:* $40.

Community Association Financial Management. Explains the budget process and financial procedures and statements necessary to operate a community association. (1.2 CEUs) *Tuition:* $115.

DIETARY MANAGEMENT

Dietary Manager Course

This course includes study of the health field, food preparation and management systems, nutritional care, and human resource management. (15 CEUs) *Tuition:* $205.

FORESTRY

Introduction to Forestry

This entry-level course describes important aspects of the science of forestry. Focuses on the forest as a historically valued resource, both aesthetically and commercially; identification of distinct forest communities; managing forest stands for specific purposes; and forest policy and planning. (1.5 CEUs) *Tuition:* $60.

Principles of Silviculture

Designed to provide an understanding of the biological management of forests. Focuses on the theory and practical skills required to establish and manage a forest in terms of the landowner's goals and management objectives. (5 CEUs) *Tuition:* $60.

Introduction to Forest Pests/Forest Insects and Tree Diseases

This two-part study acquaints students with the biology, ecology, and management of forests and urban trees in southeastern states. The two courses are offered as one enrollment; their closely linked content requires study of both parts for a thorough understanding of the subject. (10 CEUs) *Tuition:* $75.

Introduction to Forest and Wildland Firefighting

Covers basic firefighting information such as fire prevention and suppression, fire behavior, equipment, and strategies for initial attack. (4 CEUs) *Tuition:* $75.

Basic Forest and Wildland Fire Behavior

Forest and wildland fire behavior is defined as the way fire reacts to fuel, weather, and topography. Students study ways that fuels ignite, flames develop, and fire spreads and exhibits other defining characteristics. Designed for entry level personnel, this course concentrates on the fire environment, fuels, critical weather situations, suppression techniques, and the cautious firefighter. (4 CEUs) *Tuition:* $75.

Introduction to Urban and Community Forestry

Planning, establishment, and management of urban trees on community streets, in parks, and in forested greenbelts is the focus of this course in urban forestry. Topics include the use and value of community trees, ordinances to manage and protect urban trees and forests, street tree management, greenbelt silviculture, basic tree care, and tree protection.

GENEALOGY

Introduction to American Genealogical Research

This course provides the tools to conduct genealogical research. It will help you locate the records needed to study your ancestory. This course is designed to take you step-by-step through the process of filling in your family tree. Topics include the value of family records, personal knowledge of family members, and the numerous types of public and private records which must be used to compile a family history correctly. (5 CEUs) *Tuition:* $80.

HUMAN RESOURCES MANAGEMENT

Defining Human Resource Needs

Designed for individuals who would like an introduction to the field, but do not desire to take a college course. Topics include a definition of the field, its legal and social contexts, job analysis, determining human resource requirements, and recruiting, screening, and selecting employees. (2.2 CEUs)

Human Resource Functions

A continuation of the above course. Topics include orienting and training employees, appraising performance, managing careers, pay and benefits, labor relations, safety and employee assistance programs, human relations management costs and benefits, and managing international employees. (2.2 CEUs)

INSURANCE

Bail and Bail Bond Insurance in Florida

Provides fundamental information on basic principles and terminology but is not a complete program of study of the bail bond and surety fields. This course is essential for qualification for the Florida State Insurance Commissioner's examination for a limited license as a Limited Surety Agent (2-34) or Professional Bail Bondsman (2-37). In addition to this course, an 80-hour criminal justice course is a prerequisite for the state examination for the bond license. (3 CEUs)

Life, Health, and Annuity Insurance

Focuses on preparing for Florida's Life Agent qualification examination. The course complies with the Rules of the Department of Insurance on license qualification courses for Life Agents. Students who successfully complete the course qualify to take the state examination for the 2-16 or the 2-18 license. (4 CEUs)

Property and Liability Insurance

Basic course designed to equip the student with sufficient information to successfully complete the general agents licensing requirement in Florida. Introduces basic insurance terminology and explores some essential principles. (12 CEUs)

Health Insurance

Students interested in becoming Health Only agents will gain a basic knowledge of health and disability income insurance while preparing for the Florida examination for Health Insurance License (2-40). (4 CEUs)

Health Insurance

Students interested in becoming Health Only agents will gain a basic knowledge of health and disability income insurance while preparing for the Florida examination for Health Insurance License (2-40). (4 CEUs) *Tuition:* $105.

MANAGEMENT

Management Ethics

This is a beginning course for business or government managers designed to provide a basic understanding of the many conceptual, individual, and organizational issues surrounding business ethics. Although generally exploratory in nature, this class provides managers (and future managers) with some background information and basic tools, as well as provides some critical standards for approaching and evaluating ethical questions in the work place. (2.2 CEUs) *Tuition:* $80.

Principles of Supervision

Helps to prepare individuals for first-line supervision. Topics include delegating, decision making, planning, time management, organizing, staffing, directing, controlling, and labor relations. Content can be applied in all supervisory activities; course does not center on any specific occupation. (1.5 CEUs) *Tuition:* $75.

Supervisory Communications

Designed to improve the supervisor's communication skills. Topics include interpersonal communications, motivation, group communications and barriers, written communications, and speaking. (1.5 CEUs) *Tuition:* $75.

Supervisory Leadership

This course includes study of leadership role and the need to develop power and influence within that role. Different leadership approaches, skills, and styles are considered from the standpoint of understanding motivation and communication with subordinates. Relationship between effective leadership and organizational change is explored. (1.5 CEUs) *Tuition:* $75.

Managing the Problem Employee

Focuses on the theory and practical skills required for effective supervision of problem employees. Contributes to supervisor's ability to maintain a productive working environment. Teaches how to recognize the problem employee and gives strategies for managing and dealing with the problem employee. (1.5 CEUs) *Tuition:* $75.

Working Better with Your Boss

Deals with an important yet often very difficult relationship experienced by just about everyone who works in an organization: getting along with the boss. This relationship can be managed—shaped and influenced—by the subordinate. (1.5 CEUs) *Tuition:* $75.

Job Productivity

Facilitates efficiency and effectiveness in human development. Focuses on practical skills to enrich the quality of life professionally and personally by enhancing productivity and performance on and off the job. Topics include the value of self-awareness and goal setting; skills development; determining growth opportunities; developing a plan to modify nonproductive behaviors; increased performance ability through speaking and listening skills; and enhancement of significant job-productive skills. (1.5 CEUs) *Tuition:* $75.

Reports and Letters: Written Communication for Supervisors

Builds skills in the daily writing tasks required at work; includes grammar, mechanics, and organization. Reports, proposals, and business letters are emphasized. (1.5 CEUs) *Tuition:* $75.

Sexual Harassment in the Workplace

This is a beginning course for current and future managers that provides a basic understanding of the many conceptual, individual, and institutional issues that surround the subject of sexual harassment in the workplace. The course deals with such issues as changing cultural attitudes at work; the evolution of the subject; its personal, corporate, and societal ramification; profiles of typical victims and perpetrators; the changing legal definitions of harassment; and preventive measures to be taken by both individuals and organizations. (2.2 CEUs) *Tuition:* $80.

MATHEMATICS

Mathematics for Laboratory Sciences

Reviews math skills pertinent to the laboratory sciences. Basic mathematics, logarithms, conversions, systems of measure, preparation and analysis of solutions, colorimetry, and quality assurance are included. Calculations specifically related to hematology are presented for optional study. (3 CEUs) *Tuition:* $65.

PEST CONTROL

Guidelines for Structural Fumigation

Provides basic sound guidelines for performing structural fumigation. (4 CEUs) *Tuition:* $60 ($50 for National Pest Control Association members).

Guidelines for the Control of Subterranean Termites

Covers topics essential for effective subterranean termite control. (4 CEUs) *Tuition:* $60 ($50 for National Pest Control Association members).

Guidelines for Bird Management

This course provides basic sound guidelines for bird management and control. (4 CEUs) *Tuition:* $75 (&65 for National Pest Control Association members).

WASTEWATER TREATMENT

Wastewater Treatment Plant Operation, Class C

Florida's Department of Environmental Regulation recognizes this course for twelve months of constructive credit. The course has been approved by the states of Texas, Illinois, Wyoming, West Virginia, Maryland, Alaska, Georgia, and Kentucky. Teaches skills and knowledge needed for operation, maintenance, and supervision of "C" level wastewater treatment plants. (15 CEUs) *Tuition:* $110.

Wastewater Treatment Plant Operation, Class D

This course is a basic introduction to wastewater treatment. It provides basic principles of the operation of a "package wastewater treatment plant." This course is officially approved by the states of Georgia, Illinois, Wyoming, North Dakota, and Alaska. Emphasis on extended aeration type activated sludge plants. (3 CEUs) *Tuition:* $65.

Water Treatment Class C

This course is designed to train water treatment plant operators in the basic requirements of plant operation, and to help prepare them to take the water treatment state certification exam at the "C" level. After completing the course, the student will understand the responsibilities of water treatment plant operation and control, as well as develop skill in safe operational procedures sampling and laboratory testing techniques. Teaches basic biology, bacteriology, mathematics, and chemistry associated with water treatment. (14.4 CEUs) *Tuition:* $110.

WATER POLLUTION CONTROL

Activated Sludge Skills Training Program

This course assumes that the student has completed basic and intermediate operator's training. Approved by the states of Florida, North Dakota, Texas, Illinois, Georgia, Wyoming, and West Virginia. Designed to develop operator skills, this course deals with both the equipment used in activated sludge wastewater treatment and the control and troubleshooting of the biological processes that occur in the system. Developed on the basis of "need to know" principles, this course stresses those operator activities needed to manage activated sludge systems and to keep them running efficiently. The basic functions and processes of the modern activated sludge operation are covered. (12 CEUs) *Tuition:* $80.

Pumps: Operation and Maintenance Skill Training Package

Basic skills and knowledge are presented in an easily understood format. The various types of motors, motor controls, and couplings are described. The operating principles, components and maintenance of centrifugal, positive displacement, and air lift pumps are covered. (3 CEUs) *Tuition:* $80.

Anaerobic Digestion Skills Training Package

This course assumes that the student has completed basic and intermediate operator's training. The University of Florida's course for Class C Wastewater Operators or equivalent course(s) will adequately prepare one for this study. Designed to develop operator skills, this course deals with both the equipment used in anaerobic digestion wastewater sludges and the control of the biological processes involved. Developed on the basis of "need to know" principles, it describes those activities performed in the operation and management of anaerobic digestion systems. The general objective is to increase one's ability to recognize and understand the basic functions and processes of anaerobic digestion. (3 CEUs) *Tuition:* $65.

Wastewater Treatment: Sludge Conditioning, Thickening, and Dewatering Skills Training Package

This course begins with a discussion of the quality and quantity of sludge produced by different treatment processes. A detailed solids balance is performed to show how connected one treatment process is to others within a plant. Methods used to chemically condition various types of sludges are explored. The operation and control of dissolved air flotation thickeners is explained. The dewatering methods described are drying beds, centrifuges, belt filter presses, and pressure filters. (4 CEUs) *Tuition:* $65.

Wastewater Stabilization Ponds Skill Training Package

This course provides "need to know" information required to properly operate and maintain wastewater stabilization ponds (lagoons). Continuous flow-through and retention ponds are covered in the course materials. The Study Guide provides additional discussion and extensive troubleshooting guides. The course consists of four graded lessons: Ponds—Types and Processes; Pond Operation and Performance; Pond Maintenance and Laboratory Control; and Retention Pond Operation. No prior knowledge of wastewater treatment technologies is assumed. (3 CEUs) *Tuition:* $95.

Florida International University
University Park
Miami, Florida 33199   (305) 348-2000

Description:
Correspondence courses are offered through the Department of Independent Study and Distance Education of the University of Florida in Gainesville. For courses available, SEE **Florida, University of.**

Accreditations:
Southern Association of Colleges and Schools.

Florida State University
College and Copeland
Tallahassee, Florida 32306   (904) 644-6200

Description:
Correspondence courses are offered through the Department of Independent Study and Distance Education of the University of Florida in Gainesville. For courses available, SEE **Florida, University of.**

Accreditations:
Southern Association of Colleges and Schools.

Fort Hays State University
Division of Continuing Education
600 Park Street
Hays, Kansas 67601   (913) 628-5880

Description:
Correspondence courses offered by Fort Hays State University are administered by Independent Study at the University of Kansas, Lawrence, Kansas. For courses available, SEE **Kansas, University of.**

Faculty:
Lou Poirier, Assistant Dean of Continuing Education.

Accreditations:
North Central Association of Colleges and Schools.

Freed-Hardeman College
Department of Bible
Henderson, Tennessee 38340   (901) 989-6000

Description:
Freed-Hardeman College is the successor to chartered schools and colleges operated on the present campus since 1870. It is an independent Christian college providing liberal education with an emphasis on career-oriented programs.
The college offers several correspondence courses in Bible.

Faculty:
Dowell Flatt, Chairman, Department of Bible.

Academic Levels:
College

Admission Requirements:
High school graduation.

Tuition:
Contact the Department of Bible for enrollment procedure and current tuition.

Accreditations:
Southern Association of Colleges and Schools.

COLLEGE COURSES

BIBLE

Bible

For courses currently available and their descriptions, contact the Department of Bible.

Gannon University
University College
Open University Program
University Square
Erie, Pennsylvania 16451   (814) 871-7461

Description:
The history of Gannon University dates back to 1933, when a two-year junior college was established by the late Most Reverend Archbishop John Mark Gannon and named Cathedral College. In 1941, Cathedral College extended its curricula to four-year courses and changed its name to the Gannon School of Arts and Sciences. In 1979, Gannon College was designated as a university and assumed its present name.
Gannon University established the Open University Program to serve residents of the Erie metropolitan and tri-state areas. The main objective is to provide adults with the opportunity to earn credits in college academic programs for learning achieved through guided independent study. Students may attend the Open University as candidates for a degree or for personal or professional development.

The program is designed for students whose employment, family responsibilities, or geographic location prevents them from attending regular college campus classes. It is an independent study program for self-motivated students. A course manual is used to guide the student's progress through a course. It explains procedures and indicates assignments. The student mails completed assignments to the instructor, who reviews and comments on them and then returns them to the student.

Faculty:
Dr. Howard C. Smith, Jr., Dean, University College. The Open University faculty includes a blend of representatives from the business community, professional and trade organizations, health care organizations, and selected Gannon University faculty members.

Academic Levels:
College
Professional

Degree/Certificate Programs:
Associate Degree; Certificate. Gannon University offers an associate degree in Business Administration, consisting of a core of 17 courses supplemented by a concentration in a specialized area. After completing these courses, the student may transfer to the Evening Division or Day Division to complete the balance of the requirements. Also, the Open University provides a Liberal Arts program designed to enhance the student's intellectual enrichment and fulfillment, combining a solid general education base with study in areas of individual interest. This Liberal Arts program can be completed by correspondence and the student may then transfer to campus classes and complete the bachelor's degree in one of over 30 different major fields of study. A number of career-oriented certificate programs geared to develop professional expertise in a particular area are also available, such as the Health Services Administration Certificate Program, Health Services Purchasing and Materials Management Certificate Program, and Purchasing Materials Management Certificate Program. The above degree and certificate programs follow specific course requirements. However, a student may elect to take any of the courses available on a credit or noncredit basis. The courses listed below are representative of courses offered.

Admission Requirements:
Evidence of graduation from high school or the equivalent (i.e., transcript); completed application form/registration form.

Tuition:
$275 per credit. Tuition and fees subject to change; contact the Open University Program Office for current information. Deferred payment plan available (must be arranged prior to the start of the term). MasterCard accepted. If a student follows the proper procedure for withdrawal from a course, the refund schedule is: first week, 80 percent; second week, 60 percent; third week, 40 percent; fourth week, 20 percent. There will be no tuition refund after the fourth week of a term. No course may be changed for another course without the approval of the Open University Program Office; there will be no course changes after the second full week of the term.

Enrollment Period:
All efforts should be made to complete the course(s) within the semester calendar. If extenuating circumstances make completion of the requirements impossible, the following steps are necessary: (1) Requests for extensions should be made to the Open University Office prior to the last day of the semester; (2) the request is pending - subject to the approval of the course instructor; should any difficulty arise with the extension, the student will be contacted; a copy of the approval slip will be forwarded to the student; (3) the Registrar's Office will process the incomplete grade (X) which is submitted by the instructor; the incomplete grade (X) will automatically be changed to an "F" grade 30 days after the semester concludes; (4) when the course requirements are satisfied, the instructor will submit a change of grade form to the Registrar's Office converting the incomplete grade or "F" (whichever the case may be) to the appropriate letter grade.

Equipment Requirements:
Students residing outside the Erie area will receive a book list and order form for purchasing textbooks, course manuals, and other related materials through the mail from the Gannon Bookstore. A fee for postage and handling is charged to the student.

Credit and Grading:
The grading system is: A, Excellent; B, Above Average; C, Average; D, Passing; F, Failure; G, Incomplete; X, Withdrawal from a course prior to the cutoff date listed in the academic calendar, or withdrawal anytime from a course in which the student is passing. Regionally accredited courses are transferable. Examinations are administered on campus at the student's convenience. For those students who are unable to go to the campus, examinations are proctored either by regional directors or by other qualified individuals at the place of work or in the community. Credits are awarded in semester hour units.

Library Services:
The library on the Gannon University campus is available if accessible by the student.

Accreditations:
Middle States Association of Colleges and Schools; The State Board of Education, Commonwealth of Pennsylvania.

COLLEGE COURSES

ACCOUNTING
Introductory Accounting
A continuation of the study of basic accounting principles, plus special topics. (3 semester hours)

BUSINESS AND MANAGEMENT

Organizational Theory

Examination of human behavior within the framework of the organization. (3 semester hours)

Principles of Macroeconomics

This course covers macroeconomic theory and its application to such current problem areas as unemployment and inflation, the role of money in the economy and monetary and fiscal policy. (3 semester hours)

Business and Professional Writing

Study of various methods of communication used in business for audiences both within and outside the organization. (3 semester hours)

EDUCATION

Foundations of Education

The development of the school, philosophies of education. An introduction to the teaching profession. (3 semester hours)

ENGLISH

Communications

Application of the principles of logic, rhetoric, and language in written discourse. (3 semester hours)

Prose Fiction

An introduction to literature based on the short story and novel. (3 semester hours)

Research in Mass Media

An analysis of the use of logic, rhetoric, and language in mass media; principles of library research and documentation. (3 semester hours)

GEOGRAPHY

Geography of the U.S. and Canada

An analytical study of the physical and cultural geography of the U.S. and Canada. (3 semester hours)

GEOLOGY

Historical Geology

The history of the earth, including the development of life. A study of the changing nature of the surface of the earth, etc. (3 semester hours)

HEALTH SERVICES MANAGEMENT

Essentials of Health Services Financial Management

Financial requirements and sources of revenue for health services institutions. Examination of the financial aspects of daily operation (3 semester hours)

Advanced Health Services Purchasing and Material Management

A more sophisticated and advanced level relative to the concepts, techniques, skills and knowledge needed to effectively carry out the various responsibilities of the Health Services Purchasing and Materials professional. (3 semester hours)

MATERIALS MANAGEMENT

Materials Management Policy and Overview

An overview of the two discrete yet complimentary functions of Purchasing and Inventory Production Control as an integral whole. (3 semester hours)

PHILOSOPHY

Philosophy of Ethical Responsibility

Study of the main ethical systems and certain ethical questions in light of principles guiding a person's moral life. (3 semester hours)

PRODUCTION AND INVENTORY CONTROL

Basic Production and Inventory Control

A course devoted to the development, scope and objectives of production and inventory control. Topics include the material planning system and the relationship of forecasting, material planning and control, scheduling, machine loading, shop floor control techniques and organization. (3 semester hours)

PSYCHOLOGY

Introductory Psychology

The study of human personality, behavior, and adjustment. (3 semester hours)

Psychology of Human Development

A study of theories and research on evolution of complex behavior from infancy through adulthood. (3 semester hours)

Deviant Behavior

Analysis of behavior and culture conflicts which are detrimental to social harmony. (3 semester hours)

Introduction to Mental Health

An introduction to basic mental health concepts: definition of positive mental health, emotional and social adjustment, psychogenesis of emotional and mental disturbance, treatment techniques, community mental health, preventive and rehabilitative programs. (3 semester hours)

PUBLIC RELATIONS

Public Relations

Strategies and communication tools of public relations which link an institution and its publics. (3 semester hours)

PURCHASING

Intermediate Purchasing and Materials Management

An advanced introduction to, familiarization with and application of the principles, concepts and techniques relating to: (1) capital equipment buying; (2) make or buy decisions; (3) traffic management; and other topics. (3 semester hours)

RELIGION

Introduction to Sacred Scriptures

An introduction to the literature of the Old and New Testaments, with selected readings. (3 semester hours)

Theology of Moral Responsibility

Ethical responses based on God's word and the teachings of Christianity. (3 semester hours)

PROFESSIONAL COURSES

HEALTH SERVICES MANAGEMENT

Health Services Administration Certificate Program

This program requires a total of 18 credit hours. Core courses required are Health Service Delivery System, Health Services Planning, Essentials of Health Services Financial Management, Health Services Management; two courses from the following are selected by the student: Legal Aspects of Health Services Administration; Health Information Systems; Basics of Health Services Purchasing and Materials Management; Business and Professional Communications; Introductory Accounting.

Health Services Purchasing and Materials Management Certificate Program

This program requires a total of 12 credit hours. Core courses required are Basics of Health Services Purchasing and Materials Management, Advanced Health Services Purchasing and Materials Management; two courses from the following are selected by the student: Principles of Management, Professional and Business Writing, Health Services Planning.

Purchasing and Materials Management Certificate Program

A total of 18 credit hours are required for this program. Core courses required are Introduction to Purchasing and Materials Management, Intermediate Purchasing and Materials Management, Basic Production and Inventory Control, Materials Management Policy and Overview; two courses from the following are selected by the student: Introductory Accounting, Principles of Microeconomics, Professional and Business Writing, Principles of Management.

Georgia, University of
University System of Georgia Independent Study
Georgia Center for Continuing Education
1180 East Broad
Athens, Georgia 30602-3603   (706) 542-3243

Description:

The University of Georgia is a state-supported university chartered in 1785 and established in 1801. Its thirteen schools and colleges carry on the University's programs of teaching, research, and service. Thirty-three state supported institutions of higher education in Georgia are governed by the Board of Regents and are part of the University System of Georgia.

The University System of Georgia Independent Study program is a nondegree granting, academic program providing lower- and upper-division undergraduate credit courses beyond the campuses of the University System's colleges and universities. It provides students freedom from the classroom and flexibility of registration. Over 3,000 students are enrolled annually. Participating institutions include: University of Georgia, Georgia College, Georgia Southern College, North Georgia College, and Valdosta State College. Credit earned through independent study is recorded in the Registrar's office at the University of Georgia and may be used as transfer credit from the institution.

Those adults who wish to enter or re-enter an academic degree program may appeal to the Adult Advisory Service (at the above address) for advice about planning their educational futures. The University System does not have an external degree program, but one's educational future can be planned on the basis of current programs of the University.

Faculty:

Carmen Shuler White, Acting Department Head. There is a faculty of 76.

Academic Levels:

College

Degree/Certificate Programs:

Twenty-five percent of the credit requirements for a baccalaureate degree at the University of Georgia may be earned through Independent Study.

Admission Requirements:

Independent Study is open to anyone regardless of previous academic experience. Transcripts of previous college or high school work are not required for registration, and registrations are accepted at any time of the year. High school students registering for college academic credit courses must be enrolled in a college early admission or joint enrollment program before registering for Independent Study. Students may take as many courses as they wish simultaneously.

Tuition:

$53 per quarter hour for Georgia resident, nonresident $159 per credit. Additional fees for overseas airmail postage. Refund policy: An eighty percent refund of tuition will be given if the request is received within seven calendar days from the registration date; sixty percent within 14 calendar days; forty percent within 21 calendar days; and twenty percent within 28 calendar days. No refund will be issued after the 28th day.

Enrollment Period:

Correspondence courses may begin at any time. Enrollment is effective for one year from the registration date. An extension three months may be granted upon payment of a $45 fee. The minimum time to complete a course is six weeks.

Equipment Requirements:

Some courses (primarily language courses) require the use of cassette tapes and cassette player. Both must be furnished by the student. The tapes are ordered on a prepaid basis from the school. Overseas students desiring air mail return of their corrected assignments will be so billed. Textbooks must be purchased by the student, and may be ordered from the University bookstore.

Credit and Grading:

Grading system is A, B, C, D, F. The minimum passing grade is D. Averaging of final grades is based on a passing grade on any final examination. Students will not receive passing grades based on lessons alone or on an unsatisfactory examination. Students withdrawing from a course or allowing a course to expire will be assigned a grade of "W." Examinations must be monitored by an approved proctor. Correspondence credits may be transferred-in on the same basis as any other transfer credits. Credit is awarded in quarter hour units.

Library Services:

Students have access to the University of Georgia libraries on campus or through interlibrary loan.

Accreditations:

Southern Association of Colleges and Schools. Member of: National University Continuing Education Association.

COLLEGE COURSES

ACCOUNTING

Principles of Accounting

I. A study of fundamental principles applicable to the accounting cycle, asset valuation, income determination, financial reporting, basic business taxes, and owner's equity. (5 quarter hours)

II. Accounting principles and basic accounting theories as an aid to management. Cost accounting fundamentals. Analysis and interpretation of financial statements. (5 quarter hours)

Tax I

A basic Federal income tax course involving a study of history and background, general concepts of taxation, income, deductions, and federal income taxation primarily relating to individuals. This course is designed for accounting majors to emphasize the application of technical rules to factual situations such as those typically encountered by an accountant. (5 quarter hours)

AGRICULTURE

Turfgrass Management

A study of turfgrasses and growth requirements. The various operations, equipment, materials, and work program for the proper and efficient maintenance and management of turf for golf courses and other specific uses. (5 quarter hours)

Horticultural Science

An introduction to horticultural science, the biology of horticulture, the technology of crop production and marketing, the industry, geography, production systems, aesthetics, and crop types. Observations

ANTHROPOLOGY

Introduction to Anthropology

Variation in human culture and biology from the earliest beginnings to the present, including relationships between human biology, culture, and the environment, and an understanding of contemporary cultural differences by man. (5 quarter hours)

Cultural Anthropology

Concepts and methods for analysis of the institutions of nonliterate peoples and their comparison with modern societies. (5 quarter hours)

ART

Appreciation of the Visual Arts

An understanding of painting, sculpture, and architecture—both historic and contemporaneous. Emphasis on sociological and psychological factors influencing period styles and contributing to the nature of genius. The aim is to make the student both visually sophisticated and historically informed. (5 quarter hours)

Introduction to the History of Ancient and Medieval Art

A survey of world art from prehistoric through medieval times. The formal characteristics of the paintings, sculpture, architecture, and some of the minor arts will be analyzed in their stylistic and symbolic developments which will be discussed in relation to the changing cultural backgrounds. (5 quarter hours)

Introduction to the History of Art, Renaissance - Eighteenth Century

A survey of world art from the Renaissance through the eighteenth century. The formal characteristics of the painting, sculpture, architecture, and some of the minor arts will be analyzed in their stylistic and symbolic developments which will be discussed in relation to the changing cultural backgrounds. (5 quarter hours)

Introduction to Nineteenth and Twentieth Century Art

A survey of art from the late eighteenth century to the present. The formal characteristics of painting, sculpture, architecture and some of the minor arts will be discussed in relation to the changing cultural backgrounds. (5 quarter hours)

BIOLOGY

Ecology

A first course in the science of biotic populations and communities. The course covers population structure and dynamics, organization and classification of communities, nutrient and energy flows in ecosystems, and the principles of systems ecology. (5 quarter hours)

Conservation

A consideration of the basic biological aspects of the conservation of man's renewable and nonrenewable natural resources. (5 quarter hours)

BUSINESS EDUCATION

Office Management

Scientific office management: principles, equipment, supervision, information management methods and procedures, job organization and evaluation, selection and training of office personnel. (5 quarter hours)

BUSINESS LAW

Business Law I

Provides a basic appreciation of the relationships of law and society and the fundamental concepts encompassed by law as well as an investigation of contracts, Uniform Commercial Code sales and Antitrust Law. (5 quarter hours)

Business Law II

Business organization, property, bankruptcy, secured transactions, and commercial paper. (5 quarter hours)

CLASSICAL STUDIES

Classical Culture: Greece

A study of the characteristics of Greek literature, made principally through translations of selections from Greek authors. (5 quarter hours)

Classical Culture: Rome

A study of the characteristics of Latin culture made principally through translations of selections from Latin authors. (5 quarter hours)

Mythology in Classical Literature

An introduction to the myths and sagas of the Greeks and Romans, in particular through ancient literature. (5 quarter hours)

Medical Terminology

A course introducing medical terminology derived from Greek and Latin. The course will concentrate on recognizing the meanings of the components of medical terms and understanding the principles that govern their arrangement. History of ancient medicine will also be considered. (5 quarter hours)

ECONOMICS

Principles of Microeconomics

Introduction to the price and market system with applications of microeconomic theory to current economic problems. (5 quarter hours)

Principles of Macroeconomics

Income, employment and other macroeconomic theory with applications to current economic problems. (5 quarter hours)

Economic Development of the United States

American economic development from the colonial period to the present; economic factors involved in industrial growth and the resulting economic problems. (5 quarter hours)

Labor Economics

Survey of labor organizations, wages, hours, unemployment, labor legislation, and current developments in labor. Tools of economic analysis are utilized. (5 quarter hours)

History of Economic Thought

The development of contemporary economic theory from early economic ideas. A study of the development of economic methods of analysis and philosophies and their relation to current theory. (5 quarter hours)

Government and Business

A study of the interaction between business organization and government. Special emphasis on industry structure and performance. Includes government policies concerning regulation, control, and promotion of business enterprise. (5 quarter hours)

EDUCATION

Learning and Motivation

Learning theory and processes of both students and teachers, dimensions of motivation related to learning and performance. (5 quarter hours)

Career Development for Life Planning

Offers an opportunity for receiving information and developing skills necessary for effective career decision making. Processes of self-assessment, occupational exploration, and preparation for employment are explored in addition to traditional classroom activity, content is presented in an experiential manner through field trips, observations, role playing, simulation, individualized projects, and contact with resource experts. (3 quarter hours)

Adolescent Psychology

Interests, needs, and abilities of adolescents; evaluation of their total development. (5 quarter hours)

Psychology of Early Childhood

Interests, needs, and abilities of children, evaluation of their total development. (5 quarter hours)

ENGLISH

English Composition

101. Expository themes on both general and literary topics developed by basic rhetorical methods. (5 quarter hours)

102. Themes on fiction, poetry, and drama. (5 quarter hours)

Masterpieces of English Literature to 1700

Masterpieces of English literature from the beginnings to 1700. (5 quarter hours)

Masterpieces of English Literature after 1700

Masterpieces of English literature from 1700 to the present. (5 quarter hours)

Survey of World Literature I

A survey of world literature through the seventeenth century. Special attention is given to the influence of classical works on later literature, to the spread of ideas and concepts beyond national or ethnic boundaries, and to the influence of philosophical and religious views on literature. (5 quarter hours)

Survey of World Literature II

A survey of world literature from the late seventeenth century to modern times, with attention to recurrent themes, archetypal figures, and techniques of literary interpretation. (5 quarter hours)

Writing for Business

An advanced writing course, with an examination of the elements of effective writing, particularly as they apply to business and the professions. (5 quarter hours)

Survey of American Literature

A survey of American literature from the sixteenth century to the present. Assignments will be devoted to major literary figures, works, and movements in their historical contexts. (5 quarter hours)

Southern Literature

The literature of the South with special emphasis upon the Southern Renaissance, including works by Faulkner, Warren, Welty, and the Fugitive poets. (5 quarter hours)

British Romantic Literature

A survey of the major British Romantic poets and prose writers, including Blake, Wordsworth, Coleridge, Byron, Shelley, and Keats. (5 quarter hours)

The Modern Novel

A study of the twentieth-century English and American novel, focusing on such figures as Conrad, Joyce, Lawrence, Woolf, Forster, Lewis, Fitzgerald, Hemingway, Wolfe, and Faulkner. (5 quarter hours)

Medieval Literature

Masterpieces of medieval literature, exclusive of Chaucer. Most works will be read in Modern English translation. (5 quarter hours)

Children's Literature

A survey of children's stories and poems that have literary value with special attention to "classics" and to those literary types, works, and trends taught in elementary and secondary school. (5 quarter hours)

Early American

American literature from the beginning through Irving. (5 quarter hours)

Poetry and Prose of the English Renaissance

A study of the work of the major poets and prose fiction writers of the English Renaissance. (5 quarter hours)

Images in African American Literature

The course examines recurrent images, issues, and themes in African-American literature through in-depth studies of several works. Writers such as Douglass, Washington, Dunbar, Chesnutt, Wright, Walker, and Morrison will be regularly taught. (5 quarter hours)

FRENCH

Elementary French

101. Conversation, grammar, fundamentals of pronunciation and reading are taught. (5 quarter hours)

102. A continuation of the above course. (5 quarter hours)

103. A continuation of the above course. (5 quarter hours)

Intermediate French

Extensive reading of texts of literary merit. Grammar review, conversation, and pronunciation. Also prepares students to enter courses in French literature or French composition and conversation. (5 quarter hours)

GEOGRAPHY

Introduction to Human Geography

A survey of global patterns of resources, population, culture, and economic systems. Emphasis is placed upon the factors contributing to these patterns and the distinctions between the technologically advanced and less advanced regions of the world. (5 quarter hours)

Earth Science Survey

An introduction to physical geography, surveying climate, vegetation, soils, landforms, and water resources in their areal interrelations and distributions. (5 quarter hours)

Economic Geography

Location factors and principles, utilizing theoretical and empirical studies. Focus upon the spatial organization of economic production, consumption, and exchange systems. (5 quarter hours)

Meteorology

Basic principles of meteorology with applications to human activity. (5 quarter hours)

GERMAN

Elementary German

I. Introduction to essentials of grammar; acquisition of basic vocabulary; practice in reading, speaking, and writing. A cassette recorder is required for this course. (5 quarter hours)

II. A continuation of the above course with an increased emphasis on the active use of the language. (5 quarter hours)

III. A continuation of the above course. (5 quarter hours)

Intermediate German

A review of German grammar; reading of selected texts and particular emphasis on conversation and expansion of vocabulary. (5 quarter hours)

Commercial German

A career-oriented course designed to familiarize the student with the language of business, finance, and economics; active use of German; grammar review as needed. (5 quarter hours)

HEALTH

The Effects of Drug Use and Abuse

Social, moral, psychological, and physiological causes and effects of drug use and abuse. Individual, family, and community factors related to prevention and treatment. (5 quarter hours)

HISTORY

Early Modern Western Civilization

A cultural survey of Western civilization from the Renaissance to the end of the Napoleonic Era, emphasizing ideas of the period. (5 quarter hours)

Modern Western Civilization

A cultural survey of Western civilization from the Congress of Vienna to the present, emphasizing ideas of the period. (5 quarter hours)

American History to 1865

Development of the American nation from the Age of Discovery to 1865. (5 quarter hours)

American History Since 1865

Development of the American nation from 1865 to the present. (5 quarter hours)

History of Georgia

A comprehensive survey of Georgia's development from the occupation of the early Indians to the present. (5 quarter hours)

FAMILY AND CONSUMER STUDIES

Human Nutrition and Food

Relationship of nutritional needs and food choices to the optimal health of the individual during his/her life cycle. (5 quarter hours)

Introduction to Child Development

A survey of the physical, cognitive and personality development of children with emphasis upon the years two to ten. (5 quarter hours)

Principles of Family Finance

Changes in economic requirements during the family life cycle; forces affecting the economic welfare of families in this country. Focused on consumer credit, savings and investment, insurance, home ownership and estate planning. (5 quarter hours)

Development Within the Family

Individual and family development during the life cycle is considered, with special emphasis upon interpersonal relationships among family members. (5 quarter hours)

Interpersonal Relations and Marriage

Personal and social factors that influence dating, mate selection, engagement, marriage, and alternative lifestyles with emphasis on marital interaction and satisfaction. (5 quarter hours)

The Family

Family study utilizing data from the fields of anthropology, individual and social psychology, history, sociology, economics, and psychiatry. (5 quarter hours)

JOURNALISM

Mass Communications I: Survey

A survey of the structure and function of contemporary mass media from a historical and descriptive perspective, with some attention paid to problems and criticisms of the media. (5 quarter hours)

News Writing and Reporting

A study of basic reporting, writing, and editing practices with practical assignments in the various media. (5 quarter hours)

Law of Communication

A broad application of principles of law to the mass communication media, media practice, advertising, and freedom of information, including libel, contempt of court, right of privacy, copyright, and postal laws. (5 quarter hours)

Journalism in the Secondary School

A survey of news gathering, news writing, copy reading, typography, and business management, with specific relation to the high school newspaper, also school public relations. (5 quarter hours)

LATIN

Elementary Latin

I. An introduction to the Latin language: pronunciation, fundamentals of grammar, reading, and translation. (5 quarter hours)

II. An introduction to the Latin language, continued from the above course. (5 quarter hours)

III. Completion of study of Latin grammar and syntax; introduction to reading continuous Latin passages. (5 quarter hours)

The Golden Age of Latin Literature

An introduction to Golden Age Latin prose and poetry. Readings from a variety of authors, such as Cicero, Caesar, Livy, Vergil, and Horace. Review of elementary Latin grammar and syntax. (5 quarter hours)

Vergil's *Aeneid*

An introduction to Latin poetry, poetic syntax, meter, and style through reading Vergil's *Aeneid*. (5 quarter hours)

MANAGEMENT

Management and Organizational Behavior

Analysis of management functions and processes as applied to organizations, includes fundamentals of staff and operative management, management principles and techniques, application of techniques to specific fields. Study of human behavior in organizations, with emphasis on problems of organization structure, authority and responsibility, motivation and leadership. Particular attention will be given to motivation, authority relationships, and organization structure as their interactions with behavior processes make efficiency more or less difficult to achieve. (5 quarter hours)

Principles of Production/Operations Management

Production and its relationship to marketing, finance, accounting, and personnel functions are described. Forecasting demand, aggregate planning, master scheduling, capacity planning and material planning provide a basis for linking strategic plans to operations plans. Facilities design, job design, work measurement, productivity improvement, quality control, and project management are discussed. (5 quarter hours)

Small Business Management

This course is designed to acquaint the student with the aggregation of activities that are involved in the planning, establishing/entering a small business, and in the management of a small business enterprise. Special consideration will be given to the feasibility and the preparation of a plan of action for entering a new business or for entering an established business. (5 quarter hours)

Personnel/Human Resource Management

An introduction to personnel/human resource management. Topics introduced include human resource planning, staffing, training and development, compensation, safety and health, and labor relations. (5 quarter hours)

MARKETING

Principles of Advertising

Management of advertising by clients and agencies. Budgeting, research media selection, preparation of advertisements, and economic and social impact of advertising. (5 quarter hours)

Retail Store Management

A comprehensive course emphasizing the specific activities of retail management, merchandising, and promotion. (5 quarter hours)

Principles of Marketing

This course is concerned with the estimation of demand, consumer buying behavior, adaptation of products to markets, selection of channels of distribution, sales management, advertising, pricing, measurement of marketing efficiency, and procedures for planning and controlling marketing operations. The economic, social, and political forces that constantly change the market environment are stressed. (5 quarter hours)

MATHEMATICS

College Mathematics with Applications

Topics include fundamental algebra, polynomial and rational models, linear systems, matrices, sets, counting, probability, and mathematics of finance. (5 quarter hours)

Fundamentals of Algebra

Algebraic topics including polynomials, rational expressions, equations, inequalities, graphing, exponents and radicals, relations and functions through exponential and logarithmic functions. (5 quarter hours)

Trigonometry

Topics include mathematical induction, binomial theorem, circular functions, trigonometric functions, complex numbers. (5 quarter hours)

Precalculus Mathematics

The concept of function, intensive study of polynomial, rational, exponential, logarithmic, and trigonometric functions, and applications. (5 quarter hours)

Business Calculus with Applications

Systems of equations, matrices, probability, and differential calculus. (5 quarter hours)

Analytic Geometry and Calculus I

Linear analytic geometry and basic differential calculus. (5 quarter hours)

Elementary Statistics

A noncalculus introduction to descriptive and inferential statistics. Topics include graphical and numerical methods of describing data, hypothesis testing, linear regression and correlation, the normal distribution and estimation. (5 quarter hours)

PHILOSOPHY

Introduction to Philosophical Issues

A critical exploration of such topics as knowledge and belief, God and the problem of evil, freedom and determinism, the right and the good, language and meaning, mind and body, appearance and reality, and man and the world. (5 quarter hours)

Logic and Critical Thinking

Introduction to the principles and standards for thinking and communicating clearly and effectively. Topics include theories of meaning, uses of language, common causes of confusion and error in thought and argument, and evaluation of arguments. (5 quarter hours)

Symbolic Logic

A study of the methods and principles used to distinguish correct from incorrect deductive arguments, with emphasis upon contemporary techniques of analysis. (5 quarter hours)

Introduction to Ethics

A study of the major philosophical positions concerning right and wrong, ethical values, and moral responsibility. The relevance of moral philosophy to current issues of personal and social ethics will be discussed. (5 quarter hours)

POLITICAL SCIENCE

American Government

An introductory course covering the essential facts of federal, state, and local governments in the United States. (5 quarter hours)

Introduction to Criminal Justice Administration

An analysis of the actors and agencies in the administration of criminal law. The survey includes the political and legal ramifications of processes critical in the application of the criminal sanction: arrest, bail, prosecution, conviction, sentencing, and corrections. (5 quarter hours)

International Politics and Organizations

A study of the international systems of nation-states, including examination of regional alliances and the United Nations. Areas of international conflict and cooperation will also be emphasized. (5 quarter hours)

Political Parties and Elections

A study of the origins, development, and contemporary roles, structures, and problems of parties. The recruitment of candidates and the conduct of campaigns and elections are examined within the framework of the American political system. (5 quarter hours)

Comparative Political Systems

A study of democratic and autocratic political systems, with emphasis upon comparing and contrasting political structures, cultures, institutions, and leadership elites. (5 quarter hours)

Principles of Public Administration

A general survey of the field of public administration, including coverage of the executive branch, executive-legislative interactions, administrative procedures, and classical and contemporary bureaucratic problems. (5 quarter hours)

State and Local Government

The forms of organization, the functions and the operations of the fifty state governments. Special attention will be given to the growing problems in the urban areas such as the interplay of politics, pressure groups, and community power structures. (5 quarter hours)

Congress and Public Policy

A study of the structures and processes at work in Congress and their influence on the content of national policy. Attention is also given to the connection between Congress and the other branches of government. (5 quarter hours)

Minority Politics

Course develops a basic appreciation of the nature, processes, structures, and functions of African American politics in the domestic and international arena and how they differ from dominant assumptions, theories, approaches, and models in American politics. Focus on how to seek and maintain empowerment. (5 quarter hours)

National Security Policy

A study of contemporary American defense policy. Emphasis is placed on how and why national military policy is generated and its employment in international relationships. (5 quarter hours)

Latin American Politics

An examination of the major domestic and international actors in comparative Latin American political systems. Special attention and detail are given to the particular challenges posed by development, democracy, human rights, and U.S. foreign policy to the Latin American political landscape. (5 quarter hours)

Politics of the Environment

A study of how salient environmental problems interact with political dynamics, both domestically and internationally. (5 quarter hours)

The Presidency

A study of the presidential institution and the men who have occupied the Oval Office. Attention will be given to the topics of presidential roles, powers, politics, and policy making. (5 quarter hours)

Contemporary American Foreign Policy

A study of the development of American foreign policy during the twentieth century. Emphasis is placed upon America's emergence as a world power and her role of alliance leadership in the nuclear age. (5 quarter hours)

The Vietnam War

A comprehensive and in-depth study of America's longest war, with special emphasis placed on the historical background, political decisions, military strategy/tactics, and legacy associated with that conflict. (5 quarter hours)

Russian Politics and Foreign Policy

An examination of Russian political culture, foreign policy, and institutions within the framework of the Commonwealth of Independent States. (5 quarter hours)

The Politics of Japan

This course will explore both the domestic and foreign policies of contemporary Japan. Emphasis will be placed on Japan's political leadership and structures as well as those key cultural components which underlie the political-economic system of the nation. (5 quarter hours)

The Politics of the Middle East

This course focuses on the important domestic political structures and foreign policies of the key state-actors in the contemporary Middle East. In addition, the cultural and historical factors that shape the political dynamics of the region will be stressed. (5 quarter hours)

PSYCHOLOGY

Elementary Psychology

Introduction to the phenomena, laws, theories, and history of psychology. Topics include animal and human learning, motivation, perception, differential psychology, social behavior, and biopsychology. Emphasis is on fundamental principles rather than on application. Students are given the opportunity to participate in ongoing research. (5 quarter hours)

The Psychology of Adjustment

Introduction to psychological adjustment, including appropriate and inappropriate reactions to frustration and stress; solutions to conflict, fear, and anxiety; building self-concept and improving interpersonal relations. (5 quarter hours)

Abnormal Psychology

The study of the varieties of abnormal behavior; their explanation, assessment, and treatment. (5 quarter hours)

Psychology of Sex and Sexual Deviation

A survey of research in human sexual behavior. Emphasis is given to empirical findings and current personal and social implications. Topics include variations in sexual behavior, deviance, social patterns, assessment, and treatment. (5 quarter hours)

Social and Personality Development

A survey of factors that influence children's social behavior as they are integrated into adult society. Included are basic theories and research on the development of sex roles, aggression, altruism, moral standards, dependency, independence, achievement, and peer relations. (5 quarter hours)

Theories of Personality

A survey of major theories of personality, with some attention given to current research and to methodological issues in the field. (5 quarter hours)

RECREATION

Outdoor Recreation and Environmental Awareness

The organization and administration of outdoor recreation in local, county, and federal agencies with emphasis on objectives, philosophy, problems, trends, and methods of operation. (5 quarter hours)

RELIGION

Introduction to Western Religious Thought

This course represents an introductory, yet comprehensive historical and cultural survey of the Christian and Jewish experience. The contribution of both religions to ethical development in the West is another important course theme. (5 quarter hours)

Introduction to Western Religious Traditions

A study of the nature of religion and its function in Western culture. The Judeo-Christian tradition is investigated historically and analytically. (5 quarter hours)

Introduction to the Major Religious Perspectives of Mankind

A comparative and thematic study of the religious experience of the human community as expressed in the various religions or religious perspectives of the world. (5 quarter hours)

Comparative Religion

Major world religions including Hinduism, Buddhism, Confucianism, Judaism, Christianity, and Islam. (5 quarter hours)

SOCIOLOGY

Marriage and Family

Analysis of the forms and functions of marriage relationships, sex roles, marital choice, procreation, socialization; financial planning; effects of contemporary social changes. (5 quarter hours)

Introductory Sociology

An introduction to the sociological analysis of society, its origins, structure, change and problems. Emphasis is on the nature of culture, social interaction, social groups and social institutions. (5 quarter hours)

Contemporary Social Problems

A study of the major problems of our times and their social and cultural causes and consequences. The course will deal with society's perception of these social issues and attempts to resolve these problems. (5 quarter hours)

Juvenile Delinquency

An analysis of the nature, extent, and causes of juvenile delinquency with special emphasis on the juvenile justice system, evaluation research techniques, and research findings. (5 quarter hours)

Social Psychology

An analysis of group phenomena and the effects that group influence has on individual behavior. Emphasis on social perception, attitude measurement and change, authority and leadership, group productivity and prejudice; theories of socialization. (5 quarter hours)

Personality and Social Structure

A study of the foundation and development of personality; mechanisms of integration and adjustment; roles of culture, groups, and language; concepts of self; types and theories of personality; deviant personalities. (5 quarter hours)

Sociology of Occupations

A comparative study of work positions and roles in modern American society with emphasis given to such topics as occupational choice, socialization, worker adjustment, prestige, and mobility. (5 quarter hours)

SPANISH

Elementary Spanish

I. Introduction to essentials of grammar; acquisition of basic vocabulary; practice in reading, speaking and writing. A cassette recorder is required. (5 quarter hours)

II. A continuation of the above course. A cassette recorder is required. (5 quarter hours)

III. A continuation of the above course. A cassette recorder is required. (5 quarter hours)

Intermediate Spanish

A review of Spanish grammar, reading of selected texts, and particular emphasis on conversation and expansion of vocabulary. A cassette recorder is required. (5 quarter hours)

SPEECH

Oral Decision Making

An introduction to the theory and practice of democratic decision making, from researching a topic systematically in specialized library sources to reaching a workable solution through group discussion. Second phase will involve theory and practice of debating and implementing decisions through parliamentary procedure. (5 quarter hours)

Persuasion

A study of the way in which beliefs, attitudes, values, and behavior are formed and changed. (5 quarter hours)

Psychology of Speech Communication

A study of speech as a psychological phenomenon with consideration of the use of symbols, the speech personality, emotional reactions, and mental processes in speech communication, and psychological studies of language and vocal and visual symbolism. (5 quarter hours)

Communication Strategies in Social Movements

An examination of the rhetorical nature of social movements with theories of communication strategies applied in several case studies. (5 quarter hours)

VETERINARY SCIENCE

Clinical Medicine

Application of the art and science of veterinary medicine in a clinical setting. *Students who wish to register for this course should contact the College of Veterinary Medicine, telephone (706) 542-5728 for permission to enroll.* (Variable quarter hours)

WOMEN'S STUDIES

Introduction to Women's Studies

Integration of a broad range of fundamental topics in the field of women's studies, including women's legal, political, and educational position in society; the history of feminism and its relationship to women's studies; and the development of feminist theory in the United States. (5 quarter hours)

Georgia College

Independent Study
Milledgeville, Georgia 31601   (912) 453-5016

Description:

The Independent Study program of Georgia College is a service of The University System of Georgia Independent Study as offered by the Georgia Center for Continuing Education located at The University of Georgia in Athens, Georgia. For courses available, SEE **Georgia, University of.**

Accreditations:

Southern Association of Colleges and Schools.

Georgia Southern College

Division of Public Services
Independent Study
Statesboro, Georgia 30460   (912) 681-5118

Description:

The Independent Study program of Georgia Southern College is a service of The University System of Georgia Independent Study as offered by the Georgia Center for Continuing Education located at the University of Georgia in Athens, Georgia. For courses available, SEE **Georgia, University of.**

Accreditations:

Southern Association of Colleges and Schools.

Goddard College

Off Campus Study
Route 2
Plainfield, Vermont 05667   (802) 454-8311

Description:

Throughout its history, Goddard College has encouraged students to use the innumerable learning resources away from its lovely Vermont country campus in carrying out their individually planned educational programs. For the past 25 years, it has offered undergraduate education, leading to the Bachelor of Arts degree, that requires only minimal campus attendance. Graduate education, leading to the Master of Arts and Master of Fine Arts degrees, is also possible within this away-from-campus format.

The student comes to the Goddard campus for nine days (one week and two weekends at the beginning of each semester for an All College Meeting, to meet with other students, choose a faculty advisor, and plan the individual semester-long study. The student is expected to devote a minimum of 26 hours a week to his/her studies, and to be in touch with the faculty advisor by mail correspondence every three weeks. Much of this correspondence is "evaluation," finding, and defining the value to the student of his/her studies. The student creates an ongoing dialogue with his/herself and the advisor. The Goddard curriculum is listed below under broad nondepartmental headings, rather than as departments, disciplines, or subject matters.

Faculty:

Peter Burns, Director of Admissions; Ellen Codling, Assistant Director of Admissions.

Academic Levels:

College
Graduate

Degree/Certificate Programs:

Bachelor of Arts; Master of Arts; Master of Fine Arts

Admission Requirements:

Official transcripts of previous study including high school (GED or high school equivalency certificate acceptable); a personal statement in which the student writes about his/her educational goals and readiness to do independent off-campus study; an interview, if possible, at Goddard. SAT or ACT test results for undergraduate applicants who have never been enrolled in college (requested but not required). Admission is limited to mature persons whose life experience demonstrates their ability to learn independently.

Tuition:

$3,760 per semester undergraduate; $4,290 per semester graduate. Financial aid is based on financial need. Students may be eligible for a federal Pell Grant, for the federally financed College Work Study Program, or a Guaranteed Student Loan. A Financial Aid Bulletin is available from the college.

Enrollment Period:

Enrollment period is on a semester basis. Students may obtain a one semester leave of absence; thereafter, students must reapply. Students must attend a nine-day residency period each semester.

Equipment Requirements:

The student selects any learning materials required.

Credit and Grading:

Assessment of prior learning can be applied for by preparing a "prepetition" which describes the previous learning experiences. A Portfolio Preparation and Evaluation fee is charged. The student must prepare the portfolio at the same time as he/she is carrying out a full semester of study. Advanced standing from a few semester-hour equivalents to fill out an incomplete semester of transfer credit or up to two full semesters may be granted by the advisor and the Learning Progress Group may be granted. There are no examinations; written evaluations by both the student and the advisor constitute the grading system.

Library Services:

Learning resource materials are obtained by the student from those available in or near his/her home community.

Accreditations:

New England Association of Schools and Colleges.

COLLEGE COURSES

ANTHROPOLOGY

Cultural Anthropology and Multicultural Studies

The challenge in studies that have their center in this curricular area is to discover their similarities and differences as a basis for understanding and communication. Studies have focused on social and physical anthropology, comparative religion and philosophy, global ecology, and linguistics.

BUSINESS

Business, Leadership, and Community Organization

Studies in this area bout how people make a living in socially responsible ways, and make significant contributions to their communities.

EDUCATION

Teaching and Education

Studies may involve research into the great variety of problems facing schools, school boards, teachers, parents, and communities across America; comparative studies of education in various countries and cultures; studies in the history, philosophy, sociology, or economics of education; examinations of promising new educational practices and the institutions in which they are being practiced.

ENVIRONMENTAL SCIENCE

Natural and Physical Sciences, Ecological Studies

Studies with their center in this curricular area are usually interdisciplinary, for environmental and ecological problems demand examination from a multitude of perspectives.

HISTORY

History and Social Inquiry

Studies in this area often draw on ideas and information from the cultural anthropology and multicultural studies curricular area.

MASS MEDIA

Media Studies and Communication

At Goddard, the media are studied from several points of view: as art forms (especially film and video, closely related to the Performing Arts and Visual Arts areas), as social phenomena that carry both overt and covert messages (related to the History and Social Inquiry area), and as complex bodies of information and skill that can be learned and put to use (related to resources in Psychology and Counseling).

PSYCHOLOGY

Psychology and Counseling

Goddard studies in psychology are about many aspects of being human. The primary aim of some studies is increased self-knowledge, necessarily involving theories of personality and social development. Cultural and gender differences in attitudes, reactions, ways of speaking, and behavior are important subjects for research. Child, family, social, and community psychology are important at one end of a spectrum; so is physiological psychology, at the other end.

THEATRE

Performing Arts

Drama, music, and dance were originally part of religious ceremonies, and are thus deeply identified with the spiritual part of life. Goddard studies respect the performing arts as ways of giving form to feelings. Studies in this curricular area are documented in audio- and video-tapes, still photographs, and drawings or diagrams, as well as in writing. The outcomes of these studies may be presented at residencies.

VISUAL ARTS

Visual Arts

Most visual arts studies take the form of studio work: persons making art individually. Packets include sketches and photographs, as well as written reports. Studies are also possible in art history, the psychology of art, with resources from the Psychology and Counseling curricular area, or art education, with studies planned in connection with the Education curricular area.

WOMEN'S STUDIES

Feminist Studies

Off-campus studies with their center in this area may address the full spectrum of women's and feminist issues, making use of materials from any or many of the other Goddard curricular areas.

WRITING

Writing and Literature

Literature may be studied as an art form, and often has been, but its significance lies in the deeply human meanings the art conveys. It is with those meanings that Goddard studies in literature and writing are primarily concerned: studies that have at their base bringing words to life and giving life to words.

Golden Gate University
536 Mission Street
San Francisco, California 94105
(415) 442-7272

Description:

Founded in 1901, Golden Gate University is a private, nonprofit institution of higher learning and is one of the major centers in the western United States for professional education in management, public administration, and law.

The University offers a correspondence course designed to prepare the student for the State of California Insurance Agent's and Solicitor's Examinations, and the California Insurance Broker's Examination.

Academic Levels:

College

Tuition:

Contact the Dean, College of Business and Public Administration for enrollment procedure and current tuition information.

Accreditations:

Western Association of Schools and Colleges.

COLLEGE COURSES

RISK MANAGEMENT AND INSURANCE

Principles of Property and Casualty Insurance

Introductory course in all lines of non-life insurance for those entering the field with an insurance company, an agency or brokerage firm, or in risk management; other topics include all property and casualty lines and the California Insurance Code; preparation for license examination. Approved by the California Department of Insurance to meet the 90-hour educational requirement for Insurance Broker's licensing. (6 semester hours)

Governors State University

Center for Extended Learning
University Parkway
University Park, Illinois 60466 (708) 534-5000

Description:

Governors State University was chartered in 1969 in response to the dramatic growth of the Illinois community college system. The state recognized the need for an upper division, commuter university designed to allow graduates of the community college system and others in the southern Chicago metropolitan area access to baccalaureate and graduate study in a convenient location. The university is situated on a 750-acre campus.

The Office of Extended Learning provides alternative access to university programs through independent study by correspondence courses. These credit courses provide instruction for the site-bound student and extend the university's resources to underserved and/or inaccessible areas.

Faculty:

Richard Venneri, Dean, Special Programs and Continuing Education.

Academic Levels:

College
Graduate

Admission Requirements:

Enrollment on a noncredit basis is possible for some credit courses. Overseas enrollment accepted for college courses. An orientation session is required if the student lives within a 50-mile radius of Governors State University.

Tuition:

Undergraduate tuition $246 per 3 credit hours; graduate tuition $258 per 3 credit hours. Rates subject to change; contact the university for current rate information.

Enrollment Period:

Courses must be completed within the trimester for which the student has enrolled.

Equipment Requirements:

Textbooks are supplied by the student.

Credit and Grading:

Grades are determined by the instructor and letter grades are given (A, B, C, D, F). Credit is awarded in semester hour units.

Library Services:

Students have access to the University library.

Accreditations:

North Central Association of Colleges and Schools. Member of: National University Continuing Education Association.

COLLEGE COURSES

ALCOHOLISM SCIENCES

Alcoholism: A Study of Addiction

Provides an overview of the far-reaching problem of alcoholism in American society. Covers the causes, symptoms, manifestations, and treatment of alcoholism. (3 semester hours)

Alcoholism/Employee Assistance Programs in Business and Industry

(3 semester hours)

BIOLOGY

Human Evolution

(3 semester hours)

COMMUNICATIONS

Concepts in Communication

(3 semester hours)

ENGLISH

Writing Principles

Emphasizes principles, techniques, form, and style in writing. (3 semester hours)

Black Literature I: 1760–1900

Generally surveys black prose from colonial period to 1900. Covers a wide variety of works from several genres, with a major emphasis on prose embracing the slave narratives and early black fiction. (3 semester hours)

HISTORY

The History of Illinois and Its Constitution

A survey of the political, constitutional, and social history of the state of Illinois from 1700 to the present. (3 semester hours)

INTERCULTURAL STUDIES

Hispanic Experience in U.S.

Examines the historical process that led to Latino migration to the United States. Focuses on the economic, political, social, and cultural conditions which shape the life of the Latino in American society. (3 semester hours)

Ethnicity, Culture, and Politics

Explores the interrelations between ethnicity, culture, and politics in American political life. Examines these concepts in an effort to understand culture, society, race, ethnicity, and their relationship to politics and society. (3 semester hours)

MANAGEMENT

Organizational Behavior

Analyzes the behavior of people in organizations. Discusses organizational motivation, leadership, group behavior, communication, and decision making. (3 semester hours)

POLITICAL SCIENCE

Urban Politics

Analyzes critical issues of urbanization confronting American political institutions. Provides an overview of the nature and scope of the urban polity and provides a conceptual framework for analyzing and evaluating the critical issues in American urban areas. (3 semester hours)

PUBLIC ADMINISTRATION

Introduction to Public Administration

Examines theories, history, and current issues of administration in government. (3 semester hours)

SOCIAL SCIENCE

Survey of Social Science

Examination of the organizing principles and methods of the basic social sciences. (3 semester hours)

SOCIOLOGY

Family History: Legacies

(3 semester hours)

Hardin-Simmons University
Correspondence Programs
Box 984, HSU Station
2200 Hickory Street
Abilene, Texas 79698   (915) 670-1000

Description:
Hardin-Simmons University is a private institution affiliated with the Southern Baptist Church. It was established and chartered in 1891. Address inquiries regarding correspondence study to the Director of Correspondence Programs.

Faculty:
Edwin L. Hall, President.

Academic Levels:
College

Tuition:
$90 per semester hour. Tuition and fees subject to change without notice; contact the university for current information.

Enrollment Period:
Students may enroll at any time.

Enrollment Period:
Textbooks must be purchased by the student.

Credit and Grading:
Grading system is A–F. Credit is awarded in semester hour units.

Accreditations:
Southern Association of Colleges and Schools.

COLLEGE COURSES

POLITICAL SCIENCE

State and Local Government

A course designed to aid students who need a course in Texas government and the Constitution. This course satisfies the requirement of the Texas Education Agency for a course in Texas government and its Constitution for teacher certification. (3 semester hours)

Idaho, University of
Correspondence Study in Idaho
CEB 214
Moscow, Idaho 83843-4171   (208) 885-6641

Description:
Correspondence Study in Idaho is coordinated and administered by the Correspondence Study Office located at the University of Idaho. Courses are written and graded by approved faculties of the University of Idaho, Boise State University, Lewis Clark State College, and Idaho State University. The Correspondence Study Program includes college courses, high school courses, high school equivalency preparation for adults, and citizenship education for aliens. College-level courses may be taken for no credit ("auditing"). The correspondence program has been in offered for over 50 years. There are approximately 2,500 new enrollments each year.

Faculty:
Melynda Huskey, State Coordinator of Correspondence Study; Becky Stevinson, Registrar. There is a faculty of 110 from the various Idaho State Universities and Colleges.

Academic Levels:
College
Graduate
High School
Noncredit

Degree/Certificate Programs:
The University of Idaho will accept 48 credits of correspondence study toward a baccalaureate degree; Idaho State University, Lewis Clark State College, and Boise State University will accept 32 credits of correspondence study toward a baccalaureate degree.

Idaho, University of

Admission Requirements:

A student desiring to apply college credit toward a degree must satisfy the requirements of the respective college. High school students working toward a high school diploma must have written permission from the student's appropriate high school official. Those who do not wish to apply credit toward a college degree or high school diploma may register for any course in which they have an interest. However, many courses have required prerequisites and the Correspondence Study catalog should be consulted.

Tuition:

College, $59.50 per credit hour; graduate courses $85.50 per credit hour; a nonrefundable $15 study guide handling fee is charged for all college courses. High school courses $74 per one-half unit. Canada and Mexico students add $21 for air mail; Central & South America, West Indies add $44; other overseas add $50. VISA and MasterCard accepted. Refund policy: Course fee less $25 for registration costs if withdrawal is made before 2 weeks and before any lessons have been submitted; the study guide must also be returned in good condition or a deduction of $20 to cover its cost will be made. If application for refund is made after the first 2 weeks but before 30 days from the date of enrollment, 50% of the course fee less $25 registration costs and $6 for each lesson submitted will be refunded; the study guide must also be returned in good condition or a deduction of $20 to cover its cost will be made. No refunds after 30 days.

Enrollment Period:

A course should be completed within 1 year from the date of enrollment. A 6-month extension may be permitted. An extension fee of $25 must be sent with the request for renewal. After a total of 18 months, if the student is still unable to complete the course, he/she may receive 1 more full year extension by paying the total course fee again.

Equipment Requirements:

Tuition fees do not include cost of textbooks or supplies, both of which may be purchased through the school.

Credit and Grading:

A final examination is required for most classes; some courses include several examinations. A University-approved proctor must supervise the examinations. Credit is awarded in semester hour units.

Accreditations:

Northwest Association of Schools and Colleges. Member of: National University Continuing Education Association.

COLLEGE COURSES

ACCOUNTING

Introduction to Financial Accounting

Overview of the nature and purpose of general purpose financial statements provided to external decision makers; emphasis on use of financial statement information. (3 semester hours)

ADVERTISING

Reporting and Newswriting

Demands, skills, and ethics of newswriting; practice in the variety of writing tasks required of reporters. (3 semester hours)

Photo Communication

Photography as a form of communication; professionalism and ethics in photography; history and uses of the photographic media. Required photoessay. (3 semester hours)

Advertising Media Planning

Advertising media planning for all media, both broadcast and print; includes interpretation of ratings and market data, media strategies and concepts, and specific buying process in each advertising medium. (3 semester hours)

AGRICULTURAL ECONOMICS

Agriculture and Its Social and Economic Environment

Overview of American agriculture with emphasis on the economic implications of production, marketing, and prevailing government policies. Social and economic problems in agriculture are studied as they relate to the national economy, rural development, the food-population balance and agricultural trade with other nations. (3 semester hours)

Principles of Farm and Ranch Management

Decision making and profit maximization using economic principles, records, enterprise analysis, and comparison of alternative farming practices. (4 semester hours)

ANTHROPOLOGY

Museum Administration

Management of the total museum program; the concerns and responsibilities of the director, top staff, and board of trustees in the professional museum of whatever kind or size. (3 semester hours)

ASTRONOMY

Descriptive Astronomy

This nonmathematical survey will explore the historical and modern observation of the sky; physical relationships in the solar system: planets, satellites, comets, etc.; and theories of the creation of the universe and life in the universe. (3 semester hours)

BACTERIOLOGY

Elementary Microbiology and Public Health

Microorganisms and their role in health, disease, and human welfare. (3 semester hours)

BIOLOGY

Man and His Environment

Discover how humankind affects the environment with emphasis on biological, economic, and social factors. Become sensitive to the significant issues and factors in environmental decision making. (3 semester hours)

General Ecology

Ecological principles of plants and animals; structure and function of ecosystem; major ecosystems of the world. (3 semester hours)

BUSINESS

Business Communications

Provides the opportunity and motivation to improve communication skills with emphasis on their application to business. (3 semester hours)

Legal Environment of Business

Law and its relationship to society; legal framework of business enterprises; court organization and operation; private property and contract as basic concepts in a free enterprise system. (3 semester hours)

Introduction to Management

Introduction to and overview of the primary topics in management; areas of concern to modern managers, as well as the historical foundations for many of the commonly accepted fundamentals of management. (3 semester hours)

Marketing

Marketing institutions and relationships with economic, political, legal, and social environment; principles, functions, concepts, and issues of marketing within a firm and the relationship of marketing to other business disciplines. (3 semester hours)

Business Law

Course Blaw. C366. Legal concepts of agency, partnerships, corporations, securities, regulation (Securities Act of 1933 and 1934), personal property, real property, and environmental law. (3 semester hours)

Course Blaw. C466. Law of sales, negotiable instruments, security interests in properties, and business regulations dealing with competitive torts, antitrust, and federal trade regulations; business ethics. (3 semester hours)

Entrepreneurship

Process of providing solutions to identify consumer needs; characteristics of individuals who succeed; sources of venture ideas; evaluating and developing ideas; business plans; franchising. (3 semester hours)

Promotional Strategy

Marketing management point of view; objectives, methods, strategies, budgets and measures of effectiveness; campaign management including advertising, public relations, sales promotion, reseller support, personal selling. (3 semester hours)

Real Estate Law

Study of Idaho real estate law. (3 semester hours)

Real Estate Finance

Analysis of sources and methods in the financing of real property construction and development. (3 semester hours)

BUSINESS EDUCATION

Local Government Records Management and Filing

Intended to give city clerks and other city officials a knowledge of records management, microfilming, filing, and filing equipment useful in city government recordkeeping functions; acquaint yourself with the legal requirements of destruction and disposal of city records in Idaho and the practice of a number of city officials in Idaho in indexing city council meetings and maintaining city council files. (2 semester hours)

Microcomputer Applications

Computer applications course designed primarily for office administration and business teacher education students; includes hands-on experience using word processing, spreadsheet, and database management software packages; also some methodology, curriculum development, and classroom management techniques. (3 semester hours)

COMPUTER SCIENCE

Fortran Programming for Engineers

This course will introduce the process of problem solving using the computer and computer language Fortran 77. The course does not assume any previous computer experience. The overall objective of this course is to introduce the student to Fortran 77 and help to learn the basic syntax along with the development of algorithms (computer procedures) and problem solving. (2 semester hours)

CONSUMER ECONOMICS

Consumer Education

Present day social and economic problems as they affect the home. Planning the family financial security, budgets, installment buying, insurance, investments, loans, home purchases, social security, and medicare. Current information on fraud and consumer laws. (3 semester hours)

CRIMINAL JUSTICE

Introduction to Criminal Justice Administration

Study the philosophy, history, objectives, and the functions of law enforcement as an institution; institutional relationship to society; general overview of the administration of justice. (3 semester hours)

Criminal Investigation

Fundamental principles of applied criminal investigation including crime scene work, collecting physical evidence, sketching, photography, and identification techniques. (4 semester hours)

Criminology

Crime and society, theories of criminality; types and trends of crime; characteristics of offenders; social control; criminological controversies. (3 semester hours)

ECONOMICS

Principles of Economics

Econ. C201. Organization and operation of American economy; supply and demand; money and banking; employment and aggregate output; public finance and economic growth. (3 semester hours)

Econ. C202. Microeconomic principles governing production, price relationships, and income distribution. (3 semester hours)

Money and Banking

Analysis of the role of money, credit, and the financial system in the U.S. economy through the economics of commercial and central banking. Study of monetary theory and monetary policy as they affect both domestic and international economic policy goals. (3 semester hours)

EDUCATION

Elementary Language Arts

Methods of teaching the language arts, including listening, oral and written communication skills. Identifies interrelation of reading, literature, spelling, and handwriting. The role of media in language arts teaching comprises an integral part of the course. (3 semester hours)

Elementary School Science Methods

Exploration of the subject content of science programs in the elementary school with emphasis on methods and materials utilized by the classroom teacher. (3 semester hours)

Secondary Social Studies Curriculum and Instruction

Course designed as a source of ideas or guidelines for improvement of instruction in social studies in the secondary school, developed to combine theoretical and practical learning experiences for the social studies major and nonmajor student. Special emphasis is placed on unit teaching, on inquiry-conceptual approach, the critical use of varied activities and materials, and developing a democratic classroom atmosphere in order to promote learning. Substantial portions of the course are devoted to creative activities for the actual classroom situation. (3 semester hours)

ENGLISH

English Composition

Eng. C101. Basic writing skills and how to use supportive materials, source references, basic patterns of organization, and standard usage to your advantage. (3 semester hours)

Eng. C102. Advanced practice in expository writing, including analysis and interpretation of imaginative literature. Study of the relationship between literature and human experience. (3 semester hours)

World Masterpieces

Engl. C255. Examination of major works and authors in historical perspective, with emphasis upon literary and cultural backgrounds. (3 semester hours)

Engl. C256. World literature, 1700*−present.

Survey of American Literature

Engl. C277. Survey of representative developments in American literature from the Colonial Period through the Age of Romanticism, c. 1620−1865. Emphasizes critical analysis of the literature. (3 semester hours)

Engl. C278. Continuation of the above course focusing on literature from 1870s to the present. Writing intensive. (3 semester hours)

Shakespeare

Critical analysis of plot, character, and language to reveal meaning in nine representative plays. (3 semester hours)

FORESTRY

Public Relations Problems in Natural Resource Management

Introduction to the theory, tools, and practice of public relations as applied to the management of natural resources and recreation resources. The course includes considerable practical application suitable to any student's circumstances. (2 semester hours)

GERMAN

Elementary German I

Intended to bring beginning students to a standard level of proficiency of 1.2 through study and practice of communicative skills, functional grammar, and the culture of German-speaking areas. (4 semester hours)

Elementary German II

A continuation of the above course. (4 semester hours)

HISTORY

History of Civilization

Hist. C101. Great civilizations; contributions to the modern world. Beginning of civilization to 1650. (3 semester hours)

Hist. C102. Great civilizations; contributions to the modern world, 1650 to the present. (3 semester hours)

Introduction to United States History

Hist. C111. Political, diplomatic, economic, social, and cultural history; earliest times to 1877. (3 semester hours)

Hist. C112. Political, diplomatic, economic, social, and cultural history; 1877 to the present. (3 semester hours)

Idaho and the Pacific Northwest

Political, economic, social development; earliest times to the present; emphasis on Idaho and the Inland Empire. (3 semester hours)

History of the Far East

The cultures, traditions, and recent historical phenomena of East Asia; major emphasis on China and Japan; the peoples of East Asia, their intra-action and interaction with the West since 1720; their view of history, and their value system. (3 semester hours)

HOME ECONOMICS

Contemporary Family Relations

Dynamics of the major types of family relationships: marital, parent-child, sibling, and extended-family interaction in contemporary society. (3 semester hours)

Trends in Nutrition Research

Nutrition research methodology, literature critique, and recent advances in nutrition and dietetics. (3 semester hours)

LIBRARY SCIENCE

Computer Applications in Libraries

Developments and trends in library automation, especially computer applications to library work and administration. (3 semester hours)

Cataloging and Classification

Introduction to the theory and principles of classification and cataloging of book and nonbook materials; practice in using the Dewey Decimal Classification in preparing catalog cards, and in the ordering and use of Wilson and Library of Congress printed cards; assigning of subject headings, and library filing. (4 semester hours)

Acquisitions and Collection Development in Libraries

Principles of library acquisitions and collection development, including intellectual freedom, bibliographic searching, source materials, and evaluation. Provides practical training for acquiring materials such as monographs, serials, nonbook items. (3 semester hours)

The Use of the School Library

Identification of library-use skills needed by K−12 students and methods of teaching those skills. (2 semester hours)

Introduction to Reference Work

Basic information sources for school and public libraries; library reference service. (3 semester hours)

Organization and Management of Small Libraries

Management and organization of small public libraries and school library/media centers. Topics covered: mission of libraries, standards for library resources and services, library governance and finance, personnel, professional ethics, public services, material selection, technical services, automation, buildings and facilities. (4 semester hours)

Library and Media Center Practicum

Gain experience in a library or other information center under professional supervision. Ninety hours of supervised experience per credit. Student will determine the number of credits desired by submitting the equivalent credit fees. (1 to 3 semester hours)

MATHEMATICS

Finite Mathematics

Systems of linear equations and inequalities, matrices, linear programming, probability. (4 semester hours)

Mathematics for Elementary Teachers I

Mathematical development of arithmetic and problem solving as these subjects are currently taught in elementary schools. (3 semester hours)

Mathematics for Elementary Teachers II

Mathematical development of informal geometry, problem solving, and probability and statistics as these subjects are currently taught in elementary schools. (3 semester hours)

Pre-Calculus Algebra and Analytic Geometry

Algebraic, exponential, logarithmic functions; graphs of conics; zeros of polynomials; systems of equations, induction. (3 semester hours)

Survey of Calculus

This informal approach to calculus at an intuitive level will enable the student to immediately apply calculus in the areas of business and economics. (4 semester hours)

Analytic Trigonometry

Circular and trigonometric functions, inverse functions, applications including De Moivre's theorem. (2 semester hours)

Analytical Geometry and Calculus I

Functions, limits, continuity, differentiation, integration, applications, differentiation and integration of transcendental functions. (4 semester hours)

Introduction to Statistics

A beginning course in statistics for students who are not mathematics majors. However, it may also be taken by majors. Although only a small amount of algebra is needed, basic arithmetic is essential. Introduction to statistical methods and techniques as applied to the behavioral, biological, social, and managerial sciences. (3 semester hours)

MUSIC

Survey of Music

The history and appreciation of western art music from the Middle Ages until the Contemporary period, with a brief introduction to jazz and folk styles. The course stresses the relationship of music to western history and culture. (3 semester hours)

NURSING

Professional Foundations of Nursing

Discussion of nursing as a profession with a focus on history, ethics, theories, politics, and current events. Selected issues in nursing education, practice, and research are discussed, analyzed, and evaluated. (3 semester hours)

PHILOSOPHY

Ethics

Development of ethical thought. (3 semester hours)

History of Ancient Philosophy

Philosophic and political thought from the early Greeks through the Middle Ages. (3 semester hours)

History of Modern Philosophy

Philosophic and political thought from Descartes through Kant. (3 semester hours)

PHYSICAL EDUCATION

Elementary School Physical Education

Current theory in curriculum and teaching methods with practical applications. (3 semester hours)

Sport Psychology

Study how the principles and methodologies of psychology are applied to sports and athletics. Topics to be covered include philosophies of sport; motivation; personality of coaches and athletes; recreational sports for children; psychological testing; training and learning principles; mind/body relationships; the effects of anxiety, arousal, and relaxation on performance; current research in the field. (3 semester hours)

PHYSICS

Essentials of Physics

Presents, in a broad spectrum, the spirit of scientific investigation and develops an understanding of the scientific method. Methods developed can be applied to all sciences. Instills an appreciation for the physics observed around us. The student will learn how physicists have been able to discover the fundamental laws and principles of physics. Concepts are developed with reference to common, everyday experiences. (4 semester hours)

General Physics

Phys. C113. Algebra-based study of mechanics, heat, and sound. A previous course in physics is not required, but having taken high school physics makes this easier. A good understanding of algebra and trigonometry at an elementary level is most important. This course is suitable for students in forestry, architecture, biological sciences, business, and education, and for students wishing a general introductory class in physics. (3 semester hours)

Phys. C114. A continuation of *Phys. C113.* Algebra-based study of electricity and magnetism, light, atomic and nuclear physics. (3 semester hours)

Descriptive Astronomy

This nonmathematical survey will explore the historical and modern observation of the sky; physical relationships in the solar system: planets, satellites, comets, etc.; and theories of the creation of the universe and life in the universe. (3 semester hours)

POLITICAL SCIENCE

Introduction to American Politics

Basic concepts, processes, and major structural elements of the national government. (3 semester hours)

U.S. Government: Policies and Issues

Survey of major policies and issue conflicts in the United States. (3 semester hours)

Politics and Pollution

Political, governmental, and administrative aspects of overcoming air, water, and other types of pollution of our environment. (1 semester hour)

Local Government Purchasing

Recognized industry practices in the field of purchasing and the governing state laws to familiarize city clerks and county clerks with accepted purchasing practices within the State of Idaho. (2 semester hours)

American State Government

State politics, parties, interest groups, constitutions, legislative, executive, and judicial branches, federal-state relations; key issues of state politics—taxation, education, water, and welfare. (3 semester hours)

Public Administration

Environment of public administration, politics of organization, public decision making, public relations, leadership, personal administration, financial administration, administrative morality, and related topics. (3 semester hours)

PSYCHOLOGY

Introduction to Psychology

Introduction to psychological topics, including sensation and perception, learning and thinking, motivation, personality and adjustment, social processes, and psychological testing; emphasis on fundamental principles. (3 semester hours)

Statistical Methods

Survey of descriptive and inferential statistical concepts commonly used in the treatment of data in social science research. Both the understanding and the application of the concepts emphasized. Topics include measures of central tendency, measures of variability, and correlational methods and hypothesis testing up through simple analysis of variance. Mathematical competency at the high school algebra level is required. (3 semester hours)

Developmental Psychology

Conception to death; genetics, anatomy, physiology, biological changes during development, learning, socialization, cognition, and personality. (3 semester hours)

Personal and Social Development in Children

Personality and social development in children. (3 semester hours)

Psychology of Personality

Theories of personality, basic concepts, techniques of measurement methods; the normal personality. (3 semester hours)

Abnormal Psychology

Introduction to the study of abnormality through a review of the major patterns of abnormal behavior, their clinical picture, casual factors, treatments, and outcome; emphasis on biological, psychological, interpersonal, and sociocultural etiological factors and theories. (3 semester hours)

Introduction to Social Psychology

Theories, concepts and current research regarding the social causes of behavior, cognition, and social interaction. Topics of personal and social relevance such as aggression and violence, prejudice, leadership, environmental factors and behavior, prosocial behavior and application of social-psychological knowledge to human problems will be covered. (3 semester hours)

Human Sexuality

Introduction to fundamentals of human sexuality; emphasis on current trends and research (3 semester hours)

Physiological Psychology

Review of human neural physiology and anatomy, techniques used in the field, basic components and elements of neurochemistry. (3 semester hours)

Learning

An overview of various learning theories, emphasizing classical, operant, and the cognitive approaches. Both experimental and applied literature are included. (3 semester hours)

Measurement and Evaluation in Psychology

Understanding and application of psychological tests and measurements by applying the concepts of validity, reliability, norming, item analysis, and test interpretation in test construction and to the evaluation of standardized tests. (3 semester hours)

Sport Psychology

Study how the principles and methodologies of psychology are applied to sports and athletics. Topics to be covered include philosophies of sport; motivation; personality of coaches and athletes; recreational sports for children; psychological testing; training and learning principles; mind/body relationships; the effects of anxiety, arousal, and relaxation on performance; current research in the field. (3 semester hours)

Applied Behavioral Analysis

Assessment and modification of behavior in various real-world settings; experimental and self-management techniques. (3 semester hours)

Professional Issues and Ethics in Psychology

Examination of the professional and ethical dimensions of the profession of psychology. Expanding on the issues identified by the Ethical Principles of Psychologists (APA), the student will learn about and explore the dilemmas and responsibilities facing practitioners, scientists, educators, and others within this field. Some "solutions," regulatory measures, and legal precedents will also be explored. Personal appraisal of issues and the student's reactions will be solicited throughout the course. (3 semester hours)

REAL ESTATE

Fundamentals of Real Estate

Essentials of real estate practice; listings, sales, financing, land descriptions, real estate investments, brokerage, advertising, market analysis, and fundamentals arising from real estate transactions are covered in the course. (3 semester hours)

Real Estate Law

Study of real estate law. (3 semester hours)

Real Estate Finance

Analysis of sources and methods in the financing of real property construction and development. (3 semester hours)

RELIGIOUS STUDIES

Introduction to Religious Studies

Introduction to religion in today's world; emphasis on social and psychological implications for the individual. (3 semester hours)

SOCIOLOGY

Introduction to Sociology

Basic concepts, principles, processes, including socialization, primary groups, race relations, the family, religion, and population. (3 semester hours)

Introduction to Social Services

Study of the variety of problems which make us more vulnerable to the need for seeking help outside of ourselves, our family or church, and to explain the types of social services available. (3 semester hours)

Social Problems

Contemporary social issues and personal deviations; crime and delinquency, poverty and wealth, drugs, sexual variations, racism, sexism, and the environment. (3 semester hours)

Rural Sociology

Characteristics of rural society, including agricultural demography and social structure. (3 semester hours)

Collective Behavior

Analysis of such episodes of behavior as riots, demonstrations, panics, hysteria, as well as interaction of social, political, and communication processes involved in public acceptance of fashion, fads, and ideology in a mass society. (3 semester hours)

The Family: An Introduction

Study the institutions of marriage and the family in a cross-cultural perspective, and an analysis of the various factors and forces at work in out time, which are affecting relationships within the family. (3 semester hours)

Juvenile Delinquency

Extent, causes, and control of juvenile delinquent behavior. (3 semester hours)

Criminology

Crime and society, theories of criminality; types and trends of crime; characteristics of offenders; social control; criminological controversies. (3 semester hours)

SPECIAL EDUCATION

Education of People with Disabilities

Introduction to the education of exceptional children, including the mentally retarded, learning disabled, physically handicapped, deaf or hearing impaired, blind or visually impaired, emotionally disturbed/behavior disordered, communication disordered, health impaired, and gifted or talented; application to systematic instructional practices to different exceptionalities, ages, and degrees of handicapping conditions. (3 semester hours)

Classroom Applications of Learning

Introduction to classroom applications of various learning theories for behavior modification. (3 semester hours)

VOCATIONAL EDUCATION

Principles and Philosophy of Vocational Education

History, meaning, aims, administration, and place in school. (2 semester hours)

Introduction to Adult Education

Philosophy, importance, historical development, professional roles, characteristics, organization, learning problems, and issues. (3 semester hours)

Psychology of Adult Learners

Physiological, social and psychological characteristics of adult learners; relationships to family, friends, and fellow citizens. (3 semester hours)

HIGH SCHOOL COURSES

ART

Beginning Art

Designed to provide art experiences to train the beginning artist, and to develop fully literate students through these experiences. (½ unit)

CONSUMER ECONOMICS

Consumer Economics I

Basic consumer economics for individual use, and specifically adapted to the secondary student. (½ unit)

ENGLISH

Ninth English I

Develop your narrative, descriptive, and expository writing skills for personal use. The units studies include punctuation, capitalization, sentence structure, composition, paragraph writing, short story writing, and poetry. (½ unit)

Ninth English II

Development of narrative, descriptive, and expository writing for personal use. The units studied include agreement of subject and verb, agreement of pronoun and antecedent, correcting misplaced modifiers, apostrophes, common usage problems, dictionary and reference skills, expository writing, and studies of *Romeo and Juliet, The Hound of the Baskervilles* and *The Iliad.* (½ unit)

Tenth English I - Literature, Composition, and Grammar

Literature at the sophomore level focuses on exploring, understanding, and appreciating genre as a means of approaching literary works beyond students' personal experience. Composition focuses on extending narrative, descriptive, and expository writing, on expressing personal views and opinions, and on experimenting with the various genres taught in literature. (½ unit)

Tenth English II - Literature, Composition, and Grammar

A continuation of study described in *Tenth English I.* (½ unit)

Eleventh English I - American Literature and Composition

This course covers the American experience as shared by writers in their search to explain themselves and their surroundings. (½ unit)

Eleventh Grade English II - American Literature and Composition

Continuation of study of American Literature from the Civil War years to the present, emphasizing the role of the writer in society. The study of literature offers knowledge and understanding of the selections as well as insight of the human experience. Composition in this course has two division: responses to the literature in the form of written opinions and attitudes, and writing assignments which will cover appropriate forms used in the academic or post-high school world. Students are encouraged to be creative and express opinions. (½ unit)

Twelfth English I - English Literature, Composition, and Language

The study of literature offers the student not only the knowledge and understanding of the selections but also the insight of the human experience which leads to self-understanding. Composition in this course has two divisions: responses to the literature in the form of written opinions, and writing assignments which will cover appropriate forms used in the academic or post-high school world. Language study is more subjective in this course than the other two components. (½ unit)

Twelfth English II - English Literature, Composition, and Language

Continuation of the study of literature, composition, and language. This course covers at depth Neo-Classic to Modern Literature and development of full essay and critical analysis compositions. (½ unit)

HEALTH

Health Education

Study of personal wellness, focusing on positive health habits and lifestyle. Emphasis is on student self-awareness for better health and development of personal skills for health improvement. The units studied include: mental, and emotional health, fitness and nutrition, substance use and abuse, the spread and prevention of disease, safety and first aid, environmental health, life stages, personal health, and family living. (½ unit)

MATHEMATICS

Algebra I

An introductory course consisting of formulas, simple equations, signed numbers, and systems of linear equations. (½ unit)

Algebra II

A continuation of *Algebra I* including work in special products, factoring, quadratic equations, and a brief introduction to trigonometry. (½ unit)

General Mathematics I

Study of such topics as integers, fractions, decimals, management, and percentage. (½ unit)

General Mathematics II

Continuation of *General Mathematics II* with an introduction to algebra and geometry. (½ unit)

Geometry I

Fundamentals of geometry, including a study of lines, angles, planes, triangles, parallelism, inequalities, and circles. (½ unit)

Geometry II

Continuation of *Geometry I*, including a study of plane figures, an introduction to trigonometry, a study of polygons, measurement of plane figures and common solids, and loci. (½ unit)

Advanced Math I

An extension of Algebra II (second year Algebra), this course has an emphasis in trigonometry, limits, and introductory calculus topics. All major areas covered in Algebra II are reinforced at a greater depth with additional applications aided by using calculators and computers. (½ unit)

READING

Reading

Learn study skills such as note taking, outlining, and test taking; vocabulary skills of context clues and structural analysis; comprehension strategies of questioning activities, patterns of organization, inferencing, and identifying the main idea; and rate flexibility skills including skimming and scanning. This course fulfills the secondary reading requirement in Idaho. Based on the course requirements recommended by the State of Idaho, the course is written for two reading levels. (½ unit)

SCIENCE

Biology I

Study of the characteristics of living organisms, the biology of plants, the study of disease, and the study of heredity. (½ unit)

Biology II

A continuation of *Biology I* dealing with the biology of lower and higher animals, the study of reproduction, and biological conservation. (½ unit)

Earth Science I

Study the sciences of geology, physics, chemistry, and biology, including the basic physical and chemical laws that govern our universe, the internal processes of the earth, the makeup of the natural world, and the earth's distant past. Finally, the solar system and objects of the universe are covered. (½ unit)

Earth Science II

Study of the earth's environment. Map methods are developed to find locations on the earth's surface. Also, a study of the earth's air and water and the surface processes that shape the physical world. The last part of the course examines the earth's resources and the world's energy controversy and environmental problems. (½ unit)

SOCIAL SCIENCE

American History I

Survey United States' history from the age of the explorers through the Civil War and Reconstruction Periods. The emphasis is on the unique development of American culture and institutions, and the events and issues which shaped them. (½ unit)

American History II

Survey of United States' history from the post Civil War period to the modern day. The emphasis is on America's role as a world power in the twentieth century, the domestic problems faced by Americans during this time, and the challenges of the future. (½ unit)

World History

Survey of world cultures. The first seven units cover the land and people of various areas and their contribution to civilization. Units 8 and 9 deal with the world of revolution and the world of nationalism. The final unit summarizes today's world. (½ unit)

American Government I

Study of the principles of the American system of government so that high school students can understand the rights and responsibilities that come with citizenship enabling them to participate as citizens in the governmental process. The course is designed around the requirements set forth by the State of Idaho Department of Education. (½ unit)

State and Local Government II

Study of the organization and operation of the state and local governments in Idaho and the nation. (½ unit)

NONCREDIT COURSES

ELECTRICAL ENGINEERING

Elementary Electrical Theory

Basic electrical theory and circuits for electrical employees in electrical utility and general electrical areas; based upon the background of high school algebra, geometry, and physics. (Noncredit; equivalent to 2 semester hours)

MATHEMATICS

Remedial Mathematics

Remedial work in arithmetic and algebra for students who do not achieve a score on the ISU Mathematics Department placement examination sufficient to enter mathematics courses numbered 111 or higher. (Noncredit; equivalent to 4 semester hours)

Illinois, University of

GRADUATE COURSES

COUNSELING

Orientation to Counseling

Exploratory course for students considering entering counseling profession; successful completion of course is one criteria for final admission to the master's program in counseling and human services at the University of Idaho. Focus on counselors role and function, the counselor as a person, ethical considerations, and other issues; involves small group work and role playing; assessments of knowledge and skills acquired (will be asked to make VHS taped segments involving counseling situations). The VHS tape modules can only be purchased from the Correspondence Study office; additional $100 deposit on the tapes required with the enrollment fee. (2 semester hours)

PSYCHOLOGY

Profession Issues and Ethics in Psychology

Examination of the professional and ethical dimensions of the profession of psychology. Expanding on the issues identified by the Ethical Principles of Psychologists (APA), the student will learn about and explore the dilemmas and responsibilities facing the practitioners, scientists, educators, and others within this field. Some "solutions," regulatory measures, and legal precedents will also be explored. (3 semester hours)

SPECIAL EDUCATION

Physical and Medical Issues

Examination of legal and other issues; implications of physical and medical conditions; models for coordination of services provided in instructional settings; includes field component. (2 semester hours)

Augmentative and Alternative Communication Strategies for Persons with Moderate and Severe Disabilities

Develop a process for decision making, models for assessment, strategies and implementation steps for designing communications systems. Additional $100 deposit for VHS tapes. (3 semester hours)

VOCATIONAL EDUCATION

Classroom Management and Student Motivation

Techniques and strategies to motivate student interest and encourage learning. A video enhanced course. (2 semester hours)

Peer Coaching and Supervision for Educators

Observation techniques, conferencing, and feedback skills; structuring peer coaching programs. A video enhanced course. (2 semester hours)

Idaho State University

Pocatello, Idaho 83209   (208) 236-3153

Description:
The university was founded in 1901 and was established as Idaho State University in 1963. Correspondence study is available from Idaho State University, but all courses are administered by the Correspondence Study in Idaho office at the University of Idaho campus in Moscow, Idaho. SEE **Idaho, University of.**

Accreditations:
Northwest Association of Schools and Colleges.

Illinois, University of
Guided Individual Study
Office of Continuing Education and Public Service
Suite 1406
302 East John Street
Champaign, Illinois 61820   (217) 333-1321

Description:
The University of Illinois at Urbana-Champaign was founded in 1867 as a state supported, land-grant institution with a three-fold mission of teaching, research, and public service. The flagship campus of the university, it is an educational community of 34,000 students and 13,000 faculty and staff members. Correspondence study has been offered for over 50 years and courses may be taken for credit, professional development, or on a noncredit basis. For complete information, interested individuals should consult the University of Illinois correspondence course brochure which is available free of charge from the office.

Faculty:
Dr. Robert W. Batchellor, Head, Guided Individual Study.

Academic Levels:
College

Degree/Certificate Programs:
Correspondence study provides credits toward the bachelor degree. Up to 60 semester hours of correspondence and other off-campus credit may be applied toward the baccalaureate degree. This applies to credits transferred from other institutions; however, in all cases, the precise amount of credit toward a particular degree is determined by the college or department concerned.

Admission Requirements:
High school diploma, GED, or evidence of adequate background or training. Course prerequisites must be fulfilled. Students currently enrolled at colleges or universities should have the permission of their academic deans. High school seniors with superior academic records may enroll in entry level college courses with permission of their principals. Foreign students are advised not to enroll unless they have superior skills in the English language, dependable mail service, and an understanding of the credit-based system of education used in the United States.

Tuition:
$72 per semester hour of credit plus a nonrefundable $20 enrollment fee and a nonrefundable $20 course study guide fee. Fees are subject to change without notice and usually on an annual basis. Overseas students, except members of the U.S. Armed Services are required to pay a nonrefundable $30 postage fee per course for airmail return of lesson assignments. VISA, Discover, or MasterCard accepted. Veterans may be eligible for benefits under the GI Bill and/or the Illinois Veterans Scholarship. Holders of

Illinois County Child of Veteran Scholarships are eligible for the waiver of tuition.

If an application is rejected, a full refund is made. A refund of the enrollment fee less $72 $5 per lesson submitted will be made if the withdrawal request is made within six weeks of enrollment and no more than one-half of the course lessons have been submitted. A refund of one-half the enrollment fee (not to exceed the refund due during the first six weeks of enrollment) less $20 and less $5 per lesson submitted will be made if the withdrawal request is received from six to thirteen weeks of the date of enrollment and no more than one-half of the course lessons have been submitted.

Enrollment Period:

The maximum time allowed to complete a course is nine months; the minimum is six weeks. A three-month extension may be approved for an extension fee of $20. One course transfer is allowed within the first two months for a transfer fee of $20 plus a charge of $5 per lesson submitted in the original course. Any difference in enrollment fee between the original and the new course must be paid.

Equipment Requirements:

Textbooks and certain other materials required for particular courses are paid for by the student, and may be ordered from the University bookstore at the time of enrollment; the student will be billed for the costs plus postage.

Credit and Grading:

The grading system is A, B, C, D, and E (failure); a credit/no credit option is available. Generally, the final examination must be passed for credit to be awarded. A grade of C or better is required for credit. Examinations must be proctored by a University-approved proctor. Credit is awarded in semester hour credits.

Library Services:

Correspondence students may arrange to use the University libraries. Interlibrary loans from the University Library are available through many local libraries in Illinois.

Accreditations:

North Central Association of Colleges and Schools. Member of: National University Continuing Education Association.

COLLEGE COURSES

ACCOUNTING

Principles of Accounting I

Introduction to financial accounting; the communication of relevant information to external parties; includes development of accounting model, internal control, measurement processes, data classification and terminology, as well as interpretation and use of the resultant financial statements. (3 credits)

Principles of Accounting II

Introduction to managerial accounting; fundamentals of cost-volume analysis and product costing, management reporting and information for decision making; introduction to budgets and standards for planning, control, and performance measurement. (3 credits)

Intermediate Accounting

Accounting concepts, principles, and theory with an emphasis on the special problems that arise in applying these concepts for external reporting purposes; emphasizes the use of accounting information as a basis for decisions by management, stockholders, creditors, and other users of financial statements and accounting reports. (3 credits)

Cost Accounting

Use of costs for control and decision making with emphasis on standard costs, relevant costs, direct costing, nonmanufacturing costs, and responsibility accounting; for students who have already studied the basic elements of job order, process costs, and budgeting. (3 credits) (3 credits)

ADVERTISING

Introduction to Advertising

Adv. 281. A survey of advertising, its organization and functions, planning and execution, and relation to our economic and social systems. (3 credits)

Adv. 281B. Same as above course but developed for foreign students. (3 credits)

Advertising Creative Strategy

Theory and practice of advertising message planning and creation for print and broadcast media. Use of consumer and market surveys, copy-testing methods, and advertising readership studies. (3 credits)

Advertising in Contemporary Society

Advertising as an economic and social institution; its relation to the firm, individual, economy, and press system. (3 credits)

AGRICULTURAL ECONOMICS

Introduction to Agricultural Economics

Principles of microeconomics; demand, production, supply, elasticity, markets, and trade are presented and used in the analysis of decisions of individuals relating to agriculturally-oriented problems such as growth and development; recourses; trade; environment; and income. Macroeconomic concepts are also introduced. (4 credits)

ANTHROPOLOGY

Introduction to Anthropology: The Origin of Man and Culture

An introduction to and survey of human origins and early man, physical anthropology, race and racism, archaeology, and the beginning of human civilization. (4 credits)

Introduction to Cultural Anthropology

A survey of cultural anthropology which deals with the nature of culture and its various aspects including social organization, technology, economics, religion, and language among contemporary peoples with consideration of the individual in a sociocultural milieu and of the balance in any society between tradition and change. (4 credits)

Archaeology of Illinois

Traces the prehistory of Illinois from the first entry of people into the region more than 13,000 years ago until the 17th century AD and the beginning of historical records; examines subsequent cultural changes up to the 19th century and statehood from an archaeological and ethnohistorical perspective. (3 credits)

Introduction to Archaeology

Introduction to theory in archaeological research, data collection, and analysis; examines the strategies employed in the investigation of archaeological remains and how these strategies further the aims of an anthropological archaeology. (3 credits)

BUSINESS ADMINISTRATION

Purchasing Management (Undergraduate Open Seminar)

Operational dimensions of the purchasing function and the major problems involved in its management. Field projects. (3 credits)

Principles of Marketing

A course emphasizing the marketing concepts of planning, organization, control, and decision making from the viewpoint of the business executive. (3 credits)

Introduction to Management

Summary of management in a modern industrial enterprise; emphasis on motivation, small group behavior, and problems of designing and operating a formal organization structure. (3 credits)

Entrepreneurship: Small Business Formation

An applied study of the entrepreneur and of entrepreneurship. It explores entrepreneurial concepts without regard to company size or age. The course surveys broad intellectual and practical lessons for the mainstream of business. (4 credits)

Business Policy

An introduction to business planning viewed at the executive level. (3 credits)

BUSINESS AND TECHNICAL WRITING

Business and Administrative Communication

Study of communication as a tool of administration and management; practice in writing a wide variety of types and forms of communication. (3 credits)

Technical Writing

Advanced course dealing with the problems, principles, and techniques of presenting technical information. Includes reports, proposals, manuals, and technical articles. (3 credits)

ECONOMICS

Microeconomic Principles

An introduction to the functions of individual decision makers, both consumers and producers, within the larger economic system. Primary emphasis on the nature and functions of product markets, the theory of the firm under varying conditions of competition and monopoly, the study of resource markets, the distribution of income, and the role of government in prompting efficiency and equity in the economy. (3 credits)

Macroeconmic Principles

An introduction to the theory of determination of total or aggregate income, employment, output, price levels, and the role of money in the economy. Primary emphasis on monetary and fiscal policy, inflation, unemployment, economic growth, and international economics. (3 credits)

Introductory Economic Statistics

A one-semester coverage of introductory statistics as applied to economics or business: descriptive statistics; probability theory and distributions; sampling methods and distributions; estimation and hypothesis-testing; and simple and multiple regression. (3 credits)

Economic Statistics I

First half of an introductory statistics sequence as applied to economics and business: descriptive statistics; probability theory and distributions; sampling methods and distributions; and hypothesis-testing. (3 credits)

Economic Statistics II

A continuation of the above course. Emphasizes estimation and goodness of fit, single and multiple regression, correlation, Bayesian decision theory, time series analysis, and index numbers. (3 credits)

Introduction to Public Finance

A general survey of the economics of the public sector at the federal, state, and local levels, including government expenditures, public budgeting, cost-benefit analysis, principles of taxation, tax reform, and intergovernmental fiscal relations. (3 credits)

History of Economic Thought

The development of economics; the examination of contributions of individual writers and schools of thought as they influenced economic thought and national policy. (3 credits)

The Developing Economies

Analyzes the economic problems associated with newly developing nations; emphasizes their economic structures, their factor scarcities, and their programs for development. (3 credits)

The Soviet Economy

Analytical survey of Soviet economic development; structure and performance of the economy; and problems of planning and control. (3 credits)

Law and Economics

Applications of economic theory to problems and issues in both civil and criminal law and the effect of legal rules on the allocation of resources; includes property rights, liability and negligence assignment, the use of administrative and common law to mitigate market failure, and the logic of private versus public law enforcement. (3 credits)

ENGINEERING

Engineering Graphics

An integrated course in the theory and practice of engineering graphics. Topics include: graphs, sketch-made and formal drawings; pictorial, multiview orthographic, sectioned, and auxiliary views; dimensioning; and fundamental descriptive geometry. (3 credits)

EDUCATION

Educational Psychology

The basic undergraduate course in psychology of education for prospective teachers and others. (3 credits)

ENGLISH

Introduction to the Drama

Understanding of the drama through the reading and consideration of representative plays; includes selections from Greek, Elizabethan, modern English, Continental, and American drama. (3 credits)

Introduction to Film

Understanding narrative films through the viewing and discussion of a representative body of film classics drawn from the entire range of world cinema; emphasizes the basic elements of cinematic expression, and concerns major movements, periods and genres. (3 credits)

Masterpieces of English Literature

A study of representative works by major authors, including Swift, Shaw, Shakespeare, Spenser, Milton, Chaucer, and T. S. Eliot. (3 credits)

Masterpieces of American Literature

A study of representative works by major authors, including Franklin, Thoreau, Hawthorne, Melville, Twain, James, Hemingway, Faulkner, and others. (3 credits)

Introduction to Shakespeare

An introduction to Shakespeare's dramatic form, poetic language, and characteristic themes through a reading of eight plays. (3 credits)

The Modern Short Story

A study of major American and European short stories: Conrad, Joyce, Lawrence, Faulkner, Kafka, Hemingway, Crane, Roth, Ellison, Flannery O'Connor, and others. (3 credits)

The British Novel

A study of representative novels from the late eighteenth century to the present. Included are Brontë, Dickens, Conrad, Forster, Joyce, Woolf, and Murdoch. (3 credits)

American Fiction

Representative American novels and tales from James Fenimore Cooper to the present. Included are Hawthorne, Poe, Melville, Twain, James, Hemingway, Fitzgerald, and Faulkner. (3 credits)

FRENCH

Elementary French

Fr 101. Grammar, reading of modern journalistic texts, composition, translation, pronunciation. For students who have had no work in French. (4 credits)

Fr 102. Continuation of *Fr 101.* (4 credits)

Intermediate French I

Fr 103. Continuation of *Fr 102.* (4 credits)

Intermediate French II

Fr 104. Continuation of *Fr 103.* (4 credits)

GEOGRAPHY

Physical Geography I: Atmospheric Environment

An introduction to the processes responsible for the spatial variation of weather and climate with a survey of world climatic patterns. (4 credits)

Physical Geography II

Studies the physical elements of geography; designed to develop the ability to describe and understand three of the primary natural elements of the geographic landscape: soils, vegetation, and landforms. (4 credits)

GERMAN

Elementary German

Ger 101. Grammar, pronunciation, reading. For students with no work in German. (4 credits)

Ger 102. Continuation of *Ger 101.* (4 credits)

Intermediate German

Ger 103. Continuation of *Ger 102.* Modern prose and grammar review. (4 credits)

Ger 104. Continuation of *Ger 103.* Classical and modern narrative prose. (4 credits)

HEALTH EDUCATION

Contemporary Health

Examines concepts of health and health promotion in contemporary society with emphasis on health and injury control for individuals and groups. Topics include: self-care, health insurance, exercise, nutrition and weight control, sexuality, contraception, tobacco, alcohol, cardiovascular health, infectious diseases, and cancer. (3 credits)

Drug Use and Abuse

Introduction to the biological, psychological, pharmacological, and legal aspects of drug use and abuse; emphasizes personal and social actions for responsible drug use. (2 credits)

Foundations of Health Behavior

An examination of the application of the social and behavioral sciences to health and health behavior. Psychological, social psychological, and sociological approaches to health behavior will be analyzed. Topics that will be covered include the development of health attitudes and behaviors, perceptions of health and illness, methods of changing health behavior and patient-provider interaction. (3 credits)

Human Sexuality

The problems of sex and family life. (2 credits)

Health Program Development

The elements of program development and planning are presented as they pertain to various health settings including health care facilities, community agencies, and the school community. A special emphasis will be placed on student skills in developing example program plans pertinent to the student's area of interest. (3 credits)

Sexuality Program Development

Theory and practice of family life and sex education. (2 credits)

Drug Education Planning

Psychosocial, cultural, pharmacological, and legal aspects of drug use and abuse. (2 credits)

Introduction to Epidemiology

Basic concepts and methods of epidemiology; patterns of disease occurrence; applications of epidemiology to health education, health services administration and planning, health policy, and environmental health. (2 credits)

Public Health Practice

Theory and practice of community health education; adult health education through media such as radio, television, films, slides, posters, pamphlets, and newspapers; projects in preparing and using public health education materials; and evaluation of research in public health education. (4 credits)

Special Topics: Patient Education

This course emphasizes several major areas of patient education: the current status of patient education and its present direction, the relationship between education and the provision of health care, the tools and strategies of patient education, and current issues surrounding the development of patient education and its potential future directions. The course provides a theoretical and operational understanding of the various aspects of patient education and experiences of academic and professional value. (3 credits)

HISTORY

Western Civilization from Antiquity to 1660

The fundamental developments, social, economic, cultural, intellectual, and political in the history of mankind and Western society and the commercial revolution, medieval art, universities, and heresies, the Renaissance and Reformation, the Puritan Revolution, and the beginnings of the modern world. (3 credits)

Western Civilization from 1660 to the Present

The fundamental developments, social, economic, cultural, intellectual, and political in the history of mankind and Western society since 1660; includes the rise of modern science, French and Industrial revolutions, Romantic movement, growth of nationalism and socialism, imperialism, urbanization, Russian Revolution, Nazi Germany, WWI−II, and the West and the underdeveloped world. (3 credits)

History of the United States to 1877

Colonial foundations, movement for independence, early years of the republic. (3 credits)

History of the United States, 1877 to the Present

The evolution of an industrial, urbanized, and pluralistic society, grappling with domestic and global problems. (3 credits)

The United States in the Twentieth Century

One major emphasis on foreign policy, including the emergence of the United States as a great power after 1898; a second emphasis on the Progressive movement and recurrent attempts at the reform of American society; and racial and urban problems and the conservation of natural resources included. (3 credits)

Constitutional Development of the United States to 1865

An examination of the Constitution and its relationship to political, economic, and social developments and institutions from colonial beginnings through the Civil War. (3 credits)

Constitutional Development of the United States since 1865

Leading constitutional issues during the period in the historical contexts in which they were developed. (3 credits)

LATIN

Elementary Latin

Lat 101. Grammar and reading. For students who have had no work in Latin. (4 credits)

Lat 102. Grammar and reading of easy prose. (4 credits)

Intermediate Latin

Review of grammar; reading of easy narrative prose. (4 credits)

Introduction to Latin Literature

A continuation of *Intermediate Latin.* (4 credits)

MATHEMATICS

Algebra

Math. x112. Review of fundamental concepts. (3 credits)

Math x112z. Review of fundamental ideas as factoring, fractions, graphs, and exponents. Other topics are quadratics, inequalities, matrices and determinants, logarithms, progressions, and binomial theorem. (3 credits)

Trigonometry

Introduction of trigonometric functions and applications to right angles. Fundamental identities, logarithms, reduction formulas, inverse functions, the solution of oblique triangles, laws of cosines, tangents, and sines. (2 credits)

Calculus and Analytical Geometry

First course in calculus and analytical geometry. Sketching curves, differentiation with applications, and integration with applications such as finding volume. Theorem of mean value. (5 credits)

Finite Mathematics

An introduction to finite mathematics for students in the social sciences. The course covers systems of linear equations, matrices, linear programming, and probability. Problems are selected from social sciences and business. (3 credits)

Elementary Linear Algebra with Applications

Basic concepts and techniques, including linear equations, matrices, determinants, vectors in n-space, and eigenvectors with applications such as Markov processes, linear programming, economic models, least squares, and population growth. (3 credits)

Calculus and Analytical Geometry

Second course in calculus and analytical geometry. Methods of integration, infinite series, conics, polar coordinates. (3 credits)

Calculus for Social Scientists I

Introduction to basic ideas of the calculus; includes the derivative, applications of the derivative, exponential and logarithmic functions, integration, and functions of several variables. (4 credits)

Mathematics for Elementary Teachers

Systematic presentation of elementary mathematics for those preparing to teach. (3 credits)

Calculus and Analytical Geometry

Third course in calculus and analytical geometry. Vectors, geometry in space, partial differentiation, and multiple integrals. (3 credits)

Differential Equations and Orthogonal Functions

Intended for engineering students and others who require a working knowledge of differential equations. Included are techniques and applications of ordinary differential equations and an introduction to partial differential equations. (3 credits)

Linear Transformations and Matrices

An introductory course emphasizing techniques of linear algebra; topics include matrix operations, determinants, linear equations, vector spaces, linear transformations, eigenvalues, and eigenvectors. (3 credits)

PHYSICS

Theory of Mechanics, Properties of Matter, Wave Motion, Fluids, and Thermal Physics

Motion; force, dynamics, statics; momentum; work, energy, and power; rotation; gravitation and planetary motions; vibrations and waves; fluids; temperature, thermal properties, heat and heat transfer; kinetic theory of gases and thermodynamics. (4 credits)

Theory of Electricity and Magnetism, Light, and Atomic and Nuclear Physics

Electric charge, conductors and insulators; electric field, capacitors, dielectrics, and potential difference; energy and electric power; cells, resistance, current, circuits and instruments; sources and effects of magnetic fields; applied electromagnetism; radiation, light, optics, and holography; applied optics; relativity; quantum effects and duality; atomic physics; radioactivity, nuclear structure, and nuclear physics. (4 credits)

POLITICAL SCIENCE

Introduction to Political Science

Survey of major concepts and approaches employed in political science. (3 credits)

American Government: Organization and Powers

Historical development and organization of national, state, and local governments; the federal system; national and state constitutions; civil and political rights; party system; nature, structure, powers, and procedure of legislative, executive, and judicial departments in state and nation (3 credits)

Introduction to Comparative Politics

Basic concepts and principles of political analysis from a comparative perspective. (3 credits)

The Emerging Nations

An introductory comparative consideration of the patterns of political development and of the policies and problems of the emerging nations of Asia, Africa, and Latin America; emphasis on the special characteristics of countries beginning their independent nationhood and the effects of these characteristics on the political systems of these lands and their role in the community of nations. (3 credits)

Introduction to Political Theory

The nature, structure, and purposes of political theory; uses major works on the problems of political order, obedience, justice, liberty, and representation to distinguish and clarify different theoretical approaches; designed to be an introduction to ideas, not a historical survey. (3 credits)

Introduction to International Relations

The structure and processes of international relations, trends in international politics, and the future of the international system in a setting of conflict and crisis. (3 credits)

Municipal Government

Growth of cities; their legal status; and municipal politics and organization in the United States. (3 credits)

Contemporary Political Theory

Tendencies in Western political theory since 1850; conservatism and constitutionalism; the religious interpretation of the state and economic institutions; Marxism, socialism, and communism; and antidemocratic thought and totalitarian regimes. (3 credits)

PSYCHOLOGY

Introduction to Psychology

The study of human behavior with special reference to social psychology, learning, memory, thinking, emotional life, and individual differences in intelligence, aptitude, and personality. (4 credits)

Introduction to Social Psychology

Systematic study of social factors in individual and group behavior. (3 credits)

Child Psychology

Study of the psychological development of the child. (3 credits)

Cognitive Psychology

Introduction to the psychological study of human information processing and memory; acquisition, retrieval, and forgetting; and general knowledge concepts, reasoning, and related issues in cognition. (3 credits)

Perception and Sensory Processes

Survey of experimental psychology of sensory and perceptual processes and behavior; emphasis on the contribution of behavior science to understanding subjective experience of the physical and social environment. (3 credits)

Descriptive Statistics

Basic course in descriptive statistics. (3 credits)

Inferential Statistics

Basic course in inferential statistics. (2 credits)

Introduction to Statistics

Development of skill and understanding in the application of statistical methods to problems in psychological research; topics include descrip-

tive statistics, probability, estimation, basic inferential methods, regression, correlation and basic analysis of variance procedures. (5 credits)

Abnormal Psychology

Conceptions and facts about disordered behavior, including psychoses, neuroses, and other patterns of psychological disturbance. (3 credits)

Industrial Psychology

A systematic coverage of some of the most prominent areas of industrial psychology. (3 credits)

Psychology of Learning and Memory

A study of animal and human learning with special attention to the important experimental results and influential theories. (3 credits)

Psychology of Personality

A systematic study of the development, dynamics, and structure of personality, including major contributions of methodology, theory, and empirical research. (3 credits)

Behavior Modification

Introduction to behavioral approaches to human problems; overview of the basic principles of assessment and operant and respondent conditioning models; and the influence of cognitive theories on behavioral thought. (3 credits)

Modern Viewpoints in Psychology

Examines modern behaviorism, psychoanalysis, and cognitive psychology, viewed as conceptions of man, styles of theorizing and investigative strategies; critically evaluates the more influential theories and research. (3 credits)

RHETORIC

Principles of Composition

Study of the methods of exposition, problems of argument, use of evidence, and style; practice in writing with primary emphasis on exposition; research paper. (4 credits)

RUSSIAN

First-Year Russian

Russ 101. Elements of grammar, reading, writing. For students with no credit in Russian. (4 credits)

Russ 102. Continuation of *Russ 101*. Elements of grammar, reading, writing. (4 credits)

Second-Year Russian

Russ 103. Grammar review, vocabulary building. (4 credits)

Russ 104. Grammar review, vocabulary building, translation of selected texts from literature and social sciences. (4 credits)

Nineteenth-Century Russian Literature

A study of major Russian writers from Pushkin through Chekhov. No knowledge of Russian is required. (3 credits)

SOCIOLOGY

Introduction to Sociology

Introductory analysis and description of the structure and dynamics of human society. (3 credits)

Introduction to Modern Africa

An interdisciplinary introduction to Africa dealing with basic themes an problems in the politics, economics, sociology, anthropology, and history of Africa. (3 credits)

Stratification and Social Classes

Systems of social ranking with emphasis on the United States; power, prestige, privilege, culture, life styles, interests, ideologies, and interactions of classes; effects of social change and mobility. (3 credits)

Juvenile Delinquency

Historical change in definitions of delinquency, its causes and control; gangs; the juvenile justice system; treatment of offenders; and preventive programs. (3 credits)

Crowds, Social Movements, and Violence

Examines individual and collective behavior in crowds, demonstrations, riots, disasters, and social movements from social contagion, value-added, emergent norm, and social behavioral/interactionist perspectives. (3 credits)

Alcohol and Society

Social psychology of alcohol use, patterning, and abuse. Etiology and epidemiology of alcoholism. Politics of social control and treatment. History of prohibition, reform movements, and social and cultural comparisons. "Normal" and "problem" drinking socially defined. The culture of public drinking problems, relation of family, occupation, class, age, sex, ethnicity, and religion. Disease conception of alcoholism. Theories of alcoholism: medical, psychological, psychiatric, epidemiological, anthropological, sociological, and folk. Alcohol, violence, and crime in American society. Culture, alcohol, drugs, and subjective experience. (3 credits)

Family Violence

Examines the sociology of conjugal and intrafamily violence from comparative, historical, and social psychological perspectives; abuse of family members; the violent situation; interpersonal violence. (3 credits)

SPANISH

Elementary Spanish

Span 101. For students who have no credit in Spanish. (4 credits)

Span 102. Continuation of *Span 101.* (4 credits)

Span 103. Second-semester Spanish course for all students who did not take *Span 101* at the University of Illinois. (4 credits)

Reading and Writing Spanish I

Readings with written discussion in Spanish; review and development of grammar essential to competence in reading and writing. (4 credits)

Reading and Writing Spanish II

Continuation of the above course. Readings with written discussion in Spanish; continued development of writing skills. (4 credits)

NONCREDIT COURSES

ANTHROPOLOGY

Archaeology of Illinois

Anth. n610. Traces the prehistory of Illinois from the first entry of people into the region more than 13,000 years ago until the 17th century A.D. and the beginning of historical records; examines subsequent cultural changes up to the 19th century and statehood from an archaeological and ethnohistorical perspective. (Noncredit) *Tuition:* $120.

Anth. n611. Continuation of *Anth. n610.* (Noncredit) *Tuition:* $120.

BUSINESS ADMINISTRATION

Entrepreneurship: Small Business Formation

B.Adm. n620. Course is an applied study of the entrepreneur and of entrepreneurship. It explains entrepreneurial concepts without regard to company size or age. The course surveys broad intellectual and practical lessons for the mainstream of business. (Noncredit) *Tuition:* $120.

B.Adm. n621. Continuation of *B.Adm. n620.* (Noncredit) *Tuition:* $120.

BUSINESS AND TECHNICAL WRITING

Technical Writing

B.&T.W. n630. Advanced course covering the problems, principles, and techniques of presenting technical information. Includes reports, proposals, manuals, and technical articles. (Noncredit) *Tuition:* $120.

B.&T.W. n631. Continuation of *B.&T.W. n630.* (Noncredit) *Tuition:* $120.

ENGLISH

Detective Fiction: Crime Pays!

This credit-free course offers you eight different opportunities to explore detective fiction. In it, you will re-visit some favorite authors and encounter others for the first time. The course includes readings and optional written exercises you may send in for comment by the instructor, who designed the course. (Noncredit) *Tuition:* $40.

INTERNATIONAL AFFAIRS

The New Europe

Recordings by internationally acclaimed scholars examine the historical and political background of events in Eastern and Central Europe that occurred in 1992–93. The presentations and accompanying supplementary readings also analyze the social, economic, and political dimensions of: (1) the rise of nationalism and ethnic strife, (2) the breakup of the Soviet Union, (3) the impact on Germany and France, and (4) political and economic conditions in Russia. (Noncredit) *Tuition:* $120.

The Growing Spectre of Violence: A Worldwide Threat

Recordings by acclaimed scholars and researchers present ideas on the use of violence and aggression in international disputes. The presentations and accompanying supplementary readings examine individual and collective violence; violent aggression in Ireland, South Africa, and the Middle East; and ways to prevent further violence. (Noncredit) *Tuition:* $40.

Asia: Preparing for the Pacific Century

Recordings of internationally acclaimed scholars provide information about Asia in the twenty-first century. The presentations and accompanying supplementary readings focus on: (1) Asia's search for a new identity; (2) Japanese attitudes toward Westerners; (3) U.S. attitudes towards the Chinese; (4) economic cooperation among Asia-Pacific countries; (5) U.S. relations with Taiwan and China; (6) the future of Hong Kong after 1997; and (7) Asia's future. (Noncredit) *Tuition:* $40.

MATHEMATICS

College Algebra

Review of fundamental ideas as factoring, fractions, graphs, and exponents. Other topics are quadratics, inequalities, matrices and determinants, logarithms, progressions, and binomial theorem. (Noncredit) *Tuition:* $140.

Indiana State University
Independent Study
Alumni Hall 109
Terre Haute, Indiana 47809   (812) 237-2555

Description:
In 1995, Indiana State University will celebrate its 125th anniversary of the enrollment of the first class of students. ISU is a general, multipurpose, publicly supported institution of higher education.

The Independent Study program includes upwards of 70 courses. Because courses are continually being revised, on occasion one or more regular offerings may temporarily not be available. Also, new courses that were not formally offered are added as the need and faculty expertise is available. Annual enrollments are near 1,000 for credit and noncredit courses combined.

Faculty:
Dr. S. R. Wiersteiner, Director, Independent Study; Joanna Warne, Administrative Secretary. There is a faculty of 55 members.

Academic Levels:
College

Degree/Certificate Programs:
A maximum of 32 semester hours of correspondence study credit may be applied toward a baccalaureate degree. No graduate-level courses are offered through correspondence. Any course may be taken on a noncredit basis.

Admission Requirements:
High school graduation or equivalent.

Tuition:
$100 per semester hour. VISA and MasterCard accepted. Refund policy: 100 percent if withdrawal occurs within first 30 days less $15 service charge and $6 for each lesson submitted; fifty percent refund if withdrawal occurs 31 to 90 days from date of enrollment less $15 service charge and $6 for each lesson submitted. No refund granted after 90 days. The University Board of Trustees reserves the right to change fees at any time. Annual fee increases are effective with the fall semester registration each August.

Enrollment Period:
Maximum time allowed to complete a course is one year; minimum time is generally two to three months. Although one year from the date of enrollment is allowed for course completion, a six-month extension of time may be secured upon payment of an extension fee of $30 before the course expires. No course extension will be granted after a course has ' expired. If the course is not completed within a year and a half, and the student has completed 50% of the lessons, the student may request an additional extension of time. At that time, the student must choose between three or six months for completion at a cost of $50 for three months or $100 for six months.

Equipment Requirements:
Textbooks are supplied by the student and may be ordered from the Indiana State University Bookstore. There is a charge for rental of videotapes if applicable.

Credit and Grading:
Credit earned through Independent Study is of the same value as credit earned in residence and is computed in the cumulative grade-point average. Grading policy: A, B, C, D, F. Minimum passing grade is D. No credit is given if the grade is F. The final examination in most courses is heavily weighed for determining the course grade. Campus courses cannot be repeated for grade improvement. Examinations must be proctored. Credit is awarded in semester hour units.

Library Services:
Library facilities on the campus of ISU are available to correspondence students when they are in the campus area.

Accreditations:
North Central Association of Colleges and Schools.

COLLEGE COURSES

ART

Art Appreciation
An appreciation of various media and styles used by visual artists. A general education course. (2 semester hours)

Visual Arts in Civilization
A topical survey of major concepts in the visual arts and their relation to the societies which produced them. (3 semester hours)

BIOLOGY

Conversational Biology: Reproduction, Growth, and Development
Emphasis is placed on the biological aspects of human reproduction, growth, and development. Video format only. (1 semester hour)

Conversational Biology: Human Genetics
A study of basic genetic principles with emphasis on various human genetic defects. Consideration of genetic disease and counseling included. Video format only. (1 semester hour)

COMMUNICATIONS

Survey of Broadcasting
History and survey of broadcasting. Emphasis on its social, cultural, and economic implications. Required of radio-TV-film majors and minors. (3 semester hours)

Parliamentary Procedures
The principles and practices of parliamentary law. (1 semester hour)

Writing for the Broadcast Media
The techniques and philosophy, with writing of radio and television news, music continuity, public service announcements, and commercials. (3 semester hours)

CRIMINOLOGY

Criminology
A consideration of criminality, its nature and extent, particularly in the United States; and an analysis of the etiology of criminal behavior, the criminal law, and societal reaction to criminals. (3 semester hours)

Institutional, Industrial, and Commercial Security

Emphasizes prevention of security problems and the promotion and observance of effective security measures to protect lives, property, and proprietary information. (3 semester hours)

Retail Security

Emphasizes the identification and development of physical security objectives, policies, procedures, and methods necessary to achieve efficient and effective retail security measures. (3 semester hours)

Crime Prevention

Provides an overview of types of crime prevention programs that can be implemented by police departments; retail, commercial, or individual firms; and community action groups and individual citizens. (3 semester hours)

Criminal Investigation

Organization and functions of investigative agencies; basic considerations in the investigation of crime, collection, and preservation of physical evidence; elements of legal proof in the submission of evidence; investigation of specific types of offenses. (3 semester hours)

EDUCATIONAL PSYCHOLOGY

Developmental Psychology

An overview of human development from conception to death. Analysis of research and application of findings to further understanding of physiological and psychological factors affecting individuals' development and adjustment throughout life are emphasized. (3 semester hours)

Adolescent Psychology

Research on the development and behavior of adolescents is reviewed in an attempt to determine how the adult may best foster favorable growth. (3 semester hours)

ENGLISH

Introduction to Literature

Selections from prose, poetry, and drama from several historical periods and countries, with emphasis on appreciation and understanding. (3 semester hours)

Introduction to Fiction Writing

A workshop course for beginning writers of short stories or novels. (3 semester hours)

Introduction to Fiction

Representative short stories and novels from several historical periods and countries, with emphasis on appreciation and understanding prose fiction. (3 semester hours)

Children's Literature

Literature appropriate for children from preschool through junior high school age. (3 semester hours)

English Grammar

Examination of the structure of English, emphasizing basic sentence elements. (3 semester hours)

GEOGRAPHY

Introduction to Earth and Sky Sciences

Scientific method as applied to geology, oceanography, and astronomy. (3 semester hours)

World Geography

An interpretation of human activities in selected world regions. (3 semester hours)

Political Geography

Problems arising where the boundaries of sovereign states fail to separate national groups and where corporate limits fail to encompass all segments of a metropolis. (3 semester hours)

Conservation of Natural Resources

Utilization of our natural resources and the improvement in the quality of the environment, including the role of government agencies in resource management. (3 semester hours)

HEALTH

Personal Health Science and Wellness

Acquaints students with scientific data on matters of health which affect the individual, family, and society, and introduces concepts for disease prevention, health maintenance, and health resources conservation for improving the quality of life. (3 semester hours)

HISTORY

Studies in World Civilization to 1500

Studies in selected world civilizations from the beginnings to the early modern age. Those themes which have a direct bearing upon contemporary culture and society will be stressed. (3 semester hours)

Studies in World Civilization since 1500

Studies in world history dealing with the modern era and contemporary world problems. (3 semester hours)

INSURANCE

Introduction to Risk and Insurance

Basic principles of, and the intimate relations between, risk and insurance. The fundamentals of insurance as the major formal method of treating non-speculative risk. (3 semester hours)

Life and Health Insurance

Basic principles of life insurance, health insurance, and annuities. Policy provisions, policy innovations, and the role of life insurance in financial planning is examined. (3 semester hours)

JOURNALISM

Newswriting

Introduction to news and the reporter's role with intensive practice in organizing and writing news stories. Includes required laboratory assignments and experiences. Typing ability required. (3 semester hours)

Introduction to Photojournalism

The use of cameras and still pictures in print media. (3 semester hours)

Magazine Writing

A study of magazine markets and planning, gathering, organizing, and writing nonfiction articles for magazine publication. (3 semester hours)

MATHEMATICS

Intermediate Algebra

Polynomials, rational algebraic expressions, functions, graphs, inequalities, and theory of equations. (3 semester hours)

Principles of Statistics

A course for non-mathematics majors and minors. Graphical and numerical representation of data, probability, sampling, statistical inference, correlation, and regression. (3 semester hours)

Fundamentals and Applications of Calculus

Inequalities, polynomial functions, logs, and exponentials. Differential and integral calculus and applications. For students in social sciences, business, and applied areas. (3 semester hours)

Mathematics for Elementary Teachers II

Fundamental concepts in mathematics for teachers including topics in numeration, number systems, number theory, probability, and statistics. (3 semester hours)

PHYSICAL EDUCATION

Athletic Training and Emergency First Aid

Introductory course for the coach, physical educator, and athletic trainer. Successful completion of the course will lead to American Red Cross First Aid Certification (after passing the practical exam). (3 semester hours)

Foundations of Physical Education

A study of the events and people who have influenced the growth of physical education, and of the philosophies and philosophers on which the discipline is based. (2 semester hours)

Foundations of Conditioning

A course for the physical educator, coach, and athletic trainer which will introduce them to the principles underlying sound conditioning programs. Emphasis will be placed upon the development of year-round conditioning programs for specific sports. Assistance will be provided to students in the development of these sound conditioning programs and the application of sound nutritional foundations. (3 semester hours)

Sports Management

Designed to provide practical suggestions and guides for managing business affairs, athletic eligibility, contest management, facilities, intramurals, and athletic trends. (3 semester hours)

Scientific Aspects of Physical Education and Coaching

Selected principles of biology, anatomy, physiology, kinesiology related to coaching; first aid and care of injuries; training and conditioning of athletes. (3 semester hours)

Organization and Administration of Physical Education

Problems in organization and administration and an investigation of material for their solution. (2 semester hours)

Physical Education and the Law

An understanding of: what to do if involved in a lawsuit; what to expect at a trial; defenses against the negligence in sport litigation; the handicapped athlete; discrimination and the athlete; governmental immunity and proprietary function; case law relating to athletic scholarships, officials, injuries to spectators, sport facilities, and sport equipment; and sports-related medical problems relating to team physicians and athletic trainers. (3 semester hours)

POLITICAL SCIENCE

Public Personnel Administration

Organization, structure, recruitment practices, and policies of local, state, and federal departments and agencies. (3 semester hours)

PSYCHOLOGY

General Psychology

An introduction to psychology as a science, surveying learning, motivation, perception, psychobiology, cognition, intelligence, personality, etc. (3 semester hours)

Introduction to Abnormal Psychology

Encompasses personality disorders, anxiety and mood disorders, psychotic disorders, mental deficiency, and other major mental disorders. (3 semester hours)

SAFETY

Individual and Community Safety

Emphasizes the strategies designed to prevent accidents, develops the concept of self-help and mutual aid in accident and disaster occurrences, and reinforces the need to minimize losses in the social, economic, physical, and emotional criteria of human conservation. (3 semester hours)

SOCIOLOGY

Principles of Sociology

Sociology as the science of human groups. Structure, function, and processes of human groups, cultures, and institutions. (3 semester hours)

Contemporary Social Problems

Problems of social and individual maladjustment, the causes of maladjustment, and the attempted and planned efforts for the solution of these problems. (3 semester hours)

Social Conflict

An analysis of conflict and conflict resolution on interpersonal, intergroup, interorganizational, and international levels. General theories of conflict are examined in the light of selected empirical studies. (3 hours)

Indiana University
Division of Extended Studies
School of Continuing Studies
Owen Hall, Room 001
Bloomington, Indiana 47405   (812) 855-3693

Description:

Indiana University was founded in 1820, only four years after Indiana achieved statehood. It is one of the oldest universities west of the Alleghenies. Indiana University is now ranked ninth largest in the nation with an enrollment totaling over 70,000 on its eight state campuses.

The Division of Continuing Education can be traced to 1903 when several extramural courses were taught by University faculty. By 1912, college-level correspondence study became a part of the University's regular offerings. The high school correspondence program began in 1925, and external degree continuing education courses began in 1975. Indiana University has received more National University Continuing Education awards for quality independent study courses than any other school.

Toll-free telephone numbers: within Indiana, 800-822-4762; out-of-state 800-457-4434.

Faculty:

Dr. Lawrence J. Keller, Director, Division of Extended Studies. Courses are taught by regular Indiana University faculty and by certified high school teachers.

Academic Levels:

College
High School
Noncredit
Graduate

Degree/Certificate Programs:

Credit toward bachelor and associate degrees; high school diploma; certificate. An Indiana University General Studies Associate or Bachelor Degree may be earned entirely through Independent Study. The amount of independent study credit allowed toward other degrees varies with the individual school. The General Studies Degree Program requires completion of a core of arts and sciences courses—humanities, social and behavioral sciences—and a wide range of electives. The electives permit the student to explore other areas of interest and to tailor the degree to his/her individual needs.

Admission Requirements:

Open enrollment. Enrollment in an independent study course does not constitute admission to the University.

Tuition:

College-level, undergraduate $82.25 per semester credit hour, graduate $130.85 per credit hour; high school-level, $58.25 per ½ unit course. Noncredit (continuing education) courses, fee varies, see individual course descriptions below. Refund policy: for university courses, all is refunded less $15 plus $5.50 for each lesson submitted if withdrawal occurs within 30 days; between 30 and 60 days, one half is refunded less $5.50 for each lesson submitted. MasterCard and Visa accepted.

Enrollment Period:

Maximum time allowed is twelve months per course plus two six-month extensions upon payment of $20 per credit hour for each extension. Minimum time to complete a course is six weeks. Some courses require prerequisites.

Equipment Requirements:

Students pay for textbooks, supplies, and learning guides. Some cassette tapes (video or audio) are loaned to students; some must be purchased. Some slides are loaned; some purchased. Student must supply slide projector, audiocassette or videocassette player.

Credit and Grading:

Most examinations must be proctored. Grading system varies from course to course. Minimum passing grade is D-. High School English Phase Elective courses are one-half of a semester's work and are worth one-quarter unit. Indiana University is one of a number of colleges and universities participating in the DANTES program (Defense Activity for Non-Traditional Education Support) for U.S. service men and women. Military personnel should contact their Educa-

tion Officer concerning enrollment procedure. Credit is awarded in semester hour units.

Accreditations:

North Central Association of Colleges and Schools. Member of: National University Continuing Education Association.

COLLEGE COURSES

AMERICAN STUDIES

Representative Americans—Special Topic: People with Disabilities

Americans with disabilities both from a historical and a contemporary perspective. An examination of the architectural, institutional, and attitudinal environment encountered by disabled persons. Cassette tapes are utilized in this course. (3 semester hours)

ANTHROPOLOGY

Human Origins and Prehistory

Human biological evolution and prehistory from the earliest archaeological record through the rise of civilization. (3 semester hours)

Bioanthropology

Bioanthropology of man, basic biological principles, morphology, function of evolutionary history. Human evolution from lower forms, environmental factors, speciation and differentiation into varieties, mixture, growth, sexual differences, constitutional variability. (3 semester hours)

Human Variations

Variation within and between human populations in morphology, gene frequencies, and behavior. Biological concepts of race, race classification along with other taxonomic considerations, and evolutionary processes acting on humans in the past, present, and future. (3 semester hours)

Culture and Society

Introduction to the comparative study of contemporary human cultures and social processes that influence behavior. (3 semester hours)

Introduction to the Cultures of Africa

Ethnographic survey of culture areas south of the Sahara. (3 semester hours)

ASTRONOMY

The Solar System

Celestial sphere and constellations, measurement of time, astronomical instruments, earth as a planet, moon, eclipses, planets and their satellites, comets, meteors, theories of origin of solar system. (3 semester hours)

Stellar Astronomy

The sun as a star, physical properties of stars, principles of spectroscopy as applied to astronomy, double stars, variable stars, star clusters, gaseous nebulae, stellar motions and distributions, Milky Way system, external galaxies, expanding universe, cosmic time scale. (3 semester hours)

Introduction to Astronomy

Earth as a planet, satellites, and comets. The sun. Properties of stars, stellar systems. Extragalactic objects. The nature of the observable universe. (3 semester hours)

BIOLOGY

Contemporary Biology

Selected principles of biology with emphasis on issues and problems extending into everyday affairs of the student. (3 semester hours)

Biology of Women

This course examines the biological basis for bodily functions and changes that take place throughout the life of females. (3 semester hours)

BUSINESS

Introduction to Financial Accounting

Concepts and issues associated with corporate financial reporting; particular emphasis is placed on understanding the role of financial accounting in the economy and how different accounting methods affect the financial statements. (3 semester hours)

Introduction to Managerial Accounting

Concepts and issues associated with the accounting and the management of business; particular emphasis is given to understanding the role of accounting in product costing, costing for quality, cost-justifying investment decisions, and performance evaluation and control of human behavior. (3 semester hours)

Principles of Hospital Accounting

Provides a solid foundation in the basic principles and practices of accounting, with illustrations and problems relating to hospitals. Requires no previous knowledge or experience in hospital accounting. (3 semester hours)

Intermediate Hospital Accounting

Practical solutions to more difficult accounting problems arising in day-to-day hospital business operations. Uniform hospital accounting and statistics, credits and collections, third-party reimbursements, payroll accounting, inventory accounting, long-term debt and fund-raising, hospital financial statements, mechanized accounting, hospital investments. (3 semester hours)

Intermediate Accounting Theory and Problems I

Theory of asset valuation and income measurement. Principles underlying published financial statements, including consideration of enterprise assets and liabilities. (3 semester hours)

Intermediate Accounting Theory and Problems II

Application of intermediate accounting theory to problems of accounting for economic activities including long-term liabilities, corporations, earnings per share, tax allocation, pensions, and leases. Also covered are the statement of changes in financial position and inflation accounting. (3 semester hours)

Cost Accounting

Conceptual and procedural aspects of management and cost accounting. Product costing; cost control over projects and products; decision-making emphasis, profit-planning, quantitative modeling; and computer applications. (3 semester hours)

Introduction to Taxation

Internal Revenue Code and Regulations. Emphasis on the philosophy of taxation, including income concepts, exclusions from income, deductions, and credits. (3 semester hours)

Hospital Budgeting and Cost Analysis

Budgeting and cost analysis as tools to aid hospital management. Three basic methods of hospital cost analysis, third-party reimbursement formulas. Budgeting procedures illustrated are appropriate for hospitals with no prior budgeting experience, some budgeting experience, and considerable budgeting experience. (3 semester hours)

Fund Accounting

Financial management and accounting for nonprofit-seeking entities; municipal and federal governments, schools, and hospitals. (3 semester hours)

Advanced Income Tax

Internal Revenue Code and Regulations; advanced aspects of income, deductions, exclusions, and credits, especially as applied to tax problems of partnerships and corporations. (3 semester hours)

Advanced Financial Accounting

Generally accepted accounting principles as applied to partnerships, business combinations, branches, foreign operations, and nonprofit organizations. Particular emphasis is given to consolidated financial statements. (3 semester hours)

Auditing

Internal and external audits of business operations. Review of internal control including EDP systems. Concern for auditing environment and audit evidence. Verification of systems for recording and processing transactions and balance sheet and operating accounts. Basic statistical applications in auditing. Issuance of audit report. (3 semester hours)

The International Business Environment

The national and international environmental aspects of international business. Examines the cultural, political, economic, systemic, legal, regulatory, trade, and financial environments and how they impact the international business activities of firms in the U.S. and, selectively, in other countries. (3 semester hours)

International Business: Operations of International Enterprises

The administration of international aspects of business organizations through an examination of their policy formulation, forms of foreign operations, methods of organization and control, and functional adjustments. (3 semester hours)

Personal Finance

Financial problems encountered in managing individual affairs; family budgeting, installment buying, insurance, home ownership, and investing in securities. (3 semester hours)

Financial Management

Conceptual framework of the firm's investment, financing, and dividend decisions; includes working capital management, capital budgeting, and capital structure strategies. (3 semester hours)

Introduction to Managerial Economics

Microeconomic analysis and its applications to business decision making. Includes topics of demand and consumer behavior, production and costs, theory of firms and public policy towards business. Focuses on the applied aspects of microeconomics. (3 semester hours)

Principles of Urban Economics

Introduction to basic concepts and techniques of urban economic analysis to facilitate understanding of current urban problems; urban growth and structure, public provisions of urban services, housing, employment, transportation, and relationships between public and private sectors. (3 semester hours)

Legal Environment of Business

Emphasis on the nature of law through examining a few areas of general interest: duty to avoid harming others (torts), duty to keep promises (contracts), and government regulation of business (trade regulation). (3 semester hours)

Commercial Law

Focuses mainly on the law of ownership, forms of business organization, commercial paper, and secured transactions. (3 semester hours)

Introduction to Marketing

Examination of the market economy and marketing institutions in the U.S. Decision making and planning from the manager's point of view, impact of marketing actions from the consumer's point of view. (3 semester hours)

Transportation Carrier Management

Study of the marketing carrier-shipper interface with concentration on the variables of rates, service, and government regulations. Modal coverage from an integrated marketing viewpoint. An advanced course which exposes students to market-rate considerations, carrier financial problems, operational factors, and marketing opportunities. Functional analysis of all major transportation modes. Identification of major issues, analysis of alternatives, and discussion of probable future outcomes. (3 semester hours)

Retail Management

Major management problems in retail institutions. Treatment of retail/marketing strategy design and problems related to financial requirements, buying, inventory, pricing, promotion, merchandising, physical facilities, location, and personnel. (3 semester hours)

Principles of Risk and Insurance

Nature of risk, insurance as a method of dealing with risk; property-liability and life-health insurance; insurance as an economic and social institution. (3 semester hours)

Operations Management

A survey course concerned with the production and distribution of goods and services; a part of the integrated core, along with survey courses in finance and marketing. Topics include: inventory management, demand forecasting, aggregate production planning, shop scheduling, project management, quality control, and layout and process design. (3 semester hours)

Principles of Real Estate

Intended for students who plan to take only one course in the area of real estate. Topics include real estate law, brokerage, property management, appraising, mortgage finance, and investment analysis. (3 semester hours)

Business Administration: Introduction

Business administration from standpoint of manager of a business firm operating in the contemporary economic, political, and social environment. (3 semester hours)

Business Communications

Theory and practice of written communication in business; use of correct, forceful English in preparation of letters, memoranda, and reports. (3 semester hours)

Job Search Techniques

Assists students in determining employment goals and in seeking an appropriate position. Preparing the resume, organizing a job campaign, conducting the employment interview. Importance of career planning, self-assessment, and career field research are stressed. (1 semester hour)

Organizational Behavior and Leadership

Nature of human behavior in organizations as a function of the individual, the groups within which he/she interacts, and the organizational setting. Application of behavioral science concepts and findings to individual behavior and organizational performance. (3 semester hours)

Organizational Behavior and Leadership (Hospital Version)

Introduces those with supervisory or administrative positions in hospitals to important concepts, theories, and findings of organizational behavior and management theory. Builds from a behavioral foundation toward an understanding of managerial processes. Written assignments require the student to apply general concepts developed in the text to hospital settings. (3 semester hours)

CLASSICAL STUDIES

Ancient Greek Culture

Examination and evaluation of the ideas of the Greeks as reflected in their traditions and way of life, and in their intellectual and artistic achievements. Selections from general works and Greek authors in English translation. (3 semester hours)

Roman Culture

Examination and evaluation of the Romans as reflected in their traditions and way of life and in their intellectual and artistic achievements. Major topics: the person (rights, restrictions, environment), society and politics, intellectual and spiritual life. (3 semester hours)

Classical Mythology

Introduction to Greek and Roman myths, legends, and tales, especially those which have an important place in the Western cultural tradition. (3 semester hours)

Medical Terms from Greek and Latin

Basic vocabulary of some 1,000 words, together with materials for formation of compounds, enables the student to build a working vocabulary of several thousand words. Designed for those intending to specialize in medicine, nursing, dentistry, or microbiology. (2 semester hours)

COMPARATIVE LITERATURE

An Introduction to Film

Nature of film technique and film language, analysis of specific films, and introduction to major critical approaches in film studies. (3 semester hours)

Modern Literature and the Other Arts: An Introduction

Analyzes the materials of literature, painting, and music, and the ways in which meaning is expressed through the organization of the materials. Investigates similarities and differences among the arts. Examples selected from the past 200 years. No previous knowledge of any art required. Cassette tapes are utilized in this course. (3 semester hours)

COMPUTER SCIENCE

Introduction to Microcomputers and Computing

The use of computers in everyday activities. How computers work; use of packaged programs for word processing, spreadsheets, file management, communications, graphics, etc. Students must have access to an IBM-compatible 8086/8088, 80286, or 80386 computer with 640K of memory and two floppy drives or one floppy drive and one hard (fixed) drive. Two versions of this course are available: using 3½ inch disks or using 5¼ inch disks. (3 semester hours)

Introduction to Programming I

Fundamental programming constructs, including loops, arrays, classes, and files. General problem-solving techniques. Emphasis on modular programming, user-interface design, and developing good programming style. Students must have access to an IBM-compatible 8086/8088, 80286, or 80386 computer with 640K of memory and two floppy drives or one floppy drive and one hard (fixed) drive). Two versions of this course are available: using 3½ inch disks or using 5¼ inch disks. (3 semester hours)

COBOL and File Processing

Computer programming and algorithms. Application to large file processing functions of an organization. Students must have access to an IBM-compatible 8086/8088, 80286, or 80386 computer with 640K of memory and two floppy drives or one floppy drive and one hard (fixed) drive). Two versions of this course are available: using 3½ inch disks or using 5¼ inch disks. (3 semester hours)

Introduction to Computer Science

A first course in computer science for those intending to take advanced computer science courses. Introduction to algorithm design, programming, and analysis. Using SCHEME programming language, course covers procedural, data, and syntactic abstractions and use of several programming paradigms, including functional, imperative, logical, and object-oriented. Students must have access to an IBM-compatible 8086/8088, 80286, or 80386 computer with 640K of memory and two floppy drives or one floppy drive and one hard (fixed) drive). Two versions of this course are available: using 3½ inch disks or using 5¼ inch disks. (3 semester hours)

Foundation of Digital Computing

Boolean algebra and propositional logic. Set algebra including mappings and relations. Elements of graph theory and statistical analysis. Application of all topics to computer programming. Access to a computer is not required. (3 semester hours)

COBOL Programming

Basic notions of computer programming. Problems for programming and execution on a computer. Students must have access to an IBM-compatible 8086/8088, 80286, or 80386 computer with 640K of memory and two floppy drives or one floppy drive and one hard (fixed) drive). Two versions of this course are available: using 3½ inch disks or using 5¼ inch disks. (3 semester hours)

CRIMINAL JUSTICE

Introduction to Criminal Justice

Historical and philosophical background, structure, functions, and operation of the criminal justice system in the United States. Introduction to and principles of formal behavior control devices. (3 semester hours)

Theories of Crime and Deviance

Critical examination of biological, psychological, and sociological theories of crime and deviance. Examination of individual, group, and societal reactions to norm-violating behaviors. (3 semester hours)

Corrections and Criminal Justice

Historical and comparative survey of prison confinement and the various alternatives within the scope of the criminal justice system's policies and methods of implementation. (3 semester hours)

Foundations of Criminal Investigation

Physical evidence, people, and documents; their pertinence to criminal investigation. Ethical problems; impact of legal systems on investigative process; elements of effective testimony. (3 semester hours)

Child Abuse and Neglect

Cultural, societal, and personal components that lead to child abuse; approaches to treatment within a typology of abusers. (3 semester hours)

American Juvenile Justice System

Structure and operation of the juvenile justice system in the United States, past and present. Analysis of the duties and responsibilities of the police juvenile officer, the juvenile court judge, and the juvenile probation officer. (3 semester hours)

ECONOMICS

Introduction to Microeconomics

Scarcity, opportunity cost, competitive market pricing, and interdependence as an analytical core. (3 semester hours)

Introduction to Macroeconomics

Measuring and explaining total economic performance, money, and monetary and fiscal policy as an analytical core. (3 semester hours)

Introduction to Statistical Theory in Economics and Business

Review of basic probability concepts. Sampling, inference, and testing statistical hypotheses. Applications of regression and correlation theory, analysis of variance and elementary decision theory. (3 semester hours)

Survey of Public Finance

Major elements of taxation and public expenditures. (3 semester hours)

EDUCATION

Mathematics in the Elementary Schools

Emphasizes the developmental nature of the arithmetic process and its place as an effective tool in the experiences of the elementary school child. (3 semester hours)

Development of the Self-Acquired Competency Portfolio

A practical, step-by-step guide which covers how to identify and document college level learning from life experiences, how to construct a complete portfolio, and how to submit the portfolio for possible credit toward a degree in the School of Continuing Studies. (1 semester hour)

Introduction to Exceptional Children

An overview of the characteristics and the identification of exceptional children. The course presents the issues in serving exceptional children as they participate in the educational, recreational, and social aspects of their lives. (3 semester hours)

Self-Instruction in Art

A general interest course in art. Talent and past experience are not important. Students select their own topics from a range of prepared opportunities. Includes 100 lessons; students may choose strands of lessons they wish to complete, and are required to submit only four lessons for each credit hour for which they are enrolled in the course. (1 to 5 semester hours)

Human Development Opportunities for College Students

Opportunities are given for students to better understand personal development, to learn and utilize human relations skills, to access humanistic issues in both personal and societal terms, and to establish goals for the future. Course includes beginning a portfolio for personal and career development. (3 semester hours)

Managing Resources for Learning

Emphasis on time management and goal setting, textbook study, notetaking, and test taking. (1 semester hour)

ENGLISH

Introduction to the English Language

Acquaints the student with contemporary studies of the nature of language in general and of the English language in particular. (3 semester hours)

Introduction to Writing and Study of Literature I

Course L141. Literary masterpieces from Homer through Brecht. (4 semester hours)

Course L142. Murder as a literary theme examined from Texts selected thematically from Shakespeare to the present. (4 semester hours)

Literary Interpretation

Course L202. Close analysis of representative texts (poetry, drama, fiction) designed to develop the art of lively, responsible reading through learning guide discussions and writing of papers. Attention to literary design and critical methods. This section is only for students wishing to fulfill the COAS Intensive Writing Requirement. (3 semester hours)

Course L202a. Close analysis of representative texts (poetry, drama, fiction) designed to develop the art of lively, responsible reading through learning guide discussions and writing or papers. Attention to literary design and critical methods. This section does *not* fulfill the COAS Intensive Writing Requirement and is intended for students outside the Bloomington College of Arts and Sciences (COAS). (3 semester hours)

Introduction to Drama

Representative significant plays to acquaint students with characteristics of drama as a type of literature. Readings will include plays from several ages and countries. (3 semester hours)

Introduction to Fiction

Representative works of fiction; structural technique in the novel. Readings will include novels and short stories from several ages and countries. (3 semester hours)

Introduction to Poetry

Kinds, conventions, and elements of poetry in a selection of poems from several historical periods. (3 semester hours)

Women and Literature

Issues and approaches to critical study of women writers and treatment in British and American literature. Topic: Woman's search for identity. (3 semester hours)

Literary Masterpieces I

Literary masterpieces from Homer through Brecht. Aims at thoughtful, intensive reading, appreciation of aesthetic values in literature, and enjoyment of reading. (3 semester hours)

Introduction to Shakespeare

Study of ten of Shakespeare's major plays. (3 semester hours)

Science Fiction

Study of the kinds, conventions, and theories of science fiction. Course includes predominantly British and American literature. (3 semester hours)

English Literature from 1600 to 1800

Representative selections, with emphasis on major writers from Donne to Johnson, and on their cultural context. (3 semester hours)

English Literature Since 1800

Representative selections with emphasis on major writers from Blake to the present and on their cultural context. (3 semester hours)

Late Plays of Shakespeare

Close reading of eight later plays of Shakespeare. May not be taken concurrently with Introduction to Shakespeare. (3 semester hours)

19th-Century British Fiction

Forms, techniques, and theories of fiction as exemplified by such writers as Scott, Dickens, Eliot, and Hardy. (3 semester hours)

American Literature Since 1914

Readings include works by Toomer, Hemingway, Faulkner, Fitzgerald, O'Neill, Eliot, and Frost. (3 semester hours)

American Fiction to 1900

Survey of representative nineteenth-century American novels with emphasis on works of Cooper, Hawthorne, Melville, Twain, James, and Dreiser. (3 semester hours)

20th-Century American Fiction

American fiction since 1900, including such writers as London, Cather, Fitzgerald, Hemingway, Faulkner, and Doctorow. (3 semester hours)

American Drama

Main currents in American drama to the present. (3 semester hours)

Children's Literature

Historical and modern children's books and selections from books; designed to assist future teachers, parents, librarians, or others in selecting the best in children's literature for each period of the child's life. (3 semester hours)

Introductory Creative Writing

Introduction to the art of creative writing. Short assignments, independent work, and discussion of the fundamentals of writing fiction, poetry, and drama. (3 semester hours)

Critical Review Writing

Training in the preparation of critical reviews of films. (1 semester hour)

Elementary Composition

Offers instruction and practice in the reading, writing, and critical thinking skills required in college. Emphasis is on written assignments that require synthesis, analysis, and argument based on sources. (3 semester hours)

English Grammar Review

Provides a review of traditional grammar with emphasis on the sentence, parts of speech, and punctuation. (1 semester hour)

Creative Writing

Course W203a. Exploratory course in poetry. Writing and examining different forms of poetry. (3 semester hours)

Course W203b. Exploratory course in prose. Writing and examining fiction written from different points of view. (3 semester hours)

Course W203c. Exploratory course in imaginative writing. Students may choose to concentrate on poetry or prose for readings, writing assignments. (3 semester hours)

Vocabulary Acquisition

Expands vocabulary by instruction in synonyms, antonyms, analogies, idioms, common prefixes/suffixes, roots, and the use of the dictionary. (1 semester hour)

Professional Writing Skills

To develop research and writing skills required for most academic and professional activities. Emphasis on methods of research; organization; and writing techniques useful in preparing reviews, critical bibliographies, research and technical reports, proposals and papers. (3 semester hours)

Advanced Expository Writing

Course W350. Close examination of assumptions, choices, and techniques which go into a student's own writing and the writing of others. This section is only for students wishing to fulfill the COAS Intensive Writing Requirement. (3 semester hours)

Course W350a. Close examination of assumptions, choices, and techniques that go into a student's own writing and the writing of others. This course does *not* fulfill the COAS Intensive writing requirement and is intended for students outside the Bloomington College of Arts and Sciences (COAS). (3 semester hours)

FINE ARTS

Ancient and Medieval Art

A survey of major styles and monuments in art and architecture from prehistoric times to the end of the Middle Ages. (4 semester hours)

Introduction to African Art

African art in its cultural setting. Major style areas: Prehistoric Nok culture, kingdoms of Ife and Benin, Western Sudan, Guinea Coast, equatorial forests, Congo, eastern and southern Africa. Slides are utilized in this course. (3 semester hours)

Art Appreciation

To acquaint students with outstanding works of art and to provide an approach to appreciation through knowledge of purposes, techniques, form, and content. (3 semester hours)

FOLKLORE

Introduction to Folklore

A view of the main forms and varieties of folklore and the folk expression in tales, ballads, myths, legends, beliefs, games, proverbs, riddles, and traditional arts and crafts. The role of folklore in the life of man. A cassette tape recorder and blank tape are required for field work. (3 semester hours)

Introduction to American Folklore

Folklore and traditional expressive behavior within the context of American culture. Art and traditional philosophies of fold groups found in America, including ethnic groups, occupational groups, regional groups, religious groups, etc. The function of folklore within the lives of American people. Cassette tapes are utilized in this course. (3 semester hours)

Topics in Folklore: An Interdisciplinary Perspective

Covers the relationships between folklore and other disciplines such as anthropology, sociology, psychology, religion, medicine, art and architecture, literature, history, music, and popular culture. A cassette tape recorder and blank tape are required for field work. (3 semester hours)

FRENCH

Elementary French I

Introduction to French language and selected aspects of French civilization and culture. Cassette tapes are utilized in this course. (4 semester hours)

Elementary French II: Language and Culture

Basic structures of the French language and selected topics of French civilization and culture. Cassette tapes are utilized in this course. (4 semester hours)

GEOGRAPHY

Physical Systems of the Environment

Physical environment as the home of man, emphasizing the distribution and interaction of environmental variables (landforms, vegetation, soils, and climate). (3 semester hours)

Weather and Climate

Introduction to atmospheric processes responsible for weather changes. Elements of climatology and their variation in time and space. Weather forecasting, weather modification, and severe weather. (3 semester hours)

Introduction to Human Geography

Introduction to the principles, concepts, and methods of analysis used in the study of human geographic systems. Examines geographic perspectives on contemporary world problems, such as population growth, globalization of the economy, and human-environmental relations. (3 semester hours)

World Regional Geography

Analysis of population, culture, environment, and economics of major world regions. Examination of issues of global importance, including development, demographic charge, urbanization and migration, and international conflict. (3 semester hours)

Meteorology and Climatology

Fundamental atmospheric properties and interrelationships. Radiation theory, components of energy and moisture balance, atmospheric circulation, upper air-surface relationships, and global weather system. (3 semester hours)

Environmental Conservation

Conservation of natural resources including soil, water, wildlife, and forests as interrelated components of the environment emphasizing an ecological approach. Current problems relating to environmental quality. (3 semester hours)

Geography of North America

Continental and regional variations in terrain, climate, and economic and social life of the United States and Canada, with emphasis on geographical principles, sources of data, and techniques of investigation. (3 semester hours)

GEOLOGY

Earth Sciences: Materials and Processes

Introduction to origin and classification of minerals and rocks. Relationships between rock types, rock structures, surficial geological processes of running water, subsurface water, glaciation, wind, tides, and landform evolution. Geologic time. (3 semester hours)

GERMAN

Beginning German I

Intensive introduction to present-day German and selected aspects of German life. Intensive drills for mastery of Phonology, basic structural patterns, and functional vocabulary. (5 semester hours)

Beginning German II

A continuation of the above course. (5 semester hours)

HEALTH, PHYSICAL EDUCATION, AND RECREATION

Health Problems in the Community

Human ecology as it relates to interaction of social and physical phenomena in solution of community health problems. Considers the promoting of community health, programs of prevention, environmental health, and health services. (3 semester hours)

Marriage and Family Interaction

Basic personal and social factors influencing the achievement of satisfying marriage and family experiences. (3 semester hours)

Personal Health

This survey course provides a theoretical and practical treatment of the concepts of disease prevention and health promotion. Course content includes topics such as emotional health; aging and death, alcohol, tobacco, and drug abuse; physical fitness; nutrition and dieting; consumer health; chronic and communicable diseases; safety; and environmental health. (3 semester hours)

Basic Nutrition

Introduction to nutrients, their uses and food sources. Application of principles to diets for general health is covered. A review of popular topics in nutrition is emphasized. Not for students in dietetics or nutrition science. (3 semester hours)

Recreation and Leisure

An introduction to the field of recreation and leisure from the viewpoint of the individual as a consumer, and of societal agencies as providers of leisure services. Includes philosophy, history, theory and a survey of public and private leisure-service organizations. (3 semester hours)

Special Recreation Services

Discussion of the need for the provision of leisure services to special populations, including concepts and terminology resources, adaptations of programs and facilities, and gaining an awareness of needs and abilities of persons who have disabilities or handicapping conditions. (3 semester hours)

Dynamics of Outdoor Recreation

Philosophical orientation to the field of outdoor recreation; camping, outdoor education, and natural resource management, with emphasis on programs, trends, resources, and values. (3 semester hours)

Recreation Activities and Leadership Methods

Analysis of recreation program activities, objectives, determinants, and group dynamics involved in the leadership process. Identification and evaluation of equipment, supplies, and leadership techniques are included. (3 semester hours)

Recreational Sports Programming

Overview of programmatic elements and techniques in recreational sports. Topics include informal, intramural, club, and extramural programming; values of recreational sports, programming techniques, publicity and promotion, facility utilization, equipment, safety, liability, and program observation. (3 semester hours)

Tourism and Commercial Recreation

Analysis of private, commercial, and industrial recreation fields, focusing on economic impact, marketing strategies, consumer protection, and career opportunities. (3 semester hours)

Introduction to Armed Forces Recreation

Introduction to the processes and programs used by the U.S. armed forces to provide recreation services to members of the military community. (3 semester hours)

HISTORY

American Colonial History I

European background of American history; discovery and exploration of New World by Spain, France, and England. Colonization: motives, causes, types. Social and intellectual developments in English colonies in the seventeenth and eighteenth centuries. Birth of Republic, 1763—89. (3 semester hours)

American Colonial History II

A continuation of the above course. (3 semester hours)

United States 1829–1865 II

The young republic through the Civil War. Political, economic, and social conditions and changes. The Jacksonian era, the slavery conflict, and the crisis of the Union. (3 semester hours)

Recent United States History

Political, demographic, economic, and intellectual transformation 1919—45; World War I, the twenties, the Great Depression, New Deal. (3 semester hours

American Social History, 1865 to Present

America's transformation from being a predominantly rural to a predominantly urban nation and how that transformation impacted our social groups, institutions, and values. (3 semester hours)

The American West

Western expansion and development 1763—1900; economic, political, and social. Special attention to natural resources, Native American-Anglo American relations, and the role of the West in American myth and symbol. (3 semester hours)

History of Indiana I

French and English periods, revolution in the West, territorial period, statehood to 1850. (2 semester hours)

Survey of Indiana History

A survey of Indiana history and culture from the original inhabitants to recent times with emphasis on the growth of a distinctive Hoosier culture. (3 semester hours)

History of Black Americans

A survey of black life in America: the Atlantic slave trade, slavery, Afro-American culture, racism, Civil War and Reconstruction, peonage, segregation, northern migration, urban ghettos, discrimination, Harlem Renaissance, black nationalism, civil rights, black revolt, contemporary setting. (3 semester hours)

French Revolution and Napoleon

Crisis of Old Regime; middle class and popular revolt; from constitutional monarchy to Jacobin commonwealth; The Terror and revolutionary government; expansion of Revolution in Europe; rise and fall of Napoleonic Empire. (3 semester hours)

Europe in the Twentieth Century I

Economic, social, political, and military-diplomatic developments, 1900—1930. Origins, impact, and consequences of World War I, peacemaking; postwar problems; international communism and fascism; the Great Depression. (3 semester hours)

Europe in the Twentieth Century II

Economic, social, political, and military-diplomatic developments, 1930—present. Depression politics; crisis of democracy; German National Socialism; World War II; cold war, postwar reconstruction and recovery. (3 semester hours)

History of Africa

1750 to present; slave trade, European imperialism, impact of Islam and Christianity, new state formations, reassertion of African culture and identity. (3 semester hours)

The World in the Twentieth Century I

Principal world developments in the twentieth century, stressing Latin

America, Africa, Asia, and Europe; global and regional problems, political revolutions, social and cultural diversity. (3 semester hours)

Europe: Renaissance to Napoleon

Major developments in European thought during Renaissance, Reformation, scientific revolution, and Enlightenment; traditional politics, economy, and society and their transformation by Enlightened despotism, the French Revolution, and Napoleon. (3 semester hours)

Europe: Napoleon to the Present

The development of European society from the downfall of Napoleon in 1815 to the present; the impact of the industrial revolution; the rise of the middle class; changes in sex roles; liberalism, Marxism, and mass politics; nationalism and imperialism; international communism and fascism. (3 semester hours)

American History I

Evolution of American society; political, economic, social structure; racial and ethnic groups; sex roles; Native American, inter-American, and world diplomacy of the United States; evolution of ideology, war, territorial expansion, industrialization, urbanization, international events, and their impact on American history. English colonization through Civil War. (3 semester hours)

American History II

A continuation of *American History I,* 1865 to present. (3 semester hours)

The Comparative History of Religion

A study of the historic patterns of behavior of those religions for which documentation exists. Includes patterns of growth of systematic thought and ritual, patterns of religious life and reactions against them such as mysticism, salvation by faith, and the rejection of reason. (3 semester hours)

Modern East Asian Civilization

Contrasting patterns of indigenous change and response to Western imperialism in East Asia during nineteenth and twentieth centuries. China and Japan receive primary consideration; Korea and Vietnam secondary. Emphasis on the rise of nationalism and other movements directed toward revolutionary change. (3 semester hours)

Latin American Culture and Civilization I

1492–1850. African, Indian, Spanish, Portuguese heritage. Discovery and conquest. Clash of cultures. Spanish empire. Society, culture, economics, politics. Bourbon reform, independence, new republics. (3 semester hours)

American Military History

From settlement of colonies to present. European background, colonial militia, Indian fighting. Principal foreign wars and their strategic objectives. Technological changes and effect of military on American society. Army is emphasized, with some attention to navy, marines, and air force. (3 semester hours)

Sports in History

Examines the historical conditions in which sports have developed. Particular emphasis on sport in the ancient and medieval world; industrialization and sport; nationalism and sport; imperialism and sport; the state and sport; modern American society and sport. (3 semester hours)

History of Women in the United States

This introductory survey focuses on women's historical roles in the work place, the family, and politics. Material will be drawn from legal, constitutional, political, social, demographic, economic, and religious history. Course includes several borrowed video tapes. (3 semester hours)

HISTORY AND PHILOSOPHY OF SCIENCE

Scientific Reasoning

Patterns of scientific reasoning presented in a simple form useful to both nonscientists and prospective scientists for understanding and evaluating scientific information of all sorts. Illustrations in the natural, biological, behavioral, and biomedical sciences are drawn from a wide variety of historical and contemporary sources, including popular magazines and newspapers. (3 semester hours)

The Occult in Western Civilization

Critical and historical evaluation of a wide range of occult topics: superstitions, magic, witchcraft, astrology, the Cabala, alchemy, psychic phenomena (mesmerism, Spiritualism, ESP), and UFOs. Course includes a borrowed video tape. (3 semester hours)

HOME ECONOMICS

Textiles

Textile fibers, yarns, fabrication and finishes; textile processing and properties; selection and care of textiles for human use. (3 semester hours)

ITALIAN

Elementary Italian I

Introduction to contemporary Italian conversation, grammar, reading, and elementary writing. Cassette tapes are utilized in this course. (4 semester hours)

Elementary Italian II

A continuation of *Elementary Italian I.* Introduction to contemporary Italian conversation, grammar, reading, and elementary writing. Cassette tapes are utilized in this course. (4 semester hours)

JOURNALISM

The Citizen and the News

A study of the institutions that produce news and information about public affairs for the citizen of American mass society. The problems about the selection of what is communicated. Case studies. International comparisons. (3 semester hours)

Writing for Publication

A workshop for nonmajors to improve writing skills and learn basic requirements of writing for publication. Instruction in market analysis and interpreting specific editorial requirements, in gathering and researching background materials, and in preparing manuscripts. Examination of various types and styles of published writing. (3 semester hours)

LABOR STUDIES

Survey of Unions and Collective Bargaining

A survey of labor unions in the United States, focusing on their organization and their representational, economic, and political activities. Includes coverage of historical development, labor law basics, and contemporary issues. (3 semester hours)

American Labor History

A survey of the origin and development of unions and the labor movement from colonial times to the present. The struggle of working people to achieve a measure of dignity and security is examined from social, economic, and political perspectives. (3 semester hours)

Contemporary Labor Problems

An examination of some of the major problems confronting society, workers, and the labor movement. Topics cover labor-management participation (or cooperation) programs; plant closures; union avoidance and union destruction by employers; and economic development efforts and labor/community coalitions. (3 semester hours)

Labor Law

A survey of the law governing labor-management relations. Topics include the legal framework of collective bargaining; problems in the administration and enforcement of agreements; protection of individual employee rights. (3 semester hours)

Labor and the Political System

Federal, state, and local governmental effects on workers, unions, and labor-management relations; political goals; influences on union choices of strategies and modes of political participation, past and present; relationships with community and other groups. (3 semester hours)

Grievance Representation

Union representation in the workplace. The use of grievance procedures to address problems and administer the collective bargaining agreement. Identification, research, presentation, and writing of grievance cases. Analysis of relevant labor law and the logic applied by arbitrators to grievance decisions. (3 semester hours)

Labor and the Economy

Analysis of the political economy of labor and the role of organized labor within it. Emphasis on the effect of unemployment on workers, unions, and collective bargaining; investment policy and changes in technology and corporate structure. Patterns of union political and bargaining responses. (3 semester hours)

Occupational Health and Safety

Elements and issues of occupational health and safety. Emphasis on the union's role in the implementation of workforce health and safety programs, worker and union rights, hazard recognition techniques, and negotiated and statutory remedies, in particular the Occupational Safety and Health Act (OSHA) of 1970. (3 semester hours)

Collective Bargaining

The development and organization of collective bargaining in the United States, including union preparation for negotiations, bargaining patterns and practices, strategies and tactics, economic and legal considerations. (3 semester hours)

Unions in State and Local Government

Union organization and representation of state and municipal government employees, including patterns in union structure, collective bargaining, grievance representation, and applicable law. (3 semester hours)

Union Government and Organization

An analysis of the growth, composition, structure, behavior, and governmental process of U.S. labor organizations, from the local to national federation level. Consideration is given to the influences on labor institutions of industrial and political environments, to organizational behavior in different types of unions, and to problems in union democracy. (3 semester hours)

Union Organizing

Explores various approaches and problems in private and public sector organizing. Traditional approaches are evaluated in light of structural changes in labor markets and work force demographics. Topics range from targeting and assessments to committee building and leadership development. (3 semester hours)

Topics: Labor and the Media

An investigation of images of labor in the media. Topics include the media and the economy, corporate bias and the manufacturing of news, and labor's response to the corporate image. (3 semester hours)

Topics: Unions in the Construction Trades

An examination of union representation, structure, and organization in the U.S. construction industry. Topics include labor history, collective bargaining, approaches to organizing, industry economics, and construction markets. (3 semester hours)

Grievance Arbitration

Recommended only after completing *Grievance Representation*. The legal and practical context of grievance arbitration, its limitations and advantages in resolving workplace problems. Varieties of arbitration clauses and the status of awards. Participants analyze a cassette tape of a mock arbitration hearing. (3 semester hours)

Comparative Labor Movements

Labor movements and labor relations in industrial societies from historical, analytical, and comparative perspectives. Emphasis on interaction between unions and political organizations, national labor policies, the resolution of work place problems, the organization of white-collar employees, and the issues of workers' control and codetermination. (3 semester hours)

Theories of the Labor Movement

Perspectives on the origin, development, and goals of organized labor. Theories include those which view the labor movement as a business union institution, an agent for social reform, a revolutionary force, a psychological reaction to industrialization, a moral force, and an unnecessary intrusion. (3 semester hours)

Topics in Labor Studies: Philosophy of Work

A study of selected views about such topics as the value of dignity of labor; causes of alienation; impact of industrialization and automation; employees' rights and responsibilities. (3 semester hours)

Labor Studies Internship

Application of knowledge gained in Labor Studies classes to a labor organization or other public or private organization concerned with labor. (1 to 6 semester hours)

Readings in Labor Studies

This course is arranged individually between the student and the instructor. It consists of readings and papers in selected topics in Labor Studies current issues, historical development, and other labor-related concerns. Topics will vary. (3 semester hours)

Directed Labor Study

A contract course to suit the varied needs and interests of individual participants. For further information, contact the Independent Study Office. (1 to 6 semester hours)

LATIN

Elementary Latin I

Fundamentals of the language; develops direct reading comprehension of Latin. (4 semester hours)

LINGUISTICS

English Language Improvement

Designed for the international student who needs instruction in English as a second language at an intermediate to advanced level in preparation for Eng W131 (Elementary Composition). Also designed for graduate students who need help with basic skills of English composition. (3 semester hours)

Introduction to the Study of Language

A survey of perspectives on language, covering topics such as the relation between the form of words and sentences and their meanings, the sounds of languages and their dialect variations, the use of language in daily life, language in humans and animals, and the relationship between language and thought. This is not a course in English as a second language. (3 semester hours)

MATHEMATICS

Basic Algebra

Designed to provide algebraic skills needed for future mathematics courses. Operations with fractions, exponents, linear equations, inequalities, and elementary graphs. (4 semester hours)

Excursions into Mathematics

A course designed to convey the flavor and spirit of mathematics, stressing reasoning and comprehension rather than technique. Not preparatory to other courses; explores topics in the theory of games and in properties of polyhedra. (3 semester hours)

Finite Mathematics

Set theory, linear systems, matrices and determinants, probability, linear programming. Applications to problems from business and the social sciences. (3 semester hours)

Brief Survey of Calculus I

Introduction to calculus. Primarily for students from business and social sciences. (3 semester hours)

Pre-Calculus Mathematics

Designed to prepare students for Calculus I. Algebraic operations, polynomials, functions and their graphs, conic sections, systems of equations, and inequalities. (3 semester hours)

Trigonometric Functions

Trigonometric functions; identities. Graphs of trigonometric and inverse trigonometric and inverse trigonometric functions. (2 semester hours)

Calculus I

Limits, continuity, derivatives, definite and indefinite integrals, applications, techniques of integration, infinite series. (5 semester hours)

Calculus II

A continuation of the above course. (5 semester hours)

Mathematics for Elementary Teachers III

Geometric figures; measurement of line segments, areas, volumes, and angles; constructions (ruler and compass, paper folding); congruent and similar triangles; basic analytic geometry. (3 semester hours)

MUSIC

Music for the Listener

How to listen to music; art of music and its materials; instruments and musical forms. Cassette tapes are utilized in this course. (3 semester hours)

NURSING

Nutrition for Health Professionals

Emphasis on nutritional needs and eating habits throughout the life cycle, including the classification, functions, and food sources of the nutrients; the components of a balanced diet, the process by which the body utilizes food, and nutritional concerns in the U.S. (3 semester hours)

Pharmacology

The physiological action of drugs and their therapeutic use, the nurse's role in administering drugs, and the need for continuous study of drug therapy. (3 semester hours)

PHILOSOPHY

Introduction to Philosophy

Perennial problems of philosophy, including problems in ethics, in epistemology and metaphysics, in philosophy of religion. (3 semester hours)

Elementary Ethics

Some ancient, medieval, or modern philosophers' answers to ethical problems (e.g., nature of good and evil, relation of duty to self-interest, and objectivity of moral judgments). (3 semester hours)

Elementary Logic

Development of critical tools for the evaluation of arguments. (3 semester hours)

Ancient Greek Philosophy

Selective survey of ancient Greek philosophy (pre-Socratics, Plato, Aristotle). (3 semester hours)

Women in Philosophical Thought

A study of the classical and contemporary sources which influence and illustrate differing concepts of woman. The aim is for each student to clarify and assess the various concepts so as to better formulate and justify his or her own concept of woman. (3 semester hours)

Philosophy of Work

A study of selected views with regard to such topics as the value and dignity of labor; causes of alienation; impact of industrialization and automation; employees' rights and responsibilities. (3 semester hours)

PHYSICS

Physics in the Modern World

Includes elements of classical physics and the ideas, language, and impact of physics today. (4 semester hours)

Energy

A scientific approach is used to examine various aspects of energy consumption, including demand, fuel supplies, environmental impact, and alternative fuel sources. (2 semester hours)

Energy and Technology

Provides physical basis for understanding interaction of technology and society, and for the solution of problems, such as energy use and the direction of technological change. (3 semester hours)

POLITICAL SCIENCE

Introduction to American Politics

Introduction to nature of government and dynamics of American politics. Origin and nature of the American federal system and its political party base. (3 semester hours)

Introduction to Political Theory

Perennial problems of political philosophy, including relationships between rulers and ruled, nature of authority, social conflict, character of political knowledge, and objectives of political action. (3 semester hours)

Introduction to International Relations

Causes of war, nature and attributes of the state, imperialism, international law, national sovereignty, arbitration, adjudication, international organization, major international issues. (3 semester hours)

Contemporary Political Problems: Sex Discrimination and the Law

An examination of the many ways the law affects women and the advantages and disadvantages of trying to use the law to effect social change. Not a specialized law course, but does analyze some law-related articles and legal cases. (3 semester hours)

Contemporary Political Problems: Political Terrorism

Probes the evolution of terrorism from a residual event in the margins of society to almost an epidemic in the forefront of the political stage. Looks at terrorism from both a historical and theoretical aspect. (3 semester hours)

Political Parties and Interest Groups

Theories of American party activity; behavior of political parties, interest groups, and social movements; membership in groups; organizations and structure; evaluation and relationship to the process of representation. (3 semester hours)

American Constitutional Law

Nature and function of law; selected Supreme Court decisions interpreting American constitutional system. (3 semester hours)

State Politics in the United States

Comparative study in politics in the American states. Special emphasis on the impact of political culture, party systems, legislatures, and bureaucracies on public policies. (3 semester hours)

Urban Politics

Political behavior in modern American communities; emphasizes the impact of municipal organization, city officials and bureaucracies, social and economic notables, political parties, interest groups, the general public, and protest organizations on urban policy outcomes. (3 semester hours)

American Politics through Film and Fiction

The recurrent theme of power in politics is explored in depth—by means of five novels and five films. From a list of selected works, students must choose and locate the novels and videos, many of which may be borrowed from libraries. (3 semester hours)

PSYCHOLOGY

Statistical Techniques

Introduction to statistics; nature of statistical data; ordering and manipulation of data; measures of central tendency and dispersion; elementary probability. Concepts of statistical inference and decision; estimation and hypothesis testing. Special topics include regression and correlation, analysis of variance, nonparametric methods. (3 semester hours)

Introductory Psychology I

Introduction to psychology; its methods, data, and theoretical interpretations in areas of learning, sensory psychology, and psychophysiology. (3 semester hours)

Introductory Psychology II

A continuation of *Introductory Psychology I*. Developmental, social, personality, and abnormal psychology. (3 semester hours)

Psychology of Childhood and Adolescence

Development of behavior in infancy, childhood, and youth; factors which influence behavior. (3 semester hours)

The Psychology of Personality

Methods and results of scientific study of personality. Basic concepts of personality traits and their measurements; developmental influences; problems of integration. (3 semester hours)

Social Psychology

Principles of scientific psychology applied to the individual in social situations. (3 semester hours)

Abnormal Psychology

A first course in abnormal psychology, with emphasis on forms of abnormal behavior, etiology, development, interpretation, and final manifestations. (3 semester hours)

PUBLIC AND ENVIRONMENTAL AFFAIRS

Criminal Investigation

Theory of investigation, crime scene procedures, interviews, interrogations, surveillances, and sources of information; collection and preservation of physical evidence; investigative techniques in specific crimes. (3 semester hours)

Personnel Management in the Public Sector

The organization and operation of public personnel management systems, with emphasis on concepts and techniques of job analysis, position classification, training, affirmative action, and motivation. (3 semester hours)

RELIGIOUS STUDIES

Introduction to Religion in the West

Patterns of religious life and thought in the West: continuities, changes, and contemporary issues. (3 semester hours)

Introduction to Christianity

Survey of beliefs, rituals, and practices of the Christian community, with a focus on the varieties of scriptural interpretation, historical experience, doctrine, and behavior. (3 semester hours)

The Christian Church in New Testament Times

Origins of the Christian movement and development of its beliefs, practices, and institutions in the first century. Primary source is the New Testament, with due attention to non-Christian sources from the same environment. (3 semester hours)

Religion in America

Development of religious life and thought in modern America, from 1865 to the present. (3 semester hours)

SOCIOLOGY

Social Problems

Selected current "problems" of American society are analyzed through the use of basic sociological data and the application of major sociological frameworks. Policy implications are discussed in the light of value choices involved in various solutions. (3 semester hours)

Introduction to Sociology

Introduction to the concepts and methods of sociology with an emphasis on the understanding of contemporary American society. (3 semester hours)

Social Organization

Introduction to the concepts, perspectives, and theories of social organization, from the level of the dyad to whole societies and intersocietal networks. (3 semester hours)

Social Change

Introduction to theoretical and empirical studies of social change. Explores issues such as modernization; rationalization; demographic, economic, and religious causes of change; reform and revolution. (3 semester hours)

Society and the Individual

Introduction to the concepts, perspectives, and theories of social psychology from the level of the individual to collective behavior. (3 semester hours)

Population and Human Ecology

Population composition, fertility, mortality, natural increase, migration; historical growth and change of populations; population theories and policies; techniques in manipulation and use of population data; the spatial organization of populations. (3 semester hours)

The Community

Introduction to the sociology of community life, stressing the processes of order and change in community organization. Major topics include the community and society, the nonterritorial community, analysis of major community institutions, racial-ethnic differences in community behavior, community conflict, and community problems. (3 semester hours)

Sociology of Religion

The nature, consequences and theoretical origins of religion, as evident in social construction and functional perspectives; the social origins and problems of religious organizations; and the relationships between religion and morality, science, magic, social class, minority status, economic development, and politics. (3 semester hours)

Sociology of Work

Treats work roles within such organizations as factory, office, school, government, and welfare agencies; career and occupational mobility in work life; formal and informal organizations within work organizations; labor and management conflict and cooperation; problems of modern industrial workers. (3 semester hours)

Sociology of the Family

Structure and process of the conjugal family in modern and emerging societies. Focus on relationships of the family to other subsystems of the larger society, and on interaction within the family in connection with these interrelationships. Stress on development of systematic theory. (3 semester hours)

Deviant Behavior and Social Control

Analysis of deviance in relation to formal and informal social processes. Emphasis on deviance and respectability as functions of social reactions, characteristics of rules, and power and conflict. (3 semester hours)

Sociology of Law

Social origins of civil and criminal law, social bases of legal decision making, and social consequences of the application of law. (3 semester hours)

Sociology of Gender Roles

Exploration of the properties, correlates and consequences of gender roles in contemporary societies. Emphasis on defining gender roles, tracing their historical development, considering their implications for work, marriage and fertility, with cross-cultural comparisons. (3 semester hours)

Social Theory

Sociological theory, with focus on content, form, and historical development. Relationships between theories, data, and sociological explanation. (3 semester hours)

SPANISH

Elementary Spanish I

Introduction to present-day Spanish language and culture. Cassette tapes are utilized in this course. (4 semester hours)

Elementary Spanish II

This course is a continuation of *Elementary Spanish I*. Cassette tapes are utilized in this course. (4 semester hours)

Second-Year Spanish Reading I

Intensive reading of selected modern texts, both fiction and nonfiction. (3 semester hours)

Second-Year Spanish Reading II

A continuation of *Second-Year Spanish I*. (3 semester hours)

SPEECH

Public Speaking

Theory and practice of public speaking; training in thought processes necessary to organize speech content; analysis of components of effective delivery and language. Cassette tapes are utilized in this course. (2 semester hours)

Interpersonal Communication

Practical consideration of spontaneous human interaction in face-to-face situations. Special attention to perception, language, and attitudes, in dyads and small groups. Cassette tapes are utilized in this course. (2 semester hours)

Business and Professional Communication

Examines organizational communication with emphasis on skills acquisition. Developed skills include interviewing, group discussion, parliamentary procedure, and public speaking. (3 semester hours)

Freedom of Speech

A brief survey of the historical development of the concept of freedom of speech, and a close examination of contemporary free speech issues, such as those relating to national security, public order, civil rights movement, antiwar protest, obscenity, academic freedom, and symbolic speech. (3 semester hours)

TELECOMMUNICATIONS

Introduction to Mass Communications

A survey of functions, responsibilities, and influence of various mass communications media. For nonmajors. Directed toward the consumer and critic of mass media in modern society. (3 semester hours)

Living in the Information Age

Assesses how development in communications systems and technology affects our lives today and may affect them tomorrow. Reviews underlying technologies. Considers implications for individuals, institutions, and society from psychological, sociological, legal/political, business/economic, and cultural perspectives. Videotapes are used. (3 semester hours)

HIGH SCHOOL COURSES

ART

Basic Art Level I

An introductory course, in which students learn basic techniques of drawing (in both pencil and pen and ink), painting, printmaking, sculpture, and environmental design. Course assumes no previous training and is suitable for any students who want to explore or develop their artistic abilities. (½ unit)

Drawing and Storytelling

Some background in art fundamentals required. Students study storytelling art through history, practice techniques of drawing, including caricature, perspective and distortion, shading, embellishment, and calligraphy; and apply these techniques to the development of their own stories in words and pictures. (½ unit)

Art History and Appreciation

This course introduces art history and culture; it will help the student learn a way to appreciate the works of great artists of the past and present. The course provides two kinds of experience with art - critical experience, which will help gain in information from the work of art, and historical experience, which will help one understand the work's purpose and meaning. (½ unit)

BUSINESS EDUCATION

General Business

First Semester. Course serves two purposes: (1) to provide students who plan to pursue a high school business program with a basic introduction to the field of business as a background for other business courses; and (2) to provide the nonbusiness major with practical and general information about business which may be used in everyday living. Topics include what business does, business and our economic system, the consumer, banking, and career planning. (½ unit)

Second Semester. A continuation of the above course. Topics include investment, economic changes and money management, communications, transportation, taxes, labor considerations, government and business, insurance, credit, world trade, and career planning. (½ unit)

Beginning Accounting

First Semester. An introductory accounting course. Introduces accounting systems, analyzing transactions, journalizing and posting, financial statements, ledgers, checking accounts, and partnerships. Course is suitable for students who are headed immediately toward careers in business or who wish to prepare for business-related programs at the college level. (½ unit)

Second Semester. A continuation of the above course, introducing special journals, payroll accounting, depreciation, corporate accounting, voucher, petty cash, and inventory systems. (½ unit)

Beginning Typewriting

First Semester. An introduction to typewriting for personal use or as a background for further study. Includes a mastery of the keyboard, development of good typewriting techniques, centering and tabulations, and application of skills in personal/business communications, outlines, and manuscripts. (½ unit)

Second Semester. A continuation of the above course focusing on additional training for personal use and job competency; refinement of techniques; reinforcement of speed and accuracy; application of skills in business communications; manuscripts (including footnotes, tables of contents, and title pages); tabulation; letters of application and personal data sheets; business forms; and miscellaneous copy (scripts, statistics, and rough drafts). (½ unit)

Beginning Shorthand: First Semester

Focuses on the fundamentals of shorthand to help students acquire the skills necessary for rapid writing. Includes drills on common words, reading shorthand, and transcribing shorthand. (½ unit)

Beginning Data Processing

Designed to give students an understanding of the social impact of the computer, physical aspects of a computer system, and various applications of information processing in business. Students will also study the historical development of computer systems with an emphasis on future trends and career opportunities in the information processing field. (½ unit)

Business Communications

A study of communication in a working situation with emphasis on building skills in vocabulary, reading, and listening; understanding the psychology of effective business communications; speaking effectively; planning and writing letters and memos. (½ unit)

Business Law

A study of law which applies to business situations and transactions. Designed to help the student recognize legal problems he/she can handle and those requiring professional help. (½ unit)

Office Procedures

The course introduces efficient office management and procedures, including written communications from memos to business reports, telecommunications, space, records and filing, accounting, and automation. The course is suitable for any student who foresees a career in an office setting. (½ unit)

CONSUMER AND HOMEMAKING EDUCATION

Adjustment, Marriage, and the Family (Family Relations)

Designed to give individuals perspective in understanding themselves and others; provides a basis for solving and understanding everyday problems common to young people and their parents. Contains discussion on dating, courtship, marriage, and parenthood. Emphasis on personal development, marriage, and family relationships. (½ unit)

Family Management

A comprehensive course concerning management of family life situations. Topics include management of personal income, credit and savings, insurance, meal preparation, housing, consumer rights and change. Emphasis is placed on the use of money as well as other resources such as time and energy. This course is designed to help the student make wise decisions and plan for effective family living. (½ unit)

Beginning Food and Nutrition

Study of nutrients and their importance; includes food requirements during different stages of life: infancy, adolescence, adulthood, pregnancy, lactation, old age, and convalescence. Provides information of personal and practical applicability to the student's life. Course teaches not only the facts of nutrition but also the enjoyment of discovering new ways to fill nutritional needs. (½ unit)

Beginning Child Development

Designed to help individuals think about the rewards and responsibilities of being a parent. Discusses planning a family, pregnancy, childbirth, and caring for a newborn. Provides information about child development as it relates to parenting and discipline. Provides guidance in selecting substitute childcare and discusses childcare as a career. (1/2 unit)

Consumer Education

Designed to develop the student's basic economic reasoning to help him/her operate as an intelligent and efficient member of society. Emphasizes an understanding of our economic system and its interrelationships with business and government. (½ unit)

Housing and Interior Design

Designed to help students find the means to solve housing problems. Topics include evaluating housing needs, finding suitable housing, designing floor plans, and furnishing the house. Students also study the history of housing and design. (½ unit)

DISTRIBUTIVE EDUCATION

General Merchandise Retailing

Designed for those interested in owning or managing retail businesses. Topics include necessary planning in buying and selling: having the right product or service in the right quantity, in the right place, and at the right time and price to satisfy customers' needs. (½ unit)

Salesmanship

A course designed for students interested in learning about selling skills and how selling benefits our economic system. Topics include why people buy, steps in making a sale, and nonpersonal selling. (½ unit)

ENGLISH

Journalism

Introduces basic elements of journalism and its functions in society. Emphasis on a variety of projects involving reporting and media analysis. (½ unit)

Mass Media

Designed to help students understand the use of communication media—newspapers, magazines, radio, TV, and movies. Individual attention is given to types of magazines, magazine advertising, comics, radio history and radio today, the message of songs, commercials, film and TV analysis, and related topics. (½ unit)

Developmental Reading

Aimed at increasing reading power, refining reading and study habits, and developing vocabulary. Each lesson includes basic vocabulary building, "survival reading" (such as job applications, credit applications, or tax returns), and effective use of printed information (charts, parts of a book, graphs, etc.) (½ unit)

Basic Vocabulary

Through etymology, an examination of the Anglo-Saxon, Greek, Latin roots of English words, students will improve their mastery of written and spoken English. (½ unit)

Writing for Beginners

A course for high school students of any age who have little experience expressing themselves in writing. Topics include writing for different purposes and for different audiences, interviewing and writing, and writing about reading. (½ unit)

Creative Writing: Fiction

Assists new or potential writers first by bringing them in closer touch with themselves and then by dealing with the specific of short story writing. Examines problems of characterization, approach, point of view, tone, and plot. Culminates with the student writing a complete short story. (½ unit)

Speech

Introductory course in public speaking. Topics include organizing and writing speeches of these types: description, narration, information, explanation, direction, argumentation, and persuasion. Students must submit transcripts and cassette tapes of their speeches. This course is suitable for students with pressing deadlines who wish to work intensively. (½ unit)

English 9: First Semester

A study of literature, including short stories, short poems, and *The Odyssey*. Composition activities integrate the study of literature with language skills. Students review grammar, punctuation, and writing skills. (½ unit)

English 9: Second Semester

A continuation of the literature and grammar studied in the above course. Literary types studied include stories, poems, and essays. Practice writing skills, grammar, punctuation, and capitalization. (½ unit)

English 10: First Semester

Study of the continuing themes in literature, with focus on irony, private moods, and people under pressure. Instruction in grammar and composition stresses the writing of effective sentences and the planning and organization of writing. (½ unit)

English 10: Second Semester

A continuation of the above course. Grammar study focuses on usage, composition, and mechanics. (½ unit)

Library Skills and Research

Assists the student in developing the skills necessary to take full advantage of the library as a resource for independent learning. Lessons orient the student to the library, present experiences in using the library to locate specific information, and suggest strategies for gathering, organizing, and presenting information in a research report. (½ unit)

English 11: Grammar and Composition

Begins with the elements of grammar and sentence structure and progresses through paragraph construction to the general principles and organization of good writing, including essays, forms, and letters. (½ unit)

The Experience of Drama

Introduces the student to representative modern American drama through several one-act and three longer plays. Special attention is given to dramatic elements and techniques of setting, dialogue, conflict, theme, and symbolism. Students must attend and report on a play in their community (an alternate assignment will be made if attendance is not possible). (½ unit)

American Literature: First Semester (Junior-Year English)

A chronological survey of American literature from 1645 to 1900. The lives of authors and forces in the society which may have affected their writings are considered. Students also read two modern plays about early American culture. Student essays are critiqued to help evaluate progress. (½ unit)

American Literature: Second Semester (Junior-Year English)

A survey of American literature from 1900 to the present. Topics include short stories, the novel, nonfiction, poetry, and drama. (½ unit)

Women Writers: Fiction and Autobiography (Themes in Literature)

This course offers the student an opportunity to read four fictional works and one autobiography written by women. The works date from the early 19th century to the 1980s and offer a broad spectrum of attitudes toward the roles of women. Each assignment requires several short answers of approximately one paragraph. The course provides an introduction to novels and autobiographies as well as a close look at feminine roles of the last two centuries. (½ unit)

English Literature: First Semester (Senior English)

Chronological study of English literature from the Anglo-Saxon period through the eighteenth century, including Shakespeare. Historical and biographical information included to place the literature in perspective. Grammar and composition problems handled individually through criticism of student essays. (½ unit)

English Literature: Second Semester (Senior English)

A continuation of the above course, studying the "pre-Romantic" poets (Gray, Burns, and Blake) through such contemporary writers as Orwell and O'Conner; includes a Victorian novel. Grammar and composition problems handled through criticism of student essays. (½ unit)

Senior-Year Composition (Advanced Composition)

Teaches, through the reading of selected essays and stories and through the student's writing, basic characteristics of descriptive and narrative prose. Composition study includes elements of effective sentence structure, construction of paragraphs, and writing of longer themes. Emphasis given to selecting and limiting the subject, assembling materials, organization through outline, and paragraphing. Goal is to teach how professional writers practice their craft and to enable students to discover their own talents. (½ unit)

The Bible and Literature (Biblical Literature)

Examines writings of Old and New Testaments and modern literature based on biblical themes and characters. Assignments call for analysis, comparison, and interpretation of various readings. (½ unit)

Advanced Grammar and Composition (Expository Writing)

Designed to help students improve their writing by mastering the fundamentals of English grammar and usage. Practice in composing well-written, well-reasoned essays. Especially useful to college-bound students and those interested in improving their ability to express themselves through effective writing. (½ unit)

English Phase-Elective Curriculum

A phase-elective is an elective that is one-half a semester's work and worth one-quarter unit. Students entering grades 11 and 12 are increasingly faced with the responsibility of choice as it affects their own personal lives, careers, and education. It is widely recognized that no two students are quite the same, and students ought to examine their own abilities, interests, and needs. Only then may they determine which alternatives will best meet their personal circumstances. Through this process, students not only learn more responsibility for shaping their growing independence, but they are furthermore confronted, through meaningful decision making, with the necessity of a commitment of a chosen course of study. Two phase-elective courses constitute the equivalent of a full semester's work.

Four American Novels. Provides an in-depth study of four literary works. The novels are analyzed separately for content and style/technique (symbolism, imagery, development and continuity of theme/purpose, and character development). Students are encouraged to make thematic connections among the novels. All four works are concerned with the changes men and women must make in their lives—personally and as members of society—in order to survive. The student will learn to identify the conflict, the characters who deal with change and evolve, and the characters who do not and what the consequences are. (¼ unit)

Children's Literature (Genres of Literature). Acquaints the student with the world of children's books; types of books available, choosing books for a particular child, and reading and telling stories. Includes information on the developmental stages of children and their needs during those stages. Aimed at sharing with the children in one's life the comfort and pleasure found in literature. (¼ unit)

The Short Story. Provides insight into short story masterpieces and enhances reading enjoyment by studying essential elements. Topics include methods of character development; aspects of setting, plot, and conflict; examination of tone, mood, and point of view; and concepts of theme and moral. (¼ unit)

Understanding and Improving Your Memory (Basic Skills Develop-

ment). Introduction to a variety of memory techniques. Includes strategies of memorizing, using mnemonics (including link, place, and phonetic systems), and remembering names. Emphasis is toward doing more than toward knowing; the student who completes the course should have a significantly improved memory. (¼ unit)

Vocabulary Improvement. Provides practical assistance for improving vocabulary. Since no sentence can be strong without precise usage of words, this study should have direct application to writing as well as speaking and reading. (¼ unit)

Basic Composition. A study of exposition, using topics selected by the student. Lessons focus on increasing powers of observation; development of effective paragraphs; planning, writing, and revising compositions; and writing expository compositions (narration, description, explanation, and persuasion). A personal journal kept throughout the course but not submitted contributes to the course's individualized nature. (¼ unit)

Literature of the Future (Themes in Literature). Probes the shock of the future through reading high-interest novels and short stories. An underlying idea is that imaginative thought about what could happen in the future makes one more aware of life today. (¼ unit)

Mythology (Genres of Literature). Exposes students to the mythology of a number of cultures; and through mythology makes the students aware of timeless human interests paralleling their own. Since its essential characteristic is humanism, the emphasis will be on Greek mythology. (¼ unit)

Mysteries (Genres of Literature). Examines the history and structure of mystery fiction, followed by a study of the suspense story, the detective story, and the adventure mystery. Elements of mystery fiction are presented and then discussed in light of a particular work. (¼ unit)

How to Study in College (Basic Skills Development). Straightforward, practical instruction on overcoming studying difficulties, readily understood and easily applied. Focuses on practical study techniques, and covers economical ways of scheduling time, advantages and disadvantages of various methods of note taking, how to mark books, take notes, and answer exam questions. (¼ unit)

Advanced Composition. Intended for students who already have a basic grasp of composition, and feel ready for more experience in writing that will lead to greater challenges and sophistication. In addition to multi-paragraph projects, the student is introduced to the process of completing a research paper. (¼ unit)

FRENCH

French Level I: First Semester

An introductory course in which all aspects of language learning are equally important; thus, hearing and speaking French are considered as important as good reading and writing knowledge in this course. Emphasis is on these four skills. Students must tape record the oral portion of their lessons. Cassette tapes are utilized in this course. (½ unit)

French Level I: Second Semester

A continuation of the above course. (½ unit)

French Level II: First Semester

Aims at developing a greater proficiency in the basic skills: hearing, speaking, reading, and writing French. Students must tape record the oral portion of their lessons. Cassette tapes are utilized in this course. (½ unit)

French Level II: Second Semester

A continuation of the above course. Enhances the four basic skills:

hearing, speaking, reading, and writing French. Students must tape record the oral portion of their lessons. Cassette tapes are utilized in this course. (½ unit)

GERMAN

German Level I: First Semester

An introductory course on the basic four skills: hearing, speaking, reading, and writing. The student will learn both discrimination and pronunciation of the sounds of German, and will learn to understand and produce expressions found in contemporary spoken and written German. Basic structural patterns include the nominative, dative, and accusative cases; present, perfect, and future tenses; the modals; and the imperative. Students must tape record the oral portion of their lessons. Cassette tapes are utilized in this course. (½ unit)

German Level I: Second Semester

A continuation of the above course to enhance further the basic four skills: hearing, speaking, reading, and writing. Students must tape record the oral portion of their lessons. Cassette tapes are utilized in this course. (½ unit)

German Level II: First Semester

Continues development of the four skills: hearing, speaking, reading, and writing. Reviews and extends the grammatical structures and vocabulary presented in first-year German. Presents the simple past, conditional, subjunctive, passive voice, and indirect discourse. Develops active vocabulary and structures for conversation and passive vocabulary and structures for reading. Extensive work in vocabulary building through the study of word formation. Students must tape record the oral portion of their lessons. Cassette tapes are utilized in this course. (½ unit)

German Level II: Second Semester

A continuation of the above course. Completes study of German grammar, introduces German literature, and extends discussion of German culture. Students must tape record the oral portion of their lessons. Cassette tapes are utilized in this course. (½ unit)

HEALTH EDUCATION

Health and Safety Semester I: Basic Course

Fulfills the Indiana graduation requirement for health education. A general study of the factors affecting the individual's health; mental health; alcohol, drugs, and tobacco; nutrition; exercise; the environment; disease; human growth and development (includes basic structure and function of the human body, pregnancy, reproduction, and birth control). (½ unit)

Family Health Care (Human Development and Family Health)

An introduction to essential skills in recognizing both physical and mental illnesses and responding appropriately to them. Includes identification of childhood illnesses and communicable diseases; emergency care for injuries due to accidents, and care of patients at home. (½ unit)

INDUSTRIAL ARTS

Drafting: First Semester

A beginning course for students with no previous experience. Covers instruments, lettering, geometric constructions, sketching, orthographic projections, pictorial drawing, dimensioning, and sectional views. (½ unit)

Drafting: Second Semester

A continuation of the above course. Development of skills and competencies required to draw and interpret detailed assembly and production drawings used in business and industry. Emphasis on making drawings of machine parts and mechanical assemblies. (½ unit)

LATIN

Latin Level I: First Semester

A beginning course in Latin that will help enlarge a student's English vocabulary and boost SAT scores. The course introduces the very basic elements of Latin grammar and vocabulary. After acquiring a grasp of these fundamentals, the student reads brief stories, in Latin and in English, based on Roman literature and culture. (½ unit)

Latin Level I: Second Semester

A continuation of the above course to enhance mastery of the fundamentals of grammar and vocabulary and to broaden language skills. Latin reading selections are based on well-known myths and lives of famous Romans; each unit of the text includes information about Roman life and culture. (½ unit)

Latin Level II: First Semester

Reviews the basic elements of word forms and sentence structure learned in first-year Latin. More complex grammar is presented and readings are based on selections from the historian Livy and the tale of Jason and the Argonauts. (½ unit)

Latin Level II: Second Semester

A continuation of the above course with concentration on improved reading ability through readings selected primarily from Caesar's *Commentaries on the Gallic Wars*. Grammar is reviewed and vocabulary study is included in most lessons. (½ unit)

MATHEMATICS

Consumer Mathematics

Helps students build the mathematical skills needed to successfully confront these everyday situations: shopping, purchasing a car, traveling, banking; and calculating wages, insurance, rent, and taxes. (½ unit)

Business Mathematics

Provides a solid foundation in the arithmetic essential to business and one's personal affairs. All fundamentals of arithmetic with application to profit and loss, accounting procedures, buying and selling, general business operations, home ownership, insurance, installment buying, and other consumer activities will be covered. Accuracy and understanding the number system will be stressed. (½ unit)

Basic Mathematics

First Semester. Topics include whole numbers, fractions, decimals, squares and square root, and percentages. Goals are to develop computational skills in these areas and to develop ability to apply these skills correctly in a variety of practical applications. (½ unit)

Second Semester. A continuation of the above course. Topics include units of measure (lengths, angles, area, volume, capacity, weight, time and speed), informal geometry, the metric system, ratio and proportion, elementary algebra, and consumer mathematics applications. (½ unit)

Algebra Level I

First Semester. Topics include properties of the fundamental operations, operations with integers, evaluating expressions, combining like terms, removing parentheses, linear equations and inequalities, exponents, factoring, fractional expressions, and verbal problems. (½ unit)

Second Semester. A continuation of the above course; topics include rectangular coordinate system, slopes of lines, linear equations and their graphs, systems of equations and their solutions, functions and functional notation, fractional equations, complex fractions, radicals and radical equations, Pythogorean Theorem, quadratic equations, and verbal problems. (½ unit)

Algebra Level II

First Semester. Develops an understanding of the nature of fundamental operations with real numbers, equations and inequalities, graphs of points and lines, functions and variations, polynomials, rational expressions, complex fractions, irrational and complex numbers, and quadratic equations. (½ unit)

Second Semester. A continuation of the above course. Designed for greater understanding of and competence in equations in two variables; polynomial functions; analytic geometry; variation; exponential and logarithmic functions; sequences and series; trigonometric functions; triangle trigonometry; probability and statistics. (½ unit)

Geometry

First Semester. An integration of algebra and geometry to provide an appreciation of the structure of mathematics. Topics include undefined terms, basic definitions, and how both are employed to develop and prove theorems, including the application of deductive and fundamental concepts of algebra. Other topics include parallel and perpindicular lines, congruence and applications of triangles, polygons, and intensive coverage of parallelograms and other quadrilaterals. (½ unit)

Second Semester. A continuation of the above course. Comprehensive study of the right triangle (special emphasis on Pythagorean Theorem and elementary trigonometry); circles and tangents, arcs, chords, angles, and segments related to circles; areas and volumes of geometric figures and solids; basic geometric constructions with a compass and straight edge; and coordinate geometry. (½ unit)

Trigonometry

Prepares the student for college-level calculus, or for technical schools or employment in industry. Includes firm foundation in analytical and computational trigonometry; definition and graphing of circular functions, inverse functions, polar coordinates, and basic identities; solution of trigonometric equations with numerous applications; and development of computational and problem-solving skills. (½ unit)

Calculus: First Semester

A continuation for those who wish to go beyond advanced algebra and trigonometry. This course is equivalent to one semester of high school calculus. Topics include functions, limits, derivatives, and integration. The student will gain an understanding of the basic techniques of calculus and some of their most important applications. (½ unit)

Calculus: Second Semester

A continuation of the above course. Topics include logarithmic and exponential functions; techniques of integration; implicit differentiation and circular functions; and applications of the derivative and the differential. (½ unit)

SCIENCE

Introductory Earth/Space Science Level I: First Semester

Investigates three basic areas of science: astronomy, geology, and physical geography. Topics include the universe, solar system, earth-moon system, minerals, and processes of the earth's crust. (½ unit)

Introductory Earth/Space Science Level I: Second Semester

A continuation of the above course focusing on the planet earth. Topics include earthquakes and continental drift; geologic history of the planet earth; life records in rock formations; the atmosphere, and weather, the hydrosphere; and man's impact on the environment. (½ unit)

Biology Level I: First Semester

Introductory biology course concerned with the methods of science, the nature of life, and the world of living things. Examines the chemical aspects of life, the role of DNA, reproduction, and the principles of heredity and development. (½ unit)

Biology Level I: Second Semester

Concerned primarily with the study of protista, plants, and animals; the chemical and nervous control systems, population biology, and man's role in the total ecosystem. The environment receives special attention throughout the course. (½ unit)

Plant Science: First Semester

An introductory course exploring the structure and function of plants. Includes techniques for care and propagation of plants, and soil structure and conditioning. (½ unit)

Plant Science: Second Semester

A continuation of the above course. Introduces care of house plants, use of greenhouses, home landscaping, lawn care, and raising a vegetable garden. (½ unit)

Physical Science: An Introduction to Chemistry

Included in the course are the properties of matter, measurement, basics of formula and equation writing, and in-depth looks at acids, bases, salts, nuclear structures and processes, hydrocarbons, water, and the gases of the atmosphere. Concerns about environmental topics are also addressed. (½ unit)

Physical Science: An Introduction to Physics

Emphasis on basic, nontechnical understanding of the following and their relationship to our daily lives: force, motion, energy, sound, light, electricity, magnetism, and electronics. (½ unit)

Physics Level I: First Semester

Topics include basic concepts of physics and the mathematical tools required to work with them. Forces, vectors, motion, heat, energy, wave motion, kinetic theory of gases, and light are covered. (½ unit)

Physics Level I: Second Semester

A continuation of the above course. Topics include optics and light, electricity, magnetism, electromagnetism, quantum theory, and nuclear physics. (½ unit)

SOCIAL STUDIES

Psychology

Designed to acquaint the mature high school student or adult with the language and principles of psychology. Emphasis on the study of human behavior. For those who continue in college, this course serves as a basis for the study of other social sciences; for those whose education terminates at the high school level, it presents valuable information and explanation about human behavior and relationships. (½ unit)

Sociology

Covers four broad areas: socialization, institutions, stratification, and social change; topics explored to give a sense of range and development. Emphasis on operation of general social principles in a wide variety of cultures. (½ unit)

Introduction to Social Science

A basic course for students who want to find out what social science is and how social scientists work. Students engage in activities that introduce them to the methods of history, psychology, sociology, anthropology, geography, political science, and economics. (½ unit)

World History: First Semester

Introductory survey of world history from the first civilizations of the Near East to the fall of Napoleon. Topics featured: ancient Greece, the Roman Empire, the Middle Ages, the Renaissance and Reformation, the Age of Exploration and Discovery, the scientific and industrial revolutions, and the French Revolution. Emphasis on Western civilization, although attention is also given to contributions of civilizations in Africa, Asia, and America. Some study of world geography through the use of maps. (½ unit)

World History: Second Semester

A continuation of the above course through the nineteenth and twentieth centuries. Studies those movements, issues, ideas, and individuals to help the student understand the modern world and appreciate its problems. Emphasis on European civilization, but also covers Middle East, Africa, Asia, and Latin America. Maps are used to illustrate significant political information. (½ unit)

World Geography: First Semester

A regional approach to the study of topography, climate, vegetation, and resources in various countries of the world; examines the influences these elements have on human activities. Covers the United States, Canada, Latin America, and northwestern Europe. (½ unit)

World Geography: Second Semester

A continuation of the above course covering the Mediterranean, the Middle East, the U.S.S.R. and Eastern Europe, the Far East, sub-Saharan Africa, and other areas of interest. (½ unit)

United States History: First Semester

An introductory study of the history of the United States. Chronological survey of the following topics: age of discovery and founding of the colonies, struggle for independence and conflicts associated with the launching of a new system of government, the rise of nationalism, sectional strife and the Civil War, and the beginning of the Industrial Age. (½ unit)

United States History: Second Semester

A continuation of the above course. A general survey of the United States since the 1890s, including the following topics: the Spanish-American War, the Progressive Movement, World War I, the 1920s, the Depression and New Deal, World War II, and problems and promises of America today. Considerable attention is also given to the contributions of minority groups. (½ unit)

Economics

An introductory economics course. Students learn economic facts and concepts about our society and analyze materials critically and objectively. The course includes an overview of the historical development of U.S. economic processes; also includes a brief section on comparative economic systems. (½ unit)

United States Government: First Semester

The study of how people behave politically, focusing on those who are not public officials as well as those who are (the President, members of Congress, and Justices of the Supreme Court). Study of how individuals affect and are affected by the political system of this country through case studies of political behavior and analysis of that behavior. (½ unit)

United States Government: Second Semester (Citizenship/Civics)

Focuses on how to analyze and understand political problems. Emphasis on the student's ability to think critically and to analyze rationally through the study of current American problems: war, poverty, pollution, etc. (½ unit)

SPANISH

Spanish Level I

First Semester. A broad introduction to Spanish through listening, speaking, writing, and reading the language. Cassette tapes are utilized in this course. The study of Spanish culture will center around aspects of everyday life in Latin American countries. (½ unit)

Second Semester. A continuation of the above course. Cassette tapes are utilized. (½ unit)

Spanish Level II

First Semester. Builds upon the listening, speaking, writing, and reading abilities learned in the first year course, with opportunity for original expression in oral and written Spanish. The countries of Central America will be highlighted in regard to the Spanish culture. Cassette tapes are utilized. (½ unit)

Second Semester. A continuation of the above course. Cassette tapes are utilized. (½ unit)

VOCATIONAL INFORMATION

Vocational Information

Designed to help students understand their own vocational histories, become aware of job possibilities, and make some appropriate career decisions. Assignments involve locating and using community resources, learning decision-making skills, writing a job resume, arranging for an interview for a job-training opportunity or a job, and evaluating that interview. To equip students with strategies to deal with vocational decisions now and in the future, general theories and hypothetical cases are presented, as well as ample opportunity to apply those theories to the student's particular concerns. (½ unit)

Project Self-Discovery (Vocational Information)

A course in self-analysis and self-expression. Students explore directions for their future interests and careers. They master study skills and basic principles of human psychology and learn to improve their powers of self-understanding. (½ unit)

NONCREDIT COURSES

MATHEMATICS

Arithmetic for Algebra I

Reviews the building blocks of mathematics; whole numbers, fractions, decimals, addition, subtraction, multiplication, and division. For those whose arithmetic background is weak. (Noncredit) *Tuition:* $56.

Arithmetic for Algebra II

Applies knowledge of arithmetic to algebra. Study of negative numbers, absolute values, problem solving, exponents, and roots. Introduces translation of word problems into equations. (Noncredit) *Tuition:* $56.

Overcoming Math Anxiety Arithmetic for Algebra

Focuses on learning how students' anxiety about and fear of math developed and how students can rechannel this behavior into productive responses. A cassette tape is utilized in this course. (Noncredit) *Tuition:* $56.

GRADUATE COURSES

EDUCATION

Advanced Study in the Teaching of Secondary School English Language

Current programs, methods, and materials for junior high and secondary school English courses. Guided reading in teaching literature, writing, language, and media. (3 semester hours)

Advanced Study in the Teaching of Reading in the Junior High and Secondary Schools

For Secondary teachers. The developmental reading program in secondary schools, use of reading in various curriculum areas, appraisal of reading abilities, and techniques and materials for helping reluctant and retarded readers. (3 semester hours)

Writing as a Response to Reading

For elementary and secondary teachers. Explores ways to encourage quality writing and to integrate writing with both reading and the rest of the curriculum. (3 semester hours)

Advanced Study in the Teaching of Reading in the Elementary Schools

Review of the developmental reading program in the elementary school, use of reading in various curriculum areas, appraisal of reading abilities, and techniques and materials for individualized instruction. (3 semester hours)

Advanced Study in the Teaching of Language Arts in the Elementary Schools

Helps experienced teachers gain further insight into the development of the English language and how best to teach language arts. Emphasizes the basic communication skills and significant trends and materials. (3 semester hours)

Organization and Administration of a School Reading Program

Reviews principles and practices in organizing reading programs within elementary and secondary schools. Describes techniques for supervising and administering a reading program via case studies, simulation, and discussion. (3 semester hours)

Iowa, University of
Guided Correspondence Study
Division of Continuing Education
116 International Center
Iowa City, Iowa 52242-1802   (800) 272-6430

Description:

The University of Iowa is located in the southeastern section of the state. The First General Assembly of Iowa established the University in 1847, very soon after the Iowa Territory became a state. Instruction began in 1855. The Guided Correspondence Study Office is part of the Center for Credit Programs in the Division of Continuing Education. College-level correspondence study courses have been offered since 1916. There are over 5,000 enrollments yearly in 160 courses representing 40 academic departments.

A Bachelor of Liberal Studies degree program is designed for adults who have completed at least two years of college and who cannot attend classes full-time on campus. Offered by the three Iowa Regents Universities, this degree has no residence requirements and no traditional major. It may even be possible to earn the degree without leaving home.

Faculty:

Leonard Kallio, Assistant Director, Center for Credit Programs; Elizabeth Hill, Assistant Director for Student Services. There is a faculty of 120 plus 3 counselors.

Academic Levels:

College

Degree/Certificate Programs:

Up to thirty semester hours of credit earned by correspondence study may be applied toward an undergraduate degree at the University of Iowa with the approval of the dean of the student's respective college. With prior approval of a student's major department, enrolled graduate students may be allowed up to nine semester hours of correspondence study toward a graduate degree. A Certificate of Completion is awarded for specific Continuing Education Unit (CEU) courses designed for self-improvement or career enrichment. Any course may be taken for noncredit.

Admission Requirements:

Open enrollment. On-campus students enrolled in a degree program must obtain approval from the dean of his/her college before enrolling in a correspondence course. High school seniors in the upper third of the class may enroll in freshman-level correspondence courses with permission from their high school advisor or principal.

Tuition:

$74 per semester hour plus a $15 nonrefundable enrollment fee per course, payable with the application. If paying by Visa or MasterCard, students may enroll by phone (800-335-6430) or fax (319-335-2740). If enrolling by fax, the enrollment form from Guided Correspondence Study should be used. Fees for noncredit courses are individually determined. A refund of 70 percent may be granted within two months of enrollment. Courses are approved by the Veterans Administration. Some scholarships are available for Guided Correspondence Study students. These are awarded quarterly and consist of a tuition refund. Scholarships are awarded on the basis of demonstrated academic performance and financial need. Only students who have successfully completed at least one GCS course and who are not receiving any other financial aid are eligible. Write or call the GCS Office for further information and application forms.

Enrollment Period:

The maximum time allowed to complete a course is nine months. A three-month extension may be granted upon payment of a $25 extension fee. The minimum time allowed is two weeks per semester hour of credit.

Equipment Requirements:

Cost of textbooks and other supplies are in addition to fees and are the responsibility of the student.

Credit and Grading:

The grading system is the standard A, B, C, D, (for passing) and F (for failure). Minimum passing grade is D- (undergraduate), C (graduate, for credit at the University of

Iowa). Plus or minus grading in courses in the College of Liberal Arts may be used at the discretion of the instructor. Examinations are of major importance in the awarding of final grades and must be taken under the supervision of an approved proctor or at the Guided Correspondence Study Office in Iowa City. Most examinations are closed book; a few courses have open book examinations. Credit is awarded in semester hour units.

Accreditations:

North Central Association of Colleges and Schools. Member of: National University Continuing Education Association.

COLLEGE COURSES

AFRICAN AMERICAN STUDIES

Literatures of the African Peoples

Introduces the various themes and styles of selected contemporary Black writers of Africa, the Caribbean, and the United States. Stresses appreciation of the literary values of a wide range of texts, but also considers the sociopolitical contexts of writers and their works. Audiocassette tape required. (3 semester hours)

Introduction to Afro-American Culture

Familiarizes students with black literature, history, and culture since World War II. Examines the role of the Civil Rights and Black Power movements in the struggle for equality. Also considers differences among African Americans such as age, class, sexual preference, and gender. (3 semester hours)

AGING STUDIES

Human Development and Behavior

An overview of human developmental theories from a lifespan perspective. Examination of cognitive, physical, and personality development from prenatal life to old age, stressing the role of developmental process on the health and illness continuum. (3 semester hours)

Suffering, Death, and Faith

A comprehensive overview of death as seen in various cultures and historical periods. Beliefs, attitudes, behaviors, and social context concerning death and dying are explained and illustrated, as well as the significance of the dynamics of bereavement and the process of normalization after a loss. The approach is broadly ecumenical. Of special interest to health-care professionals, counselors, and social workers. Audiocassette tape required. (2 semester hours)

Multidisciplinary Perspectives on Aging

Focuses on important multidisciplinary perspectives on aging and on the functional assessment of older persons. The perspectives include social resources, economic resources, mental health status, physical health status, and activities of daily living. Attention is also given to services that are or should be available to respond to the needs of older persons. The course should be of particular interest to those professionals in social work, long-term care, home care, congregate and other housing programs, and to others working with aging and aged persons. As part of the course work students will be required to conduct interviews with two older persons. (3 semester hours)

Aging and Leisure

Considers why leisure is a burden for many older people by focusing on the economics of population, mortality, and retirement; how American society has chosen in the past to distribute work, leisure, and education over a typical life span; and current trends toward a more flexible distribution of these activities. Deals with the problems of older people who have been denied work and have been forced out of the mainstream of American life and the need for dealing with the problem of leisure as a general problem. (3 semester hours)

Selected Aspects of Social Work and Social Welfare (Sexual Health in Later Life)

Examines current knowledge about the ways that biological, sociological, and psychological aspects of aging affect sexual interest and functioning in the older adult. Explores both the dimensions of sexuality as experienced by the older person and the sociocultural factors that bear upon sexual expression in later life. The course should be of particular interest to those studying and working in the field of aging, those who provide care to the elderly, and older adults themselves. As part of the course work, students are required to visit a nursing home or other long-term care facility to assess how conductive its environment is in respecting and meeting the sexual needs of its residents. (3 semester hours)

Introduction to Biomedical Ethics

The course provides the opportunity to develop an understanding of what ethics is and what some basic methods and procedures of ethics are. These methods and procedures are then applied to ethical problems in biomedicine. Among the topics considered are suicide, experiments with human subjects, patient confidentiality, and truth-telling. (3 semester hours)

AMERICAN STUDIES

American Music (Rock and Roll)

Views rock and roll as a subculture complete with its own language, life styles, and value systems, a subculture large enough to encompass a multitude of meanings for millions of individuals whose tastes do not necessarily overlap. Analyzes what rock and roll is on aesthetic, personal, social, economic, historical, and institutional levels, with the goal of seeing how American life and rock and roll are interrelated. (3 semester hours)

Survey of American Autobiography

Considers certain aspects of American autobiography as a genre, and examines autobiographies as cultural documents. Analyzes the voices and messages of seven individuals writing out of perspectives on America that are foreign to most persons. (3 semester hours)

ANTHROPOLOGY

Introduction to the Study of Culture and Society

An introduction to the methods, concepts, and subject matter studied by sociocultural anthropologists. The course begins with basic evolutionary principles, then concentrates on the organization of contemporary societies in many parts of the world. Topics covered include kinship and religious systems, economic and political structures, and sex roles. One assignment is based on a case study of the Grand Valley Dani of New Guinea. A short term paper on the Hutterites of North America is one requirement for this course. (4 semester hours)

Anthropology and Contemporary World Problems

This course examines selected world problems from an anthropological perspective, comparing and contrasting current dilemmas with those faced by diverse human groups in recent times and the distant past. Includes problems of population, food, development, economics, politics, conflict, health, and changing male-female relationships and family patterns. (3 semester hours)

Introduction of Midwestern Prehistory (Emphasis Iowa)

This course is an introduction to the study of archaeology and midwestern prehistory. It provides a general survey of the interdisciplinary approaches to archaeology and an overview of the history of archaeology in Iowa. The prehistoric cultural sequence of Iowa is viewed against the background of North American prehistory with a discussion of current and future research. (3 semester hours)

Women's Roles: A Cross-Cultural Perspective

Examines the place of women in societies of differing levels of sociopolitical complexity. Identifies the factors that assign women "their roles," including kinship and family, belief systems, economic integration, assignment of power, and cultural change. Provides an historical overview of female roles in the Judeo-Christian tradition. (3 semester hours)

ART

Calligraphy I

Fundamentals and exercises in the use of the broad-edged pen in the making of the Fraktur letterform. Emphasis on making letters and arranging them well, plus some practice in calligraphy as applied letterform design. A one-hour videotape is required ($20 purchase fee). (3 semester hours)

Calligraphy II

Building upon the foundations of Calligraphy I, this course examines a variety of tools and letterforms, emphasizing that the look of the letter is determined by the tool that produces it. The broad-edged nib, the dip pen, the brush, and others, as appropriate, are used in the creation of the following letterforms: Merovingian, Uncial, Legend, Versals, Brushcript, Copperplate, and Dutch caps. Use of watercolor and techniques with calligraphic applications are explored. A four-hour videotape demonstrating techniques and letterforms is required (purchase only: $40). (3 semester hours)

BIOSTATISTICS

Introduction to Biostatistics

This course emphasizes the application of statistical techniques to biological data. Topics include graphs and tables, elementary probability, binomial and normal probability distributions, tests of statistical significance, confidence of data analysis and interpretation. (3 semester hours)

CHINESE

Chinese I: Non-intensive

An introduction to spoken Mandarin Chinese, with some instruction in writing Chinese characters. Assigned work consists of memorizing vocabulary and dialogues, reading and writing exercises, as well as oral exercises on tapes. Required set of audiocassette tapes ($20 purchase only). (4 semester hours)

Chinese II: Non-intensive

A continuation of Chinese I. An introduction to spoken Mandarin Chinese, with some instruction in writing Chinese characters. Assigned work consists of memorizing vocabulary and dialogues, reading and writing exercises, as well as oral exercises on tapes. (4 semester hours)

CLASSICAL STUDIES

Greek and Latin for Vocabulary Building

Section 1. This course offers a systematic approach to vocabulary building by focusing on the Latin and Greek elements in English words. Recognition of these elements is the key to understanding and remembering the meanings of thousands of English words. The course deals with a wide range of English words, from the common to the less familiar. By exploring the origins of words, their development, and their present meanings, students will improve their speaking, reading, and writing vocabularies. The ability to recognize Latin and Greek components in English words is a skill that will accompany the student far beyond the duration of the course. (3 semester hours)

Section 2. A continuation of the above course. Enables students to increase their vocabularies by introducing more Latin and Greek bases. (3 semester hours)

Medical and Technical Terminology

Offers a systematic approach to learning medical and technical vocabulary by focusing on the Latin and Greek element in English words. Knowledge of Greek and Latin elements will assist in the learning, memorization, and understanding of technical language. The primary purpose of this course is to teach the student how to determine the meaning of a scientific word by breaking down its structure in terms of prefix, stem or stems, and suffix. As an added benefit, it is hoped that students will acquire a lasting fascination with all words and their origins. (2 semester hours)

COMMUNICATIONS

Parliamentary Procedure

Designed for the person who is a member of an organization that uses parliamentary procedure as a guideline. The knowledge of parliamentary procedure will increase the chances that a person will participate in meetings and that the organization's business will run more smoothly. The course will be of benefit also to those who teach a basic course in speech communication since it is likely that a unit in parliamentary procedure/debate will be included in such a course. (1 semester hour)

Organizational Leadership

Principles and techniques of leadership in various organizations; focus on communication methods, motivation, and elements of parliamentary procedure. (3 semester hours)

Rhetoric and Politics

This course examines the modern political campaign and its major component, persuasion. It will encourage students to be alert to a political campaign, the candidates, the staffs, the volunteers, and the messages and rhetoric used to persuade voters. The course primarily focuses on the role that communication has in the campaign process. (3 semester hours)

Screenwriting

Section 1. This is a beginning course designed to develop the knowledge and skills necessary to write a film or television script. Students will complete several analytical exercises in characterization, dialogue, plot development, and visualization. (3 semester hours)

Section 2. This advanced course includes five mail-in scene assignments, two revisions, and a telephone conference with the instructor. (3 semester hours)

DANCE

Dance and Society

Explores dance as an expression of the human condition. Examines dance in relation to societal developments. Considers various forms of dance: ethnic, ballet, modern, tap, and jazz. (3 semester hours)

Iowa, University of

ECONOMICS

Principles of Microeconomics

Provides an introduction to economic principles with an emphasis on microeconomics, the study of decisions made by individual economic agents or units in the economy, such as households and business firms. Examines different types of market structures, as well as the roles of various institutions in affecting economic behavior. (3 or 4 semester hours)

Principles of Macroeconomics

Provides an introduction to macroeconomics—a study of inflation, unemployment, economic growth, and the big public-policy questions raised daily in the media. Considers operations of the national economy and its major institutions; aggregate economic measures such as income, employment, money, and inflation; monetary and fiscal policy; international monetary problems and economic growth. (3 or 4 semester hours)

Microeconomic Theory

Examines the various parts of the whole economy. Considers how a market economy determines the composition of total output (what goods are produced), the distribution of income, and the distribution of employment among alternative uses. (3 semester hours)

Macroeconomics

Demonstrates how a modern economy functions. Explains how national product, unemployment, and inflation are measured, and how national income and the price level are determined. Students learn how to analyze the impact of stabilization policies. Explores the dynamics of inflation and the problem of stagflation. (3 semester hours)

EDUCATION

Introduction to Educating Gifted Students

Provides a comprehensive introduction to the field of gifted education as well as the opportunity to apply some of the new information in work or school settings. The course is balanced between readings and papers and practical application activities. Upon completion of the course, one will have the basic foundation in issues in gifted education as well as some skills to apply directly to teaching, counseling, or administration. (3 semester hours)

Parent-Child Relationships

This course about the experience of parenting deals with such topics as: societal influences on the parenting experience; the problems and joys of parenting as children and parents grow and change; father and mother roles; parenting in differing social groups; how changes in family composition (such as blended or single-parent families) and life style affect parent-child relationships; the effects of stress and change on the parenting ability; and parenting in exceptional families. (3 semester hours)

Development and Administration of Child Care Centers

Topics in starting and managing a child care center; licensing, budgeting, health and safety, food and nutrition, parent involvement, supervising staff, maintaining quality. (3 semester hours)

Design and Organization of Curriculum

Historical overview of formal schooling and examination of social and economic issues influencing school organization, curriculum selection, and instructional practice. Special emphasis on interrelationships between all levels of formal schooling from kindergarten through postsecondary institutions, with attention to the financing of formal education and equity of educational opportunity. Designed for teachers, prospective administrators and curriculum specialists, and lay citizens seeking to broaden their perspective on the total educational endeavor. (3 semester hours)

Introduction to Education

Basic orientation in field of education: consideration of administrative organization, instructional procedures, and contemporary problems at both elementary and secondary levels. Satisfies basic foundation requirement for most teacher preparation programs. (3 semester hours)

Exceptional Persons

Intended for both regular and special educators and for those in other professions interested in learning about exceptional persons and their educational needs. This basic course deals with many types of exceptional persons (especially children and youth) and problems and approaches in educating them. (3 semester hours)

Mental Retardation

Introduction to the causes and treatment of mental retardation emphasizing educational programming for the mentally retarded and the role of schools and professional groups in teaching and training the retarded. Subjects include classification and concepts of intelligence and mental disabilities; assessment of mental retardation; etiology and psychological development; cognition, learning, and memory; the retarded child in school; retarded adults; and family, social, and legal aspects of mental retardation. (3 semester hours)

Introduction to Continuing Education

This course explores the historical and conceptual foundations of the theory and practice of continuing education, including a consideration of adult learning theory, basic terminology, the nature of adult students, and the major institutions offering educational experiences and credentials to adult learners. (3 semester hours)

Educational Psychology and Measurement

Designed as a tutorial learning experience. Topics include learning, human development, instruction, memory, educational goals, motivation, measurement, and evaluation of students. (3 semester hours)

Educational Psychology

Survey course in the psychological research on school learning. Emphasizes recent studies of development, learning, instruction, and measurement. Cognitive-science perspective is adopted throughout. (3 semester hours)

The Adolescent and Young Adult

Survey of the psychology of adolescence. Emphasizes the educational and social applications of theories of adolescent growth and development. Topics covered are concepts of adolescence and the major psychological theories of learning and development; physical and cognitive development and the genetic and biological influences on development; social, emotional, and personality development; and adolescent problems and disturbances. (3 semester hours)

Parent-Teacher Communication

The course offers an introduction to important dimensions of parent-teacher involvement: basic communication skills, assertiveness and negotiaiton, formats for involvement (including conferences, consulting, and parent education), and factors that can influence work between parents and teachers. (3 semester hours)

Introduction to Statistical Methods

Analysis and interpretation of research data; descriptive statistics (frequency distributions, central tendency, variability); introduction to statistical inference (normal curve sampling theory, simple t-test); introduction to correlation and linear regression. Although illustrative material is drawn mainly from the fields of education and psychology, most of the statistical techniques presented have general applicability to other content areas. (3 semester hours)

Educational Measurement and Evaluation Using Standardized Instruments

Tests, rating scales, questionnaires, and other standardized instruments as sources of educational data; evaluation of the reliability and validity of data-gathering techniques; interpretation of scores in individual guidance and program evaluation. Sources of test information and criticism. (3 semester hours)

ENGLISH

Selected American Works Before 1900

Introduces the student to eight major American writers of fiction, prose, and poetry in the nineteenth century: Nathaniel Hawthorne, Edgar Allan Poe, Ralph Waldo Emerson, Henry David Thoreau, Walt Whitman, Emily Dickinson, Mark Twain, and Henry James. A few other writers are briefly examined. In addition to selections in an anthology, three novels are read: Hawthorne's *The Scarlet Letter*, Twain's *Huckleberry Finn*, and James' *Portrait of a Lady*. (3 semester hours)

Shakespeare

Study of twelve of Shakespeare's plays, including works of comedy, history, tragedy, and romance. (3 semester hours)

Selected Authors (Major Nineteenth-Century British Works)

Introduces the student to the following writers of British literature in the nineteenth century: poets William Wordsworth, Percy Bysshe Shelley, John Keats, Alfred Lord Tennyson, Robert Browning, Matthew Arnold; and novelists Charles Dickens, George Eliot, and Thomas Hardy. Novels read are Dickens' *Great Expectations*, Eliot's *Adam Bede*, and Hardy's *The Mayor of Casterbridge*. (3 semester hours)

Literature and the Culture of Twentieth-Century America (1945–1990)

From the end of World War II to the end of the Cold War, America underwent dramatic changes. This course will focus on five important areas: the evolution of a youth culture, race relations, Vietnam, politics, and sexual/gender relationships. (3 semester hours)

Chaucer

An introduction to Chaucer's *Canterbury Tales* for both undergraduate and graduate English majors and non-majors. No prior knowledge of Chaucer or of Middle English is assumed. Emphasis will be on the craft of Chaucer's storytelling and the provocative insights into life and art. Reading will include the *General Prologue* and 18 tales (all in Middle English), as well as selected modern critical material. Two required audiocassette tapes are provided upon enrollment. (3 semester hours)

English Novel: Scott to Butler

Eleven masterpieces of Victorian fiction, including novels by Scott, Gaskell, the Brontë sisters, Dickens, Thackeray, Trollope, Eliot, Meredith, Hardy, and Conrad. Emphasis on understanding and appreciating the enduring appeal of nineteenth-century English fiction. (3 semester hours)

Popular Literatures (Detective Fiction)

A historical approach to the detective fiction genre, from the founders (Poe, Conan Doyle, Futrelle) through the "golden age" (Bentley, Christie, Sayers) and the "hard-boiled school" (Chandler, Hammett, Macdonald) to current authors (Sjöwall, Wahlöö, and others). (3 semester hours)

Regional Women Writers (Southern Women Writers)

This course introduces the following writers and their fiction: Kate Chopin, Zora Neale Hurston, Ellen Glasgow, Carson McCullers, Flannery O'Connor, Anne Tyler, and Gail Godwin. (3 semester hours)

Women in Literature (Representative Women Writers)

Novels include *Emma* (Austen), *Villette* (C. Brontë), *Adam Bede* (Eliot), *Barren Ground* (Glasgow), *The House of Mirth* (Wharton), *Mrs. Dalloway* (Woolf), *The Golden Notebook* (Lessing). Also stories by Katherine Mansfield. (3 semester hours)

Changing Concepts of Women in Literature

Complexities in the treatment of women in literature of the nineteenth and twentieth centuries in works by both mean and women authors: seven novels, four plays. *Jane Eyre* (C. Brontë), *Middlemarch* (Eliot), *The Bostonians* (James), *Jude the Obscure* (Hardy), *Howards End* (Forster), *The Awakening* (Chopin), *To the Lighthouse* (Woolf). Plays by Shaw and Ibsen. (3 semester hours)

Literature and Philosophic Thought (The Holocaust)

An introduction to the Holocaust, the slaughter of over 6 million Jews by Nazi Germany, focusing on the historical and human dimensions of this tragic event. Readings include historical studies and several books of personal recollections and remembrances by survivors. The course examines the roots of European anti-Semitism, the systematic development of the Nazis' genocidal campaign against the Jews, the responses of the victims, the failure of the world to stop or mitigate the destruction, the effects of this unprecedented event on Jews and Judaism, and the need to reassess the human capacity for good and evil. (3 semester hours)

Science Fiction (Historical Survey)

Brief historical survey of science fiction, beginning with Mary Shelley's *Frankenstein*, a Gothic precursor, and following with H.G. Wells, one of the "fathers" of the genre, and moving into a look at the genre as it has existed over the past fifty years. (3 semester hours)

Prose by Women Writers (Feminist Fiction)

Traces the development of the feminist novel from the late eighteenth century to today. By reading a variety of feminist novels, students will explore how the writers integrate a specific political message into fiction and the different forms and approaches possible for the feminist novel. Although the issues central to feminism will recur throughout the course, the emphasis is on reading and writing about novels. (3 semester hours)

The Interpretation of Literature

Introduces students to a wide range of American and British literature. Emphasizes the interpretation of individual works, examining basic concepts such as point of view, theme, structure, and imagery. Readings include novels, short stories, poems, and plays. (3 semester hours)

Literatures of the African Peoples

Introduces the various themes and styles of selected contemporary black writers of Africa, the Caribbean, and the United States. Stresses appreciation of the literary values of a wide range of texts, but also considers the sociopolitical contexts of writers and their works. (3 semester hours)

FINANCE

General Insurance

Theory of risk and risk bearing; arrangements for dealing with risk; insurance industry, types of insurers, functions of insurers, and government regulation of insurance; social insurance; basic features of selected insurance contracts. (3 semester hours)

FRENCH

Elementary French

Course 9:1. This is a beginning course in the French language, intended for those who have never studied French before or who seek a thorough review. It is an introduction to French grammar, sounds, and culture through the development of communication skills in speaking, listening, writing, and reading. (4 semester hours)

Course 9:2. A continuation of *Course 9:1.* (4 semester hours)

GEOGRAPHY

Introduction to Human Geography

Human geography involves both space and place, focusing on how we structure the world around us through our actions as well as how we behave within the economic, political, and physical environments we create. The course examines the following: basic concepts and social science methodology; the cultural, demographic, and physical contexts for spatial behavior; the economic and political organization of space; and the spatial structures generated by spatial behavior. (4 semester hours)

Urban Geography

Urban geography provides a social scientific understanding of urban places—towns, cities, metropolises, etc.—and insights into the significant roles such places play in our lives. The course investigates the importance of urban places not only as living and workplaces, but as hubs of various services and facilities. In addition, the course takes a multidisciplinary approach in drawing connections between urban geography and other disciplines, such as anthropology, economics, history, political science, sociology, and urban and regional planning. (3 semester hours)

GERMAN

Elementary German I

Introduction to the German language and to the culture of German-speaking countries. The course provides the opportunity to learn listening, reading, and writing skills outside of a classroom setting. Speaking skills are not heavily emphasized, but students are offered the opportunity to send audiotapes to the instructor to practice speaking. (3 semester hours)

Elementary German II

A continuation of the above course. (3 semester hours)

Intermediate German I

A continuation of beginning German, building on accumulated knowledge. This course and Intermediate German II represent the equivalent of second-year college German. Emphasizes reading, writing, and listening skills. Videotapes use material from a German television series and provide about an hour of viewing per lesson. (4 semester hours)

Intermediate German II

A continuation of the above course. (4 semester hours)

HEALTH

Health for Living

Focuses on both disease prevention and wellness. Examines the responsibility of the individual for his or her well-being. Also considers social and cultural factors that affect health and wellness. (3 semester hours)

Health Promotion in Workplace Settings

Course examines the forces and key role players behind the health-promotion boom and the designing of comprehensive health-promotion programs (e.g., health assessment, intervention programs, evaluation) for corporations, hospitals, public and private community settings. (3 semester hours)

HISTORY

Western Civilization to 1750

Evolution of western civilization up to the Napoleonic era with emphasis on political, social, economic, and cultural development of Europe as related to problems of our own time. (3 semester hours)

Western Civilization since 1750

Evolution of western civilization since the Napoleonic era with emphasis on political, social, economic, and cultural development of Europe as related to problems of our own time. (3 semester hours)

Civilizations of Asia: Premodern China and Japan (China)

An introduction to Asia through the examination of the history and culture of Eat Asia's largest country—China. Essentially a historical survey of China from its beginning to the present day. (3 semester hours)

Civilizations of Asia (Imperialism and Modern India)

Provides a broad overview of the South Asian subcontinent's history. The focus, however, is on Indian history from the Mughal empire to the present. Areas of study will include major forces that have shaped India's social, political, and cultural identity; the impact of British imperialism; and both Indian and Pakistani history since 1947. (3 semester hours)

Civilizations of Asia: Modern China and Japan (Modern Japan)

Overview of modern Japanese history from mid-nineteenth century to the recent past. Focuses on the transformation of Japan from an agricultural and semifeudal society into a modern, industrialized state. (3 semester hours)

Issues in Human History: The Vietnam War in Historical Perspective

Introduces students to the history of Vietnam over the past century. Material is organized chronologically in six units, covering traditional Vietnam, French imperialism, the Franco-Vietminh War, the Cold War, and the American War in Vietnam. (3 semester hours)

Issues in Human History: Twentieth-Century Crisis

Examines personalities and social/political movements in Germany, Russia, and the U.S. during the period 1900–1939. Considers political changes brought on by the crisis of World War I. (3 semester hours)

Great Plains

Surveys (from prehistoric times to the present) history of the Great Plains region (generally defined as that area of the continental U.S. bounded by the Rockies to the west and the prairies and timberlands to the east). Examines its inhabitants—Indian, colonizer, frontiersman, cowboy, cattleman, farmer, and others—as well as the distinctive geography and environment of the land itself. Central course theme is the adaptation made by differing cultural groups to plains life. (3 semester hours)

History of Iowa to 1900

Introduction to the environmental characteristics of the land that became the state, the aboriginal inhabitants of the land, the first contact by European explorers with the land, and the settlement and development of the land by Americans and immigrants during the last two centuries. In addition to the political and economic considerations in Iowa history, the course will examine such matters as the social, demographic, and material culture aspects of Iowa's heritage. (3 semester hours).

United States in World Affairs to 1900

Surveys American foreign relations from the Revolutionary War to 1900. Chronologically examines the periods 1775–1800, 1800–1846, 1846–1865, and 1865–1900. (3 semester hours)

United States in World Affairs 1900–1975

Surveys the growth of the U.S. as a leader in world affairs during the twentieth century; chronologically presents developments during four major periods: 1900–1920, 1921–1945, 1946–1963, and since 1964. (3 semester hours)

American History 1492–1877

Covers the period from discovery through the Civil War and Reconstruction. Emphasizes the social, economic, and political developments of the colonial era, the early republic, the antebellum period, and the Civil War and Reconstruction. (3 semester hours)

American History 1877—Present

Surveys the history of the United States from the post-Reconstruction period to the present. Examines the economic, political, and social developments of the Gilded Age, Progressive Era, and Great Depression. Considers the United States as a world power. (3 semester hours)

The New Era and the New Deal 1920–1940

Considers the social and political changes caused by prosperity and depression, changes involving federal power, political coalitions, the economic system, and foreign policy. Also considers changes in race, gender, and class relations. (3 semester hours)

The Contemporary United States 1940–Present

This course offers a survey of the history of the U.S. since 1940. It is primarily concerned with (1) developments in the Cold War and institutions waging it, (2) changes in federal power and political alignments, (3) the relationships of minority groups and social dissenters to the dominant culture, and (4) economic change. (3 semester hours)

Themes in African American History (Martin Luther King, Jr., and the Modern Civil Rights Movement

Emphasizes Martin Luther King's idea of freedom and its impact on the cultural, economic, political, and social history of America and on the lives of African Americans in particular. Focuses on a series of issues. (3 semester hours)

Medieval Civilization

Survey of European history from the fifth to the fifteenth century, with special emphasis on France, Germany, and England. Although primarily concerned with political history and the development of political institutions, the course attempts to portray the medieval world view by examining religious, economic, social, and intellectual, and cultural aspects of the civilization. Videotapes are used during the course. (3 semester hours)

Nineteenth-Century Europe

An interpretive study of European history from 1815 to 1915. Topics include the rise of the liberal bourgeois state, the 1848 revolutions, the rise of mass political parties, imperialism, the development of working-class culture, and the rise of Marxist and evolutionary socialism. Reading assignments and written work will revolve around a basic survey textbook and several major nineteenth-century novels. (3 semester hours)

Twentieth Century Europe: The Nazi Era

Europe from the turn of the century to World War II and its aftermath. The focus of this course is on the formation of the contemporary world from a European perspective. Topics given special attention are pre-1900 Europe, imperialism and colonialism, World War I, the Russian Revolution, fascism, and the nature of contemporary history. (3 semester hours)

First World War

This course examines the First World War from military, cultural, and social points of view, and assesses the impact of the war on diverse groups of people and on Western culture. The student will read a variety of texts to assess the origins of the war, the course of the war, the experience of the war for men and women who were participants on the war front and the home front, the conclusion of the war, and the significance of the war. The student will also consider various historical interpretations of the war and consider course topics from the perspective of various nations and participants. (3 semester hours)

JOURNALISM

Free-lance Reporting and Writing

Acquaints students with the process of writing and marketing freelance articles to magazines, newspapers, and other publications. Students write several articles and complete exercises involving the development of story ideas, research on periodical markets, the writing of query letters, and the revision of articles. (4 semester hours)

LATIN

Elementary Latin

Course 20:1. An introduction to Latin grammar, syntax, and vocabulary. (4 semester hours)

Course 20:2. A continuation of the above course. (4 semester hours)

Second-Year Latin I

Focuses on translating Latin prose and on reviewing morphology and grammar from the first-year course. (3 semester hours)

Second-Year Latin II

A continuation of the preceding course. Focuses on the translation of Latin poets from the first centuries B.C./A.D. and views this ancient writing as literature. Introduces students to a variety of ancient meters. (3 semester hours)

LEISURE STUDIES

Perspectives on Leisure and Play

Investigates the general question of why people play by examining theoretical explanations for play based in the social science literature, the play behavior of people in social groups, and the social-psychological dynamics of play. Also considers how societies affect and are affected by play, the question of the good life, and social responsibility in relation to outdoor recreation (the environment as playground). (3 semester hours)

Environmental Issues in Recreation

Explores contemporary environmental issues, utilizing the concept of ecosystem as a springboard for analysis. Topics include population growth, land use, endangered species, pollution, and energy resources. Students are encouraged to assess environmental impact of their own personal outdoor recreation. (3 semester hours)

Aging and Leisure

Examines the shift to an older population and the impact this shift will have on our culture. An underlying theme is that as a society, we may not be ready for the social changes that are occurring. The goal of gerontology, as we shift toward an older nation, will not be on life-span, but on health-span. The role of leisure within a health-span society will take on added significance. (3 semester hours)

LINGUISTICS

Language and Society

An introduction to sociolinguistics, focusing on the relationship between social and linguistic behavior. Topics include attitudes toward speakers of various dialects, social class dialects, regional dialects, Black English, and differences between the speech of males and females. (3 semester hours)

MASS COMMUNICATIONS

Popular Culture and Mass Communication

In this course students will explore the relationships between popular media fare and cultural realities; media formulas and communication practices in American culture. The goals are to teach the student to: (1) recognize that popular culture is often developed by and promoted with the mass media, (2) analyze popular culture characteristics as they become political and social practices in America, (3) explore how popular culture as a product of the mass mediated experience impacts your own social and cultural existence. It will examine the relationship between popular culture and the media through a number of elements: icons, stereotypes, myths, rituals, values, beliefs, legends, heroes, and formulas. (3 semester hours)

MATHEMATICS

Basic Algebra I

The real number system, linear equations and inequalities, graphing and systems of linear equations, polynomials and factoring, rational expressions, radicals, quadratic equations. (3 semester hours)

Basic Algebra II

LInear and quadratic equations, radicals, inequalities, linear functions, inverse functions, quadratic functions, polynomial functions, exponential and logarithmic functions, linear systems, matrices and determinants, conics. (3 semester hours)

Basic Geometry

Constitutes a basic course in Euclidean plane geometry along with an introduction to coordinate geometry and vectors. Emphasizes both problem solving and the development of theory. Topics include angles, triangles, polygons, Pythagorean theorem, similar triangles, circles, plane coordinates, and vectors. (3 semester hours)

Theory of Arithmetic

Study of sets, numeration, whole numbers; integers, rational numbers, and number theory. (3 semester hours)

Trigonometry

Trigonometric functions, graphs of trigonometric functions, solution of right triangles, harmonic motion, trigonometric identities and equations, addition and multiple angle formulas, sine and cosine laws, complex numbers and DeMoivre's Theorem, vectors. (3 semester hours)

Finite Mathematics

Introduction to logic, set theory, linear equations and inequalities, linear programming, matrix algebra, combinatorial probability. (4 semester hours)

Introduction to Calculus with Applications

A short course in calculus; introduction to derivatives and integrals with applications. (4 semester hours)

Quantitative Methods

Introduction to differential and integral calculus and matrix algebra; systems of linear equations, quantitative methods for treating problems in managerial and social sciences. (4 semester hours)

Calculus I

Fundamental concepts, methods, and techniques of single-variable differential and integral calculus. This is to be regarded as the first semester of a one-year course in basic calculus. (4 semester hours)

Calculus II

A continuation of the above course. Topics include applications of the integral, sequences and series, conic sections and a brief introduction to multivariable calculus. (4 semester hours)

Introduction to Linear Algebra

Presents the fundamental concepts, methods, and techniques of linear algebra. Topics include the solutions of systems of linear equations, matrices and determinants, vectors in 2-space and 3-space, general vector spaces, and linear transformations. (4 semester hours)

Elements of Group Theory

Introduction to abstract or modern algebra with emphasis on the theory of groups. Covers basic aspects of group theory: subgroups, homomorphisms and normal subgroups, factor groups, direct products, and the symmetric group. Enough theory is developed to give a complete description of all finite abelian (commutative) groups. (3 semester hours)

Fundamental Properties of Spaces and Functions

This course thoroughly covers a few of the basic concepts from calculus, such as continuity, the convergence of sequences, and series of functions. Emphasis is placed on the development of the student's ability to handle definitions, theorems, and proofs. (3 semester hours)

Foundations of Geometry

This course has been organized in a modern way to offer the opportunity of learning geometry in an interesting context that at the same time provides powerful methods and techniques for continuing the study of geometry, algebra, and other branches of mathematics. It is also designed with due account of students who are or who plan to be teachers. (3 semester hours)

History of Mathematics

Introduction to the history of mathematics. The majority of the course covers topics from elementary and high school mathematics: counting and arithmetic, Euclidean geometry, elementary algebra, trigonometry, and analytic geometry. The history of these topics should be of particular interest to teachers of elementary and secondary school mathematics. Also discusses development of calculus and its flowering in the eighteenth century, and more recent topics of modern mathematics, including non-Euclidean geometry, abstract algebra, and modern analysis. (3 semester hours)

NURSING

Human Development and Behavior

An overview of human developmental theories from a lifespan perspective. Examination of cognitive, physical, and personality development from prenatal life to old age, stressing the role of developmental process on the health and illness continuum. (3 semester hours)

Adult Development and Aging

Designed to complete the Human Development Lifespan course requirement for students who have already had a child-adolescent development class, this course focuses on physical, cognitive, and personality development in the adult and presents pressing social issues of the 1990s. (1 semester hour)

Human Sexuality

Provides an overview of human sexuality in modern American society,

216

focusing on the relationship between gender and sexuality, the ways in which society, including popular culture, constructs meaning for sexual acts and identities, and the interrelationship of sex and power. (3 semester hours)

Pathology

Introduction to the physiological and psychological disorders that commonly appear in the general population. Course emphasizes the changes that occur in the human organism when ill and some methods used to correct these changes. (4 semester hours)

NUTRITION

Nutrition

Principles of human nutrition. Designed for students in health-related fields, for teachers, and for those wishing to learn more about nutritional needs. (3 semester hours)

PHYSICAL EDUCATION

Perspectives on Leisure and Play

Investigates the general question of why people play by examining theoretical explanations for play based in the social science literature, the play behavior of people in social groups, and the social-psychological dynamics of play. Also considers how societies affect and are affected by play, the question of the good life, and social responsibility in relation to outdoor recreation (the environment as playground). (3 semester hours)

Environmental Issues in Recreation

Explores contemporary environmental issues, employing the concept of ecosystem as a springboard for analysis. Topics include population growth, land use, endangered species, pollution, and energy resources. Students encouraged to assess environmental impact of their own lifestyles. (3 semester hours)

Human Anatomy

Designed to familiarize students with body systems and the organs that are integrated into them. Covers functional aspects as well as disorders; use of correct anatomical terminology is stressed. (3 semester hours)

POLITICAL SCIENCE

The American Political System (Consent of the Governed)

Deals primarily with the national government of the United States; also discusses the relationship between the national government and the states. Studies the three branches of our government and examines the roles of various players. (3 semester hours)

Municipal Government and Politics

Designed to give insight into municipal government and politics in America in the last two decades of the twentieth century. Topics include the urban complex; urban leadership and pressure groups; elections and laws of municipalities; intergovernmental relationships; urban governmental structures; administration and finance; and urban functions and services. (3 semester hours)

American State Politics

Approaches to analysis of political behavior in American state governments with emphasis on cultures, parties, actors, processes, and issues. (3 semester hours)

PSYCHOLOGY

Elementary Psychology

Introduction to basic concepts in the study of behavior and to elementary principles of behavior. Topics include maturation, learning

and memory, thinking, emotion, perception, intelligence, personality, abnormal behavior, and attitudes. (3 or 4 semester hours)

Introduction Social Psychology

Introduction to theory and research in social psychology. After defining the realm of social psychology and the research methods used, the course covers such topics as attitude development and change, social thought, self-perception, emotion, attraction, pro- and antisocial behavior, conformity, obedience, group dynamics, social influence, and applied social psychology (environmental and health psychology). (3 semester hours)

Psychology in Business and Industry

Applications of psychology to problems in the world of work. Emphasis on personnel selection, training, attitudes, motivation, and measuring job performance. (3 semester hours)

Health Psychology

Introduction to psychological contributions to understanding etiology, prevention, and treatment of physical illness. Course covers such topics as the effects of stress on illness, personality traits and illness, the role of psychological interventions in the treatment of physical disease, and psychological adjustment to chronic illness. (3 semester hours)

Abnormal Psychology

Provides an introduction to the psychology of several types of abnormal behavior (e.g., emotional disorders, schizophrenias, developmental disorders). Course material describes each disorder, reviews research addressing causal factors, and evaluates therapies employed in treatment. (3 semester hours)

Behavior Modification

Provides an introduction to principles and procedures of behavior modification. This course has three major components. First, behavioral principles such as positive and negative reinforcement, extinction, punishment, and stimulus control are reviewed and their relevance for behavioral intervention is explained. Strategies for developing and evaluating behavioral interventions are then considered. The last part of the course teaches the student to integrate previous material to to develop comprehensive behavior change programs. (3 semester hours)

RELIGION

Religion and Society

Examines religious values as they appear in literature, science, politics, and art. An emphasis is given to contemporary culture and the ways in which the answers people give to questions of meaning have a religious dimension. Awareness will be enhanced concerning ways in which present-day culture has been influenced by religious traditions. (3 semester hours)

The Quest for Human Destiny (From Eden to 2001)

Within the frameworks of the biblical tradition (as is manifested in Genesis 1–3 and Ecclesiastes) and of ancient Near Eastern paganism (as manifested in "The Epic of Gilgamesh"), the course investigates certain "quests" for destiny, focusing primarily on the issue of human mortality. Novels by Hemingway, Hesse, Salinger, Arthur C. Clarke, Solzhenitsyn, and Edgar Rice Burroughs are considered in these frameworks to explore various responses to the perceived fundamental inadequacies of life. (3 semester hours)

Biblical Archaeology

An introduction to the archaeology of Palestine and Syria, with special attention given to the extent and type of contribution field archaeology can make to a more perceptive understanding of the Jewish and

Christian scriptures. Provides a close look at the nature, scope, and archaeological wealth of four important sites—Elba, Gezer, Qumran (Dead Sea Scrolls), and Masada. (1 semester hour)

The World of the Old Testament

Historical and intellectual background of the Old Testament; special attention given to common religious patterns in the ancient Near East, to their bearing on Israelite religion, and to their relevance for an informed contemporary understanding of the Bible; some focus on the major findings of biblical archaeology. (3 semester hours)

Prophecy in Biblical Israel

This course analyzes the prophetic movement in ancient Israel and its effect on the present from a literary, historical, and theological perspective. Although it celebrates the eighth century B.C.E. as the golden age of prophecy in biblical Israel, when Amos, Howa, Micah, and Isaiah of Jerusalem made their substantial contributions, it also considers the role of such prophets as Samuel and Elijah, who were their pioneeering predecessors, as well as the role of such prophets as Jeremiah and Ezekiel, who were their worthy successors. Moreover, the course examines the prophet's interaction with society, the forms and style of prophetic discourse, and the diverse insights regarding God, humanity, and the world that issued from both the spoken and written disclosures of biblical prophecy. (3 semester hours)

Religion and Women (Images of Women in the Bible)

Focuses on evidence of sexism and disavowals of sexism in the Bible through a comprehensive study of diverse biblical texts and their most recent interpretations. Topics include the portrayal of women in both narrative and non-narrative Old Testament texts. Jesus as a feminist, the role of women in the early church, and the relevance of the biblical tradition to the contemporary women's movement. (3 semester hours)

Literature and Philosophic Thought (The Holocaust)

An introduction to the Holocaust, the slaughter of over 6 million Jews by Nazi Germany, focusing on the historical and human dimensions of this tragic event. Readings include historical studies and several books of personal recollections and remembrances by survivors. The course examines the roots of European anti-Semitism, the systematic development of the Nazis' genocidal campaign against the Jews, the responses of the victims, the failure of the world to stop or mitigate the destruction, the effects of this unprecedented event on Jews and Judaism, and the need to reassess the human capacity for good and evil. (3 semester hours)

Introduction to Biomedical Ethics

The course provides the opportunity to develop an understanding of what ethics is and what some basic methods and procedures of ethics are. These methods and procedures are then applied to ethical problems in biomedicine. Among the topics considered are suicide, experiments with human subjects, patient confidentiality, and truth-telling. (3 semester hours)

Suffering, Death, and Faith

Examines contemporary thinking concerning our understanding of death and pain. Through assigned books, articles, and reflective writing assignments, the course asks you to evaluate your assumptions concerning suffering, death, and faith in order to better understand their mutual relationships and to reflect on how suffering transforms our understanding of the self; how awareness of death impacts self-identity; and what role faith can play in making death and suffering meaningful. The question of "health" is also explored. (3 semester hours)

RHETORIC

Accelerated Rhetoric

A freshman-level course in writing, speaking, reading, persuasion, and research that emphasizes performance, that is, learning by doing the assignments rather than by intensive study of theory. Students will do considerable writing about their own experience and considerable writing, reading, and speaking about a figure from public life. Speeches are given before assembled groups of family, friends, or associates and are recorded on audiocassette tape. (4 semester hours)

SOCIAL WORK

Introduction to Social Work

Social welfare as a social institution; settings and methodologies of social work practice; the profession of social work; historical development of American social welfare and social work. Students are encouraged to do volunteer work and are required to write a report on this work or on an approved alternative activity. A term paper may be substituted for the volunteer work or alternative activity. (4 semester hours)

Human Behavior in the Social Environment

This is a survey course, providing a foundation of knowledge concerning human behavior and development in the social and ecological systems. It includes an overview of social systemic theories, personality and life span development theories, and theories of psychosocial dysfunction. The course emphasizes theory as opposed to techniques or "how-to" exercises. (4 semester hours)

Multidisciplinary Perspectives on Aging

Focuses on important multidisciplinary perspectives on aging and on the functional assessment of older persons. The perspectives include social resources, economic resources, mental health status, physical health status, and activities of daily living. Attention is also given to services that are or should be available to respond to the needs of older persons. (3 semester hours)

Individual Study

Individual study on the subject of aging for those interested in an individualized readings course or in attending special continuing education workshops or conferences on aging. (variable semester hours)

Selected Aspects of Social Work and Social Welfare (Sexual Health in Later Life)

Examines current knowledge about the ways that biological, sociological, and psychological aspects of aging affect sexual interest and functioning in the older adult. Explores both the dimensions of sexuality as experienced by the older person and the sociocultural factors that bear upon sexual expression in later life. The course should be of particular interest to those studying and working in the field of aging, those who provide care to the elderly, and older adults themselves. As part of the course work, students are required to visit a nursing home or other long-term care facility to assess how conducive its environment is in respecting and meeting the sexual needs of its residents. (3 semester hours)

SOCIOLOGY

Introduction to Sociology: Principles

Examination of how individuals are organized into social groups, ranging from intimate groups to bureaucracies, and how these influence individual behavior; nature and interrelationships of basic social institutions such as family, education, religion, economy. (3 semester hours)

Theory, Research, and Statistics

This course focuses on the use of theories in sociology and the several research techniques and strategies sociologist typically make use of. Students will read a representative set of original theoretical writing, examine five central research approaches, and conduct a modest piece of sociological research. (3 semester hours)

Criminology

An introductory survey of criminology covering topics such as the incidence and distribution of crime; methods of studying crime and crime-related phenomena; types of crime; theories of crime causation; and societal reactions to crime. (3 semester hours)

Juvenile Delinquency

Traces the development of the American juvenile justice system with an emphasis on the "social construction of reality," i.e., changing definitions of childhood and delinquency from medieval times to the present. An overview of criminology theories whether delinquency is the result of biology, psychology, disorganized community, lack of conventional attachments, the envy of "have nots," labeling, or capitalism. Teenage suicide is linked to delinquency by a participant observation study which examines the lives of disaffected teenagers in a white middle-class suburb. (3 semester hours)

The American Family

Provides study over such topics as historical perspectives on the family, courtship, the husband-wife relationship, the role of children, the relationship of family with other societal institutions, and potential changes in and policy issues regarding the family. (3 semester hours)

SPANISH

Elementary Spanish I

A course for those who have studied no Spanish or for those whose contact with the language took place so long ago that they must start over. The primary objective is to learn to understand, read, and write Spanish. (4 semester hours)

Elementary Spanish II

Continues training in the four basic skills of reading, writing, comprehension, and speaking. (4 semester hours)

Intensive Elementary Reading Spanish

A basic beginning course for those who desire a reading knowledge of Spanish. Does not include training in writing, speaking, and listening comprehension. (3 semester hours)

Intermediate Spanish I

First half of second-year college Spanish. Provides both oral and written exercises to continue training in basic foreign language reading, writing, and oral comprehension. (4 semester hours)

Intermediate Spanish II

Second half of second-year college Spanish. Provides oral and written exercises to continue training in basic foreign language reading, writing, and oral comprehension. (4 semester hours)

STATISTICS

Introduction to Statistical Methods

Analysis and interpretation of research data, descriptive statistics (frequency distribution, central tendency, variability), introduction to statistical inference (normal curve sampling, theory, simple t-test), introduction to correlation and linear regression. Although illustrative material is drawn mainly from the fields of education and psychology, most of the statistical techniques presented have general applicability to other content areas. (3 semester hours)

THEATRE

Basic Playwriting

The purpose is to provide a basic understanding of playwriting techniques and to identify the student's playwriting talent. Eight carefully structured assignments provide analysis and practice of these techniques in writing a one-act play. (3 semester hours)

Advanced Playwriting

This course provides detailed discussion and critique of playwright's work at advanced level. The course may be taken twice, once for advanced work on a one-act play and a second time for work on a full-length play. (3 semester hours)

Shakespeare

Study of twelve of Shakespeare's plays, including works of comedy, history, tragedy, and romance. (3 semester hours)

WOMEN'S STUDIES

Religion and Women (Images of Women in the Bible)

Focuses on evidence of sexism and disavowals of sexism in the Bible through a comprehensive study of diverse biblical texts and their most recent interpretations. Topics include the portrayal of women in both narrative and non-narrative Old Testament texts, Jesus as a feminist, the role of women in the early church, and the relevance of the biblical tradition to the contemporary women's movement. (3 semester hours)

Women, Medicine, and Society

This course examines the topics of women as healers and health care personnel and women as patients and recipients of health care. It considers the impact of ideas about women's biological and social roles in particular historical and cultural settings on women as patients and health care providers. It also considers differences in class, ethnicity and sexuality and various alternatives in the healing process. Course takes an interdisciplinary approach, using historical, anthropological, fictional, biographical, and autobiographical source material. (3 semester hours)

Women's Roles: A Cross-Cultural Perspective

Social, economic, and political roles of women around the world; an analysis of sex roles with emphasis on culture change and implications for the lives of women in various societies. (3 semester hours)

Regional Women Writers (Southern Women Writers)

This course introduces the following writers and their fiction: Kate Chopin, Zora Neale Hurston, Ellen Glasgow, Carson McCullers, Flannery O'Connor, Anne Tyler, and Gail Godwin. (3 semester hours)

Women in Literature (Representative Women Writers)

Novels include *Emma* (Austen), *Villette* (C. Brontë), *Adam Bede* (Eliot), *Barren Ground* (Glasgow), *The House of Mirth* (Wharton), *Mrs. Dalloway* (Woolf), *The Golden Notebook* (Lessing). Also stories by Katherine Mansfield. (3 semester hours)

Changing Concepts of Women in Literature

Complexities in the treatment of women in literature of the nineteenth and twentieth centuries in works by both men and women authors: seven novels, four plays. *Jane Eyre* (C. Brontë), *Middlemarch* (Eliot), *The Bostonians* (James), *Jude the Obscure* (Hardy), *Howards End* (Forster), *The Awakening* (Chopin), *To the Lighthouse* (Woolf). Plays by Shaw and Ibsen. (3 semester hours)

Prose by Women Writers: Feminist Fiction

Traces the development of the feminist novel from the late eighteenth century to today. By reading a variety of feminist novels, students will explore how the writers integrate a specific political message into fiction and the different forms and approaches possible for the feminist novel. (3 semester hours)

WRITING

Nonfiction Writing

Course consists of 10 writing assignments, moving in sequence from exploratory essays with emphasis on discovery (a series of sketches) into increasingly complex, analytical, and revised essays. Assignments enable students to explore, explain, and reflect on personal experiences and philosophies. Students analyze rhetorical situations and develop appropriate styles and formats to meet the needs of specified readers. (3 semester hours)

Writing for Practical Purposes

Designed for those who are now, or will be, required to write at work. The course takes a practical approach to technical writing and aims to give confidence in approaching any writing project. The student will be asked to write with the audience as a primary consideration, and to consider purpose, pertinent information (written and graphic), persuasive strategies, organization, and clarity of prose. (3 semester hours)

Personal Writing

Using one's own life as raw material, the student will write and revise a literary letter, a memoir, a portrait, and a personal essay. The student will be introduced to and practice some technical skills that will help to make writing more mature and professional. (3 semester hours)

Creative Writing

An introduction to the process and methods of creating poems and stories. Exercises are offered to stimulate the novice writer; written work is critiqued by a participant in the University of Iowa's internationally known Writer's Workshop. (3 semester hours)

Writing for Business and Industry

Using a case study method, this course explores a wide range of situations and problems encountered when one writes in a business and professional setting. (3 semester hours)

Fiction Writing

For writers who are something more than beginners but less than experienced fictionists. (3 semester hours)

Advanced Fiction Writing

A course for writers with some experience. Students will complete 40 to 65 pages of fiction and do two 3- to 5-page story analyses. James Joyce's *Dubliners* will be used as a textbook. (3 semester hours)

Advanced Fiction Writing II

A course for experienced writers ready to design their own course of instruction. (3 semester hours)

Poetry Writing

Provides the writer with tools that will make writing poems a more rewarding experience. The writing and reading assignments stimulate thinking about poetry and provide skills that will help in exploring forms of poetry. (3 semester hours)

Advanced Poetry Writing

An intensive course in the issues and techniques of poetry writing. Explores strategies for reaching the poetic imagination through image, drama, and form. (3 semester hours)

Johnson Bible College
Correspondence Department
7900 Johnson Drive
Knoxville, Tennessee 37998   (615) 573-4517

Description:

The Johnson Bible College correspondence department offers both credit and noncredit courses. Correspondence study preceded residence study at Johnson Bible College. Ashley S. Johnson began teaching Bible by correspondence in 1886, seven years before he opened the residence college. The correspondence department has been in continuous existence, however, only since 1951, while the residence college has been in continuous existence since 1893.

Home study courses are designed with the following purposes in mind: (1) to enable Christian workers, elders, deacons, teachers, and preachers to grow and be more useful in the Lord's work; (2) to provide continuing education for mature Christian men and women who share the conviction that an individual may acquire new knowledge, understanding, attitudes, and skills as far as span of years permits; (3) to help Bible college students earn credits toward a degree, especially students who have to drop out of school temporarily, who have classroom scheduling conflicts, or who wish to accelerate their progress toward a degree by taking additional correspondence work either during or between school years. A student cannot earn a degree, a diploma, or be ordained through the correspondence department.

Faculty:

Robert E. Black, Director of Correspondence Study; Joel F. Rood, Registrar. There is a faculty of 4.

Academic Levels:
College
Noncredit

Degree/Certificate Programs:

Certificates are issued for each course completed and any credits earned are recorded on the student's official transcript. A maximum of 18 credits may be applied toward a degree at Johnson Bible College. All courses may be taken either for credit or noncredit. Normally, a student on noncredit status is not required to take a supervised final examination or to write a research paper.

Admission Requirements:

Open admission. The prospective student should submit an application form, fee, a recent photograph, and a 500-word handwritten autobiography. The photograph and personal information are for the benefit of the correspondence instructor to help give personalized instruction. The biographical information is treated confidentially and should include such information as age, education, occupation, marital status, personal ambitions, reasons for taking correspondence study, religious background, special interests, abilities, and any other personal data that the applicant thinks may be important to the instructor.

Tuition:

$65 per credit hour plus a nonrefundable enrollment fee of $10 for each course is to be paid in advance. There are no provisions for delayed payments. Tuition and fees subject to change without notice; contact the college for current information.

Enrollment Period:

The minimum time for completion of any course is eight weeks; the maximum time is twelve months. If at the end of the twelve-month period the course is not completed due to extenuating circumstances, the student may request an extension any time during the next three months. The maximum time for the extension is six months from the twelve-month expiration date. In no case will more than one extension be granted, nor will more than a total of eighteen months be allowed to complete a course. There is a $5 per month fee charged for extension of the time limit. Refunds of tuition fees are made if the request for a refund is received within thirty days of enrollment and if the correspondence materials are returned unused. An administrative fee of $10 is made in the event a refund is granted. The enrollment fee of $10 is nonrefundable. After thirty days all fees are nonrefundable.

Equipment Requirements:

The tuition fee includes the expenses of supplies such as envelopes and lesson materials as well as first class postage on materials sent to the student. Postage is not paid by the College on materials sent by the student. The cost of textbooks is not included in the tuition. Textbooks can be ordered from the publisher or from the College Bookstore.

Credit and Grading:

Final examinations for all courses taken for credit must be supervised by appropriate personnel (local college, professor, or minister). The student informs the correspondence instructor of the name and address of the person who will supervise the examination and the appropriate material and instructions will be sent to that person. There may be a fee (often $5) required for supervising the final examination and this must be the responsibility of the student. The following grading scale is used for all courses, both credit and noncredit: A, 98-100; A minus, 95-97; B plus, 92-94; B, 88-91; B minus, 85-87; C plus, 82-84; C, 78-81; C minus, 75-77; D plus, 72-74; D, 68-71; D minus, 65-67; F, 0-64. Number grades are given on examinations; letter grades given as a grade for the course. Minimum passing grade is 65 (D minus). Credits are awarded in semester hour units.

Accreditations:

Southern Association of Colleges and Schools; American Association of Bible Colleges.

COLLEGE COURSES

BIBLE

Bible Survey

This course acquaints the student with every book in the Bible. It consists of fifty lessons which alternate between the Old and the New Testaments. The lessons are based upon the content of the Bible. (3 semester hours)

Geography and Archaeology

An examination of Biblical geography and archaeology from earliest Bible times to the Bible lands of today. The student forms an acquaintance with the rivers, mountains, deserts, countries, empires, and people of the Bible. The main archaeological discoveries are studied as they relate to particular times and places. (2 semester hours)

Pentateuch

This study of the first five books of the Old Testament lays the foundation for more detailed expositional studies that are to follow. The course will provide an outlined overview and survey of this important revelation about origins. (3 semester hours)

History of Israel

This study examines the record of Israel's formation as a nation and notes their conquests and defeats, religious highs and lows, and their ultimate role as a chosen people of God. This study of Joshua through Esther provides the background for understanding other Bible studies. (3 semester hours)

History of the Hebrew Prophets

A detailed examination of the Biblical record in the books of the Hebrew Prophets. The student acquaints himself with the prophetic institution and investigates the background and content of the prophetic message from Jonah through Malachi. Careful attention is focused on the Messianic theme. (3 semester hours)

Old Testament Poetry

A study of poetry in the Old Testament with special attention being given to the major poetical books. An introduction to the style and composition of Hebrew Poetry is presented. The primary emphasis is placed on understanding the essential religious context of Job, Psalms, Proverbs, Song of Solomon, Ecclesiastes, and Lamentations. (3 semester hours)

Introduction to the Old Testament

A study designed to determine the date, authorship, and purpose of every book in the Old Testament. Attention is given to the preservation of the text and the formation of the canon. Special consideration is given to forming the answer to negative literary criticism. (2 semester hours)

Jesus and His Ministry

This study is designed to survey the life of Jesus. It will include an overview of the four gospels and emphasize the history and nature of His ministry. (3 semester hours)

Acts

A study of the early history, worship, organization, mission, and message of the church of the New Testament through an exegetical approach to the Acts of the Apostles. (3 semester hours)

John

A detailed study of the Gospel of John. Attention is focused on the Deity of Jesus and his miraculous ministry as recorded by John. (2 semester hours)

Exposition of Hebrews

A study of the meaning, doctrinal value, and historical setting of the New Testament Epistle to the Hebrews. (2 semester hours)

Romans

This course is designed especially for those who have had no special training in the Greek language. A detailed explanation of the Letter is the primary objective. The study will offer the student a splendid summary of all of the teaching of the Apostle Paul. (2 semester hours)

Introduction to the New Testament

A study designed to determine the date, authorship, and purpose of every book in the New Testament. The text and canon of the New Testament form an important part of this course. A diagnosis of the synoptic problem and a refutation of destructive critics are major concerns in this study. (2 semester hours)

Epistles

A detailed textual study of each of the New Testament letters from I Corinthians through II Thessalonians. The aim of the course is to acquire a knowledge of the text of these letters along with the historical evidences surrounding them and to review all the major doctrines of the scriptures that find their fullest expression in these writings. (3 semester hours)

Epistles and Revelation

A detailed textual study of I and II Timothy, Titus, Philemon, James, I and II Peter, and III John, Jude, and Revelation. The aim of the course is to acquire a knowledge of the text of these letters along with the historical evidences surrounding them and to review all the major doctrines that find their fullest expression in these writings. (3 semester hours)

CHRISTIAN EDUCATION

The Educational Program of the Church

This is a study of the history of the Bible School with an emphasis on how it began, its importance in the light of God's Word, the relative importance of the teacher, the student, the Word of God, and the Christ in the program of Christian Education. (2 semester hours)

CHURCH HISTORY

Restoration Movement

This course has to do with the Movement to restore the church after the New Testament pattern. It deals mainly with the life and labors of Alexander Campbell, but it also treats the work of the Haldanes, Walter Scott, Barton Stone, Thomas Campbell, James O'Kelly, and others. The course will demonstrate how essential the First Century Church is in every Twentieth Century Community. (2 semester hours)

Introduction to Missions

This course is an introduction to the whole scope of missionary endeavors. Its focus is on the world and how missionaries may function as evangelists in cross-cultural conditions. (2 semester hours)

ENGLISH

Introduction to Linguistics

A survey of the major subject areas of the discipline, including phonetics and phonemics, morphology and syntax, phonology and discourses. This study also surveys language types and linguistic groups, as well as major nonstandard dialects of English. The orientation is toward the practical use of linguistics in language teaching and learning. (2 semester hours)

Structure of the English Language

A review of the grammatical structures of the language. Some attention will also be devoted to the study of sound-formation in the major language groups of the world. (3 semester hours)

TESOL

A foundation course which trains students to *Teach English to Speakers of Other Languages*, i.e., in cross-cultural settings. Focus is on theory during the first half of the term and on practice in the second

half. Attention is given to the development and assessment of materials and methods of language teaching, as well as to the theory of testing of language competence and performance, with emphasis on the construction of testing instruments. The program also includes practice in tutoring non-native speakers of English, under college supervision. (5 semester hours)

HISTORY

American History I

A study of the social, political, economic, and cultural developments of the United States from the era of exploration and settlement through the Civil War. (3 semester hours)

American History II

A continuation of the above course. A study of the development of the United States following the Civil War to the present time. (3 semester hours)

MUSIC

Music Appreciation

This course is designed to acquaint the student having limited or no musical training with the fundamentals of musical notation and literature. Various historical periods, composers, and forms of music will be introduced. Some consideration will be given to the analysis of current musical trends within Western youth culture, and their effects upon contemporary Christian thought and behavior. (2 semester hours)

PASTORAL MINISTRIES

Church Administration

The organization of the local church to accomplish the mission addressed to the church by Christ is the primary consideration of this course. This is a study of the local church in its relation to evangelism, missions, stewardship, worship, education, membership development. (2 semester hours)

Introduction to Preaching

This course is an introduction to the basic fundamentals of sermon construction. Primary attention is given to the traditional deductive sermon format. The value of expository preaching is affirmed and a high view of Scripture is asserted. (3 semester hours)

THEOLOGY

Christian Doctrine

A study of the church with Old Testament backgrounds and New Testament fulfillment. (2 semester hours)

Systematic Theology

A study about God, the Bible, man, angels, salvation, the life of Christ, the Church, the second coming of Christ, the millenium, and the final state. (3 semester hours)

Apologetics

This is a study of the evidences of Christianity. By this study one is enabled to meet the attacks of infidels, critics, and unbelievers. Three Biblical subjects—the Creation, the Resurrection, and the Judgment—are thoroughly analyzed and the major attacks against them are answered. (2 semester hours)

Kansas, University of
Independent Study by Correspondence
Continuing Education Building
Lawrence, Kansas 66045   (913) 864-4792

Description:
Independent Study is a unit of the Division of Continuing Education at the University of Kansas. The Extension Division was formally organized in 1909 and has been operating continuously to the present. Although Independent Study is located at Lawrence and is a part of the University of Kansas, it is a statewide service mandated by the Kansas Board of Regents to serve the correspondence study needs of all Kansans. The other Regents universities taking part in this program are: Emporia State, Fort Hays State, Kansas State, Pittsburg State, and Wichita State.

Independent Study offers college courses that are similar in content to in-residence courses. Credit earned through Independent Study is transferable to other institutions and is widely accepted toward degrees. Most instructors of college courses are regular faculty members at one of the Kansas Regents universities, and in many cases they have written the study guides for the courses they instruct.

The College for High School program is designed for qualified students who wish to remain in their local high schools for four years but are prepared to pursue more advanced courses. The program allows high school juniors and seniors who have completed the necessary prerequisites to enroll in freshman and sophomore college courses with the approval of their high school principals or counselors. With permission of the high school, both high school and college credit may be obtained for the same course.

Faculty:
Nancy Colyer, Director, Independent Study; Sandra Hick, Manager, Student Services.

Academic Levels:
College
High School

Degree/Certificate Programs:
Correspondence credits applicable toward baccalaureate degree programs vary in number from 6 to 30 semester hours with the individual schools of the university. The university does not grant graduate-level credit for correspondence courses. Any course may be taken on a noncredit basis without special permission.

Admission Requirements:
College: High school graduation; completion of prerequisite courses. College for High School Program: approval of counselor or principal; prerequisites. Enrollment in an Independent Study course does not constitute official admission to resident programs at any of the seven Regents institutions.

Tuition:
$79 per semester hour. Postage and handling fee of $25 for each course. An additional charge of $18 per course is assessed for instructional materials. VISA and MasterCard accepted. A partial refund of course fees may be granted within six weeks after registration: the tuition fee, less $20 for registration and $5 for each corrected assignment. No refund is made for the instructional materials or postage fees. U.S. Armed Forces veterans and their dependents may be eligible for Veterans Administration assistance in financing Independent Study programs.

Enrollment Period:
Maximum time for completion of a course is nine months from the date of enrollment. A three-month extension can be granted upon payment of $30 fee. If the course is not completed at the end of the regular nine-month period and no extension has been secured before the expiration date, the student's enrollment in Independent Study will revert to an inactive status and will not be reinstated.

Equipment Requirements:
Some courses require use of computer diskettes and video- or audiotapes. These items are provided for each course requiring them at additional cost to the student. Textbooks are furnished by the student. Kansas residents will be charged the appropriate state sales tax.

Credit and Grading:
Supervised examinations must be proctored at an educational institution that is approved by Independent Study. The University of Kansas, in cooperation with the other six state schools, has arranged statewide examination centers for courses taken for college credit. Specific dates are set at designated testing centers, and tests are sent to the examination supervisors on request of the student. Out-of-state students may arrange to take examinations with the continuing education department, testing center, or central administrative office of a college or university in the vicinity of the student's home.

In every course for which a final examination is required, the examination must be passed in order to pass the course. Grading system is A, B, C, D, F. The minimum passing grade is D. Credit is awarded in semester hour units. Any course may be taken on a noncredit basis without special permission. Students at the University of Kansas may enroll for courses on a credit/no credit basis.

Library Services:
Independent Study students can access KU's online catalog of library holdings from computer terminals in the libraries or by remote microcomputer access to KU's campus computer network.

Accreditations:
North Central Association of Colleges and Schools. Member of: National University Continuing Education Association.

COLLEGE COURSES

AFRICAN AMERICAN STUDIES

The Black Experience in the Americas

An interdisciplinary study of the history of the African peoples of the New World, relating their cultures and institutions to the African background and to their particular reference to the U.S.A., the Caribbean, and Latin America. Topics covered include slavery, the aftermath of slavery,migration, urbanization, decolonization, civil rights and messianic movements, religion, folk culture, and the arts. (3 semester hours)

AMERICAN STUDIES

American Society

The social structure and organization of American society with special reference to long-term and recent social changes. (3 semester hours)

ANTHROPOLOGY

Fundamentals of Physical Anthropology

ANTH 104c. Covers the mechanisms and principles of Darwinian evolution with special emphasis on human and primate data. Includes genetics, variation, primate ethology, and the fossil evidence for human evolution. Mendelian and population genetics, blood group systems, quantitative morphological variation, and fossil human and primate skeletal material. (4 semester hours

ANTH 304c. A more intensive treatment than the above course. (4 semester hours)

Introduction to Cultural Anthropology

ANTH 108c. An introduction to the nature of culture, language, society, and personality. Included in this survey are some of the major principles, concepts, and themes of cultural anthropology. The variety of ways in which people structure their social, economic, political, and personal lives. Emphasized are the implications of overpopulation, procreative strategies, progress and growth of cultural complexity, developments in the Third World, and cultural dynamics in Western, as well as non-Western societies. (4 semester hours)

ANTH 308c. Same content as above course with a requirement for a research project. (4 semester hours)

Myth, Legend, and Folk Belief in East Asia

A survey of the commonly held beliefs about the beginning of the world, the role of the gods and spirits in daily life, and the celebrations and rituals proper to each season. This course presents the world view of the ordinary peoples of East Asia in contrast to their more sophisticated systems of philosophy, which are better known to the Western world. This course requires the use of audiotapes. (3 semester hours)

ART HISTORY

Introduction to Art History

Course 100c. An introduction to art and architecture in Western culture. Basic principles and problems of the visual arts are analyzed, as are the major historical trends and periods. Style, content, and cultural background are discussed and illustrated on videotape. (3 semester hours)

Course 300c. Upper-level equivalent of Course 100c. (3 semester hours)

Impressionism

A study of the development of the Impressionist style in France in the nineteenth century. The theories and techniques of Degas, Cassatt, Manet, Monet, Morisot, Pissarro, and Renoir are emphasized, though lesser-known Impressionist artists are not neglected. The impact of Impressionism on the currents of modern art is examined. (3 semester hours)

BIOLOGY

Principles of Biology

Introduces basic concepts of biology at the cellular, organismal, and population levels of organization and their applications to humans and modern society. Unifying themes include evolution, the relationship of structure to function, and laws of biological systems. (3 semester hours)

Principles of Human Physiology

Intended for students majoring in allied health curricula that require a course in human physiology, as well as those students not majoring in a science who desire some knowledge of physiology as a part of their general education. (3 semester hours)

Human Sexuality

An introduction to the field of human sexuality from a biological and physiological perspective. Topics include sexual anatomy and physiology, fertilization, pregnancy, birth and lactation, contraception, human sexual response, sexuality across the life cycle, alternatives to parenthood, sexually transmitted diseases, sexual dysfunction, and sex and the law. (3 semester hours)

BUSINESS

Supervisory Management

This course introduces and describes the supervisor's managerial functions in the organization. The primary focus is on first-level management and the link that supervisors provide between workers and management. Topics include understanding the role of supervision, applying supervisory management and communication skills, and developing an effective work environment. (3 semester hours)

CLASSICAL STUDIES

Greek and Roman Mythology

systematic examination of the traditional cycles of Greek myths and their survival and metamorphosis in Latin literature. Some attention is given to the problems of comparative mythology and the related areas of archaeology and history. No knowledge of Latin or Greek is required. (3 semester hours)

Word Power: Greek and Latin Elements in English

A study of English words drawn from Greek and Latin with attention to the needs of students of science and others interested in the sources of the English vocabulary. (3 semester hours)

COMMUNICATIONS

Introduction to Intercultural Communication

Focuses on communication as it affects culture and is affected by culture. Special emphasis on similarity and differences as they relate to the roles of verbal and nonverbal symbols, codes, and cues, stereotypes, prejudices and values, and thought patterning systems between and among cultures. (3 semester hours)

Introduction to Organizational Communication

Provides a foundation for the study of communication in organizational contexts. Introduces various organizational theories including classical, human relations, systems, and cultural approaches and examines the role of communication in each. Information flow, communication climate, communication networks, work relationships, and managerial communication are discussed, as well as organizational symbolism, conflict resolution, rituals, and ethics. Designed to heighten students' awareness of the role of communication in the organizing process and to develop their abilities to diagnose and prevent communication-related problems. (3 semester hours)

The Loving Relationship

Love as a quality of experience between persons. Focuses on the nature of the love relationship with attention to religious literature, values and traditions, popular literature and media, and some social and behavioral sciences. Analyzes various types of binding contracts characterized as loving: friendship, marriage, family, social and political units. Considers such concepts as caring, commitment, self-denial, sexuality, agape, pacifism, loyalty, and responsibility. (3 semester hours)

EAST ASIAN LANGUAGES AND CULTURES

Myth, Legend, and Folk Belief in East Asia

A survey of the commonly held beliefs about the beginning of the world, the role of the gods and spirits in daily life, and the celebrations and rituals proper to each season. This course presents the world view of the ordinary peoples in East Asia in contrast to their more sophisticated systems of philosophy which are better known to the Western world. (3 semester hours)

ECONOMICS

Introductory Economics

A nonanalytical introduction to modern economics. Emphasis on elements of economic history, the operation of economic institutions, and the formation and execution of economic policies to meet the current problems of the domestic and international economy. (4 semester hours)

EDUCATION

Teaching Reading in the Content Areas

A study of the teaching of developmental reading in the middle and secondary school. Emphasis on analysis of the reading process, with attention to such psychological factors as readiness and individual differences. Identification of basic reading skills and methods of teaching them in such subjects as language arts, social sciences, mathematics, and science. (3 semester hours)

Teaching Literature for Young Adults (Grades 7–12)

Teaching literature (novel, short story, poetry, drama, nonfiction) suitable for students in the middle school, the junior high school, and the senior high school. Ethnic literature, censorship, bibliographies, and other sources of information about books for young adults will be studied. (3 semester hours)

Foundations of Curriculum and Instruction

Basic concepts and processes of curriculum and instruction, including theories, planning models, resources for decision making, current trends, research, and proposals for improvement of curriculum and instruction. (3 semester hours)

Foundations of Education

A historical approach to the major social and philosophical foundations of American education, with an emphasis on the relation of educational theory to classroom practice. (3 semester hours)

EDUCATIONAL PSYCHOLOGY

Principles of Human Learning

An introduction to theories of human learning, motivation, and psychological and physical development that are relevant to the educational process. Theories and principles will be considered in relation to instructional strategies and skills. Atypical patterns of development will be considered. The course includes a variety of instructional activities and appropriate field experiences. (3 semester hours)

Communication and Classroom Management: Theory and Skills

Increases students' self-awareness, skill in communicating and awareness of classroom-management models and techniques. Individuals who are considering enrolling should note that this course requires classroom observation activities in school settings. (3 semester hours)

ENGLISH

Composition

Formal instruction and required practice in the basic modes of rhetorical development and argument. (3 semester hours)

Composition and Literature

An introduction to the major genres and critical approaches to literature, with continued practice in composition. (3 semester hours)

The Literature of Sports

Examines various topics and themes in the literature of sports. Focuses on the athlete in and outside sports and on the progress of teams as well as the individual athlete. Continued practice in composition. (3 semester hours)

Introduction to Fiction

The study of prose fiction—British, American, and other—with emphasis on the critical analysis of masterpieces of the genre, involving a variety of fictional types from different historical periods. (3 semester hours)

Introduction to Poetry

The appreciation and understanding of selected masterpieces of American poetry. Attention is given to various poetic forms and techniques and the relationship between the poet's life and his or her works. This course requires the use of videotapes. (3 semester hours)

American Literature I

A chronological survey of American literature from its 17th-century beginnings to 1865, with emphasis on the major writers and movements. (3 semester hours)

American Literature II

A chronological survey of American literature from 1865 to the present. Focuses on the major writers and movements of the period, with emphasis on critical analysis of individual works. (3 semester hours)

Recent Popular Literature

Study of recent bestsellers and other works of popular interest. (3 semester hours)

Shakespeare

Introduces the student to fourteen of Shakespeare's plays. Written assignments stress interpretive ability, character analysis, drawing inferences, seeing relationships within and between plays. (3 semester hours)

Writing Fiction

Practice in the craft of fiction with experience in the popular, literary, and experimental short story. (3 semester hours)

Grammar and Usage for Composition

A course in traditional grammar and principles of formal usage for students who need additional practice or development of skill in composition. (3 semester hours)

Business Writing

Designed for people already working in business or in corporate communications departments, as well as college students. Emphasizes practical writing: memos, reports, letters, press releases, letters of application and resumes, and business proposals. (3 semester hours)

Technical Writing

A study of the general principles common to all technical writing and practical exercises in writing abstracts, reviews, letters, proposals, short reports, and long reports. (3 semester hours)

Literature for Children

Wide reading in the great literature of the past and present suitable for children: folk tales, literary fantasy, realistic fiction, poetry, the picture book. Emphasis on extending the student's background and developing critical judgment. (3 semester hours)

Directed Study

Each course listed below consists of informal commentary, exchange of questions and answers, and one sustained theme. Representative works by one of the authors listed. May be repeated for a total of up to 6 hours.

Willa Cather. An introduction to the life and themes of Willa Cather through a study of her major works. (1 or 2 semester hours)

Ernest Hemingway. An introduction to one of the most influential and celebrated writers of the 20th century. Concentrates primarily on the work that Hemingway produced in the 1920s and 1930s. (1 or 2 semester hours)

Kansas Literature

A study of the literature written by Kansans during the 19th and 20th centuries. Extensive introductions provide information on the history of Kansas as well as literary analyses of the works assigned and brief biographies of the writers. Among the themes explored in the course are the frontier and pioneering, the conflict between the material and the spiritual, the relationship of people with the land, the images of Kansas in literature. (3 semester hours)

FRENCH

French for Reading Knowledge

Special course for candidates for advanced degrees in other departments and for individuals who wish to gain a reading knowledge of French. Fundamentals of grammar and reading of material of medium difficulty. Presupposes no previous study of French. Students may choose between Option A, which stresses scholarly translation, and Option B, which emphasizes developing reading skills on current topics. (3 semester hours)

Elementary French I

Introduction to the French language with an emphasis on understanding and speaking in realistic, everyday circumstances. This course requires the use of video- and audiotapes. (5 semester hours)

Elementary French II

Promotes a proficiency in spoken French, while developing skills in listening comprehension, reading, and writing. This course requires the use of video- and audiotapes. (5 semester hours)

GEOGRAPHY

Principles of Physical Geography

Discusses the components of the physical environment; familiarizes students with the distribution and dynamic nature of these components.

Major topics include the atmosphere, landforms, soils, and vegetation together with their interrelationships and their relevance to human activity. (3 semester hours)

GERMAN

Elementary German I

Essentials of grammar, practice in speaking, reading, and writing German. This course requires the use of audiotapes. (5 semester hours)

Elementary German II

Continuation of grammar; practice in conversation, composition, and reading. This course requires the use of audiotapes. (5 semester hours)

HEALTH, PHYSICAL EDUCATION, AND RECREATION

The Coaching of Basketball

Theory of basketball, including methods of coaching fundamentals; individual and team defense and offense; various styles of play and methods of coaching. (2 semester hours)

Personal and Community Health

Emphasis on healthful and intelligent living and the application of the fundamental principles of health. (3 semester hours)

Environmental Health

Overview of the interrelationship between environmental systems and humans, and the impact of the ecosystem on the health of individuals and communities. Discusses air, water, noise, chemical, nuclear, and industrial pollutants, as well as occupationally related diseases, alternate energy sources, and the "new pollutants." (3 semester hours)

Principles of Nutrition and Health

Basic principles of human nutrition as they relate to growth and development of the child, and to the maintenance of health at all ages. (3 semester hours)

Introduction to Communicable and Degenerative Diseases

Emphasizes basic concepts and principles of human health and disease causations, control, and preventive measures. (3 semester hours)

Drugs in Society

This course is designed to provide an in-depth exposure to basic drug classification, pharmacological effects, causes of drug abuse to society, common treatment modalities, and effective prevention/treatment strategies. In addition, consumer issues related to drug use, drug legislation, and drug education programs for school and community implementation will be discussed. (3 semester hours)

Advanced Concepts in Communicable and Degenerative Diseases

Emphasizes concepts and principles of human health and disease causations, control, and preventive measures. (3 semester hours)

HISTORY

World History: An Introduction

A comparative analysis of major global developments from Neolithic to modern times, illustrating some of the basic applications of the social sciences to historical explanation. Emphasis on the origins of food production, urbanism, empire building, and the great ethical and religious systems; feudalism, commerce, capitalism and industry; colonialism, imperialism, and communism. (3 semester hours)

History of the United States Through the Civil War

Historical survey of the United States from the peopling of the continent through the Civil War. This survey is designed to reflect the diversity of the American experience, to offer the student a chronological perspective on the history of the United States, and to explore the main themes, issues, ideas, and events that shaped that history. (3 semester hours)

History of the United States After the Civil War

A historical survey of the American people from Reconstruction to the present. This survey is designed to reflect the diversity of the American experience, to offer the student a chronological perspective on the history of the United States, and to explore the main themes, issues, ideas, and events that shaped that history. (3 semester hours)

Hitler and Nazi Germany

An examination of the rise of Hitler and Nazism, beginning with the breakdown of 19th-century culture in the First World War and continuing through the failure of democracy under the Weimar Republic. Discusses the impact of Nazism on Germany and how Nazism led to the Second World War and the Holocaust. (3 semester hours)

Imperial Russia and the Soviet Union

The influence of the West and Marxism on the institutional structure and the international position of Russia. (3 semester hours)

History of the American Indian

A study of Indians in the United States from colonial times to the present. Consideration will be given to the political, social, and cultural history of selected Indian tribes and to Indian-white relations with particular attention to the Indian point of view. Other topics will include a comparative study of Indian policy of nations colonizing in America, cultural intermingling and cultural conflict, and current Indian problems. (3 semester hours)

History of Kansas

The forces that have shaped the development of the state from preterritorial times to the present. Discusses economic, political, and cultural trends. (3 semester hours)

HUMAN DEVELOPMENT AND FAMILY LIFE

Principles of Environmental Design and the Family

Focuses on interrelationships among the home, landscape, materials, and the individual. Students gain experience in evaluating house plans and furnishings. Develops appreciation for the problems involved in planning and furnishing a home. (3 semester hours)

Introduction to Child Behavior and Development

Presents basic information about child behavior now available and the modifiable range of developmental patterns in growth, intellectual development, and social development. (3 semester hours)

Principles of Nutrition and Health in Development

Basic principles of human nutrition as they relate to growth and development of the child, and to the maintenance of health at all ages. (3 semester hours)

Introduction to Marriage and Family Relationships

The development of personality in the family; the courtship process; tests of compatibility and prediction of successful marriage; parental roles and child development; family rituals and patterns of interaction. (3 semester hours)

Children and Television

Concerns children's use of the television medium and the effects of mass media on them and on society. The effects of educational and prosocial programs designed to teach academic or social skills will be considered as well as the effects of violence and crime in television programming. (3 semester hours)

Adult Development and Aging

Provides a multidisciplinary overview of biological, environmental, cultural, and economic influences on adult development and aging. (3 semester hours)

JOURNALISM

Introduction to Radio, Television, and Their New Technologies

A survey of the field from traditional, transmitted radio and television to the emerging new technologies such as satellites, cable TV, and teletext. Also included are a historical perspective, an overview of technology, and an examination of the social implications of the changing media environment. (3 semester hours)

Reporting I

The role of the reporter in communicating public intelligence. The fundamental principles of gathering and writing news; practice in reporting in the community. (3 semester hours)

School Journalism and Publications

A study of the use of publications in the teaching of secondary school journalism, and analysis of problems in supervising school newspapers, magazines, and yearbooks. Topics include legal and ethical issues, scheduling and budgets, staff organization, writing and editing, advertising, and evaluating student publications. (3 semester hours)

LATIN

Elementary Latin

The basic essentials of Latin. (5 semester hours)

Latin Reading and Grammar

Latin grammar concluded, with selected readings. (5 semester hours)

Vergil's *Aeneid*

Extensive readings from Vergil's *Aeneid,* with a study of the place of this epic in literary history. Stresses the literary qualities of the *Aeneid.* (3 semester hours)

MATHEMATICS

Introductory Algebra

Designed for students who have not had at least one year of high school algebra. Presumes a good working knowledge of general mathematics, including addition, subtraction, multiplication, division, fractions, and decimals. (3 semester hours)

Intermediate Mathematics

Mathematics (primarily algebra) preparatory to the following course. (3 semester hours)

Algebra

Coordinate systems, functions, and their graphs; linear, quadratic, general polynomial, exponential, and logarithmic functions; equations and inequalities. (3 semester hours)

Trigonometry

The circular functions and their applications. (2 semester hours)

Precalculus Mathematics

An introduction to the elementary functions (polynomial, rational, exponential, logarithmic, and trigonometric) and their properties. (5 semester hours)

Mathematics for Elementary Teachers

This course is designed to give the prospective elementary schoolteacher an overview of the elementary mathematics curriculum, including probability, statistics, informal geometry, measurement, and using computers in the classroom. (3 semester hours)

Calculus I

Course 115c. Elementary differential and integral calculus, with applications to biological and social sciences. (3 semester hours)

Course 121c. Differentiation and integration of algebraic and trigonometric functions. Applications to physical sciences and engineering. (5 semester hours)

Calculus II

Continuation of *Course 115c* including exponential, logarithmic, and trigonometric functions, techniques of integration, and the calculus of functions of several variables. (3 semester hours)

METEOROLOGY

Introductory Meteorology

Introduces students to the atmospheric environment in which we live. Designed to give a better understanding of clouds, precipitation, wind systems, tornadoes, jet streams, weather forecasting and our atmosphere in general. (3 or 5 semester hours)

Unusual Weather

Designed for students with various backgrounds who are interested in understanding more about natural but unusual weather occurrences such as blizzards, hurricanes, tornadoes, and chinooks, as well as modified weather arising from urban air pollution or through the intentional activities of man such as cloud seeding. (3 semester hours)

MUSIC

Introduction to Jazz

A study of jazz in its beginning in the early 20th century to the present. (3 semester hours)

PHILOSOPHY

Introduction to Philosophy

An introductory examination, based primarily on writings of major philosophers, of such central philosophical problems as religious beliefs, the mind and its place in nature, freedom and determinism, morality, and the nature and kinds of human knowledge. (3 semester hours)

Reason and Argument

An introduction to the theory and practice of modern logical analysis. Special emphasis is placed on the logical appraisal of everyday arguments. (3 semester hours)

POLITICAL SCIENCE

Introduction to U.S. Politics

An introduction to basic American governmental institutions, political processes, and policy. (3 semester hours)

Introduction to Comparative Politics

An introduction to the comparative study of political systems emphasizing governmental structures, parties, electoral techniques, and recent trends in the field. The course also considers major differences between (1) representative and autocratic systems, and (2) developed and underdeveloped nations. (3 semester hours)

Introduction to Public Administration

Survey of public administration. Focuses on bureaucratic organizations, the democratic context of public organizations, bureaucratic politics, public management, personnel, budgeting, and intergovernmental relations. (3 semester hours)

U.S. Government and Politics

A survey of the political process, policy formation and organization of the national government in the United States. (3 semester hours)

PSYCHOLOGY

General Psychology

An introduction to the science of psychology. (3 semester hours)

Statistics in Psychological research

An introduction to statistical concepts and methods as they relate to the planning, execution, analysis, and interpretation of psychological research. (3 semester hours)

Cognitive Psychology

An introduction to contemporary research and theory in human learning and memory, relevant perceptual processes, and higher functions such as language. (3 semester hours)

Child Psychology

Psychological development of the child from conception to adolescence; emphasis on social and cognitive changes as they relate to intrapersonal changes and environmental conditions. (3 semester hours)

Social Psychology

An introduction to the psychology of social behavior with systematic consideration of such concepts as social influence, conformity and deviation, social attitudes and prejudice, socialization and personality, communication and propaganda, morale, and leadership. (3 semester hours)

Brain and Behavior

Introduces the basics of brain organization and describes the brain's microcomponents, in terms of the structure and function of individual cells and their chemical environments. Develops a conceptual framework for discussion of sensation, movement, homeostasis, biorhythms, emotion, learning, memory, thinking, consciousness, and abnormal behavior. Videotapes are utilized in this course. (3 semester hours)

The Mind

Introduces many of the recent discoveries about the mind and the brain. The course focuses on the mental activities that distinguish humans from other living creatures and that may be based on the unique capacities of the human mind. Videotapes are utilized in this course. (3 semester hours)

Children and Television

Concerns children's use of the television medium and the effects of mass media on them and on society. The effects of educational prosocial programs designed to teach academic or social skills are considered, as well as the effects of violence and crime in television programming. (3 semester hours)

Human Sexuality

An introduction to the field of human sexuality from a biological and physiological perspective. Topics include sexual anatomy and physiology, fertilization, pregnancy, birth and lactation, contraception, human sexual response, sexuality across the life cycle, alternatives to parenthood, sexually transmitted diseases, sexual dysfunction, and sex and the law. (3 semester hours)

Psychology and the Law

An application of psychological processes and concepts to the American legal system. Among the topics covered are the socialization of legal attitudes, opinions about the purposes of the criminal justice system and especially of prisons, the concept of ''dangerousness,'' the nature of jury decision making, and the rights of prisoners, patients, and children. (3 semester hours)

Psychology of Adolescence

Impact of factors of social environment and physical growth on psychological development from puberty to young adulthood. (3 semester hours)

The Psychology of Families

Study of the family as a psychosocial system. Emphasis is placed on factors affecting contemporary families including family structures, development, communication patterns, disorders, and treatment approaches. Theory, empirical evidence, and practical principles that may lead to maximizing individual growth in the family unit are discussed. (3 semester hours)

RELIGIOUS STUDIES

Living Religions of the West

An introduction to the major religious traditions of the Near East, Europe, and the Americas, with an emphasis on their development through the modern period and their expressions in contemporary life. (3 semester hours)

Understanding the Bible

An introduction to the literature of the Bible explaining the relationships among its various types of literature and the function of each type in the history and religious life of the people who produced and used them. (3 semester hours)

The Loving Relationship

Focuses on the nature of the love relationship with attention to religious literature, values and traditions, popular literature and media, and some social and behavioral sciences. Analyzes various types of binding contracts characterized as loving: friendship, marriage, family, social, and political units. Considers such concepts as caring, commitment, self-denial, sexuality, agape, pacifism, loyalty, and responsibility. (3 semester hours)

SOCIOLOGY

Elements of Sociology

The study of social life, including how human groups are organized, how they change, and how they influence individuals. Consideration is given to a variety of human organizations and social institutions and how these groups and institutions both determine, and are determined by, human beings. (3 semester hours)

Social Problems and American Values

Explores competing explanations for the causes of, and cures for, the enduring problems of American society. The course critically analyzes dominant definitions of social problems, the political and economic roots of these problems, and the public policies aimed at reducing them. (3 semester hours)

Introduction to Family Sociology

Analysis of the family as a social institution primarily in the U.S. context. Topics include current and historical changes in how the family is constituted, contrasting sociological theories of family relationships, sexuality in relation to family life, the coexistence of love and hate in families, family dissolution and reformation, and the care of children. A key theme is diversity: social class, gender, race/ethnicity, and age. (3 semester hours)

Principles of Sociology

An introduction to sociological concepts, methods, and substantive findings more intensive that provided in *Elements of Sociology*. (3 semester hours)

American Society

The social structure and organization of American society with special reference to long-term and recent social changes. (3 semester hours)

Sociology of Aging

An advanced survey of theory and research in social gerontology, giving primary attention to aging and the aged as affected by social organization, including such social institutions as familial, economic, political and health care; organizational processes such as social stratification; and living environments including community and housing. In these contexts, certain demographic, cross-cultural, social-psychological, and physiological aspects of aging will be considered. (3 semester hours)

SPANISH

Spanish Reading Course

A special course for candidates for advanced degrees designed to aid them in obtaining a reading knowledge of Spanish. Intensive study of the fundamentals of grammar, proceeding to the reading of materials of medium difficulty. Fulfills only graduate requirement of reading competency in a foreign language. (3 semester hours)

Elementary Spanish I

Introduction to the Spanish language. Equal emphasis on the development of the four skills—listening, speaking, reading, and writing—plus culture. (5 semester hours)

Elementary Spanish II

A continuation of the above course. (5 semester hours)

Intermediate Spanish I

Emphasis on reading and speaking Spanish. Basing their studies on modern Spanish and Spanish-American texts, students will be expected to do not only intensive but also extensive reading in Spanish, and to develop the ability to participate in oral discussion of the material read. A review and continuation of the study of grammar. (3 semester hours)

SPECIAL EDUCATION

Introduction to the Psychology and Education of Exceptional Children and Youth

Current practices in the identification, placement, and education of exceptional children and youth. Emphasis on patterns of social, cognitive, language, and physical development of exceptional children. Social, political, and economic advocacy issues. Individuals who are considering enrolling should note that this course requires observation activities in school settings. (3 semester hours)

Managing Behavior Problems: Concepts and Applications

Introduces principles of behavior analysis and assists in applying these principles in schools and service agencies. (2 or 3 semester hours)

SPEECH-LANGUAGE-HEARING: SCIENCES AND DISORDERS

Survey of Communication Disorders

Provides a general understanding of normal and deviant speech, language and hearing in adults and children. This course considers the normal development of communication behavior, the nature of communication disorders, and the interaction of speech pathology and audiology with allied fields (e.g., education, medicine, psychology, special education). (3 semester hours)

Language Development

Study of speech and language acquisition in children, including the phonologic, morphologic, syntactic, and semantic components. Methods of language measurement, the role of comprehension, and pragmatic aspects of language usage. (3 semester hours)

STRESS MANAGEMENT

Managing Stress: Principles and Techniques for Coping, Prevention, and Wellness

Covers major stress management techniques, helping others cope with stress, and promoting wellness. Concepts, theories and models of stress, psychological basis for stress, relationship between personality and stress, family and social stress, job stress, dissatisfaction, and burnout are discussed. (3 semester hours)

WESTERN CIVILIZATION

Western Civilization I

A program of study emphasizing the reading and discussion of some of the most influential writings and ideas that have shaped the intellectual and cultural heritage of the Western world. Includes readings from the ancient, medieval, and early modern periods. (3 semester hours)

Western Civilization II

A program of study emphasizing the reading and discussion of some of the most influential writings and ideas that have shaped the intellectual and cultural heritage of the Western world. Includes readings from the modern period. (3 semester hours)

HIGH SCHOOL COURSES

CAREER PLANNING

Career Planning

Helps individuals gain information about themselves—their interests, abilities, aptitudes, values, and leisure-time activity preferences. Provides information about the world of work, training/education, job interview skills, and resume writing. (½ unit) *Tuition:* $95.

ENGLISH

Short Story for Reluctant Readers

A selection of stories about a variety of interesting people. Designed to introduce the elements of the short story and to acquaint the student with the characteristics of good stories. (½ unit) *Tuition:* $95.

POLITICAL SCIENCE

American Government

Examines the three branches of government, political parties, civil rights and freedoms, and the forms of state and local government. (½ unit) *Tuition:* $95.

SELF DISCOVERY

Project Self-Discovery

A personal exploration designed to help students increase their general education and to improve their powers of self-understanding and self-expression. Topics include perceptions, feelings, self-confidence, abilities, success techniques, communication, and planning for the future. (½ unit) *Tuition:* $95.

Kansas State University
Division of Continuing Education
Manhattan, Kansas 66506   (913) 532-6222

Description:
Correspondence courses offered by Kansas State University are administered by Independent Study at the University of Kansas, Lawrence, Kansas. For courses available, SEE **Kansas, University of.**

Faculty:
Dr. Elizabeth Unger, Dean of Continuing Education.

Accreditations:
North Central Association of Colleges and Schools.

Kentucky, University of
Independent Study Program
1 Frazee Hall
Lexington, Kentucky 40506-0031
(606) 257-3466

Description:
The University of Kentucky is a land-grant university with an enrollment of approximately 22,000 on the main campus. The Independent Study Program enrolls 3,500 students in college courses and 6,000 students in high school courses per year.

Faculty:
Dr. Earl Pfanstiel, Director, Independent Study Program; Donna Evans, Registrar, College Division; Ester Saylor, Special Instructional Program Officer-Coordinator, High School Division.

Academic Levels:
College
High School

Degree/Certificate Programs:
The University of Kentucky will allow up to 30 semester hour credits of correspondence study toward a baccalaureate degree. No degrees or diplomas are granted through correspondence study alone. Credits may also be earned toward a high school diploma.

Admission Requirements:
Students are not required to be formally admitted to the University of Kentucky. Non-University of Kentucky degree candidates are judged on an individual basis. Students from foreign countries who use English as a second language are discouraged from enrolling and are accepted only if approved by the Director. Students at the University of Kentucky must have prior approval of their academic deans to enroll in independent study. High school students enrolling in college-level courses must secure the signed approval of their counselors or principals.

Tuition:

$91 per semester hour payable upon enrollment, plus a $5 processing charge per course. High school courses $40 for each ½ unit. Full payment required at time of enrollment. Approved by the Veterans Administration. All requests for refunds must be in writing. A refund of 75 percent will be made if cancellation is made during the first 30 days; 50 percent during 30 to 60 days; 25 percent during the 60 to 90 days. No refunds after 90 days.

Enrollment Period:

The maximum time allowed to complete a course is one year; the minimum time is 8 weeks. The enrollment period may be extended for a period of 4 months upon payment of a $25 extension fee (college courses only). This fee must be received in the Independent Study Office prior to the last working day of the last month of the student's original enrollment. Failure to apply for the extension before the expiration date will necessitate a reenrollment and payment of full tuition fees.

Equipment Requirements:

Textbooks must be furnished by the student and may be ordered from the University of Kentucky Bookstore. Some courses require access to a cassette tape player.

Credit and Grading:

Final examinations must be proctored. All Kentucky college-level students must use one of the examination centers located throughout the state. Out-of-state students must write their final examinations under the supervision of a recognized testing service or college administrator approved by the University of Kentucky Testing Officer. Grading system: A (90–100); B 80–89; C (70–79), D (60–69); E (below 60). The minimum passing grade varies with individual courses. Credit is awarded in semester hour units.

Accreditations:

Southern Association of Colleges and Schools. Member of: National University Continuing Education Association.

COLLEGE COURSES

ACCOUNTING

Principles of Accounting

Course 201. An introduction to accounting concepts and principles involved in the preparation of financial reports for internal and external use. (3 semester hours)

Course 202. An introduction to the analysis and interpretation of accounting data and its use in management planning and control. (3 semester hours)

AGRICULTURE

The Economics of Food and Agriculture

An introduction to the field of agricultural economics and some of the basic tools and concepts of decision making. Concepts are illustrated in terms of selected current social and economic issues including the role of agriculture in both a national and international dimension. (3 semester hours)

Plants and People: A Global Perspective

A survey of important world grain, oil, fiber, forage, fruit, vegetable, and specialty crop plants. Principles of plant, soil, and climatic factors governing adaptation and production of these plants are discussed and applied. Intended to provide substantial plant science background for students not majoring in the plant sciences, but is open and should appeal to beginning plant science majors as well. (3 semester hours)

Agricultural Animal Science

Relationships of food production and consumption to income of humans throughout the world; major livestock (beef and dairy cattle, sheep, swine, poultry and horses) production areas of the world; relationships between live animal merit and yield of retail cuts of meat; identification of skeletal components; identification and functions of reproductive and digestive tract components; characteristics of breeds of beef and dairy cattle, sheep, swine, poultry, and horses. (3 semester hours)

AGRONOMY

Fundamentals of Soil Science

Development of concepts and understanding of the properties and processes that are basic to the use and management of soils. (3 semester hours)

Environmentally Responsible Crop Production

A study of basic crop physiology and broadly-applicable crop production practices for key U.S. and world grain, food, and forage crops. Cropping systems case studies and greenhouse projects are used to stimulate discussion of environmentally related issues. (4 semester hours)

ANIMAL SCIENCE

Feeds and Feeding

The composition and nutritional characteristics of common feedstuffs. The digestive systems, nutritional requirements, formulated rations and economical feeding programs for farm animals. (3 semester hours)

ASTRONOMY

The Solar System

One part of the two-semester introduction to astronomy. This course is primarily about the nature, origin, and evolution of the planets of our solar system and of their satellites. Special emphasis is given to recent spacecraft studies of the solar system. Related topics include the nature of comets, the uses of astronomical telescopes, and eclipses and other solar phenomena. (3 semester hours)

Galactic and Extra-Galactic Astronomy

One part of a two-semester introduction to astronomy. This course concentrates on the universe outside our own solar system. A principle theme is the origins and evolution of stars, of galaxies, and of the universe at large. Highlights include the nature of black holes and quasars, synthesis within stars of the chemical elements essential for life, the Big Bang model of the formation of the universe, and the possible facts of the universe. (3 semester hours)

BIOLOGY

Basic Ideas of Biology

Introductory biology. Discussion topics are those relevant to both plants and animals—cell structure and function, molecules important to living things, metabolism, heredity, environment. (3 semester hours)

Animal Biology

An introduction to the major areas of interest in animal biology, e.g., life processes, the cell, development, heredity, body systems, evolution, taxonomy, phylogeny, ecology. (3 semester hours)

Introduction to Human Biology and Health

A course describing basic anatomical and physiological functions of various body cells, tissues, and organs and their interrelationships as a functioning whole. It also deals with basic information as to maintenance of health; brief description of the major and common diseases affecting man—their control and prevention. (3 semester hours)

Principles of Microbiology

This course will introduce biology and nonbiology students to fundamental microbiological principles and techniques. Emphasis is placed upon structural, functional, ecological, and evolutionary relationships among microorganisms, principally viruses, rickettsiae bacteria, and fungi and algae. (3 semester hours)

Principles of Genetics

A study of the physical and chemical aspects of the genetic material and their relationship to the expression and inheritance of the phenotype. (4 semester hours)

Evolution

Mechanisms of evolutionary change, with a brief summary of historical evolution, especially of the Metazoa. (3 semester hours)

CLASSICAL LANGUAGES AND LITERATURE

Elementary Latin

Course 101. An introduction to the study of classical Latin. Emphasis is placed on learning to read the language. Some attention is given to Latin literature and Roman civilization. (4 semester hours)

Course 102. A continuation of the above course. (4 semester hours)

Medical Terminology from Greek and Latin

Latin and Greek roots, prefixes, and suffixes as found in medical terminology. Primarily for pre-medical, pre-dental, pre-nursing, and pre-veterinary students, but others will be admitted for help in vocabulary building. (3 semester hours)

Elementary Greek

An introduction to the study of classical Greek. Emphasis is placed on learning to read the language. Some attention is given to Greek literature and civilization. (4 semester hours)

ECONOMICS

Contemporary Economic Issues

A basic course in the analysis of contemporary economic issues with emphasis on current economic topics such as inflation, poverty and affluence, urban congestion, and environmental pollution. (3 semester hours)

Principles of Economics I

The study of the allocation of scarce resources from the viewpoint of individual economic units. Topics include household and firm behavior, competitive pricing of goods and resources, and monopoly power. (3 semester hours)

Principles of Economics II

A study of how society's needs are satisfied with the limited resources available. Topics include contemporary issues such as inflation, unemployment, economic growth, international dependencies, and how public policy deals with them. (3 semester hours)

Monetary Economics

A detailed discussion of the financial sector of basic static macroeconomic models, including the views of both the monetarist and neo-Keynesian schools. Institutional aspects of the financial system are discussed. The course stresses problems of economic stabilization. (3 semester hours)

ENGLISH

Writing I

A course in writing, designed to teach students to generate and develop ideas—through significant revision—in clear, effective written English. Course includes a review of grammar, usage, punctuation, and mechanics. (3 semester hours)

Writing II

Study and practice in writing in response to written texts. Writing assignments include summary, synthesis, critique, argumentation. Instruction in library research methods and in the conventions of academic writing. (3 semester hours)

Etymology

A study of words and their fundamental values with reference to development of a writing vocabulary. (3 semester hours)

Business Writing

Instruction and experience in writing for business, industry, and government. Emphasis on clarity, conciseness, and effectiveness in preparing letters, memos, and reports for specific audiences. (3 semester hours)

Technical Writing

Instruction and experience in writing for science and technology. Emphasis on clarity, conciseness, effectiveness in preparing letters, memos, and reports for specific audiences. (3 semester hours)

Survey of English Literature I

A survey of English literature from Beowulf through Milton. The emphasis is upon the more important writers, with attention to their cultural backgrounds. (3 semester hours)

Survey of English Literature II

A survey of English literature from Dryden to the present. The emphasis is upon the more important writers, with attention to their cultural backgrounds. (3 semester hours)

Survey of American Literature I

A survey of American literature from the Colonial Era to the Civil War. Emphasis upon the more important writers, with attention to their cultural backgrounds. (3 semester hours)

Survey of American Literature II

A survey of American literature from the Civil War to the present. Emphasis upon the more important writers with attention to their cultural backgrounds. (3 semester hours)

Survey of Western Literature from the Greeks through the Renaissance

A study of works by major Western authors from the Bible and ancient Greek literature through the Renaissance. (3 semester hours)

Survey of Western Literature from 1660 to the Present

A study of works by major western authors from mid-seventeenth century to the present. (3 semester hours)

The Old Testament as Literature

A survey of the major types of Old Testament literature in English translation. While attention will be paid to historical backgrounds, the emphasis is on careful analysis of literary forms and techniques. (3 semester hours)

Shakespeare Survey

A study of ten to twelve of the major plays of Shakespeare including comedies, tragedies, and histories and covering the important phases of his career. (3 semester hours)

Studies in American Literature: 1860–1920

Studies in American writing from the Civil War to 1920, with emphasis on major writers of fiction and poetry. (3 semester hours)

FAMILY STUDIES

Personal and Family Finance

Management of personal and family financial resources throughout the lifespan. A study of individual and family finances as related to planning, credit, savings, investment, insurance, taxes, housing costs, transportation costs, retirement and estate planning. (3 semester hours)

The Individual, Marriage, and Family

Consideration of the dynamics of intimate relationships with emphasis on the individual's personal development and expectations regarding intimacy, marriage, and family. (3 semester hours)

FINANCE

Corporation Finance

An introduction to the basic principles, concepts, and analytical tools in finance. Includes an examination of the sources and uses of funds, budgeting, present value concepts and their role in the investment financing and dividend decisions of the corporate enterprise. (3 semester hours)

FORESTRY

Introduction to Wildlife Conservation

An introduction to the history, concepts, and principles of wildlife biology and management. The role of wildlife in ecological systems and human-altered environments will be discussed. (2 semester hours)

FRENCH

Elementary French

Course 101. The study of basic French through grammar, reading, and oral practice (tapes). (4 semester hours)

Course 102. A continuation of the above course. The study of basic French through grammar, reading, and oral practice (tapes). (4 semester hours)

Intermediate French

Course 201. Reading, conversation and oral comprehension are the basic aims of this course which is structured around contemporary texts. (3 semester hours)

Course 202. A continuation of the above course. (3 semester hours)

GEOGRAPHY

Physical Geography

The basic earth environment is discussed from the standpoint of process. Weather, landforms, climates, vegetation, and soils are emphasized. (3 semester hours)

Regional Geography of the World

A study of the geography of the world by region with emphasis on the world's landscapes as explained by natural and human processes. (3 semester hours)

Human Geography

A study of the spatial distributions of significant elements of human occupance of the earth's surface, including basic concepts of diffusion, population, migration, settlement forms, land utilization, impact of technology on human occupance of the earth. (3 semester hours)

Weather and Climate

Examination of the controls of climate, including air masses, ocean currents, altitude, continentality, and major patterns of precipitation and winds. Features of major climate regions are discussed. (3 semester hours)

Geography of Kentucky

A study of the cultural, economic, and environmental characteristics of Kentucky. Emphasis is placed on Kentucky geography in a regional and national context. (3 semester hours)

GERMAN

Elementary German

Course 111. The essentials of grammar with practice in reading and writing German. (4 semester hours)

Course 112. A continuation of the above course. (4 semester hours)

Intermediate German

Course 201. Systematic review of grammar and furthering of reading, writing, listening, and speaking skills based upon cultural and literary materials. (3 semester hours)

Course 202. A continuation of the above course. (3 semester hours)

HISTORY

A History of Europe Through the Mid-Seventeenth Century

This course is a survey of the development of European politics, society, and culture through the Age of Religious Conflict. (3 semester hours)

A History of Europe From the Mid-Seventeenth Century to the Present

This course is a survey of the development of European politics, society, and culture from the Age of Absolutism to the present. (3 semester hours)

History of the United States Through 1865

The course traces the nation's development through the Civil War. It is designed to meet the demands for a general understanding of American history. (3 semester hours)

History of the United States Since 1865

A continuation of the above course. (3 semester hours)

History of the British People Since the Restoration

From the Stuart period to the present. (3 semester hours)

Civil War and Reconstruction, 1860 to 1877

A study of events immediately preceding the outbreak of conflict, of the military campaigns, and of the social, economic, and political developments during the periods of war and reconstruction. (3 semester hours)

Modern American History Since 1941

An intensive study of the United States from the American entry into World War II to the present, emphasizing diplomatic, military, political, economics, and sociocultural changes. (3 semester hours)

History of the Old South

A study of the colonial beginnings and expansion of southern life, economics, and society. The growth of slavery, staple agriculture, and sectional politics constitute the major interest. (3 semester hours)

HUMAN ENVIRONMENTAL SCIENCES

Introduction to Professions in Human Environmental Sciences

An orientation to human environmental sciences, its contemporary issues, national development and philosophy, unifying concepts, areas of specialization, unique elements, leaders, and professional organizations. (1 semester hour)

JOURNALISM

Etymology

A study of words and their fundamental values with reference to development of a writing vocabulary. (3 semester hours)

MANAGEMENT

Survey of Personnel and Industrial Relations

Survey of the field of personnel and industrial relations. Introduction of the topics of manpower planning, selection, placement, training, compensation administration, labor-management relationships, hours of work, and health and safety. (3 semester hours)

MARKETING

Marketing Management

The literature and problems in the retail distribution of consumers' goods, industrial goods, sales organizations, sales promotion and advertising, and price policies. (3 semester hours)

MATHEMATICS

Intermediate Algebra

The course is remedial in nature and covers material commonly found in second year high school algebra. Specific topics discussed include numbers, fractions, algebraic expression, simplifying, factoring, laws of exponents, linear equations, simple graphs and polynomial algebra. (3 semester hours)

College Algebra

Selected topics in algebra and analytic geometry. Develops manipulative algebraic skills, required for successful calculus study. Includes brief review of basic algebra, quadratic formula, systems of linear equations, introduction to analytical geometry including conic sections and graphing. (3 semester hours)

Trigonometry

A standard course including trigonometric functions, identities, multiple analytic formulas, laws of sines and cosines and graphs of trigonometric functions. (2 semester hours)

Calculus I

A course in one-variable calculus, including topics from analytic geometry. Derivatives and integrals of elementary functions with applications. (4 semester hours)

Calculus II

A continuation of the above course primarily stressing the techniques of integration. (4 semester hours)

Elementary Calculus and Its Applications

An introduction to differential and integral calculus, with applications to business, and biological and physical sciences. (3 semester hours)

Mathematics for Elementary Teachers

Basic concepts of measurement, geometry, probability, and statistics. (3 semester hours)

MUSIC

Introduction to Music

A study of the elements of music as they apply to the listening experience; designed for the nonmusic major with no prior knowledge of music. Emphasis is placed on developing an awareness and understanding of musical styles from the Renaissance to the present. (3 semester hours)

NUTRITION

Food and Nutrition for Man

Food composition, preservation, digestion, absorption and metabolism as related to selection of nutrients essential for human life, health, growth, reproduction, lactation, and physical activity. (3 semester hours)

PHILOSOPHY

Introduction to Philosophy: Knowledge and Reality

An introduction to philosophical studies with emphasis on issues of knowing, reality, and meaning related to human existence. (3 semester hours)

Introductory Logic

A course which treats argumentation, syllogistic, and sentential logic. The focus will be on the use of formal methods in the construction and criticism of actual arguments, the aim being to inculcate standards of good reasoning, e.g., clarity, consistency, and validity. (3 semester hours)

Introduction to Philosophy: Morality and Society

An introduction to philosophical studies with emphasis on a critical study of principles of moral action and social and political values. (3 semester hours)

POLITICAL SCIENCE

American Government

A survey of national government and the political process in the United States, with emphasis on the Constitution, the President, Congress, and the judicial system. (3 semester hours)

World Politics

A study of the most significant problems of world politics, including the fundamental factors governing international relations, the techniques and instruments of power politics, and the conflicting interests in organizing world peace. (3 semester hours)

PSYCHOLOGY

Introduction to Psychology

An introduction to the study of behavior covering theories, methods, and findings of research in major areas of psychology. Topics covered will include the biological foundations of behavior; learning, perception, motivation, personality; developmental, abnormal, and social behavior; and methods of assessment. (4 semester hours)

Developmental Psychology

An introduction to the principles of developmental psychology as seen in human growth over the entire lifespan with primary focus on infancy through adolescence. Emphasis is placed on theory and data relating to the developmental aspects of cognition, language and personality. (3 semester hours)

Introduction to Industrial Psychology

Review of the functions and findings of psychology applicable to business and industry. Topics covered are employment procedures, personnel testing, attitude analysis, motivation, and morale. (3 semester hours)

Psychology of Industrial Personnel Procedure

A practical course for those preparing for personnel administration and for psychology in industry and business. A study is made of the theory and methods of position classification, job analysis, job evaluation, merit rating, supervisor selection and training, and collective bargaining. (3 semester hours)

RELIGIOUS STUDIES

Introduction to Comparative Religion

Comparative study of major world and selected regional religions with emphasis on analysis of belief, ritual, artistic expression, and social organization. Eastern and Western religions are considered. (3 semester hours)

SOCIAL WORK

Development of Social Welfare

Study of the cultural traditions, value orientations, and political and economic forces which have contributed to the emergence of present social welfare policies and systems in the United States. (3 semester hours)

SOCIOLOGY

Introductory Sociology

Introduction to the concepts and methods of sociology. Investigation of socialization, group processes, social institutions and social change. (3 semester hours)

The Family

A study of the institutions of marriage and the family and an analysis of the various factors and forces at work in our time which are affecting the individual marital relationships. (3 semester hours)

Sociology of Deviant Behavior

A systematic examination of the various types of social disorganization with particular emphasis upon the sociological explanation of underlying factors. (3 semester hours)

Criminology

A study of general conditions as to crime and delinquency, of measures of punishment and reform of offenders, of criminal procedure and its possible reform, and of measures for the prevention of crime. (3 semester hours)

Juvenile Delinquency

Studies of the extent, ecological distribution, and cause of delinquency in contemporary society, including a critical examination of trends and methods of treatment. (3 semester hours)

Dimensions of Aging

Analysis of demographic and institutional patterns, social roles, psychological and physiological changes, and rehabilitative and educational programs associated with aging. (3 semester hours)

Human Relations in Administration of Organizations

Sociological and social psychological analysis of social structure and environment, leadership, power, authority, decision making, communication, satisfaction, and stress in organizational and administrative activity. (3 semester hours)

SPANISH

Elementary Spanish

Course 141. The study of the basic principles of the language through grammar, with emphasis on rapid development of reading and comprehension skills (reading approach). (3 semester hours)

Course 142. A continuation of the above course. Selected readings. (3 semester hours)

Intermediate Spanish

Course 241. Readings of selected Spanish and Spanish American works and rapid review of principles of grammar. Emphasis is on reading comprehension. (3 semester hours)

Course 242. A continuation of the above course. Several options will be offered, including culture, literature, and contemporary problems. (3 semester hours)

STATISTICS

Statistical Method

Introduction to principles of statistics. Statistical description of sample data including frequency distribution, measures of central tendency, and measures of dispersion. Theoretical distributions, statistical estimation, and hypothesis testing. Introduction to simple linear regression and correlation. (3 semester hours)

Descriptive Statistics

Graphical and tabular description of data measures of central tendency and variation, scattergrams, correlation and best-fitting lines; index numbers. (1 semester hour)

Probability

Experiments and sample spaces; elementary and conditional probability; counting principles; random variable, distribution and expectation; normal and binomial distributions. (1 semester hour)

Sampling and Inference

Sampling; behavior of x and s squared; confidence intervals and tests of hypotheses about the mean and variance of a normal population—the x squared and the t-distributions. (1 semester hour)

TEXTILES

Textiles for Consumers

A study of textiles with emphasis on consumer applications. Properties of fibers, yarns, fabric structures, colors, and finishes as related to end use. Survey of legislation and of maintenance requirements. (3 semester hours)

HIGH SCHOOL COURSES

BUSINESS EDUCATION

Accounting

The first half of this beginning bookkeeping course covers basic bookkeeping records, the beginning balance sheet, recording income and expenses, the journal, ledger, trial balance, and interpretation of records. The student solves problems which provide a working knowledge of complete bookkeeping. The second half of the course is a continuance of the first half in which attention is given to the combined cash journals and petty cash book. (1 unit)

Business Mathematics

This is a course designed to train the individual to perform satisfactory computations and problems related to business activities. (1 unit)

Business Communications

This course is designed to help students learn how to use the English language correctly and effectively in business and industry. Skills gained in this course will aid students in communicating successfully in office occupations, in seeking jobs, and in taking job-entrance examinations. (1 unit)

Business Law

This course helps the student develop an understanding of legal rights and responsibilities in personal law and business law. Topics covered include the American legal system, court procedures, the criminal justice system, torts, the civil justice system, oral and written contracts, sales contracts, and consumer production. (½ unit)

Introduction to Business

This course is designed to introduce students to the world of business and to provide preparation for a more meaningful and beneficial interaction with business. Topics include the economic system, living in the computer age, consumer concerns, banking and financial services. (1 unit)

Consumer Education

The first half of the course is designed to help students become wise and efficient consumers. The consumers' values, goals, and decisions in the marketplace are analyzed with respect to advertising, food purchase, transportation, owning an automobile, housing, clothing, and human services. In the second half the managing of income through banking, checking, saving and investing services enables consumers to better understand the U.S. economy and their role in consumer action. (1 unit)

ENGLISH

Grammar I

This course provides instruction in terminology, punctuation, sentence structure, and clear expression of ideas. (½ unit)

Writing I

An alternative to Grammar I for student not working at grade level, this course features correct grammatical usage and written exercises to help students express ideas clearly and convincingly. (½ unit)

Literature I

This course provides a wide variety of reading experiences from some of the best works of the past and present in order to develop interpretation and comprehension skills. (½ unit)

Reading I

An alternative to Literature I for students not working at grade level, this course enables students to express in writing their interpretations of assigned readings. (½ unit)

Grammar II

This course reviews rules in grammar, usage, sentence structure, composition, and mechanics in writing. Exercises are designed to enable the student to express ideas clearly and convincingly. (½ unit)

Writing II

An alternative to Grammar II for students not working at grade level, this course provides students a variety of paragraph writing techniques with emphasis on sentence structure, punctuation, and correct use of grammar. (½ unit)

Literature II

This course covers a wide range of literature intended to stimulate the student's interest and to provide opportunities for clear and concise interpretative writing. (½ unit)

Reading II

An alternative to Literature II for students not performing at grade level, this course reviews writer's styles, literary terms and enables students to state their opinions in paragraph writing. (½ unit)

Grammar III

Reviews the rules of grammar, usage, sentence structure, and composition and focuses on the organization of materials for the preparation and writing of reports and library research. (½ unit)

Writing III

An alternative to Grammar III for students not working at grade level, this course provides students a variety of paragraph writing techniques with emphasis on sentence structure, punctuation, and correct use of grammar. (½ unit)

Literature III

This course covers a review of nineteenth-century American writers, modern fiction, nonfiction, poetry, and drama. Students will express what they have learned from these selections in style as well as factual knowledge. (½ unit)

Reading III

An alternative to Literature III for students not performing at grade level, this course reviews writer's styles, literary terms, and enables students to state their opinions in paragraph writing. (½ unit)

Grammar IV

A course designed for twelfth grade high school students. Others may enroll upon recommendation of their counselor or principal. (½ unit)

Literature IV

This course is designed to acquaint the student with the leading English authors and to help him/her acquire a deep appreciation for literature. Emphasis is placed on the relationship between the history of England and the literature that developed during each period. (½ unit)

English IV

This course is designed for students who have not yet attained mastery of grade-level language arts skills. Writing skills are developed through writing about personal experiences with emphasis on complete sentences, paragraphs, and essays. The main objective of this course is to enable students to express their thoughts in writing. (1 unit)

Mass Media

This course is designed to help the student understand the need for communication and how language, through various techniques of media, is used to appeal to and fulfill basic needs. Through the study of newspapers, magazines, comics, radio, television, and movies the student will discover how these mediums influence their decisions and opinions. (½ unit)

FRENCH

French

Emphasis on developing reading skills through lessons that focus on culture, customs, and traditions of the people. Basic grammar and skills necessary to function in the society are stressed. Students may enroll for first, second, and third courses. (1 unit)

GERMAN

German

Emphasis on developing reading skills through lessons that focus on culture, customs, and traditions of the people. Basic grammar and skills necessary to function in the society are stressed. Students may enroll for first, second, and third courses. (1 unit)

HEALTH

Health

This course is designed to give the high school student a broad view of the role health plays in modern society. The responsibility in cooperating actively and intelligently in improving his own health and that of a fellow citizen is stressed. (1 unit)

HOME ECONOMICS

Personal, Marriage, and Family Relationships

This course is designed to improve communications skills, to clarify an understanding of self, to relate personal values to the decision making process, and to help the student relate positively to family, friends, and society. Topics studied include decision making, values, relationships, conflicts, family living life styles, and group relationships. (½ unit)

MATHEMATICS

Consumer Mathematics

This course enables the student to apply skills in solving mathematical problems of consumers. Concepts of whole numbers, fractions, decimals, and percent are applied through study and problem solving in the following areas: investment, wages, commissions, buying/renting a home, taxes, travel, banking, personal care, and insurance. (1 unit)

Fundamentals of Mathematics

A remedial course for students needing more practice in developing arithmetic skills. Basic computations with fractions and decimals in problem solving in the first half are followed by a review of percentages and introduction to measures of length, weight, and volume in the second half. (1 unit)

Essentials of Mathematics

This course contains some basic content from arithmetic, algebra, and geometry. Topics include estimation, measurement, statistics, proportion/percent, transformation, probability, and logic. Problem-solving strategies are woven into the course. (1 unit)

Pre-Algebra

Topics in this course include such basic algebraic concepts as the variable, the real number system, ratio and proportion, order of operations, exponents and radicals, and geometry. The prerequisite skills, concepts, and problem-solving processes needed to help students become comfortable with and be successful in algebra are introduced. (1 unit)

Algebra I

First-year course. This course serves as an introduction to the subject and is designed to prepare students for Algebra II. (1 unit)

Algebra II

Second-year course. This course is preparation for college algebra. (1 unit)

Plane Geometry

This course comprises the equivalent of a year's high school work in plane geometry. (1 unit)

Pre-Calculus

A senior-level course for students who have completed Algebra I, Algebra II, and Plane Geometry. Trigonometric graphs, identities, and equations are included with pre-calculus topics of functions, graphs, equations, and inverse. (1 unit)

SCIENCE

General Biology

The first half introduces biology as a science. Topics covered are cell structures, heredity, genetics, classification of living beings, plants, and animals. The second half covers the way living things breathe, eat, reproduce, digest, and interact with each other and their environment. (1 unit)

General Science

A basic introductory science course. The first half focuses on life science, physical science, and developing science skills. The second half introduces earth and space and includes studies of the solar system, meteorology, oceanography, and man's role in the environment. (1 unit)

Earth Science

A combination of astronomy, geology, meteorology, and oceanography. This course enables students to gain an understanding of earth science as it related to the demands of today's society and its problems. Topics covered include scientific measurement, the solar system, time zones, atoms, minerals, rocks, messengers from space, stars, galaxies, and the universe. (1 unit)

SOCIAL STUDIES

Law and Justice

A study of the structure of our local, state, and national governments with an emphasis on the processes by which governments operate. Community life, the economy, consumer decisions, foreign policy, and the decision-making process in government are included. (1 unit)

World Civilization

This course begins with the foundations of Western civilization and touches on Asian, African, and ancient American civilizations. The first half unit includes the Renaissance, Reformation, and the Scientific Revolution. It concludes with the Napoleonic Era and the unification of Italy and Germany. The second half introduces the modern era and concludes with the 1920s. (1 unit)

World Geography

This course is designed to acquaint the student with the basic concepts of geography. The text gives a comprehensive survey of world geography from a cultural point of view and emphasizes the relationships of man and the earth in various parts of the world. Major emphasis is given to those regions which affect the geopolitical policies of the U.S. (1 unit)

U.S. History

The first half begins with the initial European settlements and includes the Revolutionary and Civil Wars. It concludes with the settlement of the West. The first half covers 1865-1900. The second half covers the growth of industry, expansion, WWI, WWII, the nation's role in world affairs to 1970, and domestic challenges brought about by rapid growth and change. (1 unit)

United States Government/Political Science

A survey of all levels of government with emphasis on the federal level. (1 unit)

Psychology

This course is designed to help the student better understand his interests, abilities, and personality growth, and to guide the student in making the best use of assets. (1 unit)

Sociology

A high school course in the field of social science called sociology with emphasis in the area of marriage and family living. (1 unit)

Kentucky Studies

A combination of geographical, historical, cultural, and recreational topics are covered. Students will have the opportunity to research and report on local points of interest as well as to become familiar with the entire state. (1 unit)

SPANISH

Spanish

Emphasis on developing reading skills through lessons that focus on culture, customs, and traditions of the people. Basic grammar and skills necessary to function in the society are stressed. Students may enroll for first, second, and third courses. (1 unit)

Kentucky Christian College
Department of Independent Study
617 North Carol Malone Boulevard
Grayson, Kentucky 41143-1199

(606) 474-6613

Description:

Kentucky Christian College is a privately supported college offering programs for the preparation of students who plan to enter Christian vocations. It was founded in 1919 by members of the Disciples of Christ. The Independent Study Department is designed to provide academic enrichment for various types of students: college students who may have classroom conflicts; local ministers who need or desire refresher courses; missionaries and native ministers who wish to achieve personal and ministry goals through continuing education; teachers who wish to increase their Biblical understanding for greater effectiveness; and anyone who wishes advanced, college-level education but is unable to attend a college for residence study.

Faculty:

Keith P. Keeran, President.

Academic Levels:

College

Degree/Certificate Programs:

A maximum of 24 semester hours of nontraditional credit may be applied to a baccalaureate degree program. No more than 12 semester hours may be applied to an associate degree.

Admission Requirements:

High school graduation or equivalent. Admission to a correspondence course is a special classification and does not necessarily qualify participants for regular admission to residence study.

Tuition:

$105 per semester hour plus $5 registration fee. Tuition and fees subject to change without notice. Contact the college for current rate information.

Enrollment Period:

Off-campus students must complete a course within one year of the date of registration.

Equipment Requirements:

Textbooks must be purchased by the student and can be ordered from the Kentucky Christian College Bookstore.

Credit and Grading:

Letter grades are used. Nonresident students should arrange with a local college, professor, or minister to proctor the final examination. Those students in military service may make arrangements with the education officer or commanding officer. Credits are awarded in semester hour units.

Accreditations:

Southern Association of Colleges and Schools; American Association of Bible Colleges.

COLLEGE COURSES

BIBLE

Survey Through the Old Testament

A survey through the Old Testament with emphasis on mastering the essential events and individuals in salvation history. The seventeen books of narrative history are surveyed in their entirety. In addition, significant representations of Poetic and Prophetic literature are considered in their historical and chronological context. (3 semester hours)

Survey Through the New Testament

Through this course the student will be exposed to the person of Jesus Christ. The student will master the key elements in His life and teachings as presented in the Gospels. Emphasis is also given to understanding the dominant themes in the Pauline Epistles. Additional literature will be surveyed to expose the student to the richness and diversity of the New Testament and prepare them for future study. (3 semester hours)

Book of Acts

An historical study of the Church of the first century including details of the missionary trips of Paul and the trip to Rome. (3 semester hours)

Pentateuch

An advanced study of the history of the Old Testament. The Pentateuch is carefully studied, with considerable emphasis on Genesis and Deuteronomy. God's chosen people and their relations with the ancient Near East are also studied. (3 semester hours)

Exposition of Roman and Galatians

An exegetical study of the books. The background, authorship, analysis, and application are covered, with the theological and practical aspects especially emphasized. (3 semester hours)

Exposition of I and II Corinthians

Similar to the above course, with both books being studied. The practical implication of problems Paul confronted in the Corinthian church are emphasized. (3 semester hours)

Exposition of I and II Thessalonians

A study of the background, authorship, and text of the books, with doctrinal and practical exegesis of the test. Special relationship of the Thessalonian letters to theology of the Second Coming is noted. (2 semester hours)

Exposition of Pastoral Epistles

A study of the place of I and II Timothy and Titus in Christian revelation, with an exegetical application of Scripture to organization and oversight of the Church today. (2 semester hours)

Exposition of Hebrews

A study of authorship, meaning, doctrine, and practical application of the book, with special emphasis on its place in Christian revelation, as clearly delineating the relationship of Christianity to Judaism. (2 semester hours)

Exposition of General Epistles

An exegetical study of James; I and II Peter; I, II, and III John and Jude. The background, discussion of authorship and authenticity is covered with each book. (2 semester hours)

Exposition of Prison Epistles

An exegetical study of the books of Philippians, Colossians, Ephesians, and Philemon, with special reference to the problem of their places in the Pauline epistolary scheme. (2 semester hours)

CHRISTIAN EDUCATION

Introduction to Christian Education

A study of the history and philosophy of Christian Education as revealed in the Bible and history. Exposure to a survey of characteristics, principles, and methods, with application to the various departments and agencies of the Church. (3 semester hours)

CHURCH HISTORY

History of the Restoration Movement

A tracing of the religious movement beginning in the early nineteenth century in the United States, which had as its purpose the uniting of all Christians by returning to the faith and practices found in the New Testament Church. Included is a study of the leaders of the Movement and their views. (2 semester hours)

MISSIONS

Studies in Christian Missions

A survey course which provides a basic study in Christian missions including motives for world evangelism, methods in promoting missions locally, history of the expansion of the Christian faith, and a survey of mission work accomplished by the American Restoration Movement. (3 semester hours)

THEOLOGY

Fundamentals of Doctrine

A thorough study of the fundamental doctrines of the Bible concerning God, Christ, the Holy Spirit, man, sin, salvation, and related topics. Also a study of the teachings of the New Testament concerning the Church, officers, name, ordinances, and stewardship, along with the duties of the members of the Church. (3 semester hours)

Biblical Theology

An advanced investigation of the New Testament and its theology, with emphasis on the life and teachings of Jesus and the work of Paul. The course will conclude with a brief introduction to contemporary theologians and their influence on Biblical studies. (3 semester hours)

Apologetics

A study of the reasoned responses of Christians to objections to the faith both past and present, with a view to developing the student's ability to demonstrate the reasonableness of his faith. (3 semester hours)

Kirkwood Community College
Adult High School Correspondence Program
Lincoln Learning Center
912 18th Avenue, SW
Cedar Rapids, Iowa 52404   (319) 366-0142

Description:

Kirkwood Community College was formally established on July 1, 1966. It is located on the south edge of Cedar Rapids, a metropolitan city situated in an area of rich agricultural production in east-central Iowa. The high school correspondence program is a development from Kirkwood's Adult High School Program. The program began in 1967 and a full-time coordinator began overseeing various functions in 1976. Any student anywhere may register for the Kirkwood Adult High School Correspondence Program.

The program is designed to assist students who: are still in high school but need make-up credits in order to graduate with their class; are no longer in school but could graduate by transferring credits to their former schools; want to earn a high school diploma through the Kirkwood Adult High School Program; would not have an opportunity to take certain courses because they have full schedules or because the classes are not available in their high school.

Faculty:
Mary Eirp, Correspondence Coordinator.

Academic Levels:
High School

Degree/Certificate Programs:
Credit is awarded for successful completion of the course(s).

Admission Requirements:
Enrollment for students who are considered actively enrolled in their local high schools is subject to the consent and approval of those schools. Prospective correspondence students who are not enrolled elsewhere may enroll in this program. There is no limit on the number of courses a student may take.

Tuition:
Iowa residents, $85 per course plus $15 processing fee; nonresidents, $110 per course plus $15 processing fee. Students must initiate the withdrawal procedure in writing stating the reason for the request to withdraw. Books and materials must be returned before any refund can be issued. If withdrawal within four weeks of the registration date, 70 percent of the tuition is refunded; within six weeks, 50 percent of the tuition is refunded; no refund is granted after six weeks. The processing fee is nonrefundable.

Enrollment Period:
The maximum time permitted for completion of a course is six months; the minimum time one month. If an extension of time is needed, a rate of $20 per month will be assessed

for a maximum of four additional months. Examinations must be proctored.

Credit and Grading:

The transfer of credit awarded for the completion of high school courses to institutions other than Kirkwood Community College is an optional matter for the accepting institution. Grading system: A, 90–100; B, 80–89; C, 70–79; D, 60–69. Minimum passing grade is D or 60 percent (final exam grades lower than 60 percent must be retaken). Credit is awarded in semester units (½ unit).

Accreditations:

North Central Association of Colleges and Schools.

HIGH SCHOOL COURSES

BIOLOGY

Biology I

Includes the study of life, simple organisms, plants, invertebrates, and vertebrates. (½ unit)

Biology II

Continues with the study of human biology, human health, heredity and genetics, changes through time, and ecology. (½ unit)

BUSINESS

Recordkeeping I

This course is designed to give attention to recordkeeping in both personal and vocational areas where the keeping of basic financial records is important. (½ unit)

Recordkeeping II

This course is designed to help students who may seek employment that will require a basic understanding of accounting procedures. It is recommended that students take *Recordkeeping I* prior to this course. (½ unit)

General Business I

Deals with product information, buying rights, check writing, using credit, loans, installment buying, and insurance. (½ unit)

General Business II

Covers social security, interest, budgeting, buying power, taxes, and career choices. (½ unit)

Consumer Economics

Deals with the consumer and the economy, earning an income, managing resources, and making wise decisions. (½ unit)

ENGLISH

Composition

Deals with the development of sentences, paragraphs, and short essays. (½ unit)

English Grammar I

Emphasizes the basic parts of speech, the parts of a sentence, and correct usage, mechanics, and spelling. (½ unit)

English Grammar II

Continues the basic parts of speech, the parts of a sentence, and correct usage, mechanics, and spelling. (½ unit)

Individualized Reading I

Requires the student to read at least six novels and write book reports on them. A specific guide is provided. (½ unit)

Literature I

Requires the reading of selected poems, selected short stories, one selected novel, and one novel of the student's choice. There are questions to answer on each section. (½ unit)

Newspaper

Includes newspaper terms, vocabulary, copyreading, proofreading, and writing in all categories from international to sports reporting. (½ unit)

Novel Study

Designed to acquaint students with the development of the novel as a special piece of literature. Student must read three novels from a selected list and complete study guides/tests on each. (½ unit)

FAMILY LIVING

Family Living I

Designed to give students insights into skills for living, living styles, and parenthood. (½ unit)

Family Living II

Includes major life problems, the world of work, money matters, and life styles. (½ unit)

HEALTH

Health I

A modern approach to making healthy choices, mental health, nutrition, and physical fitness. (½ unit)

Health II

This course covers human development, substance abuse, and modern health problems. (½ unit)

LIFE SCIENCE

Life Science I

Concepts of modern biology simply and clearly set fort. Is concerned with the nature of organisms and their environments and with natural communications and their populations. (½ unit)

Life Science II

Begins by describing man and his role in natural communities and takes up problems of population increase, heredity, selection, and the wise use of biological resources. (½ unit)

MATHEMATICS

Algebra 1a

The first semester of beginning algebra including variables, equations, signed numbers, formulas, polynomials, and factoring. (½ unit)

Algebra 1b

The second semester of beginning algebra including graphs, equations, fractions, decimals, and percents, squares and square roots, and quadratic equations. (½ unit)

Consumer Math I

Uses practical math covering the area of consumer decisions, transportation, buying food, buying clothing, family housing, and budgeting. (½ unit)

Consumer Math II

Continues with taxation, consumer credit, banking, insurance, and investments. (½ unit)

General Mathematics I

Covers addition, subtraction, multiplication, division, fractions, decimals, ratios and proportions, and percent. (½ unit)

General Mathematics II

Deals with measurements, graphing, pre-algebra and pre-geometry concepts. (½ unit)

Geometry 1a

The first semester of a basic Plane Geometry course. A student should have a basic understanding of algebra before enrolling in this course. Course covers points, lines, angles, proofs, triangles, congruent triangles, polygons, and areas. (½ unit)

Geometry 1b

A second semester of Plane Geometry. Covers ratios and proportions, similar polygons, circles, area and volume of solids, right triangles, and coordinate geometry. (½ unit)

PSYCHOLOGY

Psychology I

Includes methods of psychology, human development, heredity, environment, personality, measuring intelligence and principles of learning. (½ unit)

Psychology II

Continues with the process of thinking, perception, motivation, coping with stress, personality disorders, and social behavior. (½ unit)

SCIENCE

Earth Science I

This course provides the understanding and appreciation of our home planet, Earth. The study begins with the position of the Earth in the universe and is followed by the general characteristics of the Earth as a planet, its composition, and some of the forces that cause it to change. (½ unit)

Earth Science II

Continues with forces that cause the Earth to change into the way the Earth's surface is sculptured, the oceans, the development of North America, and the atmosphere with emphasis on the sources of weather and climate. (½ unit)

Physics

This course is an open-book course normally used by pre-nursing students. High school students may register for the course. There is no lab. A background of higher level high school math is helpful. (½ unit)

SOCIAL STUDIES

American Government

Provides factual knowledge of national, state, and local levels of government. Deals with the dynamics of political decision making. Helps give the student an appreciation of positive, active citizenship. (½ unit)

U.S. History I

Begins with the discovery of America and takes one up to 1877. (½ unit)

U.S. History II

Continues up to the 1970s. (½ unit)

World History I

Covers the beginning of civilization, classical civilizations, the world of Christendom and Islam, the worlds of Africa and the Americas, and the world of Asia. (½ unit)

World History II

Continues with the rise of the West, the Industrial Revolution, the two World Wars, and our contemporary world. (½ unit)

Sociology I

Introduces the vocabulary and methods used by the sociologist including such topics as development of personality, social adjustment, deviation, cultural ingredients/change, and understanding basic social units. (½ unit)

Sociology II

Continues with population in communities, race relationships, role and status, mass communication, collective behavior, major trends, and problems in modern society. (½ unit)

SPANISH

Spanish 1a

A first semester first year course. The course presents many of the essential rules of Spanish grammar and the fundamentals of spoken and written Spanish. (½ unit)

Lewis-Clark State College
8th Avenue and 6th Street
Lewiston, Idaho 83501   (208) 746-2341

Description:

The college was established in 1893 to train and educate teachers. It became a four-year college with a liberal arts program in 1965. Correspondence study is available from Lewis-Clark State College, but all courses are administered by the Correspondence Study in Idaho office at the University of Idaho campus in Moscow, Idaho. SEE **Idaho, University of.**

Accreditations:
Northwest Association of Schools and Colleges.

L.I.F.E. Bible College
School of Correspondence Studies
1100 Covina Boulevard
San Dimas, California 91773   (909) 599-5433

Description:

L.I.F.E. Bible College was established in 1924 by Aimee Semple McPherson. It is a four-year college offering a program leading to a Bachelor of Arts degree in Bible and Theology. The college is a professional school with the objective of training men and women for church-related ministries, e.g., Pastor, Missionary, Christian Education Director, Minister of Music, and Associate Minister.

The School of Correspondence Studies was established in 1924. Most correspondence students take one or more subjects with the view toward transferring them into the college for credit. A smaller percentage of correspondence students study for their own growth. Currently, the School of Correspondence Studies offers an Associate of Arts degree that can be earned entirely by correspondence. A minimum of 32 semester hour credits must be completed.

Graduation requirements include a 2.0 grade point average, Christian testimony consistent with scripture, fulfillment of all contracts with the school, and completion of curriculum requirements.

Faculty:

Jettie Wymore, Manager; Zoe Ann Hill, Faculty Representative.

Academic Levels:

College

Degree/Certificate Programs:

A maximum of 56 semester hours of correspondence credits may be applied toward a degree. A completion card is issued upon completion of each course in which a grade of C or above is earned.

Admission Requirements:

Minimum age of 16 or a high school graduate. Completion of correspondence studies is not a guarantee of admission to the resident program.

Tuition:

$50 per unit (semester hour). Prices are subject to change without notice. Payments are not refundable to students discontinuing a course, nor transferable to any other person.

Enrollment Period:

To remain a current correspondence student, he/she must complete a three-unit course within four months and a two-unit course within three months. If no examinations or projects are received by the school within any three-month period (without proper explanation), the course is automatically cancelled and may be renewed only by proper renewal procedures and payment of a reinstatement fee of $10. Refund for returned books is 90 percent if returned within thirty days in perfect condition. No refunds for books after thirty days from date of purchase; course syllabi not returnable.

Equipment Requirements:

In addition to the tuition costs, there is a textbook fee for each course. This fee is determined by the current cost of textbooks and syllabus. Textbook costs must be paid in advance with tuition.

Credit and Grading:

Examinations must be proctored. The grade point system is used with letter grades being translated as follows: A, 4.00; A-, 3.7; B+, 3.3; B, 3.0; B-, 3.0; C+, 2.3; C, 2.0; C-, 1.7; D, 1.0; F, 0. Correspondence courses in which a grade of D or F is earned will not be accepted for credit into the resident program. All credits are semester hour credits based on a semester of approximately 15 weeks and a class hour of 50 minutes.

Accreditations:

American Association of Bible Colleges. Member of: Association of Christian Continuing Education Schools and Seminars.

COLLEGE COURSES

BIBLE

Bible Survey

This course is designed to give the student a perspective of the Bible from Genesis to Revelation with focus on the relationships among the events, locations, and people that are a vital part of the unfolding story of redemption. (4 semester hours)

Pentateuch

A study of the first five books of the Bible in relation to Old Testament history and God's eternal divine plan of redemption through Jesus Christ. (4 semester hours)

Hebrew History

An analytical survey of the dynamics of Hebrew national history from Joshua to Nehemiah. Notable Biblical characters are highlighted and special emphasis is given to the typology of Jesus Christ. (3 semester hours)

Hebrew Prophets

An introduction to the prophetic literature of the Old Testament, including a study of the role of the prophet in ancient Israel and a survey of the books of the fifteen writing prophets. (3 semester hours)

Synoptic Gospels

An expository and historical study of the life of Christ as revealed in the first three Gospels. Jesus' life and teaching is analyzed and studied against the backdrop of the contemporary human situation in which He lived. (3 semester hours)

Acts

A study of the journeys of Paul and development of the early churches, with emphasis upon the principles which are applicable to our church life today. The ministry of the Holy Spirit is stressed. (3 semester hours)

BIBLICAL LANGUAGES

Introduction to Greek and Hebrew

This subject supplies the basic facts of the Biblical languages, Greek and Hebrew. It includes the use of the lexicon and concordance. This introduction provides word studies, sentence diagramming, and analysis of thought units. (3 semester hours)

EVANGELISM

Personal Evangelism

A study of the Biblical basis for personal witnessing, including the central tenets of the Gospel, handling excuses and objections, and establishing relationships with unbelievers. Field work will be part of the course. (2 semester hours)

International Evangelism

A basic course for all students preparing for Christian ministry, presenting the Biblical basis of worldwide evangelism, its historical development, and current status. (3 semester hours)

HISTORY

Western Civilization

A study of the social, economic, and political contributions of the ancient people of Mesopotamia, Egypt, Greece, and Rome, and the contributions of the Middle Ages and the Renaissance to Western Culture. Emphasis will be placed on the development of the Christian Church before the Reformation. (3 semester hours)

PASTORAL STUDIES

Hermeneutics I

This course covers (1) the doctrine of the Bible, including inspiration, canonization, and transmission of the Bible; (2) the study of the Bible inductively, including practical assignments in the inductive method and the application of Biblical truth to the student's personal life and ministry. (3 semester hours)

Homiletics

An introductory course designed to give the student a philosophy of preaching and a practical understanding of sermon preparation and delivery. (2 semester hours)

Spiritual Gifts and Ministries

A practical course in which the student is encouraged to participate in the ministry of the Holy Spirit, to understand the purpose of each spiritual gift, and operate in his or her "gifting." The effective working of the gifts will be examined from the individual to the assembled church. (2 semester hours)

Christian Ethics

A study of the Christian basis for personal and public morality in face of the situation motif seen in today's culture. Comparisons and contrast with secular approaches are noted as the consistency of biblical ethics is emphasized, with the practical application of the principles in one's conduct. (3 semester hours)

SCIENCE

Introduction to Science

This course is designed to help the student develop a philosophy of science that will be compatible with his/her Christian faith. Relationships between key scientific disciplines and Biblical revelations are explored, with special attention to the creation story. (3 semester hours)

THEOLOGY

Systematic Theology I

Theology: A study of the revelation God has given of Himself, His nature, His character, and His works. *Anthropology:* Studies man as God's creation, man as a sinner alienated from God by voluntary disobedience, and man as the object of God's redeeming grace. *Hamartiology:* A discussion of that part of moral theology or anthropology which deals with sin—its origin, reality, nature, extent, result, and penalty. (3 semester hours)

Systematic Theology II

Pneumatology: Covers the scriptural revelation of the person and work of the Holy Spirit. Relevant subjects discussed include His deity, divine names, symbols, as well as His work in the physical universe, in relation to Christ, and in the hearts of believers. The Pentecostal perspective is upheld. The baptism, gifts, and graces of the Spirit are emphasized as aspects of His continuing ministry in the Church today. *Angelology:* An examination of the scriptural teaching concerning the origin, nature, sphere, work, and destiny of angels. Also included is a study of the origin, activity, and doom of Satan. (3 semester hours)

Systematic Theology III

Soteriology: The doctrine of salvation; its provision through the mediatorial work of Christ, and application through the Holy Spirit. The great doctrines of the Bible such as grace, election, repentance, faith, regeneration, sanctification, union with Christ, and adoption are taught. *Ecclesiology:* The doctrine detailing origin, nature, and constitution of the Church; its local organization, ministry, ordinances, and destiny are studied. (3 semester hours)

Systematic Theology IV

Divine Healing: A study of God's provision and promises concerning physical healing. Exploration of both Old and New Testament passages confirm that healing is for today. Instruction is given from the Scripture as to how healing can be received, maintained, and ministered. *Eschatology:* The Biblical teaching regarding the last things, the second coming of Christ, and the consummation of the age, the resurrections and judgments, the millennial reign of Christ, and the final state of both the saved and the unsaved. (2 semester hours)

Louisiana State University
Office of Independent Study
106 Pleasant Hall
Baton Rouge, Louisiana 70803

(504) 388-3171

Description:
Louisiana State University began offering correspondence courses in 1924 and currently offers 150 credit courses. There is an annual enrollment of 5,000 students in the college program. Correspondence courses are available in college, high school, and certain professional, noncredit subjects. Most courses are taught by members of the regular University faculty. The college-level courses are substantially the same in scope and content as those taught on the campus. College courses can be used for degree credit; however, LSU does not offer a degree by correspondence. All courses required for taking the CPA examination in Louisiana are offered by correspondence.

Faculty:
Cynthia Jackson Lee, Registrar/Admissions Officer for Independent Study.

Academic Levels:
College
High School
Noncredit

Degree/Certificate Programs:
All courses receive college or high school credit that can apply to a degree or diploma. Up to one-fourth of the degree requirements may be accepted from correspondence courses.

Admission Requirements:
LSU students must have approval of their Dean. Louisiana high school students must have approval of their principal. Other students are accepted upon application. Individual prerequisites must be met.

Tuition:
The charge for correspondence courses includes first-class postage for sending materials (excluding textbooks). Current tuition is $55 per semester hour. Students may not enroll for more than two courses at one time, and one of these courses may not be a prerequisite for the other. Tuition for high school courses is $70 per ½ hour unit. Refund policy: A refund of 75 percent of the enrollment fee

will be made if request is received within thirty days of enrollment and no lessons have been submitted. Noncredit course fees are stated as part of the description for the specific course. As a convenience to students in foreign countries, corrected lessons will be returned via air mail upon payment of a service charge for each course: Central America, West Indies, Colombia, Venezuela, $30; all other countries $40.

Enrollment Period:

The maximum time allowed to complete a course is nine months; the minimum time is two months. An extension of three months may be granted with payment of an extension fee of $15 per course. Enrollment applications are accepted at any time.

Equipment Requirements:

Textbooks and other supplies must be provided by the student. They may be purchased locally, from the publisher, or from the LSU Bookstore, 110 Union Building, Baton Rouge, LA 70803 (504-388-5500). Some courses require the use of audiovisual materials; these are paid for by the student.

Credit and Grading:

Grades of A, B, and C are given for satisfactory work; a D is passing but unsatisfactory. An F indicated work failed. The minimum passing grade varies according to course/instructor. The final examination weighs heavily in determining course grade. Examinations are proctored by a local college administrator. Generally, LSU accepts correspondence credits from other accredited institutions. Credit is awarded in semester hour units.

Library Services:

Students living outside the Baton Rouge area should apply first to their local library for supplementary books.

Accreditations:

Southern Association of Colleges and Schools. Member of: National University Continuing Education Association.

COLLEGE COURSES

ACCOUNTING

Introductory Financial Accounting

Principles and methods of accounting primarily concerned with financial data gathering and presentation in the form of general purpose external financial statements; legal and ethical obligations of the accounting profession. (3 semester hours)

Introductory Managerial Accounting

Principles and methods of accounting primarily concerned with data gathering and presentation for purposes of internal management evaluation and decision making. (3 semester hours)

Intermediate Accounting

Part I. Accounting concepts and principles underlying preparation of financial statements; their application in measurement and reporting of selected balance-sheet items and related revenue and expense recognition. (3 semester hours)

Part II. A continuation of Part I. Accounting for liabilities, income

taxes, pensions, leases, stockholders equity, earnings per share, accounting charges and corrections, income and balance-sheet presentations. (3 semester hours)

Part III. A continuation of Part II. Statement of changes in financial position, financial reporting, and changing prices; financial statement analysis and disclosure; partnerships and not-for-profit accounting. (3 semester hours)

Cost Analysis and Control

Nature, objectives, basic systems, and procedures of cost accounting and control for manufacturing firms; cost-volume-profit relationships; standard costs and variance analysis; direct costing; relevant costs; introduction to capital budgeting. (3 semester hours)

Income Tax Accounting I

Fundamentals of federal income taxation with respect to individuals, income inclusions and exclusions, and statutory deductions in arriving at tax liability. (3 semester hours)

Auditing

Nature of public accounting; auditing theory, procedures, and problems; internal control; internal auditing; development of audit programs; evidential matter; and reporting. (3 semester hours)

Advanced Accounting

Completion of the core financial accounting sequence; business combinations; consolidated financial statements; segment reporting; Securities and Exchange Commission procedures. (3 semester hours)

ANTHROPOLOGY

Introduction to Physical Anthropology and Prehistory

Origin and evolution of people; evolution and its physiological bases; human prehistory; human diversity; origin and development of human culture through the rise of civilization. (3 semester hours)

Introduction to Cultural and Social Anthropology

Diversity of human cultures; nature of culture, social organization, subsistence patterns, economics, law, politics, religion, language, and other institutions of culture viewed in cross-cultural perspective. (3 semester hours)

Archaeology

Archaelogical goals, methods, techniques, and interpretations; particular prehistoric cultural sequences or projects; relationship of archaeology with other social, life, and earth sciences. (3 semester hours)

ASTRONOMY

The Solar System

Fundamental principles of the solar system. (3 semester hours)

Stellar Astronomy

Fundamental principles of stellar astronomy. (3 semester hours)

BIOLOGY

General Biology

BIOL 1001. General concepts in cell biology, genetics, ecology, and evolution. (3 semester hours)

BIOL 1002. Diversity, interactions, and life histories of microorganisms, fungi, plants, and animals. (3 semester hours)

BUSINESS EDUCATION

Keyboarding

Development of the touch system of typing. (1 semester hour)

Keyboarding Applications

Basic formatting of common business documents, including letters, tables, and reports; improving speed and accuracy. (2 semester hours)

Document Production

Introduction to word processing concepts and applications; formatting advanced business documents. (3 semester hours)

Beginning Shorthand

Basic principles of reading and writing shorthand. (3 semester hours)

Records Management

Principles of records creation, retention, transfer, and disposal; organization and management of stored records; coding, microfilming, and retrieval of information; use of manual, mechanical, and computer means of storing and retrieving information. (3 semester hours)

Office Management

Emphasis on facilitating office work through management of environment, organization, communication, personnel, systems, productivity, and cost factors. (3 semester hours)

CLASSICAL STUDIES

Greek and Roman Mythology

Survey of the principal myths of the Greeks and Romans. (3 semester hours)

COMPUTER SCIENCE

Introduction to Pascal Programming

Computer programming using Pascal. (3 semester hours)

COBOL Programming and Business Data Processing Systems

COBOL programming; its use in business data processing systems. (3 semester hours)

DAIRY SCIENCE

Elements of Dairying

Fundamentals of dairy production and manufacturing. (3 semester hours)

ECONOMICS

Economic Principles and Problems

ECON 2010. Nature of economics, economic concepts and problems; economic systems, and role of government; accounting, analytical, and policy aspects of national income and product; the money and banking system. (3 semester hours)

ECON 2020. A continuation of basic economics; theories of production, determination of prices in regulated and unregulated industries, functional distribution, international economics, and problems of economic development. (3 semester hours)

Economic Principles

Economic understanding of both micro- and macroeconomic principles; economic problems associated with monetary policy, fiscal policy, public finance, government and business, labor, international trade, economic growth, and comparative economic systems. (3 semester hours)

Money, Banking, and Macroeconomic Activity

The role of commercial banks, other financial institutions, and the central bank in affecting the performance of the economy; relationships of money and fiscal policy to prices, production, and employ-ment; internal and external effects on U.S. fiscal and monetary policy. (3 semester hours)

Business Finance

Finance function within business enterprises; tools and techniques of financial management, concepts of capital structure and dividend policy, working capital management, capital budgeting, institutional environment of the firm. (3 semester hours)

EDUCATION

Evaluation of Instruction

Principles and techniques in development, administration, scoring, and evaluation of classroom and standardized tests. (2 semester hours)

Characteristics of Exceptional Children

Individual differences of various types of exceptional children; characteristics, educational programs, and resources for treatment. (3 semester hours)

Books and Audio-Visual Materials for Children

Development and selection of all types of books and non-book materials for children; methods of reading guidance. (3 semester hours)

ENGLISH

English Composition

ENGL 1001. Introduction to writing in simpler forms of expressive and informative discourse. (3 semester hours)

ENGL 1002. Introduction to writing persuasive, evaluative, and other forms of argumentative discourse. (3 semester hours)

Advanced English Composition

Theory and practice of exposition, description, and narration. (3 semester hours)

Business Writing

Preparation of business documents, such as reports, articles, and letters. (3 semester hours)

Descriptive English Grammar

Analysis of the sentence from the perspective of transformational grammar; includes a brief survey of various approaches to the study of language. (3 semester hours)

A Survey of English Literature from the Beginnings to 1798

(3 semester hours)

A Survey of English Literature from 1798 to the Present

(3 semester hours)

Introduction to Fiction

Study and appreciation of the short story and the novel. (3 semester hours)

Introduction to Drama and Poetry

Study and appreciation of these types of literature. (3 semester hours)

Major American Writers

Important authors from Irving to Hemingway. (3 semester hours)

Technical and Professional Writing

Training in skills required of practicing scientists, engineers, and technical managers. (3 semester hours)

ENVIRONMENTAL STUDIES

Environment and Technology, A Perspective on Environmental Problems

Environmental quality problems involving water, air, and land; representative ecological stresses analyzed to develop awareness of their fundamental nature and interrelationships; society's response to alleviate such problems. (3 semester hours)

FINANCE

Business Law

Development of the Anglo-American common law, the American constitutional system, and the Louisiana civil law system; the law of contracts and agency; social and ethical facets of the legal environment; case materials used to demonstrate problem analysis and solution. (3 semester hours)

Commercial Transactions for Accountants

Legal concepts underlying sale of goods; commercial paper; security interests, partnerships, corporations, and bankruptcy; application of the Uniform Commercial Code and preparation for CPA examination. (3 semester hours)

Principles of Real Estate

Principles of purchasing, owning, and operating real estate relative to interest in realty, liens, contracts, deeds, titles, leases, brokerage, management. (3 semester hours)

Business Finance

The finance function within the business enterprise; tools and techniques of financial management, concepts of capital structure and dividend policy, working capital management, capital budgeting, institutional environment of the firm. (3 semester hours)

FRENCH

Elementary French

FREN 1001. Basic lexicon and structure of French; emphasis on communicative language use; supplementary work in language lab. (4 semester hours)

FREN 1002. Basic lexicon and structure of French; emphasis on communicative language use; supplementary work in language lab. (4 semester hours)

Intermediate French

FREN 2101. A continuation of *Elementary French*. Structures and lexicon of French; additional emphasis on reading and writing. (3 semester hours)

FREN 2102. A continuation of the above course. Structures and lexicon of French; additional emphasis on reading and writing. (3 semester hours)

GEOGRAPHY

Human Geography

GEOG 1001. Culture traits—such as languages, religious beliefs, and cultural transformations of natural landscapes—as a basis for dividing the earth's surface into its most significant parts; the seven culture worlds and their development, present situation, and interaction. (3 semester hours)

GEOG 1003. A continuation of GEOG 1001. (3 semester hours)

GEOLOGY

General Geology: Physical

Earth materials and landforms; processes at work on and within the earth. (3 semester hours)

General Geology: Historical

History of the earth and life on it, as deciphered from study of its rocks and fossils. (3 semester hours)

GERMAN

Elementary German

GERM 1101. Basic lexicon and structures of German; emphasis on communicative language use. (4 semester hours)

GERM 1102. A continuation of the above course. (4 semester hours)

Intermediate German

GERM 2101. Reading, conversation, composition, review of lexicon and structure. (3 semester hours) grammar review and presentation of new material. (5 semester hours)

GERM 2102. A continuation of the above course. Reading, conversation, composition; emphasis on lexicon of spoken German. (3 semester hours)

Readings in German Literature

Analysis of literary text; expansion of lexicon, comprehension, composition skills. (3 semester hours)

HISTORY

Western Civilization to 1500

Ideas, trends, and institutions in western civilization from earliest times to the Reformation. (3 semester hours)

Western Civilization since 1500

Development of western civilization from the Reformation to the present. (3 semester hours)

England from Roman Times to the 1688

(3 semester hours)

Britain from 1689 to the Present

(3 semester hours)

U.S. History to 1865

(3 semester hours)

U.S. History from 1865 to the Present

(3 semester hours)

Louisiana

Political, economic, social, and cultural development of Louisiana. (3 semester hours)

Colonial America, 1607–1763

Political, economic, cultural, and military developments in the thirteen colonies. (3 semester hours)

The American Revolution, 1763–1789

Political, intellectual, economic, and military developments in the formation of a permanent American union. (3 semester hours)

African-American History since 1876

Life and history from the end of Reconstruction to the present; emphasis on the 20th century as an era of change. (3 semester hours)

INDUSTRIAL EDUCATION

Occupational Safety

Identification and appraisal of accident-producing conditions and practices; evaluation of accident problems in plant facilities, materials handling, machine safeguarding, hand tools, and occupational health. (3 semester hours)

KINESIOLOGY

Personal and Community Health Problems

Content and theory related to basic health information; critical health issues; improving and maintaining optimal health. (3 semester hours)

Principles of Conditioning

Current methods and concepts of training and conditioning; role of physical fitness activities in the physical education program; participation in selected activities designed to promote fitness; planning programs for physical fitness for educational and social institutions. (2 semester hours)

Human Sexuality

Historical, semantic, religious, social, medical, and comparative cultural aspects of human sexuality from childhood to senility. (3 semester hours)

Community Safety Education

Covers all grade levels in the school health program; community programs; home, traffic, and recreational safety; emphasis on organization and administration of these programs. (3 semester hours)

LATIN

Elementary Latin

Classical Latin; emphasis on comprehension rather than grammar; repetition of controlled vocabulary and contextual clues used to read extensive passages of simple Latin. (5 semester hours)

Intermediate Latin

Reading comprehension approach to language continued in extensive passages of moderate difficulty; increases vocabulary levels and completes introduction to basic Latin grammatical constructions. (5 semester hours)

MANAGEMENT

Principles of Management

Management functions, including planning, organizing, staffing/human resource management, leading/interpersonal influence, and controlling. (3 semester hours)

Human Resource Management

Human resource functions; including planning, recruitment, selection, development, utilization, maintenance, and reward of employees; relationships with environment and employee associations. (3 semester hours)

Management and Organized Labor Relationships

Impact of organized labor on personnel and management practices; emphasis on nature of union organizations; union certification and decertification elections, contract administration, and government regulation of labor-management relationships. (3 semester hours)

Human Behavior in Organizations

Behavior sciences applied to understanding human dynamics in organizations; individual, interpersonal, group, and intergroup behavior as organizational variables; impact of human behavior in organizations; dynamics and success. (3 semester hours)

MARKETING

Principles of Marketing

The field of marketing; marketing environment, functions, and institutional structure at a macro level; marketing strategy and policies at a micro level; problems of cost and productivity at both macro and micro levels; viewpoint of society, consumer, and marketing manager. (3 semester hours)

Consumer Analysis and Behavior

Nature and dynamics of consumer markets and significance of these markets to marketing executives; concepts and constructs employed to identify and measure market segments and to analyze behavioral patterns of these segments as a basis for marketing strategy. (3 semester hours)

Marketing Research

Formulation of marketing policies; theories, concepts, and methodology involved in applying research to marketing problems. (3 semester hours)

Marketing Communication: Promotion

Nature and contributions of personal selling and advertising to the firm's problems of demand stimulation; principles and concepts related to integration and organization of promotional effort to facilitate communication programs for products and/or services. (3 semester hours)

Retailing Management

Store organization, operation, and management; retail method of inventory; problems connected with retail buying and selling. (3 semester hours)

Business Marketing

Strategies developed by manufacturers to compete for markets; differences between industrial and final consumer markets; function of industrial purchasing with regard to selection of sources of supply and development of purchasing policies; strategic overview of marketing; how companies buy and sell from each other; not confined to industrial companies. (3 semester hours)

International Marketing

Global marketing environment and analytical processes; global marketing as all-encompassing (import-export, joint ventures, foreign subsidiaries, licensing, management contracts); marketing systems in various countries; strategies for international and multinational operations. (3 semester hours)

MATHEMATICS

Preparation for College Mathematics I

Real numbers, elementary equations, and inequalities; polynomials and basic factoring; algebraic fractions; graphing linear equations. (4 semester hours)

Preparation for College Mathematics II

Liner equations and inequalities, polynomials and factoring, algebraic fractions, operations on radical expressions, rational exponents, quadratic equations, graphing. (4 semester hours)

Mathematics for Prospective Elementary School Teachers I

Logic; counting numbers, integers, rational numbers, real numbers, with emphasis on field properties; set nomenclature and some number theory; units of measurement. (3 semester hours)

Mathematics for Prospective Elementary School Teachers II

A continuation of the above course; measurement, informal geometry, systems of equations, introduction to probability and statistics. (3 semester hours)

Basic Mathematics and Applications

Basic mathematical skills of graphing, formulas for geometric measurement, systems of linear equations and inequalities, review of quadratic equations, logarithms and application to exponential growth and decay, triangle trigonometry and its application to geometry and measurements. (3 semester hours)

College Algebra

Quadratic equations, systems of linear equations, inequalities, functions, graphs, exponential and logarithmic functions, complex numbers, theory of equations. (3 semester hours)

Plane Trigonometry

Trigonometric functions and identities, inverse trigonometric functions, graphs, solving triangles and equations, complex numbers, polar coordinates. (3 semester hours)

Mathematics of Commerce

Interest, discount, annuities, depreciation, and insurance. (3 semester hours)

The Nature of Mathematics

Logic; the algebra of logic, computers, and number systems; networks and combinatorics; probability and statistics. (3 semester hours)

Calculus with Business and Economic Applications

Differential and integral calculus of algebraic, logarithmic, and exponential functions; applications to business and economics, such as maximum-minimum problems, marginal analysis, and exponential growth models. (3 semester hours)

Mathematics for Business Analysis

Sets and counting; probability, including conditional probability, discrete and continuous random variables, variance, and normal distributions, matrices and echelon method for solving systems of equations; functions of several variables and partial derivatives. (3 semester hours)

Analytic Geometry and Calculus I

Analytic geometry, limits, derivatives, integrals. (5 semester hours)

Analytic Geometry and Calculus II

Conics, arc length, transcendental functions, coordinate systems, infinite series. (5 semester hours)

Multidimensional Calculus

Three-dimensional analytic geometry, partial derivatives, multiple integrals. (3 semester hours)

Linear Algebra

Systems of linear equations, vector spaces, linear transformations, matrices, determinants. (3 semester hours)

Elementary Differential Equations with Linear Algebra

First order differential equations, linear differential equations with constant coefficients, and systems of differential equations; vector spaces, linear transformations, matrices determinants, linear dependence, bases, systems of equations, eigenvalues and eigen vectors. (4 semester hours)

MECHANICAL ENGINEERING

Dynamics

Vectorial treatment of kinematics and kinetics of particles and rigid bodies; force, mass, acceleration; impulse and momentum; work and energy. (3 semester hours)

MUSIC

Music Appreciation

MUS 1751. The art of music, with emphasis on listening skills; a nontechnical approach to understanding vocabulary and materials of music; correlation of musical literature with other disciplines in the humanities. (3 semester hours)

MUS 1752. The varied facets of the musical arts: folk music, symphony, opera, ballet, vocal, and chamber music. (3 semester hours)

Music of the Middle Ages and the Renaissance

History of music from ca. 800 to 1600. (2 semester hours)

Music of the Baroque and Classic Eras

History of music from ca. 1600 to 1815. (2 semester hours)

Music of Romantic and Modern Eras

History of music from ca. 1815 to the present. (2 semester hours)

NUTRITION

Introduction to Human Nutrition

Nutrition needs of people; meeting these needs in different ways; weight control, evaluating dietary faddism. (3 semester hours)

PHILOSOPHY

Introduction to Philosophy

Major works on such basic themes as appearance and reality, man and the world, nature of knowledge, relation of mind and body, right and good, existence of God, and freedom and determinism. (3 semester hours)

Introduction to Philosophy: Elementary Logic

Formal and informal reasoning; includes traditional syllogistic logic, modern deductive logic, and scientific method in the natural and social sciences. (3 semester hours)

Introduction to Symbolic Logic

Propositional and elementary predicate logics; formal methods of proof; interpretation and translation to and from natural language; philosophic assumptions underlying logic; relevance of formal logic to philosophic questions. (3 semester hours)

PHYSICAL SCIENCE

Physical Science

PHSC 1001. The first half of a two-semester survey course in the physical sciences. Topics in the first semester are taken primarily from the field of physics. (3 semester hours)

PHSC 1002. The second half of a two-semester survey course in the physical sciences. Topics in the second semester are taken primarily from the fields of astronomy, chemistry, and geology. (3 semester hours)

PHYSICS

General Physics

PHYS 2001. Mechanics, heat, and sound. (3 semester hours)

PHYS 2002. A continuation of the above course. Electricity, magnetism, light, and topics in modern physics. (3 semester hours)

POLITICAL SCIENCE

American Government

Principles, structures, processes, and functions of American government; emphasis on national government. (3 semester hours)

Contemporary Political Systems

Government and politics in democratic, communistic, and developing systems (Britain, France, Soviet Union, China, Latin America, Africa); emphasis on political culture, parties, governmental institutions. (3 semester hours)

Public Policy Making: An Introduction

Sequential process of policy making from problem identification through policy formulation, adoption, implementation, and evaluation of impact; application to civil rights, welfare, urban affairs, taxation, and government spending. (3 semester hours)

Political Parties in the United States

Structure and function of political parties at local, state, and national levels; voting studies of presidential elections. (3 semester hours)

PSYCHOLOGY

Introduction to Psychology

Understanding, prediction, and control of human behavior. (3 semester hours)

Psychology of Adjustment

Adjustment mechanisms in normal adults; broad areas of abnormal behavior and major personality theories. (3 semester hours)

Educational Psychology

Principles of learning, motivation, development, and evaluation as related to the educative process. (3 semester hours)

Developmental Psychology of the Life Span

Survey of developmental processes across the life span. (3 semester hours)

Child Psychology

Psychological and social development of the child. (3 semester hours)

Adolescent Psychology

Adolescent behavior considered in terms of psychological, social, and physical development. (3 semester hours)

QUANTITATIVE BUSINESS ANALYSIS

Statistical Methods and Models I

Statistical description and inference; data distributions, descriptive measures, index numbers, time series analysis; review and extension of probability theory; probability distributions; standard distributions, including normal and binomial; sampling distributions. (3 semester hours)

Introduction to Management Science

Methods of operations research; decision theory, elementary classical optimization techniques, linear programming, critical path models, other relevant topics. (3 semester hours)

Conceptual Foundations for Statistical Analysis

Foundations for advanced work in statistical inference; probability, probability distributions, expected value, sampling distributions, application of sampling distributions to problems of estimation and control. (3 semester hours)

Operations/Production Management

Designing, operating, and controlling productive systems; product design; facility location and layout; inventory control; forecasting; material requirements planning; aggregate planning; scheduling and quality control. (3 semester hours)

REAL ESTATE

Principles of Real Estate

Principles of purchasing, owning, and operating real estate relative to interest in realty, liens, contracts, deeds, titles, leases, brokerage, management. (3 semester hours)

SOCIOLOGY

Introduction to Sociology

Major subject areas and principles of sociology. (3 semester hours)

Current Social Problems

Sociological analysis of major social problems in contemporary society; focus on both the institutional and personal causes and consequences. (3 semester hours)

Marriage and Family Relationships

Current issues and trends in marriage and family relationships. (3 semester hours)

Criminology

Crime, the criminal justice system, and penology. (3 semester hours)

Sex Roles in Contemporary Society

Changes in sex roles and sex-related behavior of males and females, including institutional and structural changes. (3 semester hours)

SPANISH

Elementary Spanish

SPAN 1101. Basic lexicon and structures of Spanish; emphasis on communicative language use. (4 semester hours)

SPAN 1102. A continuation of the above course. (4 semester hours)

Intermediate Spanish

SPAN 2101. A continuation of elementary Spanish. Additional emphasis on reading and writing. (3 semester hours)

SPAN 2102. A continuation of the above course. (3 semester hours)

Readings in Spanish Literature

Interpretive reading of Spanish texts; development of competency in written Spanish. (3 semester hours)

SPEECH

Interpersonal Communication

Theories and research in human communication; one-to-one interaction. (3 semester hours)

Argumentation and Debate

Principles of argumentation and debate, including analysis, briefing, evidence, reasoning, and refutation. (3 semester hours)

VOCATIONAL EDUCATION

Foundations of Vocational Education

Overview of programs and practices; history, philosophy, and purposes of vocational education. (3 semester hours)

Safety Practices and Industrial Hygiene

(3 semester hours)

ZOOLOGY

Human Physiology

Elements of human physiology; controls and functions of the various organ systems. (3 semester hours)

HIGH SCHOOL COURSES

ART

Art I, 1st Semester

Introductory art course for students in grades 9 through 12; basic lessons in appreciating the visual arts and in creating art forms as a means of personal expression. (½ unit)

Art I, 2nd Semester

A continuation of the above course. (½ unit)

BUSINESS EDUCATION

Introduction to Business (General Business), 1st Semester

Background for further business and economics studies in high school or college; business and economic affairs affecting an individual's well-being; personal financial management; routine computational skills essential to evaluate financial affairs. (½ unit)

Introduction to Business (General Business), 2nd Semester

A continuation of the above course. (½ unit)

Clerical Practice

Skills needed to master office duties; mailing, handling the public, telephone and telegraph services, copying and duplicating; emphasis on qualifications of office workers. (½ unit)

COMPUTER LITERACY

Computer Literacy

Impact of the computer on our lives during the twentieth century; introduction to computer programming. (½ unit)

ENGLISH

English I, 1st Semester

Improvement of reading, writing, listening to, and understanding the English language. (½ unit)

English I, 2nd Semester

A continuation of the above course. (½ unit)

English II, 1st Semester

Writing of unified, well-developed, coherent paragraphs; organization of short, multi-paragraph composition; basic rules of grammar, capitalization, punctuation, and other mechanical matters. (½ unit)

English II, 2nd Semester

Essays, plays, poetry, and Shakespeare's *Julius Caesar.* (½ unit)

English III, 1st Semester

Longer and more complex writing assignments than in 10th grade English; effective use of sentences; selections from the writings of well-known American authors from the seventeenth century to the end of the nineteenth century; important concepts used in analyzing literary works. (½ unit)

English III, 2nd Semester

Examples of the main types of twentieth-century American literature; the short story, poetry, essay, biography, and drama. (½ unit)

English IV, 1st Semester

Major uses of language; opportunity to practice with most uses; uses requiring logical thinking; problems which confront a writer in planning and writing lengthy papers; selections from the writings of the best British authors from Anglo-Saxon times through the eighteenth century, including a play by Shakespeare. (½ unit)

English IV, 2nd Semester

Selections from British authors of the nineteenth and twentieth centuries. (½ unit)

Business English, 1st Semester

Basic communication skills; emphasis on the writing of clear sentences using formal standard language. (½ unit)

Business English, 2nd Semester

A continuation of the above course. (½ unit)

FINE ARTS

Fine Arts Survey: Music and Dance

A nontechnical introduction to various facets of music and dance as art forms; basic terms and concepts; personalities and history of music and dance. (½ unit)

Fine Arts Survey: Art and Drama

Introduction to visual and dramatic arts; development, history, philosophy, and principles of art; production of art work in various media; elements of drama and their interrelationships. (½ unit)

FRENCH

French I, 1st Semester

Beginning French, with emphasis on development of pronunciation, listening comprehension, reading, and writing skills; recorded exercises used for drill in pronunciation and listening comprehension. (½ unit)

French I, 2nd Semester

Development of pronunciation, listening comprehension, reading, and writing skills; recorded exercises used for drill in pronunciation and listening comprehension. (½ unit)

French II, 1st Semester

Development of pronunciation, listening comprehension, reading and writing skills. (½ unit)

French II, 2nd Semester

A continuation of the above course. (½ unit)

HEALTH

Health Education: A Social Approach

Basics of health science, including consumer health, care of the human body, nutrition, mental health, and substances that modify behavior (drugs, tobacco, alcohol). (½ unit)

Health Education: A Physical Approach

Basics of health science, including prevention of disease, chronic health conditions, environment and community health, accident prevention, and family life and sex education. (½ unit)

HOME ECONOMICS

Home and Family

Understanding of self and others, maintaining physical health, dressing properly, looking toward marriage (dating, engagement), marriage, becoming a parent (discipline and guidance in child development). (½ unit)

Consumer Education

New products and services, varied lifestyles, government involvement, and changing economic conditions that influence consumers; emphasis on understanding consumer behavior and on developing knowledge of principles of buymanship for household goods, personal services, and collective goods. (½ unit)

Nutrition Education

Basic understanding of nutritional needs; making wise choices in snacks and providing adequate diets for families in the future; needs for a balanced diet; purchasing, preparing, and serving food. (½ unit)

Child Development

Emphasis on children's physical, social, and emotional development; children's needs at specific developmental stages; accepted principles of child care. (½ unit)

MATHEMATICS

Mathematics I, 1st Semester

Arithmetical computations associated with whole numbers, decimals, and fractions; simple linear equations and inequalities. (½ unit)

Mathematics I, 2nd Semester

Operations on integers and rational numbers; fractions, decimals, and percents; simple linear equations and inequalities; interest problems; English and metric conversions. (½ unit)

Algebra I, 1st Semester

Essential fundamentals such as relationships between quantities as expressed by formulas, equations, graphs, fundamental operations, factoring, fractions, problem solving, etc. (½ unit)

Algebra I, 2nd Semester

A continuation of the above course. (½ unit)

Business Mathematics, 1st Semester

Personal cash and bank records, buying problems, personal finance, commission income, savings, life insurance. (½ unit)

Business Mathematics, 2nd Semester

Travel and transportation, taxes, small business problems, retail buying and selling, wholesaling, manufacturing, and business ownership. (½ unit)

Geometry, 1st Semester

Study of points, lines, planes, measurement, angles and perpendiculars, congruent triangles, triangle inequalities, and parallels. (½ unit)

Geometry, 2nd Semester

Study of polygons, similarity, right triangles, circles and spheres, area and volume. (½ unit)

Algebra II, 1st Semester

Fundamental operations, products and factoring, inequalities; first-degree equations; algebraic fractions and exponents; radicals. (½ unit)

Algebra II, 2nd Semester

Quadratic equations having one variable; conics; complex numbers; analytic geometry; logarithms. (½ unit)

Trigonometry

Fundamental concepts of trigonometry; applications to everyday situations. (½ unit)

Consumer Mathematics, 1st Semester

Includes personal finances, transportation, and housing; computational skills and applications stressed. (½ unit)

Consumer Mathematics, 2nd semester

Taxes, insurance, investment, budgeting, and measurement. (½ unit)

Analytic Geometry

Study of vectors, lines, circles, functions, graphing, and conic sections in the plane; vectors, lines, planes, surfaces, and curves in three dimensions. (½ unit)

MUSIC

Music Appreciation

A nontechnical introduction to music; emphasis on history and humanities. (½ unit)

SCIENCE

General Science, 1st Semester

Introduction to matter; physical and chemical changes; atomic structure; matter in action; energy; sound; electricity and magnetism; force and motion. (½ unit)

General Science, 2nd Semester

The solar system; the earth and its composition, oceans, and atmosphere; characteristics of life; the human body; the environment. (½ unit)

Environmental Science, 1st Semester

Concepts concerning ecosystems; their functions, stability, and evolution; human population issues; importance and management of resources. (½ unit)

Environmental Science, 2nd Semester

Sources, effects, and control procedures for the major kinds of pollutants; emphasis on Louisiana's concerns; environmental decision making; risk assessment; toxins and environmental health. (½ unit)

Physical Science, 1st Semester

The nature of science; measurement, motion, machines, energy, heat, sound, light, and electricity. (½ unit)

Physical Science, 2nd Semester

A continuation of the above course with emphasis on chemical properties of elements. (½ unit)

Biology, 1st Semester

Basic terminology and concepts of biology; cellular and multicellular life. (½ unit)

Biology, 2nd Semester

A continuation of the above course. Sponges and coelenterates; worms, arthropods, and vertebrates, including fish, amphibians, mammals, birds, human biology. (½ unit)

Earth Science, 1st Semester

Topics include atmosphere, seasons, weather, oceanography, earth-moon systems, matter, minerals, rocks, erosion, and water systems. (½ unit)

Earth Science 2nd Semester

Topics include glaciers, earthquakes, landforms, geologic time scale, renewable and nonrenewable resources, the universe, stars, solar system, and energy. (½ unit)

Chemistry, 1st Semester

Introduction to principles of modern chemistry; properties of elements and compounds; role of chemistry in modern world. (½ unit)

Chemistry, 2nd Semester

Chemical reactions, including reaction energy, reaction kinetics, and equilibrium; electropositive elements; electronegative elements; transition metals; natural and artificial radioactivity. (½ unit)

Physics, 1st Semester

Review of scientific methods and problem solving; topics in mechanics such as motion, acceleration, vectors, and gravitation; properties of matter. (½ unit)

Physics, 2nd Semester

Survey of the various types of energy including heat, sound, light, electricity, and magnetism. (½ unit)

SOCIAL SCIENCE

World Geography, 1st Semester

The world today; affairs of the nations of the world. (½ unit)

World Geography, 2nd Semester

A continuation of the above course. (½ unit)

Civics

For students completing requirements under the new BESE guidelines. (½ unit)

Civics, 1st Semester

Privileges and responsibilities of citizenship; participation in the world community; needs of individuals adjusting to their environment; readings from current publications and optional assignments on recent developments. (½ unit)

Civics, 2nd Semester

Introduction to and understanding of the economic life of the American citizen. (½ unit)

World History, 1st Semester

Social, economic, and political developments which gave rise to succeeding world conditions; development of the student's power of observation and reference; history from the earliest civilization through the Renaissance. (½ unit)

World History, 2nd Semester

A continuation of the above course. History from the time of the Renaissance. (½ unit)

American Government

Governmental system of the United States; historical foundations; emphasis on functions of local, state, and federal governments; delegation of powers among the executive, legislative, and judicial branches; role of the citizen in American government. (½ unit)

American History, 1st Semester

Social and economic phases of U.S. development; growth of democracy and democratic institutions; historical developments through 1900. (½ unit)

American History, 2nd Semester

A continuation of the above course. Begins with the Industrial period. (½ unit)

Sociology, 1st Semester

Basic concepts of sociology; social and cultural relationships; social structure and organization, institutions, and functions. (½ unit)

Sociology, 2nd Semester

The individual in society; socialization process; changing society and social movements; social problems and adjustments; utilization of concepts introduced in the first semester. (½ unit)

Free Enterprise System

Basic principles of a free enterprise economic system; major institutions of the American economy. (½ unit)

Anthropology

Study of basic techniques and approaches in the field of anthropology; perspectives on a variety of cultures, including our own. (½ unit)

SPANISH

Spanish I, 1st Semester

Beginning course in Spanish with emphasis on development of pronunciation, listening comprehension, and reading and writing skills; cassette tape recorded exercises used for drills in pronunciation and listening comprehension. (½ unit)

Spanish I, 2nd Semester

A continuation of the above course. (½ unit)

Spanish II, 1st Semester

A continuation of *Spanish I*. (½ unit)

Spanish II, 2nd Semester

A continuation of the above course. (½ unit)

STUDY SKILLS

Dynamics of Effective Study

Identification of each student's study needs; time management; organization; note taking; and critical thinking. (½ unit)

NONCREDIT COURSES

BOOKKEEPING

Fundamentals of Accounting

Basic bookkeeping principles as used in a business enterprise. (Noncredit) *Tuition:* $50.

Fundamentals of Accounting - Advanced Course

A continuation of the above course. Covers the accounting cycle of a corporation. (Noncredit) *Tuition:* $50.

COMPUTER LITERACY

Computer Literacy

An introduction to the basic concepts of computers; how they work, how they are used, terminology, and a brief history of computers. (Noncredit) *Tuition:* $50.

COMPUTER SCIENCE

Computer Science - BASIC Programming

Fundamentals of structured programming using the BASIC language including the use of read and data statements, designing interactive programs, using controlled loops and sorting. (Noncredit) *Tuition:* $50.

ELECTRICITY

Experiences in Electricity, Unit I - Direct Current

Designed to improve your understanding of electrical principles, this course covers basic electrical concepts including current, voltage, power, resistance, and conduction. (Noncredit) *Tuition:* $30.

Experiences in Electricity, Unit II - Alternating Current

Continuation of Unit I, this course introduces you to an understanding of alternating current that includes transformers, inductors, and capacitors. (Noncredit) *Tuition:* $30.

ENGLISH

Preparation for College English - Grammar

This course is an intensive review of basic grammar skills, and focuses on the parts of a sentence, types of sentences, punctuation, and capitalization. (Noncredit) *Tuition:* $50.

Preparation for College English - Writing

An introduction to the principles of writing. Students will begin by writing unified, coherent, specific paragraphs and move on to writing adequately developed essays appropriate for beginning college students. (Noncredit) *Tuition:* $50.

FIREMANSHIP TRAINING

Firefighter, Level I

This course is addressed toward the recruit who has recently entered the Fire Service and is geared toward the development of basic fire fighter skills. Including a study of the behavior of fire, this course looks at the care and protection of the fire fighter and his/her equipment and role in providing emergency service to the community. (Noncredit) *Tuition:* $40.

Firefighter, Level II

Continuation of Firefighter, Level I. Second of three courses designed to bring the new fire fighter to a level of competence and confidence where he or she would require a minimum of supervision. (Noncredit *Tuition:* $40.

Firefighter, Level III

The final course in the Fire Fighter series, it prepares you to be a company officer. It covers the testing of equipment, rescue and safety, and inspections. (Noncredit) *Tuition:* $40.

Fire Service Instructor I

Designed to assist the company-level officer meet the criteria of NFPA 6U1041, *Fire Service Instructor Professional Qualifications* and to prepare for the certification examination. (Noncredit) *Tuition:* $50.

Fire Service Officer I

Aimed at the fire fighter who has the potential to be promoted to Lieutenant or Captain, this course discusses the impact of community dynamics on the fire department: budgets, accident investigations, safety precautions, and service injuries. The course can also prepare you for completing a nationally recognized certification exam for Fire Officer as outlined in NFPA 1021. (Noncredit) *Tuition:* $50.

GREEK AND ROMAN MYTHOLOGY

Greek and Roman Mythology

Introduction to the world of the gods and goddesses of classical mythology. (Noncredit) *Tuition:* $80.

LAW ENFORCEMENT

English for Law Enforcement Officers

Designed for law enforcement officers, this course guides the student through the principles of correct English grammar and focuses on improving writing skills. (Noncredit) *Tuition:* $40.

MATHEMATICS

Refresher Mathematics

Intended to provide a comprehensive review of the fundamentals of basic mathematics, this course addresses the computational skills needed in everyday living including whole numbers, fractions, decimals, percents, and measurement. (Noncredit) *Tuition:* $40.

A Study of Fractions

A basic review of fractions and their uses, this course covers improper fractions and mixed numerals, adding and substracting fractions, multiplying and dividing fractions, applying the use of fractions. (Noncredit) *Tuition:* $25.

A Study of Decimal Fractions

This course covers decimals and decimal fractions and their uses including the multiplication, division, addition, and subtraction of decimal fractions. (Noncredit) *Tuition:* $25.

A Study of Basic Algebra

A review of basic concepts in algebra including: signed numbers, rules for solving equations, combining terms, ratio and proportion, and applications. (Noncredit) *Tuition:* $25.

A Study of Selected Geometry Topics

This course includes a basic review of those geometrical formulas you may find useful in your daily living including the formulas for surface area, volume, and right triangle solutions. (Noncredit) *Tuition:* $25.

A Study of Intermediate Algebra

A review of intermediate algebra including solving equations in one and two variables, solving quadratic equations, and solving equations with radical signs. (Noncredit) *Tuition:* $25.

Preparation for College Mathematics I

Real numbers, elementary equations, and inequalities; polynomials and basic factoring; algebraic fractions; graphing linear equations. (Noncredit) *Tuition:* $125.

Preparation for College Mathematics II

Linear equations and inequalities, polynomials and factoring, algebraic fractions, operations on radical expressions, rational exponents, quadratic equations, graphing. (Noncredit) *Tuition:* $125.

SOCIAL WORK

Basic Human Biology for Social Work

Basic information concerning human biology beginning with the components of a cell and moving through the different biological systems. (Noncredit) *Tuition:* $90.

STUDY SKILLS

Dynamics of Effective Study

This course looks at various ways of managing your time, organizing and outlining your notes, using references, and taking tests. Designed to improve your methods of studying. (Noncredit) *Tuition:* $50.

Martin Luther College
Correspondence Study Program
Division of Special Services
1884 College Heights
New Ulm, Minnesota 56073   (507) 354-8221

Description:

Martin Luther College, owned and operated by the Wisconsin Evangelical Lutheran Synod, was founded by the Evangelical Lutheran Synod of Minnesota and other states. During its 1883 convention the Minnesota Synod resolved to establish an educational institution for the purpose of supplying ministers of the Gospel to its congregations and mission fields. Besides the ministerial course, other courses were to be included in the curriculum. The new college was located in New Ulm and was ready for dedication and occupancy in the fall of 1884.

The Division of Special Services offers programs which supplement those of the regular academic year: summer school, the certification program offered in conjunction with the summer session, workshops, independent study projects, extension courses, and a correspondence study program. In an effort to serve better the Church and more specifically the members of the Wisconsin Evangelical Lutheran Synod, the correspondence program was established in the early 1960s. The program is intended to provide opportunity for additional study for men and women to become better qualified as teachers in Christian day schools and high schools or as lay leaders in congregations.

Faculty:

Dr. John Isch, Director of Special Services. There is a faculty of 3.

Academic Levels:

College

Noncredit

Degree/Certificate Programs:

The content, work requirement, and credit offered for courses in the correspondence program are equivalent to the same courses in the regular program of the college. Credit is applicable to the synodical certification program for teachers.

Admission Requirements:

Open enrollment. If the demand for correspondence courses available should exceed the manpower available, preference will be given to those who are working toward the synodical certification program for teachers. Application for correspondence study may be made at any time.

Tuition:

The fee for a three-credit correspondence course is $235. Refund policy: One-third of tuition is nonrefundable as well as $6 per completed lesson. No refunds granted after four months or after one-half of the lessons have been completed.

Enrollment Period:

Each student is allowed to take only one course at a time. A student is expected to complete the work required by a specific correspondence course within one year from the date of acceptance. A six-month extension for a fee of $40 will be granted if the application is made prior to the termination date.

Equipment Requirements:

Textbooks, materials, and mailing expenses are supplied by the student. Textbooks may be purchased from the Martin Luther College Bookstore. Arrangements to rent books for supplementary reading may be made with the Director of Special Services.

Credit and Grading:

Normally, a three-credit correspondence course is divided into 24 lessons. The course may have two or three examinations. Each examination should be taken within two weeks from the date of the return of the last lesson required. If more time is required, a student may ask for a deferment

and an extension of time by giving the reasons for such delay to the Director of Special Services. A student enrolled in a correspondence course should make arrangements with a local pastor or principal of a Lutheran elementary or high school to proctor the examination. A student may also take the examination at the college. Letter grades are used: A, B, C, D, and F. Minimum passing grade is C-. Credit is awarded in semester hour units.

Accreditations:

North Central Association of Colleges and Schools.

COLLEGE COURSES

RELIGION

The Life of Christ

This course is directed to the Gospel of the life of Christ rather than to a biographical harmony of the four Gospels. The Gospels are treated separately to discover in each book the form and content of its unique testimony of Christ. (3 semester hours)

Christian Doctrine I

A study of those truths which the Bible, as the divinely inspired source of doctrine, presents concerning the Author, the object, and the Mediator of salvation. The doctrines included are: (a) the doctrine of the Word of God (inspiration); (b) the doctrine of God, the Author of salvation; (c) the doctrine of Man, the object of salvation; (d) the doctrine of Christ, the Mediator of salvation. (3 semester hours)

Christian Doctrine II

The Scriptural truths concerning the blessing the Holy Ghost showers on believers, individually and collectively, in the presentation and appropriation of the gift of salvation. The doctrines included are the following: (a) the doctrine of conversion, (b) the doctrine of justification, (c) the doctrine of sanctification; (d) the doctrine of election, (e) the doctrine of the Means of Grace, (f) the doctrine of the Church, (g) the doctrine of the final consummation of salvation in heaven. (3 semester hours)

Mary Hardin-Baylor, University of
Correspondence Department
Belton, Texas 76513   (817) 939-4508

Description:

The University of Mary Hardin-Baylor was chartered in 1845 by the Republic of Texas as the female division of Baylor University. The school moved from Independence to Belton in 1886. In 1917, the name was changed from Baylor Female College to Baylor College for Women. In 1934, it was renamed Mary Hardin-Baylor College in honor of Mrs. Mary Hardin of Burkburnett who, with her husband John G. Hardin, made substantial gifts to the school. In 1978, Mary Hardin-Baylor College became the University of Mary Hardin-Baylor.

Correspondence courses are principally for use of current students.

Faculty:

R. W. Montgomery, Registrar. Regular faculty of 65 are involved in the correspondence program.

Academic Levels:
College

Degree/Certificate Programs:
Up to 31 semester hour credits may be applied to the bachelor's degree.

Admission Requirements:
Admission to the University is required for enrollment in correspondence courses.

Tuition:
$125 per semester hour. All tuition is paid at the time of registration. Tuition is fully refunded within the first 2 weeks provided no lessons have been turned in for grading and all course materials are returned. Thereafter, no refunds will be made.

Enrollment Period:
Registration for correspondence courses is for one year. No course may be completed in less than six weeks. The first lesson should be submitted within 30 days after enrollment and others should follow at regular intervals. Only six lessons may be submitted in one week and no more than three at one time. A course which is not completed within 12 months may be extended for three months upon request and payment of a $20.00 fee.

Equipment Requirements:
The student provides textbooks which may be purchased from the UMHB Bookstore.

Credit and Grading:
Examinations which count for 75 percent of the grade must be taken within one month of the date the last lesson is received by the Correspondence Department, unless the course expires before that time. If it is not practical for the student to travel to the campus, the examination may be sent to another institution for administration. A proctoring institution may charge a fee for administering the final examination. Grading system: A, B, C, D, F. Minimum passing grade is D. Credit is awarded in semester hour units.

Library Services:
Correspondence students have complete access to the campus library.

Accreditations:
Southern Association of Colleges and Schools.

COLLEGE COURSES

BUSINESS

Principles of Management
(3 semester hours)

Risk Management and Insurance
A study of the principles and practices in the fields of life, fire, marine, and casualty insurance. (3 semester hours)

Principles of Microeconomics
A broad introductory course of fundamental principles in the field of economics, emphasizing microeconomics. (3 semester hours)

Principles of Macroeconomics
A continuation of the above course in the study of fundamental principles of economics, emphasizing macroeconomics. (3 semester hours)

Principles of Marketing
Introduces students to basic concepts, practices, and analytic techniques of contemporary marketing. (3 semester hours)

Personnel Management
A study of the managing of manpower in modern society; the behavior of people in their employment relationships. (3 semester hours)

Marketing Management
A study of the relationship between the firm and the consumer as seen from the point of view of the marketing manager, including consumer behavior, marketing research, and the social and legal environment. (3 semester hours)

Organizational Behavior
A survey of case studies dealing with human relations problems in business management. An extensive study of human behavioral patterns and motivational techniques in business. (3 semester hours)

Principles of Real Estate
Principles of real estate finance, brokerage, land economics, building and construction, marketing, appraising, and real estate law. (3 semester hours)

EDUCATION

Social Studies in Elementary School
Designed to give the prospective teacher a basic understanding of the content, methods, and materials of teaching the social studies in the elementary school. (3 semester hours)

Human Growth and Development
Designed to give a comprehensive picture of human growth, development, and learning from early childhood to late adolescence, based on studies of the physical, emotional, social, moral, and mental factors involved in development. Special emphasis is directed to child development. (3 semester hours)

The Exceptional Learner
(3 semester hours)

ENGLISH

Survey of English Literature to 1790
Historical survey of the development of English literature to 1790. Careful study of representative selections and development of types. Parallel reading in novel and drama. (3 semester hours)

Survey of English Literature since 1790
A continuation of the above course with special emphasis upon the nineteenth and twentieth centuries. (3 semester hours)

American Literature to 1900
Historical survey of the major American writers from colonial times to 1900. Emphasis on the nineteenth century. (3 semester hours)

HEALTH EDUCATION

Health Education in Elementary School
Health problems and interests of elementary school children, promotion of the healthful school environment, and understanding of health appraisal of school children and curriculum construction. (3 semester hours)

HISTORY

History of Western Civilization to 1715

A study of the western tradition from the early pre-literary period to the death of Louis XIV in 1715, including the civilizations of the Fertile Crescent, Egypt, Greece, Rome, and medieval and early modern Europe. (3 semester hours)

History of Western Civilization since 1715

European history since 1715, including the development of nation-states, the expansion of Europe, the French Revolution and Napoleon, nineteenth century nationalism and imperialism, and the power politics and wars of the twentieth century. (3 semester hours)

Unites States History through 1865

A survey of the social and political history of the United States through 1865, including European backgrounds, colonial development, the American Revolution, the making of the U.S. Constitution, the growth of political parties, sectionalism, and the War Between the States. (3 semester hours)

MATHEMATICS

Mathematics for the Elementary Teacher

A course designed for elementary teachers including the basic concepts of algebra and informal geometry. (3 semester hours)

Geometry

Incidence and separation properties of planes and space, metric apparatus, inequalities, the parallel postulate, circles and constructions with rule and compass. (3 semester hours)

NURSING

Terminology Used in Nursing

Designed to provide basic information regarding terminology essential for communication between the nurse and other health care professionals. (3 semester hours)

The Nursing Role in Pharmacotherapeutics

Designed to emphasize the nursing role in drug therapy. There is a focus on drugs in the context of their principal uses, their effects on biochemical or physiological processes, and guidelines for nursing intervention indicated by these effects. (3 semester hours)

PHYSICAL EDUCATION

Tests and Measurements in Physical Education

Use, interpretation, evaluation and administration of tests in health and physical education. Analysis and application of statistical procedures. (3 semester hours)

Principles of Adapted and Therapeutic Physical Education

A survey of orthopedic deviations, faculty, body mechanics, and subfitness. Experience in the administration, recording, and interpretation of findings of screening and physical fitness tests. Field trips to rehabilitation centers, hospitals, and related areas. (3 semester hours)

POLITICAL SCIENCE

State and Federal Government I

A study of the federal and state constitutions and governments with emphasis on elections, political parties, and interest groups. (3 semester hours)

State and Federal Government II

A study of the federal and state constitutions and governments with emphasis on governmental structures, processes, and policy making. (3 semester hours)

PSYCHOLOGY

History and Systems of Psychology

A survey of the major theories and theoretical systems and their historical development. Includes an integration of the Christian beliefs and the student's own philosophical presuppositions, and current psychological theories. (3 semester hours)

Developmental Psychology

Development of the human being from birth through old age, studied in terms of basic psychological principles. Major theories of child development will be considered. (3 semester hours)

Abnormal Psychology

An introduction to the symptomatology and etiology of the behavioral, emotional, and mental disorders, with consideration of modern therapeutic approaches. (3 semester hours)

Social Psychology

A background in historical and contemporary social psychological theories. An analysis of social factors at work in the development of the individual through childhood, adolescence, and adulthood. (3 semester hours)

Memory Learning and Problem Solving

Taking the cognitive point of view, this course treats man as an active processor of information. Methods to improve memory, learning, and problem solving are shown from both the informational and practical perspectives. (3 semester hours)

RELIGION

Old Testament Survey

A general survey of the Old Testament with special emphasis being given to great characters, events, and religious teachings. (3 semester hours)

New Testament Survey

A course intended to introduce the student to the New Testament, and to an intelligent and appreciative understanding of the life and teachings of Jesus Christ, the early Christian movement, and the doctrinal concepts and ethical ideals of Christianity. (3 semester hours)

SOCIOLOGY

Social Psychology

A background in historical and contemporary social psychological theories, indicating the growing need combining the individual and social approaches to the study of the development of man. An analysis of social factors at work in the development of the individual through childhood, adolescence, and adulthood. (3 semester hours)

SPANISH

Elementary Spanish I

Beginning Spanish consisting of fundamentals of grammar and composition with strong emphasis on oral comprehension and conversation. (4 semester hours)

Elementary Spanish II

A continuation of the above course. (4 semester hours)

Intermediate Spanish I

Readings of moderate difficulty from representative Spanish authors with oral discussion in Spanish of the reading selections. Review of composition and certain grammatical principles. (3 semester hours)

Intermediate Spanish II

A continuation of the above course. (3 semester hours)

Survey of Spanish Literature I

A survey course covering the history and development of Spanish literature from the Middle Ages to the present time. (3 semester hours)

Survey of Spanish Literature II

A continuation of the above course. (3 semester hours)

Advanced Grammar

A course designed especially for students who plan to teach in high school and for those interested in translation. (3 semester hours)

Survey of Spanish American Literature II

A survey course covering the history and development of Spanish American literature from its beginning to the present time. Reading of selected works. (3 semester hours)

Maryland, University of
Open Learning Program
University College
University Boulevard at Adelphi Road
College Park, Maryland 20742 (800) 888-8682

Description:

The University of Maryland University College is primarily for adults who prefer to pursue part-time study. Instruction is offered at more than thirty sites in Maryland and the District of Columbia metropolitan area.

Open Learning for the Fire Service (OLFS) is an independent study program for fire service personnel throughout the country. The student is provided with the option of taking an individual fire course or pursuing a planned degree route. If qualified, a Bachelor of Science degree can be earned. Classroom attendance is not required. Funded and sponsored by the Federal Emergency Management Agency/National Fire Academy, OLFS is a consortium of seven colleges and universities that offer the program. The University of Maryland University College serves OLFS students in Delaware, Maryland, New Jersey, North Carolina, Washington (DC), West Virginia, and Virginia.

Faculty:

JoAnne Hildebrand, Director, OLFS, University College.

Academic Levels:

College

Degree/Certificate Programs:

To earn a Bachelor of Science degree a student must be classified as a degree student. For those students who wish to pursue a particular subject, individual courses may be taken for credit. National Fire Academy certificates are awarded for successful completion of six courses.

Admission Requirements:

Open Learning courses are junior-senior level. Credits may be transferred in for approval and application to the baccalaureate degree.

Tuition:

Contact the university for current Open Learning tuition costs.

Equipment Requirements:

Textbooks must be purchased by the student.

Credit and Grading:

A–F. Examinations must be proctored. Credit is awarded in semester hour units.

Accreditations:

Middle States Association of Colleges and Schools.

COLLEGE COURSES

FIRE SERVICE

Fire Dynamics

Study of fluid mechanics and thermodynamic principles of fire propagation. Variables in pre- and post-flashover fire development. Study of geometric, material, gaseous, fluid flow, and thermodynamic parameters. Compartment and building fire models. (3 semester hours)

Political and Legal Foundations of Fire Protection

An analysis of the legal, political, and social variables of the government's role in public safety. Includes legal limitations and responsibility, liability of fire prevention organization and personnel. (3 semester hours)

The Community and the Fire Threat

The sociological, economic, and political characteristics of communities and their impact on the fire problem. Includes a study of community profiles and structures with consideration of the economic, geographic, and sociological variables of the fire threat. Examination of functional basis of the community, the diverse social roles of community agencies, and study of the fire service as a complex organization within the community. (3 semester hours)

Applications of Fire Research

Understanding of fire research, its application, and the transfer and implications of available research results for fire prevention and protection programs. National and international studies. Maintaining awareness of research developments. (3 semester hours)

Incendiary Fire Analysis and Investigation

Examination and procedures and techniques for collection, comparison and analysis of the physical evidence relative to the area of fire origin. Principles of evidence or ignition phenomena, and propagation variables. Legislative, economic, psychological and sociological variables of incendiary fire. Role of insurance and government programs. Data analysis and prediction techniques, including pattern analysis. (3 semester hours)

Fire Protection Structure and Systems Design

Design principles involved in structural fire protection with empirical or analytical tests and prediction procedures. Includes control detection and suppression design practices. Fundamentals of the hydraulic design of sprinkler and water spray systems with recent innovations. (3 semester hours)

Fire Related Human Behavior

Human behavior in fire incidents related to fire protection variables. Includes practices, programs, codes and ordinances, concepts of role, personal invulnerability, risk and group dynamicrelated to design aspects of buildings and the mitigation effects of fire in the modern society. (3 semester hours)

Fire Prevention Organization and Management

An overview of the techniques, procedures, programs, and agencies involved in fire prevention. Topics include public and private fire prevention functions, licenses, permits, zoning, legal aspects, inspection, investigation, planning, arson and incendiary diary analysis. (3 semester hours)

Analytic Approaches to Public Fire Protection

Systems analysis and its use and limitations in fire protection and other problem areas. Illustrated with case studies and models using the system approach to fire suppression and prevention. (3 semester hours)

Personnel Management for the Fire Service

Personnel management procedures and problems in the fire service. Includes manpower planning, labor relations, recruitment, selection, testing, performance appraisals, classification, motivation, politics, and management. (3 semester hours)

Advanced Fire Administration

An overview of organization and management techniques in the fire service. Topics include management of equipment and personnel, fire department functions, planning, resource development, labor relations, communication, financial management, and community relations. (3 semester hours)

Disaster and Fire Defense Planning

The concepts and principles of community fire risk assessment, as related to group fires and natural disasters. Includes regional and cooperative procedures and plans, the relationship of structural, climatic, and topographical variables to group fires, conflagrations, and natural disaster. (3 semester hours)

Marywood College
Off-Campus Degree Program
2300 Adams Avenue
Scranton, Pennsylvania 18509 (800) 836-6940

Description:

Marywood College was founded by the Sisters, Servants of the Immaculate Heart of Mary in 1915. The college is a private, coeducational institution offering both undergraduate and graduate programs. The size of the on-campus student body at Marywood averages about 3,500. In 1975, Marywood College made higher education a possibility for those adults who cannot attend classes on campus. This program of correspondence study developed into the Marywood College Off-Campus Program. A student may earn a Bachelor of Science degree in Accounting or Business Administration through a coordination of independent study and 2 two-week residencies on campus. Credits are generally transferable from other accredited institutions as well as through work assessment evaluation and the College Level Examination Program (CLEP). The program is fully structured from start to finish and provides flexibility as to starting time, selection of course sequence, and scheduling of study time. Nearly 300 students are enrolled in the Off-Campus Degree Program.

Faculty:

Peggi Munkittrick, Director, Distance Education; Sr. Dolores Filicko, I.H.M., Registrar; Melissa A. Cottone, Coordinator of Student Enrollment and Retention, Off-Campus Degree Program. The faculty for the Off-Campus Degree Program numbers 25.

Academic Levels:

College

Degree/Certificate Programs:

Baccalaureate. The Marywood Off-Campus Degree Program offers the Bachelor of Science degree in Accounting or Business Administration. In the course description section below, the courses are detailed under their respective headings. With the required exception of two six-credit residency periods of two weeks each, the entire degree may be earned through correspondence study.

Admission Requirements:

High School graduation or state-approved GED equivalency certificate. Student must reside outside a 25-mile radius of the campus and be at least 21 years of age.

Tuition:

$187 per credit; course materials $75. Deferred payment plan available. Monthly payment plan for employer-sponsored deferred tuition plan is also available; contact the Off-Campus Degree Program office for information. Approved by the Veterans Administration. Pro rata refund policy.

Enrollment Period:

A student must work within the format of two six-month semesters, in each of which a student would register for three courses or nine credits. The scheduled study time is two months per course. Two campus residencies of two weeks duration each (six credits awarded for each residency) are required at Marywood College. A student may obtain a leave of absence from the program for a valid reason.

Equipment Requirements:

Independent study course materials, student guides, and textbooks are supplied by the College and included in the tuition.

Credit and Grading:

The method of examinations is a combination of proctored and the honor system; course final examinations are proctored, while course lesson examinations are open-book, non-proctored. Transfer credit from other accredited institutions accepted as well as credits earned through the College Level Examination Program (CLEP). The minimum passing grade is 65 percent. Grading system: A, 95–100; B-plus, 90–94, B, 85–89; C-plus, 80–84; C, 75–79; D-plus, 70–74, D, 65–69; F, failure. The minimum passing grade is D (65). A total of 126 semester hours is required for graduation; 66 of these must be in the liberal arts; 60 must be in the major (Accounting or Business Administration). Credit is awarded in semester hour units.

Library Services:

The Marywood Electronic Library may be accessed by students.

Accreditations:

Middle States Association of Colleges and Schools.

COLLEGE COURSES

ACCOUNTING

Accounting I

An introductory course in accounting emphasizing nature and preparation of basic statements, basic accounting cycles, and basic concepts and principles that underlie accounting thought. (3 semester hours)

Accounting II

Continues the application of accounting principles to partnerships and corporations. Includes stockholders' equity, long-term investments in corporate securities, cash flows, analysis and interpretation of financial statements. (3 semester hours)

Intermediate Accounting I

Presents the objectives of accounting and the principles that have evolved in response to the objectives; presentation and disclosure problems surrounding the general purpose financial statements; valuation and recording of working capital as well as non-current items; analysis and interpretation of accounting data; development of financial statements from incomplete records. (3 semester hours)

Intermediate Accounting II

A continuation of the above course. Includes the study of liabilities, long-term debt, securities and owner's equity. Also on the agenda: a discussion of revenue recognition, accounting for leases and statement of cash flow. (3 semester hours)

Cost Accounting

Presents the principles of cost accounting, beginning with the nature and purpose of cost accounting in the manufacturing environment. The major areas of job order and process cost accounting are presented along with the application of these techniques to manufacturing and other environments. Finally, the use of cost accounting as a management tool is explained. (3 semester hours)

Financial Management

Deals with institutions, problems, organizations, and analytical procedures that are unique to financial management. (3 semester hours)

Federal Taxation

Detailed study of federal income taxation and regulations, including a major emphasis upon the federal income tax provisions having common application to all types of taxpayers. (3 semester hours)

Business Law I

After introductory material on sources of law, court systems, civil procedure and tort liability, a substantial part of this course is devoted to the law of contracts. Also discussed at length are business organizations, namely partnerships, limited partnerships, and corporations. (3 semester hours)

Business Law II

A continuation of Business Law I; agency and employment, bankruptcy, secured transactions, commercial paper, and the Uniform Commercial Code. (3 semester hours)

Statistics for Business Decisions

Designed to yield statistical insight into business problems. Presents basic probability theory, random sampling and sampling distributions and statistical estimations. Other topics include organization of statistical data, regression and correlations analysis, and testing hypothesis with sample data. (3 semester hours)

Advanced Accounting

Covers the more complex topics in accounting such as governmental accounting, nonprofit entities, partnerships including nonprofit entities, partnerships including ownership changes and liquidations and business combinations. Emphasis is given to consolidated financial statements and the problems involving intercompany transactions and special issues in accounting for subsidiaries. (3 semester hours)

Auditing Principles and Procedures

Provides an understanding of concepts that underline the principles, standards, and procedures involved in the conduct of an audit. An analysis of the auditing profession, the audit process and reporting of problems is presented through the use of an integrated case study. Landmark legal cases; official pronouncements such as SASs, SSARs, FSABs, and industry audit guides are discussed. (3 semester hours)

Organizational Communication

Covers the role of communication of organizations, as well as the different communication approaches organizations use. Discusses business communication, personality variables in communication, communication conflicts, and small group communication. (3 semester hours)

Management Information Systems

The historical development of computers, systems planning, systems studies, flexibility studies, computer operations, computerized management systems, auditing aspects of computer management considerations in computer planning, and accounting implications in the computer age. (3 semester hours)

Managerial Decision Making

Emphasis upon the decision making process as a whole. A process model will be used to show why and how a decision materializes. Interdisciplinary sources affecting decision making, including the environment, psychology, sociology, and constraints placed upon the decision maker are discussed. (3 semester hours)

Principles of Marketing

Fundamentals of marketing management, including marketing decision making, product strategy, promotion, pricing and distribution. Market analysis and consumer behavior, as well as marketing planning and organizations will be stressed. (3 semester hours)

Money and Banking

An initial understanding of money, its definition, supply, importance, and control by the central bank is the starting point for this course. Following that is a concentration on developing an understanding of the relationship between monetary and fiscal policy and inflation and government spending and the effects of all of these on investment and savings. (3 semester hours)

International Business Management

Presents an overview of international business, including the diversity of international environment. Considers the governmental impact on American overseas operations and discusses conflicts with nationalism and national interest along with global business strategy, organization, and administration. (3 semester hours)

Taxation of Business Entities

Income taxation of corporations, tax implications of the formation of a corporation, corporate distributions not in complete liquidation, corporate distributions in complete liquidation. Subchapter S corporations and partnership taxation. (3 semester hours)

BUSINESS ADMINISTRATION

Principles of Marketing

Fundamentals of marketing management, including marketing decision making, product strategy, promotion, pricing, and distribution. Market analysis and consumer behavior, as well as marketing planning and organization will be stressed. (3 semester hours)

Introduction to Human Resources Management

Introduces the student to current corporate human resources practices. Discusses human resources problems and presents alternative solutions to such problems. (3 semester hours)

Personal Financial Planning

The importance of setting and organizing objectives for an individual or family is covered. The process of converting these and implementing alternative plans is discussed. Protection against personal risk, capital accumulation, provision for retirement, investment and property management, and planning for business interests are addressed. (3 semester hours)

Marketing Management

Introduces managerial decisions in the realm of marketing and approaches to making those decisions. Includes such topics as market opportunity and targets, buyer behavior and marketing decisions. Also considers how to make products available and stimulate demand in the marketplace. (3 semester hours)

Principles of Economics I - Macroeconomics

Introduces principles of economic theory as applied to the aggregate economy (macroeconomics); compares the United States economy to other economic systems; evaluates the performance of the United States economy and of institutions within that economy; applies Keynesian analysis; traces the effect of various types of monetary and fiscal policy. (3 semester hours)

Operations Management

An introduction to the basics of production/operations management. The material is organized around the planning, organizing, and controlling theme. Topics covered include forecasting, capacity planning, facility location planning, layout planning, organizing for operations, job design, inventory control, material requirements planning, and quality control. (3 semester hours)

Managerial Decision Making

Emphasis upon the decision making process as a whole. A process model will be used to show why and how a decision materializes. Interdisciplinary sources affecting decision making, including the environment, psychology, sociology, and constraints placed upon the decision maker are discussed. (3 semester hours)

Personnel Management

Examines the changing responsibilities of a personnel manager within an organization; addresses human and interorganizational behavior. Discusses processes and philosophies of obtaining personnel, developing their abilities, rewarding them monetarily, aligning group and individual interests with organizational goals and preserving the health of the work force. (3 semester hours)

Money and Banking

An initial understanding of money, its definition, supply, importance, and control by the central bank is the starting point for this course. Following that is a concentration on developing an understanding of the relationship between monetary and fiscal policy and inflation and government spending and the effects of all of these on investment and savings. (3 semester hours)

Small Business Management

Focuses on such topics as planning a new business and the external sources of information needed by the entrepreneur. Also covers purchasing an existing business as well as raising funds for a new business, tax aspects, and relevancy of franchising. (3 semester hours)

International Business Management

Presents an overview of international business, including the diversity of international environment. Considers the governmental impact on American overseas operations and discusses conflicts with nationalism and national interest along with global business strategy, organization, and administration. (3 semester hours)

Principles of Management

Fundamentals of management theories and philosophies. Includes planning, decision making, organizing, personnel staffing, directing, and controlling. (3 semester hours)

ECONOMICS

Principles of Economics I - Macroeconomics

Introduces principles of economic theory as applied to the aggregate economy (macroeconomics); compares the United States economy to other economic systems; evaluates the performance of the United States economy and of institutions within that economy; applies Keynesian analysis; traces the effect of various types of monetary and fiscal policy. (3 semester hours)

Principles of Economics II - Microeconomics

Offers theoretical and empirical evaluation of market power with respect to prices, production, and employment in specific industries (microeconomics); examines the distribution of income and pricing of economic resources; analyzes trade and finance among nations. (3 semester hours)

ENGLISH

Composition and Rhetoric

The purpose of this course is to make the student a better writer. The course is offered to help students learn the basic principles of writing as a communication medium; to analyze examples of successful writing; and to improve writing skills through practice. (3 semester hours)

FINE ARTS

Art in the Modern Era

A study of the interdisciplinary factors that help shape the phenomenon we call modern art. The total effect on art since the 1950s will be experienced. (3 semester hours)

FRENCH

Elementary French

Course 101. Emphasizes the acquisition of communication skills within a culturally significant context. Course planned specifically for the student who has not studied the language previously. (3 semester hours)

Course 102. A continuation of the above course. Emphasizes the acquisition of communication skills within a culturally significant context. (3 semester hours)

HISTORY

Roots of the Modern World

A study of the pivotal events and achievements of modern humankind stressing the period from the European intellectual revolution to World

War I and relating them to the life of humankind in contemporary times. (3 semester hours)

Global Resources and Scarcities

Presents historical and ecological perspectives on humankind's common heritage of resources and the use of them. Analyzes contrasting interpretations of past and present experiences and competing solutions for the future. (3 semester hours)

Perspectives on the Pursuit of Peace

An interdisciplinary analysis of the historical, sociological, and philosophical perspectives on the pursuit of peace throughout the centuries. Emphasis is placed on twentieth-century approaches to peace, such as nonviolent resistance, disarmanment, and international cooperation. (3 semester hours)

LITERATURE

The Classics in World Literature

Studies the works of Homer, Virgil, Ovid, Sophocles, Dante, Chaucer, Shakespeare, and others. Includes essay examinations. (3 semester hours)

World Literature and the Modern Age

Studies the works of Moliere, Swift, the British Romantics, Whitman, Melville, Flaubert, Tolstoy, Kafka, Eliot, Sartre, and Camus. Includes essay examinations. (3 semester hours)

American Short Fiction

Provides an in-depth examination of the initiation theme organized to enable the student to recognize, identify, and appreciate the varying styles of major American authors. Pays much attention to irony, paradox, symbol, motif, and foreshadowing in the works of Nathaniel Hawthorne, Ambrose Bierce, Henry James, Stephen Crane, and Edith Wharton. (3 semester hours)

MATHEMATICS

Mathematics for Contemporary Society

This course presents the fundamentals of finite mathematics in a basic, introductory style but at the same time covers the subject matter in sufficient depth so that the student can see a rich variety of realistic and relevant applications. Topics include: logic, probability, linear programming, matrices, functions and relations, and computers. (3 semester hours)

PHILOSOPHY

Introduction to Philosophy

An introduction to the broad range of historical and systematic thought which is philosophy. Topics covered include a history of philosophy from the ancient period to the contemporary period and philosophical problems—ethics, political philosophy, religion, theory of knowledge and metaphysics. (3 semester hours)

Ethics

This is a study of the nature of the good life and what constitutes good and bad, right and wrong human conduct. (3 semester hours)

Perspectives on the Pursuit of Peace

This course is a philosophical analysis of relevant primary sources in terms of possible personal contributions to a more compassionate, just, and peaceful world. (3 semester hours)

Political Philosophy

An examination of the assumptions underlying the world's major political ideas and systems. Emphasis is placed on a presentation of the fundamental ideas of the major political philosophers and the significance of these ideas in terms of the present. (3 semester hours)

PHYSICAL EDUCATION

Lifetime Fitness: The American Way

This course is designed to give practical insight in the following areas: cardiovascular fitness, diet and weight control, stress management, and strength and flexibility. (3 semester hours)

PSYCHOLOGY

General Psychology

A broad-based investigation of the nature of behavior, stressing general scientific principles, the complexity of human motivation, and potential of psychology for the student's self-realization. (3 semester hours)

PUBLIC RELATIONS

Public Relations: Principles and Practice

The nature of public relations; processes of researching and influencing public opinion; analysis of public relations programs; responsibilities of the public relations practitioner to the media and to the public. (3 semester hours)

RELIGIOUS STUDIES

Jesus in the Twentieth-Century Perspective

A many-faceted look at Jesus the Christ under the light of contemporary biblical and theological scholarship. Issues examined include, among others, his human consciousness, connection with the Essenes, death and resurrection, and redemptive work. (3 semester hours)

Paths of Belief

A discussion of the world's faiths apart from affections and disaffections. This course includes, but is not limited to, a critical review of the beginnings of Indian religion, Buddhism, Hinduism, Chinese and Japanese religion, Judaism, Islam, Catholicism, and Protestantism. (3 semester hours)

Religious Thought in America

An examination of key theories on the role of religion and a discussion of some major religions in America and how they continue to influence American life. (3 semester hours)

SCIENCE

Ecology

An investigation of the relationship between living organisms and their natural environment. Emphasis is placed on the existence of natural species and their relationship to other life forms. (3 semester hours)

Matter, Energy, and Technology

Introductory course which provides a sound basis for understanding basic theories of biology, chemistry, and physics. Topics covered include motion and mechanics, energy, chemistry, magnetism, electricity, sound, astronomy, and space science. (3 semester hours)

SOCIAL SCIENCE

Introductory Sociology

Introduces fundamental sociological concepts and interpretations of human behavior. Explores the social dimensions of culture, social structure, and the relationship of human personality to society. Includes the topics of childhood socialization, sex roles, deviance, social classes, social institutions, and social change. (3 semester hours)

SPANISH

Spanish for the Business Person I

The first part of this course presents a discussion of the geographic, social, economic, and political differences between the countries of Latin America. The second part of the course is designed to improve business communication skills through an introduction to the fundamentals of Spanish grammar, drill in pronunciation, conversation, and reading. (3 semester hours)

Spanish for the Business Person II

A continuation of the above course and designed to increase the level of student communication skills in Spanish. Course content is designed to stimulate the spontaneous use of vocabulary and forms used in commerce. (3 semester hours)

Mayville State College
Mayville, North Dakota 58257 (701) 786-2304

Description:
Mayville State College is one of North Dakota's original colleges. It was established in 1889 with a two-year program; this was expanded to a four-year program in 1925.

Correspondence study is offered on an emergency basis only. Credits earned through such study may be applied to the requirements for a degree, provided that the number of such credits does not exceed one-eighth of the total number required for completion of the curriculum concerned. As a rule, correspondence work is not offered during the summer months.

Faculty:
Robert Schwieso, Academic Dean.

Academic Levels:
College

Admission Requirements:
Enrollment is restricted to matriculated students at Mayville State College.

Tuition:
Contact the Academic Dean for enrollment procedure and current resident tuition information.

Enrollment Period:
All lessons are expected to be completed by June 30. Contact the Academic Dean for courses available.

Credit and Grading:
A, B, C, D, F. Credit is awarded in quarter hour units.

Accreditations:
North Central Association of Colleges and Schools.

Memphis State University
Open Learning Fire Service Program
University College
Memphis, Tennessee 38152   (901) 678-2716

Description:
Established as West Tennessee State Normal School in 1912, the university adopted its present name in 1957.

Open Learning for the Fire Service (OLFS) is an independent study program for fire service personnel throughout the country. The student is provided with the option of taking an individual fire course or pursuing a planned degree route. If qualified, a Bachelor of Science degree can be earned. Classroom attendance is not required. Funded and sponsored by the Federal Emergency Management Agency/National Fire Academy, OLFS is a consortium of seven colleges and universities that offer the program. Memphis State University serves OLFS students in Alabama, Arkansas, Kentucky, Mississippi, Tennessee, and South Carolina.

Faculty:
Dr. Susanne Darnell, Director, OLFS, University College.

Academic Levels:
College

Degree/Certificate Programs:
To earn a Bachelor of Science degree a student must be classified as a degree student. For those students who wish to pursue a particular subject, individual courses may be taken for credit. National Fire Academy certificates are awarded for successful completion of six courses.

Admission Requirements:
Open Learning courses are junior-senior level. Credits may be transferred in for approval and application to the baccalaureate degree.

Tuition:
Contact the university for current Open Learning tuition costs.

Equipment Requirements:
Textbooks must be purchased by the student.

Credit and Grading:
A–F. Examinations must be proctored. Credit is awarded in semester hour units.

Accreditations:
Southern Association of Colleges and Schools.

COLLEGE COURSES

FIRE SERVICE

Fire Dynamics

Study of fluid mechanics and thermodynamic principles of fire propagation. Variables in pre- and post-flashover fire development. Study of geometric, material, gaseous, fluid flow, and thermodynamic parameters. Compartment and building fire models. (3 semester hours)

Political and Legal Foundations of Fire Protection

An analysis of the legal, political, and social variables of the government's role in public safety. Includes legal limitations and responsibility, liability of fire prevention organization and personnel. (3 semester hours)

The Community and the Fire Threat

The sociological, economic, and political characteristics of communities and their impact on the fire problem. Includes a study of community profiles and structures with consideration of the economic, geographic, and sociological variables of the fire threat. Examination of functional basis of the community, the diverse social roles of community agencies, and study of the fire service as a complex organization within the community. (3 semester hours)

Applications of Fire Research

Understanding of fire research, its application, and the transfer and implications of available research results for fire prevention and protection programs. National and international studies. Maintaining awareness of research developments. (3 semester hours)

Incendiary Fire Analysis and Investigation

Examination and procedures and techniques for collection, comparison and analysis of the physical evidence relative to the area of fire origin. Principles of evidence or ignition phenomena, and propagation variables. Legislative, economic, psychological and sociological variables of incendiary fire. Role of insurance and government programs. Data analysis and prediction techniques, including pattern analysis. (3 semester hours)

Fire Protection Structure and Systems Design

Design principles involved in structural fire protection with empirical or analytical tests and prediction procedures. Includes control detection and suppression design practices. Fundamentals of the hydraulic design of sprinkler and water spray systems with recent innovations. (3 semester hours)

Fire Related Human Behavior

Human behavior in fire incidents related to fire protection variables. Includes practices, programs, codes and ordinances, concepts of role, personal invulnerability, risk and group dynamic related to design aspects of buildings and the mitigation effects of fire in the modern society. (3 semester hours)

Fire Prevention Organization and Management

An overview of the techniques, procedures, programs, and agencies involved in fire prevention. Topics include public and private fire prevention functions, licenses, permits, zoning, legal aspects, inspection, investigation, planning, arson and incendiary diary analysis. (3 semester hours)

Analytic Approaches to Public Fire Protection

Systems analysis and its use and limitations in fire protection and other problem areas. Illustrated with case studies and models using the system approach to fire suppression and prevention. (3 semester hours)

Personnel Management for the Fire Service

Personnel management procedures and problems in the fire service. Includes manpower planning, labor relations, recruitment, selection, testing, performance appraisals, classification, motivation, politics, and management. (3 semester hours)

Advanced Fire Administration

An overview of organization and management techniques in the fire service. Topics include management of equipment and personnel, fire department functions, planning, resource development, labor relations, communication, financial management, and community relations. (3 semester hours)

Disaster and Fire Defense Planning

The concepts and principles of community fire risk assessment, as related to group fires and natural disasters. Includes regional and cooperative procedures and plans, the relationship of structural, climatic, and topographical variables to group fires, conflagrations, and natural disaster. (3 semester hours)

Messiah College
Department of Religion and Philosophy
Grantham, Pennsylvania 10727 (717) 766-2511

Description:

Messiah College was founded in 1909 by the Brethren in Christ Church in Harrisburg, Pennsylvania. Until 1972, the College was owned and operated by the Brethren in Christ Church. Legal control has now been transferred to a self-perpetuating Board of Trustees. Today, the College and Church hold a covenant relationship, and each party works to further the ministry of the other.

Several Bible and religion courses are available in correspondence format.

Faculty:

Dr. Luke L. Keefer, Jr., Chairman, Department of Religion and Philosophy.

Academic Levels:

College

Tuition:

Contact the Department of Religion and Philosophy for enrollment procedures and current tuition information. Students withdrawing will receive a prorated refund.

Credit and Grading:

Credit is awarded in semester hour units. Grading system: A, B, C, D, F.

Accreditations:

Middle States Association of Colleges and Schools.

COLLEGE COURSES

BIBLE

Bible

For courses currently available and their descriptions, contact the Chair of the Department of Biblical and Religious Studies.

RELIGION

Religion

For courses currently available and their descriptions, contact the Chair of the Department of Biblical and Religious Studies.

Metropolitan State College of Denver
Extended Campus Program
5660 Greenwood Plaza Boulevard
Englewood, Colorado 80111   (303) 721-1313

Description:

Metropolitan State College of Denver is a state institution that shares a campus and facilities with the Community College of Denver-Auraria Campus and the University of

Colorado at Denver. Metro State participates in the Colorado Consortium for Independent Study which is composed of the independent study offices of six institutions of higher education in Colorado: Adams State College, Colorado State University, University of Colorado, University of Northern Colorado, University of Southern Colorado, and Metropolitan State College of Denver. The Consortium strives to provide quality independent study opportunities and to avoid duplication of courses offered by Consortium members. The correspondence student should consult the listings in this *Guide* of all member schools of the Consortium for a complete offering of subject matter.

Faculty:
Gwen Thornton, Director.

Academic Levels:
College

Admission Requirements:
Open enrollment.

Tuition:
$70 per semester hour. Fees subject to change without notice. Refund allowed within 40 days minus an administrative fee. Specific information about the institution's policy will be sent to the student with the course material.

Enrollment Period:
The maximum time allowed to complete a course is 1 year; minimum time is 2 weeks per semester hour. A 12-month extension may be granted upon payment of an extension fee.

Equipment Requirements:
Textbooks and supplies must be purchased by the student and can be ordered from the Metropolitan State College of Denver-Auraria Book Center, 955 Lawrence Street, Denver, CO 80204.

Credit and Grading:
Grading system is A, B, C, D, F with plus and minus recorded and averaged. Minimum passing grade is D. Credit is awarded in semester hours.

Accreditations:
North Central Association of Colleges and Schools. Member of: National University Continuing Education Association.

COLLEGE COURSES

BIOLOGY

Ecology for Non-Majors

This course familiarizes the student with the fundamentals of human ecology of North America. Classical concepts of ecology and modern environmental pressures will be brought together to give both a background to and a discussion of existing environmental problems. (3 semester hours)

COMPUTER SCIENCE

Introduction to Computers

A study of the hardware, software, and general characteristics of computer systems. Develops knowledge of computer concepts and skills through the use of Microsoft Works 3.0. Students will study word processing, data management, how to create graphics from spreadsheets, microcomputer interfaces, the DOS operation systems, data communications, computer crime and ethics, and how to select, purchase, and maintain a computer. In order to participate in this instructional program, the student must have access to the following: a PC-compatible computer capable of running Microsoft Works 3.0 and a printer. A mouse is optional. (3 semester hours)

CRIMINAL JUSTICE

Introduction to the Criminal Justice System

An overview of the American criminal justice system, covering the continuum of criminal justice from police, through the courts, to corrections. This course is offered by computer, and students must have a computer and modem. (3 semester hours)

Constitutional Law

Covers the U.S. Constitution and the function of the U.S. Supreme Court. Includes readings of decisions in the areas of speech, religion, civil rights, privacy, and other fundamental rights. (3 semester hours)

Juvenile Law

An analysis of the social-legal operation of the Juvenile Court, substantive and due process rights of minors; analysis of legal reasoning underlying juvenile law operating at all levels of government. (3 semester hours)

Probation and Parole

The history, development, principles, and operation of probation and parole, including selection, supervision, and prediction of success, experimental programs and current trends. (3 semester hours)

Civil Law for Criminal Law Administration

A study of the fundamental concepts found in civil law with an emphasis on civil liability commonly occurring in criminal justice. Designed to help persons in criminal justice and related fields to plan for and prevent civil liability as well as deal with it when it arises. (3 semester hours

Penology

The history and development of the American system of prisons; the inmate and the prison community; custody; discipline; treatment; and alternatives to incarceration. (3 semester hours)

EDUCATION

Project Wild II—Advanced

This course is designed for students who have previously completed a Project Wild workshop (beginners level) and have a copy of the Project Wild activity guidebook. Students will increase their knowledge of wildlife education and research resources; identify supplemental materials for wildlife education; and become familiar with wildlife educational field sites. (1 semester hour)

HISTORY

Survey of African History

This course surveys the major developments on the African continent from ancient times to the modern period. The course focuses on political and cultural developments in African civilizations from ancient Egypt to the contemporary period. (3 semester hours)

Issues in European History: Spain

A study of the development of the Spanish nation with special emphasis on the political and cultural aspects of the empire, and on social development which culminated in the Civil War and the Franco Era. (3 semester hours)

Women in European History

An historical analysis of the role of, and contributions made by, women in the development of western civilization from neolithic times to the present. (3 semester hours)

Modern Middle East

This course explores the volatile history of the Middle East region with special emphasis on the post-World War II period. (3 semester hours)

Biography as History: Western Heroes and Villains

Examines the lives, personalities, and historical importance of some of the West's most colorful characters. From the Spanish explorations through the early 20th century, each significant era of the West's lively past is examined through the eyes of approximately 30 of the region's most important figures. Emphasis is on the lively aspects of each personality, as well as their importance in shaping the destiny of the West. (3 semester hours)

SPANISH

Destinos Beginning Spanish I

This course is designed for beginning students of Spanish and uses the video course, *Destinos: An Introduction to Spanish.* Basic skills addressed include listening, speaking, reading, writing, and culture. The course is conducted primarily in Spanish, using English to clarify essential points. (4 semester hours)

Michigan, University of

Extension Service
Department of Independent/Correspondence Study
200 Hill Street
Ann Arbor, Michigan 48104-3297
(313) 764-5310

Description:

The University of Michigan is a public university with three campuses (Ann Arbor, Flint, and Dearborn) and an enrollment of over 42,000 students. The Independent/Correspondence Study Program is a function of the University of Michigan Extension Service. The program has been in effect for more than 40 years.

Faculty:

Glenda K. Radine, Interim Director, Extension Service; Janet M. Baylis, Program Associate.

Academic Levels:

College
Noncredit
Graduate

Degree/Certificate Programs:

Fifteen hours of credit can be applied toward an undergraduate degree at the University of Michigan.

Admission Requirements:

Anyone may enroll who has a desire to continue an educational program, or, to test his/her ability to do university level work, or, to seek the challenge of learning something new, or, who cannot matriculate on campus during the time courses are regularly offered. No enrollment restrictions other than the student must meet the prerequisites for the course.

Tuition:

$211 per credit hour for undergraduate credit; $358 per credit hour for graduate credit. Infrastructure fee $150. American Express, MasterCard and Visa accepted. A $50 administrative fee is charged if the student drops a course within the first two months of the enrollment period; student receives remainder of fee as a refund. No refund is given if the student drops the course after the two-month period. Persons 65 years of age or older may enroll in any of the courses listed below at a fee equal to 50 percent of the announced fee for the course, exclusive of any special charges. Tuition must be paid in full at the time of enrollment. Students can apply for Veterans benefits. All students enrolling from foreign countries should add $30 to the cost of the course for airmail postage.

Enrollment Period:

The maximum time to complete a course is one year from date of enrollment. The minimum time for course completion is eight weeks from date of enrollment. Under unusual circumstances, a six-month extension to complete a course may be granted upon payment of a $15 extension fee.

Equipment Requirements:

Students must purchase textbooks and records. For those courses requiring use of cassette tapes, a $20 deposit must be paid for the tapes of which $15 will be refunded upon their return to the Department of Independent/Correspondence Study.

Credit and Grading:

The Admissions Office makes the decision regarding the transfer of correspondence credits from another institution. The course(s) for which transfer is sought should be equivalent to and have the same requirements as one offered on the University of Michigan campus. Examinations must be proctored. Students are given letter grades on their courses; D is the minimum passing grade. Credit is awarded in semester hour units.

Library Services:

Students may use the University of Michigan libraries by presenting their receipt and a library authorization form to the library.

Accreditations:

North Central Association of Colleges and Schools. Member of: National University Continuing Education Association.

COLLEGE COURSES

ASIAN STUDIES

Asia Through Fiction

Selected novels and short stories by Asian writers and by westerners writing about Asia. Readings focus on India, Ceylon, Southeast Asia, Japan and China. (3 semester hours)

COMMUNICATIONS

Preparation of Radio and TV Continuity

Instructs students on the goals and basics of writing non-dramatic material for radio, television, and motion pictures. Primarily, the course focuses on writing exercises intended for the broadcast/cablecast media of radio and television. (3 semester hours)

ECONOMICS

Principles of Economics

Course 201. Covers principles of microeconomics. Theory behind the workings of markets for goods and services will be investigated. The theories will then be applied to specific problems such as the effect of business monopoly, role of the government and the distribution of income. (4 semester hours)

Course 202. Covers principles of macroeconomics. Theory behind the workings of the national economy will be investigated. The theories will then be applied to specific problems such as the effect of changes in the spending of consumers, firms and government, or the impact of changes in the supply of money. Also covered: the role of the government as an agent with the power to tax, spend, and print money. (4 semester hours)

ENGLISH

The Contemporary Novel

The American novel since 1945. Readings from Barth, Bellow, Morris, Gass, Pynchon, Mailer, and Heller. Course includes cassette tapes of biographical sketches and background of the authors. (3 semester hours)

Studies in Individual Authors: Hemingway and Fitzgerald

Analysis of the principal works of Hemingway and Fitzgerald. Includes transcribed lectures. Cassette tapes of lectures optional. (3 semester hours)

FILM ARTS

Film Analysis

Aesthetics of film art, artistic elements in creating a film, historical evaluation, stylistic movements, and the place and impact of film in society. Explored through a film screening, reading, and criticism. (4 semester hours)

FRENCH

First Special Reading Course

Basic principles of grammar essential to intelligent reading, plus minimal competence in pronunciation. Designed for students wishing to pass the language requirement for the doctorate. No credit will be given until the student has successfully completed the Second Special Reading Course. (4 semester hours)

Second Special Reading Course

Continued examination of grammatical forms and construction essential to comprehension and translation. (4 semester hours)

GERMAN

First Special Reading Course

A study of German grammar and syntax. Designed for and open to graduate students aiming to fulfill the German language requirements for the doctorate. No credit will be given until student has successfully completed the Second Special Reading Course. Cassette tape used. (4 semester hours)

Second Special Reading Course

Continuation of the above course. An intensive study of syntactical patterns to promote rapid understanding. Directed reading in fields of specialization for research purposes. (4 semester hours)

HISTORY

Topics in Asian and African History: Palestine and the Arab-Israeli Conflict

The focus of the course content is on Palestinians and Israelis. Topics include: differences among Jewish Israelis (Zionists, non-Zionist, and anti-Zionist as well as western and eastern), and among Palestinian-Israelis, Palestinians under occupation, and Palestinians in the Arab world and elsewhere. The course will examine the conflict spillover into Lebanon as well as the Palestinian intifada and regional peace efforts. (4 semester hours)

MATHEMATICS

Analytic Geometry and Calculus I

A well-rounded picture of what calculus is about, with an application to problems in geometry and the physical sciences. (4 semester hours)

Analytic Geometry and Calculus II

Continuation of the above course. One of the standard sequence courses in calculus and geometry. (4 semester hours)

NATURAL RESOURCES

The Environment and the Citizen, Part I

First of a two-course sequence which focuses on the total environment (natural and man-made). Includes three core units: Man and the Environment, Population and Urbanization, and Ecology, plus the selection of two of the remaining ten elective units: Economics and the Environment, Urban and Regional Planning, Soil Resources, Tree Resources, Fishery Resources, Wildlife Resources, Air Pollution, Outdoor Recreation, and the Role of the Citizen. *May be elected for graduate credit.* (2 semester hours)

The Environment and the Citizen, Part II

Continuation of the above course. Consists of five of the remaining eight units not selected by the student in Part I. *May be elected for graduate credit.* (2 semester hours)

PSYCHOLOGY

Introduction to Psychology

Covers areas such as human development, how we learn, how people differ from one another, the effects of stress on behavior, mental illness, and psychology as a science. (4 semester hours)

Psychology of Aging

Normal and abnormal changes in behavior that occur between early and late maturity, with emphasis on sensation and perception, intelligence, learning and personality, as well as social roles and the impact of environmental changes on older people. (3 semester hours)

Introduction to Behavior Therapy

Principal concepts of behavior modification both as a technique and as a theory of human interaction. *May be elected for graduate credit.* (3 semester hours)

WOMEN'S STUDIES

Introduction to Women's Studies

Overview of women's studies covering present status of women in American society through considerations of history of women, nature of U.S. culture and institutions and prospects for future change in status. (4 semester hours)

Gender and Society: Hierarchies in Social Organization

Course explores the history of women; examines the basic theory of male dominance as an approach to understanding the status of women; examines how religion and economics affect women's status, and then studies the position of women in several Asian, African, and American countries. (3 semester hours)

Women in Literature and the Arts

Introduces women artists, women's art and women's creative potential, giving the student the background to understand women in the arts and the ability to participate in the women's art movement as creator, appreciator, supporter; or all of these. (3 semester hours)

Mid-America Bible College

External Studies
3500 S.W. 119th Street
Oklahoma City, Oklahoma 73170
(405) 691-3800

Description:

Mid-America Bible College is a private college affiliated with the Church of God. It was established as South Texas Bible Institute in 1953 and adopted its present name in 1985 upon its move to Oklahoma City.

External Studies correspondence courses are offered to those who wish to advance their education for greater effectiveness, or for those who find it impossible to attend regular classes.

Faculty:
Forrest Robinson, President.

Academic Levels:
College
Noncredit

Degree/Certificate Programs:
A maximum of eighteen hours may be earned by external studies and applied toward a degree.

Admission Requirements:
For degree-seeking status, high school graduation or equivalent. Courses taken for noncredit courses may be pursued by anyone.

Tuition:
Contact the college for current tuition and fees. Special discount is available to groups that enroll in extension courses. If no lessons have been submitted and withdrawal occurs within ten days of the time materials are received, 100% of tuition will be refunded provided all lesson

materials are returned in new condition. After ten days, whether the course is completed or not, there will be no refund.

Enrollment Period:
For college credit, a course must be completed within six months from the date of enrollment. To extend this time limit, permission must be received from the Academic Dean and an additional $100 fee will be required.

Equipment Requirements:
Textbooks must be purchased by the student.

Credit and Grading:
A–F. Credit is awarded in semester hour units.

Accreditations:
North Central Association of Colleges and Schools; American Association of Bible Colleges.

COLLEGE COURSES

BIBLE

Introduction to the Old Testament

A general introduction to the background and history of the Hebrew people in the Old Testament period. This embraces the sacred writings, prophets, and culture of the Hebrew people against the historical, social, political, literary, economic, and religious background of mankind to the end of the Old Testament period. (3 semester hours)

Introduction to the New Testament

An introduction to the intertestamental period to the beginnings of Christianity will be surveyed. A survey of the content and meaning of each New Testament book will be studied against the religious, literary, social, political, and economic background of the first century. (3 semester hours)

The Gospel of John

An intensive study of the Gospel of John with emphasis on major themes or motifs and special textual and theological features of the writing. It includes consideration of the Gospel's literary structure, its portrayal of Jesus and His ministry, and some comparison with Synoptic accounts. (3 semester hours)

Synoptic Gospels (Matthew, Mark, Luke)

Attention is given to Synoptic relationships, oral tradition, authorship, date and message of Matthew, Mark, and Luke, along with exposition of each Gospel. (3 semester hours)

Acts

A study of the Book of Acts with emphasis upon its origin and relationship to the New Testament writings. This study on Acts focuses particularly on the function of the apostolic ministry and the working of the Holy Spirit in the early church. (3 semester hours)

Romans

An exegetical and expository study of the book of Romans which also includes an introduction to the subject of justification by faith in the book of Galatians. The date and place of writing, destination, occasion, are studied but primary emphasis centers on discussion and studies which will directly help the student appreciate the value, strength, and theological importance of this particular letter. (3 semester hours)

Isaiah

A study of Isaiah and his contribution to Hebrew prophecy. An analytical treatment of the book of Isaiah, including its history, critical problems, main ideas, and thought. Particular attention is given to the Messianic passages. (3 semester hours)

CHURCH HISTORY

Church History

Course 3703. A study of the historical founding and development of the Christian church from apostolic times to the events of the Protestant Reformation. This will include study of the persons and movements significant to the spread of Christianity and its effects on world history. (3 semester hours)

Course 3803. A continuation of the above course from the Reformation of 1517 to the present with a special study of the development of Christianity in America. The history and traditions of the Church of God Reformation Movement will be examined. (3 semester hours)

ENGLISH

Survey of American Literature

Course 2503. This is a study of the development of American literature from colonial times to the present showing its relationship to the cultural and social history and philosophy of the various periods. (3 semester hours)

Course 2603. This is a study of the development of American literature from colonial times to the present showing its relationship to the cultural and social history and philosophy of the various periods. (3 semester hours)

HISTORY

American History

Course 2103. A survey course of the United States covering the period from the discovery of America to the Civil War. (3 semester hours)

Course 2203. A continuation of the above course covering the period from Reconstruction following the Civil War to the present. (3 semester hours)

History of World Civilization

Course 1103. Significant events, persons, details, and cultural patterns from the beginnings of civilization. (3 semester hours)

Course 1203. A continuation of the above course to the present time. (3 semester hours)

PSYCHOLOGY

Principles of Counseling

This class is designed to introduce students to the principles and practices of the counseling process. The techniques of major religious and secular approaches to counseling will be studied. (3 semester hours)

SOCIOLOGY

Introduction to Sociology

A study of the nature of social relations, social institutions, and social processes, and of the products of these relationships. The nature of culture, communication, socialization, mobility, social control, and other sociological concepts are considered. (3 semester hours)

THEOLOGY

Systematic Theology

Course 2103. An introductory study of what it is possible for us to know about God, humanity, sin, salvation, sanctification, the Church, and the end of the world. (3 semester hours)

Course 2203. A continuation of the above course with primary emphasis on soteriology—the source and plan of salvation and the sanctifying work of the Holy Spirit. The nature of the Church and future things are studied. (3 semester hours)

Minnesota, University of
Independent Study
Continuing Education and Extension
77 Pleasant Street S.E.
Minneapolis, Minnesota 55455 (612) 624-0000

Description:

The University of Minnesota began as a preparatory school and was chartered in 1851, seven years before the Territory of Minnesota became a state. It is publicly supported and now offers programs on five campuses: Minneapolis-St. Paul, Duluth, Morris, Crookston, and Waseca. The Department of Independent Study offers by correspondence over 350 degree credit courses in approximately 70 disciplines. High school courses are also offered. In selected courses, students have the option of submitting assignments and receiving instructor evaluations/comments by e-mail. Contact the Department of Independent Study for specific information.

Faculty:

Deborah L. Hillengass, Director, Independent Study.

Academic Levels:

College
High School
Noncredit

Degree/Certificate Programs:

Programs include credit courses that may apply toward associate and bachelor degrees, and certificates. The individual school at the University of Minnesota determines the number of correspondence courses allowed toward degree programs. It is possible to attain the associate degree completely from correspondence credits, and approximately half of the required credits toward the bachelor's degree. A complete certificate program can be completed through correspondence. Any course may be taken for noncredit. The Department of Independent Study offers high school correspondence courses as an educational service to the state of Minnesota. With the approval of high school authorities, Independent Study courses may be used to fulfill requirements for high school graduation. The high school diploma is not granted by the Department of Independent Study, but by the school board only. High school courses listed below use the quarter and the semester as the basis of credit evaluation.

Admission Requirements:

Open enrollment; an Independent Study course can be started at any time. Some courses require prerequisites; consult the Independent Study bulletin. The University of Minnesota is approved for DANTES (Defense Activity for Non-Traditional Education Support) for members of the military forces. Eligible service members should check with their respective Education Officers for information.

Tuition:

Tuition varies with number of credits, college, undergraduate/graduate, etc. ($79.50 per quarter hour credit for 0000- and 1000-level courses). The tuition for 3000- and 5000-level courses varies by school. Prices subject to change without notice. For cost of noncredit courses, contact Department of Independent Study. There is a partial payment plan available. High school courses $45 per quarter credit, $90 per semester credit. A tuition assistance plan is also available; consult the Independent Study Office. Texts and materials must be paid in full at the time of purchase. A refund plan is available up to three months from registration. Financial assistance plans available for Minnesota residents.

Enrollment Period:

The maximum time allowed to complete a course is one year. A one-year extension may be permitted upon approval of request and payment of a $40 fee. Minimum time for completion of a course is six weeks.

Equipment Requirements:

Textbooks and materials costs are in addition to tuition and must be paid for by the student.

Credit and Grading:

Examinations include a final and one or more midcourse exams, all of which must be proctored, either at one of the University of Minnesota campuses or by a local school official or librarian. The university uses two grading systems: A–F and S–N (satisfactory-not satisfactory). Minimum passing grade is D. Credit is awarded in quarter hour units.

Library Services:

Independent Study students may borrow books from the University of Minnesota Libraries.

Accreditations:

North Central Association of Colleges and Schools. Member of: National University Continuing Education Association.

COLLEGE COURSES

ACCOUNTING

Introduction to Financial Reporting

Basic concepts of measurement and valuation that underlie the development of financial reports for external users. Financial statement preparation, analysis of alternative valuation approaches, interpretation of financial statement information. (5 quarter hours)

Introduction to Management Accounting

A broad overview of management accounting as the main information collection and analysis technology of an organization. Topics include analysis of cost-volume-profit relationships, budgeting and analysis of variances from budgeting performance, and issues relating to decentralized organizational design. (4 quarter hours)

Income Tax Accounting

The more common and important provisions of the federal income tax system as applied to individuals and corporations. Begins with a consideration of which types of income are taxable and which are not. Consideration is then given to business deductions, personal deductions, gains and losses, nontaxable exchanges, deferred compensation, and taxation of business entities. Covers recent tax laws, including those enacted through the end of 1991. (4 quarter hours)

AFRICAN AMERICAN STUDIES

Introduction to African Literature

A survey of 19th- and 20th-century African literature, including oral narratives, written poetry, short stories, novels, plays. All readings in English. (4 quarter hours)

AGRICULTURAL ECONOMICS

Financing State and Local Governments

Examination of problems and issues in financing state and local public services in the United States; state and local revenue systems; debt and expenditures; intergovernmental fiscal relations; and budget analysis. (4 quarter hours)

AMERICAN INDIAN STUDIES

American Indian History I: From the Mid-15th Century to 1850

Explores the history of Native North American groups from the pre-European-contact period to about the mid-19th century. Addresses central themes relating to various Native American cultures, as well as their interactions with various European invaders. Brief case studies highlight the complexity and diversity of Native American groups. Stresses the integrity and viability of Native American societies, the dynamism of their largely self-directed culture change in response to contact with other Native American groups and European invaders, and the duality of the culture change—European invaders were also profoundly changed by the clash of cultures. (4 quarter hours)

American Indian History II: 1850 to the Present

Completes American Indian history form pre-contact to the present. Stresses general themes in Native American history and focuses on the efforts of Native American nations to control their cultural destiny against the efforts of the U.S. government to forcibly assimilate them into European culture. Discusses the ways change is incorporated within the belief systems of Native American cultures from the perspective of members of those cultures, connects U.S. Indian policy to national and international persistence and incorporation of change within both Native American and European American cultures. (4 quarter hours)

AMERICAN STUDIES

American Cultures

Interdisciplinary study of American cultures, from the colonial era through the mid-19th century. Major topics: diversity in colonial America, struggles for independence and equal rights (the Revolutionary War; women's fight for a public, political role; and the battle against slavery), and the frontier. Explores experiences and beliefs of European Americans, Native Americans, African Americans, Asian Americans, and Chicanos. (4 quarter hours)

American Cultures II

Interdisciplinary study of the diversity of American cultures, 1890-1945. Major topics: urban life and leisure, changing family and gender roles, race and national identity. Explores experiences and cultural products of European Americans, Native Americans, African Americans, Asian Americans, and Chicanos. (4 quarter hours)

American Cultures III

Interdisciplinary study of diversity of American cultures, 1945 to present. Major topics: family practices and gender roles, social change movements (civil rights movement, American Indian movement, women's movement), and the politics of popular culture (music, television, fashion, art). Explores experiences and cultural products of European Americans, Native Americans, African Americans, and Chicanos. Video rental required. (4 quarter hours)

Topics in American Studies: Ellery Queen and the American Detective Story

Surveys American detective fiction, both classic and hard-boiled, to suggest reasons for its continued popularity. Novels and stories by the major writers (Poe, Hammett, Ellery Queen, Rex Stout, and others) will be assigned for reading and discussion. Audiocassettes focus on Ellery Queen as an example of the changing style of the genre. (4 quarter hours)

Topics in American Studies: The Meanings of Place

This course provides direct experiences in analyzing the cultural and psychological messages of our surroundings. With guidance from a cultural historian and a landscape architect, students will observe and explore various settings to discover what present day environments can reveal about the past and to gain a better understanding of the connections between sense of place and feelings of well-being. Places picked for analysis include the Minneapolis and St. Paul central districts, selected Twin Cities neighborhoods, village and small town settings inside and outside Minnesota, and various landscapes of the open countryside. Video rental required. (4 quarter hours)

Directed Study: American Architecture to 1860

Selective examination of building forms and patterns in America, with attention to Old World antecedents and their vernacular expressions during the pre-Revolutionary period. The scope of this course extends into the mid-nineteenth century, covering the birth of a national style (architecture as politics). (4 quarter hours)

ANTHROPOLOGY

Human Origins

World prehistory as investigated by archaeologists is the major topic of this course. The methods and concepts employed by archaeologists in the study of human origins and prehistoric biological and cultural development are also considered. (5 quarter hours)

Understanding Cultures (1102

Study of cultures in all parts of the world, directed toward a broad understanding of how people view their world, cope with their environments, and organize their lives. (5 quarter hours)

Understanding Cultures (V112)

Introduction to the ways the cross-cultural, comparative, and holistic study of contemporary societies and cultures across the world can provide an understanding of human diversity, adaptation, and condition. Considers social, political, economic, technological, and religious institutions. Video rental required. (5 quarter hours)

Psychological Anthropology

Examines the relation between culture and personality, with emphasis on recent work in psychoanalytic anthropology. Topics include human nature, child development, personality, mental illness, group psychodynamics, religious ritual and symbolism, and war. (4 quarter hours)

ARCHITECTURE

The Meanings of Place: City, Town, and Countryside

This course provides direct experiences in analyzing the cultural and psychological messages of our surroundings. With guidance from a cultural historian and a landscape architect, students will observe and explore various settings to discover what present day environments can reveal about the past and to gain a better understanding of the connections between sense of place and feelings of well-being. Places picked for analysis include the Minneapolis and St. Paul central districts, selected Twin Cities neighborhoods, village and small town settings inside and outside Minnesota, and various landscapes of the open countryside. Video rental required. (4 quarter hours)

Directed Study: American Architecture to 1860

Selective examination of building forms and patterns in America, with attention to Old World antecedents and their vernacular expressions during the pre-Revolutionary period. The scope of this course extends into the mid-nineteenth century, covering the birth of a national style (architecture as politics). (4 quarter hours)

ART

Introduction to the Visual Arts

Considers the basic issues of art. Examples of painting and sculpture are analyzed to illustrate the roles of art in society. Problems of design, materials, and technique are presented topically rather than chronologically. Video rental required. (4 quarter hours)

ASTRONOMY

Physical Science: Solar System Astronomy

An introductory survey of the solar system, including a study of the earth, planets, satellites, asteroids, comets, and meteorites. Topics include the celestial sphere, coordinate systems, time intervals, motions and physical attributes of planets in the solar system, and instruments used by the astronomer. Observations of the night sky included. (5 quarter hours)

Physical Science: Stellar Astronomy

An introductory survey of the large scale structures of the universe, including the definition of certain properties of stars (magnitude, luminosity, brightness). Topics: the sun, the spectral classification of stars, white dwarfs, neutron stars, black holes, clusters, nebulae, galaxies, quasars, cosmology, and cosmogony. Observation of the night sky included. (5 quarter hours)

BIOLOGY

General Biology

An introduction to the general principles of biology. Topics: the cell, metabolism, heredity, reproduction, ecology, and evolution. Eight new or revised lab exercises, most of which students can perform in their own kitchens. (5 quarter hours)

Heredity and Human Society

Principles of heredity and their social and cultural implications. Explanation of the use and misuse of genetics. Overview of Mendelian and molecular genetics, and the relationships between genetics, evolution, and individual and social behavior. An audiocassette course. (4 quarter hours)

Environmental Studies

Principles of ecology and current environmental issues including air and water pollution, human population growth, toxic and hazardous wastes, urbanization, land use, biological diversity, energy, environmental health, conservation history, attitudes towards nature, environmental politics, and ethics. (4 quarter hours)

Cell Biology

Structures and functions of membranes, organelles, and other macromolecular aggregates found in plant, animal, and bacterial cells. Cell form and movement, intercellular communication, transport, and secretion. (3 quarter hours)

Genetics

Introduction to the nature of genetic information, its transmission from parents to offspring, its expression in cells and organisms, and its course in populations. Graduate credit is available for a different version of this course. (4 quarter hours)

BUSINESS

United States: Law in Society

In order to give students an appreciation of the role of law in our changing society, the legal aspects of current topics are discussed: court and court systems; grand and petit juries; corrections; consumer issues including insurance (no-fault auto and life); and wills and probate procedures. A civil law suit is explained. (4 quarter hours)

Introduction to Business and Society

Intended for both business and general education, this course provides an overview of the economic environment in which business operates. Major functions of a business organization are surveyed, including production, finance, personnel, and marketing. (4 quarter hours)

Small Business Fundamentals

The importance of small business in the United States, and the challenges, pitfalls, and procedures related to starting and operating a small business. Emphasizes analysis of the economic environment, strategic planning, internal analysis of a potential firm's strengths and weaknesses versus the competition, writing a business plan. Considers accounting, finance, marketing, management. (4 quarter hours)

Practical Law

Designed to acquaint students with common legal problems. Topics: definition and sources of law; formation and discharge of contracts; torts (personal injury and property damage suits); criminal law; bailments; nature and classification of real and personal property; joint ownership and tenancy. (4 quarter hours)

Accounting Fundamentals

I. The first of a two-part introductory course in college accounting, designed for both business and nonbusiness students. Considers balance sheet and income statement methodology, the accounting cycle for both service and merchandising businesses, and examination of special journals, inventories, receivables, and accounting for plant assets. (4 quarter hours)

II. Topics: handling dividends, retained earnings and treasury stock, debt, investments, financial reporting, and sources and uses of working capital. Also examines financial statements, accounting for manufacturing operations, and cost analysis problems. (4 quarter hours)

Marketing: Introduction

Emphasizes application of the fundamentals of marketing through case study and decision making. Topics: target markets, segmentation analysis, marketing mix, and strategic marketing. Optional video rental. (4 quarter hours)

Marketing: Principles of Management

Emphasis on the principles of management as explored through the classical, behavioral, and management science schools. Topics: the environment in which managers operate, including the ethical environment and social responsibility, planning, decision making, organizing, controlling, motivation, leadership, group dynamics, and total quality management. Video rental required. (5 quarter hours)

Business and Society: Ethics and Stockholder Management

Basic economic and social goals, and various attempts to meet them. Emphasis on American society. Business as an institution; its relationships to other institutions and society. Ethical and practical conflicts in the role of the firm and the manager examined in the context of the public policy process. Current social issues and their impact on business. (4 quarter hours)

International Business

World business, with emphasis on international concepts, comparative cultures and environments, global business strategies, multinational corporations, and management operations in the global scene. The international constraints in the multinational corporation are examined. (4 quarter hours)

BUSINESS LAW

Introduction to Law, and the Law of Contracts and Sales Contracts

Study of the origin of law, its place in and affect upon society; the history and development of law; the systems of courts; and legal procedure. An extensive study of the law of contracts as the basic law affecting business transactions; and law affecting the the sale of goods contracts. (4 quarter hours)

Agency, Partnerships, Corporations, and Commercial Paper

A study of law affecting the relationship between principal and agent, master and servant, and employer and employee. Topics: partnership and corporate forms of business entities (including the methods of creating the relationships), the law developed to regulate and control these organizations and their members, and contracts referred to as commercial papers (negotiable instruments), with emphasis on effect of the Uniform Commercial Code. (4 quarter hours)

Law of Personal Property, Real Property, Wills and Estates

Study of the basic concepts of personal property, including rights of possessors, bailee, finders and holders of security interests. Also includes study of the basic concepts and principles of real property law; transfers of ownership, control of and encumbering such interests. Concludes with a brief study of the law of wills and estates in passing rights to property in event of death. (4 quarter hours)

CHEMISTRY

Physical Science: Principles of Chemistry

Fundamental principles and laws of chemistry; problem-solving techniques applied to chemistry. Topics: classification of matter, elements, atomic and molecular structure, compounds and chemical bonding, mole calculations, percent composition and empirical formulas, chemical equations, reactions, and stoichiometry, solutions and solution concentrations, acids and bases, gases and gas laws, and organic chemistry. (5 quarter hours)

CHILD PSYCHOLOGY

Introductory Child Psychology

Designed to provide an understanding of children and their development, the methods used by child psychologists, and the critical evaluation of research. Topics: personality and social behavior, biological bases and cognitive development, and the work of Jean Piaget. (4 quarter hours)

Infancy

Perceptual, motor, emotional, social, and cognitive development during the first two years of life; the developing infant in his or her social and physical environment. (4 quarter hours)

Introduction to Social Development/Processes of Social Development

Processes of individual change from infancy through adolescence. Development of capacities for and influences of social relations. Research methodology, and theoretical perspectives. (4 quarter hours)

Adolescent Psychology

Survey of the behavior and psychological development of the adolescent including biological factors, cognition and creativity, moral development, parent-child relations, peers, ego identity, sexual development, school adjustment, social-cultural considerations, and the adolescent subculture. (4 quarter hours)

Behavior Problems of Children

This course deals with the identification of maladaptive behavior in children, and suggests ways of coping with children demonstrating such behavior. The focus is the child at home, at school, and in social relationships. Examines the effects of heredity, family experience, peer pressure, and socioeconomic class on the development of behavior problems in children. (4 quarter hours)

CHINESE

Introduction to Chinese Literature

Survey of major Chinese literary movements from the emergence of the early Confucian canon to the 13th century. All reading are in English. (4 quarter hours)

CLASSICAL STUDIES

Magic, Witchcraft, and the Occult in Greece and Rome

Magic and witchcraft in classical literature and mythology. The practice of magic as observed from papyri, epigraphical and literary evidence. Beliefs and practices concerning prophecy and the interpretation of dreams. Also explores the changing role of witchcraft and divine possession from early to later antiquity, and the relation of these phenomena to changes in economic and social conditions. An audiocassette course. (4 quarter hours)

The Age of Constantine the Great

Change and continuity in the Roman Empire from its zenith in the 2nd century through the 3rd century crisis to the New Empire of Diocletian and Constantine, the first Christian emperor (circa A.D. 180 to 363). Proscription of classical paganism; Christianity as imperial religion. (4 quarter hours)

Greek and Latin Terminology in the Medical and Biological Sciences, and the Humanities

Presentation in English contexts of Greek and Latin prefixes, suffixes, and root words in modern technical vocabularies; special attention to medical terminology. (2 quarter hours)

Directed Studies: Roman Realities: Life and Thought in the Roman Empire

The eruption of Vesuvius buried and preserved the Italian cities of Pompeii and Herculaneum so quickly and completely that excavations now enable us to construct a vivid picture of life at that time. Using this evidence and other research, this course focuses on social history through the study of art, archaeology, literature, dream interpretation, medical writing, and magic. An audiocassette course. (4 quarter hours)

Eroticism and Family Life in the Graeco-Roman World

Analysis of Greek and Roman family life in the shaping of personality; diachronic change in modes of erotic expression; narcissism and homosexuality; the status and roles of women; evolving views of sexual morality in the ancient world compared to present trends. Representative views taken for analysis and discussion from art and literature. Development of early Christian attitudes toward sexuality. An audiocassette course. (4 quarter hours)

Madness and Deviant Behavior in Greece and Rome

Definitions of madness in Greece and Rome and theories of its etiology; assessment of predisposing factors in Greece and Rome; examples of madness from mythology, legend, and history; cross-cultural comparison with contemporary United States. (4 quarter hours)

COMPOSITION

Writing Practice I

The novice, rusty, or insecure writer learns 22 ''don'ts''—common errors of the beginning writer—and gains a clear, confident, college-level approach to writing. (5 quarter hours)

Introduction to Technical and Business Communication

Introduction to the processes used to define a topic, draft, and rewrite reports for business, government, and technical fields. This is not a general-purpose composition course. Projects will be situated in a business, engineering, government, or technical setting. (2 quarter hours)

Writing About Literature

Developing a critical argument about literary texts (novels, poems, plays, short stories) with attention to use of secondary sources. Examination and use of different modes of explication and criticism. (4 quarter hours)

Writing in the Humanities

Emphasizes writing about the kind of texts ordinarily encountered in philosophy, history, cultural anthropology, social work, and interdisciplinary fields. The critical reading strategies applied in several short writing assignments help students become more effective interpreters of literary and nonliterary texts. Topics: effective analysis and argument, including the proper use and presentation of textual evidence, with attention paid to the evaluation of sources. (4 quarter hours)

Writing For the Arts

Descriptions of painting, film, music, architecture, and other types of art (other than literature) as the basis for analysis. Initial emphasis will be on developing concise and unambiguous descriptions of art objects or performances. The chief emphasis will be on how descriptions serve as the basis for more complicated writing assignments, such as formal analyses, reviews, and review-based research. (4 quarter hours)

Writing in the Social Sciences

Strategies for expressing quantitative or statistical information in clear prose. How statistical tables and summaries interact with written text. How to develop narrative and descriptive techniques for producing case studies and histories. Emphasizes the proper use of qualitative information and case histories in the analysis of complex situations, and how writing should change for different audiences. (4 quarter hours)

Writing About Science

Designed to improve the writing ability of students interested in science, this course focuses on writing about science (general) and writing for science (special). The various tasks and forms of science writing are discussed and practiced. Also considers the writing process and what makes for rhetorical effectiveness: organization, support, clarity, cleanliness, and appropriateness for the audience. (4 quarter hours)

Critical Reading and Writing for Management

This course develops general strategies for engaging texts critically, both as a reader and as a writer. The major assignments—abstract, critique, and synthesis—gradually teach the skills needed for precise understanding of texts, critical analyses of texts, and sophisticated use of them. (4 quarter hours)

Technical Writing for Engineers

Emphasizing the writing process, this course helps students learn about technical writing for different audiences and ways to achieve it. Also introduces various formats for technical writing (e.g., instruction manual, memo, formal report). (4 quarter hours)

Preprofessional Writing for Business

Focus on content, form, and style of business writing in reports, job-search materials, and correspondence. Case studies and practical examples. (4 quarter hours)

COMPUTER SCIENCE

Perspectives on Computers and Society

The impact of computers on society—partnership or confrontation? History of development, potential for use, computer utility, benefits and potential problems, chip technology and computer-aided design, software development and maintenance, networks, use and misuse, graphics, artificial intelligence, computer-based education, applications in the office, business, and industry. Study guide available in print, braille, and on audiocassette. (4 quarter hours)

Introduction to Microcomputer Applications

Introduction to IBM microcomputer applications, including microcomputer components, operating system (DOS), word processing, spreadsheet, and database management software. This hands-on laboratory course emphasizes solving problems using popular microcomputer applications software. Several disks are included with the course materials; students must indicate whether they want 5¼ 25 or 3½ inch disks. All assignments are done on computers. Software (i.e., the word processor, spreadsheet, and database management programs) is provided with the course materials, but students must have access to an IBM PC or compatible microcomputer or be able to use the microcomputers in one of the university's computer labs. (5 quarter hours)

Introduction to Computer Programming

Students design, write, code, and run computer programs written in the BASIC computer language. Emphasizes writing properly structured and documented programs to solve problems from the social and natural sciences. Topics: problem-solving techniques as applied to computing, elements of BASIC, external data file manipulation, writing structured programs, and integration of programming with data created by other applications. Gives background for further programming courses. Students must have access to an IBM or IBM-compatible computer with a BASIC interpreter or be able to use the microcomputers in one of the University's computer labs. Two disks are included with the course materials; student must indicate whether they want 5¼ or 3½ inch disks. (5 quarter hours)

CULTURAL STUDIES

Discourse and Society I: Reading Culture

The foundation course of the Cultural Studies Program. Prepares students to speak, write, and think critically about different forms of cultural production by studying art, literature, mass media, social history, and cultural theory. Students examine the discursive practices through which meanings, values, beliefs, and identities are constructed. Focuses on cultural artifacts drawn from Western "high art," folk culture, and mass culture, selected to prompt students to reflect on how discourses organize their behaviors, desires, and concepts. Helps students to develop the intellectual confidence to assert themselves as cultural producers and consumers. (4 quarter hours)

Discourse and Society II: Meaning and History

Examination of historically grounded case studies—early 18th-century art, two novels, a historical work, an anthropological work, an opera, examples of mass culture, and analysis of advertising. Ways social and political conflicts of particular moments and specific locations are represented in the discourse of these case studies. Students relate the discourses in the case studies to the socio-historical conditions out of which they arise by learning to apply Marxist critical theory, discourse theory, ideological critique, theories of gender and race. (4 quarter hours)

European Folktales

This course is devoted to the folktales of Germany, Scandinavia, France, Russia, and England. Discusses the structure, message for adults and children, and origins of folktales as a genre, and compares the tales of different nations and states. Folktales are analyzed within the broader context of oral literature and folklore. (4 quarter hours)

DANISH

Beginning Danish I

Development of reading, writing, and speaking skills. An audiocassette course. (5 quarter hours)

EAST ASIAN STUDIES

Religions of East Asia

A survey of the religious traditions of China and Japan, exploring beliefs and practices from antiquity to modern times. Course covers elements of Confucianism, Taoism, Buddhism, and Shintoism, and examines the general role of religion in East Asian society. Readings include both primary and secondary materials. (4 quarter hours)

ECOLOGY

Introduction to Ecology

Basic concepts in ecology; organization, development, and functioning of ecosystems; population growth and regulation. Human impact on ecosystems. (4 quarter hours)

ECONOMICS

Economics and Society

General description of the economy of the United States and analysis of contemporary economic problems. Provides a simple framework used by economists for analysis of these issues and problems. (4 quarter hours)

Principles of Macroeconomics

Determinants of national income, national income accounting, unemployment and inflation. Classical and Keynesian theories. Money and banking, monetary and fiscal policy, international economic relations, and less-developed nations. (4 quarter hours)

Principles of Microeconomics

A study of basic economic principles of pricing and resource allocation. Includes demand and supply; consumer choice; costs of production and efficient input combination competition, monopoly, oligopoly; determination of wages, rent, interest, profits; income distribution; farm and urban problems. (4 quarter hours)

Macroeconomic Theory

Factors determining price level, amount of employment and unemployment, total spending by consumers. Business investments, total savings, national income, and the effects of government spending, taxes, and monetary policy on price level. Employment, output, and national income. (4 quarter hours)

Money and Banking

Money, banks, and financial intermediaries as economic institutions; the mechanics of monetary transactions; the value of money; international monetary relationships; issues relating to monetary policy. (4 quarter hours)

EDUCATION

A Systematic Approach to Designing Instruction

Instructional materials design in accordance with systems principles, including design of a specific unit of courseware. Students watch videos edited from live classroom lectures and discussions. Video rental required. (3 quarter hours)

Introduction to Computer-Based Instructional Design

Introduction to designing computer-based instructional programs through programming. Students learn to use the application Authorware Professional, a state-of-the-art authoring language developed for designing computer-based presentations, drills, tutorials, games, and simulation. Must have access to a Macintosh computer with System 7. Video rental required. (4 quarter hours)

Second Languages and Young Children: Like Child's Play

Examines current approaches to teaching second languages to young children, with emphasis on innovative curricular models. Provides information about the way young children acquire language and the effects of bilingualism on child development, and presents rationales, advantages, and pedagogical theories of various program models, from full immersion to programs that emphasize cultural understanding. Video rental required. (4 quarter hours)

Creating Social Studies Curriculum Materials

Using historic sites and related materials to create new social studies curricula. Implementing and evaluating living history learning experiences in the classroom. (3 quarter hours)

Directed Study: Inventing the Future—Living, Learning, and Working in the 1990s

This field-based course is for managers, human services and health services workers, counselors, teachers, and upper-division or graduate students in many fields. Topics: trends in work, leisure, education, technology, health, spirituality, home life, and more. (4 quarter hours)

Personal Time Management and Effective Administration

This course is designed for any individual who "doesn't have enough time." It teaches practical, pragmatic approaches - using examples and samples of proven techniques—to the problems of scheduling, organizing work, delegating, setting priorities, handling interruptions and meetings, doing the distasteful and the difficult, setting up filing systems that work, and finding the time to do those things that one really wants to do, but doesn't have time for. (2 quarter hours)

EDUCATIONAL PSYCHOLOGY

Knowing, Learning, and Thinking

Principles of human information processing; issues in memory and thought; discussion of mental operations in comprehension and understanding; analysis of intellectual structures supporting problem solving in applied settings. (4 quarter hours)

Psychology of Student Learning

How to improve learning comprehension, memory, managing group behavior, intelligence, problem solving, and motivation. (3 quarter hours)

Workshop: Counseling Psychology—Integrative Career Planning

Based on profound changes occurring in work, technology, education, family, and society, this course provides students with an in-depth approach to career planning called "Integrative Life Planning" (ILP). Up-to-date information about labor market trends and workforce and work pattern changes is combined with the latest knowledge of how to plan for work and other life roles in the 21st century. Other topics: life span career development, assessing individual and cultural identities, career socialization and sterotyping, and career change/transitions. Video rental required. (4 quarter hours)

Education of the Gifted and Talented

Origin and development of terms such as *giftedness, creativity, genius, talent,* and *intelligence*; implications for educational practice; current issues and trends. Video rental required. (3 quarter hours)

ENGINEERING

Deformable Body Mechanics

Introductory treatment of stress and strain at a point. Stress-strain relationships in two dimensions. Linear theory of torsion. Bending stresses. Deflection of determinate and indeterminate beams. Instability. (4 quarter hours)

ENGLISH

Introduction to American Literature: Some Major Figures and Themes

Introduction to some major themes and writers in American literature. Readings from Faulkner, Malamud, Melville, Fitzgerald, Chopin, Ellison, Henry James, and Dickey are complemented by audiocassette programs by Professor Edward Griffin. Emphasizes the American experiences, myths of the American wilderness, dreams of innocence and freedom, and social responsibility for relations among the varied peoples of the New World. (4 quarter hours)

Introduction to Modern Poetry

A study of modern British and American poetry organized around themes (war, the city, nature, death, love, etc.) and including such writers as Yeats, Thomas, Auden, Eliot, Frost, cummings, and Stevens. (4 quarter hours)

Introduction to Modern Drama

A study of modern drama, including plays by Ibsen, Strindberg, Chekov, Synge, Shaw, O'Neill, Pirandello, Brecht, Williams, Miller, Ionesco, and Beckett. (4 quarter hours)

Introduction to Literature: Science Fiction and Fantasy

The evolution of modern science fiction and fantasy from their 19th-century roots to the popular literature and mass phenomenon of today. Considers such major themes as religion, sexuality, the future of technology in the works of Ursula K. Le Guin, Frank Herbert, and Robert Heinlein, among others, and the contributions of such eminent fantasists as J.R.R. Tolkien, George Lucas, and Steven King. (4 quarter hours)

Literature of American Minorities

Fiction, autobiography, and poetry by award winning African American, American Indian, Asian American, and Chicano/Chicana writers. Introduction to social and literary issues affecting minority group identity and individual writers. Offers perspectives on American minorities through the lens of modern and contemporary literature. (4 quarter hours)

Techniques of Literary Study

Training and practice in the analysis of various literary forms, with a special emphasis on poetry. Use of argument, evidence, and documentation in literary papers; introduction to major developments in contemporary criticism. (4 quarter hours)

Survey of English Literature

I. A historical survey of the major figures, movements, and trends in English literature and culture during the Middle Ages and the Renaissance. Chaucer, Shakespeare, Marlowe, and the metaphysical poets, along with topics such as attitudes toward women and generic development of the sonnet and drama, are featured. (4 quarter hours)

II. This course focuses on the literature of the Restoration and the 18th century (Age of Reason), especially Milton, Johnson, Swift, Austin, and Pope. (4 quarter hours)

III. Explores the literature of the Romantic and Victorian periods (19th century), especially Wordsworth, Keats, Wollstonecraft, Tennyson, the Brownings, the Shelleys, and Dickens. (4 quarter hours)

Shakespeare I

Study of Shakespeare's early and middle comedies, tragedies, and history plays (*Romeo and Juliet, A Midsummer Night's Dream, Henry IV Part I, Henry V, Much Ado About Nothing, Julius Caesar,* and *Hamlet.* An audiocassette course. (4 quarter hours)

Shakespeare II

Study of Shakespeare's middle comedies and tragedies and late romances with attention to history, literary values, and theater performance. Students read *As You Like It, Macbeth, King Lear, Antony and Cleopatra, Coriolanus, The Winter's Tale,* and *The Tempest.* An audiocassette course. (4 quarter hours)

Major American Writers: Fitzgerald and Hemingway

An examination of the short stories of two contemporary early 20th-century writers—F. Scott Fitzgerald and Ernest Hemingway—in the context of Jazz Age literary, cultural, and artistic developments. An audiocassette course. (4 quarter hours)

Major American Writers: Voices and Visions in American Poetry

A study of major American poets, such as Whitman, Dickinson, Frost, Pound, Hughes, and Plath, through an analysis of representative works and video programs on the life, times, and poems of each poet. Video rental required. (4 quarter hours)

Survey of American Literature to 1850

The development of American literature and thought from pre-Columbian days through the early American Renaissance. Authors studied include Native American and African American writers from the colonial and early national periods, together with such major white writers as Poe, Emerson, and Hawthorne. (4 quarter hours)

Survey of American Literature, 1850 to 1900

Literature and thought from the American Renaissance through the 19th century. Authors studied include Whitman and Dickinson as poetic giants, Twain and Chopin as experimental novelists. (4 quarter hours)

Survey of American Literature, 1900 to 1960

American literature during the breakup of social and literary norms caused by two world wars, feminism, and the emergence of the civil rights movement. Authors studied include Frost and Eliot, Fitzgerald, Hurston and Hughes, Wright, Olsen, and Rich. An audiocassette course. (4 quarter hours)

American Short Story

Historical developments of the literary forms of the short story in American culture. Students read the works of Irving, Poe, Melville, Crane, Cather, Hemingway, Updike, Cheever, and other authors. (4 quarter hours)

The English Language

An introduction to the English language and English linguistics, examining structure (phonetics, phonology, morphology, syntax, semantics), language acquisition, historical change, dialect variation, and aspects of the social life of English. Video rental required. (4 quarter hours)

Topics in the English Language: The Origin of English Words

An introduction to the origins of English words. Explains how the words of English emerged, clashed, combined, lost their initial freshness, and died, to give way to upstarts whose day will come. (4 quarter hours)

Topics in English and North American Literature: The Celtic World

A wide-ranging introductory survey of the history, music, folk ways, and traditional oral culture of the six Celtic countries (Brittany, Cornwall, Ireland, Isle of Man, Scotland, and Wales). Topics: ancient culture; tribal society; saints, druids, bards, poets; the age of King Arthur; languages; and the future of Celtic culture. An audiocassette course. (4 quarter hours)

Topics in English and North American Literature: D.H. Lawrence and Freud

An intensive reading of the prose fiction and poetry of D.H. Lawrence alongside key texts by Freud. The course examines modern culture and its discontents as interpreted by these two writers. An audiocassette course. (4 quarter hours)

Topics in Anglophone Literature: Modern Women Writers

Fiction and poetry by British and American women writers from 1900 to the present—Kate Chopin, Edith Wharton, Virginia Woolf, Doris Lessing, Eudora Welty, Sylvia Plath, Anne Sexton, Toni Morrison, Audre Lorde, and Adrienne Rich. Emphasizes how these writers perceived themselves as women and as artists, their analyses of the roles of women in modern society, and the formal literary qualities of their works. (4 quarter hours)

Figures in English and North American Literature: The Woman Writer: 19th Century Fiction

Short stories and novels by 19th-century women writers—Jane Austen, Elizabeth Gaskell, Charlotte Brontë, Harriet Beecher Stowe, George Eliot, Sarah Orne Jewett, Mary E. Wilkins Freeman, and Charlotte Perkins Gilman. Emphasizes the ways women writers' professional roles evolved during the 19th century, the conflicts they faced as their careers developed, the extent to which their wiring satisfied the requirements of their audiences, and the formal literary qualities of their works. (4 quarter hours)

Figures in English and North American Literature: Hemingway

The course covers what most critics consider the most impressive segment of Hemingway's career, the period between 1922 and 1929. Students will read two novels from this period—*The Sun Also Rises* and *A Farewell to Arms*—and two collections of stories: *In Our Time* and *Men without Women.* (4 quarter hours)

20th Century English Novel

A study of the British novel in the 20th century, emphasizing some of its main ideas, techniques, and relationships to the history of the novel.

Authors of historical or representative importance include Forster, Joyce, Lawrence, Woolf, Waugh, Cary, Amis, Sillitoe, and Murdoch. (4 quarter hours)

Modern Drama to 1920: Pirandello to Pinter

Introduction to the themes and techniques of modern drama since the 1920s. Topics: the nature of the theatrical play, the ''modernism'' in modern drama, and thirteen important plays written from 1920 to 1960 by ten major playwrights—Pirandello, Anouilh, Giradoux, O'Neill, Miller, Lorca, Williams, Brecht, Beckett, and Pinter. (4 quarter hours)

James Joyce

An introduction to the life and works of Joyce, including the epiphanies, the poems, the play *Dubliners*, and the novels *Portrait of the Artist as a Young Man*, and *Ulysses*, and bits of *Finnegan's Wake*. An audiocassette course. (4 quarter hours)

American Poetry

An examination of American poetry from 1890 to 1940. Includes historical and intellectual background, and poetic theory. Poets discussed include Frost, Stevens, Pound, Eliot, Moore, and Williams. (4 quarter hours)

Literatures of the United States

A historic survey and analysis of nearly thirty giants of American fiction. Students examine the development of the form of the short story in America to enhance their understanding and appreciation of a wide range of writers, from Irving's early sketches to Barthelme's and Coover's present-day experiments. (4 quarter hours)

Literature: Reading Short Stories

This course encompasses ideas about the human experience by American, British, and Continental authors. (4 quarter hours)

African-American Literature

Students read and evaluate the poetry, drama, folklore, short stories, and longer fiction of black authors. Students assess the artists' perceptions and interpretations of black culture in America from colonial times to the present. (4 quarter hours)

Asian-American Literature

The challenges presented to Asian immigrants and their children are examined, with attention to the clash between ethnic identity and American situation. Students analyze both historical and contemporary works produced by writers such as Carlos Bulosan, Louis Chu, Joy Kogawa, and Amy Tan. amd others. (4 quarter hours)

Intermediate Fiction Writing: The Short Story

Students explore the craft of the short story by writing, reading, and listening. The tapes contain a discussion of craft and content with several writers. An audiocassette course. (4 quarter hours)

Intermediate Poetry Writing

Offers students a variety of exercises and readings to help them develop an awareness of the way they use language to describe the worlds of experience and imagination. Substantial reading in contemporary poetry to help students focus on image, diction, voice, tone, and structure in their own poems. (4 quarter hours)

Topics in Creative Writing: Journaling into Fiction

An exploration of the links between private and public writing. Students build on the strengths and skills already present in their private writing as they move more fully into the world of the imagination to create fiction, poems, or song. Writing assignments illustrate the ways private journaling may be turned into fiction, using techniques such as dreams, prose poems, stream of consciousness, found art, and others. An audiocassette course. (4 quarter hours)

Journal and Memoir Writing

Students read selected journals and memoirs, as well as complete exercises based on the readings. The journal writing process—informal and fragmentary—is the basis of all writing suggestions; students are encouraged to work from memory and personal experience. The student course project is to write a memoir or autobiography and not the originating journal exercises. An audiocassette course. (4 quarter hours)

Journal and Memoir Writing II: Memory in Different Modes

Using the process of writing from brainstorming to drafting to revision, this course guides students to involve memory in writing several genres: poems, traditional memoir essays, and fiction. The course also considers how cultures shape memory differently, suggesting work from Native American, Hispanic, Asian American, and African American writers. (4 quarter hours)

Introduction to Professional Editing

Beginning editing, from substantive editing to the nature of the editor-writer relationship: manuscript reading, author queries, rewrite and style, extensive discussion of different kinds of editing including substantive editing and mechanical editing. Students develop editing awareness and skills by working on varied writing samples. (4 quarter hours)

ENTOMOLOGY

Honey Bee Biology and Management

This course is useful to both nonexperienced and experienced beekeepers. Topics: history of beekeeping, life history and behavior of honey bees; colony and apiary management; pollination and hive products; honey bee diseases and their control. (4 quarter hours)

FAMILY STUDIES

Human Sexual Behavior

Exploration of biological, psychological, and social aspects of human sexuality. Topics: sexual development over the life span; anatomy and physiology; reproduction; birth control and abortion; sexual response, arousal, and communication; love; sex research; gender roles and sex differences; heterosexuality, homosexuality, and bisexuality; sexual variations and economics; sexual coercion and abuse; dysfunction and therapy; sexually transmitted diseases; ethics, religion, and law; and sex education. (5 quarter hours)

Family Systems

Examination of the family as an institution and system of relationships. Current developments in the study of family, changes in American society, and their influence on family life. The course includes lectures, simulated family interaction, and participation of a studio audience on videocassettes. Video rental required. (5 quarter hours)

Special Topics in Family Social Science: Violence in the Family

This course focuses on the various forms of abuse (physical, psychoemotional, sexual) found among family members—spouses, parents and children, siblings. Attention is given to the factors that bring about or inhibit family violence, and to prevention and treatment strategies. (4 quarter hours)

Special Topics in Family Social Science: American Families in Transition

Through interviews with family scholars, this course presents a comprehensive view of family life and examines historical and contemporary family issues. The focus is on rapid changes in family life. An audiocassette course. (4 quarter hours)

Racial and Ethnic Minority Families

Sociological overview of family structures and family values of various American racial and ethnic groups, including African Americans, Native Americans, Mexican Americans, Jews, and Asian Americans. Combines a study of research and case studies with individual projects to develop and enrich understanding of cultural diversity. (4 quarter hours)

Home Life: Parent-Child Relationships

An interdisciplinary course to help students develop their own philosophy of childrearing—attitudes, principles, perspectives—that will guide them in their relations to their children and performance of their parental responsibilities. Focuses on helpful information related to crises of parenthood. Research emphasizes principles of parent-child relations and prepares students for the tasks of parenthood. (4 quarter hours)

FINANCE

Finance Fundamentals

A comprehensive, analytical introduction to the principal concepts of finance. All major business financial decisions are discussed: balance sheet and income statement management, the general business environment, valuation theory, financial management decisions concerning uses and sources of funds, and a survey of the nation's financial markets. (4 quarter hours)

FINNISH

Beginning Finnish I

Teaches the beginnings of the Finnish language skills of listening, speaking, reading, and writing. Offers a two-tier approach to Finnish: communicative skills and the basics of vocabulary and grammar. Emphasizes social situations for which students learn useful/helpful phrases. Includes some composition. First in a series of three courses. An audiocassette course. (5 quarter hours)

Beginning Finnish II

A continuation of the above course. (5 quarter hours)

Begining Finnish III

A continuation of the above course. (5 quarter hours)

FOOD SCIENCE

Technology of Food Processing

Introduction to the technology of processing and distribution of foods, with reference to the prevention of biological, physical, and chemical deterioration. Changes in food composition, microbiological safety, food laws and regulations, technologies of the major food processes (canning, freezing, drying), and cereal and oilseed processing are considered. (4 quarter hours)

FORESTRY

Conservation of Natural Resources

Current status, utilization, and sound management of natural resources with emphasis on the ecological approach. Conservation principles and their application to soil, water, forests, grasslands, wildlife, minerals, and energy sources. (3 quarter hours)

FRENCH

Beginning French

I. Thirteen episodes of the video series *French in Action*, in which a young American man meets and interacts with a young French woman in Paris. Vignettes taken from French films, television, advertising, and cartoons. The audiotapes, texts, workbook, and study guide will help you learn authentic language for basic conversation and familiarize you with French culture. Video rental required. (5 quarter hours)

II. A continuation of the above course. (5 quarter hours)

III. A continuation of Beginning French II. (5 quarter hours)

French Literary Texts: Novel, Poetry, Drama

Provides training in reading literary works of poetry, drama, prose. Completely in French. (4 quarter hours)

Literature in English Translation: Flaubert and Modern Writing

An intensive reading in English of major works by Flaubert in the context of Freudian criticism and modern writing. (4 quarter hours)

GEOGRAPHY

The Language of Maps

Study of various phases of the process of using maps to communicate ideas. Ways of describing location, distance, direction, area, and other basic spatial concepts. Data classification, map symbols, methods of analyzing patterns on maps. Use of maps to inform and/or persuade. (5 quarter hours)

Geography of the United States and Canada

Learn the tools of geographic analysis through readings and exercises focused on ten major regions of the United States and Canada. Emphasis on comparison and analysis of road maps, landform maps, and thematic maps to decipher the cultural, physical, and economic nuances that make all locations geographically unique. (4 quarter hours)

Geography of Minnesota

The changing geography of Minnesota and the Upper Midwest. Explores the legacy from the railroad era, transformation in the auto-air age, and the emerging future. A videocassette course. (4 quarter hours)

Geography of Latin America

Provides an opportunity to study and evaluate the character and diversity of Mexico, Central America, the Caribbean, and South America. Individual countries and major regions within them are analyzed. The influence of both cultural and physical elements on people and their use of the land is emphasized. Problems are considered on both a national and regional basis. A videocassette course. (4 quarter hours)

Russia and Environs

An introduction to the diverse characteristics and regions of the former Soviet Union. Emphasizes a topical analysis of the physical, cultural, and economic phenomena in the U.S.S.R., including the impact of present political and economic trends. (4 quarter hours)

Environmental Problems

Defining and "solving" environmental problems; implementing "solutions." (4 quarter hours)

The Meaning of Place: City, Town, and Countryside

Graduate credit is available for this course. (4 quarter hours)

GEOLOGY

The Dynamic Earth: An Introduction to Geology

An introduction to general geology. Survey of the main features of the physical world and the processes that have evoked them. Topics: plate tectonics, rock formation, weathering, soils, deserts, oceans, and the phenomena of earthquakes, glaciers, and volcanoes. (4 quarter hours)

Historical Geology

Evolution of the earth and its inhabitants from their origins to the present, with emphasis on the past 600 million years. The first part of the course outlines the fundamentals of geology, evolution, and paleontology. (4 quarter hours)

GERMAN

Beginning German

I. Introduction to reading through familiarity with "survival" situations; beginning listening with videos of everyday events; introduction to the frequently used constructions of German through a text and a computer tutorial on a 3.5-inch disk. Students must have access to a Macintosh or and IBM-compatible with 256K. Video rental required. (5 quarter hours)

II. A continuation of the above course. Building reading comprehension through expansion of topics related to travel and recent history; expanding listening comprehension with videos relating to broader topics; reviewing German constructions with a text and computer tutorial. Equipment requirements the same as for Beginning German I. Video rental required. (5 quarter hours)

III. A continuation of the above course. Pushing reading comprehension to the intermediate level with a work of popular fiction; intermediate listening comprehension practice with videos depicting contemporary German life; reviewing German constructions with a text and computer tutorial. Equipment requirements the same as for Beginning German I. Video rental required. (5 quarter hours)

German Authors and/or Topics in Translation: Post-War Developments as Seen Through Works of Heinrich Boll

Through reading Boll's novels and short stories, students will gain an understanding of the development of West German society since 1945. Students learn about postwar Germany through extensive study notes and some outside reading. Students are also asked to use media resources (films, magazines, videotapes, as available) to round out their knowledge of contemporary Germany. (4 quarter hours)

GREEK

Beginning Classical Greek I

An introduction to Homeric and Classical Greek language: alphabet, vocabulary, and idioms. Selected readings from *Iliad* and *Odyssey* of Homer and classical Greek selections of moderate difficulty. Written translation exercises, oral exercises, and introduction to scansion and meter. (5 quarter hours)

HISTORY

Introduction to Modern European History since the Middle Ages

Course 4737. Survey of European history to the 18th century. Emphasizes the rise of the nation-state and the role of Christianity and exploration in its development. (4 quarter hours)

Course 4738. Survey of European history in the 18th and 19th centuries. Emphasizes the struggle for control of the state, the Age of Reason, and the French Revolution. (4 quarter hours)

Course 4739. Survey of European history in the 19th and 20th centuries. Emphasizes the impact of industrialization on 19th-century civilization and the international problems of the 20th century. (4 quarter hours)

Introduction to World History I

Case studies of different periods of ancient and medieval history, including civilizations in Mesopotamia, Egypt, India, and China; the first classical empires of China and India, Imperial Rome, as well as premodern empires in Mali, Mexico, and Peru; and universal religions—Hinduism, Buddhism, Christianity, and Islam. (5 quarter hours)

Introduction to World History II

Continuation of the above course. Explores world civilizations in the era of global contact, 1450 to 1950, from a comparative perspective. Topics: linking the globe through trade and migration; cultural, racial, and religious contact and clash in the Americas, Africa, and Asia; colonialism, industrialization, nationalism, independence movements, and decolonization. Video rental required. (5 quarter hours)

Introduction to World History III

Continuation of the above course. Covers the 50 years since World War II. The course themes of ecology and human rights are used to investigate how larger events, such as the cold war and economic development, affected the identity and livelihood of individuals. Other topics include destabilization, decolonization and national independence, different strategies for economic development, race relations, social movements, apartheid, international division of labor, urbanization, and the environment. (5 quarter hours)

English History to the 17th Century

First of a two-part sequence. Covers the history of England from earliest times to the death of Queen Elizabeth I. (4 quarter hours)

English History from the 17th Century to the Present

Second of a two-part sequence. Covers the period from the Stuart Accession through the Cold War. (4 quarter hours)

American History

I. U.S. history from colonial times through Reconstruction. Emphasizes political, economic, social, and diplomatic history. Assignments cover a wide variety of topics, including the witchcraft trials of Salem, slavery and the American Republic, the Revolution, the Civil War. Video rental required. (5 quarter hours)

II. U.S. history from 1880 to the present. Students will study "Captains of Industry" and the rise of industrial America; the populist and progressive reform movements; the world wars; the depression and the New Deal; the cold war, the civil rights movement, the women's movement, the Vietnam War, and the Reagan years. A videocassette course. (5 quarter hours)

Cultural Pluralism in American History

A survey of the development of American society focusing on the roles of African Americans, Native Americans, Asian Americans, and Hispanic Americans. Issues of cultural pluralism, empowerment, racism, and intergroup relations are explored within a comparative historical framework. An audiocassette course. (4 quarter hours)

Survey of Civilizations in Ancient Asia

Ancient societies in East, South, and West Asia. (4 quarter hours)

Survey of Latin American History: Colonial Period to 1800

Pre-Hispanic and colonial period to 1800, with emphasis on social, cultural, and economic aspects. Settlement of the Americas by Europeans and Africans. Exploitation of the Americas. Responses of dominated people in the Americas. Video rental required. (4 quarter hours)

Survey of Latin American History: 1800–1929

Covers the period from independence to the early 20th century and examines the formation of the nation-states that emerged from the disintegration of the Spanish and Portuguese empires in the Americas. Topics: the difficulty in reestablishing the legitimacy of authority enjoyed by Spain and Portugal before independence; the transformation from a corporatist society to one based on liberalism; and the social impact of African slavery and its abolition on Latin American societies. (4 quarter hours)

Survey of Latin American History: 1929 to Present

Provides students with an understanding of 20th-century Latin American social, economic, and political history focusing on the struggles staged by the popular classes. Particular attention paid to the activities of peasants and workers as well as to the movements for national liberation and civil rights. (4 quarter hours)

Topics in European History: Columbus and the Age of Encounter

This course places the familiar figure of Columbus in the context of the world of the late 15th century. Readings examine Europe and the rest of the known world, the New World of the Western Hemisphere, the motives and means through which Europeans expanded their interests around the globe, and the far-reaching consequences of Columbus's voyages. (4 quarter hours)

Topics in European History: The Life and Times of Peter the Great

A study of tsar Peter the Great of Russia and his impact both on his country and Europe as a whole. In looking at Peter's 43-year reign, two major themes will be explored—his efforts to westernize Russia and his constant wars against his neighbors, especially Sweden. Topics: early years; various wars, battles, and peace treaties; and the reforms he introduced into Russian life. (4 quarter hours)

Topics in European History: Sweden, 1560–1721: Experiment in Empire

Study of the formation and dismantling of Sweden's Baltic empire between 1560 and 1721 highlights the administrative, economic, demographic, and social foundations of the experience, as well as the politics and diplomacy of the period. Students will work with primary sources in translation as well as several scholarly texts. (4 quarter hours)

Civil War and Reconstruction

Integrates scholarly readings with the award-winning PBS video series, *The Civil War*. The course covers politics and society from 1848 to 1877. Topics include: sectional differences and the causes of the war; the military aspects of the conflict; slavery, emancipation, and how the slaves helped transform the war into a revolutionary struggle; and Reconstruction politics. Video rental. (4 quarter hours)

The United States in the 20th Century: 1932–1960

The Great Depression and the New Deal; the challenge of fascism and the coming of World War II; the origins of the Cold War; the great red scare; the politics and culture of the Eisenhower era; the origins of the civil rights movement; labor relations. A videocassette course. (4 quarter hours)

American Business History

Exploration of the role of business leaders such as James J. Hill, Carnegie, Rockefeller, Morgan, and Ford; the development of business institutions; and the interaction of business with economic developments, social values, and government economic policies. A videocassette course. (4 quarter hours)

American Indian History I: Pre-Contact to 1830

Explores the history of Native North American groups from the pre-European-contact period to about the mid-19th century. Addresses central themes relating to various Native American cultures, as well as their interactions with various European invaders. Brief case studies highlight the complexity and diversity of Native American groups.

Stresses the integrity and viability of Native American societies, the dynamism of their largely self-directed culture change in response to contact with other Native American groups and European invaders, and the duality of the culture change—European invaders were also profoundly changed by the clash of cultures. (4 quarter hours)

American Indian History II: 1830 to the Present

Completes American Indian history form pre-contact to the present. Stresses general themes in Native American history and focuses on the efforts of Native American nations to control their cultural destiny against the efforts of the U.S. government to forcibly assimilate them into European culture. Discusses the ways change is incorporated within the belief systems of Native American cultures from the perspective of members of those cultures, connects U.S. Indian policy to national and international persistence and incorporation of change within both Native American and European American cultures. (4 quarter hours)

History of American Foreign Relations, 1760–1865

Foreign policy and diplomacy during the period of independence and territorial expansion. Topics: diplomacy of the American Revolution, the War of 1812, the Monroe Doctrine and territorial expansion, American commercial expansion, foreign relations with American Indians, the Mexican War, and the diplomacy of sectionalism and the Civil War. (4 quarter hours)

History of American Foreign Relations, 1865–1945

An examination of American foreign policy and diplomacy from the end of the Civil War to the end of World War II. Topics: American economic expansion and imperialism of the late 19th century; the Spanish-American War; the Open Door and China; Theodore Roosevelt, the Big Stick, and the Panama Canal; American entry into World War I; isolationism; the United Nations; and World War II. (4 quarter hours)

History of American Foreign Relations 1945–1995

American foreign relations from the end of World War II to the most recent international affairs. Examines the cold war and the changes that have recently taken place with the end of that ideological conflict. Primary issues: the decision to drop the atomic bomb; American-Soviet relations; the Vietnam War; the Reagan years and the fall of communism, and the present concerns regarding trade and international economic issues. (4 quarter hours)

Topics in American History: A Century of American Immigration: 1884–1984

History of a century of American immigration. Considers migration patterns, ethnic communities and conflict, maintenance of ethnic cultures, immigration legislation, social mobility, and the emergence of a pluralistic America. Students will compare immigrant experiences in both urban and rural settings. (4 quarter hours)

American Constitutional History I

The origins and developments of constitutional government in America with emphasis on the role of constitutional politics in the evolution of public policy. This course focuses on the English and colonial background through the Reconstruction period. (4 quarter hours)

American Constitutional History II

A continuation of the above course. Emphasizes the Constitution and the rule of law in modern America. Includes an optional videocassette with discussion of the Constitution by eminent judges and scholars. (4 quarter hours)

HORTICULTURE

Home Horticulture: Landscape Gardening and Design

Working knowledge of propagation and culture of common landscape materials: turf, flowers, trees, and shrubs. Principles and practices of gardening; prepared for beginners, but also valuable for the advanced or experienced gardeners. Text assignments and home projects with plants for the garden are required. Topics: planting, transplanting, seeds, soils, fertilizers, preparing beds and planting areas, selecting a good garden site, controlling garden pests, weeding, watering, cultivating, vegetable gardening, and landscape maintenance. Discusses annuals, perennials, bulbs, and roses for northern gardens. The final project provides the fundamentals for home landscape design. (4 quarter hours)

HUMANITIES

Humanities in the Modern West

I. Exploration of 18th-century Enlightenment and Romanticism. The main themes are reason, human nature, and the problem of evil. Authors discussed include Marlowe, Pope, Voltaire, Rousseau, and Goethe. (4 quarter hours)

II. Industrial Revolution, romanticism, socialism, individualism. Selected documents of economic and socialist theory and the romantic movement; representative works by Zola, Ibsen, Dostoevsky, Tolstoy. (4 quarter hours)

III. Focuses on the late 19th century. Topics: evolution (Darwinism) and the beginnings of existentialism. Authors discussed include Kierkegaard, Nietzsche, Turgenev, Thomas Mann, and Chekhov. (4 quarter hours)

European Heritage: Greece

This course traces the development of Greek thought and literature from the Homeric epic, through Greek tragedy and comedy, to the dialogues of Plato. (4 quarter hours)

European Heritage: Rome

This course deals with major texts of Roman culture and the early development of Christianity. Reading assignments include works by Plutarch, Vergil, the Stoics, Lucretius, St. Augustine, and the New Testament. (4 quarter hours)

INDUSTRIAL RELATIONS

Topics in Industrial Relations: Teaching Labor Relations in the Schools

This course enables elementary and secondary school teachers to incorporate the study of labor unions and collective bargaining into their lesson plans. Also assists teachers to discuss labor issues with their students when national and local developments demand a response. Provides a knowledge of the labor relations process as it affects the teaching profession. (4 quarter hours)

Collective Bargaining and Labor Relations

An introduction to collective bargaining and labor-management relations. Examines the historical evolution of trade unions in the United States, the structure and administration of trade unions, and the processes of collective bargaining and contract administration. The coursework incorporates case exercises that provide students with insights into the real world nature of labor-management relations. (4 quarter hours)

INFORMATION SCIENCE

Fundamentals of Information Development and Use

Explores the concepts and skills necessary to understand data and how it can be acquired and used. Topics: computing, data handling, formal use of data in problem solving and decision making, and managing information and information resources. Students need access to a computer. (4 quarter hours)

ITALIAN

Beginning Italian

Equal emphasis is given to four skills: listening, speaking, reading, and writing. Instructional materials also introduce many cultural aspects of contemporary Italian life. An excellent preparation for the traveler to Italy. (5 quarter hours)

JEWISH STUDIES

Introduction to Judaism

Concepts, movements, and institutions in the development of classical Judaism, as manifested in the literature and festivals of the Jewish people from Second Commonwealth times to the present. A videocassette course. (4 quarter hours)

Modern Judaism

Explores the roots of modern Judaism in Eastern Europe, the immigration experience, and the formation of American Judaism as a distinctive religious system with its major components: the rabbi, the community, Israel, religious obligations, and theology. (4 quarter hours)

The Holocaust

Nazi destruction of Jewish life in Europe, 1933–1945. Historical background of European communities. Anti-Semitism and Nazism. Ghettos under Nazi rule; social and cultural organization, and government. Nazi terror and destruction; Jewish resistance; historical consequences. An audiocassette course. (4 quarter hours)

JOURNALISM

Introduction to Mass Communications

A survey of the means of delivering information, opinion, and entertainment. Historical roots, current structures, principal issues in modern mass media. An audiocassette course. (4 quarter hours)

The Media in American History and Law: Case Studies

Using a case-study approach, this course focuses on ethical and legal issues, examining the media in the cultural-socioeconomic-political and technological context of a specific historical period: the Vietnam War. (4 quarter hours)

Magazine Writing

Writing nonfiction feature articles for adult consumer and trade publications is covered, as is a study of marketing one's free-lance writing, including the construction and submission of query letters. Students write, revise, and submit three articles to magazines or newspaper feature sections of their choice. (4 quarter hours)

Communication and Public Opinion I

Theories of mass communication, models of the communication process, and research on public opinion and persuasion. The course also explains in nontechnical terms some of the methods used in the scientific study of the mass media and of public opinion, including polling. (4 quarter hours)

History of Journalism

This course covers First Amendment rights, press credibility and governments seeking cover from "sunshine" laws, muckracking, informationals, and advertorials, fictionalized documentaries, video newspapers, 500 cable choices, and other influences that keep reshaping journalism and the events and trends it records. Attention is given to improving writing skills and identifying job opportunities. (4 quarter hours)

Literary Aspects of Journalism

A study of the literary aspects of journalism as exemplified in, and influenced by, works of English and U.S. writers, past and present—John Hersey, Lillian Ross, Joan Didion, Truman Capote, Tom Wolfe, and others. Explores the relationship between journalism and literature and how this relationship has figured in the development of U.S. journalism. Written assignments focus on analysis of readings; also, students may opt to write a piece of their own literary journalism. An audiocassette course. (4 quarter hours)

LATIN

Beginning Latin

I. Basic grammar and vocabulary, practice in reading and writing Latin, workbook exercises, easy Latin readings, and Roman legends in *38 Latin Stories*. (5 quarter hours)

II. Continuation of above course. Similar in content and method, leading to connected reading in *38 Latin Stories*. (5 quarter hours)

Selections from Latin Literature

A review of the elements of the above two courses, with a shift of emphasis to longer passages of continuous reading in *38 Latin Stories*. A considerable amount of historical and literary background is presented in English to orient the student to the material. (5 quarter hours)

Latin Prose and Poetry: Caesar and Others

Selections from Cicero, Livy, and Ovid are read. In addition to the review of Latin grammar, which will be incorporated in the readings, the readings familiarize students with the legends of Rome's founding and early heroes, the defeat of its army by Hannibal at Cannae, the first important speech of its most brilliant orator, Cicero, his correspondence after the assassination of Julius Caesar, and Ovid's poetic interpretation of several Greek myths. Literary and historical background material is provided in English. (5 quarter hours)

Latin Poetry: Cicero

The complete speech "Pro Rabirio." (5 quarter hours)

Latin Poetry: Vergil's Aeneid

Readings of selections from Books I-II; background material about Roman life and thought is included in the text. (5 quarter hours)

Readings of selections from Books I–II; background reading in Roman life and thought is included in the text. (5 quarter hours)

LINGUISTICS

The Nature of Human Language

A survey of the nature of human language, its properties, its possible origins, and how it differs from animal communication. Methods of describing the sounds, structures, and meanings of language are also examined, along with a consideration of the relationship between language, and the different roles of language in society. Whenever possible, points are illustrated with examples from the everyday use of English. A videocassette course. (4 quarter hours)

Sociolinguistics

Focuses on the relationship between language and social identity; how we define ourselves and others through the use of language. Close examination of various regional, social, ethnic, and gender varieties of American English. Introduction to linguistic field methods and practical applications to teaching and testing. A videocassette course. (4 quarter hours)

MANAGEMENT

Fundamentals of Management

Leadership and management functions such as those required to establish goals, policies, procedures, and plans. Motivation, planning, and control systems, and concepts of organizational structure and behavior. (4 quarter hours)

Psychology of Management

Development and application of behavior principles, methods, and skills that underlie managerial competencies in preventing and solving problems within and between individuals and groups, and aid in effective use of human resources. Projects and procedures are used to highlight concepts, methods, and skills, and to give practice in applying them to management problems. (4 quarter hours)

Business Policy: Strategy Formulation and Implementation

Focuses on how companies develop business-level and corporate strategies and implement and revise these strategies in complex environments. Students apply the tools and techniques of industry and competitive analysis, company situation analysis, and diversification analysis to twenty business cases. Video interviews with managers and others from the cases emphasize the "real-world" nature of the course material. (5 quarter hours)

Entrepreneurship and the Smaller Enterprise

Assessment of opportunities and constraints in establishing and managing one's own firm; structuring a new venture, buying into an existing enterprise, owning an enterprise versus becoming a principal employee in a new venture. Case method. Designed to accommodate both the undergraduate students who want course credit and nondegree-seeking entrepreneurs who want information/planning guidelines to help them start and manage their own small business. (4 quarter hours)

MARKETING

Principles of Marketing

Focuses on marketing as a process of managing exchanges. Students learn the environmental factors that impact the strategic marketing process and explore interrelationships between strategic and tactical marketing issues concerning product/service, price, promotion, and distribution decisions. (4 quarter hours)

MATHEMATICS

Trigonometry

Analytic trigonometry, identities, equations, properties of functions; right and oblique triangles without logarithmic computations. Calculator with trig and inverse trig functions necessary. (4 quarter hours)

College Algebra and Analytic Geometry

Functions, graphs, quadratic equations, inequalities, complex numbers, theory of equations, permutations and combinations, probability, systems equations, graphing linear and quadratic equations, conic and standard position, logarithms. (5 quarter hours)

Short Calculus

For students in pre-business administration, pre-pharmacy, and others requiring a minimal amount of calculus. (5 quarter hours)

Precalculus

Inequalities; analytical geometry; complex numbers; binomial theorem; mathematical induction; functions and graphs; trigonometric, exponential, and logarithmic functions. Intended for students who need to review high school higher algebra and trigonometry before taking a calculus sequence. (5 quarter hours)

Calculus I

Analytical geometry and calculus of functions of one variable. Also available in a video version. (5 quarter hours)

One-Variable Differential and Integral Calculus I

Calculus of functions of one variable and related geometry and applications. (4 quarter hours)

One-Variable Differential and Integral Calculus II

Calculus of functions of one variable and related geometry and applications. (4 quarter hours)

Calculus III

Vectors, matrices, linear algebraic equations, Gaussian elimination, determinants and their applications, linear transformations, subspaces, quadratic forms, rigid motions, and orthogonal matrices. (4 quarter hours)

Elementary Differential Equations

Equations of first order, applications; linear equations with constant coefficients, Laplace transforms, simultaneous equations, and series solutions. (4 quarter hours)

Introduction to Linear Algebra and Linear Differential Equations

Vectors, systems of linear equations, matrices, determinants, bases, eigenvalues. Linear differential equations and systems with constant coefficients, initial value problem and general solution, variation of parameters for inhomogeneous equations, applications. (5 quarter hours)

Multivariable Differential Calculus

Differentiation of parametric curves. Partial differentiation and the derivative as a local linear approximation. The chain rule. Application to max/min problems with attention to boundaries and constraints include Lagrange multipliers. Taylor's theorem (multivariable) and the second derivative test. (4 quarter hours)

Multivariable Integral Calculus

Double and triple integrals; change of variable procedures emphasizing polar and spherical coordinates; mass and centoid; integration on curves and surfaces; vectors fields and the theorems of Green, Gauss, and Stokes. (4 quarter hours)

MUSIC

Fundamentals of Music

Explores topics in musical pitch and rhythm, as well as skills such as singing, playing the piano, clapping rhythms, and discriminative listening. Recommended for students who have an avocational interest in music or who will use basic music skills in their careers. (4 quarter hours)

Fundamentals of Music II

Basic procedures for harmonizing melodies, including chord construction and succession, voice-leading, and stylistic considerations. Development of basic listening and sight-singing skills. Rigorous review of music fundamentals. (4 quarter hours)

The Avant-Garde

The course centers on composers of the American musical avant-garde, ca. 1950–1970, including John Cage and Pauline Oliveros, in their sonic and social contexts. Attention is given to the recent impact on music from non-Western culture. Assignments—which include reading, listening, journal writing, original composition, and performance—are designed to be achievable by people with no prior musical training. (4 quarter hours)

American Music: Twentieth-Century American Music

Analysis of American music during this century: folk, popular and classical, black and Chicano, opera and symphony, contemporary. Background knowledge of musical terms necessary. (4 quarter hours)

NORWEGIAN

Beginning Norwegian I

An introduction to basic Norwegian grammar, pronunciation, sentence structure, reading, and writing. Emphasis placed on vocabulary and expressions used in everyday situations, while providing a foundation for further study. (5 quarter hours)

Beginning Norwegian II

A continuation of the preceding course. (5 quarter hours)

Beginning Norwegian III

A continuation of the preceding course with emphasis on reading and writing skills. (5 quarter hours)

Intermediate Norwegian I

Further development of reading, writing, listening, and speaking skills. Grammar review. Students will be exposed to a wide variety of sources, including newspaper and magazine articles, songs, folktales, short stories, poetry, travel brochures. Lessons center on specific aspects of Norwegian life and culture. An audiocassette course. (5 quarter hours)

Intermediate Norwegian II

A continuation of the above course with particular emphasis on reading, writing, and listening skills. Authentic Norwegian texts are made more accessible with prereading strategies and reading/comprehension tasks appropriate at this level. An audiocassette course. (5 quarter hours)

Intermediate Norwegian III

A continuation of the above course that includes more advanced texts that center on social issues. Comprehension and expression of critical thought are promoted through reading and writing tasks. Pronunciation and grammar review. Advanced points of grammar. An audiocassette course. (5 quarter hours)

NURSING

Life Span Growth and Development I

Introductory course that incorporates biological, sociological, and psychological perspectives of human life span development from conception through adolescence. A videocassette/audiocassette course. (2 quarter hours)

Life Span Growth and Development II

Introductory course that incorporates biological, sociological, and psychological perspectives of human life span development from young adulthood through aging and the death experience. A videocassette/audiocassette course. (2 quarter hours)

NUTRITION

Principles of Nutrition

A study of fundamental nutritional concepts (human nutritional requirements, the function of nutrients, and nature of deficiencies). Vegetarianism, weight loss, fad diets, activity, obesity, cancer, heart disease, food processing, safety, and world food problems. (4 quarter hours)

PHILOSOPHY

Introduction to Logic

Rules and procedures of sound argument and valid inference. Relationship of formal patterns of reasoning to such uses of ordinary language as argument, propaganda, and persuasion. How formal logic can be employed as a tool for critical thinking. (5 quarter hours)

Introduction to Philosophy

For much of its history, Western philosophy has been largely a matter of attempting to provide an unshakable foundation for either morals or the natural sciences. Most Western philosophers have spent their intellectual careers trying to define what knowledge and certainty are for the benefit of these two areas of knowledge. Course traces the history of that endeavor by looking at philosophers who are usually cited as pillars of the Western theory of knowledge and metaphysics: Plato, Descartes, Hume, Kant, Wittgenstein, and Kuhn. (5 quarter hours)

Introduction to Ethics

Three classic philosophical theories, by Aristotle, Immanuel Kant, and John Stewart Mill, of how to do the right thing on any occasion. Application of the three theories to actions of characters in the novel *Middlemarch*, by George Eliot, and to actions of Native American characters in the novel *The Surrounded*, by D'Arcy McNickle, exploring any difficulties in applying the theories to cultures different from the ones the theories' authors were familiar with. (5 quarter hours)

Philosophy: Problems of Ethics

The course aims at providing the student with an understanding of the development of moral thought in Western civilization and the problems generated by changing views about the nature of human beings and their behavior. The emphasis of the course is on showing how thinking clearly about the various factors in the development of moral thought in the West is relevant to contemporary moral practice. (4 quarter hours)

PHYSICS

The Physical World

Fundamental laws and principles of the physical world discussed in the context encountered in modern science and technology. Topics: motion of particles, laws of motion, momentum conservation, energy conservation, gravity, fluids, temperature, heat, wave motion, the nature of light, optics, electricity, electric circuits, and magnetism. (4 quarter hours)

The Changing Physical World

Introduces the nonscientist to the changing world of 20th-century physics. Against a background of history and philosophy, it highlights the new ideas and discoveries of relativity, cosmology, and quantum theory as seen from the vast scale of stars and galaxies through the everyday realm of matter and energy, to the submicroscopic level of atoms and nuclei. A videocassette course. (4 quarter hours)

Introductory Physics

I. Topics: uniformly accelerated motion, Newton's laws of motion, work, energy, motion of rigid bodies, mechanical properties of matter, temperature, gas law, thermal properties of matter, thermodynamics, vibratory motion, wave motion, and sound. (4 quarter hours)

II. Topics: electric fields, direct current circuits, magnetism, electromagnetic induction, alternating currents, electromagnetic waves, properties of light, optical devices, interference, diffraction, atomic structure, the atomic nucleus, and physics of the universe. (4 quarter hours)

Introductory Physics Laboratory

I. Laboratory experiments in conjunction with the course Introductory Physics I (see above). Experiments include graphical analysis of data, geometry of motion, gravitational field, energy, power, and sound waves. (1 quarter hour)

II. Laboratory experiments offered in conjunction with the course Introductory Physics II (see above). Experiments: probability and statistics, direct current circuits, magnetic fields, optics, optical instruments, and diffraction. (1 quarter hour)

General Physics

Course 7733. Topics: motion, Newton's laws, work and energy, momentum and the pressure of gases, mechanical properties of matter, temperature, thermal properties of matter, thermodynamics, sound, entropy. (4 quarter hours)

Course 7734. Topics: fluid statics, fluid dynamics, elastic properties of solids, vibration, traveling waves, standing waves, sound waves, reflection and refraction of light, optical instruments, interference, electric fields, and electrical energy. (4 quarter hours)

Course 7735. Topics: direct-current circuits, capacitors, magnetic fields and forces, alternating-current circuits, special relativity, wave-particle duality, Bohr model of the atom, quantum mechanics, nuclear physics, and elementary particle physics. (4 quarter hours)

Comprehensive Introductory Physics with Calculus I

Calculus-level general physics stressing the use of fundamental principles. Topics: vectors, kinematics in two and three dimensions, partical dynamics, work, energy, collisions, and gravitation. (4 quarter hours)

Comprehensive Introductory Physics with Calculus II

Calculus-level general physics stressing the use of fundamental principles. Topics: rigid-body kinematics and dynamics, statics, elasticity, oscillations, mechanical waves, sound, fluid statics and dynamics, heat and thermodynamics. (4 quarter hours)

Comprehensive Introductory Physics with Calculus III

Calculus-level general physics stressing the use of fundamental principles. Topics: the electric field, electric potential, capacitors, dielectrics, DC circuits, magnetic fields, induction, magnetic materials, and AC circuits. (4 quarter hours)

Comprehensive Introductory Physics with Calculus IV

Calculus-level general physics stressing the use of fundamental principles. Topics: Maxwell's equations, electromagnetic waves, nature and propagation of light, reflection, refraction, lenses, mirrors, optical instruments, interference, diffraction, special relativity, quanta, atomic spectra, nuclei, fission, and fusion. (4 quarter hours)

Modern Physics

Descriptive modern physics. Topics: quantum mechanics, hydrogen atom, multi-electron atoms, molecular structure, quantum statistics, thermal radiation, solid state physics, nuclear physics. (4 quarter hours)

POLITICAL SCIENCE

American Government and Politics

An introduction to the ways in which the goals of political actors and the structures of government combine to influence American national policy making. Attention given to the major actors (both institutions and individuals), the mechanics of elections and governing, and the values and standards of democratic rule in the United States. Concludes with two case studies of recent events in American politics. (5 quarter hours)

Contemporary Political Ideologies

A systematic survey of the major competing ideologies of the 20th century, including communism, conservatism, liberalism, fascism, "liberation" and "green" ideologies, and other. Special emphasis is placed on the historical sources, philosophical foundations, and argumentative structure of these influential ideologies. A videocassette course. (4 quarter hours)

The United States Congress

Internal organization, committee system, party leadership, norms, recruitment; legislative policymaking; relationship with the president and bureaucracy; interest group, political party, and constituency influences on the congressional process. (4 quarter hours)

Judicial Process

Structure of the American judiciary; selection of judges; process of litigation; influences on judicial decisions; impact of and compliance with decisions; role of the Supreme Court in the American political system. (4 quarter hours)

Topics in International Politics and Foreign Policy: Understanding War: Its Causes and Consequences

Normative and ethical issues surrounding international violence; types and causes of war between the 18th and 20th centuries; mechanisms for creating peace and limiting future violence. (4 quarter hours)

Politics of Russia and the Commonwealth of Independent States

Analysis of politics in the former USSR, including the political heritage, the impact of Marxism-Leninism, the principal institutions, historical development since 1917; foreign policy, political elites, the decision-making process; political socialization, and selected economic and political issues. (4 quarter hours)

Chinese Government and Politics

An exploration of China since the Communist revolution and Chinese political shifts from 1950 to 1980; their attempts at modernization, achieving a high quality of life for the Chinese people, and achieving a major role in international politics. Topics: Chinese political ideology, developmental policies and plans, the political and economic impact of developmental plans, and the contemporary Chinese international role. (4 quarter hours)

American Political Parties

Party activities in the United States—recruiting, nominating, and campaigning. Parties in power. Party organization and membership, party identification, third parties, and independents. Party reform and the functions of parties. Attention throughout to the impact of parties on democratic government. (4 quarter hours)

PORTUGUESE

Directed Studies: The Everpresent Past in Spanish and Portuguese Culture

The course investigates how the concept of "regenerationism" has retained and exerted cultural force in the Iberian nations, forming a part of their cultural systems—and how it continues to exert that force today. Course materials chronologically structured around the development of the notion that, in Spain and Portugal, there are no beginnings—only "re-beginnings." Selections from literature, philosophy, and social commentary illustrate this sense of a lost past of imperial greatness and the need to recreate it. Begins with the Portuguese poet Luis de Camoes' epic poem of 1578 and ends with the documents about the Spanish "nationalities" of the post-Franco era. Most readings are in the original language. (4 quarter hours)

PSYCHOLOGY

Introduction to Psychology

Introduction to the study of human behavior. Topics: biological foundations of behavior; learning and memory; cognition, thinking, language and social development; individual differences and measurement; and personality, psychopathology, and psychotherapy. This course is also available in a computer version. (5 quarter hours)

Introduction to Biological Psychology

An introduction to the biology of behavior. Topics: basic neuroanatomy and neurophysiology; the neural basis of learning, memory, and motivation; biology of abnormal behavior, dementia, and drug addiction. Explores how behavior can be analyzed by studying the nervous system. (4 quarter hours)

Introduction to Personality

Introduction to the study of personality—how people are and how they got that way. A look at how the major theorists explain personality development; a review of important research; a discussion of how different schools of personality study and assess individual personality and do psychotherapy. Exploration of some special topics in the field. (4 quarter hours)

Introduction to Abnormal Psychology

Focuses on the theoretical causes of human behavior, the description of behavioral disorders, the etiologies of behavioral disorders, and treatment alternatives. (4 quarter hours)

Directed Studies: Stress Management

The concept of stress, various ways of measuring stress levels, the concept of coping, and various methods of coping. Information will be incorporated from diverse medical and psychological research to show how the brain, beliefs, moods, and thoughts affect one's physical and psychological well-being. Techniques for dealing with stress directly and for health maintenance. (4 quarter hours)

Psychology of Human Development

Explores the growth and development of an individual from conception through old age. Emphasizes physical, motor, social, emotional, and psychological growth. Integration of facets of development is made in order to understand a human being as a complex organism functioning in a complex environment. (4 quarter hours)

PUBLIC HEALTH

Dying and Death in Contemporary Society

Provides basic background information on concepts, attitudes, ethics, and lifestyle management in relation to dying, death, grief, and bereavement. Emphasis placed on the educational aspects of these topics for community health and helping professionals and educators. (3 quarter hours)

Toward an Understanding of Child Sexual Abuse

The 10 programs of this course deal with a historical understanding of child sexual abuse, including definitions, dynamics, effects on the victim, how society intervenes, and prevention methods. The course is aimed at the future or current professional in public health, health sciences, social work, education, or law. A videocassette course. (4 quarter hours)

Child Abuse and Neglect

This course is a survey of the basic concepts and knowledge of child abuse and neglect. It includes a historical overview and the issue of balance of rights between children and their parents. Includes examples of child abuse and neglect; discussion of why it occurs, its consequences, and how society can intervene and prevent. A videocassette course. (3 quarter hours)

RELIGIOUS STUDIES

Religions of South Asia

Introduction to Hinduism, Buddhism, and Jainism. A videocassette course. (4 quarter hours)

Introduction to Judaism

Concepts, movements, and institutions in the development of classical Judaism, as manifested in the literature and festivals of the Jewish people from Second Commonwealth times to the present. (4 quarter hours)

RETAILING

Introduction to Retail Merchandising

General aspects of retailing, including types of retailers, market research, management, buying, promotion, and trends. Focuses on aspects of retailing careers within the structure of existing retail firms. Students will develop a retail portfolio that will assist them in networking, including opportunities to conduct interviews with practitioners in the field. (4 quarter hours)

RHETORIC

Writing in Your Profession

Projects in writing professional reports. Analysis of audience and situation; writing effectively to meet the needs of particular readers. Assignments include writing instructions, feasibility report, proposal, memorandum, letter of application, and resume. (4 quarter hours)

Document Design

How to design a document to meet users' needs, complete a draft, and evaluate the effectiveness of the document (forms and software documentation). For databases, decision aids, computer-aided instruction, online programs (Internet and others), visual displays. (4 quarter hours)

RUSSIAN

Beginning Russian

I. A multipurpose program of instruction in the fundamentals of the Russian language. Acquaints students with all four basic language skills: listening, reading, speaking, and writing. Optional use of computer materials in IBM or Macintosh format. (5 quarter hours)

II. A continuation of the above course. (5 quarter hours)

III. A continuation of Beginning Russian II. (5 quarter hours)

Literature: Middle Ages—Dostoevsky in Translation

The history of Russian literature from its beginning (about A.D. 1000) to the middle of the 19th century. Covers Pushkin, Gogol, and Dostoevsky. Students read both literary works (in English) and scholarly materials (historical, biographical, critical commentary) and complete 9 five-to-eight page writing assignments. (4 quarter hours)

Literature: Tolstoy to the Present in Translation

Introductory study of literary movements represented by well-known writers and their selected works from the second half of the 19th century to the Perestroika (Restructuring). Students read both literary works (in English) and scholarly material (historical, biographical, critical commentary). (4 quarter hours)

SCANDINAVIAN

The Scandinavian Fairy Tale as Literature

An exploration of Hans Christian Andersen's stories and tales (in English). An audiocassette course. (4 quarter hours)

SOCIAL WORK

Introduction to American Social Welfare and Community Services

Survey of social services and their components, including many fields of practice, multiple auspices and dependencies; numerous levels of participation, differing ideologies and methods of approach to social problems, and the dynamics of change from social movements to institutionalizations inherent in American social service delivery systems. Course is primarily about the "frames of reference" within which help is offered in American social services, public and private. The uneasy relationship between social service policies and professional social work practice. (5 quarter hours)

Social Work with Involuntary Clients

Designed for students and professionals practicing with involuntary clients in many fields, such as chemical dependency, mental health, public schools, criminal justice and those in nursing, social work, psychology, and psychiatry. Helps students and practitioners understand the dynamics of involuntary status and improve their contact with clients in involuntary situations. A videocassette course. (3 quarter hours)

SOCIOLOGY

Sociology and Social Problems

Provides students with the tools of the sociological imagination. Introduction to the process by which sociological theories are developed and tested and shows how those theories may be applied usefully to major social problems. A videocassette course. (5 quarter hours)

Topics in Social Structure: Women in Muslim Society

Introduction to the role of women in Muslim society from a sociological perspective. Explores what it is to be a woman in a society that is dominated by Islamic religious values and third world cultures. Covers the literature of women's studies in general. Islamic values in regard to the status of women in particular, and the sociological theories of sex roles. Provides insightful and sociological comparison of the effects of different political and economic structures on the roles of women in different muslim societies, including some African, Asian, and Middle Eastern countries. Readings in anthropological and sociological literature, and the autobiographies of Muslim women. (5 quarter hours)

Introduction to Sociology

An intensive examination of the major issues in social psychology. Covers substantive areas of self, personality, person perception, interpersonal attraction, attitudes, social influence, presocial behavior and aggression, small groups, and collective behavior. Emphasis on application of theories and concepts to everyday life. (4 quarter hours)

SPANISH

Beginning Spanish

I. Fundamentals of Spanish. Students develop listening and speaking skills by means of tapes, and learn to read and write basic Spanish in the cultural context of Spain and Spanish America. (5 quarter hours)

II. A continuation of the preceding course. (5 quarter hours)

III. A continuation of the preceding course. (5 quarter hours)

Intermediate Spanish I

Speaking and comprehension; development of reading and writing skills based on materials from Spain and Spanish America. Grammar review; compositions. (5 quarter hours)

Intermediate Spanish II

A continuation of the preceding course. (5 quarter hours)

Intermediate Spanish III

A continuation of the preceding course. (5 quarter hours)

Topics in Spanish-Portuguese Civilization and Culture

The course investigates how the concept of ''regenerationism'' has retained and exerted cultural force in the Iberian nations, forming a part of their cultural systems—and how it continues to exert that force today. Course materials chronologically structured around the development of the notion that, in Spain and Portugal, there are no beginnings—only ''re-beginnings.'' Selections from literature, philosophy, and social commentary illustrate this sense of a lost past of imperial greatness and the need to recreate it. Begins with the Portuguese poet Luis de Camoes' epic poem of 1578 and ends with the documents about the Spanish ''nationalities'' of the post-Franco era. Readings in English translation. (4 quarter hours)

STATISTICS

Introduction to the Ideas of Statistics

Survey of statistical ideas that emphasizes concepts over computation—controlled versus observational studies; presentation and description of data; correlation and causality; sampling; accuracy of estimates; tests. (4 quarter hours)

Statistics

Introduction to modern statistics, emphasizing exploratory data analysis. Topics: methods of organizing, graphing, and interpreting data; measures of center and variability; sampling; probability and probability distributions; estimation, correlation, and hypothesis testing. (5 quarter hours)

SWEDISH

Beginning Swedish

I. An introduction to written and spoken Swedish through basic grammar, workbook exercises, and easy composition. Vocabulary useful to everyday situations is covered. (5 quarter hours)

II. A continuation of the above course. Continued development of basic skills in reading, writing, and speaking. Exercises also include grammar and oral assignments. (5 quarter hours)

III. A continuation of foundation skills in reading, writing, and listening. (5 quarter hours)

Intermediate Swedish

I. Further development of reading, writing, and listening skills; grammar review; composition. (5 quarter hours)

II. Intended to allow the student to gradually begin to master Swedish in advanced contexts. Texts by various Swedish writers. Grammar exercises cover a systematic overview of prepositions, word order, and sentence structure. (5 quarter hours)

III. Advanced texts focusing on four themes: Swedish history, Swedish culture, and Swedish-American immigration. Systematic review of grammar, as well as advanced points of grammar. (5 quarter hours)

Readings in Swedish Literary Texts

Swedish immigrants and discussion of Swedes in America will be used to develop reading and writing skills. Samples from taped interviews are available on audiocassette. (4 quarter hours)

THEATRE

Introduction to the Theatre

An eclectic overview of Western drama from Aeschylus to August Wilson, from Shakespeare to Sam Shepard, focusing of the plays, playwrights, and players that have shaped today's theatre, film, and television. Students are required to attend theatre performances and to enhance their critical skills and understanding of the processes and forms of drama and production. A videocassette course. (4 quarter hours)

Playwriting

Designed to introduce the craft of writing for the theatre to students who have no experience in playwriting. Provides a forum in which students complete their first one-act play, emphasizing the technical elements, vocabulary of playwriting, the nature of the writing experience—from germinal idea to completed script—and strategies for taking a new play to market. (4 quarter hours)

WOMEN'S STUDIES

Northern Minnesota Women: Myths and Realities

This course examines the stereotypes and realities of life for Northern Minnesota Indian, Yankee, and immigrant women from the times of early settlement to the present day. (3 quarter hours)

Topics in Women's Studies: Women Between Victorianism and Emancipation

This course explores continuity and change in the history of Anglo-American women from the late Victorian era to the present. Topics: the Victorian legacy, women and work, women's education, female sexuality, reproduction, and women and politics. (4 quarter hours)

Biology of Women

A study of the biological aspects of the female life cycle. Special attention given to early development, menstrual cyclicity, gestation and childbirth, sexuality, menopause, the aging process, and diverse health conditions. (4 quarter hours)

HIGH SCHOOL COURSES

BUSINESS

Accounting, Part A

A simple accounting cycle for a small service business is worked out in 11 lessons and two application projects. Students will use debits, credits, balance sheets, general journals, ledgers, cash journals, work sheets, and income statements. This course will give an individual some of the basics of accounting. (1 semester credit)

General Business, Part A

Designed to acquaint students with the role of business in our economic system. Students also explore their relationships as consumers to business and our economic system. Topics: business and our economic system; money, credit, and banks; earning an income; labor and management; taxation; economic problems; and citizenship as it relates to the free enterprise system. (1 semester credit)

General Business, Part B

A continuation of Part A, with emphasis on the role of the consumer in our economic system. Topics: money management; the art of spending; consumer protection; consumer credit; making money payments; building financial security; and insurance. (1 semester credit)

ENGLISH

Ninth Grade English, Part A

A review of short story elements, emphasizing plot, character, setting, point of view, theme and unity; an introduction to the epic, focusing on themes and patterns in Homer's *Odyssey*. (1 semester credit)

Ninth Grade English, Part B

This course includes reading and writing about poetry, nonfiction (such as biography and articles), and drama (*Romeo and Juliet*). (1 semester credit)

Tenth Grade English, Part A

An exploration of encounters with others, ourselves, and our environment. Students relate to selected poetry and prose to their own lives and analyze the nature of our language and how it works in communicating experiences and ideas. (1 semester credit)

Tenth Grade English, Part B

A continuation of Part A. (1 semester credit)

Eleventh Grade English, Part A

Begins with three lessons in language study (fact versus opinion, explaining ideas in paragraphs, and writing a persuasive essay). The last six lessons examine major types of American literature (short stories, poetry, nonfiction, and drama, including the classic play *Our Town*). The open-book final exam (essay) focuses on conflicts such as good versus evil and hope versus despair. The study guide materials emphasize important relationships between ideas in literature and the experiences we face in our lives today. (1 semester credit)

Eleventh Grade English, Part B

A continuation of Part A, this course focuses on the historical development of American literature and culture. Includes Native American writing, Puritanism, early New England writers (Thoreau), major poets (Emily Dickinson, Walt Whitman), Mark Twain, and modern realistic writers (Jack London, Stephen Crane). The open-book final exam has essay choices about such elements of the American Dream as materialism, individualism, and our democratic ideals. (1 semester credit

Twelfth Grade English, Part A

A thematic approach to the study of Western literature. Topics: ways of looking at literature, the conflict of wills, choices and consequences, and the personal essay. Students will explore these topics in the works of Orwell, de Maupassant, Sophocles, Moliere, Chaucer, Plato, Hardy, Greene, Woolf, Tolstoy, Camus, and others. (1 semester credit)

Twelfth Grade English, Part B

A continuation of Part A. Topics: appearance versus reality, protest against injustice, and the search for meaning in life. Students will explore these topics in the works of Ibsen, Kafka, Auden, Lawrence, Swift, Mansfield, Zola, Conrad, Joyce, and others. (1 semester credit)

Straight Thinking

An examination of the important differences between clear and unclear thinking. Barriers to clear thinking, such as assumptions, opinions, and common fallacies, are identified and analyzed. Language, viewpoint, and experience, as they affect thinking, are also investigated. (½ semester credit)

Youth in Conflict

The course examines, through two novels and a musical play, the reactions of young people to violence, war, and the conflicts associated with seeking and finding one's identity. (½ semester credit)

Meaning and Self-Discovery in Literature

In examining the viewpoints of three authors, this course traces the actions of characters in two novels and a play as they search for, and attempt to define, the meaning of their own lives and of life in general. (½ semester credit)

Practical Writing

Provides practical writing experience in important types of everyday communication. Writing assignments; describing scenes, telling a story, explaining ideas in an organized essay, comparing or contrasting ideas, judging or evaluating the worth of something, and persuading. Emphasis on revising drafts encourages writers to improve their writing skills in such areas as standard English usage, sentence structure, and subordination, and essay parts (how to introduce a topic, develop the main ideas, and come to a conclusion). (½ semester credit)

Advanced Composition

Designed for students who want additional practice in expository writing—offers experience in composing essays of description, persuasion, comparison/contrast, criticism, interpretation, and stylistic imitation. One assignment involves analyzing a newspaper article. (1 semester credit)

Creative Writing

A comprehensive introduction to various types of creative writing. Students explore the sources of creative writing and learn how to describe a scene, reveal character, tell a story, and write poetry, a short script, and an article or personal essay. (1 semester credit)

Contemporary Literature/Contemporary Problems

A presentation of literature with a view to understanding contemporary problems, this course permits students to gain insight into the problems of Indians, blacks, women, ecology, and the future. (1 semester credit)

The Black American Experience

Through literature, this course provides an examination of the African heritage and the slave experience of black Americans. Students read short stories, an autobiography, and poetry written by black authors. (1 semester credit)

The American Dream in American Drama

Examines the notion of America as the "Promised Land" offering wealth, security, equality, and opportunity to all citizens. The American Dream is explored in 11 modern plays (1920–1972). Among the plots and themes are the story of a successful winegrower who needs a bride, African Americans' aspirations, and contemporary alienation. (1 semester credit)

Basic Strategies for Writing

A course of five units with two lessons each. The first lesson leads students through prewriting activities to help them form a starting place and directs them through the organization of a first draft. The second lesson focuses on revision. Students write personal narratives, descriptive essays, character sketches, persuasive essays, and compare/contrast essays on WAC computer software, obtainable from Independent Study on registration. A computer-based course. (1 semester credit)

GERMAN

Beginning German, Part A

This is the course for you if German is not offered in your high school. Discover how easily you can ask and answer basic questions about yourself, your friends, and family; count; and tell time in German. Equivalent of the first half-year of German. (1 semester credit)

MATHEMATICS

Elementary Algebra, Part A

Designed to acquaint students with basic algebraic notation, sets and variables, properties and operations of real numbers, equations and inequalities in one and two variables, and systems of linear equations and inequalities. (1 semester credit)

Elementary Algebra, Part B

A continuation of Part A. (1 semester credit)

Plane Geometry, Part A

Topics: points, lines and planes, proofs, angles, theorems, parallel lines, proving lines parallel, proving triangles congruent, congruent segments and angles, applying congruent triangles, inequalities, definitions and properties of similar polygons, working with similar triangles, Pythagorean theorem, and ratios, proportion, and similarity. (1 semester credit)

Plane Geometry, Part B

A continuation of Part A, this course emphasizes the Pythagorean theorem, circle relationships, areas and volumes, solids, cylinders, cones, spheres, distance, midpoint, slope formulas, coordinate geometry, and geometric constructions and transformations. (1 semester credit)

Higher Algebra, Part A

An extensive review of concepts learned in elementary algebra. Further development of topics in linear equations, factoring, fractions, exponents, complex numbers, and quadratic equations. (1 semester credit)

Higher Algebra, Part B

A continuation of Part A. Covers functions, radicals, graphical methods, systems of quadratics, determinants, ratio and variation, binomial theorem, factorials, logarithms, and progressions. (1 semester credit)

RUSSIAN

Beginning Russian, Part A

Reading, writing, translation, and grammar of the Russian language. (1 semester credit)

Beginning Russian, Part B

A continuation of Beginning Russian, Part A. (1 semester credit)

SCIENCE

Biology, Part A

Topics include the cell, basic biological processes, and comparative anatomy and physiology as they relate to evolution and human biology. (1 semester credit)

Biology, Part B

A continuation of Part A. General topics include human inheritance, embryology, and evolution; viruses, molds, yeasts, and bacteria and their importance to humans; and green plants and their functions. (1 semester credit)

Physics, Part A

Basic principles and laws of physics; motion, causes of motion; forces and interactions; work, energy, momentum; kinetic theory of matter, heat transfer; and interaction of heat and work. (1 semester credit)

Physics, Part B

Second part of the physics sequence. Considers the electromagnetic spectrum, the nature of light, geometric optics, diffraction and polarization, electrostatics, D.C. circuits, and electromagnetic induction. (1 semester credit)

SOCIAL STUDIES

Problems of American Democracy, Part A

A basic introduction to the theory and reality of American social problems, this course is equivalent to the first half of 12th grade social studies. Topics include society and culture, the process of socialization, problems of social mobility, and problems of continuity, and change. (1 semester credit)

Problems of American Democracy, Part B

Equivalent of the second half of 12th grade social studies. Topics include principles and practices of government, the political processes, national government, financing government, and the United States and world affairs. (1 semester credit)

World Geography, Part A

Introduces students to geographic issues in the United States and around the world. Students use maps, tables, and graphs to learn geographic analysis techniques, and develop an awareness of important geographic issues. (1 semester credit)

World Geography, Part B

A continuation of the above course. (1 semester credit)

General Psychology, Part A

A survey of psychology and psychological methods designed to acquaint students with the manner in which psychologists examine and attempt to explain human behavior. Topics: sensation, perception, learning, motivation, behavior. (1 semester credit)

General Psychology, Part B

A continuation of Part A. Topics include verbal behavior, cognitive processes, frustration and conflict, individual differences, personality, behavior pathology, social psychology, and foundations of behavior. (1 semester credit)

Project Self-Discovery

Through introspective assignments, students gain a better understanding of themselves and their world. Designed to encourage students to grow to see themselves in positive ways, perceive themselves and their world accurately and realistically, and learn to identify with and relate to other people. (1 semester credit)

NONCREDIT COURSES

DRAFTING

Introduction to Drafting

Beginning architectural instruction in the use of drafting instruments. Emphasis on drafting fundamentals: lines, lettering, introduction to orthographic and paraline drawings. Introduction to architectural symbols and vocabulary as related to interior design. (Noncredit)

FRENCH

Reading French

Fundamentals of grammar; reading of appropriate prose. Prepares for graduate reading examination in French. (Noncredit)

MATHEMATICS

Introduction to Basic Mathematics

In-depth review of basic mathematics from whole numbers to geometry. Emphasizes computation and understanding the basic concepts. (Noncredit)

Elementary Algebra

For students with a strong arithmetic background who are ready to study elementary algebra. Topics: signed numbers, algebraic expressions, equations, inequalities, rational expressions, exponents, polynomials, factoring, graphing, 2x2 systems, radical expressions, and word problems from these areas. (Noncredit)

Plane Geometry: Programmed Study

Elements of plane geometry with some geometry of solids. Equivalent to one year of high school plane geometry. (Noncredit)

Intermediate Algebra, Part I

For students needing additional preparation in algebra before Part II. Sets, real numbers, linear equalities, linear inequalities, absolute values, polynomials, rational expressions, exponents, roots, quadratic equations, relations and functions, systems of equations, word problems. (Noncredit)

Intermediate Algebra, Part II

Assumes basic knowledge of linear and quadratic equations and inequalities, exponents, factoring, rational expressions, roots, radicals, complex numbers, and graphing. Topics: quadratic equations, matrix solutions, general inequalities, conic sections, functions, logarithmic and exponential functions, introduction to sequences, series, and binomial theorem. (Noncredit)

SPANISH

Reading Spanish Students

Prepares students primarily for reading, and especially reading general and technical nonliterary prose. (Noncredit)

Minot State University
Continuing Education
500 University Avenue West
Minot, North Dakota 58707   (701) 857-3817

Description:
A state-supported public institution, Minot State University was founded in 1913. It offers associate, baccalaureate, and master degrees.

Work done by correspondence is supervised by Minot State University instructors and is of the same standard as that maintained in resident work.

Faculty:
Dr. James Croonquist, Dean of Graduate School and Continuing Education; Dr. Kathleen Corak, Registrar/Admissions Officer. There is a faculty of 30 members.

Academic Levels:
College

Degree/Certificate Programs:
Minot State University will accept up to 16 semester hours of credit earned by correspondence study toward a degree.

Admission Requirements:
High School graduation or GED.

Tuition:
Contact the university for current tuition and fees. VISA or MasterCard accepted. Refund policy: if a student formally withdraws from a course within thirty days of enrollment, the fee less $20, less amount paid to the instructor for graded lessons, will be refunded; if a student formally withdraws from a course within three months of enrollment, one-half the fee less $20, less amount paid to the instructor for graded lessons, will be refunded; no refunds after three months from the date of enrollment.

Enrollment Period:
The maximum time allowed to complete a course is one year.

Equipment Requirements:
Textbooks must be paid for by the student; the cost is not included in the tuition. Books may be ordered from the University Bookstore.

Credit and Grading:
The grading system is A, B, C, D, F. Seventy percent (D) is the minimum passing grade. The final examination must be proctored, either at Minot State University, or by a local school official. To obtain transfer credits for a Minot correspondence course, the student must submit a statement of approval from the accepting institution that it will honor the credits. Transfer-in correspondence credits are accepted the same as institutionally-earned credits. It is recommended that students do not enroll for correspondence work while in residence at any institution. Credits and grades earned through correspondence are not used in computing grade point averages. Credit is awarded in semester hour units.

Accreditations:
North Central Association of Colleges and Schools.

COLLEGE COURSES

BIOLOGY

Medical Terminology

Study of the common prefixes, stems, and suffices used in medical terms. (1 semester hour)

Biogeography

Principles of plant and animal distribution, including causality and the role of man. (3 semester hours)

Freshwater Biology

Biological, chemical, and physical characteristics of inland waters, including origins, interrelationships, and the effect of civilization. (3 semester hours)

Systematic Botany

Classification and taxonomy of seed plants with emphasis on local flora. (3 semester hours)

Soils

Principles of soils, including formation, properties, chemistry, fertilizers, and classification. (3 semester hours)

BUSINESS

Accounting Principles I

Introduces the fundamental principles of accounting, including the classification of accounts, debits/credits, the basic financial statements, adjusting/closing entries, special journals, cash, receivables/payables, inventories, plant and intangible assets, payroll, and a manual or computerized practice case. (3 semester hours)

Accounting Principles II

Concludes the principles sequence by addressing accounting theory, partnership accounting, corporate capital, bonds payable, investments in stocks/bonds, statement of cash flows, financial statement analysis, manufacturing accounting, decision making, and income taxes. (3 semester hours)

Fundamentals of Management

Focuses on the nature of management, the evolution of management thought, strategic management and planning concepts, decision making and creative problem solving, and motivation and leadership in a changing environment. (3 semester hours

Personnel Management

Includes personnel policies, programs and procedures, standards, employment, staffing, wage and salary administration, personnel laws, and personnel research. (3 semester hours)

Organizational Behavior

Introduces the principles, concepts, and processes that interpret human relations in management at the individual, group, and organizational levels. (3 semester hours)

Legal Office Terminology

The study of legal terminology, dictation, and transcription with guides to punctuation, capitalization, Latin and French terms and phrases that are commonly used, legal allocations, and correct methods of typing legal subject matter. (3 semester hours)

Legal Office Procedures II

The scope of the course is broadened to include not only legal office procedures, but the exercise of judgment and independent action. (3 semester hours)

Electronic Office Procedures

A classroom course designed to develop skills and procedures necessary to function efficiently in today's office as an administrative support person. (3 semester hours)

DRIVER EDUCATION

Driver and Safety Education

Driver and traffic safety education are introduced in this course. Various high school textbooks and other teaching tools will be reviewed. (3 semester hours)

Readings in Traffic Safety

This is an independent research course. It is designed to broaden the knowledge of the student in several different subjects. The world of traffic safety is ever changing, and there is a need for studies and research of these changes. (1 semester hour)

Organization and Administration of Safety Education

Basic concepts and development of the four-phase program: dual-controlled car, simulator, multiple car driving range, and classroom. (2 semester hours)

Advanced In-Car Instruction

Physical skills are important but they are easily mastered by almost anyone. The difficult part of driving involves the mental abilities of observing, evaluating, and deciding how to best control the speed and position of the car. Involved also are social responsibilities and the assessment of risks. This course will help to prepare instructors to teach driving skills in a planned, safe, and effective manner. (3 semester hours)

ENGLISH

Freshman English I

Reading, writing, and reasoning based on expository prose. (3 semester hours)

Freshman English II

Reading, writing, reasoning, and research based on imaginative literature. (3 semester hours)

Introduction to Literature

Introductory study of literary forms, such as the short story, the novel, poetry, and drama; literary criticism and techniques. Special emphasis is given to basic critical vocabulary. (3 semester hours)

Literature for Children

Introductory study of poetry, folk and fairy tales, myths and legends, modern realistic stories, historical, biographical, and science books for children in the first six grades. (3 semester hours)

Approaches to Grammar

Comparative study of descriptive English grammars, including traditional grammar, with emphasis on preparing teachers for secondary schools. (3 semester hours)

Advanced Composition

This course is concentrated instruction and practice in writing. (3 semester hours)

Professional and Technical Writing

This course concentrates on instruction and practice in technical and job-related expository writing. (3 semester hours)

World Literature I

Study of the representative literature other than American and English. (3 semester hours)

World Literature II

Acquaints the student with some of the most important and interesting works of literature from around the world, excluding British and American writers, in more recent time. (3 semester hours)

MATHEMATICS

Algebra

Real numbers, simple algebraic expressions, linear equations, graphs, factoring, quadratic equations. (4 semester hours)

College Algebra

Linear and quadratic equations, radicals, exponents and logarithms, rational expressions, systems of linear equations, matrices and determinants, sequences, series, function rotations and graphing. (4 semester hours)

Precalculus

Trigonometric functions, solving triangles, analytic geometry, theory of equations, sequences, series and induction. (4 semester hours)

College Geometry

Euclidean geometry for secondary teachers. Incidence, distance, betweenness, separation, congruency, geometric inequalities, parallel postulate, similarity, circles and hyperbolic geometry. (4 semester hours)

SOCIAL SCIENCE

Western Civilization to 1789

A survey of the political, intellectual, social, and economic trends of

Western Civilization from the Classical Age to the French Revolution. (3 semester hours)

The U.S. Government

Origin and development of the U.S. national government. Growth of the national government and its impact on our daily lives. An analysis of the major institutions of government. (3 semester hours)

State and Local Government

Comparison of the structure, organization, and interrelationships of American federal, state, and local governments. Special attention will be given to North Dakota government. (3 semester hours)

Introduction to Sociology

The study of society; its culture, organization, groups, roles, and processes. (3 semester hours)

Changing American Family

History, structure, and functions of the family as a social institution. Emphasis is placed on changing patterns of dating, mate selection, cohabitation, marriage, gender roles, dual career families, divorce, and remarriage. (3 semester hours)

Mississippi, University of
Department of Independent Study
Center for Public Service and Continuing Studies
P.O. Box 729
University, Mississippi 38677-0729
(601) 232-7313

Description:

The University of Mississippi was chartered in 1844 and began its first session on November 6, 1948. The University has occupied a position of educational leadership not only in the state but also in the South and the nation. It pioneered in the accreditation of high schools in Mississippi, was a charter member of what is now the Southern Association of Colleges and Schools (a regional accrediting agency), and helped to found the National Association of State Universities and Land Grant Colleges. Independent study courses have been offered since 1926. Approximately 1,200 students enroll each year in courses offered by 26 academic departments in the Schools of Accountancy, Business Administration, Education, and Liberal Arts.

The University of Mississippi's Independent Study courses are offered primarily for students who want to continue their formal education but are unable to attend classes. The Independent Study student is supported by the educational resources of the University to the same extent as the student who works on campus.

Faculty:

Joan G. Popernik, Coordinator of Independent Study. There is an faculty of 48 members.

Academic Levels:

College
Noncredit

Degree/Certificate Programs:

A student who expects to earn an undergraduate degree from the University of Mississippi should consult his/her dean in regard to the maximum number of hours that may be earned through independent study. A student seeking a degree from another institution should consult that institution's catalog or the dean of the school from which he/she expects to receive a degree to determine the applicability of credit earned in independent study courses.

Admission Requirements:

Open enrollment. Some courses have required prerequisites. With the approval of the high school principal or counselor, high school juniors and seniors may enroll for college-level courses on a credit basis.

Tuition:

$65 per semester hour plus a $10 nonrefundable mailing and handling fee for each course, payable at registration. A $25 postage fee is charged for students who wish to have their materials mailed to destinations outside of the United States and who are not served by an A.P.O. or F.P.O. address. Payment by MasterCard or Visa accepted. A refund is allowed if no more than one month has elapsed since enrollment. The amount of this refund is eighty percent of the enrollment fee submitted, less a $5 charge for each lesson graded. Refunds are made only under the conditions stated above and with the understanding that the student will pay the full amount of the fee if he/she should ever again enroll for an independent study course.

Enrollment Period:

Maximum time allowed for course completion is one year; minimum time for course completion is six weeks. If a course is not completed within one year from the date of enrollment, a three-month extension of time may be granted for a fee of $15. An application for an extension of time must be received in the office of Independent Study prior to the expiration of the on-year enrollment period. Under unusual circumstances, a second extension of time may be granted.

Equipment Requirements:

Textbooks must be purchased by the student for all independent study courses. Some courses require cassette tape players. Cassette tapes may be rented by the student from the Department of Independent Study. Students may purchase textbooks in the editions specified for independent study courses from The Ole Miss Bookstore, The University of Mississippi, Box 9, University, MS 38677, (601) 232-7131.

Credit and Grading:

To obtain credit, the student is required (1) to write a test after submitting a specified number of lessons and (2) to write a final examination. A passing grade in the final exam is required for credit in the course. Grading system: A, B, C, D, F. Students residing in Mississippi are tested at any one of the approved examination centers in the state. Out-of-state students write tests under the supervision of an approved education official. Credits are awarded in semester hour units.

Library Services:

No library facilities/services offered for nonresident students.

Accreditations:

Southern Association of Colleges and Schools. Member of: National University Continuing Education Association.

COLLEGE COURSES

ACCOUNTING

Introduction to Accounting Principles

Course 201. Accounting principles and procedures for proprietorships, partnerships, and corporations; preparation of financial statements; management's use of accounting data. (3 semester hours)

Course 202. A continuation of the above course. (3 semester hours)

Administrative Accounting

Planning and control through accounting; information systems; cost determination; financial statement analysis and interpretation. (3 semester hours)

ART

Art Appreciation

For all students interested in acquiring an understanding of the visual arts. An introductory survey of painting, sculpture, and architecture. (3 semester hours)

BIOLOGY

Inquiry into Life—Human Biology

A survey course, intended for nonbiology majors, introducing basic principles and emphasizing the function of the human body, including diseases, cellular processes, respiration, muscular system, reproduction, development, immunity, and inheritance. (3 semester hours)

Inquiry into Life—The Environment

A survey course, intended for nonbiology majors, emphasizing the relationships of humans to the environment, including origin and diversification of life, behavior, ecology, role of plants, and environmental concerns. (3 semester hours)

CHEMISTRY

Environmental Chemistry

Course 201. A general survey of the chemical basis of the natural water, oxygen, nitrogen, and carbon dioxide cycles, water pollution, essential and processed foods, and food additives. (3 semester hours)

Course 202. Human population growth, agricultural chemicals, energy consumption, air pollution, household chemicals, and drugs and their relationship with the environment. (3 semester hours)

COMPUTER SCIENCE

Computer Science Survey

An introduction to computers and computing for students with no prior knowledge of computers. (3 semester hours)

ECONOMICS

Principles of Microeconomics

The nature of economics, economic concepts and institutions; the role of the price system in directing the production of goods and services; distribution of income; and comparative economic systems. (3 semester hours)

Money and Banking

Nature and functions of money and banking; relation of money and credit to the American political system, the Federal Reserve System, and national economic goals. (3 semester hours)

EDUCATION

Career Education

The process of teaching career education and economic awareness to students in elementary and secondary schools. (3 semester hours)

EDUCATIONAL PSYCHOLOGY

Educational Psychology

Application of principles of general and developmental psychology to the science of teaching; learning, motivation, psychological testing. (3 semester hours)

Psychology of Adolescence

Psychological principles underlying the mental, emotional, and socio-moral stresses of the preadolescent and adolescent. (3 semester hours)

Psychology of Human Growth and Development

General survey of various aspects of psychological development from infancy through adolescence with emphasis on those conditions which enhance the growth of the individual. (3 semester hours)

ELEMENTARY EDUCATION

Science in the Elementary School

Practical instructional experiences as they relate to concepts, curriculum, and evaluation in science education. Emphasis on objectives, content, materials, and methods of science teaching in elementary schools; supervised experiences with children. (3 semester hours)

Arithmetic in the Elementary School

Modern methods and techniques for teaching computation, measurement, geometry, problem solving, and consumer arithmetic; diagnosis of error patterns; practicum experience included. (3 semester hours)

ENGLISH

English Composition

Course 101. Instruction in composition, grammar, and reading, with particular emphasis on actual practice in writing. (3 semester hours)

Course 102. A continuation of the above course. (3 semester hours)

Introduction to Literature

Survey of techniques and terminology of literary analysis, including practice with poetry, prose, and drama. (3 semester hours)

Masterworks of English Literature

Readings in nine major English writers from Chaucer to the present. (3 semester hours)

Masterworks of American Literature

Readings in nine major American writers from Franklin to the present. (3 semester hours)

Shakespeare

Course 301. Representative plays written before 1600. (3 semester hours)

Course 302. Representative plays written after 1600. (3 semester hours)

Survey of American Literature to the Civil War

Prose and poetry from the Colonial beginnings to the end of the New England dominance in the nineteenth century. (3 semester hours)

Survey of American Literature Since the Civil War

Prose and poetry from Walt Whitman to the present. (3 semester hours)

Survey of English Literature From the Beginning Through the Eighteenth Century

Selected prose and poetry from the beginning through the eighteenth century. (3 semester hours)

Survey of English Literature From the Romantic Period to the Present

Selected prose and poetry from the Romantic period to the present. (3 semester hours)

Advanced Composition

A practical course for students who desire additional instruction and experience in writing. Special emphasis on developing techniques of effective written communication. (3 semester hours)

Advanced English Grammar

Morphology and syntax with emphasis on traditional scholarly approaches to usage. (3 semester hours)

Background of American Literary Culture, 1800 to 1900

American cultural ideas as reflected in literature. (3 semester hours)

The Fiction of Faulkner's Yoknapatawpha County

Reading and study of selected novels by William Faulkner. (3 semester hours)

History of the English Language

The development of the language from Old English to the present with particular attention to phonology and morphology. (3 semester hours)

The American Novel Before 1914

Development of the American novel, including the work of Brown, Cooper, Simms, Hawthorne, Melville, Mark Twain, Howells, James, Crane, Norris, and others. (3 semester hours)

FINANCE

Money and Banking

Nature and functions of money and banking; relation of money and credit to the American political system, the Federal Reserve System, and national economic goals. (3 semester hours)

Risk and Insurance

Basic principles of risk management and insurance; recognition, evaluation, and treatment of risk. An overview of the field. (3 semester hours)

FRENCH

Elementary French

Course 101. Grammar, conversation, and reading. (3 semester hours)

Course 102. A continuation of the above course. (3 semester hours)

Second Year French

Course 201. Reading, writing, aural comprehension, with a review of grammar. (3 semester hours)

Course 202. A continuation of the above course. (3 semester hours)

GERMAN

Ph.D. German

Instruction in reading German. Adequate preparation for reading knowledge examinations given Ph.D. candidates. (Noncredit)

Elementary German

Course 101. Grammar, aural comprehension, reading, and writing. (3 semester hours)

Course 102. A continuation of the above course. (3 semester hours)

Second Year German

Course 201. Reading, writing, aural comprehension, with a review of grammar. (3 semester hours)

Course 202. A continuation of the above course. (3 semester hours)

HEALTH AND SAFETY

Personal and Community Health

A comprehensive health course including principles and practices of healthful living for the individual and community; major health problems; responsibilities of home, school, health agencies. (3 semester hours)

First Aid

Methods and procedures of first responder aid and emergency care appropriate for common injuries, illnesses, health emergencies, and disasters. (3 semester hours)

Safety Education

Principles, procedures, and materials for teaching safety in school, home, and community. (3 semester hours)

HISTORY

Western Civilization from the Earliest Times to 1648

Political, cultural, social, and economic development. (3 semester hours)

Western Civilization Since 1648

A continuation of the above course. (3 semester hours)

The United States to 1877

Political, cultural, social, and economic development. (3 semester hours)

The United States Since 1877

A continuation of the above course to the present. (3 semester hours)

Mississippi History, 1540 to the Present

The political, economic, and cultural development of the state. (3 semester hours)

Women in the South

A historical survey of Southern women with emphasis on research through documentary sources and history. (3 semester hours)

HOME ECONOMICS

Nutrition

Fundamental principles of human nutrition; application to needs of individuals and families at all stages of the life cycle. (3 semester hours)

Child Care and Development

The physical, mental, social, and emotional development of the child from birth to six years. (3 semester hours)

Human Development Across the Lifespan

Life span human development including physical, intellectual, emotional, and social development; the needs of individuals throughout the life span; and the formation and maintenance of human relationships. (3 semester hours)

Marriage and Family Relationships

A functional approach to the interpersonal relationships of mate selection, marriage, and family life. (3 semester hours)

Fashion Merchandsing and Marketing

In-depth study of the fashion business, includes the production of fashion, major and regional marketing centers, the retail distribution of fashion, and buyer responsibilities. (3 semester hours)

Human Sexuality

Physiological, psychological, and ethical aspects of sexuality. The human sexual system, cultural perspectives, sexual roles, behavior and deviations, gender identity, decision making, and childhood experiences. (3 semester hours)

JOURNALISM

Introduction to Advertising

Principles; technical phases of planning and preparing campaigns; advertising research, layout, and copy writing. (3 semester hours)

School Publications

Problems and purposes of school newspapers and other scholastic publications; production techniques; selecting and directing a staff; financial and ethical problems. (3 semester hours)

KINESIOLOGY

Psychomotor Assessment

Evaluation of health status, physical fitness, and other psychomotor parameters using appropriate laboratory and field techniques and focusing on administration and interpretation of results. (3 semester hours)

LATIN

Introduction to Latin

Course 101. Essentials of grammar, training in translation. (3 semester hours)

Course 102. A continuation of the above course. (3 semester hours)

Intermediate Latin

Course 201. Continuation of grammar and reading of selections from representative authors. (3 semester hours)

Course 202. A continuation of the above course. (3 semester hours)

Latin Review and Reading

Review of grammar. (3 semester hours)

LIBRARY SCIENCE

Children's Literature, K–8

Selection, examination and effective utilization of literature for children from kindergarten through grade 8. (3 semester hours)

LINGUISTICS

Advanced English Grammar

Morphology and syntax, with emphasis on traditional scholarly approaches to usage. (3 semester hours)

History of the English Language

The development of the language from Old English to the present with particular attention to phonology and morphology. (3 semester hours)

MARKETING

Marketing Principles

Basic principles and methods of marketing consumer and industrial goods; functions and institutions involved in marketing processes. (3 semester hours)

Introduction to Advertising

Advertising principles, consumer trends affecting advertising, media selection, layout techniques, and advertising research. (3 semester hours)

Buyer-Seller Communications

Fundamentals of communication theory and correct sales principles needed for a successful career in sales; insight into the importance of communications in buyer-seller relations. (3 semester hours)

Introduction to Retailing

Principles underlying the successful operation of retail stores, particularly single-line or independent-unit, department, and chain stores. (3 semester hours)

MATHEMATICS

Elementary Statistics

Descriptive statistics; probability distributions; sampling distributions; estimation; hypothesis testing; and linear aggression. (3 semester hours)

College Algebra

(3 semester hours)

Trigonometry

(3 semester hours)

Mathematics for Elementary Teachers I

Introduction to sets; the real numbers system and its subsystems. (3 semester hours)

Mathematics for Elementary Teachers II

Informal geometry; measurement and the metric system; probability and statistics. (3 semester hours)

Unified Calculus and Analytic Geometry

Course 261. Differential and integral calculus with analytic geometry. (3 semester hours)

Course 262. A continuation of *Course 261.* (3 semester hours)

Course 263. A continuation of *Course 262.* (3 semester hours)

Course 264. A continuation of *Course 263.* (3 semester hours)

Calculus for Business, Economics, and Accountancy

Differential and integral calculus with an emphasis on business applications. (3 semester hours)

MUSIC

Introduction to Music Literature

An overall historical perspective including style recognition and familiarity with the major composers and compositions. (3 semester hours)

Opera

An introduction to opera as an art form. (1 semester hour)

PHILOSOPHY

Contemporary Philosophical Problems

Philosophical issues in recent social topics, e.g., whether computers think, "politically correct thinking," and the new sexuality. (3 semester hours)

Logic

Principles and methods of sound reasoning, emphasizing analysis of everyday arguments. (3 semester hours)

History of Philosophy

Course 301. Major philosophers from the Pre-Socratics through the Medieval Period. (3 semester hours)

Course 302. Major philosophers from the Renaissance through the early 20th century. (3 semester hours)

Philosophy of Religion

Philosophical questions in religious thought and practice, e.g. the problem of evil, the existence of God, the nature of religious belief and experience. (3 semester hours)

Business Ethics

Ethical problems in business theory and practice, e.g., the myth of amoral business, conflicts of interest, and employer-employee rights and obligations. (3 semester hours)

POLITICAL SCIENCE

Contemporary Terrorism

A systematic study of transnational terroristic disorder. Societal manifestations, prophylaxix and survival. (3 semester hours)

PORTUGUESE

Elementary Portuguese

Course 101. (3 semester hours)

Course 102. A continuation of the above course. (3 semester hours)

Second-Year Portuguese

Course 201. (3 semester hours)

Course 202. (3 semester hours)

PUBLIC ADMINISTRATION

Criminal Investigation

Criminal investigation procedures, including theory of investigation, case preparation, specific techniques for selected offenses, questioning of suspects and witnesses, and problems in criminal investigation. (3 semester hours)

READING

Foundations of Reading Instruction

Survey of the knowledge base necessary for teaching reading; emphasis on basics, word recognition, comprehension, and study skills. (3 semester hours)

Diagnosis and Remediation of Reading Disabilities

Fundamentals of diagnosis and remediation of reading disabilities and application of the principles studied with emphasis on causes of reading disabilities. (3 semester hours)

Methods and Materials for Teaching Reading in Elementary School

The reading process as it applies to the elementary curriculum. Organizational patterns, approaches, and materials for teaching word recognition, comprehension, and functional skills. Correlates reading with the content areas and encompasses teaching reading to the exceptional child. (3 semester hours)

Reading in the Secondary School

The reading process as it applies to junior and senior high school curricula. Emphasis on preparing pre-service content-area teachers to meet the needs of students with widely varying levels of reading achievement. (3 semester hours)

REAL ESTATE

Principles of Real Estate

A study of principles of land economics, the law dealing with property rights, agency, contracts and transfer of title; Mississippi Licensing Law, the Code of Ethics, and basic mathematics pertaining to the real estate industry. (3 semester hours)

Real Estate Valuation and Appraisal

A study of the theories of value as applied to both residential and income properties, determinants of value, underlying principles of valuation, and consideration of selected problems in appraisal with emphasis on residential property. (3 semester hours)

RECREATION

Foundations of Leisure

Analysis of the leisure field to provide a basic understanding of leisure as an increasingly important component of our society. (3 semester hours)

Outdoor Recreation

A study of the roles and responsibilities of local, state, and federal governments in providing appropriate locations, facilities, programs, and leadership. (3 semester hours)

Special Programs in Therapeutic Recreation

An introduction to adapted fitness programs and therapeutic recreation services for special populations, with emphasis on modifying programs and activities to meet individual needs. (3 semester hours)

RELIGIOUS STUDIES

World Religions

A comparative study of major religions from prehistoric times to the present. (3 semester hours)

New Testament Thought

Themes of the gospels and epistles reinterpreted according to contemporary critical findings. (3 semester hours)

Philosophy of Religion

Philosophical questions in religious thought and practice, e.g., the problem of evil, the existence of God, the nature of religious belief and experience. (3 semester hours)

SOUTHERN STUDIES

Women in the South

A historical survey of Southern women with emphasis on research through documentary sources and oral history. (3 semester hours)

SPANISH

Elementary Spanish

Course 101. Grammar, aural comprehension, reading, and writing. (3 semester hours)

Course 102. A continuation of the above course. (3 semester hours)

Second-Year Spanish

Course 201. Reading, writing, aural comprehension, with a review of grammar. (3 semester hours)

Course 202. A continuation of the above course. (3 semester hours)

SPECIAL EDUCATION

Survey of Exceptional Children

An introduction to the special education of the exceptional child including the etiological, psychological, educational and vocational aspects of exceptionality. Emphasis is on the needs of exceptional youth and current issues in instruction and management techniques. (3 semester hours)

TELECOMMUNICATIONS

Introduction to Telecommunications

Interdisciplinary analysis of technological developments and regulatory, political, financial, social, and other forces influencing electronic information management. (3 semester hours)

NONCREDIT COURSES

GERMAN

Ph.D. German

Instruction in reading German. Adequate preparation for reading knowledge examinations given Ph.D. candidates. No previous knowledge of German required. (Noncredit) *Tuition:* $165.

Mississippi State University

Independent Study Program
Division of Continuing Education
P.O. Drawer 5247
Mississippi State, Mississippi 39762-5247
(601) 325-2652

Description:

Mississippi State University began as The Agricultural and Mechanical College of the State of Mississippi, one of the national Land-Grant Colleges established after Congress passed the Morrill Act in 1873. It was created by the Mississippi Legislature on February 28, 1878. The Division of Continuing Education coordinates an educational service connecting the University, its scholars, research, and resources with the people and communities of Mississippi.

The Independent Study Program is one of the many services of the Division of Continuing Education. The program offers a wide variety of high school and college-level credit courses designed for individuals who have need for further learning experiences but who are unable to participate in regularly scheduled classes.

Faculty:

Robert B. Leiter, Dean of Continuing Education; Greg Carlyle, Coordinator of Independent Study.

Academic Levels:
College
High School

Degree/Certificate Programs:

The State of Mississippi allows up to two units of correspondence study to be applied toward high school graduation; prior approval of the student's high school principal required. Mississippi State University will allow up to 20 percent of the total credits for an undergraduate degree to be from correspondence study.

Admission Requirements:

For high school courses, the principal of student's present high school or high school from which student seeks graduation must give prior approval. For college courses, graduation from an accredited high school or equivalent.

Tuition:

High school, $55 per one-half unit plus $10 postage and handling; College, $50 per semester credit hour plus $10 handling fee. $20 airmail postage fee for courses mailed to foreign countries. Tuition is due at time of registration. A refund of 80 percent is allowed up to one month after registration if no lessons have been submitted.

Enrollment Period:

The maximum time allowed to complete a high school course is one year for one-half unit. Two three-month extensions may be allowed with a $10 extension fee for each extension. For college courses, the maximum time allowed is one year. Two three-month extensions may be allowed with a $10 fee for each extension. Minimum times are 30 days for one course, 45 days for two courses (this applies to both high school and college courses).

Equipment Requirements:

Textbook costs are not included in the tuition. They may be purchased from the MSU Bookstore. High school course texts sometimes may be obtained from a local high school.

Credit and Grading:

All tests must be supervised by a school official. College students residing in Mississippi must take exams in one of the 22 examination centers in the state; out-of-state students, under the supervision of a school official. Minimum passing grade is 60 percent. Credit is awarded in semester hour units for college credit, ½ units for high school credit.

Accreditations:

Southern Association of Colleges and Schools. Member of: National University Continuing Education Association.

COLLEGE COURSES

ACCOUNTING

Principles of Financial Accounting

Financial accounting fundamentals including accounting cycle, accounting systems, cash flow, assets, liabilities, equity, and forms of business organizations. (3 semester hours)

Principles of Managerial Accounting

Managerial accounting fundamentals including interpretation and use of management reports, cost behavior, cost accumulation, budgeting, financial statement analysis, responsibility accounting. (3 semester hours)

Cost Accounting

Cost accounting principles and techniques as applied to cash, receivables, inventories, plant and equipment and intangible assets, accounting working papers and financial statements. (3 semester hours)

BUSINESS STATISTICS

Business Statistical Methods I

Methods of describing numerical data; probability in business decisions; random variables; sampling distributions; introduction to estimation and hypothesis testing; computer statistical packages applied. (3 semester hours)

COMPUTER SCIENCE

Basic Computer Concepts and Applications

Basic concepts of computing using large-scale and microcomputers. Introduction to operating system commands, applications software (word processing, spreadsheets, communications, etc.), and rudimentary BASIC programming. (3 semester hours)

COUNSELOR EDUCATION

Introduction to Counseling

Overview of counseling as a profession including specialty areas. Theories and techniques used in counseling. (3 semester hours)

Developmental Counseling and Mental Health

Methods of identifying and meeting normal emotional and social needs of children and adults. Emphasis on maintaining better mental health conditions in schools. (3 semester hours)

ECONOMICS

Principles of Economics I

Introduction to macroeconomics: free enterprise principles, policies, institutions; national income, employment, output, inflation, money, credit, business cycles, and government finances. (3 semester hours)

Principles of Economics II

Introduction to microeconomics: emphasizes American industrial structure, demand and supply, pricing and output, income distribution, factor pricing, international trade. (3 semester hours)

EDUCATION

Modern Concepts and Methods of Teaching Mathematics in the Elementary and Junior High Schools

A study of the new concepts in mathematics with emphasis on proper grade placement and techniques of presentation. (3 semester hours)

EDUCATIONAL PSYCHOLOGY

Human Growth and Development

Psychological principles in the study of the child from birth to puberty; acquisition of motor skills; advance in perception; language, reasoning, and social behavior. (3 semester hours)

Psychology of Adolescence

Physical, intellectual, emotional, and social growth processes from late childhood toward early adulthood; pubertal problems; mental hygiene of adolescence; family and peer relationships. (3 semester hours)

Principles of Educational Psychology

Application of psychological principles to the educational process; topics covered include learning, humanism, motivation, cognitive development, creativity, intelligence, exceptionality, classroom management, measurement, and evaluation. (3 semester hours)

Personality Adjustment in Educational and Related Settings

Personality development with special attention to motivation, culture, and interpersonal relations; personality problems in educational settings; corrective techniques. (3 semester hours)

Application of Learning Theories in Educational and Related Settings

Critical review of literature on learning in applied settings. (3 semester hours)

Measurement and Evaluation

Measurement and evaluation of learning activities and achievement of elementary school pupils and high school students; standardized tests; test construction; statistical techniques. (3 semester hours)

FINANCE

Money and Banking

Money; banks; banking systems; the effects of bank action on the economic system, international financial considerations; and macroeconomic analysis. (3 semester hours)

Business Finance

Study of objectives, tools, methods, and problems of financial management; financial analysis, planning, control, sources/uses of funds, capital budgeting decisions, and working capital. (3 semester hours)

FOOD SCIENCE

Principles of Processing Fruits and Vegetables

History and scope of the industry, equipment, methods, and techniques employed in commercial processing. (3 semester hours)

Current issues in Food Science

Maintaining or improving food quality and adapting to new techniques is an ever present challenge. This course is designed to study recent topics of interest in the food science fields and is structured to provide information about controversial and new topics in food safety and nutrition. (3 semester hours)

Food Products Evaluation

Basic principles and applications in food product measurements, including physical, chemical, and sensory tests. Methods such as container evaluation; flavor, color and odor; viscosity and solids texture; water activity and pH and acidity are discussed. (3 semester hours)

FRENCH

Intermediate French

Course FLF 1133. Rapid review of French grammar; oral-aural practice; reading of intermediate texts. (3 semester hours)

Course FLF 1143. Oral-aural practice; reading of intermediate texts. (3 semester hours)

HISTORY

Early Western World

A survey of western world history from ancient times to about 1600. (3 semester hours)

Modern Western World

A continuation of the above course, covering the period from the 17th century to the present. (3 semester hours)

Early United States History

A survey of U.S. history through the Civil War. (3 semester hours)

Modern United States History

A continuation of the above course, covering the period from Reconstruction to the present. (3 semester hours)

Mississippi History

A survey of Mississippi history examining economic, social, political, geographical, and cultural aspects of the state's past. (3 semester hours)

HOME ECONOMICS

Individual and Family Nutrition

Fundamental principles of human nutrition and the practical application of this knowledge in the selection of adequate diets. (3 semester hours)

MARKETING

Retailing

Survey of the nature, procedure, and results of trade at the retail level. (3 semester hours)

Principles of Marketing

A general survey of the functions, processes, institutions, and costs in distribution of goods and services from producers to users. (3 semester hours)

MATHEMATICS

College Algebra

Review of fundamentals; linear and quadrative equations; inequalities; functions; simultaneous equations; topics in the theory of equations. (3 semester hours)

Trigonometry

The trigonometric functions: identities; trigonometric equations; applications. (3 semester hours)

Finite Mathematics and Introduction to Calculus

Matrices and systems of linear equations; introduction to calculus. (3 semester hours)

Structure of the Real Number System

The nature of mathematics, introductory logic; metric system; structure and development of the real number system. (3 semester hours)

Informal Geometry and Measurement

Measurements; graphs; informal geometry. (3 semester hours)

Calculus I

Analytic geometry; functions; limits; continuity; derivatives of algebraic functions; applications of the derivative. (3 semester hours)

Calculus II

Anti-differentiation; the definite integral; applications of the definite integral; differentiation and integrations of transcendental functions. (3 semester hours)

MICROBIOLOGY

Elementary Microbiology

A survey of the microbes, their influence on hygiene, disease transmission, higher plants, animals, agriculture and industry. (3 semester hours)

Science of Public Health

Factors contributing to health and disease, and air purification and to new frontiers in public health. (3 semester hours)

Communicable Disease Control

Provides a description of microorganisms, how to identify them and the active role they have in producing and transmitting disease between organisms. (3 semester hours)

Foodborne Disease Control

Covers facts underlying foodborne illnesses by identifying the causative agents and the reasons for their presence, survival and multiplication in food. Discussion is given to the operation of an effective food sanitation program. (3 semester hours)

Vectorborne Disease Control

Studies diseases transmitted by arthropods, flies, mosquitoes, fleas, lice, ticks, mites, and rodents: control methods for this transmission. Includes identification of insecticides and insecticidal formulations. (3 semester hours)

Waterborne Disease Control

Discusses the causative agent, distribution, channels of transmission, incidence, water sources and conditions implicated, and characteristic host reactions, for each of a number of diseases which may be transmitted by water. (3 semester hours)

Microbial Ecology of Food

Influence of environmental factors on food safety and quality. Emphasis on safety, quality assurance, and practical situations. (3 semester hours)

PHYSICAL EDUCATION

Principles and Methods of Elementary School Health and Physical Education

Principles and methods of teaching health and physical education to elementary school children. (3 semester hours)

General Safety Methods

Analysis of accident causes and methods of prevention. Home, school, industry, farm, water, pedestrian problems considered. (3 semester hours)

PHYSICS

Physical Science Survey

Course PHI 1013. Designed for the nontechnical student who desires a knowledge of physical science. A survey of the fundamental laws of physics and astronomy. (3 semester hours)

Course PHI 1023. For the nontechnical student. A survey of the fundamental laws of chemistry, meteorology, and geology. (3 semester hours)

Descriptive Astronomy

The solar system; description and evolution of stars and the universe; methods of obtaining astronomical information; applications of astronomical knowledge. (3 semester hours)

POLITICAL SCIENCE

American Government

The evolution of American governmental institutions and the organization and operation of the U.S. government today. (3 semester hours)

Introduction to International Relations

This course examines through case studies the basic concepts of international politics such as nation, state, power, influence, bipolarity, deferrence, nonalignment, alliances, and diplomacy. (3 semester hours)

Comparative Government

Study of various governmental systems. (3 semester hours)

PSYCHOLOGY

General Psychology

The study of human behavior, heredity and growth; motivation; feeling and emotion; frustration; conflict; learning; language; thinking; attention; sensation; perception; intelligence; aptitudes; social influences. (3 semester hours)

REAL ESTATE

Principles of Real Estate

A survey in the problems involved in the acquisition, transfer, operation, and management of real estate. (3 semester hours)

RUSSIAN

Elementary Russian

Course FLR 1113. An introduction to conversational Russian. (3 semester hours)

Course FLR 1123. Conversational Russian. Reading of graded texts. (3 semester hours)

SOCIOLOGY

Introduction to Sociology

The nature and development of culture, social aspects of personality; analysis of community life, population trends, social classes, institutions, processes, and organization; culture change. (3 semester hours)

Marriage and Family

A study of dating, mate selection, marriage and parenthood, with emphasis on the contemporary American family. (3 semester hours)

SPANISH

Intermediate Spanish

Course FLS 1133. Rapid review of Spanish grammar; oral-aural practice; reading of intermediate texts. (3 semester hours)

Course FLS 1143. Oral-aural practice; reading of intermediate texts. (3 semester hours)

SPECIAL EDUCATION

Psychology and Education of Exceptional Children and Youth

Introduction to exceptional children and youth who deviate from the average in physical, mental, emotional, and social characteristics. Program planning is surveyed. (3 semester hours)

Working with Parents of Exceptional Children

A study of the development, goals, and objectives of organized parent education groups. A study of problems of parents of the handicapped. (3 semester hours)

Teaching the Disadvantaged Child

The study of the disadvantaged child in terms of theories, concepts, cultures, and techniques of teaching and exploration of curricular innovation. (3 semester hours)

WILDLIFE MANAGEMENT

Introduction to Aquaculture

Provides a foundation for understanding the principles of aquatic ecology, fish biology, engineering, economics, and marketing that will be required to successfully culture any aquatic animal, or to assist fish

producers with technical information and educational programs. (3 semester hours)

HIGH SCHOOL COURSES

BUSINESS

Business Dynamics

Part 1. (½ unit)

Part 2. (½ unit)

Business Law

(½ unit)

COMPUTER SCIENCE

Computer Education

Part 1. (½ unit)

Part 2. (½ unit)

ENGLISH

English 1 - Ninth Grade

Part 1. (½ unit)

Part 2. (½ unit)

English 2 - Tenth Grade

Part 1. (½ unit)

Part 2. (½ unit)

English 3 - Eleventh Grade

Part 1. (½ unit)

Part 2. (½ unit)

English 4 - Twelfth Grade

Part 1. (½ unit)

Part 2. (½ unit)

FRENCH

French 3

Part 1. (½ unit)

Part 2. (½ unit)

HEALTH EDUCATION

Health Education

Part 1. (½ unit)

Part 2. (½ unit)

HOME ECONOMICS

Family Living and Parenthood

(½ unit)

LATIN

Latin 1

Part 1. (½ unit)

Part 2. (½ unit)

Latin 2

Part 1. (½ unit)

Part 2. (½ unit)

MATHEMATICS

Algebra 1

Part 1. (½ unit)

Part 2. (½ unit)

Algebra 2

Part 1. (½ unit)

Part 2. (½ unit)

Consumer Mathematics

Part 1. (½ unit)

Part 2. (½ unit)

General Mathematics 1

Part 1. (½ unit)

Part 2. (½ unit)

General Mathematics 2

Part 1 (½ unit)

Part 2. (½ unit)

Geometry

Part 1. (½ unit)

Part 2. (½ unit)

Advanced Mathematics

Part 1. (½ unit)

Part 2. (½ unit)

Trigonometry

(½ unit)

SCIENCE

Biology

Part 1. (½ unit)

Part 2. (½ unit)

General Science

Part 1. (½ unit)

Part 2. (½ unit)

Applied Life Science

Part 1. (½ unit)

Part 2. (½ unit)

Consumer Science

Part 1. (½ unit)

Part 2. (½ unit)

SOCIAL STUDIES

Economics

(½ unit)

Geography

(½ unit)

Psychology

(½ unit)

Mississippi State and Local Government

(½ unit)

Mississippi History

(½ unit)

Problems in American Democracy

(½ unit)

U.S. Government

(½ unit)

United States History

Part 1. (½ unit)

Part 2. (½ unit)

World History

Part 1. (½ unit)

Part 2. (½ unit)

SPANISH

Spanish 3

Part 1. (½ unit)

Part 2. (½ unit)

Spanish 4

Part 1. (½ unit)

Part 2. (½ unit)

Mississippi Valley State University

Correspondence Studies Program
P.O. Box 125
Itta Bena, Mississippi 38941   (601) 254-9041

Description:

Mississippi Valley State University was formally opened in 1950. As A state-supported institution of higher learning, the University provides training in intellectual and technical skills and performs educational services in terms of the needs that the people of Mississippi have envisioned.

Through the Correspondence Studies Program, University courses are made available to persons who wish to pursue course work for the baccalaureate degree or for renewal of license but are unable to follow the regular University class schedule. The quality of education received by students in correspondence courses parallels that received by students in the regular academic courses. Faculty members are required to have on file course outlines similar to those for regular academic courses. All courses are supervised by a full-time faculty member and are based on and agreed upon by contract between the student and the instructor.

Prospective correspondence students should contact the Correspondence Studies Program at the above address for complete information regarding courses available.

Faculty:

Fred Williams, Acting Director of Continuing Education; C.P. Hicks, Registrar/Admissions Officer. Faculty of 32; 7 subject specialists; 3 counselors.

Academic Levels:

College

Degree/Certificate Programs:

Only work taken at an institution which is accredited by its State Department of Education may be used for transfer credit. Mississippi Valley State University allows 24 semester hours of correspondence credit to be applied toward a bachelor's degree.

Admission Requirements:

Mississippi Valley State University welcomes applicants who have the ability to do university work, the determination for self-development, a desire for liberal education, and sound academic preparation; high school graduation or GED. Student must not be on probation any institution of higher learning.

Tuition:

Contact the university for current tuition and fees. Tuition must be paid by cashiers check or money order when paying through the mail; no personal checks accepted. No fees will be refunded after registration has been completed and course materials mailed to applicant. A student may register for no more than six semester hours per year.

Enrollment Period:

Correspondence course may be begun after consultation between the student and the instructor. The minimum time for completion of a three semester-hour course is thirty days from the date of application. The minimum time for completion of two courses of three semester hours each, taken concurrently, is forty-five days from the date of application. The maximum time for completion of a course is one year from the date of application. An extension of three months may be granted upon payment of an extension fee; an extension of time must be requested from the correspondence coordinator before the expiration of the allotted year.

Equipment Requirements:

All textbooks and materials must be supplied by the student. Purchasing information accompanies lessons and assignments.

Credit and Grading:

Acceptability of credits transferred-in will be determined by the head of the department in which the student intends to major. Letter grades are used: A, 90–100; B, 80–89; C, 70–79; D, 60–69; F, 59 and below. Minimum passing grade is D. Credit is awarded in semester hour units.

Accreditations:

Southern Association of Colleges and Schools.

COLLEGE COURSES

ANTHROPOLOGY

Introduction to Anthropology
(3 semester hours)

CRIMINAL JUSTICE

Juvenile Justice Process
(3 semester hours)

The Police Process
(3 semester hours)

Police Administration and Operation
(3 semester hours)

EDUCATION

Introduction to Education
(3 semester hours)

Arithmetic for Children
(3 semester hours)

Behavior Management
(3 semester hours)

Career Education
(3 semester hours)

Education Reform in Mississippi
(3 semester hours)

General Psychology
(3 semester hours)

Human Growth and Development
(3 semester hours)

Language Arts and Skills
(3 semester hours)

Literature for Children
(3 semester hours)

Science in the Elementary School
(3 semester hours)

Social Science for Children
(3 semester hours)

Psychology of the Exceptional Child
(3 semester hours)

Organizational Procedures
(3 semester hours)

Teaching the Severely and the Profoundly Handicapped
(3 semester hours)

ENGLISH

World Literature
Course 201. (3 semester hours)
Course 202. (3 semester hours)

FINE ARTS

Art Appreciation
(3 semester hours)

Art History
Course 310. (3 semester hours)
Course 311. (3 semester hours)

FRENCH

Elementary French
Course 101. (3 semester hours)
Course 102. (3 semester hours)

Intermediate French

Course 201. (3 semester hours)

Course 202. (3 semester hours)

GEOGRAPHY

Fundamentals of Geography

(3 semester hours)

Geography of North America

(3 semester hours)

GERONTOLOGY

Psychology of Aging

(3 semester hours)

Health and the Institutional Elderly

(3 semester hours)

Physiology, Nutrition, and Aging

(3 semester hours)

Providing Services to the Elderly

(3 semester hours)

HEALTH, PHYSICAL EDUCATION, AND RECREATION

Comprehensive Health

(3 semester hours)

Marriage, Family Living, and Sex Education

(3 semester hours)

HISTORY

Afro-American History

(3 semester hours)

Early American History

(3 semester hours)

Early Western Civilization

(3 semester hours)

History of England

(3 semester hours)

Late Western Civilization

(3 semester hours)

Mississippi History

(3 semester hours)

Modern American History

(3 semester hours)

MATHEMATICS

College Algebra

(3 semester hours)

General College Mathematics

Course 101. (3 semester hours)

Course 102. (3 semester hours)

Mathematics for Elementary Teachers

(3 semester hours)

Mathematics for Junior High Teachers

(3 semester hours)

Plane Trigonometry

(3 semester hours)

PHYSICAL SCIENCE

Earth and Space Science

(3 semester hours)

POLITICAL SCIENCE

American National Government

(3 semester hours)

Comparative Government

(3 semester hours)

Constitutional Law I

(3 semester hours)

International Relations

(3 semester hours)

Public Administration

(3 semester hours)

State and Local Government

(3 semester hours)

Western Political Philosophy

(3 semester hours)

SOCIOLOGY

Introduction to Sociology

(3 semester hours)

Problems of the Family

(3 semester hours)

Social Problems

(3 semester hours)

Social Psychology

(3 semester hours)

Sociology of the Community

(3 semester hours)

Seminar in Sociology

(3 semester hours)

Missouri, University of
Center for Independent Study
136 Clark Hall
Columbia, Missouri 65203   (314) 882-2491

Description:

The University of Missouri was established in 1839 as the sole public university in Missouri. The University of Missouri System includes campuses in Columbia, Kansas City, Rolla, and St. Louis. The university has a commitment to diversity and comprehensive education at both the undergraduate and graduate levels. As a part of University Extension, the Center for Independent Study serves over

17,000 persons annually in university, high school, and noncredit independent study courses. The center has the administrative responsibility for coordination of all correspondence instruction offered by each of the four University of Missouri campuses.

The Center for Independent Study is now offering Video Credit Courses. Tapes may be viewed at Viewing Centers, through home use, through group enrollment, or over television. In addition, tapes for some of the courses are available through local libraries and commercial video stores. Students enrolling in video credit courses must submit a special video form and indicating thereon how they wish to view lesson tapes (i.e., home use, Viewing Center, television broadcast, or group enrollment.

Faculty:

Dr. Roger G. Young, Director, Center for Independent Study; Dr. Dale D. Huffington, Associate Director; C. Alex Phillips, Operations and Student Services; Susanne Darcy, Editorial and Instructional Services.

Academic Levels:

College
High School
Noncredit
Graduate

Degree/Certificate Programs:

The number of semester hours of credit accepted for a degree varies among the colleges within the University of Missouri. The University does not grant a high school diploma, but offers an extensive high school curriculum. The student's high school principal or counselor must grant prior approval for a student to take a University of Missouri high school course for credit. Certain selected college-level courses are available for high school seniors, also requiring prior approval.

Admission Requirements:

For university credit, high school diploma or equivalent. For high school courses, completion of the eighth grade or be at least eighteen years of age. No restrictions for noncredit courses.

Tuition:

$101 per semester hour for undergraduate courses; $127.80 semester hour for graduate courses; $69 per half-unit high school courses; $68 per CEU for noncredit courses. Prices subject to change without notice and usually on an annual basis. Air mail postage fee extra for foreign students. Tuition must be paid at enrollment. Requests for withdrawal from a course must be made in writing. A refund of 70 percent will be made if postmarked within first month after enrolling; 50 percent if postmarked within second month after enrolling; no refund after second month of enrolling.

Enrollment Period:

The maximum enrollment period for each course is 9 months. One 3-month extension granted upon payment of an extension fee of $30 for university courses, $15 for high school courses, $15 for noncredit courses.

Equipment Requirements:

Textbooks must be purchased separately by the student. They may be purchased locally or through the Center for Independent Study. Some courses require supplementary reference books, equipment, audio- or videotapes which are available on a rental basis plus refundable deposit from the Center.

Credit and Grading:

Examinations are proctored. College courses: residents of Missouri must take examinations at one of the Extension Centers. Nonresidents must be proctored by an education official. High school courses: examinations must be proctored by a high school official. The A, B, C, D, F system of grading is used. The grade F carries no credit. D carries no credit in Graduate School. Credit is awarded in semester hour units.

Library Services:

More than 35 public and private colleges and universities throughout Missouri will permit Independent Study students to use their libraries.

Accreditations:

North Central Association of Colleges and Schools. Member of: National University Continuing Education Association.

COLLEGE COURSES

ACCOUNTING

Accounting I

An introduction to the field of accounting, this course covers the fundamentals of financial accounting. (3 semester hours)

Accounting II

This course covers the fundamentals of managerial accounting and additional topics in financial accounting. (3 semester hours)

AGRICULTURAL ENGINEERING

Surface Water Management

Topics in this course include water management and its role in maintaining soil productivity; farm surveying and the design and layout of terrace systems. (3 semester hours)

ANIMAL SCIENCE

Applied Nutrition

Feed composition and utilization; ration formulation; feed evaluation and identification; and practical problems. (3 semester hours)

Horse Production

This course covers horse production; students learn proper ways to breed, feed, and manage horses. (3 semester hours)

ANTHROPOLOGY

General Anthropology

This is a general course that surveys fields of anthropological concern: archaeology, cultural anthropology, physical anthropology, linguistics;

it emphasizes underlying concepts and principles in these fields. Examples from peoples of the world are included. (3 semester hours)

ASTRONOMY

Cosmic Evolution/Introductory Astronomy

This course highlights several topics. Planets: a brief survey of their motions and properties. Stars: observations, including stellar spectra and colors; stellar evolution and star clusters. Galaxies: structure and content of the Milky Way galaxy, its relationship to other galaxies. Cosmology: the origin and evolution of the universe. (4 semester hours)

ATMOSPHERIC SCIENCE

Introductory Meteorology

Physical processes of atmosphere in relation to day-to-day changes in weather. (3 semester hours)

BIOLOGY

General Biology

This course covers general principles of biology; it studies the cell through organisms, ecosystems, and humans. (3 semester hours)

General Genetics

This course studies the principles of heredity and reasons for variation in plants and animals. A study of Mendelian principles and population genetics with emphasis on the human is included. (3 semester hours)

CLASSICAL STUDIES

Classical Civilization

This course examines how the myths of Greece and Rome as an aid in the interpretation of literature and art. (3 semester hours)

COMMUNICATIONS

Introduction to Mass Media

This course introduces the oral, print, and electronic media of communication; emphasis is on history, theory, and criticism of the mass media as cultural institutions. (3 semester hours)

COMPUTER SCIENCE

Introduction to BASIC

An introduction to Microsoft and IBM PC BASIC, this course emphasizes language syntax, structured programming, and problem solving; it is designed for teachers and persons in related occupations. (3 semester hours)

Software Applications on the PC

An introduction to operating systems, word processing, spreadsheets, and database manipulation. This is a postbaccalaureate course designed for teachers and persons in related occupations. (3 semester hours)

CRIMINAL JUSTICE

Introduction to Criminology and Criminal Justice

This is a survey of the historical development and the current status of American criminal justice. Processes, institutions, and significant problems of the various components are analyzed. (3 semester hours)

Corrections

This course studies the correctional setting as an aspect of the criminal justice system; it analyzes the administrative involvement and studies the modes of organization and management that seem applicable to this type of setting. (3 semester hours)

Rights of the Offender

This course addresses the constitutional protection of the accused, including an analysis of the rights guaranteed under the Fourth, Fifth, Sixth, and Fourteenth Amendments. (3 semester hours)

ECONOMICS

Principles of Macroeconomics

This course surveys macroeconomic principles and their application to contemporary economic issues. (3 semester hours)

Introduction to the American Economy

An introduction to economic analysis that examines the development and operation of the American economy, this course studies its evolutions, institutions, and principal problems. (3 semester hours)

Introduction to Economics II

This course focuses on microeconomics, firm analysis, the principles of supply and demand, elasticity, price determination, costs, income distribution, market structures, trade, and other related social and economic issues. (3 semester hours)

Money and Banking

This course discusses American monetary and banking systems and their influence on economic activities. (3 semester hours)

EDUCATION

Art Activities in the Elementary School

This course studies the vital role of art activities and creative experiences in the growth and development of children. (2 semester hours)

Teaching of Reading

This course studies the materials and methods used in teaching reading in elementary grades. (3 semester hours)

Teaching Reading in the Content Areas

This course addresses specific ways teachers can help students improve skills at reading in content areas. (3 semester hours)

Photography for Teachers

Course topics include basic 35mm photography techniques and processes, photo publications, and basic slide/tape production as they apply to educational settings. (3 semester hours)

Seminar: Teaching of Reading Comprehension

This course reviews the most current research on reading comprehension. Particular emphasis is given to classroom applications and the role of the teacher. Specific techniques for the improvement of reading comprehension are discussed and illustrated in the context of the typical classroom setting. While designed primarily for elementary teachers, the concepts and techniques taught in this course also can be applied to middle- and senior-high level reading programs. Includes 14 half-hour video lessons. (3 semester hours)

Issues and Trends in Reading Instruction

Provides intensive study of significant issues and current trends in reading on all instructional levels. (3 semester hours)

The Secondary School Curriculum

For secondary school principals, teachers, superintendents. Present trends in curricular change and methods of curricular investigation. (3 semester hours)

Career Visions: A Career Planning Course for Adults

This course, written by educators and career planning professionals, is designed for adults who are interested in their own career planning.

Through readings and exercises, students learn about adult developmental issues and dealing with life's transitions. They assess barriers to their career planning; determine their interests, skills, and work values; and explore career options and lifestyle patterns. Students learn survival and enhancement skills for college, resume writing and interviewing skills and job hunting strategies. (3 semester hours)

Learning and Instruction

This course examines the nature of human learning processes and includes implications for instruction; emphasis is on the bases of learning, readiness for learning, types of learning, memory, and other related topics. (2 semester hours)

Child Development

The psychological, intellectual, social, and physical development of children is studied in this course. (2 semester hours)

Adolescent Development

The psychological, intellectual, social, and physical development of adolescents is studied in this course. (2 semester hours)

Educational Measurement

This course studies the basic concepts of standardized testing evaluation techniques, and interpretation of test scores. It addresses ways that these concepts can improve the instructional process. (2 semester hours)

Foundations of Educational and Psychological Measurement

Basic principles of educational and psychological measurement including test construction, validity, reliability, item analysis, and derived scores are addressed in this course. (3 semester hours)

Special Topics (Preventing School Failure)

This course is designed to provide teachers with practical methods for preventing school failure. Much of the course centers on the self-esteem of both the student and the teacher. Strategies for enhancing self-esteem are provided, as well as methods and materials for motivating students. Unique programs that have worked at certain schools in the past are highlighted throughout the course. A two-day seminar is required. (3 semester hours)

Special Topics (Cooperative Classroom Management

This course is designed to provide teachers with practical methods for dealing with discipline problems in the classroom. Discipline approaches are drawn primarily from the Adler-Dreikurs Model, as well as from Thomas Gordon, B.F. Skinner, William Glasser, and Lee Canter. Why students behave as they do is also thoroughly examined. A two-day seminar is required. (3 semester hours)

Special Topics (Introduction to Educating the Gifted)

Surveys the history and philosophy of gifted education and examines characteristics of gifted learners and teachers of the gifted. (3 semester hours)

Special Topics (A Changing World—A Changing Classroom: Dealing with Critical Situations in the School)

Examines a range of current social problems, such as drug abuse, school violence, divorce, suicide, and illiteracy, and their effect on classroom management and school curriculum. Coping strategies are suggested through exemplary presentations in the area of class management and person-to-person interactions. (3 semester hours)

Special Topics (Coping with Student Problems in the Classroom: Dealing in Discipline)

Designed to help teachers deal more effectively with interpersonal conflicts and disruptive behavior in the classroom, this course examines behavioristic methods, humanistic methods, and methods designed to foster self-control and responsibility in students. Each method is applied to simulated classroom situations at both the elementary and secondary levels. Ways of dealing with drug problems and special situations in urban schools are examined, and basic information on an educator's legal rights and responsibilities is provided. (3 semester hours)

Special Topics (Developing a Personal System of Discipline)

This course is designed to help educators build a personal system of discipline, tailored to meet their own special needs and those of their students. Such a system will be developed after examining eight current models of discipline and after viewing four outstanding theatrical films, including *The Breakfast Club*. A two-day seminary is required. (3 semester hours)

Special Topics (Working With Students At Risk)

This course examines the problems of students of all ages. The first part of the course presents strategies for dealing with at-risk students at various grade levels. The second part of the course deals with what schools and teachers might do to help students who are substance abusers, who have suicidal tendencies, or who are pregnant. The readings are supplemented with five theatrical films and one short film dealing with AIDS, which was designed for use in schools. A two-day seminar is required. (3 semester hours)

Historical Foundations of American Education

This course discusses the development of American educational institutions and the ideas and the social forces that have influenced them. (3 semester hours)

Topics in Educational Administration I (The Role of the Mentor Teacher)

This course studies the role of the mentor teacher, with emphasis on the elements necessary for a successful relationship between the mentor teacher and the beginning teacher. It discusses the nature and purpose of induction programs, and it gives instruction on how to establish the mentor relationship; begin the school year; manage time; develop student motivation; deal with stress; and meet the needs of at-risk students. A video enhanced course. (3 semester hours)

Organizational Analysis in Higher and Adult Continuing Education

This course analyzes the organizational chracteristics and principles in higher and continuing education. Topics include: organizational theories and models, organizational culture, communication, innovation, planning, leadership, power and influence, and external environmental influences. (3 semester hours)

Educational Statistics I

This course introduces statistical techniques employed in education: descriptive statistics, correlation, simple regression, and hypothesis testing. (3 semester hours)

ENGINEERING

Engineering Graphics

This course covers lettering, drafting equipment, CAD equipment, technique, and standards; engineering measurement, multiview and pictorial drawing, sketching, and interpretation; three-dimensioning, sectioning, and production drawings; and 3D database creation, analysis, and visualization. (3 semester hours)

Accounting I

This course uses the problem approach to cover accounting principles in relation to business papers, journals, ledgers, balance sheets, income statements, trial balances, and worksheets. A video enhanced course. (3 semester hours)

Management for Engineers

This course teaches students how to adjust to the transition from engineer to manager; course topics include team building and motivation; techniques of control and communications; and time management. Students learn how to organize technical activities and manage special projects. (3 semester hours)

Engineering Mechanics-Statics

This course applies the principles of mechanics to engineering problems of equilibrium. Topics include resultants, equilibrium, friction, trusses, center of gravity, and moment of inertia. (3 semester hours)

Engineering Mechanics-Dynamics

This course applies the principles of mechanics to engineering problems of motion and acceleration. Topics include plane motion, force, mass and acceleration, work and energy, and impulse and momentum. (2 semester hours)

ENGLISH

Fundamentals of Composition

Stresses sentence-level skills and the construction of coherent paragraphs. Students study elements of composition and usage crucial to their ability to meet the university's standards of correct and effective writing. (3 semester hours)

Exposition and Argumentation

Stresses writing as a process, with due attention given to critical reading and thinking skills needed to succeed in college. Course covers inventing, drafting, revising, and rewriting skills as well. (3 semester hours)

Creative Writing: Poetry

This course introduces different poetic forms and basic elements of poetry, including sound, rhyme, meter, and figurative language. Students will apply these elements to their own poetry. (3 semester hours)

Technical Writing

This course teaches advanced composition dealing with the fundamentals and applications of technical writing; it includes work with proposals, progress reports, and formal reports. (3 semester hours)

Literary Types

This course introduces the student to the various literary types, including poetry, drama, and the short story. (3 semester hours)

American Poetry: A Survey

In this course, students read and evaluate works by ten poets, dating from the mid-19th century to the 1960s. A video enhanced course. (3 semester hours)

Experiencing American Cultures in the Contemporary Novel

This multicultural course features novels and memoirs by contemporary Native American, African-American, Mexican-American, and Chinese-American writers. In addition to reading the novels, students listen to audiocassettes containing selected readings and interviews with the writers. (3 semester hours)

Gothic Fiction

A survey of English and American Gothic fiction from the 18th century to the present, this course examines major novels and short stories that define the Gothic tradition in literature. (3 semester hours)

Women's Experiences in Modern Fiction

A survey of modern fiction by and about women, this course includes related essays, many of which are written by the women whose fiction is studied. (3 semester hours)

African-American Literature

Using a socio-historical approach, this course surveys the writing of black authors from the mid-19th century to the 1960s. (3 semester hours)

Literature of the New Testament

This course presents a comprehensive understanding of the New Testament; its literary background and its significance for Western civilization. (3 semester hours)

Literature of the Old Testament

This course analyzes representative stories, themes, and concepts of the Old Testament by examining nineteen of its books from a literary perspective. (3 semester hours)

Shakespeare

This course studies Shakespeare's life and includes a reading of thirteen of his major plays—histories, comedies, and tragedies—that represent all phases of his development. Students will read *Hamlet, Romeo and Juliet, King Lear, Macbeth*, and other Shakespearean plays. (3 semester hours)

American Literature

A survey of major American writers from colonial days to the present, this course provides an overall view of the development of American literature. (3 semester hours)

Introduction to Folklore

This course introduces the study of folklore, including the methodology, approaches, and genres of folklore. (3 semester hours)

Survey of British Literature: Beginnings to 1784

This course follows the development of English literature from the Middle Ages through the 18th century; students will read and analyze representative works of major writers. (3 semester hours)

Introduction to British Literature I

Covers the same material as the above course. (3 semester hours)

Introduction to British Masterpieces I

Covers the same material as the above course. (3 semester hours)

English Literature I

Covers the same material as the above course. (3 semester hours)

Themes and Forms in Literature (Shakespeare)

This course is designed to give students a better understanding of Shakespearean drama in performance. Using the BBC-TV video series, this course examines the following plays: *A Midsummer Night's Dream, Richard III, Romeo and Juliet, The Merchant of Venice, Julius Caesar, Hamlet, Othello, King Lear, Measure for Measure,* and *The Winter's Tale*. A video enhanced course. (3 semester hours)

ENTOMOLOGY

Insects in the Environment

This course introduces the study of insects, with emphasis on those species important to humans and on the general principles of integrated insect control. This course is designed for students interested in a study of insects and how they are affecting the environment. (3 semester hours)

EXTENSION EDUCATION

Program Development and Evaluation

This course examines the principles and procedures of program development and evaluation used in extension and other adult education agency; it includes a review of concepts found useful in curriculum development. (3 semester hours)

Extension Organization and Administration

This course studies the principles of administration and organization and their application to extension work. (3 semester hours)

Fundamentals of Extension Teaching of Adults

This course examines the special needs of adult students in extension education, including a study of classroom techniques. (3 semester hours)

FINANCE

Principles of Finance

Course topics include budgeting, taxes, housing and auto loan credit, insurance, mutual funds, stocks and bonds, and retirement planning. (3 semester hours)

FRENCH

Elementary French I

This course gives an introduction to French grammar and composition; students practice hearing and speaking French through the use of audiocassette tapes. (5 semester hours)

Elementary French II

A continuation of Elementary French I. (5 semester hours)

GEOGRAPHY

Regions and Nations of the World I

This introductory course studies regional character; spatial relationships; major problems of Europe, Anglo-America (United States and Canada), and Latin America. It is organized around basic geographic concepts. (3 semester hours)

Regions and Nations of the World II

This introductory course studies regional character; spacial relationships; and major problems of the Commonwealth of Independent States, the Middle East, the Orient, Africa, and the Pacific world. It is organized around basic geographic concepts. (3 semester hours)

Introductory Meteorology

This course examines the physical processes of the atmosphere in relation to day-to-day changes in weather. (3 semester hours)

Physical Geography

This is an introductory study of the physical environment; maps, landforms, water, elements of climate, climatic types, soils, and vegetation. The course examines the effects of human behavior on natural environmental systems. (3 semester hours)

Geography of Missouri

Course topics include the physical, human, economic, and political geography of Missouri; the course also studies how geography applies to current state issues. (3 semester hours)

GEOLOGY

Physical Geology

This course studies the materials of the earth's crust; structures and geologic features of the earth's surface; common minerals and rocks; and topographic and geologic maps. (4 semester hours)

Earth Science

This is a general study of the earth; its origin; the development of its crustal features and the processes that shape them; its oceans; its climates; and its neighbors in the solar system. A video enhanced course. (3 semester hours)

GERMAN

Elementary German I

Covers the basics of speaking, reading, and writing German. (5 semester hours)

Elementary German II

A continuation of Elementary German I. (5 semester hours)

Elementary German III

A continuation of Elementary German II. (5 semester hours)

HEALTH EDUCATION

Elements of Health Education

Health needs of university students and school-aged children are investigated in this course through an examination of personal and community health problems. (2 semester hours)

HEALTH SERVICES MANAGEMENT

Topics in Health Services Management for Health Care Executives

This course presents the basic theories, concepts, and tools of economics that can be used to evaluate systematically the characteristics, utilization patterns, delivery strategies, and financing mechanisms of an individual, organization, or industry. (3 semester hours)

The American Health Care System

Student is provided with a basic understanding of the major components (financing, planning, and regulating) of the American health care system. Emphasis on current issues and their impact on the delivery system. (3 semester hours)

HISTORY

Foundations of Western Civilization

This course studies the development of characteristic ideas and institutions of Western cultural tradition, from origin of civilization in ancient Near East to beginning of rapid social, political, intellectual transformation of Europe in the 18th century. (3 semester hours)

History of Modern Europe

This course covers selected major themes in European history from the French Revolution to recent times. Topics include the breakdown of traditional institutions and ideas; political and social revolution; industrialization, nationalism, imperialism, and world wars; democratic and totalitarian ideologies and movements; the quest for national order; and European unity. (3 semester hours)

American History to 1877

An introduction to U.S. history through the Civil War, this course surveys political, economic, social, and cultural development of the American people. (3 semester hours)

American History Since 1877

An introduction to U.S. history since 1877, this course surveys political, economic, social, and cultural development of the American people. (3 semester hours)

Survey of American History to 1865

An introduction to U.S. history through the Civil War, this course surveys political, economic, social, and cultural development of the American people. (3 semester hours)

Survey of American History Since 1865

An introduction to U.S. history since 1865, this course surveys political, economic, social, and cultural development of the American people. (3 semester hours)

American Civilization

An introduction to U.S. history through the Civil War, this course surveys political, economic, social, and cultural development of the American people. (3 semester hours)

American Civilization Since 1865

An introduction to U.S. history since 1865, this course surveys political, economic, social, and cultural development of the American people. (3 semester hours)

The War in Vietnam and the U.S.

This course provides an understanding of the political experience and the lessons and legacies of the war in Vietnam both in Vietnam and in the United States. Includes 15 one-hour video lessons. (3 semester hours)

Britain, 1688 to the Present

This course surveys modern Britain from the era of Restoration and Glorious Revolution (1660–1689) to the present. Major themes include the social, intellectual, cultural, political, and economic aspects of modern and contemporary Britain. (3 semester hours)

Modern England, 1714–Present

Covers the same material as the above course. (3 semester hours)

Making of Modern Britain

Covers the same material as the above course. (3 semester hours)

Western Civilization Since 1600

This course studies modern western civilization from the 17th century to the present, with special emphasis on the philosophical, political, social, and economic backgrounds of modern society. (3 semester hours)

Modern Western Civilization

Covers the same material as the above course. (3 semester hours)

Topics in European Civilization: 1715 to the Present

Covers the same materials as the above course. (3 semester hours)

History of Missouri

This course surveys Missouri's political, social, economic, and cultural development from the beginning of settlement to the present. (3 semester hours)

History of Science

This course surveys science from ancient times to the 20th century, focusing on the leading conceptual developments within science, the scientific revolution, and science's role in society. (3 semester hours)

America, 1945–Present

Traces the role of America since World War II. Topics include aid to Europe; the Korean War; domestic, political, and cultural changes through the Eisenhower years; the New Frontier; the Great Society; and the changes in the 1970s and early 1980s; the civil rights crisis; and the development of the welfare state. (3 semester hours)

Revolutionary America, 1754–1789

This course studies the causes and consequences of the American Revolution. Emphasis is placed upon the social conditions in America that contributed both to the Revolution and to the writing of the 1787 Constitution. (3 semester hours)

History of the Old South

This course studies the history of the American South to 1860. (3 semester hours)

History of the American South I

Covers the same material as the above course. (3 semester hours)

American Foreign Relations

Following a rapid survey of major principles and actions in American diplomatic affairs before 1900, this course analyzes developing principles, problems, methods, and factors in American foreign relations since that date. Attention is given to the interrelationships of domestic factors and foreign relations with an attempt to discover principal influences that have shaped this area of American development. (3 semester hours)

HORTICULTURE

Basic Home Horticulture

This course includes discussions and scientific rationale of the current cultural practices for growing of home horticultural plants. (3 semester hours)

Plant Propagation

This course discusses the principles and practices of the propagation of horticultural plants. (3 semester hours)

HUMAN DEVELOPMENT AND FAMILY STUDIES

Administration of Programs for Children and Families

This course examines the design, operation, and evaluation of family programs. (3 semester hours)

JOURNALISM

History of American Journalism

Examines the American mass media from colonial days to the present in the context of social, economic, and political change. (3 semester hours)

High School Journalism

Provides a basic background in journalism and guidelines on how to teach it at the secondary level. Analysis of problems facing scholastic journalism. (2 semester hours)

LIBRARY SCIENCE

Library Materials for Children and Youth

This course studies the background of library materials for children; psychology of children; the characteristics of print, nonprint material; and current publishing trends. Other course topics include readers' guidance, book talks, and story-telling resources. (3 semester hours)

MANAGEMENT

Fundamentals of Management

This organizational course introduces the basic concepts of management and their application to operations and human resource management. (3 semester hours)

Introduction to Business Law

This course introduces the legal aspects of business related to society—the legal system; constitutional, criminal, and tort law; contracts and sales law cases and problems; and administrative regulation of business and consumer issues. (3 semester hours)

Human Resource Management

Topics in this course include workforce policies and procedures of the business enterprise. (3 semester hours)

Organizational Theory

This course examines what an organization is and how it functions. Course topics include theories and practical information about organizations; models for decision making; and environmental factors and their effects on organizations. (3 semester hours)

MARKETING

Principles of Marketing

This course studies institutions, processes, problems involved in transferring goods from producer to consumer; emphasis is on the economic and social aspects of the transfer. (3 semester hours)

MATHEMATICS

Intermediate Algebra

This course prepares students for college algebra. It covers graphs, functions, linear equations, inequalities, polynomials, systems, exponents, and quadratic equations. Problem solving is emphasized. (3 semester hours)

Trigonometry

This course covers the basics of trigonometry. (2 semester hours)

College Algebra

Review of topics from elementary algebra, quadratics, systems of linear equations with introduction to determinants, graphing, inequalities, complex numbers, polynomials, and logarithms. (3 semester hours)

Elements of Calculus

Introductory analytic geometry, derivatives, and definite integrals. (3 semester hours)

Analytic Geometry and Calculus I

This course gives an introduction to the differentiation and integration of algebra functions, elementary analytic geometry, functions, limits, continuity, derivatives, antiderivatives, and definite integrals. (5 semester hours)

Calculus with Analytic Geometry I

Covers the same material as the above course. (5 semester hours)

Introductory Algebra

Topics in this course include numbers and their arithmetic properties, introduction to elementary algebra including exponents and radicals, elementary geometry and formulas, linear and quadratic functions including their graphs, and equations with two unknowns. (3 semester hours)

Calculus II

Course 175. This course discusses select topics from plane analytic geometry and calculus. (5 semester hours)

Course 220. Covers the same material as the above course. (4 semester hours)

Calculus with Analytic Geometry II

This course discusses select topics from plane analytic geometry and calculus. (5 semester hours)

Analytic Geometry and Calculus II

Covers the same material as the above course. (4 semester hours)

Calculus III

Course 201. Topics in this course include vectors, solid analytic geometry, calculus of several variables. (3 semester hours)

Course 250. Covers the same material as the above course. (4 semester hours)

Calculus with Analytic Geometry III

Topics in this course include vectors, solid analytic geometry, calculus of several variables. (4 semester hours)

Analytic Geometry with Calculus III

Covers the same material as the above course. (5 semester hours)

MILITARY SCIENCE

The War in Vietnam and the U.S.

This course provides an understanding of the political experience and the lessons and legacies of the Vietnam war both in Vietnam and the United States. Includes 15 one-hour video lessons. (3 semester hours)

MUSIC

Music Appreciation

Designed for the student with little or no music background, this course emphasizes the basic elements of music and the historical and stylistic periods, which are illustrated by examples of different genre. (3 semester hours)

PARKS, RECREATION, AND TOURISM

Introduction to Leisure Studies

This course examines the history of recreation and the leisure movement; the theories and philosophies of play, recreation, and leisure; and the developmental stages of leisure services to their contemporary status. (3 semester hours)

Delivery Models in Therapeutic Recreation

An investigation of therapeutic recreation service delivery models of the ill and disabled in both institutional and community settings, this course emphasizes advanced leadership and therapeutic interactional skills and dynamics. (3 semester hours)

Operation of Therapeutic Recreation: Procedures and Principles

This course covers the theories and principles of leadership and programming as they apply to recreation services for the ill, handicapped, and aged. (3 semester hours)

Problems

This course provides an independent investigation of special topics. It is necessary for the student to consult with a faculty member in the department for the design of the problem to be investigated and the designation of the appropriate credit. (1 to 3 semester hours)

PEST MANAGEMENT

Theory and Concepts of Plant Pathology

This course investigates the diseases of plants. Topics include viruses, prokaryotes, fungi, gene regulation, plant metabolism, and the genetics of plant disease. (3 semester hours)

PHILOSOPHY

General Introduction to Philosophy

This course presents an introduction to traditional philosophical problems and to methods of philosophical inquiry. Consideration is given to different philosophical theories on reality, man, nature, and God; knowledge and how it is acquired; values; and social issues. (3 semester hours)

Foundations of Philosophy

Covers the same material as the above course. (3 semester hours)

Introduction to Philosophy

Covers the same material as the above course. (3 semester hours)

Major Questions in Philosophy

Covers the same material as the above course. (3 semester hours)

Introduction to Logic

A study of the basic rules of both informal and symbolic logic; it includes discussion on the types of argumentation; methods of reasoning; valid reasoning; inductive and deductive reasoning as used in the sciences and in communication. (3 semester hours)

Foundations of Logic and Scientific Method

Covers the same material as the above course. (3 semester hours)

Logic and Language

Covers the same materials as the above course. (3 semester hours)

Ethics and the Professions

This course examines ethical issues confronted by individuals in professions such as medicine, law, business, journalism, and engineering. (3 semester hours)

PHYSICS

The Mechanical Universe

This course is an introduction to classical physics. The discipline's three components—mechanics, electromagnetics, and thermodynamics—are the emphasis of this course. Topics studied include motion, vectors, gravity, work and energy, engines, waves, and angular momentum. A video enhanced course. (3 semester hours)

PLANT PATHOLOGY

Theory and Concepts of Plant Pathology

This course investigates the diseases of plants. Topics include viruses, prokaryotes, fungi, gene regulation, plant metabolism, and the genetics of plant disease. (3 semester hours)

POLITICAL SCIENCE

American Government

Topics in this course include the Constitution, federalism, civil liberties, political attitudes, interest groups, political parties, nominations, elections and campaigns, voting behavior, Congress, the Presidency, and the judiciary. (3 semester hours)

Introduction to Political Science

This course introduces the scope and content of politics, and it studies the theory and operation of democratic and nondemocratic governments. (3 semester hours)

International Relations

This course provides theories and analyses on various international topics. Included are three schools of thought in the area of international relations: idealism, realism, and transnationalism. The concept of power and how political leaders use it to achieve goals is studied, as well as the role of the public in shaping foreign policy. In addition, the arms race and nuclear deterrence is discussed, with commentary on the Cuban missile crisis, the cold war, and the Persian Gulf War. The course concludes with a look at current problems in the world; population growth, depletion of resources, environmental pollution, and food shortage. (3 semester hours)

State Government

This course studies government and politics at the state level, with an emphasis on the state of Missouri. (3 semester hours)

Introduction to Public Administration

This course surveys recurring themes, conceptual problems, and substantive findings in public administration literature, with particular attention to U.S. public bureaucracies. (3 semester hours)

Congress and Legislative Policy

A study of legislative institutions, procedures, and behavior; emphasizes the role of the U.S. Congress in the context of theories of political representation. Includes 26 video programs. (3 semester hours)

Congressional Politics

Covers the same material as the above course. (3 semester hours)

The American Constitution

This course examines leading constitutional principles as they have evolved through important decisions of the U.S. Supreme Court. Includes 16 video programs. (3 semester hours)

U.S. Defense Policy Making

This course follows the evolution of United States defense policy making since World War II; special emphasis is given to strategic policies and weapon systems, and to the political processes through which these are selected and implemented. (3 semester hours)

The Politics of the Third World

This course explores the processes and problems of the developing nations of the world. It examines the internal political processes of third world nations, as well as the position of the third world in international affairs. (3 semester hours)

American Political Thought

This course studies American political ideas, with an emphasis on current problems and conflicts and on intellectual responses to social change. (3 semester hours)

The War in Vietnam and the U.S.

This course provides an understanding of the political experience and the lessons and legacies of the Vietnam War in both Vietnam and the United States. A video enhanced course. (3 semester hours)

PSYCHOLOGY

General Psychology

This course gives a historical background of the psychology and principles of human behavior. It includes an introduction to human growth and development, intelligence, motivation, psychological measurement, emotions, personality development and adjustment, and related research methods. (3 semester hours)

Child Psychology

This course introduces the scientific study of the physical, cognitive, and psychosocial development of the child from the point of conception until adolescence. (3 semester hours)

Social Psychology

This course studies the social bases of behavior and the behavior of individuals in social situations. 3 semester hours)

Human Learning

This course studies the principles of learning and forgetting and the factors that affect human learning and retention. (3 semester hours)

Industrial Psychology

This course examines the principles involved as employees interact with the social and physical events in their industrial work environment. (3 semester hours)

Abnormal Psychology

This course provides an introduction to major symptom complexes, theories of etiology, and treatment of behavior disorders. (3 semester hours)

Adolescent Psychology

This course studies the principles of biological, behavioral, and personality development from puberty to maturity. (3 semester hours)

Environmental Psychology

This course studies the psychological effects of various environmental and socially relevant problems. Course topics include: environmental perception, attitudes toward the environment, effects of the environment on work performance, environmental stressors, crowding, and the effects of urban environments on interpersonal relations. (3 semester hours)

Animal Behavior

This course presents a comparative study of animal behavior. It teaches how behavior relates to bodily structure and environment. (3 semester hours)

Psychology of Sensation and Perception

This course studies the general characteristics of the senses and the basic conditions and principles of human perception, with an emphasis on auditory and visual perception. The role of sensation and perception on affectivity and motivation is stressed. (3 semester hours)

Perception

Covers the same material as the above course. (3 semester hours)

Cognitive Psychology

This course focuses on basic research on human perception, memory, attention, and thought. (3 semester hours)

Thinking and Cognition

Covers the same material as the above course. (3 semester hours)

RURAL SOCIOLOGY

Rural Sociology

This course introduces the student to the sociology of rural and small towns. The structure, functioning, and trends of rural society are discussed. Basic sociological principles are also emphasized. (3 semester hours)

Urban Sociology

This course studies urbanism as a world phenomenon; the ecological, demographic characteristics of cities; and the organization of urban society. Urban topics include status systems, occupational structure, formal and informal associations, racial and cultural relations, forms of communication, housing, city planning. (3 semester hours)

RUSSIAN

Elementary Russian

This course covers the basics of speaking, reading, and writing Russian. Audiocassettes are utilized on a rental basis. (5 semester hours)

SOCIAL WORK

Social Welfare and Social Work

This course examines the nature of social welfare institutions and social work, and the relationship between them. It focuses on policy issues, with special reference to poverty, racism, and sexism. (3 semester hours)

Social Justice and Social Policy

Based on the concepts of human need and social justice, this course provides a historical and analytical approach to social welfare policies and programs. (3 semester hours)

Policy and Service Delivery in Social Welfare

Based on the concepts of human need and social justice, this course provides a historical and analytical approach to social welfare policies and programs. A graduate level course. (3 semester hours)

SOCIOLOGY

Introduction to Sociology

This course examines the organization and activities of human groupings such as family, community, crowd, social class; the structure and function of institutions; and the social influences that shape personality, behavior, social change. (3 semester hours)

Criminology

Topics in this course include the sociology of law; the constitutional, psychological, sociological theories of criminal behavior; the process of criminal justice; the treatment of corrections; and the control of crime. Includes 13 video programs. (3 semester hours)

Urban Sociology

This course studies urbanism as a world phenomenon; the ecological and demographic characteristics of cities; and the organization or urban society. Urban topics include status systems; occupational structure; formal and informal associations; racial and cultural relations; forms of communication; housing; and city planning. (3 semester hours)

Social Organization of the City

Covers the same material as the above course. (3 semester hours)

Urban and Rural Sociology

Covers the same material as the above course. (3 semester hours)

Aging in Contemporary Society

Topics in this course include attitudes and stereotypes associated with the aged; the status of the aged in American society; the social psychology of the aging process; and the response of social institutions such as the family and political system to the aging of the population as a whole. (3 semester hours)

SPANISH

Elementary Spanish I

Course 1. This course gives an introduction to the Spanish language. Students practice hearing and speaking Spanish through the use of audiocassette tapes. (5 semester hours)

Course 110. The goals of this course are to be able to speak and understand simple (spoken) Spanish, as well as to read and write simple prose. A video enhanced course (eight video programs). (4 semester hours)

Elementary Spanish II

A continuation of the above course. Students practice hearing and speaking Spanish through the use of audiocassettes. (5 semester hours)

Elementary Spanish III

This is a multi-skill course following *Elementary Spanish II* that highlights cultural/literary readings; it includes a grammar review and practice in the spoken language, as well as some practice in written expression. (3 semester hours)

SPECIAL EDUCATION

Introduction to Special Education

This is a study of special children and youth: their characteristics, prevalence, and etiological background. The legal ramifications and other considerations, such as methodological approaches and staff responsibilities of special education programs, are discussed. (3 semester hours)

The Psychology and Education of Exceptional Individuals

This course studies the psychology and education of individuals with special problems and/or abilities. It surveys theories and strategies for the learning-teaching process and sources of assistance to educators and parents. (3 semester hours)

Introduction to Mental Retardation

This introductory course describes the characteristics, classification, and causes of mental retardation and severe handicaps. (3 semester hours)

STATISTICS

Elementary Statistics

Topics in this course include the collection and presentation of data; averages; and dispersion. This course also provides an introduction to statistical inference, estimation, hypothesis testing, and correlation. (3 semester hours)

THEATRE

The Theatre in Society

This course examines the role and scope of the theatre in the modern world community. (2 semester hours)

WOMEN'S STUDIES

Women's Experiences in Modern Fiction

A survey of modern fiction by and about women. Includes related essays, many of which are written by the women whose fiction is studied. (3 semester hours)

Women in Popular Culture

Drawing on the theoretical framework created by feminist scholars, this course investigates the ways women are portrayed in today's media. Topics include women in television and film, women's magazines, fashion and beauty, self-help books, advertising aimed at women, psychology and women, and ways to reverse traditional views of women. (3 semester hours)

HIGH SCHOOL COURSES

AGRICULTURE

Introductory Agriculture

First half. This course gives a general introduction to American agriculture, with a focus on Missouri agriculture. Includes a survey of livestock production. (½ unit)

Second half. Focuses on crop production, soil-and-water conservation, and forest management. (½ unit)

Introductory Horticulture

First half. This course is designed to introduce students to the science of horticulture and its practical applications for home and industry. (½ unit)

Second half. The second half of this course further introduces students to the science of horticulture and its practical applications to home and industry. (½ unit)

ANTHROPOLOGY

Anthropology

This course focuses on the cultural aspects of social groups. Included in this study are such topics as language, food-getting, economics, social stratification, sex, marriage, family, religion, and the arts. Examples from specific societies are used to illustrate the discussion of these topics. (½ unit)

Indians of Missouri

This course traces the history of the American Indians in the area that is now the state of Missouri. Ancient as well as recent Indian cultures are investigated. Modern archaeological methods are described, and the importance of the Indian culture is discussed. (½ unit)

ART

Art I

Designed for the beginning student in art, this course covers the basic principles of design and the elements of art: line, color, shape, texture, and form. Emphasis is placed on the quality of the students' art work; their understanding and appreciation of art; and their application of design elements. (½ unit)

Art Appreciation

This course provides information about and experiences with visual art. Students will learn to respond to works of art through the use of description, analysis, interpretation, and critical judgment. (½ unit)

BUSINESS EDUCATION

Accounting

First half. This course is an introduction to the basic accounting principles and procedures applied to businesses operating in a private enterprise economy. It describes the types of on-the-job activities required of entry-level accounting workers and the use of computers in maintaining accounting records. Students will work through an accounting cycle for a sole proprietorship. Other topics include cash control and banking activities, accounting for sales on account, and accounting for cash payments. (½ unit)

Business and Personal Law

This course addresses the practical aspects of the law; it focuses on situations involving legal questions that students are most likely to encounter. The first section of the course surveys the American legal system; the second section gives detailed attention to contacts. (½ unit)

Business Mathematics

This course covers the various aspects of consumer-oriented business practices, which include keeping financial records; figuring pay rates, benefits, and commissions; understanding metric measures; and borrowing, saving, and investing money. Practice problems in the course promote proficiency in dealing with everyday mathematical situations. (½ unit)

Consumer Economics: The Economic Environment

This course demonstrates how economics principles influence the daily lives of Americans. Consumer spending, borrowing, saving, and investing are explored. (½ unit)

Economics: Making Decisions

This course studies how individuals and societies make decisions about the use of natural resources, labor, time, and money. The student is introduced to economic terminology and to the everyday application of basic economic principles. (½ unit)

Electronic Office Systems

This course acquaints the student with the fundamental systems and concepts of office technology and the organization of the modern office. (½ unit)

Introduction to Business

First half. An introduction to basic economic theories and principles, this course emphasizes the individual's role as wage earner, consumer, and citizen. (½ unit)

Second half. Topics explored in the second half unit of this course include: the wide use of credit, insurance, investments, communication, transportation, the government's role in our economy, labor, world trade, career planning, and job seeking. (½ unit)

Introduction to Computers

This beginning computer course acquaints students with computer vocabulary and concepts. It discusses the historical background of computers, how computers work, computer applications, and the social implication of computers. (½ unit)

Keyboarding/Typewriting

First half. This introductory course teachers correct typing techniques that promote accuracy and speed, proofreading notation, standard formats used in business and professional documents, and reports and tables. (½ unit)

Second half. This course teaches more complex forms of the basic materials covered in the first half unit and emphasizes improved typing proficiency—techniques, speed, and accuracy. (½ unit)

Principles of Marketing

This course explores the many marketing practices and their roles in today's business world. It also describes several career positions in marketing. (½ unit)

Advanced Marketing

This course covers the economics of marketing and introduces basic math skills for figuring discounts, sales taxes, and shipping charges. Students will create their own advertisements; they will study stock and inventory control, and they will evaluate various management skills. (½ unit)

You and the World of Work

This course introduces the student to the work world. It examines the intellectual tools needed to perform in the marketplace; the impact of technology in the business world; and the personal time and money management skills required to succeed in the workplace. (½ unit)

CIVICS

Civics: Government and Citizenship

This course describes organization and function of our government at the local, state, and national levels. It also covers the rights and responsibilities of citizenship. Instruction and evaluation on both United States and Missouri Constitutions are included. (½ unit)

You and the Law

This course surveys criminal law, consumer law, family law, housing law, environmental law, and individual rights. (½ unit)

CONSUMER HOMEMAKING

Food for Fun and Fitness

This course provides an overview of the importance of a balanced diet to one's physical and emotional health. The role of each nutrient is described, as well as the ways in which the body uses each nutrient. Lessons are also included on weight control, eating out, and proper techniques for buying, preparing, and storing food. (½ unit)

Housing Decisions

This course discusses the factors that affect home-related decisions. Housing decisions discussed in the course range from deciding whether to rent or purchase a home to deciding how to decorate and accessorize a home. (½ unit)

Parenting and Child Development

This course looks at the realities and responsibilities of parenthood. It also studies the development of the child from the prenatal period to adolescence. (½ unit)

Personal Adjustment, Dating, and Marriage

This course examines contemporary health and lifestyle issues and options. Personality development, communication skills, and decision-making processes are stressed. (½ unit)

CONTEMPORARY ISSUES

Societal Issues in the Contemporary World

Topics studied in this course include the freedom of speech, the drug epidemic, violent crime, the public debt, the environmental crisis, and the U.S.-Commonwealth of Independent States relationship. (½ unit)

DRIVER EDUCATION

Driver Education

This course educates students about driving strategies, driving maneuvers, and traffic laws. Designed to promote a positive attitude toward safety, the course does not provide behind-the-wheel instruction; it does, however, prepare the student to acquire practical skills. (½ unit)

ECONOMICS

Economics: Making Decisions

This course studies how individuals and societies make decisions about the use of natural resources, labor, time, and money. The student is introduced to economic terminology and to the everyday application of basic economic principles. (½ unit)

ENGLISH

9th Grade English

First half. A thorough examination of the elements of English grammar; emphasis is on the development of writing skills. Literature sections in each lesson introduce and discuss literary genres including poetry, the short story and its sub-genres, and Shakespearean drama in *Romeo and Juliet.* (½ unit)

Second half. Continues the examination of the elements of English grammar with an emphasis on composition. Literature sections introduce and discuss the western and fantasy short story sub-genres, prose essays; and Charles Dickens' *Great Expectations.* (½ unit)

10th Grade English

First half. Continues the study of composition from the ninth-grade courses. The reading assignments are designed to enhance the student's understanding and appreciation of literature; the writing assignments are designed to familiarize the student with a variety of expressive techniques. (½ unit)

Second half. Continues the study of composition and literature with more emphasis on developing the student's writing skills. (½ unit)

11th Grade English

First half. This course analyzes the progression of the American Dream and its influence on literature. In addition, English mechanics, usage, and the methods of writing are emphasized. Students will write narrative, persuasive, and expository essays, which culminate in a literary analysis. (½ unit)

Second half. This course examines the themes of journeys and initiations in literature. Students will read a variety of short stories and poems as well as a novel. The grammar sections focus on improving the foundations of vocabulary, sentence structure, and critical thinking to improve both creative and practical writing skills. (½ unit)

12th Grade English

First half. In addition to presenting a thorough review of of general writing skills, this course surveys selections from the Anglo-Saxon, medieval, and Elizabethan periods and from the seventeenth and eighteenth centuries. (½ unit)

Second half. This course surveys selections from the Romantic and Victorian Ages and gives students the opportunity to express themselves in writing by responding to the reading selections. (½ unit)

African-American Literature

This course is a survey of the black experience in the United States beginning in the antebellum period and ending with contemporary drama. Readings are taken from a variety of genres—autobiography, poetry, the novel, the short story, and drama—and time periods—antebellum, Reconstruction, the Harlem Renaissance, the Depression, the 1950s, and contemporary. (½ unit)

Creative Writing

An introduction to short story writing, this course takes students step-by-step through the creative writing process and helps them develop their imaginations and communication skills. Topics covered include finding story ideas, inventing fictional characters, moving action and creating plot, and revising a rough draft. (½ unit)

English Literature Through Shakespeare

This course follows the development of English literature from its earliest known epic *Beowulf*, through *Canterbury Tales*, to Shakespeare's tragedy *Macbeth*. A brief exploration of how English developed and some historical background are included for study. (½ unit)

Grammar, Spelling, and Vocabulary

This course is especially designed for students who need to learn or review the basic elements of grammar: parts of speech, types of clauses and phrases, and usage. Punctuation, capitalization, spelling, and vocabulary are also included. (½ unit)

Improving Reading and Study Skills

This course is especially designed for students having difficulty with reading. It stresses reading for speed and accuracy, how to locate information, and how to acquire memory skills and test-taking skills. (½ unit)

Introduction to Journalism

This course covers the fundamentals of modern journalism. Students will learn about writing styles, copyediting, proofreading, typography, page makeup, photojournalism, advertising, and journalism ethics. (½ unit)

King Arthur and the Middle Ages

This course traces the early Celtic tales through the French variations and 14th- and 15th-century English interpretations. It examines Arthur as both a historical and legendary figure. (½ unit)

Man and Myth

This course studies Greek, Norse, and medieval mythology starting with the Greek view of creation and ending with King Arthur and Merlin the magician. (½ unit)

Mystery Fiction

This course discusses the genre of mystery fiction, with an emphasis on the detective story. The plots and character of several stories and one short novel are examined. (½ unit)

Readings in the American Novel

This course traces the development of the American novel by examining five well-known works. Major American themes that occur in these novels are discussed. (½ unit)

Readings in Science Fiction

This course defines science fiction as a literary genre, identifying and exploring common themes and motifs in four classic science fiction novels and examining how those themes relate to people and politics in the real world. (½ unit)

Readings in the Short Story

This course presents an introduction to the short story. The first half of the course explores elements of fiction such as plot, theme, and irony; the second half focuses on the historical development of the American short story. (½ unit)

Science Fiction for Reluctant Readers

Students who are not avid readers are able to explore science fiction by reading various short stories in this course. (½ unit)

Search for Identity Through Literature

This course examines two aspects of the individual's search for identity. It explores relationships people have with their peers, their families, and society as a whole, and it probes the struggles individuals have with their consciences and with the obstacles that prevent them from realizing their full potential. (½ unit)

Short Stories for Reluctant Readers

This is an introductory course for students who do not usually enjoy reading. By reading and analyzing short, high-interest stories, students will learn to recognize the major elements of fiction, such as plot, characterization, and theme. (1/2 unit)

Thinking Clearly: Making Sense

This course shows how thinking and life-style can be influenced by "word magic." Students learn how to evaluate what they read and hear by applying logic to language. (½ unit)

FRENCH

French I

First half. This course provides and introduction to the principles of French grammar and composition. Audiocassette tapes are used throughout the course. (½ unit)

Second half. This course continues with a study of the principles of French grammar and composition introduced in the first half unit, and it explores the culture of France. Audiocassettes used throughout the course. (½ unit)

French II

First half. This course studies the principles of French grammar and composition while exposing the student to French life and culture. It is designed for students who have had one year of French. Audiocassettes used throughout the course. (½ unit)

Second half. This course continues the study of the principles of French grammar and composition begun in the first half unit. Audiocassettes used throughout the course. (½ unit)

GEOGRAPHY

World Geography: Europe, Middle East, Africa

This course examines the relationship of human beings to their geographic environment, and it emphasizes how climate and geographic features influence human activities. Descriptions of the various climatic and geographic regions of the world are included, and special attention is given to the basic concepts of geography. (½ unit)

World Geography: Asia, the Pacific, North America, South America

This course examines the relationship of human beings to their geographic environment, and it emphasizes how climate and geographic features influence human activities. Descriptions of the various climatic and geographic regions of the world are included, and special attention is given to the basic concepts of geography. (½ unit)

GERMAN

German I

First half. This course introduces the basics of German grammar and composition and discusses some aspects of German life and culture. (½ unit)

Second half. This course continues with a study of the principles of German grammar and composition introduced in the first half unit, and it explores additional aspects of German culture. (½ unit)

German II

First half. This course is designed for students who have completed one year of German. It expands on reading, writing, listening, and speaking skills. Students also study cultural aspects of German-speaking countries. (½ unit)

GOVERNMENT

American Government

This course studies the basic principles, structure, and operation of national, state, and local government. It also discusses topics such as participation in the political system, policy-making, and contrasting economic and political systems. (½ unit)

International Relations

This course studies how nations interact in war and peace. It focuses on how force is used when negotiations fail in the time period of 1870 to the present. (½ unit)

HEALTH AND PHYSICAL EDUCATION

Health

This course provides an overview of health. It studies the effect that life-style can have on one's overall wellness and the ways in which people can maximize their physical, emotional, and social health through positive life-style choices. (½ unit)

Fitness for Well-Being

This course is designed to provide students with information on how to enhance their lives through exercise and a balanced diet. Cardiovascular fitness, muscular fitness, flexibility, nutrition, and weight control are among the topics discussed. (½ unit)

Physical Education for Special Needs

This course explains the rules and playing procedures of many sports and recreational activities that can be adapted to meet the special needs of individual students. Emphasis is placed on participation in physical education regardless of physical ability. (½ unit)

HISTORY

American History Through Reconstruction

This course presents the values, ideals, and attitudes of Americans at different times in our history. Major topics include colonial settlement, the Revolutionary War, the new government, the rise of sectionalism, the Civil War, and Reconstruction. (½ unit)

American History Since Reconstruction

This course studies events that occurred in the time period beginning immediately after Reconstruction and ending in the mid-1980s. Topics discussed include industrialization, the reform movement, the the First World War, Franklin Roosevelt, the Second World War, and contemporary international and domestic developments. (½ unit)

Medieval History

This course surveys the development of Western civilization from the fall of the Roman Empire in the West to the end of the Middle Ages (A.D. 450–1500). (½ unit)

Missouri History

This course provides a history of the state of Missouri. Students learn about the contributions of Missouri and Missourians to the history of the United States. (½ unit)

World History to the American Revolution

This course gives a brief overview of world history from the Stone Age to 1776. Course topics include the rise of civilization, the Greeks and Romans, early Asian empires, African and American cultures, the spread of Islam, the development of Europe through the Middle Ages and Renaissance, and the European colonial system. (½ unit)

World History Since the American Revolution

This course gives an overview of important events in world history. Topics of discussion include the French Revolution, the Industrial Revolution, Latin American revolutions, the Western influence on the world, decolonization, World War I, World War II, the Korean War, and the Persian Gulf War. (½ unit)

INDUSTRIAL ARTS

Amateur Radio

Starting with the basic rules and procedures, essential electronic concepts, and how to use communications radios, this course gives students a step-by-step introduction to radio. Morse code is taught with audiotapes, and students are given practical applications of selected electronics theory. This course covers information students will need to know in order to take an F.C.C. license exam for an amateur radio operator license. (½ unit)

DC Electronics

Designed for students with no background in electronics, this course covers the fundamentals of electricity, including a close examination of direct current electronics. Students will complete undgraded lab exercises in order to learn the procedures discussed. (½ unit)

General Drafting

First half. This course describes drafting instruments and equipment and it teaches students drafting concepts and techniques that enable them to visualize and draw in three dimensions. (½ unit)

Second half. A continuation of the above course. (½ unit)

Technical Drafting

This is an advanced course for students who have successfully completed an introductory course in drafting. It is designed to improve skills in manipulating drafting equipment and in expressing ideas graphically. It also teaches students how to read and interpret advanced drawings correctly. (½ unit)

MATHEMATICS

Algebra I

First half. This course reviews the essential skills of arithmetic as they relate to the study of algebra. The first half unit begins with real numbers and their properties, and it shows how these properties can be used to solve equations. The course concludes with problems related to inequalities, linear functions, and graphing linear inequalities. (½ unit)

Second half. Building on mathematical operations taught in the first half, this course presents linear systems in two variables; it continues with problems that require the student to factor polynomials and solve open sentences involving rational expressions. The course concludes with a study of square roots; rational and irrational numbers; and radicals. (½ unit)

Algebra II

First half. The course begins with matrices and a review of the essentials of algebra. Then it presents linear functions; linear equations and inequalities; and linear equations in three variables. It concludes with the factoring of polynomials and the solving of quadratic equations. (½ unit)

Second half. Building on the operations covered in the first half unit, this course presents sequences and series; radicals and irrational numbers; complex numbers; and polynomial functions. It concludes with quadratic relations and systems; exponents; and logarithms. (½ unit)

Business Mathematics

This course covers the various aspects of consumer-oriented business practices including keeping financial records, figuring pay-rates, benefits and commission, understanding metric measures; and borrowing, saving, and investing money. Practice problems promote proficiency in dealing with everyday mathematical situations. (½ unit)

Fundamentals of Statistics and Probability

This course provides a solid background in probability and statistics that can be used as the basis for data analysis and decision making. (½ unit)

General Mathematics

First half. The basic needs for mathematics in everyday life are introduced in the first half of this course. It is designed to help the student understand mathematical concepts. Computational skills are taught using whole numbers, decimals, fractions, and mixed numbers; metric conversions are also discussed. (½ unit)

Second half. The second half of this course includes a review of computation with fractions, the metric system, geometry, probability and estimation. The exercises are designed to improve the student's ability to read, analyze, and work useful problems. (½ unit)

Applied Math

First half. This course builds on the skills the student has learned in general math courses. Topics include integers, variables and expressions, equations and problem solving, rational numbers, fractions, probability, decimals, and percentages. (½ unit)

General Mathematics II

Second half. This course offers an advanced study in algebra, geometry, and business mathematics concentrating primarily on geometry and business math. (½ unit)

Geometry

First half. This course in informal geometry covers such topics as geometric art and constructions, inductive reasoning, congruence, and circles. (½ unit)

Second half. This is a continuation of the above course and covers topics such as the concepts for understanding circles and their relations (tangents, radii, arcs, chords and central angles, secants); basic constructions and locus; formulas to determine the area of plane figures and the area and volume of solid figures (with descriptions for the sources of these formulas); coordinate geometry; and the concepts

and properties of transformational geometry (mapping, translation, reflection, rotation, dilations, and similarity ratios). (½ unit)

Precalculus

First half. This course covers coordinate geometry, polynomials, inequalities, the function of graphs, exponents, logarithms, trigonometric functions, and triangle trigonometry. (½ unit)

Second half. A continuation of the above course covers graphing; trigonometric formulas; polar coordinates and complex numbers; conic sections; vectors; matrices and determinants; sequences and series; and rules of differentiation. The course also introduces the student to calculus. (½ unit)

Trigonometry

This course covers trigonometric functions and their graphs; trigonometric identities; trigonometry and triangles; inverse functions and equations; circular functions and applications; complex numbers; sequences and series. (½ unit)

MUSIC

Music Appreciation

This course explores the concepts, styles, techniques, instruments, and history of music from the Medieval through the Classical eras. Audiocassette tapes are used to provide listening examples of various types of instruments and forms of music. (½ unit)

PERSONAL DEVELOPMENT

Career Planning: Charting Your Future

Students identify their own interests, values, assets, skills, and goals. They then choose some careers they wish to explore and investigate those careers. (½ unit)

Parenting and Child Development

This course looks at the realities of parenthood and its responsibilities. It also focuses on the development of the child from the prenatal period to adolescence. (½ unit)

Personal Adjustment, Dating, and Marriage

This course examines contemporary health and lifestyle issues and options. Personality development, communication skills, and decision-making processes are stressed. (½ unit)

Planning for College

The purpose of this course is to assist students who are planning to attend college by teaching them basic college survival skills: how to choose and apply to a college, where to look for financial aid, how to improve study habits, and how to adjust to social life on campus. (½ unit)

Project Personal Development

This course helps students to get to know themselves better and enhance their personal development. Through the use of case studies, students apply what they learn about motivation, behavior, peer pressure, responsibility, values, self-esteem, choices, personality, goals, and determination. (½ unit)

PHOTOGRAPHY

Introductory Photography

This course covers the basics of black and white photography, including the technical processes and equipment used. In addition to learning how to take pictures, develop film, and print photographs, the student will learn to critically evaluate photographs. (½ unit)

PSYCHOLOGY

Psychology: Foundations of Human Behavior

This course introduces the basic concepts of psychology; what psychology is and how psychologists arrive at psychological principles. Course topics include biological, environmental, and hereditary influences on behavior; personality; learning; thinking; and measurements of personality and intellectual ability. (½ unit)

Introduction to Personal and Social Psychology

This general psychology course concentrates on the "why" of human behavior. It examines sensation, perception, emotions, motivation, and frustration as they affect human behavior. Social influences on individual and group behavior are considered and the techniques used in the treatment of personality disorders are also presented. (½ unit)

Psychology and Everyday Topics

This psychology course gives a general background of psychological concepts and then applies these concepts to everyday topics: love, death, the women's movement, crime, drug abuse, and prejudice. (½ unit)

RELIGIOUS STUDIES

World Religions

This course provides a detailed survey of the major religions of the world—their histories, origins, and contemporary status. Judaism, Christianity, Islam, Hinduism, Buddhism, and the religions of China and Japan are examined. (½ unit)

SCIENCE

Aerospace: Crossing the Space Frontier

This course provides an explanation of many of the scientific principles of space technology and a history of how those technologies developed out of the political turmoil of the 20th century. (½ unit)

A Survey of the Living World

An introduction to biology that emphasizes the interdependence of all living things, this course provides general information on plants and animals, from one-celled organisms to the most developed forms. (½ unit)

Astronomy

First half. This introductory astronomy course presents the terminology, a historical perspective, and current thinking about our universe. The first half unit provides an understanding of the solar system, the night sky, and some practical aspects of astronomy. (½ unit)

Second half. The second half unit of this course presents a description of the universe beyond the solar system. Topics include star formation, star death, galaxies, the general structure of the universe, and the possibility of other intelligent life in the universe. (½ unit)

Chemistry

First half. An introduction to the science of chemistry, this course studies scientific measurement, matter, and the mole, chemical formulas, chemical reactions, solids, liquids, and gases. (½ unit)

Second half. A continuation of the first half unit, this second half studies atomic structure; electron clouds and probability; periodic properties of elements; chemical bonding; molecular structure; energy and disorder. Brief introductions to general chemistry topics such as redox equations and pH determinants, are included. (½ unit)

Conservation of Natural Resources

This survey course examines the nature of our environment, discusses environmental problems, and explains the principles of conservation. (½ unit)

Physical Science

First half. By explaining the properties and structure of matter, this course introduces physical science. Chemical, electrochemical, and nuclear reactions are studied. Students learn how to balance equations, formulate hypotheses, use the scientific method, and analyze the periodic table. (½ unit)

Second half. This course includes coverage of such topics as the laws of motion; work and heat; waves and sounds; light; electric charges and current; electromagnetism; and our present energy needs. (½ unit)

Physics

First half. This course presents the basic concepts of physics. Measurement and problem solving, velocity, acceleration, motion, forces, work, power, heat, and temperature are among the concepts studied. (½ unit)

Special Topics in Geology

This course introduces the science of geology with special emphasis on the mutual effects of geologic processes and human life. (½ unit)

Special Topics in Life Science

Four specialized areas of biology are studied in this course: human anatomy and physiology, genetics, evolution, and ecology. (½ unit)

The Underground World of Caves

A theoretical and practical approach to caves, this course examines the geology and ecology of these formations and it describes safe methods of cave exploration. (½ unit)

SOCIOLOGY

Sociology

An introduction to the field of sociology, this course examines such topics as culture and the family, social structure, education, religion, and change in society. (½ unit)

SPANISH

Spanish I

First half. This course introduces the principles of Spanish grammar; students practice building simple sentences, and learn common idioms. The culture, religious practices, and family traditions of Spanish-speaking peoples are discussed. Audiocassette tapes are used throughout the course. (½ unit)

Second half. A continuation of the study of Spanish grammar, as well as the study of the cultural, religious, and family traditions of Spanish-speaking peoples. (½ unit)

Spanish I - Video

First half. This course introduces the principles of Spanish grammar; students practice building simple sentences, and learn common idioms. The culture, religious practices, and family traditions of Spanish-speaking peoples are discussed. Includes 8 video programs. (½ unit)

Second half. A continuation of the study of Spanish grammar, as well as the study of the cultural, religious, and family traditions of Spanish-speaking people. Includes 7 video programs. (½ unit)

Spanish II

First half. This course is designed for students who have completed one year of Spanish. It expands on speaking, writing, and reading skills. (½ unit)

Second half. This course continues the study of speaking, writing, and reading skills, as well as the study of the cultural and family traditions of Spanish-speaking people. (½ unit)

NONCREDIT COURSES

HEALTH CARE ADMINISTRATION

An Orientation to Health Maintenance Organizations

This course gives an overview of the American health care system and the rise of HMOs, and it discusses the characteristics of HMOs and how they are different from other health care delivery systems. Departmental operations of HMOs and the relationships between an HMO, its members, and its providers are also covered. (.5 CEU) *Tuition:* $36.

NURSING

Advances in the Recognition and Treatment of Depressive Disorders

The diagnosis and treatment of depressive disorders are covered in this course. Included are discussions of the types and symptoms of depressive disorders; suicide; the use of antidepressants; drug reactions and interactions; and new developments in treatments and antidepressants. (.5 CEU) *Tuition:* $36.

An Overview of HIV Infections and AIDS: 1993

This course covers the transmission of the human immunodeficiency virus, ways to prevent transmission, the special problems HIV patients face, and current methods of treatment of HIV and opportunistic diseases. (.5 CEU) *Tuition:* $36.

Basics of Cancer Chemotherapy

This course is a practical overview of chemotherapy as a treatment for cancer. It covers such issues as the action and classification of chemotherapeutic agents, the principles of safe administration of chemotherapeutic agents, and selected nursing practices related to helping patients undergoing chemotherapy. (1.5 CEUs) *Tuition:* $108.

Cardiovascular Pharmacology: 1993

This course provides recommended dosages, mechanisms of action, sites of action, and clinical considerations for specific drugs used in treating and managing the patient who has cardiovascular disease. It also provides basic information on cardiovascular anatomy, physiology, and hemodynamics. The goal of this course is to increase understanding of the various medication therapies prescribed by physicians. (1.5 CEUs) *Tuition:* $108.

Common Gynecologic Disorders and Procedures: 1992

This course discusses prevention, symptoms, and treatment of various gynecologic disorders, including sexually transmitted diseases. Some common gynecologic procedures are also covered along with related nursing strategies. (.5 CEU) *Tuition:* $36.

EKG Interpretation: 1992

This course allows nurses to review the principles of electrocardiography and to interpret normal and abnormal waveforms, including 20 cardiac dysrhythmias. The correct way to apply EKG leads is explained. (1 CEU) *Tuition:* $72.

Health Care of the Mature and Older Woman: 1992

This course gives an overview of the psychological and physiological changes that occur as a part of menopause and aging, and it presents nursing strategies for providing health care to women in the latter stages of their lives. (.5 CEU) *Tuition:* $36.

Introduction to Cardiovascular Disease: Assessment and Management: 1993

This course examines ways in which the nursing professional can intervene to help patients at risk lessen their chances of developing heart disease. It discusses some barriers that may keep patients from heeding dietary and lifestyle changes, and it studies methods of evaluating patients, including history and diagnostic tests to uncover early heart disease. (1 CEU) *Tuition:* $72.

Major Issues in Gerontological Nursing: 1993

This course gives an overview of aging and discusses issues related to providing health care to the elderly, including disease processes, drug therapy, dementia, and nutritional problems. (1 CEU) *Tuition:* $72.

Normal and Abnormal Breath Sounds: 1990

This course explains the normal respiratory physiology. Through the use of an audiocassette containing more than 40 breath sounds, the student learns how to recognize abnormal and normal breath sounds. Proper auscultatory sites and appropriate documentation are also discussed. (.5 CEU) *Tuition:* $36.

Nursing Ethics

This course defines ethics in a health care context, particularly in relation to a nurse's role, and it discusses how ethical problems are solved. Topics such as the right to informed consent, the right to refuse treatment, and limiting life-prolonging treatment are covered, as is institutional ethics. (1.5 CEUs) *Tuition:* $108.

Nursing Skills for the Management of Head, Spinal, Chest, Abdominal, and Orthopedic Trauma: 1991

This course reviews the basic pathology initiated with trauma and discusses appropriate nursing intervention for specific traumatic injuries. (1 CEU) *Tuition:* $72.

Nutritional Needs of the Elderly in Health and Disease: 1990

This course examines the nutritional needs of the elderly, including how requirements for certain nutrients change as people age and the effect of diet-medication interactions affect people as they age. Other course topics include the factors that affect nutritional intake, the need for specialized nutritional support, and recommendations for a rational diet for the elderly. (.6 CEU) *Tuition:* $43.

Overview of Anesthesia for Nurses: 1992

This course is designed to de-mystify anesthesia by addressing common misconceptions and outlining all aspects of anesthesia care, including risk factors, pre- and post-anesthesia medications, and the preparation of patients for anesthesia. Discussions of general, regional, and local anesthesia and intravenous sedation are included. Nursing diagnoses and strategies for patients experiencing anesthetic emergencies are outlined. (.5 CEU) *Tuition:* $36.

Overview of Nursing for Women's Health: 1992

This course provides an overview of nursing in relation to women's health. Topics covered include the history and future of women's health, the stages of a woman's development, well women's health care, cancer in women, and the special types of stressors and challenges women face. (1 CEU) *Tuition:* $72.

The Modern Assessment and Management of Pain: 1990

The emphasis of this course is on the management of acute pain, chronic pain, and pain in the pediatric patient. The classifications, pathophysiology, and assessment of pain are also discussed. (.5 CEU) *Tuition:* $36.

The New Threat of Drug-Resistant Microbes: 1993

This course provides the necessary information for identifying the major drug-resistant microbes that have recently gained notoriety. Ways to identify personal protective measures that may prevent exposure to hepatitis B, hepatitis C, tuberculosis, and HIV are explained. (.5 CEU) *Tuition:* $36.

POLITICAL SCIENCE
City and County Planning and Plan Implementation

This course was developed in an effort to make governmental officials, planning commissioners, and the public aware of the importance of comprehensive planning as a function of local government. The course covers such subjects as the legal foundation of planning, zoning, and subdividing land; planning techniques; capital improvement programming; and plan implementation. Each person completing this course will receive a certificate signed by the Chancellor of the University of Missouri. (2 CEUs) *Tuition:* $26.

PUBLIC AND COMMUNITY SERVICES
Wildland/Urban Interface Fire Protection: A National Problem with Local Solutions

This course is designed to help fire service personnel and related professionals assess their local wildland/urban interface fire problem, recognize the protection strategies that have proven effective, and implement these solutions in their own communities and wildlands. (2 CEUs)

RELIGIOUS STUDIES
Introduction to the Old Testament

This course discusses the literature, history, and thought of the Old Testament; it introduces scholarly theories necessary for academic study of the Bible. It covers the traditions of creation, selection, covenant, monarchy, prophecy, and post-exilic Judaism. (Noncredit) *Tuition:* $52.

Major World Religions

This course studies the different ways in which the great world religions interpret life and reality; it surveys the basic ideas in Confucianism, Taoism, Shintoism, Hinduism, Jainism, Buddhism, Judaism, Zoroastrianism, Christianity, Sikhism, and others. (Noncredit) *Tuition:* $52.

Missouri, University of - Kansas City
5100 Rockhill Road
Kansas City, Missouri 64110   (816) 276-1000

Description:
Correspondence courses offered by the University of Missouri at Kansas City are administered by the Center for Independent Study in Columbia, Missouri. The Center for Independent Study has administrative responsibility for coordination of all correspondence instruction offered by each of the four University of Missouri campuses. For courses available, SEE **Missouri, University of.**

Accreditations:
North Central Association of Colleges and Schools.

Missouri, University of - Rolla
Rolla, Missouri 65401   (314) 341-4164

Description:
Correspondence courses offered by the University of Missouri at Rolla are administered by the Center for Independent Study in Columbia, Missouri. The Center for

Independent Study has administrative responsibility for coordination of all correspondence instruction offered by each of the four University of Missouri campuses. For courses available, SEE **Missouri, University of.**

Accreditations:
North Central Association of Colleges and Schools.

Missouri, University of - St. Louis
8001 Natural Bridge Road
St. Louis, Missouri 63121   (314) 453-5451

Description:
Correspondence courses offered by the University of Missouri at St. Louis are administered by the Center for Independent Study in Columbia, Missouri. The Center for Independent Study has administrative responsibility for coordination of all correspondence instruction offered by each of the four University of Missouri campuses. For courses available, SEE **Missouri, University of.**

Accreditations:
North Central Association of Colleges and Schools.

Moody Bible Institute
Independent Studies
Center for External Studies
820 North LaSalle Drive
Chicago, Illinois 60610   (312) 329-2080

Description:
Independent Studies was begin in 1901. It offers an accredited Associate of Biblical Studies degree along with a continuing education program entitled the Adult Bible Study certificate program. Enrollment figures for both credit and noncredit are over 20,000 per year and represent a worldwide student body.

Faculty:
Dr. Randall Dattoli, Director of Administrative Affairs; Christopher Mincey, Registrar. The faculty includes 32 members and subject specialists.

Academic Levels:
College
Noncredit

Degree/Certificate Programs:
Associate of Biblical Studies; Certificate. A residency requirement of 12 semester hours must be completed for the Associate of Biblical Studies program.

Admission Requirements:
To enroll for credit in a college credit course, the student must have a high school diploma or hold the General Educational Development (GED) equivalency. High school seniors of high academic standing may enroll upon the approval of the Registrar. Enrollment in the Correspon-

dence School does not constitute admission to the Moody Bible Institute Day School.

Tuition:

Contact the institute for current tuition and fees. Courses include all tests, exams, study guides, workbooks, instructional services and other materials. No refund will be made unless materials are returned in resalable condition. If materials are returned within thirty days, refund will be payment price less postage/handling fee and any service charges; if returned after thirty days and before one year, refund will be payment price less $15 restock fee, postage/handling fee, and service charges. No refund after one year.

Enrollment Period:

Maximum time to complete a course is twelve months; students may apply for a six-month extension.

Equipment Requirements:

Textbooks, course outlines, examinations supplied by the school. Student must supply a Bible and cassette player for courses in Greek and Preaching.

Credit and Grading:

The graduation requirements for the Associate in Biblical Studies includes the completion of the specified 29 credit hour curriculum; satisfactory involvement in Practical Christian Ministry for two additional semesters; a residency of 12 semester hours at MBI from either Day School, Evening School, or Summer School; transfer credit will be considered up to half of the required credits; transfer credits must be earned in an accredited school (the courses comparable to Moody courses) and the grade must be at least a C. The Certificate in Biblical Studies requires the completion of the specified 31 credit hour curriculum in college credit courses; cumulative grade average of at least 2.0 (C); satisfactory involvement in Practical Christian Ministry for two semesters; three personal references, one of whom is the student's pastor, that give evidence of Christian character; membership in an evangelical Protestant church (documented by the church to the registrar); and personal affirmation and signing of the MBI Doctrinal Statement. Final examinations for college credit courses must be proctored. All other examinations are open book. Grading system for college credit courses: A, 94–100; B, 86–93; C, 76–85, D, 70–75; F, below 70. Minimum passing grade is D.

Accreditations:

North Central Association of Colleges and Schools; American Association of Bible Colleges.

COLLEGE COURSES

BIBLE

Old Testament Survey I

Survey I covers Genesis through Esther, showing how the law of Moses and the historical books fit together. Shows historical perspective and gives foundation for interpreting the rest of Scripture. (3 semester hours)

Old Testament Survey II

Survey II covers Job through Malachi. Provides a synthetic study of poetry, wisdom literature, and prophecy. Helps the student see the whole patterns which emerge from the various authors. (3 semester hours)

New Testament Survey

Presents an overview of the Gospels, early church and epistles. Enables the student to grasp the New Testament as a whole and each book as a unit. (4 semester hours)

Elements of Bible Study

Introductory course which emphasizes the inductive approach to Scripture study. Teaches Bible study tools and basic, interpretive principles and methods. (2 semester hours)

John

Analytical study of Christ's deity and saving work. Focuses on His life and ministry. (2 semester hours)

Acts

Study of the relationship of Acts to the Gospels. Presents Jesus Christ's continuing ministry through the Holy Spirit. Emphasizes the ministries of Peter, Paul, and other leading personalities in the early church. (2 semester hours)

Biblical Hebrew I

Teaches the Hebrew alphabet, vowel pointings, basic vocabulary, grammar tenses, and sentence structure. Readings are assigned from the Old Testament. Designed to provide first-year proficiency in Hebrew. (4 semester hours)

Biblical Hebrew II

Advanced course in Hebrew includes identification of verbs and nouns; grammatical and syntactical principles to aid in translation and interpretation. Students translate passages from Genesis and Psalms. (4 semester hours)

New Testament Greek Grammar I

Teaches the Greek alphabet, the essentials of Greek grammar, and some constructions of the Greek sentence. Enhances Bible study by promoting familiarity with the language of the New Testament. (4 semester hours)

New Testament Greek Grammar II

Offers advanced experience with conjugations, third declension nouns, and grammatical constructions. The Greek text of I John is used for translation assignments. (4 semester hours)

Bible Study Methods

Learn how to study the Bible for better understanding. Ten study methods include the synthetic, historical, topical, and analytical. (2 semester hours)

Romans

Stresses this epistle's contribution to the doctrines of salvation, sanctification, and the place of the Hebrew and Gentile in the divine plan. Applies principles for Christian living to our contemporary society. (4 semester hours)

CHRISTIAN EDUCATION

An Introduction to Christian Education: Church at Work in the World II

Introduction to Christian education in which the nature of biblical ministry is developed. Emphasizes issues and functions of the educational ministry as related to home, school, and church. (3 semester hours)

Biblical Philosophy of Education

Outlines distinctly evangelical educational philosophy with specific implications for the Christian school. Helps students articulate a personal educational philosophy. (3 semester hours)

EVANGELISM

Personal Evangelism

Presents the biblical principles of effective evangelism. Includes an overview of discipling, emphasizing the analysis of follow-up techniques and materials. Also surveys selected cults focusing on their basic tenets, personalities, publications, and enlistment strategies. (3 semester hours)

MISSIONS

An Introduction to Christian Missions: Church at Work in the World I

Gives attention to the nature of the church and its biblical basis of missions. Also covers the church's cross-cultural mission, historical dynamic of its mission today, and the role of the local church in world evangelization. (3 semester hours)

PASTORAL STUDIES

Biblical Preaching

Organized presentation of the principles of preparing, outlining, and delivering an effective, biblical sermon. (3 semester hours)

THEOLOGY

Christian Life and Ethics

A study of the Christian's position and practice. Attention given to the development of a biblical world view, the spirit-filled life, the body life of the church, and health interpersonal relationships. (3 semester hours)

Biblical Eschatology

Studies the biblical answers to questions about the future. Topics include physical death, the second coming of Christ, resurrection, the tribulation, millenium, judgments, heaven and hell. (2 semester hours)

Church History

Reviews the story of the church through the centuries, from its founding in Jerusalem to today. Teaches how God works through people to fulfill His purposes. (3 semester hours)

NONCREDIT COURSES

BIBLE

Christian Life Series

First Steps in the Christian Faith. A study of the assurance of salvation and forgiveness for sin. Also explores the significance of baptism and communion and instructs how to get the most from Bible reading and prayer. (1 CEU)

The Bible Says. Discloses the basics of the Christian faith. Topics include: God, Christ, the Holy Spirit, the Trinity, Christian heritage, the inspiration of the Bible, and living the Christian life. (1 CEU)

God's Will for Your Life. Teaches what the Bible says about discovering God's will. Lessons give practical instruction on waiting on God, pleasing Him and developing a relationship with the Lord. (1 CEU)

John. Study of the Gospel in which Christ reveals more of Himself than any other book in the New Testament. (1 CEU)

How to Understand the Bible. Includes a survey of how we got the Bible, the conflict of science and the Bible, and the tools and methods necessary for deeper understanding of God's Word. (1 CEU)

The Life of Christ. A comparative analysis of the four Gospels which reconstructs Jesus' life and ministry in chronological order. (1 CEU)

Old Testament Studies Series

Survey of the Old Testament I. Genesis through Esther. Gives attention to individual books; shows their relationship to the entire Bible. (1 CEU)

Survey of the Old Testament II. Job through Malachi. Studies the books of poetry and prophecy. Teaches the relationship of each book to the entire Bible. (1 CEU)

Genesis. The study of beginnings, tracing man's roots back to the origin of time. Subjects covered are creation, sin, death, sacrifices, languages, and the nations. (1 CEU)

Exodus. A study of redemption which shows the drama of Israel's deliverance from slavery. Lessons include: origins of the Jewish Passover feast, the giving of the Ten Commandments, and the Tabernacle. (1 CEU)

Psalms. Analyzes these songs of prayer and praise and highlights main themes and prophetic content. Also distinguishes various types of Psalms. (1 CEU)

Joshua, Analyzes Israel's conquest of the Promised Land. Provides moral and spiritual lessons. Joshua's key to victory over the enemy is a key for victorious Christian living. (1 CEU)

New Testament Studies Series

Survey of the New Testament. An overview of the entire New Testament. Provides a link between the Life of Christ, the birth of the church, and the doctrines expounded throughout. (1 CEU)

Matthew. Emphasizes Jesus as the promised Messiah and King of Israel. Probes the meaning of Christ's rejection and God's program following that rejection. (1 CEU)

Romans. Reveals Paul's complete and logical statement of God's plan of salvation. Presents deep doctrinal truths that are applicable to Christian living. (1 CEU)

I Corinthians. Examines contemporary issues that face today's church such as: women's roles in church, church discipline, marriage and divorce, civil rights, and spiritual gifts.

Hebrews. Highlights passages on Christ's deity. Clarifies His high priestly ministry as a fulfillment of Old Testament types and shadows. (1 CEU)

I and II Peter. Discusses Peter's letters to Christians suffering persecution. Contains practical guidelines for dealing with family, business, or social relationships. (1 CEU)

Personal Ministries Series

Acts. Studies the birth of the Christian church and focuses on the relationship of Acts to the Gospels. Examines the ministries of Peter, Paul, and other early church leaders. (1 CEU)

Successful Soul-Winning. Explains what the Bible teaches about a Christian's responsibility to witness. Includes training, technique, problems, and victories. (1 CEU)

The Biblical Basis of Missions: Mission Today. An introduction to the study of Christian missions using Bible teaching as a guide. A practical course recommended for those interested in missions. (1 CEU)

The Cults Exposed. Exposes the doctrinal errors of cults such as Mormonism, Jehovah's Witnesses, Christian Science, Spiritism, Unity,

Oriental Cults, and The Way International. Designed to sharpen Bible knowledge and strengthen witnessing skills. (1 CEU)

The Doctrine of the Holy Spirit: Person and Work of the Holy Spirit. Emphasizes the personality, deity, and activities of the Holy Spirit. Examines the Spirit's role in creation, revelation, and inspiration of Scriptures. (1 CEU)

Memorize the Word. A memorization course that benefits the student by helping personal and group Bible study, witnessing and other areas of Christian service. Provides proven techniques for memorization of Scripture. (1 CEU)

Christian Education Series

First Steps in the Christian Faith. A study of the assurance of salvation and forgiveness for sin. Also explores the significance of baptism and communion and instructs how to get the most from Bible reading and prayer. (1 CEU)

The Bible Says Discloses the basics of the Christian faith. Topics include: God, Christ, the Holy Spirit, the Trinity, Christian heritage, the inspiration of the Bible, and living the Christian life. (1 CEU)

Teaching—With Results. A study of the principles of Christian teaching and learning, personal Bible study, steps in lesson preparation and planning, classroom management and evaluation. (1 CEU)

Understanding Students. Explores the physical, mental, social, emotional, and spiritual characteristics of human development from birth through adulthood. (1 CEU)

Building a Successful Sunday School. Identifies how to organize and implement an effective Sunday school ministry. Explains how to set up departments, train teachers, and solve problems. (1 CEU)

Being a Christian Leader. Examines the biblical principles of leadership in the Old and New Testament. Designed to equip men and women for leadership. (1 CEU)

Prophetic Series

Bible Prophecy. Explains principles of prophecy as well as specific prophecies from a logical, biblical perspective. Covers topics such as God's dealings with Israel, the Antichrist and Christ's second coming. (1 CEU)

Daniel. An account of the sovereignty of God, this course reveals the course of gentile world empires and the ultimate deliverance of God's covenant people. (1 CEU)

Judges and Ruth. Study of Israel's moral downfall and also the story of Ruth and Boaz. Provides insights into the Kinsman-Redeemer theme, the weakness of human character, and the nature of God's grace. (1 CEU)

Ephesians. Examines how to become a mature child of God. Topics covered are: unity of believers, spiritual gifts within the church and relationships at home or work. (1 CEU)

Isaiah. This great prophet was the conscience of his generation with profound messages for his backsliding and embittered people; his book is filled with detailed predictions of the first and second comings of Christ. (1 CEU)

Revelation. A well-documented study that examines the close of history. Discusses many elements of the drama of the last days. (1 CEU)

Electives

The Good News. Provides a simple explanation of God's plan of salvation. Ideal for unsaved people, new believers or those who need assurance of salvation. (1 CEU)

The Life of David. Biographical study of one of the greatest heroes of the Old Testament. Includes maps and charts to trace the messianic

line from Adam to David to Christ. David's life teaches practical lessons on faith, repentance, and godliness. (1 CEU)

Christians in a Scientific World: Science Asks, God Answers. Bible-centered course on questions about science, archaeology, evolution, and creation. The issue about the Bible's inspiration is addressed. (1 CEU)

Jude. Reveals the definition, thought, and demeanor of an apostate. Indicates how Christians are to act toward apostates. (1 CEU)

Keys to Happy Family Living. Prepared by a Christian psychologist, the course teaches the keys to a Christ-centered personality, marriage, and parenting. Lessons include: unity, communication, the husband and wife's responsibilities and training in love. (1 CEU)

Proverbs. Offers wisdom for living. Students learn to apply biblical wisdom to everyday life situations. Topical studies include relationships with society, family, and God. (1 CEU)

Colossians. Exposes false doctrine, worldly teachings, and the pitfalls of man's philosophies. A relevant study for the twentieth-century church. (1 CEU)

James. Presents important lessons on resisting evil, enduring temptation and avoiding evil speech and gossip. A practical course on how our actions reflect our faith. (1 CEU)

Galatians. Focuses on the believers' freedom in Christ. Students learn the purpose of the law and understand elements of a life truly pleasing to God. (1 CEU)

A Holy Life and How to Live it. Provides biblical steps that lead to greater freedom from sin. Covers basic principles of moral action with emphasis on practical implications. (1 CEU)

Scofield Bible Course

Designed specifically for Sunday school teachers, Bible students, pastors, evangelists, and missionaries, this course offers a deeper knowledge and understanding of God's Word. More than 100,000 Christian workers and lay persons have enrolled in the Scofield Bible Course, choosing to learn in their own homes at their own pace. This is a non-college course.

Scofield Old Testament. Volume 1, Introduction; Volume 2, The Old Testament. (9 CEUs)

Scofield New Testament. Volume 3 and 4, The New Testament. (9 CEUs)

Scofield Bible Doctrine. Volume 5, Twenty-Six Great Words of Scripture; Volume 6, Doctrine of God, Man, Last Things. (9 CEUs)

Murray State University
Distance Learning/Correspondence Study
Center for Continuing Education and
Academic Outreach
305 Sparks Hall
P.O. Box 9, University Station
Murray, Kentucky 42071-0009 (502) 762-4159

Description:

Murray State University recognizes that educational needs cannot always be fully met with the regular schedule of classes. To serve these individuals, the Center for Continuing Education and Academic Outreach offers a variety of courses to nonresident students, enabling them to complete work for degrees, to acquire new skills, and to pursue special interests for professional and cultural enhancement.

Faculty:

Dr. Viola P. Miller, Dean, Continuing Education/Academic Outreach; John M. Yates, Director, Correspondence Study; Karen Mills, Secretary.

Academic Levels:

College

Degree/Certificate Programs:

Not more than 32 semester hours of the requirements for a baccalaureate degree from Murray State University may be earned by correspondence; 122 semester hours of correspondence study may be applied to the Bachelor of Independent Study degree.

Admission Requirements:

A student may enroll for a course any time during the calendar year. Each student desiring to earn credit by correspondence must assume full responsibility for registering for proper courses and should check carefully with the registrar of his/her college to determine if these courses will fulfill the requirement for the degree of certificate.

Tuition:

$70 per semester hour. Refunds for independent study courses are granted if requested within six weeks from the date of enrollment. The amount of refund is equal to three-fourths of the fee, less a fee for each lesson of work submitted. After six weeks of enrollment, no refund will be made.

Enrollment Period:

The minimum time within which one three-semester-hour course may be completed is five weeks; two three-semester-hour courses, ten weeks; one two-semester-hour course, four weeks; two two-semester-hour courses, eight weeks; one three-semester-hour course plus one two-semester-hour course, nine weeks. Maximum time to complete a course is one year from date of enrollment.

Equipment Requirements:

All texts and instructional materials are paid for by the student. Texts may be ordered through Murray State University Bookstore or purchased from local bookstores.

Credit and Grading:

A final examination is required at the completion of each course and must be taken within thirty days from the time the last lesson is completed. Examinations must be proctored. The proctor must make a signed statement to the Center for Continuing Education to the effect that the examination was taken under normal conditions and without the student's receiving assistance from any source. Grading system: A - Exceptionally high quality, valued at four points for each credit; B - Good, valued at three points for each credit; C - Fair, valued at two points for each credit; D - Barely satisfactory, valued at one point for each credit. The minimum passing grade is D.

Library Services:

A student should write directly to the Murray State University Library for books needed in a course requiring book reports or reference books. Students may use the University Library if he/she is on campus.

Accreditations:

Southern Association of Colleges and Schools. Member of: National University Continuing Education Association.

COLLEGE COURSES

AGRICULTURE

Animal Science

This is a basic course in animal science including the importance and place of livestock in agriculture; types, market classes, and grades of beef, sheep and swine; origin and characteristics of breeds; and the judging of beef, sheep, and swine. (3 semester hours)

Poultry Science

The fundamental principles and practical application of poultry science to general farm conditions and commercial production is studied. Breeding, incubation and brooding, selecting and culling, feeding, housing, and common disease prevention and control are emphasized. (3 semester hours)

Crop Science

A study of the fundamental principles underlying the production of agricultural crops. (3 semester hours)

BUSINESS

Business Law I

This course involves a presentation of the basic principles of law as they are applied to business. The areas studied include contracts, agency, and partnerships. (3 semester hours)

Business Law II

The areas of business law studied include corporations, property, sales, commercial paper, credit, and economic relations. (3 semester hours)

Records Management

A study of the principles and concepts of records management including creation (design, layout, and composition of technical documents with flowchart procedures) use, maintenance, and destruction. The course includes consideration of storage facilities, records classification, graphic analysis, forms and report control, protection of vital records, and micrographic systems. (3 semester hours)

ENGLISH

Composition

Instruction and practice in writing expository prose. (3 semester hours)

Composition and Research

A study of more advanced composition skills, with emphasis on techniques of research. (3 semester hours)

Appreciation for Literature

A course designed to develop a broad literary appreciation and understanding. This course provides for the study of various genres, including fiction, poetry, and drama. (3 semester hours)

Technical Writing for Industry and Technology

Theory of and practice in the writing of technical letters and reports for industry and technology students. (3 semester hours)

HEALTH

Personal Health

This course is designed to educate students about wellness through the acquisition of knowledge, attitudes, and behaviors. The major health-related problems of society are addressed, as well as an understanding of individual developmental patterns and health needs. Personal fitness is assessed and activities that promote lifelong fitness are practiced. A broad range of factors affecting wellness, including identification of risk and health promotion behaviors, is covered. Topics include, but are not limited to, substance use and abuse, nutrition, sexually transmitted diseases, health risk factors, mental and emotional health, exercise. (2 semester hours)

HISTORY

American Experience to 1865

A thematic approach to the history of the United States to 1865, designed as a general education social science elective. Three basic themes will be included: the transplantation of European and African cultures to America and their interaction with the cultures of native American Indians; the emergence of distinctive American values and institutions and the establishment of the American nation; and the stresses that culminated in the Civil War. (3 semester hours)

American Experience since 1865

A thematic approach to the history of the U.S. since 1865, designed as a general education social science elective. Students will examine three themes: the forces that transformed America from a predominantly rural, agricultural society to a predominantly urban, industrial one; the rising political consciousness of various American groups and the expanding regulatory role of the federal government; and the emergence of America as a world power. (3 semester hours)

INTERDISCIPLINARY STUDIES

World Civilizations I

An interdisciplinary survey of the origins of man; the emergence of civilized life; the evolution of and interaction among the environmental, social, economic, and political influences in the major civilizations of the world prior to 1500 A.D. (3 semester hours)

World Civilizations II

An interdisciplinary survey of the evolution of and interaction among the environmental, social, economic, and political influences in the major civilizations of the world since 1500, and a consideration of the causes and consequences of the emergence of a global civilization in the modern world. (3 semester hours)

MASS MEDIA

New Technologies

Rules and regulations at the federal, state, and local levels, plus the basics of systems planning, design, operation, and management. All the new technologies and delivery systems will be covered. (3 semester hours)

MATHEMATICS

College Algebra

Modern college algebra. (4 semester hours)

PHILOSOPHY

Logic

Studies of inductive and deductive forms of arguments and inferences. Also, examination of terms, propositions, truth-functions, quantificational logic, the language of logic, probability, Mill's methods, definitions, division, and classification. (3 semester hours)

PHYSICAL EDUCATION

Introduction to Recreation and Leisure Services

An introduction to the philosophy, history, and objectives of the recreation and leisure profession. (3 semester hours)

POLITICAL SCIENCE

American National Government

The American political system, its constitution, institutions, and processes. (3 semester hours)

State and Local Politics

Study of the three branches of state government coupled with an examination of the politics, organization, and functions of counties, townships, and special districts. (3 semester hours)

Introduction to International Relations

The nature of the international society and the forces affecting the behavior of states in their relations with one another. (3 semester hours)

Kentucky Government and Politics

A meaningful examination of the political processes and governmental machinery essential to an adequate understanding of government and politics in Kentucky. (3 semester hours)

PSYCHOLOGY

General Psychology

A basic survey course introducing the student to the methods, concepts, and terminology of the field. (3 semester hours)

Independent Study: Research Methods

Individual programs involving readings or conducting a research project in psychology. (3 semester hours)

SOCIOLOGY

The Family

A study of the family as a social institution. (3 semester hours)

Social Gerontology

A study of the development and group behavior of adults, and the causes and consequences of having older people in the population. (3 semester hours)

Nebraska, University of - Lincoln
Department of Distance Education
269 Nebraska Center for Continuing Education
33rd and Holdrege Streets
Lincoln, Nebraska 68583-9800 (402) 472-4321

Description:
The University of Nebraska Departments of Independent Study and Academic Telecommunications merged in 1993 to form the Department of Distance Education. The staff of the department can employ the delivery system that best meets a student's or client's need, whether it is via print-based independent duty, video, satellite, microwave, or face-to-face instruction. Instructors for courses are

appointed upon the recommendation of the participating department chairpersons.

Faculty:

Monty E. McMahon, Director; James E. Sherwood, Associate Director; James E. Schiefelbein, Assistant Director and Independent Study High School Principal; Marie A. Barber, Coordinator of Curriculum and Services.

Academic Levels:

College

High School

Noncredit

Degree/Certificate Programs:

The University of Nebraska - Lincoln offers an accredited diploma through the Independent Study High School. A college student may receive credit for from 25 to 60 credit hours of correspondence study toward a diploma at UNL, depending upon the degree sought.

Admission Requirements:

The College Program is open to anyone with a high school diploma or equivalent. For the High School Program, students under the age of 18 must have written permission from their local school administrator; students age 18 or over may enroll in the diploma program by submitting a transcript of previous high school courses or may take a GED test for evaluation. The University of Nebraska is a participating institution in the DANTES program. Members of the military forces should consult with their Education Officer regarding information about this program. High school students earn five credit hours or one-half Carnegie unit by successfully completing a one-semester course. Two and one-half credit hours or one-fourth Carnegie unit are awarded for successfully completing a one-half semester course. No credit or transcript will be forwarded if a financial balance due remains on the student's record.

Tuition:

College: $77.75 per undergraduate credit hour, $91 per graduate credit hour. High school: nonresident $83 per ½ unit, resident $79 per ½ unit. A handling fee of $18 per course enrollment is charged for shipment of course materials. MasterCard, Visa, and American Express cards are accepted. The College Program is eligible for Veteran's benefits. Refund policy: If students cancel an enrollment or drop a course, tuition will be refunded on receipt of a written request up to 60 days from the date of enrollment; $20 will be deducted for processing as well as $10 for each assignment or test evaluated. No refunds are given for handling fees or transportation charges.

Enrollment Period:

The maximum time allowed to complete a course is one year; the minimum time is five weeks. An extension of one year may be granted upon a written request and payment of a $50 extension fee for a college course or $35 for a high school course.

Equipment Requirements:

Textbooks are not included in the tuition fees and may be purchased from the Division of Continuing Education. Some courses require access to a cassette tape player.

Credit and Grading:

Any college level credit course may be taken on a noncredit basis. Examinations must be taken in the presence of an approved proctor (usually a local school official). The grading system for High School courses is A–F. The minimum passing grade varies depending up on the course. Credit is awarded in semester hour units.

Accreditations:

North Central Association of Colleges and Schools. Member of: National University Continuing Education Association.

COLLEGE COURSES

ACCOUNTING

Introductory Accounting

Course 201x. Develops fundamentals of accounting reporting and analysis that are helpful in understanding managerial and business concepts and practices, and provides a foundation for many advanced courses. (3 semester hours)

Course 202x. A continuation of the above course. (3 semester hours)

Managerial Accounting

Internal accounting as a tool to generate information for managerial planning and control. Conventional and computer problem materials are used to develop understanding of operating and capital budgets, standard costs, incremental concepts, relevant costs, transfer pricing, and responsibility and profit center reports as a means of analysis as well as techniques of measurement. (3 semester hours)

ART

Introduction to Art History and Criticism

A survey of history of art from the earliest times to the end of the Medieval period. (3 semester hours)

BIOLOGY

Principles of Ecology

A study of the structure and dynamics of populations and communities of organisms in relation to each other and to their environments. Emphasis on the concepts describing how populations of plants and animals grow and interact within communities. Includes an introduction to the quantitative description of ecological processes. Discussion of the application of ecological principles to natural resource management and environmental problems. (3 semester hours)

BROADCASTING

Broadcast Writing

Intensive training in writing style and techniques for news broadcasting. (3 semester hours)

Advanced Broadcast Writing

Techniques of planning, preparing, and writing radio, television, and motion picture scripts including announcements, interviews, talk programs, features, editorials, investigative reports, and dramatic adaptations. (3 semester hours)

CLASSICAL STUDIES

Scientific Greek and Latin

Study of scientific and technical terminology derived from Greek and Latin. (2 semester hours)

ECONOMICS

Principles of Macroeconomics

An introduction to the nature and methods of economics. Topics include economic systems, measurement and analysis of aggregate variables, such as national income, consumption, saving, investment, international payments, employment, price indices, money supply, and interest rates. Fiscal, monetary, and other policies for macroeconomic stabilization and growth are evaluated. (3 semester hours)

Principles of Microeconomics

Continuation of an introduction to economic methods with emphasis on analysis and evaluation of markets. Topics include demand, supply, elasticity, production costs, consumption utility, monopoly, competition, monopolistic competition, oligopoly, allocative and technical efficiency, and income distribution. The analysis is applied to resource markets, unions, antitrust laws, agriculture, international trade, and to other economic problems and policies. (3 semester hours)

Statistics

An introduction to the collection, analysis, and interpretation of statistical data used in economics and business. Topics include probability analysis, sampling, hypothesis testing, analysis of trends and seasonality, correlation, and simple regressions. (3 semester hours)

Elementary Quantitative Methods

An introduction to modern quantitative methods used in decision making in business and economics. Topics include linear models, simplex method, network and scheduling models, inventory models, decision theory, and others. (3 semester hours)

Principles of Insurance

The fundamentals of risk management and insurance including the nature and treatment of pure loss exposures, legal principles, property and liability insurance, life and health insurance, social insurance, and the functional and financial operation of insurance companies with emphasis on personal lines of insurances. (3 semester hours)

Introduction to International Economics

An intermediate survey of international trade and factor movements; balance of payments; commercial policy; economic integration; international monetary system and institutions; exchange rates; and open economy macroeconomics. (3 semester hours)

EDUCATION

Teaching Social Studies in the Elementary School

Emphasizes the role, content, materials, and trends of social studies in childhood education; selection and use of learning experiences; development of lesson plans and/or teaching unit. (3 semester hours)

EDUCATIONAL PSYCHOLOGY

Fundamentals of Psychology for Education

Fundamental concepts and principles of psychology with special reference to the development of human personality from infancy through childhood, adolescence, and later life. Major emphasis upon the biosocial forces that shape behavior. (3 semester hours)

Learning in the Classroom

The conditions (factors) essential to learning and its facilitation and transfer. Measurement of learning aptitude, achievement, and other aspects of human development. (3 semester hours)

ENGLISH

Composition I

Course for beginning students in the study and practice of composition, emphasizing the development of personal, professional, and academic writing in the context of local and regional issues. (3 semester hours)

Twentieth-Century Fiction

Selected readings in the novel and short story, mainly American, British, and European, from 1900 to the present. (3 semester hours)

Shakespeare

Introductory study of a representative sample of Shakespeare's works. (3 semester hours)

Composition

Course for intermediate students in the study and practice of composition. (3 semester hours)

Business Writing

Study and practice of written communication in situations typical of business, government, and other large organizations. (3 semester hours)

Special Topics in Writing

Course for intermediate students in the study and practice of composition. (2 semester hours)

FINANCE

Principles of Insurance

The fundamentals of risk management and insurance including the nature and treatment of pure loss exposures, legal principles, property and liability insurance, life and health insurance, social insurance, and the functional and financial operations of insurance companies with emphasis on personal lines of insurances. (3 semester hours)

Finance

Scope and content of the finance specialization; survey of the major theoretical issues; study of the financial instruments; analysis of the capital management problems; and development of criteria for financial decision making. (3 semester hours)

Real Estate Principles and Practice

The real estate market: ownership, interests, sales, leases and agencies, special financing institutions, financial aspects of ownership, managerial aspects of brokerage, property valuation and real estate appraising. (3 semester hours)

Real Estate Finance

Consideration of procedure, instruments, techniques, and trends in financing urban real property; an examination of realty credit markets and sources of funds (private and public); valuation of real property for lending and investment purposes; and measurement of investment performance. (3 semester hours)

GEOGRAPHY

Introductory Economic Geography

Basic factors influencing the location of economic activity. An examination of world and regional patterns in the context of differing environmental systems. (3 semester hours)

Introductory Human Geography

The study of human populations, cultures, and landscapes, with particular attention to human-environment relations and global interconnections. (3 semester hours)

Physical Geography

A systematic examination of the basic elements of the physical environment. The first portion of the course provides an introduction to the fields of climatology and meteorology through an examination of atmospheric processes. The second portion of the course examines landforms and the processes responsible for their creation. At appropriate points during the course, the modifying work of people within the natural environment will be reviewed. (3 semester hours)

Geography of the United States

An introduction to the regional geography of the United States. Attention to the significance of location, advantages and limitations of the natural environment, population distribution, and economic development considered regionally. (3 semester hours)

HEALTH

Elements of Health

Discusses the scientific foundation of personal health and the role of behavior in advancing individual levels of health. Stresses the principles of disease prevention in understanding the basic elements of accident prevention, substance abuse, nutrition, mental health, family planning, infection control, chronic disease prevention, sexually transmitted diseases, and organization of health services. (3 semester hours)

HISTORY

Western Civilization to 1715

This course will explore topically the essential ideas and practices that have shaped the development of the Western World from the Greeks and Romans to the Enlightenment. (3 semester hours)

Western Civilization since 1715

This course will analyze on a topical basis the impact of social, economic, political, and intellectual change upon Europe from the Enlightenment and will describe the dramatic rise of Europe to prominence in the world and the equally dramatic demise of European domination in the twentieth-century age of war and destruction. (3 semester hours)

Latin American Culture and Civilization

A topical and analytical survey of the development of Latin American culture and civilization. The themes to be discussed include race relations, war and peace, and the struggle for a better life. (3 semester credits)

Introduction to East Asian Civilization

A survey of the traditional cultures and modern history of China and Japan. Emphasis is on political systems, intellectual and religious history, and cultural developments. (3 semester credits)

American History to 1877

A survey of American history from the age of discovery through the Civil War. Emphasis on political, economic, and social problems in the growth of the American nation. (3 semester hours)

American History after 1877

Emphasis on the political, economic, and social problems accompanying America's rise as an industrialized world power. (3 semester hours)

History of the Middle Ages

The transition from ancient to Medieval civilization; the so-called Dark Ages; the late Medieval Renaissance and the dawn of the modern era. (3 semester hours)

History of Early Modern Europe: Renaissance to the French Revolution

The beginning of the modern era, with much attention to the secularization of European society from the Renaissance through the Age of Enlightenment. (3 semester hours)

Nebraska History

Survey of the political, economic, and social development of Nebraska from the earliest explorations to the present. (3 semester hours)

HUMAN DEVELOPMENT AND THE FAMILY

Human Development and the Family

A developmental life cycle approach to the study of the individual from conception to death, Each stage of life is studied from the perspective of how individual development is fostered within the family system. (3 semester hours)

INDUSTRIAL ENGINEERING

Engineering Economy I

An introduction to economic comparisons of engineering alternatives. Concepts of time, value of money, methods of evaluating alternatives, depreciation, and taxes. (3 semester hours)

MANAGEMENT

Elementary Quantitative Methods

An introduction to modern quantitative methods used in decision making in business and economics. Topics include linear models, simplex method, network and scheduling models, inventory models, decision theory, and others. (3 semester hours)

Operations and Resources Management

A study of analytical management techniques for: (1) ascertaining demand for the organization's goods and services; (2) justifying and acquiring the necessary resources; and (3) planning and controlling the transformation of resources into goods and services. Course discussion includes application in both large and small organizations, private and public enterprise, and service as well as manufacturing organizations. (3 semester hours)

Personnel Administration

A study of personnel administration as an integral part of all activities and functions of an organization. Emphasis is on the principles of personnel administration: the environmental factors that influence personnel policies and practices and the organizational practices relating to the procurement, development, maintenance, and utilization of a work force. (3 semester hours)

Administrative Policy

Formulation and application of management policy; involves analysis and simulation of cases in which students use knowledge acquired in such basic courses as marketing, accounting, finance, personnel and economics. The course demonstrates the complexity of business problems and the interrelationships of business functions. (3 semester hours)

International Management

This course is taught from the perspective of American enterprises operating in foreign nations. The manner in which cultural, economic, political, and social differences affect the management of business, governmental, military, and other enterprises is considered. Stress is given to the problems in managing in Latin America, Europe, and the Far East. (3 semester hours)

MARKETING

Marketing

Examination of the marketing system, its relations with the socioeconomic system, and the influences of each upon the other. Study of the evolution and present structure of marketing institutions and processes. Consideration of customer attributes and behavioral characteristics, and how a marketing manager responds to these in the design of marketing strategies, using research, product development, pricing, distribution structure, and promotion. (3 semester hours)

MATHEMATICS

Intermediate Algebra

Course 95x. A review of the topics in a second-year high school algebra course taught at the college level. Topics include: real numbers, 1st and 2nd degree equations and inequalities, linear systems, polynomials and rational functions, exponents and radicals, functions and relations, exponentials and logarithms. (Noncredit)

Course 100x. A review of the topics in a second-year high school algebra course taught at the college level. Topics include: real numbers, 1st and 2nd degree equations and inequalities, linear systems, polynomials and rational functions, exponents and radicals, functions and relations, exponentials and logarithms. There is a heavy emphasis on problem-solving strategies and techniques throughout the course. (3 semester hours)

College Algebra

Real and complex numbers, exponents, factoring, linear and quadratic equations, absolute value, inequalities, functions, graphing, polynomial and rational functions, exponential and logarithmic functions, analytic geometry, systems of equations. (3 semester hours)

Trigonometry

Trigonmetric functions, identities, trigonometric equations, solution of triangles, inverse trigonometric functions, graphs, logarithms, and exponential functions. (2 semester hours)

Calculus for Managerial and Social Sciences

Rudiments of differential and integral calculus with applications to problems from business, economics, and social sciences. (3 semester hours)

Analytic Geometry and Calculus I

Functions of one variable, limits, differentiation, related rates, maximum-minimum, and basic integration theory with some applications. (5 semester hours)

Analytic Geometry and Calculus II

Exponential, trigonometric and inverse trigonometric functions; techniques of integration; indeterminate forms; improper integrals; sequences; infinite series; polar coordinates, and vectors. (5 semester hours)

NUTRITION

Introduction to Nutrition

A survey of the science of human nutrition and relationships between nutrition and health of individuals and groups throughout life and in special nutritional problems. (3 semester hours)

PHILOSOPHY

Introduction to Logic and Critical Thinking

An introduction to the principles of correct reasoning and their application. The emphasis is on improving the skills of thinking and reading critically, analyzing and evaluating arguments objectively, and constructing sound arguments based on relevant evidence. (3 semester hours)

Introduction to Modern Logic

An examination of the methods of deductive thinking, with applications to deductive inferences in science and everyday life. Emphasis on the applications of logic in other areas such as mathematics and morality. (3 semester hours)

Philosophy of Religion

An introduction to the philosophical understanding of religion. Topics include a number of views on the nature of God, on the possibility of God's existence through either argumentation or religious experience, and on the relation between religion and morality. (3 semester hours)

PHYSICS

Elementary General Physics

Course 141x. Mechanics, heat waves, and sound. Students must complete the laboratory experiments to earn five hours of credit. (4 semester hours)

Course 142x. Electricity, magnetism, optics, relativity, atomic and nuclear physics. Students must complete the laboratory experiments to earn five hours of credit. (4 semester hours)

General Physics

Course 211x. A calculus-based course intended for students in engineering and the physical sciences. Mechanics, fluids, wave motion, and heat. (4 semester hours)

Course 212x. A continuation of *Course 211x.* Electricity, magnetism, and optics. (4 semester hours)

POLITICAL SCIENCE

American Government

A survey of the organization and working of national government in the United States. (3 semester hours)

Contemporary Foreign Governments and Their Problems

A description and analysis of the principal types of modern political systems, including types of democracies and dictatorships found in Western systems, Eastern systems, and the Third World. Occasional comparison will be made with American institutions and political processes. The course will deal both with structures and major policy problems confronting these political systems: the politics of education, human rights, demands for regional autonomy, ethnic conflict and diversity, political violence, demand for welfare services, crises in agriculture, and other topics of relevance. (3 semester hours)

Introduction to Public Administration

A study of the administrative aspect of government, concentrating on approaches to the study of public administration, aspects of public organization and structure, and administrative powers and responsibility. (3 semester hours)

Political Parties and Election Campaigns

A review of the relationships among political parties, interest groups, and public relations firms in the electoral process. Emphasis will be given to proposals to reform the election system and to stimulate effective citizen involvement. (3 semester hours)

PSYCHOLOGY

Introduction to Psychology

Introduction to concepts and research in the areas of personality, attitudes, emotion, learning, memory, perception, and physiological bases of behavior. (4 semester hours)

Psychosocial Aspects of Alcoholism

Historical, social-psychological, and physiological aspects of alcohol use and abuse. Examines alcoholism definitions and typologies. Discusses theoretical approaches to the development of this disorder including constitutional, psychological, and sociological conceptualizations. Treatment, prevention, and intervention procedures used to cope with the problem of alcoholism. (3 semester hours)

REAL ESTATE

Real Estate Management

Managing residential, cooperative, office, commercial, shopping, special purpose properties; merchandising space, tenant selection and relations; maintenance; owner relations. (3 semester hours)

Real Estate Principles and Practice

The real estate market; ownership, interests, sales, leases and agencies, special financing institutions, financial aspects of ownership, managerial aspects of brokerage, property valuation and real estate appraising. (3 semester hours)

Real Estate Investments

Coursework devoted to a better understanding of the analytical tools available for real estate investment analysis and decision making to include application of investment principles to various types of properties (apartments, office buildings, and other commercial property). (3 semester hours)

Fundamentals of Real Estate Appraisal

Fundamentals of real property valuation techniques, methods, and approaches, including factors affecting value; principles of real property valuation; characteristics and functions of real estate markets; steps in the valuation process; locational analysis; land valuation methods; types and methods of estimating depreciation and obsolescence; sales comparison analysis; gross rent multiplier and income capitalization analysis; statistical tools and their applications to appraisal analysis; valuation of special classes of residential property; four case study student responses with emphasis on single-family appraising are required. (3 semester hours)

Real Estate Finance

Consideration of procedure, instruments, techniques, and trends in financing urban real property; an examination of realty credit markets and sources of funds (private and public); valuation of real property for lending and investment purposes; and measurement of investment performance. (3 semester hours)

SOCIOLOGY

Introduction to Sociology

An introduction to the sociological study of human behavior, especially social organization, culture, and the social institutions that comprise society. Attention also will be given to social change, differentiation and inequality, and other social issues. (3 semester hours)

Social Problems

Treatment of the principal "problem" areas in contemporary society. Analysis of processes of disorganization in society, with some attention to contrasting processes by which social structures are formed and perpetuated. (3 semester hours)

Sociology of Crime

An introduction to the sociological approach to the study of crime, including the definition of crime, approaches to its measurement, and the major theories of crime. The course also covers the social institutions intended to prevent or correct criminal behavior. (3 semester hours)

Marriage and the Family

Historic marriage and family patterns. The American family, past and present. The husband-wife relationships. The parent-child relationships. The family-society relationships. (3 semester hours)

HIGH SCHOOL COURSES

AGRICULTURE

General Agriculture 1

Students are introduced to the agricultural industry. They study life in rural communities; caring for the farmstead; farm production resources, and livestock management. (½ unit)

General Agriculture 2

Students learn about producing farm crops and managing the farm business. Students also examine agriculture cooperatives, the changing rural scene, and careers in agriculture. (½ unit)

Horticulture, Lawn and Plant Care

In this course, students learn how to plant and maintain a bluegrass lawn. They also learn how to prune flowering shrubs, evergreens, and shade trees. (½ unit)

Horticulture, Landscaping

Students learn how to plan a landscape for a home and how to plant and care for annual flowers and vegetables. They select and maintain equipment for landscaping and gardening. (½ unit)

ART

General Art

Students learn the basic tools, terms, and techniques used in art. They study and then practice the use of lines, shape, texture, and pattern. The focus of this course is on developing well-designed compositions and on enhancing students' powers of observation and their ability to use basic elements of art and design. (½ unit)

Drawing and Composition

This course is an introduction to techniques for drawing, emphasizing compositional design and creative expression. Students learn the premises of self-critique and evaluation and apply them to further learning experiences. (½ unit)

Advanced Drawing

The emphasis of this course is the student's production of finished drawings stressing creativity, individuality, aesthetics, and skills for self-critiques. Students are encouraged to experience various drawing techniques and begin to develop their own individual style. (½ unit)

Watercolor Studies

Specific projects and problem-solving exercises are developed by the instructor based on the student's needs, knowledge, and experience. Students experiment with a variety of watercolor approaches and techniques. Principles and techniques for matting and framing watercolors will be presented. This course stresses the development of well-designed compositions, creativity, individuality, aesthetics, and skills for effective self-critiques. (½ unit)

Acrylic Painting

This course addresses various techniques that may be used in acrylic painting with an emphasis on creativity and individual expression while stressing the development of well-designed compositions, as well developing skills for effective self-critiques. Students will submit paintings on primed canvas sheets; the method for stretching canvas and basic principles and techniques for framing paintings are presented. (½ unit)

BUSINESS

Learning to Type with One Hand

This beginning course in typing is designed for students who have no formal typing experience and who need to type with either the right or left hand. Students practice the fundamentals of touch typing to develop moderate speed and accuracy. The course includes problems in typing that apply to personal, school, and office tasks. (½ unit)

Beginning Typing 1

Students develop basic typing skills for personal use at home, in school, and at work. After learning to control the keyboard by touch, students practice formatting techniques as they type reports, letters, tables, and other documents. In a reinforcing sequence of language arts exercises, students apply rules for correct word division, capitalization, punctuation, and number style. They also learn to detect, mark, and correct errors in typewritten copy. Balanced drills provide the practice necessary for typing with moderate speed and accuracy. (½ unit)

Beginning Typing 2

In this second-semester typing course, students focus on business formatting while improving their keyboarding skills. They prepare reports, letters, tables, and business forms in the correct format from a variety of input modes. At the same time they practice the correct use of punctuation, capitalization, and numbers in typewritten communication; proofread copy for errors; and edit copy for revision. Keyboarding speed and accuracy are emphasized. In the last unit, students learn how to compose and type the documents they are likely to need when applying for a job. (½ unit)

Advanced Typing 1

In the second year of typing, students continue to improve keyboarding speed and accuracy and to develop production skills. They are introduced to advanced formatting procedures for typing special kinds of business communications. Language arts exercises emphasize the correct use of colons, hyphens, dashes, abbreviations, and plural forms. A series of simulated "in-basket" projects at the end of the course provides experience in establishing priorities and making formatting decisions to complete a related set of typing jobs in a typical office situation. (½ unit)

Advanced Typing 2

Students prepare for the keyboarding and formatting tasks they will encounter in various work settings while increasing their efficiency in establishing priorities, arranging and editing copy, and choosing appropriate formats. Exercises focus on accurate spelling, subject-verb agreement, contractions, and possessive terms. (½ unit)

Business English and Communication

Students need to have a knowledge of basic grammar to be successful in this course. They focus on the common language skills necessary to good expression in such business communications as letters, memos, and reports. Coherent writing, sentence structure, and vocabulary building are stressed. (½ unit)

Office Systems

Students will become familiar with the processes involved in dealing with filing and office machine systems; incoming and outgoing funds and bank statements; sales and accounts payable, inventory control and report, and payroll systems. (½ unit)

Beginning Shorthand 1

The fundamentals of Gregg shorthand and dictation are presented. Students transcribe shorthand exercises to cassette tapes and take dictation at graduated speeds from cassette tapes. Upon completion of this course, they should be able to read shorthand and take dictation with moderate speed and accuracy. (½ unit)

Beginning Shorthand 2

Students strengthen their knowledge of Gregg shorthand, increase their speed in taking dictation, and become more accurate in transcribing it. In addition, they learn about the duties assigned to and performed by secretaries. After completing this course, students should be able to take dictation consisting of elementary business correspondence with speed and accuracy. They also should be able to transcribe the dictation into appropriate formats. (½ unit)

Consumer Education

Students learn about their rights and responsibilities as consumers. They discover how personal goals and values affect their choices; how they can develop reliable decision-making skills for spending, saving, and investing; how they can evaluate alternatives in the marketplace; and how they can get the most for a given expenditure of resources. Specific lessons on personal finance include earning money, spending and saving money, working with money, and getting and using credit. (½ unit)

Introduction to Business

This course gives an overview of business in America. Students learn about the place of business in society, the relationship of business and government in our economic system, the place of banks and credit in the economy, personal money management, consumer rights and responsibilities, and the use of credit. (½ unit)

Beginning Accounting 1

Studies in accounting terminology, concepts, principles, and practices give students a solid foundation both for a career and for financial success. After becoming acquainted with the various applications, they reinforce their understanding of accounting procedures by working through realistic accounting cycles for a proprietorship and for a partnership. (½ unit)

Beginning Accounting 2

Students learn that effective business decisions can be made only when their information is current, accurate, and complete. They apply their knowledge of business decision-making processes while studying the accounting system of a corporation that uses special journals. The final section emphasizes the functions of accounting control systems. (½ unit)

Economics

Students gain an understanding of basic economic concepts by examining historical and current examples of economic principles at work. They study the role and workings of the market in modern capitalistic economies and analyze how government controls the market in response to the will of society. Finally, other economic systems are compared to the market systems in free societies. (½ unit)

Business Law

Students are introduced to basic concepts of business law in the United States. They study contracts, civil law, criminal law, the court system, personal property and bailments, commercial paper, employment, credit agreements, and insurance. Students gain an understanding of legal rights and responsibilities in business dealings. (½ unit)

Personal Finance

Students taking this course discover some of the basic principles involved in financial planning and financial decision making. Students receive a firm foundation in economic practice as they study about interest, insurance, and bank accounts. In this course, students follow a programmed approach to financial planning. They put into practice what they have learned about decision making and good economic practices as they develop their own financial plan. (½ unit)

CAREER PLANNING

Career Planning

As students follow the pathway of self-discovery, they become aware of their potential for entering various fields of work. They are helped to weigh their own interests, values, aptitudes, and abilities against the characteristics required of people who perform various jobs. This course is designed to increase students' awareness of career development issues and to familiarize students with resources that can help them reach their career goals. They learn what steps they should take in planning their future careers and how to apply self-assessment skills in a lifelong process of achieving career satisfaction. (½ unit)

COMPUTER SCIENCE

Computer BASICs

This covers the development, uses, and components of computers. Students learn the vocabulary and syntax of the BASIC language and write simple programs in BASIC. (½ unit)—

DRIVER EDUCATION

Driver Education

Students focus on becoming responsible drivers, learn basic decision-making steps, and study the importance of driving defensively. This course meets the 30 hours of classroom instruction required for a student discount by most insurance companies and for student licensing by most states. Students also need six hours of actual driving instruction. (½ unit)

ENGLISH

Basic Grammar

Students learn the terminology and structure of the English language in an easy-to-understand, step-by-step fashion. Parts of speech, sentence structure, choice and use of words, capitalization, and punctuation are covered. (½ unit)

Intermediate Grammar

This course challenges students with an in-depth study of grammar. Students review parts of speech and usage, sentence patterns, basic punctuation, and capitalization. They study clauses, phrases, and sentence problems; and complex pronoun, verb, and adverb forms. (½ unit)

Effective Reader Skills

The intent of this course is to help students become more effective readers by emphasizing strategies that help them improve their basic language and literacy skills. They study about central themes, main ideas, major and minor details, inferences, fact and opinion, context clues, and vocabulary. (½ unit)

General Literature 1

This course fosters in students the desire to read and the ability to express their ideas about what they read. Students read various books. The themes of the books appeal to the interests and concerns of teenagers. The reading material is not difficult, but the books do have literary merit. (½ unit)

General Literature 2

This course is similar to *General Literature 1*. Students read various books. The required books are somewhat more difficult and should be considered junior- and senior-level reading. (½ unit)

Multicultural Literature

This course fosters in students the desire to read and the ability to express their ideas about what they read. Students read short stories and novels (including sport, detective, and science fiction) that introduce multicultural themes of interest to teenagers. The reading material is not difficult but does have literary merit, and ranges from freshman through junior level. (½ unit)

The Short Story

The form of the short story is the central concern of this course. As students read the assigned stories, they will study such aspects of form as plot, character, and theme. (½ unit)

The American Short Story

Students become familiar with the basic literary elements of short stories and with techniques for analyzing short stories. They learn about the development of the American short story during the past 150 years by analyzing stories that exemplify the characteristics of the Romantic, Realistic, Naturalistic, and Modern periods. The stories in this course are more difficult than those in *The Short Story* course. (½ unit)

Basic Expository Writing

This course presents the basics of expository writing. Students practice a step-by-step process in learning to write unified, coherent papers. In the process of learning to write, students learn to think in an organized, systematic fashion. They also study effective uses of language, as well as methods of connecting ideas and expanding ideas by means of details and examples. (½ unit)

Writing Research Papers

Because the search for information is a lifelong activity that cuts across many disciplines, the primary emphasis in this course is on the variety of techniques that can be used to find information. Students also explore the wide range of sources of information, alternate ways of presenting the results of their search for information, and at least two of the many possible formats for documenting resources. (½ unit)

Ninth Grade English 1

This course introduces three aspects of language arts: literature, grammar, and composition. In the literature segments of the course, students read short stories, poetry, drama, and selections from the *Odyssey*. The emphasis is on enjoying and understanding various types of literature.In the grammar and composition lessons, students deal with parts of speech, characteristics of sentences, and paragraph development. (½ unit)

Ninth Grade English 2

Students review basic approaches to literature and fundamentals of grammar and composition before learning new information about these elements. In the literature lessons, students read short stories, essays, biographies, *Romeo and Juliet*, and selections from *Great Expectations*. In the grammar and composition lessons, students concentrate on punctuation; on the structures and purposes of sentences, and on developing specificity and coherence in paragraphs. (½ unit)

Tenth Grade English 1

Students continue to develop their skills in the three aspects of language arts. In the literature segments of the course, students read short stories, poetry, drama, and tales of King Arthur and his Knights of the Round Table. In the grammar and composition lessons, students study the parts of speech, basic parts and characteristics of sentences, capitalization and punctuation, and the step-by-step development of a paper. (½ unit)

Tenth Grade English 2

Students review before learning new information about the fundamentals of grammar and composition and the study of literature. In the literature lessons, students read short stories, essays, and biographies, *Julius Caesar*, and John Steinbeck's *The Pearl*. In the grammar and composition lessons, students concentrate on the patterns, structures, kinds, and purposes of sentences; on additional ways to punctuate sentences; and on developing polished papers. (½ unit)

Eleventh Grade English 1

The historical development of American literature from the colonial period to 1900 is the central theme of this course. Students gain an understanding of the ideas that fostered the growth of the United States and of the ways in which its literature became distinctively American. Students develop composition skills not only through analysis of the literary selections but also through application of the basic organizational pattern of a good essay. (½ unit)

Eleventh Grade English 2

In this course, student study the development of 20th-century American literature from 1900 to the present, noting both the ways literary forms have changed and the ways literature reflects the period in which it is written. Instruction in grammar and composition with emphasis on writing, punctuating, and revising sentences and on writing and polishing expository essays is provided. (½ unit)

Twelfth Grade English 1

Students read many of the great works from the Anglo-Saxon period through the 18th century. They gain an understanding of the development of English literature as they study Shakespeare's *Macbeth* and selections from *Beowulf, The Canterbury Tales,* and *Paradise Lost.* Students work on improving their writing skills by preparing papers that analyze the literary works. (½ unit)

Twelfth Grade English 2

In this course, students further their understanding of the historical development of English literature as they read selections by major authors of the Romantic Age, the Victorian Age, and the twentieth century. They apply and improve their writing skills as they analyze the many facets of the literary selections they read. (½ unit)

FRENCH

French 1

Students are introduced to the basic grammatical concepts necessary to develop reading and writing skills in French. They become acquainted with French culture through a variety of readings in both French and English. Students also have the opportunity to develop speaking and listening skills as they hear French and speak it themselves. This course covers the basic sentence structure of positive and negative statements, commands and questions, and the present and future tenses. (½ unit)

French 2

This course reinforces and augments the grammatical concepts presented in *French 1*. Students build new vocabulary, learn more advanced grammar concepts, increase their reading comprehension skills, and develop their knowledge of several essential parts of speech and a number of commonly used French idioms and expressions. (½ unit)

French 3

In this course, students look at the United States from the French perspective and take an imaginary tour of Paris. After reviewing the grammar and rules presented in *French 1* and *French 2*, students study indirect objects; emphatic, interrogative, and reflexive pronouns; and

verbs in the reflexive voice, the imperfect tense, and the conditional mood. (½ unit)

French 4

Students are introduced to famous people and events and study the broad social, economic, and political forces that shaped French culture. Students study the *subjonctif* and are introduced to the *passé simple*. They also increase their awareness of the subtleties of the language as they learn specific strategies and helpful techniques for reading and listening. (½ unit)

GERMAN

German 1

The reading selections are designed to familiarize students with German as it is written and spoken. New words and grammatical constructions are introduced gradually in the readings and are explained with straightforward definitions and examples. Students study nouns, articles, personal pronouns, possessive adjectives, and prepositions; uses of nominative, accusative, genitive, and dative cases; agreement; and positions of direct and indirect objects. The analysis of verbs is confined to the present tense forms of regular, irregular, and reflexive verbs. Students also study normal and inverted word order in sentences, learn to connect independent clauses with coordinating conjunctions, and become familiar with rules of spelling, capitalization, and punctuation. (½ unit)

German 2

Students learn about the legends, customs, and daily lives of the German people. Idiomatic expressions receive considerable attention in the course, while periodic reviews reinforce points that students may have forgotten. Among the topics emphasized are plurals of nouns and articles in the genitive and dative cases; declension of nouns and articles; uses of *der-* and *ein-* words; "doubtful" prepositions; and uses of *da-* and *wo-* compounds. The forms and uses of the past, perfect, past perfect, and future tenses of regular, irregular, and reflexive verbs in the active voice also are introduced. (½ unit)

German 3

The reading selections included in this course help students develop an understanding of German culture and its contributions to Western civilization. A concise review of the principles presented in the previous two German course lays the foundation for more advanced study of German grammar and sentence structure. Students consider expressions of time; declension of adjectives; degrees of adjectives and adverbs; past tense of modal auxiliaries; modal auxiliaries with dependent infinitives; principal parts of separable, inseparable, and mixed verbs; and intransitive verbs with dative objects. (½ unit)

German 4

In this course, students not only further their appreciation of German history and culture but also practice and extend their skills in reading, writing, and speaking German. Because mastery of verbs is essential to mastery of the German language, much of the grammar pertains directly or indirectly to the forms and uses of verbs, infinitives, and modal auxiliaries. By the end of this course, students should have a German vocabulary of approximately 1,300 words, know the meaning of approximately 150 idioms, and have a firm grasp of German sentence structure. (½ unit)

HOME ECONOMICS

Social Protocol: Family and Personal Etiquette

Students receive information and guidelines on the behavior and manners appropriate in a variety of situations. (½ unit)

Career Protocol: Business and International Etiquette

Students receive information and guidelines on the behavior and manners appropriate in a variety of business situations, when meeting or hosting international visitors, or when traveling to other countries. (½ unit)

General Homemaking: Home Management

Students are introduced to the basic principles of personal development and home management. These concepts are reinforced through practical experience. Students develop skills in home and family living through units on family, child development, and personality development. (½ unit)

General Homemaking: Clothing and Foods

Clothing and foods receive equal emphasis in the this course. After studying principles of clothing design, selection, and care, students complete a simple sewing project. The units on foods help students plan and prepare simple recipes. Students will prepare and serve a complete meal. (½ unit)

Personal Adjustment and Family Living

In this course, students develop the ability to understand and solve everyday problems common to them, their parents, and others. Students deal with dating, courtship, and marriage issues and analyze the development of healthy interpersonal relationships. (½ unit)

Introduction to Nutrition

Students are introduced to the fundamental ideas of personal nutrition. The focus of the course is on individual dietary management. Special emphasis is placed on the changing nutritional needs of individuals throughout the life cycle. After successfully completing this course, students will be able to make informed dietary choices. Among the topics discussed are digestion, weight control, and the function of nutrients. (½ unit)

Introduction to Interior Design

In this challenging course, students learn the basics of interior design and decorating. They discover the elements that help create an attractive and functional living space and learn the proper use of color, texture, pattern, and shape in designing and organizing living areas. Students put the skills they learn into practice through a series of design projects. (½ unit)

INDUSTRIAL EDUCATION

General Shop 1

Students learn about operations performed by woodworkers and metalworkers. This course is useful even for students who do not plan a career in these fields. Access to a workshop is important. Students are encouraged to perform the operations described in the course. (½ unit)

General Shop 2

In this course, students are introduced to the skilled crafts. They are presented with general information about graphic arts, plastics, leathers, electricity, power mechanics, and home maintenance. (½ unit)

Small Engine Care and Operation

Students are introduced to two- and four-cycle engines—the gasoline-powered, single-cylinder machines that power lawn mowers, chain saws, and motorcycles. They learn to care for and safely operate these engines. Access to common shop tools and a small engine is recommended. (½ unit)

Small Engine Maintenance and Repair

Students learn to maintain and repair gasoline-powered, single-cylinder machines. Instructions for maintaining specific models are included. Access to common shop tools, used parts, and small engines is recommended. (½ unit)

Automotive Mechanics

Students learn about the operation and repair of the automobile engine. They study in detail the procedures and tools used to overhaul an engine. Safety is stressed throughout this course. (½ unit)

LATIN

Latin 1

The Latin readings for this introductory course, adapted from ancient history and mythology, deal with the Trojan War and Aeneas' journey to Italy. Students work intensively on nouns, adjectives, and verbs; study first, second, and third declension nouns in all cases; and learn to form the six tenses of Latin verbs in the active voice for all four conjugations. (½ unit)

Latin 2

The readings for this course are based on the founding of Rome and its early history as a monarchy and then a republic. The grammar includes pronouns, passive voice of verbs, infinitives, adverbial expressions, participles, deponent verbs, and indirect statement. Students are provided with numerous opportunities to practice individual grammar concepts and to use their developing vocabulary skills. By the end of this course, students will have a firm grasp of basic Latin grammar and an extensive Latin vocabulary. (½ unit)

Latin 3

The Latin readings for this course are adaptations of the historian Livy's account of Hannibal's exploits during the Second Punic War. Considerable attention is given to verbs in the subjunctive mood. In addition, students become familiar with tense sequences and the construction of dependent clauses. (½ unit)

Latin 4

Selections from Caesar's *Gallic Wars* that are appropriate to students' growth and depth in the language are presented. Students also read selections from Suetonius and Apuleius, and they identify the characteristic and unusual aspects of syntax and grammar found in these readings. (½ unit)

MATHEMATICS

Basic Mathematics 1

This course is specifically designed for students who need to develop understanding and skill in using basic arithmetic. After studying each of the four basic operations—addition, subtraction, multiplication, and division of whole numbers—students learn to solve word problems involving that operation. Interpretation of word problems is covered thoroughly and understandably. Topics such as estimating, rounding, and factoring are introduced to provide a foundation for further study in the second semester of basic mathematics. (½ unit)

Basic Mathematics 2

After reviewing operations with whole numbers, students are introduced to the meaning of fractions and operations with fractions, operations with decimals, and problems involving money and percentages. Word problems are used extensively to relate these concepts to practical situations. Topics covered in the first semester of basic mathematics are thoroughly reviewed before further expansion and clarification. Students practice each concept in a step-by-step manner before moving on to more complex topics. (½ unit)

General Mathematics 1

Students develop an understanding of fractions, decimals, and percentages, as well as developing skill in using these mathematical operations. They learn to handle data through graphs, scientific notation, and means of comparison; and they apply their understanding of concepts, operations, and data analysis to practical problems dealing with interest, insurance, taxes, banking, and budgeting. (½ unit)

General Mathematics 2

Students extend their use and understanding of basic mathematics. They study positive and negative numbers, square roots, formulas, the Cartesian coordinate system, simple equations, and sets, the metric system, measurement, area, and volume, and begin to use a ruler and compass. (½ unit)

Business and Consumer Mathematics 1

Students develop arithmetic skills that apply to common business activities, operations, and transactions. The topics include whole numbers, fractions, decimals, percentages, ratios, proportions, basic statistics, graphs, discounts, merchandising, bank services, and interest. (½ unit)

Business and Consumer Mathematics 2

In this course, students study installment financing, charge accounts, taxes, automobile ownership, budgeting, stocks, bonds, home financing, and homeowner's insurance. (½ unit)

Beginning Algebra 1

Students become acquainted with basic algebraic concepts, such as integers, linear equations, linear inequalities, factoring, and fractions. (½ unit)

Beginning Algebra 2

In this course, students receive instruction in linear sentences, algebra in a plane, linear systems, functions, fractional equations, real numbers, equations with real solutions, and plane trigonometry. (½ unit)

Geometry 1

Students develop reasoning skills using geometric terms and processes, concepts of logic, and applied problem solving. Topics include parallel lines and planes, congruent triangles, inequalities, and quadrilaterals. Geometric concepts are analyzed using formal, paragraph, and indirect proofs. The lab kit contains compass, protractor, ruler, graph paper, and manipulative materials needed to do laboratory activities in the course. (½ unit)

Geometry 2

Students continue developing their reasoning skills while studying similarity, areas and volumes, right triangles, circles, coordinate geometry, and transformations. Current mathematical standards involving problem solving, communication, reasoning, and connections are carefully followed in this course. The lab kit contains compass, protractor, ruler, graph paper, and manipulative materials needed to do laboratory activities in the course. (½ unit)

Advanced Algebra 1

Such concepts as integers, polynomials, factoring, rational expressions, real numbers, equations, and inequalities are presented and related to practical problems encountered in daily living. (½ unit)

Advanced Algebra 2

Students complete an in-depth study of logarithms and trigonometry. Included is the study of conic sections, progressions and series, trigonometric functions, graphing, and problem solving. Students receive a good foundation for the future study of mathematics, chemistry, physics, or engineering. (½ unit)

Precalculus 1: Analytic Geometry and Algebra

Analytic geometry and advanced topics in algebra are presented in this course. Students study functions, including algebraic, logarithmic, exponential, and matrix functions. Drawings and graphs are presented to clarify essential mathematical principles. (½ unit)

Precalculus 2: Trigonometry

Students are presented with a thorough treatment of trigonometric concepts and applications. They study proofs of trigonometric identities, solutions or right and oblique triangles, solutions of trigonometric equations, logarithms, vector applications, and complex numbers. (½ unit)

MUSIC

Beginning Piano 1

Students learn to read music and to play simple selections in the keys of C and G major. They develop their skills through study of the keyboard, basic terminology, musical notation, scales, rhythm, and simple transposition. As a concluding project, students present a recital for their family. (½ unit)

Beginning Piano 2

Students learn to play scales, arpeggios, chords, cadences, and simple selections in the keys of C, G, D, A, and E major. Their skill development continues as they study terminology, rhythm, and transposition. As a final project, students arrange and present a recital for friends and family. (½ unit)

Intermediate Piano 1

Students build on their ability to read and play simple compositions in major keys. They improve their piano technique and extend their musical knowledge through study of terminology, major scales, triads, and their inversions, rhythm, tempo, transposition, and pedal effects. Students also present a recital. Students use the recorded audiocassette tape for ear-training exercises. (½ unit)

Intermediate Piano 2

Students continue to develop their skills through study of terminology, major and minor scales, rhythm, transposition, accompaniment, and ensemble playing. They are exposed to different periods of music (including the twentieth century), a variety of composers, and various styles of music. As a final project, students arrange and present a recital for friends and family. Students use the recorded audiocassette tape for ear-training exercises. (½ unit)

Advanced Piano Performance 1

There is no syllabus for this course; instead the student receives a project guide that includes background information for some projects and directions for working with the ISHS music teacher. The instructor designs the projects to fit the needs of each student, concentrating on technique and interpretation of a wide variety of piano literature. The final project is a public recital. (½ unit)

Advanced Piano Performance 2

There is no syllabus for this course; instead the student receives a project guide that includes background information for some projects and directions for working with the ISHS music teacher. The instructor designs the projects to fit the needs of each student, with emphasis given to solo, accompaniment, and ensemble performance. Arranging and presenting a public recital is the culminating project. (½ unit)

Music Theory

Through study of the elements of music theory, students increase their understanding and enjoyment of music. They study musical notation, major and minor scales and key signatures, intervals, triads, rhythm, and fundamental terminology. (½ unit)

Harmony

Advanced instruction in keys and key signatures, scales, intervals, chords and their inversions, modulations, and nonharmonic tones is provided in this conventional harmony course. Students study and apply rules for harmonizing melodies and bass lines; for writing four-part harmony for soprano, alto, tenor, and bass; and for writing simple accompaniments. (½ unit)

PHOTOGRAPHY

Photography

This course presents a comprehensive overview of photography with strong emphasis on the practical aspects of taking good pictures. Beginning photographers will be guided into the subject by a brief introduction to the history and theory of photography. Students then study camera types and accessories, learn to compose photos and evaluate photographic composition, and examine color photography. (½ unit)

SCIENCE

Health Science 1

Students are introduced to medically accepted means of promoting physical and mental well-being. Among the subjects addressed are grooming, emotional health, drug abuse, and the functions of the nervous and endocrine systems. (½ unit)

Health Science 2

Students expand their understanding of basic human physiology as it applies to health practices. They learn about exercise and fatigue; nutrition; the digestive, respiratory, and circulatory systems; infections and chronic disease; public health and the environment; and human sexuality and heredity. (½ unit)

Biology I

This entry-level course in biology introduces students to fundamental concepts and relates scientific material to the students' everyday lives. Students study organisms and their relationship to their environment. They explore cell organization, reproduction, heredity, mutation, and adaptation. In addition, they study various aspects of ecology and conservation; consider the methods of classifying and naming living organisms; and learn about bacteria, protozoa, algae, and fungi. (½ unit)

Biology 2

This course continues the study of the four kingdoms in the classification system of living things. Students further their understanding of fundamental biological concepts and principles as they learn about the characteristics of representative members of various phyla and classes of the plant and animal kingdoms. Students learn about the anatomy and physiology of the human body and also consider such health-related topics as nutrition, disease, and harmful drugs. (½ unit)

Biology 3

A systems approach to living organisms is used in this course. Students learn about the characteristics of living organism, and the classification, basic chemistry, cellular organization, biochemistry, and energy production and release of living systems. They apply this knowledge base while examining specific biological processes including gas exchange, food utilization, and excretion. (½ unit)

Advanced Biology

Students begin their study of the animal kingdom by considering the differences between plants and animals, by studying the principles of biological nomenclature and classification, by surveying major phyla

of the animal kingdom, and by reviewing the fossil record of animal development. Students compare the digestive, respiratory, excretory, and transport processes of various multicellular animals, including humans, as well as the nervous and endocrine systems that help coordinate those processes. They also study patterns of reproduction and embryological development in animals. (½ unit)

Basic Electricity and Electronics

In this introductory course, students gain a broad, general understanding of electrical and electronic phenomena and devices and develop an appreciation for the role that electricity plays in their lives. The course provides a readable, nontechnical survey of static electricity and electronic devices. The experiments in the course give students practical experience in constructing simple circuits and measuring electrical quantities. (½ unit)

Chemistry 1

The course presents an introduction to principles and procedures in chemistry. Students study scientific measurements, chemical names and formulas, states of and changes in matter, numerical relationships in chemical reactions, trends expressed in the periodical table, and the behavior of gases. They calculate empirical and molecular formulas, write and balance equations, determine mole and mass, interpret chemical equations, and gain insight into the various models of the atom. (½ unit)

Chemistry 2

Students study equilibrium and solubility; oxidation-reduction, acid-based reactions; electron energy levels, molecular structure, transition elements, and carbon compounds. (½ unit)

Physical Science 1

This course presents basic concepts, logical methods, and practical applications of chemistry through a nonmathematical approach. Students study the properties of matter; the atomic and molecular structure of matter; the nature of gases, acids, bases, salts, and carbon compounds; and the behavior of nuclear particles. They perform experiments and study the applications of chemistry to a variety of processes. (½ unit)

Physical Science 2

This course presents basic concepts, logical methods, and practical applications of physics. The approach is essentially nonmathematical, but many of the problems presented require simple computational skills. Students carry out simple experiments and learn to understand force, work, power, energy, sound, light, magnetism, electricity, and other concepts. (½ unit)

Physics 1

This course uses historical examples and common phenomena to illustrate the questions raised by physicists and the methods used to answer them. As students consider the concepts of motion, force, vectors, work, and heat, they will carry out simple experiments that allow them to observe the physical phenomena related to these concepts. (½ unit)

Physics 2

In this course, students continue to investigate questions raised by physicists and the methods used to answer those questions. Students study energy, kinetic theory, electrostatics, optics, and the particle and wave nature of light. In the process, they carry out simple experiments that permit them to directly observe the physical phenomena associated with the concepts under examination. (½ unit)

SOCIAL STUDIES

Civics

In this course students will develop an understanding of their role as American citizens. They consider their role as citizens of the United States and examine their rights and responsibilities in state and local governments, in the home and school, and in the world. Through the examination of certain contemporary problems, students acquire the ability to analyze critically the social and political issues of a democratic society. (½ unit)

Sociology

In this course, students learn about social development of individuals in a society and consider the effects that culture, language, and status have on this development. Special attention is given to mechanisms of social control and to forces of social change. Through the analysis of social institutions and the examination of contemporary social problems, students develop an understanding of the characteristics of social interaction in a complex, modern society. (½ unit)

Psychology

This introduction to psychology covers a broad range of topics, including learning processes, the development of personality, mental and emotional problems, the psychology of group behavior, and social attitudes. (½ unit)

World Geography 1

This course explores relationships between people and their physical environment. While studying about the United States, Canada, and Latin America, students study the general characteristics of each region before analyzing interactions between the culture and geography of selected nations. (½ unit)

World Geography 2

This course deals with four geographic regions: Europe, Africa, Australia and Oceania, and Asia. Students learn how the topography, climate, and natural resources of each region influence the lives of people. They also learn how the people of a region raise their standard of living by reacting to and modifying their natural surroundings. Throughout the course students use such basic geographic skills as reading and drawing maps, analyzing charts and diagrams, and interpreting technical vocabulary. (½ unit)

World History 1

Students learn about both the history and cultures of Western and non-Western worlds. Special attention is given to the civilizations that developed in India, China, Africa, and Latin America from ancient to recent times. The contributions that each culture made to world civilization are stressed. (½ unit)

World History 2

The history of the Western and non-Western worlds from about 1750 to the present is the subject of this course. Students begin the course by examining the social and political upheavals that revolutionized Western civilization and signaled the end of absolutism. Then they consider the growth of democracy and nationalism, the causes and effects of the Industrial Revolution, the "new" imperialism, and the two world wars. They conclude with a discussion of postwar problems and recent developments that have had global impact. (*/12 unit)

American History 1

The history of the United States from the European background to settlement through the Civil War is presented in this course. Students begin by examining the definition of history and its value. The readings stress important themes and events and include excerpts from the primary sources of each period considered. Self-check exercises are used as a device to reinforce the facts and issues presented in the textbook and syllabus. (½ unit)

American History 2

This course traces the major historical developments in the United States from 1865 to the present. Students examine the causes and effects of the Industrial Revolution, immigration, reform movements, the two world wars, and other historical phenomena that have influenced American society since the Civil War. The readings include excerpts from primary sources. Social history is emphasized throughout. (½ unit)

American Government: Theories, Policies, and Politics

Students analyze the American federal system of government as outlined by the Constitution of the United States. They study state and local government and examine the structures of the 50 state governments. The constitutional rights guaranteed to American citizens, as well as the relationship of citizens to states. are discussed in detail. (½ unit)

American Government: National Level

Students learn about the functions, powers, and structures of the three branches of the national government of the United States. They consider the constitutional systems of separation of powers and checks and balances. In addition, students examine the role that the national government plays in the solution of specific foreign and domestic problems. (½ unit)

Modern Problems

Significant social and political issues that are of special concern to today's students are examined in this course. Students analyze several of these issues through an in-depth study of the following five topics: education and opportunity, cities in crisis, poverty in an affluent society, voices of dissent, and peace or war. (½ unit)

Ethnic Studies and Human Relations

The ability to relate to one another is (and probably always has been) one of the most important issues for humankind. In examining the histories and cultures of a variety of Americans (including those of European, African, Asian, Hispanic, and Native American descent), this course provides the background necessary to the understanding of attitudes toward ethnicity that have existed and exist today in the United States. Students examine the roles of economics, Eurocentrism, and ethnocentrism as they clarify their own views toward a pluarlistic and diverse society. (½ unit)

SPANISH

Spanish 1

Students develop a good grasp of fundamental Spanish grammar that enables them to read simple stories and to compose simple paragraphs. They also develop an understanding of the culture and geography of Mexico. Basic sentence structure, parts of speech, regular and irregular verbs in the present tense are covered. Students develop vocabulary related to clothing, the house, time, weather, the calendar, numbers, and family relationships. (½ unit)

Spanish 2

Through discussion of such diverse topics as entertainment, traditional Hispanic foods, and geography and travel, students increase their vocabulary, their understanding of grammatical constructions, and their ability to read and write Spanish. Students focus on the study of stem-changing and irregular verbs, possessive adjectives, comparison of adjectives, and the preterite tense. (½ unit)

Spanish 3

Students increase their ability to read, write, and speak Spanish as they systematically study more advanced language concepts. A thorough review of regular, irregular, and stem-changing verbs in the present and preterite tenses leads smoothly and naturally into a study of reflexive and spelling-change verbs and the imperfect, present progressive, and present perfect tenses. Students expand their ability to write complex sentences in Spanish using reflexive, direct object, and indirect object pronouns and increase their knowledge of Spanish culture as they read and hear about special occasions, holidays, and practices observed by the Spanish people. (½ unit)

Spanish 4

Students thoroughly review regular, irregular, and stem-changing verbs in the present, preterite, and imperfect tenses before beginning a study of the future, conditional, and present subjunctive tenses. (½ unit)

STUDY SKILLS

Effective Methods of Study

This course is designed to improve study skills, habits, and attitudes through experimentation with new study procedures and through application of established study methods. (½ unit)

NONCREDIT COURSES

BUILDING INSPECTION

Field Inspection and Plan Review

This course covers the basic principles of building inspection and building code administration. Fire safety and nonengineering structural provisions of the Uniform Building Code are presented and related to practical situations. The content of the course also is applicable to other model code documents. (Noncredit) *Tuition:* $160; materials $123.

ENGLISH

Adult Basic Skills English

This course provides a review of basic language arts and literacy skills necessary for success in college and in business. A focus on sentences and the ways in which effective sentences convey meaning, with particular emphasis on the relationships between clauses and phrases, leads into an exploration of strategies for effective reading. (Noncredit) *Tuition:* $210; materials $95.

MATHEMATICS

Adult Basic Skills Math

This course provides a review of computational mathematics and elementary algebra necessary for success in college-level work and in the business world. Students review basic arithmetic and algebraic operations and learn to solve problems involving these concepts. (Noncredit) *Tuition:* $210; materials $50.

Geometry 1

Students develop reasoning skills using geometric terms and processes, concepts of logic, and applied problem solving. Topics studied include parallel lines and planes, congruent triangles, inequalities, and quadrilaterals. Geometric concepts are analyzed using formal, paragraph, and indirect proofs. The lab kit contains compass, protractor, ruler, graph paper, and manipulative materials needed to do laboratory activities in the course. (Noncredit) *Tuition:* $233.25; materials $102.

Geometry 2

Students continue to develop their geometry skills while studying the topics of similarity, areas and volumes, right triangles, circles, coordinate geometry, and transformations. Current mathematical standards involving problem solving, communication, reasoning, and connections are carefully followed in this course. The lab kit contains compass, protractor, ruler, graph paper, and manipulative materials needed to do laboratory activities in the course. (Noncredit) *Tuition:* $233.25; materials $102.

Intermediate Algebra

A review of the topics in a second-year high school algebra course taught at the college level. Topics include: real numbers, 1st and 2nd degree equations and inequalities, linear systems, polynomials and rational functions, exponents and radicals, functions and relations, exponentials and logarithms. (Noncredit) *Tuition:* $233.25; materials $102.

PROFESSIONAL COURSES

REAL ESTATE

Real Estate Settlement Procedures Act

This course is designed primarily for professionals in the real estate field. It introduces the law governing real estate settlement procedures and emphasizes the information regarding costs of settlement that must be provided to consumers. This course also deals with prohibited practices, the rules covering required escrow deposits, and enforcement of the Real Estate Settlement Procedures Act. (Noncredit) *Tuition:* $65; materials $17.

Fair Housing Laws

This course is designed primarily for professionals in the real estate field. It covers the various fair housing laws designed to eliminate unlawful discrimination practices in real estate transactions and emphasizes the Fair Housing Act of 1968. (Noncredit) *Tuition:* $65; materials $15.

Truth in Lending Act

This course is designed primarily for professionals in the real estate field. It introduces the primary piece of legislation governing consumer credit transactions. It also covers the rights of consumers of credit regarding disclosure of specific information and cancellation of some credit transactions, the use of uniform terminology in the disclosures, and the required uniform methods of computing the cost of credit in connection with consumer credit transactions. (Noncredit) *Tuition:* $65; materials $15.

Contracts and Agency Relationships

This course is designed primarily for professionals in the real estate field. It covers the legal agreements that are used for the sale of real estate (listing agreements, purchase agreements, and land installment contracts). This course also examines the agency relationships that govern the conduct of real estate agents with their principals. (Noncredit) *Tuition:* $65; materials $15.

Legal Documents Used in Real Estate

This course is designed primarily for professionals in the real estate field. It provides a general review of the types of documents used in real estate. Topics included are contracts, liens, deeds, leases, security documents, and closing documents. (Noncredit) *Tuition:* $65; materials $20.

Closing the Real Estate Transaction

This course is designed primarily for professionals in the real estate field. It focuses upon various aspects of closing a real estate transaction. Topics covered are sources of professional assistance necessary or helpful in executing a real estate closing, the seller's and buyer's responsibilities in preparation for closing, the effect of the Real Estate Settlement Procedures Act on closings, and activities during the actual closing transaction. (½ unit) *Tuition:* $65; materials $15.

Commercial Real Estate Leases

This course is designed primarily for professional in the real estate field. It focuses on the provisions of commercial real estate leases. (Noncredit) *Tuition:* $65; materials $15.

Real Estate Sales and Brokerage

This course is designed to benefit persons who wish to enter the field of real estate sales and licensed salespersons who wish to become brokers. The course emphasizes practical knowledge. Students will learn about actual problems and proven techniques for solving them. The major topics covered are professional requirements and basic techniques, product and customer evaluation, the sales process, and professional brokerage. (Noncredit) *Tuition:* $210; materials $62.

Income Property: Advanced Appraisal Methods

This course is designed to benefit newcomers who want to enter the field of real estate appraisal or individuals who need continuing education credits. The course emphasizes practical knowledge. Students will encounter actual problems and learn to use proven techniques for solving them. The major topics covered are appraisal methods dealing with income property. (Noncredit) *Tuition:* $175; materials $25.

Nebraska, University of - Omaha
60th and Dodge Street
Omaha, Nebraska 68182   (402) 554-2200

Description:

Formerly the Municipal University of Omaha, an institution founded in 1908, this University came under the direction of the University of Nebraska Board of Regents in 1968.

A series of independent study courses in Real Estate were developed through a cooperative relationship between the Nebraska Real Estate Commission, the Department of Finance of the University of Nebraska - Lincoln, and Department of Real Estate and Land Usage Economics at the University of Nebraska - Omaha.

These courses carry credit from the University of Nebraska - Omaha but are administered by the Division of Continuing Studies at the University of Nebraska - Lincoln. For a description of the Real Estate courses, SEE **Nebraska, University of - Lincoln.**

Accreditations:

North Central Association of Colleges and Schools.

Nevada, University of - Las Vegas
4505 Maryland Parkway
Las Vegas, Nevada 89154   (702) 739-3443

Description:

The William F. Harrah College of Hotel Administration of the University of Nevada, Las Vegas offers courses which are open to anyone 15 years of age or older or who presents evidence of high school graduation.

The College of Health Sciences program in health care administration offers a course on health care systems.

The courses listed below are administered by the Independent Study Department of the University of Nevada, Reno, but credit for the courses will be from the University of Nevada, Las Vegas. For enrollment and tuition information, SEE **Nevada, University of - Reno.**

Accreditations:

Northwest Association of Schools and Colleges.

COLLEGE COURSES

HEALTH CARE ADMINISTRATION

U.S. Health System: Policies and Programs

Survey of the policies and structures of the U.S. health care system. Historical analysis of the development of the current system. Overview of the organization and administration of health care services today and for the future. (3 semester hours)

HOTEL ADMINISTRATION

Introduction to the Hospitality Industry

A survey of the history, likely direction, and organizational structure of the hospitality industry and the place of the hotel in the local and national economy. (3 semester hours)

Lodging Operations

A study of front office procedures, including forms and machines, and interpersonal dynamics from reservations through the night audit. (3 semester hours)

Hospitality Purchasing

Basic principles of purchasing food and beverage, as well as nonfood items, with particular attention to product identification and to the receiving, storing, and issuing sequence. (3 semester hours)

Executive Planning for Housekeeping Operations

Application of various systems, procedures, and controls associated with a modern hotel or hospital housekeeping department. Emphasis on management delegation, scheduling systems, routines, and equipment requirements. Laundry operations and hotel recreation departments are also reviewed. (3 semester hours)

Hotel Marketing I

The organization of the hotel marketing function; its role and responsibility in developing an integrated marketing program. (3 semester hours)

Convention Sales and Service Management

Practical insights into the different kinds of meetings and conventions, the types of organizations that stage such events, and the people who hold the key to site selection. Includes how to reach, sell, and service these important groups and people. (3 semester hours)

Organizational Theory Applied to the Service Industries

The interaction of people in the work environment, examination of organizational behavior and structures, with special application to the service industries. (3 semester hours)

Mathematics of Casino Games

Develops the techniques and methods for computing the probabilities, expected values, and house percentages of casino games and analyzes the effects of changes in playing rules and playoff odds. (3 semester hours)

International Tourism

A study of international travel and tourism. Focus on the economic, social, political, and environmental considerations of international tourism management and development. (3 semester hours)

Hotel Advertising and Sales Promotions

A practical approach to contemporary advertising for hotels, restaurants, and tourist destinations. Focuses on the distinctive aspects of hospitality, advertising principles, strategies, techniques, and their application to industry situations. Emphasis on providing the hospitality manager with a working knowledge in the areas of planning, developing, and implementing effective advertising campaigns. (3 semester hours)

Catering Operations and Sales

Study of hotel catering including operation, sales, and relationships with other departments and outside vendors. Emphasis on logistical operations and seeking servicing from various market segments. (3 semester hours)

Nevada, University of - Reno
Independent Study by Correspondence
Division of Continuing Education
1041 North Virginia Street, Room 225
Reno, Nevada 89557-0081   (800) 233-8928

Description:

The University of Nevada, Reno is a land-grant institution which offers opportunity for higher education to qualified applicants. It was established by the Nevada State Constitution of 1864. The university actually began operation in 1874.

The University of Nevada, Reno, through its Independent Study Department, offers college-level correspondence courses for both regular credit and noncredit. The Independent Study Department began in the 1940s.

Faculty:

Catharine D. Sanders, Director, Independent Study by Correspondence; Kerri M. Garcia, Assistant Director.

Academic Levels:

College
High School
Noncredit

Degree/Certificate Programs:

The University of Nevada, Reno will allow up to 60 semester credits through correspondence study toward a baccalaureate degree.

Admission Requirements:

Eighteen years of age or high school graduate for university credit. Superior high school students by special permission. Approval of high school principal for high school credit. Some courses have required prerequisites.

Tuition:

$60 per credit. All courses also have special stationery, handling, and postage fees. These fees vary by course. High school courses $70 per one-half high school credit. VISA,

Discover, or MasterCard accepted. No refunds for course fees are made after a lesson has been submitted or two months have elapsed. If a student withdraws from a course within two months of the original date of enrollment and has not turned in any lessons, a partial refund is allowed. An administrative fee of $25 per course is charged.

Enrollment Period:

One year is allowed for completion of a course; one six-month extension may be allowed upon payment of a $15 extension fee. The minimum time allowed to complete a college course is 4 weeks per credit; high school courses 8 weeks for each ½ unit course.

Equipment Requirements:

Textbooks are not included in the course fee and must be purchased separately. Other required materials such as tape cassettes, slides, and science kits must be purchased separately. Cassette players and slide projectors must be furnished by the student. A deposit (varies by course) is required for courses requiring the use of tapes or cassettes; upon completion of the course when all tapes are returned in a satisfactory condition, a refund for the full amount of the deposit will be made.

Credit and Grading:

Courses for credit require supervised progress tests and a mid-course examination in most cases. All courses taken for credit require a proctored final examination. The grading system uses the letter grades: A, Excellent; B, Above Average; C, Average; D, Passing; F, Failure. Minimum passing grade is D. The student may opt for pass/fail at the beginning of the course. Only two courses at the same time are allowed. Credit is awarded in semester hour units.

Library Services:

Students have access to the Getchell Library on the Reno campus as well as the Learning Resource Centers at Truckee Meadows Community College and Western Nevada Community College.

Accreditations:

Northwest Association of Schools and Colleges. Member of: National University Continuing Education Association.

COLLEGE COURSES

ACCOUNTING

Elementary Accounting I

Purpose and nature of accounting, measuring business income, accounting principles, assets, and equity accounting for external financial reporting. (3 semester hours)

Introductory Accounting II

Forms of business organizations; cost concepts and decision making; break-even analysis, fixed and variable costs, budgeting for internal reporting. (3 semester hours)

ANTHROPOLOGY

The Human Experience

Introduction to human culture and society. Understanding human diversity through comparative study of politics, religion, economics, and kinship. (3 semester hours)

Archaeology

Uses of archaeology to understand and interpret major stages of human cultural development from beginnings to first civilizations. (3 semester hours)

CURRICULUM AND INSTRUCTION

Curriculum Development in Environmental Education

Development of the school curriculum in the area of environmental education. Special emphasis is given to school and school-camp programs. Activities for promoting the acquisition of environmental concepts are demonstrated. (2 or 3 semester hours)

Special Problems in Curriculum and Instruction

Science Teaching and the Development of Reasoning. Designed to acquaint the student with formal and concrete reasoning patterns of children in the area of science. Presents a three-part strategy for introducing new material in any subject area in the classroom. (3 semester hours)

Five Teaching Skills. Five teaching skills practiced in microteaching situations and coding from an audio tape. A method of self-analysis of classroom interactions. (1 semester hour)

Volcanic Landscapes - South. Specialized instruction designed to develop breadth of understanding in current curriculum and instruction topics for elementary, secondary, and special education teachers. (1 semester hour)

ECONOMICS

Principles of Macroeconomics

Introduction to the determination of levels of national income, employment and prices, and the basic causes of fluctuation of these levels. (3 semester hours)

Principles of Microeconomics

Introduction to the theory of relative prices; the allocation of productive resources among alternative uses in the production of national output and its distribution. (3 semester hours)

Principles of Statistics I

Probability and major probability distributions; sampling theory; descriptive statistics; measures of central tendency and dispersion; index figures; time series. (3 semester hours)

Principles of Statistics II

Statistical inference: estimation; hypothesis testing; simple linear regression and correlations; analysis of the variance. (3 semester hours)

ENGLISH

Oral English for Non-Native Speakers

Individualized practice in the oral properties of English for persons who need to improve their fluency (requires access to a learning laboratory or cassette recorder). (3 semester hours)

Introduction to Literature

Introduction to fiction, poetry, and drama. (3 semester hours)

Vocabulary and Meaning

Problems of meaning, word derivation, and word formation are investigated with a view to enlarging and refining a working English vocabulary. (2 semester hours)

Introduction to Fiction

Significant works of fiction from various languages, with attention to the novel and the short story as literary forms. (3 semester hours)

Introduction to Drama

Reading of a variety of plays, with attention to special characteristics of drama. (2 or 3 semester hours)

Introduction to Poetry

Reading and discussion of selected British and American poems with attention to form and content. (2 or 3 semester hours)

Introduction to Language

Nature and function of language, including an introduction to the linguistic subsystems of modern English and the development of the English language. (3 semester hours)

Descriptive Grammar

Modern English grammar and usage. (3 semester hours)

Theories of Second Language Acquisition

Survey of major theories of second language acquisition and their potential applications to language teaching. Topics include: language and behavior, language acquisition in children and adults, social and psychological factors. (3 semester hours)

Teaching English as a Second Language

Current methods and materials in ESL with emphasis on curriculum models and applications. Class observation at primary, secondary, and university levels. (3 semester hours)

Language Testing

Theories of defining and assessing competence in English as a second language. Preparation and administration of various tests with attention to cultural bias in testing. (3 semester hours)

Linguistics

Studies in general linguistics. (3 semester hours)

ENVIRONMENT

Man and Environment

Interdisciplinary introduction survey of the ecology of natural systems, with emphasis on the relation of man to the environment. (3 semester hours)

FRENCH

Elementary French I

Introduction to the language through the development of language skills and through structural analysis. Includes an introduction to French culture. (4 semester hours)

Elementary French II

Introduction to the language through the development of language skills and through structural analysis. Includes an introduction to French culture. (4 semester hours)

Reading French I

Development of reading skills, including vocabulary building, verb recognition, and sentence structure. Reading of selected texts for comprehension. (2 semester hours)

Reading French II

Continuation of development of reading skills with emphasis on comprehension. Practical readings in the humanities, social science, and natural sciences, with individualized assignments when appropriate. (2 semester hours)

GEOGRAPHY

Introduction to Cultural Geography

Systematic consideration of the spatial aspects of human culture. Major theses: spatial history and morphology, society-land relations, and economics development and resource utilization. (3 semester hours)

Regional Geography of the Underdeveloped World

Synthesis of the geographic factors (human, economic, environmental, political) which give distinctive character to specific areas of the underdeveloped world. Emphasis on international awareness. (3 semester hours)

GERMAN

Elementary German I

Introduction to the language through the development of language skills and through structural analysis. Includes an introduction to German culture. (4 semester hours)

Elementary German II

Introduction to the language through the development of language skills and through structural analysis. Includes an introduction to German culture. (4 semester hours)

Reading German I

Development of reading skills, including vocabulary building, verb recognition and sentence structure. Reading of selected texts for comprehension. (2 semester hours)

Reading German II

Continuation of development of reading skills with emphasis on comprehension. Practical readings in the humanities, social sciences, and natural sciences with individualized assignments when appropriate. (2 semester hours)

HISTORY

European Civilization

Course C105. Development of Western civilization from the dawn of history to 1648. (3 semester hours)

Course C106. Development of Western civilization from 1648 to the present. (3 semester hours)

Nevada History

Nevada history from early exploration to the present. Includes examination of the Nevada Constitution and satisfies the Nevada Constitution requirement. (3 semester hours)

England and the British Empire

C393. History of England and its empire: social, economic and political development. Background of English literature and law. (3 semester hours)

C394. Begins at Elizabethan Age. (3 semester hours)

HUMAN DEVELOPMENT AND FAMILY STUDIES

Child Development

Overview of growth and development from the prenatal period through adolescence. (3 semester hours)

ITALIAN

Elementary Italian I

Introduction to the language through the development of language skills, and through structural analysis. Includes an introduction to Italian culture. (4 semester hours)

Elementary Italian II

A continuation of the above course. (4 semester hours)

Second Year Italian

Course C203. Structural review, conversation and writing, readings in modern literature. (3 semester hours)

Course C204. A continuation of the above course. (3 semester hours)

JOURNALISM

Introduction to Journalism

Survey of the role of newspapers, radio, television, advertising, and public relations organizations. Interpretation of the day's news and analysis of media performance. (3 semester hours)

Corporate Communications

Principles of successful advertising and public relations for commercial and nonprofit organizations. Planning, media selection, copy writing, and graphics. Social responsibilities of advertisers and agents. (3 semester hours)

Magazine Writing

Writing and marketing of articles for magazines. Analysis of general interest and specialized magazines. (2 semester hours)

MANAGEMENT

Corporate Finance

Business and corporate finance, investments and international finance. (3 semester hours)

Marketing Principles

Objectives and policies of marketing managers as influenced by marketing institutions, the functions performed, and consumer wants and needs in a diverse culture. (3 semester hours)

Investments

Analysis of investment risks, media and investment portfolios with relation to requirements and policies of individual investors. (3 semester hours)

MATHEMATICS

Intermediate Algebra

Basic properties of the real numbers; standard algebraic techniques, including exponents, factoring, fractions, radicals, problem solving; linear and quadratic equations; the concept of graphing. (3 semester hours)

Plane Trigonometry

Trigonometric functions and their identities; solution of triangles. (2 semester hours)

Fundamentals of College Mathematics

Equations and inequalities; relations and functions; linear, quadratic, polynomial, exponential, and logarithmic functions; circles, lines, and parabolas; right-triangle trigonometry; finite probability measures; some statistical concepts. (3 semester hours)

College Algebra

Relations, functions, graphing; equations; linear, quadratic, polynomial systems; matrices and determinants; sequences, mathematical induction, compound interest and amortization, binomial theorem; the complex numbers, logarithms; combinatorics. (3 semester hours)

Algebra and Trigonometry

Equations, relations, functions, graphing; polynomial, rational, exponential, logarithmic, and circular functions with applications; coordinate geometry of lines and conics; analytic trigonometry; matrices, determinants; binomial theorem. (5 semester hours)

Analytic Geometry

Coordinization of the plane; linear, quadratic, polynomial, rational, exponential, and logarithmic functions; lines, slope, parallelism, perpendicularity; vectors, parabolas, ellipses, hyperbolas; translation and rotation; the complex numbers. (3 semester hours)

Elementary School Mathematics I

Mathematics needed by those teaching new-content mathematics courses at the elementary school level with emphasis on the structure of the real number system and its subsystems. (3 semester hours)

Elementary School Mathematics II

A continuation of the above course. (3 semester hours)

Mathematics of Finance

Interest, annuities, sinking funds, depreciation and amortization. (3 semester hours)

Elements of Calculus I

Fundamental ideas of analytic geometry and calculus, plane coordinates, graphs, functions, limits, derivatives, integrals, the fundamental theorem of calculus, rates, extrema, and the applications thereof. (3 semester hours)

Calculus I

Fundamental concepts of analytic geometry and calculus; functions, graphs, limits, derivatives, and integrals. (4 semester hours)

MEDICAL TERMINOLOGY

Medical Terminology

Self-learning approach to terminology used in the medical professions. Emphasis on understanding of word roots and building vocabulary. (1 semester hour)

NUTRITION

Human Nutrition

Introduction to the principles of nutrition and their application to well-balanced diets. (3 semester hours)

POLITICAL SCIENCE

Constitution of Nevada

Nevada Constitution, including the historical development of Nevada from territory to statehood. (1 semester credit)

American Politics: Process and Behavior

American government and the discipline of political science; surveys, participation, pursuit and use of power, and contemporary political issues. (3 semester hours)

Principles of American Constitutional Government

Constitutions of the United States and Nevada with additional attention to various principles and current problems of government. (3 semester hours)

PSYCHOLOGY

Introduction to Psychology as a Social Science

Presents psychology as a science concerned with the actions of organisms in a social and cultural context. (3 semester hours)

Child Psychology

Psychological aspects in the development of children through preadolescence. Examination of behavioral, social, cognitive, af-

fective, and cultural factors. Theory and research on developmental stages. (3 semester hours)

Psychology of Adolescence

Psychological and social psychological growth and development during adolescence in contemporary Western society. Covers puberty to early adulthood. (3 semester hours)

Educational Psychology

Educational applications of psychology to learning, discipline and social, emotional and intellectual behavior. Educational and psychological tests and measurements. (3 semester hours)

Personality

Survey of major theories of personality. Personality development, structure and dynamics. Examination of major areas of research on personality. (3 semester hours)

Abnormal Psychology

Psychology of abnormal behavior—primarily neuroses and psychoses—stressing symptomatology, etiology, dynamics, and problems in diagnosis. (3 semester hours)

SOCIOLOGY

Principles of Sociology

Sociological principles underlying the development, structure, and function of culture, society, human groups, personality formation, and social change. (3 semester hours)

Social Problems

Selected social problems, their causation and proposed solutions. (3 semester hours)

SPANISH

Elementary Spanish I

Introduction to the language through the development of language skills, and through structural analysis. Includes an introduction to Spanish and Latin American culture. (4 semester hours)

Elementary Spanish II

A continuation of the above course. (4 semester hours)

Reading Spanish I

Development of reading skills, including vocabulary building, verb recognition, and sentence structure. Reading of selected texts for comprehension. (2 semester hours)

Reading Spanish II

Continuation of development of reading skills with emphasis on comprehension. Practical readings in the humanities, social sciences, and natural sciences, with individualized assignments when appropriate. (2 semester hours)

WESTERN TRADITIONS

Foundations of Western Culture

Introduction to Greek, Roman, and Judeo-Christian traditions through the Middle Ages. (3 semester hours)

WOMEN'S STUDIES

Introduction to Women's Studies

Interdisciplinary analysis of women in culture and society from historical and cross-cultural perspectives. (3 semester hours)

HIGH SCHOOL COURSES

BIOLOGY

Introductory Biology I

The elementary facts pertaining to the organization and function of living systems, dealing primarily with the functional and structural aspects of living organisms. Presents the broad sweep of biology in a reasonably integrated manner with fundamental concepts stressed. Looks at a large number of specific biological facts within a framework of concepts and basic principles. (½ unit)

Introductory Biology II

Continuation of the above course. The functional and structural aspects of living organisms. Specific topics: genetics, plants, animals and their reproduction, growth, and behavior. (½ unit)

COMPUTER LITERACY

Computer Literacy

An introduction to the world of computers presenting the student with special terms used with computers and new knowledge on hardware and software commonly used in business and industry today. Includes an introduction to BASIC programming. (½ unit)

ENGLISH

English 1A

A thorough examination of the elements of English grammar, including parts of speech: nouns, verbs, subjects, and pronouns. Structure of the simple sentence, its parts, and punctuation. (½ unit)

English 1B

Continues the examination of the elements of English grammar with emphasis on the structure and punctuation of compound and complex sentences. Includes assignments on developing writing skills, creating power paragraphs, and organizing short papers. (½ unit)

English 2A

Continued study of English grammar. Emphasis also on composition and vocabulary building. Literature segments introduce and discuss literary genres including poetry and the short story. (½ unit)

English 2B

Continued study of English grammar including sentence fragments, correct verb usage, subject-verb agreement, and modifiers. Practice in writing compositions. Enriches vocabulary and illustrates techniques of analyzing and interpreting short stories. (½ unit)

English 3A

A survey of American literature from the early beginnings of this country through the American Civil War and Reconstruction. Includes a study of the major writers from the explorers to Mark Twain. Presents a wide range of literature to include journals, short stories, and poems. (½ unit)

English 3B

Continues the study of American literature from 1880 to the present day. Includes the study of poems, short stories, and dramatic plays including *Our Town* and *The Glass Menagerie*. Emphasis on literary terms and their application to different genres of literature. (½ unit)

English 4A

A survey of English literature from the Anglo-Saxon era through the Age of Enlightenment. This course includes a study of the major writers and poets to include Chaucer and Shakespeare. Presents a wide range of literature including short stories, poems, and plays. (½ unit)

English 4B

Continues the study of English literature from the Romanticists to modern day writers. Writers to be studied include Wordsworth, Coleridge, Keats, Tennyson, Browning, and many others. Presents a wide range of literature including poems and short stories. Selections portray a look at English society and how writers and their audiences coped. (½ unit)

GOVERNMENT

American Government 1A

The principles, origins, structure, and basic theories of American government. Discusses different forms of government worldwide and examines the U.S. Constitution and the functions of the executive branch. Includes analysis of foreign and domestic policy. Overview of Congress and the fiscal budget. (½ unit)

American Government 1B

Continues the study of the principles and basic theories of American government. Examines the independent agencies of government and their specific contributions. Explores the origins and structure of the judicial branch and the court system. Discusses civil rights and provides an in-depth overview of the American political process. (½ unit)

HISTORY

American History 1A

Survey of American political, economic, social, and cultural development from European heritage through contemporary times. Examines the historical forces that shaped American society. Major topics include colonization and the American Revolution, War of 1812, the Civil War, and the opening of the Western frontier. (½ unit)

American History 1B

Begins with an analysis of the American economy at the end of the 20th century. Overview of the American people as a rich and varied culture, the Civil Rights Act of 1960, and political developments from post-Civil War period to present. Concludes with a survey of American foreign policy, the Cold War era, and an outline of the Korean and Vietnam Wars. (½ unit)

World History 1A

Traces the world's political, economic, social, and cultural development from the Stone Age to the French Revolution and the growth of democracy in the 19th century. Emphasis on the development of Western Civilization, but also includes the early civilizations and the Middle Ages in the Far East. Covers such topics as the Renaissance, Reformation, and Napoleonic era. (½ unit)

World History 1B

Continues to trace the world's political, economic, social, and cultural development to contemporary times. Covers important historical events like the Industrial Revolution, Imperialism, World Wars I and II, and the Russian Revolution. Concludes with an overview of the United Nations and scientific developments during the Cold War era. (½ unit)

MATHEMATICS

Applied Mathematics 1A

A problem-solving approach to the study of fractions and decimals. Intended as either an introduction to a review of these basic concepts and emphasizes their application in everyday living. (½ unit)

Applied Mathematics 1B

A continuation of the problem-solving approach of the above course, covering such areas as ratio and proportion, graphs, percentages, and introductory consumer math. Application of these skills in everyday living is stressed. (½ unit)

Algebra 1A

Introduction to the definitions of terms, operations, and formulas needed in pursuing the concepts covered. Includes integers, absolute values, methods to solve algebraic expressions, open equations, sets, and factoring. Concepts important in the study of advanced mathematics and science, as well as vocational and technical fields. (½ unit)

Algebra 1B

Continuation of the above course. Introduces exponents, polynomials, binomials, trinomials, problem-solving applications, rational expressions, number roots, radicals, and quadratic functions. (½ unit)

Algebra 2A

The first of two courses designed to reinforce the concepts covered in *Algebra 1A* and *1b*. Topics: the real number system, linear equations in one variable, graphing linear inequalities, and solving linear systems. Emphasis on improving problem-solving skills. (½ unit)

Algebra 2B

Reviews and reinforces all the essential concepts of algebra including the real number system, equation solving, and integers. Introduces word problems and equation solving with three variables, graphing and solving linear equalities, solving absolute inequalities, graphing equations and direct variation. (½ unit)

Calculus I

Examines calculus as a mathematics tool used to solve problems involving change and motion. Presents functions, formal differentiation, Mean Value Theorem, and integration. (½ unit)

Calculus II

Includes definite integrals, transcendental functions, and methods of integration. (½ unit)

SOCIAL SCIENCE

Sociology

An introduction to the field of sociology. Explains sociological concepts, discusses subcultures, socialization, and social stratification. Examines groups, societal trends, differences, and specific institutions present within society. (½ unit)

NONCREDIT COURSES

CITIZENSHIP

Citizenship for New Americans

A course for non-citizens who are unable to attend regular classes. (Noncredit) *Tuition:* $60 (plus $8 stationery and handling fee).

EDUCATION

Legal Foundations of Education

Historical development of paramount issues in contemporary education. Emphasizes legal aspects of emerging educational patterns. (3 CEUs) *Tuition:* $120 (plus $17 stationery and handling fee).

MATHEMATICS

Fundamentals of the Metric System

An easy to follow treatment of the fundamentals needed to use and understand the metric system of measurement. Practical applications requiring knowledge of metric vocabulary; linear measure; liquid measure; metric mass (weight); area and volume; temperature; household measurements; sizes of wearing apparel and shoes; travel; common conversion tables; history and background of the metric system. (2 CEUs) *Tuition:* $60 (plus $8.50 stationery and handling fee).

New Mexico, University of
Independent Study Through Correspondence
Division of Continuing Education and
Community Services
1634 University Boulevard, NE
Albuquerque, New Mexico 87131-4006
(505) 277-1604

Description:
The University of New Mexico's Division of Continuing Education and Community Services, formerly the Division of Extension, was established in 1928 and has been conducting instruction by correspondence and extension courses continuously since that date. Independent Study Through Correspondence courses are organized to parallel as closely as possible the courses offered in residence at the university.

Academic Levels:
College

Degree/Certificate Programs:
Up to thirty semester credit hours of correspondence study may be applied toward a bachelor degree at the university.

Admission Requirements:
High school graduate or over 21 years of age. Students working toward a degree at the university may enroll in correspondence courses with the written permission of the dean of their college. Only two correspondence courses at a time are permitted. Courses for graduate credit are not offered by Independent Study.

Tuition:
$90 per semester hour. Refund policy: Full, minus $10 within 60 days of enrollment. No refund will be made after a lesson has been submitted or after 60 days have passed since date of registration.

Enrollment Period:
The maximum time allowed to complete a course is one year; the minimum is two months. A 90-day extension is allowed for good reason upon payment of a $20 fee per course. A maximum of two extensions will be granted. No enrollments may be extended beyond the six months of extra time allowed, and no extensions will be granted for a discontinued or revised course.

Equipment Requirements:
The cost of textbooks is not included in the tuition and they may be ordered from the U.N.M. Bookstore.

Credit and Grading:

Examinations must be proctored. The grading system is A, B, C, D, F. The minimum passing grade is D. Credit is awarded in semester hour units.

Accreditations:

North Central Association of Colleges and Schools. Member of: National University Continuing Education Association.

COLLEGE COURSES

ANTHROPOLOGY

Cultures of the World

Basic concepts and methods of cultural anthropology. Selected cultures, ranging from preliterate societies to aspects of urban civilization. The purpose of this course is to prepare students to better understand the nature and varieties of human cultures in different parts of the world and at different levels of technological development. (3 semester hours)

ASTRONOMY

Introduction to Astronomy

The theme is cosmic evolution. It provides a guided tour of the universe to find out where and when we are in the cosmos. The presentation is descriptive and nonmathematical. It starts with an overview into people's ideas about the universe. After an inquiry into the origin and evolution of the solar system, a study of stars is made to find the place of the solar system in the Milky Way Galaxy. Finally, a history is presented of the physical, chemical, and biological evolution of the universe, from its beginning in a big bang to the possibility of life elsewhere in the Galaxy. Special topics may include black holes, interstellar communication, UFOs, and missions to the planets. No preparation is assumed. Important concepts of physics, chemistry, and biology are introduced in the context of the course. (3 semester hours)

General Astronomy

Course Astr 270C. The solar system, stellar astronomy, the galaxy, extragalatic systems, cosmology. (3 semester hours)

Course Astr 271C. The solar system, stellar astronomy, the galaxy, extragalatic systems, cosmology. (3 semester hours)

Refresher Course in Astronomy for Teachers

To update and enrich your background in astronomy, and to provide you with astronomical resources that may be used in the classroom. (3 semester hours)

ECONOMICS

Principles and Problems

Introduction to macro-theory and money and banking. Emphasis on contemporary economic problems, e.g., inflation, unemployment, poverty. (3 semester hours)

Principles of Economics

Introduction to micro-theory, international trade theory, economic growth and development. A continuation of the above course. (3 semester hours)

Money and Banking

Principles of money, credit and banking; organization and operation of the banking system; and the relationship between money, banking, and the level of economic activity. (3 semester hours)

EDUCATION

Teaching Reading in the Elementary School

Establishing a theoretical framework for exploring various approaches to reading/language development, instruction and evaluation in multicultural classroom settings. (3 semester hours)

Children's Literature

A survey course of the field of children's literature. Focuses on knowledge and practice of literature, literary response, and classroom programs. (3 semester hours)

ENGLISH

Composition I: Exposition

Expository writing and reading. Concentrates on organizing and supporting ideas in writing. (3 semester hours)

Composition II: Analysis and Argument

Practice writing analytic and argumentative essays based on expository and literary readings. (3 semester hours)

Expository Writing

An intermediate course with emphasis on rhetorical types, structure and style. (3 semester hours)

Survey of Earlier English Literature

From Old English to 1798. A study of the principal literary and intellectual movements, and selected writers and literary works from Beowulf through Johnson. (3 semester hours)

Survey of Later English Literature

From 1798 to present. Study of principal literary and intellectual movements, and selected writers and literary works. (3 semester hours)

American Literature

A general survey to the present. (3 semester hours)

History of the English Language

Etymology, morphology, phonetics, and semantics of English; relation between linguistics and cultural change. (3 semester hours)

GEOLOGY

Physical Geology

Materials composing the earth, work of agencies, both external and internal, modifying its surface, and rock-forming processes. (2 semester hours)

Historical Geology

History of the earth and the evolution of continents and ocean basins; evolution of life. (3 semester hours)

HEALTH

Personal Health

Exploration of the major areas of health information pertinent to understanding how to achieve, maintain, and promote positive health. Topics covered include mental health, drugs, human sexuality, prevention and control of diseases, nutrition, consumer health, and ecology. (3 semester hours)

Fundamentals of Human Sexuality

Basic knowledge about human sexuality including anatomical, physiological, psycho-social, and ethical components. Reproduction, contraception, sexually transmitted diseases, sexual health, and sexual dysfunctions are among areas examined. (3 semester hours)

HISTORY

Western Civilization

Course 101c. Ancient times to 1648. (3 semester hours)

Course 102C. 1648 to present. (3 semester hours)

History of the United States

Course 161C. Survey of the economic, political, intellectual, and social development of the United States, including the place of the U.S. in world affairs from 1607 to 1877. (3 semester hours)

Course 162C. Survey of the economic, political, intellectual, and social development of the United States, including the place of the U.S. in world affairs from 1877 to present. (3 semester hours)

History of New Mexico

Survey from Cabeza de Vaca to the present. (3 semester hours)

Military History of the United States

Survey of U.S. military and naval history from colonial times to present, with emphasis upon technological, managerial, and political developments that have affected the armed services. (3 semester hours)

History of the Southwest Spanish Period

Spanish exploration and occupation of the Southwest; colonial government and missions. (3 semester hours)

MATHEMATICS

Mathematics for Elementary and Middle School Teachers I

The intuitive and logical background of arithmetic; properties of sets; algorithms of arithmetic in base ten and other bases; properties of the integers; mathematical terminology; elements of number theory; problem solving. (3 semester hours)

Mathematics for Elementary and Middle School Teachers II

The properties of the rational number system; extension to the irrationals; decimal and fractional representation of real numbers; intuitive geometry and measurement. (3 semester hours)

Mathematics for Elementary and Middle School Teachers III

Topics from probability and statistics, geometry, and algebra; some applications of mathematics; elements of logic; enrichment topics for the classroom. Introduction to BASIC and Logo. (3 semester hours)

Intermediate Algebra

Covers linear equations and inequalities, polynomials, factoring, exponents and radicals, fractional expressions and equations, quadratic equations. (3 semester hours)

College Algebra

Includes the study of equations, inequalities, graphs, functions, exponential and logarithmic functions, systems of equations and inequalities, and polynomials. (3 semester hours)

Advanced College Algebra

Includes a study of functions with emphasis on graphs, equations, inequalities, exponential and logarithmic functions. (3 semester hours)

Calculus I

Derivative as a rate of change, intuitive, numerical and theoretical concepts applications to graphing, trigonometric and exponential functions, integral as a sum, relation between integral and derivative, applications, mean value theorem. (4 semester hours)

Calculus II

Applications of the definite integral, transcendental functions, tech-

niques of integration, numerical methods of integration, and finite series. (4 semester hours)

Calculus III

Vector representation of curves and surfaces, partial derivatives, gradient, tangent planes, directional derivative, multiple integrals, cylindrical and spherical coordinates, applications. (4 semester hours)

Vector Analysis

Vector algebra, lines, planes; vector valued functions, curves, tangent lines, arc length, line integrals; directional derivative and gradient; divergence, curl, Gauss' and Stokes' theorems, geometric interpretations. (3 semester hours)

NURSING

Nursing Pathophysiology I

A beginning course in human pathophysiology for pharmacy and nursing students. (2 semester hours)

Nursing Pathophysiology II

This course includes basic knowledge of pathophysiology in the following areas—cardiac, respiratory, renal, digestive tract, and endocrine. (2 semester hours)

Care of Aging Client

Theoretical study of the basic roles of nursing. Emphasis placed upon aspects of the health care delivery system applied to aging clients who are coping with dysfunction related to normal aging changes or chronic disease. (2 semester hours)

Human Responses to Changed Health Status

Theoretical study of human responses to changes in health status. Emphasis on understanding behavioral responses to health status, treatment modalities and the nurse's role. (2 semester hours)

PHILOSOPHY

Introduction to Philosophical Problems

Philosophical issues and methodology illustrated through selected problems concerning values, knowledge, reality; and in social, political, and religious philosophy. (3 semester hours)

Introduction to Logic and Critical Thinking

Emphasis is placed on development of ability to understand, analyze, and critically use various forms of argument. (3 semester hours)

POLITICAL SCIENCE

The Political World

An introduction to politics, with emphasis on the ways people can understand their own political systems and those of others. (3 semester hours)

American Politics

Survey of American politics, including political behavior of the American electorate, the theory of democracy, the structure and function of American political institutions, and contemporary issues. (3 semester hours)

Law in the Political World

Introduction to the role of law and legal institutions in politics and society. (3 semester hours)

Constitutional Law: Powers

The separation of powers and federalism. Includes an introduction to the Supreme Court as an institution. (3 semester hours)

Constitutional Law: Rights

Freedom of speech, freedom of religion, privacy, procedural justice, equal protection of the laws, and other issues in and around the Bill of Rights. (3 semester hours)

PSYCHOLOGY

Abnormal Behavior

Review of the historical, scientific, and ethical issues in the field of psychopathology. Categorization of deviant behavior is regarded as less important than theories of abnormal behavior development, systems of therapy, and relevant research. (3 semester hours)

SOCIOLOGY

Introduction to Sociology

Basic concepts, topics, and theories of contemporary sociology. (3 semester hours)

Social Problems

Sociological approaches to problems such as poverty, crime and delinquency, mental disorders, drug use, corporate power, and other issues selected by the instructor. (3 semester hours)

Sociology of Mass Communications

Mass communication in society with emphasis on Western industrial societies, impact of mass communication on social movements and on sectors of the social structure; social psychology of mass communications. (3 semester hours)

The Urban Community

The forms and development of urban community; demographic, spatial, functional, and temporal patterns; metropolitan development and city-hinterland relations. (3 semester hours)

North Carolina, University of

Independent Studies
Division of Continuing Education
Campus Box 1020, The Friday Center
Chapel Hill, North Carolina 27599-1020
(919) 962-1104

Description:

The University of North Carolina, provided for in the state constitution of 1776 and chartered in 1789, opened its doors to students in 1795. It was the first state university in the United States to award state university diplomas to the students.

Independent Studies is a joint effort by eight institutions of the University of North Carolina. College-level correspondence courses and other opportunities for individualized study at a distance from university campuses are offered. Participants in the program are: Appalachian State University, East Carolina University, Elizabeth City State University, North Carolina State University, University of North Carolina at Chapel Hill, University of North Carolina at Greensboro, Western Carolina University, and Winston-Salem State University. In the consortium arrangement, each institution originating a course provides instruction and awards academic credit, while responsibility for admin-

istration of the program lies with the office of Independent Studies at UNC Chapel Hill.

Faculty:

Norman H. Loewenthal, Senior Associate Director for Independent Studies.

Academic Levels:

College
Noncredit

Degree/Certificate Programs:

Correspondence study credit is allowed toward a bachelor degree, but the number of credits varies among member schools of the consortium.

Admission Requirements:

Open enrollment; some courses have required prerequisites.

Tuition:

$55 per semester hour. Students residing outside the United States Canada, and Mexico must include an additional $35 to cover the cost of mailing graded assignments. This extra charge does not apply to APO and FPO addresses. Refund policy: a partial refund will be granted provided the request is made within two months of the enrollment date. The actual cost of graded assignments will be deducted as well as a fee for the expense of processing the enrollment (1-semester hour courses, $22; 2-semester hours courses, $44; 3-semester hours courses, $66; 4-semester hours courses, $88). Military personnel should consult with their Education Officer for enrollment through DANTES. Contact Independent Studies for cost of noncredit courses.

Enrollment Period:

The maximum time allowed to complete a course is nine months. One extension of four months may be granted upon payment of a $20 renewal fee. The minimum time to complete a course is eight weeks from the date of enrollment.

Equipment Requirements:

Textbooks must be purchased separately by the student. They may be ordered through the Student Stores, CB 1530 Daniels Building, UNC-Chapel Hill, NC 27599-1530 (919-962-2430).

Credit and Grading:

The grading system of the specific campus offering an independent study course will be used. Generally, the grades are A, B, C, D, and F (Failure). A student may request a pass-fail option (no letter grade). Final examinations, required for credit, must be supervised at an accredited institution. Credit is awarded in semester hour units.

Library Services:

Interlibrary loans are available to North Carolina residents from the North Carolina State Library.

Accreditations:

Southern Association of Colleges and Schools. Member of: National University Continuing Education Association.

COLLEGE COURSES

ACCOUNTING

Accounting I - Concepts of Financial Reporting

Financial reporting concepts, the accounting information generating process, reporting practices, financial statement preparation, and the interpretation and analysis of financial statements. Basic accounting principles and concepts, the accounting cycle, income measurement, and internal controls. (3 semester hours)

Accounting II - An Introduction to Managerial Accounting

The analysis of accounting data that are useful in managerial decision making and in the control and evaluation of the decisions made within business organizations. An introduction to basic models, financial statement analysis, cost behavior analysis and cost control procedures. (3 semester hours)

ANTHROPOLOGY

Cultural Anthropology

Comparative study of contemporary human culture, social institutions and processes that influence behavior. The range of human cultural variation shown throughout the world, including the student's own culture system. (3 semester hours)

ART

History of Western Art I

A systematic survey of Western art from the Egyptians to Giotto. This course includes painting, sculpture and architecture. (3 semester hours)

History of American Art

A history of American art (painting, sculpture, and architecture) from the Colonial Period through the twentieth century. (3 semester hours)

ASTRONOMY

Conceptual Astronomy

An introduction to astronomy. Students will gain a knowledge of the day and night sky by using binoculars, telescopes, and other simple instruments and will learn how to observe and measure properties of astronomical objects. Basic concepts of the solar system, stellar evolution, and cosmology are covered. Mathematics is minimized and understanding is emphasized. (3 semester hours)

BIOLOGY

Principles of Biology

An introduction to the fundamental principles of biology, including cell structure, chemistry and function, genetics, evolution, adaptation, and ecology. (3 semester hours)

Frontiers in Biomolecular Science

This course is designed to assist secondary science educators in keeping current with new knowledge in the rapidly evolving field of molecular science. Emphasis is placed on cell, developmental, and molecular biology which are fields where this new knowledge will have the greatest impact on our daily lives. (4 semester hours)

BUSINESS ADMINISTRATION

Basic Accounting Principles

Role of accounting, basic concepts and methodology, mass data processing, valuation and income determination principles, management and internal control problems, basic financial statement components. (3 semester hours)

Management Accounting

Structure of financial statements and related accounting reporting problems; compound interest problems; analysis and interpretation of accounting data; income tax planning. (3 semester hours)

Business Communications

Specific instruction designed to develop competence in business communication: written communications, including letter, memorandum, and report writing; oral communications (individual and group); legal and ethical communication issues; and the electronic office. (3 semester hours)

CHEMISTRY

Introduction to Chemical Concepts

A course emphasizing simple mathematical techniques in a chemistry setting. Emphasis is on chemical reactions, stochiometry (simple and complex), and the periodic chart. (2 semester hours)

General Descriptive Chemistry I

Topics covered include atoms, molecules, ions, chemical formulas and equations, thermochemistry, gases, electronic structure of atoms, periodic table, properties of elements, chemical bonding, an introduction to organic chemistry, liquids and solids, phase changes, and solutions. (3 semester hours)

General Descriptive Chemistry II

Topics covered include rates of reactions, chemical equilibria, precipitation reactions, acids and bases, acid-base reactions, spontaneity of reaction, electrochemical cells, oxidation-reduction reactions, complex ions, coordination compounds, and nuclear reactions. (3 semester hours)

CLASSICAL STUDIES

Medical Word Formation and Etymology

This course is a practical introduction to the scientific language of medicine. It aims to acquaint the student with the classical (Greek and Latin) roots of that language and the ways these roots combine to form most of the important terms in use today. (Mastery of a relatively small number of roots will enable the student to make sense of thousands of such terms). The historical development of medical terminology is also considered. (3 semester hours)

Word Formation and Etymology

This course is an introduction to the Latin and Greek elements which make up over half the vocabulary of the English language. It is designed to improve vocabulary skills, promote precision of expression in writing and speaking, and increase the student's appreciation of the historical developments of his language. (3 semester hours)

COMPUTER SCIENCE

Computer Literacy

This course is designed for those with little or no computer experience. Topics include: physical components of computers, how computer programs are created, how computers are integrated into complete systems to solve problems, common computer applications, and ways in which computers affect our society. No access to computers is required. (3 semester hours)

Computer Laboratory

This introductory, hands-on course in basic microcomputer applications includes word processing, spreadsheet, database, graphs, and outlining. Students will use an integrated software package and associated text. Access to an IBM-compatible computer with MS-DOS 2.xx or higher and a printer is required.(1 semester hour)

ECONOMICS
Introduction to Economics I
Scarcity, production possibilities, and opportunity cost. Supply and demand analysis, free markets, the price system, and government policy. Microeconomic analysis of business decisions in competitive and noncompetitive markets. Macroeconomic analysis of production, employment, the price level, inflation, and economic growth. Monetary policy, fiscal policy, and stabilization of the economy. (3 semester hours)

Intermediate Microeconomics
The functioning of the market economy. The role of prices in determining the allocation of resources, the functioning of the firm in the economy, and forces governing the production of economic goods. (3 semester hours)

EDUCATION
Reading Education for Secondary and Special Subject Teachers
This course is designed to prepare secondary and special subject teachers to meet the literacy needs of students who exhibit a variety of reading levels. Emphasis is placed upon content reading skills which enable students to comprehend printed materials used in secondary courses. Instructional strategies and study methods are introduced to help secondary readers develop vocabulary, comprehend texts, write reports, and take tests. (2 semester hours)

Reading in the Elementary School
A course designed to give experienced teachers study in depth of the reading process as a fundamental aspect of the entire school curriculum. Newer media, techniques, and practices will be examined and evaluated. (3 semester hours)

ELECTRICAL ENGINEERING
Electric Circuits I
Introduction to theory, analysis, and design of electric circuits. Circuit parameters and elements: voltage, current, power, energy, resistance, capacitance, inductance. Kirchoff's laws and circuit-analysis techniques. Linearity, superposition, Thevenin's theorem. Active circuit elements and elementary amplifiers. Transient response of energy-storage circuits. Periodic functions, RMS values, phasors. Sinusoidal-steady-state response, resonance, Q bandwidth. Introduction to frequency response. (3 semester hours)

ENGLISH
Composition and Rhetoric
Basic forms and principles of expository and argumentative writing. Grammar and conventions of standard written English. Strategies for generating, organizing, and revising papers. Procedures of library research and use of evidence. (3 semester hours)

Composition and Reading
Continued study of forms and principles of expository and argumentative writing. Emphasis on academic writing. Interpretation, analysis, and evaluation of literary and nonliterary works, with skills in critical reading being connected to improvements in writing. A research paper is required. (3 semester hours)

English Composition and Rhetoric
ENGL 11. This course emphasizes the writing of effective paragraphs and their combination into longer papers, culminating in a study of the research paper. Coincidental to the development of writing facility will be the development of improved skills in the close reading of essays. (3 semester hours)

ENGL 12. This is a composition course focusing on persuasive writing; it includes a controlled resource paper. (3 semester hours)

A Survey of English Literature from Chaucer Through Pope
A study of representative works of Chaucer, Shakespeare, Spenser, Donne, Milton, Swift and Pope. Drama, poetry and prose are considered. (3 semester hours)

Introduction to Fiction
Students study the practice of basic fiction techniques and write numerous short papers as well as one complete story. Students read and analyze literary stories by well-known writers. Each student keeps a journal for which supplementary assignments are made. Emphasis is on creative work and a tutorial relationship with the instructor. (3 semester hours)

Contemporary Literature
The literature of the present generation. (3 semester hours)

Business Writing
This course teaches the skills of effective business communication. The course's introductory unit reviews grammar and focuses on fundamental business writing strategies. The course's second unit asks the student to apply the skills acquired in Unit 1 to specific types of business documents, including informative and positive messages; negative messages; persuasive messages; sales and fund-raising letters; and job-search documents. The course's third unit guides the student through the process of creating a substantial business report. (3 semester hours)

Creative Writing
The course builds on the short story writing skills introduced in *Introduction to Fiction*. Exercises allow students to develop the beginning, middle, and end of stories, to work with imagery, and to listen for their own voice and style. In addition to these exercises, students write two complete short stories and revise one. (3 semester hours)

Advanced Creative Writing
This course seeks to discover and develop the student's creative abilities in the planning and preparing of short stories. There are no set assignments, but students accomplish the equivalent of three semester hours' work by writing five or six stories. (3 semester hours)

Advanced Poetry Writing
There are no set assignments, but the student accomplishes the equivalent of three semester hours' work in a tutorial relationship with the instructor. (3 semester hours)

English Grammar
This course is an introduction to linguistics—the descriptive study of language. Examples are drawn from present-day English; and the student is introduced to such aspects of language as the sounds of English, the way words change in sound and meaning, systems of analyzing language patterns, and the varieties of English appropriate to different audiences and circumstances. (3 semester hours)

Shakespeare
A study of Shakespeare's major dramatic works, selected from the comedies, histories, and tragedies. The student will develop a critical appreciation of the plays themselves and learn about Shakespeare's dramatic technique and the intellectual and political background of

Elizabethan England by reading 12 plays and writing about them. (3 semester hours)

American Literature to 1865

This survey course begins with a brief examination of selected works of such figures as Anne Bradstreet, Benjamin Franklin, and Washington Irving, but the major focus of the course falls upon Emerson, Thoreau, Poe, Hawthorne, Melville, and Whitman. (3 semester hours)

Foundation Composition

This course is designed for transfer students and other upperclassmen who have encountered difficulty in meeting required college standards for composition. The writing process is divided into three phases: composing and organization, stylistics, and editing. Revision is stressed. (3 semester hours)

Fundamentals of Teaching English as a Second Language

A study of current trends and techniques in teaching English as a second language, including strategies for teaching listening, speaking, reading, and writing; measurement techniques for determining proficiency and progress of limited English Proficiency Students; adaptation of instructional materials for teaching ESL through the content areas; and aspects of English language and American culture that affect language learning among non-native speakers. (3 semester hours)

Writing for Business and Industry

Students will practice the kinds of writing they will be required to do throughout their careers. Early assignments include writing letters and memos; later assignments require a formal proposal and a formal report. Work is evaluated on the basis of content, style, organization, format, credibility, and appearance. (3 semester hours)

ENVIRONMENTAL SCIENCE

General Environmental Science

A comprehensive examination of population, resources, and environment as they relate to the well-being of human populations. The course looks at water, air, and soil pollution, and searches for ways to avoid misusing the earth's environment. Strategies are proposed for reversing environmental degradation and maintaining a healthful and sustainable earth. (3 semester hours)

FRENCH

Elementary French

This course has been designed to follow the basic format of the first semester course in elementary French given at UNC-Chapel Hill. Carrying four semester hours of credit, it has the same primary goals as the program upon which it is modeled: to give the beginning student a solid grasp of the underlying structures and vocabulary of modern French, and to systematically develop the four basic skills of listening, speaking, reading and writing. Audiocassette tapes are required, and the student must have access to an audiocassette tape recorder. (4 semester hours)

GEOGRAPHY

Cultural Geography

An introductory game/project-oriented course concerned with the characteristics, description, development, and spatial arrangement of world cultures or "way of life." (3 semester hours)

Physical Geography

An assessment of the occurrence, characteristics, and interrelationships of the earth's climates, landforms, natural vegetation and soils, especially as they influence man's attempt to utilize his environment. (3 semester hours)

North America's Landscapes

A survey of the cultural and physical landscapes of the United States and Canada. Emphasis on landscape evolution, present distributions, and interactions between people and their environment. (3 semester hours)

GEOLOGY

Introductory Geology and Laboratory

The nature and origin of minerals and rocks, volcanoes, earthquakes, earth's interior, mountains, soil, ground water, landscapes and the geologic work of glaciers, streams and wind are covered in this course. The topics of continental drift and the relationship between geology and man's environment also are considered. (4 semester hours)

Evolution of Life

Origin and evolution of life as examined from the perspectives of earth history and the fossil record, including theories of evolution, invertebrates, plants, and vertebrates. (3 semester hours)

Geology I: Physical

Systematic consideration of processes operating on and below the earth's surface and the resulting features of landscape, earth structures, and earth materials. Occurrences and utilization of the earth's physical resources. (3 semester hours)

GERMAN

Elementary German

1. In German 1 and 2, the student will acquire some elementary communication skills and get a systematic introduction to the basic grammatical patterns of the German language. While reading and writing will get the major emphasis, tape recordings will make it possible to also practice listening and speaking. This use of all four basic skills enables the student to approach the new language from every possible angle and thus to lay the foundation for future reading or conversation courses. Audiocassette tapes are required, and the student must have access to an audiocassette tape recorder. (3 semester hours)

2. A continuation of the above course. By the end of the course the student will have learned all fundamentals of German grammar. The student will also receive an introduction to simple literary texts. Students must have access to an audiocassette tape recorder in order to progress with listening and speaking skills. (3 semester hours)

Intermediate German

3. Designed to give students a thorough grammar review and to develop speed and accuracy in reading German prose. The course will acquaint the student with some of the twentieth century's outstanding German-language writers. (3 semester hours)

4. Designed to extend the student's ability to read German quickly and accurately. Readings include short stories by twentieth century authors and a play by Friedrich Durrenmatt. (3 semester hours)

HEALTH ADMINISTRATION

Field Training in Health Policy and Administration, I and II

This course provides an intensive field experience in a long-term care facility, working under the direction of an approved perceptor. In consultation with the course instructor, the preceptor and student design a program of activities specifically suited to the student's experience and in keeping with the needs of the facility. Over the course of the internship, the student spends time in each major functional area of the facility—administration, human resources and personnel management, nursing and health care services, rehabilitation, medical and patient records, activities, social services and admissions, business and financial management, dietary, housekeeping and laundry, and environmental management and maintenance. (6 semester hours)

Long-Term Care Administration I

Introduction to administration of long-term care facilities. Evolution of long-term care, survey of the current field. Examination of state and national requirements. (3 semester hours)

Long-Term Care Administration II

Advanced study of the administrative aspects of managing long-term care facilities. Emphasis on financing and patient care administration. (3 semester hours)

Management of Health Resources

Covers concepts of resource management in health care delivery and the supervision process and related skills as applied in various health-related facilities. (3 semester hours)

HISTORY

Western Civilization Since 1400

A survey of the development of Western civilization from the Renaissance to the present. (3 semester hours)

Ancient World to 180 A.D.

The ancient cultures of the Middle East, Greece, and Rome, including Mesopotamian, Egyptian, Hebrew, Phoenician, Greek, and Roman societies and cultures. (3 semester hours)

History of Western Civilization I

The emergence of Western civilization from antiquity to the mid-seventeenth century. (3 semester hours)

History of Western Civilization II

The development and spread of Western civilization since about 1650. A study of the ideas, institutions, and developments that have created the modern world. (3 semester hours)

Ancient History

Dealing with the history of the Orient, Greece, and Rome to the time of Constantine, this course pays particular attention to social and economic conditions, and cultural and religious developments. (3 semester hours)

Modern European History, 1500–1815

An introductory survey of the history of Europe from about 1450 to 1815. (3 semester hours)

Modern European History Since 1815

The reactions of European society to the problems created by industrialization, nationalism, revolutionary movements, the world wars, and the decline of Europe. (3 semester hours)

The World Since 1945

This course provides an introduction to the social, economic, and political history of the world since 1945. The course focuses on international problems and on case studies of individual countries. (3 semester hours)

American History to 1865

This course is a general survey of the history of the United States from the settlement of America to the emergence of the United States as an industrial nation. The emphasis throughout is on making relationships between important facts and drawing conclusions from them. (3 semester hours)

American History since 1865

This course is a general survey of the history of the United States from the end of the Civil War to the present. Particular emphasis is placed upon politics, economics, and the significant legislation of the period. (3 semester hours)

English History to 1688

A survey of English history from the earliest times to 1714, this course includes the Anglo-Saxon period, the Norman conquest, the feudal period, the Tudor monarchy, the constitutional struggles of the seventeenth century, and the end of the Stuart monarchy. (3 semester hours)

English History since 1688

This course deals with the Hanoverians, the American Revolution, the Napoleonic era, the Industrial Revolution, and the great social and economic changes of the nineteenth and twentieth centuries as England changed from a laissez-faire economy to a welfare state. (3 semester hours)

History of Russia from 1861 to the Present

This course enables the student to obtain some insight into the political and cultural trends which underlie the development of Russian state and society and their positions in the modern world. (3 semester hours)

Diplomatic History of the United States: 1900 to the Present

The course traces the development of American foreign relations from 1914 to the present with an eye to understanding the role of the United States in its world setting. It is hoped that the course will provide students with an understanding of the forces shaping twentieth-century diplomacy, the complex nature of decision making, and the historical background of present-day problems. (3 semester hours)

INTERDISCIPLINARY STUDIES

American Studies: The South in History and Literature

This course is a combination of American history and literature, and the topic is the American South. Students should gain a deeper knowledge and appreciation of the South and its relations with the larger society and culture, and an understanding of the questions and problems associated with the study of the South. Students will read primary historical accounts and outstanding short literary works. (3 semester hours)

ITALIAN

Elementary Italian

1. This course is designed to introduce the student to the most essential elements of Italian structure and vocabulary, as well as some basic aspects of Italian culture. All four language skills are stressed: listening comprehension, speaking, reading, and writing. Audiocassette tapes are required and the student must have access to an audiocassette tape player/recorder. (3 semester hours)

2. A continuation of the above course. The emphasis of this course will be still placed on developing the four basic skills of listening, speaking, reading, and writing and all major grammatical points will be covered. Audiocassette tapes are required and the student must have access to an audiocassette tape player/recorder. (3 semester hours)

Intermediate Italian

3. The Italian language is studied with emphasis on reading and writing. (3 semester hours)

4. A thorough knowledge of the Italian language is gained through reading a varied spectrum of Italian contemporary prose and writing in Italian on a variety of given topics. (3 semester hours)

LATIN

Elementary Latin

1. The principles of Latin necessary for the translation of Latin into English are introduced. A pronunciation tape is required. (3 semester hours)

2. Development of the ability to read and translate Latin prose is the primary aim of this course. Two books of Caesar's *Gallic Wars* will be read. (3 semester hours)

Intermediate Latin

3. In translating Cicero's *First Oration Against Catalus and in Defense of Archias*, attention is given to vocabulary, grammatical forms and syntax, and to the basic stylistic devices of Cicero's prose. (3 semester hours)

4. This course has a dual purpose: to polish the student's ability to translate Latin prose and to introduce him/her to Latin poetry. The work includes careful translation of selected lines and verses, and an introduction to the scansion of Latin heroic poetry and a thorough review of Latin forms and syntax, an analysis of certain creative techniques encountered in Ovid and Livy. (3 semester hours)

LIBRARY SCIENCE

Research Skills

Introductory course emphasizing search strategies and basic library resources, both traditional and computer. Useful to students writing research papers, speeches, or projects. Students are required to select a college library (either a community college, technical institute, or four-year college) in which to complete the assignments. (1 semester hour)

MATHEMATICS

Mathematics of Finance

Simple and compound interest, annuities and their application to amortization and sinking fund problems, installment buying, and calculation of premiums of life annuities and life insurance. (3 semester hours)

Precalculus Algebra and Trigonometry

Functions and their graphs (special attention to polynomial, rational, exponential, logarithmic, and trigonometric functions), and analytic trigonometry. (3 semester hours)

Elements of Calculus

Emphasis on concepts and applications of calculus, along with basic skills. Algebra review functions, graphs, limits, derivatives, integrals, logarithmic and exponential functions, functions of several variables, applications in biological and social sciences. (4 semester hours)

Analytic Geometry and Calculus I

First of three semesters of a unified analytic geometry and calculus sequence. Functions, graphs, limits, derivatives of algebraic and trigonometric functions, indefinite and definite integrals, fundamental plane analytic geometry. (4 semester hours)

Analytic Geometry and Calculus II

Second of three semesters of a unified analytic geometry and calculus sequence. Differentiation and integration of exponential, logarithmic, and inverse trigonometric functions. Techniques of integration. Complex numbers. Elementary differential equations. Sequences, series, power series, and Taylor's Theorem. (4 semester hours)

Analytic Geometry and Calculus III

Third of three semesters of a unified analytic geometry and calculus sequence. Vectors and vector functions. Analytic geometry of three dimensional space. Functions of several variables, partial derivatives, gradients, directional derivatives, maxima and minima. Multiple integration. Line and surface integrals, Green's Theorem, Divergence Theorem. (4 semester hours)

Algebra

This course provides a review of the basics of algebra. Basic algebraic expressions, functions, exponents, and logarithms are included with an emphasis on problem solving. (3 semester hours)

Calculus for Business and Social Sciences

An introductory survey of differential and integral calculus with emphasis on techniques and applications of interest for business and social sciences. (3 semester hours)

Trigonometry and Analytic Geometry

Covers the basis concepts of trigonometry and analytic geometry. Covered are the trigonometric functions and their graphs, relationships, and applications. Basic analytic geometry topics include the conics, translations, and rotations. Basic ideas of vector geometry are introduced. (3 semester hours)

MUSIC

Fundamentals of Music I

Musical notation, major and minor scales, key and time signatures, rhythms, simple keyboard chord progressions, and melody-writing are included. Optional material on the guitar. (3 semester hours)

Masterworks of Music

This course is directed primarily to students with little or no formal background in music. A grounding in the fundamentals of music theory is given in the first two lessons. The main body of the course teaches music appreciation through a study of the main periods of music history and through detailed examination of representative works from each period. The course seeks to lay a foundation for the understanding and enjoyment of music of any period or genre. (3 semester hours)

NUTRITION

Introduction to Human Nutrition

Presented as an integrated body of knowledge derived from several disciplines. Functions and sources of man's food. Nutrient requirements and their relation to health and disease. The relevance of nutrition to individual well-being, social welfare, and economic development. (3 semester hours)

PHILOSOPHY

Main Problems in Philosophy: An Introduction

This course is an introduction to Western philosophy with an historical approach. Readings include brief selections from Plato, Aristotle, Descartes, Locke, Berkeley, Hume, Kant, and Peirce. In addition to metaphysics and epistemology, the course treats theories of truth and the mind-body problem. (3 semester hours)

Introductory Symbolic Logic

Using a standard notation of symbolic logic, this course teaches principles and techniques for determining the validity and invalidity of arguments. The course covers truth-function theory and quantification theory. (3 semester hours)

Introduction to Ethics

An introduction to the study of moral issues and philosophical questions concerning morality. (3 semester hours)

Bioethics

The ethical basis of moral and legal problems generated or made acute by advances in biology and medicine, such as abortion, euthanasia, patient rights, experiments with human subjects, and genetic manipulation. (3 semester hours

PHYSICS

General Physics

Course 204. Introduction to physics, including the study of mechanics, sound, heat, and thermodynamics. The analytical approach is employed, with emphasis on problem solving. (3 semester hours)

Course 207. Introduction to physics, including the study of electricity and magnetism, optics, and modern physics. The analytical approach is employed, with emphasis on problem solving. (3 semester hours)

POLITICAL SCIENCE

Introduction to Government in the United States

This course is a broad introduction to government in the United States. It examines the foundations of American government, the politics and actions of citizens, and the political institutions of the U.S. government. Founding principles, the Constitution, civil rights and civil liberties, elections and political parties, public opinion and the media, interest groups, Congress, the presidency, bureaucracy and courts, and the policy process are covered. (3 semester hours)

State and Local Government

This is an introductory course on the politics and policies of subnational governments in the United States. The course devotes some attention to localities but concentrates on the states. Emphasis is placed on the role of states and localities in the federal system and the importance of recent political changes affecting them. (3 semester hours)

Politics in Western Europe

This course provides an overview of European politics through an understanding of parliamentary democracy, political parties, political institutions, and the ways in which governments respond to diversity within their borders. Students will learn how European political systems differ from the American system, and how to interpret the changes that have occurred in Europe with the fall of Communism in the East and increased integration through the European Community. (3 semester hours)

Introduction to Political Thought—Ancient and Medieval

Survey course tracing the political ideas of major Western philosophers from Plato in the fourth century B.C. through Thomas Aquinas in the thirteenth century A.D. It introduces students to the origins and evolution of some of the political values and ideas that have helped shape our world. Authors whose works will be used in the course are Aeschylus, Thucydides, Plato, Aristotle, St. Paul, St. Augustine, and Thomas Aquinas. (3 semester hours)

Urban Politics

The focus of this course is on the policy arena of urban politics. The course also traces the evolution and current status of our cities. Specific problems of the cities will be addressed: the political content and structure of urban government; the social and economic context in which local policies are made; race and poverty; and taxation and spending in urban America. (3 semester hours)

Introduction to American Government

The American federal system, integrating national and state governments, with emphasis on constitutional principles, major governmental organs, governmental functions, and the politics and machinery of elections. Some attention to other types of political systems, and comparisons where relevant. (3 semester hours)

United States Foreign Policy

This course surveys the process of United States foreign policy making and the sources which influence its formulation. Implementation is examined through study of recent foreign policy issues. Emphasis is placed upon the role of the United States in world affairs since World War II. (3 semester hours)

POULTRY SCIENCE

Poultry Production

This course is the lecture portion of *Poultry Science 201* and does not include the laboratory aspects. Fundamental principles of broiler, turkey, and egg production including poultry physiology, breeding, incubation, housing, nutrition, disease control, management, and marketing. (3 semester hours)

PSYCHOLOGY

Introduction to Psychology

Survey of basic principles for the understanding of behavior and experience including development, learning, cognition, biological foundations, perception, motivation, personality, behavior foundations, perception, motivation, personality, behavior abnormalities, measurement of individual differences, and social processes. The value of scientific observation and experimentation to the development of psychological understanding is emphasized. (3 semester hours)

General Psychology

This course is designed as an introduction to the basic methods, theories, and applications of psychology to a wide range of issues. Areas reviewed will include biological, developmental, cognitive, clinical, social, and personality psychology. (3 semester hours)

REAL ESTATE

Real Estate Principles and Practices

This course is designed as an introductory-level offering. It provides a comprehensive view of all factors which affect real estate decisions, and emphasizes components of real estate law, brokerage, appraisal, license law, finance, and closing procedures. (3 semester hours)

RECREATION ADMINISTRATION

Introduction to Parks, Recreation, and Tourism

Introduction to the professional field of recreation by presenting the basic principles, fundamentals and concepts of recreation as related to such factors as: recreation history and objectives, sociological and economic aspects of recreation, leadership qualities, and facility provision, and settings for organized recreation in modern society. (3 semester hours)

RELIGIOUS STUDIES

Introduction to Old Testament Literature

An introduction to the literature of the Old Testament. (3 semester hours)

Introduction to New Testament Literature

A basic guide to the history and literature of the New Testament and to the central figures and ideas of earliest Christianity. (3 semester hours)

RUSSIAN

Elementary Russian

1. This is an introductory course designed to lay the foundation of grammar and to convey basic reading and pronunciation skills. (3 semester hours)

2. The second semester of an introductory course designed to continue with the laying of the foundation of grammar. (3 semester hours)

Intermediate Russian

3. The objective of this course is the completion of the basic Russian grammar. Extensive exercises are designed to consolidate the knowledge acquired in the first two courses, especially of the more difficult grammar. (3 semester hours)

4. The Russian grammar is thoroughly reviewed. At the same time, the student is exposed to short readings in Russian literature. (3 semester hours)

SOCIOLOGY

Criminology

The processes whereby behavior is defined as crime and persons are identified as criminals. Includes a sociological investigation of agencies of law enforcement, adjudication, correlations, and prevention; patterns of criminal behavior; explanations of variations in criminality with emphasis on sociocultural and sociopsychological theories. (3 semester hours)

Juvenile Delinquency

Nature and extent of juvenile delinquency; measurement problems; and biogenic, psychogenic and sociogenic theories of delinquency causation. Policy implications of delinquency theories for treatment and prevention. Evaluation of treatment and prevention programs. (3 semester hours)

American Society

This course introduces the essentials of contemporary sociology. It asks two basic sociological questions: What holds society together? and How are individuals related to society? and explores answers through the study of the specific substantive fields of sociology. (3 semester hours)

Black-White Relations in the United States

Designed to introduce the student to minority relations as a field of study, to assist in providing a perspective in which to view contemporary black-white relations, and to challenge the student to rely upon disciplined and scientific inquiry in this subject. This course places major emphasis upon the power relationships which exist between a large dominant group and a smaller minority group. (3 semester hours)

Crime and Delinquency

This course takes a step back from our everyday notions of crime and begins to examine the more complex social factors associated with crime and delinquency. The definitions, various patterns, and possible causes of crime and delinquency will be scrutinized during this course, culminating in an examination of possible solutions to the crime problem. Introductory terms and concepts concerning the criminal justice system will be introduced and then built upon to gain a better understanding of how our criminal justice system is supposed to work, and how it actually does work. (3 semester hours)

Family and Society

The family is studied as a social institution which has economic and political ties and overtones. A study is made of the similarities and differences which are found in various societal contexts. (3 semester hours)

SPANISH

Intermediate Spanish

SPAN 3. The two-semester sequence of Spanish 3, 4 is designed to increase reading and writing skills. An introduction to representative literary works and study of the finer points of Spanish structure are included. (3 semester hours)

SPAN 4. This course is designed to increase reading and writing skills. An introduction to representative literary works and study of the finer points of Spanish structure are included. (3 semester hours)

SPEECH

Social Dialects

Students will study language diversity in the United States. They will learn about dialects as well as language of immigrant groups and about the interaction of languages in contact. They will also study the role language plays in education, law, and medicine and the various language policies in the United States. (3 semester hours)

STATISTICS

Introduction to Statistics for Engineers

Statistical techniques useful to engineers and physical scientists. Includes elementary probability, frequency distributions, sampling, variation, estimation of means and standard deviations, confidence intervals, significance tests, elementary least squares curve fitting. (3 semester hours)

Basic Statistics

Collection and handling of data; measures of central tendency and variability; correlation, sampling and probability; analysis of variance; introduction to research design. (3 semester hours)

NONCREDIT COURSES

ENGLISH

English Composition and Grammar

A basic course in English that presupposes no previous study of either composition or grammar. Its purpose is to increase awareness of language, to provide skills necessary for effective writing, and to clarify common trouble spots in grammar and mechanics. The course is flexible enough to serve a student just beginning high school, someone needing a college preparatory refresher course, or an adult seeking a review of fundamental English for his or her own satisfaction. (Noncredit) *Tuition:* $165.

FAMILY DAY CARE

Family Day Care Independent Study

Consisting of two courses, this certificate program is designed for persons currently providing family day care in their own homes and desiring additional training in this field. The courses cover basic entry level material on twelve key day care topics, six focusing on management and six on quality programming. Reading material for the program is contained in an introductory information packet and six topical packets for each course. A manual for each course guides the student through the packets and assigns reports on activities to be undertaken in the learner's home in the normal course of providing day care.

Course 1: Family Day Care Management. This course provides the caregiver with basic information on managing a family day home. Included are practical suggestions for working with parents, keeping business records, creating a healthy and safe environment, providing nutritious food, understanding cultural diversity and making use of community resources. (Noncredit) *Tuition:* $50 plus $15 for materials.

Course 2: Building quality in Family Day Care. This course provides information on how to set up the environment and activities in a family day home so that children benefit from the experience both emotionally and intellectually. Topics include the use of space for play and learning, child development and growth, planning activity programs, handling behavior problems, care for the school-aged child, and working with children with special needs. (Noncredit) *Tuition:* $50 plus $15 for materials.

MATHEMATICS

Review of Algebra

A contemporary approach to the algebra of real and complex numbers, this is the equivalent of what was formerly called Intermediate Algebra in the secondary schools. The manner in which the subject is treated is in line with the new approach now being introduced into the schools at both the elementary and secondary levels. (Noncredit) *Tuition:* $165.

NURSING

Nursing Refresher Course

This course is part of the Nursing Refresher Program which also includes a clinical practicum. The Program is designed to address a full range of common nursing problems. Medical surgical concepts as well as psychosocial aspects of nursing care are presented. The correspondence course includes 33 modules on topics in the field of nursing. The program is open to nurses who haven't worked in five years or more or who have a lapsed or inactive license, and who would like to return to nursing either full or part-time. You must arrange for the clinical portion of the Program before enrolling in the correspondence course. Nurses who complete the entire program, including the correspondence course and the practicum, will be eligible to apply for reinstatement of the North Carolina nursing license. (14 CEUs) *Tuition:* $250.

North Carolina, University of - Greensboro
1000 Spring Garden Street
Greensboro, North Carolina 27412
(919) 379-5243

Description:
The University of North Carolina at Greensboro was established in 1891 as the State Normal and Industrial College. It later became the North Carolina College for Women and from 1932 was the Woman's College of the University of North Carolina. Its present name was adopted in 1963 and it became coeducational in 1964. UNC-G is a participant in a consortium of eight institutions within the University of North Carolina System offering college-level correspondence courses and other opportunities for individualized study at a distance from the university campuses. In the consortium arrangement, each institution originating a course provides instruction and awards academic credit, while responsibility for administration of the program lies with the office of Independent Studies at the University of North Carolina at Chapel Hill. SEE **North Carolina, University of - Chapel Hill.**

Faculty:
Karen Hogarth, Member of UNC Independent Studies Advisory Committee.

Accreditations:
Southern Association of Colleges and Schools.

North Carolina State University
Raleigh, North Carolina 27607 (919) 737-2434

Description:
North Carolina State University was founded in 1887 as a land-grant institution and began operations as the North Carolina College of Agriculture and Mechanic Arts in 1889. It is a participant in a consortium of eight institutions within the University of North Carolina System offering college-level correspondence courses and other opportunities for individualized study at a distance from the university campuses. In the consortium arrangement, each institution originating a course provides instruction and awards academic credit, while responsibility for administration of the program lies with the office of Independent Studies at the University of North Carolina at Chapel Hill. SEE **North Carolina, University of - Chapel Hill.**

Faculty:
John Cudd, Member of UNC Independent Studies Advisory Committee.

Accreditations:
Southern Association of Colleges and Schools.

North Dakota, University of
Department of Correspondence Study
Division of Continuing Education
P.O. Box 58201
University Station
Grand Forks, North Dakota 58201
(701) 777-3044

Description:
The University of North Dakota began its service of correspondence courses in 1910 and the program has been in continuous operation since then. Over 3,000 students are enrolled in the 80 courses available for both credit and noncredit.

Faculty:
Karen Berthold, Director, Correspondence Study; Diana Latexier, Registrar. There is a faculty of 35 members.

Academic Levels:
College
Noncredit

Degree/Certificate Programs:
The University of North Dakota will allow up to 30 semester hours of correspondence credit toward an under-

graduate degree; it will not accept correspondence credit toward a graduate degree.

Admission Requirements:

Correspondence study courses are open to all interested persons. Some courses have required prerequisites. Superior high school students may enroll in a college course upon written approval of their superintendent.

Tuition:

$70 per semester hour payable in full at the time of registration. There is also a $15 administrative fee per course. Variable tuition charges for noncredit courses (contact the Department of Independent Study for current tuition). Fees are subject to change without notice and are usually on an annual basis. If a request for withdrawal is submitted within one month from the date of enrollment, the course fee will be refunded less a $15 administrative fee and a charge for each lesson graded. If the request for withdrawal is received between one and two months of the date of enrollment, one-half of the course fee will be returned less a $15 administrative fee and a charge for each lesson graded. No refunds will be authorized after two months from the date of enrollment.

Enrollment Period:

The maximum time allowed to complete a course is one year; only three lessons can be submitted per seven-day period. A six-month extension may be allowed with payment of a $25 extension fee.

Equipment Requirements:

The cost of textbooks is not included in the tuition. They may be ordered separately from the University Bookstore. Visa and MasterCard are accepted.

Credit and Grading:

One or more examinations are required in most courses taken for credit and must be supervised by a proctor acceptable to the Department of Correspondence Study. The final examination must be taken within one month of the completion of the course. Letter grades are awarded in the majority of credit correspondence courses. However, students also have the option of Satisfactory/Unsatisfactory (S/U) grading based on restrictions outlined in the University of North Dakota undergraduate catalog. Credit is awarded in semester hour units.

Library Services:

Students are required to use local library facilities.

Accreditations:

North Central Association of Colleges and Schools. Member of: National University Continuing Education Association.

COLLEGE COURSES

ACCOUNTING

Elements of Accounting

Course 200. Basic principles of the complete accounting cycle. (3 semester hours)

Course 201. Partnerships and corporations with special emphasis on accounting procedures for the assets and liabilities commonly found in business. (3 semester hours)

ANTHROPOLOGY

Introduction to Cultural Anthropology

The nature and development of culture, utilizing illustrative data drawn from literate an nonliterate people of the world. (3 semester hours)

Introduction to Biological Anthropology

Introduction to field of biological or physical anthropology. This course will provide a general background in human evolution biology. (3 semester hours)

Medical Anthropology

An examination of the human biological and cultural responses to health and disease as seen from an anthropological perspective. (3 semester hours)

CHEMICAL ENGINEERING

Stoichiometry

Introductory principles of stoichiometry with emphasis directed to material and energy balances involved in chemical processes. (3 semester hours)

COMPUTER SCIENCE

Introduction to Computers

An introductory course for students who do not plan to take advanced courses in Computer Science. This course is designed for students who have a limited mathematical background. Introduction to computers, problem-solving and the BASIC language. (2 semester hours)

Introduction to Computers Laboratory

A computer literacy course. Hands-on use of word processors, spreadsheets, databases, and BASIC language for microcomputers will be included. (1 semester hour)

Computer Programming I

An introduction to computer programming in a high-level language, with emphasis on problem solving and logical thinking. Students learn to design, implement, test, and debug programs for small-scale problems using elementary data types and control structures. (3 semester hours)

ECONOMICS

Elements of Economics

Survey of economic principles for students planning no further formal study of economics. Analysis of factors influencing aggregate levels of output, employment, and prices; introduction to U.S. monetary system; price determination and resource allocations under competitive and monopolistic conditions. Review of selected contemporary economic issues. (3 semester hours)

Principles of Microeconomics

Nature, method, and scope of economic analysis: economic scarcity, resources, specialization and division labor, supply and demand, production and cost, technology, product and resource market structures, distribution of income, and international trade. (3 semester hours)

Principles of Macroeconomics

Analysis of aggregate levels of income and employment, inflation, monetary and fiscal policy, economic growth and development, international finance, and comparative economic systems. (3 semester hours)

ENGINEERING

Engineering Graphics

Analysis and representation of planes and solids in orthogonal and axonometric projection; graphical expression and communication of three dimensional objects by technical sketching, instrumental delineation, size specification and fundamental applications of interactive, computer-aided drawing. (2 semester hours)

Descriptive Geometry

Graphical analysis, synthesis and, solutions of three dimensional design problems via technical drafting and an introduction to computer-generated imagery. Point, line, and plane relationships as related to basic engineering and geological applications are studied by using both the successive auxiliary view approach and revolution methods. (2 semester hours)

ENGLISH

Composition I

Guided practice in writing, with emphasis on thoughtful analysis of one's subject matter, clear understanding of the writing situation, flexible use of rhetorical strategies, and development of stylistic options. (3 semester hours)

Composition II

Guided practice in writing with emphasis on more demanding writing situations. (3 semester hours)

Technical and Business Writing

(2 semester hours)

Introduction to Fiction

Fiction studied as a literary type, for understanding and for critical appreciation. (2 semester hours)

Survey of American Literature

ENGL 303. The literature of the United States from its beginnings to the Civil War. (3 semester hours)

ENGL 304. The literature of the United States from the Civil War to the twentieth century. (3 semester hours)

Black American Writers

Writings by black Americans studied for understanding and critical appreciation. (3 semester hours)

FINE ARTS

Introduction to Fine Arts

Preparatory presentation and discussion sessions combined with attendance at a variety of art events to provide understanding and appreciation of the fine arts and their importance to the individual and the community. (3 semester hours)

FRENCH

Beginning French

Course 101. Fundamentals of French grammar, oral use of the language and reading of easy French. The audio-oral approach through tapes is required. (4 semester hours)

Course 102. Continued study of fundamentals of French grammar, oral use of the language, and reading of easy French. The audio-oral approach through tapes is required. (4 semester hours)

Second Year French

Course 201. Review of the structure of the language; readings in French, practice in oral and written expression. (4 semester hours)

Course 202. A continuation of the above course. (4 semester hours)

GEOGRAPHY

Cultural Geography

A systematic analysis of man's cultural regions including settlement patterns and change via migration and diffusion. (3 semester hours)

World Regional Geography

Development of the concept of region with analysis of the relationship of physical and cultural features to the contemporary world situation. (3 semester hours)

Geography for Teachers

Geographical concepts and basic philosophy including a survey of the literature which forms the basis for analysis and application of current techniques in the field of geography. (2 semester hours)

Geography of Canada

A regional and topical analysis of the physical, cultural, and economic features of Canada. (3 semester hours)

Geography of North Dakota

An analysis of the development and distribution of the physical, cultural, and economic characteristics of the state. (3 semester hours)

GERMAN

Beginning German

Course 101. Fundamentals of German grammar, oral use of the language and reading of easy German. The audio-oral approach through tapes is required. (4 semester hours)

Course 102. Continuing study of fundamentals of German grammar, oral use of the language, and reading of easy German. The audio-oral approach through tapes is required. (4 semester hours)

HISTORY

Western Civilization to 1500

An interpretative survey of cultural continuity from 3000 B.C. to the end of the European Middle Ages. (3 semester hours)

Western Civilization Since 1500

An interpretative survey with emphasis on movements common to Western Europe from the Reformation through World War II. (3 semester hours)

United States to 1877

A survey of early American history, including old world background, transformation of British institutions into American institutions, revolution, and the establishment of the Union with its temporary breakup in the Civil War. (3 semester hours)

United States since 1877

A survey of the last century of American history, including the transformation of an isolationist, agrarian nation into an urban, industrial, and world power, with emphasis upon the resulting domestic maladjustments. (3 semester hours)

HOME ECONOMICS

Fundamentals of Nutrition

Basic principles of nutrition with applications for individuals and family groups. (3 semester hours)

HUMANITIES

Humanities I

This course is designed to introduce beginning university students to the modes of expression of the major disciplines of the humanities: imaginative literature, philosophy, history, religion, drama, music, and art. A central theme provides the focus of the course and in approaching that theme through each of the humanistic disciplines, the way is opened to a perception of the value structure of our cultural tradition. (4 semester hours)

Humanities II

This course is structurally the same as *Humanities I*, and has the same general goals, but differs from it in that its subject matter is the culture of classical Greece. The authors read in the course include Homer, Aeschylus, and Plato along with varying selections from other poets, dramatists, philosophers, and historians. (4 semester hours)

INDUSTRIAL TECHNOLOGY

Industrial Safety

The major safety concerns and problems commonly associated with the industrial and occupational environment are addressed. Emphasis is placed on management of technology and people for optimum safety conditions and productivity. (2 semester hours)

MANAGEMENT

Managerial Concepts

This course is designed to expose the student to a variety of concepts presented within the framework of the traditional functions of management. The various approaches to planning, decision making, organizing, motivation, work groups, authority, personnel staffing, leadership, change/conflict, communications, and controlling are explored in the context of supervisory personnel development. (3 semester hours)

MATHEMATICS

Intermediate Algebra

For students with high school algebra or who feel the need to review high school algebra before going on in mathematics. Covers fractions, exponents, radicals, graphing, equations, inequalities, systems of equations, functions, variations, and other topics. S-U grading only. (3 semester hours)

Finite Mathematics

An elementary introduction to some of the mathematical techniques which have applications in the management, life, and social sciences. Topics covered include systems of linear equations and inequalities, matrices, linear programming, mathematics of finance, and elementary probability. (3 semester hours)

Trigonometry

(2 semester hours)

Discrete Mathematics

Introduction to set theory, functions and relations, permutations and combinations, logic, Boolean algebra, induction, difference equations. Other topics from graphs, finite, automata, and formal languages. (3 semester hours)

Calculus I

(4 semester hours)

Calculus II

(4 semester hours)

Calculus III

(4 semester hours)

METEOROLOGY

Introduction to Radar Meteorology

Introduction to principles and theory of microwave radar and its use as a meteorological observation or research tool. Includes laboratory. (4 semester hours)

MUSIC APPRECIATION

Introduction to the Understanding of Music

Music appreciation for student without an extensive background in music. (3 semester hours)

NORWEGIAN

Beginning Norwegian

Course 101. Grammar, pronunciation, reading and translation, oral and written exercises. The audio-oral approach through tapes is required. (4 semester hours)

Course 102. Grammar, pronunciation, reading and translation, and written exercises. (4 semester hours)

Second-Year Norwegian

Grammar, selected readings, translation, and conversation. (4 semester hours)

OCCUPATIONAL THERAPY

Introduction to Occupational Therapy

History, scope, objectives, and functions of occupational therapy. (2 semester hours)

Medical Terminology

Knowledge of medical terminology. (1 semester hour)

PHARMACOLOGY

Human Pharmacology

A survey of the more important drugs used in medicine, including basic principles, clinical use, and possible adverse effects. (3 semester hours)

Drugs Subject to Abuse

Biochemical, pharmacological, behavioral, and therapeutic aspects of substance abuse. (2 semester hours)

PHILOSOPHY

Contemporary Moral Issues

A study of decision making based on contemporary value systems as applied to key social and personal concerns in America, namely business ethics, medical-moral problems, truthtelling in the public and private sectors, environmental ethics, racism, poverty, war and peace, etc. (3 semester hours)

Death and Dying

An examination of various perspectives on death and dying in our own and other cultures with a view to coping with the problems of mortality and immortality. Medical, psychological, philosophical, and religious aspects contributing to an understanding of the meaning of death will be offered by resource people whose experience will lend assistance to the students confronting the reality of death and dying. (2 semester hours)

PSYCHOLOGY

Introduction to Psychology

Nature and scope of psychology as a science and a profession. (3 semester hours)

Introduction to Statistics

Descriptive and inferential statistics as applied to psychological measurement and experimentation. (4 semester hours)

Developmental Psychology

Intellectual, emotional, and social development of the normal individuals; significance of childhood experience for later development. (4 semester hours)

Abnormal Psychology

Systematic study of behavior pathology, with primary emphasis on etiology and symptomatology. (3 semester hours)

Adulthood and Aging

Basic findings and theoretical issues in the study of human aging from biopsychological and sociopsychological persepectives with an emphasis on the individual. (3 semester hours)

Introduction to Personality

Examination of basic concepts in the field of personality. (3 semester hours)

RELIGIOUS STUDIES

Introduction to Religion (West)

A survey of the classical stories, rituals and symbols of religious culture in Western civilization from ancient times to the present. (3 semester hours)

World Religions

A general survey of major world religions including Hinduism, Buddhism, Confucianism, Taoism, Islam, Judaism, and Christianity. Stress on the major tenets of these religions. (3 semester hours)

SOCIOLOGY

Introduction to Sociology

An introductory analysis of the nature of society, the interrelationships of its component groups, and the process whereby society persists and changes. Interpretation of human behavior from the standpoint of the group. (3 semester hours)

Social Problems

A sociological analysis of major social problems in America. (3 semester hours)

Rural Sociology

A survey of sociological principles as they relate to rural society with emphasis on rural change and rural development. (3 semester hours)

The Family

Structure and function of the family, comparative family systems, sociology of family life stages (such as courtship, marriage, parenthood, old age), contemporary trends and problems of the family. (4 semester hours)

Aging

Socialization theory and its implication for the aging process. (3 semester hours)

Sociology of Death and Dying

The study of social aspects of death and dying as they involve the individual, the family, organizations, and life-and-death decisions. (3 semester hours)

Social Psychology

The study of individual behavior in its social context: how the individual acts upon the social environment, is acted upon by the environment, and interacts with other individuals. (4 semester hours)

SPANISH

Beginning Spanish

Course 102. Continued study of pronunciation and fundamental grammatical principles through the development of skill in listening, comprehension and speaking, followed by practice in reading and writing. The audio-oral approach through tapes is required. (4 semester hours)

VISUAL ARTS

Introduction to Drawing and Color Materials

Introduction for nonmajors to drawing and color media and techniques. Includes working from still-lifes, models, and landscapes. (3 semester hours)

Special Topics: Visual Thinking

Develop an enriched appreciation of the world around us and creativity through a study of how we perceive—right brain, left brain—and how perceptions can be used creatively. (3 semester hours)

VOCATIONAL EDUCATION

Coordinating Techniques

Guidance, selection, and placing students in training stations; assisting in job adjustments; developing training agreements and training plans; evaluation; follow-up; state reports; advisory committees; public relations; labor laws; program justifications; organization and supervision of cooperative programs. (2 semester hours)

Philosophy of Vocational Education

Theory and practice of vocational education in secondary and postsecondary schools. Interrelationship of vocational education programs. Funding for vocational education programs. Relationship between general education and vocational education. (3 semester hours)

North Georgia College
Independent Study
Dahlonega, Georgia 30597   (404) 864-3391

Description:
    The Independent Study program of North Georgia College is a service of the University System of Georgia Independent Study as offered by the Georgia Center for Continuing Education located at the University of Georgia in Athens, Georgia. For courses available, SEE **Georgia, University of.**

Accreditations:
    Southern Association of Colleges and Schools.

Northern Colorado, University of
College of Continuing Education
Greeley, Colorado 80639   (303) 351-2944

Description:

The University of Northern Colorado, formerly Colorado State College, was founded in 1890. Although teacher education was its original purpose, the university now offers programs in the liberal arts, preprofessional, and vocational programs. The university participates in the Colorado Consortium for Independent Study which is composed of the independent study offices of six institutions of higher education in Colorado: Adams State College, Colorado State University, University of Colorado, University of Northern Colorado, University of Southern Colorado, and Metropolitan State College of Denver. The consortium strives to provide quality independent study opportunities and to avoid duplication of courses offered by consortium members. The correspondence student should consult the listings in this *Guide* of all member schools of the Consortium for a complete offering of subject matter.

Faculty:

Sharol L. Darling, Independent Study Program Manager.

Academic Levels:

College

Degree/Certificate Programs:

Up to thirty correspondence credits may be applied toward the baccalaureate degree.

Admission Requirements:

Open enrollment. Some courses require prerequisites.

Tuition:

$70 per semester hour credit plus course fee if applicable. Fees subject to change without notice. Refund allowed within forty days of enrollment minus an administrative fee.

Enrollment Period:

The maximum time allowed to complete a course is 1 year. A 12-month extension may be granted upon payment of a fee of $20 per semester hour.

Equipment Requirements:

Textbooks and supplies must be purchased by the student.

Credit and Grading:

Grading system is A, B, C, D, F with plus and minus recorded and averaged. The minimum passing grade is D. Examinations must be monitored by an approved proctor. Credit is awarded in semester hours.

Library Services:

Correspondence students may use the University of Northern Colorado Library upon presentation of course receipt at checkout desk. Students are encouraged to use local libraries and interlibrary loan as necessary.

Accreditations:

North Central Association of Colleges and Schools. Member of: National University Continuing Education Association.

COLLEGE COURSES

BIOLOGY

Exploring Biology

An exploration of biological principles of concern to the educated layperson. Topics include ecology, evolution, the cell, organs and systems, inheritance and disease. (3 semester hours)

ECONOMICS

Money and Banking

The study of monetary theory, monetary policy, money, banking, and the Federal Reserve System. (3 semester hours)

Urban Planning Economics

Students will study economic problems relevant to urban areas including land use, congestion, housing, and poverty. The role of the private and public sector in resolving these problems will be analyzed. (3 semester hours)

Comparative Economic Systems

Analysis of capitalism, socialism, communism, as types of economic systems; origins, historical development, major characteristics, successes and failures, and future development of prominent world economies. (3 semester hours)

Industrial Organization

Theoretical and empirical study of the structure, organization, and conduct of firms on economic performance and welfare. (3 semester hours)

Intermediate Microeconomics

The theory of consumer choice, of the business firm, and resource allocation. (3 semester hours)

Women and the Economy

Explore the economic status of women, the institutions that have affected their economic decisions, and impact on the performance of the economy. (3 semester hours)

Labor/Management Economics

Examine American Labor Movement, development of labor laws and policy, economics of labor markets, employment of collective bargaining practice, union impact on contemporary industrial organization. (3 semester hours)

Public Finance

Government financing at federal, state, and local levels as reflected in expenditures, revenues, and debt. (3 semester hours)

International Trade

Analyze theoretical underpinnings of international trade and their relevance to practical issues. Trade impediments, trade policies and institutions which have evolved in a dynamic international system are also discussed. (3 semester hours)

International Finance

Analyze theories and functions of the international financial system, stressing balance of payments and national income problems, adjustment mechanisms, exchange rates, and capital flows. (3 semester hours)

Economics of Growth and Development

Analyze the theory, processes, and history of economic growth and development, emphasizing resource use and productivity in less developed areas. (3 semester hours)

Contemporary Economic Problems

Learn the contribution of economic models and techniques in understanding current issues facing society. Analyze the efficiency and equity impact of alternative solutions. (3 semester hours)

Economic History of the United States

Review the historical changes in U.S. economic institutions. Assess U.S. history based on macroeconomic and microeconomic pressures. Emphasis is on post-Civil War period. (3 semester hours)

History of Economic Thought

Trace the evolution of economic thinking from the seventeenth century to modern day. See roles played by certain ''schools'' of economic thinkers, the genesis of their ideas, and their contributions. (3 semester hours)

EDUCATION

Achieving Effective Instruction in Developmental Reading

Teaching/learning strategies, reading materials, selection, lesson planning, and organizing for instruction in reading across the total curriculum constitute the focus of the course. This course meets the reading requirement for Colorado teacher certification at the elementary level. (3 semester hours)

Reading and Writing in the Content Area

Develop understanding of cognitive affective needs of middle and secondary students in reading and writing to learn. Develop sensitivity to individual needs. This course meets the reading requirement for Colorado teacher certification at the secondary level. (3 semester hours)

Exceptional Students in the Regular Classroom

Provides information on handicapped and gifted students, identification procedures, and teaching techniques. (2 semester hours)

Seminar in Mainstreaming: Exception Students in the Regular Classroom

Survey course for non-special education graduate students concerning mainstreaming and accommodation of handicapped students in regular classrooms. Emphasis placed on solving classroom problems relating to graduate students' previous experiences with handicapped persons. (3 semester hours)

Neurology and Learning

Explore key neurological concepts and their application to the classroom. Concepts will illuminate behavioral issues and clarify cognitive issues facing teachers and learners from pre-birth through childhood to adult learning patterns. (3 semester hours)

ENVIRONMENTAL STUDIES

Environment, Politics, and Law

Analysis of the causes and proposed solutions of environmental problems and of the environmental issues and their political resolution. (2 semester hours)

GEOGRAPHY

World Geography

Introduction to the complex relationships that link humans with their physical, cultural, and spatial environments. Students will investigate these diverse relationships through a variety of worldwide examples. (3 semester hours)

Geography of the United States and Canada

An analysis of the cultural and environmental patterns of North America, with emphasis on the geographic processes that shape them. (3 semester hours)

Colorado

Study of the geographical and human resources of Colorado, including physical features, climate, landform regions, and natural resources and their utilization and conservation. (3 semester hours)

GERONTOLOGY

Introduction to Gerontology

Survey of the field of gerontology with attention to the physical, psychological, social, economic, and cross-cultural aspects of aging. (3 semester hours)

HEALTH

Issues in Health

Analyze the variety of forces which currently affect the well-being of human population groups on a national level. (3 semester hours)

Health and Lifestyles Among the Elderly

A survey of the psychosocial and biomedical dimensions that affect the health of the elderly. Current theories and scientific research on the aging process will also be discussed. (3 semester hours)

Human Nutrition

For students of any major. Investigation of the principles of nutrition as applied to humans. (3 semester hours)

Introduction to Human Rehabilitation Services

Overview of human rehabilitative service delivery systems such as rehabilitation, social services, mental health, and corrections. Orientation to current practices of the rehabilitative services professional. (3 semester hours)

MATHEMATICS

Intermediate Algebra

Elementary concepts of algebra through quadratic equations with emphasis on the function concept and consideration of systems of linear equations. (3 semester hours)

Plane Trigonometry

Study circular functions and their applications, inverse trigonometric functions and identities, and complex numbers through DeMoivre's Theorem. (3 semester hours)

Introduction to History of Mathematics

Survey of history of mathematics from antiquity to the present, emphasizing both development of mathematical concepts and the people involved. (2 semester hours)

MEDICAL TERMINOLOGY

Medical Terminology

For students of any major. Terminology used in medical sciences. Development of medical vocabulary. (2 semester hours)

NURSING

Pathophysiology

A systems approach to alteration and disruption of physiologic functions. Focus on differentiation of pathophysiologic findings and identification of treatment modalities. (3 semester hours)

EKG Interpretation

An introduction to the basic concepts of EKG and arrhythmia recognition. (2 semester hours)

OCEANOGRAPHY

Oceans and Mankind

You will study various aspects of people and technology concerning the oceans, including foods and minerals, coastal erosion, submersibles, diving, recent technological developments, pollution, and international political implications. This course is available on computer using the Phoenix System at the University of Northern Colorado in addition to the regular Independent Study format. (3 semester hours)

PHYSICAL EDUCATION

Introduction to Coaching - ACEP Level I

Designed to help coaches develop an appropriate coaching philosophy and to assess and enhance communication, motivation, teaching, and supervisory skills. Also addresses the basics of conditioning, sport nutrition, and injury prevention, treatment, and rehabilitation. (2 semester hours)

Sport Injuries for Coaches - ACEP Level II

Designed to emphasize situational decision making, this course presents prevention, recognition and immediate care of injuries, and illnesses and conditions specific to athletic participation. The course teaches the ability to recognize a situation, to evaluate the signs and symptoms that are present, and to take necessary action. Orthopedic types of injuries are the focus of concentration in this class, and the important areas of environmental conditions, emergency planning, and procedures and therapeutic exercises are also included. (2 semester hours)

Sport Law for Coaches - ACEP Level II

This course explains a coach's legal responsibility in easy to understand terms and gives practical advice for improving standards of care and safety for athletes. (2 semester hours)

Sport Physiology for Coaches - ACEP Level II

Principles and methods of developing muscular and energy fitness. Provides coaches with the information and guidance to develop training programs appropriate for particular sports and athletes. (2 semester hours)

Sport Psychology for Coaches - ACEP Level II

Motivation, communication, stress management, the use of mental imagery, and other topics for enhancing coach-athlete relationships and for stimulating improved sport performance. (2 semester hours)

Teaching Sport Skills for Coaches - ACEP Level II

Provides coaches with an understanding of how athletes learn and how coaches can improve their teaching effectiveness. Includes information on planning and organizing practices and seasons, establishing learning goals for practices and seasons, and evaluating practices and seasons. (2 semester hours)

Time Management for Coaches - ACEP Level II

Develops knowledge and skills in time management. Coaches learn how to select priorities and set realistic goals, organize a season plan, and reduce interruptions in their working environment. In addition, the course includes recommendations for managing potentially stressful situations and avoiding burnout. (2 semester hours)

Sport Law

Study of the law and implications relative to physical education and sport. Emphasis on safety procedures, preventative measures, and legal responsibilities of physical education teachers, coaches, and activity directors. (3 semester hours)

POLITICAL SCIENCE

United States National Government

Identification and analysis of principal rules, actors, and institutions of national politics and explanation of their development. (3 semester hours)

Introduction to Political Science

A comparative survey of political institutions and processes and of the various approaches to the explanation of politics. (3 semester hours)

Colorado Politics

Examination of Colorado state and local politics including the institutions and processes of policymaking from a comparative perspective. (3 semester hours)

The Presidency and Congress

An examination of the processes and policies of the executive and legislative branches of the U.S. national government and of the relationship between them. (3 semester hours)

Comparative Public Policy

Cross-nationally compare public policy in such areas as education, transportation, taxation, population, and income maintenance. Identify and explain differences and similarities across policy areas within one country and cross-nationally. (3 semester hours)

Northern Iowa, University of
Guided Correspondence Study
Continuing Education and Special Programs
124 Student Health Center
Cedar Falls, Iowa 50614-0223 (800) 772-1746

Description:

The University of Northern Iowa was established in 1876 as the Iowa State Normal School. Its original mission was the preparation of public school teachers. Over the years the role has expanded to include undergraduate and graduate degree programs in the liberal and vocational arts, as well as in education.

Guided Correspondence Study is a college program with more than sixty courses and over 1,000 enrollments. Instructors are regular university faculty members. Some courses have the option of lower-level graduate credit; however, they cannot be applied towards graduate degrees at the University of Northern Iowa.

Faculty:

Dr. James Bodensteiner, Director, Credit Programs. There are 48 faculty members for correspondence courses.

Academic Levels:

College

Degree/Certificate Programs:

No more than one-fourth of the work required for an Iowa Teaching License or for a B.A. degree may be earned through correspondence study. However, an external degree (Bachelor of Liberal Studies) is designed primarily for correspondence students.

Admission Requirements:

Those who meet the university's admission requirements may enroll for correspondence study and may be permitted to continue correspondence study so long as a 2.00 grade index (C) is maintained. Admission to the Guided Correspondence Study program does not constitute admission to the University. High school seniors with superior academic records may enroll for university-level correspondence courses.

Tuition:

$74 per semester hour plus a nonrefundable $13 enrollment fee per course. An 80 percent refund will be made when the student cannot continue with the course because of illness, certified by a statement from a physician, within one year of the date of enrollment. A 70 percent refund will be made when the student chooses to withdraw from a course for any other reason during the first six weeks of enrollment. The request must be in writing and must be postmarked no later than six weeks after the enrollment date. When a refund is made, a charge of $7.50 will be deducted for each lesson and examination corrected. All course materials must be returned to the Correspondence Study Office. The $13 enrollment fee in nonrefundable.

Enrollment Period:

The maximum time allowed to complete a course is one year. A three-month extension may be granted upon payment of a renewal fee of $15. The minimum time allowed is two weeks for each credit hour.

Equipment Requirements:

Textbooks and supplementary materials are not included in the tuition. They may be purchased through the University Book and Supply Store, 1009 West 23rd Street, Cedar Falls, Iowa 50613.

Credit and Grading:

Correspondence study courses may not be taken on a pass/fail basis. No credit is given for a course partially completed. Examinations must be proctored. The grading system is A, B, C, D, F, with D being the minimum passing grade. Credit is awarded in semester hour units.

Library Services:

Students who are enrolled in correspondence courses may request reference books from the Correspondence Study Office. The Correspondence Secretary will order the books from the UNI Library. The student is responsible for getting the books returned to the library on time.

Accreditations:

North Central Association of Colleges and Schools. Member of: National University Continuing Education Association.

COLLEGE COURSES

ACCOUNTING

Principles of Accounting I

Introduction to basic language, principles, and procedures of ac-

counting; emphasis on collection of data for external reporting. (3 semester hours)

Principles of Accounting II

Emphasis on accounting for the corporate form of business, managerial accounting for decision making, financial statement analysis, and accounting for manufacturing firms. (3 semester hours)

ANTHROPOLOGY

Human Origins

Introduction to the physical and prehistoric development of humankind, including primate and human evolution, modern races, and the archaeological cultures of the world. (3 semester hours)

DESIGN, FAMILY, AND CONSUMER SCIENCES

Basic Nutrition

Study of nutrition in relation to growth development, and maintenance of the body. (2 semester hours)

Human Identity and Relationships

Use of social science theories and research to understand the physiological, psychological, and sociocultural influences on human identity, development of self, and interpersonal relationships. Emphasis placed on methodologies for obtaining valid research information and application of such information to facilitating positive individual growth and effective interpersonal relationships. (3 semester hours)

Management of Family Resources

Management of human, economic, and environmental resources available to individuals and families through the life cycle; application of management processes toward goal achievement. (3 semester hours)

ECONOMICS

Economics for General Education

An overview of economics, including a look at how a market system functions and how national income, output and employment are determined. The focus is primarily (though not exclusively) on the U.S. economy. (3 semester hours)

EDUCATIONAL FOUNDATIONS

Group Evaluation Techniques

Principles of educational measurement and evaluation. Use of standardized instruments designed to measure achievement, aptitude, and interest; some applications to teacher-made tests. (3 semester hours)

History of Education

The purpose of this course is to give the professional educator and interested student an insight into education as a historical and social process. A study of important social and educational theories and practices will be considered. There will also be an in-depth study of the crucial issues and perennial problems of education. A portion of the course work will be structured so the students can study independently an educational concern in which they are interested. (3 semester hours)

EDUCATIONAL PSYCHOLOGY

Child Psychology

Developmental concepts and principles applied to physical, intellectual, moral, and social behaviors of children age 6 to 12; emphasis on practical application of psychological principles. (2 semester hours)

Development of Young Children

The growth and development of the young child with emphasis on research having important implications for the care and education of young children. (3 semester hours)

Psychology of Adolescence

Adolescence as a period of change. New mental capabilities, physical and sexual changes, and social influences across social classes affecting behavior and self-concept. The development of psychosexual maturity, identity, and moral values. Implications for helping professions and caretakers. (2 semester hours)

Social Psychology, Education

A study of the experience and behavior of individuals in relation to other individuals, groups, and cultures. The areas of communication, attitudes, group processes, conformity, aggression, and leadership will be investigated and application of these concepts made to the area of education. (3 semester hours)

ELEMENTARY EDUCATION

Applications in Elementary Science Teaching

Examination of current curriculum and trends in the teaching of science in the elementary school. The course also includes an overview of science content commonly found in elementary science programs and appropriate teaching strategies for presenting this content. (2 semester hours)

Applications in Elementary Social Studies Teaching

Recent research will be examined as a basis for current trends in curriculum design and methods for the teaching of social studies in the elementary schools. Learning theory, changing cultural patterns, and interpersonal relationships are studied for their implications in planning teaching strategy and selecting instruction materials. (3 semester hours)

ENGLISH

Introduction to College Writing

This course offers students practice in the process of personal, opinion, report, and analytical type writing. (3 semester hours)

Introduction to Literature

Understanding and appreciating the basic forms of imaginative literature. (3 semester hours)

Twentieth-Century British Novel

Designed to acquaint the student with the major novelists in the modern English tradition: Conrad, Forster, Lawrence, Joyce, Woolf, Huxley, Waugh, Greene, Orwell, and Ford Madox Ford. These selected writers represent the most accomplished achievements in both traditional and experimental fiction of this century and their many visions of human experience record the aspirations of the modern age. The students will read one major work by each of the novelists. (3 semester hours)

British Novel to 1900

The rise of the novel form in eighteenth-century England (Fielding, Richardson, Stern, and Smollot). A continued study of the great Victorian novelists (Austen, Dickens, Thackeray, and others). The chief purpose is to provide the student, through the actual reading of a set of novels, a deeper appreciation and understanding of the complexity and value of the British novel. (3 semester hours)

Literature for Young Adults

The purpose of this course is to provide an opportunity for wide reading and analysis of the various types of literature written especially for the adolescent. The novel will be stressed: Western, sports, mystery, science fiction, romance, and adventure. Included will be a study of the reading interests of young adults and ways to use adolescent literature in the classroom, grades 7–12. (2 semester hours)

GEOGRAPHY

World Geography

A study of variations over the surface of the earth of such aspects as physical, cultural, and economic characteristics. (3 semester hours)

Political Geography

Geographic factors in the origin, development, behavior, and interaction of states. (3 semester hours)

HEALTH

Personal Health

Provides students with an opportunity to increase their health knowledge, develop self-awareness regarding their health decision-making processes and achieve a higher level of freedom from negative health influences. Topics covered are health behavior, stress, mental health, parenting, substance abuse, nutrition, weight control, exercise, cardiovascular health, disease, aging, and death. (2 semester hours)

Community and Public Health

Public health activities concerned with protection and care of the individual; focuses on factors that may be inimical to human being. (3 semester hours)

Consumer Health

Issues surrounding the purchasing of health goods and services: quackery, nontraditional health care and sources of consumer protection in the health marketplace. (2 semester hours)

HISTORY

U.S. History to 1877

Foreign relations, westward expansion, development of democracy, growth of nationalism, and sectional controversies to the end of Reconstruction. (3 semester hours)

U.S. History since 1877

Rise of big business, reform movements, the emergence of the United States as a world power, and wars and other crises to the present. (3 semester hours)

Modern Europe to 1815

France, Spain, England, Prussia, Austria, the Netherlands, and the Italian states to 1815. (3 semester hours)

Modern Europe Since 1815

Major topics to be studied include: Peacekeeping after the French Revolutionary wars and the Napoleonic Wars; Conservatism and Liberalism; Great Britain's leadership of Europe after 1815; nineteenth-century nationalism and imperialism; capitalism vs. socialism; the origins of World War I; consequences of the defeat of Germany; the rise of the USSR; the rise of Fascism and National Socialism; World War II; Europe since 1945; the United Nations; the European Market. (3 semester hours)

Recent U.S. History

A history of the American people since 1945, with emphasis on domestic affairs. The course is designed for upper-level undergraduate or graduate students. It is intended for the student who wishes to become more familiar with the immediate background of the world in which we live, and for the teacher who wants to bring American history courses up to the present. (3 semester hours)

HUMANITIES

Humanities I

A survey of major developments in the Western world from the civilization of the Ancient Near East to seventeenth-Century Europe. Particular emphasis is placed on the literature from the Greek civilization, the early Christian period, and the Renaissance and Reformation. (4 semester hours)

Humanities II

This course covers the seventeenth century to the present, dealing with major events, ideas, and trends in the political, social, economic, artistic, philosophical and religious components of Western civilization during the past four centuries. (4 semester hours)

India

An overview of Indian culture since 2500 B.C. to modern period, discussion of major religions in India—Hinduism, Buddhism, Islam, and other significant aspects of Indian society (family, festivals, marriage, caste) and politics. (3 semester hours)

Middle East

An overview of the Middle Eastern Culture—Islam, Judaism, and other important sociopolitical aspects of the Middle Eastern societies (family, political, social, village institutions). (3 semester hours)

MANAGEMENT

Quality Management

Management of quality in manufacturing and service operations. Process control, acceptance sampling, vendor relations, product reliability, equipment maintenance, organizational issues affecting product quality. (3 semester hours)

MARKETING

Principles of Marketing

A survey course dealing with the world of marketing in society, customer determination and selection, product management, channels of distribution, pricing concepts, and promotional activity within an economic and business environment. (3 semester hours)

Consumer Behavior

Recent findings of psychologists, sociologists, anthropologists, and marketers in relationship to internal and external influences on buyer behavior and marketing-related decision making. (3 semester hours)

MATHEMATICS

Mathematics in Decision Making

A survey of math ideas of particular use in analyzing information and in forming and analyzing hypotheses. Topics include logical statements, probability, statistics, graphs, interest, and matrices. (3 semester hours)

Metric System and Measurement

The course is intended to make the student familiar with basic ideas of measurement and methods of teaching. It also attempts to teach the common metric units and their uses as well as the advantage of the metric system over others. The course is a laboratory type course in which the student will conduct various experiments at home. (2 semester hours)

Statistical Methods

The course involves some work with descriptive statistics, including graphical representations, measures of location and dispersion and correlation and regression. A major portion of the course is devoted to an intuitive approach to probability and statistical inference including problems of estimation and the testing of statistical hypotheses. The prospective student in this course should have a good understanding of high school algebra. (3 semester hours)

MUSIC

Our Musical Heritage

Exploration of music within the context of revolving Western culture. Music fundamentals and vocabulary. Repertories from the medieval world through the post-Romantic era. (3 semester hours)

Introduction to Music Theory

Basic skills and vocabulary. Designed for non-music majors with limited background in music fundamentals or as preparation for music major theory courses. Emphasis on notation, key/time signatures, rhythm, and aural training. (2 semester hours)

POLITICAL SCIENCE

Introduction to American Politics

The political behavior of Americans as shaped, channeled, and fostered by political beliefs and institutions. (3 semester hours)

American Government in a Comparative Perspective

A comparison of contemporary political institutions, processes, and ideas in the United States and other selected countries. (3 semester hours)

PSYCHOLOGY

Introduction to Psychology

This course provides a foundation for psychological understanding. Topics to be studied include biological basis of behavior, sensation and perception, motivation and emotion, learning and memory, maturation and development, personality and abnormal behavior, and social psychology. (3 semester hours)

Introduction to Developmental Psychology

Theory and research methods used in the study of development of organisms (especially human); developmental perspective as part of the process of psychological inquiry. (3 semester hours)

Introductory Social Psychology

Overview of social psychology from perspective of general psychology; includes social perception, attraction and liking, affiliation, social influence, group dynamics, and attitude formation and changes. (3 semester hours)

Psychology of Aging

An introduction to the principles of adult development and aging. Emphasis is placed on age-changes in interpersonal relationships, personality, cognition, biological, and mental health processes. (3 semester hours)

RELIGION

Religions of the World

The course will study the living world religions with emphasis on their interpretations of existence, the problem of meaning and values, and human destiny. Inasmuch as religious people affirm that life is meaningful, the course is concerned with the reasons these people give for their affirmation. (3 semester hours)

Individual Readings in Religion

Directed readings and written reports in any area of religion. The student determines the particular area in which he/she wishes to read by sending a proposal to the instructor. A bibliography is then set up by the student in conjunction with the instructor. There are no examinations as such, but the proposal will necessitate at least one research paper to bring to focus the reading project. This course may be repeated for a maximum of 6 hours. (1 to 3 semester hours)

SOCIAL SCIENCE

American Civilization

This course introduces students to the history and culture of the American people over the past four centuries, using a thematic approach. The major themes emphasized will be: race and ethnicity, wealth and poverty, religion, gender, reform tradition, and war and peace. (3 semester hours)

SOCIOLOGY

Criminal Justice System

The genesis, transformation, and day-to-day operation of criminal justice within our society; emphasis on interrelationships between specific stages in the crime-control process and the differences between U.S. and other criminal justice systems. (3 semester hours)

American Racial and Ethnic Minorities

This course surveys American minorities, including Hispanics, Blacks, Asians, and native Americans. Multidisciplinary study with emphasis on geographic origins, linguistics, economics, folkways, and mores of each group. (3 semester hours)

Principles of Sociology

Principal social processes and institutions involved in the development of the individual and of society; methods of self and social control. (3 semester hours)

Social Problems

An analysis of the nature and range of social problems arising in modern industrial society. Consideration given to the conditions creating them and the methods by which society seeks to cope with them. (3 semester hours)

Statistics for Social Research

Introduction and application of statistical methods to problems in social research; classification and presentation of statistical data, measures of central tendency and variability, measures of relationships, linear correlation and regression, probability, hypothesis testing and statistical inference. (3 semester hours)

The Family

Origin, development, and problems of the modern family and marriage. (3 semester hours)

Social Deviance and Control

Causes and consequences of socially disapproved behavior; role of social control agencies in recruitment of deviant identities; management of and the reaction to deviance; dynamics of labeling processes and examination of the social meaning of non-normative behavior. (3 semester hours)

Corrections and Punishment

Origin, development, and characteristics of corrections in the United States. Corrections as part of the criminal justice system, community-based corrections, short- and long-term correctional institutions, the handling of criminal offenders, and the future of corrections are also emphasized. (3 semester hours)

Juvenile Delinquency

This course studies the types of juvenile delinquents, causes of delinquent behavior, social institutions and their effect upon delinquency, prevention, and control of delinquent behavior. (3 semester hours)

Minority Group Relations

An analysis of the psychological, sociological, and economic roots of racial, ethnic, and sexual oppression. A world-wide view of the "cycle of race relations" with special emphasis on industrialization and its relationship to the colonized world. (3 semester hours)

Northern Michigan University
Independent Study
Department of Continuing Education Credit Programs
Cohodas Administrative Center
Room 410
Marquette, Michigan 49855   (906) 227-1439

Description:

Northern Michigan University was established in 1899 in Marquette by the Legislature of the State of Michigan as a Normal School to provide teachers for Michigan's Upper Peninsula. A four-year collegiate program was introduced in 1918 and university status was achieved in 1963.

Correspondence courses which are completed satisfactorily carry the same amount of credits as if taken as a classroom course, but honor points are not awarded.

Faculty:

Kathleen Harrington, Programs/Procedures Coordinator; Gerald Williams, Registrar.

Academic Levels:

College

Degree/Certificate Programs:

A candidate for the bachelor's degree may not present more than 16 credit hours by independent study for the degree. Associate degree candidates may not present more than 8 credit hours by independent study for the degree.

Admission Requirements:

Applicants for correspondence courses are required to meet the same entrance qualifications as those enrolling for regular classroom-type courses. New enrollments may be made at any time. Students should plan for at least one on-campus meeting (if possible) with their assigned instructor.

Tuition:

Contact the university for current tuition and fees. A full tuition refund payment is made (less a $25 administrative processing fee) if the student submits a written request to the department within 40 days of course registration provided *no* lessons have been sent in for evaluation. No refund is made available unless the above requirements have been fulfilled.

Enrollment Period:

Correspondence courses must be completed within one calendar year from the date of registration. A student may request one extension of up to six months if at least 25 percent of the lesson assignments have been completed.

Equipment Requirements:

Students are recommended to purchase textbooks from the Northern Michigan University Bookstore to ensure obtaining the correct editions.

Credit and Grading:

All courses require a final written examination (or equivalent requirement). If there are valid reasons why the examination cannot be taken on campus, students may make arrangements for having the exam proctored by a local public school official. Grading system: A through F with plus and minus. Minimum passing grade is D. Credit is awarded in semester hour units.

Library Services:

Students may call the University library and with proper identification have qualified reference materials mailed to them for a specific period of time.

Accreditations:

North Central Association of Colleges and Schools.

COLLEGE COURSES

CRIMINAL JUSTICE

Police Operations

Line activities of law enforcement agencies with emphasis on the patrol function and the prevention of crime; includes traffic, vice, investigative, juvenile, and other specialized operational units. (4 semester hours)

Survey of Corrections

Introductory survey to philosophy, theory, and practice involved in treatment of convicted offenders; appraisal of treatment and post-correctional practices; functions of probation and parole are analyzed. (4 semester hours)

ENGLISH

College Composition I

Development of students' abilities to read and discuss, and to write paragraphs and short essays about significant subjects. Each student writes a minimum of 5,000 words for this course. (4 semester hours)

Technical and Report Writing

Readings and writing assignments treating subjects appropriate for students in scientific, technical, or business fields. Formal expository writing and the preparation of reports are emphasized. (4 semester hours)

HISTORY

History of Western Civilization to 1500

The development of western civilization from the earliest times to 1500. Emphasis is distributed among the ancient, medieval, and renaissance worlds. (4 semester hours)

History of Civilization Since 1500

Survey of the development of western civilization from 1500 to the present. Cultural, social, economic, and political ideas and institutions are traced as background to the understanding of contemporary type problems. (4 semester hours)

The United States to 1865

Survey of American history from the colonial period through the Civil War. Major emphasis is placed upon political development within a broad economic, social, and cultural context. (4 semester hours)

The United States since 1865

Survey of the history of modern America from the period of Reconstruction to the present. The political, economic, education, social, cultural, and diplomatic facets of the American experience are emphasized. Study of these major historical elements is pursued in an effort to help students better understand the problems and challenges of contemporary American life and the role of America in a thermonuclear world. (4 semester hours)

History of the American Indian

Historical study of the American Indians from their origins to the present. The central theme is the remarkable persistence of cultural and personality traits and ethnic identity in Indian societies in the face of white conquest and efforts at elimination or assimilation. (4 semester hours)

Northern State University
Office of Continuing Education
Independent Study by Correspondence
1200 South Jay Street
Aberdeen, South Dakota 57401
(605) 622-2486

Description:

Through its Office of Continuing Education, Northern State University offers Independent Study by Correspondence courses prepared and taught by regular members of Northern's faculty who teach or have taught similar courses on campus.

Faculty:

Marc Barnes, Associate Director, Continuing Education.

Academic Levels:

College

Degree/Certificate Programs:

At Northern State University a student may apply credit earned through Independent Study by Correspondence not to exceed a total of 25 percent of the total semester hours required for graduation.

Admission Requirements:

Enrollment in courses by correspondence is open to all students without official admission to the college. Enrollment by this method does not, however, constitute admission to the college.

Tuition:

$72 per semester hour. Fees must be paid at the time of application. There is no refund after six months have passed from the enrollment date; 60% of the tuition will be refunded if 25% or less of the work is completed; 30% of the tuition will be refunded if 25.1% but less than 50% of the work is completed before the six-month cutoff.

Enrollment Period:

The maximum time allowed to complete a course is one year; four lessons per week are permitted. An extension of three months may be granted upon payment of a $20 fee. Reinstatement, allowing an extension of one more year, is possible upon payment of a reinstatement fee.

Equipment Requirements:

Textbooks are not included in tuition and must be purchased separately. They may be ordered from the University Bookstore or obtained locally.

Credit and Grading:

Examinations must be proctored by a local school official or taken at the University Extension Office. Both the final examination and the quality of the submitted lessons will be considered when awarding the final grade. All correspondence courses are graded on a satisfactory/unsatisfactory basis. This system merely means that credit earned will not be included when honor point computations are made. Credit is awarded in semester hour units.

Accreditations:

North Central Association of Colleges and Schools.

COLLEGE COURSES

ASTRONOMY

Descriptive Astronomy

The study of coordinate systems, solar systems, eclipses, time, space, and stars. (3 semester hours)

BUSINESS ADMINISTRATION

Mathematics for Business

A review of the fundamentals of arithmetic with emphasis on their application to business problems. (3 semester hours)

American Business Systems

Introduces students to major business functions including management, accounting, marketing, organization, law and governmental regulations. (3 semester hours)

Marketing

A study of the principles, origin, development and extension of the market. (3 semester hours)

Retail Management

An analysis of the organization and management of retail establishments with consideration given to the customer. (3 semester hours)

Organizational Behavior

A study of the behavior of individuals in an organizational setting which stresses the importance of understanding perceptions, decision making, creativity, attitudes, group behavior, communications, power, and conflict in developing an effective management style. (3 semester hours)

ECONOMICS

Principles of Economics

Course 201. Fundamental concepts such as production, consumption, national income and accounting, business organization, government finance, money and banking and economic growth. (3 semester hours)

Course 202. A continuation of the above course with emphasis on

pricing and allocation of resources, distribution of national income, and international economics. (3 semester hours)

EDUCATION

Educational Psychology

The effects of both innate and acquired characteristics on individual behavior, utilizing the needs of the individual in motivating learning, laws of learning, and individual differences. (3 semester hours)

HEALTH

Personal Health

A study of the application of the laws of health to the welfare of the individual. (2 semester hours)

School Health

Consideration is given to health instruction in the schools, medical and nursing services, nutrition, school lunch programs, safety, mental hygiene, and environmental sanitation. (2 semester hours)

HISTORY

History of Civilization

Course 121. A survey of world history to 1700. (3 semester hours)

Course 122. A survey of world history from 1700 to present. (3 semester hours)

United States History

Course 241. American history from the period of exploration to 1870. (3 semester hours)

Course 242. American history from 1870 to the present. (3 semester hours)

South Dakota History and Government

The state, county, and local government of South Dakota and its historical development. (3 semester hours)

INDUSTRIAL EDUCATION

Metric Measurement

A course designed to provide the student with the concepts and knowledge necessary to use and/or teach metric measurements as they will be used by the International Standards and are being adopted by the United States. (An additional charge in excess of tuition must be made for this course because of a special kit of metric materials needed to complete the course. Please contact the Office of Extension concerning this extra charge). (2 semester hours)

Technology and Society

A course designed to introduce the student to the concepts of technology. Emphasis will be on the historical, social, and economic impact of the past, present, and future. Praxeological knowledge will also be included. (3 semester hours)

MATHEMATICS

College Algebra

An introduction to the structure of the real number system. Polynomials, roots, factorization, solution of quadratic equations, mathematical induction, binomial theorem, combinations, permutations, inequalities, exponential and logarithmic functions. (4 semester hours)

Trigonometry

A study of trigonometric functions, radian measure, special angle formulas, functions involving more than one angle, identities, trigonometric equations, inverse functions, graphs of trigonometric functions, logarithms, solution of triangle. (3 semester hours)

Calculus and Analytic Geometry

A study of analytic geometry of the plane functions, limits, derivatives, conic sections, maximum and minimum, related rates, the mean value theorem, antiderivatives, solution of differential equations, and definite integrals. (4 semester hours)

Foundations of Mathematics

A study of the basic principles underlying the elementary school program. An introduction to sets, numeration systems, properties of integers, nonmetric geometry, and the properties of rational and irrational numbers. (3 semester hours)

Algebra and Geometry for Elementary Teachers

This course includes a study of computations with rational numbers, metric geometry, functions, transformation geometry, probability, statistics, and topics from number theory. (3 semester hours)

Analytic Geometry and Calculus

An introduction to indeterminate forms, improper integrals, infinite series, vectors, solid analytic geometry, partial derivatives, and multiple integration. (4 semester hours)

POLITICAL SCIENCE

American Government

The organization and functions of our national government; selected problems of national government. (3 semester hours)

State and Local Government

A study of state and local governments with emphasis on no particular state. (2 semester hours)

PSYCHOLOGY

General Psychology

A representative survey of modern scientific psychology. To assist the student in developing insights into his own psychological processes and those of others. To suggest principles and procedures by which psychological knowledge is applicable to the solution of personal and social problems. (3 semester hours)

Human Growth and Development

A systematic presentation of the facts and generalizations concerning human development from infancy through adulthood. The emphasis is on human development as a whole with major divisions of the course dealing with physical, mental, social and emotional development. (3 semester hours)

SOCIOLOGY

Principles of Sociology

An introduction to sociology. The interrelationships of personality, society and culture; major sociological concepts, social processes and institutions. (3 semester hours)

Courtship and Marriage

Mate selection as the keystone to the family as a social institution; the problems and advantages of the American dating scene; love and sexual patterns in the United States; the institution of marriage; conflict and adjustments in a paired relationship; becoming parents. (3 semester hours)

Social Disorganization and Deviant Behavior

Major problems of social maladjustment; the processes underlying individual and social disorganization. (3 semester hours)

Population Problems

A study of the history of the world's population and the social significance of different population sizes and growth rates; emphasis upon the social determinants of fertility, morality and migration. (2 semester hours)

The Family

The family as a social institution; its origin and its place in American culture; the rural family; the impact of urbanization on family life; family functions; and comparison of families in different cultures. (3 semester hours)

Social Gerontology

A study of the process of aging, with an emphasis on the social process. An analysis of the effects of a growing senior citizen population on society and the world. A concentration on the social problems of senior citizens and consideration of programs designed to meet those problems. (3 semester hours)

Northwood University
Independent Study/Correspondence Program
3225 Cook Road
Midland, Michigan 48640-2398

(800) 445-5873

Description:

Northwood University (formerly Northwood Institute) is a nonprofit, private, tax-exempt, independent, coeducational business- and management-oriented college actively allied to both business and the arts. Founded in 1959, the "Northwood Idea" is to incorporate the teachings of the American free enterprise system into college classrooms. The name Northwood is a familiar one to automotive professionals throughout the country. It is the premier school in automotive programs and have earned this reputation over many years of quality education to automotive students and a close working relationship with dealers. The Michigan campus of Northwood University houses both the Automotive Hall of Fame and the National Automobile Dealers Education Center.

Northwood offers programs to complete associate and bachelor's degrees in many business areas. There are campuses in Midland, Michigan; Cedar Hill, Texas; and West Palm Beach, Florida. Northwood also offers an external degree program.

Any student admitted to Northwood University may earn credit through the Independent Study Program. Courses which are completed satisfactorily will carry credits equal to those earned on campus.

Faculty:
Sheryl Beyer, Director.

Academic Levels:
College

Degree/Certificate Programs:

A maximum of 20 credit hours may be earned through independent study toward the associate and bachelor degrees. Correspondence credits transferred-in will be accepted if they meet Northwood's class requirements.

Northwood University

Admission Requirements:

2.00 Grade Point Average if currently enrolled at Northwood; if not, $15 nonrefundable application fee and the tuition payment are due at the time of enrollment.

Tuition:

$195 per credit hour (subject to change). Normally no refund for withdrawal except in exception cases.

Enrollment Period:

All courses should be completed within 90 days of payment and receipt of all materials; after 90 days, a grade of "I" will be entered. The student must remove the "I" within 90 days or it will automatically become an "F."

Equipment Requirements:

Textbooks must be purchased by the student and may be secured from the Northwood Bookstore.

Credit and Grading:

Most Individual Learning courses require proctored final exams. If students cannot take the exams on the campus, they may send the name, title, professional address, and telephone number of a professional educator who is willing to proctor the exam as a favor to the student. Northwood Institute grades on a 4.0 scale: A=4, B=3, C=2, D=1. Students, to be in good standing, must maintain a 2.0 or above academic average. Students below 2.0 are placed on probation. Students whose average falls below a 1.5 are dismissed. Students on probation are given two terms to show improvement before dismissal. Those students academically dismissed may re-apply for admission after one academic year if they have shown the ability to do college level work at some other institution or have been successful in a professional position. Students who expect to use Northwood Institute courses at another institution should have written approval from the school. Northwood is a participant in the Michigan Uniform Guest Student plan sponsored by the Michigan Association of Collegiate Registrars and Admissions Officers. Credit is awarded in quarter hour units.

Accreditations:

North Central Association of Colleges and Schools.

COLLEGE COURSES

BUSINESS LAW

Business Law I

Basic principles of law applicable to the business world, emphasizing contract, sales, bailments, negotiable instruments, agency, partnerships, corporations, insurance, and real estate. (4 credit hours)

Business Law II

An in-depth study of contract law with special emphasis on those points of law which would be of particular importance to those students planning a career in accounting (especially those considering qualifying as a CPA). (4 credit hours)

ENGLISH

Introduction to World Literature III

World literature of modern authors illustrating realism and naturalism with an introduction to symbolism and the modern school. (4 credit hours)

Report Writing

The study and practice of composing various types of business reports, including analytical, progress, letter, and short reports. Proposal writing, thesis composition, and professional techniques are also stressed. (4 credit hours)

FINANCE

Financial Management

Study of the theoretical and conceptual framework that the financial manager uses to reach decisions. Particular emphasis is given to the finance function and its relevance to the management of a business firm. Analysis, problem-solving techniques, and decision-making tools are emphasized. (4 credit hours)

GEOGRAPHY

North American Geography

A regional study of selected regions of North America (north of the Rio Grande River) in terms of the resources, economic activities, population/urban patterns, physical geography and interregional/international relationships. (4 credit hours)

HISTORY

Current World Problems

Analysis and discussion of the significant current world problems, causes of selected persistent problems, and various organizational attempts to solve world problems. (4 credit hours)

HOTEL, RESTAURANT, AND INSTITUTIONAL MANAGEMENT

Hotel-Restaurant Purchasing

Methods and materials of purchasing and control of all items involved in the sales and service functions of the industry; includes maintenance, repair, and replacement needs. (4 credit hours)

Housekeeping Operations

Study of housekeeping practices dealing with recruiting, selecting, and placing employees. Includes work in training, work improvement techniques, organizing, planning and scheduling. Study of cleaning equipment, materials, methods, and agents. Types of linen, draperies, carpeting, bedding, and furniture are discussed. Methods of inventory control are stressed. (4 credit hours)

HUMANITIES

Introduction to Philosophy

The development of thought and wisdom from ancient to modern concepts as described in the writings of the great philosophers. (4 credit hours)

Introduction to Art

Art past and present with emphasis on personal expression and application to everyday living. (4 credit hours)

Introduction to Music

The study of music from the past and present, and its impact on our culture. Included is a survey of music from historic periods and the relationship of this auditory art form to other areas of the humanities. (4 credit hours)

Introduction to Modern Art

An introduction to significant aspects and concepts in modern artistic expression. (4 credit hours)

Business Design Management

A comprehensive probe into the psychology and theory of design and color; the historic application of each toward visual and volumed form; the professional application of each in the marketing and merchandising of furnishing elements and interior concepts. (4 credit hours)

MARKETING

Industrial Marketing

The role of industrial marketing in the economy, including concepts, problems and strategies of marketing capital goods, raw and semi-fabricated materials, industrial supplies, component parts and services to business and industry. (4 credit hours)

Advertising Management

An in-depth study of management of the advertising function. Explores how advertising fits into the marketing communication areas of American and multinational business; also explores the management of advertising agencies and small business advertising. (4 credit hours)

Marketing Research

The role of research in the solution of marketing problems, with emphasis on available data analysis, non-parametric statistical procedures, sampling, variable analysis and field research methodology. (4 credit hours)

Marketing Management

A capstone, managerial analysis of marketing policy strategy, organization and administrative structures to facilitate the marketing function. Includes procedures of demand analysis, product planning policy, pricing and physical distribution. Emphasizes the integration of marketing activities and its planning and direction. (4 credit hours)

MATHEMATICS

Business Mathematics

Mathematical processes and their business applications. (4 credit hours)

Introductory Algebra

Elementary algebra, radicals, exponents, linear and quadratic equations, graphing, ratio, proportion, and variation. (4 credit hours)

College Algebra

Progressions, complex numbers, logarithms, permutations, combinations, probability, induction, and binomial theorem. (4 credit hours)

Statistics

Sources and methods of presentation of data. Measures of central tendency, measures of variability and skewness. Basic probability concepts applied to business. (4 credit hours)

Marketing Research Statistics

Upon completion of the course, the student will have a working knowledge of hypotheses testing, ANOVA, chi-square, and correlation and regression analyses. Computer programs will be used to facilitate calculations. The emphasis is on the use of and the interpretation of statistical information. (4 credit hours)

NATURAL SCIENCE

Environmental Science

A broad presentation of environmental science integrating technical and social issues. The legal, economic, and social aspects of current issues are scrutinized from a scientific base. (4 credit hours)

PHILOSOPHY

Philosophy of American Life and Business

Development and methods of American capitalism; nature, origins, and evolution of private property and free markets in agriculture, industry, trade, and finance, with special reference to the United States, and their meaning in relation to American life, institutions, and especially to business. (4 credit hours)

Philosophy and Ethics

Analysis of the moral and ethical principles of our civilization and consideration of topics such as moral influence, responsibility, and the Judaic-Christian traditions, humanism, and law and order. (4 credit hours)

Critical Philosophical Problems

Critical philosophical problems of man with emphasis on the current status. Problems include the relationship of the increase of knowledge and the use of science and technology in the life of man; human rights, war, peace, poverty, prosperity, private property, government control, religion, and other selected philosophical problems with international significance, implications, and relationships. (4 credit hours)

POLITICAL SCIENCE

Introduction to American Government

Development of the American political system with emphasis on decision making in the Legislative, Executive, and Judicial departments. (4 credit hours)

PSYCHOLOGY

Personality and Adjustment

Dynamics of adjustment and personality, motivation and emotion; significance of clinical and organizational psychology. (4 credit hours)

Applied Psychology

Theories, principles, and methods of general and applied psychology and specific procedures and problems in business, education, government, and other institutions. Emphasis is placed on the understanding of appropriate use of methods of selection, evaluation, training, supervision, and motivation of individuals in a variety of situations. (4 credit hours)

SOCIOLOGY

World Culture and Customs

Origin and background of peoples, social organizations, culture, and customs of specific areas of the world, such as the Latin Americans, Europeans, *et al.* (4 credit hours)

Ohio University
Independent Study Program
302 Tupper Hall
Athens, Ohio 45701-2979   (614) 593-2910

Description:

Ohio University is a coeducational, state-assisted institution which offers undergraduate study in more than 120 areas and numerous graduate programs. Chartered in 1804, the University currently has five regional campuses in addition to its main campus in Athens. The Ohio University Independent Study program was begun in 1924 and currently serves about 6,000 students each year through a variety of delivery systems. The purpose of the Independent Study program is to provide a number of flexible options by which persons capable of pursuing college-level work can earn college credit without some of the limitations imposed by the traditional university structure. Ohio University offers a variety of two- and four-year degree programs in selected areas that can be completed through Independent Study options.

Faculty:

Dr. Richard W. Moffit, Director, Independent Study Program. There is a faculty of 160 members.

Academic Levels:

College

Noncredit

Degree/Certificate Programs:

Bachelor and associate degrees. There is no limit in the number of credit hours earned through correspondence study which can be applied toward degree requirements at Ohio University.

Admission Requirements:

Independent Study is open to anyone who can profitably pursue the program. Formal admission to Ohio University is not required; present Ohio University students must receive permission from their college to enroll in independent study. Capable high school juniors and seniors who are recommended by their guidance counselors or principals may enroll in courses for college credit. Acceptance in an independent study course does not constitute admission to Ohio University. No overseas enrollment in courses that require slides or videotape.

Tuition:

$53 per quarter credit hour, plus nonrefundable $10 enrollment fee per course, payable at enrollment. Visa, MasterCard, and Discover accepted. Approved for Veterans Benefits; students may also qualify for individual tuition assistance from their place of employment. A full refund is given if student is refused enrollment or if course is not available for enrollment. Request for withdrawal within one month of enrollment, refund of course fee less $25 and a charge for each lesson graded. Request for withdrawal after one month but less than two months, refund of half of course fee less a charge for each lesson graded. No refund after two months.

Enrollment Period:

The maximum time allowed to complete a course is 12 months. An extension of three months may be granted upon payment of a $25 fee.

Equipment Requirements:

Certain courses require access to calculator, cassette player, VCR, or slide projector which must be supplied by the student. The cost of textbooks is not included in the tuition.

Credit and Grading:

Final grades are generally determined by grades on written lessons and supervised examinations; reported on A to F scale. Minimum passing grade is generally 60 percent. Method of grading is explained in detail in each course guide. Examinations must be supervised by an approved proctor. Credit is awarded in quarter hour units. All credit earned from regionally accredited institutions with a grade of C- or higher is accepted as transfer credit and can be applied to degree requirements in the same manner as credit earned at Ohio University (all University and departmental restrictions on transfer credit for particular courses also apply to correspondence transfer credits).

Library Services:

Students living in an area near an Ohio University campus may use the campus library, although borrowing privileges may be restricted. No other services are offered, although students are encouraged to use local library facilities and interlibrary loan services to obtain information and materials.

Accreditations:

North Central Association of Colleges and Schools. Member of: National University Continuing Education Association.

COLLEGE COURSES

ACCOUNTING

Financial Accounting

Introduction to accounting principles and practices and data accumulation. (4 quarter hours)

Managerial Accounting

Uses of accounting information for making managerial decisions. Study of cost behavior. Overhead costs allocation, basic cost accumulation systems, elementary capital budgeting, master and flexible budgets, and cost control. (4 quarter hours)

Financial Accounting Procedures

Course 103. Fundamental accounting principles for service businesses and merchandising enterprises; debits, credits, and double entry; journalizing and posting; accounting systems and special journals; accounting for purchases and sales, cash, receivables, interest, revenue and expense; financial statement preparation, including adjusting and closing procedures. (4 quarter hours)

Course 104. ccounting procedures for inventory, plant assets, intangible assets, long-term investments, current liabilities, accounting procedures for owners' equity in single proprietorship, partnership, and corporation. (4 quarter hours)

Course 105. Financial statement analysis, annual reports, statement of cash flow, managerial accounting concepts and principles, job order cost systems, process cost systems. (4 quarter hours)

ANTHROPOLOGY

Introduction to Cultural Anthropology

Basic concepts; introduction to various world cultures; nature of cultural diversity; evolution of sociocultural systems. (5 quarter hours)

AVIATION

Private Pilot Ground Instruction

Forty hours of ground instruction covering radio navigation, meteorology, FAA regulations, communications, aircraft construction and performance data to meet requirements of private pilot's written exam. (4 quarter hours)

Advanced Aeronautics for Commercial Pilot Ground Instruction

Forty hours of ground instruction covering advanced aerodynamics, radio navigation, FAA regulations, aircraft construction and performance, theories of flight, weight and balance, and instruments to meet requirements of commercial written exam. (4 quarter hours)

Instrument Ground Instruction and Air Traffic Control

Forty hours ground instruction covering various navigation systems and procedures, aircraft radios and communications, instrument flying, and air traffic control procedures. Includes functions of ATC centers, approach control, towers, and flight service stations. FAA regulations included. Meets all requirements for instrument pilot written exam. (4 quarter hours)

BIOLOGY

Human Biology

Humans as living organisms; our origins, ecology, and inheritance; and functioning of our bodies' systems. (5 quarter hours)

Human Physiology

Functions of various systems as applied to humans. Special reference to physiological adaptations to environment and regulatory functions. (4 quarter hours)

Bioethical Problems in Biology and Medicine

Ethical problems arising from rapid advances in biological and biomedical research. Topics include: human experimentation, fetal research, informed consent, death with dignity, euthanasia, biological engineering, reproductive advances, sex control, test tube babies, surrogate mothers, behavioral modification with drugs, electronics and surgery, health care delivery, mental health, and genetic screening. (5 quarter hours)

Biology and the Future of Man

Course covers human sexuality, physiological effects of environmental pollutants, drugs of abuse, and introduction to advances in biological technology that influence the future of humans. (5 quarter hours)

Principles of Biology

Principles of cell biology, physiology, ecology, genetics, and evolution. (4 quarter hours)

BUSINESS ADMINISTRATION

Business and Its Environment

Nature of business and of economic, social, and political environments of business firm. Emphasis on ways in which such surroundings affect business policies and operations. (4 quarter hours)

Small Business Administration

Place and role of small business firms; problems they face; opportunities involved and competitive considerations. (4 quarter hours)

BUSINESS LAW

Law and Society

Conceptual approach to origin, nature, structure, functions, and procedures of law with study of ethics and introduction to constitutional, administrative, criminal, tort, contractual, international, and environmental law, as well as business organizations. (4 quarter hours)

Law of the Management Process

Conceptual framework of legal nature of organizations, particularly corporations and partnerships; rights, powers and limits of managers in relation to duties and responsibilities to their organizations, owners, creditors, employees, customers, state and public. (4 quarter hours)

Law of Commercial Transactions

Legal aspects of commercial paper, consumer credit, and bankruptcy. (4 quarter hours)

Law of Health Care

Analysis of public-private constraints in foundation health agencies; experimentation and risk assumption; medical records; hospital liability; governmental regulations. (4 quarter hours)

Environmental Law

Legal aspects of both individual environmental and societal environmental rights and duties with respect to constitution, private property, nuisance, negligence, statutes, regulatory agencies, and court decisions. Emphasis upon case study of federal, state, and local laws which shaped existing law and those which are likely to shape future legislative and administrative action. (4 quarter hours)

Law of Property and Real Estate

Property law as an institution and analysis of creation, transfer, and relation of various legal interests in property, especially land. (4 quarter hours)

BUSINESS MANAGEMENT TECHNOLOGY

Introduction to Management

Nature of managerial concepts, managerial functions, and organizational structure, with emphasis on current issues. (4 quarter hours)

Mathematics in Business

Application of basic math to business problems. Special emphasis on compound interest, installment buying, and depreciation. Elementary applications of probabilities and statistics. Introduction to computer programs commonly used in business math applications. (4 quarter hours)

Concepts of Marketing

Introduction to problems of manufacturers, wholesalers, and retailers as they relate to modern marketing, market, and product. (4 quarter hours)

Elements of Supervision

Concepts of modern-day supervision. Emphasis on supervisor's major functions and development of sensitivity to human facets in management, using behavioral science findings. (3 quarter hours)

Small Business Operations

Prepares students for selection and operation of small business. Balanced look at all major aspects confronting small-business operator; including finance, personnel, sales, and success and failure factors. (4 quarter hours)

Introduction to Business Computing

Computer applications used in business and industry. Students do computer assignments using DOS operating system, WordPerfect, Lotus 1-2-3, and Harvard Graphics. Extra-credit lesson covers dBase IV. (4 quarter hours)

Managing Finance in Business

Introduction to basic concepts, principles, and analytical techniques of financing. Emphasis on planning and managing assets. (4 quarter hours)

Concepts of Purchasing Management

Analysis of purchasing operation's structure and procedure. Descriptions of quality, quantity, value analysis, sources of supply, and procurement controls. Vendor/buyer relationships, make-or-buy decisions, inventory control, buyer training, materials handling, records, and budgets. (4 quarter hours)

Concepts of Sales

Policies and procedures pertaining to planning sales effort, and control of sales operations. Personality development and role of selling in society, careers, and psychology and philosophy as related to selling. (3 quarter hours)

Practical Personnel Procedures

Hiring, training, assignment of work, employee counseling, promotion, wage and salary administration. Leadership, motivation, and direction of employees toward management/employee-oriented goals. (3 quarter hours)

Business Report Writing

Practice in planning and writing effective business letters, memoranda, and reports. (4 quarter hours)

Advertising Concepts

General course in advertising which emphasizes psychology, advertising agency, media research, brands, and labels. (4 quarter hours)

Managerial Planning

In-depth coverage of the planning process with emphasis on strategic planning. The case study approach is employed to develop skill in complex and difficult decision making. Applications in management science to assist in the decision process are covered. (4 quarter hours)

Concepts of Labor and Management Relations

A broad overview of micro- and macroeconomic theory as applied to the labor factor of production; the many problems related to the full utilization of human resources and government policies addressing these problems; the effects of unionism and labor-management relations including collective bargaining. (4 quarter hours)

Government and Business

Business and government relations, with emphasis on analysis of selected areas involving public policy and business. (3 quarter hours)

Computer Applications for Management

Completes business plan begun in *Managerial Planning*. Utilizes integrated software package in comprehensive case-studies approach in business. Spreadsheet, data base management, word processing, and graphics applications used to create comprehensive business report that ties together overall curriculum. Students must have access to IBM or compatible computer system. Software will be provided. (4 quarter hours)

CHEMISTRY

Principles of Chemistry I

Introduction to chemistry through study of atomic and molecular structure, periodic table, and states of matter. (3 quarter hours)

Principles of Chemistry II

Introduction to descriptive inorganic chemistry through study of solutions and concept of equilibrium. (3 quarter hours)

ECONOMICS

Principles of Microeconomics

Basic theory and economic analysis of prices, markets, production, wages, interest, rent, and profits. (4 quarter hours)

Principles of Macroeconomics

Basic theory of national income analysis. Monetary and fiscal policies of the federal government. Causes of unemployment and inflation. (4 quarter hours)

Microeconomics

Price system as an allocative mechanism. Price and production policies of individual firms and consumers under alternative market conditions and analysis of these policies on social efficiency of resource allocation. Students expected to have an understanding of elementary algebra and geometry. (4 quarter hours)

Macroeconomics

Factors determining level of nation's economic activity and responsible for growth and stability in nation's economy. Part of course devoted to measures of national income while remainder consists of analysis of interrelationships among production, price levels, relative prices, employment and capital formation. Students expected to have an understanding of elementary algebra and geometry. (4 quarter hours)

Labor Economics

Economic forces generating modern labor problems. History of labor movement; labor in politics; labor-management relations; wages and full employment. (4 quarter hours)

International Trade

International trade patterns, theories of absolute and comparative advantage, classical and modern trade theory, tariffs, quotas, nontariff barriers, and preferential trading arrangements. (4 quarter hours)

Money and Banking

Role of money and banking system in determination of national income and output. Monetary theory and policy emphasized. An optional videotape is used for further explanation and examples. (4 quarter hours)

EDUCATION

Life and Career Experiences Analysis

The course is designed to assist adults to analyze and document college-level learning acquired from experience in employment, community volunteering, and homemaking. Successful completion of the course provides the student with a portfolio of materials which can be submitted to various academic departments of the University for assessment and possible award of credit. *Prerequisite:* Admission to the External Student Program through the Adult Learning Services Office and permission. Students may not enroll in this course without confirmation of admission to the program. The course must be completed within six months after enrollment. (4 quarter hours)

ENGLISH

Developmental Writing Skills

Intensive, voluntary, fundamental program in writing, punctuation, grammar, sentence formation, usage and paragraphing skills. Attention to agreement, fragments, pronoun reference, modifiers, tense forms, subordination, etc. (4 quarter hours)

Freshman Composition: Writing and Rhetoric

Focuses on writing expository essays which are well organized and logically coherent. Students write approximately 10 essays. Essay topics come from personal experience or from reading nonfiction. Not a grammar course; those with major writing deficiencies should take Fundamental Usage Skills. (5 quarter hours)

Freshman Composition: Writing and Reading

Focuses on writing expository essays which are well-organized and logically coherent. As preparation for the papers required, students will read fiction, poetry, and drama focused on common themes and discuss their understanding of issues and works presented. (5 quarter hours)

Freshmen Composition: Women and Men in Literature

Readings used to examine depiction of women and men in literature. Students encouraged to think and write about how, in both literature and life, women and men see themselves and each other, how people learn what society expects of them, and about such topics as sexuality, marriage, friendship, and rebellion against sex roles. (5 quarter hours)

Introduction to Literature

Approaches to reading and interpretation of literature, emphasizing skills, techniques, and language of interpretation. (4 quarter hours)

Critical Approaches to Fiction

Critical foundations of fiction; close textual analysis of several short novels by twentieth-century authors. (4 quarter hours)

Critical Approaches to Poetry

Critical foundations of poetry; close textual analysis of works of poetry. (4 quarter hours)

Critical Approaches to Drama

Critical foundations of drama; close textual analysis of plays from classical Greece to the twentieth century. (4 quarter hours)

Introduction to International Literature III: The Modern Tradition

Selected literary works which provide background for and express modern sensibility in western literature. (5 quarter hours)

Shakespeare, The Histories

History plays. (5 quarter hours)

Shakespeare, The Comedies

Comedies. (5 quarter hours)

Shakespeare, The Tragedies

Principal tragedies. (5 quarter hours)

Technical Writing

Focuses on writing on clear and concise proposals, feasability reports, progress reports, and descriptions of mechanisms and technical processes. (4 quarter hours)

Advanced Composition

Aim: to increase skills and expertise in writing of discursive prose. Method: regular practice and evaluation, supplemented by attention to professional prose and concepts in rhetoric and style. (5 quarter

English Literature, 1500–1660

Authors, works, and genres of Renaissance English literature. (4 quarter hours)

English Literature, 1660–1800

Authors, works, and genres of Restoration and 18th-century English literature. (4 quarter hours)

English Literature, 1800–1900

Authors, works, and genres of Romantic and Victorian English literature. (4 quarter hours)

American Literature to the Civil War

Authors, works, and genres of American literature before the Civil War. (4 quarter hours)

American Literature Since the Civil War

Authors, works, and genres of American literature from the end of the Civil War to the end of World War I. (4 quarter hours)

American Literature: 1918 to Present

Authors, works, and genres of American literature from the end of World War I to the present. (4 quarter hours)

American Literature

American authors, themes, genres, etc., usually in 19th- and 20th-century literature. (4 quarter hours)

Creative Writing: Fiction

Beginning course in short fiction with emphasis on invention, craft, and criticism of student writing and published fiction. (4 quarter hours)

Creative Writing: Poetry

Beginning course in poetry with emphasis on invention, craft, and criticism of student writing and published fiction. (4 quarter hours)

ENVIRONMENTAL AND PLANT BIOLOGY

The World of Plants

Survey of variety of plants, and how they affect and are affected by humans. This course requires use of a videotape. (4 quarter hours)

Plant Biology

Structure of seed plants as related to function. Survey of plants, with emphasis on classification, life histories, and relationships of selected plant groups. (5 quarter hours)

FINANCE

Managerial Finance

Role of financial management in business enterprise; financial analysis; planning needs for short-term and long-term funds; planning for profits; capital budgeting; internal management of working capital and income; raising funds to finance growth of business enterprises. (4 quarter hours)

FOREIGN LITERATURE IN ENGLISH

Spanish Literature in English

Course 336A. A study of *Don Quixote* in modern English translation. (4 quarter hours)

Course 336B. Reading and analysis of *One Hundred Years of Solitude* by Gabriel Garcia Marquez in modern English translation. (4 quarter hours)

GEOGRAPHY

Elements of Physical Geography

Systematic survey of temperature, precipitation, atmospheric and oceanic circulation, and global systems of climate, soils, natural vegetation and landforms. (5 quarter hours)

Human Geography

Examination of spatial dimensions of culture, emphasizing patterns of variation of selected cultural elements—language, religion, population, settlement, political and economic landscapes, and human/environmental interactions. (4 quarter hours)

GREEK

Beginning Greek

Course 111. Grammar, vocabulary and reading of ancient Attic Greek. (4 quarter hours)

Course 112. A continuation of *Course 111.* (4 quarter hours)

Course 113. A continuation of *Course 112* with readings from the *Dialogues* of Plato, *Histories of Thucydides* and *Herodotus* and Aesop's *Fables.* (4 quarter hours)

HEALTH

Health Sciences and Lifestyle Choices

Practices and appreciation of means whereby health of individual and group may be maintained. (4 quarter hours)

Introduction to Health Care Organizations

Focuses on U.S. health system, describing health care institutions, providers, payment practices, and significant health legislation. Discusses trends and future perspectives against historical background. Assists manager to develop panoramic view of health care organizations. (4 quarter hours)

Teaching of Health

Instruction, principles, and curricula used in presenting health information to pupils in elementary and secondary schools. (5 quarter hours)

HISTORY

Western Civilization in Modern Times

Course 101. Renaissance to 1648: Renaissance, Reformation, origins of national state system, diplomacy and imperialism as applied to Portugal, Spain, and Hapsburg Empire, and commercial and scientific revolutions. (4 quarter hours)

Course 102. A continuation of *Course 101.* Covers 1648–1848: absolutism, constitutionalism, operation of coalition diplomacy, and imperialism as applied to France and Britain; westernization of eastern Europe, enlightenment, French Revolution, agricultural, commercial, and industrial revolutions and growth of ideologies—liberalism, socialism, and nationalism. (4 quarter hours)

Course 103. A continuation of the *Course 102.* Covers 1848 to present: continued industrial revolution and spread of liberalism, socialism and nationalism; rise and fall of German bid for power in two world wars; new ideologies of materialism, positivism. Social Darwinism, irrationalism, totalitarianism; Russian and Chinese revolutions and international communism; rise and fall of western empires in Africa and Asia. (4 quarter hours)

American History to 1828

Political, diplomatic, social, and economic development of American history. Covers 1607–1828: colonial America, founding of new nation, and early national period. (Use of cassette tapes is essential in this course; tapes may be borrowed from the Independent Study office for a deposit of $21; $9 is refunded when the tapes are returned in good condition). (4 quarter hours)

History of the United States, 1828–1900

Political, diplomatic, social, and economic development of American history. Covers 1828–1900: Jacksonian democracy, territorial expansion, sectionalism and controversy, Civil War, reconstruction, and impact of expanded Industrial Revolution. (Use of cassette tapes is essential in this course; tapes may be borrowed from the Independent Study office for a deposit of $35; $15 is refunded when tapes are returned in good condition). (4 quarter hours)

History of the United States Since 1900

Covers 1900 to present: progressive movement, WW I, prosperity and depression, WW II, and problems of cold war era. (Use of cassette tapes is essential in this course; tapes may be borrowed from the Independent Study office for a deposit of $35; $15 is refunded when the tapes are returned in good condition). (4 quarter hours)

History of Blacks in America Since 1865

Concerns Emancipation and its continuing effects of black person in America. Life in South, migration to North, and conservative and radical attempts by black community to deal with these problems. (Use of cassette tapes is essential in this course; tapes may be borrowed from the Independent Study office for a deposit of $70; $30 is refunded when tapes are returned in good condition). (4 quarter hours)

Ohio History to 1851

Ohio to 1851; prehistoric Ohio, early exploration, settlement, government; statehood and economic development; political parties, antislavery movement, constitutional change. (4 quarter hours)

Ohio History Since 1851

Ohio since 1851; pre-Civil War politics, Civil War. Economic and political transition during post-Civil War. 20-century problems. Biographical sketches. (4 quarter hours)

Early Christianity: East and West

Will investigate historical development and spread of Christianity from its origin to about A.D. 600. Content includes Greek and Hebraic backgrounds, early church fathers of east and west, ecumenical councils, early heresies, and development of church doctrine. (4 quarter hours)

HUMAN AND CONSUMER SCIENCES

Introduction to Nutrition

Nutrients, their food sources and functions in body, application to planning adequate diet throughout life cycle. (4 quarter hours)

Introduction to Child Development

Fundamental patterns of development and behavior during prenatal period through early childhood. (4 quarter hours)

Introduction to Residential Design

Practical and aesthetic study of residential design, including design theory, materials and finishes, selection, and arrangement of furniture and accessories. (3 quarter hours)

Family Consumer Economics

Management of personal and family financial problems. Emphasis on consumer's role in economy. (3 quarter hours)

HUMANITIES

Humanities - Great Books

Course 107. Ancient classics of Western civilization (Greek, Roman, Biblical) leading toward an understanding of cultural heritage. Guidance in critical thinking, reading, and writing about those works. (4 quarter hours)

Course 108. A continuation of *Course 107.* Medieval and Renaissance classics of Western civilization. (4 quarter hours)

Course 109. A continuation of *Course 107, 108.* Modern classics of Western civilization (18th–20th centuries). (4 quarter hours)

Course 307. Ancient classics of Western civilization (Greek, Roman, Biblical) leading toward an understanding of cultural heritage. Guidance in critical thinking, reading, and writing about those works. (4 quarter hours)

HUMAN RESOURCE MANAGEMENT

Human Resource Management

Survey of human resource management practices in areas of human resource planning, recruitment, selection, training and development, performance appraisal, compensation, discipline, safety audits, and personnel research. Includes applications in employment law and discussion of interface of line and staff responsibilities in organizations. (4 quarter hours)

HUMAN SERVICES TECHNOLOGY

Deaf Language and Culture

Course is designed to teach basic sign language and to examine the problems faced by hearing-impaired persons, as well as their capabilities and contributions. Course is especially designed for persons in helping and service professions. The course uses a VHS videotape which students purchase for $20. (3 quarter hours)

Intermediate Deaf Language and Culture

A continuation of the above course with emphasis on building vocabulary and fluency in sign language, adapting print materials for hearing-impaired, and researching problems and resources in student's own community. Course requires VHS videotape which is purchased by the student for $20. (3 quarter hours)

INTERPERSONAL COMMUNICATION

Fundamentals of Human Communication

Introductory analysis of oral communication in human relationships with focus on variety of contexts including: dyadic, small group, and public communication experiences. Serves as survey of human communication processes. (4 quarter hours)

Fundamentals of Public Speaking

Principles of public speaking, practice in presenting informative and persuasive speeches with emphasis on communicative process. Students must have use of VHS format color camera and videotape player (VCR) to videotape some lesson assignments. (4 quarter hours)

Introduction to Communication Theory

Survey of selected humanistic and scientific approaches to communication studies. Emphasis on philosophical bases of communication theory. (5 quarter hours)

JOURNALISM

Introduction to Mass Communication

All forms of mass communication including newspapers, magazines, radio-television, book publishing, public relations, advertising, and photojournalism. Begins with analysis of communication process. (4 quarter hours)

LATIN

Beginning Latin

Course 111. Grammar, vocabulary, and reading. (4 quarter hours)

Course 112. A continuation of *Course 111.* (4 quarter hours)

LAW ENFORCEMENT TECHNOLOGY

Introduction to Law Enforcement Technology

Philosophy and history of law enforcement; overview of crime and police problems; organization and jurisdiction of local, state, and federal law enforcement agencies; survey of professional career opportunities and qualifications required. (3 quarter hours)

Constitutional, Criminal, and Civil Law

Study of the U.S. Constitution and amendments thereto by text material and case method system; major emphasis on freedom of speech, search and seizure, arrest and detention, interrogation and confession, self incrimination, right to counsel, double jeopardy and due process situations. (3 quarter hours)

Interviewing and Report Writing

Examination of interviewing and interrogation procedures employed by law enforcement and security personnel for obtaining information plus practical experience in use of methods. Mechanics of writing reports, including collecting information and taking statements, writing descriptive narratives and report revision. (3 quarter hours)

Criminal Investigation

Fundamentals of investigation; crime scene search and recording; collection and preservation of physical evidence, scientific aids, *modus operandi*, sources of information, interviews and interrogation, follow-up, and case preparation. (3 quarter hours)

Law Enforcement and the Deaf

Course is designed specifically for needs of law enforcement personnel in communicating with hearing impaired. Covers fingerspelling and limited vocabulary of signs and information related to specific situations encountered in law enforcement. Videotape required ($50). (4 quarter hours)

LIBRARY SCIENCE

Basic Acquisitions of Media

Basic procedures in ordering, receiving, organizing, processing of printed library materials. Visit to a library required. Videotape required. (4 quarter hours)

MANAGEMENT

Introduction to Management

Nature of managerial concept, managerial functions and organizational structure, with emphasis on current issues. (4 quarter hours)

Management

Students are assumed to have background in economics, accounting, business law, and statistics. Understanding of and practice in solving problems facing managers and administrators using concepts and principles from behavioral sciences and other applicable disciplines. (4 quarter hours)

Business Communications

Introduction to basic concepts of organizational communication and practice with written communication forms (letters and reports). Brief consideration given to oral communication. (4 quarter hours)

Organization Behavior - Micro Perspective

Conceptual framework of behavioral sciences applied to management and organizations. Motivation and leader behavior within organizational settings. (4 quarter hours)

Organization Behavior - Macro Perspective

Organizational theory and behavior emphasizing formal organizations theory and work group behavior. Concentrates on interaction between organization, its environment and its members, and influences of informal work groups on member behavior. (4 quarter hours)

MARKETING

Marketing Principles

Principles of marketing management with emphasis on practices and problems of marketing manager; analysis of marketing environment; supplemented with cases. (4 quarter hours)

MATHEMATICS

Basic Mathematics

A fundamental course in arithmetic and elementary algebra for students with unusually weak backgrounds. (4 quarter hours)

Algebra

Review topics in high school algebra including linear and quadratic equations and inequalities, factoring, fractions, radicals and exponents and simple graphing techniques. (5 quarter hours)

Precalculus

Graphs, inverses, and operations of functions. Study of polynomial, rational, exponential, logarithmic, and trigonometric functions. Additional topics from trigonometry and analytic geometry. (5 quarter hours)

Elementary Topics in Mathematics

Course 120. (4 quarter hours)

Course 121. (3 quarter hours)

Course 122. (3 quarter hours)

Plane Analytic Geometry

Straight lines, circles, conic sections, functions and graphing of functions studied. (3 quarter hours)

Introduction to Calculus

Course 163A. Presents survey of basic concepts of calculus. (4 quarter hours)

Course 163B. A continuation of *Course 163A.* (3 quarter hours)

Elementary Linear Algebra

Solutions to linear systems, matrices and matrix algebra, determinants, n-dimensional real vector spaces and subspaces, bases and dimension, linear mappings, eigenvalues and eigenvectors, diagonalization. Emphasis is on techniques and computational skills. (4 quarter hours)

Finite Mathematics

Elementary probability and introduction to statistics. (4 quarter hours)

Analytic Geometry and Calculus

Course 263A. Limits and differentiation, including trigonometric functions with applications. (4 quarter hours)

Course 263B. A continuation of *Course 263A.* Integration, logarithmic, exponential, and other transcendental functions. (4 quarter hours)

MUSIC

History and Literature of Music

Course 321. History of music with survey of musical literature to 1600. Course requires use of cassette tapes. Students purchase the tapes for a fee of $8. (3 quarter hours)

Course 322. History of music with survey of musical literature, 1600–1750. Students must have access to cassette tape recorder. (3 quarter hours)

Jazz History

Study of various musics collectively known as jazz, using textbook and recordings. Topics covered include background and history of various jazz styles, characteristics of various styles, identities of major composers, arrangers, and performers of jazz. (3 quarter hours)

OPERATIONS MANAGEMENT

Principles of Operations

Emphasis on conceptual understanding of the operations function and includes the following topics: product/process selection and design, facility location and layout, capacity, materials and inventory management, quality, etc. (4 quarter hours)

PHILOSOPHY

Fundamentals of Philosophy

Survey of selected basic problems, concepts and methods in philosophy. (5 quarter hours)

Principles of Reasoning

Basic concepts of logic and techniques for judging validity of arguments introduced. System for symbolizing arguments and deriving conclusions from premises employed. Topics also covered: informal fallacies in reasoning, syllogistic or Aristotelian logic; Venn diagrams, truth tables. Students may purchase an optional videotape for $20 which gives additional assistance with course material. (4 quarter hours)

Introduction to Ethics

Discussion of classic and/or modern philosophical views of human values, ideals and morality. Provides introductory survey of some main problems, concepts and results of ethics including selected philosophers of the past and present. (4 quarter hours)

Philosophy of Art

Conceptual analysis of common assumptions, attitudes, theories, and ideas about arts, their criticism, and appreciation. (4 quarter hours)

Philosophy of Religion

Problems in nature of religion, existence, and nature of God; problem of evil, immorality, and religious language. (4 quarter hours)

Introduction to Philosophy

Analysis of typical philosophical problems arising in study of nature, society, and religion for purpose of developing thoughtful and consistent intellectual perspective. (3 quarter hours)

Philosophy of Culture

Philosophical studies of man as culture-creating being. (5 quarter hours)

Hinduism

Vedic religion, Hinduism, Jainism. (4 quarter hours)

Islam

Introduction to basic ideas, history, and background. A VHS videotape is an optional supplement to the course. Students may borrow the tape from the Independent Study office for a deposit of $35; $15 is refunded when the tape is returned in good condition. (4 quarter hours)

PHYSICAL EDUCATION

History and Principles of Physical Education

History of sport and physical education from ancient to modern times. Principles underlying physical education in modern program of education. A set of slides accompanies this course for which the student pays a charge of $35 of which $25 is refunded when slides are returned in good condition. (4 quarter hours)

Organization and Administration of Physical Education

Organization and administration of physical education, intramural and athletic programs in elementary and secondary schools. (4 quarter hours)

PHYSICAL SCIENCE

Survey of Astronomy

Topics covered: origins and history of astronomy; nature of astronomical observations and instruments; solar systems; comets, meteors, and meteorites; sun and stars; origin and evolution of stars; structure of our galaxy; pulsars; quasars; galaxies; expanding universe; cosmology. (4 quarter hours)

Physical World

Course 101. Fundamental ideas of measurement, motion, electricity and magnetism, heat, atomic and nuclear physics. Introduction to relativity and quantum phenomena. (4 quarter hours)

Course 121. Fundamental ideas of measurement, motion, energy, sound, light, electricity, and magnetism and astronomy. Topics in astronomy include solar system, time, moon phases, tides, eclipses, sun, and galaxies. (3 quarter hours)

Color, Light, and Sound

Designed for nonscience majors. Physical nature of light and sound, including transmission, absorption, reflection, interference, and resonance. Applications include analysis of musical instruments, acoustics, optical systems, perception of color and sound. (4 quarter hours)

The Metric System

Introduction to international (metric) System of Units (SI) through lecture and laboratory experience. Topics include history of and rationale for SI; SI and its rules for use; metric computation and conversion techniques. (1 quarter hour)

PHYSICS

Introduction to Physics

Course 201. First course in physics; open to students from all areas. Students should have high school level algebra and trigonometry, but no calculus required. Recommended for students in liberal arts, architecture, industrial technology, botany, geology and premedicine. Mechanics of solids and liquids. (4 quarter hours)

Course 202. A continuation of *Course 201.* Includes electricity, magnetism, heat, thermodynamics, waves and sound. (4 quarter hours)

Course 203. A continuation of *Course 202.* Includes light, relativity, quantum, atomic, and nuclear physics. (4 quarter hours)

POLITICAL SCIENCE

American National Government

Constitutional basis and development, political processes, and organization of American national government. (4 quarter hours)

State Politics

Comparative analysis of state political systems. Emphasis on structure and process of policymaking of states within federal context. (5 quarter hours)

PSYCHOLOGY

General Psychology

Introduction to psychology. Survey of topics in experimental and clinical psychology including physiological bases of behavior, sensation, perception, learning, memory, human development, social processes, personality, and abnormal behavior. (5 quarter hours)

Elementary Statistics for the Behavioral Sciences

Measures of central tendency, variability, correlation; sampling distributions and statistical inference; simple test of hypotheses. (5 quarter hours)

Psychology of Adjustment

Dynamics, development, and problems of human adjustment. (4 quarter hours)

Educational Psychology

Application of psychological theories and models to educational settings (emphasis on schools). Major topics include goals of education; cognitive and behavioral models of learning; motivation; individual differences; effects of social class, ethnicity, gender, and cultural deprivation on learning and development; tests and evaluation. Emphasis is on the role of teachers and parents as facilitators of learning and development. (4 quarter hours)

Abnormal Psychology

Behavior disorders, their cause and effects on person, family, and society. (4 quarter hours)

Environmental Psychology

Natural and built environments of everyday as factors of human behavior, cognition, and choice. Research concerning environmental design and evaluation from psychological standpoint emphasized. (4 quarter hours)

Social Psychology of Justice

Theory and research on the interface of psychology and the legal system (with an emphasis on social psychology). Specific topics include dilemmas faced by psychologists in the legal system; legality vs. morality; the socialization, training, and ethics of lawyers and police; perception, memory, and error in eyewitness testimony; hypnosis; lie detection and confessions; rights of victims and accused; rape and rapists; arrest and trial; jury selection; jury dynamics and deliberations; insanity and the prediction of dangerousness; sentencing; death penalty; rights of special groups; theories of crime. (4 quarter hours)

Psychology of Adulthood and Aging

Behavioral change and continuity over the adult years through old age. Emphasis on the interaction of psychological, sociocultural, and biological variables as they contribute to behaviors of aging individuals from perspective of developmental framework. (4 quarter hours)

QUANTITATIVE BUSINESS ANALYSIS

Introduction to Business Statistics

Sampling plans, point and interval estimation. Classical (hypothesis testing) decision theory. Contingency table analysis, simple regression, correlation analysis, and nonparametric statistics. Computer programs are used to aid analysis when appropriate. (4 quarter hours)

SECURITY/SAFETY TECHNOLOGY

Introduction to Protective Services

Gives an overview of private security profession. Student will be able to relate private security's function to its proper perspective in today's complex society and to see where private security and its various functions fit into criminal justice system. (3 quarter hours)

Physical Security Systems

Physical security requirements and standards. Course includes study of various physical security systems plus technical devices employed in industrial, retail, and institutional security operations. (3 quarter hours)

Occupational Safety and Health

Analysis and implementation survey of federal laws pertaining to occupational safety and health standards and criteria. (3 quarter hours)

Fire Safety and Fire Codes

Function and objective of fire prevention programs, *e.g.*, recognition and correction of fire hazards; enforcement of codes and ordinances; knowledge of federal, state, and local fire laws and codes. Further emphasis on fire prevention and fire protection. (3 quarter hours)

Loss Prevention in Modern Retailing

Detailed study of use of proper controls in loss prevention and loss detection in retailing industry. Emphasis to provide students with sound background for determining their needs in such areas as: physical security, inventory security, security surveys, personnel screening, risk analysis and loss prevention as total systems approach. (3 quarter hours)

Analysis of Security Needs - Survey

Methodology used in making security surveys, *e.g.*, selection of scope, team composition, design of survey, compiling data, evaluation of planning, implementation and results of corrective measures. (3 quarter hours)

Information and Data Systems Security

This course covers the ways that information and data can be attacked in computer-based systems, and then discusses the human and technological safeguards that can be used to forestall these attacks or lessen their impact. Content includes consideration of Right to Privacy laws. (3 quarter hours)

Security Administration

Introduction to corporate security administration including historical and legal framework for security operations as well as detailed presentation of specific security processes and programs utilized in providing security. (3 quarter hours)

Current Problems in Security

Analysis of special problem areas in security such as: security education and training, community relations, labor problems, and disaster planning. Other specific areas analyzed for further research by individual students. These areas may include bank security, campus security, computer security, hospital security, and various other areas. (3 quarter hours)

Analytical Accounting

Specifically designed for security administration majors. Covers areas such as audit tracing, cash flow analysis, inventory system analysis and other auditing principles used to protect assets and discover losses. (3 quarter hours)

Special Area Studies: Terrorism

This course presents methods by which industry, business and government can combat the threat of terrorism. The political, psychological, and sociological parameters in which terrorism can exist are explored. (3 quarter hours)

Special Area Studies: Law and Security

This course explores the legal ramifications of decisions that security personnel must make and provides a framework for security organizations to operate in vis-a-vis our society's legal structures. (3 quarter hours)

SOCIOLOGY

Introduction to Sociology

Nature of human society and factors affecting its development. Fundamental concepts of sociology; culture, personality, socialization, groups, institutions. (5 quarter hours)

Elementary Research Techniques

Research techniques in sociology. Research design; collection, recording, and analysis of data. (4 quarter hours)

Criminology

Theories and research in criminal behavior and societal reaction to criminality. Causes and consequences of crime. (4 quarter hours)

Juvenile Delinquency

Theories and research in delinquency. Causes and consequences of delinquent behavior among juveniles. (4 quarter hours)

STUDY SKILLS

Effective Study Skills

Helps students assess present study behaviors and attitudes and adopt techniques that increase their effectiveness in managing time, taking notes, reading and organizing text material, and preparing for exams. Emphasizes regular practice and use of skills taught. (2 quarter hours)

College Reading Skills

Focuses on improving comprehension, interpretation, and evaluation of reading materials that are typical of college courses. Moves from short passages to longer selections. Includes speed reading techniques and vocabulary building. Emphasizes practice and application of skills. (2 quarter hours)

THEATRE

Theater History I

Development of theater and drama in prehistoric, Greek, and Roman periods. (4 quarter hours)

Theater History II

Development of theater and drama in medieval and Renaissance periods. (4 quarter hours)

Theater History III

Development of theater and drama from Renaissance to modern. (4 quarter hours)

WOMEN'S STUDIES

Introduction to Women's Studies

Study of female experience, drawing on materials from literature, autobiography, philosophy, history, law, myth, religion, and social sciences. Looks at cultural beliefs about women's nature and role in different times and places, representation of women and their relationships with others in myth and literature, and women's efforts to define new identity through work, creative activity, and through feminism, both historically and at present. Current issues explored. (4 quarter hours)

The New Scholarship on Women: The Question of Difference

Question of sexual differences has both plagued and motivated contemporary feminist analyses. Course explores what new scholarship on women going on in diverse disciplines contributes to question of differences between women and men. (4 quarter hours)

Oklahoma, University of
Independent Study Department
College of Continuing Education
1700 Asp Avenue, Room B-1
Norman, Oklahoma 73072   (405) 325-1921

Description:

The University of Oklahoma Independent Study Department has been offering correspondence courses since 1910.

The department offers 210 college, 80 high school, and 30 noncredit courses. There were 5,822 enrollments during fiscal year 1994.

Faculty:

Larry Colbert, Interim Director; Charles B. Williams, Project Specialist; Patty Fotinos, College Enrollments; Donna Rushing, High School Enrollments and Records. There is a faculty of 120 members of which 80 percent teach college courses.

Academic Levels:

College

High School

Noncredit

Degree/Certificate Programs:

Correspondence credits may be applied toward the bachelor degree. In general, a University of Oklahoma student may meet up to one-fourth of total degree requirements through any combination of correspondence, testing-out, and extension credits. Individual colleges and departments frequently impose limitations more stringent than those given as a general rule.

Admission Requirements:

High school students must have the approval of their respective school principals or superintendents. Admitted University of Oklahoma students need the approval of their respective college deans. Non-University of Oklahoma students seeking college usually must have a high school diploma or the equivalent, but need not apply to the University for admission. Noncredit students have no restrictions on admission/enrollment.

Tuition:

College courses, $55 per semester hour plus a $5 records fee for each academic term in which the students enroll; high school courses, $70 per ½ unit course; noncredit course fees vary. Additional fees may be applicable. Tuition must be paid at time of registration. VISA and MasterCard accepted. Refund of 80 percent is made if withdrawal occurs within 30 days of enrollment; 50 percent is refunded if within second 30 days of enrollment; thereafter no refund is made. When applicable, deduction is made for any grading of lessons.

Enrollment Period:

The maximum time allowed to complete a course is one year; a 6-month extension may be granted upon payment of an extension fee of $30. The minimum time allowed to complete a course is 2 weeks per semester hour for college courses; 6 weeks for high school courses. The minimum times begin with submission of first lesson; work must be pro-rated according to number of lessons.

Equipment Requirements:

The cost of textbooks is not included in the tuition and must be purchased by the student, either locally or through the Independent Study Department; there is a refund plan for the return of used books. Some courses have additional equipment requirements such as the purchase of cassette tapes and access to a tape player. Foreign students must pay for airmail postage of materials and lessons.

Credit and Grading:

Most college credit and high school examinations receive letter grades (A–F on a four-point scale); noncredit examinations, Satisfactory (S) or Unsatisfactory (U). The minimum passing grade is D (S for noncredit courses). Students may request Pass/No Pass grading for letter-graded courses, but must do "C"-level work or better to receive a Pass grade. Generally, the final grade is based entirely on the results of the examination. All examinations must be supervised by an approved proctor. Credit is awarded in semester hour units.

Library Services:

On-campus students have access to the University library system. With a few exceptions, most courses require no access to library facilities/services.

Accreditations:

North Central Association of Colleges and Schools. Member of: National University Continuing Education Association.

COLLEGE COURSES

ACCOUNTING

Fundamental Financial Accounting

Basic principles of financial accounting. Emphasis on the preparation and use of the income statement, balance sheet, and statement of funds flow for corporations. Coverage includes the analysis and recording of transactions involving cash, inventories, fixed assets, bonds, and capital stock as well as closing, adjusting, and reversing entries for revenue and expense items. (3 semester hours)

Fundamental Managerial Accounting

Introduction to managerial accounting. Analysis of cost behavior and the use of this knowledge for both short and long term decisions. An introduction to budgeting and the accumulation of product costs for planning and performance evaluation. Specific coverage includes cost-volume-profit analysis, capital budgeting, allocations, variances from standard costs and the measurement of divisional performance. (3 semester hours)

Intermediate Accounting I

Valuation and other theoretical problems in accounting for cash, temporary investments, receivables, inventories, long-term investments, plant and equipment, intangible assets. (3 semester hours)

Intermediate Accounting II

Stockholder's equity, dilutive securities, investments, issues related to income determination including revenue recognition, accounting for income taxes, pensions, leases and error analysis, preparation and analysis of financial statements, including price level changes and statement of changes in financial position. (3 semester hours)

Cost Accounting

Basic cost principles. Job order costing, process and joint costing, estimated costs. (3 semester hours)

Governmental Accounting

Study of governmental and nonprofit accounting. An analysis of funds that reflect activity for governmental units, including various enterprise funds such as hospitals and educational institutions. (3 semester hours)

ANTHROPOLOGY

Mythology and Folkore

The course will focus on two major areas: (1) the nature and function of myth and folklore in human societies, and (2) the uses to which the study of folklore have been put by anthropologists in both functional and culture-historical analyses of preliterate societies. (3 semester hours)

Maya, Aztec, and Inca: High Civilizations of Ancient America

An archaeological and ethnological study of pre-Spanish cultures of Mesoamerica and the Central Andes, primary emphasis to Maya of Yucatan, Aztec of Mexico, and Inca of Peru. (3 semester hours)

ART

Public School Art

Theory and objectives for art teaching in the elementary schools. Experimentation with a variety of materials and techniques. (2 semester hours)

ASTRONOMY

General Astronomy

Introduction to the concepts of modern astronomy. The solar system, the sun and stars, the Milky Way and other galaxies, current theories of the origin, evolution, and fate of the universe. (4 semester hours)

BUSINESS ADMINISTRATION

Real Estate Principles

Introduces the student to the broad field of real estate. Topics covered in the course include real estate valuation, investment analysis, ownership forms, conveyancing, productivity analysis, development, marketing, financing, and governmental regulation. (3 semester hours)

BUSINESS COMMUNICATIONS

Advanced Business Communication

The dynamics, qualities, functions, and methods of administrative communication; problems and practice in preparing effective material; practical application, including the construction of primary research tools. (3 semester hours)

BUSINESS LAW

Legal Environment of Business

The legal environment of business organizations with ethical considerations and the social and political influences affecting such environments. (3 semester hours)

Real Property

General law of real property, historical development, acquisition of title to personal property, estates and land, landlord and tenant relationships, easements, deeds, mortgages, adverse possessions, wills, and trusts. (3 semester hours)

CHEMISTRY

Chemistry for Non-Science Majors

Principal concepts and theories of chemistry are critically examined, in chronological order, from the layman's viewpoint. Non-technical and non-mathematical. (4 semester hours)

Organic Chemistry

Course 3053. Two-course sequence covering the fundamental concepts or organic structure and reactions of the principal functional groups. Reaction mechanisms. (3 semester hours)

Course 3153. A continuation of the above course. (3 semester hours)

CHINESE

Beginning Chinese

Course 1115. An elementary curse in understanding, speaking, reading, and writing Chinese. (5 semester hours)

Course 1225. A continuation of the above course. (5 semester hours)

CLASSICAL STUDIES

Latin Derivatives

Designed to enlarge the student's English vocabulary through the study mainly of important Latin verbal bases and their combinations with prefixes and suffixes that appear frequently in learned English works. Considerable practice in analysis. Knowledge of Latin not required. (2 semester hours)

Classical Mythology

The origins and development of Greek and Roman myths indispensable for understanding of ancient and modern literature; with allusion to their influence on art and religion. (3 semester hours)

Medical Vocabulary

Designed to be of special use to students of the biological sciences. Study of basic Greek and Latin elements of medical terminology through the analysis of select vocabularies and word lists. (2 semester hours)

Hebrew Civilization in Ancient Times

A topical survey from 1400 B.C. to 425 A.D., dealing critically with the main institutions and their historical background from early tribal theocracy to the end of the Rabbinic Patriarchate under Rome. (3 semester hours)

DRAMA

History of the Theatre

Course 2713. To acquaint the student with the development of drama, theatre, and production procedures through the ages from 500 B.C. to the eighteenth century. (3 semester hours)

Course 2723. To acquaint the student with the development of drama, theatre, and production procedures from the eighteenth century to the present. Requires access to the 1991 film version of *Cyrano de Bergerac.* (3 semester hours)

ECONOMICS

Economic History of the United States: Development of American Economic System and Institutions

Agriculture, industry, and commerce of the United States; organization of our economic life. (3 semester hours)

Principles of Economics—Macro

The functioning and current problems of the aggregate economy; determination and analysis of national income, employment, inflation and stabilization; money and banking, monetary and fiscal policy; and aspects of international interdependence. (3 semester hours)

Principles of Economics—Micro

Goals, incentives, and allocation of resources resulting from economic behavior with applications and illustrations from current issues; operation of markets for goods, services, and factors of production; the behavior of firms and industries in different types of competition and income distribution. (3 semester hours)

Elements of Statistics

Basic statistical techniques emphasizing business and economic applications. Topics include data summary techniques, elementary probability, theory, estimation, hypothesis testing, simple regression, time series and index numbers. (3 semester hours)

International Trade Theory and Problems

Benefits of trade, determination of the direction and level of trade, commercial policy and trade barriers, international trade problems and issues. (3 semester hours)

World Economic Development

The economics of the developing nations; a review and analysis of common problems and issues. (3 semester hours)

EDUCATION

Education of Exceptional Learners

A comprehensive overview of learners with exceptionalities—including the student who is physically/health impaired, visually impaired, learning impaired, speech/language impaired, mentally retarded, learning disabled, gifted, emotionally disturbed or multiple handicapped. (3 semester hours)

ENGINEERING

Thermodynamics

First and second laws of thermodynamics are developed and applied to the solution of problems from a variety of engineering fields. Extensive use is made of partial differential calculus to interrelate the thermodynamic functions. (3 semester hours)

Electrical Science

Formulation and solution of circuit equations, network theorems, sinusoidal steady-state analysis, simple transients. (3 semester hours)

Fluid Mechanics

Coverage of the fundamentals of fluid statics and dynamics. Formulation of the equation of fluid flow, i.e. Navier Stokes equations, Euler's equation, Bernoulli equations, etc., and their application. Ideal fluid flow and viscous fluid flow. (3 semester hours)

Hydrology

An applied course on hydrology dealing with environmental water problems; principles of hydrologic systems, their structure and components; methods of analysis and their application to various purposes of water resources planning and development. (3 semester hours)

ENGLISH

Principles of English Composition

Course 1113. Systematic analysis of the components of effective writing and study of expository prose models. Drill on the whole composition, paragraph, and sentence. (3 semester hours)

Course 1213. A continuation of the above course. Study of literary types and themes. (3 semester hours)

World Literature to 1700

A reading of literary works, by types, from classical antiquity to 1700. (3 semester hours)

World Literature, 1700 to Present

Masterpieces of world literature from 1700 to the modern period. (3 semester hours)

English Literature from 1375 to 1700

A survey of major writers and literary movements from Chaucer through Dryden. (3 semester hours)

American Literature

Course 2773. A survey of major American writers and literary movements from the colonial period to the Civil War. (3 semester hours)

Course 2883. A continuation of the above course. A survey of major American writers and literary movements from the Civil War to the present.

The Bible as Literature

Interpreting the Bible as literature. Discussion of readings of individual books. A number of critical issues that affect the ways we approach the project of understanding the Bible will also be considered. (3 semester hours)

History of the English Language

Traces the development of the English language from its Indo-European origins through its present state. Special attention will be paid to changes in grammar and vocabulary. (3 semester hours)

FINANCE

Personal Finance

Problems and applications in personal finance, financial planning and budgeting covering savings, thrift institutions, financial sources, interest rates, life, property, and casualty insurance, personal investments, tax planning, real estate financing, public annuities, and retirement and estate planning. (3 semester hours)

Business Finance

An introductory course in financial administration of the firm. The finance function, concepts of sources and uses of funds, analysis and estimation of need for funds, short and long term; short term sources, working capital management policy; long term sources; capital structure policy and implementation, capital budgeting and the cost of capital. (3 semester hours)

Financial Markets

A survey of financial markets and institutions. Includes the nature, functions, creation and destruction of money and credit. Analytics of term, default, and tax structures of interest rates emphasized. Special emphasis on the commercial banking system and the Federal Reserve. Analysis of the growing futures and options markets and interaction of the U.S. financial system with the rest of the world. (3 semester hours)

FRENCH

Beginning French

Course 1115. An elementary course in understanding, speaking, reading, and writing French. Cassette recorder required. (5 semester hours)

Course 1225. An elementary course in understanding, speaking, reading, and writing French. A continuation of the above course. (5 semester hours)

Intermediate French

Course 2113. The systematic cultivation of increased depth and control in the basic skills of listening, speaking, reading, and writing French. (3 semester hours)

Course 2223. A continuation of *Course 2113.* (3 semester hours)

French Conversation and Culture

Conversation practice based on elementary readings in selected topics from traditional and contemporary French culture, with the objective of developing additional active vocabulary and increased oral fluency while obtaining basic concepts about the French culture. (3 semester hours)

French Conversation and Literature

Conversation practice based on modern literary texts, with the objective of improving reading speed, vocabulary and comprehension, and increased oral fluency, while obtaining an expanded appreciation of French literary texts. (3 semester hours)

Advanced French Composition

The inculcation of proper writing habits, at an advanced level, toward the achievement of idiomatic French. (3 semester hours)

Survey of French Literature to 1800

Course 4153. Reading and discussion of major French works and their background from the Middle Ages to the French Revolution. (3 semester hours)

Course 4163. Reading and discussion of major French works and their background from 1800 to the present day. (3 semester hours)

French Civilization I

The political and social background of French literature from its beginning to the French Revolution. (3 semester hours)

French Civilization II

The political and social background of French literature from the French Revolution to the present day. (3 semester hours)

GEOGRAPHY

Political Geography

Identifies and evaluates distinctive geographical patterns resulting from political behavior; examines the geographical bases of political conflict at scales ranging from urban to international and evaluates methods of conflict resolution; surveys patterns of political systems, territorial administration, and voting. (3 semester hours)

GEOLOGY

Physical Geology for Science and Engineering Majors

Plate tectonics, the makeup of continents and mountain building. Heat flow, magnetism, gravity, rock deformation, earthquakes and the earth's interior. Surface process including weathering, erosion, transport, and deposition. Landforms, rivers, groundwater, glaciers, ocean processes, and volcanoes. Minerals and rocks. Application of geology to land-use, ground water, mineral and fossil fuel exploration. (4 semester hours)

Historical Geology

Physical history of the earth from its origin as a planet through the Great Ice Age; origin and growth of continents and ocean basins; systematic survey of the history of continents with emphasis on North America; growth and leveling of mountain chains, rift valleys, transgressions and regressions of seas; continental fragmentation, assembly and relative motions; plate tectonics, particularly as it relates to continent history; climate and evolutionary changes through geologic time; principles and methods used to interpret earth history and date rocks; geologic time; lab includes historical studies of specific regions, study of maps and fossils. (4 semester hours)

GERMAN

Beginning German for Reading

Course 1013. Designed as initial preparation for the advanced degree reading examination. (3 semester hours)

Course 1023. A continuation of the above course. (3 semester hours)

Beginning German

Course 1115. An elementary course in understanding, speaking, reading, and writing German. Cassette player/recorder required and must be provided by the student. (5 semester hours)

Course 1225. A continuation of the above course. (5 semester hours)

Intermediate German

Course 2113. Develops reading skills and control of grammar. Emphasis on expansion of vocabulary and strong reinforcement of grammatical structures. Reading and discussion of texts of literary and cultural interest. (3 semester hours)

Course 2223. A continuation of the above course. (3 semester hours)

German Composition and Conversation

Exercises in oral and written German. Reading of cultural and literary texts of contemporary interest. Emphasis on writing and speaking German. (3 semester hours)

Scientific German

Course 3013. Training in the reading of scientific material of gradually increasing difficulty. (3 semester hours)

Course 3123. A continuation of the above course. (3 semester hours)

GREEK

Beginning Greek

Course 1115. Introductory study of the vocabulary and grammar of the Greek language. Some practice in the reading of simple New Testament prose. (5 semester hours)

Course 1215. A continuation of the above course. (5 semester hours)

New Testament Greek

The reading of substantial portions of the New Testament, chosen to illustrate its literary qualities and to exhibit the characteristics of its language. (3 semester hours)

HEBREW

Beginning Hebrew

Course 1114. An elementary course in understanding, speaking, and writing Hebrew. (4 semester hours)

Course 1214. A continuation of the above course. (4 semester hours)

Intermediate Hebrew

Readings in classical and post-classical Hebrew with emphasis on independent and accurate translation. (3 semester hours)

HISTORY

Europe: 1500 to 1815

An introductory survey of Europe in the early modern period. Topics include Reformation, development of the nation-state, the Enlightenment, and the French Revolution, Napoleon. (3 semester hours)

Europe Since 1815

An introductory survey of Europe from 1815 to the present. Examines the major political, economic, social, and cultural trends in the major countries and European foreign affairs and overseas expansion. (3 semester hours)

United States, 1492 to 1865

General survey of U.S. history from its colonial origins to end of Civil War, with emphasis on national, political, diplomatic, economic, constitutional, social and intellectual developments. (3 semester hours)

United States, 1865 to the Present

A general survey of U.S. history from the Civil War to the present, with emphasis on national, political, diplomatic, economic, constitutional, social, and intellectual developments. (3 semester hours)

Western Civilization I

History and culture of western civilization from origins of Greek society to end of religious wars in the seventeenth century. (3 semester hours)

Western Civilization II

History and culture of western civilization between 1660 and the present. Emphasis will be placed on western institutions and ideas, their evolution, and their influence elsewhere. (3 semester hours)

History of East Asian Civilization to 1800

A general survey of the history of China, Japan, Korea, and Vietnam from earliest times to 1800. Development of Chinese civilization— including political forms, thought, religions, and society—and its dissemination to nearby kingdoms. (3 semester hours)

History of Modern East Asia Since 1800

A general survey of the history of the modern transformation of East Asia in response to the West. Revolution in China, modernization of Japan, the rise of nationalism in Korea and Vietnam. (3 semester hours)

World Civilizations to 1600

Deals with the entire globe rather than with some one country or region; deals with all peoples, not just with Western or Non-Western peoples. Focuses on historical forces or movements of worldwide influence. Comparative history. (3 semester hours)

World Civilizations Since 1600

Deals with the entire globe rather than with some one country or region; deals with all peoples, not just with Western or Non-Western peoples. Focuses on historical forces or movements of worldwide influence. Comparative history. (3 semester hours)

England to 1688

A survey covering the Roman, Anglo-Saxon, and Norman periods and later medieval and Tudor England. Attempts to delineate the unique nature of English development as it was exported to English colonies. (3 semester hours)

England since 1688

Attempts to delineate the time period from monarchy to the democratic welfare state. (3 semester hours)

Colonial Hispanic-American History, 1492–1810

The founding and development of the Spanish and Portuguese empires in America with special attention to the conquest of native civilizations and to the political, economic, social and intellectual institutions of the colonial period. (3 semester hours)

History of Hispanic-American Nations, 1810 to Present

The emancipation and development of the Spanish-American nations (and of Brazil) with special attention to the movements for national independence, political unification, economic development and social welfare. (3 semester hours)

History of Islam

Survey of the history of Islamic civilization in the Near East, North Africa, India, and Malaysia from the advent of the Prophet to the modern period. (3 semester hours)

History of Oklahoma

A survey of Oklahoma history from its beginning to the present, including its Indian background, formation into territories, achievement of statehood, and general cultural, economic, and political development. (3 semester hours)

Hebrew Civilization in Ancient Times

A topical survey from 1400 B.C. to 425 A.D., dealing critically with the main institutions and their historical background from early tribal theocracy to the end of the Rabbinic Patriarchate under Rome. (3 semester hours)

United States Diplomatic History to 1900

A survey of American diplomatic history from the War for Independence to 1900, emphasizing problems of expansion and relations with major European, Latin American, and Far Eastern countries. (3 semester hours)

United States Diplomatic History in the Twentieth Century

A survey of American diplomatic history since 1900, emphasizing relations with major European, Latin American, and Asian countries, and the increasing problems of the United States as a world power. (3 semester hours)

History of Modern Japan Since 1800

Japan's response to the West, with emphasis on the opening of Japan, the Meiji Restoration, modernization, imperialism, intellectual currents, and recent economic growth. (3 semester hours)

HUMAN RELATIONS

Introduction to Human Relations

Designed to introduce students to the breadth and depth of the field of human relations. Emphasis is on the processes of communication, problem solving, decision making, conflict and change as they occur in individuals, interpersonal, group, and intergroup relations. (3 semester hours)

JAPANESE

Beginning Japanese

Course 1115. An elementary course in understanding, speaking, reading, and writing Japanese. (5 semester hours)

Course 1225. A continuation of the above course. (5 semester hours)

JOURNALISM

Introduction to Advertising

Survey of the field of advertising and career areas within the field with emphasis on the relationship between marketing and advertising and the media which serve as channels of advertising communication. (3 semester hours)

Principles of Public Relations

The history, scope, ethics, and functions of public relations. Particular attention is given to ways of gaining public support for an activity, cause, movement, or institution. (3 semester hours)

Professional Writing: Fundamentals

Basic theory, orientation and fundamental techniques of fiction writing. (4 semester hours)

Professional Writing: Approaches to Fiction

Technique and theory of fiction writing and plots, with emphasis on current American short stories. (4 semester hours)

Professional Writing: Magazine Writing

Research, preparation, technical devices, marketing of the nonfiction article or book. Study of current trends with emphasis on magazine nonfiction. (4 semester hours)

Professional Writing: The Novel

Analysis of the practical creative problems involved in writing novels. Instruction in specific approaches and techniques useful in plotting, characterization, setting, scene, etc. Supervised writing of a novel by each student. (4 semester hours)

Supervision of Secondary School Publications

Sources of news for school publications; techniques for writing news stories, feature articles and editorials; preparation of copy and selling advertising; production techniques; function, planning and production of the school yearbook; recruiting and organizing staffs for newspaper and yearbook. (3 semester hours)

LATIN

Beginning Latin

Course 1115. Introductory study of the vocabulary and grammar of the Latin language with practice in reading sentences and connected prose from selected Latin authors. (5 semester hours)

Course 1215. A continuation of the above course. 5 semester hours)

Intermediate Prose: Cicero's *Orations*

Reading designed mainly to increase the student's proficiency in rapid translation of excerpts from the prose writings of major Latin authors. (3 semester hours)

Advanced Poetry: Vergil

Reading of extended passages from Vergil's *Aeneid.* Practice in scansion, occasional lectures on Vergil's life, the historical and literary aspects of the *Aeneid* and Vergil's place in the epic tradition. (3 semester hours)

LIBRARY SCIENCE

Use of the Library and Information Resources

The general process of defining information needs in selecting appropriate information sources. Intended to make students more knowledgeable consumers of information. Exercises in the use of information resources stressing the full range of sources and services available in libraries and information centers. (3 semester hours)

Children's Literature

Survey, evaluation, and selection of materials for children; interests and needs of various age groups; methods of stimulating reading and listening. Reading of books for children is emphasized. (3 semester hours)

MANAGEMENT

Principles of Organization and Management

An introductory course presenting the basic principles and practices of management both private and public. Historical development of management; basic definitions and philosophy; fundamental managerial functions, including planning, organization, staffing, directing, and controlling; a survey approach to quantification in organizational life; current trends in management; possible future developments in organization and administration. (3 semester hours)

Personnel Management

A foundation course which systematically combines the research findings of the social sciences and the prevailing practices of personnel management. Emphasizes the responsibilities of managers for human resources of their organizations. (3 semester hours)

MARKETING

Principles of Marketing

Focuses on the relationship between the firm and its customers and the other members of the channel of distribution. Introduces students to the marketing function of an organization; the environmental factors influencing marketing decisions; the discovery of marketing opportunities; the development of marketing strategy; and the development of marketing programs. (3 semester hours)

MATHEMATICS

Intermediate Algebra

Properties of real numbers, equations and inequalities, algebra or rational expressions, exponents and radicals, introduction to quadratic equations, functions and graphs, systems of linear equations. (3 semester hours)

Introduction to Elementary Functions

Review of linear equations and quadratic equations; systems of equations; inequalities; polynomial and rational functions; introductory trigonometry; mathematical induction; permutations and combinations. (3 semester hours)

Elementary Functions

Covers algebra skills, trigonometry, exponential and logarithmic functions, emphasizing the functions concept as an organizing theme. (3 semester hours)

Trigonometry

A study of the analytical development of the trigonometric functions. (2 semester hours)

Calculus I for Business, Life and Social Sciences

Topics in differentiation and integration of polynomial functions. Introduction to exponential and logarithmic functions. Applications to the business, life, and social sciences. (3 semester hours)

Calculus II for Business, Life and Social Sciences

Differentiation and integration of exponential and logarithmic functions; simple differential equations; partial derivatives; double integrals; probability. Applications to business, life and social science. (3 semester hours)

Analytic Geometry

Topics include Cartesian coordinates, polar coordinates, conic sections, translation and rotation of axes, lines and planes in space. (2 semester hours)

Calculus and Analytic Geometry I

Topics covered include equations of straight lines; conic sections; functions, limits and continuity; differentiation; maximum-minimum theory and curve sketching. (3 semester hours)

Calculus and Analytic Geometry II

Integration and its applications; the calculus of transcendental functions; techniques of integration; and the introduction to differential equations. (3 semester hours)

Calculus and Analytic Geometry III

This course opens with a section on parametric equations which studies the notion of curve length using different coordinate systems including polar coordinates. There are major sections devoted to the study of sequences and series. It is here that is found the basis for many numerical algorithms used in calculators and computers. The course concludes with a section on vector techniques applied to analytic geometry. (3 semester hours)

Arithmetic for Elementary Teachers I

A systematic analysis of arithmetic and a presentation of intuitive algebra and geometry. (3 semester hours)

Arithmetic for Elementary Teachers II

Algebra and the structure of number systems, functional relationships, informal geometry. (3 semester hours)

Linear Algebra

Systems of linear equations, determinants, finite dimensional vector spaces, linear transformations and matrices, characteristic values and vectors. (3 semester hours)

MUSIC

The Understanding of Music

Open to non-music majors to satisfy Humanities requirement. A course in music appreciation covering all of the important fields of music, with opportunity for the students to listen to recordings. (3 semester hours)

Experiencing Music

Develops and understanding and appreciation of music through a study of its elements (melody, rhythm, harmony, tempo, dynamics, form, timbre, style and texture). The elements will be explored through lecture notes, reading and listening and other participatory activities. Music studied highlights how various multicultural folk songs influenced 20th-century American classical music. (2 semester hours)

PHILOSOPHY

Introduction to Philosophy

Basic problems of philosophy explored through a consideration of selected philosophers. (3 semester hours)

Introduction to Logic

A survey of traditional techniques with a look at contemporary techniques for evaluating deductive arguments. The application of these techniques is stressed and common errors and fallacies in reasoning are discussed. (3 semester hours)

Introduction to Ethics

Basic issues in moral philosophy examined through a consideration of selected philosophers, including a sampling of normative theories as well as an introduction to issues of metaethics. (3 semester hours)

History of Ethics

A survey of the major figures in the history of moral philosophy with emphasis on their interrelations, influences on each other and effect on contemporary philosophy. (3 semester hours)

History of Medieval Philosophy

A study of philosophers and movements in philosophy from the patristic through the high scholastic period, that is, from ca. 400–ca. 1300 A.D. (3 semester hours)

History of Modern Philosophy

A survey of modern European philosophy with concentration on selected readings from the Renaissance through Kant. (3 semester hours)

PHYSICAL EDUCATION

Elementary Nutrition

An evaluation of basic composition of nutrients and accessory factors required for adequate human nutrition. Application of nutritional principles to the planning of normal and special dietary regimens. (3 semester hours)

Personal Health

Emphasizes the health knowledge and practices needed for effective living. Has a holistic focus on personal health and provides both informational and behavioral basis for health promotion and disease prevention. (3 semester hours)

Theory of Baseball

The science of coaching baseball. Thorough coverage of the basic fundamentals of defensive and offensive baseball; coaching and teaching techniques; strategy and administrative duties of the baseball coach. (2 semester hours)

Theory of Basketball

History and techniques of the game, basic teaching and coaching of fundamental skills; methods of training and care of equipment. Advanced techniques in offensive and defensive strategy; psychology of handling personnel; scouting assignments. (2 semester hours)

Theory of Track and Field

History and technique of track and field events. A study in the theory, methods, and mechanics of coaching track and field events. Organizing and conducting track meets. (2 semester hours)

Theory of Wrestling

The history and developments of wrestling in the United States and the world; rules of college and high school wrestling; building a high school and a college wrestling program; the anatomical and physiological benefits derived from wrestling. (2 semester hours)

Recreation Resources—Leisure Environment

The historical and philosophical basis of leisure and recreation in modern society; the recreation environment from a regional and urban perspective; and critical issues that face recreation and urban planners and designers. Incorporates population geography and environmental health issues into an analysis of the physical and social environment that supports recreational programming and facility development. Focuses on urban development and the relationship of recreation resources to the aesthetic and mechanics of modern metropolitan areas. (3 semester hours)

Physical Activities for Special Populations

The organization and administration of programs of physical activity for atypical populations. A detailed study of specific abnormalities commonly found in a special population with recommended procedures for accommodating these individuals in the special program. (2 semester hours)

Management in Health and Sport Sciences

The philosophy and methodology of organizing and administering the physical education aspect of the total school program. Thorough study of the policies and procedures necessary to carry out the program. (3 semester hours)

Psychology of Sport

Understanding the psychological dimensions of behavior of the participant in sport; analyzing the effect of internal and external stimuli on sport participants; observing individual and group relationships to competition; and critically reviewing the motivational, achievement, anxiety, aggressive, and social facilitation aspects of sport. (3 semester hours)

Assessment in Health, Physical Education, and Recreation

The theory of measurement in health and physical education, the selection and administration of appropriate tests, and the interpretation of their results by fundamental statistical procedures. (3 semester hours)

Drug Education

Beneficial and harmful uses and effects of drugs. Motivations behind drug abuse, especially among youth, and the implications of this problem on the individual, school, and society. Consideration given to legislative and educational efforts. Investigation of interpersonal skills and communication interaction techniques. The use of values-clarification techniques. (3 semester hours)

POLITICAL SCIENCE

Government of the United States

A study of the structure, organization, and powers of the executive, legislative, and the judicial branches including relationships between state and national governments. Emphasis upon political processes and popular governments; elections, political parties, pressure groups, voting behavior. (3 semester hours)

Introduction to Political Science

An introduction to political science as a whole and to its various fields. Especially designed for political science majors and students considering it for a major. Additional focus on career opportunities such as public affairs and government service, foreign service, and international affairs, law and law enforcement. (3 semester hours)

Introduction to Public Administration

General concepts of public administration and the significance of administration in the modern state. Analysis of administrative theory, structure, and organization; dynamics of management; fiscal, personnel, and operational administration. (3 semester hours)

Introduction to International Relations

Analysis of the nature of international politics as well as the study of the factors that govern the interaction of states such as nationalism, power, ideology, law, and organization. (3 semester hours)

Introduction to Law Enforcement and Criminal Justice

A survey of law enforcement including historical and developmental aspects; the role of the police in a democratic society; and a survey of other agencies whose mission is the administration of criminal justice. (3 semester hours)

The Government of Oklahoma

Oklahoma government and politics, organization, structure, functions, and administrative problems of Oklahoma state and local governments; constitution of Oklahoma; legislative, executive, and judicial departments; political parties; election system; fiscal and administrative systems. (3 semester hours)

Urban Government and Politics

Structure and function of urban governments and analysis of politics in urban areas. (3 semester hours)

State Government

The organization, structure, functions, and administration of American state and local governments; federal-state relations; constitutions and legal systems; legislative, executive, and judicial departments; a study in the political process; problems of metropolitan areas; fiscal and administrative systems. (3 semester hours)

American Political Parties

A descriptive and critical examination of the political processes in the United States, with special reference to the role and organization of political parties and their relationship to voter behavior and the popular control of government. (3 semester hours)

United States Diplomatic History to 1900

A survey of American diplomatic history from the War for Independence to 1900, emphasizing problems of expansion and relations with major European, Latin American, and Far Eastern countries. (3 semester hours)

Police Administration I

The police as a functional aspect of the criminal justice process; principles of police organization and administration; administration of staff and auxiliary units including records, detention, personnel administration and training, internal investigation, inspection, planning and research, communication, intelligence, and legal branch; executive responsibilities; policy development and its implementation; supervision and discipline, and complaints against the police. (3 semester hours)

Principles of Criminal Investigation

Interviewing complainants and witnesses and interrogation of suspects; crime scene searches; collection and preservation of physical evidence; surveillance; use of scientific aids and role of the laboratory; fingerprints; ballistics, documents, serology, photography, neutron activation. (3 semester hours)

Criminal Legal Procedure

Criminal procedure and courtroom practices most commonly confronted by law enforcement officers in the administration of criminal law; inquests, indictments, warrants, arrest, preliminary examination, bail; pleadings, trial, appeals, search and seizure; use of force; evidence. (3 semester hours)

Elementary Criminal Law

An introduction to the study of crimes, attempts and conspiracy; classification and nature of crimes, intent in crimes, defenses to crimes including mistake of law or fact, double jeopardy, entrapment, and the statute of limitations. (3 semester hours)

PSYCHOLOGY

Elements of Psychology - Beginning Course

A survey of the scientific study of human behavior. Emphasis is placed upon scientific method, basic life processes, mechanics of adaptation, individual differences, and group behavior. (3 semester hours)

Introduction to Personality

Process of personality formation and development. "Normal" and "neurotic" personalities; basic principles of personality development. (3 semester hours)

Introduction to Life-Span Developmental Psychology

Survey of the psychological changes across the life span; the changes in cognitive, social, and emotional, physiological development from conception to death will be included. (3 semester hours)

Industrial Psychology

A study of the application of psychological principles, methods, and techniques in business and industry. (3 semester hours)

Principles of Psychopathology

An examination of the major clinical and research findings in the field of abnormal psychology. Topics include studies of conflict, anxiety, neurosis, character disorders, schizophrenia, and psychotherapy. (3 semester hours)

RUSSIAN

Beginning Russian

Course 1115. An elementary course in understanding, speaking, reading, and writing Russian. (5 semester hours)

Course 1225. A continuation of the above course. (5 semester hours)

Masterpieces of Russian Literature in Translation

Acquaints students with Russian literature (in English) from the classical period. (3 semester hours)

Beginning Business Russian

This course is intended to enable Russian students to read, write, and translate business Russian. Readings in the course will consist of translating contracts, agreements, and other areas of commercial correspondence. (3 semester hours)

Advanced Business Russian

Intended to enable Russian reading and translation of more advanced Russian business texts. Reading will consist of translating business order, contracts, agreements, and other areas of commercial correspondence. (3 semester hours)

Scientific Russian

Course 3203. Training the reading of scientific material of gradually increasing difficulty. (3 semester hours)

Course 3213. A continuation of the above course. (3 semester hours)

SOCIOLOGY

Introduction to Sociology

The fundamental concepts of sociology; foundations of group life; social change, processes, and problems. (3 semester hours)

The Sociology of Crime and Delinquency

A study of the nature and causes of various forms of illegal activity. Emphasis on the role of social factors in the genesis of deviant motivation and on the question of how this motivation comes to be expressed as crime and delinquency. (3 semester hours)

Sociology of the Family

The sociological study of the family as an institution; the origin and development of the family; the interrelationships of the family and the larger society; the environmental conditions which seem to favor the development and continuance of the major family forms; the rise of the modern democratic family; characteristic patterns of change in the contemporary family. (3 semester hours)

SPANISH

Beginning Spanish

Course 1115. An elementary course in understanding, speaking, reading, and writing Spanish. (5 semester hours)

Course 1225. A continuation of the above course. (5 semester hours)

Spanish Reading

Course 2113. The cultivation of facility in reading modern literary texts. (3 semester hours)

Course 2223. A continuation of the above course. (3 semester hours)

Spanish Composition

A systematic review of Spanish grammar, with a view toward improving the student's control of written Spanish. (3 semester hours)

Advanced Spanish Composition

The inculcation of proper writing habits, at an advanced level, toward the achievement of idiomatic Spanish. (3 semester hours)

Readings in Spanish Literature

Designed to improve reading comprehension and to introduce the language techniques of literary analysis. Representative works from the various literary genres will be studied. (3 semester hours)

Survey of Spanish-American Literature

Course 4093. A study of representative works from the colonial period to 1888. (3 semester hours)

Course 4103. A study of representative works from 1888 to the present day. (3 semester hours)

Survey of Spanish Literature

Course 4153. A study of representative works from the beginnings to the Neo-Classic period. (3 semester hours)

Course 4163. A study of representative works from 1700 to the present day. (3 semester hours)

Spanish Civilization

Spanish cultural heritage from the beginnings to the present day. (3 semester hours)

HIGH SCHOOL COURSES

ART

Calligraphy

Exercises in the use of Speedball points and lettering. Includes spacing, proportion, Roman lettering, and letter design. (½ unit)

Beginning Drawing

A sequence of exercises to encourage the sense of discovery and to teach discipline in handling tools. This leads to studies from nature and to figurative representation. (½ unit)

Art Understanding

An introductory course in appreciating and understanding art, in "looking," not drawing. Provides information on how to develop art understanding and assists in developing a philosophy of art. (½ unit)

Drawing II

Drawing methods, "line" and "blocking in," proportion, composition, perspective, the human figure, detail, outdoor subjects. Explains visual subjects, experiments with mixed media. (½ unit)

COMPUTER LITERACY

Introduction to Computer Literacy

A basic course designed to introduce students to computers. Includes a review of the history of computers, the impact computers have on our daily working and personal lives, an examination of different computer models and applications and an analysis of the computer revolution from mechanical origins to high tech utilization. (½ unit)

COMPUTER SCIENCE

Computer Operations

Designed for students interested in learning basic computer terminology and operation. Includes word processing, database, and spreadsheet applications for Apple II computers. Access to Apple II computer, printer, and AppleWorks required. (½ unit)

ENGLISH

Basic English Grammar and Usage

A remedial course in English. This course teaches the fundamentals of English usage, spoken or written. Concentrates on English grammar, parts of speech, phrases and clauses, and word choice. (½ unit)

Ninth Grade English

First Semester. Appreciation of literature, elementary composition, and grammar review. (½ unit)

Second Semester. (½ unit)

Tenth Grade English

First Semester. Literary appreciation and grammar. (½ unit)

Second Semester. (½ unit)

Eleventh Grade English

First Semester. Introduction to American literature through the study of the works of modern American authors; exercises in grammar. (½ unit)

Second Semester. (½ unit)

Twelfth Grade English

First Semester. English literature and poetry from its beginning in 1798. Grammar review. (½ unit)

Second Semester. (½ unit)

Business English

A refresher course in grammar, punctuation, and composition. Designed for the person who needs a general course that reviews English usage, spoken or written, and fundamental business communications. (½ unit)

FRENCH

First Year French

First Semester. Beginning course emphasizes grammar, vocabulary, and translation of French to English and English to French. (½ unit)

Second Semester. (½ unit)

Second Year French

First Semester. (½ unit)

Second Semester. (½ unit)

GERMAN

German, First Year

First Semester. Beginning course with emphasis on basic vocabulary and grammar. Pronunciation included with three cassette tapes. Student must have access to cassette tape player. (½ unit)

Second Semester. A continuation of the above course. (½ unit)

German, Second Year

First Semester. A continuation of the above course. Student must have access to cassette tape player for lessons and exams. (½ unit)

Second Semester. A continuation of the above course. (½ unit)

HOMEMAKING

Etiquette Manners for Today

Standard rules of good manners adapted to situations encountered by today's young people. (½ unit)

Relationships and Child Growth

Designed to help the students better understand themselves and those around them as they grow to maturity. (½ unit)

Clothes

Modern clothing, fibers, fabrics, and yarns from manufacture to use and care. (½ unit)

Food

Covers nutrition, food management, food preparation, career opportunities, foods of America and other countries. (½ unit)

Furnishings

Covers all phases of home furnishing from furniture to major appliances. Includes interior design and care of furnishings. (½ unit)

JOURNALISM

Creative Prose Writing

Examines the basic techniques of article and story writing for high school students interested in developing an understanding of and skill in self-expression. (½ unit)

LATIN

First Year Latin

First Semester. Beginning course, emphasizing grammar, vocabulary, and translation from Latin into English and from English into Latin; stressing the value of Latin as background for the study of English. (½ unit)

Second Semester. (½ unit)

Second Year Latin

First Semester. Latin grammar, vocabulary, derivation of English words, correlation of English and Latin grammar. (½ unit)

Second Semester. Based on Caesar's *Gallic Wars.* Attention to grammar is limited as much as possible, consistent with the needs of accurate translation; emphasis is given to the story itself in its historical setting. (½ unit)

MATHEMATICS

Algebra

First Semester. Understanding of the process is stressed; attempts to gradually develop the ability to solve verbal problems. (½ unit)

Second Semester. A continuation of the above course. (½ unit)

Third Semester. For students who have had two semesters of algebra and two semesters of geometry. (½ unit)

Fourth Semester. (½ unit)

Modern Geometry

First Semester. Covers elements of geometry, induction-a method of discovery, deduction and proof, angle relationships, perpendicular lines, parallel lines and planes, congruent triangles. (½ unit)

Second Semester. Covers similar polygons, trigonometry, circles, arcs, angles, constructions and loci, coordinate geometry methods, coordinate geometry proofs, areas of polygons and circles, areas and volumes of solids. (½ unit)

Trigonometry

(½ unit)

Pre-Calculus and Analytic Geometry

(½ unit)

General Mathematics

First Semester. For anyone who wishes to renew background for arithmetic. Contains an introduction to sets, various numeration systems, and some work in basic arithmetic. (½ unit)

Second Semester. A continuation of the above course. (½ unit)

SCIENCE

Biology

First Semester. Covers the nature and continuity of life. Includes a study of biology as a science, the chemical and structural bases of life, photosynthesis, respiration, protein synthesis, cellular reproduction and basic and applied genetics. (½ unit)

Second Semester. Covers microbiology (viruses, bacteria, protozoa, fungi and algae) and the multicellular plants (mosses, ferns, and the seed plants as well as their parts and processes). (½ unit)

Physics

First Semester. Covers basic physics concepts and principles that form a foundation for most studies of science and technology. Includes motion, forces, vectors, momentum, work, energy, gas laws and states of matter. (½ unit)

Second Semester. Covers sound, light mirrors and lenses, electricity (fields and circuits), magnetics, the atom, and nuclear physics. (½ unit)

Science C

A course in good health practices for the high school and adult student. Study of the complex systems of the body; survey of human physiology, sexuality; prevention and cure of disease; and sound safety practices. (½ unit)

SOCIAL STUDIES

Aerospace Education

Covers aerospace history and environment and aircraft flight and navigation. (½ unit)

Conservation of Natural Resources

A survey of the natural resources in the United States, their availability, use, depletion, and effect on the environment. (½ unit)

Basic Economics

Basic economic problems. (½ unit)

World Geography

First Semester. World geography by regions. (½ unit)

Second Semester. A study of the economic, cultural and physical features of Europe, Africa, Asia, South America, and Australia. Includes such aspects of geography as physical features, languages, religions, industry, natural resources and governments of the countries of these continents. (½ unit)

American Government

Powers of federal government; relationships among branches, organizations and functions. (½ unit)

American History

First Semester. From the discovery of America through the aftermath of the Civil War. (½ unit)

Second Semester. (½ unit)

World History

First Semester. A study of the world from the beginning of recorded history. Includes the early civilizations in the Middle East, the Greek and Roman Empires, the Far East and European civilizations into the nineteenth century. Map work is emphasized. (½ unit)

Second Semester. Includes the early civilizations of Africa and the Americas, Europe and Asia in the nineteenth and twentieth centuries and concludes with the world as it was in 1975. (½ unit)

Peer Counseling I: Knowing Myself and Helping Others

Designed to help students know themselves, view the world from others' perspectives, use communication skills positively, learn basic leadership skills and demonstrate ability to perform group-oriented tasks. (½ unit)

Peer Counseling II: Project Self-Discovery

Students examine the effects of peer pressure on themselves and society and the impact of interpersonal skills on all aspects of life, and assess personal behavior in terms of long- and short-range, life and career goals. (½ unit)

Oklahoma History

Study of people, places, and things in the State of Oklahoma. (½ unit)

Psychology

A general introduction to the field, focusing on psychology and the individual, theories of human behavior, realms of the unconscious, social change, social problems, and education. (½ unit)

Sociology

Sociology is a study of how groups and individuals relate to one another in our society. Cultural similarities and differences are examined in this course. The course is useful to anyone who wishes to make decisions based on valid understanding of the interrelated nature of today's world. (½ unit)

SPANISH

First Year Spanish

First Semester. Beginning course with emphasis on basic vocabulary, grammar and pronunciation. Student must have access to a cassette tape player. (½ unit)

Second Semester. (½ unit)

Second Year Spanish

First Semester. (½ unit)

Second Semester. (½ unit)

STUDY SKILLS

Vocabulary Building

Basic vocabulary building for high school students. (½ unit)

Vocabulary Building II

Vocabulary building for students who plan to pursue their education beyond high school. (½ unit)

NONCREDIT COURSES

ART

Calligraphy

This course covers the basic principles of lettering, care of materials, and ten letter styles. (Noncredit)

Drawing I

Fundamentals of drawing including line variations, contour drawing, detail drawing, shading, stipple drawing, simplification and use of wet media. (Noncredit)

Drawing II

Drawing methods—"line" and "blocking in." Proportion, composition, perspective, the human figure, detail, outdoor subjects. Explains visual subjects, experiments with mixed media. (Noncredit)

COMPUTER LITERACY

Introduction to Computer Literacy

A basic course. Introduces students to computers. Reviews the history and impact of computers on our working and personal lives, examines computer models and applications, analyzes the computer revolution from its mechanical origins to high tech use. (Noncredit)

COMPUTER SCIENCE

Computer Operations

Designed for those interested in learning basic computer terminology and operation. Includes word processing, database, and spreadsheet applications for Apple II computers. Access to Apple II computer, printer, and AppleWorks required. (Noncredit)

ENGLISH

Basic English - Grammar and Usage

Course concentrates on English grammar, parts of speech, phrases and clauses, and word choice. (Noncredit)

English Review

Basic course in fundamentals of English grammar and usage. Directed to those students who need reinforcement in basic English skills and older students who need refresher courses. (Noncredit)

Vocabulary A

Basic vocabulary building for high school level readers. (Noncredit)

Vocabulary B

Post-high school study of vocabulary, including Latin and Greek prefixes and roots and Italian, French, and Spanish borrowings. (Noncredit)

MATHEMATICS

Pre-Calculus and Analytic Geometry

(Noncredit)

Basic Algebra for College Students

A review of beginning algebra. (Noncredit)

RUSSIAN

Conversational Russian for Tourists

Practically oriented. For those with no previous knowledge of Russian and who would like to use the basic language in communicating with Russians during trips to the Commonwealth of Independent States. (Noncredit)

WRITING

Creative Prose Writing

Basic techniques of article and story writing for developing understanding and skill in self-expression. (Noncredit)

How to Write Children's Books

Teaches how to rediscover childhood memories and experiences necessary to write children's books, how to select and use the proper viewpoint, character development, plotting, how to begin the story, determining proper viewpoint, character development, plotting, how to begin the story, determining age appropriateness, manuscript preparation, editing, and marketing. The picture book, choose-your-own-adventure stories and other specialties also included. (Noncredit)

How to Write Your Life Story

Teaches methods to jog your memory, organize material, and communicate naturally and clearly. Explains how to choose photos and other memorabilia, how to reproduce your life story for family members and how to expand your story into a family history. (Noncredit)

Professional Writing I: Fundamentals

Aims at shortening the apprenticeship of the beginning writer by giving point of view and methods of professional, selling writers. (Noncredit)

Professional Writing II: Approaches to Fiction

Study of fiction techniques in plotting and story mechanics. (Noncredit)

Professional Writing III: The Novel

Studies novel-writing techniques. (Noncredit)

Professional Writing IV: Non-Fiction and the Modern Magazine

Study of non-fiction methods, practices, marketing articles, development of marketable ideas. (Noncredit)

Technical Writing for Science, Business, and Industry

A reader-oriented approach to teaching science and industry professionals to write letters, proposals, reports, and product instructions for those outside their fields and nonprofessionals. (Noncredit)

Oklahoma State University
Independent and Correspondence Study
001 Classroom Building
Stillwater, Oklahoma 74078   (405) 744-6390

Description:

Oklahoma State University was founded in 1890 and now has an enrollment of approximately 28,900 students. Its library houses 1,800,000 volumes. The university offers Bachelor, Master, and Doctoral degrees in a large number of fields. The Independent and Correspondence Study program is designed to meet the needs of students both on and off campus. The courses are available to all qualified persons who are interested in academic, cultural, career, and professional advancement.

Faculty:

Charles Feasley, Director; Imogene Stanford, Registrar. There is a faculty of 125 members.

Academic Levels:
College
High School
Noncredit

Degree/Certificate Programs:

Up to one-fourth of the required semester hours for the baccalaureate degree may be earned through correspondence courses. The university does not offer high school diplomas, but credits earned through correspondence study will be transferred to any high school allowing such credits. Continuing Education Units (CEUs) are granted for specified courses. All correspondence work is on the undergraduate level.

Admission Requirements:

Any person who is a graduate of a high school or who is 21 years of age may enroll in correspondence work for credit at OSU. Admission to the university is not a requirement for enrolling in correspondence work. Members of the Armed Forces may apply through DANTES and should consult their respective Education Officers for information.

Tuition:

$55 per semester hour credit for college courses; $70 per ½ unit for high school courses. MasterCard and Visa accepted. If a student withdraws from a correspondence course within 30 days after enrollment, the refund is 80 percent of tuition minus the cost of any grading. If this withdrawal occurs after 30 days from enrollment but no more than 60 days from enrollment, the refund is 50 percent of the tuition minus any grading costs. No refund after 60 days. Veteran's benefits are available for both high school and college courses. Employee tuition assistance plans are welcome.

Enrollment Period:

Maximum time allowed to complete a course is one year. A three-month extension may be granted for a fee of $20 per semester hour. The minimum time allowed is 30 days after the first assignment.

Equipment Requirements:

Charges for materials (textbooks, syllabus, etc.) are in addition to the tuition and are listed for each course in the OSU Independent and Correspondence Study catalog; the individual course listing should be referred to before enrolling.

Credit and Grading:

Final examinations or equivalent projects are required for all courses and comprise a substantial part of the final grade. A student must pass at least one proctored exam in order to receive a passing grade. Proctors may be local education personnel. Grading system: A, B, C, D, and F. Minimum passing grade is D. Credit is awarded in semester hour units.

Library Services:

Correspondence students may take advantage of OSU's text rental service. A deposit of the cost of the book is made and refunded minus the rental charge unless the student chooses to keep the book.

Accreditations:

North Central Association of Colleges and Schools. Member of: National University Continuing Education Association.

COLLEGE COURSES

ACCOUNTING

Principles of Accounting

ACCTG 2103. Financial accounting covering the accounting process and principles of accrual accounting. (3 semester hours)

ACCTG 2203. Managerial accounting concepts and objectives, planning and control of sales and costs, analysis of costs and profits. (3 semester hours)

AGRICULTURAL EDUCATION

International Programs in Agricultural Education and Extension

World hunger and its root causes. The function of international agencies, organizations, foundations and churches in improving the quality of life for people of the developing nations. Roles of agricultural education and extension at all levels for enhancing the effectiveness of indigenous programs of rural development and adult education. (3 semester hours)

AGRONOMY

Fundamentals of Soil Science

Principal physical, chemical, and biological properties of the soil related to plant growth; soil testing and fertilizer usage; formation and classification of soils; rural and urban land use. (4 semester hours)

ANIMAL SCIENCE

Livestock Feeding

Nutrients and their functions, nutrient requirements of the various classes of livestock; composition and classification of feed stuffs and ration formulation. (3 semester hours)

Principles of Animal Nutrition

Basic principles of animal nutrition including digestion, absorption, and metabolism of the various food nutrients; characteristics of the nutrients; measure of body needs; ration formulation. (3 semester hours)

Agricultural Animals of the World

The production and utilization of agricultural animals by human societies. (3 semester hours)

ANTHROPOLOGY

Cultural Anthropology

Introduction to culture, various sub-disciplines of cultural anthropology, anthropological concepts and capsule enthnographies of assorted ethnic groups. (3 semester hours)

ART

Introduction to Art

An introduction to the analysis and interpretation of visual arts. Visual, emotional, and intellectual aspects of art in painting, sculpture, printmaking, and architecture. (3 semester hours)

ASTRONOMY

Elementary Astronomy

Methods of observation and analysis. Current interpretations of observational data in regard to the solar system, Milky Way galaxy and the universe. (4 semester hours)

BUSINESS ADMINISTRATION

Introduction to Small Business Management

An introduction to investigating and evaluating business opportunities, marketing products or services, managing business finances, and managing people. (3 semester hours)

Small Business Management

Problems faced in the creation and early growth periods of business enterprises. Accounting, finance, opportunity recognition, legal constraints, management, marketing, taxation, and procedural problems. (3 semester hours)

BUSINESS COMMUNICATIONS

Written Communication

Analysis of business communication in terms of generally accepted communication principles. Practice in written messages; specifically, special goodwill letters, neutral and good-news, disappointing, persuasive, and employment messages. (3 semester hours)

Organizational Communication

Communication theory and process; common and special problems associated with interpersonal and organizational communication affecting business decisions and operations. Principles and methods of basic and applied research in business and communication; practice in administrative report writing. Analysis of selected business cases. (3 semester hours)

Business Report Writing

Fundamentals of writing business reports, including coverage of mechanics, content, and structure of business reports. Practice in writing business reports. (3 semester hours)

BUSINESS LAW

Legal and Regulatory Environment of Business

General concepts regarding the nature of the legal system, ethical issues in business decision making, dispute resolution processes, basic constitutional limitations on the power of government to regulate business activity, the nature of government regulation, fundamental principles of tort and contract law. (3 semester hours)

COMPUTER SCIENCE

Introductory BASIC Programming

A beginning course in the art and science of computer programming. (2 semester hours)

Computer Programming

Programming in a high-level programming language. Introduction to algorithms, problem-solving techniques, and structured programming. Examples of applications from various areas such as business, science, or engineering. Students should have passed college algebra and have use of a computer with a PASCAL compiler. (3 semester hours)

Computer Science I

Nonnumerical algorithms, string processing, programming style, and documentation. Introduction to internal searching and sorting methods; linear linked lists. (3 semester hours)

ECONOMICS

Introduction to Macroeconomics

The functioning and current problems of the aggregate economy: determination and analysis of national income, employment, inflation and stabilization; monetary and fiscal policy; and aspects of international interdependence. (3 semester hours)

Introduction to Microeconomics

Goals, incentives, and outcomes of economic behavior with applications and illustrations from current social issues; operation of markets for goods, services and factors of production; the behavior of firms and industries in different types of competition; income distribution; and international exchange. (3 semester hours)

EDUCATION

The World of Work for Adult Learners

Assists off-campus, adult students in exploring career options through increased understanding of self and expanded knowledge of occupational information. Includes a study of the decision-making process and a look at the present and future changing world of work. (2 semester hours)

Psychological Foundations of Childhood

The child from conception to puberty focusing on educational implications of development in cognitive, affective, and psychomotor domains. (3 semester hours)

Education of Exceptional Learners

Learning characteristics, needs, and problems of educating the ex-

ceptional learner in the public schools. Requires class observation and access to professional journals. (2 semester hours)

Psychology of Adolescence

The adolescent from pubescence to adulthood focusing on educational implications of development in cognitive, affective, and psychomotor domains. (3 credit hours)

Measurement and Evaluation in the School

Construction and selection of classroom tests. Contrasts between criterion-referenced and norm-referenced measurement strategies. Grading techniques, rudiments of standardized test selection and score interpretation, and the basic statistics used to summarize and analyze test results. (2 semester hours)

Human Learning in Educational Psychology

Instructional psychology focusing on the study of teaching and learning theory as part of an instructional program to deal with individual, cultural, and environmental differences. Case studies emphasizing motivation, planning, evaluation, classroom problems, and management. (3 semester hours)

ELECTRICITY

Fundamentals of Electricity

Elementary principles of electricity covering basic electric units. Ohm's Law, Kirchoff's Law, circuit solutions, network solutions, magnetism, inductance and capacitance. (4 semester hours)

Pulse and Digital Techniques

Electronic circuits used in digital control and computation. Pulse generation, Boolean algebra and logic circuits. (4 semester hours)

ENGINEERING

Statics

Resultants of force systems, static equilibrium of rigid bodies, and statics of structures. Shear and moment diagrams. (3 semester hours)

Thermodynamics

Properties of substances and principles governing changes in form of energy. First and second laws. (3 semester hours)

ENGLISH

Freshman Composition I

The fundamentals of expository writing with emphasis on structure, development and style. (3 semester hours)

Freshman Composition II

Expository composition with emphasis on technique and style through intensive and extensive readings. (3 semester hours)

Introduction to Technical Writing

Technical literature and publications in the student's area of specialization. Emphasis on clarity, simplicity, and careful organization. (3 semester hours)

Introduction to Literature

Fiction, drama/film, and poetry. Written critical exercises. (3 semester hours)

Survey of American Literature I

The Puritans through the Romantic Period. (3 semester hours)

Fiction Writing

Directed readings and practice in writing fiction with special attention to techniques. Course structure builds on successive assignments so multiple submissions are prohibited. (3 semester hours)

Poetry Writing

Directed readings and practice in writing poetry with special attention to techniques. (3 semester hours)

Technical Writing

Applied writing in areas of specialization. Intensive practice in professional writing modes, styles, research techniques and editing for specialized audiences and/or publications. (3 semester hours)

Short Story

Origins, development, theory, and craft of the short story. (3 semester hours)

English Grammar

The traditional terminology and concepts of English grammar leading or evolving into the several current systems of descriptions. (3 semester hours)

American Poetry Post 1900

Genre development. Major writers and their works. (3 semester hours)

Shakespeare

Major plays and selected criticism. (3 semester hours)

American Novel to 1900

Genre development. Major writers and their works. (3 semester hours)

FAMILY RELATIONS

Human Development Within the Family: A Lifespan Perspective

Human development within the family system from a lifespan perspective. The principles of development and dynamics of behavior and relationships are included. (3 semester hours)

Human Sexuality and the Family

Sexual development emphasizing personal adjustment and interaction with family and culture. (3 semester hours)

Marriage

Consideration of courtship and marriage with special emphasis on building a health paired relationship; communication and decision making; and coping with such problems as money, sex, role taking, in-laws, and children. (3 semester hours)

FIRE PROTECTION AND SAFETY TECHNOLOGY

Structural Designs for Fire and Life Safety

Building construction standards and codes to assure maximum life and property safety from fires, explosions and natural disaster. Egress design specifications, occupancy and construction classifications and fire protection requirements for building construction and materials. (3 semester hours)

Fire Protection Management

Applied human relations, technical knowledge and skills for achieving optimum effectiveness from a fire protection organization. (3 semester hours)

Fire Protection Hydraulics and Water Supply Analysis

Fluid flow through hoses, pipes, pumps, and fire protection appliances. Water supply and distribution analysis using hydraulic calculations. Testing techniques to detect anomalies in design or performance capabilities. (3 semester hours)

Radiological Safety

Ionizing radiation problems; detection and measurement, shielding and exposure-limiting, radiation health aspects, storage, handling and disposal. (3 semester hours)

Hydraulic Design of Automatic Sprinkler Systems

Hydraulic calculation technique for the design and analysis of automatic sprinkler fire extinguishing systems. (3 semester hours)

Industrial Fire Pump Installations.

Applications, design, and analysis of industrial fire pump installations. Graphical analysis of fire pump contributions to existing fire protection water supply systems emphasized. (3 semester hours)

Sprinkler System Design for High Piled and Rack Storage

Specific design techniques for sprinkler system protection of commodities stored in solid piles or racks over 12 feet in height. (3 semester hours)

FRENCH

Elementary French I

Main elements of grammar and pronunciation, with work on the four basic skills of listening comprehension, speaking, reading, and writing. (5 semester hours)

Elementary French II

A continuation of *Elementary French I*. (5 semester hours)

GEOGRAPHY

Introduction to Geographic Behavior

The major organizing concepts of economic and cultural geography. Man's geographic behavior in terms of his spatial organization to the earth's surface and his development of regional and political systems. (3 semester hours)

Physical Geography

Distribution and analysis of natural features of the earth. Landforms, soils, minerals, water, climates, flora and fauna. Emphasis on man-environment relations where appropriate. (4 semester hours)

Meteorology

Physical elements which cause and influence weather. Nonmathematical survey. (3 semester hours)

Geography of Oklahoma

Geographic interpretation of physical, economic, historical and scenic features. (3 semester hours)

Geography of Music

Geographical and historical analysis of music as a cultural trait. The cultural significance of music and how it varies from place to place as well as how it helps shape the character of a place. (3 semester hours)

GEOLOGY

Geology and Human Affairs

The influence of geology and related earth sciences on the human environment. Emphasizes energy and material resources, beneficial and hazardous natural processes, and the planetary and biological evolution of earth. (4 semester hours)

GERMAN

Elementary German I

Main elements of grammmar and pronunciation, with work on the four basic skills of listening comprehension, speaking, reading, and writing. (5 semester hours)

Elementary German II

A continuation of *Elementary German I*. (5 semester hours)

HEALTH

Total Wellness

Knowledge, attitudes, and practices related to self-direction of health behavior for total well-being. (3 semester hours)

HISTORY

American History to 1865

From European background through the Civil War. (3 semester hours)

American History Since 1865

Development of the United States including the growth of industry and its impact on society and foreign affairs. (3 semester hours)

Western Civilization to 1500

History of Western civilization from the ancient world to Reformation. (3 semester hours)

Western Civilization after 1500

History of Western civilization from the Reformation to present. (3 semester hours)

Oklahoma History

Early exploration and establishment of Indian Territory; the rise and demise of the Five Indian Nations; and the organization and development of the 41st state to the present. (3 semester hours)

Ancient Near East

The ancient world from the beginnings of recorded history through the Egyptian, Mesopotamian, Hebrew, and Persian civilizations, in addition to the minor civilizations of the area. (3 semester hours)

Ancient Greece

The Greek world from the Bronze Age through Alexander the Great with special emphasis on politics, culture and institutions of classical Greece. (3 semester hours)

Ancient Rome

Political, social, economic and cultural history of the Roman Republic and Empire. (3 semester hours)

East Asia Since 1900

Impact of the Occident on China, Japan, and Southeast Asia. Problems of trade and diplomacy; political and industrial transformation of Japan; revolutionary process in China; the rise of nationalism in Southeast Asia. (3 semester hours)

Modern Japan

Modernization process in Japan since 1868. (3 semester hours)

Modern China

Response of China to the West since 1840, with stress on economic, social, and intellectual currents. (3 semester hours)

Studies in History: Traditional Japan

The formation of Japanese society and culture and its development in pre-modern Japan. (3 semester hours)

HORTICULTURE

Principles of Horticultural Science

Basic physical and physiological processes that are responsible for plant dormancy, growth, flowering, fruiting, and senescence with respect to the science and art of production, cultivation, utilization, and/or storage of horticultural plants. Current research associated with various horticultural commodity groups is also discussed. (3 semester hours)

HUMANITIES

Masterworks of Western Culture: Ancient and Medieval

Ideas and values of Western culture as revealed through literary, artistic, historical, and philosophical contexts from Greek, Roman, and Medieval periods. (3 semester hours)

Masterworks of Western Culture: Modern

Ideas and values of Western culture as revealed through literary, artistic, historical, and philosophical contexts from the Renaissance to the Modern period. (3 semester hours)

JOURNALISM

Feature Writing for Newspapers and Magazines

Newspaper features and special articles for business and trade journals; sources, materials, markets and other factors pertinent to nonfiction writing. (3 semester hours)

MANAGEMENT

Management

Management principles and techniques of analysis. Decision making as applied to management systems, organizations, interpersonal relationships, and production. (3 semester hours)

Organizational Behavior and Management

Behavioral science concepts relevant to the study of organizational and managerial behavior. Provides an understanding of the components and dynamics of organizational behavior essential to any manager. Managerial applications stressed. (3 semester hours)

Human Resource Management

Policies and practices used in personnel management. Focuses upon the functions of a human resource management department. (3 semester hours)

Organization Theory and Development

The design of formal organizations with an emphasis on topics related to organizational and managerial effectiveness. Focus on what is known about managerial and organizational effectiveness and how this knowledge may be applied. (3 semester hours)

Production and Operations Management

Production/operations management utilizing a management science approach. Management decision-making techniques and their application to problems in production and operations management. (3 semester hours)

MARKETING

Marketing

Marketing strategy and decision making. Consumer behavior, marketing institutions, competition, and the law. (3 semester hours)

Sales Management

Sales planning and control, organization of the sales department, developing territories, motivating salesmen and control over sales operations. (3 semester hours)

MATHEMATICS

Intermediate Algebra

Review of fundamental operations of algebra, rational expressions, exponents and radicals, simple equations and inequalities, introduction to quadratic equations, inequalities, introduction to analytic geometry. This course does not count for college credit hours.

College Algebra

Quadratic equations, functions and graphs, inequalities, systems of equations, exponential and logarithmic functions, theory of equations, sequences, permutations and combinations. (3 semester hours)

Trigonometry

Trigonometric functions, logarithms, solution of triangles and applications to physical sciences. (3 semester hours)

College Algebra and Trigonometry

An integrated course in college algebra and trigonometry. (3 semester hours)

Elementary Calculus

An introduction to differential and integral calculus. For students of business and social sciences. (3 semester hours)

Calculus for Technology Programs

Functions and graphs, differentiation, and integration with applications. (3 semester hours)

Calculus I

An introduction to derivatives, integrals and their applications, including introductory analytic geometry. (5 semester hours)

Differential Equations

Methods of solution of ordinary differential equations with applications. First order equations, linear equations of higher order, series solutions, and Laplace transforms. (3 semester hours),

Special Studies: Metric System

An elementary introduction to the metric system with respect to length, weight, volume and temperature. (1 semester hour)

Special Studies: Basic Mathematics with the Calculator

Designed to use the hand-held calculator to teach fundamental math applications for business, household, and financial transactions. Students must have use of a hand-held calculator. (2 semester hours)

Linear Algebra

Algebra and geometry of finite-dimensional linear spaces, linear transformations, algebra of matrices, eigenvalues and eigenvectors. (3 semester hours)

MERCHANDISING

Profitable Merchandising Analysis

Relationship analysis of profit and loss statement. Retail mathematical calculations necessary to plan and control merchandising results—open-to-buy, mark-up, mark-down, turnover, stock-sales ratio. (3 semester hours)

NUTRITION

Basic Human Nutrition

Functions of the nutrients in human life processes. Nutrient relationship to health as a basis for food choices. (3 semester hours)

PHILOSOPHY

Philosophical Classics

Basic works by great thinkers, including Plato, Descartes, and Hume. (3 semester hours)

Philosophies of Life

Introductory ethics and social philosophy. Moral decision making, the good life, social values, freedom and responsibility. (3 semester hours)

POLITICAL SCIENCE

American Government

Organization, processes and functions of the national government of the United States. (3 semester hours)

Governments and Politics in the Middle East

Analysis of political institutions and processes with emphasis on selected countries of the Middle East; the social and economic basis of politics; nationalism, political development, and factors of instability and change. (3 semester hours)

State and Local Government

Political processes, government, and administration of American states, cities, and counties; special emphasis on Oklahoma. (3 semester hours)

Problems in Government, Politics and Public Policy: War and Peace in the Nuclear Age

Special problem areas of government, politics, and public policy concentrating on topics not covered in other departmental course offerings. (3 semester hours)

PSYCHOLOGY

Introductory Psychology

Principles, theories, vocabulary and applications of the science of psychology. (3 semester hours)

Social Psychology

Theories and applications of social cognition, the self, pro-social and aggressive behavior, groups, attitudes and the environment. (3 semester hours)

History of Psychology

History of psychology as an aspect of European intellectual history. Psychological thought from early philosophical roots to modern conceptions of psychology as a science. (3 semester hours)

SOCIOLOGY

Introductory Sociology

The science of human society. Emphasis on basic concepts. Assists the student in understanding the social influences of day-to-day life. (3 semester hours)

Social Problems

Exploration in selected social issues in contemporary American society, such as deviance, poverty, sexism, racism, and ageism. (3 semester hours)

Juvenile Delinquency

Juvenile delinquency behavior in relation to family, school, church, peers, community and institutional structures. The extent of delinquent expressions, varieties of delinquency, comparative international perspectives and new trends of females in delinquency and gang behavior. (3 semester hours)

Sociology of Aging

Sociological problems of aging, including the analysis of the behavior of the aged within the framework of social institutions. (3 semester hours)

Social Ecology and Life Processes

Human interdependencies and interrelationships with the social and physical environments, with special focus on the mutual impact of human values, human environment and life phases. (3 semester hours)

Oklahoma State University

SPANISH

Elementary Spanish I

Pronunciation, conversation, grammar, and reading. (5 semester hours)

Elementary Spanish II

A continuation of *Elementary Spanish I*. (5 semester hours)

SPEECH PATHOLOGY

Survey of Communication Disorders

The normal development of speech and language. The characteristics, diagnosis, and treatment of speech, language, and hearing disorders among all age groups. Suggestions for related professions involved with communication disorders. (3 semester hours)

STATISTICS

Elementary Statistics

An introductory course in the theory and methods of statistics. Descriptive measures, elementary probability, samplings, estimation, hypothesis testing, correlation, and regression. (3 semester hours)

Elementary Statistics for Business and Economics

Basic statistics course for undergraduate business majors. Descriptive statistics, basic probability, discrete and continuous distributions, point and interval estimation, hypothesis testing, correlation and simple linear regression. (3 semester hours)

Intermediate Statistical Analysis

Applications of elementary statistics, introductory experimental design, introduction to the analysis of variance, simple and multiple linear regression, nonparametric statistics, survey sampling, time series, and Bayesian analysis. (3 semester hours)

STUDY SKILLS

Effective Study Skills for School Success

Designed to provide a structured, systematic program that allows students to evaluate their study skills, knowledge, and needs. Techniques to improve study habits are topics covered in the course. (1 semester hour)

THEATRE

Introduction to Theater in Western Civilization

Character, plot, thematic, historical, and production analyses of various types of play scripts; understanding the work of various theater artists; developing appreciative audiences. (3 semester hours)

ZOOLOGY

Human Heredity

The impact of genetics on human endeavor. (3 semester hours)

HIGH SCHOOL COURSES

BUSINESS EDUCATION

Accounting

1A. Students learn basic accounting concepts and principles for a service type business and for a small merchandising business. (½ unit)

1B. Students work through the accounting cycle using combination journal and subsidiary ledgers and special journals. Instruction is included for payroll systems, introduction to automated data processing and accounting for sales tax, bad debts, and depreciation. (½ unit)

Business Math 1A

Students apply basic math principles to transact simple business procedures such as checkbook accounts, unit and multiple pricing, preparing budgets, figuring commissions, purchasing insurance and making simple investments. (½ unit)

Salesmanship

1A. Provides knowledge and skills needed for a career in selling. Methods of selling, the buying and selling process, customer motives, and product information. (½ unit)

1B. Sales techniques including preparation of sales forms, operation of cash register, handling of money, telephone selling, industrial selling, and how to get a job in selling. (½ unit)

ENGLISH

English 10

2A. Study of characteristics of the short story, poetry, and drama, with emphasis on similarities and differences in style and content. Student increases writing abilities through skill-building exercises. (½ unit)

2B. A continuation of *English 2A*. Introduces Greek drama, prose forms, Shakespeare, and the novella and gives the student a review of English grammar and usage. (½ unit)

Science Fiction

Readings deal with popular science fiction; students study reasons for science fiction's popularity and its cultural relevance to our society. (½ unit)

The Short Story

Course designed to help students understand the essential elements of a short story, including plot, characters, setting, point of view, theme and style. (½ unit)

FRENCH

French

1A. First semester course that helps develop skills necessary to communicate in French in both oral and written form, with emphasis on vocabulary, grammar, and pronunciation while studying cultural aspects of life in French-speaking countries. (½ unit)

1B. A continuation of *French 1A*. (½ unit)

GEOGRAPHY

World Geography

1A. A comprehensive survey of the geographic factors in the environment. (½ unit)

1B. A comprehensive survey of the countries and peoples of the world. (½ unit)

GUIDANCE

Careers/Exploration: Project Self Discovery

Designed for high school students to encourage honest self-appraisal by submitting perceptions and opinions to a Project Counselor who acts as an interested "listener." All such exercises are completely confidential. Counselor is qualified to evaluate and encourage students as they confront their future and grow in personal development. (½ unit)

Knowing Myself and Helping Others

Designed to help students understand themselves, use communication skills positively, learn basic leadership skills, and demonstrate ability to perform group-oriented tasks. (½ unit)

HISTORY

American History

1A. The European background for the beginning of American history through the Emancipation Proclamation, industrial development and the rise of big business. (½ unit)

1B. A continuation of *American History 1A.* Studies of how our nation became a world power, covers both world wars, and explains rapid technological and cultural changes affecting country up to present. (½ unit)

Oklahoma History

Traces the history of the state from the early European explorers, through the Indian era, to statehood and the present, with emphasis on the people involved in its development. (½ unit)

World History

1A. Traces the development of civilization in different parts of the world, from ancient times through the 1700s. (½ unit)

MATHEMATICS

Geometry

1A. First semester of basic geometry with focus upon understanding simple plane forms and introducing proofs to solve problems. (½ unit)

1B. Second semester of basic geometry using more complex forms and working with advanced proofs; builds upon first semester course. (½ unit)

Trigonometry

A simple yet thorough introduction to the fundamentals of trigonometry. (½ unit)

SCIENCE

Biology

1A. Study of life processes beginning with cellular level through the development of plant life, alluding to genetics and the diversity of life forms. (½ unit)

1B. A continuation of *Biology 1A* including invertebrate and vertebrate animals, human anatomy and physiology, ecology, population dynamics, and environmental problems. (½ unit)

NONCREDIT COURSES

ACCOUNTING

Basic Accounting Techniques

I. Designed to teach basic accounting concepts and principles needed for a service type business and for a small merchandising business by stressing practical application of bookkeeping procedures and elementary accounting. (4 CEUs) *Tuition:* $85; materials $51.50

II. Continuation of first course designed to work through the accounting cycle using combination journal and subsidiary ledgers, including instruction for processing payrolls, computing sales taxes, bad debts, and depreciation costs. (4 CEUs) *Tuition:* $85; materials $51.50

COMPUTER PROGRAMMING

Introduction to Computer Programming Using BASIC

A beginning course in the art and science of computer programming. Requires having access to a computer with BASIC interpreter or compiler and a printer. Programming examples are executed on DEC System 20, Apple, IBM PC, TRS-80, and PET/Commodore 64, but computers with different versions of BASIC can be used. (5 CEUs) *Tuition:* $115; materials $36

FIRE PROTECTION AND SAFETY TECHNOLOGY

Industrial Fire Pump Installations

Designed to help fire protection specialists determine under what conditions fire pumps are needed and how to install, maintain, test and inspect such installations; familiarity with basics of automatic sprinkler protection as well as standpipe and hose systems helpful in order to successfully complete the course. (5 CEUs) *Tuition:* $170; materials $41

GENEALOGY

Genealogical Research

Designed for the beginning to intermediate student wishing to understand and implement the basic concepts of tracing lineage. (3 CEUs) *Tuition:* $45; materials $14

HOUSING

Earth-Sheltered Housing

Designed for the general public covering basic issues to be considered in designing and planning an earth-sheltered structure. (2 CEUs) *Tuition:* $40; materials $20

RADIOLOGICAL SAFETY

Radiological Safety for Hospitals and Clinics

Course provides instruction about how to handle radiation sources, how to detect characteristics of radiation emission, and how to protect against adverse effects. Basic knowledge of science and math helpful in making course meaningful, though not required. (6 CEUs) *Tuition:* $170; materials $34.50

REAL ESTATE

Real Estate Modules

Thirteen courses offering continuing education credit for real estate licensees, each equivalent to three contact hours of instruction. Modules available on the following subjects: Abstracting and Title Insurance Contract for Deed; Fair Housing; Land Descriptions; Landlord/Tenant Relations; Market Analysis; Overview of Agency Law; Overview of Contract Law; Overview of Real Property Management; Trust Accounts; Real Estate Valuation; The Investigations; Undisclosed Dual Agency. (.3 CEUs for each module) *Tuition:* $45 for each module

SPRINKLER SYSTEMS

Hydraulic Calculation of Automatic Sprinkler Systems

Course designed to guide students through the different steps in designing and calculating needs for the installation of automatic sprinkler systems in various types of settings. (6 CEUs) *Tuition:* $170; materials $37

Sprinkler System Design for High-Piled and Rack Storage

Course provides instruction and assistance in establishing and using the proper criteria and specifications for the hydraulic design of automatic sprinkler systems for the protection of high-piled and rack storage. A working knowledge of the hydraulic design and calculation process is necessary in order to successfully complete the course. (5 CEUs) *Tuition:* $170; materials $82.50

TECHNICAL WRITING

Technical Writing

Designed to help persons master applied writing skills for specific subjects, including intensive practice in professional writing modes, styles, and research techniques leading to a technical report. (5 CEUs)
Tuition: $170; materials $53

Oral Roberts University

Center for LifeLong Education
Tulsa, Oklahoma 74171   (918) 495-6238

Description:

Recognizing that learning is an ongoing, lifelong process, Oral Roberts University has created the Center for LifeLong Education to enable mature adults to complete their college training through nonresidential studies. The program is for adult learners who are seeking to better equip themselves educationally, but find it impossible to leave their homes, jobs, and ministries to relocate in Tulsa, Oklahoma. All courses are designed by the ORU faculty. In many cases they are identical to on-campus courses, but where appropriate, some have been specially adapted for this program.

Faculty:

Jeff L. Ogle, Dean, Center for LifeLong Education; Ann Craig, Director, Correspondence Studies.

Academic Levels:

College
Noncredit

Degree/Certificate Programs:

Degree-seeking students may major in Church Ministries, Elementary Christian School Education, Christian Care and Counseling, and Business Administration. Courses are also available to assist those teachers in Christian schools who are seeking certification from the International Christian Accrediting Association.

Admission Requirements:

If enrolling in a degree program, students must be at least 22 years of age (except full-time military personnel) and be a high school graduate or a recipient of a GED; meet all ORU admission requirements. Non-degree seeking students is not required to present the full entrance requirements.

Tuition:

$105 per credit hour. VISA, MasterCard, or Discover accepted. Refund policy: The amount of refund is determined by the date the study guide was mailed and the date a written request for refund was received. If 1–4 weeks, 75% of tuition refunded; 5–6 weeks, 50%; 7–8 weeks, 25%; after 8 weeks, no refund.

Enrollment Period:

Students have four months from the date of enrollment to complete a course.

Equipment Requirements:

Textbooks must be purchased by the student.

Credit and Grading:

Grades are recorded as A, B, C, D, or F. Credit is awarded in semester hours.

Library Services:

The Center for LifeLong Learning provides access to ORU library resources.

Accreditations:

North Central Association of Colleges and Schools.

COLLEGE COURSES

ACCOUNTING

Principles of Financial Accounting

A conceptual study of the principles of financial accounting that emphasizes the balance sheet, income statement, and the basic bookkeeping system. The course specifically includes deferrals and accruals, adjusting, and closing entries, special journals, the voucher system, and payroll accounting. (3 semester hours)

Principles of Financial/Managerial Accounting

A continuation of financial accounting as it relates to partnerships and corporations with a movement into the managerial accounting area, including manufacturing accounting, control accounting, CVP relationships, financial statement analysis, funds statement, consolidated statements, and special management reports. (3 semester hours)

Quantitative Analysis

A study of quantitative analysis; interpretations of data for business decision making; probability theory, linear programming, special purpose algorithms, inventory models, PERT/CPM, simulation forecasting, and other quantitative methods. (3 semester hours)

BIBLE

Survey of the Old Testament

A historical-thematic survey of the Old Testament. Special attention will be given to the cultural background, to the theological and contextual perspectives, as well as to the practical application of major Old Testament themes. (3 semester hours)

Survey of the New Testament

An examination of the New Testament and of the historical, social, economic, and religious background out of which Christianity arose. (3 semester hours)

Historical Geography of the Holy Land

A study of the geography and history of Palestine since antiquity, especially in relation to the nation of Israel and the Early Church. (3 semester hours)

Old Testament Introduction

A general introduction to the books of the Old Testament, dealing with problems of canon, authorship, composition, date of writing, and the geographical, archaeological setting in which the Bible events occurred. (3 semester hours)

New Testament Introduction

A general introduction to the background and inspiration of the NT, the formation of its canon, the NT apocryphal writings, as well as the various approaches to NT criticism. The student will also be introduced to the historical, literary, and textual issues pertinent to each NT writing. (3 semester hours)

Jesus and the Gospels

A study of the life and teachings of Jesus Christ as presented in the Gospels and early Christian literature. (3 semester hours)

Biblical Eschatology

A study of Old and New Testament teachings on eschatology, including those aspects of the Kingdom of God which are already present and those yet to be fulfilled. Specific attention will be given to concepts such as Messiah, resurrection, tribulation, millennium, judgment, signs of the times, and Kingdom of God. (3 semester hours)

Life and Teachings of Paul

A study of the life and teachings of the Apostle Paul as recorded in the book of Acts and the Pauline Epistles. Special attention will be given to the beginnings and growth of the church. (3 semester hours)

Hebrews and General Epistles

A study of the New Testament books of Hebrews, James, 1 and 2 Peter, and Jude. Particular attention will be given to the major teachings of these books as they fit into their original historical contexts as they speak to us today. (3 semester hours)

Hermeneutics

A study of the problems and methods of biblical interpretation, including the factors of presuppositions, grammar, literary and historical context, and the appropriate handling of the various kinds of literature found in the Bible. (3 semester hours)

Pentateuch

A study of the first five books of the Old Testament, commonly known as the Pentateuch. Emphasis will be placed on the historical, cultural, and geographical milieu of these books. (3 semester hours)

Hebrew Prophets

A study of the origin and development of prophecy among the Hebrews during the first half of the first millennium B.C. Emphasis will be placed on the messages of the prophets, historical background, and the social and religious implications of their teaching. (3 semester hours)

Poetical Literature

A study of the poetical books of the Old Testament including Job, Psalms, Proverbs, Ecclesiastes, Song of Solomon, and Lamentations, with emphasis on Hebrew poetry and its relation to other ancient literatures. (3 semester hours)

BIOLOGY

Principles of Biology

A study of principles of plant and animal life, with emphasis on ecology, human nutrition, reproduction, development, genetics, the creation/evolution controversy, and the interrelationship of science and faith. (3 semester hours)

Principles of Biology Laboratory

A study providing direct, active, low-technology experience with biological experimentation and discovery of plant and animal life in a realistic environmental perspective. Experiments will emphasize scientific processes (methods). Discoveries (explorations) in local ecosystems will develop an appreciation for the beauty and complexity of our biological world. They will also equip you for informed stewardship in your community. (1 semester hour)

BUSINESS ADMINISTRATION

Principles of Economics I (Macroeconomics)

A study to introduce the student to the development of the modern economic system and of its basic principles, theories, and institutions. (3 semester hours)

Principles of Economics II (Microeconomics)

Theory of markets, price mechanism, production, distribution and resource allocation; application of marginal analysis and equilibrium theory to the price and output decisions of the individual firm in pure competition, monopolistic competition, oligopoly and monopoly; agriculture; labor, rent, interest and profit theory; international trade; the economics of change. (3 semester hours)

Money and Banking Finance

A study of the forms and functions of money, credit, financial institutions, theory of prices and income, interest rate, and monetary policy in theory and practice. (3 semester hours)

Business Law I

A study of the basic principles and concepts of business law, its source and development regarding the individual and society generally, with particular emphasis upon the laws governing contracts., personal property, and bailments. Also, a review of the Administrative Procedures Act and its effect on the business community through such acts and agencies as the Federal Trade Commission, the Clayton Act, Sherman Act, Fair Labor Practices Acts, Interstate Commerce Commission, Federal Power Commission, National Labor Relations Board, the Securities and Exchange Commission, and the Internal Revenue Service. (3 semester hours)

Business Law II

A continuation of the above course with emphasis upon the Uniform Commercial Code, the Uniform Consumers' Code, and the Truth in Lending Act, and their effect on sales, consumer loans, disclosure statements, limitations on consumer liability, home solicitation sales, and consumer and creditor remedies. Also, the study of the law of agency, partnerships, special ventures, corporations, and real property. (3 semester hours)

Financial Management

A study of the basic principles and theories of business finance, including the tax environment, cash-flow analysis, working capital management, effects of financial and operational leverage, capital budgeting, cost of capital analysis, investment banking, mergers, acquisitions, reorganizations, and liquidations. (3 semester hours)

CHRISTIAN CARE AND COUNSELING

Introduction to Christian Caregiving

A study designed to examine the "caring" aspect of the Christian life from theoretical, theological, and practical perspectives. The integration of the theoretical and theological perspectives with practical experiences will be implemented and evaluated. (3 semester hours)

Issues and Identify of the Caregiver

A study of the ethics, values, and litigation that affect the counseling field and professionals in that field. The role of the professional counselor is examined. (3 semester hours)

Introduction to Human Behavior

A survey of the basic principles of psychology, including development, motivation, emotion, learning, intelligence, physiological aspects, sensory processes, perception, attention, measurement, and personality. (3 semester hours)

Biblical Counseling I

An introduction to basic concepts and procedures of biblical counseling. Its purpose is to acquaint the student with a biblically-oriented approach to people helping. The knowledge and skills gained may then be integrated into the student's personal counseling style and serve as a basis for training laymen as people helpers. (3 semester hours)

Christian Approaches to Counseling

A study designed to acquaint students with the four basic paradigms of Christian counseling: insight-oriented, behavioral, cognitive, and faith-healing. The philosophic assumptions and uses of specific techniques with each will be explored. (3 semester hours)

Foundations of Personality Development

A study of the principle interpretations of personality development, description, dynamics, and determinants. (3 semester hours)

Life-Span Development

A study of human behavior in the social environment and the effect that environmental and psychological variables have upon the development of humans from conception to death. Special attention is given to the development of behaviors, attitudes, and problems specific to different sub-cultural and age groups, including the elderly. (3 semester hours)

Developing Helping Skills

A study of the major theoretical concepts of counseling psychology presented with practical applications of those concepts in terms of counseling strategies and techniques. The student is expected to formulate appropriate hypotheses concerning representative client problems and propose competent methodologies/strategies for addressing those problems. (3 semester hours)

Crisis Intervention

A study to acquaint the student with the nature and dynamics of crisis situations. Emphasis is placed upon intervention principles and procedures in the context of situational crises. The approach includes the concept of training laymen for basic crisis intervention. (3 semester hours)

Abnormal Human Behavior

This course is designed as an introduction to abnormal and maladaptive behavior. Theoretical perspectives, a classification and assessment system as well as the application of this information to the clinical setting will be given. (3 semester hours)

Practical Applications of Helping Skills I

The counseling practicum is designed to provide students with an opportunity to become acquainted with the practice of counseling. Working in various settings, students will interact with counseling professionals and become familiar with counseling as it is practiced within an agency. (3 semester hours)

Practical Applications of Helping Skills II

On-the-job experience in applying helping skills. Students are placed in agencies under the direct supervision of practicing counselors. (3 semester hours)

Marriage and Family

This course is a study to explore the dynamics of family relationships, particularly from the viewpoint of family counseling and therapy. The course focuses on knowledge and skills such as the theology of marriage and the family, problems of divorce and remarriage, courtship and mate selection, and the theory and technique of family therapy, including a historic overview, systems theory, psychodynamic theory, behavioral theory, communications theory, structural theory, and strategic theory. (3 semester hours)

Group Dynamics

This course involves participation in small groups. It includes an investigation of small group process through reading and surveying research literature. (3 semester hours)

Assessment and Evaluation

Assessment is designed as an introductory course for counselors. Its objective is to promote knowledge of and skills in assessment and evaluation. (3 semester hours)

Substance Abuse

This course presents the theological, ethical, moral, and practical considerations important in counseling those who are chemically dependent. (3 semester hours)

Special Issues in Counseling

This course is devoted to the study of contemporary problems, trends, or innovative developments in Christian counseling. (3 semester hours)

CHURCH MINISTRIES

Educational Ministries of the Church

A study designed to introduce the student to the historical, philosophical, and theological basis of the educational ministries of the church. Includes a study of the basic principles and practices of organization and administration of these ministries with emphasis on implementing programs to meet the needs of the learner throughout his/her life-span. The roles of the Director/Minister of Christian Education, the Board of Christian Education, and the volunteer staff member will also be examined. (3 semester hours)

Teaching the Bible

Fundamental and advanced methods of Bible study relating to teaching situations in the church are studied. Through consideration of background information will be encouraged for proper understanding of biblical situations and applied to our present time. (3 semester hours)

Introduction to Christian Missions

A study designed to provide an overview of God's eternal purpose—the preparation of a people for Himself from all the nations of the earth. By examining the biblical foundation, the historical development, the cultural considerations, and the strategic demands of God's work in the world, the student is challenged to the primary role of missions in the church. (3 semester hours)

Missionary Internship

A study designed to provide the student with practical exposure to the missionary enterprise. It allows the student to experience the administrative, home base operation that is essential to any missionary endeavor, to develop ministry skills through evangelism and church ministry, and to participate in a short-term cross-cultural mission. (3 semester hours)

Sermon Preparation

This course is designed to instruct the student in the proper interpretation and presentation of biblical material through preaching. Basic communication skills and sound principles of hermeneutics of scripture will be addressed, and attention will be given to the biblical perspective of preaching, principles of sermon construction, and sermon delivery. (3 semester hours)

Church Growth

An introduction to the biblical basis, the spiritual dynamics and the social factors which are concerned with how people are converted and brought into the fellowship of the church. (3 semester hours)

Evangelism

A course dealing with the evangelistic dimensions of the pastoral ministry in preaching, counseling, teaching, visitation, and training the laity for outreach. (3 semester hours)

Church Administration

A study designed to introduce the student to the practical aspects of administration within the church setting. This includes organization, planning, staff selection, motivation and training, evaluation and general leadership principles and problems. Administrative procedures are centered on the biblical and theological purposes of the church. (3 semester hours)

Senior Practicum/Project

Designed for seniors to obtain practical experience and to pursue research in the area of Church Ministries. (3 semester hours)

COMMUNICATIONS

Oral Communication

The course provides a practical interweaving of communication theory, principles, and practice as it explores many of the communication situations you will encounter in your career. (3 semester hours)

COMPUTER SCIENCE

Microcomputers in Business

An introduction to commercially available software packages commonly used in business environments. Representative packages include word processors, spreadsheets, and databases. This course provides a foundation for computer applications encountered in upper-level business courses. (3 semester hours)

EDUCATIONAL FOUNDATIONS

Educational Methods, Materials, and Media

Comprehensive foundations for majors in the School of Education and various teacher preparation programs. Includes an introduction to reading in the content areas. In addition, includes a study of educational media as they relate to the teaching/learning process. (3 semester hours)

Philosophy and History of Christian Education

The aim of this course is to make a study of Christian Education in general and the Christian School Movement in particular. (3 semester hours)

Human Growth and Development

A study of the human life cycle from conception to death. Emphasis is placed on the continuity of developmental phases of children, adolescents, adults, delineating the interrelationships among various aspects of development-biological, cognitive, emotional, social—emphasizing the many factors influencing development. (3 semester hours)

Christian School Curriculum (Early Childhood–Grade 8)

An in-depth study of current Christian School curriculum models and programs including goals, content, methodology, and evaluation. Also, strategies and techniques for developing computer-based instruction are discussed. (3 semester hours)

Exceptional Individuals

A study of the developmental characteristics and needs of the exceptional individual and the implications for teacher and counselor on the local, state, and national level. (3 semester hours)

Microcomputers in Education

This course will present through didactic and pragmatic segments how microcomputers operate, how to select and evaluate software programs, applications of microcomputers in various education environments, and how to conduct computer-assisted instruction and define

the various types of computer languages with the introductory programming of BASIC language by class members. (3 semester hours)

Classroom Management

A study of the various approaches in behavior management. Emphasis will center on behavior modification techniques. Parents and teachers will be introduced to token learning principles and how they apply to behavior management in the classroom. (2 semester hours)

Evaluation

Theory of educational evaluation and testing; criteria, construction, and evaluation of teacher-designed tests; elementary statistical concepts, and their values and limitations; a survey of individual and group tests used to measure general abilities, aptitudes, interests, and personality characteristics. (3 semester hours)

Methods and Student Teaching

Students devote 12 weeks in class observation, teacher assistance, and student teaching under professional supervision of cooperating teacher and college supervisor. Students engage in both curricular and extracurricular programs. Methods of teaching kindergarten through grade 3 are included. (5 semester hours)

Methods and Student Teaching Grades 4–8

Students devote 12 weeks in class observation, teacher assistance, and student teaching under professional supervision of cooperating teacher and college supervisor. Students engage in both curricular and extracurricular programs. Methods of teaching grade 4 though grade 8 are included. (5 semester hours)

ELEMENTARY EDUCATION

Language Arts: Early Childhood–Grade 8

A study of the scope and sequence of skill development in language arts—listening, speaking, reading, and writing with emphasis on grammar in traditional and innovative school programs. (3 semester hours)

Teaching the Bible

Fundamental and advanced methods of Bible study relating to teaching situations in the church are studied. Thorough consideration of background information will be encouraged for proper understanding of biblical situations and applied to our present time. (3 semester hours)

Foundations of Reading and Language Development

Basic principles of reading and language development; teaching strategies; materials; readiness for reading; word recognition; comprehension; vocabulary development and study skills for developmental reading from early childhood through elementary. (3 semester hours)

Children's Literature and the Library

Designed to acquaint the student with outstanding authors and illustrators of the best literature for children, with emphasis upon its proper use in meeting their emotional, intellectual, and aesthetic needs. (3 semester hours)

Elementary Reading Methods

A study of the scope and sequence of reading in the elementary school. Includes methods, materials, testing, and evaluation procedures in traditional and innovative school programs. A practicum is included. (3 semester hours)

Art: Early Childhood–Grade 8

Theory and methods of teaching art early childhood through grade 8. Discusses presentation and projects suitable to be taught. (2 semester hours)

Music: Early Childhood–Grade 8

This course will strongly emphasize skills as well as materials, methods, and philosophy of music to meet needs of the early childhood through grade 8 classroom teacher. Singing, creating, listening, music reading, rhythm experiences, and playing instruments are activities provided. (3 semester hours)

Mathematics: Early Childhood–Grade 8

A study of content, methods, and materials used in the teaching of arithmetic early childhood through grade 8. Modern concepts in mathematics are stressed, and observation in school classrooms is required. (3 semester hours)

Health, Nutrition, Motor Learning, Games and Activities: Early Childhood–Grade 8

This course emphasizes health and nutrition knowledge and practices needed for effective school and community living. Major health problems will be considered. This course is further designed to develop a knowledge in motor learning, elementary games, and activities essential to the growth and development of the elementary age child. Knowledge, skills, and techniques for instruction in a variety of activities will be discussed. Practicum experiences will enhance and reinforce class learning. (2 semester hours)

Science: Early Childhood–Grade 8

A course designed to familiarize students with the scientific concepts normally encountered in the school curriculum and the laboratory materials and equipment required in teaching early childhood through grade 8 science. (3 semester hours)

Social Studies: Early Childhood–Grade 8

A study of content, methods, and materials used in the teaching of social studies early childhood through grade 8. Trends in concept development and problem solving. Construction of teaching plans and units. Provision for observation in school classrooms. (3 semester hours)

Diagnosis and Correction of Reading Deficiencies

Diagnosis and assessment of reading disabilities of individuals emphasizing the interpretation of data obtained. Development of case reports, including recommendations and remediation. Corrective and remedial instruction utilizing appropriate materials and methods for individuals having reading problems. Instruction is designed to accommodate student needs through special techniques and adaptations of instructional materials. (3 semester hours)

ENGLISH

Reading and Writing in the Liberal Arts

A study designed to teach writing based on short informative or imaginative selections. Students will write in response to activities and assignments in analytical thinking and critical reading with emphasis on organization and expression. The students' ability to read critically, think logically, and write with precision and clear purpose is expected to increase. The student will also review grammar and mechanics. (3 semester hours)

Reading and Writing in the Disciplines

A study designed to emphasize content in the various disciplines. Students will participate in the following activities: exercises in critical reading, reasoning skills, writing in response to readings in a chosen discipline; assignments in writing to incorporate paraphrase, summary, quotation; practice in argument and persuasion; brief evaluative or critical essays in the readings; and research preparatory to writing a major research essay; writings based on library research; emphasis on ethical incorporation of borrowings. (3 semester hours)

GOVERNMENT

American Government and Politics

This course is an introduction to the study of (and participation in) government and politics in the United States. It analyzes (1) the governing process, (2) how people affect and are affected by government, (3) the major institutions of U.S. government, (4) some important issues that affect peoples' lives and what government might do about them, and (5) a Christian understanding of liberty and justice. (3 semester hours)

HEALTH AND PHYSICAL EDUCATION

Health Fitness I

A study designed with two overall purposes: first to assist the student to analyze his life and health; spiritually, physically, and emotionally, and to realize God's desire for his total well being; secondly, to provide practical guidelines for obtaining a complete Christian lifestyle of health—physically, spiritually, and emotionally. (1 semester hour)

Health Fitness II

A study to provide an understanding and personal appreciation of the relationship of physical activity and fitness to health, so that the individual will select an appropriate personal life-style necessary to produce optimal life-long health and well-being. This is a continuation of Health Fitness I. The main emphasis is on nutrition, muscular-skeletal fitness, and cardiorespiratory fitness. (1 semester hour)

Fitness for Life I

A study to provide students the opportunity to continue developing, implementing and monitoring their personal fitness program. Textbook assignments are included to build on the fitness knowledge base and thus to make the core requirements more meaningful. (1 semester hour)

Fitness for Life II

A study to provide the students the opportunity to continue developing their personal fitness program implemented in Fitness for Life I. Emphasis in this course is placed upon flexibility, strength, and weight control. (1 semester hour)

HISTORY

American History Survey: 1760 to Present

A study to examine the political, economic, social, and cultural development of the United States of America from the late colonial period to the present. (3 semester hours)

HUMANITIES

Introduction to Humanities I

Survey and synthesis of the history, literature, culture, and world views of Greco-Roman Classical and Medieval Christian cultures. (3 semester hours)

Introduction to Humanities II

Survey and synthesis of the history, literature, culture, and world views of the Renaissance, Reformation, and Enlightenment periods in Western Civilization. Some attention is given to the major world civilizations whose ideas, values, and cultures were beginning to influence western experience. (3 semester hours)

Modern Humanities I

Survey and synthesis of the history, literature, culture, and views significant to Western civilization from the French Revolution through World War I. Increased attention is given to the interaction among world civilizations. (3 semester hours)

Modern Humanities II

Survey and synthesis: landmarks, from World War I to present, in the history, literature, culture, and world views of various modern world civilizations from the perspective of Western civilization. (3 semester hours)

LEARNING ASSESSMENT

Prior Learning Assessment

A study designed to assist the student who is seeking college credit for prior learning experiences. Experiential learning is defined, and the steps of the assessment process are explored. The student is guided in the production of the first draft of a prior learning assessment portfolio. The course is a prerequisite to applying for prior learning assessment and credit. (3 semester hours)

MANAGEMENT

Principles of Management

The process of management is described and analyzed within the traditional framework of planning, organizing, staffing, directing (leading), and controlling. These functions of management are studied to determine causal relationships between managerial action and subsequent attainment of organizational objectives. Moral, ethical, and theological concepts will be considered. Special study is made of management by objectives. (3 semester hours)

Strategic Management

Designed to develop logical thinking and to give experience in the written and oral presentation of solutions to problems requiring business decision-making. Integrates the fields of marketing, finance, accounting, economics, law, and industrial management into a management concept of business decision making. Case studies, films, and computer simulations are used to bridge the gap between theory and practice. (3 semester hours)

MARKETING

Principles of Marketing

A study is made of the structure and analysis of consumer and industrial markets and the behavior of business firms in the competitive economy. Included are marketing policies and practices, marketing consumer goods, and marketing industrial goods. (3 semester hours)

MATHEMATICS

Introduction to College Mathematics

A study designed to introduce the student to college mathematics by building on knowledge already accumulated and by bringing new concepts into focus to strengthen the student's critical thinking process. (3 semester hours)

Elementary Statistics

A study designed for students of social studies, psychology, economics, and business administration. It includes both descriptive and inferential statistics and treats the fundamental concepts exemplified by frequency distributions, measures of central tendency and of variability, reliability and validity of measures, the interpretation of results, and hypothesis testing. (3 semester hours)

PHYSICAL SCIENCE

Principles of Physical Science

A study designed to examine the many topics which go together to make up the physical sciences. Also includes a study in the basic principles of scientific thought and investigation. The physical sciences are the non-biological sciences, but the scope is limited to physics, chemistry, and astronomy. (3 semester hours)

Principles of Physical Science Laboratory

Laboratory exercises to provide practice, manipulation, and visualization which supplements the lecture for the above course. (1 semester hour)

STUDY SKILLS

Study Skills

A study designed to acquaint the student with the nature of the external degree approach and format and with various study strategies. It is also designed to acquaint the student with the nature, philosophy, and lifestyle of Oral Roberts University. (3 semester hours)

THEOLOGY

Holy Spirit in the Now

President Oral Roberts analyzes biblical concepts and principles that reveal the Person and work of the Holy Spirit. Parallels of the dynamic ministry of the Spirit in today's world are clearly drawn. (3 semester hours)

Christian Faith and Ministry

A cursory exploration of the biblical truths and teachings of the Christian church. Emphasis is placed on the charismatic interpretation of these truths, especially as expounded by President Oral Roberts. (3 semester hours)

Contemporary Religions in America

This course is designed to introduce the student to the historic background and theologies of the various cultic groups that exist today. The student will learn about the historical settings out of which each group emerged, who lead these movements, the distinctive doctrines that each group developed, and the methods used by the groups to secure followers. (3 semester hours)

Systematic Theology I

Covers the idea of theology, the existence of God; Scriptures as revelation; the nature, works, and decrees of God. (3 semester hours)

Systematic Theology II

Doctrine of the Trinity. Decrees of God, Creation, and Providence. (3 semester hours)

Study and Research Strategies

This course is intended for all students in the Church Ministries and Christian Care and Counseling majors. It explores with the student reading, writing, and research strategies. It introduces students to the expected writing level in their course of study and the various formal styles which are expected of all students. (3 semester hours)

American Christianity

A study designed to investigate the life and thought of the churches in America in the context of American historical, theological, and cultural developments from the colonial settlement to the present. Attention will be given to Puritanism, the evangelical awakenings, and conservative and liberal traditions. (3 semester hours)

Signs and Wonders

This course is designed to allow students to study the manifestation of signs and wonders in the history of the Church, to learn from those servants of God whose ministries are characterized by signs and wonders, and to experience signs and wonders in their own lives and ministries. (3 semester hours)

Contemporary Theology

A study of mid-19th and 20th-century trends in theological thought from Schleiermacher to modern theologians with special reference to theological options of the present day. (3 semester hours)

Charismatic Theology

A study which focuses on the history and teaching of the doctrine of the Holy Spirit within the context of the Pentecostal and Charismatic movements of the twentieth century. Contemporary theological expressions of the Holy Spirit's supernatural gifts and the teaching of classical Pentecostalism, the denominational renewal movement among Protestants and Catholics and the independent Charismatic movements will be investigated. (3 semester hours)

History of Christianity I, Early and Medieval

A study of the development of the Christian Church from its birth up to the Reformation, with emphasis upon the major historical movements, leaders, and theological issues of the period. (3 semester hours)

History of Christianity II, Reformation to Present

Survey of expression from the Reformation era with emphasis on the reformers, the impact made politically and economically; special reference to the great missionary expansion. (3 semester hours)

Prayer

A study designed to assist the student in evaluating and developing a life of prayer. Various approaches to prayer that have been described in Scripture and by Christian leaders are explored. (3 semester hours)

Divine Healing

A study to examine the biblical, theological, and historical roots of healing in the Christian Church. Includes a study of the principles and patterns of healing demonstrated by Jesus and His disciples. Explores various models for healing ministries and how each of us can be healed and can be instruments of healing for others. (3 semester hours)

Oregon, University of
Eugene, Oregon 97403   (503) 686-3111

Description:

Correspondence courses offered by the University of Oregon are administered by the Office of Independent Study of the Oregon State System of Higher Education in Portland, Oregon. For courses available, SEE **Oregon State System of Higher Education.**

Accreditations:

Northwest Association of Schools and Colleges.

Oregon Institute of Technology
Oretech Branch Post Office
Klamath Falls, Oregon 97601 (503) 882-6321

Description:

Correspondence courses offered by the Oregon Institute of Technology are administered by the Office of Independent Study of the Oregon State System of Higher Education in Portland, Oregon. For courses available, SEE **Oregon State System of Higher Education.**

Accreditations:

Northwest Association of Schools and Colleges.

Oregon State System of Higher Education
Office of Independent Study
c/o Portland State University
P.O. Box 1491
Portland, Oregon 97207   (503) 725-4865

Description:

Correspondence study was begun by the University of Oregon in 1907. The Oregon State System of Higher Education was organized in 1932. For its first 20 years it was one of the top ten in size in the United States. Situated on the University of Oregon campus in Eugene until 1973 when it relocated to Portland, the Independent Study program currently offers college, noncredit, and high school courses. There are approximately 3,000 students enrolled in high school and college courses. Independent Study courses are offered by one or more of the colleges and universities of the Oregon State System of Higher Education, as follows: Eastern Oregon State College (La Grande), Oregon Health Sciences University (Portland), Oregon Institute of Technology (Klamath Falls), Oregon State University (Corvallis), Portland State University (Portland), Southern Oregon State College (Ashland), University of Oregon (Eugene), and Western Oregon State College (Monmouth). Toll-free telephone number: 1-800-547-4909, extension 4865. FAX (503) 725-4840.

Faculty:

Dr. Paul A. Wurm, Director, Independent Study. There is a faculty of 52 members.

Academic Levels:
College
High School
Noncredit

Degree/Certificate Programs:

Up to 60 quarter hours earned through independent study may be applied toward a baccalaureate degree. All Independent Study credits are treated as "transfer credit" and evaluated in that manner. Students should consult with their institutions for the number of credits allowable and transferable.

Admission Requirements:

Open enrollment. Some courses have required prerequisites. High school students must have approval from local school authorities in order for credits to apply toward graduation requirements.

Tuition:

College courses are $61 per quarter hour credit; high school courses are $100 per course. Refund of 100 percent if course is cancelled within one month following enrollment. Between one month and six months, a $20 per course administrative fee is withheld. No refunds after six months. In all cases an appropriate reduction is made for any lessons or examinations submitted for grading.

Enrollment Period:

Maximum time allowed to complete a course is one year; minimum time is three months. Two six-month extensions may be allowed upon payment of $15 for each extension.

Equipment Requirements:

Textbooks must be supplied by the student and are not included in the tuition. College/university textbooks may be purchased from the Textbook Department, PSU Bookstore, 1880 SW 6th, Portland, OR 97207. High school textbooks may be purchased from the Office of Independent Study, Portland State University, 1633 SW Park Avenue, Portland, OR 97207. Some language courses require access to a cassette tape player.

Credit and Grading:

Examinations must be proctored. The grading system is A through F, or on a Pass/No Pass option. Minimum passing grade is D (C or better for Pass. Credit is awarded in quarter hours; Carnegie units for high school courses.

Accreditations:

Northwest Association of Schools and Colleges. Member of: National University Continuing Education Association.

COLLEGE COURSES

ANTHROPOLOGY

Native North Americans

Indian and Eskimo life in North American before white contact, contemporary life. (3 quarter hours)

Native Central Americans

Contact period and contemporary ethnography of native peoples. Ecological adaptation, socioeconomic organization, and culture change. (3 quarter hours)

Native South Americans

Contact period and contemporary ethnography of native peoples. Ecological adaptation, socioeconomic organization, and culture change. (3 quarter hours)

ART

Introduction to Drawing

Introduction to expressive modes of drawing and composition as related to media and technique. Enrichment of visual vocabulary. (3 quarter hours)

ATMOSPHERIC SCIENCE

Introduction to Atmosphere

Course in meteorology employs basic physical principles in explaining the structure of the atmosphere, weather processes, structure of storms, observation, instruments, weather reporting and depiction, climate elements and weather modification. Comprehensive preparation for more advanced professional studies in meteorology. (4 quarter hours)

Weather Analysis Laboratory (Synoptic Meteorology)

Series of practical exercises in weather analysis provides the student with the major experiences essential to performing technical analysis of data and charts representing the structure and properties of the atmosphere in specific weather situations. Analyze air masses, locate fronts, draw surface and upper air charts, analyze weather satellite data and construct cross-sections. Middle latitude and tropical systems are included. Analysis of a weather situation proposed by the student provides a final project using techniques and concepts from the earlier exercises of the course. (4 quarter hours)

Project in Synoptic Meteorology

An analysis of data gathered on a weather situation proposed by the student. After approval of the project by the instructor, an analysis is conducted by the student utilizing appropriate techniques learned in the above course (Project in Synoptic Meteorology).

BUSINESS ADMINISTRATION

Intermediate Accounting

BA 317. Basic accounting theory and practice, financial statements, revenue recognition, concepts of valuation of current assets. (4 quarter hours)

BA 318. Concepts of valuation of liabilities, income taxes, pension plans, leases. (4 quarter hours)

BA 319. Concepts of valuation of owners equity, earnings per share, changes in financial position, disclosure requirements, alternatives to conventional financial reporting, analysis of financial statements. (4 quarter hours)

Cost Accounting I

Cost behavior, profit planning and budgeting, motivation and control, cost accounting systems, standard costing. (4 quarter hours)

Accounting for Not-For-Profit Organizations

Planning, budgeting, and controlling the operations of government and not-for-profit entities; review of fund accounting. (3 quarter hours)

Auditing I

Environment and professional nature of auditing. Concepts of testing, evidence, internal control, analysis of client accounting systems. (4 quarter hours)

CHEMISTRY

Nutrition

Nutritive value of foods from the standpoint of newer scientific investigations; nutritional requirements for normal human beings; selection of an optimal diet for health; present-day problems in nutrition; recent trends in American dietary habits. Meets prenursing, premedicine requirements. (3 quarter hours)

ECONOMICS

Principles of Economics (Micro)

A study of the market system involving the essentials of demand and supply analysis, competition and monopoly, labor, public policy towards business, and the distribution of income. (3 quarter hours)

Principles of Economics (Macro)

A study of factors affecting the level of national income, the essentials of money and banking, and the role of government expenditure and taxation in achieving economic stability and growth. (3 quarter hours)

EDUCATION

Breakthrough Strategies to Teach and Counsel Youth

A course offering state-of-the-art strategies to more effectively help troubled youth succeed emotionally, socially, and academically. Through audiocassettes and workbook materials, participants learn innovative techniques that actually train and motivate youth to become successful students with vital social and emotional skills. (1 quarter hour)

ENGLISH

Shakespeare

Eng 201. The early period, 1564–1594: early comedies, histories, and tragedies. (3 quarter hours)

Eng 202. Major plays of the middle period. (3 quarter hours)

Eng 203. Major plays of the late period. (3 quarter hours)

Survey of American Literature

American literature from Puritan beginnings to the middle of the nineteenth century, including Melville, Hawthorne, Emerson and Thoreau. (3 quarter hours)

American Fiction

Sixteen chapters on major American novelists of the twentieth century (Hemingway, Faulkner, Steinbeck, Wolfe, etc.) or on types and movements (the realistic-naturalistic novel, the historical novel). Student selects and reports on eight titles chosen from those discussed in the syllabus. (3 quarter hours)

Contemporary Literature

A study of fiction of the twentieth century, chiefly British and continental, with an emphasis on its relation to intellectual and cultural backgrounds and on its responses to the great events of the century. Syllabus is a series of chapters, some on major figures (such as Mann, Gide, Hesse), others on trends or movements embodying several figures (such as the stream of consciousness novel or existentialist literature). Report on six titles chosen from syllabus. (3 quarter hours)

Contemporary Literature (Drama)

Plays of the twentieth century. Study from the works of dramatists including dramatists including Ibsen, Shaw, Pirandello, O'Neill, and Brecht. Read eight plays and will submit a report on each as described in the syllabus. (3 quarter hours)

American Folklore

A study of native American folklore and its connections in American history and culture including the role of folk music. Methods of folklore collection are discussed. Students are required to submit a collection of folklore items. (3 quarter hours)

English Composition

Wr 121. Fundamentals of expository prose, frequent written themes. Special attention to substance and structure in written discourse. (3 quarter hours)

Wr 122. Advanced expository prose, frequent written themes. Emphasis on the relationship between style and content in exposition. (3 quarter hours)

The Research Paper

Basic college-level research writing course which emphasizes organization, logic, support of generalizations, and the special skills needed for writing a research paper, including analyzing sources, note taking, outlining, integration of source material into the student's own writing, and correct documentational form. (3 quarter hours)

Short Story Writing

Emphasizes the fundamentals of short story writing. A knowledge of English fundamentals equivalent to at least one year of college composition is essential. Students discover his/her talent through the writing of stories, analysis and comparison of stories. (3 quarter hours)

Poetry Writing

Verse writing: study of various verse forms as a media of expression. Analysis of class work. (3 quarter hours)

GEOGRAPHY

Introductory Geography

Emphasis on understanding and distribution of landforms of the earth. (3 quarter hours)

Pacific Rim

Interpretation of contemporary Asian developments with reference to past traditions and comprehension of the diverse physical, cultural, political, and economic geography of Pacific Asia and the Pacific basin. Particular emphasis is placed on the roles of the United States and Japan in the emerging Pacific economy. This course uses the 10-part PBS video series developed during 1990-92 by the Pacific Basin Institute. Requires a $50 deposit for videotapes with $30 refunded when the tapes are returned. (3 quarter hours)

GEOLOGY

General Geology

Geol 101. Processes of nature affecting the surface of the earth; formation of economic geologic deposits; the main events in the history of the earth. Sequence does not include laboratory exercises. (3 quarter hours)

Geol 102. A continuation of *Geol 101.* (3 quarter hours)

Geol 103. A continuation of *Geol 102.* (3 quarter hours)

Volcanoes and Earthquakes

The mechanisms that cause earthquakes and volcanoes, relation to plate tectonics, associated hazards, geothermal resources, examples in Oregon. (3 quarter hours)

Introduction to Oceanography

Physical, chemical, and biological process of the world's oceans. History and geology of the ocean basins. (3 quarter hours)

Geology of Oregon

Geologic and tectonic history of Oregon. Plate tectonic processes responsible for its evolution. Open to students in any field. (3 quarter hours)

The Fossil Record

Life on earth from the first protein synthesis reactions 3 billion years ago up to the dominance of mammals today. Geologic use of plant and animal fossils and their role in the interpretation of the history of the earth. All manner of fossil life: protozoa, plants, and animals. For those without extensive science/math backgrounds. (3 quarter hours)

HEALTH

Personal Health Problems

An in-depth study of personal health problems and current health topics, with the examination of decision-making processes regarding choices of behavior. (3 quarter hours)

HISTORY

History of Western Civilization

Hst 101. Covers the period from the Stone Age to about 1500 A.D. This course and Hst 102, 103 constitute a review of the great civilizations from ancient times to present. (3 quarter hours)

Hst 102. A continuation of the above course to the early 19th century. (3 quarter hours)

Hst 103. A continuation of the above course to recent times. (3 quarter hours).

History of the United States

Hst 201. This course and Hst 202, 203 constitute the standard one-year undergraduate review of the history of the United States from colonial times to the present day. (3 quarter hours)

Hst 202. A continuation of Hst 201. (3 quarter hours)

Hst 203. A continuation of Hst 202. (3 quarter hours)

JUSTICE ADMINISTRATION

Criminal Justice Process

An open system analysis of the decisions made in the criminal justice process. Contemporary problems and issues, prevailing ideologies, and current operational practices will be analyzed focusing around these critical decisions. Alternatives and the dilemmas of change in policing, prosecution, court administration and correctional programs are considered. (3 quarter hours)

Juvenile Justice Process

A general overview of the various activities and decisions involved in the processing of young law violators, with some examination of the historical evolution of the juvenile court and of contemporary issues and trends. (3 quarter hours)

Criminal Law and Legal Reasoning

Study of the basic concepts related to criminal law, including: historical development, legal elements of crime and proof; defenses and mitigation, reasonable doubt, and presumptions of fact; with particular emphasis on the application of logical reasoning to make legal decisions. (3 quarter hours)

Constitutional Criminal Procedures

A critical examination of the legal controls on the administration of criminal justice, with special attention to current court decisions related to such issues as search and seizure, admissions and confessions, wiretapping and eavesdropping, right to counsel, fair trial, self incrimination, cruel and unusual punishment. (3 quarter hours)

Court Procedures

General review of the major activities and procedures involved in the conduct of criminal trials, with extensive use of mock trial exercises. (3 quarter hours)

MATHEMATICS

Introduction to College Math

Mth 111. Introductory college algebra. Axioms of algebra, algebraic expressions, functions, linear and quadratic equations, systems of linear equations, solution of linear inequalities and logarithms. (4 quarter hours)

Mth 112. Standard college course: theory of trigonometric functions and their application in solving triangles, polynomials, and sequences. (4 quarter hours)

Calculus for Management and Social Sciences

An introduction to differential and integral calculus, the course is intuitive in approach and emphasizes applications. While intended as a terminal course, the interested student may follow it by the more extensive and rigorous calculus sequence. (4 quarter hours)

Calculus

Mth 251. Standard college course in differential calculus and analytic geometry. (4 quarter hours)

Mth 252. A continuation of *Mth 251*. Standard college course in integral calculus. (4 quarter hours)

PHILOSOPHY

Quests for Meaning: World Religions

A survey of major world religions: Hinduism, Buddhism, Confucianism, Taoism, Shinto, Judaism, Christianity, and Islam. An examination of the origin, founder, basic beliefs and history—stressing how each proposes to deal with the universal human quest for meaning. (4 quarter hours)

PHYSICAL SCIENCE

Foundations of Physical Science

GS 104. Branches of the physical sciences, their basic terminology, fundamental laws, procedures, and interrelations. The three-term sequence of GS 104, GS 105, and GS 106 is a survey of astronomy, chemistry, geology, and physics. This first course in the sequence covers the history of the universe, astronomy and the solar system, heat, molecular motion and property of matter. (3 quarter hours)

GS 105. A continuation of *GS 104*. Electricity, magnetism, and the beginning of modern physics. (3 quarter hours)

GS 106. A continuation of *GS 105*. Chemistry is covered in this final sequence. (3 quarter hours)

POLITICAL SCIENCE

Oregon Politics

Current issues in Oregon politics at the city, county, and state levels. Contending views which shape the political system. Audiocassettes highlight the classic debates in Oregon politics, and include recorded interviews with selected leaders. (3 quarter hours)

PSYCHOLOGY

Psychology as a Social Science

Introduction to the field of psychology with major emphasis on what psychological findings can currently contribute to our understanding of human behavior on a social level. Includes extensive coverage of personality and social psychology. (3 quarter hours)

Psychology as a Natural Science

Methods and criteria by which experimental psychology makes observations and constructs theories. Basic findings in physiological psychology, perception, learning, thinking, and motivation. (3 quarter hours)

Human Development

Development of the child and adolescent as an individual and as a member of social groups., Included is a comparative study of different home and school environments as they influence psychological growth throughout the life span. (3 quarter hours)

Introduction to Psychopathology

Various forms of unusual behavior, including anxiety states, hysteria, hypnotic phenomena, and psychoses. Normal motives and adjustments considered in their exaggerations in the so-called neurotic person. (3 quarter hours)

SOCIOLOGY

Introduction to Sociology

Presents the basic findings of sociology concerning the individual, culture, group life, social institutions, and factors of social change. Consideration of fundamental concepts and research methodologies. (3 quarter hours)

Oregon State System of Higher Education

Institutions and Social Change

A continuation of the above course. (3 quarter hours)

Social Problems and Issues

Examination of social problems with a particular focus upon American society. Sociological perspectives on the definition, description, and analysis of contemporary and recurrent problems in industrialized societies. Investigation of sources and responses to social problems considered in their societal context. (3 quarter hours)

Women in China

Explores the roles and status of Chinese women in historical and contemporary society. The historical background of the Chinese Women's liberation movement, the role of Chinese women in current reforms, the difficulties that must be met and overcome in Chinese women's work, study, and lives. Provides a basis for understanding the contribution of Chinese women to democratic life and to social progress. (3 quarter hour)

HIGH SCHOOL COURSES

BIOLOGY

Biology I

Provides a survey of the world of living things by examining their relationships to one another and their environment. Ecosystems, communities, populations, genetics, as well as an overview of the variety of organisms in the biological world are studied. (½ unit)

Biology II

A continuation of *Biology I* which involves a more detailed study of plant and animal functions, such as their reproduction and development. (½ unit)

BUSINESS

Introduction to Accounting (Bookkeeping) I

The aim of this course is to give the student instruction in practical methods of bookkeeping and information concerning principles underlying all accounting records. It includes a study of business relationships as affecting accounting records, recording of transactions in the more simple forms of books or original entry, posting of ledgers and preparation of financial statements. (½ unit)

Introduction to Accounting (Bookkeeping) II

A continuation of *Introduction to Accounting (Bookkeeping) II*. (½ unit)

Personal Finance

A new course incorporating all Oregon Personal Finance guidelines in a one-semester course. Topics include: credit, money management, banking, savings, investment, purchase of goods and services, employment, and the rights and responsibilities of the consumer in the marketplace. (½ unit)

Personal Finance Decisions

An in-depth personal finance course, emphasizing personal budgeting, consumer law and government services for consumers. Also included: purchasing cars, food, clothes, health services, appliances, homes, insurance, and financial services. (½ unit)

Career Education

A practical course designed to assist each student in creating systematic procedure for obtaining and keeping satisfactory employment. Points of emphasis include career research, job search, application and interview procedure, and career readjustment. (½ unit)

EARTH SCIENCE

Earth Science I

First semester of Earth Science introduces the tools scientists use for problem solving, including hypotheses, scientific method, and measurements. The emphasis is on the study of the earth (geology) including plate tectonics, building the crust, weathering and erosion, ice, wind, and waves. Earth's history, resources, rocks, and minerals are also included. (½ unit)

Earth Science II

The second semester of Earth Science covers air, water, and weather. Oceanography, the study of the oceans and the earth's surface below the oceans is explored. The section on astronomy studies the sun, our solar system, stars, and galaxies. (½ unit)

ECONOMICS

Principles of Economics

A one-semester course providing an understanding of economics by examining the production, distribution, and consumption of goods and services. Focuses on the foundations of economics, microeconomics, macroeconomics, and world economics through a theoretical approach to the study of economics. (½ unit)

ENGLISH

Ninth Grade Grammar and Composition

Covers parts of speech, phrases, clauses, sentences, capitalization and punctuation, paragraphs, and short expository compositions, summaries, and reports. (½ unit)

Tenth Grade Grammar and Composition

Exercises covering parts of speech, phrases, clauses, sentence structure, punctuation, use of pronouns, modifiers, verbs, study of agreement, spelling and vocabulary will strengthen writing mechanics. Course materials review the writing process, exposition, persuasion, and business letters then introduce library and dictionary skills, narration and description. (½ unit)

Tenth Grade Literature

Covers poetry, short story, drama, essay. (½ unit)

Eleventh Grade Grammar and Composition

Review of grammar and mechanics in writing. Composition practice in sentences, paragraphs, essays, and in expository primary source paper. Students can improve skill in effective word choice, sentence structure, and organization of ideas. (½ unit)

Eleventh Grade American Literature

The second semester of third-year high school English. Short story, essays, the novel, poetry, drama, colonial writing. (½ unit)

Twelfth Grade Grammar and Composition

The first semester of fourth-year high school English. Parts of speech, agreement of subject and verb, correct use of pronouns, correct use of verbs, modifiers, punctuation, and capitals. Coordination and subordination, clear reference and placement of modifiers, parallel structure and unnecessary shifts in sentence, sentence conciseness and sentence variety, writing the effective paragraph, the research paper, vocabulary, and spelling. (½ unit)

Twelfth Grade English Literature

The second semester of fourth-year high school English. The Anglo-Saxon Period, the Norman Period, the Elizabethan Age, *Macbeth*, Seventeenth and Eighteenth Centuries, Romantic Age, Victorian Age, modern short story, modern poetry, two British plays, book report. (½ unit)

Corrective English

A programmed course in grammar, sentence building, correct usage and punctuation. (½ unit)

Business English

Basic drill in standard English usage demanded for success in the business world. Use verbs, nouns, pronouns and modifiers correctly, and punctuate acceptably for clear meaning. Learn the forms of business letters, the parts of the business letter, proper punctuation and capitalization of each part, and the effective use of such characteristics as brevity, completeness, tact, and courtesy necessary to produce desired results. (½ unit)

English Review

Understanding the structure of the sentence, using verbs, pronouns and modifiers correctly, punctuation, singular and plural possessives of nouns, developing improvement in vocabulary and capitalizing correctly. (½ unit)

GLOBAL STUDIES

Global Studies I

Focusing on Africa, China, Japan, and India, the importance of physical environment, history, and religion is stressed. Ethnic diversity, the arts, and daily living are also covered. (½ unit)

Global Studies II

Latin America, Middle East, Soviet Union, and Western Europe. Topics covered: importance of physical environment, history, religion, ethnic diversity, the arts, and daily living. (½ unit)

GOVERNMENT

Government

Provides an understanding of types of governments, background and importance of the U.S. Constitution, current U.S. governmental structure and state and local government. (½ unit)

HEALTH

Personal Health I

The main objective of this first semester basic health education course is to have students develop an awareness of issues relevant to living a healthy lifestyle. Emphasis is placed on the following areas: the wellness continuum, fitness, nutrition, growth and development, safety, self-concept building, stereotyping and prejudices, drugs and alcohol, sexuality and AIDS and other diseases. (½ unit)

Personal Health II

The second semester health education course is a continuation of a general first year course. It will emphasize a more in-depth study of basic health areas. A greater focus will be placed on the following areas: self-enhancement, stereotyping and prejudices, relationships, sexuality, AIDS and STD's, drugs and alcohol, nutrition and fitness. (½ unit)

HISTORY

United States History I

First semester of a one-year course in U.S. history beginning with the exploration of the Americas. The course includes economic development and ethnic contributions along with traditional U.S. history themes. It concludes with the domestic progressive period of the early twentieth century. (½ unit)

United States History II

Second semester of a one-year course in U.S. history beginning with United States involvement in international affairs (1800) up to the present. The course covers U.S. history events emphasizing economic, social, and international influences on twentieth-century U.S. history. (½ unit)

World History I

This course covers prehistory, all early civilizations, Greece, Rome, and the development of Christianity and Islam. Also included are the histories of India, Asia, Latin America, and Africa up to the 1600s. The course concludes with nation-building in Europe and the Renaissance, Reformation, and Age of Discovery. (½ unit)

World History II

Begins with the age of Revolution beginning in 1600. It moves to European nationalism, the industrial revolution, and democratic reform. Imperialism, World War I and II and their aftermaths are covered. It concludes with Europe, the Western Hemisphere, Middle East, Africa, and Asia to the present. (½ unit)

MATHEMATICS

General Math I

First semester of a one-year general math course. Topics covered include addition, subtraction and multiplication, division, whole numbers, decimals, graphs, statistics, number theory and computation with fractions. (½ unit)

General Math II

Second semester of a one-year general math course. Topics covered include measurement, ratio, proportion, percent, consumer problems, perimeter, area, volume, probability, integers, and an introduction to algebra. (½ unit)

Algebra I, First Semester

First semester of a one-year high school Algebra I course. Topics covered include basic concepts, addition and subtraction in algebra, multiplication and division in algebra, and solving linear sentences. The text integrates concepts from arithmetic, probability, statistics, and geometry whenever possible. (½ unit)

Algebra I, Second Semester

Second semester of a one-year high school Algebra I course. Topics covered include graphing lines, equations of lines, finding distance and slope, working with exponents, polynomials, systems and quadratic equations. The text integrates concepts from arithmetic, probability, statistics, and geometry whenever possible. (½ unit)

Geometry I

First semester of a one-year high school geometry course. Topics covered include points, lines, definitions, "if-then" statements, angles, reflections, polygons, transformations, and congruence. (½ unit)

Geometry II

Second semester of a one-year high school geometry course. Topics covered include triangles, measurement formulas, three dimensional figures, areas, volumes, coordinate geometry, and similarity. (½ unit)

Algebra II, First Semester

First semester of a one-year high school Algebra II course. Provides instruction in the language of algebra, variation, linear relations, sequences, matrices, systems, parabolas, quadratic equations, and functions. (½ unit)

Algebra II, Second Semester

Second semester of a one-year high school Algebra II course. Provides instruction in powers, roots, exponents, logarithms, trigonometry, polynomials, second degree equations, series, combinations, and probability. (½ unit)

Consumer Mathematics

Apply computational skills to real-life situations. Topics include: purchasing skills, travel planning, investing dollars, consumer credit, managing personal income, and independent living. (½ unit)

PSYCHOLOGY

General Psychology

This course examines the behavior of humans through the study of approaches to psychology; the brain, body, and awareness; cognitive process; human development; personality, adjustment and conflict; psychological disorders; self and social influences; and the scientific method. (½ unit)

SOCIAL SCIENCE

Current Issues

A course that examines the current issues through reading and writing about articles found in newspapers, magazines, and some library resources. Areas of study include business and economics, our multicultural society, public education, history, law and criminology, medicine, politics and technology. (½ unit)

SOCIOLOGY

General Sociology

A social science survey course that emphasizes the study of society and its component social relations, organizations, and change. Some specific topics to be focused on include families, parenthood, divorce, sex roles, relationships, prejudice, poverty, crime, and urban problems. Case studies are used in examining these and other phenomena. (½ unit)

NONCREDIT COURSES

ENGLISH

Corrective English

For mature persons who feel the need of a thorough review of all facts and principles of grammar which have practical application in relation to punctuation and good usage. (Noncredit)

MATHEMATICS

Elements of Algebra

Thorough review of all the facts and principles of first-year high school algebra. (Noncredit)

Intermediate Algebra

Fundamentals of algebra. For those entering college with less than two years of high school algebra. (Noncredit)

Oregon State University

Corvallis, Oregon 97331   (503) 754-4331

Description:
Correspondence courses offered by Oregon State University are administered by the Office of Independent Study of the Oregon State System of Higher Education in Portland, Oregon. For courses available, SEE **Oregon State System of Higher Education.**

Accreditations:
Northwest Association of Schools and Colleges.

Pennsylvania State University
Department of Independent Learning
128 Mitchell Building
University Park, Pennsylvania 16802-3601
                                    (800) 252-3592

Description:
Penn State's Department of Independent Learning has been offering courses to the nontraditional learner since the very early 1900s. It offers individual courses, both credit and noncredit, certificate programs, and degree opportunities. A recent annual enrollment reached 16,000 students. These students came from every county in Pennsylvania, every state in the Union, and from a number of foreign countries.

Faculty:
Dr. James H. Ryan, Vice President and Dean for Continuing and Distance Education; Tammy Myers, Registration Supervisor. Approximately 100 faculty members; 2 counselors.

Academic Levels:
College
Noncredit

Degree/Certificate Programs:
Correspondence courses provide credits toward a certificate, associate degree, and baccalaureate degree. There is no limit to the number of correspondence credits which may be applied toward a degree. Correspondence transfer credits from other institutions may be accepted if the course fits a degree program, has a grade of C or better, and was taken at a regionally accredited institution.

Admission Requirements:
High school diploma or GED to take college credit courses; no requirements for noncredit courses, other than meeting course prerequisites. When enrolled in a Penn State course, the student is considered a degree student only if he/she has been officially admitted into a degree program by the University Admissions office. This classification also includes those students admitted on a provisional basis. All other persons, including students enrolled at other institutions, are considered nondegree students.

Tuition:
$98 per semester college-credit. Noncredit course tuition varies. A nonrefundable $28 processing fee is required for each course enrollment. Full payment must accompany registration. Visa and MasterCard accepted. Telephone Courses with video components have an additional media fee as well as videocasette rental fee. If the student withdraws from an Independent Learning course, he/she will receive a refund of 80 percent if withdrawal occurs up to 18 days from enrollment date; 60 percent if 19 to 36 days from enrollment date; 40 percent if 37 to 54 days from enrollment date; 20 percent if 55 to 72 days from enrollment date. No refund will be granted after the 72nd day. No refund for course materials will be given if lessons

have been submitted. A complete refund for materials is given if no lessons have been submitted and the materials are neither marked nor damaged in any way.

Enrollment Period:

Nondegree students have one year to complete a course; degree or provisional students are required to complete a course in six months. A maximum of two six-month extensions beyond the first year for completion may be granted upon payment of a $15 fee for the first six-month extension and a $20 fee for the second.

Equipment Requirements:

The school rents some lab kits, audiocassettes, and videocassettes; textbooks and other materials are purchased by the student, either from local bookstores or from the Department of Independent Learning at registration. A number of courses have video components and require a refundable videotape deposit plus a nonrefundable media fee. To enroll in these courses, the student must have access to a videocassette recorder (VCR) or if the student is in the vicinity of the University Park campus, the videos may be viewed at the Sparks Building Learning Center.

Credit and Grading:

The grading system is A, A-, B+, B, B-, C+, C, D, F with D being the minimum passing grade. Examinations must be proctored by a University-approved proctor. Credit is awarded in semester hour credits.

Library Services:

All Penn State libraries on campuses throughout Pennsylvania are available to the Independent Learning student.

Accreditations:

Middle States Association of Colleges and Schools. Member of: National University Continuing Education Association.

COLLEGE COURSES

ACCOUNTING

Introductory Financial Accounting

Fundamentals of the collection, recording, summarization, and interpretation of accounting data. (3 semester credits)

Introductory Managerial Accounting

Actual and standard cost systems; managerial uses of cost data. (3 semester credits)

AGRICULTURE

Job Placement Skills and Strategies

Strategies and skills designed to identify career/life goals and implement career decisions. Video component. (1 semester credit)

AMERICAN STUDIES

Introduction to American Studies

A study of selected attempts to identify and interpret movements and patterns in American culture. (3 semester credits)

ANTHROPOLOGY

Introductory Anthropology

Prehistoric and traditional peoples and cultures; traditional customs and institutions compared with those of modern society. (3 semester credits)

Introduction to Archaeology

This course surveys basic approaches used by archaeologists to interpret prehistoric human cultural patterns. (3 semester credits)

Cultural Anthropology

Beginnings of human culture; primitive economic life, society, government, religion, and art among traditional peoples. (3 semester credits)

ART HISTORY

The Arts

Develop critical perception, knowledge, and judgments through an examination of the basic concepts common among the arts. Video component. (3 semester credits)

Survey of Western Art

General survey of major monuments and trends in the history from prehistory through the late Gothic period. Video component. (3 semester credits)

Survey of Western Art II

Survey of the major monuments and trends in the history of art from the Renaissance to the modern era. (3 semester credits)

Special Topics: African Art

This course will examine the art of various African peoples in historical, religious, sociological, and geographic contexts. Contemporary African art, the influence of African art, and Afro-American art will also be major topics. Video component. (3 semester credits)

Japanese Art

(3 semester credits)

ASTRONOMY

Astronomical Universe

Nonmathematical description of the astronomical universe and the development of scientific thought. Video component. (3 semester credits)

BIOLOGICAL SCIENCE

Genetics, Diversity, and Evolution

How living organisms pass on their inheritance, how plants and animals came to be what they are, and how they react. (3 semester credits)

Environmental Science

Kinds of environments; past and present uses and abuses of natural resources; disposal of man's wastes; prospects for the future. (3 semester credits)

BIOLOGY

Plants, Places, and People

Useful and dangerous plants; historical (archaeological), cultural (ethnological), and economic (anthropocentric) aspects, including structural and chemical characteristics of botanical importance. (3 semester credits)

Physiology

Normal functions of the animal body, with special reference to those of man. (3 semester credits)

Introduction to the Biology of Aging

Examination of human aging from a biological perspective, causes of physiological and pathological changes, and factors that contribute to life propagation. (3 semester hours)

BUSINESS ADMINISTRATION

Business and Society

Various interrelationships, philosophies, and viewpoints regarding business in society are examined, including selected issues in the context of social responsibility. (3 semester credits)

BUSINESS LAW

Legal Environment of Business

Social control through law: courts, basic policies underlying individual and contractual rights in everyday society. Video component. (3 semester credits)

BUSINESS LOGISTICS

Business Logistics Management

Management of logistics function in firm, including physical supply and distribution activities such as transportation, storage facility location, and materials handling. Video component. (3 semester credits)

Transport Systems

Conceptual model of a transport system, environmental relationships; modal components and managerial conditioning, with special application to the United States. (3 semester credits)

Traffic Management

Analysis of the traffic function in the logistics system. Evaluation of routes, rates, and shipping document procedures. (3 semester credits)

CHEMISTRY

Chemical Principles

Chem 012 (DN). Basic concepts and quantitative relations. (3 semester credits)

Chem 013 (DN). A continuation of the above course including an introduction to the chemistry of the elements. (3 semester credits)

Organic Chemistry

Introduction to organic chemistry, with emphasis on the properties of organic compounds of biochemical importance. (3 semester credits)

CIVIL ENGINEERING

Water Pollution

Water pollutants; quality of municipal and industrial water; processes for water pollution control and water purification; water distribution; wastewater collection. (3 semester credits)

Fluid Flow

Elementary theory of fluid flow; hydrostatics; flow through orifices, Venturi meters, and pipes; flow in open channels; theory of the centrifugal pump. (3 semester credits)

CLASSICAL STUDIES

English Vocabulary from Latin and Greek

An introduction to English etymology stressing the most frequently occurring Latin and Greek elements and their English derivatives. (3 semester credits)

Greek and Roman Literature

Selected readings with a chronological and thematic context of significant and influential masterworks of Greece and Rome. (3 semester credits)

COMPARATIVE LITERATURE

Masterpieces of Western Literature Through the Renaissance

Universal themes and cultural values in works by such writers as Homer, Sophocles, Chaucer, Dante, Boccaccio, Rabelais, and Cervantes. (3 semester credits)

Masterpieces of Western Literature Since the Renaissance

Universal themes and cultural values in works by such writers as Voltaire, Goethe, Ibsen, Flaubert, Doestoevsky, Unamuno, Mann, and Borges. (3 semester credits)

Myths and Mythologies

The myths of non-Western and Western cultures based on selected mythologies from around the world. (3 semester credits)

COMPUTER ENGINEERING

Introduction to Digital Systems

Introduction to switching theory; study of basic TTL circuits, microprocessors, and assembly language programming. (3 semester credits)

Computer Organization and Design

Introduction to major components of a computer system, how they function together in executing a program, how they are designed. (3 semester credits)

Introduction to Computer Architecture

Principles of computer architecture; memory hierarchies and design, I/O organization and design, CPU design and advanced processors. (3 semester credits)

DIETETIC FOOD SYSTEMS MANAGEMENT

The Profession of Dietetics

Introduction to the profession and exploration of the roles and responsibilities of dietetic professionals. (1 semester credit)

Sanitation Practices in Food Service Operations

Practical applications related to the management of the sanitation subsystem within a food service operation. (3 semester credits)

Food Service Management: Theory and Practice

Professional functions of the hospital food service system, relationships with the nutrition component of food service system, and organization served. (3 semester credits)

Field Experience in Community Dietetics

Planning, preparation, and field experiences in community dietetic programs. (2 semester credits)

Human Resource Management in Food Service Operations

Theories and principles of supervision and training of food service employees for overall operational effectiveness. (3 semester credits)

Quantity Food Production Management

Systems approach to managing quantity food production functions in health care settings; included are quantity food production principles and standards. (4 semester credits)

Management of Food Service Operating Systems

Major principles related to managing the purchasing, food, and labor subsystems of a health care food service system. (4 semester credits)

Quality Assurance for Dietetic Management

Theories, principles, and methods of managing quality dietetic services. (3 semester credits)

Professional Staff Field Experience

Method of, practice in, the client-oriented dietetic systems in health care facilities. (4 semester credits)

Field Experience in Dietetic Management

Supervised experience in a department of dietetics: analysis of food service systems. (1 to 4 semester credits)

Marketing of Food Services in Health Care Facilities

Theories and applications of marketing principles to the design of consumer-oriented dietetic services. (3 semester credits)

EARTH SCIENCE

Out of the Fiery Furnace

A history of materials, energy, and humans, with emphasis on their interrelationships. For nontechnical students. Video component. (3 semester credits)

ECONOMICS

Introductory Microeconomic Analysis and Policy

Methods of economic analysis and their use; economic aggregates; price determination; theory of the firm; distribution. (3 semester credits)

Introductory Macroeconomic Analysis and Policy

National income measurement; aggregate economic models; money and income; policy problems. (3 semester credits)

Principles of Economics

Analysis of the American economy, emphasizing the nature and interrelationships of such groups as consumers, business, governments, labor, and financial institutions. (3 semester credits)

Intermediate Microeconomic Analysis

Allocation of resources and distribution of income within various market structures, with emphasis on analytic tools. (3 semester credits)

Intermediate Macroeconomic Analysis

Analysis of forces that determine the level of aggregate economic activity. (3 semester credits)

Labor Economics

Economic analysis of employment, earnings, and the labor market; labor relations; related government policies. (3 semester credits)

Environmental Economics

Environmental pollution, the market economy, the optimal resource allocation; alternative procedures; levels of environmental protection and public policy. (3 semester credits)

EDUCATIONAL PSYCHOLOGY

Educational Psychology for Professional Effectiveness

Principles of educational psychology applied to self-understanding and on-the-job leadership. (3 semester credits)

Introduction to Statistics in Educational Research

The foundations of statistical techniques used in educational research; distributions, central tendency, variability, correlation, regression, probability, sampling, hypothesis testing. Students must have access to the MINITAB program to enroll in this course. It may be purchased from Independent Learning and is available for either a Macintosh or MS-DOS computer with hard disk drive. (3 semester credits)

EDUCATIONAL THEORY AND POLICY

Sociology of Education

The theoretical, conceptual, and descriptive contributions of sociology to education. (3 semester credits)

History of Education in the United States

American educational ideas and practice critically examined in terms of their historical development and contemporary significance. (3 semester hours)

Introduction to Philosophy of Education

Introduction to the examination of educational theory and practice from philosophical perspectives, classical and contemporary. (3 semester credits)

ELECTRICAL ENGINEERING

Signals and Circuits I

Introduction to signals, signal processing, energy, power, electrical circuit analysis, linear networks, transient and steady-state responses. (3 semester credits)

Signals and Circuits II

Polyphase circuits; complex frequency; frequency response; bode diagrams; magnetically coupled circuits; power transformers; two-part networks; Laplace transforms; circuit applications. (3 semester credits)

ELECTRICAL ENGINEERING TECHNOLOGY

Fundamentals of Electrical Circuits

Fundamental theory of resistance, current, and voltage. Direct-current concepts from simple series circuits through Thevenin's Theorem. (3 semester credits)

Electrical Circuits Laboratory

Introduction to electrical apparatus, including instruments, their interconnection into basic circuits, observation of circuit behavior, and report writing. (1 semester credit)

Electrical Circuits

Direct-current analysis; introduction to basic magnetism and magnetic currents; single-phase circuit fundamentals. (3 semester credits)

A.C. Circuits

Application of network theorems, laws, and methods to alternating-current circuits; balanced and unbalanced polyphase systems. (2 semester credits)

ENGINEERING GRAPHICS

Introductory Engineering Graphics

Multiview projections, pictorial drawings, dimensioning, engineering standards, and working drawings. (1 semester credit)

Engineering Design Graphics

Introduction to creative design, space analysis, graphs, graphical mathematics, vector analysis, and design implementation. (1 semester credit)

ENGINEERING MECHANICS

Statics

Equilibrium of coplanar force systems; analysis of frames and trusses;

noncoplanar force systems; friction; centroids and moments of inertia. (3 semester credits)

Dynamics

Motion of a particle; relative motion; kinetics of translation, rotation, and plane motion; work-energy; impulse-momentum. (3 semester credits)

Strength of Materials

Axial stress and strain; torsion; stresses in beams; elastic curves and deflections of beams; combined stress; columns. (3 semester credits)

ENGLISH

Understanding Literature

Explores how major fiction, drama, and poetry, past and present, primarily English and American, clarify enduring human values and issues. (3 semester credits)

Basic Writing Skills

Intensive practice in writing sentences and paragraphs and instruction in grammar, usage, and punctuation. Designed for students with deficient preparation. (3 semester credits)

Rhetoric and Composition

Instruction and practice in writing expository prose that shows sensitivity to audience and purpose. (3 semester credits)

Introduction to Creative Writing

Practice and criticism in the reading, analysis, and composition of fiction, nonfiction, and poetry writing. (3 semester hours)

English Language Analysis

An examination of English sounds, words, and syntax using traditional, structural, and transformational grammar. (3 semester credits)

Effective Writing: Writing in the Social Sciences

Instruction in writing persuasive arguments about significant issues in the social sciences. (3 semester credits)

Effective Writing: Business Writing

Writing reports and other common forms of business communications. (3 semester credits)

Introduction to Article Writing

Written exercises in, and a study of, the principles of article writing; practice in the writing of specific articles. (3 semester credits)

American Literature from 1865

Introduction to literary history and analysis. Writers such as Twain, James, Crane, Frost, Eliot, O'Neill, Fitzgerald, Faulkner, and Hemingway. (3 semester credits)

Reading Poetry

Elements of poetry, including meter, rhyme, image, diction, and poetic forms in British, American, and other English-language traditions. (3 semester credits)

EXERCISE AND SPORT SCIENCE

History, Orientation, and Principles of Health and Physical Education

General scope, purpose, history, growth, and development of health, physical education, and athletics. (3 semester credits)

Adapted Physical Education

Basic concepts of planning and conducting physical education programs for children with physical, sensory, and/or intellectual impairments. (3 semester credits)

The Modern Olympic Games

An analysis of the modern Olympic Games from their inception to the present. Video component. (3 semester credits)

Intramural Athletics

Programs of activities, types of competition, scoring, awards, schedules, organization, publicity, and other topics related to intramural athletics in schools and colleges. (3 semester credits)

Organization and Administration of Health and Physical Education in Schools

Organization and administration guidelines and standards pertaining to health, physical education, intramurals, and athletics in the schools. (2 semester credits)

Principles, Ethics, and Issues of Athletic Coaching

Integration of the practical and theoretical knowledge necessary for effective coaching, through classroom and field experiences. (3 semester credits)

FINANCE

Introduction to Finance

The nature, scope, and interdependence of the institutional and individual participants in the financial system. Video component. (3 semester credits)

Personal Finance

Personal management of budgets, bank accounts, loans, credit buying, insurance, real estate, and security buying. (3 semester credits)

Security Markets

Analysis of the organization and operation of stock and bond markets; security speculation, brokerage houses; exchange relations with other institutions; security price behavior, exchange regulation. (3 semester hours)

Corporation Finance

The acquisition and management of corporate capital; analysis of operations, forecasting capital requirements, raising capital, and planning profits. (3 semester credits)

FRENCH

Elementary French I

Grammar, with reading and writing of simple French; oral and aural work stressed. Prerecorded audiocassettes must be rented. (4 semester credits)

Elementary French II

Grammar and reading continued; oral and aural phases progressively increased. Prerecorded audiocassettes must be rented. (4 semester credits)

Intermediate French

Grammar, reading, composition, oral and aural exercises. Prerecorded audiocassettes must be rented. (4 semester credits)

France and the French-Speaking World

An introduction to the culture of France and its impact on the world. (3 semester credits)

GEOGRAPHY

Human Geography: An Introduction

Spatial perspective on human societies in a modernizing world; regional examples; use of space and environmental resources; elements of geographic planning. (3 semester credits)

GEOSCIENCE

Planet Earth

Nontechnical presentation of earth processes, materials, and landscape. Practicum includes field trips, study of maps, rocks, dynamic models, and introduction to geologic experimentation. Video component. (3 semester credits)

GERMAN

Elementary German I

Listening, speaking, reading, writing; introduction to basic structures and vocabulary through dialogs and literary and cultural readings. Prerecorded audiocassettes must be rented. (4 semester credits)

Elementary German II

Listening, speaking, reading, writing; introduction to basic structures and vocabulary through dialogs and literary and cultural readings. Prerecorded audiocassettes must be rented. (4 semester credits)

Intermediate German

Continued skill development; readings consisting of short literary and journalistic writings; increased attention to German cultural context. Prerecorded audiocassettes must be rented. (4 semester credits)

HEALTH EDUCATION

Health Aspects of Sport

Basic principles and concepts of safety, health, and fitness for recreation and sport. (1 semester credit)

Health and Disease

Essentials of communicable and chronic disease control. (1 semester credit)

Drugs in Society

An exploration of the health-related aspects of drug use and abuse. (1 semester credit)

Introduction to Health Aspects of Human Sexuality

An examination of health concerns related to sexuality and sexual behavior. (1 semester credit)

Consumer Health

Essentials for determining credibility of claims for particular health services and products from a consumer's perspective. (1 semester credit)

Principles and Practices of Healthful Living

Facts and principles as related and applied to the science of living serve as a basis for health instruction and student guidance. (3 semester credits)

Special Topics: Issues in Sports Medicine

Designed to familiarize the student with various health aspects of sport, including such topics as risks related to sport participation, fitness, and exercise. (3 semester credits)

Development of Stress Management Programs for Health Education

Planning, developing, and implementing strategies for stress management programs for health education professionals in school, community, and corporate settings. (3 semester credits)

Consumer Health Education

Orientation of school and community health education opportunities to the consumer task of selection of health products and services. (3 semester credits)

Health Education Practicum

Field health education experience under the supervision of University faculty and qualified personnel within a health agency or clinical setting. (3 to 13 semester credits)

HEALTH POLICY AND ADMINISTRATION

Introduction to Health Services Organization

Examination of social, political, economic, historic, and scientific factors in the development and organization of the medical care health services. (3 semester credits)

HISTORY

The Western Heritage I

A survey of the Western heritage from the ancient Mediterranean world to the dawn of modern Europe. (3 semester credits)

The Western Heritage II

A survey of the Western heritage from the dawn of modern Europe in the seventeenth century to the present. (3 semester credits)

American Civilization to 1877

An historical review of the American experience from its colonial beginnings through the Civil War and Reconstruction. (3 semester credits)

American Civilization Since 1877

An historical survey of the American experience from the emergence of urban-industrial society in the late nineteenth century to the present. (3 semester credits)

Medieval Civilization

(3 semester credits)

History of Communism

Marxism, Leninism, and evolution of the Soviet Union; formation and development of the Communist bloc; impact of Chinese communism. (3 semester credits)

History of Fascism and Nazism

The study of right-wing totalitarianism in the twentieth century, with special emphasis on Fascist Italy and Nazi Germany. (3 semester credits)

History of the American Worker

A study of the American worker from the preindustrial era to the present. (3 semester credits)

Vietnam at War

Rise of nationalism and communism; origin of conflict; United States involvement; impact on postwar regional and international politics; contemporary Vietnam. (3 semester credits)

Introduction to the Middle East

Origins of Islamic civilization; expansion of Islam; the Ottoman Empire; the Middle East since 1918. (3 semester credits)

HORTICULTURE

Plant Propagation

Principles and practices of asexual and sexual plant propagation. (3 semester credits)

Commercial Floral Design

Techniques of commercial floral design for private and public social and religious events. (2 semester credits)

HUMAN DEVELOPMENT

Field Projects

Independent study and research in a human service program; written and oral summary of rationale, procedures, findings. (1 to 6 semester credits)

HUMAN DEVELOPMENT AND FAMILY STUDIES

Introduction to Individual and Family Development

Introduction to psychosocial and family development at all stages of the individual and family life cycle. (3 semester credits)

Personal and Interpersonal Skills

Conceptions of life-span personal and interpersonal skill enhancement. (3 semester credits)

Infant and Child Development

Theory, research, and methods of social/behavioral/biological sciences related to developmental processes and intervention during infancy and childhood. (3 semester credits)

Adult Development and Aging

Physiological, psychological, and social development and intervention from young adulthood through old age. (3 semester credits)

Special Topics: Child Maltreatment

Designed for anyone, including those in the social services, who is interested in defining, treating, and preventing child maltreatment. Emphasis is placed on the advantages of adopting family-oriented services to enhance parental functioning. (1 semester credit)

Family Development

Family functions over the life course; family from a multidisciplinary perspective, emphasizing adaptation and change. (3 semester credits)

INDUSTRIAL EDUCATION

Safety Education for Vocational Teachers and Industrial Trainers

Principles and practices of accident prevention in vocational-industrial schools and industrial training environments. (3 semester credits)

JUSTICE ADMINISTRATION

Introduction to the American Criminal Justice System

Criminal justice system, including formulation of laws, extent of crime, processing and correction of offenders, victims. Video component. (3 semester credits)

Introduction to Security and Loss Control

A general introduction to the field of private security and asset protection. (3 semester credits)

Probation, Parole, and Pardons

Examination of community treatment in the correctional process; contemporary usage of presentence investigation, selection, supervision, release of probationers and parolees. (3 semester credits)

Violent Crime in the United States

The impact of violent crimes on victims, their families, and communities; the police process as it relates to violent crime. (3 semester credits)

Correctional Institutions and Services

Intensive analysis of intramural and extramural programs for juvenile and adult offenders; professional functions in the total correctional process. (3 semester credits)

Seminar, Criminal Justice Agency Administration

Relates theoretical concepts to practical approaches currently operational on national basis; controversial issues identified, suggestions for resolution explored. (3 semester credits)

Policing in America

This course will focus on the current status of law enforcement in the United States. Video component. (3 semester credits)

Supervision of Law Enforcement Personnel

This course is designed to give officers a better understanding of the role of the first-line supervisor in law enforcement. Special attention is paid to the performance of subordinate personnel and its importance to the organization. Students are also made aware of how the supervisor's role will be redefined and modified as law enforcement organizations face the twenty-first century. Video component. (3 semester credits)

LABOR AND INDUSTRIAL RELATIONS

Industrial Relations

Introductory analysis of the employment relationship and of the interrelated interests of managements, workers, unions, and the public. (3 semester credits)

History of the American Worker

A study of the American worker from the preindustrial era to the present. (3 semester credits)

LINGUISTICS

The Study of Language

A nontechnical introduction to the study of human language and its role in human interaction. Video component. (3 semester credits)

Introduction to Language

Language and culture; language and the mind; mental processes of the bilingual; child's acquisition of language; communication systems of animals. (3 semester credits)

MANAGEMENT

Survey of Management

Introduction to organizational factors relevant to management processes, including leadership, motivation, job design, technology, organizational design and environments, systems, change. (3 semester credits)

Organizational Behavior

Theories, concepts, applications appropriate to the study of the individual and small group in organizations. (3 semester credits)

Organization Design and Development

The analysis of fundamental processes and structures of organizations, focusing on the organization as the unit of analysis. (3 semester credits)

Human Resource Management

Introduction to the strategic planning and implementation of human resource management, including staffing, development, appraisal, and rewards. (3 semester credits)

Contemporary Issues in Management

Advanced treatment of topics of current managerial significance. (3 semester credits)

MANAGEMENT INFORMATION SYSTEMS

Introduction to Management Information Systems

Business computer systems and their impact on management decision making. (3 semester credits)

MARKETING

Contemporary American Marketing

Social and economic aspects; movement of goods and services from producers to consumers; analysis of marketing functions, systems, and institutions. (3 semester credits)

MATHEMATICS

Basic Skills

(3 semester credits)

Intermediate Algebra

Algebraic expressions; linear, absolute value equations and inequalities; lines; systems of linear equations; integral exponents; polynomials; factoring. (3 semester credits)

Finite Mathematics

Introduction to logic, sets, probability. (3 semester credits)

Elementary Linear Algebra

Matrices and vectors; transformations; systems of linear equations; convex sets and linear programming. (3 semester credits)

College Algebra I

Quadratic equations; equations in quadratic form; word problems; graphing; algebraic fractions; negative and rational exponents; radicals. (3 semester credits)

College Algebra II and Analytic Geometry

Relations, functions, graphs; polynomial, rational functions, graphs; word problems; nonlinear inequalities; inverse functions; exponential, logarithmic functions; conic sections; simultaneous equations. (3 semester credits)

Plane Trigonometry

Trigonometric functions; solutions of triangles; trigonometric equations; identities. (3 semester credits)

General View of Mathematics

Survey of mathematical thought in logic, geometry, combinatorics, and chance. Video component. (3 semester credits)

Insights into Mathematics

Examples of mathematical thought in number theory, topology, theory of symmetry, and chance. Video component. (3 semester credits)

Technical Mathematics

Algebraic expressions, exponents, radicals, equations, graphs, systems of equations, trigonometric functions, solution of right triangles, vectors, complex numbers. (5 semester credits)

Technical Mathematics and Calculus

Logarithms, inverse trigonometric functions, trigonometric identities, inequalities, series, limits, differentiation, higher order derivatives, implicit differentiation, applications, integration, areas, volumes, differential equations. (5 semester credits)

Techniques of Calculus I

Functions, graphs, derivatives, integrals, techniques of differentiation and integration, exponentials, improper integrals, applications. (4 semester credits)

Techniques of Calculus II

Analytic geometry, partial differentiation, maxima and minima, differential equations. (2 semester credits)

Calculus with Analytic Geometry I

Functions; limits; analytic geometry; derivatives, differentials, applications. (4 semester credits)

Calculus with Analytic Geometry II

Derivatives, integrals, applications; sequences and series; analytic geometry; polar coordinates; partial derivatives. (4 semester credits)

Calculus of Several Variables

Analytic geometry in space; differential and integral calculus of several variables. (2 semester credits)

Number Systems

Introduction to sets and logic, properties of the natural numbers, integers, rational and real numbers, algorithms, applications to geometry. (3 semester credits)

Matrices

Systems of linear equations; matrix algebra; eigenvalues and eigenvectors; linear systems of differential equations. (2 semester credits)

Integral Vector Calculus

Multidimensional analytic geometry; potential fields; flux; Green's, divergence, and Stokes' theorems. (2 semester credits)

Ordinary Differential Equations

First- and second-order equations; numerical methods; special functions; Laplace transform solutions; higher order equations. (3 semester credits)

Ordinary and Partial Differential Equations

First- and second-order equations; numerical methods; special functions; Laplace transform solutions; higher order equations; Fourier series; partial differential equations. (4 semester credits)

MECHANICAL ENGINEERING TECHNOLOGY

Kinematics

Graphical and analytical studies of relative motions, instant centers, velocity and acceleration in plane motions, slider crank mechanisms, cams, gears, gear trains, and flexible connectors. (3 semester credits)

Product Design

Design of machine elements, including levers, bearings, shafts, clutches, springs, and gears; selection of ball bearings and belts; design of small mechanical devices. (3 semester credits)

MECHANICAL TECHNOLOGY

Mechanics for Technology: Statics

Forces; moments; resultants; two- and three-dimensional equilibrium of force systems; friction; centroids and moment of inertia of areas. (3 semester credits)

Strength and Properties of Materials

Axial stress and strain; shear; torsion, beam stressed, and deflections; combined axial and bending stresses; columns, ductility, resilence, and toughness. (3 semester credits)

METEOROLOGY

Weather and Society

Nontechnical treatment of fundamentals of modern meteorology;

effect of weather and climate on man and his activities. (3 semester credits)

Introductory Meteorology

Nontechnical treatment of fundamentals of modern meteorology; effect of weather and climate on society and its activities. (3 semester credits)

Tropical Meteorology

Atmospheric processes in the tropics; mass, heat, energy, momentum, water vapor budgets, cumulus convection, hurricanes, and other disturbances. (3 semester credits)

Applications of Statistics to Meteorology

Distribution of scalars and vectors; sampling; regression and correlation in two and three dimensions; time series; statistical forecasting; forecast verification. (3 semester credits)

MUSIC

Rudiments of Music

Introduction to the elements of music: notation, scales, meter, rhythm, intervals, basic chord structure. For non-music majors. (3 semester credits)

An Introduction to Western Music

A general survey of art music in Western society highlighting important composers and stylistic developments. (3 semester credits)

Evolution of Jazz

Study of origins and development of jazz as an art form. (3 semester credits)

NUCLEAR ENGINEERING

Understanding Health Effects of Ionizing Radiation

NUC E 297C. Basic nuclear science, the types and sources of ionizing radiation, and the somatic and genetic effects of ionizing radiation on human tissues. Video component. (3 semester credits)

NUC E 497C. Basic nuclear science, the types and sources of ionizing radiation, and the somatic and genetic effects of ionizing radiation on human tissues. Video component. (4 semester credits)

NURSING

Organization and Administration for the Nurse Manager

(3 semester credits)

Data Management for Nurse Managers

(3 semester credits)

Nursing Management of Human Resources

(3 semester credits)

NUTRITION

Introductory Principles of Nutrition

The nutrients: food sources and physiological functions as related to human growth and well-being throughout life; current nutrition issues. (3 semester credits)

Contemporary Nutrition Concerns

Interpretation of nutrition principles in relation to contemporary problems in selecting food for growth, development, and health. (1 semester credit)

Diet Therapy and Nutrition Care in Disease

Principles of nutrition care to meet therapeutic needs, inpatient care, and rehabilitation. (4 semester credits)

Nutrition Component of the Food Service System

Introduction to basic nutrition principles and their application in a food service system. (3 semester credits)

Nutrition Care of the Elderly

Introduction to the psychosocial, nutritional, and physiological needs of the elderly with emphasis on the delivery of nutrition care. (3 semester credits)

Independent Studies: Nutrition in Action

Nutrition instruction for elementary school teachers to use in the classroom. Video component. (3 semester credits)

PHILOSOPHY

Basic Problems in Philosophy

Issues such as the foundations of knowledge, the existence of God, the problem of freedom, and the nature of reality. (3 semester credits)

Major Figures in Philosophy

Introduction to philosophy through the study of the writings of representative thinkers in the history of philosophy. Video component. (3 semester credits)

Critical Thinking and Argument

Principles of correct thinking; deductive and inductive inference; use and misuse of language in reasoning. (3 semester credits)

Elements of Symbolic Logic

Translating arguments into symbolic form and establishing validity. For nonscience majors. (3 semester credits)

Existentialism

Exploration of a controversial modern mode of philosophizing about life, death, absurdity, and faith. (3 semester credits)

Ethics and Social Issues

Ethical issues such as war, privacy, crime and punishment, racism and sexism, civil liberties, affirmative action, abortion, and euthanasia. Video component. (3 semester credits)

Medical Ethics

(3 semester credits)

PHYSICAL SCIENCE

Physical Science

Development of physics, including modern physical concepts and their relationship to the careers of physical scientists. (3 semester credits)

PHYSICS

The Science of Physics

Historical development and significance of major concepts and theories, with emphasis on the nature of physical science and its role in modern life. (3 semester credits)

General Physics

PHYS 201 (DN). Mechanics. (4 semester credits)

PHYS 202 (DN). General physics (without lab). Electricity and magnetism. (4 semester credits)

PHYS 203 (DN). Wave motion and thermodynamics. (3 semester credits)

Introduction to Quantum Physics

Relativity and quantum theory applied to selected topics in atomic, molecular, solid state, and nuclear physics. (3 semester credits)

POLISH

Beginning Polish

POL 001. An elementary course to enable the student to achieve a measure of proficiency in reading and speaking Polish. (4 semester credits)

POL 002. A continuation of the above course. (4 semester credits)

Polish Culture and Civilization

Survey of Polish culture and civilization from 966 to the present. (3 semester credits)

POLITICAL SCIENCE

Introduction to American National Government

Introduction to development and nature of American political culture, constitutional/structural arrangements; electoral/policy processes; sources of conflict and consensus. (3 semester credits)

American Public Policy

Examination of selected areas of public policy in America. Analysis of policy content, alternatives, and impact. (3 semester credits)

Introduction to Comparative Politics

Introduction to study of comparative government and politics; normative/empirical theories; governmental functions in modern societies; representative structures and processes. (3 semester credits)

International Relations

Characteristics of modern nation-states and forces governing their international relations; nationalism; imperialism; diplomacy; current problems of war and peace. (3 semester credits)

American Local Government and Administration

Organization, powers, functions, and problems of American cities and metropolitan areas; modern trends and developments. (3 semester credits)

Political Science Internship

Combining experience in government offices, related agencies, or law firms, with appropriate readings and a research paper/report. (1 to 6 semester credits)

PSYCHOLOGY

Psychology

Introduction to general psychology; principles of human behavior and their applications. Video component. (3 semester credits)

QUANTITATIVE BUSINESS ANALYSIS

Introduction to Statistics for Business

Statistical inference: estimation, hypothesis testing, correlation, and regression; application of statistical techniques to economic and business problems. (3 semester credits)

Quantitative Methods for Business Decisions

Introduction to quantitative methods for conceptualizing business and management problems. (3 semester credits)

RELIGIOUS STUDIES

Introduction to World Religions

A historical and comparative survey of the principal beliefs and practices of the world's major religions. (3 semester credits)

Introduction to the Religions of the East

Religious experience, thought, patterns of worship, morals, and institutions in relation to culture in Eastern religions. (3 semester hours)

Jewish and Christian Foundations

Introduction to the perspectives, patterns of worship, morality, historical roots, and institutions of the Judaeo-Christian traditions; their relationships to culture. (3 semester credits)

SCIENCE, TECHNOLOGY, AND SOCIETY

Critical Issues in Science, Technology, and Society

An overview of the interactions of perspectives from humanities, sciences, and technology, and their integration in addressing social policy issues. (3 semester credits)

SOCIOLOGY

Introductory Sociology

The nature and characteristics of human societies and social life. (3 semester credits)

Introductory Social Psychology

The impact of the social environment on perception, attitudes, and behavior. (3 semester credits)

Social Problems

Current social problems such as economic, racial, and gender inequalities; social deviance and crime; population, environmental, energy, and health problems. (3 semester credits)

Introduction to Social Research

Fundamental concepts and problems in social science research; design, measurement, sampling, causation, validity, interpretation. (3 semester credits)

Urban Sociology

City growth and decline; impact of city life on individuals, families, neighborhoods, and government; urban life-styles. (3 semester credits)

Sociology of the Family

Family structure and interaction; functions of the family as an institution; cross-cultural comparisons. (3 semester credits)

Sociology of Education

The theoretical, conceptual, and descriptive contributions of sociology to education. (3 semester credits)

SPANISH

Intermediate Spanish

Audio-lingual review of structure; writing; reading. (4 semester credits)

Masterpieces of Spanish American Literature in English Translation

Emphasis on works and authors of international importance. Lectures, readings, and written work in English. (3 semester credits)

SPEECH COMMUNICATION

Effective Speech

Principles of communication, demonstrated through analysis and evaluation of messages made by others, with some attention to preparing your own speech. Video component. (3 semester credits)

STATISTICS

Elementary Statistics

Descriptive statistics, frequency distributions, probability, binomial and normal distributions, statistical inference, linear regression, and correlation. (4 semester credits)

THEATRE

Principles of Playwriting

Structure, dramatic effect, characterization, and dialogue; the writing, reading, and criticism of original one-act plays. (3 semester credits)

VISUAL ARTS

The Visual Arts and the Studio: An Introduction

Introduction to the visual arts; the practice of the visual arts; social, cultural, and aesthetic implications of studio activity. Video component. (3 semester credits)

Introduction to Drawing

The study and practice of basic drawing as a way of understanding and communicating. (3 semester credits)

WOMEN'S STUDIES

Women and the American Experience

(3 semester credits)

NONCREDIT COURSES

ARCHITECTURAL ENGINEERING

Plan Reading and Architectural Details

An informal course covering principles of drawing interpretation applied to working drawings for buildings; architectural symbols and conventions; drafting of typical construction details. (2.4 CEUs)

ART

Introduction to Calligraphy

A stroke-by-stroke guide to the art of hand lettering with exemplars for such alphabet hands as Roman, Uncial, Blackletter, and Italic. (3.6 CEUs)

CIVIL ENGINEERING

Water Pollution Control

Water pollutants; quality of municipal and industrial water; processes for water pollution control and water purification; water distribution; wastewater collection. (4.5 CEUs)

ENGINEERING GRAPHICS

Engineering Graphics

Technical skills and drafting room practices; fundamental to theoretical graphics; orthogonal, oblique, and perspective projections; working and schematic drawing. (6.4 CEUs)

ENGLISH

Introduction to Article Writing

Written exercises in, and a study of, the principles of article writing; practice in the writing of specific articles. (3 CEUs)

HOTEL AND FOOD SERVICE

Sanitation Certification

This course is designed to provide an understanding of the basic sanitation principles applicable to all forms of food service operations. (4 CEUs)

INDUSTRIAL ENGINEERING

Basic Supervision

Designed for front-line supervisors (foremen, etc.) of production, construction, or service industries. Duties and responsibilities, planning, communicating, keeping records and preparing reports, setting performance standards, selecting and inducting new employees, training workers and developing subordinates, improving work methods, cost control, safety, and the background of human nature. (2 CEUs)

Advanced Supervision

A course in supervision, more advanced than Basic Supervision but entirely at a level for middle management. Designed for supervisors (foremen, etc.) of production, construction, or service industries who have completed a course in basic motivation, grievance handling, counseling the worker, developing teamwork, decision making, personnel rating, understanding the boss, customer relations, leadership, the management team, and self-development. (2 CEUs)

MATHEMATICS

Basic Mathematics

Operations with whole numbers, fractions, decimals, integers; ratio, proportion, percents, unit conversions, estimates, graph and table reading. Emphasis on applications. Video component. (Noncredit) *Tuition:* $185.

NUCLEAR ENGINEERING

Understanding Health Effects of Ionizing Radiation

Basic nuclear science, the types and sources of ionizing radiation, and the somatic and genetic effects of ionizing radiation on human tissues. (3.2 CEUs)

NUTRITION

Fat Chance!

This course provides a guide for families and the family meal planner for promoting healthy food selection, establishing proper eating patterns, and encouraging proper exercise. This course is for families but is easily adapted for use by an individual. (Noncredit) *Tuition:* $54.

PETROLEUM AND NATURAL GAS ENGINEERING

Petroleum and Natural Gas Exploration

Geologic factors and exploration procedures related to the production of petroleum and natural gas. (3 CEUs)

Oil and Gas Production Practice

Production practices from initial drilling for oil and gas through secondary recovery of oil. (3 CEUs)

PHILATELY

Beginning Stamp Collecting

The first course in a comprehensive series of credit-free courses in stamp collecting. Structured to accommodate the limited background and mobility of a young collector. (Noncredit) *Tuition:* $40.

Beginning Stamp Collecting for Adults

The course covers the same content as the course above, but it is structured to appeal to the adult beginning collector. (Noncredit) *Tuition:* $60.

Intermediate Stamp Collecting I

Topics include sources, the reference collection, auctions, condition and value, and stamp shows. (Noncredit) *Tuition:* $65.

Intermediate Stamp Collecting II

The second course at the intermediate level of stamp collecting in the philately series. Course content deals primarily with the tools and techniques of collecting, and the development of a reference collection dealing with printing, production, counterfeits, forgeries, covers, postal history, topicals, and specializing. (Noncredit) *Tuition:* $72.

Printing Methods and Techniques

The major methods of printing and their relationship to stamp design and production are discussed. Students will assemble a reference collection to learn how a stamp's method of printing can be used to identify counterfeits by their physical characteristics. (3 CEUs)

WILDLIFE MANAGEMENT

Wildlife Ecology and Management

General principles of wildlife management; population dynamics; managing wildlife for harvest; endangered and extinct species; refuges, parks, and reserves. Video component. (4.4 CEUs)

Pennsylvania State University - College of Agricultural Sciences

Department of Independent Learning
128 AG Mitchell Building
University Park, Pennsylvania 16802-3693
(814) 865-5403

Description:

The College of Agricultural Sciences of Pennsylvania State University first offered correspondence courses in 1892 and has continued without interruption since that time. More than 270,000 people from all 50 states and more than 30 foreign countries have participated in this program.

Instruction is provided in the sciences that underlie agriculture and in their application to agricultural practice. Responsibility for preparing the courses rests with the various departments in the College of Agriculture and the Cooperative Extension Service. Because qualified faculty members prepare and organize the subject matter, the lessons in any given field contain the latest information available to the various departments. Some courses are prepared by Cooperative Extension Service specialists, some by college faculty, and some through joint authorship. The courses are intended to meet the needs of people at home, on their jobs, on farms, and in their gardens.

Faculty:

Lamartine F. Hood, Dean, College of Agricultural Sciences.

Academic Levels:

Noncredit

Degree/Certificate Programs:

Regular college credit is not given for courses. However, when a student completes courses valued at a total of 60 or more study points, with an average of C or better for each course, he/she is eligible to receive a Certificate of Accomplishment.

Admission Requirements:

None.

Tuition:

See individual course listings below (prices include tuition, study guide, mailing, and handling). Courses are mailed under a special fourth-class book rate. Delivery may take two to four weeks in the United States, depending upon the distance from University Park. For each course sent air mail, there is a $15 mailing and handling charge for the initial mailing of course materials. If the actual costs of mailing the materials exceeds $15, the student will be billed for the additional amount. If the actual cost is less than $15, the balance will be refunded. All courses and course fees are subject to change without notice. Students are sent entire courses upon receipt of check or money order. No refunds or exchanges of courses are made.

Enrollment Period:

Students may enroll at any time by filing an application form with the the Department of Independent Learning.

Equipment Requirements:

Basic material presented in most courses covers the subject adequately without requiring supplemental textbooks; however, students who can do supplemental reading will find the courses more rewarding. Lessons are designed to present material in an interesting and concise form. The lessons are 8½ by 11-inch bound sheets, illustrated with photographs and drawings. Some courses have video components. To enroll in these courses the student must have access to a videocassette recorder.

Credit and Grading:

Minimum passing grade is 70. Examinations are open book. Credit is awarded in study points.

Accreditations:

Middle States Association of Colleges and Schools.

NONCREDIT COURSES

AGRICULTURAL ECONOMICS AND RURAL SOCIOLOGY

Farm Management

This course is useful for nonfarmers who want to improve their understanding of the business of farming; for beginning farmers who need an outline of basic knowledge and an efficient approach to farm management; and for established farmers who want a review and summary. (8 study points) *Tuition:* $21.

Parliamentary Procedure for Common Use

This course briefly, yet clearly, covers parliamentary procedures. The lesson content is sometimes presented in outline form for the reader's convenience and ready reference. The course is not meant to replace the more authoritative, detailed reference material necessary for some groups. (3 study points) *Tuition:* $28.

Farm Law

This course provides detailed information on deeds, mortgages, agreements, leases, wills and estates, eminent domain, and water rights. The course is intended to help the individual to understand the laws and learn when to seek the advice of an attorney. (5 study points) *Tuition:* $21.

Developing Your Leadership Potential

This course is intended to help potential leaders understand their groups and present group activities, and to develop leadership skills in group members. (12 study points) *Tuition:* $28.

Farm Management for Part-Time and Small Farmers

The pros and cons of part-time farming for individual farm families are considered in this course. Land, labor, management, capital, market requirements and the advantages and disadvantages of 18 livestock and 18 crop enterprises are discussed. Lessons on record-keeping, tax considerations, budgeting, and insurance needs are geared to the part-time farm and the small farm business. (11 study points) *Tuition:* $24.

Farm Financial Management

Farmers, large users of capital, find it impossible to finance their needs from their own capital resources. This course discusses where to find credit; how to get it, how to use it effectively, the cost of using it, why costs differ among different types of lending agencies, and the legal aspects of using credit. Financial budgeting as a tool for planning profitable adjustments in production practices and farm organization are explained and illustrated. (10 study points) *Tuition:* $20.

Estate Planning for Farm Families

This course aims to help families understand the need for the terms of estate planning. It helps families to understand their alternatives and make sound decisions. (12 study points) *Tuition:* $23.

AGRICULTURAL AND BIOLOGICAL ENGINEERING

Farm Buildings

This course explains the planning of farm buildings and the requirements for sound construction. Special emphasis is given to foundation design and framing techniques. Building materials, such as wood, concrete, insulation, roofing, and paint, are considered. The course is valuable to anyone interested in planning or constructing farm buildings. (9 study points) *Tuition:* $23.

Farm Refrigeration

This course covers the fundamentals of farm refrigeration and their application to milk coolers, egg coolers, air conditioners, and frozen food cabinets. Lessons aid in the selection, application, operation, and maintenance of farm refrigeration equipment. (8 study points) *Tuition:* $20.

Electrical Tips for Everyone

This course provides a practical explanation of the function and use of electrical wiring in the home. Motors and controls constitute an important part of this course. Troubleshooting and do-it-yourself jobs are discussed. Drawings and photographs are used frequently to illustrate the subject matter. (15 study points) *Tuition:* $31.

Everyday Measurements and Calculations in the Metric System

This course examines the metric system of measurements, which has advantages over the English system and is being adopted in the United States. The course should enable people to answer questions involving numbers used daily. It is designed to help the reader deal more confidently with common math problems, using the metric units. Easy-to-understand tables and problems are used to simplify conversion from conventional to metric and metric to conventional units. (15 study points) *Tuition:* $25.

AGRONOMY

Soil and Water Conservation

Principles of soil and water conservation and their practical application through proper land use, soil management, and runoff and erosion-control practices are considered in this course. (7 study points) *Tuition:* $17.

Soil Fertility and Management

Objectives of this course are to study: (1) the factors which influence the growth of plants; (2) the various materials used for the nutrition of plants; and (3) the influence of soil and other factors affecting the use of fertilizer materials. (7 study points) *Tuition:* $24.

Home Lawns

Methods of establishing, fertilizing, and maintaining turf on home lawns are detailed. The course discusses initial planning, provision for drainage and irrigation, and the characteristics of the commonly used lawn grasses. Steps in soil preparation are outlined, and rates and methods of seeding are given for various grasses and mixtures. Instruction also covers caring for new seedings and maintaining and repairing established lawns. (8 study points) *Tuition:* $25.

ANTIQUES AND COLLECTIBLES

Antiques and Collectibles: Treasures in the Home

See course description below under **Family Living.**

CAMPGROUND DEVELOPMENT

Campground Development

This course explains how to establish a private campground as a family enterprise. It analyzes current trends in recreation and discusses the potential market as well as other factors to be considered by the operator, such as location, type of terrain, health requirements, and personal characteristics. The course discusses the cost of developing campgrounds; offers suggestions for water, sewage, and electrical installations; and provides specific plans for site development. (10 study points) *Tuition:* $22.

CAREER DEVELOPMENT

Waiter/Waitress Training - Guidelines for a Profession

This course is intended for use in waiter/waitress training sessions, for the employed professional or for persons considering employment in the food service industry. Guidelines are given for self-improvement, finding a job, and serving the public. Detailed directions on how to serve food and alcoholic beverages, types of restaurants, tipping, and how to be a professional on the job are included. (8 study points) *Tuition:* $17.

DAIRY AND ANIMAL SCIENCE

Sheep Husbandry

The following subjects are presented in this course: sheep management, including economics and future potential; housing and equipment; nutrition and feeding; forage program; and diseases and parasites. Lamb marketing, hothouse lambs, wool and wool grades, and plants poisonous to sheep are also discussed. (10 study points) *Tuition:* $20.

Stock Feeding

This course discusses briefly the digestive organs; the functions of food in the economy of the body; the classification of feeds and their constituents; feeding for the production of meat, milk, and wool; the computation of rations; and the use of roughages. (7 study points) *Tuition:* $22.

Beef Production

This course considers the economically important traits of beef cattle, the origins and merits of the different beef breeds, and management practices dealing with diseases, feeding, and record-keeping of beef cattle. Also covered are principles of reproductive physiology as they relate to beef production. (12 study points) *Tuition:* $26.

Genetics and Animal Breeding

The early history and present knowledge in the field of applied animal breeding and artificial breeding are the major subjects of this course. Inbreeding, linebreeding, and crossbreeding advantages and disadvantages are reviewed. (7 study points) *Tuition:* $21.

Breeds of Dairy Cattle

This course discusses the origins, development, and characteristics of Jersey, Guernsey, Ayrshire, Holstein, Brown Swiss, and minor dairy breeds, and the purposes for which they are adapted. (9 study points) *Tuition:* $18.

Silos and Silage

This course covers the following topics: the history of ensilage; the construction of approved types of silos; and cultivating, harvesting, and storing corn and grass crops used for silage. Feeding of silage is also included. (5 study points) *Tuition:* $14.

Dairy Goats

This course explains the origins, characteristics, and adaptations of breeds of milk goats. Breeding and feeding are fully covered; special attention is given to care and management. Illustrations of equipment and housing are included. (9 study points) *Tuition:* $20.

Dairy Cattle Feeding

Feed nutrients, digestion of feed, uses of feed in the animal body, characteristics of common feeds, general rules used in feeding, and formulating grain mixtures are topics discussed in comprehensive lessons. (3 study points) *Tuition:* $16.

Light Horses

More people are turning to horseback riding for pleasure and relaxation, and an increasing number of people own light horses for enjoyment. This course is designed to help the beginner, and to to provide a review for the more experienced person. Horse selection, feeding, care, management, housing, equitation, and equipment are topics included. (8 study points) *Tuition:* $25.

ENTOMOLOGY

Beekeeping

This course covers in detail the life history and habits of the honeybee, methods for successful production of comb and extracted honey, seasonal management, rearing of queens, control of bee diseases and enemies of the honeybee, preparing the comb or extracted honey for market, and marketing methods. (8 study points) *Tuition:* $38.

Basic Insect Science and Management

This course discusses the importance, value, and history of insects and their relationship to man. In addition, insect anatomy, classification, identification, life cycle, reproduction, and control are covered. (8 study points) *Tuition:* $26.

FAMILY LIVING

Home Furnishing

This course discusses ways to make your home attractive so that it reflects your family members' tastes. Emphasis is given to skillful use of resources (space, furnishings, and money). Also covered are design principles and their relationship to home decorating, arrangement of furnishings, and using accessories in a room. Readers are encouraged to use this course to help solve their decorating problems. (10 study points) *Tuition:* $20.

Improving House and Grounds

Practical ideas are offered for making homes more livable and home grounds more attractive. Included are floor plans of efficient bathroom, kitchen, and storage areas, as well as seven steps to more beautiful home grounds. (7 study points) *Tuition:* $21.

Ways with Windows

This course is designed to help homemakers develop creative window treatments that will fit into the home furnishings plan. Information is provided on principles of interior design, kinds of window treatments, and suggestions for basic and "problem" windows. Instruction is given in installing window hardware, selecting fabric, figuring yardage, and sewing curtains and draperies. (10 study points) *Tuition:* $22.

Physical Fitness for Modern Americans

Discussed in this course are the following: the conditioning effect of exercises; heart disease and physical fitness; obesity, overweight, and physical activity; dieting, pills, fad diets, caloric intake; developing physical fitness; and stress, strain, and physical exercise. Many myths about exercise are dispelled, and the readers are encouraged to survey what is currently happening in their lives. This course is a companion to *Mental Fitness for Modern Americans.* (8 study points) *Tuition:* $17.

Mental Fitness for Modern Americans

Getting to know oneself and forming good relationships with others are the keynotes of this course. The reader is directed step by step in ways of improving self-image and self-esteem as well as close and casual relationships with others. This course is a companion to *Physical Fitness for Modern Americans.* (8 study points) *Tuition:* $18.

Antiques and Collectibles: Treasures in the Home

This course surveys antiques and collectibles that may be part of the intimate scene of family living or individual life. The emphasis is on those objects of historical and aesthetic value and interest that people can enjoy every day in their own homes. Topics include identifying, locating, and evaluating antiques and collectibles; principles of collecting, including motivation and developing an appreciation for design, style, and historical periods; tips for beginners; buying and selling antiques and collectibles; using and caring for antiques and collectibles; heirlooms of the future; surveys of antiques and collectibles; and bibliographies. (12 study points) *Tuition:* $24.

FOOD SCIENCE

Basic Milk and Dairy Technology

This course covers dairy chemistry; dairy microbiology quality tests; food value of milk; milk and public health; handling milk and cream and manufacturing or preparing buttermilk; concentrated milks and other special products. This course provides a foundation for more specialized courses in market milk, ice cream, and cheese. (12 study points) *Tuition:* $26.

Dressing and Curing Meat

Discussed in this course are dressing and cutting the carcass, locating different cuts and preparing them for the table, and curing and handling different kinds of meats for future use. Methods of making meat products, such as the common kinds of sausage and scrapple, are fully described. (8 study points) *Tuition:* $25.

Canning and Food Preservation

This course explains the boiling-water-bath and pressure-canner methods for canning fruits, vegetables, and meats. It provides directions and recipes for making jellies, pickles, and relishes. Instruction is given on selecting appropriate foods and containers, freezing fresh and cooked foods, and cooking frozen foods. Daily food requirements of home-preserved foods are outlined. Also discussed are the drying and storing of foods, and directions are included for making a small dehydrator for home use. (7 study points) *Tuition:* $26.

Food: Selection and Preparation

Among the topics discussed in this course are basic food facts, menu plans, recipes, meat grades and carving methods, children's diets, lunch-box meals, and food costs. Each lesson is designed to help the homemaker prepare more appetizing and nutritious meals. (7 study points) *Tuition:* $21.

Market Milk

Commercial handling and processing of market milk from the farm to the consumer are discussed from the viewpoint of the milk processor or dealer. The course covers sanitary production, transportation, the receiving station, processing plant methods, pasteurization, special products, and distribution. (15 study points) *Tuition:* $31.

Ice Cream Manufacture

This course is intended for persons who are engaged in the ice cream business or who intend to enter the business. Lessons cover the manufacture of commercial ice cream, ices, and sherbets. Special attention is given to making and freezing of the mix and to problems in mix calculations and standardization. (12 study points) *Tuition:* $28.

Cottage Cheese Making—Home and Commercial

Many small dairy plants could make their own cottage cheese profitably. This course describes starter propagating, calculating and preparing the bulk starter, testing for acidity, manufacturing by both the "long-set" and "short-set" methods, creaming cottage cheese, and determining defects and their causes. (4 study points) *Tuition:* $15.

Meal Planning for Young Homemakers

This course is designed to help young homemakers plan and serve more nutritious meals, make the best use of their time and money, develop good food habits in family members, and learn to consult reliable nutrition information sources. The topics covered include nutrition for children and teenagers, leanness and longevity for family members, the homemaker's figure, and food fads. (7 study points) *Tuition:* $16.

Maintaining Desirable Weight

Living at desirable weight has its rewards in health, personality, growth, and careers. This course discusses how food habits developed in infancy apply to food quantity as well as quality, how food habits are difficult to change, and how individuals tend to gain weight at certain times in the life cycle. Other topics discussed are ideal weight for heart- and circulatory-risk candidates, losing weight, the delusion of fad diets, and how to eat and exercise to stay at best weight. (8 study points) *Tuition:* $18.

FORESTRY

Small Woodlot Forestry

This course recommends ways to establish, maintain, manage, and use farm woodlots. The distinction between the woodlot and park and picnic grounds is discussed and methods of propagation and renewal are fully described. (8 study points) *Tuition:* $18.

HORTICULTURE

Plant Life

This is a basic course for those who work with or are interested in plants. The lessons briefly discuss such matters as the structure of plants, their water and nutrient requirements, growth, reproduction, and ways to improve crop plants. Considering these fundamentals is essential for understanding the varied and complex world of plant life. (8 study points) *Tuition:* $24.

Propagation of Plants

Plant propagation is the basis of two industries in agriculture: nursery and seed production. This course presents a comprehensive discussion of: (1) seed production, including genetics, breeding, and seed processing; (2) seed sowing and transplanting of seedlings; (3) vegetative propagation, including cuttings, division and separation, layering, grafting, and budding; and (4) nursery management. (15 study points) *Tuition:* $22.

Home Garden Fruits

This course includes the following topics: underlying principles of fruit culture, site selection, planting, approved methods of treating soil and applying fertilizers, pruning principles, and selection of varieties. Methods of harvesting and packing fruits and types of storage houses are fully treated. This course addresses the needs of people with small home orchards. (8 study points) *Tuition:* $18.

Small Fruits

This course describes the production and marketing of strawberries, raspberries, blackberries, currants, gooseberries, blueberries, and grapes. It covers propagation, cultivation, pruning, disease and insect control, harvesting, packing, and shipping. Detailed instructions are useful to both beginners and general farmers who grow berries for home use or as a sideline. (10 study points) *Tuition:* $21.

Home Vegetable Gardening

This course is intended primarily for persons who produce vegetables for home use rather than for market. Instructions apply equally to the home garden on the farm and to the backyard garden of the town or city dweller. (6 study points) *Tuition:* $20.

Home Floriculture

This course considers the common annual and perennial plants and some of the shrubs most easily grown for ornamental purposes. One lesson covers roses, and one covers houseplants. Directions are given for growing the spring- and summer-flowering bulbous plants. (12 study points) *Tuition:* $31.

Flower Arrangement

Step-by-step procedures are given for developing well-proportioned flower arrangements by considering color, design, and containers. Information on preserving flowers covers the use of borax, silica gel, and glycerine, and hanging and pressing methods. Directions are provided for making corsages and corsage bows. (9 study points) *Tuition:* $20.

Landscape Planning for Small Properties

Carefully planning a property requires understanding community relations, using critical judgment to choose a home site, knowing how to move soil to create living areas, placing buildings, and making decisions on walks, drives, walls, and steps, as well as other structures. This course considers these requirements on an equal basis with good planting techniques. A recommended list of trees and shrubs for Pennsylvania is included. (12 study points) *Tuition:* $24.

Rhododendrons and Azaleas

This course describes the selection, planting, and care of plants requiring acid soil. Included are rhododendrons, azaleas, and other members of the heath family. (5 study points) *Tuition:* $14.

Trees for Home Grounds

This course is designed to help homeowners select tree species for various purposes. Instructions are given on buying, planting, pruning, fertilizing, watering, and identifying and controlling diseases and insects. Included is a discussion of laws pertaining to shade trees. (11 study points) *Tuition:* $21.

Shrubs for Home Grounds

This course is for the do-it-yourself home-landscaper. It describes foliage, flower, and fruit characteristics and growth habits of almost 200 woody plants. Pruning and pest control recommendations are given for each kind of shrub. (10 study points) *Tuition:* $23.

Vines, Ground Covers, and Espaliers

This course deals with plants which grow as vines and are used as ground covers, or are trained to grow in a predetermined pattern, a technique known as espaliering. Plant varieties and cultural methods are reviewed. (5 study points) *Tuition:* $14.

Bulbs for Your Flower Garden

Care and propagation of narcissus, tulip, lily, iris, and dahlia bulbs. (10 study points) *Tuition:* $18.

Annuals for Your Flower Garden

This course describes the cultural and varietal characteristics of over 80 annual plants grown for their attractive flowers. (8 study points) *Tuition:* $18.

Houseplant Culture

This course explains good horticultural practices in houseplant culture. It discusses ways of providing a suitable environment for a variety of houseplants through natural and/or artificial lighting, heat and humidity control, suitable soil mixes, diseases, and containers and terrariums. (6 study points) *Tuition:* $15.

Perennials and Biennials for Your Flower Garden

Cultural needs and growth habits of almost one hundred plant species are described in this course. (9 study points) *Tuition:* $21.

Rose Gardening

Anatomy; most popular cultivars; planting and pruning; how to propagate and feed roses; identifying and treating insects and diseases that attack roses. (4 study points) *Tuition:* $28

Edible Nut Production

This course describes home-grounds production of chestnuts, walnuts, hickories, hazels, and filberts. Improved varieties, soil and fertilizer needs, diseases and insects and their control, and propagating methods are presented. (10 study points) *Tuition:* $24.

Commercial Fruit Tree Production

This course is intended for those interested in growing tree fruits as a business. It covers location, planting, soil management, pruning, packing, and marketing. Apples, peaches, pears, plums, cherries, and quinces are the fruits emphasized. (15 study points) *Tuition:* $22.

Disease and Insect Problems in the Commercial Orchard

This companion course to *Commercial Fruit Tree Production* is intended for those interested in tree fruits as a business. The course covers the major diseases and insects of apples, pears, peaches, cherries, plums, and other deciduous tree fruits. It describes symptoms and damages and suggests such controls as varietal resistance and sanitation. Specific chemical controls should be obtained from current state and U.S. Department of Agriculture publications. (5 study points) *Tuition:* $17.

Selection of Indoor Plants

This course describes plants that can be grown successfully under varying home conditions. It discusses foliage plants for shade and low-light intensities; plants for semi-sun; plants for full sun; forcing bulbs

to bloom indoors in winter; succulents; and greenhouse plants. (11 study points) *Tuition:* $20.

MICROBIOLOGY

Microbiology

This course contains an introduction to microbiology as well as an elementary survey of its more important applications. There are lessons on the significance of microorganisms in water, sewage, soils, milk, food, fermentation, and disease. (11 study points) *Tuition:* $28.

POULTRY SCIENCE

Poultry Keeping

The characteristics and useful qualities of the more common breeds of poultry are briefly discussed. Topics that are considered fully are the location, construction, and care of buildings; incubation, brooding, and diseases; the selection and care of eggs and rearing stock; feeding for egg production; artificial illumination; and approved practices in marketing. (16 study points) *Tuition:* $26.

Production of Market Turkeys

This course explains types of turkeys that markets want; the market advantages of different varieties and strains; methods of marketing; ways of producing turkeys for markets, including breeding, brooding, feeding, and dressing; and vices and ailments of turkeys. (10 study points) *Tuition:* $20.

Rabbit Production

This course gives instruction in breed selection, housing, equipment, feeding, care, and breeding of rabbits for meat. Diseases and pests are fully covered. Special attention is given to killing, skinning, and marketing. (7 study points) *Tuition:* $21.

RADIATION PROTECTION

Radiation Protection for Family, Food, and Farm

This course begins with a nontechnical overview of radiation and atomic structure to help the reader understand how these two topics are related to nuclear power. The course then provides information about the health effects of radiation, followed by a discussion about how nuclear power plants operate and the safety of such operations. Also outlined in the course are protective actions that one can take in the event of a nuclear emergency, including actions pertaining to farm management. The last lesson describes microwave radiation and the safe use of microwave ovens. (10 study points) *Tuition:* $17.

WILDLIFE RESOURCES

Wildlife Ecology and Management

General principles of wildlife management; population dynamics; managing wildlife for harvest; endangered and extinct species; refuges, parks, and reserves. (4.4 CEUs) *Tuition:* $160.

Pittsburg State University
Division of Continuing Education
1701 South Broadway
Pittsburg, Kansas 66762   (316) 231-7000

Description:

Correspondence courses offered by Pittsburg State University are administered by Independent Study at the University of Kansas, Lawrence, Kansas. For courses available, SEE **Kansas, University of.**

Faculty:
Peggy Czupryn, Acting Dean of Continuing Education.

Accreditations:
North Central Association of Colleges and Schools.

Portland State University
724 S.W. Harrison
Portland, Oregon 97201   (503) 229-3511

Description:
Correspondence courses offered by Portland State University are administered by the Office of Independent Study of the Oregon State System of Higher Education in Portland, Oregon. For courses available, SEE **Oregon State System of Higher Education.**

Accreditations:
Northwest Association of Schools and Colleges.

Purdue University
Self-Directed Learning Programs
Continuing Education
1586 Stewart Center, Room 116
West Lafayette, Indiana 47907-1586
                                              (800) 359-2968

Description:
Purdue University is land-grant university established in 1869. It has four campuses with an enrollment of 47,000 students. The Self-Directed Learning Programs include professional courses in the fields of food plant pest management and pest control technology.

Faculty:
Jennifer L. Towler, Coordinator.

Academic Levels:
Professional

Degree/Certificate Programs:
Noncredit; Certificate.

Admission Requirements:
None.

Tuition:
Food Plant Pest Management for U.S. and Canada: $244.95 total for course and book; outside U.S. and Canada: $284.95 total for course, book, and airmail postage. Pest Control Technology for U.S. and Canada: $184.95 total for course and book; outside U.S. and Canada $224.95 total for course, book, and airmail postage. VISA and MasterCard accepted.

Enrollment Period:
Students may enroll at any time. Maximum time for completion of a program is one year. An extension of six months may be granted upon payment of a fee.

Equipment Requirements:
Textbooks are supplied with each course and included with the enrollment fee.

Credit and Grading:
A numerical grading system is used. Minimum passing grade is 70 percent. Examinations must be proctored. The courses described below are offered on a noncredit basis; however, many states have endorsed them for continuing education credit.

Accreditations:
North Central Association of Colleges and School. Member of: National University Continuing Education Association.

PROFESSIONAL COURSES

PEST MANAGEMENT
Food Plant Pest Management
This course offers a specialized, in-depth training program for managing pests in food processing and pharmaceutical plants, as well as large food handling facilities. Topics include introduction to entomology; insect development, classification and identification; principles of pest management in food processing plants; sanitation and GMPs relating to pest management; pest management environmental inspections and insect monitoring; pesticides used in food processing plants; pesticide applications in food processing plants; space treatments for food processing plants; safety and environment; pest-proofing of food processing plants; cockroach management; stored product pests; fly pest management; insect light traps; ants and other hymenopterous pests; rodent pest management; bird pest management; fumigation principles for food processors; warehouse pest management.

The course was developed and written by Robert M. Corrigan and John H. Klotz, both of the Department of Entomology at Purdue University. Supplemental readings cover specialized topics such as sanitation, food laws and regulations, pesticide applications in food plants, pest-proofing for food plants, fumigation practices for food plant operations, and warehouse pest management. Distilled from leading trade publications, academic journals, and textbooks, the readings provide up-to-the minute information while saving student the expense of additional textbooks and time in library research. (Noncredit)

Pest Control Technology
This course provides an opportunity for service technicians, managers, and owners in the pest control industry, and public health to improve their ability to manage insect, rodent, and various other pest problems in structural situations. The course was developed by Professor Gary W. Bennett, and Research Assistant Michael Scharf, both of the Department of Entomology at Purdue University. The following topics are presented: importance of urban pest management and the pest control industry; introduction to entomology and principles of pest management; insect development, classification, and identification; pesticides; safety and the environment; equipment; cockroaches; subterranean termites; nonsubterranean termites and other wood destroying organisms; ants and other hymenopterous pests; stored product pests; fleas, ticks, and other ectoparasites; occasional invaders and miscellaneous pests; fabric insects; flies and mosquitoes; rats and mice; birds; urban wildlife; sanitation and pest management in food processing plants; pest management in specialized facilities; fumigation.

The course meets the standards set forth for certification by the Environment Protection Agency. Evaluation under an EPA contract showed that the course significantly improved the level of knowledge of supervisory personnel. Whether preparing for certification or simply improving skills, students enrolled in this correspondence course have found it of high practical value. If the student is using the course to prepare for certification, he/she must contact the appropriate state's certifying agency to arrange for the certification examination. (Noncredit)

Reformed Bible College

Correspondence Studies
3333 East Beltline N.E.
Grand Rapids, Michigan 49505
(616) 363-2050

Description:

Reformed Bible College was founded by a group of pastors and laymen in 1939 to provide biblical and theological training for students interested in working in mission, evangelism, and church education. It began as a three-year institution and provided instruction for hundreds of students interested in church vocation. In 1970, the Reformed Bible Institute became a four-year college and awarded its first Bachelor of Religious Education degrees in 1971.

The correspondence program began primarily for on-campus students who needed flexibility in scheduling courses. Currently, 139 students are enrolled in correspondence courses. Opportunity for systematic study is offered to anyone who is interested in expanding his/her knowledge of Scripture.

Faculty:

Marge De Young, Director of Correspondence Studies; Dorothy Hostetter, Director of Admissions. There is a faculty of 5 members.

Academic Levels:

College

Degree/Certificate Programs:

All credits earned by correspondence can be applied toward fulfillment of degree requirements at Reformed Bible College.

Admission Requirements:

High school graduation or the equivalent.

Tuition:

Contact the college for current tuition and fees. Tuition will be fully refunded, less a service charge of $25.00, if withdrawal occurs within 30 days of enrollment; half of tuition paid will be refunded within 60 days, less the service charge; no refund will be given after 60 days. Full refund for textbooks and materials if returned without markings or damage and in saleable condition.

Enrollment Period:

Students may enroll at any time. The maximum time to complete a course is 1 year. An extension of an additional year may be granted upon application.

Equipment Requirements:

Textbooks, study guides, and cassettes must be purchased by the student and can be ordered from Correspondence Studies.

Credit and Grading:

Examinations must be proctored. Grading system is by letter grades, A, B, C, D, F with plus and minus. Minimum passing grade is D-. Credit is awarded in semester hour units.

Accreditations:

American Association of Bible Colleges.

COLLEGE COURSES

BIBLE

Introduction to Biblical Interpretation

A course designed to enable the student to discover the message of the Bible and teach it to others. Special attention is given to fundamental techniques of Bible study and to basic issues of interpretation. (3 semester hours)

Old Testament Survey

An introduction to Old Testament history and biblical theology, with assignments in reading and writing of reports. (3 semester hours)

New Testament Survey

A survey course in New Testament history and biblical theology, with particular emphasis on individual Bible book outlines, research assignments, and overall impact of the New Testament for today. (3 semester hours)

Acts

A study of the book of Acts. Historical, exegetical, and theological issues are studied. (3 semester hours)

Gospels

A study of the four gospels. Particular attention is given to the characteristics of each gospel and to the fundamental features of the life of Jesus that the gospels portray. (3 semester hours)

Pentateuch

A study of the first five books of the Old Testament. Historical, exegetical, and theological issues are studied. Modern critical problems as they apply to these books are also considered. (3 semester hours)

Revelation

A study of the New Testament apocalypse. The basic themes of the book will be explored and attention will be given to various ways the book has been interpreted throughout the history of the church. (3 semester hours)

THEOLOGY

Christian Doctrine I

The first course in the study of Biblical doctrine. It concentrates on Biblical teaching about God (theology), humanity (anthropology), and the person and work of Christ (Christology). (3 semester hours)

Roosevelt University

Reformed Confessions

An examination of the historical setting and theology of the Belgic Confession, Heidelberg Catechism, and the Canons of Dort. (3 semester hours)

Roosevelt University
External Studies Program
430 South Michigan Avenue
Chicago, Illinois 60605   (312) 341-3866

Description:

Roosevelt University was founded in 1945 as an independent, nonsectarian, coeducational institution of higher learning. Since 1947, Roosevelt University's home has been the famous Auditorium Building on Michigan Avenue overlooking Grant Park and Lake Michigan. Class schedules are flexible (courses are offered from early morning until late at night as well as on weekend) and class sizes are small. Moreover, the Roosevelt faculty number of 450 full- and part-time members is accessible to students. Many of the nearly 700 foreign students attracted to Roosevelt polish their English in the University's English Language Program which is rated one of the country's best. Roosevelt was also a forerunner in developing techniques for teaching preschool children and in the education of teachers for urban schools. A large segment of Chicago area teachers and administrators received their training at Roosevelt University. Student enrollment currently approximates 7,000 of which more than one-third are pursuing graduate studies.

For those students wishing to enroll in undergraduate courses but who are unable to attend classes on campus, the External Studies Program offers an alternative. Under the direction of a Roosevelt faculty member—with whom the student maintains contact by telephone, mail, or individual meetings—the student proceeds through a series of "modules," or study materials specifically designed for each course. Generally, a three-semester-hour course consists of three modules. Thousands of students have taken external courses since the program was developed at Roosevelt University in 1974. There are currently 1,200 students enrolled.

Faculty:

Arny Reichler, Director, External Studies Program; Bill Smyser, Registrar.

Academic Levels:

College

Degree/Certificate Programs:

All correspondence study credits may be applied toward a baccalaureate degree if appropriate to the individual's program. Coursework completed externally applies to the fulfillment of the University's minimum 30 semester hour residence requirement.

Admission Requirements:

Applicants for admission must pass Roosevelt University's entrance examination or have complete 12 semester hours of credit with a grade of C or better from an accredited academic institution. Individual courses may be taken by out-of-state students enrolled in another accredited university.

Tuition:

$300 per credit hour. Students who find that they are unable to complete an External course should present or mail to the External Studies Director a signed copy of their Change of Program Form. The amount of a refund depends on the number of days between registration and official withdrawal, as follows: before first module issued, 100 percent; 1–30 days, 90 percent; 31–45 days, 60 percent; 46–60 days, 30 percent; more than 60 days, no refund.

Enrollment Period:

Enrollment in correspondence study allowed any time during the academic year (September through May). Up to six months is allowed to complete a course; an extension of six months may be permitted.

Equipment Requirements:

The cost of textbooks is not included in the tuition. Texts may be purchased locally or through the University Bookstore.

Credit and Grading:

The grading system is A, B, C, D, F; D is the minimum passing grade (C in English); pass/fail option available. Examinations must be proctored. Credit is awarded in semester hour units.

Library Services:

The Roosevelt University Library is available to external students.

Accreditations:

North Central Association of Colleges and Schools.

COLLEGE COURSES

COMMUNICATION SKILLS

Grammar Skills: Learning to Learn

This module focuses on improving the basic skills necessary for academic success: reading, note-taking, exam-taking, critical evaluation and analysis. The basic goal is to make students aware of the concentration and thinking skills they most need, and to provide practice in these areas. (1 semester hour)

Grammar Skills: Exploring the Shape of Words

This module provides students with rules of grammar, and methods of learning grammar concepts and ways of bringing them into everyday writing. (1 semester hour)

Composition Skills: Writing for Business and Academic Success

This module helps the student to write clearly and with impact. The module begins with business writing and then focuses on academic writing. (1 semester hour)

Argument and Persuasion

This course provides an introduction to the terms and analytical skills necessary for critically evaluating an argument, as well as constructing one's own argument. (1 semester hour)

Communication Skills

This course examines the various facets of the communication process and how it works. It identifies communication barriers and how we can overcome them by developing basic skills in writing and speaking and by understanding the importance of interpersonal communication. (1 semester hour)

The Critical Report/Review

This is a module which gives the student a step-by-step guide to writing a critical/report review. (1 semester hour)

Research Skills

A practical guide to problems of selecting, ordering, researching, and developing a topic for the research paper. Invention, or the selection and limiting of a topic, is followed by lessons on how to find materials of different kinds in libraries, how to develop the paper once research is completed, and how to annotate the paper in the proper form. (1 semester hour)

COMPUTER SCIENCE

Data Processing Fundamentals

(3 semester hours)

Module I. Computer Systems. This module gives an appreciation of the power of computers, with illustrations drawn from business and scientific applications. It discusses the electronic data processing cycle, techniques for data entry, output, and auxiliary storage. it describes computer codes, types of computers such as microcomputers, minis, and mainframes, with basic explanations of how they function. Students are also shown various data communication systems and their importance in the modern data processing environment. The module emphasizes understanding of basic concepts and vocabulary buildup.

Module II. Computer Systems. This module explains what a computer program is and the characteristics of a good program. It provides an introduction to flowcharting and program design using a heuristic device drawn from robotics. Structured programming and other modern program development approaches are also discussed. The characteristics, advantages and disadvantages, and uses of the main computer languages are given, with worked examples. An introduction to operating systems is included to give appreciation of the complexity of the modern data processing environment. The module emphasizes understanding of basic concepts and vocabulary build-up.

Module III. Information Systems. This module defines the tasks of a system analyst and the environment in which he works. It explains the various steps of the life cycle development of a system or subsystem, including analysis, design, testing, implementation, and documentation. A payroll system is described in some detail. The module introduces system flowcharts and other tools. A sample cost-benefit calculation is given. The various types of files are discussed as well as the organization of a database. The need for database management is explained, as well as its pitfalls. The staffing requirements of data processing departments are reviewed as well as the trends in the market for data processing personnel. The module emphasizes understanding of basic concepts and vocabulary buildup.

Introduction to Programming Techniques

This three-module course provides the student with an introduction to program design with the emphasis on the general problem-solving process. The concepts of top-down design and structured programming are introduced and emphasized. Programming in BASIC using microcomputer. (3 semester hours)

COBOL Programming

In this three-module course students learn to design and code COBOL programs properly (Structured Coding) utilizing the latest computer equipment and software. (3 semester hours)

Business Applications on the IBM PC/XT

In this three module course, students will receive hands-on experience with word processing, database, and spreadsheet software. Other topics to be covered include purchasing hardware and software, local area networks, BASIC programming, accounting applications, and data communications. (3 semester hours)

Systems Analysis and Design I

This three-module course introduces the student to the methods and procedures for the development of a computer-based information system; the life cycle concept of systems development and the phases involved; documentation requirements and controlling project development. (3 semester hours)

Telephone Communication Systems

Covered in this three-module course are telecommunications development, concepts, and management. Topics will include the history of telecommunication; the regulatory environment and its impact on the industry; telecommunications technology and examples of applications, telephony, voice communications and standards. Other topics will include examples of network management, operations and network design. Future directions and trends within the industry will be emphasized throughout the course. (3 semester hours)

Small Computer Data Processing

The programming experience using microcomputers and the BASIC language is the objective of this course. Six programs will be completed by the student. Programs range from the simple to the moderately complex. Structured programming techniques, documentation, and adherence to specifications will be emphasized. Professional programming standards are applied as to correctness, neatness, maintainability, and meeting deadlines. (3 semester hours)

Advanced COBOL Programming

In this three-module course, students will design, code, and test five computer programs using advanced COBOL techniques. (3 semester hours) communications. (3 semester hours)

ECONOMICS

Introduction to Economics I

This is a course in introductory macroeconomics. Macroeconomics aims at explaining the determination of national product, employment, inflation, interest rates, and the business cycle. Such explanations are then used as guides for the formulation and analysis of national economic policy. (3 semester hours)

ENGLISH

Introduction to Composition

(3 semester hours)

Module I. Designed to introduce the art of composing into words your own ideas, thoughts, feelings, and emotions. Explores the need and advantages of writing always with a sense of audience and purpose and introduces a variety of ways for discovering subjects and topics on which to write.

Module II. Introduces, defines, and illustrates traditional types of essays: narration, description, and exposition.

Module III. Introduces, defines, and illustrates the remainder of the expository modes: cause and effect; comparison and contrast; process analysis; and definition.

Argumentation, Analysis, Research

(3 semester hours)

Module 1. Introduces the student to basic research and analytical techniques.

Module 2. Focuses on the practical skills needed to do effective library research.

Module 3. Introduces the syntheses and the critical paper.

Review of Composition

(3 semester hours)

Module I. Designed as an overview of the writer's considerations and the differences between writing and speaking.

Module II. This module begins with a discussion of the purpose and functions of paragraphs. Explains the order of paragraph development and the principles of paragraph coherence.

Module III. This module deals with persuasion and the process of revision.

GEOGRAPHY

Physical Geography I

(3 semester hours)

Module I. This module begins with an introduction to the historical development of geography as a field of study and to the use of maps. The second part examines the components and zones of the atmosphere with special attention to human degradation of the atmosphere.

Module II. Three different, but interrelated, topics are presented. The factors affecting temperature on earth are examined in the context of the use of solar energy. Next, the wind systems of the earth which redistribute heat energy are examined. The module closes with a discussion of the hydrologic cycle and the precipitation patterns of the earth.

Module III. The elements of climate are discussed in the context of human habitation of various climatic zones. Major topics include hurricanes and tornadoes, the influence of climate upon house design, the climate of urban areas, and human attempt to modify climate.

Module IV. Two general topics are presented: the geography of soil and natural vegetation zones of the earth. The discussions revolve around agricultural practices in different parts of the world. There is also an in-depth look at the rigorous environments of the desert, rain forest, and arctic tundra.

Physical Geography II

(3 semester hours)

Module I. This module presents an introduction to tectonic activity (volcanism and mountain-building) and its relationship to the rock types of the earth. Other non-tectonic processes involved in determining rock type are also examined. Minerals important to human economic activity (especially coal and petroleum) are discussed. semester hours)

Module II. This module presents an overview of the relationship between water and rocks. Ground water and surface water are examined in terms of their influence on the configuration of the landscape. Other topics revolve around human activity: attempts to change the flow characteristics of streams; sanitary landfills; and water pollution.

Module III. Three topics are discussed: human response to natural hazards and to landscape esthetics; the use of remote sensing (aerial photography and satellite imagery) in geography and environmental studies; the determinist and possiblist viewpoint on the influence of the

physical environment upon human cultural and economic development.

Urban Geography

This module examines the phenomenon of the city from a geographical point of reference, covering the role of cities and problems faced by people in cities past, present, and future. The specific challenges posed by the ongoing process or urbanization, especially in American society, are analyzed in some detail. Topics covered include the historical origins and background of the city, the structure of the urban place, problems facing cities of today, and prospects for the urban future. (3 semester hours)

Political Geography

(3 semester hours)

Module I. Political Geography. This module introduces political geography, defines it within the physical and social sciences, and discusses the discipline's origins and history.

Module II. The State as the Paradigm of a Politically Organized Area. Based on the introduction provided in the previous module, this exploration of political geography focuses on the state. The state is defined and its principal elements considered—location, shape, size, boundaries, resources, and population. The influence of these elements on the state's development, power, and vitality is examined, and the importance of its boundaries assessed. The role of the capital city in the life of the nation is also considered.

Module III. Political Geography. The first two chapters of the module concern the human resources of a state (population density, population distribution according to age, sex, race, ethnicity, etc.) as well as the population problems characterizing modern states (overpopulation, urbanization, etc.) and population policies followed by diverse governments. The power of a state is scrutinized from both a material and an ethical point of view. The last three chapters analyze the geographical aspects of relations between states in the context of the struggle between Western-type democratic societies and the authoritarian and totalitarian systems of government in the Communist and some Third World countries.

GENERAL STUDIES

Introduction to the Humanities

This module provides a general introduction to humanities study by examining three broad categories of cultural expression: that which is produced anonymously within a culture itself (such as mythology, folk and fairy tales); that which is supported economically by patrons or governments (such as much classical music and poetry); and that which is supported fully by the individual consumer (such as popular movies, television, and bestsellers). (1 semester hour)

Television: The Issues and the Art

Specific topics explored include the power of the ratings, the objectivity of TV news, educational television, blacks and women on and in television, children's TV, and the new technology, especially cable and the "videocassette revolution." Includes a history of the medium and analyzes the art of television. (1 semester hour)

Aesthetics: Philosophies of Art

An historical study of several philosophies of art, leading to the student's writing his/her own philosophy of art in a final essay. The course begins with a survey of ideas about art from the Classical period to the present. This is followed by a discussion of the relative roles of the artist and the audience and a consideration of the critic's role. The course examines the question of whether all the arts are really alike at all, or if the term "art" used freely to apply to painting, music, film, literature, etc., is being misused. (1 semester hour)

The Storyteller's Art

An analysis and history of storytelling, from earliest oral myths down to current experiments in literature and film. A brief discussion of the elements of story is followed by an historical survey which includes discussions and analyses of the texts. (1 semester hour)

Encounters with New Worlds

This course uses readings with a common theme—the experience of human beings encountering new worlds—to explore the ideas involved in this theme. The course also considers the art in which these experiences are expressed and uses the readings to illustrate various skills necessary to all students. (1 semester hour)

A Cherished Pledge: The Individual and the State

In this module the relation between the individual and the state in Western culture is explored. The module emphasizes the common, continuing conflict between the individual's belief and rights and the interests of the state; and the common, continuing will on the part of Western men and women to resolve this same conflict. (1 semester hour)

Men/Women Relationships: War or Peace?

This module studies the differences between women and men, particularly the psychological and biological differences and the differences in moral decision making. (1 semester hour)

Elements of Research

This module provides a review of the integral steps in research projects, from invention of a topic to completion of the final paper. While mechanics are stressed, the larger issue of the importance of information and its successful manipulation is also discussed. The course culminates with a brief research paper on a topic selected and developed by the student. (1 semester hour)

Genetics: The Language of Life

This course begins with a simplified description of the cell, the basic unit of living things, and the two processes by which cells divide to form new cells. Mendel's laws of heredity are presented and explained with examples. Human heredity is discussed. The composition of chromosomes and mutation are presented. (1 semester hour)

Pollution of Our Environment

In this course, an outline of the factors in pollution is presented. The perspective is that of Barry Commoner, one of the leading anti-pollution prophets. In addition to the technical aspects of pollution, the socioeconomic aspects are discussed, including Commoner's hypothesis of the ultimate cause of pollution. (1 semester hour)

Science and Society

This course is concerned specifically with the interaction between science and society: social, economic, and legal interactions with science. Information is presented on what research is, how it is supported by public money, how decisions on project funding are made, how research in the U.S. relates to that done in other countries, how scientists see their responsibilities to society, and unanticipated consequences of new technology. (1 semester hour)

Earthquakes, Continental Drift, and Plate Tectonics

The theory of plate tectonics—that the continents move slowly across the face of the earth on huge plates—developed during the late 1960s. (1 semester hour)

Machines and Society

This courses focuses on the origins of industrial technology, the way innovators create inventions, the role of science in industry. It also studies the ways in which modern industrial technologies have changed cities and have affected warfare, non-Western societies, and the lives of ordinary Americans. (1 semester hour)

Women's Work

This course addresses the subject of women's work, past and present, and the impact of these changes upon American society. Among the aspects considered are: biological determinism vs. technological and political change; jobs vs. family; femininity vs. assertiveness in business careers; job-sharing, flex-time, and part-time work; women in traditionally male occupations; and the impact or equal opportunity legislation. (1 semester hour)

Mankind Against Disease

This course examines one of mankind's critical problems, that of health, in its social context. The readings will focus on the impact of illness on human societies and how different societies have coped with health problems at different stages of history. The connections between disease and socioeconomic, political, even religious and psychological phenomena will be discussed. The profound impact of the biomedical and public health revolution of the past century will be seen in the perspective of history. The course will incorporate the finds of history, sociology, and social psychology. (1 semester hour)

Governing the City

This course analyzes the development of urban political structures and relationships from the colonial town meetings through the weak mayor, the strong mayor, and the city manager systems. The connections between political structures and machine rule will be analyzed with Chicago as a model. Metropolitan government and community control are examined. (1 semester hour)

HISTORY

History of Chicago

(3 semester hours; individual modules may be taken for 1 semester hour)

Module I. From Trading Post to Metropolis. This module emphasizes the importance of geography and technology to the growth of Chicago from an outpost fort to the second largest urban center in the U.S. The module explores the development of water and rail transportation and the accompanying establishment of the trading, processing, manufacturing, and retail enterprises. This module's coverage runs from the ethnically diverse city's pre-Fort Dearborn beginnings through its "rebirth" after the Great Fire of 1871.

Module II. Immigrants and Politics, Chicago—1871–1919. This module covers the growth of ethnic politics in Chicago.

Module III. Chicago History—1920–1987. The emergence of Chicago as the capital of gangland corruption with the "wide open city" of the 1920s. The module examines the linkages between corrupt politicians and gangsters during the Prohibition era. The module ends with the political turmoil that followed the death of Chicago's first black mayor.

Topics in American Social History

(3 semester hours; individual modules may be taken for 1 semester hour)

Module I. A Survey of Social Developments: The Effects of Immigration and Migration Upon the Fabric of Social Development.

Module II. A Survey of Social Developments: America "Settles In"—The Consumer and Technology.

Module III. Women and Work: The Continuous Revolution. Topics include the history of working women; the effect of race and class on employment patterns; housework, clerical work, and the professions;

and current issues concerning comparable worth, government family policy, and the media.

American Labor History

(3 semester hours; individual modules may be taken for 1 semester hour)

Module I. Labor Free and Unfree. A Survey of Major Labor Systems of Colonial and Early National Periods and Their Evolution. The objective of this module is to examine in detail slavery, indentured servitude, and free labor in colonial America and in the early national period up to the Civil War.

Module II. Labor in an Expanding Industrial Society 1860−1920. The major objective of this module is to learn the structural differences among the Knights of Labor, AFL, and IWW and the limitations in organizing imposed by each structure.

Module III. Labor in an Advanced Industrial Society. A Survey of Developments from World War I to the Present. A major objective of this module is to explore the effects of the anti-union drive of the 1920s, the depression of the 1930s, and World War II on the labor movement and working conditions in general. It covers the founding of the CIO and its structural and philosophical differences with the AFL as well as the basis for their eventual reunion. Other major topics are the increased role of government in labor relations and current trends and problems of the labor movement.

The Holocaust in Literature

This module provides a brief history and overview of literature concerning the Holocaust in Europe from 1933−1945, followed by discussions of three major novels on this theme. (1 semester hour)

JOURNALISM

Introduction to Public Relations

(3 semester hours)

Module I. This module discusses the history of public relations from the early 1900s to the 1980s, both in this country and abroad.

Module II. Tasks common to everyone in public relations, as well as specialized responsibilities.

Module III. The student learns how to perform the basic work of public relations.

MATHEMATICS

Finite Mathematics

(3 semester hours)

Module I. Background and Miscellany. Graphing points, functions, and equations; first degree equations and straight line graphs; linear inequalities; linear programming; mathematics of finance (optional topic).

Module II. Linear Systems—Equations and Matrices. Three (first degree) equations in three variables; matrix representation of 3 x 3 and m x n systems; multiplication of matrices; Leontief's input-output model of the economy (optional topic).

Module III. Probability. Sets and counting; permutations and combinations; sample spaces and basics of probability; conditional probability; Bayes Theorem; Bernoulli trials and expected value (optional topic).

NATURAL SCIENCE

Seminar in the Natural Sciences

The emphasis in this seminar is on the development of an understanding of the philosophy of science and of the methods used to obtain scientific knowledge. The course will deal with three areas: the methodology of science, specific branches of science, and with contemporary scientific problems. There are six modules required; students may include either 2A or 2B below. (6 semester hours)

Module 1A. What is Science?

Module 2A. The Structure of Matter.

Module 2B. Earthquakes, Continental Drift, and Plate Tectonics.

Module 3. Genetics: The Language of Life.

Module 4. Pollution of Our Environment.

Module 5. Science and Society.

Module 6. Contemporary Scientific Problems.

PSYCHOLOGY

Coping With Stress

(3 semester hours)

Module I. What are Stress and Stress Management?

Module II. Action-Oriented Stress Management.

Module III. Relaxation Dynamics.

Behavioral Medicine

(3 semester hours)

Module I. This is a course on stress theory and research. Considers basic stress concepts including the history of the study of stress, life events, the stress arousal response, cognitive models of stress, and the transactional perspective.

Module II. Topics include: personality and illness; stress and illness; stress, risk behavior, and illness; crises, catastrophes, and disasters; stress, the life span, and the family; job stress; and stress, the environment, and society.

Module III. This module reviews major approaches to stress management, including relaxation as well as behavioral, cognitive, and combination approaches to active coping. Examines theory and research underlying these approaches.

SOCIAL SCIENCE

Social Sciences Seminar

This seminar is designed to acquaint students with some of the major ideas and methods used by economists, historians, political scientists, psychologists, sociologists, and other social scientists. (6 semester hours)

SOCIOLOGY

Introduction to Sociology

The three modules of this course provide a basic introduction to sociology and sociological thinking, and an overview of basic topics in the field. Emphasis is placed on helping the student discover the relevance of sociological knowledge for his or her everyday life. (3 semester hours)

Research Methods in the Social Sciences

(3 semester hours)

Module I. Research Methods in the Social Sciences.

Module II. Additional Techniques of Data Gathering.

Module III. A Closer Look.

Saint Joseph's College

Distance Education Program
278 White's Bridge Road
Standish, Maine 04084-5263   (800) 742-4723

Description:

Saint Joseph's College is a private coeducational liberal arts college in southern Maine. Founded in 1912 by the Sisters of Mercy, Saint Joseph's (the only Catholic college in Maine), the 165-acre campus is located on the shore of Sebago Lake, 18 miles from Portland.

In 1976, a special program was established to provide the adult learner an alternative approach to traditional education. This approach is basically a method of delivering conventional college courses in a convenient format. The External Degree was added to the academic offerings to meet the educational needs of students whose field of endeavor requires a degree. It serves the adult learner who cannot leave the local situation and one whose educational background may be incomplete or fragmented. The External Degree provides a directed independent study learning program enhanced by a campus residency session for each student. During directed independent study, students are assigned a faculty instructor for individualized guidance and evaluation throughout each course. Even at a distance from the campus, students maintain regular personal contact with faculty, staff, and counselors through telephone conferences and written communications.

There are currently over 5,000 students enrolled from fifty states and fifty foreign countries.

Faculty:

Dr. Patricia M. Sparks, Dean, Distance Education; Edward J. Rielly, Assistant Dean; Jamie Morin, Director, Enrollment Management. There is a faculty of 74 member plus 15 counselors and 8 academic advisors.

Academic Levels:

College
Graduate

Degree/Certificate Programs:

The following degree programs are available:

Bachelor of Science in Professional Arts, Bachelor of Science in Business Administration, Bachelor of Science in Health Care Administration. Credits are earned by completing off-campus modules and on-campus residency courses.

Master in Health Services Administration. Students can earn a graduate degree in Health Services Administration by completing a minimum of 42 semester hours of credit through off-campus courses and on-campus residency courses. Associate Degree requirements are a total of 66 semester hours credits of which a minimum of 24 semester hours through Saint Joseph's College (9 of these credits must be earned at the required 3-week summer residency). A total of 18 semester hours is required for completion of a Certificate Program (no summer residency required). Individual evaluation of transfer credit is based on prior learning in accordance with guidelines established by the American Council on Education.

Admission Requirements:

Applicants for the BSBA and BSHCA degree programs must have earned a high school diploma or its equivalent; applicants for the BSPA degree program must be registered nurses that have earned an associate degree or have graduated from a two- or three-year professional or technical hospital-based program. All bachelor-degree-seeking students in the External Degree Programs must successfully complete at least five modules of independent study (valued at 30 semester hours) and one summer residency session (9 semester hours). A total of 128 semester hours is required for graduation. Applicants to the Master in Health Services Administration program should have a baccalaureate degree from an accredited institution of higher learning; a minimum of two years' experience, preferably administrative, in a health-related field; and the equivalent of twelve semester hours in health care management/systems or related subjects.

Tuition:

Undergraduate tuition $170 per credit hour ($190 per credit hour on campus); graduate tuition per credit $205 per credit hour ($225 per credit hour on campus. Application fee, $50; graduation fee $50. Payment is accepted by check, money order, American Express, VISA, Discover, or MasterCard. Students who choose to withdraw must make their request in writing to the Dean, Distance Education Program, prior to their course completion date. Refund of tuition is made according to the following schedule: withdrawal within 30 days, 95 percent of tuition; withdrawal within 60 days, 50 percent of tuition; withdrawal after 60 days, no refund.

Credit and Grading:

Letter grades are used with plus and minus. Minimum passing grade is D. Credits in transfer are accepted from other accredited colleges and universities if appropriate to the program of studies and if grade of C or better has been attained. The maximum number of credits accepted are 89 semester hours for the baccalaureate degree; 42 semester hours for the associate degree, and 6 semester hours for a certificate. Examinations must be proctored. Credit is awarded in semester hour units.

Library Services:

The college provides a useful supplement to the student's local or interlibrary borrowing systems. Copies of periodicals and journals are available for a nominal fee. All requests must be made in writing to the campus librarian.

Accreditations:

New England Association of Schools and Colleges. Member of: National University Continuing Education Association.

COLLEGE COURSES

BUSINESS ADMINISTRATION

Financial Accounting

Involves a study of the fundamental principles of accounting as they relate to management. Emphasis is given to the development and analysis of basic financial statements, the development of budgets, and other techniques of financial analysis for management decision making. (3 semester hours)

Managerial Accounting

Takes the student through cost methods and systems, operational and capital budgeting, divisional performance measurement and control as well as analysis of financial statements. (3 semester hours)

Introduction to Microeconomics

Includes an examination of the market structures of pure competition; monopolistic competition, oligopoly, and monopoly; analysis of the role of labor and unions; public goods and the public sector; discussion of the problems of foreign aid, poverty, pollution, and tax reform. It explores international economics, trade and lending, tariffs, quotas and free trade, international adjustments and the balance of payments problems. (3 semester hours)

Introduction to Macroeconomics

Gives the student an understanding of how the United States allocates resources, and produces, distributes, and consumes its goods and services. Equips the student to analyze economic events of the present. Topics include the national income accounts, aggregate supply and demand, aggregate income, employment, inflation, determinants of consumption and investments, the role of money and the federal reserve, and monetary and fiscal policies. (3 semester hours)

Business Law I

Explores what constitutes "law," and follows with a study of its basic principles: contracts, agency, partnerships, sole proprietorships, personal and real property. (3 semester hours)

Business Law II

Examines the Uniform Commercial Code, with special attention to sales, secured transactions, commercial paper, creditors' rights, and bankruptcy. (3 semester hours)

Business Ethics

This course examines the application of ethics to various components of business, including organizational, marketing, personnel, and financial matters. (3 semester hours)

Business, Government, and Society

A study of the interrelationships between business organizations, the various local, state, and federal governments, and other segments of society. (3 semester hours)

Introduction to Management

Examination of the decision-making process as it affects individuals and groups. It discusses principles and techniques of business as they relate to the planning, organizing, coordinating, leading, directing, and controlling of the business enterprise. It reviews the day-to-day problems faced by managers, focusing on how to solve them. (3 semester hours)

Business Communications

Develops the students' written and verbal communication ability in the business environment, stressing an understanding of the communication process through identifying how words are used as basic symbols of human communication. (3 semester hours)

Operations Management

Provides an introduction to the planning and controlling of operations within an organization. The course deals with analytical methods employed, the design of the system, and the control devices for both quality and quantity. (3 semester hours)

Human Resources Management

Emphasizes principles, methods and procedures in personnel management and labor relations. Topics include job analysis and description, employee motivation, performance appraisal, and union-management relations as they evolve within the business organization. (3 semester hours)

Financial Management

Explores the concepts and techniques for determining the need for the acquisition and management of capital resources for firms including financial analysis, forecasting, leverage, capital budgeting, time value of money, investment banking, common and preferred stock, financing and bond evaluation. (3 semester hours)

Small Business Management

Explores the role of the small business in the American economy. The various forms of business ownership, financing, risk management, human resource management, marketing and the necessary information systems will be examined in depth. Emphasis is placed on the formulation of a comprehensive business plan. (3 semester hours)

Organizational Analysis

Develops the skills necessary to understand the structure and processes of interaction between formal and informal organizations; examines bureaucratic, matrix, cost-centered, global, and post-industrial models; examines the role informal structures play in organizational adaptation through contemporary case analysis. (3 semester hours)

Introduction to Marketing

Emphasizes basic decision-making tools and analytic processes employed by the marketing manager. Topics include product policy and new product development; distribution channels and systems; personal and mass selling techniques; pricing; promotion; and marketing program implementation. (3 semester hours)

Marketing Research

Reviews the identification, collection, and analysis of data for the marketing process. Strengths, limitations, environment, and evaluation of research in the marketing process are covered. (3 semester hours)

Marketing Management

Presents an in-depth study of marketing principles, enabling the student to make effective decisions for all or part of an organization's marketing efforts. Text readings and case studies expose the student to a broad range of marketing problems, large and small, profit and nonprofit, in the retail, wholesale, and manufacturing businesses. (3 semester hours)

COMPUTER SCIENCE

Introduction to Computers

Provides an introduction to computers and the MS-DOS and UNIX operating systems. Word processing, text management programs, spreadsheet and database programs are emphasized. (3 semester hours)

EDUCATION

Educational Psychology

Studies the learning process based upon theories, principles and applications; explores methods and concepts relating to teacher-student interaction; uses case studies to view the teaching process from various perspectives. (3 semester hours)

Adult Learning

Provides a conceptual framework and presents practical considerations important to those engaged in the planning, administration, and delivery of adult education and training programs. (3 semester hours)

Theory and Practice

Involves the student in the development of instructional resources for adult learning, based on the theories and practices presented in *Adult Learning*. (3 semester hours)

Measurements and Evaluation

Covers the basic principles of measurement; characteristics of measurement instruments; administration and scoring of standardized tests; practice in the construction of informal objective tests; statistical treatment and interpretation. (3 semester hours)

The History and Philosophy of American Education

A history of American education from colonial times to the present, emphasizing the basic development and principles of educational philosophy. (3 semester hours)

Theories and Practices of Curriculum Development

Presents a broad overview of the nature, theory, history, and organization of curriculum trends and issues. The course applies acquired knowledge and skills to the development of a relevant curriculum and plan of instruction. Offered in summer residency only. (3 semester hours)

Principles of Teaching

Designed to assist educators involved in instructional roles with varied learning populations, especially adults. Models, strategies, and techniques to make the instructional process optimally effective are emphasized. Students then apply course principles to develop appropriate teaching methodologies. Offered in summer residency only. (3 semester hours)

Educational Administration

Orients prospective educational administrators to the role of management personnel. The course focuses on the role of the administrator, and the behavior, systems analysis, and administration of the school as a social system. Internal operations as well as external social forces which affect the operation of a school system are examined. (3 semester hours)

Practicum for School Nurses

Provides a field experience in a school setting that emphasizes the administrative and education role of the school nurse, with opportunity to integrate concepts and knowledge in practice. Individualized course objectives and evaluation are developed with the student to meet particular state certification requirements. Participants must be registered nurses. (3 semester hours)

ENGLISH

English Composition I, II

Acquaints the student with the principles of grammar and syntax and provides a basis for effective written and interpersonal communication skills. Methods of rhetoric and essay writing, advanced grammar and usage skills are progressively introduced, culminating with preparation and completion of a term paper. The courses must be taken sequentially. (6 semester hours)

English Composition

This is a prerequisite course assigned to students who have completed three semester hours of composition and grammar, expository writing and/or an analogous course, but need an additional three semester hours to satisfy the English requirement. (3 semester hours)

ETHICS

Ethics

A critical study of the most important competing ethical theories enabling students to learn to formulate rational responses to the most pressing practical ethical questions. (3 semester hours)

Basic Two-Dimensional Art

Establishes a foundation in art by introducing the fundamentals, elements, and principles of design. Theories stemming from the context of art history are integrated with practical design problems of the present day. This introductory course gives the necessary background for appreciating art in a variety of media and settings in our contemporary world. (3 semester hours)

HEALTH CARE ADMINISTRATION

American Health Care Systems

An overview of American health care systems. This overview includes an historical perspective of its growth and development, and an assessment and analysis of its current status and future prospects. It focuses on a basic understanding of its diverse and complex subsystems; respective professional and allied health roles; conflicts and contributions in the political, legislative and economics domains, and their complex interdependency. (3 semester hours)

Social Issues in Health and Illness

Encompasses economic, ethical, psychosocial, legal, political, and cultural aspects of people in health and illness. These aspects are specifically analyzed in relationship to access to health care for specific populations including the elderly, the poor, and the homeless in health and illness. The AIDS epidemic is examined along with the responsibilities of health care providers, victims, and high risk populations. Potential strategies for health care administrators are examined, compared, and contrasted in relationship to social issues in health and illness, and the health care delivery system. (3 semester hours)

Aging in America

Presents concepts related to physiological, psychological, and social factors important in the aging process and their implications for health services. Includes an in-depth exploration of the social, political, economic, and ethical parameters of alternative approaches to services delivery. (3 semester hours)

Medical Care Concepts

Explores basic structures and functions of the human body along with related medical terminology. It also discusses conventional medical practice and institutional protocol. It is designed for those students who do not have clinically-oriented education or experience. It will prepare them for work in the health care field, and allow them to better understand other health care courses. (3 semester hours)

Issues in Occupational Health

Provides an overview of the occupational health field, with attention to industrial hygiene, toxicology, epidemiology, and safety engineering. The course concentrates on the development and management of occupational health services by health professionals. Discussions will focus on the identification of problems, creation of strategies and implementation of realistic solutions that address health and safety issues in a variety of occupational settings.

Health Care Administration I

Provides management theory in the health care setting. Focus is placed on the management functions of planning, organizing, staffing, directing, and controlling. Cases are provided for application of management functions within health care. (3 semester hours)

Health Care Administration II

Brings together the current thinking about the management of health care organizations. It is a multidisciplinary approach covering leadership, motivation work design, power, influence, and organizational change. (3 semester hours)

Organizational Analysis

Develops the skills necessary for understanding formal and informal organizational structures and processes. Formal models examined include bureaucratic, matrix, cost-centered, global and post-industrial. The roles of informal organizations in industrial, political and associational institutions are also explored through contemporary case studies. (3 semester hours)

Leadership in Health Administration

Designed to help students assess their current leadership styles and abilities, as well as stimulate further development of their administrative potential and skills. The focus is on the identification of leadership skills needed for management and supervisory roles in a variety of health care settings. The application of theories and skills to realistic situations is emphasized through use of case studies, analysis of the students' experiences, and other teaching methods. (3 semester hours)

Introduction to Public Health

A basic public health course that focuses on administration and practice. Students examine the roots of public health; the bases for public health in sociology, economics, philosophy, government and law; and the management of public health programs. Major emphasis is placed on the concepts of epidemiology, health planning, and community diagnosis illustrated by case studies. Health and the environment are stressed. Environmental hazards, occupational health, and environmental health programs are examined. Maternal and child health, school and adolescent health, aging and behavioral health, (mental health and illness, alcoholism, substance abuse and violence) are addressed. Health care services are discussed and the future of public health is debated. (3 semester hours)

Introduction to Health Policy and Planning

Focuses on policy processes, namely health issues and how they are acted on in government. Students examine the nature of the political process in this country and the issues it generates. Major emphasis is placed on the American way of making policy: problem identification, proposed development, the decision-making process, program results, implementation, and evaluation. The federal budget is analyzed as an inventory of major issue areas. Case studies are used to illustrate areas of the public policy process. Detailed case studies are further analyzed by the student in the areas of problem identification and problem definition, forecasting public options, pricing and public policy, cost-effectiveness and cost-benefit analyses. The concept of planning is interwoven throughout the study of public policy processes to enable the student to understand and use public policy processes as a health care administrator. (3 semester hours)

Foundations of Financial Management in Health Administration

Introduces the student to basic accounting concepts and terminology, providing an overview of accounting principles and procedures. (3 semester hours)

Applied Financial Management in Health Administration

Applies the principles of financial and managerial accounting to the health environment. Mechanisms of rate setting, reimbursement, appli-

cation of budget principles and working capital management are included. (3 semester hours)

Health Care Economics

Introduces the quantitative and qualitative aspects of economics as they apply to the health care system. Government regulation, the effects of inflation, and public policy are explored in detail. (3 semester hours)

Introduction to Long-Term Care

An overview of the long-term care system, with an emphasis on developing an understanding of the populations needing service, available service options, and current issues relating to quality, access, and cost. Also included is a discussion of the relationships among components of the long-term care system and between the long-term care system and other health and social systems. (3 semester hours)

Issues in Long-Term Care Policy

Examines system-wide policy issues involved in the provision of long-term care. The relationship between public and private efforts are considered, as well as the appropriateness of institutional vs. community-based services. There is strong emphasis on issues dealing with access to services, cost of providing those services, and the relationship between cost and access. Medical, socioeconomic, and ethical aspects of long-term care are reviewed relative to potential modifications in health manpower, reimbursement, and public health policy that might improve such care delivery. (3 semester hours)

Long-Term Care Administration

A study of the administration and management of long-term care facilities and organizations. It applies management concepts and techniques learned in prior general management and health care administration courses to the particular problems and needs of long-term care organizations. (3 semester hours)

Long-Term Care Laws and Regulations

Acquaints students with the current state of long-term care regulations as well as the dynamics behind them. It specifically addresses the new federal OBRA (Omnibus Budget Reconciliation Act) regulations which require major changes in the way in which long-term care is delivered. It requires students to demonstrate familiarity with state and local statutes and regulations. (3 semester hours)

Legal Aspects of Health Care Administration

Provides an introduction to law and the legal process as it relates to health administration. It includes areas of public accountability, liability and health care providers, rights of patients, and administrative and business law for health care organizations. (3 semester hours)

Strategic Planning in Health Care Organizations

Presents the student with an introduction to and overview of strategic planning and management. The course will discuss the applicability of strategic planning and management concepts to a variety of organizational situations, with particular emphasis on the health care field. Students learn the steps in the planning process and how to apply that process to actual situations through the use of case studies. (3 semester hours)

Ethics in Health Care

Addresses the application of ethics to various components of the health care delivery system, health care providers as well as administration in institutions. It discusses codes of ethics and handling of ethical problems. (3 semester hours)

Nursing Home Administrator-in-Training

Specifically designed for nursing home administrators. The course requires the student: to develop a program for familiarization with a nursing home, to spend time with, or otherwise become knowledgeable about the functional areas or departments of a nursing home, and to complete six assignments relating to that experience. Content areas covered include: general administration and governance, residence care, personnel management, financial management, physical resource management and safety, marketing, and public/community relations. The length of the AIT period may vary by state, but follow the same standardized guidelines, and include the same number and type of assignments. (6 semester hours)

HISTORY

Western Civilization

A study of the principal civilizations of the world and their basic contributions to the development of a Western tradition. Emphasizes an understanding of the contemporary world and an appreciation of its diverse cultures. (6 semester hours)

History of the United States

Traces the development of the nation from colonial times to the present with specific emphasis on its national formation and expansion; the Civil War and Reconstruction; industrial growth, foreign policy, and world-power status. (6 semester hours)

HUMANITIES

Introduction to Literature

Provides a survey designed to deepen understanding and appreciation of the forms of literature, especially the novel, short story, poetry, and drama. (3 semester hours)

American Literature I

Includes a review of selected religious and political writings of the colonies and continues with a major focus on works by major authors of the nineteenth century, including Hawthorne, Poe, Melville, Emerson, and Thoreau. (3 semester hours)

American Literature II

Studies selected readings by late nineteenth- and twentieth-century authors up to the present, with an emphasis on works that are representative of central trends in modern fiction, including regionalism, realism, naturalism, and psychological realism. (3 semester hours)

Major British Writers I

Studies the chief literary periods and major writers of English literature from Old English times to the twentieth century. (3 semester hours)

Major British Writers II

Studies the chief literary periods and major writers of English literature from the Romantic period to the twentieth century. (3 semester hours)

Military History to the Present Age

A survey of military history which traces the evolution of warfare, military technology, strategy, and tactics to the present. It is not necessary for students to be familiar with military history in order to benefit from the course, although prior familiarity with historical thinking would be helpful. The course complements the history of Western civilization by placing its subject, war and militarism, in a mixed context of culture, science, technology, economics, and administration. Militarism is seen as a process which occurs in combination with many other factors and forces. (3 semester hours)

Comparative Religions

An introductory-level course which describes the world's major religions. Neither esoteric nor sectarian, it acquaints the student with historical and literary aspects of Hindu and Buddhist thought, moving to Western religions. It considers the nature of other religions and cults, devoting the final segment to the study of the Judeo-Christian tradition. (3 semester hours)

MATHEMATICS

College Mathematics

Employs algebra as the basis for further study, emphasizing applicability to accounting, statistics, and business administration. (3 semester hours)

Elementary Statistics

An introduction to statistical methods of data analysis. Topics include descriptive statistics, elementary probability theory, random variables and probability distributions, hypothesis testing and inferential statistics, nonparametric methods, analysis of variance, and regression. (3 semester hours)

MUSIC APPRECIATION

Music Appreciation

Discusses the principles of musical structure, media of performance and characteristic styles to develop intelligent habits of listening. Representative works by outstanding composers of each stylistic period are reviewed. Attendance at a symphony concert is required. (3 semester hours)

NATURAL SCIENCE

Human Ecology I

Addresses environmental problems created by man's activities—use of land, agricultural policy, and exploitation of resources. Problems and potential solutions are examined from ecological, economic, and ethical perspectives; course readings are drawn from each of these areas. (3 semester hours)

Human Ecology II

A continuation of the above course focusing attention on human health and the man-made environment. It entails a survey of environmentally-caused diseases, their prognosis and treatment, and the role of government and industry in their prevention. (3 semester hours)

Nutrition

Studies the principles of normal nutrition, including digestion, absorption, and metabolism of nutrients. Assessment of nutritional status and the normal nutrient requirements of different age levels are explored. Nutritional principles are then applied to therapeutic diets used in diseased states. (3 semester hours)

PHILOSOPHY

Introduction to Philosophy

Studies the most important philosophers in the history of philosophy with an emphasis on the seminal ideas that have shaped western culture. Includes topics in logic, philosophy of being, philosophy of knowledge, philosophy of God, and social and political philosophy. (3 semester hours)

Philosophy of Human Nature

Studies the nature of human existence and its relationship to reality. Includes topics in metaphysics, epistemology, and ethics. (3 semester hours)

PSYCHOLOGY

Introduction to Psychology

An introduction to the basic concepts in psychology. Topics will include research methods, learning, memory, intelligence, personality, abnormal psychology, and social processes. (3 semester hours)

Developmental Psychology

A review of major theories of the development of social, cognitive, moral, and symbolic functioning in children. Focus will be on the works of Freud, Baldwin, Piaget, Kohlberg, as well as contemporary cultural-context theory. (3 semester hours)

Psychopathology

An overview course in introductory psychopathology. Theoretical, empirical, and clinical discussion of some "disorders" and discussion of diagnosis and therapy are presented in a unified view. (3 semester hours)

Personality Theory

This course will critically examine the major theoretical approaches to understanding personality, including the works of Freud, Jung, Skinner, Maslow, and Rogers. Methods of assessment such as self-report and projective testing will be discussed. The theories, methodologies, and research results pertinent to a number of topics in the psychology of personality will be addressed. (3 semester hours)

Learning

An intensive examination of how behavioral potentiality is acquired and maintained. The course focuses on Pavlovian and operant conditioning in animals and human subjects. Special topics include the application of these principles to psychotherapy, drug addiction, self-control, and biological influences and constraints on learning. (3 semester hours)

Social Psychology

Examines the way individuals are affected by and interact in social situations. Topics include attitude formation and change, the attribution process, intergroup conflict and conflict resolution, leadership, the social psychology of health and aging. (3 semester hours)

Adolescent Psychology

A theoretical exploration of adolescents' development in light of the physiological, cognitive, and social changes of this period. Class discussions and student assignments will serve to relate the research and theory presented in the text with tangible adolescent behaviors. (3 semester hours)

Educational Psychology

Studies the learning process based upon theories, principles and applications. Explores methods and concepts relating to teacher-student interaction. Uses case studies to view the teaching process from various perspectives. (3 semester hours)

Introduction to Counseling

This course is an examination of major forms of counseling and psychotherapy, including the psychoanalytic, cognitve-behavioral, humanistic, and existential approaches. There is an emphasis both on techniques of therapy and on the underlying theoretical rationale for the various methods. (3 semester hours)

Human Relations in Business

Examines psychological principles as applied to problems of communication, group dynamics, morale, and executive leadership. (3 semester hours)

Death and Dying

Views death as an issue for the living, who must contend with personal attitudes toward death, grieving, loss of loved ones, and their own notions or absence of notions about immortality. Personal and societal issues are explored along with the notion of death as a passage into another form of life. Those who do not have a notion of immortality are invited to share their perspectives, thereby broadening a collective outlook. (3 semester hours)

Measurements and Evaluation

Covers the basic principles of measurement; characteristics of measurement instruments; administration and scoring of standardized tests; practice in the construction of informal objective tests; statistical treatment and interpretation. (3 semester hours)

Industrial Psychology

Emphasizes the application of psychological principles to the industrial setting. Emphasis will be on a practical understanding of the problems of personnel motivation; communication; leadership; industrial organization; group dynamics; and attitude formation and change. Current principles, theories, and practices relating to the psychological assessment of employees and executives are addressed. (3 semester hours)

RADIOLOGIC TECHNOLOGY

Current Topics in Radiology

Examines the leading developments in the field of radiology and x-ray technology, including such topics as nuclear accident management; radon as a health hazard; total quality management; and quality assurance, including organization and record keeping. (3 semester hours)

Senior Seminar

Examines case studies and published research in preparation for discussion on topics such as workers' rights, including workplace conduct; EEOC regulations; employee/employer rights; leadership and supervision, ethical considerations, medical billing, and equipment purchase. (3 semester hours)

RELIGIOUS STUDIES

Introduction to the New Testament

Introduces the cultural, historical, and religious milieu in which Christianity emerged, emphasizing the Gospels of Matthew, Mark, Luke, and John. (3 semester hours)

Introduction to the Old Testament

Examines the literature and ideas of the Hebrew Bible (Old Testament), focusing on creation, election, and covenant. (3 semester hours)

Faith in the Contemporary World

Studies the Biblical and traditional meaning of faith with special emphasis given to the New Testament concept of faith. The personal structure rather than merely propositional character of faith is stressed as the distinctive feature of the faith required of the Christian in today's society. Offered in summer residency only. (3 semester hours)

SOCIOLOGY

Principles of Sociology

Examines the concepts and methods of research used to understand human life within the social groups which make up society. A study of culture, socialization, and social organization is undertaken in order to understand the social institutions (family, religion, education, economic, and political order). Students also examine issues which surface in medicine and health care, war and peace, gender, ethnicity, race and age. Finally, students study a variety of social processes which facilitate social change. (3 semester hours)

Social Problems

Examines the major social problems and issues in a modern industrial and post-industrial society. The course explores both sides of each issue and critically evaluates proposed solutions. The student will be given the opportunity to develop skills in the analysis of social problems, and to make informed judgments about their causes and solutions. Special emphasis is given to problems of current interest. (3 semester hours)

Social Psychology

Examines the way individuals are affected by and interact in social situations. Topics include attitude formation and change, the attribution process, intergroup conflict and conflict resolution, leadership, the social psychology of health and aging. (3 semester hours)

The Family

Examines the social theory relevant to contemporary family life. The focus includes the changing relationships between the family and society along the following dimensions: dating and courtship behaviors, husband and wife sex roles, parenting, socialization processes, family forms, coping with conflict, dissolution of the family and alternative life-styles. (3 semester hours)

Modern Community

Involves an analysis of the American community as a social system. This course draws on the rich sociological literature in community studies. Topics include culture and personality, local institutions, adaptive change, social class, power, conflict and community development. (3 semester hours)

Criminology

Examines various theories purported to explain social disorder as manifested in crime and delinquency. Methods of crime prevention, theories and practices for the punishment and treatment of criminals are emphasized. (3 semester hours)

Aging in America

Presents concepts related to physiological, psychological, and social factors important in the aging process and their implications for health services. Includes an in-depth exploration of the social, political, economic, and ethical parameters of alternative approaches to services delivery. (3 semester hours)

Race and Ethnic Relations

Explores patterns of intergroup relationships between various religious and ethnic groups that comprise American society. Processes of racial and cultural contact between peoples, especially in regard to the origin and development of American minority groups are explored. Focus is on integration, segregation, and cultural pluralism. Social theories of racial and ethnic aggression and minority responses to oppression are also examined. (3 semester hours)

Organizational Analysis

Develops the skills necessary for understanding formal and informal organizational structures and processes. Formal models examined include bureaucratic, matrix, cost-centered, global and post-industrial. The roles of informal organizations in industrial, political, and associational institutions are also explored through contemporary case studies. (3 semester hours)

GRADUATE COURSES

HEALTH SERVICES ADMINISTRATION

United States Health Care Systems

Provides a comprehensive overview of the overlapping health care systems in the United States. It describes and assesses the various system levels, components, and the interrelationship of these elements to the total organization of health services delivery. The student is expected to develop an appreciation for the complexities and subtleties of health services and understand the biological, behavioral, cultural and organizational factors affecting the use, organization, and outcome of health care resources. The roles of hospitals, public health agencies, proprietary interests, and other service systems are examined. Current system dilemmas and issues are identified. (3 semester hours)

Organization Theory and Behavior

Examines major theories of organization and considers implications of these concepts for managerial effectiveness. Motivation, incentives, group dynamics, learning models, and control are reviewed, together with other aspects of organizational behavior. Approaches to organizational change and development are emphasized. Students develop a greater capacity to perceive organizational phenomena, address administrative problems, and better understand the implications of leadership. (3 semester hours)

Health Care Administration

Introduces students to operations management. Topics, such as organizational structure; management planning; use and control of resources; problem solving; information; decision making; and the roles of senior managers are studied in the context of different health care delivery settings. Goal-setting and coordination, among key health care workers, are studied in connection with professional values, conflict resolution, and quality assessment. (3 semester hours)

Management Information Systems

Focuses on the analysis of health care information needs and decision-making processes, and the development of appropriate information to meet these needs. Major types of information systems, including financial, patient care and strategic management are examined. Students design and plan the implementation of a management information system, including data base construction and report presentation. (3 semester hours)

Health Care Financial Management

This course is oriented to the contemporary role of a senior health services manager, and is designed to give the student both conceptual understanding and applied skills in financial management. The course reviews accounting concepts and procedures, and internal control. It emphasizes the interpretation of financial statements and operational budgeting. It examines cost analysis, cost allocation, capital budgeting, and rate setting. The strategic role of financial management in today's health care organization is the unifying theme of the course. This is a required residency course and is held on campus during the summer. (3 semester hours)

Research Methods

Examines methods for planning and conducting research and analyzing data. Particular attention is given to data collection techniques, and the application of findings to the study of health needs or management systems. Statistical methods of data analysis applicable to health research interests are reviewed. This is a required residency course and is held on campus during the summer. (3 semester hours)

Health Economics

Discusses economics as a basic set of concepts for understanding of public policy issues in health care. The relationships between economic analysis and value judgments underlying different public policies and issues are covered in detail. The course emphasizes the financing and delivery of personal medical services, health care costs, and national health insurance. It also examines public policies appropriate to achieving economic efficiency and equity in the financing and delivery of personal health services. (3 semester hours)

Health Care for the Aged

Examines the types of acute and chronic illness that prevail among elderly persons, together with their physical and social manifestations. It identifies modes of health service that predominantly serve the elderly problems of coherence in their delivery, and their linkage with other services throughout the health care system. Public policies and financing mechanisms will be reviewed as to their impacts on service delivery and health status of the aged. Students consider a model health care system for the aged, incorporating the delivery of long-term and acute services. (3 semester hours)

Ethical and Legal Perspectives

Considers ethical questions involving inpatient care and the management of health services. A professional ethic is defined through an examination of the relationships between health providers and patients and the norms appropriate to their respective conduct. Issues relating to clinical ethics, informed consent of the patient, use of life support systems, and care of the profoundly retarded, critically injured, premature infants, and the elderly are discussed from moral, legal, and religious perspectives. Particular attention is given to the legal issues inherent in the provision of health services. Means of anticipating, preventing, or responding to legal issues are considered and the appropriate role of the health manager in legal matters is examined. (3 semester hours)

Health Care Marketing

This course relates key marketing functions to the health care industry. It integrates health care services development with promotion activities, pricing, and the distribution of services. Emphasis is placed on the managerial aspects of marketing strategies necessary for survival in a competitive marketplace. Further attention is given to the design of services and programs that respond to market interests and consumer preferences. (3 semester hours)

Human Resources Management

The course addresses the management of personnel in health care organizations, including organizational structure, staffing, unionism, worker productivity, and performance evaluation. Managerial tools used in recruitment, personnel supervision, organizational control, and leadership are reviewed. Case studies are used to engage the student in the practical application of theories and practices of personnel management, quality of work life, manpower planning, management development, and compensation systems. (3 semester hours)

Labor Relations

This course historically reviews the growth of the American labor movement and examines contemporary issues and problems connected with the collective bargaining process, wages, productivity, seniority, and union security. Characteristics of American unions and their influence upon managerial functions and the bargaining process are examined. (3 semester hours)

Ambulatory Care Administration

Focuses on the growing provision of health services by practitioners and health care delivery organizations outside of the institution. The relationship between ambulatory care programs and inpatient hospitalization is examined. Staffing, payment for services, quality assurance,

physical facilities, continuity of care, and current strategic developments are studied. (3 semester hours)

Medical Sociology

The course addresses attitudes and beliefs about health and illness; social factors in the incidence and distribution of illness; and the development of formal and informal organizations that affect a society's overall mental and physical well-being. Social, cultural, and historical dimensions of disease; individual and group responses to disease; and mechanisms established to prevent, treat, and monitor disease are considered. (3 semester hours)

Gerontology

Discusses current theories of psychosocial and biological processes of aging, and how these interact and affect the aging individual. It examines the environment of the older person, including housing, transportation, and access to support services. Special issues involving rural, urban, minority, and poor elderly persons will be examined. The emerging implications of leisure, as well as employment of the elderly, are considered. (3 semester hours)

Environmental Health

Explores the effects of human-environmental interaction on physical, mental, and social well-being. Environmental conditions that minimize transmission of communicable diseases, exposure to toxic substances, hazardous working conditions, and accidents are included. The course reviews health control programs and public policy decisions necessary to create an appropriate environment. (3 semester hours)

Seminar in Health Management

This course must be taken in summer residency. It is an integrative seminar designed to synthesize learning from previous courses. Health care systems theories, concepts, policies, and practices are reviewed in a series of case studies which emphasize problem solving and decision making. Students have an opportunity, in an interactive setting with faculty and peers, to sharpen their skills and understanding. Issues of administrative ethics, organizational politics, and management effectiveness are also examined. (3 semester hours)

Strategic Management

This is an advanced course in management concepts and theory. It summarizes the state of the art of business policy and strategic management, synthesizing both prescriptive and descriptive ideas of theorists, practitioners, and researchers. An overview of current practices and notable advances in strategic management is emphasized. Case studies applied to health care management assist students facing the managerial challenges of the 1990s and beyond. (3 semester hours)

Health Policy and Politics

The course is designed to increase the student's understanding of policy formulation which impacts the provision of health services. The course discusses problems of defining and analyzing policy, so that decision makers can better assess the consequences of their actions. An examination is made of the forces of change in society as they affect policy formulation. It explores how political choices must be made with respect to social needs and the relationship of cultural values to proposed solutions. (3 semester hours)

Applied Research Paper/Project

This course aims to integrate the curriculum, enabling the student to demonstrate mastery of subject matter leaned from various courses, as will as skills in research, reasoning, and writing. The student works directly with the instructor in a customized applied research experience that draws on the student's interests and abilities. (3 semester hours)

Sam Houston State University
Correspondence Course Division
Sam Houston Avenue
P.O. Box 2359
Huntsville, Texas 77341-2359 (409) 294-1005

Description:
Founded in 1879, Sam Houston State University is a publicly-supported liberal arts and teacher training institution. It provides the opportunity for qualified individuals to obtain college credit through correspondence course study. This service has proven highly beneficial for those who have chosen to drop out of school for a time and desire to continue their college work; for teachers who wish to take courses leading toward additional certification or who are in the need of additional study in the disciplines they teach; and for citizens who wish to broaden their learning. Hundreds of students both off and on campus have earned college credit over the years through the method of independent study.

Faculty:
Gail M. Wright, Coordinator, Correspondence Course Division. A faculty of 36 serves the correspondence course program.

Academic Levels:
College

Degree/Certificate Programs:
A maximum of eighteen semester hours of correspondence study may be applied toward a baccalaureate degree at the University. Correspondence study may also lead to a certificate or diploma. Correspondence credits transferred-in must be approved by the Director of Admissions.

Admission Requirements:
Entrance requirements are the same for correspondence courses as for any other college course. Students must be eligible for admission to resident work before they are eligible to enroll in a correspondence course. Students must furnish official transcripts for each college attended other than Sam Houston State University.

Tuition:
$135 per course; each course carries 3 semester hours. All fees payable at time of enrollment. MasterCard and Visa accepted. Refund policy: before the enrollment is complete, 100 percent; one week or less, 80 percent; between one and two weeks, 60 percent; between two and three weeks, 40 percent; between three and four weeks, 20 percent; no refund after four weeks.

Enrollment Period:
Maximum time allowed to complete a course is one year. Minimum time is sixty days. Extension of time for three months may be granted upon payment of a fee; only one extension allowed. Students may begin a course at any time. It is recommended that correspondence students enroll in only one course at a time.

Equipment Requirements:
All textbooks are paid for by the student and are in addition to the tuition fees. They may be ordered from the University Bookstore.

Credit and Grading:
A final examination will be given in each course. All examinations must be taken at the University or an approved institution. Grading system: A through C. Minimum passing grade is C.

Library Services:
All enrolled correspondence students have access to the Newton Gresham Library (in-house only); no check-out privileges are granted.

Accreditations:
Southern Association of Colleges and Schools. Member of: National University Continuing Education Association.

COLLEGE COURSES

ACCOUNTING
Principles of Accounting
Course 231. A study of the conceptual framework which explains financial accounting with an emphasis on the business and economic information generated in the accounting process. Students are encouraged to understand the increasing prominence of accounting in virtually all aspects of business activity. (3 semester hours)

Course 232. The study of financial accounting is continued from the course above. Partnership and corporation accounting, cost accounting, and analysis of financial statements are the areas emphasized. An introduction to managerial uses of accounting is included. (3 semester hours)

Managerial Accounting
Further development of financial accounting concepts and interpretation and further study of management uses of accounting data. It includes a study of basic accounting concepts; interpretation of accounting reports, cost control and analysis and methods of measuring performance. (3 semester hours)

AGRICULTURE
Principles of Agriculture Economics and Marketing
This course is designed to give the student an introduction to economic problems related to agriculture at the farm or ranch and national level. (3 semester hours)

Introduction to Marketing of Agricultural Products
General principles involved in the movement of agricultural commodities from farmer to consumer. Use of outlook information, market price determination, and methods of selling farm products. (3 semester hours)

Agribusiness Organization and Management
Principles of management relevant to agribusiness firms, i.e., procurement of inputs, processing, merchandising, storage, pricing, and transportation. (3 semester hours)

ART
Introduction to the Visual Arts
The presentation of the theory and philosophy of art through an

analysis of the principles, problems, and techniques of the artist. (3 semester hours)

Pre-Renaissance Art History

A survey of prehistoric, ancient, and medieval art. (3 semester hours)

BUSINESS ADMINISTRATION

Business Principles

The purposes of this course are to give students a general survey course in business and to give prospective business workers an intelligent understanding of common business transactions. (3 semester hours)

Business Legal Environment

This course covers legal environment in which individuals and businesses operate. The specific subjects of Origin and Source of Law, Court Systems, Constitutions, Business Entities, Torts, Administrative Agencies, and Consumer Law are covered. (3 semester hours)

Business Law

The focus of this course is on areas of modern commercial law faced by businesses and business-related professions. Specific subjects covered include Contracts, Sales, Commercial Paper, Real Property, Personal Property, Bankruptcy, Wills, and Secured Transactions. (3 semester hours)

Real Estate Law

This course covers the legal aspects of real estate including the legal principles and the legal instruments used in real estate transactions. (3 semester hours)

CHEMISTRY

Introductory Inorganic and Environmental Chemistry Lecture

The elements and their compounds are considered from a nontechnical standpoint with emphasis placed on more familiar materials. (3 semester hours)

Introductory Organic and Biochemistry Lecture

An orientation in organic chemistry is given in the first part of the course to allow treatment of the chemistry of nutrition and other biochemical aspects given in the last part. (3 semester hours)

ECONOMICS

Introduction to Economics

This course combines microeconomics and macroeconomic principles so that students will be introduced to many aspects of a modern market economy. Student will be exposed to material to help them develop an understanding of economic thinking, and how to use economic theory and principles to critically evaluate economic problems, issues, and controversies. (3 semester hours)

Principles of Microeconomics

Basic economic principles including price theory, analysis of the firm, competition and monopoly, and the distribution of income. (3 semester hours)

Principles of Macroeconomics

The economic role of government, public finance and taxation, national income analysis, national income theory, money and banking, economic fluctuations and growth, and international trade and finance. (3 semester hours)

ENGLISH

Readings in Literature of the Western World

Readings in the classical, medieval, and modern masterpieces of the Western World. (3 semester hours)

Readings in Literature of Great Britain and Its Commonwealth

A study of a variety of works of poetry, fiction, and drama by the literary masters of England, Scotland, and Ireland. (3 semester hours)

Readings in Literature of the United States

A study of American literary works from various genres and periods. (3 semester hours)

Introduction to Technical Writing

A course in the special problems of technical literature and technical report writing. (3 semester hours)

American Masterworks

Outstanding short fiction, selected novels, selected poetry, selected nonfiction; the best of four genres in American literature. (3 semester hours)

Shakespeare

A survey of Shakespeare's major work. (3 semester hours)

Introductory Creative Writing

Directed writing in fiction, poetry, and drama. (3 semester hours)

Early English Masterworks

A study of the major figures of English literature from the beginning until 1798. (3 semester hours)

Later English Masterworks

A study of the major figures in English literature from 1798 to the present. (3 semester hours)

American Literature: 1820s to 1860s

A study of the emergence of a distinctive American literary art, including such writers as Poe, Emerson, Thoreau, Hawthorne, Melville, and Whitman. (3 semester hours)

Drama of Shakespeare's Contemporaries

The development of the drama in England, the predecessors and contemporaries of Shakespeare. (3 semester hours)

FINANCE

Personal Finance

A study of the problems of personal financial management. Topics include savings, risks, investment considerations, insurance, taxation, governmental programs in financial planning, etc. (3 semester hours)

Financial Institutions and Markets

This course will explore the structure of the financial system with emphasis on the role, operations, and regulations of financial institutions and markets, including international. The nature, participants, instruments, and relationships of the money and capital markets will be examined. (3 semester hours)

Life Insurance

Principles of life insurance, business and personal uses of life insurance, classification and analysis of policies, reserves and policy values, organization and administration of life insurance companies are studied. (3 semester hours)

GEOGRAPHY

Geographic Skills

An introductory course designed to acquaint students with the basic principles of geography. Attention will be focused upon the spatial interrelationships which exist between man and his environment, the geographic region and selected geographic skills to include latitude and longitude, earth-sun relations, time, map scale, graphs, and the use of roadmaps and the atlas. (3 semester hours)

Cultural Geography

An evolutionary examination of man as an agent of change within the environment. Innovation, development, and diffusion of agriculture, language, religion, music, sport, and other attainments and institutions will be examined for their expression of the landscape. (3 semester hours)

GEOLOGY

Physical Geology

An introduction to the materials, processes, and structure of the earth. Topics include earthquakes, volcanoes, plate tectonics, mountain building, weathering and erosion, glaciation, oceans, and mineral resources. (3 semester hours)

Historical Geology

An introduction to the history of the earth and its past inhabitants. This course gives a broad overview of the various kinds of animals and plants that have existed on earth in the geologic past as revealed by the fossil record. Past land-sea relationships and ancient environments are also discussed. (3 semester hours)

HEALTH EDUCATION

Lifestyles and Wellness

This course explores a variety of health issues which influence the well-being of an individual throughout the life cycle. The student is given an opportunity to develop a personal philosophy of wellness and self responsibility for health through self assessment, investigation of personal environmental and social factors affecting one's health and examination of alternatives in lifestyles. (3 semester hours)

Child and Adolescent Health

This course will focus on the causes, recognition, and assessment of health among children and adolescents: pattern of growth and development, common childhood illnesses and health problems, and factors which influence the maintenance of health and the prevention of illness among youth. This course is designed for any student who is likely to be working with young people. (3 semester hours)

HISTORY

United States History to 1876

The colonial origins of the United States and growth of the Republic to 1876. (3 semester hours)

United States History Since 1876

Continuing survey of the history of the United States to the present. (3 semester hours)

World History from the Dawn of Civilization Through the Middle Ages

A survey of world history from the dawn of civilization in Mesopotamia, China, India, Egypt, and Mesoamerica through the Middle Ages in Europe and Asia. The Middle Ages, Renaissance, and Reformation, as well as the rise of nation states and the commercial economy are stressed as background to modern history. (3 semester hours)

World History from the Renaissance to the Age of Imperialism

A survey of world history since the sixteenth century. Special attention is given to European expansion overseas, imperialism and colonization, the Industrial Revolution, the Enlightenment, the French Revolution, nineteenth century nationalism and democracy, and the colonial rebellions in Africa, Latin America, and Asia. Such 20-century problems as World War I, World War II, the Cold War, and the collapse of the Soviet Union are also considered. (3 semester hours)

Texas and the Southwest

As a study of the Greater Southwest, this course surveys Spanish expansion and the Spanish-French rivalry in the lower Mississippi region and Texas. Special emphasis is given to geographic factors and cultural developments. (3 semester hours)

HOME ECONOMICS

Consumer Education

Study of consumer goods and services as related to the home. It includes the study of family purchasing, advertising, commodity information, merchandise standardization, branding, grading, marketing, and consumer legislation. (3 semester hours)

INDUSTRIAL EDUCATION

Engineering Drawing

This is a recognized standard course in beginning drawing for engineering and industrial education. (3 semester hours)

KINESIOLOGY

Foundations of Kinesiology

This course serves as a base for all kinesiology courses. Units will include historical development, philosophical implications, physical fitness, scientific bases of movement, and educational values of kinesiology. (3 semester hours)

Administration of Kinesiology and Recreation

The first half of this course is concerned with the organization and administration of physical education and recreation in the public schools; the second half, with the organization, administration, and business management of a high school athletic program. (3 semester hours)

MANAGEMENT

Principles of Management

This course is concerned with the principles and methods used in managing and operating business and industrial enterprises. A study is made of the activities of planning, organizing, and controlling the functions essential for business operation. (3 semester hours)

Human Behavior in Business

Advanced study of individual and group behavior in organizations and how it affects the achievement of organizational objectives. (3 semester hours)

Personnel Management

Personnel policies and administration, job classification and analysis; wage plans and employment procedure; employment interviewing and testing; employee training and evaluation; labor turnover; legislation affecting labor problems are studied. (3 semester hours)

MARKETING

Principles of Marketing

This course includes marketing functions, transportation, assembling, storage, trade channels, cost, cooperative marketing, trade association, price policies, and market analysis, marketing structures and agencies, types of middlemen, international marketing, and current marketing practices. (3 semester hours)

Retailing

The evolution of retailing, the scope of retailing, store location, store layout, organization, the customer, buying markets, receiving and marketing merchandise, mark-up, stock control, merchandise plan, fashions, retail credit, accounting, insurance, advertising, and sales promotion are studied in this course. (3 semester hours)

MATHEMATICS

College Algebra

Topics include a brief review of introductory algebra, variation, elementary theory of equations, functions (including exponential and logarithmic), inequalities, systems of equations, and other related topics. (3 semester hours)

Plane Trigonometry

Topics include coordinate systems, circular functions, solutions of triangles, identities, trigonometric equations, and inverse functions. (3 semester hours)

Elementary Mathematics of Finance

Mathematical principles and techniques are applied to problems which arise in finance. Topics include simple interest, compound interest, installment buying, annuities, and perpetuities. (3 semester hours)

PHILOSOPHY

Introduction to Philosophy

A general examination of the fields and issues of philosophy as discussed by both classical and modern philosophers. Philosophical problems discussed include the existence of God, the nature of knowledge and truth, the issue of human free will, and theories of moral judgment. (3 semester hours)

Critical Thinking

Designed to improve students' ability to think critically. This course covers the fundamentals of deductive reasoning, the identification of common fallacies, and an introduction to inductive reasoning, as well as sensitizing the students to some of the ways information is distorted, e.g., by advertising and news management. (3 semester hours)

PHOTOGRAPHY

History of Photography

A study is made of the history of photography from its earliest beginnings. Technical, visual, aesthetic and social aspects are considered. (3 semester hours)

POLITICAL SCIENCE

Principles of American Government - National and State

This course deals with the origin, development, and Constitution of the American governmental system, citizenship and civil rights, suffrage, the national party system, the national executive, organization of congress, national judiciary, federal-state relations, and the Constitution of the State of Texas. This course meets the legislative requirement for a course on the Constitutions of the United States and Texas for teacher certification. (3 semester hours)

American Public Policy

This course is a study of national and state policy. Topics include foreign relations, labor, agriculture, civil liberties, and environmental policy. (3 semester hours)

PSYCHOLOGY

Introduction to Psychology

This course is designed to be a broad survey of the field of psychology covering such topics as learning, perception, personality, development, psychopathology, etc. It covers both the theoretical basis and the empirical content of these areas. (3 semester hours)

Psychology of Adjustment

A study is made of the dynamics of human behavior applying psychological theory to the development of the wholesome, well adjusted personality. Techniques for managing stress, reducing anxiety, coping with anger, increasing assertiveness, and achieving self-control are considered. (3 semester hours)

SOCIOLOGY

Principles of Sociology

Introduction to the discipline with a focus on concepts and principles used in the study of group life, social institutions, and social processes. (3 semester hours)

Social Problems

Application of sociological principles to major problems of the contemporary society. Special attention is given to mental disorders, use and abuse of drugs and alcohol, sexual deviance and crime and delinquency; problems of youth and the family in contemporary society; institutionalized aspects of inequality, prejudice and discrimination; and population and environmental concerns. (3 semester hours)

Physical Anthropology and Archaeology

Origins and relationships of extinct forms of nonhuman primates and man. Special attention is given to a survey of the methods of archaeological investigation. (3 semester hours)

Cultural Anthropology

Cultural and social organization among primitive or preliterate societies, marriage, property, religion, magic, and tribal control; significance of the study of primitive cultures for understanding of urban industrial civilizations. (3 semester hours)

Sociological Theory

A historical survey of the development of sociological thought. Emphasis is placed upon the growth of sociology as a discipline, major areas of interest, and major contributors. (3 semester hours)

Marriage and the Family

An sociological examination of marriage and family life. Problems of courtship, mate selection, and marriage adjustment in modern American society. (3 semester hours)

Minority Relations

A sociological description, analysis, and interpretation of racial and ethnic relations in America. Special emphasis is placed upon: key sociological concepts relative to the processes of intergroup relations—assimilation, conflict, segregation and stratification; facts and myths about race; and reactions of minority groups to their status of disadvantage. (3 semester hours)

Indians of North America

Anthropological approaches are used in examining the origin and comparative development of native Indian cultures from the earliest peopling of the continent. Special attention is placed upon ecological and cultural factors as antecedent to the study of selected tribes of contemporary North America. (3 semester hours)

Savannah State College

Department of Correspondence Study
112-C Hill Hall
P.O. Box 20372
Savannah, Georgia 31404   (912) 356-2243

Description:

Savannah State College is a unit of the University System of Georgia offering both undergraduate and graduate programs. Correspondence courses are offered through the Coastal Georgia Center, a joint effort of Armstrong State College and Savannah State College.

Faculty:

Rosemary Banks, Program Specialist. Faculty of 12.

Academic Levels:

College

Degree/Certificate Programs:

All correspondence courses are equivalent to 5 quarter hours or 3⅓ semester hours of undergraduate credit. Up to 45 quarter hours may be applied to a degree at Savannah State College; no more than 50 percent of required courses for the major or minor may be by correspondence.

Admission Requirements:

Graduation from an accredited high school or a high school approved by Savannah State College; GED accepted. Resident students of Savannah State College are required to secure permission for enrollment from the Vice President of Academic Affairs.

Tuition:

Average tuition $165 per course. Contact the college for current tuition and fees. Refund of tuition less a withdrawal fee if withdrawal is within six weeks and if no more than three lessons have been submitted; no refunds after six weeks. Federally funded grant programs available; contact the Vice President for Business and Finance, Savannah State College.

Enrollment Period:

The maximum time to complete a course is one year; a six-month extension may be granted upon payment of an extension fee.

Equipment Requirements:

Textbooks and materials are to be obtained from the College Bookstore at the student's expense.

Credit and Grading:

Examinations must be proctored.

Accreditations:

Southern Association of Colleges and Schools. Member of: National University Continuing Education Association.

COLLEGE COURSES

BUSINESS

Introduction to Business

(5 quarter hours)

GEOGRAPHY

World and Human Geography

(5 quarter hours)

HISTORY

History of World Civilization (to 1500)

(5 quarter hours)

History of World Civilization (since 1500)

(5 quarter hours)

History of the United States and Afro-Americans through the Civil War

(5 quarter hours)

History of the United States and Afro-Americans since the Civil War

(5 quarter hours)

History of Early Europe (to 1789)

(5 quarter hours)

History of Modern Europe (since 1789)

(5 quarter hours)

MATHEMATICS

College Algebra

(5 quarter hours)

POLITICAL SCIENCE

American Government

(5 quarter hours)

American Constitutional Law

(5 quarter hours)

Black Politics

(5 quarter hours)

The American Political Process

(5 quarter hours)

PSYCHOLOGY

General Psychology

(5 quarter hours)

SOCIOLOGY

Introduction to Sociology

(5 quarter hours)

Saybrook Institute

Option for Non-Matriculated Students
1550 Sutter Street
San Francisco, California 94109
                    (415) 441-5034

Saybrook Institute

Description:

Saybrook Institute is a graduate school and research center designed specifically for adult learners interested in producing innovative work which challenges mainstream assumptions about the study of human beings and social systems. The master's and doctoral programs in Psychology and Human science are characterized by: (1) faculty and student inquiry in the field of human science, (2) innovative teaching, and (3) the development of new methods of research. The curriculum is structured within the larger framework of the human sciences. The human science approach asserts that human beings and human nature have a uniqueness which natural science methodologies alone cannot fully capture and delineate.

Another unique aspect of Saybrook Institute is its at-a-distance-learning format, structured to meet the personal and professional needs of adult learners. This format expands upon the European tutorial model which emphasizes a one-to-one teaching/learning process. Using learning guides, students complete coursework at home. Progress is guided by faculty, who communicate by telephone, mail, or computer telecommunication. Relationships between students and faculty are established and renewed at semiannual residential meetings. The National Meetings provide a week of intense and enriched learning. This structure works especially well for mature students who wish to control the pace, the scope, and the process of learning.

Students may concentrate their studies in the areas of: Consciousness Studies, Health Studies, Clinical Inquiry, Systems Inquiry, Interarea Studies. Non-matriculated students may enroll in the only one course per semester.

Faculty:

Dr. J. Bruce Francis, President; Joan Sugata, Coordinator, Non-Matriculation Program.

Academic Levels:

Graduate

Degree/Certificate Programs:

Participation in the non-matriculated program does not guarantee admission into a degree program. Non-matriculated students may transfer up to 30 units of previously completed graduate-level coursework to the required 72 units for a doctoral degree, and 6 graduate units of the required 30 units for a master's degree. Non-matriculated students may transfer an additional 12 units of Saybrook credit for either a doctoral degree or a master's degree.

Admission Requirements:

To receive graduate credit, students must have a baccalaureate degree or equivalent. Non-matriculated students may enroll in one course per semester. Students may take any course offered during a given semester as long as space is available.

Tuition:

$6,825 per year. Contact the school for current tuition rate. A student's official withdrawal date is the day the institute receives first notification of the student's intention to withdraw. Fees are refunded according to the following: 100 percent if prior to beginning of semester; 50 percent within the first 3 months; no refund after 3 months.

Enrollment Period:

Enrollment is on a semester basis; courses must be completed within the semester. Applications deadline for the fall semester is August 15; for the spring semester, February 15.

Equipment Requirements:

Each course at Saybrook has a learning guide which provides a conceptual overview of the field of study, outlines the study plan and required materials, discusses the assignments, and includes suggestions for further readings and an extensive bibliography. Instructors are a resource for discussing ideas, for clarifying topics, and for evaluating assignments.

Credit and Grading:

Course completion is determined by satisfactorily finishing, as judged by the course instructor, the assignments outlined in the course learning guide. Saybrook does not give letter grades. Instead, a written evaluation by the instructor is included in the student's permanent file.

Accreditations:

Western Association of Schools and Colleges.

GRADUATE COURSES

CLINICAL INQUIRY

Introduction to Clinical Inquiry

This course is a review and assessment of the clinical work that students have been involved with. It will explore the belief systems that they hold as therapists and the theoretical concepts that they have used utilizing case examples as a main source of material. The goal is to expand the students' theoretical thinking about clinical material and to assist them to discern those areas of practice that need added attention. A systemic point of view will be used to facilitate this type of exploration. A first-level course. (3 semester units)

Assessing Persons

Assessing persons well can contribute to these goals: (1) knowledge and self-knowledge of the client; (2) prediction of future scenarios; (3) indication of intervention strategies. Assessing persons poorly, on the other hand, can directly impugn one's professional competence. This course introduces technical issues bearing on these concerns, and considers interviews, as well as structured and projective techniques. (3 semester units)

Clinical Research

This is a course designed to train students to do research in clinical settings. Emphasis will be placed upon discovery-oriented methods rather than hypothesis-testing ones (although the latter are not excluded). The basic orientation will be that of qualitative methodology because such a perspective interferes minimally with the ongoing psychological processes and yet tries to capture what took place as faithfully as possible. While the phenomenological approach will be emphasized, other types of qualitative approaches will also be taught. (3 semester units)

Functional and Dysfunctional Behavior

This course provides an overview of the major schools of thought that have shaped modern thinking about various aspects of psychopathology, e.g., behavioral, biophysical, intrapsychic, phenomenological, and social. Consideration is given to etiology, development, pathological patterns, psychotherapy, and critical evaluations of the field. Dysfunctional behavior is studied in the larger context of functional behavior, self-actualization, and the development of human capacities. (3 semester units)

Human Sexuality

This course presents an investigation of sexuality within the larger context of human experience. Emphasis is placed on the study of human sexual development, dimensions of sexual behavior, sex education, health issues, sex therapy, ethical and legal aspects of sexuality, and art and sexuality. (3 semester units)

Structure and Dynamics of the Family

This course explores the nature of families and human systems and some of the approaches to therapeutic change within them. The theoretical work of Bateson, Haley, Hoffman, Minuchin, and Nagy are highlighted. The goal of the course is to offer a framework for thinking about families and understanding the nature of family processes. (3 semester units)

CONSCIOUSNESS STUDIES

Cognitive Psychology

This course presents major theories and concepts in the psychology of learning, thinking, and perceiving. Readings encompass neurological development, sense perception, memory, information processing, affective motivation, intelligence, problem solving, decision making, the formation and use of symbols, and linguistic representation and communication. The purpose of this course is to explore the relationship of thought and behavior (mind and body) in human existence. (3 semester units)

Consciousness and Society

This course describes and explores the potential significance that contemporary technologies and research applications in the field of consciousness studies have for local and global societies. Material is drawn from current social trends in holistic health, transpersonal encounter, bioregional and planetary awareness, informative economics, and intercultural exchange. Approaches to community activism, economic design, and transcultural appreciation from a consciousness perspective are offered, as well as thoughts about the social potential of consciousness research using computers, biofeedback, altered states, and accelerated learning programs. (3 semester units)

Dimensions of Creativity

This course examines the creative process, the creative person, and the creative product. The many dimensions of scientific and artistic creativity are studied, as well as the way creativity relates to social-cultural influences, family background, personality factors, and cognitive styles. Imagery and symbolization, intrapsychic experience, and aesthetic productivity are explored. Recent creativity research and theories of creative development are considered. (3 semester units)

Eastern Psychologies

This course examines the great systems of Eastern thought. (3 semester units)

Introduction to Neuropsychology

This course focuses upon the study of neurological mechanisms, on brain-behavior relationships, and the diagnosis and treatment of neuropsychological disorders. (3 semester units)

Introduction to the Psychology of Consciousness

This course is an overview of the current state of the field. Topics include current research paradigms, methodological issues, and the attempts to synthesize intellectual knowledge. Results of research are summarized and evaluated in dream, hypnotic, psychedelic, psychotic, biofeedback-induced, and parapsychological domains of consciousness. Attention is also given to the varieties of religious experience and the psychology of meditation, the contrast of Eastern/Western approaches and the therapeutic implications of imagery research. (3 semester units)

Neuropsychology and Learning Disabilities

This course provides a critical view of the neuropsychology contributions to a learning disabilities epistemology. Focusing on brain development and brain functioning in children, and drawing on recent animal and human research, brain-behavior relationships are identified and analyzed within an environmental context. Internal factors (e.g., genetics) and external factors (e.g., infant stimulation) are studied as mediators of neuropsychological functioning. Consideration is given to the interactive effects of neuropsychological physiological, and sociological factors on learning differences and on learning disabilities. (3 semester units)

Models of Consciousness

This course emphasizes a critical approach to the study of current phenomenological and theoretical models of consciousness, such as those proposed by Hilgard, Tart, Ornstein, Penfield, and Wilber. Attempts at the synthesis of more adequate models are encouraged by drawing from brain research data, cognitive psychological and psychobiological theory, algorithmic information processing approaches, and behavioral approaches, as well as the traditional descriptions of Eastern and Western religious experience. Consideration is given to the relationship of model to theory, and theory to model. (3 semester units)

Psychology of Shamanism

This course takes a cross-cultural approach in studying the ways in which shamans change their conscious states as well as their techniques of diagnosing and treating disease. Personality studies of shamans are reviewed, and their role in developing countries and among ethnic minorities of developed nations is surveyed. The roles of expectancy, placebo effect, and suggestion in their work are discussed as well as the place of ritual, myth, music, and art. (3 semester units)

Contemporary Issues in Psychology

This course provides faculty members an opportunity to share with students scholarly work and research in which they are currently engaged. Topics reflect problems or challenges in both theory and applied work in the human science fields. Topics and instructors change each semester. (3 semester units)

Contemporary Issues in Human Science

This course provides faculty members an opportunity to share with students scholarly work and research in which they are currently engaged. Topics reflect problems or challenges in both theory and applied work in the human science fields. Topics and instructors change each semester. (3 semester units)

HEALTH STUDIES

Health Psychology

This course examines ways that a person's life-crisis, life-style, self-beliefs, and values influence health, illness, and recovery. (3 semester units)

Introduction to Health Studies

This course will explore the factors that are swinging the pendulum away from technological factors in medicine and healing, toward the human dimensions of the process. Topics include new models of healing; values, purposes, and ethics in medicine; the doctor/patient relationship; personal responsibility and illness; cultural and social relations applied to prevention and healing; and the emergence of the field of health psychology. (3 semester units)

Psychophysiology

This course examines and assesses hypotheses, theories, and models concerning mind/body interaction, and explores practices which use the body to promote mental health. Areas covered include: the endocrine system, the respiratory system, and the nervous system as mediators of the mind/body relationship; the role of body image in illness; the power of physical posture and movement in consciousness transformation; and the implications of body-oriented therapies, such as biofeedback, autogenic training, neurolinguistic programming, etc. (3 semester units)

Systems of Healing

This course requires a critical assessment of the major health care practices within various cultural systems and historical eras. The focus is on the essential nature of the healing process. A wide range of healing systems is examined, including non-allopathic systems such as Chinese medicine, Yoga, shamanism, and "faith healing," as well as alternative and traditional practices currently used within our own culture. Students are required to compare and contrast these various practices and to formulate common principles of healing. (3 semester units)

INQUIRY THEORIES

Introduction to Theories of Inquiry

This course focuses on the philosophical foundations (epistemology) of the inquiry process. Readings are chosen to clarify: (1) the evolution of twentieth-century thinking about the nature of knowledge and scientific method; (2) psychological and sociological factors affecting definitions of knowledge and science; and (3) the definition and rationale for a human science approach to inquiry and research. (3 semester units)

Critical Theory

The focus of this course is issues concerning the current theoretical and research status of humanistic psychology and the human science approach to the social sciences. The founders of the Frankfurt School (Adorno, Horkheimer, etc.), Habermas, and other contemporary critical theorists will guide the critical review of basic epistemological assumptions commonly held among humanists. The broader social and political issues that affect the study of human life, potential ideological biases, and the consequences for the work we do will be explored. (3 semester units)

Metaphor and Human Understandings

This course examines metaphorical reasoning as a dominant logic of human science. The relationship of metaphor and theory is explored. Readings are transdisciplinary and draw from works by anthropologists, philosophers, linguistic analysts, and political scientists, as well as psychologists. Assignments give students experience doing interpretive analysis which is a necessary skill for conducting phenomenological and hermeneutic research. (3 semester units)

Critical Thinking and Argument Analysis

This course will prepare students for research in human science and psychology by exploring the rules of evidence, the nature and process of social-scientific argument and writing, and the ways to consider alternative sets of data. And, by identifying the necessary ingredients of research proposals, this course will enable students to develop the skill of sound reasoning and argumentative writing. (3 semester hours)

METHODOLOGIES AND METHODS

Overview of Methods for Disciplined Inquiry

This course reviews the major characteristics of disciplined inquiry. It provides introductory coverage of a variety of methods which an investigator could consider in addressing a specific question, problem or issue. Methodological issues and decisions, strategies of inquiry, research designs, data collection procedures, and the interface among inquiry concepts are emphasized. (3 semester units)

Experimental Research Methods

This course involves asking questions and defining problems; generating hypotheses and selecting research designs which involve the manipulation of variables; investigating six major designs and data analyses used with these designs; designing, extending and evaluating experiments; and relating hypothesis testing and problem solving. (3 semester units)

Non-Experimental Research Methods

This course examines research methods of inquiry that are primarily descriptive and exploratory in character. These methods include naturalistic observation, participant-observation, unobtrusive measures, survey research, intensive interviewing, and the use of archival and other written documents. (3 semester units)

Phenomenology and Interpretive Research

This is a second-level methods course with emphasis on teaching the practical skills necessary for interpretive research work. Philosophical inquiry will be kept in the background, but will be focused on, if necessary. The course will examine salient issues: intentionality, perception, language, and human action. Standards for doing valid research work will be critically examined throughout the course. (3 semester units)

PSYCHOLOGY

Developmental Psychology

The processes and significant transition points for adult, early childhood, and adolescent development are considered in this course. Major theories of development are contrasted by examining principal concepts and uncovering their assumptions about what motivates behavior and development, what the nature of development is, and what the primary influences on development are. Specific topics such as mother-infant attachment, sex-role socialization, cognitive and moral development, and reciprocal effects in parent-child interaction are reviewed. (3 semester units)

Ethics in Psychotherapy and Psychological Research

This course focuses on the ethical issues that arise in the practice of psychotherapy and in designing and carrying out psychological research. Assignments ask students to critically evaluate APA Ethical Principles and State laws governing psychologists and to examine the ethical implications of their personal beliefs and values on their work. (3 semester units)

History and Systems of Psychology

This course attempts to find an explanation of the persistent problems in psychology, and examines the evolution of answers to these problems. The focus of the course is on the contemporary development of psychology as a separate scientific discipline.

Personality Theory and Research

This course provides an overview of classical and contemporary theory and research in personality. Topics include an examination of various theories including contrasts among psychoanalytic, social learning, and humanistic perspectives; current theoretical controversies; the function and evolution of theory; and major methodological issues. Special attention is given to new theories and research on aspects such as intrinsic motivation, emotions, locus of control, prosocial behavior, self-concept, and personality change. (3 semester units)

Socialization and Personality

Students of socialization focus on the processes by which individuals develop into competent members of society (and thereby uphold the continuation of societal values and norms), and at the same time develop into autonomous individuals who possess unique personalities. This course includes literature representative of each of these areas, socialization processes as they affect both children and adults, and the individual's active role in the socialization process. (3 semester units)

Study of Women

The focus of this course is on the development of non-alienating theory and methods in human science. Deficiencies in existing theories and methods are examined as they relate to the psychological and social understanding of women's experience. Topics include: the family in social and historical perspective; feminine protest, anger, and deviance; psychological depression; and creative productivity as manifested in women's art and literature. (3 semester units)

SYSTEMS INQUIRY

Introduction to Systems Inquiry

This course is designed to be a comprehensive introduction to general systems theory and its applications in the social and behavioral sciences. It will present the pioneering work of Van Bertalanffy, Ackoff, Boulding, Emery and Trist, Waddington, and Jantsch, as well as the more recent work of such theorists as Bateson, Wilden, and Miller. Students will gain a basic vocabulary of systems concepts and learn how to diagnose and analyze systems problems. (3 semester units)

Systems Behavior

This course introduces programs and approaches to: (1) describe the behavior of a selected Human Activity System (HAS); (2) construct a process model of a particular HAS; and (3) characterize the critical processes that contribute to the effectiveness of the selected HAS. (3 semester units)

Systems Design

This course aims at generating an understanding of the theoretical, philosophical, and methodological perspectives of systems design, and develops entry professional level competence in carrying out design in the context of human activity systems. With the combination of guided and self-directed learning experience, students will be assisted to: (1) characterize and model a systemic context of the selected design problem; (2) organize their own design theme; (3) select design approaches, methods, and tools appropriate to the system to be designed; (4) construct and evaluate a model of the system to be designed and developed. (3 semester units)

Systems Development

The design proposal developed in the Systems Design course provides the functional context within which (1) the processes of design will be introduced and the characteristics of the various types of design systems elaborated. The student then will complete the design tasks embedded in the design proposal and present a design model of the system to be developed. Following an examination of the model, a developmental plan will be constructed which sets forth the implementation of the design model. (3 semester units)

South Carolina, University of
Independent Learning
915 Gregg Street
Columbia, South Carolina 29208
1-800-922-2577

Description:
Chartered in 1801 as South Carolina College, the University of South Carolina is among the oldest state universities, the first to be supported continuously by annual state appropriations. In recent years the University has emerged as a leading educational institution of 16 academic units, enrolling over 35,000 on all campuses. Distance Education at the University of South Carolina is a part of the undergraduate program, and the courses are designed primarily for college credit work, but may also be used for general learning. High school courses are also available.

Faculty:
Susan E. Bridwell, Dean of Distance Education; Carolyn Champion, Associate Director, Student Support Services; Todd Oswald, Student Services Coordinator. Seventy regular members of the University faculty teach correspondence courses.

Academic Levels:
College
High School
Noncredit

Degree/Certificate Programs:
In most programs of study, no more than 30 semester hours earned through correspondence study may be applied towards an undergraduate degree at the University of South Carolina.

Admission Requirements:
High school graduation is required for admission to college courses. Some courses have required prerequisites. Formal admission to USC is not required of students who enroll in correspondence study courses. Members of the military service should contact their Education Officer for information regarding correspondence courses through DANTES.

Tuition:
$75 per semester hour; $75 per 1/2 unit high school course. A nonrefundable rental fee is charged for all courses that require audio- or videocassettes. Pro rata refund plan: 75 percent refunded if official request is received in writing prior to an enrollment of 1 month, course materials are returned undamaged, and no assignments have been submitted for grading. MasterCard and Visa acceptable for payment of tuition.

Enrollment Period:
The maximum time allowed to complete a course is 12 months. No course may be completed in less than 2 months from the date of enrollment. One extension of 3 months may be allowed with payment of a $10 extension fee for

each college or noncredit course, $5 for each high school course.

Equipment Requirements:

Textbook costs are in addition to tuition; books may be purchased separately by the student from the University Bookstore. A rental fee is charged for audiocassette tapes required by some courses; the student must furnish a audiocassette player for these courses. VHS Videocassette courses require the signing of a usage agreement and a usage fee payable upon enrollment.

Credit and Grading:

Grading system for college courses A through F with plus and minus values. Minimum passing grade is D. A numerical grading scale is used for high school courses. Failure of the final examination means a failing grade for the course. Examinations must be supervised by a University of South Carolina-approved proctor. Correspondence study credits may be used for initial or renewal of Teacher Certification. Credit is awarded in semester hour units.

Library Services:

Students in-state can contact the university campus nearest their location for use of materials provided at local libraries or for access to systemwide resources through the online catalog and interlibrary loan.

Accreditations:

Southern Association of Colleges and Schools. Member of: National University Continuing Education Association.

COLLEGE COURSES

ASTRONOMY

Descriptive Astronomy I

A survey of the main points of knowledge in astronomy with an emphasis on ''how.'' Briefly covers all the universe from the earth to the distant galaxies. Special studies of space travel, the moon, the sun and pseudoscience. (3 semester hours)

Descriptive Astronomy IA

Early astronomy, the earth as a planet, space exploration and modern non-optical astronomical techniques are considered. (1 semester hour)

Descriptive Astronomy II

Stars and their evolution, galaxies and their structure, the evolution of the universe and the possibilities of extraterrestrial life are the main emphasis of this course. (3 semester hours)

Descriptive Astronomy IIA

Makes a study of our solar system—its structure, the structure and surfaces of the planets and other objects in the solar system and how the solar system was formed. (1 semester hour)

BUSINESS ADMINISTRATION

Fundamentals of Accounting

External financial reporting for business entities, including income measurement and determination of financial position. (3 semester hours)

Fundamentals of Accounting II

Internal managerial and cost accounting, including budgeting, cost determination, and analysis. (3 semester hours)

Careers in Business

An introduction to career opportunities and the career placement process in business. (1 semester hour)

Survey of Commercial Law

Basic legal concepts and the judicial system, with emphasis on business law. (3 semester hours)

Management of Risk and Insurance

A management approach to the handling of nonspeculative risks faced by individuals and organizations. Analysis of the nature and uses of private and social insurance as well as other methods for achieving economic security. Tactics, techniques, and strategies for managers of life, health, property, and liability insurance programs. (3 semester hours)

Marketing

Marketing functions, trade channels, price policies, expenses and profits of middlemen, and public policy with respect to marketing practices. (3 semester hours)

Buyer Behavior

The study of the consumer decision process. (3 semester hours)

Introduction to Real Estate and Urban Development

Real estate analysis and administration; basic principles, concepts, terminology, and institutional factors related to real estate decisions in the urban environment. (3 semester hours)

Personal Finance

Life insurance, health insurance, wills, trusts, Social Security, stocks, bonds, real estate, mutual funds, and other uses of funds. (3 semester hours)

Principles of Management

A comprehensive survey of the basic principles of management applicable to all forms of business. The course provides the student with a basis for thinking about complex business situations in the framework of analysis of the management process. (3 semester hours)

Personnel Management

Contemporary concepts and practices of personnel administration. (3 semester hours)

Financial Accounting I

Accounting theory and practice as it relates to preparation of financial statements. (4 semester hours)

Financial Accounting II

A continuation of the above course. (3 semester hours)

Cost/Managerial Accounting I

Cost accounting systems, planning, and control. (3 semester hours)

Commercial Law I

Contracts, agencies, and partnerships. (3 semester hours)

Commercial Law II

Corporations, bankruptcy, and the Uniform Commercial Code. (3 semester hours)

Auditing I

Principles of independent, internal, and governmental auditing. (4 semester hours)

Marketing Communications and Strategy

The promotion process for consumer and industrial products. (3 semester hours)

Personal Selling and Sales Management

Principles of selling and their relationship to the management of a sales force. (3 semester hours)

Commercial Bank Practice and Policy

The fundamental principles underlying the employment of bank funds are emphasized. Attention is devoted to the allocation of funds among the various classes of loans and investments, to bank operating costs and earnings, and to changing bank practices. (3 semester hours)

Governmental and Nonprofit Accounting

Accounting principles and procedures for local, state, and federal governmental units and for private nonprofit organizations. (3 semester hours)

Retailing Management

A comprehensive course emphasizing the specific activities of management, merchandising, and promotional functions required of the retail outlet with a competitive business environment. (3 semester hours)

ECONOMICS

Principles of Economics I

Macroeconomic analysis: basic definitions and concepts including scarcity, the circular flow of economic life, mechanics of pricing, and the fundamentals of American capitalism; national income economics emphasizing national income accounting, income and employment theory and monetary and fiscal policy. (3 semester hours)

Principles of Economics II

Microeconomic analysis: theory of the firm, cost output and determination, market pricing; income distribution in a capitalistic economy; international economics. (3 semester hours)

Commercial and Central Banking

A study of the history, structure, functions, and operations of our commercial and central banking systems. Emphasis is placed on the influence and operation of the Federal Reserve System. (3 semester hours)

Financial Institutions

A study of the functions and operations of financial institutions and their relationships to the commercial banking system and the general economy. Attention is devoted to savings institutions, insurance companies, rural and urban real estate credit, consumer credit, and associated topics. (3 semester hours)

Government Policy Toward Business

An analysis of public policy toward business in the United States. Emphasis is on the desirability of various policies in light of their consequences for the general welfare. (3 semester hours)

ENGLISH

Composition

Learn the process of composition with attention to invention, arrangement, and style, and supervised practice in reading and writing essays. (3 semester hours)

Composition and Literature

A introduction to literature and writing expository and critical essays including a research paper. (3 semester hours)

American Literature

Survey of American literature: major authors, genres, and periods. (3 semester hours)

Vocabulary and Language

Native and borrowed sources of the English vocabulary, with attention to the language relationships, changes in the pronunciation and meaning of words, and history and linguistic function of dictionaries. (3 semester hours)

Topics in American Literature: Flannery O'Connor

An intensive study of the short stories of O'Connor. (3 semester hours)

Children's Literature

Reading and evaluating representative works appropriate for the elementary school child. (3 semester hours)

Adolescent Literature

Reading and evaluating representative works appropriate for the adolescent reader. A study of the characterization of adolescents in literature and of the historical development of the writing of literary works expressly for adolescent readers. (3 semester hours)

Principles of Modern Literary Theory

Major 20th-century approaches to texts, from New Criticism to the present. (3 semester hours)

English Grammar

A study of traditional, structural, and generative systems of English grammar. (3 semester hours)

Development of the English Language

This course examines the development of the English language, from its Indo-European family through the Germanic branch and into Old English, Middle English, and Modern English. This historical view shows that language constantly changes in its vocabulary, its grammar, its usage, and its pronunciation. No previous knowledge of Old English or Middle English is necessary. (3 semester hours)

The Teaching of Writing

Theory and methods of teaching composition and extensive practice in various kinds of writing. (3 semester hours)

Technical Writing

Preparation for and practice in types of writing important to scientists, engineers, and computer scientists, from brief technical letters to formal articles and reports. (3 semester hours)

Business Writing

Extensive practice in different types of business writing, from brief letters to formal articles and reports. (3 semester hours)

FRENCH

Beginning French

Course C-109. Introduction to grammar and practical vocabulary necessary for fundamental communication skills. (3 semester hours)

Course C-110. A continuation of Course C-109. (3 semester hours)

GEOGRAPHY

Introduction to Geography

A survey of the principles and methods of geographic inquiry. (3 semester hours)

Introduction to Weather and Climate

The interrelationship of weather elements and controls and the spatial distributions of climate and vegetation. (4 semester hours)

Human Impact on Environment

A spatial consideration of the processes, effects and trends in environmental change resulting from man's activity. The problems of resource management and the implications for man's future habitation of the earth are emphasized. (3 semester hours)

Geography of North America

Physical and cultural geography of North America with emphasis on the United States. (3 semester hours)

GOVERNMENT AND INTERNATIONAL STUDIES

The United States and World Problems: Global Perspectives

Principal forces and factors influencing world affairs, with emphasis on the role of the United States in issues relating to resources, food, arms control, human rights, the environment, rich and poor countries, the development gap, and detente. (3 semester hours)

The United States and World Problems: Regional Perspectives

Principal forces and factors influencing world affairs, with emphasis on the problems and policy perspectives of foreign countries and regions. (3 semester hours)

American National Government

Formation and development of the national government, its organization and powers. (3 semester hours)

Theories of International Relations

International political behavior and institutions. (3 semester hours)

Economic Aspects of International Politics

Economic problems and policies in international politics including theory of comparative advantage; international economic aid, trade, and monetary issues; the United States' role in the international economy; and the functions of international economic institutions. (3 semester hours)

HEALTH EDUCATION

Personal and Community Health

Principles of personal hygiene; physiological systems of the body with emphasis on nutrition, physical fitness, stress control, consumer health, sexuality, and self-care skills. (3 semester hours)

Health Education for the Elementary School

Methods and materials for elementary schools. Integration and correlation of materials with school subjects. Sample content of material developed for primary, intermediate, and upper grades. (3 semester hours)

HISTORY

History of the United States from Discovery to the Present Day

Course C-111. A general survey of the United States from the era of discovery to 1865, emphasizing major political, economic, social, and intellectual developments. (3 semester hours)

Course C-112. A continuation of Course C-111 covering from 1865 up to the present. (3 semester hours)

The Rise of Industrial America, 1877–1917

A survey of recent United States history with emphasis on the economic, social, and literary developments from 1877 to 1917.

History of South Carolina, 1670–1865

A study of South Carolina origins and developments. (3 semester hours)

History of South Carolina Since 1865

A survey of recent South Carolina history with emphasis on social and institutional development. (3 semester hours)

LATIN

Beginning Latin I

Introduction to grammar and practical vocabulary necessary for fundamental skills. (3 semester hours)

Beginning Latin II

A continuation of Beginning Latin I. (3 semester hours)

MARINE SCIENCE

Oceans and Man

A nontechnical introduction to human interactions with the marine environment: marine organisms, marine systems, and the physical and chemical characteristics of oceans and estuaries. (3 semester hours)

MATHEMATICS

An Introduction to Elementary Mathematics

Topics include review of arithmetic, algebra, and geometry. (3 semester hours)

Basic College Mathematics

Basic college algebra; linear and quadratic equations, inequalities, functions and graphs of functions, exponential and logarithmic functions, systems of equations. (3 semester hours)

Trigonometry

Topics in trigonometry: circular functions, analytic trigonometry, applications of trigonometry. (2 semester hours)

Precalculus Mathematics

Topics in algebra and trigonometry: subsets of the real line, absolute value; polynomial, rational, inverse logarithmic, exponential functions; circular functions, analytic trigonometry. (4 semester hours)

Calculus for Business Administration and Social Sciences

Derivatives and integrals of elementary algebraic, exponential and logarithmic functions. Maxima, minima, rate of change, motion, work, area under a curve, and volume. (3 semester hours)

Finite Mathematics

Elementary matrix theory; systems of linear equations; permutations and combinations; probability and Markov chains; linear programming and game theory. (3 semester hours)

Basic Concepts of Elementary Mathematics I

The meaning of number, fundamental operations of arithmetic, the structure of the real number system and its sub-systems, elementary number theory. (3 semester hours)

Basic Concepts of Elementary Mathematics II

Informal geometry and basic concepts of algebra. (3 semester hours)

MUSIC

Introduction to Music

Perceptive listening and appreciation of musical elements, forms and style periods, including composers' lives, individual styles and representative works. Emphasis is on classical music, but jazz and American popular music is also included. Students must have access to a compact disc player. (3 semester hours)

PHILOSOPHY

Introduction to Philosophy

An introduction to the main problems of philosophy and its methods of inquiry, analysis and criticism. Works of important philosophers will be read. (3 semester hours)

Introduction to Logic I

The nature of arguments: fallacies, criteria and techniques of valid deductive inference; applications. This is a self-guided computer-assisted course. Students must have access to an IBM or IBM compatible computer with a 3.5'' disk drive. (3 semester hours)

PHYSICAL EDUCATION

Measurement and Evaluation in Physical Education

The historic background of measurement in physical education; statistical techniques to be used in scoring and interpreting tests; evaluation of measures now available in the field; and the administration of a testing program. (3 semester hours)

Organization and Administration of Physical Education

Organization of instructional, intramural, interscholastic and recreational programs with emphasis on criteria for evaluation and selection of activities. (3 semester hours)

PHYSICS

General Physics I

Part I of an introductory course sequence. Topics include mechanics, wave motion, sound, and head. (3 semester hours)

General Physics II

Continuation of General Physics I. Includes electromagnetism, relativity, quantum, atomic, and nuclear physics. (3 semester hours)

PSYCHOLOGY

Introduction to Psychology

Organized introduction to psychology, the science of individual human and animal behavior. (3 semester hours)

Psychology of Adjustment

The effort of the human organism to accommodate himself to the physiological and psychological stresses and strains to which he is exposed. (3 semester hours)

Psychology of Marriage

The psychological, physiological and social characteristics of marriage. (3 semester hours)

Health Psychology

Application of psychological theories and assessment and treatment methodologies for health maintenance, and the diagnosis and treatment of illness. (3 semester hours)

Abnormal Behavior in Children

Theories, description, and assessment of child behavior problems and disorders; psychological and educational methods of intervention. Covers aggression, hyperactivity, early infantile autism and childhood schizophrenia, fears, social withdrawal, enuresis, retardation, and related problems. (3 semester hours)

Psychology of Child Development

The objectives of this course are to acquaint the student with the basic determinants of child behavior, the ways in which child behavior differs from adult behavior, and the ways in which childhood influences adulthood. (3 semester hours)

Psychology of Adolescence

Mental, emotional, and social development with aspects of adjustment. (3 semester hours)

Psychology of the Exceptional Child

Mentally deficient, physically handicapped, and unusually bright children; characteristics, causes, needs, and guidance. (3 semester hours)

Specific Learning Disabilities of School Children

Children with average or above average intelligence and specific learning impairments; diagnostic and remedial techniques. (3 semester hours)

RETAILING

Merchandising

Decision making and budgets. (3 semester hours)

SOCIAL WORK

Foundations of Social Welfare

Social welfare agencies; the education and ethical code of social workers; principles, theories, and research underlying social work practice and methods. (3 semester hours)

Social Welfare Services for Children and Youth

Social welfare services available to children and youth and the referral processes involved. (3 semester hours)

Social Welfare Services for Families and the Aged

Social welfare services available to families, ranging from counseling services to specialized services for aged citizens. (3 semester hours)

Social Welfare Services for Women and Minorities

Social services available for women and minorities and the forces that shape these services. (3 semester hours)

Independent Study

Completion of a research project in the student's community. (3 semester hours)

Interviewing

Major concepts, principles, and methods in professional social work practice. (3 semester hours)

SOCIOLOGY

Introductory Sociology

An introduction to sociological facts and principles: an analysis of group-making processes and products. (3 semester hours)

Sociology of Delinquent Youth Behavior

Social factors in the development, identification, and treatment of delinquents. (3 semester hours)

Sociology of Sport

Theories, methods, and substantive issues in the study of sport in contemporary societies. (3 semester hours)

STATISTICS

Elementary Statistics

An introductory course in the fundamentals of modern statistical methods. Topics include descriptive statistics, probability, random sampling, tests of hypothesis, estimation, simple linear regression, and correlation. (3 semester hours)

South Carolina, University of

HIGH SCHOOL COURSES

BUSINESS EDUCATION

Business English and Communication

The student should have some knowledge of basic grammar before enrolling in this course. The course emphasizes the common language skills necessary for good expression in business communications, such as letters. Coherent writing, unity of thought, sentence structure, and vocabulary building are stressed. (½ unit)

Office Systems

Students will become familiar with the processes involved in dealing with filing and office machine systems; incoming and outgoing funds and bank statements; and sales and accounts payable; inventory control and report, and payroll systems. (½ unit)

Consumer Education

This is a one-semester course designed to give students a better understanding of their rights and responsibilities as consumers in the free enterprise system. It explains how personal goals and values affect consumers' choices; how consumers can develop reliable decision-making skills for spending, saving, and investing; how they can evaluate alternatives in the marketplace; and how they can get the most from a given expenditure of resources. Specific lessons on personal finance include earning money, spending and saving money, working with money, and getting and using credit. Of particular interest are lessons on how consumers can get the most for their money when they buy food, drugs, cosmetics, clothing, transportation, housing, and home furnishings. Lessons on financial protection provide helpful information on purchasing life, health, and property insurance. (½ unit)

Introduction to Business

This course gives an overview of business in our society. The topics covered include the place of business in society, the relationship of business and government in our economic system, the place of banks and credit in the economy, personal money management, consumer rights and responsibilities, and the use of credit. (½ unit)

Business Law

Students are introduced to basic concepts of business law in the United States. They study contracts, civil law, criminal law, the court system, personal property and bailments, commercial paper, employment, credit agreements, and insurance. Students gain an understanding of legal rights and responsibilities in business dealings. (½ unit)

CAREER PLANNING

Career Planning

This course is designed to increase students' awareness of career development issues and to familiarize students with resources that can help them reach their career goals. They learn what steps they should take in planning their future careers and how to apply self-assessment skills in a lifelong process of achieving career satisfaction. (½ unit)

ENGLISH

Basic Grammar

This course is designed to help students to learn the terminology and the structure of the English language. The material is presented in an easy-to-understand, step-by-step fashion. Students can enter the course with little or no previous instruction in formal grammar. Parts of speech, sentence structure, choice and use of words, capitalization, and punctuation are covered in this course. (½ unit)

Intermediate Grammar

Students will review parts of speech and usage, sentence patterns, basic punctuation, and capitalization. They will study new material, such as clauses, phrases, sentence problems and effective sentences, complex and compound sentences, and complex pronoun, verb, and adverb forms. (½ unit)

Effective Reader Skills

The intent of this course is to help students become more effective readers by emphasizing strategies that help them improve their basic language and literacy skills. They study about central themes, main ideas, major and minor details, inferences, fact and opinion, context clues, and vocabulary. (½ unit)

The American Short Story

The primary objectives of this course are to familiarize students with the basic literary elements of short stories and to provide students with techniques for and experience in analyzing short stories. The secondary objective is to help students understand the development of the American short story over the past 150 years through analysis of stories that exemplify the characteristics of the Romantic, Realistic, Naturalistic, and Modern periods. (½ unit)

Composition I: Basic Expository Writing

This course presents a systematic approach to the basics of expository writing. Students will practice a step-by-step process in learning to write unified, coherent papers. In the process of learning to write, students will learn to think in an organized, systematic fashion. They will also study effective uses of language, as well as methods of connecting ideas and expanding ideas by means of details and examples. (½ unit)

Ninth Grade English

First Semester. This course introduces three phases of language arts: literature, grammar, and composition. In the literature segments of the course, students read short stories, poetry, drama, and selections from the *Odyssey*; the emphases are on enjoyment and on techniques for better understanding of these types of literature. In the grammar and composition lessons, parts of speech, basic parts and characteristics of sentences, and paragraph development are emphasized. (½ unit)

Second Semester. Students review basic approaches to literature and fundamentals of grammar and composition before learning new information about these elements in the study of English. In the literature lessons, students read short stories, essays, and biographies, *Romeo and Juliet* and selections from *Great Expectations*. In the grammar and composition lessons, students concentrate on punctuation; the parts, structures, kinds, and purposes of sentences; and on developing specificity and coherence in paragraphs. (½ unit)

Tenth Grade English

First Semester. This course further develops students' skills in three phases of language arts: literature, grammar, and composition. In the literature segments of the course, students read short stories, poetry, drama, and tales of King Arthur and his knights of the Round Table. The emphases are on reading for enjoyment and on developing techniques for better understanding these types of literature. In the grammar and composition lessons, parts of speech, basic parts and characteristics of sentences, capitalization and punctuation, and the step-by-step development of a paper are emphasized. (½ unit)

Second Semester. Students review basic approaches to literature and fundamentals of grammar and composition before learning new information about these elements in the study of English. In the literature lessons, students read short stories, essays, and biographies, *Julius Caesar*, and John Steinbeck's *The Pearl*. In the grammar and composition lessons, students concentrate on the patterns, structures, kinds and purposes of sentences, as well as on additional ways to punctuate sentences, and on developing clear, specific, coherent, and polished papers. (½ unit)

Eleventh Grade English

First Semester. The roots and historical development of American literature from the colonial period to 1900 are the central elements of this course. Students will gain an understanding of the ideas and perspectives that fostered the development of our country and of the ways in which our literature became distinctively American. In addition to studying the literature, students will review the proper grammatical constructions of sentences before focusing on such topics as punctuating sentences and correcting sentence problems. Students' composition skills will be developed, not only through analysis of the literary selections but also through study and application of the basic organizational pattern of a good essay. (½ unit)

Second Semester. In this course, students will study the development of American literature from the Civil War to the present, noting both the ways in which literary forms have changed and the ways in which literature reflects the period in which it is written. Instruction in grammar and composition, with emphasis on writing, punctuating, and revising sentences, and on writing and polishing expository essays, is also provided. (½ unit)

Twelfth Grade English

First Semester. In this course students will read many of the great works that have formed our English literary heritage from the Anglo-Saxon period through the eighteenth century. They will gain an understanding of the development of English literature as they read Shakespeare's *Macbeth* and selections from *Beowulf, The Canterbury Tales, Paradise Lost,* and other literary works. Students will have the opportunity to improve their writing skills as they apply good writing practices in analyzing the literary works. (½ unit)

Second Semester. In this course students will further their understanding of the historical development of English literature as they read selections by major authors of the Romantic Age, the Victorian Age, and the twentieth century. They will continue to apply and improve their writing skills as they analyze the many facets of the literary selections that they read. (½ unit)

ETIQUETTE

Etiquette

In this course, students receive information and guidelines on the behavior and manners appropriate in a variety of situations. (½ unit)

FRENCH

First Year French

First Semester. In this first semester course, students are introduced to the basic grammatical concepts necessary for them to develop reading and writing skills in the French language. Students will become acquainted with the French culture through a variety of readings in both French and English. They will also have the opportunity to develop speaking and listening skills as they hear the French language and speak it themselves. This course covers basic sentence structures used in expressing positive and negative statements, as well as commands and questions, in both present and future tenses. Both vocabulary building and grammar are stressed as the student studies several essential parts of speech and a number of commonly used French idioms and expressions. (½ unit)

Second Semester. This second semester course is a continuation of the above course. It reinforces and augments all of the grammatical concepts previously studied. At the same time, it provides new

material that builds new vocabulary, introduces more advanced grammar concepts, and increases reading comprehension skills. (½ unit)

Second Year French

First Semester. In this course, students look at the United States from the French perspective and take an imaginary tour of Paris. After reviewing the grammar and rules presented in First Year French, students study indirect objects; emphatic, interrogative, and reflexive pronouns; and verbs in the reflexive voice, the imperfect tense, and the conditional mood. (½ unit)

Second Semester. Students are introduced to famous people and events and study the broad social, economic, and political forces that shaped French culture. Students study the *subjunctif* and are introduced to *passe simple.* They also increase their awareness of the subtleties of the language as they learn specific strategies and helpful techniques for reading and listening. (½ unit)

MATHEMATICS

Basic Mathematics

First Semester. This course is specifically designed for students who need to develop understanding and skill in using basic arithmetic. After studying each of the four basic operations—addition, subtraction, multiplication, and division of whole numbers—students learn to solve word problems involving that operation. Interpretation of word problems is covered thoroughly and understandably. Topics such as estimating, rounding, and factoring are introduced to provide a foundation for further study. (½ unit)

Second Semester. After reviewing operations with whole numbers, students are introduced to the meaning of fractions and operations with fractions, operations with decimals, and problems involving money and percent. Word problems are used extensively to relate these concepts to practical situations. (½ unit)

General Mathematics 1

Students develop an understanding of fractions, decimals, and percentages as well as developing skill in using these mathematical operations. They learn to handle data through graphs, scientific notation, and means of comparison; and they apply their understanding of concepts, operations, and data analysis to practical problems dealing with interest, insurance, taxes, banking, and budgeting. (½ unit)

General Mathematics 2

In this course students extend their use and understanding of basic mathematical skills and concepts. They study positive and negative numbers, square roots, formulas, the Cartesian coordinate system, simple equations, and sets. The metric system, measurements, area, volume, and beginning constructions with a ruler and compass are also presented. (½ unit)

Business and Consumer Mathematics

First Semester. Students will develop arithmetic skills that apply to common business activities, operations, and transactions. The topics include whole numbers, fractions, decimals, percents, ratios, proportions, basic statistics, graphs, discounts, merchandising, bank services, and interest. (½ unit)

Second Semester. The topics presented are installment financing, charge accounts, taxes, automobile ownership, budgeting, stocks, bonds, home financing, and homeowner's insurance. (½ unit)

Beginning Algebra

First Semester. Students will become acquainted with basic algebraic concepts such as integers, linear equations, linear inequalities, factoring, and fractions. This course provides opportunities for students of various levels of ability to be successful and to develop knowledge and skills commensurate with their capacity and desire to learn. (½ unit)

Second Semester. Instruction in linear sentences, algebra in a plane, linear systems, functions, fractional equations, real numbers, equations with real solutions, and plane trigonometry is provided in this course. (½ unit)

Geometry

First Semester. Students develop reasoning skills using geometric terms and processes, concepts of logic, and applied problem solving. Topics include parallel lines and planes, congruent triangles, inequalities, and quadrilaterals. Geometric concepts are analyzed using formal, paragraph, and indirect proofs. (½ unit)

Second Semester. Students continue to develop geometry skills while studying similarity, areas and volumes, right triangles, circles, coordinate geometry, and transformations. Current mathematical standards involving problem solving, communication, reasoning, and connections are carefully followed in this course. (½ unit)

Advanced Algebra

First Semester. Such concepts as integers, polynomials, factoring, rational expressions, real numbers, equations, and inequalities are presented and related to practical problems encountered in daily living. (½ unit)

Second Semester. Logarithms and trigonometry are presented in depth. Included is the study of conic sections, progressions and series, trigonometric functions, graphing, and problem solving. The subject matter provides a good foundation for the future study of mathematics as well as for chemistry, physics, or engineering. (½ unit)

Precalculus: Analytic Geometry and Algebra

Analytic geometry and advanced topics in algebra are presented in this course. The emphasis is on functions, including algebraic, logarithmic, exponential, and matrix functions. Drawings and graphs are presented frequently to clarify essential mathematical principles. (½ unit)

Pre-Calculus: Trigonometry

This course presents the student with a thorough treatment of trigonometric concepts and applications. Among the subjects included are proofs of trigonometric identities; solutions of right and oblique triangles; solutions of trigonometric equations; logarithms; vector applications; and complex numbers. (½ unit)

SCIENCE

Health Science

First Semester. This course introduces students to medically accepted means of promoting physical and mental well-being. Among the subjects addressed are grooming, emotional health, drug abuse, and the functions of the nervous and endocrine systems. (½ unit)

Second Semester. This course will expand the student's understanding of basic human physiology as it applies to health practices. Topics covered include exercises and fatigue; nutrition, the digestive, respiratory, and circulatory systems; infections and chronic disease; public health and the medical profession; and human sexuality. (½ unit)

Biology 1

This entry-level course in biology introduces the student to fundamental biological concepts and relates scientific material to the student's everyday life. Basic concepts, ideas, facts, and scientific terms are presented in easy-to-understand language. The course begins with a presentation of the nature of science and the role of biology. The course emphasizes the study of living things and their relation to their environment. Students will explore basic concepts related to cell organization, reproduction, heredity, and mutation and adaptation. In

addition, they will study various aspects of ecology and conservation; consider the methods of classifying and naming living things; and learn about bacteria, protozoa, algae, and fungi. (½ unit)

Biology 2

This course continues the study of the four kingdoms in the classification system of living things. Students will further their understanding of fundamental biological concepts and principles as they study characteristics of representative members of various phyla and classes of the plant and animal kingdoms. Considerable attention is devoted to the study of human biology. Students will learn about the anatomy and physiology of the human body and also consider such health-related topics as nutrition, disease, and harmful drugs. (½ unit)

Physical Science

First Semester. This course contains a balanced presentation of basic concepts, logical methods, and practical applications of chemistry through a nonmathematical approach. The following subjects are discussed in some detail: the properties and changes in matter; the atomic and molecular structure of matter; the nature of gases, acids, bases, salts, and carbon compounds; and the behavior of nuclear particles. The practical nature of science will become apparent to students as they perform experiments and study the applications of chemistry to water purification, textile manufacture, steel production, and other processes. (½ unit)

Second Semester. This course contains a balanced presentation of basic concepts, logical methods, and practical applications of physics. Although the approach used is essentially nonmathematical, many of the problems presented require simple computational skills. As students carry out simple experiments, they will develop an understanding of force, work, power, energy, sound, light, magnetism, electricity, and other basic concepts. (½ unit)

SOCIAL STUDIES

Civics

In this course, students will develop an understanding of their role as American citizens. Not only will they consider their role as citizens of the United States, but students will also examine their rights and responsibilities in state and local governments, in the home and school, in the economy, and in the world. Through the examination of certain contemporary problems, students will acquire the ability to analyze critically the social and political issues of a democratic society. (½ unit)

Sociology

In this course, students will study the social development of individuals in a society, and they will consider the effects that culture, language, and status have on this social development. Special attention is given in this course to mechanisms of social control and to forces of social change. Through the analysis of such social institutions as the family, government, church, and school and through the examination of such contemporary social problems as poverty, urban decay, delinquency, and discrimination, students will develop an understanding of the characteristics of social interaction in a complex, modern society. (½ unit)

Psychology

This introduction to psychology covers a broad range of topics, including learning processes, the development of personality, mental and emotional problems, the psychology of group behavior, and social attitudes. Study of these topics will help students to develop an awareness and an understanding of the many forces that influence their behavior. (½ unit)

World Geography

First Semester. This course explores relationships between people and their physical environment. Students learn how natural surroundings influence the way people live and how people modify their surroundings to make their lives easier. While studying about the United States, Canada, and Latin America, students learn the general characteristics of each region before they analyze the interaction between the culture and geography of certain nations. (½ unit)

Second Semester. This course deals with four geographic regions: Europe, Africa, Australia and Oceania, and Asia. Students learn how the topography, climate, and natural resources of each region influence the lives of the people of the region. They also learn how the people of the region raise their standard of living by reacting to and modifying their natural surroundings. Throughout the course, students use such basic geographic skills as reading and drawing maps, analyzing charts and diagrams, and interpreting technical vocabulary. (½ unit)

Economics

This course leads to a better understanding of basic economic concepts by examining historical and current examples of economic principles at work. Students will study the role of the market in modern capitalistic economies and how it functions. The market system as a pure concept and the market system as it functions with government control and restraint will be examined. Students will analyze how government promotes and curbs the market in response to the will of society. Finally, the variety of alternate economic systems adopted in some parts of the world will be compared to the market systems in free societies. (½ unit)

World History

First Semester. Emphasis on the history and cultures of both the Western and non-Western worlds is an important feature of this course. Special attention is given to the civilizations that developed in India, China, Africa, and Latin America from ancient to recent times. The contributions which each culture made to world civilization are stressed throughout the course. (½ unit)

Second Semester. This course examines the history of the Western and non-Western worlds from about 1750 to the present. The social and political upheavals which revolutionized Western civilization and signaled the end of absolutism are examined first, and then the consequent growth of democracy and nationalism is considered. Considerable attention is given to the causes and effects of the Industrial Revolution, the "new" imperialism, and the two world wars. The course concludes with a discussion of postwar problems and recent developments that have worldwide impact. (½ unit)

American History

First Semester. The history of the United States from the European background to settlement through the Civil War is presented in this course. Students begin by examining the definition of history and its value. The readings stress important themes and events and include excerpts from the primary sources of each period considered. Self-check exercises are used as a device to reinforce the facts and issues presented in the readings and in the syllabus materials. (½ unit)

Second Semester. This course traces the major historical developments in the United States from 1865 to the present. Students will examine the causes and effects of the Industrial Revolution, immigration, reform movements, the two world wars, and other historical phenomena that have influenced American society since the Civil War. The readings include excerpts from primary sources. Social history is emphasized throughout the course. (½ unit)

American Government: Theories, Policies, and Politics

This course contains an in-depth analysis of the American federal system of government as it is outlined by the Constitution of the United States. In addition, students will study state and local government and will analyze the similarities and differences that exist in the structures of the governments of the fifty states. By helping students increase their understanding of the principles of national, state, and local government in the United States, this course helps prepare the student for responsible citizenship. The constitutional rights that are guaranteed to an American citizen as well as the relationship of citizens to the states are discussed in detail. (½ unit)

American Government: National Level

In this course the role, functions, powers, and structures of the three branches of the national government of the United States are analyzed in detail. The student will consider the constitutional systems of separation of powers and checks and balances and will study the relationships that actually exist among the President, Congress, and the Supreme Court. In addition, the student will study the role that the national government plays in the solution of specific foreign and domestic problems. (½ unit)

SPANISH

First Year Spanish

First Semester. The primary purpose of this course is to provide students with a good grasp of fundamental Spanish grammar that will enable them to read simple stories and to compose simple paragraphs. The secondary purpose is to help students develop an understanding of the culture and geography of the Spanish speaking world. Basic sentence structure, parts of speech, and regular and irregular verbs in the present tense are covered. Students will develop a basic vocabulary related to clothing, the house, time, weather, the calendar, numbers, family relationships, and other topics of conversation. (½ unit)

Second Semester. Against a cultural backdrop that includes discussion about such diverse topics as jobs and entertainment, traditional Mexican foods, and Spanish history and travel, students will increase their vocabulary, their understanding of grammatical constructions, and their ability to read and write the Spanish language. The course builds on the information about the Spanish culture and language presented in the first semester. Students focus on the study of stem-changing and irregular verbs, possessive adjectives, comparison of adjectives, and preterite tense. (½ unit)

Second Year Spanish, First Semester

Students increase their ability to read, write, and speak the Spanish language as they review the vocabulary and language structure presented in the first-year courses and as they systematically study more advanced language concepts. A thorough review of regular, irregular, and stem-changing verbs in the present and preterite tenses leads smoothly and naturally into a study of reflexive and spelling-change verbs and the imperfect, present progressive, and present perfect tenses. Students also expand their ability to write complex sentences in Spanish using reflexive, direct object, and indirect object pronouns. Students increase their awareness of Spanish culture as they read and hear about special occasions, holidays, and practices observed by the Spanish people. (½ unit)

Second Year Spanish, Second Semester

Students increase their ability to read, write, and speak Spanish as they review the vocabulary and language structures presented in the first-year courses and as they systematically study more advanced language concepts. A thorough review of regular, irregular, and stem-changing verbs in the present, preterite, and imperfect tenses leads smoothly and naturally into a study of the future and conditional tenses, as well as the present subjunctive tense and stem-changes in the subjunctive. Students increase their awareness of Spanish culture as they read and hear about special occasions and practices observed by the Spanish people. (½ unit)

STUDY SKILLS

Effective Methods of Study

This course is designed to improve study skills, habits, and attitudes through experimentation with new study procedures and through application of established study methods. (½ unit)

South Dakota, University of
Independent Study Division
State-Wide Educational Services
414 East Clark Street
Vermillion, South Dakota 57069-2390
(800) 233-7937

Description:

The University of South Dakota was founded in 1882 and now has a resident enrollment of over 5,000 students. With the introduction of correspondence courses in 1915-16, the university initiated its program of bringing the university to the people of the state. Also founded in 1915 was the National University Extension Association, of which the University of South Dakota was a charter member, "to serve colleges and universities engaged in extension work..." The NUEA, dedicated to continuing education and improved public service, is now the National University Continuing Education Association.

The Extension Division of the University was formally established in 1918. In 1967, the Division was designated as State-Wide Educational Services; the Center for Continuing Education was constructed and opened for use in 1971. State-Wide Educational Services provides a variety of services including high school and college independent study (formerly called correspondence), off-campus extension classes, workshops, institutes, and short courses for credit and noncredit.

Faculty:

Jane Doyle Bromert, Dean, State-Wide Educational Services; Kathleen Skotvold, Office Supervisor, Independent Study; Lori Blodgettt, Staff Assistant, Independent Study.

Academic Levels:
College
High School
Noncredit

Degree/Certificate Programs:

A total of thirty credits of correspondence study may be applied toward a baccalaureate degree; not more than twelve may be in any one area.

Admission Requirements:

Open enrollment; many courses have prerequisites. High school students must have approval of an officer from the school awarding the diploma.

Tuition:

$72 per credit hour. Contact the university for high school course tuition. Prices subject to change on an annual basis. MasterCard and Visa accepted. Refund policy: College tuition, within 30 days of enrollment, 75% refund less $5 per corrected lesson; within 60 days, 50 percent refund minus $5 per corrected lesson; after 60 days, no refund.

Enrollment Period:

The maximum time to complete a course is one year; the minimum time three months. One six-month extension may be permitted upon payment of an extension fee.

Equipment Requirements:

The costs of textbooks and syllabi are the responsibility of the student, as are cassette player/recorders and blank tapes.

Credit and Grading:

Examinations must be proctored; letter grades A-F are awarded, with D- as the minimum passing grade. The last thirty credit hours for a degree must be earned on the University of South Dakota campus. Credit is awarded in semester hour units.

Library Services:

Interlibrary loan available.

Accreditations:

North Central Association of Colleges and Schools. Member of: National University Continuing Education Association.

COLLEGE COURSES

ACCOUNTING

Principles of Accounting

ACCT 210. A study of the theory and application of financial accounting for service, wholesale and retail business organized as sole proprietorships. Coverage of double entry accounting, accrual basis, with emphasis on financial statement preparations. (3 semester hours)

ACCT 211. Study of partnerships' and corporations' accounting methodology. Emphasis is on long-term debts and investments. In addition, the basic concepts of managerial accounting for managerial decision making are emphasized. (3 semester hours)

ART EDUCATION

Elementary Art Methods

This course includes fundamental work in art projects suited to the needs of grade school teachers with an emphasis on the selection of materials and methods of instruction. (2 semester hours)

ASTRONOMY

Elementary Astronomy II

A general nonmathematical introduction to some of the more important ideas and concepts in modern astronomy. The emphasis will be on solar system astronomy, but also readings and studies will take the student on a voyage through star clusters and galaxies, black holes and gasses that swallow light. Consideration will also be given to practical observations which do not require equipment. (3 semester hours)

ECONOMICS

Microeconomics

The emphasis of this course is on microeconomic topics which are specific units of an economic system—industries, firms, and households—and their roles in the economy. Students will concentrate on the relationship between these individual units and the output or price of specific products, the number of workers employed in a single firm, and the revenue and expenditures of a given industry. Topics include market structures, government regulations, the distribution of income, and current economic problems. (3 semester hours)

EDUCATIONAL PSYCHOLOGY

Adolescent Growth and Development

The focus of this course is understanding the issues of behavior and physiological adjustments that adolescents experience during puberty and their junior and senior high school years. Issues addressed include: family roles and relationships, drug addiction, teen pregnancy, sexuality, peer pressure, and others. (3 semester hours)

ELEMENTARY EDUCATION

Geography for Elementary Teachers

This course is designed as an introduction to the breadth and excitement of the field of geography. The focus of the course is centered around a series of topics that will enable students to understand our planet earth. Topics will include: location, physical, and cultural attributes; place similarity and regions; and other topics deemed essential for understanding the earth. (2 semester hours)

ENGLISH

Composition

The course focuses on theme writing, principles of grammar and diction, preparation of a research paper, and critical reading of illustrative material. (3 semester hours)

Introduction to Literature

The main purpose of this course is to show the relationship between literature and the human experience. Readings in the genres of fiction, poetry, drama, and nonfiction will include the themes of innocence and experience, love and hate, and conformity and rebellion. Students will become acquainted with basic elements of literature such as theme and point of view. (3 semester hours)

English Grammar

This course is designed to improve the sentence level writing skills. The course stresses sentence construction, correct grammar, and punctuation. (3 semester hours)

Advanced Composition

This upper division composition course is designed to improve the student's basic writing skills. Assignments range from essays to practical applications such as letters and grammatical skills. (3 semester hours)

Business Writing

Writing for the world of work. The course emphasizes reader-based writing, language, format, and organization appropriate for real-life business/administrative situations. Students write a variety of memos and letters, a resume, and report. (3 semester hours)

Survey of British Literature I

This course introduces the great works of British literature beginning with the earliest known work and ending with the 18th century. Students will become familiar with historical and literary trends and also analyze individual pieces from the Anglo-Saxon, Medieval, Elizabethan, Puritan, Cavalier, Restoration, and 18th-century periods. (3 semester hours)

Survey of British Literature II

A continuation of the above course. Surveys British literature beginning with the Romantics, followed by the Victorians, and ending with 20th-century literature. (3 semester hours)

Survey of American Literature I

This course surveys the works of significant American writers from the colonial period through the mid-19th century, using a variety of critical approaches. Emphasis is on the growth of American thought and the development of literary or spiritual haven, legacy and loss, and the individual's place in society. Longer works include *The Scarlet Letter* and *Walden*. (3 semester hours)

HEALTH EDUCATION

Personal Health and Behavioral Change

A generalized study of health on a personal level as well as its dynamic applications to modern life and a rapidly changing environment. The concept of wellness is applied to topics like stress, mental health, sexuality, alcoholism, smoking, psychoactive drug use and abuse, nutrition, diet and weight control, exercise, health consumerism, cardiovascular health, cancer, safety, death and dying, and aging. Emphasis is on behavioral change and self-responsibility. (3 semester hours)

HISTORY

American History

HIST 151. The course surveys the political, economic, social, and cultural aspects of American history from 1492 to the end of Reconstruction in 1877. (3 semester hours)

HIST 152. This course surveys the political, economic, social, and cultural aspects of American history from 1877 to the present. (3 semester hours)

MATHEMATICS

Math Review

This course is designed as a review of basic algebra and to prepare a student for college algebra. The course includes symbols, the number system, properties, equations, inequalities, graphing, exponents, polynomials, factoring, rational expressions, roots and radicals, quadratic equations and functions. (4 semester hours)

College Algebra

Math 111. (4 semester hours)

Introduction to Finite Mathematics

An introduction to topics such as mathematics of finance probability, statistics, combinatorics, and linear programming. (4 semester hours)

Trigonometry

The theory and use of definitions, equations, identities, and graphs of trigonometric functions, the solutions of triangles and applications. (2 semester hours)

Linear Algebra

Systems of linear equations, vector spaces, linear transformations, matrices, quadratic forms and orthogonal and unitary transformations. (3 semester hours)

Foundations of Mathematics

Symbolic logic, set theory, mathematical induction, number theory and numeration. (3 semester hours)

POLITICAL SCIENCE

American Government

This fundamental course offers the opportunity to explore the what, how, and why of the American political system so that the student can better cope with future questions of American public policy. (3 semester hours)

PSYCHOLOGY

Personal Adjustment

This course is a thorough discussion of human personality development in terms of both family and individual modes of adjustment and psychological growth. It focuses on the everyday challenges of life and effective ways of adjusting to those challenges. (3 semester hours)

SECONDARY EDUCATION

Reading Development in Content Areas

This course is intended to help preservice teachers work more effectively with readers at the secondary level. Major emphases of the course include: (1) a better understanding of the reading process; (2) a better understanding of the strengths and needs of secondary readers; (3) a greater familiarity with effective instructional practices and programs for these readers; and (4) a better understanding of instruments and procedures for evaluation of student growth in reading. (3 semester hours)

SOCIAL WORK

Social Work Practice II

Emphasis in this course is placed on the indirect aspects of practice. Resource use and development in the nonmetropolitan community is the underlying theme. (3 semester hours)

SOCIOLOGY

Introduction to Crime and Delinquency

The sociology of criminal behavior and juvenile delinquency, with an emphasis on what causes these characteristics. The extent and forms of crime are considered together with the characteristics of offenders. (3 semester hours)

Criminology

This course covers basic and advanced study of the course of crime, the detection of crime, and the prevention of crime. The course discusses criminals and crime in America. (3 semester hours)

Penology

A study of the history and theory of justice and the treatment of the juvenile offender. The roles of legal and other social agencies are considered. The sentencing process and new methods are also discussed. (3 semester hours)

Juvenile Delinquency

This course studies the juvenile delinquent and the effect of the juvenile justice system on the delinquent. It starts with the study of the juvenile and how he/she becomes delinquent. Various theories are given in an attempt to explain delinquent behavior. The juvenile court is discussed and evaluated. (3 semester hours)

Women, Crime and Justice

This course looks at the crimes of women and the role women play in criminal justice. It includes frank discussions about women as criminals, victims, and professionals and how they have broken into a previously male-dominated profession. Also included is coverage of women as victims of rape and abuse and what we have failed to do to stop it. (3 semester hours)

Female Criminals of the World

This course looks at female crime around the world. It discusses the role of women in various societies and how that role relates to their crime patterns. The course offers a chance to see how societies where women are still considered property have dealt with women criminals. Also, in societies where women are approaching equality, the student looks at the growth of women's crime rates. (3 semester hours)

STATISTICS

Introduction to Statistics

The course emphasizes concepts and applications. Included in the course are the following: descriptive statistics, basic probability and probability distribution concepts, estimation, testing hypotheses, chi-square test for independence, contingent table, basic analysis of variance, and basic regression analysis. (3 semester hours)

HIGH SCHOOL COURSES

ART

Beginning Drawing and Painting

This course introduces the student to the use of pencil, lithograph crayon, pastel, ink, and watercolor. The course provides instruction in the drawing of still life, the human figure, animals, landscapes, and action pictures. Emphasis is placed on development of the student's creativity and natural artistic ability. (½ unit)

BUSINESS EDUCATION

Beginning Typing

First Semester. This course is designed to help students develop basic typing skills for personal use at home, in school, and at work. After learning to control the keyboard by touch, students practice formatting techniques of centering, spacing, and alignment as they type reports, letters, tables, and other documents. In a reinforcing sequence of language arts exercises, students apply rules for correct word division, capitalization, punctuation, and number style. They also learn to detect, mark, and correct errors in typewritten copy. Balanced drills provide the practice necessary for typing with moderate speed and accuracy. (½ unit)

Second Semester. This course focuses on business formatting while it improves keyboarding skills. Students continue to prepare reports, letters, tables, and business forms in the correct format from a variety of input modes. At the same time they practice the correct use of punctuation, capitalization, and numbers in typewritten communication; proofread copy for errors; and edit copy for revision. Keyboarding speed and accuracy are emphasized throughout the course. In the last unit, students lean how to compose and type documents they are likely to need when applying for a job. (½ unit)

Business English

The course emphasizes the common language skills necessary to good expression in business communications, such as letters. Coherent writing, unity of thought, sentence structure, and vocabulary building are stressed. (½ unit)

Consumer Education

This one-semester course is designed to give students a better understanding of their rights and responsibilities as consumers in the free enterprise system. It explains how personal goals and values affect consumers' choices; how consumers can develop reliable decision-making skills for spending, saving, and investing; how they can evaluate alternatives in the marketplace; and how they can get the most for a given expenditure of resources. Specific lessons on personal finance include earning money, spending and saving money, working with money, and getting and using credit. (½ unit)

General Business

This course gives an overview of business in our society. The topics covered include the place of business in society, the relationship of business and government in our economic system, the place of banks and credit in the economy, personal money management, consumer rights and responsibilities, and the use of credit. (½ unit)

Beginning Accounting

First Semester. As a foundation for preparing for a career, a successful personal financial future, or both, students study accounting terminology, concepts, principles, and practices. After students become acquainted with the various applications, they use their skills and reinforce their understanding of accounting procedures through practical experience in working through realistic accounting situations. One of the projects involves using a journal in completing an accounting cycle for a sole proprietorship; another involves using a journal in completing an accounting cycle for a partnership. (½ unit)

Second Semester. This course emphasizes the principle that effective business decisions can be made only when the information is current, accurate, and complete. It focuses on accounting terminology, concepts, and procedures as they relate to automated accounting systems. Reinforcement of basic and new learning is provided for students through their study of the accounting system of a corporation that uses special journals. The final section of the course emphasizes the functions of accounting control systems. (½ unit)

Economics

The fundamental concepts of scarcity and choice, and cause-and-effect relationships in the American economic system are analyzed. Through the study of real-life problems, such as strip mining and burning coal, students gain insight into the relationships between social and economic goals in an industrialized, technological society today. (½ unit)

ENGLISH

Basic English I

This course is designed to help students learn the terminology and the structure of the English language. The material is presented in an easy-to-understand, step-by-step fashion. Students can enter the course with little or no previous instruction in formal grammar. Parts of speech, sentence structure, choice and use of words, capitalization, and punctuation are covered in this course. (½ unit)

Composition 1: Basic Expository Writing

This course presents a systematic approach to the basics of expository writing. Students will practice a step-by-step process in learning to write unified, coherent papers. In the process of learning to write, students will learn to think in an organized, systematic fashion. They will also study effective uses of language, as well as methods of connecting ideas and expanding ideas by means of details and examples. (½ unit)

General Literature 1

This course is intended to foster in students the desire to read and the ability to express their ideas about what they read. (½ unit)

General Literature 2

This course is similar in design and intent as the above course. (½ unit)

The Short Story

The form of the short story is the central concern of this course. As students read the assigned stories, they will study such aspects of form as plot, character, and theme. (½ unit)

Ninth Grade English

First Semester. This course introduces three phases of language arts: literature, grammar, and composition. In the literature segments of the course, students read short stories, poetry, drama, and selections from the *Odyssey;* the emphases are on enjoyment and on techniques for better understanding of these types of literature. In the grammar and composition lessons, parts of speech, basic parts and characteristics of sentences, and paragraph development are emphasized. (½ unit)

Second Semester. Students review basic approaches to literature and fundamentals of grammar and composition before learning new information about these elements in the study of English. In the literature lessons, students read short stories, essays, and biographies, *Romeo and Juliet,* and selections from *Great Expectations.* In the grammar and composition lessons, students concentrate on punctuation; the parts, structures, kinds, and purposes of sentences; and on developing specificity and coherence in paragraphs. (½ unit)

Tenth Grade English

First Semester. This course further develops students' skills in three phases of language arts: literature, grammar, and composition. In the literature segments of the course, students read short stories, poetry, drama, and tales of King Arthur and his knights of the Round Table. The emphases are on reading for enjoyment and on developing techniques for better understanding these types of literature. In the grammar and composition lessons, parts of speech, basic parts and characteristics of sentences, capitalization and punctuation, and the step-by-step development of a paper are emphasized. (½ unit)

Second Semester. Students review basic approaches to literature and fundamentals of grammar and composition before learning new information about these elements in the study of English. In the literature lessons, students read short stories, essays and biographies, *Julius Caesar,* and John Steinbeck's *The Pearl.* In the grammar and composition lessons, students concentrate on the patterns, structures, kinds, and purposes of sentences, as well as on additional ways to punctuate sentences, and on developing clear, specific, coherent, and polished papers. (½ unit)

Eleventh Grade English

First Semester. The roots and historical development of American literature from the colonial period through the Civil War era are the central elements of this course. Students will gain an understanding of the ideas and perspectives that fostered the development of our country and the ways in which our literature became distinctively American. In addition to studying literature, students will review the proper grammatical constructions of sentences before focusing on such topics as punctuating sentences and correcting sentence problems. Students' composition skills will be developed, not only through analysis of the literary selections, but also through study and application of the basic organizational pattern of a good essay. (½ unit)

Second Semester. In this course, students will study the development of American literature from the Civil War to the present, noting both the ways in which literary forms have changed and the ways in which literature reflects the period in which it is written. Instruction in grammar and composition, with emphasis on writing, punctuating, and revising sentences, and on writing and polishing expository essays, is also provided. (½ unit)

Twelfth Grade English

First Semester. In this course students will read many of the great works that have formed our English literary heritage from the Anglo-Saxon period through the eighteenth century. They will gain an understanding of the development of English literature as they read Shakespeare's *Macbeth* and selections from *Beowulf, The Canterbury Tales, Paradise Lost,* and other important literary works. Students will have the opportunity to improve their writing skills as they apply good writing practices in analyzing the literary works. (½ unit)

Second Semester. In this course students will further their understanding of the historical development of English literature as they read selections by major authors of the Romantic Age, the Victorian Age, and the twentieth century. They will continue to apply and improve their writing skills as they analyze the many facets of the literary selections that they read. (½ unit)

FRENCH

First Year French

First Semester. This is a course designed to help students develop reading skills and writing skills in French. It also offers opportunities for students to develop speaking skills. (½ unit)

Second Semester. This course is a continuation of the first semester course in which French sentence structure, grammar, idiomatic expressions, and vocabulary are introduced through a series of stories about an American student in France. In addition to being presented in written form in the syllabus, the reading selections are recorded on cassette tapes. (½ unit)

Second Year French

First Semester. The course material is presented through reading selections written entirely in idiomatic French. These selections written by the author describe scenes of Parisian and French life. Included are reading selections about the French theatre, the metric system, French cooking, proverbs, and the effect of the two world wars on France. In addition to being presented in written form in the syllabus, reading selections are recorded on cassette tapes. (½ unit)

Second Semester. This course is an historical survey of French civilization from its origins to the present. Students will be introduced to famous people and events and will study the broad social, economic, and political forces that shaped French culture. Students who have successfully completed this fourth semester of French will have acquired a knowledge of French vocabulary, grammar, and sentence structure that will enable them to read a variety of French books without difficulty. (½ unit)

GERMAN

First Year German

First Semester. The reading selections present everyday situations, stories, and historical anecdotes in the form of dialogue and narrative prose; they are designed to familiarize students with the German language as it is written and spoken. New words and grammatical constructions are introduced gradually in the readings and are explained with straightforward definitions and examples. (½ unit)

Second Semester. Through the reading selections, students will learn more about the legends, customs, and daily lives of the German people. The emphasis on acquisition of vocabulary continues, and idiomatic expressions receive considerable attention. Periodic reviews of vocabulary and grammar reinforce points that students may have forgotten. (½ unit)

Second Year German

First Semester. The variety of reading selections included in the second year courses in German will help students develop an understanding of German culture and its contributions to Western civilization. This course consists of a concise review of the principles of pronunciation and grammar presented in the first year courses and lays the foundation for more advanced study of German grammar and sentence structure. (½ unit)

Second Semester. Through the reading selections for this course,

students will not only further their appreciation of German history and culture, but also practice and extend their skills in reading, writing, and speaking the German language. By the end of their second year of German, students should have a German vocabulary of approximately 1,300 words, know the meaning of approximately 150 idioms, and have a firm grasp of German sentence structure. (½ unit)

HOME ECONOMICS

Etiquette

This course is designed to give the student common-sense information on correct behavior and guidelines for proper etiquette. (½ unit)

General Homemaking

HME 003H 055. This homemaking course introduces students to basic principles of personal development and home management and reinforces these concepts through practical experience. Units of the family, child development, and personality development lead students to new understandings and skills in home and family living. Other units emphasize planning in home management and the wise use of consumer resources. (½ unit)

HME 004H 055. Clothing and foods receive equal emphasis in this introductory course in homemaking. After studying principles of clothing design, selection, and care, students practice basic sewing skills, including hand- and machine-stitching techniques. They are required to demonstrate their skills by completing a simple sewing project. The units on foods are designed to help students understand the importance of the four basic food groups and to apply that knowledge in planning meals, purchasing foods, and preparing simple recipes. As a final cooking project, students are required to prepare and serve a complete meal. (½ unit)

Clothing Construction

The focus of this course is on the development of basic sewing skills for personal use. After studying equipment, patterns, and fabrics, students learn to make their own clothes through a series of four sewing projects. The principles of the bishop method of clothing construction—grain perfection, accuracy in preparing, cutting and marking fabric, cutting to fit, and perfection in stitching and pressing—are applied throughout the course. (½ unit)

Personal Adjustment, Marriage, and Family Living

This course is planned to give students a perspective in understanding and solving everyday problems common to them, their parents, and others. Discussion of dating, courtship, and marriage is included. The development of healthy interpersonal relationships is emphasized. (½ unit)

MATHEMATICS

Basic Mathematics 1

This course is specifically designed for students who need to develop understanding and skill in using basic arithmetic. After studying each of the four basic operations—addition, subtraction, multiplication, and division of whole numbers—students learn to solve word problems involving that operation. Interpretation of word problems is covered thoroughly and understandably. (½ unit)

Basic Mathematics 2

After reviewing operations with whole numbers, students are introduced to the meaning of fractions and operations with fractions; operations with decimals; and problems involving money and percent. (½ unit)

General Mathematics 1

Emphasis is placed on developing the students' understanding of fractions, decimals, and percents, as well as on developing skill in using these mathematical operations. Ways of handling data, through graphs, scientific notation, and means of comparison, are also presented. Student apply their understanding of concepts, operations, and data analysis to practical problems dealing with interest, insurance, taxes, banking, and budgeting. (½ unit)

General Mathematics 2

In this course, students will extend their use of the basic mathematical skills and their understanding of the concepts studies in General Mathematics 1. In addition, they will study positive and negative numbers, square roots, formulas, the Cartesan coordinate system, simple equations, and sets. The metric system, measurement, area, volume, and beginning constructions with a ruler and compass are also presented. (½ unit)

Business and Consumer Mathematics

First Semester. The student will develop arithmetic skills that apply to common business activities, operations, and transactions. The topics include whole numbers, fractions, decimals, percents, ratios, proportions, basic statistics, graphs, discounts, merchandising, bank services, and interest. (½ unit)

Second Semester. The topics presented are installment financing, charge accounts, taxes, automobile ownership, budgeting, stocks, bonds, home financing, and homeowner's insurance. (½ unit)

Beginning Algebra

First Semester. Students will become acquainted with basic algebraic concepts, such as integers, linear equations, linear inequalities, factoring, and fractions. This course provides opportunities for students of various levels of ability to be successful and to develop knowledge and skills commensurate with their capacity and desire to learn. (½ unit)

Second Semester. Instruction in linear sentences, algebra in a plane, linear systems, functions, fractional equations, real numbers, equations with real solutions, and plane trigonometry is provided in this course. (½ unit)

Geometry

First Semester. Both plane geometry and coordinate geometry are presented. Topics covered include definitions of geometric terms, assumptions, theorems, congruence of triangles, perpendicularity, and parallelism. (½ unit)

Second Semester. The main topics include space geometry, non-Euclidean geometry, similar triangles, coordinate geometry, vector geometry, the circle, the locus, and inequalities. (½ unit)

Advanced Algebra

First Semester. Such concepts as integers, polynomials, factoring, rational expressions, real numbers, equations, and inequalities are presented and related to practical problems encountered in daily living. (½ unit)

Second Semester. Logarithms and trigonometry are presented in depth. Included is the study of conic sections, progressions and series, trigonometric functions, graphing and problem solving. The subject matter provides a good foundation for the future study of mathematics as well as for chemistry, physics, and other mathematically related subjects. (½ unit)

SCIENCE

Health Science

SCI 001H 055. This course introduces students to medically accepted means of promoting physical and mental well-being. Among the subjects addressed are grooming, emotional health, drug abuse, and the functions of the nervous and endocrine systems. Students will become familiar with the language used to describe the vital aspects of personal health. (½ unit)

SCI 002H 055. This course will expand the student's understanding of basic human physiology as it applies to health practices. Topics covered include exercise and fatigue; nutrition; the digestive, respiratory, and circulatory systems; infections and chronic disease; public health and the medical profession; and human sexuality. (½ unit)

Basic Biology

First Semester. This entry level course in biology introduces the student to fundamental biological concepts and relates scientific material to the student's everyday life. Basic concepts, ideas, facts, and scientific terms are presented in easy-to-understand language. The course begins with a presentation of the nature of science and the role of biology among the sciences. The course emphasizes the study of living things and their relation to their environment. (½ unit)

Second Semester. A continuation of the study of the four kingdoms in the classification of living things. Students will further their understanding of fundamental biological concepts and principles as they study characteristics of representative members of various phyla and classes of the plant and animal kingdoms. Considerable attention is devoted to the study of human biology. Students will learn about the anatomy and physiology of the human body. They will also consider such health-related topics as nutrition, disease, and harmful drugs. (½ unit)

Physical Science

First Semester. This course contains a balanced presentation of basic concepts, logical methods, and practical applications of chemistry through a nonmathematical approach. The practical nature of science will become apparent to students as they perform experiments and study the applications of chemistry to water purification, textile manufacture, steel production, and other processes. (½ unit)

Second Semester. This course contains a balanced presentation of basic concepts, logical methods, and practical applications of physics. Although the approach used is essentially nonmathematical, many of the problems presented require simple computational skills. As students carry out simple experiments, they will develop an understanding of force, work, power, energy, sound, light, magnetism, electricity, and other basic concepts. (½ unit)

SOCIAL STUDIES

World Geography

First Semester. This course explores relationships between people and their physical environment. Students learn how natural surroundings influence the way people live; they also learn how people modify their surroundings to make their lives easier. After students examine the principles of physical geography, they apply what they have learned about landforms, climate, vegetation, and soils to the study of specific geographic regions. The United States, Canada, and Latin America are dealt with in this course. (½ unit)

Second Semester. This course deals with four geographic regions: Europe, Africa, Australia and Oceania, and Asia. In this course, students learn how the topography, climate, and natural resources of each region influence the lives of the people of the region. Students learn how the people of the region raise their standard of living by reacting to and modifying their natural surroundings. Throughout the course, students use such basic geographic skills as reading and drawing maps, analyzing charts and diagrams, and interpreting technical vocabulary. (½ unit)

World History

First Semester. Emphasis on the history and cultures of both the

Western and non-Western worlds is an important feature of this course. Special attention is given to the civilizations that developed in India, China, Africa, and Latin America from ancient to recent times. The account of Western development begins with the ancient civilizations of the Middle East, Greece, and Rome; continues with the political, social, and economic developments in the Middle Ages; and concludes with the changes that occurred during the Age of Discovery, the Age of Absolutism, and the Age of Reason. The contributions that each culture made to world civilization are stressed throughout the course. (½ unit)

Second Semester. The history of the Western and non-Western worlds from about 1750 to the present is the subject of this course. The social and political upheavals that revolutionized Western civilization and signaled the end of absolutism are examined first, and then the consequent growth of democracy and nationalism is considered. Considerable attention is given to the causes and effects of the Industrial Revolution, the "new" imperialism, and the two world wars. The course concludes with a discussion of postwar problems and recent developments that have worldwide impact. (½ unit)

American History

First Semester. The history of the United States from the European background to settlement through the Civil War is presented in this course. Students begin by examining the definition of history and its value. The readings stress important themes and events and include excerpts from the primary sources of each period considered. (½ unit)

Second Semester. This courses traces the major historical developments in the United States from 1865 to the present. Students will examine the causes and effects of the Industrial Revolution; immigration; reform movements; the two world wars; and other historical phenomena that have influenced American society since the Civil War. The readings include excerpts from primary sources. Social history is emphasized throughout the course. (½ unit)

American Government

SST 035H 002. This course contains an in-depth analysis of the American federal system of government as it is outlined by the Constitution of the United States. In addition, the students will study state and local government and will analyze the similarities and differences that exist in the structures of the governments of the 50 states. By helping students increase their understanding of the principles of national, state, and local government in the United States, this course will prepare the student for responsible citizenship. The constitutional rights that are guaranteed to an American citizen as well as the relationship of citizens to the states are discussed in detail. (½ unit)

SST 036H 002. In this course the role, functions, powers, and structures of the three branches of the national government of the United States are analyzed in detail. The student will consider the constitutional systems of separation of powers, and checks and balances and will study the relationships that actually exist between the President, the Congress, and the Supreme Court. In addition, the student will study the role that the national government plays in the solution of specific foreign and domestic problems. (½ unit)

Modern Problems

Significant social and political issues that are of special concern to today's students are examined in this course in contemporary problems. Students will analyze issues through an in-depth study of six topics: Prejudice and Discrimination; the Drug Scene; Poverty in an Affluent Society; Peace or War; Voices of Dissent; Propaganda, Polls, and Public Opinion. (½ unit)

SPANISH

First Year Spanish

First Semester. The primary purpose of this course is to provide students with a good grasp of fundamental Spanish grammar that will enable them to read simple stories and to compose simple paragraphs. The secondary purpose is to help students develop an understanding of the culture and geography of Spain, Mexico, and Latin America. (½ unit)

Second Semester. Against a cultural backdrop that includes discussion about such diverse topics as Christmas customs in Spanish-speaking countries, traditional Mexican foods, and Spanish history, students will increase their vocabulary, their understanding of grammatical constructions, and their ability to read and write the Spanish language. (½ unit)

Second Year Spanish

First Semester. Students will increase their ability to read, write, and speak the Spanish language as they review the vocabulary and language structures presented in the first year courses and as they systematically study more advanced language concepts. Students will also enhance their awareness of the Spanish culture as they read and hear about special occasions and practices observed by the Spanish people. (½ unit)

Second Semester. Continuing emphasis is placed on reading in the Spanish language and on understanding Spanish-speaking people. Composition and writing skills are also stressed. Students will continue to improve their listening and speaking skills. (½ unit)

STUDY SKILLS

Effective Methods of Study

This course is designed to improve study skills, habits, and attitudes through experimentation with new study procedures and through application of established study methods. (½ unit)

PROFESSIONAL COURSES

REAL ESTATE

Real Estate Prelicensing Study

State-Wide Educational Services, in cooperation with the University of South Dakota School of Business and the South Dakota Real Estate Commission, offers three noncredit independent study courses for prelicensing study. The courses meet the statutory requirement for contact hours and have been approved by the South Dakota Real Estate Commission.

Real Estate I. This first 40-hour educational requirement serves as a course of study for the sales license. *Tuition:* $150 plus books, tax, and handling.

Real Estate II. This course is a study of legal instruments and relationships in real estate law. These instruments include titles, purchase, agreements, deeds, liens, conveyances, and other types of contracts. *Tuition:* $150 plus books, tax, and handling.

Real Estate III. This course places special emphasis on those problems that confront the broker in his or her business. The economic environment that determines the conditions of the real estate market is covered as well as the effects of political decisions as reflected in taxes and zoning. *Tuition:* $150 plus books, tax, and handling.

Real Estate Appraisal. This course aids you in completing the regulatory educational requirements and acquiring skills necessary to become an appraiser. The course is designed to cover the basic theories and methods of real estate appraisal, with particular attention being given to the areas of study deemed necessary for an applicant to possess the South Dakota Real Estate Appraiser's License issued by the Real Estate Commission. *Tuition:* $150 plus books, tax, and handling.

South Florida, University of

4202 Fowler Avenue
Tampa, Florida 33620   (813) 974-4030

Description:

Correspondence courses are offered through the Department of Independent Study and Distance Education of the University of Florida in Gainesville. For courses available, SEE **Florida, University of.**

Accreditations:

Southern Association of Colleges and Schools.

Southeastern Bible College

External Studies Department
3001 Highway 280 East
Birmingham, Alabama 35243   (205) 969-0880

Description:

Southeastern Bible College was founded in 1935 and offers Christian higher education in a thorough-going Biblical framework. The College takes its place with similar institutions throughout the country in offering training with a high academic standard coupled with a balanced spiritual emphasis. The College is not denominationally affiliated.

The External Studies Department began at Dallas Bible College in Texas in 1959. The Department was transferred to Southeastern Bible College in January 1986. There are currently 300 students enrolled in independent study by correspondence.

Faculty:

Dr. Ray E. Baughman, Dean of External Studies.

Academic Levels:

College
Noncredit

Degree/Certificate Programs:

Bachelor, Associate, Certificate, Diploma. Transfer of credit from other colleges will be considered upon receipt of an official transcript.

Admission Requirements:

High school graduation or GED. Enrollment is restricted to students in the United States, Canada, the Armed Forces, and U.S. missionaries.

Tuition:

$75 per semester hour. Textbooks and tapes are not included in tuition. Students may make a down payment of one third of tuition and the cost for all books and materials with the balance to be paid in four months. Refund policy: Written notification must be submitted. If no lessons have been sent in and withdrawal is within ten days of the time materials were received, 100 percent will be refunded; between 11–31 days, 60 percent; 4–6 weeks, 40 percent; 7–8 weeks, 20 percent; 9 weeks or over, no refund.

Enrollment Period:

Students may enroll at any time during the year. A maximum of one year is allowed to complete a course. If an extension of time is necessary, the student may apply for a six-month extension for a fee of $10. The minimum time to complete a course is six weeks.

Equipment Requirements:

Textbooks must be purchased by the student. Some courses require the purchase and use of VHS and audio tapes; access to videocassette and/or audiocassette players is necessary.

Credit and Grading:

Grading system is A–F. The minimum passing grade is D. Examinations must be proctored.

Accreditations:

American Association of Bible Colleges.

COLLEGE COURSES

BIBLE

Bible Study Methods

In this course the student will study eight different methods of Bible study and then learn to correlate them into the mastery of a Bible book. The student will be instructed in the use of *Young's Concordance*, commentaries, and modern translations. In the second part of the course, the student will do assignments from the Book of I Peter. The purpose of this section is to use the methods to develop skills in doing an analytical study of a Bible book for one's self. (3 semester hours)

Bible Survey I: God's Plan of the Ages

A course to help the student visualize God's plan of the ages, from eternity to eternity. The student will study Bible history and prophecy in order to have a framework in which to study each book of the Bible, to understand its relationship to other books of the Bible, and to see the Bible as a whole. There is also an emphasis upon Bible geography. (3 semester hours)

Bible Survey II: Old Testament

Attention is given to the theme, principal teachings, background, author, recipients, date, and geography of each book of the Old Testament. (3 semester hours)

Bible Survey III: New Testament

Attention is given to the theme, principal teachings, background, author, recipients, date, geography and how the New Testament related to the Old Testament. (3 semester hours)

Bible Exposition: Acts

From the ascension of Christ and the birth of the church to the end of the first church generation in A.D. 63, the unfolding revelation of God is studied in its chronological order and in its geographical and historical setting. The emphasis is put upon studying the Scripture itself. This is accomplished by the use of certain Bible study methods and the interaction of the student with his resource materials. The student is continually asked to make applications of the truth that he has studied to his own life and ministry. (2 semester hours)

Bible Exposition: Daniel

This course is a detailed, analytical study of the Book of Daniel. This book gives a basic framework for the study of prophecy. It is the fountainhead of the great prophetic themes concerning the "times of the Gentiles" and God's program for Israel. (2 semester hours)

Bible Exposition: Exodus

This course leads the student into a detailed study of the "Book of Redemption." It shows how God redeemed His people from Egypt by blood and by power. It also illustrates many of the conflicts, trials, and testings that a believer experiences. (2 semester hours)

Bible Exposition: Genesis

The book of Genesis is of primary importance because it is the "seed plot" of the Bible. The beginning of every very important doctrine is found in it. The student will study the historical, geographical, and chronological settings, the covenants, key people, and key events: creation, temptation, fall, flood, and entrance into Egypt. Key chapters are studied in detail. (2 semester hours)

Bible Exposition: Hebrews

This course is designed to bring many of the Old Testament theological concepts and relate them to the New Testament. It shows how Jesus Christ is the fulfillment of these promises and prophecies. (2 semester hours)

James and Galatians

This course is an expositional study of these Bible books. The student will do 33 analytical studies. (2 semester hours)

James and Galatians Practicum

In addition to the work done in the *James and Galatians* course, the student will prepare 13 lesson plans, teach the lessons in a class, record the classes, and evaluate them. The lesson plans must include: behavioral objectives, introduction, teaching outline with audiovisuals. The class may be in Sunday school, midweek, or home Bible class (approved by Southeastern Bible College). (4 semester hours)

Bible Exposition: Gospel of John

This key book of the Bible will be studied verse-by-verse. By tape the student will listen to eight key lectures by the late Dr. Martin O. Massinger who taught this course for over 30 years at Dallas Bible College. (2 semester hours)

Bible Exposition: Joshua

A detailed analytical study of the Book of Joshua that examines the development of Israel as a theocratic nation as it enters and possesses the promised land. This will include the historical background, the military campaigns, the tribal allotments, and the character qualities of Joshua and other persons in this period. Attention will be given to the application of spiritual truth to the believer's life. (2 semester hours)

Luke and John

Each of the Gospels emphasize a certain aspect of Jesus. In this course, instruction is given Bible practicum series. The practicums unite analytical Bible study and Christian ministry. The student will make analytical studies of the books and develop ministry assignments from them: devotionals, sermon outlines, lecture outlines, and discipleship assignments. Emphasis is placed upon learning Bible book methods of study and the presentation. (4 semester hours)

Bible Exposition: Revelation

A detailed analytical study of the Book of Revelation with special emphasis upon the historical and eschatological significance of the book as it relates to the premillennial, pretribulational, dispensational system of interpretation. Problem passages and other systems of interpretation will be dealt with. (3 semester hours)

Bible Exposition: Romans

The Book of Romans is a doctrinal treatise of supreme importance. It is really a condensed doctrinal course in the subjects of grace, propitiation, righteousness of God, justification, reconciliation, identification, adoption, sanctification, spiritual gifts, and glorification. The student will be asked to apply the truths of the book to the spiritual experience of the student. (3 semester hours)

I and II Thessalonians, Philippians

A detailed study of the books of I and II Thessalonians and Philippians. Emphasis is given to the study of the principles of evangelism, care of new believers, spiritual life, the Lord's return for His church, the Day of the Lord, and the doctrine of Christology. (2 semester hours)

I and II Timothy

This course is an analytical study of the two pastoral epistles that Paul sent to Timothy. (2 semester hours)

I and II Timothy Practicum

This practicum includes the analytical study of the *I and II Timothy* course with the study of adult education. The student will prepare 13 lesson plans, teach the lessons, record the classes, and evaluate them. This class may be in a Sunday School, training hour, midweek service, Christian college, or home, but it must be approved by Southeastern Bible College. (4 semester hours)

Life of Christ

This is a presentation of the Lord's earthly life in both a chronological and geographical order. The student will gain an understanding of the progression and interrelation of the events in the life of Jesus. Six major themes are traced through the Gospels. (2 semester hours)

Missionary Methods in Acts

This course is an inductive study of the Book of Acts. There is a special emphasis upon the philosophy and methods of the church as it begins to fulfill the great commission. Most of the assignments will be in the Book of Acts studying the goals, spiritual dynamics, personnel communication, opposition, and internal crises as the church evangelizes, trains leadership, and plants new churches. (3 semester hours)

EDUCATION

Educational Psychology

The scientific study of learning and other human behavior that is relevant to education. Educational objectives, learner characteristics, learning theories, learning principles, creativity, motivation, discipline, memory, measurement and evaluation, and educational innovations are studied. (3 semester hours)

ENGLISH

English Grammar and Composition

This is a course in grammar, correct usage, and punctuation. The programmed textbook takes the student through the material a step at a time. Additional assignments are given related to the structure and writing of paragraphs. Three themes or writing assignments are written during the course. (3 semester hours)

English Composition

This course is a continuation of *English Grammar and Composition* with emphasis on composition. The analysis of compositions and writing of short compositions are preparation for the writing of a research paper. Lessons emphasize style, organization of materials, research techniques, documentation of sources, and bibliographical preparations. (3 semester hours)

GREEK

Greek I

This course gives an introduction to New Testament Greek and Greek language tools. It is a practical course designed to enrich a teaching and preaching ministry. Many memory helps are supplied. The student will study the alphabet, parts of speech, sentence structures, verb tenses, and substantive cases. There will be word studies with special attention given to synonyms. The textbooks are tools that the student will use in a lifetime of study. The course may be taken with or without the video. (3 semester hours)

Greek II

This course is a continuation of *Greek I*. Each lesson will include three areas of study: a review of grammar, analysis of selected Greek verses, and vocabulary study. In the vocabulary study, the student will do word studies with special attention given to synonyms. (3 semester hours)

HEBREW

Introduction to Biblical Hebrew

This course gives an introduction to Hebrew and Hebrew language tools. It is a practical course designed to enrich a teaching and preaching ministry. The student will study the alphabet, parts of speech, word formation, sentence structures, and synonyms. A unique method of verb identification is presented. Rote memory work has been kept to a minimum. The textbooks are tools that you will use in a lifetime of study. Most assignments are taken from the Psalms. This course is not designed to make the student a Hebrew expert, but to help in understanding the experts and the tools they have prepared. (3 semester hours)

MATHEMATICS

College Math

This course is designed for those working toward teacher certification in elementary education, or for those who need a math course in their program. It presumes little prior knowledge of mathematics and is presented in a semi-programmed work-text format that allows the students to progress at their own pace. (3 semester hours)

MISSIONS

Introduction to Missions

This course is a study of the biblical and theological basis for missions as given in the Bible. Consideration is given to the missionary call; stress is placed upon the biblical response to universalism and syncretism. The history of missions is surveyed through missionary biographies. The course examines the basic means and opportunities of missions, selected ministries through church and parachurch entities, and trends in missions today. (2 semester hours)

PASTORAL STUDIES

Personal Evangelism

This course is a study of the theology, principles, and methods designed to equip students to share with others a saving knowledge of Jesus Christ. A part of the course is related to the follow-up of new Christian. The student will listen to eight lectures by Evangelist James Dixon and submit a tape of the student's presentation of the gospel. (2 semester hours)

Pastoral Practicum

The Pastoral Practicums are designed to give the student guided experiences in the local church ministry.

PA-412. This course concentrates on the qualifications of a pastor, the call, licensing/ordination, pitfalls, and visitation of church members, prospects, shut-ins, bereaved, and nursing home and hospital patients. A plan for premarital counseling will also be prepared. It is the student's responsibility to obtain permission from his pastor to do the ministry required in this course. (2 semester hours)

PA-442. This course concentrates on the public ministry of the pastor: baptisms, funerals, Lord's supper, weddings, prayer meetings, worship services, and outreach programs. It is the student's responsibility to obtain permission from his pastor to do the ministry required in this course. (2 semester hours)

PSYCHOLOGY

Introduction to Psychology

This course is a study of human behavior and mental activity. Major theories of behavior are explored and evaluated. Assignments include personal applications and experiments. Modern methods of educational theory are used in the study of this course. (3 semester hours)

Counseling

This course surveys counseling theories, examines the role of the Christian counselor, and introduces the student to the basic techniques and methods of personal counseling. The student will learn to know when and where to refer people who have problems too serious for the counselor to handle. The student also will be studying spiritual as well as psychological principles. Problem areas that will be studied include: anxiety, depression, suffering, guilt, loneliness, rejection, self-discipline, and personal relationships. (2 semester hours)

Introduction to Human Development

This course is an introduction to the self-actualization of a person so that, under God, he is doing what he is best fitted to do, becoming all that he is capable of becoming, and achieving his greatest potential in the plan and program of God. Spiritual, psychological, and social aspects of human development are studied. The student will take the Daisy Temperament Analysis and Ministry Quotient Analysis, to help better understand one's self. (3 semester hours)

Marriage and Family Counseling

Principles and techniques available to the counselor are explored and evaluated. A part of this course is made up of selected tape lectures from counseling seminars. (2 semester hours)

SOCIOLOGY

Marriage and Family

This course introduces the student to what the Bible says about marriage and the family. The student will study the role of the husband and wife, communication in the home, parent-child relationships, dating and courtship, and perils to marriage and the family. Eight key lectures by Mervin Longenecker, selected reading assignments, and several short research projects are required. (2 semester hours)

SPEECH

Speech

Basic principles of effective speech are studied with emphasis on voice, general appearance, method of delivery, and preparation of various types of speeches. The assigned speeches will vary from 3 to 10 minutes and are to be given in connection with a church ministry or civic club. Cassette tapes are used for instruction in voice development, to give examples of the different kinds of speeches, to record the student's speeches, and to record the instructor's evaluation of the student's speeches. Students may submit speeches on audio or VHS video cassettes. (3 semester hours)

THEOLOGY

Doctrine: Bible Introduction

This course is a study of how the Bible came from God to man. It is divided into three basic parts: the various doctrines of inspiration, canonicity or determining what books should be in the Bible, and how the message of the original autographs has been transmitted to us today. (3 semester hours)

Bible Introduction Practicum

In addition to what is accomplished in *Doctrine: Bible Introduction,* the student will actually teach a 13-lesson course on this subject from the material that the student has prepared. It can be a Sunday school class, midweek service, or a home Bible class (Southeastern Bible College approval is needed). (4 semester hours)

Doctrine: Eschatology

This is a study of biblical prophecy, the basis of interpretation, God's plan of the ages, biblical covenants, dispensations, prophecies of this age and its end, the tribulation, the second advent, the kingdom, and the eternal state. Also studied is the relationship of this life to positions and activities of eternity. (2 semester hours)

Doctrine: Spiritual Life

This course introduces the student to the promise of the Spirit-filled life and the ministry of the Holy Spirit to the believer. (2 semester hours)

Doctrinal Summary

This course is a systematic study of the whole field of Christian doctrine: Bibliology (the Bible), Theology (God), Christology (Christ), Soteriology (salvation), Anthropology (man), Pneumatology (the Holy Spirit), Ecclesiology (the church), Angelology (angels) and Eschatology (things to come). (3 semester hours)

Theology I

This course is a systematic survey of Bible doctrines: Bibliology, Theology, Christology, Pneumatology. It is designed to carefully orient the student in the field of Systematic Theology and to help the student relate the studies to one's personal life. (3 semester hours)

Theology II

This course is a systematic survey of Bible doctrines: Angelology, Satanology, Anthropology, Harmatiology, Soteriology, Ecclesiology, and Eschatology. It is designed to carefully orient the student to the field of Systematic Theology and to help relate the studies to the personal life. (3 semester hours)

Doctrinal Position Paper

Those in the Bachelor of Science Degree program will take this course in their final semester. The student will demonstrate his comprehension of Bible Doctrine. This paper is to have a clear, accurate declaration of the student's personal beliefs with adequate defense. (1 semester hour)

Southeastern College
Thomas G. Wilson Institute for Distance Learning
1000 Longfellow Boulevard
Lakeland, Florida 33801   (800) 854-7477

Description:
Southeastern College was founded in 1935 and is a four-year undergraduate college owned and operated by the seven southeastern districts of the Assemblies of God. The College seeks to provide educational opportunities for the personal growth and development of all students by integrating an understanding of the Bible with other areas of study.

Southeastern College has offered correspondence courses since 1982 and an external degree program since 1986. The courses offered are related to ministerial training with four majors: Bible, Missions, Christian Education, and Pastoral Ministries. Approximately 900 external degree students are enrolled in more than 2,000 courses per year.

The External Degree Program provides a student with the opportunity to earn an accredited Bachelor of Arts degree without any resident requirements. All courses can be provided by the college and completed by the student at his/her place of residence. Courses listed below are available either by correspondence format or by Guided Instruction Via Telephone and Mail format. The latter format is indicated at the end of the course description.

Faculty:
Dr. Charles W. Spond, Director for Distance Learning; Elaine G. Newman, Admissions Secretary. The resident college faculty supports the correspondence program.

Academic Levels:
College

Degree/Certificate Programs:
Baccalaureate degree.

Admission Requirements:
High school graduation or equivalent. Correspondence courses may be taken without entering the External Degree Program. Transfer-in credits may be accepted if from a regionally accredited institution.

Tuition:
$60 per credit hour. External Degree Program admission fees: $135. MasterCard and Visa accepted. Refund may be given if withdrawal occurs within 15 days of enrollment. Veterans benefits may apply for qualified applicants. Military personnel may enroll through DANTES.

Enrollment Period:
The maximum time to complete a course is one year. An extension of six weeks may be granted upon request and payment of a $20 extension fee.

Equipment Requirements:
Textbooks must be purchased by the student. Study guides are included in tuition.

Credit and Grading:
Letter grades are assigned. Examinations must be supervised by an approved proctor.

Library Services:
External Degree student have access to the college library by mail and are required to identify appropriate library resources within their locale.

Accreditations:

Southern Association of Colleges and Schools; American Association of Bible Colleges; American Association of Christian Schools International.

COLLEGE COURSES

BIBLE

Old Testament Survey

A synthetic study of the books of the Old Testament giving students an appreciation of each book as a unit and of its contribution to God's plan of redemption as it develops in the Old Testament. (3 semester hours)

Isaiah

A careful study of the life of Isaiah, with emphasis given to his times, his message to Israel, and his Messianic prophecies. Attention is given to the problem of authorship. Telephone/Mail format. (2 semester hours)

Pentateuch

Advanced study of the first five books of the Bible. Special attention is given to critical problems, the early history of Israel, to Mosaic laws, and to ethical values and abiding principles. (3 semester hours)

Old Testament History I

An analysis of the history of Israel from the conquest of Canaan through the destruction of Jerusalem and the beginning of the Babylonian captivity. Special attention will be given to the impact of the prophetic movement on various stages in this period of ancient history as well as the impact of foreign cultures and powers on Israel. Telephone/mail format. (3 semester hours)

Old Testament History II

An analysis of the history of Israel from the Babylonia captivity through the Maccabean period. Special attention will be given to Daniel's experiences in the exile, the reconstruction of the Temple, the rebuilding of Jerusalem, the contribution of some of the Minor Prophets, and the impact of the foreign cultures and powers on Israel. Telephone/Mail format. (3 semester hours)

Biblical Hermeneutics

A course designed to familiarize the student with the science of interpretation as related to the Biblical text. Emphasis is placed upon the principles of exegesis, particularly the interpretation of scripture in light of its historical, grammatical, and theological content. (2 semester hours)

Genesis

An exegetical treatment of the first book of the Bible. The four events relating to origins are emphasized in Genesis 1–11 while the four personalities of Genesis 12–50 focus attention on the Abrahamic Covenant and the chosen people of God. Telephone/Mail format. (2 semester hours)

Jeremiah

A study of the life and ministry of the prophet Jeremiah who lived during the last days of the Jewish kingdom. Special application is given to the true nature of prophetic ministry in the Old Testament. Telephone/Mail format. (2 semester hours)

Teaching the Bible

A survey of various Bible study methods and their application to teaching the Bible are explored. Students will examine portions of Old Testament passages, Galatians, James, and prepare teaching plans using various Bible study methods. (3 semester hours)

Hebrew Poetry

A study of poetry in the Old Testament with special emphasis given to Psalms and Song of Solomon. There will also be an analysis of the rhythm of thought and parallelism characteristic of Hebrew poetry. (2 semester hours)

Hebrew Wisdom Literature

An examination of the wisdom literature of the Old Testament with special emphasis given to Proverbs and Ecclesiastes. Telephone/Mail format. (2 semester hours)

Exodus

An exegetical course in Exodus which gives consideration to the deliverance of Israel, the law, the tabernacle, and the priesthood. Israel's history and culture are discussed in the light of the theology of Ancient Israel. Telephone/Mail format. (2 semester hours)

Leviticus

An exegetical course which deals with the Old Testament covenant and the Levitical laws relating to the various offerings, the operations of the tabernacle, and the cleanliness and purity of the people of God. Telephone/Mail format. (2 semester hours)

Ezekiel

An analysis of the ministry of the man who preached to Israel during the period of exile in Babylon. Special attention is given to those prophecies which have to do with the judgment and restoration of Israel. Telephone/Mail format. (2 semester hours)

The Book of Job

An analysis of the problem of evil and suffering in relation to a sovereign God as presented in the book of Job. Telephone/Mail format. (2 semester hours)

Minor Prophets

The last twelve books in the Old Testament canon are studied in the light of the circumstances which confronted the prophets, and cover the content of their messages as a revelation of the will of God. (3 semester hours)

Apocalyptic Literature of the Old Testament

An exegetical and historical analysis of the apocalyptic literature of the Old Testament and the nature of apocalyptic literature. Special emphasis will be given to the apocalyptic literature of Daniel, Ezekiel 38–48, and Zechariah 9–14. Telephone/Mail format. (2 semester hours)

New Testament Survey

A synthetic view of the books of the New Testament emphasizing how each book and group of books contribute to the working out of the plan of redemption which was begun in Genesis and was consummated in Revelation. (3 semester hours)

Life of Christ

A study of the life and teachings of Jesus as recorded in the gospels in light of the historical, cultural, geographical settings of the first century. The course will emphasize the ministry of John the Baptist, the proclamation of the Kingdom of God, the miracles and parables of Jesus, the passion, the resurrection, and messianic titles. (2 semester hours)

Acts

A detailed study of the origin and development of the apostolic church and of the ministry of the ascended Christ as carried on through the church by the power of the Holy Spirit. (2 semester hours)

Matthew

A study of Matthew's gospel emphasizing the Sermon on the Mount and other discourses such as the parables of the Kingdom, the Church, and eschatological passages. Attention will be given to Matthew's unique presentation of Jesus as the Messiah. Telephone/Mail format. (2 semester hours)

Luke

A study of Luke's gospel showing the portrayal of Jesus as the universal Savior. Topics of study will include Luke's literary style, his social interest, prayer, and the Holy Spirit. Telephone/Mail format. (2 semester hours)

Earlier Epistles of Paul

An analytical study of Galatians and I and II Thessalonians, with emphasis on the relationship of faith and works, the transmission of authoritative teaching, and the teaching on the *parousia*. Telephone/Mail format. (2 semester hours)

Mark

A study of Mark's distinctive portrayal of Jesus' ministry as the servant of Yahweh and his Gentile emphasis. A chapter-by-chapter analysis of the text reflecting on Mark's themes and characteristics will be conducted. Telephone/Mail format. (2 semester hours)

Prison Epistles

An analytical, expository treatment of Ephesians, Philippians, Colossians, and Philemon. Telephone/Mail format. (2 semester hours)

Pastoral Epistles

An expository study of First and Second Timothy and Titus. Consideration is given to the authorship, date, the threat of Gnosticism, and the significance that these epistles have for church organization and for the function of the pastor in the local church. (2 semester hours)

Biblical Introduction

A study of the inspiration, canonization, and transmission of the Biblical text. The course includes a review of the history of the English Bible. Trustworthiness of the text is supported by a consideration of archaeological discovery and correlation with secular historical data. Telephone/Mail format. (2 semester hours)

Corinthian Correspondence

An analysis and exposition of First and Second Corinthians stressing the historical background with special exegetical treatment of I Corinthians. (3 semester hours)

Romans

An intensive study of the Pauline Epistle in light of the principles of sound exposition. Special attention is given to the theological concepts of law, righteousness, justification, and sanctification, as well as the place of Israel in God's plan. (3 semester hours)

General Epistles

An outlined study of the letters of James, Peter, John, and Jude, with special attention given to historical background, structure, and distinctive teachings of each book. Telephone/Mail format. (2 semester hours)

Revelation

An analysis of the historical setting, language, and special symbolism in Revelation. Special attention will be given to the apocalyptic language and the end-time images described in the book. Telephone/Mail format. (2 semester hours)

Epistle to the Hebrews

An expository study with a discussion of the authorship, date, and destination of this epistle. Emphasis is placed on the priestly work of Christ. Telephone/Mail format. (2 semester hours)

Gospel of John

A study of the Johannine Christology, the relation of the Gospel to the Synoptics, the distinctive place of the Gospel, and the person and ministry of Jesus Christ in the Gospel. (2 semester hours)

BIBLICAL LANGUAGES

Introduction to Biblical Languages

A basic course introducing students to rudiments of classical Hebrew and Koine Greek. Designed to help students in use of various study tools and/or to prepare them for more advanced study of one or both the languages. (3 semester hours)

Greek Ia

This course is an introduction to the language in which the New Testament was originally written. The student begins with pronunciation and basic reading and writing, then progresses to basic rules of grammar and syntax. Additional vocabulary words are included in each lesson, along with basic translation exercises from Greek to English and English to Greek. (4 semester hours)

Greek Ib

In this course, the student completes his study of Machen's text. Principles of grammar and syntax are more advanced, moving the student to the point of reading basic Biblical passages and doing rudimentary exegesis. (4 semester hours)

Greek IIa

In preparing for serious study of the New Testament, the student begins to focus on syntax, concentrating on nouns, verbs, and clauses. Supplementary vocabulary learning is also required. (3 semester hours)

Greek IIb

The student continues the study of Greek syntax while continuing to expand his vocabulary. (3 semester hours)

Hebrew Ia

This course is an introduction to the primary language of the Old Testament. Following a study of consonants, vowel points and pronunciation, the student advances to crucial vocabulary and basic rules of grammar and syntax. Translation exercises are also included with the lessons. By the end of the course, the student is able to translate certain basic Biblical passages. (4 semester hours)

Hebrew Ib

In this course, the student reviews basic principles of Dr. Mansoor's book, then progresses to a more detailed study of grammar and syntax. (4 semester hours)

Hebrew IIa

The student begins a practical application of his study of Hebrew by focusing on the book of Genesis. Continuation of vocabulary building. (3 semester hours)

Hebrew IIb

Through practice in composing in Hebrew, the student deepens his understanding of syntax, develop vocabulary, and prepares for advanced exegesis of Biblical passages. (3 semester hours)

Reading in the Greek New Testament

This reading course is designed to develop the student's ability to read the Greek New Testament. Observation of the formative elements of the various word forms noting their syntactical functions will be emphasized. (2 semester hours)

Principles of Exegesis

This course will consider a sound methodology for searching out the truth which the New Testament authors intended to communicate. Exegetical resources will be considered. (2 semester hours)

BUSINESS

Economic Principles I

This course explains the organization, operation, and goals of the U.S. economic system with emphasis on basic principles and concepts; the measurement, determination, and stabilization of national income; and the management of money. Telephone/Mail format. (3 semester hours)

Economic Principles II

This course is a continuation of basic principles of economics with particular emphasis on the nature and application of those concepts bearing on decision-making within a household, firm, or industry, including consideration of problems respecting the composition and pricing of the national product, distribution of income, pricing, and output of factors of production and international trade. (3 semester hours)

Principles of Management

A study of the fundamentals of administration and management. Content will include these management functions: planning, organizing, staffing, leading, and controlling. The course seeks to integrate the functions of management with appropriate quantitative and behavioral concepts. (3 semester hours)

Human Resources Management

Principles and practices related to human resources management, based on current business practices, the behavioral sciences, and biblical values. Consideration will be given to personnel sources, selection and placement of personnel, workers' environments, compensation, training, promotion, health and safety, benefit plans, relations between management and employees. (3 semester hours)

Principles of Finance

A study of basic principles and theories of business finance, to include taxes as related to the church environment, cash flow management, capital management, banking, interest, investments, and insurance. (3 semester hours)

Business Communications

Principles of effective communication in a business environment. The course includes the preparation of letters, reports, and other forms of business writing on the computer, a study of communication variables and barriers to effective communication in a business organization. (3 semester hours)

Business Law

Designed for the teacher, churchman, educational administrator, businessman, or any citizen who would like to increase his understanding of those legal principles which apply to normal business transactions. Contracts, agency, property, insurance, wills and trusts, and torts are among the topics discussed. (3 semester hours)

CHRISTIAN EDUCATION

History and Polity of the Assemblies of God

The factors which contributed to the origin of the General Council of the Assemblies of God; its growth and development at home and abroad; its organizational structure and government. (2 semester hours)

Church Music for Ministers

A study of the relationship of music to the services of the church, planning and management of the church music programs, and organizational methods for the development of children, youth, and adult choirs and programs. (1 semester hour)

Social Foundations of Education

A study of the principles and philosophy of education with emphasis on historical and social forces affecting the development of American education with its opportunities and requirements. Surveys teacher organizations, professional ethics, and school law. (3 semester hours)

Psychological Foundations of Education

A study of the principles and philosophy of human growth and development, and learning theory applied to teaching. An overview of various models and methods of classroom management. Construction, evaluation, and interpretation of formal and informal educational tests and measurements. (3 semester hours)

Developmental Psychology

A study of the human growth and development from conception to death. The course emphasizes the physical, mental, emotional, social, and personality growth with special attention given to guidance toward acceptable behavior, responsible adult control of relevant phases of nurture, modes of interpersonal interaction, and the aging process. Telephone/Mail format. (3 semester hours)

Teaching the Bible

A study of the objectives, organization of materials, and methods of teaching as related to teaching Bible. (3 semester hours)

Teaching Principles and Competencies

Focus on generic teaching competencies and the principles underlying successful teaching (K−12), including lesson planning classroom management, instructional organization, presentation of subject matter, communication, and evaluation of pupil achievement. A teaching unit will be developed by each student. Includes 20 hours of field-based observation/participation in local school setting. Telephone/Mail format. (2 or 3 semester hours)

Children's Ministries

A specialized study of children's ministry as it pertains to specific programs as Children's Church, Kids' Crusades, Story Hour, Vacation Bible School, camps, retreats, etc. Involves special emphasis on the principles of Christian Education as applies to these areas. Telephone/Mail format. (2 semester hours)

Administration of Christian Education

A survey of the historical development, philosophy, and principles of Christian education and an emphasis upon administrative methods as they apply to the total educational work of the local church. (3 semester hours)

Instructional Media for Christian Education

A course designed to develop skills and techniques needed for the utilization and production of classroom instructional materials and equipment. Telephone/Mail format. (1 semester hour)

Organizational Behavior and Leadership Styles

A theology of leadership is developed upon which current trends in church organization and leadership techniques are assessed. The history of organizational and management theory is developed, as well as organization, leadership, and group process theories. Planning, programming, budgeting, and evaluation are considered in relation to congregational programs. Other areas of management are presented on an introductory basis, such as planning and managing change in an organization, systems analysis, conflict management, and review of leadership traits. Telephone/Mail format. (3 semester hours)

Family Ministries

A course designed to equip a leader with the knowledge and skills of how to minister to families in the church. It includes an analysis of trends and issues of the contemporary family, formulation of strategies and administration of family ministries. Telephone/Mail format. (2 semester hours)

Pastoral Counseling

A study of Biblical basis for pastoral counseling, the basic techniques of pastoral care, a general introduction to the major areas of pastoral concern, counseling the sick, the grief-stricken, teenagers, the aged, those in crisis. (3 semester hours)

Youth Ministries I

A study of the needs and characteristics of young people relating to their place in the home, school, church, and society. An investigation of methods and techniques to win and hold teens through a sound Christian education program and youth worship service. (2 semester hours)

Multiple Staff Ministry

The meaning and forms of multiple-staff ministry will be developed on Biblical values with the objectives of creating effective multiple-staff ministries and staff collegiality. The course will assist the participant in the development of concepts and values that will lead to commitments of shared ministry. Ways of dealing with concerns and issues which create conflict and interfere with staff collegiality will be examined. (2 semester hours)

Conflict Management

Based upon Biblical and behavioral concepts, this course is designed to equip religious leaders with an understanding of conflicts, and the skills to deal with them. It is based upon the premise that conflicts are inherent in begin human and that salvation does not involve the absence of conflict, but the realization of redemptive outcomes in conflicts. The goals to be achieved are interpersonal acceptance and group effectiveness. Telephone/Mail format. (2 semester hours)

Organization and Administration of Christian Schools

A study of the basic organization and administration of Christian schools. Emphasis placed on the areas of organizing, staffing, and financing, as well as on the functions of various departments. Telephone/Mail format. (3 semester hours)

CHURCH HISTORY

Church History I

A study of the background, establishment, and development of the Christian church and its influence in world history, including the factors leading to the Reformation. An emphasis is placed on the development of theological concepts and their effect on the church. (3 semester hours)

Church History II

A study of modern church history, beginning with the Reformation and continuing to the present, observing theological trends and ecclesiastical developments in European and American Christianity and examining the interrelationships between church and society. Emphasizing those factors which contributed to the twentieth-century pentecostal revival and analyzing the impact of other contemporary ecclesiastical events. (3 semester hours)

Introduction to Historical Theology

An introduction to the study of historical theology. The approach will be that of surveying the historical development of several key theological themes; e.g., the doctrine of God, the doctrine of Christ, the doctrine of the Holy Spirit, etc. Telephone/Mail format. (2 semester hours)

American Religious History

An examination of the development and significance of religion in the United States. Emphasis will be given to the influence of the church and society upon each other. Emphasis will also be given to American revivalism and its contribution to the pentecostal movements of the twentieth century.

History of Religious Renewal Movements

A survey and analysis of revival/renewal movements and spiritual awakenings throughout the history of the Christian church. Emphasis will be given to the reasons for their development, their significance, and their impact upon society and the reasons for their continuation or decline. Telephone/Mail format. (3 semester hours)

COMMUNICATIONS

Parliamentary Law

A course designed to acquaint both the layman and the minister with principles and procedures for the formation of organizations, the conducting of business meetings, the preparation of constitution and by-laws, the appointment and function of committees. (1 semester hour)

EDUCATION

Introduction to School Programs/Education Practicum

Overview of school programs (K−12), school organization and administration, and general curriculum. Telephone/Mail format. (3 semester hours)

Philosophy of Christian School Education

A course in the distinctive philosophy of Christian day schools. Attention is given to the writing of a clearly articulated statement of Christian school philosophy. (1 semester hour)

Teaching Principles and Competencies/Practicum

Focus on generic teaching competencies and the principles underlying successful teaching (K−12), including lesson planning, classroom management, instructional organization, presentation of subject matter, communication, and evaluation of pupil achievement. A teaching unit will be developed by each student. Telephone/mail format. (3 semester hours)

Exceptional Student Education

A course designed to equip the regular classroom teacher with the knowledge and skills needed in working with exceptional students. Emphasis on causes, terminology, diagnosis, characteristics, problems, and educational implications. Telephone/Mail format. (2 semester hours)

Social Foundations of Education

A study of the principles and philosophy of education with emphasis on historical and social forces affecting the development of American education with its opportunities and requirements. Surveys teacher organizations, professional ethics, and school law. (3 semester hours)

Psychological Foundations of Education

A study of the principles and philosophy of human growth and development, and learning theory applied to teaching. An overview of various models and methods of classroom management. Construction, evaluation, and interpretation of formal and informal educational tests and measurement. (3 semester hours)

Introduction to Humanities

An integrated course designed to increase the students' understanding and appreciation of great and vital ideas in Western culture through the study of representative materials in art, music, literature, and philosophy. Telephone/Mail format. (3 semester hours)

Instructional Media for Education

A course designed to develop skills and techniques needed for the selection, utilization, and production of classroom instructional materials and for application and integration of educational technology to all areas of the curriculum. Telephone/Mail format. (2 semester hours)

Speech and Communications Skills in Educational Settings

Provides prospective teachers with theory, techniques and practice in effective verbal and noverbal communication skills; emphasis includes planning, organizing, and participating in various speaking situations that involve interaction and communication in educational settings. Telephone/Mail format. (2 semester hours)

The Adolescent

Emphasis is on understanding the physical, psychological, social, emotional, intellectual, and ethical development of the adolescent. Application of knowledge in planning organizational structures, curriculum, and teaching/learning activities appropriate in various educational settings. Telephone/Mail format. (3 semester hours)

Teaching Language Arts Skills in the Primary/Elementary School

Approaches in building a language arts program. Focus on skills in teaching handwriting, spelling, oral and written communications. Telephone/Mail format. (2 semester hours)

Teaching Mathematics in the Secondary School (6–12)

An analysis of instructional methods, content, objectives, and materials appropriate for teaching mathematics in the secondary schools (6–12). Telephone/Mail format. Telephone/Mail format. (2 to 3 semester hours)

Children's Literature

An investigation of genres in literature, with emphasis on numerous award-winning children's books and authors. Strategies for motivating students to interact with literature are demonstrated, and preparation of learning activities for the elementary classroom is mandatory. (3 semester hours)

Teaching Health and Physical Education in the Primary/Elementary School

A consideration of healthful school living, school health services, health instruction, and their relationships to the growth and development of the child and the learning process. Telephone/Mail format. (2 semester hours)

Teaching Reading in the Content Areas

The study of methods, materials, and techniques of teaching reading in the content areas, focusing on the incorporation of vocabulary, comprehension, and study skills into the content curriculum. Telephone/Mail format. (2 semester hours)

Foundations of Primary Education (Early Childhood I)

Emphases will include principles of child growth and development and the major philosophies of early childhood education and their educational implications. Focus is on the major models of early childhood education with evaluation of the degree to which each is developmentally appropriate for young children. Additional focuses include the influence of children's home lives on their development and the unique individual needs of all children, including those from multicultures. (3 semester hours)

Teaching English in the Secondary School

A study of instructional methods, content, objectives, and materials for teaching secondary level English. Field-based pre-student teaching experiences required. Telephone/Mail format. (2 semester hours)

Foundations of Primary (K–3)

Emphases will include principles of child growth and development and the major philosophies of early childhood education and their educational implications. Focus is on the major models of early childhood education with evaluation of the degree to which each is developmentally appropriate for young children. Additional focuses include the influence of children's home lives on their development and the unique individual needs of all children, including those from multicultures. Telephone/Mail format. (2 semester hours)

Foundations of Primary (K–3) Observation/Practicum

Field experience involving 20 hours of observation/participation in K–3 settings. Telephone/Mail format. (1 semester hour)

Curriculum Design for Primary/Elementary Grades (Early Childhood II)

A course with emphasis on the total classroom functioning within primary (K–3)/elementary (1–6) schools. The course includes the integration of knowledge across the curriculum through application of problem-solving and critical thinking skills; evaluation and adaption of materials, instruction, and assessment methods using a variety of developmentally appropriate approaches to knowledge building; definition of routines, records, and environments for effective functioning of primary and elementary classrooms; and examination of standardized tests and measurement and their application in the total school, as well as the classroom. (3 semester hours)

Methods of Teaching Math in the Primary/Elementary School

Emphases on fundamental concepts of mathematics and various strategies for teaching math. Telephone/Mail format. (2 to 3 semester hours)

Language Acquisition and Language Arts in Primary (K–3)

Emphases on theories of language acquisition and the planning and development of learning environments that are print and language rich. Other emphases include integration of language into other areas of the curriculum, whole language, aiding children to develop communication and listening competencies, and providing appropriate language models for young children. Telephone/Mail format. (2 to 3 semester hours)

Teaching Social Studies in the Primary/Elementary School

Curriculum instructional approaches and materials for teaching social studies in grades K–6. Emphasis placed on helping prospective teachers acquire background and skills in developing and teaching units of work. Telephone/Mail format. (2 semester hours)

Methods of Teaching English to Speakers of Other Languages ESOL

An overview of curriculum, materials, and instructional methods for teaching English to speakers of other languages (K–12 and Adult Education). Emphasis is on cross-cultural communication processes and the selection and development of appropriate instructional strategies and materials. Telephone/Mail format. (3 semester hours)

Teaching Social Studies in the Secondary School

A study of the objectives, organization of materials and methods of teaching social studies in the secondary school. Emphasis is given in this program to development of content materials, current issues and trends. Field-based pre-student teaching experience required. Telephone/Mail format. (2 semester hours)

Introduction to Reading

An approach to teaching reading utilizing diagnosis, prescription, assessments, and a management system. Phonics terminology and procedures for teaching skills in the following areas are presented: auditory discrimination, visual discrimination, word recognition, comprehension, and reference and study skills. Opportunities for demonstration of eight teacher competencies are provided. Telephone/Mail format. (3 semester hours)

Diagnosis and Remediation of Reading

This course explores evaluation of student strengths and weaknesses in the elementary classroom through the use of criteria-referenced assessments and norm-referenced tests. Teacher-made activities to be used for remediation are developed, and commercial materials are selected for use in the instructional process. Field-based pre-student teaching experiences required. Telephone/Mail format. (3 semester hours)

Teaching Art for the Primary/Elementary Teacher

Art through laboratory practice in painting, drawing, design, graphics, and various crafts with particular reference to their appropriateness for teaching in the elementary school. Telephone/Mail format. (2 semester hours)

Teaching Science in the Primary/Elementary School

Emphasis placed on service content, methods, and materials as related to teaching science in elementary schools. Telephone/Mail format. (2 semester hours)

Teaching Physical Education in the Secondary School 6−12

Emphases will be placed on the methods, measurements, philosophy, and curriculum for teaching physical education in grades 6−12. Telephone/Mail format. (2 to 3 semester hours)

Music for the Primary/Elementary Teacher

A course designed for elementary education majors to give the teacher a knowledge of music teaching methods and materials for use in the classroom. Telephone/Mail format. (2 semester hours)

Curriculum Design K−12

An overview and evaluation of school programs and the underlying philosophy of curriculum K−12, with emphasis on the teacher's role in the organizational structure, and techniques, and problems of curriculum development at the primary (K−3), elementary (1−6), middle grades (5−9), and secondary (6−12) levels. Telephone/Mail format. (2 to 3 semester hours)

Organization and Administration of Christian Schools

A study of the basic organization and administration of Christian schools. emphasis placed on the areas of organizing, staffing, and financing, as well as on the functions of various departments. Telephone/Mail format. (3 semester hours)

Student Teaching

A full-time practice teaching experience in the student's area of study involving planning, organization, and use of instructional materials in a classroom. One-half semester of field experiences and seminars during the senior year under supervision of a qualified in-service teacher and college supervisor providing continuous evaluation of teaching experiences. Telephone/Mail format. (6 semester hours)

ENGLISH

English Composition I

Study and practice in the skills of writing and reading with attention given to grammar. (3 semester hours)

English Composition II

A study of literary forms of composition and style in writing. Practice in reading for adequate comprehension at the collegiate level and

methods of research are covered. A research paper is required. (3 semester hours)

English Literature I

Reading and discussion of selected English classics from Beowulf to the end of the eighteenth century, with emphasis on literature as the expression of the times. (3 semester hours)

Major British Authors

An analytical introduction to the major writers of British literature that focuses on the lives and times of the authors as well as on their writings. Telephone/Mail format. (3 semester hours)

Advanced Grammar

This course is designed to enable students to develop proficiency in analyzing almost all types of sentences and grammatical structures. The traditional method of diagramming sentences is used extensively. Telephone/Mail format. (3 semester hours)

Advanced Expository Writing

This course is designed to enable the student to develop proficiency in various forms of writing with emphasis on exposition. Writing exercises in class will be evaluated by both students and instructor for practical advantage. Telephone/Mail format. (3 semester hours)

Contemporary Literature

A study of selected American, English, and world literature of the twentieth century with emphasis given to literature of the last three decades. Telephone/Mail format. (3 semester hours)

American Literature

A survey of prose and poetry with attention to sociopolitical backgrounds and growth of American thought as expressed through selected authors from the colonial period to 1950. (3 semester hours)

Creative Writing

Study and practice in narrative, poetical, and dramatic writing. The course will include reading and discussing student work in groups and in conferences with the instructor. Telephone/Mail format. (3 semester hours)

Adolescent Literature

A critical study of literature for the adolescent reader with attention given to its role in the secondary and middle school English curriculum. Telephone/Mail format. (3 semester hours)

Contemporary Christian Writers

A critical study of fictional works by selected authors: C.S. Lewis, Graham Greene, Alexsandr Solzhenitzyn, Walker Percy, Flannery O'Connor, Frederick Buechner, and Harold Fickett. Telephone/Mail format. (3 semester hours)

Introduction to Shakespeare

A course designed to introduce students to Shakespeare's comedies, histories, tragedies, and romances by the studying of selected plays. Telephone/Mail format. (3 semester hours)

The American Novel

A course designed to familiarize the students with the growth and development of the American novel beginning with early American novels and concluding with the great novelists of the 1920s (Hemingway, Fitzgerald, and Faulkner). Telephone/Mail format. (3 semester hours)

World Literature

A study that focuses on the classics of world literature, including the Old Testament, Homer's writings, the Greek and Roman tragedies and philosophers, a cross section of primarily non-English writers from the time of the Old Testament to the present, and that requires personal critical reaction and evaluation. (3 semester hours)

HISTORY

Western Civilization I

A survey of the great epochs of civilization from early Mesopotamian and Egyptian beginnings to the beginning of the Renaissance, including the development of social, economic, religious, and political institutions. Telephone/Mail format. (3 semester hours)

Western Civilization II

A survey from the beginning of the Renaissance to the present with an emphasis on the factors which have resulted in the problems of our current world society. Telephone/Mail format. (3 semester hours)

Latin American History and Culture

A survey of the European impact upon the peoples of the Caribbean, Central America, South America, and their development since the wars of liberation, together with the basic elements of present culture. Telephone/Mail format. (3 semester hours)

Modern European History to 1870

A history of Europe from 1600 to 1870 with an emphasis on the factors leading to and resulting in new national monarchies and the development of worldwide (European) colonialism. Telephone/Mail format. (3 semester hours)

Modern European History since 1870

A history of Europe from 1870 to the present with an emphasis on the factors leading to the World Wars and the present tension between East and West. Telephone/Mail format. (3 semester hours)

The Ancient World

A study of the Greek and Roman civilizations, considering the body of classical knowledge developed by such Greek writers as Erastosthenes, Archimedes, Protagoras, Socrates, Aristotle, Plato, Hippocrates, Thucydides, and Herodotus. A study of such Roman writers as Vergil, Tacitus, and Cicero. Telephone/Mail format. (3 semester hours)

American History I

The first course in a sequential survey of American history examines the social, economic, and political development of the United States through the Civil War. Major themes from English settlement at Jamestown to the Civil War introduce students to the growth patterns in the American experience over nearly four centuries, formative years in which many of the characteristics of modern America took shape. (3 semester hours)

American History II

The second half of a sequential survey of American history traces the social, economic, and political development of the United States from Reconstruction of the South after the Civil War to the present. Major themes of America's transformation from an agrarian nation and minor member of the international community to an industrial world power are examined to help students understand the nature of current national issues. (3 semester hours)

Modern American History

A survey of the recent history of the United States: World War I and II and the inter-war period, the post-war period, the Cold War, the Marshall Plan, the Korean War, the proliferation of nuclear arms, the Sino-Soviet split, the Vietnam Conflict, the New Frontier, and the Great Society, Watergate, and Reaganomics. Telephone/Mail format. (3 semester hours)

JOURNALISM

Journalism

A communication course designed to give the student an introduction to writing for various forms of news media (radio, television, newspapers, church publication, bulletins, periodicals). Other phases of journalism, such as interviewing, editing, and proofreading are also considered. Public relations as related to journalism is stressed throughout the course. Telephone/Mail format. (3 semester hours)

MATHEMATICS

Basic College Math

This course stresses the fundamental concepts and applications of mathematics. Topics include logical systems, arithmetic, number bases and groups, algebra, graphing, functions, exponents, and algebraic techniques, geometry, and statistics. (3 semester hours)

College Algebra

Intended to provide a link between a variety of mathematical techniques and methods of solving problems and the more abstract point of view required in calculus. Few of the subjects covered will be entirely new, but many of them are treated in more generality, and explanations for what were previously mysterious techniques are furnished. At the conclusion of the course the student should be able to apply all of basic algebra with confidence and understanding. (3 semester hours)

Geometry

Emphasis on Euclidean geometry with elements of projective geometry. (3 semester hours)

Abstract Algebra

Groups, rings, polynomials, and fields. (3 semester hours)

Mathematics II for Teachers

The focus of this course will be real numbers, measurement, geometry, similarity and congruence, coordinate geometry, graphing, and algebra. Problem solving will be stressed. (3 semester hours)

Introduction to Statistics

Hypothesis testing, chi-square, probability distributions, regression, and correlation. (3 semester hours)

Number Theory

Euclidean algorithm, greatest common divisor, common multiple, congruence, and quadratic residues. (3 semester hours)

Introduction to Probability Theory

Probability spaces, random variables, expectations, and limit theorems. (3 semester hours)

Symbolic Logic

Axiomatic development of the sentential nature of symbolic logic. Applications to mathematical systems. (3 semester hours)

Finite Mathematics

Statements, sets, permutations, combinations, probability, and matrices. (3 semester hours)

Introduction to Analysis

Real numbers, limits, completeness and compactness, continuity. (3 semester hours)

Trigonometry and Analytic Geometry

Numerical trigonometry, identities and equations, the straight line, circle and graphs of elementary functions. (3 semester hours)

History of Mathematics

A historical survey of the unfolding of mathematical thought. (3 semester hours)

MISSIONS

Missionary Field Work

A short term missionary field project supervised by the college. The project involves literature distribution and evangelism of the community, children, and youth programs, and ministry in the churches. Telephone/Mail format. (3 semester hours)

Theology of Missions

An introduction to the theology of the Christian Mission in the Old Testament and New Testament, and a study of the responsibility of the individual, the pastor, and the church in its implementation. Telephone/Mail format. (3 semester hours)

Comparative Religions

A comparative study of the major religions in the world. Telephone/Mail format. (3 semester hours)

Introduction to Language Learning

The use of phonetics as a tool in the study of foreign languages. Telephone/Mail format. (3 semester hours)

Area Study: Latin America

A general introduction to the area in matters of geography, historical development, religious and cultural development; and the spread of the gospel and development of the church. Telephone/Mail format. (3 semester hours)

Missionary Life and Work

A study of the missionary motive, objective, call, qualifications, and preparation of the missionary candidates; spiritual and cultural life of the missionary in the field; the administration of missions at home and abroad; and methods used in planting indigenous churches. Telephone/Mail format. (3 semester hours)

Missions History I

A survey of the expansion of the church from apostolic times to the period of Carey (19th century). Study is made of the historical background, and of the contributions and methods of the principal missionaries of this period. Telephone/Mail format. (3 semester hours)

Missions History II

A historical survey of missions during the 19th and 20th centuries noting the problems and challenges of today's church. Attention will be given to the development and spread of Assemblies of God missions. Telephone/Mail format. (3 semester hours)

Anthropology

A survey of man and his culture. Special study is made of primitive groups in the world today. Telephone/Mail format. (3 semester hours)

Area Study: Europe

A general introduction to the area in matters of geography, historical development, religious and cultural development, and the spread of the gospel and development of the church. Telephone/Mail format. (3 semester hours)

The Urban Context for Ministry

An analysis of the city from a standpoint of demographics, lines of communications, slow and rapid change, which provides the backdrop for the church planting and church revitalization. Examples of various cities in foreign countries will be used also to enhance an awareness of the necessity for flexible strategies. Telephone/Mail format. (2 semester hours)

Area Study: Middle East

A general introduction to the area in matters of geography, historical development, religious and cultural development and the spread of the gospel and development of the church. Telephone/Mail format. (3 semester hours)

Area Study: Asia

A general introduction to the area in matters of geography, historical development, religious and cultural development, and the spread of the gospel and development of the church. Telephone/Mail format. (3 semester hours)

Area Study: Africa

A general introduction to the area in matters of geography, historical development, religious and cultural development; and the spread of the gospel and development of the church. Telephone/Mail format. (3 semester hours)

Contemporary Issues in Missions

This course allows specialized studies of issues related to the field and to Church Missions interaction. A formal research paper is required. Telephone/Mail format. (3 semester hours)

Inter-Cultural Communications

The principles and processes of communicating from one culture to another with a focus on the relevance of incarnation as the model for the communication of the Gospel. Telephone/Mail format. (3 semester hours)

MUSIC

Music Theory I

A study of fundamental musical concepts with emphasis on interpretation of pitch and rhythmic notation, key signatures, scales, intervals, melodic composition and analysis, and introduction to harmonic materials. (3 semester hours)

Church Music for Ministers

A study of the relationship of music to the services of the church, planning and management of the church music programs, and organizational methods for the development of children, youth, and adult choirs and programs. Telephone/Mail format. (3 semester hours)

Church Music Organization and Administration

A study of the administrative role of the minister of music in a fully-developed music program at the local level. This course is designed for the upper division student in church music. Telephone/Mail format. (3 semester hours)

PHILOSOPHY

Introduction to Philosophy

A systematic survey of the fundamental concepts of philosophy with special attention given to the problems of knowledge, being, the existence of God, the freedom of will, and good and evil. Intended to familiarize the student with the method of abstract thinking. (3 semester hours)

Apologetics

A philosophical study and defense of the Christian faith as it is related to naturalistic science and humanism with emphasis on the necessity of the deity of Christ, His supernatural incarnation, His substitutionary death, and His physical resurrection. Telephone/Mail format. (2 semester hours)

Principles of Ethics

A survey of the theory of value as applied to human goals and behavior, with Christian ethics compared to other systems. Telephone/Mail format. (3 semester hours)

History of Philosophy

A survey of the ideas underlying western civilization from Thales to the present. Special emphasis is given to Descartes, Leibniz, and Kant. Telephone/Mail format. (3 semester hours)

PHOTOGRAPHY

Photography

An introductory course in camera operation and picture composition. Emphasis is placed on still photography techniques with exposure to darkroom procedures and video recording to enable the prospective K−12 teacher, communications director, missionary, and minister to apply and integrate this technology. Field assignments will occupy approximately half of the course experience. Each student is required to have access to a 35mm adjustable camera. Telephone/Mail format. (2 semester hours)

Photography Practicum

Laboratory work involving still photography/video projects and/or programs for schools, publications, churches, or other ministries. Telephone/Mail format. (1 semester hour)

PRACTICAL MINISTRY

Evangelistic Work of the Church

A study of conversion; of the steps to take in leading a soul to Christ; of techniques and methods used in personal witnessing, street meetings, house-to-house visitation, and evangelization as it applies to rural and urban areas. Special attention given to the memorization of Scriptures which are vital and basic in witnessing. (2 semester hours)

History and Polity of the Assemblies of God

The factors which contributed to the origin of the General Council of the Assemblies of God; its growth and development at home and abroad; its organizational structure and government. (2 semester hours)

Christian Spirituality

This course is designed to help students understand and engage in spiritual growth, and centers on one's relationship with God. The course addresses such areas as prayer, Bible study, fellowship, trials, the grace of God and the need to be obedient to God. Students will also become acquainted with various perspectives on spiritual life from the area of Historical Theology. Telephone/Mail format. (2 semester hours)

Healing: A Ministry of the Holy Spirit

The Biblical basis for a doctrine of divine healing will be investigated. An historical survey will demonstrate the continuation of divine healing throughout the history of the Church. Emphasis will be placed on the opportunity and privilege of availing oneself of the Spirit's ministry of healing in today's Church. Recent and contemporary practices related to divine healing will be addressed. Telephone/Mail format. (3 semester hours)

Evangelism and the Gifts of the Holy Spirit

A study of the use and importance of the gifts of the Holy Spirit in the evangelism of the New Testament Church, especially in the Acts of the Apostles. After establishing the connection between the manifestation of the supernatural gifts and the spread and acceptance of the Gospel message in the New Testament, students will explore the impact these gifts could have on modern-day evangelism. Telephone/Mail format. (3 semester hours)

Modern Cults

A study of modern cults, their doctrinal positions, and defections from historical Christianity. Telephone/Mail format. (3 semester hours)

Royal Ranger Leadership Training

A course designed to train potential Royal Ranger leaders in the local church. Emphasis is placed on organizing an outpost, counseling boys, coordinating the outpost meetings, and the camping programs. Telephone/Mail format. (2 semester hours)

Church Planting

This course provides the general framework for establishing new churches. Special attention will be given to the Decade of Harvest Goals, the General Council services available, and the individual District Programs for Church Planting. It will provide both general and specialized help for establishing a new church in a community. The various proven methods, such as ''Mothering'' and ''District Sponsoring,'' will be examined. Telephone/Mail format. (2 semester hours)

Worship and the Gifts of the Holy Spirit

A theology of worship will be developed based on both the Old and New Testament models. Attention will be focused on worship and the exercise of spiritual gifts with particular interest in developing a New Testament order of worship. The course will include an historical review of worship as experienced by the Church, including an analysis of the present state of Pentecostal worship as related to the gifts of the Holy Spirit. A basic intent of the course is to encourage the operation of the gifts in congregational worship. (3 semester hours)

Special Programs

A course designed to acquaint the student with the various church-related programs of Christian education, service, and outreach of the Assemblies of God, including Christ's Ambassadors, men's and women's ministries, and each department's related programs. Telephone/Mail format. (2 semester hours)

Administration of Christian Camping

A course designed to train potential youth leaders in the local church. Emphasis is placed on administration and organization; selection of campsite, facilities and equipment; program planning for various age levels; responsibilities for personnel; counseling and problem solving. Telephone/Mail format. (2 semester hours)

Homiletics I

A basic course in sermon preparation dealing with the parts of the sermon structure and delivery. Attention is given to audience analysis, proper use of the vocal mechanism, and other speech principles. The primary emphasis in the development of the sermon structure is given to topical preaching, utilizing propositional outlines. (3 semester hours)

Homiletics II

An intermediate course dealing with the theological foundations, historical perspectives and contemporary objectives of preaching. The analysis and interpretation of biblical passages in relation to sermon development is addressed. Several types of sermon structures are utilized in relationship to biblical preaching. (3 semester hours)

Pastoral Theology I

A study of the Biblical materials as they relate to the pastoral ministry. The course includes an overview of the pastor's call, the church call, the pastor's life, general administrative duties, church community and district responsibilities. (3 semester hours)

Pastoral Theology II

An in-depth study of the church and its program by means of a simulated church model. The class is organized as a church with all offices and organizations. A thorough examination of all church-related experiences such as business meetings, committees, building programs, mission conventions, and special meetings are simulated by the class. Lectures concerning the nurture and care of the church complement the practical functioning of the class. (3 semester hours)

Organizational Behavior and Leadership Styles

A theology of leadership is developed upon which current trends in church organization and leadership techniques are assessed. The history of organizational and management theory is developed, as well as organization, leadership, and group process theories. Planning, programming, budgeting, and evaluation are considered in relation to congregational programs. Other areas of management are presented on an introductory basis, such as planning and managing change in an organization, systems analysis, conflict management, and review of leadership traits. Telephone/Mail format. (3 semester hours)

The Gifts of the Holy Spirit: An Experiential Theology

The course will cover the discovery, operation, use, and purpose of spiritual gifts. Focus will be on gift operation within the life of the individual and within the life of the Church body and ministry. The Biblical foundation for gifts and the practical operation of gifts within Biblical boundaries will be discussed. Examples and case studies of how gifts have been exhibited and utilized within the operation of the Church will be examined. Telephone/Mail format. (3 semester hours)

Leadership Development

A theological rationale based upon the doctrine of the priesthood of the believer and the gifts of the Holy Spirit is developed with practical application for the recruitment and development of lay persons for ministry within the congregation and to the community. The course focuses on the identification of individual gifts and talents that persons may possess and the training of those individuals for various ministries. Styles of leadership, administrative functions, and multi-staff relationships are considered. Telephone/Mail format course. (2 semester hours)

Pastoral Counseling I

A study of Biblical basis for pastoral counseling, the basic techniques of pastoral care, a general introduction to the major areas of pastoral concern, counseling the sick, the grief-stricken, teenagers, the aged, those in crisis. (3 semester hours)

Pastoral Counseling II

A study of verbatims, case studies, clinical situations with special attention given to pre-marital, marital, and family counseling. (3 semester hours)

Youth Ministries

A study of the needs and characteristics of young people relating to their place in the home, school, church, and society. An investigation of methods and techniques to win and hold teens through a sound Christian education program and youth worship service. (2 semester hours)

Church Business Administration

A study of the various areas of pastoral responsibilities including board administrations and organizations, committee organization, leadership training, budgeting, financing, planning, auxiliary organizations and their relationship to the total church program. (2 semester hours)

Multiple-Staff Ministry

The meaning and forms of multiple-staff ministry will be developed on Biblical values with the objectives of creating effective multiple-staff ministries and staff collegiality. The course will assist the participant in the development of concepts and values that will lead to

commitments of shared ministry. Ways of dealing with concerns and issues which create conflict and interfere with staff collegiality will be examined. (3 semester hours)

Biblical Foundations of Counseling

The course provides for an intensive study of the Scriptures enabling the student to formulate a Biblical view of human behavior and to utilize the Scriptures effectively in counseling and as a change-agent in people's lives. (3 semester hours)

Conflict Management

Based upon Biblical and behavioral concepts, this course is designed to equip religious leaders with an understanding of conflicts, and the skills to deal with them. It is based upon the premise that conflicts are inherent in being human and that salvation does not involve the absence of conflicts, but the realization of redemptive outcomes in conflicts. The goals to be achieved are interpersonal acceptance and group effectiveness. Telephone/Mail format. (2 semester hours)

Counseling and Contemporary Issues

Course content deals with controversial issues of alternative lifestyles. These include homosexuality, occultism, drug and alcohol addiction, divorce and remarriage. Relevant Biblical values and current psychological data will be the basis for student study and discussion for developing a pastoral counseling approach to these issues. Telephone/Mail format. (3 semester hours)

Church Jurisprudence

A study of the laws in various administrative areas affecting clergymen and churches. The study includes pastoral contracts, rights, liabilities, restriction, negligence, taxation, administration of private schools, church and state and laws of the church. Telephone/Mail format. (2 semester hours)

Group Process in the Church

This course is designed to provide a theoretical and practical understanding of the use of groups and group process within the church setting. Philosophies of small group ministry will be explored, along with srategies for beginning groups and maintaining them in a church, training leaders, and the dynamics of small group interaction. (3 semester hours)

Church Growth

An introduction to and study of church growth as effective evangelism. Attention will be given to its theological bases and methodological principles. Telephone/Mail format. (2 semester hours)

Advanced Youth Studies

A study of youth ministry and how to build an effective youth program. Attention is given to such things as management and funding of a youth ministry; having an educational and worship ministry to youth; the pastoral ministry to youth; youth discipleship, evangelism, and counseling (family, preventative, and crisis); building Christian character in youth; and resources. Telephone/Mail format. (3 semester hours)

Evangelizing and Discipling Youth

This course offers a brief history of youth awakenings; strategies for evangelizing and discipling youth (small groups ministry, one on one, campus ministry); insights into understanding spiritual growth and development of youth; and resources. Telephone/mail format. (2 semester hours)

Theology of Pastoral Care

This course deals with the implications of various theological perspectives relative to pastoral care. It addresses the purposes and practices of pastoring as described in the Scriptures and in moral and systematic theology. Special emphasis is placed upon the approach of theology to specific pastoral problems. (3 semester hours)

PSYCHOLOGY

Introduction to Psychology

An introduction to the field of psychology. (3 semester hours)

Psychology of Adjustment

The application of principles of psychology to the everyday life with an aim to assist in developing a wholesome self-concept and understanding of one's role in society. (3 semester hours)

Industrial and Organizational Psychology

A survey of the specialized fields of psychology to the everyday life with an aim to assist in developing a wholesome self-concept and understanding of one's role in society. Telephone/Mail format. (3 semester hours)

Theories of Personality

A study of the nature, development and adjustment of personality. Points of view representing the various systems of psychology are represented. The work of the major theorists are reviewed, evaluated, and systematized. Telephone/Mail format. (3 semester hours)

Marriage and Family

A study of the history, purpose, and problems of the family. Special attention is given to social conditions influencing courtship, marriage, divorce, and family life with emphasis upon materials of value to counselors. Telephone/Mail format. (3 semester hours)

Developmental Psychology

A study of the human growth and development from conception to death. The course emphasizes the physical, mental, emotional, social, and personality growth with special attention given to guidance toward acceptable behavior, responsible adult control of relevant phases of nurture, modes of interpersonal interaction, and the aging process. (3 semester hours)

Abnormal Psychology

A study of the nature, causes, and treatment of abnormal behavior including personality disorders, neuroses, psychoses, stress reaction, and other dysfunctions. Elements contributing to mental health and well-integrated personality are also considered. (3 semester hours)

History and Systems of Psychology

A tracing of psychology from early concepts to its present status with emphasis on theoretical systems. Telephone/Mail format. (3 semester hours)

Psychology of Religion

A study of historical development, the current trends and the major contributions of the psychological studies of religious experience and development. A study of how the church has contributed to the psychological welfare of man through religious experience and how the church can function to facilitate mental health. Telephone/Mail format. (3 semester hours)

Integration of Psychology and Theology

A study of the contemporary evangelical efforts to integrate psychology and theology, focusing on the value of an integrative effort to both the theory and practice of psychology and theology. Discussion includes matters of behavior, cognition, emotion, and motivation. Telephone/Mail format. (3 semester hours)

Psychotherapy I

A discussion of various theoretical approaches to the practice of counseling and psychotherapy with normal and disturbed clients. Focus will be on the psychoanalytic, cognitive, behavioral, and phenomenological approaches. Telephone/Mail format. (3 semester hours)

Psychotherapy II

An advanced course covering issues of relevance including the clinician as a person and professional, ethical and competency issues, and the integrative perspective. Older and newer approaches to psychotherapy will be integrated with emphasis on the student's personality and values in an emerging personal eclectic style. Telephone/Mail format. (3 semester hours)

Social Psychology

A review of theories of interpersonal behavior and group dynamics emphasizing the influence of groups and group membership upon individual behavior including aggression, attitudes, attribution, conformity, altruism, communication, propaganda, morale, and other aspects of interpersonal relationships. Telephone/Mail format. (3 semester hours)

Physiological Psychology

A study of the biological basis of human behavior, including in-depth treatment of relationships between the activity of the nervous and endocrine systems and behavior. Telephone/Mail format. (3 semester hours)

Experimental Psychology

A study of methods and problems in psychological experimentation. Emphasis is on the study of techniques used with specific reference to defining variables, stating hypotheses, designing experiments with adequate controls, and reporting findings. The student is expected to carry out several experiments during the semester. Telephone/Mail format. (3 semester hours)

Marital and Family Therapy

A study of typical marriage and family problems including communications, roles, and sexual dysfunction. Various counseling techniques related to marital maladjustment and principal approaches to conjoint marital therapy and family therapy will be emphasized. An overview of family systems approach will be given. Telephone/Mail format. (3 semester hours)

Directed Readings and Research in Psychology

Provides the student with the opportunity for extensive study through in-depth reading in a specific topic of his/her choosing under the guidance of the Psychology Department. An intensive synopsis of readings or a formal research paper is required. Telephone/Mail format. (1 to 3 semester hours)

SCIENCE

Planet Earth

Insights and discoveries of the past two decades as internationally known scientists share their theories about the formation of the earth—its oceans and climate—and the universe beyond. Telephone/Mail format. (3 semester hours)

Physical Science Survey I

The more essential and practical phases of physics and chemistry are covered in this course. Telephone/Mail format. (3 semester hours)

Fundamentals of Biology

A brief overview of cell structure, physiology, genetics, origins, ecology, and classification of living forms. (3 semester hours)

SOCIAL SCIENCE

Introduction to Sociology

A study of the social organization, institutions, and social forces of our society. It considers the nature of man and his culture, the development of institutions, and the problems of social change. (3 semester hours)

Marriage and Family

The course begins with a brief view of approaches to studying the family and a look at definitions and varieties of U.S. families. It then explores the family life cycle—parenting, mate selection, and three major aspects of marriage itself. The last section of the course looks at some of the problematic aspects of the U.S. family including stress, divorce, and the elderly. (3 semester hours)

World Geography

A study of the geographic regions, inhabitants, resources, physical characteristics, and economy of the world. Telephone/Mail format. (3 semester hours)

United States Constitution

A study of the legal culture in the United States including the British common law system, the origins of the U.S. Constitution, the amendments, and the landmark cases. Telephone/Mail format. (3 semester hours)

United States Government

A study of American politics; the constitutional basis, organization, and function of our government. Telephone/Mail format. (3 semester hours)

Geography and Resource Use

A survey of the nature and use capabilities of the natural and human resources of the United States and in particular of Florida. An emphasis is placed on the wise utilization of these resources. (3 semester hours)

SPEECH

Fundamentals of Speech

A study of the voice, its training and use, the forms of speech, and their preparation and delivery. (3 semester hours)

Parliamentary Law

A course designed to acquaint both the layman and the minister with principles and procedures for the formation of organizations, the conducting of business meetings, the preparation of constitution and by-laws, the appointment and function of committees. (1 semester hour)

Communication Theory

An in-depth study of the various approaches to communication and their application. Telephone/Mail format. (3 semester hours)

Oral Interpretation

Examination of techniques involved in the recreation of literature for an audience with emphasis on individual interpretation and presentation of literary expression. Telephone/Mail format. (3 semester hours)

SYSTEMATIC THEOLOGY

Introduction to Theology

An introduction to Christian doctrine based upon the "Statement of Fundamental Truths" listed by the General Council of the Assemblies of God. (2 semester hours)

Systematic Theology I

An introduction to theology (its meaning and purpose), a study of the doctrine of Scripture (revelation, inspiration, and canon), and a study of the doctrine of God (His existence, attributes, works, and the Trinity). (2 semester hours)

Systematic Theology II

A study of the doctrine of Christ (His person, nature, and works), and the doctrine of the Holy Spirit (His personality, deity, and work). (2 semester hours)

Systematic Theology III

A study of the doctrine of man (his origin, nature, original state and fall), the doctrine of sin (its origin, nature, and consequences), and the doctrine of salvation (its provision and application to man). (2 semester hours)

Systematic Theology IV

A study of the doctrine of the church (its definition, organization, function, and ordinances), the doctrine of angels (their creation, nature, fall, and work), and the doctrine of last things (physical death, second coming, resurrection, judgments, and final state). (2 semester hours)

The Doctrine of the Holy Spirit

A study of the distinctive Pentecostal doctrine of the Holy Spirit, focusing on baptism in the Spirit, the fruit and gifts of the Spirit. Special attention will be given to terminology used by Pentecostals (filled, baptized, anointed, etc.).

The Doctrine of God

An in-depth study of the doctrine of God, considering His existence, names, nature, attributes, works, and the Trinity. Telephone/Mail format. (2 semester hours)

Old Testament Theology

A study of the doctrinal content of the Old Testament in its progressive unfolding of the nature of God and His plan of redemption. Attention will be given to the theme of promise as it runs through the Old Testament. (2 semester hours)

New Testament Theology

A study of the major doctrinal material of the New Testament. Attention will be given to the teaching of Jesus, the proclamation of the early church, the theological ideas of the Pauline and Johannnine writings. (2 semester hours)

The Doctrine of Salvation

A study of the doctrine of salvation, including an emphasis on regeneration, justification, and the Christian life. Telephone/Mail format. (2 semester hours)

The Doctrine of Scripture

An in-depth study of the doctrine of the Scripture, focusing on revelation, inspiration, and canonization. (2 semester hours)

The Doctrine of Christ

A study of the person and work of Jesus Christ, including consideration of His names, natures, humiliation, exaltation, offices, and atoning death. Telephone/Mail format. (2 semester hours)

Doctrine of Last Things

A study of the doctrine of last things. Consideration will be given to physical death, immortality of the soul, the rapture, the second coming of Christ, the resurrection of the dead, and the final judgment. Telephone/Mail format. (2 semester hours)

Southeastern Massachusetts University
Division of Continuing Studies
Old Westport Road
North Dartmouth, Massachusetts 02747
(617) 999-8775

Description:
The state-supported institution of higher learning was established in 1960 as the Southeastern Massachusetts Technological Institute by the General Court of the Commonwealth of Massachusetts. The present name was adopted in 1969 and university status was granted.

The Division of Continuing Studies and Special Programs offers professional education for nurses by means of self-paced home study courses in cooperation with Health Update of Lakewood, Colorado. Course titles change with each semester. Courses described below are representative of those offered. Contact the Director of Special Programs for current offerings.

Faculty:
Kevin J. Garganta, Director, Special Programs.

Academic Levels:
Professional

Degree/Certificate Programs:
Certificate. A CEU Certificate for successful completion of each course will be awarded by Health Update.

Admission Requirements:
Applicants must be Registered Nurses. State of licensure is requested when registering for the courses.

Tuition:
Contact the Director of Special Programs for current tuition rates.

Enrollment Period:
Students may enroll up to June 1 (spring semester) and January 1 (fall semester) for the home study courses available in the particular time period.

Equipment Requirements:
A complete packet of materials for each course will be sent within two weeks of enrollment.

Credit and Grading:
Each course must be completed within three months after receipt of the program. A post-test will be graded and the student will receive individualized feedback from the instructor.

Accreditations:
New England Association of Schools and Colleges; American Nursing Association.

PROFESSIONAL COURSES

NURSING

Assessment of the Geriatric Patient

This course is intended to teach students to develop an individualized assessment instrument to guide them in assessing elderly patients or clients in their clinical practice. Special emphasis is given to distinguishing between symptoms of disease vs. those of the normal aging process; developing an assessment guideline for clinical practice using physical psychosocial, and medical parameters; and recognizing certain nursing considerations which are critical in obtaining an accurate assessment. (.6 CEUs)

Avoiding Medication Errors

This course concentrates on the most common causes and contributing factors to medication errors, and on how to avoid them. It is designed both for clinical nurses who wish to avoid errors themselves as well as for those administrative nurses who would like to help others decrease errors. (.6 CEUs)

Clinical Time Management

This self-paced program will teach methods to accomplish more work while gaining more personal rewards. The science of time management, as it applies specifically to nurses in clinical, educational, or administrative settings, will be covered. (.6 CEUs)

Southeastern Oklahoma State University
Correspondence Courses
Office of the Registrar
Durant, Oklahoma 74701   (405) 924-0121

Description:
Southeastern Oklahoma State University was founded in 1909 as Southeastern State Normal School. Four-year programs began in 1939 and university status was achieved in 1974.

Correspondence courses offered at the University are directed by regular members of the University faculty. Each course is outlined to provide a systematic and progressive presentation of the subject matter in a series of assignments.

Faculty:
Mary A. Castleberry, Registrar.

Academic Levels:
College

Admission Requirements:
During any one term, the amount of credit earned through correspondence courses is limited to 6 semester hours and to 12 semester hours during any one calendar year. No student is permitted either to begin or to continue correspondence or extension courses while taking work in residence at Southeastern or any other institution except upon the written consent of those institutions and Southeastern.

Tuition:
Contact the Office of the Registrar for current tuition information.

Enrollment Period:
The student is encouraged to complete at least one assignment per week and is expected to complete a course within one calendar year. If the course is not completed

within one year from the date of enrollment, the course is automatically cancelled.

Equipment Requirements:
Textbooks must be purchased by the student.

Credit and Grading:
As soon as possible after the last assignment has been received by the University, the student must take a final examination at Southeastern, administered by the Office of the Registrar or the instructor of the course; or at the college nearest the student's home, if arrangements are satisfactory to the instructor.

Accreditations:
North Central Association of Colleges and Schools.

COLLEGE COURSES

EDUCATION

Science in the Elementary School
Methods and materials in presentation of elementary science. Field experiences. (3 semester hours)

Social Studies in the Elementary School
Identification and implementation of teaching strategies and instructional materials for social studies in elementary school. Field experiences. (3 semester hours)

HISTORY

American History to 1876
A survey of American history from discovery to 1876. (3 semester hours)

Early Western Civilization
Ancient and medieval civilization in its cultural, political, and economic aspects. (3 semester hours)

Modern Western Civilization
European civilization detailing the growth and the development of European institutions. (3 semester hours)

Oklahoma History and Government
(3 semester hours)

SAFETY

General Safety Education
Review of the safety education program. Areas include pedestrian, bicycle, traffic, vocational, home, farm, fire, and disaster. (1 semester hour)

SOCIOLOGY

Principles of Sociology
A survey course to introduce students to the science of human behavior. (3 semester hours)

SPANISH

Modern Spanish Novel
Intensive and extensive reading of representative works. (3 semester hours)

Survey of Spanish-American Literature
Intensive and extensive reading of representative works. (3 semester hours)

Southern Colorado, University of
Division of Continuing Education
2200 Bonforte Boulevard
Pueblo, Colorado 81001-4901 (719) 549-2316

Description:
The University of Southern Colorado was established as San Isabel Junior College and offered first instruction in 1933. Formerly known as Southern Colorado State College, the present name was adopted in 1978. The university participates in the Colorado Consortium for Independent Study which is composed of the independent study offices of six institutions of higher education in Colorado: Adams State College, Colorado State University, University of Colorado, University of Northern Colorado, University of Southern Colorado, and Metropolitan State College of Denver. The consortium strives to provide quality independent study opportunities and to avoid duplication of courses offered by consortium members. The correspondence student should consult the listings in this *Guide* of all member schools of the Consortium for a complete offering of subject matter.

Faculty:
Dr. Gary Means, Dean.

Academic Levels:
College

Admission Requirements:
Open enrollment.

Tuition:
$70 per semester hour. Rate subject to change without notice. Refund allowed within forty 40 days minus an administrative fee. Specific information about the institution's policy will be sent to the student with the course material.

Enrollment Period:
The maximum time allowed to complete a course is 1 year; minimum time is 2 weeks per semester hour. A 12-month extension may be granted upon payment of an extension fee.

Equipment Requirements:
Textbooks and supplies must be purchased by the student and can be ordered from the USC Bookstore, University Center, Pueblo, CO 81001.

Credit and Grading:
Grading system is A, B, C, D, F with plus and minus recorded and averaged. Minimum passing grade is D. Credit is awarded in semester hours.

Accreditations:
North Central Association of Colleges and Schools. Member of: National University Continuing Education Association.

COLLEGE COURSES

EDUCATION

Current Issues in Education

Contemporary problems in education, their historical development and philosophical implications. The student will identify the range and kinds of issues of educational policy that are currently confronting American education. Selected issues(s) of most concern to the student will be intensively researched, developed, and presented. Upon registration, the student will receive course guidelines outlining suggested topics and format for producing one final report. (2 semester hours)

ENGLISH

Literature of Science Fiction

In-depth study of selected significant novels, short stories, and poetry from fantasy to ''hard'' science fiction. Reading and analysis of works chosen by the student from a bibliography provided by the instructor. (3 semester hours)

Special Projects: Audio Books, Tuned in Tutoring. Hear! Hear!

At home, in the car, on the run, listen to the classics, fiction, nonfiction. Design your own course of literary study from libraries of taped books. Have a ''class'' anytime, any place; learn at your own pace. Intended to promote active listening and lifelong literacy; materials focus on oral, written, and performed literature, listening skills, multiple ways of learning and being intelligent. (2 semester hours)

Special Topics - Ways of Knowing: Science, Technology, and Fiction

Interrelationships among science, technology, and fiction: their impact on modern society, utilizing appropriate subject-matter readings in a variety of social and technological specialties. (3 semester hours)

HISTORY

Special Topics: La Chicana

The course will focus on the history and development of Chicanas and contemporary issues faced by Chicanas in the United States. It is intended to be a literary analysis of Chicana history in terms of the intersections of race, class, and gender relations including an examination of contemporary social class status. Historical influences such as the European invasion of the Aztec society by the Spaniards followed by the infiltration of the Anglo into the then developing Indo-Spanish culture will be examined. The effects of the colonization process and its effects on La Chicana will be a primary goal of analysis for this course. Chicanas' roles in this historical process will be highlighted throughout the course. Stereotypes and myths concerning the character of Chicanas and their historical roles will be examined and reframed. (3 semester hours)

NURSING

Ethical Issues in Health Care

Selected theories which influence ethical choice in Nursing practice. Areas of philosophy, law, and the legal system which affect the public's health will be discussed. Topics to be included are related to current ethical issues and nursing decision making. (Offered through NLN accredited BSN program). (3 semester hours)

Research in Nursing

Introduction to the steps of research methodology. Analysis of research studies provides the basis for determining integration of appropriate research into nursing practice. (3 semester hours)

Professional Issues in Nursing

This course explores the professional, ethical, and legal issues related to professional nursing. Attention is given to professional and political issues as they influence nursing practice. (2 semester hours)

Gerontological Nursing

An elective theory course which focuses on nursing interventions for both well and ill older adults. (3 semester hours)

POLITICAL SCIENCE

Understanding Human Conflict

This course will focus on the conflict and cooperation between individuals and groups. Special attention will be paid to ethnic conflict and international war with regard to conflict management and solution. (3 semester hours)

Comparative Politics

The study of comparative politics is the investigation of people and their political arrangements throughout the world. It focuses on, but is not limited to, the state level of analysis. A series of questions will be posed applicable to any country of the world in an effort to compare the efficiency and effectiveness of different systems of government. The three major areas of inquiry are: (1) inputs to governments (leadership, ideology, interest groups); (2) the institutions of government (executive, judicial, military arrangements); and (3) the output of government (public policies-both domestic and international). Rates, directions, and forces of change will also be examined. (3 semester hours)

World Issues

In this course the student will study the major issues facing the contemporary world. It will have an analytical, problem-solving orientation where information, critical reasoning, and creative thinking are emphasized. Subjects will include such topics as population growth, military intervention, child labor, refugee issues, water, energy, resources, and other current topics. (3 semester hours)

Area Study: Latin America

This course will introduce the student to the political, economic, social, and military processes and structures of Latin America. Special emphasis will be placed on contemporary issues with regard to economic development and democratization. (3 semester hours)

Area Study: Asia and the Pacific

This course will introduce the student to the political, economic, social, military processes and structures of Asia and the Pacific Rim. Special emphasis will be placed on contemporary issues with regard to economic development of the region in this decade. (3 semester hours)

Topics: United States Foreign Policy

This course is designed to acquaint the student with the process, management, and underlying principles that govern U.S. foreign policy. The process and management will include an understanding of the relationship between the President, the professional bureaucracy, and the legislature. The principles will include the ethical and moral values that guide U.S. policymakers in the conduct of foreign policy. The Constitutional basis for foreign policy and the rules which reflect and guide foreign policy will be discussed. (3 semester hours)

SOCIAL WORK

Techniques of Analysis

The student will learn about descriptive and inferential statistics—

what they are and how to apply them to either research or accountability in the social work field. Additionally, the course will cover mean, mode, median, standard deviation, chi square, and Pearson's correlation coefficient. (3 semester hours)

Special Projects: Historical Perspectives of the Social Work Profession

In this course the student will learn how the profession of social work has evolved through the ages, and how this evolution fits the states of society's development. The course will cover: the evolution of social work tenets during the preprofessional years; how social work became a profession; and the impact social work has had on society. (3 semester hours)

Special Projects: Effective Management of Relationships for Social Workers

In this course the student will learn how to identify and cope with the many varieties of difficult types of people that can interfere with productive social work task completion. The course will also address the practical analyses of various leadership styles that social workers may encounter during their careers. (3 semester hours)

SOCIOLOGY

Crime and Delinquency

Nature of crime and delinquency in contemporary American society; emphasis on causation and treatment. A review of relevant criminological theories and current trends and issues. (3 semester hours)

Crime and Women

Exploration of theoretical, historical, social, cultural, and political variables that create both women victims and criminals. Course will further explore career opportunities for women in the field of criminal justice to include historical and current philosophies of corrections and women within corrections. This course, through the use of current-day hands-on materials and resources, will provide the student with a good working insight into women as criminals, victims, and correctional professionals. (3 semester hours)

Social and Cultural Theory

The course will examine from the classical to contemporary theory in sociology and anthropology, and will include historical perspectives into the events that were occurring during the times that major writers were developing their theories. (3 semester hours)

Film and Society

An in-depth look at the images of social life and social relationships contained in popular movies. The course will also explore the influence of media upon social relationships. Requirements and listing of movies will be provided. (3 semester hours)

Poverty

Poverty in the United States, its measurement and extent, perpetuating conditions, lifestyle, and anti-poverty programs. The course will also explore both liberal and conservative viewpoints on the causality of poverty as well as the proposed remedies for eliminating poverty. Current programs, both public and private, will be examined. (3 semester hours)

Family Violence

The extent, seriousness, and impact of the major forms of domestic violence. This course will explore the theoretical, historical, social, and cultural ties of family dynamics and violence. Current research as well as forms of intervention will be explored as well. (3 semester hours)

Victimology

Study of the victim's role in criminal transactions. Examination of individuals and groups as victims of officially defined crime, as well as other social injuries not officially defined as crime. Review of theoretical background and current issues (i.e., post-traumatic stress syndrome) will be included. (3 semester hours)

Advanced Criminological Theory

Examination of major theories of crime and their policy implications; focus on sociohistorical factors in theory development. Review of current literature and application to trends in criminal behavior will also be included. (3 semester hours)

Southern Illinois University at Carbondale
Division of Continuing Education
Individualized Learning Program
Mailcode 6705
Carbondale, Illinois 62901-6705

(618) 536-7751

Description:

Southern Illinois University at Carbondale (SIUC) is one of two universities in the Southern Illinois University system. It was established in 1869. The university has educational programs in operation at several campuses in the Carbondale area. The Individualized Learning courses offered through the Division of Continuing Education are designed to be completed without the need for attendance at scheduled class meetings. Students receive a course Study Guide developed by an SIUC instructor to serve as the framework for the course and study at a time and place of their choosing. Currently there are 44 courses available with over 1,750 students enrolled.

Faculty:

Richard C. Crowell, Coordinator-Credit Programs.

Academic Levels:

College

Degree/Certificate Programs:

All courses are fully accredited and are entered on SIUC transcripts the same as any other SIUC course. Enrollment on a noncredit basis is accepted.

Admission Requirements:

High school graduation or GED equivalent. Enrollment is on a semester basis; courses available may vary each semester.

Tuition:

$65 per credit hour, payable at the time of registration. Students who officially withdraw from a course within three weeks of registration and/or class beginning will receive a credit to the University account. No refund of tuition and fees is made for a withdrawal after the official deadline, except for entry into military service, in which case special consideration is given. Withdrawal must be in writing in order to receive a refund minus a handling charge. Nonsubmission of assignments in an Individualized Learning course does not constitute withdrawal.

Enrollment Period:

Enrollment is on a semester basis. Students living more than 35 miles from campus can mail assignments to the Division of Continuing Education and take exams under an approved hometown proctor.

Equipment Requirements:

Textbooks and study guides must be purchased by the student. The average cost per course of instructional materials is approximately $60. Some courses make use of audiovisual materials for which there is a $10 handling charge. Students are responsible for obtaining appropriate playback equipment.

Credit and Grading:

In the event that the student is unable to complete a course by the end of the semester, he/she may receive an "incomplete," and the student will have 1 year to remove the "incomplete" before academic penalty is imposed.

Library Services:

Students within travel distance have access to the Learning Resources Center in Morris Library.

Accreditations:

North Central Association of Colleges and Schools. Member of: National University Continuing Education Association.

COLLEGE COURSES

AGRICULTURE

Introduction to Computers in Agriculture

An introductory course about the use and role of computers in agriculture. The major thrust includes a basic understanding and application of microcomputers in agriculture with special emphasis on how to save time, money, and increase efficiency in agriculture. (3 semester hours)

ALLIED HEALTH

Medical Terminology

Introduciton to the study of medical language with a working knowledge of the most common word roots, prefixes, suffixes in medical terminology. Emphasis placed on spelling, pronunciation, use of the medical dictionary, vocabulary building, common abbreviations and charting terms. (2 semester hours)

ART

Survey of 20th Century Art

A survey of the major developments in painting, sculpture, architecture, and other selected areas of the visual arts from the beginning of the 20th century to the present. These developments are examined in relation to the other significant cultural, scientific, and philosophical events of the 20th century. (3 semester hours)

Meaning in the Visual Arts

Designed to provide students with a broad understanding of the history of art and its relation and implications to contemporary culture. Emphasis is placed on the relation of art to all disciplines, historical and contemporary. (3 semester hours)

BIOLOGY

History of Biology

The interrelationships between the development of biological knowledge and the history of the human races. (3 semester hours)

CONSUMER ECONOMICS

Consumer Problems

Study of family income and expenditure patterns, selection of commodities and services, and an analysis of consumer proteciton devices. (3 semester hours)

CRIMINAL JUSTICE

Introduction to Criminal Law

The nature and theories of law and social control; legal reasoning and case analysis; simple legal research; statutory construction; principles and history of punishment; consitutional, historical, and general legal principles applicable to the criminal law. (3 semester hours)

Criminal Procedure

An introduction to the procedural aspects of criminal law pertaining to police powers in connection with the laws of arrest, search and seizure, the exclusionary rule, civil liberties, eavesdropping, confessions, and related decison-making factors. (3 semester hours)

ELECTRONICS TECHNOLOGY

Introduction to Electronics

A nonmathematical introduction to the world of electronics. The uses of electricity and control devices for its use. Laws and theories which govern electronics. Devices and circuits which make up today's electronic system. Current flow through the conductors and devices which make up electornic circuits. (3 semester hours)

Computer Systems Applications

Analysis and working knowledge of numbering systems, Boolean algebra, logic gates, pulse shaping circuits, and various timing circuits used in computers, microprocessors, and other digital systems. (3 semester hours)

FINANCE

Insurance

Fundamentals of insurance and risk management, including a study of selected insurance contracts and alternative methods of controlling risk exposures. (3 semester hours)

Small Business Financing

Financing problems involved in raising venture capital, debt type funds, expansion funds, and government sponsored funding. Budgeting, working capital management, and fixed asset planning are covered. (3 semester hours)

HISTORY

Modern American from 1877 to the Present

A general survey of the political, social, and economic development of the United States from 1877 to the present. (3 semester hours)

HUMANITIES

East Asian Civilization

An introduction to East Asian cultural traditions. Literature, philosophy, history, and art of China and Japan. (3 semester hours)

JOURNALISM

The Law of Journalism

Legal limitations and privileges affecting the mass media to include the law of libel, development of obscenity law, free press and fair trial, contempt of court, right of privacy, advertising and antitrust regulations, copyright, and access to the press. (3 semester hours)

LAW ENFORCEMENT

Introduction to Security

An introduction to public and private security issues with a directed emphasis on industrial and retail security, loss prevention, physical security, and design. (3 semester hours)

LOGIC

Elementary Logic

Study of the basic forms of reasoning, with emphasis on the evaluation of arguments encountered in everyday life. (3 semester hours)

MANAGEMENT

Small Business Management

Identification of small business, its importance and relationship to the United States economy and the opportunities and requirements unique to operation and management. Personal characteristics, interpersonal relationships, organizational systems, and decision-making processes are examined for their contribution to the success or failure of the firm. (3 semester hours)

MATHEMATICS

Intermediate Algebra

Properties and operations of the number system. Elementary operations with polynomials and factoring. Elementary operations with algebraic fractions. Exponents, roots, and radicals. First and second degree equations and inequalities. Functions and graphing. Systems of equations and inequalities. Exponential and logarithmic functions. (3 semester hours)

Technical Mathematics

TC 105A. Will enable the student to solve problems within the context of engineering technologies. Emphasizes the use of algebraic equations and geometric relationships and formulas, and right triangle trigonometry. The use of an electronic calculator with scientific functions is required. (2 semester hours)

TC 105B. Emphasizes the applicaiton of trigonometric relationships to problems in applied technologies, and contains additional topics in algebra including linear systems, quadratic equations, and exponential and logarithmic functions. The use of an electronic calculator with scientific functions is required. (2 semester hours

METEOROLOGY

Understanding the Weather

Introduction to the processes that create the world's weather and its seasonal and geographic variations; basics of weather forecasting; issues of managing the atmospheric environment, including air pollution meteorology, causes and hazards of storms, human-induced climatic change, weather modification. (3 semester hours)

MUSIC

Music Understanding

The aural perception of musical sound events, relationships, and structures. Helps the student to become a more sensitive and perceptive listener. Listening assignments include a wide variety of styles and kinds of music. Not historically oriented. (3 semester hours)

PHILOSOPHY

Existential Philosophy

Surveys the two main sources of existentialism, the philosophies of Kierkegaard and Nietzsche, with occasional reference to thinkers such as Sartre, Heidegger, Buber, Marcel, and others. (3 semester hours)

Problems in Philosophy

Introductory survey of some main philosophic problems concerning people, nature, society, and God, as discussed by major Western thinkers. (3 semester hours)

Moral Decision

Introduction to contemporary and perennial problems of personal and social morality, and to methods proposed for their resolution by great thinkers of past and present. (3 semester hours)

PHYSICS

Applied Physics

TC 107A. Places emphasis on basic and applied physics at a level consistent with technical education objectives. The student will learn laws and principles and solve problems pertaining to mechanics and the structure of matter. (2 semester hours)

TC 107B. The student will learn laws and principles and solve problems pertaining to heat and electricity. (2 semester hours)

PHYSIOLOGY

Princples of Physiology

A comprehensive introductory analysis of the functional machinery of the living body, with emphasis on human physiology. (3 semester hours)

POLITICAL SCIENCE

Introduction to American Government and Politics

An introduction to American government including the cultural context, structure and functions of the national political system, and some attention to subnational politics. (3 semester hours)

Politics of Foreign Nations

Politics and the societies and cultures that shape them, Western democracies, Third World, communist countries. (3 semester hours)

Introduction to Public Administration

An introduction to the study of public bureaucracy. Theoretical, political, and practical issues of organization, staffing, financing, and other matters are surveyed. United States administration and organizational behavior are stressed. (3 semester hours)

Poltical Systems of the American States

The state level of government viewed with emphasis on recent developments and current research. (3 semester hours)

Public Financial Administration

An examination of governmental revenues and expenditures, with emphasis on state and local governments. Special attention is given to patterns of taxation and expenditure, intergovernmental fiscal relations, municipal debt, and administrative decision making. (3 semester hours)

REAL ESTATE

Real Estate

Problems of real estate ownership, management, financing, and development. (3 semester hours)

Real Estate Appraisal

The techniques and art of real estate valuation using market comparison, cost, and income approaches. Includes appraisal principles, procedures, and applications. (3 semester hours)

RUSSIAN

Soviet Russian Literature

Major fiction writers and literary trends since 1917. Lectures, readings, and reports. Taught in English. (3 semester hours)

Soviet Civilization

Soviet culture and civilization is studied primarily through literary works, journalistic materials, and excerpts from nonliterary works as general background reading. Taught in English. Readings are in English and in bilingual edition. (3 semester hours)

Russian Realism

Authors in 19th-century Russian literature. Special attention to stylistic devices. Lectures, readings, and individual class reports. (4 semester hours)

SOCIOLOGY

The Sociological Perspective

An examination of the range of social relationships among people; basic sociological concepts and theories, social groups, social institutions, social and cultural change, and social deviance. (3 semester hours)

TECHNICAL STUDIES

Applications of Technical Information

This course is designed to increase student competence in analyzing and utilizing the various types of technical information encounted by managers in technical fields. (3 semester hours)

TOURISM

The Hospitality and Tourism Industries

Introduction to the diverse aspects of the hospitality and tourism industries and the interrelationships between them. Historical development of the industries, trends, current issues, and career opportunities will be examined. (3 semester hours)

Front Office Management

Principles and concepts of effective front office management in the lodging industry. (3 semester hours)

Food and Beverage Management

Examination of the managerial responsibilities of the food and beverage manager in the hospitality operation. Management methods in budgeting, forecasting, controlling costs, and establishing operational policies. (3 semester hours)

Southern Mississippi, University of
Office of Independent Study
Box 5056
Hattiesburg, Mississippi 39406 (601) 266-4206

Description:
The University of Southern Mississippi opened in 1912 as the Mississippi Normal College. Its present name was adopted in 1962. The Division of Lifelong Learning provides such educational opportunities as extension courses, conferences, workshops, special interest courses, and Independent Study.

Faculty:
Clifford Rudder, Coordinator; Lisa Carpenter, Registrar.

Academic Levels:
College
High School
Noncredit

Degree/Certificate Programs:
Up to one-fourth (33 semester hours) of the requirements for the bachelor's degree at the University of Southern Mississippi may be met through correspondence courses. The Department of Independent Study does not issue a high school diploma, but issues credit through an accredited high school.

Admission Requirements:
Open enrollment. Students in attendance at any institution of higher learning are urged to obtain permission from their deans before enrolling for correspondence study. Admission to the University is not required. A student registering for high school credit must have the principal's written approval for a course to count toward high school credit.

Tuition:
University courses, $195 per three semester hours; high school courses, $55 per half unit. There is a $5 first class mailing fee for each course. A refund of 80 percent is allowed if no more than one month has elapsed since registration and if no lessons have been submitted.

Enrollment Period:
The maximum time allowed to complete a correspondence course is one year from the date of acceptance of the application. The minimum time for completion of a course is one month from the date of registration, provided assignments are sent in two or three at a time at regular intervals proportionately spaced over the minimum time. A three-month extension beyond the one-year limitation will be granted upon payment of $20 before the expiration date. Students are allowed one three-month extension for each course.

Equipment Requirements:
Textbooks must be paid for by the student and may be purchased locally. They may also be purchased through the USM Bookstore. Certain used books are available at a reduced price. Cassette tapes for some classes are on a loan basis.

Credit and Grading:
Grades are A, B, C, D, F. The minimum passing grade for a course is D (70 percent). Independent college courses

may be taken on a pass/fail option. Credit is awarded in semester hour units. Examinations must be proctored. Independent Study Examination Centers are located at various locations throughout Mississippi.

Library Services:

Students may use on-campus facilities with a library card provided by the Department of Independent Study.

Accreditations:

Southern Association of Colleges and Schools. Member of: National University Continuing Education Association.

COLLEGE COURSES

ANTHROPOLOGY

Introduction to Anthropology

An overview of the field of anthropology. (3 semester hours)

BIOLOGY

Zoogeography

A descriptive analytical study of the distribution of plants and animals. (3 semester hours)

BUSINESS ADMINISTRATION

The Legal Environment of Business

A study of the Mississippi and Federal Court systems, torts, and contract law. The course is designed to reflect the impact of law upon society. (3 semester hours)

COMPUTER SCIENCE

Introduction to Computing

Personal computer concepts, uses of computers in society, introduction to software packages for word processing, data management, spreadsheets, graphics, and introduction to programming using BASIC. (3 semester hours)

CRIMINAL JUSTICE

Introduction to Criminal Justice

An introduction to the fundamentals of police operations from the police image to apprehension of the criminal. (3 semester hours)

Traffic law

(3 semester hours)

Introduction to Criminal Corrections

(3 semester hours)

Introduction to Juvenile Justice

(3 semester hours)

ECONOMICS

Introduction to Economics

A basic overview of the determination of national income, employment, prices, economic growth and the laws of production, distribution, and allocation. (3 semester hours)

Principles of Economics I

An examination of the basic institutional environment of American capitalism and the determination of the level of national income, employment, prices, and growth. (3 semester hours)

Principles of Economics II

An examination of the laws of production and their influence on costs and output. Also, a study of product and factor price determination under varying degrees of competition. (3 semester hours)

EDUCATION

Principles of Guidance

An introductory course dealing with fundamental philosophy, methods, and organization of guidance services in the public secondary schools. (3 semester hours)

ELECTRONICS ENGINEERING TECHNOLOGY

Electric Power Generation and Distribution

(3 semester hours)

ENGINEERING TECHNOLOGY

Engineering Economics

Mathematical techniques used to simplify economic comparisons in the acquisition and retirement of capital goods in industry. (3 semester hours)

ENGLISH

Writing I

Stresses clear, effective writing with special attention to syntactical and organizational skills. (3 semester hours)

Writing II

Refines compositional skills and stresses additional rhetorical and research methods. (3 semester hours)

Fiction Writing II

(3 semester hours)

Fiction Writing III

(3 semester hours)

Poetry Writing II

(3 semester hours)

Poetry Writing III

(3 semester hours)

Survey of Literature of the South

(3 semester hours)

GEOGRAPHY

World Geography

An introductory course in world regional geography. (3 semester hours)

Introduction to Geography

An introduction to geography focusing on the basic elements and concepts. (3 semester hours)

Geography of the United States and Canada

(3 semester hours)

HEALTH

Personal Wellness

An examination of the relationships of various lifestyle components to various levels of wellness. (3 semester hours)

Community Health

Community control of environmental health hazards, community control of diseases, health agencies. (3 semester hours)

Marriage and Human Sexuality

Physical, emotional, and medical basis for successful courtship, marriage, and parenthood. (3 semester hours)

HISTORY

World Civilization to 1648 A.D.

(3 semester hours)

World Civilization Since 1648 A.D.

A continuation of the above course. (3 semester hours)

United States to 1877

(3 semester hours)

United States Since 1877

A continuation of the above course. (3 semester hours)

HOME ECONOMICS

Nutrition for Living

(1 semester hour)

INDUSTRIAL AND VOCATIONAL EDUCATION

Engineering Drawing I

(3 semester hours)

Engineering Drawing II

(3 semester hours)

Architectural Drawing

(3 semester hours)

MANAGEMENT

Management for Organizations

(3 semester hours)

MARKETING

Principles of Marketing

An integrated managerial-systems approach to the study of marketing functions in organizations. Development of marketing concepts, institutions, functions, and policies are analyzed within the framework of the competitive, legal, economic, and social environment. (3 semester hours)

MATHEMATICS

College Algebra

Polynomials, factoring, functions and graphs, linear and quadratic equations and inequalities. (3 semester hours)

Plane Trigonometry

(3 semester hours)

Calculus I with Analytic Geometry

Functions, limits, derivatives, application of the derivative, and selected topics from analytic geometry. (3 semester hours)

Calculus II with Analytic Geometry

Definite and indefinite integrals, applications of the integral transcendental functions, and selected topics from analytical geometry. (3 semester hours)

Calculus III with Analytic Geometry

Techniques of integration, infinite series, L'Hôpital's rule, improper integrals. Taylor's formula, and selected topics from analytic geometry. (4 semester hours)

Calculus for the Business and Social Sciences

Basic concepts and techniques of calculus at an appropriate level for the mathematically inexperienced student. Aims to demonstrate how calculus can be used to build mathematical models in management and economics. More emphasis is placed on applications than on the underlying theory. (3 semester hours)

Mathematics for Teachers of Junior High School Mathematics

The real number system and major subsystems, introduction to algebra, informal geometry, consumer mathematics, and an introduction to BASIC programming. (3 semester hours)

PHILOSOPHY

Introduction to Philosophy

(3 semester hours)

Logic

This course is designed to sharpen skills in critical thinking and generally broaden the ability to reason. Three major areas will be studied: (1) traditional deductive logic, (2) symbolic logic, and (3) logic and language with the emphasis on informal fallacies. (3 semester hours)

Ethics

This course deals with the nature of morality, important representative thinkers and topics of serious ethical concern. Some representative issues are: medical ethics (e.g., euthanasia, abortion), capital punishment, suicide, violence, environmental ethics, authority and responsibility. (3 semester hours)

PHYSICAL EDUCATION

Organization and Administration of Health and Physical Education

A study of the scope of the problem of administration in physical education and athletics. (3 semester hours)

POLITICAL SCIENCE

American Government

An introductory course in the principles and practices of American government and politics. (3 semester hours)

Introduction to Political Science

(3 semester hours)

State and Local Politics

A study of state and local governments in the United States. (3 semester hours)

PSYCHOLOGY

General Psychology

An introduction to the scientific study of human behavior and experience. (3 semester hours)

Child Psychology

Study of child through the elementary school years, emphasizing principles and problems of development. (3 semester hours)

Adolescent Psychology

Psychological development of the individual through the adolescent years. (3 semester hours)

REAL ESTATE

Real Estate Principles

Introduces the student to the field of real estate with topics such as real estate finance, residential and income appraisal, property management, law, brokerage, and others covered. (3 semester hours)

Real Estate Law

The law of real property and the law of real estate brokerage. It is designed to meet the requirements for salesperson's or broker's licensing. (3 semester hours)

RECREATION

Theory of Recreation Leadership

A study of the theory, methods, and techniques for leading individuals in small and large group activity, and performing the function of professional leadership within the community and non-community recreational settings. (3 semester hours)

RELIGION

Introduction to Religion

An introduction to religions of the world, historic and contemporary. (3 semester hours)

The Life of Jesus

A study of the life of Jesus as presented in the first three gospels. (3 semester hours)

SOCIOLOGY

Introduction to Sociology

A course designed to give the student a general overview of the content and methodology of sociology. (3 semester hours)

The Family

An analysis of the structure and functions of the family as an institution and the factors making for family change. (3 semester hours)

Criminology

A study of causes, treatment, and prevention of crime. The presentation deals with criminology, penology, and criminal legislation in ancient and modern times. (3 semester hours)

SPEECH COMMUNICATION

Business and Professional Speaking

(3 semester hours)

SPORTS ADMINISTRATION

Organization and Administration of High School Athletics

The organizational and administrative procedures of major and minor sports programs. (3 semester hours)

Basic Fundamentals of Coaching Basketball

The theoretical study of offensive and defensive concepts. A study of philosophy, terminology, strategy, and individual techniques in basketball. (3 semester hours)

Advanced Techniques of Coaching Basketball

The criteria of player selection with emphasis on the area of theory, principles, and techniques of offensive and defensive planning and strategy. (3 semester hours)

HIGH SCHOOL COURSES

BUSINESS

Accounting I

First Half. A beginning course which will teach the basic bookkeeping concepts as they apply to the techniques used in the business world. (½ unit)

Second Half. A continuation of the above course. (½ unit)

Business Mathematics

This course presents three distinct types of subject matter: business problems, fundamental operations, and mental arithmetic. It is designed so that the student may gain a deeper understanding of number operations and relationships and obtain a firmer grasp of the meaning and use of fractions, decimals, and percents. (½ unit)

Business Communications

The course presents fundamental skills necessary for the writing of effective business correspondence. Drills are given in building the sentence and paragraph units so that the student should be able to write a satisfactory letter of any type. (½ unit)

Business Law

The course is designed to give the student a practical understanding of the law and of the legal framework that has grown up around it. This practical understanding of the law should help determine if and when a lawyer should be consulted. (½ unit)

Business Dynamics

First Half. A course in which the student acquires information about business and its services (transportation, communication, banking, insurance, etc.) and information which is important in the everyday life of persons. (½ unit)

Second Half. A continuation of the above course.

Shorthand I

First Half. This course, based on the new Gregg Series 90, is prepared for the student who desires to learn the fundamentals of Gregg shorthand. Upon completion of the course, the student will have a knowledge of all Gregg shorthand principles and will have read and copied much printed shorthand with some degree of speed and accuracy. (½ unit)

Second Half. A continuation of the above course. (½ unit)

Typewriting I

First Half. A course in the fundamentals of touch typewriting for the purpose of mastering the keyboard and operative parts of the machine; also gives practice and training in the preparation of a variety of business papers. Student must have access to a typewriter. (½ unit)

Second Half. A continuation of the above course. (½ unit)

Typewriting II

First Half. This course is organized to give the student experience in the preparation and understanding of varied typing problems of increasing difficulty and to develop vocational competency in office procedures. (½ unit)

Second Half. A continuation of the above course. (½ unit)

ENGLISH

English I

First Half. A ninth-grade level course to give a review in the use of the tools of basic grammar and elementary composition. (½ unit)

Second Half. A ninth-grade level course to give an appreciation of literature. (½ unit)

English II

First Half. A tenth-grade level course to give an appreciation of literature, elementary composition, and grammar review. (½ unit)

Second Half. A continuation of the above course. (½ unit)

English III

First Half. An eleventh-grade level course which introduces the student to American literature through the study of modern fiction, nonfiction, poetry, and drama. The course also presents the fundamentals of grammar to be used in writing. (½ unit)

Second Half. A continuation of the above course. (½ unit)

English IV

First Half. A twelfth-grade level course which provides a review of English grammar as well as the opportunity to practice good writing skills. (½ unit)

Second Half. This course surveys English literature from the Anglo-Saxon period through the eighteenth century. (½ unit)

JOURNALISM

Introduction to Journalism

A course to give a basic understanding of journalism and skills in writing for high school newspapers; fosters appreciation of good journalism. (½ unit)

FRENCH

French I

First Half. An introduction to the principles of grammar, pronunciation, and reading. (½ unit)

Second Half. A continuation of the above course. (½ unit)

French II

First Half. Continued grammar drill, with more extensive reading and translation. (½ unit)

Second Half. A continuation of the above course. (½ unit)

HOME ECONOMICS

Home Economics I

First Half. This introductory course in homemaking is designed to give a student general information in understanding himself, his family, and his social relationships. (½ unit)

Second Half. This course has combined scientific knowledge of a balanced diet with its practical application of meal planning. (½ unit)

Home Economics II

First Half. This course is primarily concerned with basic sewing skills and the evaluation and management of a wardrobe. (½ unit)

Second Half. This is an introductory course in home planning, furniture and equipment buying, the selection of accessories, and the choice of style and design. (½ unit)

Family Living and Parenthood

This study of family living includes personality development, dating problems, engagement, marriage, laws, marriage adjustments, family finances, divorces, and preparation for parenthood. (½ unit)

Child Development

The major purpose of this course is to focus on children—their physical, emotional, and intellectual growth. (½ unit)

MATHEMATICS

Algebra I

First Half. This course reflects the recent advances in the teaching of mathematics and the content of modern mathematics. Mathematical concepts are taught for an understanding of the numbers systems with some attempts to illustrate the uses of mathematics in the modern world of science and technology. (½ unit)

Second Half. A continuation of the above course. (½ unit)

Algebra II

First Half. This course is a continuation of Algebra I. The topics include: a review and extension of topics previously studied, binomial theorem, complex numbers, theory of equations, algebraic and graphical solution of simultaneous quadratic equations in two unknowns, ratio, proportion, variation. (½ unit)

Second Half. A continuation of the above course. (½ unit)

Consumer Math

First Half. The very basic of the high school math classes, Consumer Math is intended to prepare non-college students with practical math application in a variety of areas. Topics of studies include estimation, the work force, recreation, purchasing goods, checking and savings, accounts, credit, auto expenses, transportation, taxes, housing expenses, and an overview of a variety of the use of mathematics in professions. (½ unit)

Second Half. A continuation of the above course. (½ unit)

General Mathematics I

First Half. This course provides a mathematical background which is directly related to everyday life. The topics include a review and extension of arithmetic with applications to everyday living; the fundamental processes with integers, fractions, and decimals; percentage; scale drawings, graphs, formulas; budgeting and spending, banking and saving money. (½ unit)

Second Half. A continuation of the above course. (½ unit)

General Mathematics II

First Half. This is a continuation of Fundamental Mathematics I. Review and extension of algebra to include the formula, signed numbers, equations of first degree in one and two unknowns, and problems; applications of mathematics to home and community life, to science and technical work. (½ unit)

Second Half. A continuation of the above course. (½ unit)

Geometry

First Half. This course deals with modern geometry as it is used in today's world. It is a study of geometry in the context of the space age, lines and planes in space, angles and triangles, geometric inequalities, congruences, along with deductive and indirect proof. (½ unit)

Second Half. A continuation of the above course. (½ unit)

Mathematics, Advanced

First Half. This is a modern pre-calculus course which includes a study of advanced algebra with an emphasis on functions and the analytic aspect of trigonometry. (½ unit)

Second Half. A continuation of the above course. (½ unit)

SCIENCE

Biology

First Half. This course attempts to make the student aware of interrelationships of living things and their environmental adaptations and to have a clear comprehension of the significance and importance of life to human welfare. (½ unit)

Second Half. A continuation of the above course. (½ unit)

Chemistry

First Half. This course is designed to provide introductory material on atomic structure, the Periodic Table, and chemical bonding. (½ unit)

Second Half. A continuation of the above course. (½ unit)

General Science

First Half. This is a course which presents an insight into the study of air, water, matter and energy, understanding man, heat, weather and astronomy. (½ unit)

Second Half. A continuation of the above course. (½ unit)

Physics

First Half. This course examines the fundamental relationships of matter and energy. (½ unit)

Second Half. A continuation of the above course. (½ unit)

SOCIAL STUDIES

Economics

The primary emphases of this course are the study of tools of economic analysis and their application to contemporary economic issues. (½ unit)

Geography

A primary objective in this course is to gain an understanding of the interdependence of people and places, and the physical and economic factors which affect each. (½ unit)

Government, Mississippi, State and Local

This course is primarily concerned with citizenship and the part that a responsible citizen should play in his community, county, state, and country, as well as his/her place in the community of the world. (½ unit)

Government, United States

A study of the basic principles of American government; the organization, process, and functions of the national and state levels of government are covered. (½ unit)

History, United States, 1877 to Present

First Half. (½ unit)

Second Half. A continuation of the above course. (½ unit)

Sociology

This course is concerned with how people behave in groups and how group interaction influences their behavior. (½ unit)

World History

First Half. This course deals with the rise and growth of civilization from the time that man appeared on earth to the present. (½ unit)

Second Half. A continuation of the above course. (½ unit)

SPANISH

Spanish I

First Half. An introduction to the principles of grammar, pronunciation, and reading. (½ unit)

Second Half. A continuation of the above course. (½ unit)

Spanish II

First Half. (½ unit)

Second Half. A continuation of the above course. (½ unit)

NONCREDIT COURSES

SPORTS ADMINISTRATION

Basketball Officiating

(Noncredit)

Football Officiating

(Noncredit)

Southern Oregon State College

1250 Siskiyou Boulevard
Ashland, Oregon 97520   (503) 482-6411

Description:

Correspondence courses offered by Southern Oregon State College are administered by the Office of Independent Study of the Oregon State System of Higher Education in Portland, Oregon. For courses available, SEE **Oregon State System of Higher Education.**

Accreditations:

Northwest Association of Schools and Colleges.

Stephens College

Stephens College Without Walls
Campus Box 2083
1200 East Broadway
Columbia, Missouri 65215   (800) 388-7579

Description:

A liberal arts college for women, Stephens College was established in 1833. Stephens was a member of the original University Without Walls consortium in the early 1970s. Stephens College Without Walls was established to provide adult students the opportunity to continue their education with minimal disruption to work and family. The external degree (independent study) program is one of three programs of academic study for women and men 23 years of age and older.

Over 1,400 students have graduated from the program. Many have continued their education in graduate and professional schools. Students may select from a wide variety of majors and can expect excellence in teaching and continual academic support. Liberal arts, business, and professional courses are available through correspondence study, with a required residence seminar at the beginning of the program. This seminar is held in double weekend format or an seven-day format with many assignments completed at home prior to and after the actual time on campus.

Faculty:

Rosemary Allen, Interim Director; LuAnna Andrews, New Student Coordinator. All campus faculty members are involved as teachers or counselors.

Academic Levels:

College

Degree/Certificate Programs:

Certificate, Associate degrees, and Baccalaureate degrees. Residency is met by a minimum of ten courses with the Stephens faculty; this includes the required Liberal Studies Seminar and independent guided study courses through Stephens. The list of courses available changes, evolves, and grows to meet student needs. Independent contract studies are available when students want specific course content which is not already available. In contract studies, the student and faculty member(s) design a course, including goals and objectives, content, and evaluation process. Because new courses are being designed continuously, the student is advised to contact the Stephens College Without Walls office for more detailed information about available courses.

The required Liberal Studies Seminar includes a 3-semester-hour course, consisting of orientation to the program, advising and degree planning, and self-assessment workshops.

Admission Requirements:

Student must be 23 years of age or older; open enrollment. Official transcripts from: all previous accredited colleges or universities; official transcript from previous training programs if no college, official high school transcript, or GED certificate; CLEP results and ACE-evaluated courses transcripts; TOEFL scores as applicable. Majors in Health Information Management must be Accredited Record Technicians. Student must be enrolled in a degree program at Stephens and must participate in an entrance Liberal Studies Seminar which involves attendance on campus or at other locations for either two weekends or eight consecutive days. Remaining coursework may be completed by independent study.

Tuition:

Application fee, $50. Tuition $208.33 per semester hour credit. VISA and MasterCard accepted. Textbooks are not included in tuition. Other fees may apply for on- or off-campus seminars. Refund policy varies according to course format.

Enrollment Period:

Maximum time to complete a course is one year; minimum time is six months.

Equipment Requirements:

Textbook costs are not included with tuition. Grading system is 4.00 scale (A-4.00, B-3.00; C-2.00; D-1.00; F-0.00. Minimum passing grade varies by course. Examinations must be proctored. Credit is awarded in semester hours (three semester hours for the successful completion of each course).

Library Services:

Students have access to the Stephens College Library. They will also receive a letter of introduction from the Stephens College Librarian for admission to local libraries in the student's home town.

Accreditations:

North Central Association of Colleges and Schools; Health Information Management program accredited by the American Health Information Management Association and the American Medical Association.

COLLEGE COURSES

BUSINESS ADMINISTRATION

Introduction to Business

An introduction to the structure and functions of contemporary business enterprise. Emphasis placed on career possibilities and the skills and knowledge necessary for specific careers. (3 semester hours)

Conceptual Foundations of Accounting

This course will provide a study of accounting as the language of business, providing an introduction to the uses of financial data in decision making. It is intended to give the student an appreciation of the functions accounting performs in the business world and in society in general. (3 semester hours)

Accounting I

This course is a study of accounting theory and techniques used in the accumulation and disclosure of accounting data resulting from business transactions in proprietorships, partnerships, and corporations. (3 semester hours)

Accounting II

An introduction to managerial accounting. The preparation, use, and interpretation of internal accounting data in the managerial functions of planning, organizing, controlling, and decision making. (3 semester hours)

Principles of Management

Study of the basic principles of management, including organizational designs and the use of groups, leadership, communication, planning, decision making, and controlling. (3 semester hours)

Marketing

An introductory course for those taking their first and perhaps only course in marketing. Both macro- and micro-marketing topics will be approached. The course includes the study of consumer behavior and traditional decision-making areas of the marketing manager: product, price, distribution, and promotion. (3 semester hours)

Retailing

A study of the principles involved in the management of the functional areas of any retail organization: merchandising, promotion, personnel, operations, and control. Special attention given to the role of the retailer in the social milieu, to ethical considerations and to current issues in the industry. (3 semester hours)

Personnel Management

This course is designed to acquaint the student with the theory and techniques of effectively managing human resources in modern organizations. Topics covered will include the following: personnel planning, and staffing, training and development, performance appraisal, government regulations affecting personnel, and labor relations. (3 semester hours)

Principles of Finance

An introduction to finance from a corporate perspective. Topics include financial markets, capital budgeting, working capital, and financial statement analysis. (3 semester hours)

Business Law

A study of the laws of contracts, agency, and employment, with emphasis on contract formation, consumer protection, and remedies. (3 semester hours)

Social and Ethical Issues in Business

This is an applied ethics course in which techniques of moral reasoning are applied in the analysis of moral issues in business. The course covers such broad issues as the moral justification of our economic system, the moral responsibility of corporations, and the role of business in a global society. We will also address more contemporary and pressing issues such as employee rights, affirmative action, and environmental issues. (3 semester hours)

Special Studies and Projects in Business

An in-depth investigation of a topic of special interest to the student on the application of theory, methodology and analysis to a practical organizational setting. Students should submit proposals to the faculty member they wish to sponsor the project. (1½ or 3 semester hours)

Senior Seminar: Business Policy and Strategy

This is a capstone course in Business Administration. Students will be expected to draw from all business functional areas in the process of analyzing complex organizational cases. The course is designed to encourage a comprehensive appreciation of organizations and their many environments (e.g., social, technological, political, competitive, and economic), and an understanding of the effects and interdependencies of the various business functional areas. The course focuses on the key role of business strategy and policy decisions in determining individual, organizational, and societal outcomes. (3 semester hours)

CHILD DEVELOPMENT

Child Development: Infancy

A study of physical, intellectual, social, and emotional development of infants from conception to age two for the future parent and/or teacher. (1½ semester hours)

The Child: Lifespan and Cross-Cultural Perspective

A study of the physical, psychosocial, cognitive development of the child within a lifespan and cross-cultural perspective. Emphasis on the early childhood and elementary years is supported by observation of and participation with children in a variety of settings. (3 semester hours)

Child Development: The Adolescent Years

A study of the developmental segment spanning the junior high, senior high, and early college or post-high school years. These years are studied from the four traditional areas of child development—physical, social, emotional, and intellectual. The course provides the student with an understanding of the whole adolescent. It develops knowledge, skills, and attitudes and encourages the student to study and interact with adolescents. (1½ to or 6 semester hours)

Creative Activities for Children

Course content is designed for all those who wish to stimulate their creative expression and to develop their visual and manipulative skills. Students research, develop, and present creative curriculum particularly in art and natural science, along with their own exploration of materials and concepts in all levels of human development. Open to all students: parents, teachers, and many others, and requires no previous formalized training in the arts. (3 semester hours)

Literature for Children: Person, Place, Time

An intercultural approach to the study of literature for children which recognizes that this world literature reflects human experience shaped by time and place. Includes extensive reading of children's books, application of appropriate evaluation criteria and a consideration of various issues which have meaning for individuals and societies. (3 semester hours)

Programs, Philosophies, and Issues in Early Childhood Education

The course is a study of a variety of types of programs for children through age 8, using the perspective of the past, the reality of the present, and the trend toward the future as the broad base for reading and first-hand experience. Emphasis is placed on day care, and other community-based programs, and regular participation in one of these programs is expected. Current issues in the field and the use of research tools in independent study relevant to the class topics are emphasized. (1½ to 3 semester hours)

ENGLISH

Literary Studies: Science Fiction

The impact of scientific developments on existing moral and social orders; the possible outcomes of present social and political forces; the high adventure of encounters with alien life forms and intellectual systems—these form the basic concerns of science fiction. This course explores science fiction as a literary form, its relation to futurology, and its value as a form of thought. (3 semester hours)

Literary Studies: Fairy Tale and Fable

Underlying modern narrative forms (novels, short stories, and autobiographies), we often find structures reminiscent of primitive or fold narratives—especially fairy tales and fables. This course explores some traditional collections of these forms, their distinctive characteristics, their psychological value both as expression and as experience; their sociological and political impact, and their persistence in the structures of selected modern works. (3 semester hours)

Literary Studies: Women in Love

The theme of romantic love as it shaped and tested women just before our time—and as it shaped our own notions of what love is. (3 semester hours)

Elizabethan Shakespeare

This course involves a study of the following plays and works: *The Taming of the Shrew, A Midsummer Night's Dream, Romeo and Juliet, The Merchant of Venice, Richard III,* and selected sonnets. (3 semester hours)

Advanced Literary Studies: Feminism and the Literary Imagination

This course explores the reasons why writers (male and female) responded as they did to efforts to affirm, assert or enforce equality (by whatever definition) between men and women. The course attempts to reconstruct the contexts within which writers have been obliged to confront the efforts of women to realize themselves. In some cases, this will involve the study of evasions, in others, of repression, in others, of supportive or encouraging gestures. (3 semester hours)

Advanced Literary Studies: Austen, Brontë, Burney, Eliot

(3 semester hours)

Eighteenth- and Nineteenth-Century International Literature

Eighteen- and nineteenth-century men and women of letters were more profoundly involved in public affairs—and had a more direct impact on them—than has been true of writers before or since. this course, through selected readings by English and European writers of these periods, explores the interaction of literature and public life and the impact of writers on the development both of modern literary forms and of modern political and social structures. (3 semester hours)

Major Works of Dostoevsky

A selection from Dostoevsky's major novels for a study of his themes, characters, and development. (3 semester hours)

FASHION

Topics in Fashion

The Fashion Department will negotiate contract studies with individual students upon request. (variable semester hours)

Foundations of Fashion Merchandising

An introductory course which provides an overview of fashion retailing functions with special emphasis on merchandising and management activities. (3 semester hours)

Fashion Merchandising Strategies and Decision Making

A course designed to interpret fashion merchandising principles through the case analysis method. Students are encouraged to analyze and develop alternative courses of action for a variety of situations. (3 semester hours)

GEOLOGY

Geology

The Geology courses listed below are designed to meet the needs of students who have an interest in geology but have had no previous training in that subject. The courses may be selected without regard to order but merely according to the students' interests; one, several, or all may be taken. All course materials including text and specimens are provided. With each course, a set of slides is provided for visual interpretation. Outside readings will be done from a prepared bibliography and, therefore, library resources will be necessary.

Geology I: Caves and Caverns

A basic study of the subject including underground water generally or certain phases, e.g., geysers and hot springs, cold water springs, or other possible topics. (3 semester hours)

Geology I: Historical Geology

Deals primarily with the major events through which the earth has passed since its origin, as well as study of the kinds of animals which have lived since our planet was born. Special concern is given to the evolution of life through the geologic past. Some time is given to studying specimens of a few common types of fossils. A set of fossils will be sent as part of the materials of this course. Readings will be done from a prepared bibliography with evaluation by reports on readings and examination at the end of the course. (3 semester hours)

Geology I: Oceans

A basic study of the geologic work of the oceans (and sedimentary rocks) or more specific phases of oceanography (or sedimentary rocks), e.g., the West vs. East Coast of the U.S., or other possible topics. (3 semester hours)

Geology I: Rivers

A basic study of the work done by rivers or more specific phases of river work, e.g., canyons, waterfalls, or other possible topics. (3 semester hours)

Geology I: Volcanoes

A basic study of the volcanism or certain phases of volcanism, e.g., those of North America, intrusive volcanism, extrusive volcanism or other possible topics. (3 semester hours)

Conservation of Natural Resources

The course is basically concerned with the current environment crisis. Subjects covered include the energy crisis, water pollution, air pollution, soil, range, or grasslands, forest, wildlife, population, etc. (3 semester hours)

Astronomy

An introduction to descriptive astronomy covering the major types of sky objects. It includes methods of observing the location as well as natural history. (3 semester hours)

Alternative Forms of Energy

Students may become involved in a local alternative energy project such as solar or wind energy. (3 semester hours)

Introduction to Meteorology

An introduction to the study of the weather. In addition to readings, the student makes her/his own weather station for recording and predicting the weather. Emphasis on field observations as well as basic theory. (3 semester hours)

Environmental Ethics

Environmental issues have aroused a conflicting variety of economic, scientific, and political interpretations. The course considers values at stake and offers concerned citizens an ethical framework with which to formulate and implement ecological decisions. Endangered species, coal mining, nuclear energy, and chemical pollution are discussed and analyzed. (3 semester hours)

HEALTH INFORMATION MANAGEMENT

Human Anatomy and Physiology - Lecture

A basic introductory course in human anatomy and physiology which is organized into five principal areas of concentration: (1) organization of the human body, (2) principles of support and movement, (3) control systems, (4) maintenance of the human body, and (5) continuity. In each area, emphasis is placed on the interrelationship of structure and function in each of the organs which comprise the major systems of the human body. Students may take Human Anatomy and Physiology - Laboratory before or after completion of this course. The intensive lab is offered during the summer for five days on the Stephens College campus. (3 semester hours)

Introduction to Statistics

This is a study of elementary statistics as used in psychology, business, or information management. Topics include organization of data, measures of central tendency and variability, the normal distribution, sampling distributions, estimation, hypothesis testing, regression, and correlation, differences between samples, and chi-square tests. The course is also available for reduced credit and content. (3 semester hours)

Pathophysiology I

An in-depth study of the general principles of disease and the disorders that affect the body as a whole. The disease processes affecting the human body are studied via an integrated approach to specific diseases. Each disease is studied in relation to its etiology, pathology, physical signs and symptoms, treatment, and prognosis and public health aspect. (3 semester hours)

Pathophysiology II

A continuation of *Pathophysiology I:* an in-depth study of the general principles of disease and the disorders that affect the body as a whole. The disease processes affecting the human body are studied via an integrated approach to specific diseases. Each disease is studied in relation to its etiology, pathology, physical signs and symptoms, treatment, and prognosis, and public health aspect. (3 semester hours)

Accounting I

This course is a study of accounting theory and techniques used in the accumulation and disclosure of accounting data resulting from business transactions in proprietorships, partnerships, and corporations. (3 semester hours)

Accounting II

An introduction to managerial accounting. The preparation, use, and interpretation of internal accounting data in the managerial functions of planning, organizing, controlling, and decision making. (3 semester hours)

Principles of Management

Study of the basic principles of management, including organizational designs and the use of groups, leadership, communication, planning, decision making, and controlling. (3 semester hours)

Legal and Ethical Issues in Health Information: A Contemporary Perspective

Study of selected legal and ethical issues which relate to health care professionals. Legal theories and general ethical principles are applied to analyze and evaluate issues in health information management in particular and health care delivery in general. (3 semester hours)

Nosologic Systems

A survey of the history and purpose of a variety of nomenclature and classification systems available in the health care field. Attention is paid to evaluation of these systems and their appropriateness in various health care settings; registries; training programs (in-service and commercial); data quality control concerns and Diagnosis Related Groups. Data quality and coding under the prospective payment system is emphasized also. (3 semester hours)

Integrated Quality Management

History, principles, and techniques of retrospective, concurrent, and prospective review programs; review of utilization of health care and other cost containment programs; application of evaluation techniques in different health care settings; risk management. (3 semester hours)

Personnel Management

This course is designed to acquaint the student with the theory and techniques of effectively managing human resources in modern organizations. Topics covered will include the following: personnel planning, and staffing, training and development, performance appraisal, government regulations affecting personnel, and labor relations. (3 semester hours)

Management of Health Information Centers

Study of the application of management principles and personnel administration to the delivery of health information services. Emphasis on leadership styles, communication processes, performance evaluation and disciplinary measures, interviewing skills, financial concepts of health care delivery, and the development of work standards and productivity monitors. (3 semester hours)

Comparative Health Record and Information Systems

Investigation of health record and information systems in alternative care settings and health-related agencies. (3 semester hours)

Internship in Health Information Management

Individualized learning experience in management and administration of health information centers in various health care facilities. Individual assignments will be planned prior to the assignment in conjunction with the student and clinical instructor. All students must complete a four-week internship in management. Temporary relocation may be necessary. At lease two consecutive weeks of practice must be in residence at a major medical center other than where employed. The center must be accredited by JCAHO or AOA. The medical record department must be under the direction of a Registered Record Administrator. The remaining two weeks are assigned in a minimum of three alternative health care facilities and/or related agencies or educational institutions. The days spent fulfilling this portion of the internship need not be consecutive, as long as ten days are spent in at least ten sites. (3 semester hours)

HUMAN ECOLOGY

Ecological Community: Introduction

An introduction to the world's population and energy problems. A look into the causes and the predicted future of the population explosion and energy shortages. Emphasis on what man can do as an organized group and on an individual basis in order to survive the crisis. (3 semester hours)

Ecological Community: Politics and Ecology of Housework

This course will focus on the constant and intimate link between women and domesticity in American society. Because of their domestic connections, women are in an unusual position to facilitate change toward an appropriate and ecologically responsible lifestyle. An historical, contemporary and futuristic framework will illuminate female influence on housework, consumerism, family life, domestic architecture, transportation needs, socialization patterns, etc. Students should gain an increased understanding of the significant role women can play in the future of planet Earth. (3 semester hours)

Ecological Community: Ethics and Values

This course will inquire into the values needed to guide personal, political, and social decision making in an ecological age. The course will focus upon the discovery, testing, and acting out of a personal ecological ethic that has impact on personal habits and insights, as well as institutional policies and structures. (3 semester hours)

Ecological Community: Special Study

This is a special study providing an opportunity for the student to have a learning experience in a setting in which efforts for the making of profit are secondary to the humanistic, nontraditional nature of the enterprise, i.e., co-op people's radio station, nonprofit food and supply stores, etc. (3 semester hours)

HUMANITIES

The Humanities: Arts and Knowledge

This course offers an introduction to the arts with emphasis on basic concepts and terms in the fine arts (literature, painting, sculpture, architecture, and music) with some information about the applied and performing arts. Useful for students who have no background in arts or for those who know one art form in isolation from other arts, as this course brings together some general ideas about the arts as a medium of human expression, plus specific terms and examples from specific art media. (3 semester hours)

The Bible and the Arts

This course involves a close study of the Bible as a literary document which forms the inspiration or basis for art works of many kinds. Emphasis is on what the King James translation of the Old and New

Testaments and Apocrypha (any good translation) contain. The instructor will supply detailed study notes in the form of an outline, and three tests will be based on these study suggestions and the assumption that the student will also read all "literary" portions of the King James Bible and assigned parts of the Apocrypha. (3 semester hours)

LIBERAL AND PROFESSIONAL STUDIES

Experiential Learning Outcomes: A Portfolio

This course instructs the student with significant life experiences how to identify those with college-level learning and how to analyze each prior experience for the learning components. Through the development of a written portfolio, the learning outcomes of each experience or experiences are described in competency statements and documented according to faculty evaluator guidelines. Each area of knowledge from prior learning is then related to the student's degree proposal either in the selected major, minor, or in electives. The amount of credit gained through the prior learning process is variable. Credits are placed on the transcript when the course is completed. (No credit given for this course)

Loneliness and Love in Adult Life

Students in this course will explore in-depth how periods of loneliness can help a person move toward more authenticity, more honesty, and toward more meaningful love relationships with other human beings. Special attention will be given to such issues as the following: our need for fulfillment through work, marriage, intellectual accomplishment, sex, feeling love and appreciation for yourself. Concerns of adulthood will also be discussed: security vs. freedom, decision making and re-decision making after age forty, our sense of time, urgency, loss of innocence, motives in conflict, and the new narcissism. Readings will include examples from fiction, poetry, and psychological studies of today's women and men who are conducting their own risky experiments in living, using the only material they have at hand—their own lives. (3 semester hours)

MATHEMATICS

Introduction to Statistics

This is a study of elementary statistics as used in psychology, business, or information management. Topics include organization of data, measures of central tendency and variability, the normal distribution, sampling distributions, estimation, hypothesis testing, regression, and correlation, differences between samples, and chi-square tests. The course is also available for reduced credit and content. (3 semester hours)

NATURAL SCIENCE

Photography Through the Microscope

A chance for the student to learn photography through the microscope by practical experience. Student must have access to a microscope and a 35mm single lens reflex camera or other type that can be adapted. (3 semester hours)

Wildlife Photography

Methods of photographing wildlife, including techniques in photography as well as animal habits and behavior. The student should own a reflex type 35mm camera and be willing to spend up to $50 for a suitable telephoto lens. (3 semester hours)

Wildflower Photography

A chance for the student to learn to identify wildflowers through close-up photography. Student should own or have use of a 35mm single lens reflex camera. (3 semester hours)

Bird Study

The student develops a schedule of field trips for making bird observations and identification. A bird list and field notebook must be kept. Tapes for aids in learning will be supplied by the instructor (songs, etc.). (3 semester hours)

Identification of Weeks, Wildflowers, and Trees

The student collects and identifies local plants, pressing them, and preparing traditional herbarium sheets. A study is made of techniques of plant taxonomy and the history of herbaria in plant science. The local library can be a source of plant identification books and manuals plus books on herbaria. (3 semester hours)

Biology of Aging

The study of aging in humans as to what is meant by aging and what happens during the process. Such topics as theories of aging, factors affecting the rate of aging, and sexuality of aging are covered. (3 semester hours)

AIDS: Facts and Issues

A study of the medical facts and social issues surrounding AIDS. (3 semester hours)

Topics in Nutrition and Health

Pre-Menstrual Tension. A study of all that is known about a phenomenon which affects 50 to 60 percent of all women. Causes, effects, and the role of diet, vitamins, exercise, and hormonal therapy are covered. (3 semester hours)

Children's Nutrition. A study of proper nutrition for children. The course considers a complete, easy-to-follow, nutritional program that ensures a child's physical and mental well-being from infancy through adolescence. Included in the course is a prevention diet that eliminates antinutrients. (3 semester hours)

Psycho-Nutrition. A study of the vital role of diet and vitamin therapy in preventing and curing mental illness. The deficiencies that cause neurosis and psychosis. Nutritional programs for a productive, normal life. (3 semester hours)

The Biological and Medical Effects of Pollution

A study of pollutants and their effects on life in general and, in particular, on the human organism. (3 semester hours)

Human Nutrition

A scientific study of human diet as to what constitutes a proper diet. What foods, vitamins, and minerals are important and why? A discussion of some of the nutritional controversies and dangers of today's world. (3 semester hours)

Population Control in Animals

Most animal populations maintain fairly constant population levels, while others have cyclic pulses of abundance. Still others progressively increase or decrease in numbers. The purpose of this study is to identify diverse representative examples from the variety of population patterns and to interpret the controlling mechanisms. (3 semester hours)

Human Anatomy and Physiology - Lecture

A basic introductory course in human anatomy and physiology which is organized into five principal areas of concentration: (1) organization of the human body, (2) principles of support and movement, (3) control systems, (4) maintenance of the human body, and (5) continuity. In each area, emphasis is placed on the interrelationship of structure and function in each of the organs which comprise the major systems of the human body. Students may take Human Anatomy and Physiology - Laboratory before or after completion of this course. The intensive lab is offered during the summer on for five days on the Stephens College campus. (3 semester hours)

PHILOSOPHY

Introduction to Philosophy

The aim of this course is to develop critical habits of thinking by studying major philosophical methods, concepts, thinkers, and questions. (3 semester hours)

Logic/Critical Thinking

The course teaches the basic strategies for critical thinking and logical argument, by focusing on the natural structures of arguments and analyzing them through methods of class logic and the identification of commmon fallacies. Additional topics include deductive and inductive reasoning, immediate inferences, argument proofs, and truth tables. Computer tutorial instruction is available for those with access to an IBM or IBM-clone system. (3 semester hours)

The Japanese Cult of Efficiency

The course probes the phenomenon of Japanese economic success: how do they do it? The readings for the course focus on the following topics: the economic success of Japan and its costs; Japanese management concepts and practices; the relation of Japanese economic values to social realities and ancient cultural values. (3 semester hours)

Philosophy and Law Seminar

An introduction to the philosophy of law, the course promotes critical reflection on the concepts undergirding the rule of law. Students study the logical structures of legal reasoning and review ethical criticism of the American legal system and legal profession. The main course work involves examining and evaluating important contemporary court decisions in the light of logical criteria and ethical principles. (3 semester hours)

Biomedical Ethics

This course aims to help health care personnel to understand philosophically and become responsible for the ethical issues and values involved in their work. Modern medicine has forced new and deeply complex moral problems upon them. These problems range from the delivery of health care to the complex issues of killing and letting die, abortion, birth defects, coercion, and paternalism. By looking at the major ethical standards of philosophy and applying them to case studies, the student will learn to sort out and identify the value choices that are involved. (3 semester hours)

Social and Ethical Issues in Business

This is an applied ethics course in which techniques of moral reasoning are applied in the analysis of moral issues in business. The course covers such broad issues as the moral justification of our economic system, the moral responsibility of corporations and the role of business in a global society. Also addressed are more contemporary and pressing issues such as employee rights, affirmative action, and environmental issues. (3 semester hours)

Ethical Issues

A brief introduction to the principles of philosophical ethics with application to major current issues. The student will be asked to take three major areas and consider possible ethical choices in them: sexuality, medical ethics, and business and social ethics. (3 semester hours)

Philosophy of Education

This course examines the basic beliefs and their consequences that underlie different educational views. In this course, students see how different views are translated into educational practice and move toward developing our own philosophy of education for a changing world. (3 semester hours)

Death and Human Existence

This course studies death and dying using the resources of psychology, sociology, literature, and philosophy, in order to provide breadth as well as depth in one's personal and professional understanding of thanatology. Special emphases of the course are: one's personal attitudes toward death, the dying process and the environment, ethics of intervention, and cataclysmic death (nuclear warfare). (3 semester hours)

PSYCHOLOGY

Basic Psychology

Basic psychology is a survey of the methods, concepts, and findings of contemporary psychology. The basic areas covered are: perception, motivation and emotion, learning and cognition, the biological aspects of behavior, consciousness, and development and personality. This diversity gives the student the opportunity to become somewhat familiar with the various fields of psychology today, and to prepare for taking further courses in psychology and related areas. (3 semester hours)

Educational Psychology

The course is a study of the nature and conditions of human learning, methods of assessing relevant intellectual and personality characteristics of pupils, and personality and social dynamics as they enter into the learning process. (3 semester hours)

The Adult Years

A study of the development of normal individuals from late adolescence through old age. Stress is upon the developmental tasks and psychosocial crises of this period. The psychological development of women is given special attention. Some attention is also given to adult development in other cultures. (3 semester hours)

Psychology of Leadership

The course is designed to give students knowledge and understanding of the basic principles of group dynamics, leadership, and interpersonal communication. Through reading, the student is expected to learn how to become more effective in human relation skills, including the ability to express ideas and feelings, listen and respond empathetically to others and act assertively in situations where rights and responsibilities are involved. (3 semester hours)

Psychology of Women

This course will survey research findings and theory on the psychology of women and sex differences. Physiology, developmental psychology, personality theory, and social theory will be studied. (3 semester hours)

Readings in Experimental Psychology

This course covers both methodological issues in doing different kinds of psychological research, and certain content areas of psychology such as learning, perception, thinking and memory, where there has been considerable psychological experimental work. The basic concepts, distinguishing features, advantages and disadvantages of various forms of psychological research are covered, from naturalistic observation, correlational studies, to strictly experimental forms of research. In addition, the relationship between experimental work and theory is covered. Finally, students review in some depth selected areas of psychological experimental research to evaluate the relationship between what is known and how it was established. (3 semester hours)

Social Psychology

The exploration of major topics of social psychology, emphasizing the process of attitude formation and change, the nature of social motives, the socialization of the individual, and the dynamics of social change, with special attention being given to changing sex roles. (3 semester hours)

Psychology of Personality

A study of personality as an organized psychological entity that develops through different stages from birth to adulthood and of the concepts and propositions, taken from different theories, which describe the influence of biological, psychological, and social processes on the formation of personality. (3 semester hours)

Abnormal Psychology

A survey of the field of abnormal behavior. Reviews the history and present status, concentrating on the various approached to the etiology and treatment of the neuroses and functional psychoses. (3 semester hours)

History and Systems of Psychology

Study of the history of the major schools and concepts of modern psychology and of the people who developed them. Attention is primarily on the emergence of modern psychology from the work in philosophy and physiology in the time period, seventeenth to twentieth centuries, and mostly in Europe. (3 semester hours)

Psychological Testing and Personality Assessment

This is a standard, basic course in the theory of psychological testing, the statistical concepts for understanding and using psychological tests and a survey of current standardized tests and assessment procedures. This is a key course in any clinical-counseling program, and it represents psychology's unique contribution in the clinical field. This course is important for everyone involved in administering, interpreting, or dealing with the results of standardized tests in education and other applied areas. (3 semester hours)

Counseling I

This course is designed with the intent that the student, upon completion, will have an appreciation for and understanding of the theoretical basis underlying many of the current counseling and psychotherapy approaches. (3 semester hours)

Health Psychology

Health Psychology is an emerging area that covers the many ways, direct and indirect, that psychological factors may affect the course of health and illnesses. It is based on the premise that the body is a psychobiological unity. Hence different psychological factors may participate in different ways in the different phases of an illness, from its origin to its endpoint. In this course the student considers many aspects of this complex process: psychological factors affecting the incidence of different illnesses, psychological gains and losses from being sick, the doctor-patient relationship, behavioral forms of treatment, and the psychological factors affecting the chances for and rate of recovery. (3 semester hours)

Interviewing/Case Study

The course includes a review of some of the concepts of the interview, practice at interviewing, and write-up of case histories, three from published material and one from the student's own interviews. (3 semester hours)

Group Procedures

A study of the social and psychological basis for group participation and organization. The student will survey the numerous models of groups including Gestalt, T-Groups, Encounter Groups, Behavior Therapy, Tavistock, and Rational Encounter. The course is designed for the student in the clinical-counseling sequence who wishes to learn about the principles and processes of group dynamics. (3 semester hours)

Behavior Modification

Designed to assist the student to gain an appreciation of behavior modification through a study of its theoretical basis and its practical application. (3 semester hours)

RELIGIOUS STUDIES

Introduction to Religion

Introduces the student to the universal and particular elements of religion by comparing her or his autobiographical experience with development of religion from personal experience to major beliefs and institutional forms including brief study of the major religions of the world and types of religious experience represented in major religious figures. (3 semester hours)

Paths in World Religions

An introduction to the study of religion in personal and social experience, the course briefly surveys the great traditions of the East and West. Following the survey, the student moves in depth to study two traditions or two themes or two issues of particular interest to her/him. Buddhism and Christianity might be studied and compared, or the themes of suffering and the after-life probed, or the issues of women in the religious community or of the live of nonviolence examined in some depth. (3 semester hours)

Meditation and Contemplation

A seven-week program of instruction in basic and intermediate meditation. Techniques from relaxation and concentration exercises to advanced exercises in sense-training and interpersonal awareness. (1½ semester hours)

Religion in America

Study of the role of religion in the development of American society, including the history and beliefs of its major groups, influence of religious ideas and institutions in American character and culture, and the issues raised by separation of church and state, civil religion and pluralism. (3 semester hours)

Topics in Religion: Visions of Peacemaking—The Personal and the Political

This course will investigate, through psychological, sociological, and feminist writings, the roots of violence in human interactions. Through this analysis, connections will be drawn to larger national and international interactions and policies that reflect the roots of violence in the human psyche, especially in regard to gender differences and social institutions. Integral to this study will be a personal exploration into our fears and responses to threat and into how we can learn to move beyond fear and despair. The main focus of the course will be on alternatives (primarily feminist) to violence, both theoretical and practical, that lead to visions of possibilities for peace in interpersonal, social, and global dimensions. Hence, new views of child rearing, the human individual, family structures, gender identity, power, conflict resolution, and global community will be explored for what they can offer to a vision of peacemaking. (3 semester hours)

Topics in Religion: Albert Schweitzer and Reverence for Life

A study of the life and philosophy of Albert Schweitzer dealing with his theology, humanitarian service, and his relevance to contemporary problems in religion, ecology, and international relations. (3 semester hours)

Science and Religious Beliefs

A comparison of the method, language, and communities of science and religion, treatment of the various contemporary theories of science and their implications for religion including the theory of indeterminacy in physics, the genetic code, biology and evolution in an expanding universe. (3 semester hours)

SOCIAL STUDIES

Popular Culture in 20th-Century America

A survey and analysis of the popular arts and mass amusements; their social and cultural significance; and their audience in America since the very late nineteenth century. Attention given to definitions of the field, methods of studying the popular arts, the high culture/mass culture controversy, and case studies of particular examples of twentieth-century popular culture. (3 semester hours)

The Heritage and Material Culture of Women

This course will provide students with the theoretical background necessary to allow them to identify and explain specific examples of the female heritage and material culture. Students will be encouraged to draw from the wealth of their own material heritage and personalize this learning by collecting examples of the female domestic arts (e.g., quilt patterns, handicrafts, kitchen tools, clothing, photographs, etc.). Students may also explore other female cultural influences in American society (e.g., gothic/romance literature, soap operas, women's magazines, female rituals/ceremonies/customs, etc.). (3 semester hours)

American Feminism: Defining Woman's Place

This course will examine American feminism over time, focusing on the frequent conflict between sociocultural prescriptive gender roles and the reality of individual behavior. Building from the past, evaluating the present, and speculating about the future; students will deal with woman's changing place and behavior in society relative to feminism, both as a movement and an ideology. (3 semester hours)

Social Housekeepers: Women and Reform in America

This course will examine the relationship between women and the impulse to reform in American society. Students will study the influences of these "social housekeepers" in historical and contemporary crusades for abolitionism/civil rights, women's rights/suffrage, health and diet reform, birth control, social purity, education, communitarianism, peace, ecological and nuclear responsibility, etc. (3 semester hours)

Women and Medicine: A Cultural Perspective

This course will examine the relationship between medicine and cultural influences, with a specific focus on the roles women have played across time. Students will investigate the state of women's health along with medical theories and therapies focusing on hysteria, pregnancy and childbirth, birth control, sexuality, dress reform, exercise, diet and related issues. Special attention will be paid to the cultural implications and influences on the development of scientific theory and the professionalization of medical practice during the nineteenth century. From that historical base, students will move on to explore the various controversies involving women and medicine in modern society. (3 semester hours)

Women's Lives

In this course, biography and autobiography will be used to illuminate women's prescriptive and behavioral roles in American society. Selected works should cover a wide spectrum of time to show continuity and change throughout American history. Students may choose biographical and autobiographical materials with an eye toward examining the variety inherent in the female experience or focus their reading on the lives of women in a particular field, e.g., the arts, politics, science, reform, education, business, etc. (3 semester hours)

Intentional Communities

This course examines real and literary utopian efforts across time and place and inquires into the meaning of intentional communities within a larger social context. From Plato's *Republic* to modern communes, students will analyze past and present models of society. This course will also offer a special focus on the role of women relative to utopianism. (3 semester hours

Voluntary Human Services and Associations

The course utilizes an experiential approach to the study of the community. Students work as volunteers in a human service agency or as members of a voluntary association for 85 hours. (3 semester hours)

Personal and Family Finance

An examination of American economic forces and institutions and their impact on our personal and family lives. Money management, budgeting, insurance, taxes, borrowing, banking, transportation, investment principles, housing and real estate, consumer products and protection, retirement, wills, trusts, and estate planning. (3 semester hours)

Human Sexuality

A study of the physiological, psychological, and ethical aspects of sexuality. The human sexual system, cultural perspectives, sexual roles and behavior, and decision making are considered with special relevance to women and ethnic minorities. (3 semester hours)

Family in Social Context

This course is designed to help the preprofessional or professional person with the conceptual framework necessary for understanding and working with families in teaching, public health work, social agency programs, community development, family life education, counseling, and research. Emphasis is on the stages of growth and change that characterize the life of the contemporary American family. A minimum of four hours a week for ten weeks will be spent working in a social agency or activity of the student's choice. The field work must relate to direct social involvement with people. It can be on a volunteer or paid basis. (3 semester hours)

Marriage and the Family

A study of the biological, psychological, and sociological aspects of marriage and family life. Tradition, social change, dating and mate selection, marital sexuality, sex role behavior, pregnancy and childbirth, the influence of childhood experiences on adult life, managing the financial partnership, and terminating intimate relationships are considered. (3 semester hours)

American History: Colonial Period

The course concentrates on the growth of a distinctive society, culture, economy, and political system in the thirteen British colonies which became the United States. It pays particular attention to the nature and meaning of the American revolutionary experience, including an in-depth study of the revolution's impact on American women's lives. (3 semester hours)

American History: Civil War Period

The course studies the causes, nature, and consequences of the Civil War, including postwar Reconstruction, over the period 1845–1877. It deals with important themes in American history which continue to have great relevance in the late twentieth century: the meaning and obligations of democracy; the nature of the American federal union and the Constitution, especially the division of powers among the central government and the states; and race relations in a democratic-capitalist society. The student will examine such questions through readings which include an eminent historian's synthesis, contemporary documents of various kinds, and fiction. (3 semester hours)

Recent U.S. History: 1929 to Present

The course introduces the student to the major social, political, and economic events and interpretations since the Great Depression (1929). Opposing points of view are examined and evaluated. The student should become aware of the different interpretations of recent U.S. history and the difficulties involved in writing good history. (1½ to 3 semester hours)

The American West

A study of the American West, the westward movement as a force in American history, and the concepts of region, sectionalism, and frontier, with emphasis on the region west of the Mississippi in the nineteenth and twentieth centuries. Topics of inquiry include the role of the federal government and the corporation in exploration and economic development; western responses to real or assumed "exploitation" by "outsiders," including corporations and the government in Washington, D.C.; the changing western ecology; changing gender roles in this region popularly associated with rugged male qualities; minority-majority and minority-minority relations (White, Native American, Chicano, Black, Asian) in this diverse "melting pot;" and the West in American popular culture. (3 semester hours)

Japanese Culture and Society

An historical survey and exploration of the high culture and social institutions of Japan, from the Heian culture of ninth-century Kyoto, through the rise of the shoguns and Zen culture, until the "Great Peace" of the Tokugawa that prepared the groundwork for a modern Japan. As part of the course, students are asked, where possible, to view videotape versions of Japanese movie classics illustrating historical periods and cultural values, especially the films of Kurosawa. (3 semester hours)

The American South

A study of the southern region and the concepts of region and sectionalism within the American context from the earliest days of settlement (1607) to the present. Topics of inquiry include definitions of southern uniqueness over time; economic change from the antebellum plantation economy to modern hi-tech industries of the Sun Belt; race relations from slavery through the segregation era to the civil rights movement; and changing gender relations. (3 semester hours)

American Women's History

This course will focus on recent scholarship aimed at replacing women in American history. The course materials examine women's roles within changing historical and diverse cultural contexts. Students will gain new insight into the complexities of women's lives from the colonial period to the Civil War. (3 semester hours)

American Women's History Since the Civil War

Students in this course will examine the changing cultural images and realities of women's lives across time and place, with special consideration of the issues of race, class, and ethnicity, toward the goal of better understanding the complex nature of woman's multiple roles throughout this period of American history. (3 semester hours)

F.D.R. and Truman

A study of the political, economic, and social conditions between 1932 and 1952 with an evaluation of the leadership of F.D.R. and H.S.T. (3 semester hours)

Kennedy and L.B.J.

A study of the political, economic, and social conditions between 1960 and 1968 with an evaluation of the leadership of J.F.K. and L.B.J. (3 semester hours)

Your Roots in 20th-Century America: Family History and National History

This course integrates national history with family history in the American twentieth century. The readings and an intensive personal research project into the student's own family history try to make American history since 1900 more meaningful by making it more personal and relevant. (3 semester hours)

Race and Ethnic Relations

This course, approached from a sociopsychological orientation, is designed to explore the various racial and ethnic groups who make up our complex society. It is intended to enlarge the student's understanding of minority group relations and to explode some of the destructive myths that contribute to prejudice and provincialism. Special attention is given to the effects of minority group phenomenon on women. (3 semester hours)

Modern Japan Seminary

A study of modern Japan's cultural and social transformations in a comparative analysis with the United States. Special topics include: business and economic practices, education, roles and status of women, "groupism" vs. "individualism," value structures and the modernization process. (3 semester hours)

The Contemporary Woman and Crime

This course is concerned with the extent and type of female participation in criminal activity and with the treatment the woman offender receives at various stages of the criminal justice process. (3 semester hours)

WOMEN'S STUDIES

Growing Up Female

A study of the psychological, physical, and intellectual development of women, the effects of family, language, education, and mass media as socializing forces on women's upbringing, and the possibilities and methods the student may find for creating a health, fulfilling, and meaningful life for herself and other women in today's world. The student will examine her experiences, her behavior, her values, and her attitudes in relation to course content and consider how social institutions have affected her development, both positively and negatively as a woman. The student will also learn about the experiences of women whose culture and lives are different from her own. (3 semester hours)

Women's Studies Topics: Women and Aging

The course is designed to present an analysis of the sociological and psychological issues of women's aging. The materials will be approached from the feminist perspective. Some of the topics to be explored are demographic factors, the double standard of aging, myths about growing older, political and social legislation affecting the older population—especially women, cultural variations in the roles and expectations for older women, and women as agents of change. (variable credit)

Issues in the Women's Movement

This course is an introductory study of the issues of the women's movement and their significance for individual women and their society. Common assumptions about women are questioned and attitudes about women and attitudes held by women are assessed. (3 semester hours)

Cultural Images of Women

This course is an introductory study of the cultural images by which woman defines herself and by which she is defined by society.

Common assumptions about women are questioned and attitudes about women and by women are assessed. (3 semester hours)

Development of Feminist Thought

This course focuses on the variety and changing expressions of feminist thought over the past four centuries, in dealing with the conflict between the social prescription and the reality of behavior for women during this time. The lives and works of prominent, influential women feminist theorists, as well as the experiences of women who spoke through actions rather than words, will be studied within several cultural and historical contexts. This study should inform students as to the dynamic nature of women's participation in society and emphasize the diversity inherent within the feminist continuum. (3 semester hours)

Contemporary Feminist Thought

This course will deal with a comparative study of the diverse expressions of feminism among various groups within the United States and in other countries of the world. Specific attention will be focused on continuity and change in gender issues across time and culture. Each student will be encouraged to examine her own beliefs in comparison with others and arrive at a personal position statement relevant to her definition of woman's nature and role in society. (3 semester hours)

Topics in Religion: Visions of Peacemaking—The Personal and the Political

This course will investigate, through psychological, sociological, and feminist writings, the roots of violence in human interactions. Through this analysis, connections will be drawn to larger national and international interactions and policies that reflect the roots of violence in the human psyche, especially in regard to gender differences and social institutions. Integral to this study will be a personal exploration into our fears and responses to threat and into how we can learn to move beyond fear and despair. The main focus of the course will be on alternatives (primarily feminist) to violence, both theoretical and practical, that lead to visions of possibilities for peace in interpersonal, social, and global dimensions. Hence, new views of child rearing, the human individual, family structures, gender identity, power, conflict resolution, and global community will be explored for what they can offer to a vision of peacemaking. (3 semester hours)

The Contemporary Woman and Crime

This course is concerned with the extent and type of female participation in criminal activity and with the treatment the woman offender receives at various stages of the criminal justice process. (3 semester hours)

Women and Technology

This course will explore the relationship between technology, the philosophical, cultural, and practical applications of scientific discoveries, and women. Technology will include aspects which specifically affect women and aspects which affect all of society in general. Technology which specifically affects women includes both the personal role (reproductive and birth technologies) and the traditional role (domestic technologies, architecture, and transportation technologies). Other technologies affecting women and society include office/work technologies, energy production, military and weapons technology, space technology, nuclear technology, and computer science developments. (3 semester hours)

Women's Spirituality

A study of women's expression of their own spirituality begins with a study of the meaning of spirituality. Each student selects materials referred to in the texts as the starting point for her own exploration of spirituality. Biblical texts, novels, poems, spiritual writings or rituals

may be selected. A journal will be kept throughout the period of the course. In addition to commentary on the required readings, the journal may include meditations, poems, drawings, records of conversations, descriptions of ritual movement and dance, etc. (1½ semester hours)

The Heritage and Material Culture of Women

This course will provide students with the theoretical background necessary to allow them to identify and explain specific examples of the female heritage and material culture. Students will be encouraged to draw from the wealth of their own material heritage and personalize this learning by collecting examples of the female domestic arts (e.g., quilt patterns, handicrafts, kitchen tools, clothing, photographs, etc.). Students may also explore other female cultural influences in American society (e.g., gothic/romance literature, soap operas, women's magazines, female rituals/ceremonies/customs, etc.). (3 semester hours)

American Feminism: Defining Woman's Place

This course will examine American feminism over time, focusing on the frequent conflict between sociocultural prescriptive gender roles and the reality of individual behavior. Building from the past, evaluating the present, and speculating about the future; students will deal with woman's changing place and behavior in society relative to feminism, both as a movement and an ideology. (3 semester hours)

Social Housekeepers: Women and Reform in America

This course will examine the relationship between women and the impulse to reform in American society. Students will study the influences of these "social housekeepers" in historical and contemporary crusades for abolitionism/civil rights, women's rights/suffrage, health and diet reform, birth control, social purity, education, communitarianism, peace, ecological and nuclear responsibility, etc. (3 semester hours)

Women and Medicine: A Cultural Perspective

This course will examine the relationship between medicine and cultural influences, with a specific focus on the roles women have played across time. Students will investigate the state of women's health along with medical theories and therapies focusing on hysteria, pregnancy and childbirth, birth control, sexuality, dress reform, exercise, diet and related issues. Special attention will be paid to the cultural implications and influences on the development of scientific theory and the professionalization of medical practice during the nineteenth century. From that historical base, students will move on to explore 1the various controversies involving women and medicine in modern society. (3 semester hours)

Women's Lives

In this course, biography and autobiography will be used to illuminate women's prescriptive and behavioral roles in American society. Selected works should cover a wide spectrum of time to show continuity and change throughout American history. Students may choose biographical and autobiographical materials with an eye toward examining the variety inherent in the female experience or focus their reading on the lives of women in a particular field, e.g., the arts, politics, science, reform, education, business, etc. (3 semester hours)

Senior Colloquium

This course asks learner to address the impact of their educational experience on their own process of intellectual and emotional growth and the impact of the learnings that they have gained as Stephens College Without Walls students on their professions, their communities, and the world in which they live. The study of the process of social and personal change that was begun in the entry Liberal Studies Seminar will be integrated in this concluding seminar. The learner will be expected to demonstrate that he or she can be a facilitator of change. (1½ or 3 semester hours)

Syracuse University
University College
Independent Study Degree Programs
301 Reid Hall
610 East Fayette Street
Syracuse, New York 13244-6020
(315) 443-3284

Description:

Syracuse University was founded in 1870. It is a private institution organized into 21 major academic units including University College, the continuing education unit. The Independent Study Degree Programs department was founded in 1966 as a subdivision of University College. The department has programs for eleven degrees offered in cooperation with various campus academic departments.

It is during the short required residency periods that the student's ongoing work is directed and disciplined. When the student leaves the campus after a residency period, he/she takes with them all the study materials needed. Assignments are completed according to the schedule established with professors. These assignments are mailed or faxed to the professors for evaluation.

Faculty:

Robert D. Colley, Director, Independent Study Degree Programs; Roberta Jones, Associate Director.

Academic Levels:

College

Graduate

Degree/Certificate Programs:

Degree programs include the Associate (A.A.) and Bachelor of Arts (B.A.) in Liberal Studies; Bachelor of Science (B.S.) in Business Administration; Criminal Justice, Restaurant and Foodservice Management, and Business Administration; Master of Library Science (M.L.S.); Master of Business Administration (M.B.A.); Master of Science in Nursing (M.S.); Master of Social Science (M.S.Sc.); and Master of Arts with emphasis in either advertising design or illustration.

Admission Requirements:

Admissions criteria vary, depending on the degree program. Applicants are evaluated on the basis of their credentials: past academic records, recommendations, performance on a standardized test, professional experiences, and interview/portfolio review. Those interested should contact the Independent Study Degree Programs office. Overseas students welcome.

Tuition:

$290 per semester hour credit for undergraduate programs; $479 per semester hour credit for graduate programs.

Enrollment Period:

Time limit requirements are flexible, depending upon the student's situation. Each course requires a residence portion at the beginning of each semester, of one to two weeks, depending upon the student's individual program.

Equipment Requirements:

Textbook costs are not included in the tuition. Housing and meal costs during the residence portion are extra.

Credit and Grading:

Examinations are administered on campus during the resident portions. Grading system is A through F; the minimum passing grade for bachelor degrees is D, for graduate degrees, C. Credit is awarded in semester hour units.

Job Placement Assistance:

Correspondence students have full access to the services of the University's Placement Office.

Accreditations:

Middle States Association of Colleges and Schools.

COLLEGE COURSES

BUSINESS ADMINISTRATION

Bachelor of Science in Business Administration

The student must complete 120 credits for the degree. Up to 90 credits may be transferred in, leaving a minimum of 30 credits that must be completed at Syracuse University. All core courses must be completed (36 credits). The program is split into two parts: 57 credits from Management, and 63 from Liberal Studies and free electives. 21 credits of upper division management coursework must be completed beyond the core.

CRIMINAL JUSTICE

Bachelor of Science in Criminal Justice

The criminal justice program is designed primarily as an upper level course of study so that professionals with associate's degrees in the field can complete their baccalaureate degrees. 120 credits are required for the degree.

LIBERAL STUDIES

Associate in Arts

The A.A. program requires a week in residence on the Syracuse campus for each semester of enrollment. 60 credits must be completed for the degree.

Bachelor of Arts in Liberal Studies

The student must complete 120 credits for the degree. Up to 90 credits may be transferred in, leaving a minimum of 30 credits that must be completed at Syracuse University.

RESTAURANT AND FOODSERVICE MANAGEMENT

Bachelor of Science in Restaurant and Foodservice Management

The student must complete 124 credits for the degree. Up to 90 credits may be transferred in, leaving a minimum of 34 credits that must be completed at Syracuse University. Contact Independent Study Degree Programs for specific course requirements.

GRADUATE COURSES

ADVERTISING DESIGN

Master of Arts in Advertising Design or Illustration

To be eligible for admission to this program, the student must have an undergraduate degree and at least three years of professional experience. To obtain the degree, 30 credits must be earned at Syracuse. No transfer credit is permitted and three two-week residence periods are required.

BUSINESS ADMINISTRATION

Master of Business Administration

If the student comes into the program with no transfer credits or waivers, he/she must complete 54 credits for the degree. The M.B.A. curriculum consists of two elements: a core of 15 essential management courses (39 credits) and an additional 15 credits of electives. A week in residence on the Syracuse campus is required at the beginning of each semester.

COMMUNICATIONS MANAGEMENT

Master of Science in Communications Management

Designed specifically for experienced public relations practitioners, the Master of Science in Communications Management is a newly created program that draws from three of Syracuse University's premiere academic divisions: the S.I. Newhouse School of Public Communications, the Maxwell School of Citizenship and Public Affairs, and the School of Management. This 36-credit program is notable for its interdisciplinary approach to the advanced education of public relations practitioners, based on the development of key management abilities critical to success in this evolving profession. The program consists of four core areas: public relations, management, electives, and cumulative experience. Three one-week long residency periods yearly are required.

LIBRARY SCIENCE

Master of Library Science

This degree program requires 36 credits of coursework. Subject to approval, up to six credits of relevant graduate coursework completed within the past five years. Three two-week summer sessions are required. A major specialization within the M.L.S. is the school media program.

NURSING

Master of Science in Nursing

The 36-hour degree program requires four summer residencies. A total of 30 credits are earned in core courses and 6 in electives.

SOCIAL SCIENCE

Master of Social Science

The student must complete 30 credits for the degree. Up to 6 credits may be transferred provided they were taken at the graduate level of an accredited institution and the student received a grade of B or better. The courses must be relevant to the M.S.Sc. curriculum.

Taylor University

Institute of Correspondence Studies
1025 West Rudisill Boulevard
Fort Wayne, Indiana 46807   (800) 845-3149

Description:

Taylor University merged with Summit Christian College in 1992. Founded in 1904, Summit Christian College (formerly Fort Wayne Bible College) provided degree programs in the fields of Biblical, general, and professional education. As a result of the merger, the Institute of Correspondence Studies is now directed by Taylor University. Full transfer credit is granted by Indiana University for work applicable to university programs. Taylor University is committed to the conservative and evangelical interpretation of the Christian faith. The student body is interdenominational.

Taylor University's correspondence courses are designed to help students who need extra courses, ministers who want refresher courses, missionaries who wish to achieve personal and ministry goals, teachers who wish to increase their effectiveness, and all who wish advanced education. The Institute of Correspondence Studies began in 1970 when the college took over the correspondence program of Judson College.

Faculty:

Heather Y. Zenk St. Peters, Director.

Academic Levels:

College

Degree/Certificate Programs:

Courses are offered for 2 to 4 credit hours. These credits may be transferred to the college specified by the student. Most colleges or universities do have a determined number of external credits allowable toward any degree program. A certificate is awarded after completion of 32 credit hours.

Admission Requirements:

High school graduate. Some courses have prerequisites.

Tuition:

$65 per semester hour plus nonrefundable $10 enrollment fee for each course. Students from Canada add $10 and from other countries add $20 to cover postage. VA benefits; discounts to prisoners, missionaries. Course may be returned unused within thirty days for full refund minus $10 refund fee.

Enrollment Period:

A maximum of one year is allowed for the completion of any one course. If necessary, an extension of time may be granted upon request, for which an extension fee of $10 is charged.

Equipment Requirements:

Textbooks must be purchased by the student; books may also be rented for an initial four-month period at the rate of $8 per text (if the course is not completed at the end of four months, the student will be billed for the balance of the textbook's list price; any book with a list price of under $10 must be purchased). Typewritten lessons are preferred.

Credit and Grading:

A proctored final examination is required in each course. Minimum passing grade is generally 70 percent but is dependent upon requirements of individual institution accepting the credits. The grading system is on a 12-point scale (A plus = 12 points; D minus = 1 point). Credit is awarded in semester hour units.

Accreditations:

North Central Association of Colleges and Schools; American Association of Bible Colleges.

COLLEGE COURSES

BIBLE

Old Testament Survey

A survey of the entire Old Testament through a book-by-book approach to the narrative. It includes a study of the distinctive message, the characters and the events of each book in their relation to the historical sequence, and some applications of Old Testament teaching to contemporary Christian living. (2 or 3 semester hours)

New Testament Survey

A survey of the entire New Testament, including the life of Christ, the establishment of the Church, the life and letters of Paul, and the remaining letters of the New Testament. (2 or 3 semester hours)

Pentateuch

A study of the first five books of the Bible, dealing with problems of authorship, date and critical theories. Special attention is given to the creation, the fall, and the flood. Jewish foundations, law and history are treated throughout the Mosaic period. (3 semester hours)

Historical Books

A study of the books of Joshua through Esther, with emphasis on Biblical history, geography, chronology, and spiritual implications. (3 semester hours)

Poetic and Wisdom Literature

A study of the wisdom and poetical literature of the Old Testament, including an analysis and exposition of the major themes of Job, Psalms, Proverbs, Ecclesiastes, and Song of Solomon. (2 semester hours)

Genesis

A detailed study of this "book of beginnings," giving attention to its authorship, authenticity, chronology and content in light of the findings of science and archaeology. (3 semester hours)

The Gospels

A thorough study of the four Gospels in harmony with parallel study of the historical and sociological background of the life of Christ. (3 semester hours)

Hebrews, General Epistles, Revelation

A detailed study of the doctrinal and practical aspects of the last 13 books of the New Testament, including Hebrews, the non-Pauline Epistles, Pastoral Epistles, and the Apocalypse. (3 semester hours)

Matthew

An exegetical study of this gospel with an emphasis on the mastery of its contents, on the use of its message in evangelism in contemporary culture, and on its contribution to biblical and systematic theology. (2 semester hours)

Acts and the Early Church

A comprehensive study of apostolic Christianity, its origin and early development, with emphasis on the place of Christ and the Holy Spirit. (2 semester hours)

Pauline Epistles

Attention is given to the life, ministry, and writings of Paul. The doctrinal, pastoral, and personal epistles of Paul are studied with reference to their geographical and historical settings, the organization of the Apostolic Church, and the development of Christian doctrine. Careful exegesis is made of selected portions of each epistle. (3 semester hours)

The Gospel of John

An analytical study of the content of the fourth gospel, with special emphasis on the distinctive elements of John's message. (2 semester hours)

Romans

A detailed analysis and exegesis of the teaching of Romans, with special emphasis on the development of thought throughout the entire book. (3 semester hours)

BIBLICAL LANGUAGES

Elementary Old Testament Hebrew I

A study of the fundamentals of accidence and basic syntax of Biblical Hebrew. An emphasis on translation from English to Hebrew. A translation of selected portions of the Hebrew Old Testament. (2 semester hours)

Elementary Old Testament Hebrew II

A continuation of the above course. (2 semester hours)

Elementary Old Testament Hebrew III

A continuation of the above course. (2 semester hours)

Elementary New Testament Greek I

A study of the fundamentals of accidence and basic syntax of Koine Greek. A translation of selected portions of the Greek New Testament with emphasis on development of ability in translation. (3 semester hours)

Elementary New Testament Greek II

A continuation of the above course. (3 semester hours)

Elementary New Testament Greek III

A continuation of the above course. (3 semester hours)

Analysis of the Greek New Testament: Mark

A mastery of the basic principles of syntax with emphasis on noun cases. Translation of the first nine chapters of Mark's Gospel. Vocabulary building. (3 semester hours)

Analysis of the Greek New Testament: I Corinthians

A continuation of the basic principles of syntax with emphasis on verb tenses and participles. Translation of the Epistle of I Corinthians. Vocabulary building. (3 semester hours)

Analysis of the Greek New Testament: Galatians

A careful application of the principles of syntax and exegesis covered in Mark and I Corinthians. Translation of the Epistle to the Galatians. Vocabulary building. (3 semester hours)

Advanced Analysis of the Greek New Testament: Romans

An advanced study of the principles of Greek syntax and exegesis through a translation of the book of Romans. This course should help the student discover nuggets of truth from the Greek text which are hidden from the Bible student who does not have Greek as a usable tool. (2 semester hours)

Advanced Analysis of the Greek New Testament: James

An advanced study of the principles of Greek syntax and exegesis through a translation of the Epistle of James. Designed to help the student discover nuggets of truth from the Greek text that are otherwise hidden from the one who does not have Greek as a usable tool. (2 semester hours)

Advanced Analysis of the Greek New Testament: Hebrews

An advanced study of the principles of Greek syntax and exegesis through a translation of the Epistle of Hebrews. (2 semester hours)

CHRISTIAN EDUCATION

Ministry to Children

A study of ways of ministering effectively to all age groups of children within the church and of evaluating and structuring church programs so as to strengthen both the home and the church. The student will learn principles of effective, creative programming geared to helping children with their needs. (3 semester hours)

Ministry to Youth

A study of the contemporary youth culture and developing techniques in programming and structuring of a youth ministry in the local church. (3 semester hours)

Ministry to Adults

A study of the psychological and spiritual needs of adults with a view to establishing objectives of adult Christian education. Attention is given to programming and new methods designed to enhance the spiritual growth process among adults. (3 semester hours)

Leadership Development

A course structured to provide an overview of the field of Christian education, concerned with the organization, administration and supervision of the total church program of Christian education. A study of the roles of both professional and lay leadership in the local church. (3 semester hours)

Educational Psychology

A study of the development of the learning process from early childhood through adolescence. Psychological theories are considered on the basis of biblical principles. (3 semester hours)

CHURCH HISTORY

Early Christianity Through Medieval Times

A study of the beginning of the Christian movement and its contact with Judaism, paganism, and Greek philosophy, the Roman empire, and the Renaissance, including the great personalities, documents, and developments of the Church up to the Reformation. (3 semester hours)

Reformation Christianity

A study of the history of Christianity from 1500 to 1650, dealing with the achievements of Luther, Zwingli and Calvin; the expansion of Protestantism in Germany, Switzerland and England; the Anabaptist movement; the Catholic Reformation and the religious wars up to the Treaty of Westphalia. (3 semester hours)

European Christianity: 1650 to Present

A study of the development of Christianity across Europe from 1650 to the present. (3 semester hours)

American Religious History

A study of the history of American Christianity from its beginnings in 1607 to the present time. It is designed to give the student not only a knowledge of the development of Christianity in our nation, but also an understanding of the social, cultural, political and economic forces which influence American religious life, and the impact of Christianity upon American society. (3 semester hours)

FINE ARTS

Introduction to Art

A study of art through an historical survey. This course is designed to give the student an introduction to the great masters of the past, the art periods, as well as broaden the student's appreciation for and understanding of art. A video course. (2 semester hours)

HISTORY

World History I

A survey of the history and culture of early times, from the beginnings of civilization through the Reformation. Special attention is given to racial traits, customs and institutions which make up civilized ways of life. Cultures and political developments are studied against the background of ethnographic materials. (3 semester hours)

World History II

A study of modern civilization from 1650 to present, including industrial and political revolutions; democracy; development of modern thought, art, and literature; growth of the Americas; European and American contacts with the Orient; the World Wars and their aftermath. Special attention is given to the interplay of culture, the rise of new social and political ideas, and the influence of modern science. (3 semester hours)

United States History I

A survey of the United States history from its beginning to the Civil War, with attention to geographic expansion and the development of political, social, religious and economic institutions. (3 semester hours)

United States History II

A continuation of the survey of United States history from the Civil War to the present. (3 semester hours)

JOURNALISM

Journalism

An introduction to newspaper journalism with emphasis upon the writing of news articles and feature articles. (3 semester hours)

LITERATURE

American Literature

A survey of American literature from its beginning to the present, marking the transition from the Romantic period in American literature to the Realistic period. A continuation through the naturalistic trends to the contemporary era gives attention to major writers and works throughout. (3 semester hours)

British Literature

This course provides the student with a foundational understanding of English literature, surveying major British authors from antiquity to the present and examining the historical, sociological, and psychological forces that have shaped English literature. (4 semester hours)

MISSIONS

Modern Cults

A course designed to enable Christian workers to identify and to meet the specious arguments of modern cults. The history, methods, growth and policies of modern cults are studied, with special emphasis on how to deal with those threatened or ensnared by them. (3 semester hours)

Perspectives on the World Christian Movement

An introduction to the theology, history, strategy, and priorities of contemporary evangelical mission work. (3 semester hours)

World Religions

A study of the main religious systems of the world, including Hinduism, Islam, Judaism, Confucianism, Taoism, Buddhism, Shintoism, Sikhism, Jainism, and Christianity. The religions are seen in historical, cultural perspective and translations of their writings are examined. (3 semester hours)

Cross-Cultural Evangelism

A study of the principles of cross-cultural communication and their application to the task of communicating the biblical gospel in a relevant way to people of other cultures and religions. (3 semester hours)

MUSIC

Music Fundamentals - Beginners

A course designed for the musical novice. It provides an understanding of the basic tools of the printed musical page and correct usage of each. Covers an in-depth study of note reading, intervals, and major scales, plus minor scales, primary chords, and their proper voicing. (2 semester hours)

Music Fundamentals - Intermediate

A course involving a more advanced study of the tools of music and their use. It is designed to follow *Music Fundamentals - Beginners*. The course includes a more advanced study of scales, chords, intervals, melody writing, and harmonization. (3 semester hours)

Music Appreciation

A course designed to develop greater understanding and appreciation for music of the various historical periods. An introduction to the art of music and its materials. Considerable attention is given to listening to recordings and studying the lives of leading composers. (2 semester hours)

Hymnology and Church Liturgy

A study of hymns, hymn writers, the historical background connected with the writing of hymns, and the interrelating of hymns and songs to the entire music program of the church. (2 semester hours)

NATURAL SCIENCE

Biological Science Survey

An introduction to the principles of plant and animal life. Major sections of the course deal with the cell, multicellular plants, multicellular animals, man, heredity and evolutionary theory. The latter is examined in the light of biblical revelation. (3 semester hours)

Physical Science Survey

An introduction to the basic physical sciences of astronomy, physics, chemistry, meteorology and geology. Each is considered in relation to the others and its influence on man. (3 semester hours)

Physical Geography

A study of the physical environment, major landform categories, and the processes which form them. (3 semester hours)

Human Anatomy and Physiology

A comprehensive study of the human body and its various systems, with special emphasis upon mental and physical health and fitness. (3 semester hours)

PASTORAL STUDIES

Worship

A study of the biblical, historical, and practical basis of worship. Includes the study of various liturgies and the development of a worship style relevant to the student. (2 semester hours)

Evangelism and Discipleship

A study of the principles of lifestyle evangelism and one-on-one discipleship. In addition to written assignments, practical experience is employed. There is some memorization of scripture. (3 semester hours)

Introduction to Preaching

Principles of the preparation and delivery of sermons with experience in both writing and delivery. Emphasis on expository preaching and the development of a basic sermonic process. A detailed introduction to this course is given on the first of four cassette tapes included with the course. (3 semester hours)

Pastoral Theology

A basic course for pastors. This course looks at the pastor's call, his work in the church, and his personal life. Particular emphasis is given to the pastor's study and pulpit ministry. (3 semester hours)

PHILOSOPHY

Introduction to Philosophy

A survey course in philosophy that seeks to introduce the student to some core topics, such as: methods, assumptions, knowledge, truth, origins, values, purpose, and religion. The study includes an overview of the answers offered by naturalism, idealism, and Christianity to key philosophical questions. (3 semester hours)

Apologetics

An examination of the nature and methodology of Christian apologetics with particular attention to the philosophical defense of the truth of the Christian faith. (3 semester hours)

Introduction to Logic

A study of the principles and methods of correct reasoning as employed in the logical appraisal of argument. (3 semester hours)

Contemporary Issues

An explanation of the basis and nature of the major ethical approaches. The strengths and weaknesses of each approach are discussed in the light of biblical teachings. Examples are presented, illustrating the practical implications of each theory. (3 semester hours)

PSYCHOLOGY

General Psychology

An introduction to the subject matter and methods of psychology. Emphasis is given to the integration of psychological science and the Christian faith. (3 semester hours)

Research in Psychology

This course surveys a variety of research methods in psychology including the experiment, naturalistic observation, interviews, questionnaires, and archival research. Topics include ethics in research and writing the research article. Practical assignments in research are given. (3 semester hours)

Integration of Psychology and Christianity

A course designed to examine the relationship between psychology and the Christian world view. Topic areas include the presuppositions of modern psychology, the Christian view of human nature, models of the integration of psychology and Christianity, and tension areas between psychology and theology. (3 semester hours)

Theories of Personality

A study of the norms of mental health; the various mental mechanisms; the influence of habits formed in early childhood on behavior during adolescence and later life; the psychological principles for effective living. Includes coverage of self-esteem, identity, social responsibility, coping, and mastery. (3 semester hours)

Fundamentals of Counseling

This course will provide an analysis of the major theories and approaches to counseling, and will correlate them with counterpart theories of personality and learning. Each major theory will be dealt with in light of biblical revelation. As a result, the student is encouraged to formulate a tentative theory of counseling consistent with biblical truth. (3 semester hours)

SOCIAL SCIENCE

Social Problems

A course that assists the student in developing a critical understanding of the social problems which face our society today and a framework for analyzing problems which will arise in the future. (3 semester hours)

Cultural Anthropology

An introduction to cultural anthropology, its theory and method. The culture concept is examined. The social, economic, religious, aesthetic and linguistic aspects of culture are treated distinctly, as in the process of cultural dynamic and the development of anthropological theory. The course is designed especially to prepare students for ministry in a cross-cultural setting. (3 semester hours)

THEOLOGY

Theology I

A detailed study of *Bibliology* (the Bible: divine revelation, inspiration, illumination, and authority), *Theology* (God: His person, attributes, names, and works, plus the Trinity), and *Angelology* (angels, demons, and Satan). This course is foundational to all systematic theology. (3 semester hours)

Theology II

A detailed study of *Christology* (the person and work of Jesus Christ: His incarnation, ministry, and fulfillment of Messianic prophecy), *Pneumatology* (the person and work of the Holy Spirit: His attributes, names, symbols, and relation to the Godhead, creation, and the believer), *Anthropology* (the study of man, his creation, nature, and the fall), and *Harmatiology* (the study of sin: its nature, origin, and effect). (3 semester hours)

Theology III

A detailed study of *Soteriology* (the doctrine of salvation: its accomplishment and application in the life of the believer), *Ecclesiology* (the study of the church: its origin, mission, composition, ordinances, and final destiny), and *Eschatology* (the study of the last things, the consummation of God's redemptive purpose). (3 semester hours)

Tennessee, University of
Department of Independent Study
420 Communications Building
Knoxville, Tennessee 37996-0300

(800) 670-8657

Description:

The correspondence course program at the University of Tennessee was initiated in 1923 as the Department of Correspondence Instruction. At that time, the university consisted of only two campuses, the main campus in Knoxville and the medical campus in Memphis. In 1973, when the university had grown to a five-campus, multipurpose, statewide institution, the department was renamed the Center for Extended Learning, and a year later, in keeping with range and adaptability of instructional procedures used, the term "correspondence instruction" was changed to "independent study." The emphasis was thus placed not on the medium by which courses are extended but on the method of instruction: step-by-step learning for individual students. Each year there are approximately 3,000 enrollments.

Independent Study courses for college credit are prepared and taught by faculty members of four campuses of the University of Tennessee: Chattanooga, Knoxville, Martin, and Memphis. Correspondence courses from all four campuses are administered by the Department of Independent Study. The content and study requirements closely parallel those of similar courses taught in residence and are fully acceptable toward degree requirements within the limits set by each college.

Faculty:

Dr. David F. Holden, Director, Department of Independent Study. A faculty of 80 from four campuses teach the correspondence courses.

Academic Levels:
College
High School
Noncredit

Degree/Certificate Programs:

Up 30 semester hours or equivalent of the requirements for a degree at the University of Tennessee may be transferred from Independent Study. Credits may also be earned toward Certificates and Diplomas.

Admission Requirements:

Independent Study courses may be taken for credit or noncredit by anyone; there are no admission requirements. For credit purposes, the same eligibility applies that would apply for regular residence classes. Students enrolled in a degree program on a University of Tennessee campus must have the approval of their college dean before enrolling in an Independent Study course. High school students must have the approval of the principal if the course is to be used for credit toward a high school diploma.

Tuition:

$76 per semester hour. Fees for high school courses are $60 per ½ unit (a one-semester course). There is a $10 charge per course to cover the cost of mailing course materials and graded assignments to the student. Costs for textbooks and materials are extra and are listed in the Independent Study Catalog. All fees must be paid in full at the time of enrollment. MasterCard, Visa, and Discover accepted. VA Benefits accepted. Overseas students should contact the Department of Independent Study for postage rates. A refund may be requested within sixty days of the date of enrollment. Requests must be made in writing or in person. For college course, a charge of $24 will be made if no lessons have been submitted in the course. A charge of $58 will be made if one or more lessons have been submitted. For noncredit courses, a charge of $24 will be made if no lessons have been submitted; $43 if one or more lessons have been submitted. The postage and handling fee is not refundable.

Enrollment Period:

Enrollment may begin at any time during the year. The maximum time allowed to complete a college course is nine months; minimum time is eight weeks. One three-month extension may be allowed upon payment of a $24 extension fee. High school courses have an enrollment period of nine months from date of enrollment; if additional time is needed, the student may request a three-month extension for $24. The maximum time for completing a high school course, including the paid extension, is twelve months from the original date of enrollment.

Equipment Requirements:

Some courses require an audiocassette player. Textbooks are not included in tuition charges and must be purchased by the student.

Credit and Grading:

A through F, numerical grades, or, at the student's option, Satisfactory/No Credit in college courses. No grades are given in noncredit courses. A through F in high school courses. Minimum passing grade: D on the A through F scale; C (Satisfactory) on the Satisfactory/No Credit scale. Examinations must be proctored by an approved official if student does not live within 50 miles of a University of Tennessee campus. Credits are awarded in semester hour units.

Library Services:

Correspondence students have borrowing privileges at the University libraries if the student lives near one of the four campuses.

Accreditations:

Southern Association of Colleges and Schools. Member of: National University Continuing Education Association.

COLLEGE COURSES

ACCOUNTING

Principles of Financial Accounting

Introduction to financial accounting theory and practice with emphasis on preparation and reporting of financial information. (3 semester hours)

Principles of Managerial Accounting

Introduction to managerial and cost accounting concepts with emphasis on uses of accounting data by managers in planning operations, controlling activities, and decision making. (3 semester hours)

Intermediate Financial Accounting

Course 311K. Theory, principles, and procedures related to the valuation of assets, liabilities, and equities; measurement of periodic income; and preparation of financial statements. (3 semester hours)

Course 312K. A continuation of the course described above. (3 semester hours)

Cost and Managerial Accounting

Analysis of costing for products, projects, and management control. Topics include cost behavior, cost prediction, budgeting, and responsibility accounting. (3 semester hours)

AGRICULTURAL ECONOMICS

Introduction to Agricultural Economics

Application of economic principles of demand, supply, price determination, and market structure to agriculture, natural resources, rural community development, and international trade and development. Economic aspects of current issues and problems associated with production, marketing, consumption, resource use, and government intervention in the agricultural, rural, and international sectors. (3 semester hours)

Natural Resource Economics

Nature of natural resources; economic efficiency as a basis for natural resource use; externalities in natural resource use; factors influencing environmental quality; alternative public policy tools for influencing natural resource use or improving environmental quality. (3 semester hours)

ANTHROPOLOGY

Human Origins

Survey of humanity's background, fossil primates, fossil human remains, and living races of humankind. (3 semester hours)

Cultural Anthropology

Major concepts and methods in the study of culture; survey of cross-cultural similarities and differences in subsistence, social organization, economic, political, and religious institutions; language, ideology, and arts. Contributions of anthropology to resolving contemporary human problems. (3 semester hours)

BIOLOGY

Medical and Scientific Vocabulary

An introduction to the immediate constituents of medical and scientific vocabulary building and recognition through study and analysis of the most common technical prefixes, combining forms, and suffixes. (2 semester hours)

BUSINESS MANAGEMENT

Management Concepts, Theory and Practice

Inter- and intra-group relations in administration with special emphasis on superior-subordinate relations in a business environment. Comparison of classical concepts of leadership, structure, and development with contemporary research. (3 semester hours)

Human Resource Management

Principles and policies involved in the effective administration of personnel. (3 semester hours)

CHEMISTRY

Chemistry and the Environment

Basic concepts and methods of investigation with applications of chemical principles to the environment. (3 semester hours)

CHILD AND FAMILY STUDIES

Introduction to Early Childhood Education

History, philosophy, current trends, issues, programs, program models. Includes observation. (3 semester hours)

Human Sexuality

Sexuality through cultural, social, familial, and psychological factors. (3 semester hours)

Adulthood and Aging

Adult life in society from youth through elderly; adjustment to internal, environmental changes through adulthood; interrelationships among various aspects of development: physical, cognitive, emotional, social. Includes observation. (3 semester hours)

CRIMINAL JUSTICE

Philosophical and Ethical Issues in Criminal Justice

An investigation into the implications for criminal justice theory and practice of selected philosophical positions and perspectives. (3 semester hours)

CURRICULUM AND INSTRUCTION

Education in the United States

Organization and historical development of education in the United States, philosophical concepts and their influences on contemporary education; current issues. (3 semester hours)

The Teaching of Reading in the Elementary School

Survey of methods, strategies, diagnostic-prescriptive procedures, and materials for teaching reading. Field component included. (3 semester hours)

The Teaching of Reading in the Secondary School

Integrating reading skills and teaching strategies with the teaching of content area subjects. This course is available in a 3-semester hour version and a 4-semester hours version according to the student's needs. (3 or 4 semester hours)

Diagnostic and Prescriptive Teaching of Reading

Field-based, classroom diagnostic-prescriptive teaching; in-depth study of selected assessment instruments, instructional strategies, materials, and management procedures. Contact with a school is required. (3 semester hours)

ECONOMICS

Principles of Economics: Macroeconomics

A study of national income and its determination, money and banking, economic fluctuations, fiscal and monetary policy, economic growth, and international economics. (3 semester hours)

Principles of Economics: Microeconomics

A study of the market system, the price system, forms of business organization, government and business, labor and distribution. (3 semester hours)

Money and Banking

Development and analysis of the American monetary system and commercial and central banking; special attention to analysis and evaluation of monetary policies. (3 semester hours)

Intermediate Macroeconomic Theory

Introduction to contemporary theory of income and employment; emphasis on the essential principles and concepts used in the determination of the level on income and employment, the rate of economic growth, and the general price level. (3 semester hours)

ELECTRICAL ENGINEERING

Circuits I

Fundamental laws of circuit analysis. Ohm's Law, Kirchoff's current and voltage laws, the law of conservation of energy, circuits containing independent and dependent voltage and current sources, resistance, conductance, capacitance, and inductance analyzed using mesh nodal analysis, super-position and source transformations, and Norton's and Thevenin's Theorems. Steady state analysis of DC and AC circuits. Complete solution for transient analysis for circuits with one and two storage elements. (3 semester hours)

ENGLISH

English Composition I

Strategies for written argumentation, critical reading, and discussion; emphasis on audience analysis, the invention and arrangement of ideas, and revision of style and mechanics; typical assignments include formal essays, journals and collaborative projects. (3 semester hours)

English Composition II

Critical strategies for reading and writing about literature; emphasis on documented essay, library skills, and continued development of style and voice; typical assignments include analytical essay, annotated bibliography, journals, and collaborative projects. (3 semester hours)

British Literature I: Beowulf through Johnson

Major literary works from three periods: Middle Ages, Renaissance, and Restoration and Eighteenth Century. Writing-emphasis course. (3 semester hours)

British Literature II: Wordsworth to the Present

Major literary works from three periods: Romantic, Victorian, and the Twentieth Century. Writing-emphasis course. (3 semester hours)

American Literature I: Colonial Era to the Civil War

Development of American literature from its beginnings to the Civil War. Writing-emphasis course. (3 semester hours)

American Literature II: Civil War to the Present

Development of American literature from the Civil War to the present. Writing-emphasis course. (3 semester hours)

Introduction to Creative Writing

Practice in writing poetry and fiction, combined with study of models and techniques. Writing-emphasis course. (3 semester hours)

World Literature

A survey of world masterpieces (excluding American and British writers) from the beginnings through the eighteenth century. (3 semester hours)

Technical Writing

Introduction to written media in engineering, business, and industry. Writing and referencing of technical reports. Topics include proposals, feasibility reports, brochures, manuals, the letter of application, status reports and inter-office memoranda. (3 semester hours)

Introduction to Shakespeare

A study of Shakespeare's artistry as exhibited in ten plays—comedies, histories, tragedies, and dramatic romances. (3 semester hours)

Women in Literature

A survey of women writers since classical times, with attention to the critical reception of their works and to the characterization of women in literature. (3 semester hours)

FORESTRY, WILDLIFE, AND FISHERIES
Introduction to Forestry, Wildlife, and Fisheries

History of natural resources policies and practices; social perspectives and attitudes concerning natural resources and their use; techniques of integrated natural resources management, ecological principles, current policies, social trends, and forest and wildland resource use. (3 semester hours)

FRENCH
Elementary French

First Semester. Introduction to French. Must be taken in sequence. (3 semester hours)

Second Semester. A continuation of *First Semester.* Must be taken in sequence. (3 semester hours)

Intermediate French

First Semester. Sequence stresses the reading, writing, listening, and speaking of French to prepare for upper division courses in the language. Must be taken in sequence. (3 semester hours)

Second Semester. A continuation of *First Semester.* Must be taken in sequence. (3 semester hours)

Elements of French for Upper Division and Graduate Students

First Semester. Elements of language, elementary and advanced readings. Open to graduate students preparing for language examinations, and upper division students desiring reading knowledge of the language. (3 semester hours)

Second Semester. A continuation of *First Semester.* (3 semester hours)

History of French Literature

Course 311K. Chronological view of French literature in relation to the specific historical developments that have influenced it. (3 semester hours)

Course 312K. This is a directed readings course. (3 semester hours)

Aspects of French Literature

Study of masterpieces from the great literary movements and countermovements. (3 semester hours)

French Literature of the Sixteenth Century

Highlights of sixteenth-century French literature. Excerpts from Rabelais and Montaigne; readings of poems from the writers from Lyon and members of the Pléiade. (3 semester hours)

French Literature of the Seventeenth Century

Masterpieces of seventeenth-century French literature. (3 semester hours)

French Literature of the Eighteenth Century

Major works of the Enlightenment. (3 semester hours)

GEOGRAPHY
World Geography, First Semester

Selected topics and problems of contemporary interest to illustrate geographical points of view, concepts, and techniques. (3 semester hours)

GERMAN
Elementary German

First Semester. Must be taken in sequence. (3 semester hours)

Second Semester. Must be taken in sequence. (3 semester hours)

HEALTH
Personal Health

Significant data and facts helpful in making intelligent decisions concerning personal health: crucial issues of personal, family, and social living. (3 semester hours)

Consumer Health

Major consumer health care providers and health care services; selecting, purchasing, evaluating, and financing medical and health care services/products. (3 semester hours)

Death, Dying, and Bereavement

Aspects of dying, death, and handling the trauma of loss. Medical, financial, physical, legal, and social implications of death. (3 semester hours)

HISTORY
Development of Western Civilization

Course 151K. Historical survey of the civilization of the western world. Ancient world to 1715. Writing-emphasis course. (3 semester hours)

Course 152K. Historical survey of the civilization of the western world. 1715 to present. Writing-emphasis course. (3 semester hours)

History of the United States

Course 251K. Settlement to 1877. (3 semester hours)

Course 252K. 1877 to present. (3 semester hours)

History of Tennessee

Tennessee's history from the eighteenth century to the present. (3 semester hours)

LIBRARY SCIENCE
Children's Literature

Examination and study of materials suitable for children in grades K–9 to use for leisure time or classroom activities. Criteria for selecting books, magazines, recordings, films, and related materials. Storytelling and other devices for encouraging literacy. (3 semester hours)

Books and Nonprint Materials for Adolescents and Adults

Examination and study of materials suitable for young adults in grades 10–12 to use for leisure time or classroom activities and for adults' recreational and informational reading. Criteria for selecting books, magazines, recordings, films, videos, and computer software. Strategies for encouraging literacy and principles of materials selection. (3 semester hours)

MATHEMATICS
Statistical Reasoning

An introduction to probability and statistics without calculus. (3 semester hours)

College Algebra

A review of algebraic functions, equations, and inequalities for students who satisfy the course prerequisites for *Calculus A* but whose placement test scores indicated additional preparation is necessary. (3 semester hours)

Calculus A

For students not planning to major in science, engineering, mathematics, or computer science. Calculus of algebraic, exponential, and logarithmic functions, with applications. (3 semester hours)

Calculus B

A sequel to *Calculus A*, including elementary matrix algebra, multi-variable calculus, and optimization. (3 semester hours)

Precalculus I

Review of algebraic, logarithmic, exponential, and trigonometric functions for students who satisfy the course prerequisites for *Calculus I* but whose placement test scores indicate additional preparation is necessary. (4 semester hours)

Calculus I

Standard first-year course in single variable calculus, especially for students of science, engineering, mathematics, and computer science. Differential and integral calculus with applications. (4 semester hours)

Calculus II

A continuation of *Calculus I*. (4 semester hours)

Calculus III

Calculus of functions in two or more dimensions. Includes solid analytic geometry, partial differentiation, multiple integration, and selected topics in vector calculus. (4 semester hours)

Structure of the Number System

Problem solving, sets and relations, numeration systems, integers, elementary number theory, rational numbers and decimals. (3 semester hours)

Probability, Statistics, and Euclidean Geometry

Probabilities in simple experiments, measures of central tendency and variation. Basic plane and three-space geometry, congruence and similarity, constructions with compass and straightedge, transformations, area and volume measurement. Turtle graphs. (3 semester hours)

Differential Equations I

First course, emphasizing solution techniques. Includes first-order equations and applications, theory of linear equations, equations with constant coefficients, Laplace transforms, and series solutions. (3 semester hours)

NUTRITION

Introductory Nutrition

Principles of nutrition and applications to everyday life with focus on wellness and assessments for personal fitness. (3 semester hours)

PHILOSOPHY

Medical Ethics

Ethical issues in medicine such as abortion, euthanasia, human experimentation, fairness in health care delivery and the doctor-patient relationship. (3 semester hours)

POLITICAL SCIENCE

United States Government and Politics

Introduction to fundamental institutions and processes of American National Politics including the constitution, voting, presidency, congress, and the courts. (3 semester hours)

International Relations

Principles of theory and practice of international politics. Fundamentals of national power study, diplomacy, foreign policy, as well as the social, cultural, legal and economic aspects of relations among nations. Discussion on several major current international problems. (3 semester hours)

PSYCHOLOGY

General Psychology

Introduction to primary approaches to the study of human behavior and experience. (3 semester hours)

Biological Basis of Behavior

Survey of theories and research concerning the role of genetic factors, nervous and endocrine systems, and other biological influences on behavior. (3 semester hours)

Behavior and Experience: Humanistic Psychology

Behavioral and phenomenological analysis of individuals and their development in natural environments. (3 semester hours)

Child Psychology

The normal child from conception through infancy, childhood, and adolescence. Physical, cognitive, social, and emotional development. (3 semester hours)

Learning and Thinking

Survey of theory and findings of research concerning both humans and nonhumans. (3 semester hours)

Abnormal Psychology

Individual and environmental factors in deviant and maladaptive behavior; neurotic and psychotic reactions. Contemporary methods of treatment. (3 semester hours)

Social Psychology

Theories, methods, and findings of research concerning individual behavior in a social context. (3 semester hours)

Statistics in Psychology

Descriptive statics; logic of hypothesis-testing and statistical inference. Basic parametric and nonparametric tests. (3 semester hours)

Methods of Research in Psychology

Fundamentals in the design, conduct, and interpretation of research, including systematic observation, experiments, quasi-experiments, and program evaluations. Focus on both laboratory and natural settings. (3 semester hours)

RELIGIOUS STUDIES

Images of Jesus

Major portrayals of Jesus Christ from the first century to the twentieth within the context of the cultural milieu which gave birth to each. (3 semester hours)

Medical Ethics

Ethical issues in medicine such as abortion, euthanasia, human experimentation, fairness in health care delivery, and the doctor-patient relationship. (3 semester hours)

SAFETY

General Safety

Principles, practices, and procedures in general safety. Safety problems in schools, traffic, recreation, industry, home, and other public areas. (3 semester hours)

SOCIOLOGY

General Sociology

Major concepts and theoretical approaches of sociology with emphasis on culture, socialization, social organization, and social stratification. (3 semester hours)

Social Problems and Social Change

Increasingly acute and intense problems such as alcoholism, violence, crime, inequality, life-style preferences, and environmental abuse within the context of social change. (3 semester hours)

Marriage and Family

The relationships of the family structure to social organization. Particular emphasis focused on the family historically, mate selection, marital adjustment, marital happiness, and divorce in a changing society. (3 semester hours)

Collective Behavior and Social Movements

Collective phenomena leading to social change. Response to disaster, popular crazes, and social protests and development, organization, and function of social movements. Emphasis on American cases. (3 semester hours)

Criminology

Systemic inquiry into alternative definitions of crime, statistical distribution of different types of crime causation, and responses to crime, primarily by the police. (3 semester hours)

Juvenile Delinquency

Critical assessment of historical and contemporary nature of the delinquency problem. Major theories of delinquency. Current issues in juvenile justice. (3 semester hours)

The City

The revolutionary impact of cities and city life as seen from an ecological perspective. The organization of life in cities into communities, neighborhoods, and other territories. Urban planning and problems. (3 semester hours)

Social Psychology

Social psychological analysis of social behavior emphasizing its acquisition, its enactment, and its dynamic nature. (3 semester hours)

Sociology of Aging

How roles and statuses change with age in relation to the major social institutions; the impact that the rapidly increasing number of older people has on society, the effect of society on older people. (3 semester hours)

Criminal Justice

A critical assessment of the criminal justice apparatus and its components. Brief examination of the police, with most of the emphasis on the criminal courts and institutions and programs such as the prison, probation, and parole. Analysis of their operation and impacts. (3 semester hours)

SPANISH

Elementary Spanish

First Semester. Introduction to Spanish. Must be taken in sequence. (3 semester hours)

Second Semester. A continuation of the course above. Must be taken in sequence. (3 semester hours)

Intermediate Spanish

First Semester. Reading, writing, listening, and speaking of Spanish to prepare for upper division courses in the language. Must be taken in sequence. (3 semester hours)

Second Semester. A continuation of the course above. Must be taken in sequence. (3 semester hours)

SPECIAL EDUCATION

Introduction to Special Education

A survey of special education with emphasis placed upon consideration of the history of special education; federal involvement and leaderships; and the global characteristics of the target population. (3 semester hours)

HIGH SCHOOL COURSES

ART

Visual Art - Basic Cartooning

An introduction to the fundamentals of drawing, from rudimentary anatomy and figure drawing to picture composition and the use of perspective. Much emphasis will be placed on finding your own style and developing techniques that will make your work unique. (½ unit)

Visual Art - Advanced Cartooning

This course focuses on the details of story-telling: how to present a punch-line visually, how to simplify your drawing, and how to further emphasize one's own particular style. The similarities between cartooning and illustration will be discussed and the differences explored. (½ unit)

BUSINESS EDUCATION

Accounting I

First Semester. Beginning course introducing the language of business, methods of keeping good personal records, including those for income tax purposes, banking, social security, a future vocation, or as an asset in other business positions. (½ unit)

Second Semester. A continuation of the above course. (½ unit)

Business Communication

First Semester. Designed for the business major or other students interested in an intensive review of effective business communication practices. (½ unit)

Second Semester. A continuation of the above course. (½ unit)

Business Law

First Semester. Introduces basic concepts of law and law enforcement related to business. Topics include contracts, using credit, renting and owning real property. (½ unit)

Second Semester. A continuation of the above course. (½ unit)

Business Mathematics

First Semester. Business transactions of the consumer in daily life and applications of good business principles to savings and investments, home ownership, travel, and transportation. (½ unit)

Second Semester. A continuation of the above course. (½ unit)

General Business

First Semester. Designed to help prepare individuals to make decisions in their inter-related roles as consumers, wage earners, and citizens. Examination of basic economic principles and theories; encourages students to develop competence to apply this economic knowledge to practical ends. (½ unit)

Second Semester. A continuation of the above course. (½ unit)

Office Procedures

This course is intended to prepare students for employment in clerical jobs in a business office. Information on handling the mail, filing, reception duties, and keeping personal records. Requires access to typewriter or word processor. (½ unit)

Recordkeeping

This course will teach the student how to maintain a good record system in a modern business. Topics include storing data, recording receipts, keeping a checking account, petty cash, and budget records (including family budgets), sales and accounts receivable records, and computerized records systems. (½ unit)

ENGLISH

9th Grade Language Skills

Basic grammar, punctuation, and sentence structure. (½ unit)

10th Grade Language Skills

Basic grammar, punctuation, and sentence structure. (½ unit)

11th Grade Language Skills

Grammar, punctuation, sentence structure, and paragraphing. (½ unit)

12th Grade Language Skills

Grammar, punctuation, sentence structure, paragraphing, outlining, and theme writing. (½ unit)

9th Grade Reading Skills

Basic skills in vocabulary, dictionary, and sentence meaning. (½ unit)

10th Grade Reading Skills

Further development in vocabulary, sentence meaning, inferences. (½ unit)

11th Grade Reading Skills

Vocabulary development, dictionary skills, reading essays and literature for meaning. (½ unit)

12th Grade Reading Skills

Advanced skills in vocabulary, flexibility, and reading for meaning. (½ unit)

English Language Arts I (9th Grade)

First Semester. A study of grammar rules, spelling, and punctuation. (½ unit)

Second Semester. A study of different types of literature and literary techniques. One novel is assigned reading. (½ unit)

English Language Arts II (10th Grade)

First Semester. A study of grammar rules, spelling, punctuation, and paragraph writing. (½ unit)

Second Semester. A study of a novel, a play, poems and short stories which the student analyzes with regard to techniques. (½ unit)

English Language Arts III (11th Grade)

A study of grammar rules and paragraph writing. A term paper is assigned. (½ unit)

English Language Arts IV (12th Grade)

First Semester. A study of composition and grammar. A term paper is assigned. (½ unit)

Second Semester. A study of themes in British literature. (½ unit)

FRENCH

French I

First Semester. First year high school French covering basic grammar and vocabulary. Reading, writing, and oral skills. Student must have access to a cassette audiotape player-recorder. (½ unit)

Second Semester. A continuation of the above course. (½ unit)

French II

First Semester. Second year high school French. Reading and writing skills are emphasized. Oral skills also included. Student must have access to a cassette audiotape player-recorder. (½ unit)

Second Semester. A continuation of the above course. (½ unit)

HEALTH

Health Education

First Semester. A study of personal health. The interrelatedness of physical health, mental health, exercise, and drugs. (½ unit)

Second Semester. A continuation of the above course. (½ unit)

HOME ECONOMICS

Consumer Education and Resource Management

This course helps students develop practical consumer skills used everyday in the marketplace: money management, comparison shopping, budgeting, financial planning, investing, and buying insurance. The interaction of the individual and the economy as a whole is considered. (½ unit)

Nutrition and Food I

A basic study of the foods we eat and their effect on our bodies. This course focuses on each of the major food groups in terms of their nutritional value and on ways of using the food in well-balanced meals. Also included is a unit on planning for special dietary needs. (½ unit)

JOURNALISM

Journalism

Introduction to journalism with emphasis on print media. Topics include history and responsibilities of journalism, news, sports, features, and editing. Development of good writing style. (½ unit)

LATIN

Latin I

First Semester. Introduction to elementary Latin—the language itself and Roman mythology. Emphasis on reading and writing. Must be taken in sequence. (½ unit)

Second Semester. A continuation of the above course. (½ unit)

Latin II

First Semester. Grammar, culture, and translation. Must be taken in sequence. (½ unit)

Second Semester. A continuation of the above course. (½ unit)

MATHEMATICS

Algebra I

First Semester. First year algebra. Introduction to basic concepts of algebra. (½ unit)

Second Semester. A continuation of the above course. (½ unit)

Algebra II

First Semester. Second year algebra. A continuation of the study of algebra. (½ unit)

Second Semester. A continuation of the above course. (½ unit)

Arithmetic

First Semester. General mathematics. Includes study of place value, addition, subtraction, multiplication, division, and decimals. (½ unit)

Second Semester. Further study of fractions, mixed numbers, ratios, proportions, decimals, percentage, averages, and basic geometry. (½ unit)

Geometry

First Semester. Introduction to plane geometry. (½ unit)

Second Semester. A continuation of the above course. (½ unit)

Trigonometry

An introduction to the fundamentals of trigonometry. (½ unit)

SCIENCE

Biology I

First Semester. Introduces the general areas of botany, zoology, and human biology. Biological developments of the past as well as a consideration of the future are stressed. Must be taken in sequence. (½ unit)

Second Semester. A continuation of the above course. (½ unit)

Physical Science

First Semester. Introduction to science and the scientific method. Topics covered include basic properties of matter, how energy affects matter, and the production and use of energy. (½ unit)

Second Semester. Topics include: how our planet is changing, properties of the living world, and the environment. (½ unit)

SOCIAL STUDIES

Civics

First Semester. Democracy on the local, state, and national levels. (½ unit)

Second Semester. Relations of citizenship to economic life; natural resources; government and business; trades and professions. (½ unit)

Economics

First Semester. Designed to help students develop skills needed for continual growth in interpreting and understanding economic problems in an expanding economy, the developing of natural and human resources, and a spirit of individual freedom. (½ unit)

Second Semester. A continuation of the above course. (½ unit)

Psychology

First Semester. Studies include human growth and development, theories of personality, learning, and behavior. (½ unit)

Second Semester. A continuation of the above course. Studies frustration and conflict, personality disturbances, group dynamics, and the development of attitudes. (½ unit)

Alternate Semester. In a systematic way, explore and develop your own personal strengths. Understand your attitudes, interaction with others, and your personal and vocational goals. (½ unit)

Sociology

This course focuses on how people behave in groups and how group interaction shapes their behavior. (½ unit)

United States Government

First Semester. Local, state, and national government; role of United States in the community of nations. (½ unit)

Second Semester. A continuation of the above course. (½ unit)

United States History

First Semester. The story of our country as it developed. From early exploration and through the Reconstruction Period. (½ unit)

Second Semester. From the end of Reconstruction to the present. (½ unit)

World Geography

First Semester. Introductory studies in human relationship to physical features, resources, climate, regional characteristics of the world. Practice in using maps, atlases, etc. (½ unit)

Second Semester. A continuation of the above course. (½ unit)

World History

First Semester. A survey course beginning with the study of prehistoric cultures and continuing through the Americas. (½ unit)

Second Semester. Surveys chronologically the Renaissance and Reformation through the world problems of today. (½ unit)

SPANISH

Spanish I

First Semester. First year high school Spanish, covering basic vocabulary, pronunciation, and elementary grammar. Must be taken in sequence. (½ unit)

Second Semester. A continuation of the above course. (½ unit)

Spanish II

First Semester. Second year Spanish. Reading and writing skills are emphasized. Must be taken in sequence. (½ unit)

Second Semester. A continuation of the above course. (½ unit)

NONCREDIT COURSES

CARTOONING

Cartooning I - Basic Cartooning

This course explores the fundamentals of figure drawing and the basic concepts of graphic storytelling. Exercises help the student improve his/her craftsmanship while he/she develops individual style. (Noncredit) *Tuition:* $80.

Cartooning II - Advanced Cartooning

This course helps the student discover his/her potential in the field of cartoon art. Advanced work in storytelling, rendering, and caricature draws heavily upon editorial art, comic books, and newspaper strips. The student's development of an individual style is emphasized. (Noncredit) *Tuition:* $80.

MATHEMATICS

Everyday Mathematics

A refresher course in general mathematics; an aid in preparing for the General Equivalency Diploma (G.E.D.) test. Includes fractions, mixed numbers, percentage, interest, square roots, ratios, taxes, decimals, weights and measurements. (Noncredit) *Tuition:* $80.

Refresher Algebra

Fundamental operations of algebra, factoring, squares, odd and even powers, fractions, exponents, radicals, trinomials. (Noncredit) *Tuition:* $80.

Trigonometry

Plane trigonometry including trigonmetric equations, polar coordinates, and other preparatory techniques for calculus plus applications to a variety of physical problem situations. (Noncredit) *Tuition:* $80.

NURSING

Shock: A Nursing Perspective

An in-depth review of the complex syndrome of shock. Topics include introduction to shock and overview of major classifications; the four stages of shock; the therapeutic tools to manage the shock patient; the nursing implications for prevention, assessment, and planning of patient care. (2 CEUs) *Tuition:* $80.

Patient Medication Records Review for Nurses

Designed specifically for nurses. An introduction to a systematic method of reviewing patient medication records to detect potential problems. Topics include problems with therapeutic regimens; duplication in therapy; drug interaction; inappropriate doses, routes, schedules, and dosage forms; adverse effects; and drug-disease interactions. (3 CEUs) *Tuition:* $69.

SELF DISCOVERY

Project Self-Discovery

General principles and self-analysis to help the student recognize his/her strengths and weaknesses and to develop his/her own program of personality improvement. (Noncredit) *Tuition:* $80.

STUDY SKILLS

How to Study

Major aspects of the psychology of studying and learning; specific directions and techniques for mathematics, foreign languages, examinations, and note-taking. (Noncredit) *Tuition:* $65.

WRITING

How to Write Almost Anything

This course teaches you to write simply and clearly. You will learn to put words into correct and coherent form so you can express yourself. Topics include description, details, revising, persuasion, grammar, and letter writing. (Noncredit) *Tuition:* $130.

Creative Writing I - Articles

This course contains tested methods for writing publishable articles of 100 to 1800 words. Beginning with the filler (short verse and anecdote), the student will learn the process of writing and marketing the humorous, inspirational, self-help and personal article along with specific tips of tailoring magazine articles to meet an editor's approval. (Noncredit) *Tuition:* $130.

Creative Writing II - Writing Short Stories

This course offers students a practical guide to the basic techniques of fiction writing. Through a series of exercises, students learn sound methods for developing their skills at combining description, narration, dialogue, scenes, point of view, plotting, etc. into a unified piece of fiction. (Noncredit) *Tuition:* $130.

Creative Writing III - Writing Poetry

An introduction to the basics of writing poetry for personal pleasure or publication. Among the topics covered are rhythm, sound, rime, traditional forms, free verse, sources of ideas for poems, writer's block, revision, and submitting poems for publication. (Noncredit) *Tuition:* $130.

Tennessee, University of - Chattanooga
615 McCallie Avenue
Chattanooga, Tennessee 37403 (615) 755-4111

Description:
Founded in 1886 as the University of Chattanooga, it later merged with the Chattanooga City College to become part of the University of Tennessee. It is a member with the campuses at Memphis, Knoxville, and Martin of a University of Tennessee consortium for the purpose of administering their correspondence courses from a central agency, the Department of Independent Study, located at the University of Tennessee at Knoxville. For courses available and registration procedures, SEE **Tennessee, University of.**

Faculty:
Dr. Jack Reese, Chancellor; Dr. Gerald Weeks, Dean, Continuing Education.

Accreditations:
Southern Association of Colleges and Schools.

Tennessee, University of - Martin
Martin, Tennessee 38238   (901) 587-7000

Description:
The history of the University traces back to when the Baptists of Martin and the Beulah Association established the Hall-Moody Institute in 1900. It gained junior college status in 1927 when it joined the University of Tennessee system and became a senior college in 1951. It is a member with the campuses at Memphis, Chattanooga, and Knoxville of a University of Tennessee consortium for the purpose of administering their correspondence courses from a central agency, the Department of Independent Study located at the University of Tennessee at Knoxville. For courses available and registration procedures, SEE **Tennessee, University of.**

Faculty:
Dr. Margaret N. Perry, Chancellor; Dr. John Eisterhold, Director, Extended Services.

Accreditations:
Southern Association of Colleges and Schools.

Tennessee, University of - Memphis
800 Madison Avenue
Memphis, Tennessee 38163   (901) 577-4000

Description:
The University of Tennessee at Memphis, formerly named the University of Tennessee Center for Health Sciences, offers programs in medicine, dentistry, basic medical sciences, nursing, pharmacy, and allied health. It is a member with the campuses at Chattanooga, Knoxville, and Martin of a University of Tennessee consortium for the purpose of administering their correspondence courses from a central agency, the Department of Independent Study located at the University of Tennessee at Knoxville. For courses available and registration procedures, SEE **Tennessee, University of.**

Faculty:
Dr. William R. Rice, Chancellor.

Accreditations:
Southern Association of Colleges and Schools.

Texas, University of - at Austin
Independent Learning
Extension Instruction and Materials Center
Division of Continuing Education
P.O. Box 7700
Austin, Texas 78713-7700   (512) 471-7716

Description:

The University of Texas at Austin has been offering correspondence courses since 1909. Approximately 12,000 students are enrolled annually enrolled in college, high school, and career-development courses. A toll-free number to reach Independent Learning is 1-800-252-3461.

Faculty:

Dr. Thomas M. Hatfield, Dean of Continuing Education; Dr. Judy Copeland Ashcroft, Director, Extension Instruction and Materials Center; Sharon Montgomery, Director, Independent Learning; Olga Garza, Supervisor, Student Services. There is faculty of 90 members for correspondence study courses.

Academic Levels:

College
High School
Noncredit

Degree/Certificate Programs:

Most academic divisions at the University of Texas at Austin allow students to earn up to thirty percent of required credit toward a baccalaureate degree by independent study. Requirements vary with the individual colleges. Students are advised to confirm specific degree plans. It is not possible to attain a degree solely by correspondence study.

Admission Requirements:

Open enrollment; regular admission to the University of Texas at Austin is not required. Some courses require prerequisites. Resident students at UT at Austin must have prior approval of their academic deans to enroll in an independent study course. Military personnel interested in correspondence study through DANTES should contact their Education Officer for information.

Tuition:

College-level courses $170 per three-hour course; $250 per five-hour course. High school-level courses average $85 per course. There is a $25 administrative/postage charge per course. Some courses require audiocassette tapes that can be rented for the period of enrollment. VISA or MasterCard accepted. Seventy-five percent of the tuition charge, less an administrative and grading fee for each lesson submitted, is refundable if a written request for refund is received within thirty days of the official enrollment date; fifty percent of the tuition charge, less a grading fee for each lesson submitted, is refundable if a written request for refund is received within sixty days of the official enrollment date; the unused portion of the foreign postage charge is refundable when other refund conditions have been met; no refunds after sixty days.

Enrollment Period:

Maximum time allowed is 9 months; only one extension of 3 months will be allowed upon payment of a $25 extension fee. The minimum time for completion of a course is 2 to 3 months.

Equipment Requirements:

Required textbooks must be purchased by the student. Textbooks may be purchased from Wallace's Book Store, Drawer M, University Station, Austin, Texas (512) 477-6141). Some courses make use of cassette tapes which require a partially refundable deposit. Cassette players must be furnished by the student.

Credit and Grading:

Grading system is: A (Excellent), B (Above Average), C (Average), D (Pass), F (Failure), CR (Credit) when enrolled on a pass/fail basis. Minimum passing grade is D (usually 60 percent). High school grading follows a numerical system (70 is the minimum passing grade). To receive credit for a correspondence course all students must pass a supervised final examination under an approved proctor. Credit is awarded in semester hour units.

Library Services:

Persons enrolled in correspondence study may obtain materials from the Circulation Services Department of the Perry-Castaneda Library by obtaining a courtesy borrower's card for a small fee.

Accreditations:

Southern Association of Colleges and Schools. Member of: National University Continuing Education Association.

COLLEGE COURSES

ANTHROPOLOGY

Physical Anthropology

Human evolution, race, heredity, the organic basis of culture; culture history through the Paleolithic stage. (3 semester hours)

Cultural Anthropology

The concept of culture, social and political organization of primitive peoples, language, the supernatural and elementary cultural theory. (3 semester hours)

Human Origins and Evolution

Detailed examination and analysis of morphological trends evident in the hominid fossil record. (3 semester hours)

ART EDUCATION

Art Education

An introduction to museum education designed primarily (though not exclusively) for the student interested in a museum career. Topics include development of museum education in America, training docents, developing youth and adult programs, educational exhibitions, resource centers, grant writing, and research. Primarily for those employed in art museums. (3 semester hours)

ART HISTORY

Introduction to the Visual Arts

Visual elements, their nature, functions, and relationships in painting, sculpture, and architecture. (3 semester hours)

ASTRONOMY

Introductory Astronomy

A descriptive astronomy course for nonscience majors. This self-paced course emphasizes how we interpret astronomical evidence to deduce the properties of objects in the sky, especially stars. It covers properties of light and atoms, telescopes, the birth and death of stars, galaxies, and the universe. A brief examination of the solar system also explores the topic of life in the cosmos. (3 semester hours)

CURRICULUM AND INSTRUCTION

Human Learning and Development: The Adult Years

Designed for practitioners who work with adult learners and for adults who desire a better awareness and insight into their potential as learners. Key concepts of adult development and the interactive physical, psychological and social factors will be explored and related to the adult learner and the specific learning environment. Readings and applications exercises will provide the student with opportunities to both gain an understanding of the adult learner and gain skill in applying adult learning theory to practical learning situations. (3 semester hours)

CZECH

First-Year Czech I

An introduction to the fundamentals of Czech grammar and vocabulary. Access to a cassette recorder is required. (5 semester hours)

First-Year Czech II

Textbook assignments will be supplemented with selected readings. Access to a cassette recorder is required. (5 semester hours)

ECONOMICS

Introduction to Macroeconomics

Analysis of the economy as a whole (its organization and basic forces influencing its growth and development); money and banking; national income, national income, public finance, and international linkages. (3 semester hours)

Introduction to Microeconomics

Analysis of the economic behavior of individual consumers, firms, and workers; special attention to the role of markets. (3 semester hours)

Elementary Economics of the Third World

Economic principles in relation to the less developed nations of the world. (3 semester hours)

Development Problems and Policies in Latin America

Description of the Latin American economy; business and market organizations; problems of growth (involving credit, public finance, trade, investment aspects). (3 semester hours)

EDUCATIONAL PSYCHOLOGY

Psychological Foundations of Education

Scientific contributions to the understanding of human behavior and educational processes: cultural influences, processes of learning and socialization, classroom management, development, intellectual functioning, and educational achievement. (3 semester hours)

Introduction to Statistics

Measures of central tendency and variability; correlation and regression; probability and statistical inference; analysis of variance; nonparametric statistics. (3 semester hours)

ENGLISH

Rhetoric and Composition

A composition course that provides basic instruction in the writing and analysis of expository prose; includes an introduction to logic and the principles of rhetoric. (3 semester hours)

Topics in Writing

Literature and Composition. Reading and writing about a specific subject, with emphasis on the evaluation of information, analytical reading, and critical writing. (3 semester hours)

Black Literature

Introduction to black literature, focusing on the works of black Americans with one short unit on African literature. Special assignment options are available for education majors and teachers and for those interested in creative writing. (3 semester hours)

Masterworks of Literature: American

Introduction to masterpieces of the literary tradition, emphasizing historical, generic, thematic connections. Major American writers in poetry, prose, and drama. One audio tape. (3 semester hours)

Masterworks of Literature: British

Introduction to masterpieces of the literary tradition, emphasizing historical, generic, thematic connections. Major English writers in poetry, prose, and drama. (3 semester hours)

Masterworks of Literature: World

Introduction to masterpieces of the literary tradition, emphasizing historical, generic, thematic connections. Major European writers from biblical times to the 20th century in poetry, prose, and drama. (3 semester hours)

Technical Writing

A course designed to meet the technical writing needs of students or practitioners in the following fields: engineering, business, accounting, and the health professions. Provides a review of basic writing skills. (3 semester hours)

Shakespeare: Selected Plays

A representative selection of Shakespeare's best comedies, tragedies, and histories. (3 semester hours)

Introduction to Criticism

Introduction to major terms, issues, and approaches in literary criticism, and their application to the reasoned discussion of poetry, fiction, and drama. (3 semester hours)

Creative Writing

A study of the techniques of writing fiction and poetry. Reading and analysis of examples, with emphasis on the creative work of the student. Half the lessons devoted to fiction; half to poetry. (3 semester hours)

American Literature: From the Beginnings to 1865

A survey of major writers, poetry, and prose. (3 semester hours)

American Literature: From 1865 to the Present

A survey of major writers, poetry, and prose. (3 semester hours)

The Modern Short Story

Extensive readings and analyses of stories by major modern writers, such as Faulkner, Hemingway, Joyce, Chekhov, and Kafka, as well as contemporary writers. (3 semester hours)

Modern Poetry: Representative Poets of the Twentieth Century

Poets studied include Eliot, Auden, Stevens, and Thomas. (3 semester hours)

American Science Fiction

Covers the development of American science fiction from the 1920s to the 1980s. Texts read in this course range from the naive adventure stories of the "pulp era" in the 1920s to the cynical cyberpunk fiction of the 1980s. Basic course structure follows the historic development of the genre. Students also focus on particular themes and various theoretical approaches to science fiction. (3 semester hours)

FRENCH

First-Year French I

Basic grammar with emphasis on reading and translation. Access to a cassette recorder is required. (5 semester hours)

First-Year French II

Continuation of grammar study with emphasis on reading and translation. Access to a cassette recorder is required. (5 semester hours)

Second-Year French I: Four Skills

Emphasis on the four skills: listening, speaking, reading, writing. Ten required audiocassette tapes. (3 semester hours)

Second-Year French II: Four Skills (Literature)

Emphasis on the four skills: listening, speaking, reading. Texts are literary works of nineteenth and twentieth centuries. Ten required audiocassette tapes. (3 semester hours)

GEOGRAPHY

The Human World: An Introduction to Geography

An introductory survey of the human geography of the earth, major cultural divisions, and selected regions and countries. (3 semester hours)

GERMAN

First-Year German I

Basic training in grammatical patterns and usage of modern German. Stress is on pronunciation through use of a comprehensive tape program, with fundamentals of grammar, word order, and basic vocabulary. Student must have access to a cassette tape recorder. (5 semester hours)

First-Year German II

Advanced training in grammatical patterns and usage of modern Germany. Student must have access to a cassette tape recorder. (5 semester hours)

Second-Year German I: Readings in Humanities and Social Sciences

Reading of representative works of modern authors, practice in German composition, and a thorough grammar review. (3 semester hours)

Second-Year German II: Readings in Humanities and Social Sciences

Part of the reading is assigned for intensive work and part for rapid reading, including one or more of the classic prose or verse works of German literature. (3 semester hours)

GOVERNMENT

Texas Government

A brief survey course in Texas politics and government. Topics include the Texas Constitution; political parties and interest groups; elections; the legislative, executive, and judicial branches; local government; taxing; and spending. (1 semester hour)

American Government

National and state government with special reference to Texas. The origins and development of the American political system; nature of the U.S. and Texas constitutions; federalism, including local government; basic freedoms, equality under law, and citizenship; public opinion and political behavior; interest groups, political parties, and elections. (3 semester hours)

Issues and Policies in American Government

Topic 1: The Constitutional Debates. A closer look into the foundations of American government by considering the debates surrounding the ratification of the Constitution in the late 1780s. Focus is specifically on the Federalist debate. (3 semester hours)

Topic 2. American Political Behavior. An examination of American political behavior; emphasis on the development and methods of political behavior as a field. Mass political behavior and elite political behavior, including section on leadership and persuasion. (3 semester hours)

International Politics since the Second World War

An examination of some of the major attributes of the international political system in the postwar period; special emphasis is placed upon such interrelated issues as power, equality, and the challenge of change in the international political arena. (3 semester hours)

Public Opinion and American Politics

The nature of and major influences on public attitudes, the measurement of public opinion, and the role of public opinion in government. (3 semester hours)

Religion and Politics in American Thought

Study of religion and politics in American thought from the colonial era to the present. Covers religion in American Constitutional jurisprudence and the "culture" war between American secularism and its critics. Also covers contemporary social issues such as religion and racial justice, civil disobedience, war and peace, and religion and economic life. (3 semester hours)

American Foreign Relations

The aims, methods, and accomplishments of United States foreign policy since World War II, by geographic areas and by special problems. (3 semester hours)

GREEK

First-Year Greek I

Ancient Greek. (5 semester hours)

First-Year Greek II

Ancient Greek. Completion of grammar and some reading from Plato. (5 semester hours)

New Testament Greek: The Gospels

The Greek text of the Gospels with attention to problems of syntax, word studies, and techniques of literate translation. May be repeated for credit when topics vary. (3 semester hours)

Topic 1: The Gospel of John.

Topic 2: The Synoptic Gospels. Primarily a study of the Gospel of

Luke with comparison of parallel passages in the Gospel of Matthew and Mark.

New Testament Greek: The Gospels, Acts of the Apostles, and Paul's Epistles

The advanced reading course in New Testament Greek with an introduction to the methods of textual criticism and exegesis intended for those who would like to read the sacred texts of Christianity unbiased by an ecclesiastical interpretation. (3 semester hours)

HEALTH EDUCATION

Human Sexuality

Analysis of the physiological, psychological, and social factors of human sexuality. Focus on sexuality throughout the life cycle, examining basic anatomy as well as the psychosocial factors which play a part in determination of changing patterns of sexual behavior. Various issues that influence sex roles, sexual behavior, and the delivery of sexual health care will be explored. (3 semester hours)

HISTORY

English Civilization before 1603

Prehistoric and Roman Britain; the invasions and settlements made by the Angles, Saxons, and Danes; the conversion of Britain to Christianity; the Norman Conquest; the manorial system; the Hundred Years' War; the Reformation; literature; and the reign of Elizabeth. (3 semester hours)

English Civilization since 1603

The British Civil War; Oliver Cromwell, the Restoration; the Glorious Revolution; the Second Hundred Years' War with France; the Industrial, American, and French revolutions; Parliamentary reform; the British Empire; and the World Wars. (3 semester hours)

Western Civilization in Medieval Times

The growth of European civilization from prehistory to the end of the seventeenth century. (3 semester hours)

Western Civilization in Modern Times

A study of European civilization from 1700 to the present. (3 semester hours)

The United States, 1492–1865

Fulfills legislative requirement for American history. (3 semester hours)

The United States since 1865

Fulfills legislative requirement for American history. (3 semester hours)

Latin America before 1810

Basic survey course designed as an introduction to Latin American history in the colonial period. (3 semester hours)

LATIN

First-Year Latin I

A systematic introduction to Latin literature through the study of the forms of the language; practice in reading and translation of selected easy Latin sentences. (5 semester hours)

First-Year Latin II

A continuation of the above course leading to and including a survey of various Roman writers—Catullus, Horace, Martial, Cicero, and Pliny. (5 semester hours)

Second Year Latin II: Virgil's *Aeneid*

A study of the Augustan Age and one of the great epic poems of the western world. (3 semester hours)

MATHEMATICS

College Algebra

Designed for students who need to improve their ability to handle algebra before proceeding to calculus or other courses. Topics include a brief review of elementary algebra; linear, quadratic, exponential, and logarithmic functions; polynomials; systems of liner equations; applications. (3 semester hours)

Mathematics of Investment

Topics, formulas, and procedures for applications of mathematics in the area of finance and investment. Emphasis is on rationales, rather than proofs. Topics covered: simple interest and simple discount, compound interest (with special attention given to the concepts of compound interest, discounting with compound interest, equivalent rates, and equations of value, which are the foundation for the rest of the course); simple annuities; amortization and sinking funds; general annuities; and bonds. (3 semester hours)

Trigonometry

A precalculus course with emphasis on the special functions of calculus: the circular functions (sin, cos, etc.) and their inverses (arcsin, arccos, etc.), the exponential functions and the inverses (the logarithmic functions). Covers measurement of angles. (3 semester hours)

Applicable Mathematics

An entry-level course for the nontechnical student, dealing with some of the techniques that allow mathematics to be applied to a variety of problems. Topics include linear and quadratic equations, systems of linear equations, matrices, probability, statistics, exponential and logarithmic functions, and mathematics of finance. (3 semester hours)

Elementary Functions and Coordinate Geometry

Study of elementary functions, their graphs and applications, including polynomial, rational, and algebraic functions, exponential, logarithmic, and trigonometric functions. (3 semester hours)

Calculus I for Business and Economics

Differential and integral calculus of algebraic, logarithmic, and exponential functions with applications; introduction to mathematics of finance. (4 semester hours)

Calculus II for Business and Economics

Introduction to applications of differential and integral calculus, including functions of several variables. Topics will include problems involving maxima and minima, techniques of integration, differential equations, series, probability, linear programming, and matrices. (4 semester hours)

Differential and Integral Calculus

Introduction to the theory and applications of differential and integral calculus of functions of one variable; topics include limits, continuity, differentiation, the mean value theorem and its applications, integration, the fundamental theorem of calculus, and transcendental functions. (4 semester hours)

Sequences, Series, and Multivariable Calculus

Introduction to the theory and applications of sequences and infinite series, including those involving functions of one variable, and to the theory and applications of differential and integral calculus of functions of several variables; topics include parametric equations, sequences, infinite series, power series, vectors, vector calculus, functions of several variables, partial derivatives, gradients, and multiple integrals. (4 semester hours)

Linear Algebra and Matrix Theory

Linear equations and matrices, linear mappings, determinants, eigenvalues, quadratic forms. (3 semester hours)

Foundations of Arithmetic

An analysis, from an advanced perspective, of the concepts and algorithms of arithmetic, including sets; numbers; numeration systems; definitions, properties, and algorithms of arithmetic operations; and percents, ratios, and proportions. Problem solving is stressed. (3 semester hours)

Foundations of Geometry, Statistics, and Probability

An analysis, from an advanced perspective, of the basic concepts and methods of geometry, statistics, and probability, including representation and analysis of data; discrete probability, random events, and conditional probability; measurement; and geometry as approached through similarity and congruence, through coordinates, and through transformation. Problem solving is stressed. (3 semester hours)

Introduction to Number Theory

Properties of integers, divisibility, linear and quadratic forms, prime numbers, congruences and residues, quadratic reciprocity, and number theoretic functions. (3 semester hours)

Structure of Modern Geometry

Basic ideas of plane and solid geometry; ruler and compass constructions; representation of space objects by plane projections; use of these ideas in teaching plane and solid geometry. (3 semester hours)

NURSING

Specialized Topics in Nursing - Statistical Methods in Psychology

Introductory descriptive and inferential statistics designed for the student who knows relatively little mathematics. Recommended for majors who plan to do graduate work in psychology or related fields. Measures of central tendency and variability; statistical inference; correlation and regression. (3 semester hours)

NUTRITION

Introductory Nutrition

Essential food components and their functions in life processes. (3 semester hours)

PHILOSOPHY

Contemporary Moral Problems

Primarily for lower-division students. Philosophical examination of selected moral problems arising out of contemporary society and culture. (3 semester hours)

Introduction to Philosophy

A survey of major philosophical problems, with readings from classical and modern philosophers. (3 semester hours)

Introduction to Logic

Logical structure of sentences; deductive and inductive arguments; principles of reasoning; fallacies, practical applications. (3 semester hours)

PHYSICS

Mechanics

Designed for students who intend to major in science or mathematics. (3 semester hours)

General Physics - Technical Course: Mechanics, Heat, and Sound

Terminal technical course for Allied Health Majors and others - not recommended for premedical students. (3 semester hours)

General Physics - Technical Course: Electricity and Magnetism, Light, and Atomic and Nuclear Physics

Terminal technical course for Allied Health majors and others—not recommended for premedical students. (3 semester hours)

Elementary Physics for Nontechnical Students: Mechanics, Heat, and Sound

Designed for students who do not intend to do further work in science, engineering, or medicine. This section emphasizes reading in science over problem solving. No laboratory is required. (3 semester hours)

Elementary Physics for Nontechnical Students: Electricity and Magnetism, Light, and Atomic and Nuclear Physics

Designed for students who do not intend to do further work in science, engineering, or medicine. This section emphasizes reading in science over problem solving. No laboratory is required. (3 semester hours)

PSYCHOLOGY

Introduction to Psychology

Basic problems and principles of human experience and behavior. (3 semester hours)

Introduction to Child Psychology

Psychological and behavioral development from conception through childhood. (3 semester hours)

Personality

Research and theory concerning personality structure, dynamics, development, and assessment. (3 semester hours)

Statistical Methods in Psychology

Introductory descriptive and inferential statistics designed for the student who knows relatively little mathematics. Measures of central tendency and variability; statistical inference; correlation and regression. (3 semester hours)

Social Psychology

Theory and research on the analysis of human conduct in social settings. (3 semester hours)

Abnormal Psychology

Biological and social factors in the development and treatment of psychopathology. (3 semester hours)

RADIO-TELEVISION-FILM

Development of the Motion Picture

Survey of significant movements and schools of filmmaking through viewings and discussions of representative motion pictures; critical approaches to performance, sociological impact, and visual aesthetics Course includes one video tape. (3 semester hours)

SOCIOLOGY

Introduction to the Study of Society

The nature of human societies, social processes, social interaction, and the sociological approach. (3 semester hours)

The Nuclear Threat

Provides an introduction to one of the major social issues of the century and the debates surrounding it. Major topics include an overview of nuclear warfare, origins of the arms race, consequences of the nuclear arms race, prevention of nuclear war, and the fate of planet Earth. (3 semester hours)

Racial and Ethnic Relations

The place of minorities in the social order; comparative studies of race relations in the United States in other societies. (3 semester hours)

SPANISH

First-Year Spanish I

Understanding both written and spoken Spanish is the course object. Access to a cassette recorder is required. (5 semester hours)

First-Year Spanish II

Continued practice in reading and comprehension of spoken Spanish. Access to a cassette recorder is required. (5 semester hours)

Second-Year Spanish I: Oral Expression, Reading, and Composition

Access to an cassette recorder is required. (3 semester hours)

Second-Year Spanish II: Oral Expression, Reading, and Composition

A continuation of the above course. The course continues to reinforce fundamental structures of language and vocabulary expansion through more challenging cultural and literary readings. Access to a cassette recorder is required. (3 semester hours)

Advanced Composition

Translation from English texts into Spanish and free composition; special attention to idiomatic expressions and grammatical and syntactical features. (3 semester hours)

SPECIAL EDUCATION

Orientation to Teaching in Special Education

Offers one semester hour of credit for the successful completion of 30 hours of supervised volunteer work involving people with disabilities. Students keep a journal and respond to questions relating to their volunteer work. The purpose of the course is to allow students to explore the field of special education. (1 semester hour)

HIGH SCHOOL COURSES

BUSINESS EDUCATION

Accounting, First Semester

Covers the first three parts of the textbook—Accounting as a Career, Accounting for a Service Business, and Accounting for a Merchandising Business. (½ unit)

Accounting, Second Semester

Covers the last three parts of the textbook—An Automatic Accounting System, An Accounting System with Special Journals, and Accounting Control Systems. (½ unit)

ECONOMICS

Economics

Covers various aspects of the U.S. economic system, including the nature of a free enterprise system, a mixed-market economy, and government in relation to the mixed-market economy. Also covers international economics and income tax. (½ unit)

ENGLISH

English 1, First Semester

Various forms of literature are studied with emphasis on developing writing, reading, and analytical skills. Also emphasizes development of grammar skills through exercises. Incorporates grammar activities with writing assignments. Introduces literary concepts and terms, and encourages students to build communication skills. Each lesson contains a substantial writing component. Reading selections include modern and classical fiction and nonfiction emphasizing cultural diversity. (½ unit)

English 1, Second Semester

A continuation of English 1; integrates classical and modern literature with the study of writing, reading, and communication skills. Lessons include sections devoted to analysis, grammar, and vocabulary development. Writing process stressed with focus on grammar skills. Reading selections reflect diverse cultures. (½ unit)

English 2, First Semester

English 2 is a course that incorporates the study of both grammar and literature. A strong writing component includes activities that encourage the development of grammar skills. Workshop-style writing assignments focus on standard modes of writing. Assignments and exercises are based on a diverse group of readings from the text. Readings include fiction, nonfiction, and poetry. (½ unit)

English 2, Second Semester

A continuation of English 2, incorporating the study of both grammar and literature. A strong writing component includes activities that encourage the development of grammar skills. Journal entries encourage creative writing and reflection on the diverse text selections including fiction, nonfiction, and poetry. Workshop-style writing assignments focus on standard modes of writing. (½ unit)

English 3A: Junior Grammar and Composition

Incorporates many of the essential elements that pertain to literature (student reads two American novels) into a course based on a composition text. (½ unit)

English 3B: Junior Literature

Covers the essential elements that pertain to literature in the junior year, plus compositions. (½ unit)

English 4, First Semester

A survey course of British literature from the Anglo-Saxon period through the 19th century, including an intensive study of *Macbeth*. Lessons stress reading for understanding and analysis, and writing/composition skills, with attention to the writing process. Also integrated into the lessons are exercises for vocabulary development and grammar review. (½ unit)

English 4, Second Semester

The first half of the course surveys 20th-century British literature, and the second half surveys works from African and Hispanic writers. Like English 4, First Semester, this course stresses reading skills and vocabulary, but places even greater emphasis on writing. (½ unit)

GERMAN

German 1, First Semester

Beginning study of the German language through the development of skills in listening, speaking, reading, and writing. Introduces the student to the history and culture of German-speaking peoples. Student must have access to a cassette tape recorder. (½ unit)

German 1, Second Semester

Continuation of the above course through the development of skills in listening, speaking, reading, and writing. Student must have access to a cassette recorder. (½ unit)

German 2, Fist Semester

Intermediate study of the German language through continued development of listening, speaking, reading, writing skills, and exposure to German culture and language structure. Student must have access to a cassette tape recorder. (½ unit)

German 2, Second Semester

Further intermediate study of the German language through development of listening, speaking, reading, writing skills, and exposure to German culture and language structure. Student must have access to a cassette tape recorder. (½ unit)

HEALTH

Health Education

Covers the essential elements for Health Education. Requires some community research work and access to a library. (½ unit)

HOME ECONOMICS

Individual and Family Life

Introduces students to the complexities of family life, including the concepts and skills related to the individual's role within the family, family life patterns, adult roles, management in family life, parenting, and special concerns of the family. (½ unit)

MATHEMATICS

Algebra 1, First Semester

Presents the fundamentals of algebraic operations, equations of first degree, graphs, ratios, and proportion. (½ unit)

Algebra 1, Second Semester

Presents the fundamentals of algebraic operations, equations of first degree, graphs, ratios, and proportion. (½ unit)

Algebra 2, First Semester

Presents coordinates of points, quadratic equations, factoring and theory of equations, fractions and fractional equations, exponents and radicals, and logarithms. (½ unit)

Algebra 2, Second Semester

Presents coordinates of points, quadratic equations, factoring and theory of equations, fractions and fractional equations, exponents and radicals, and logarithms. (½ unit)

Elementary Analysis

Includes linear relations; polynomial functions; matrices, determinants, and vectors; arithmetic and geometric series; relationship between rectangular and polar coordinates; logarithmic and exponential functions; properties and graphs of the straight line and conics; probability and statistics; and intuitive calculus. (½ unit)

Geometry, First Semester

Presents most of the classical topics of plane, Euclidean geometry together with some topics of solid geometry (especially those emphasizing space perception). Offers the logical development of the subject from undefined terms, postulates, and definitions. (½ unit)

Geometry, Second Semester

A continuation of the above course. (½ unit)

Pre-Algebra, First Semester

Covers operations on fractions and on decimals, solution of equations, using formulas to solve problems, using graphs to organize data, and an introduction to the metric system of measurement. (½ unit)

Pre-Algebra, Second Semester

Covers percent, statistics, ratio and proportion, operations with integers and rational numbers, solving equations and inequalities, geometric properties, and coordinate geometry. (½ unit)

Trigonometry

Includes computational and analytical portions of trigonometry. (½ unit)

PHYSICAL EDUCATION

Physical Education 1A: Orientation to Physical Education

Introduces students to the basic concepts of physical education and requires performance of physical activities and various fitness tests. *Note:* This course requires physical exertion equal to that of the regular classroom. Students who have doubts as to their physical condition should consult a physician before attempting this course. (½ unit)

Physical Education 1B: Lifetime Sports

Bowling. Introduces a walking or jogging program and requires research and participation in a lifetime sport. Responsible adult must verify participation in required activities. Students need to have access to equipment necessary for bowling. (½ unit)

Golf. See previous course description. Students need to have access to equipment necessary for golf. (½ unit)

Tennis. See course description above. Students need to have access to equipment necessary for tennis. (½ unit)

SCIENCE

Biology 1, First Semester

Study of physical and chemical characteristics of living things, makeup and functions of humans. One outside reading book is required. Students must have access to microscope. This is a laboratory course. (½ unit)

Biology 1, Second Semester

Includes study of health, changes in living things, genetics, and conservation. This is a laboratory course. (½ unit)

Physical Science, First Semester

Reading and laboratory course for beginning students. (½ unit)

Physical Science, Second Semester

Reading and laboratory course for beginning students. (½ unit)

SOCIAL STUDIES

Basic United States Government

This course satisfies the state requirement for U.S. and Texas government. Especially designed for students with reading difficulties. (½ unit)

U.S. Government

This course satisfies the state requirement for U.S. and Texas government. (½ unit)

U.S. History, First Semester

Covers the period from 1877 to approximately 1929. Includes social, economic, and political history. (½ unit)

U.S. History, Second Semester

A continuation of the above course. Covers U.S. history from approximately 1929 to the present. The two semesters together cover the essential elements for the required course in U.S. history. (½ unit)

World Geography Studies, First Semester

Covers geography skills plus three geographical areas—Anglo-America, North Africa/Southwest Asia, and Latin America. (½ unit)

World Geography Studies, Second Semester

Covers eight areas—Sub-Saharan Africa, Australia, Europe, Japan, China, Southeast Asia, Soviet Union, and India. (½ unit)

World History Studies, First Semester

Covers the period of world history from ancient Egypt through the French Revolution (1789). Map skills and other social studies are taught. (½ unit)

World History Studies, Second Semester

Covers the period from 1789 to the present. Social studies skills are taught. (½ unit)

SPANISH

Spanish 1, First Semester

Beginning study of the Spanish language through the development of skills in listening, speaking, reading, and writing. Introduces the student to the history and culture of Spanish-speaking peoples. Student must have access to a cassette tape recorder. (½ unit)

Spanish 1, Second Semester

Continuation of beginning study of the Spanish language through the development of skills in listening, speaking, reading, and writing. Introduces the student to the history and culture of Spanish-speaking peoples. Students must have access to a cassette tape recorder. (½ unit)

Spanish 2, First Semester

Intermediate study of the Spanish language through continued development of listening, speaking, reading, writing skills. Study of the Spanish language as well as exposure to the culture of Spanish-speaking peoples. Students must have access to a cassette tape recorder. (½ unit)

Spanish 2, Second Semester

Continued intermediate study of the Spanish language through development of listening, speaking, reading, and writing skills, with emphasis on speaking and writing skills. Student must have access to a cassette tape recorder. (½ unit)

SPECIAL EDUCATION

Orientation to Special Education

This one-hour college course in special education is especially well suited to high school students in grades 11 and 12 who are interested in working with disabled people and who are considering professions in such areas as special education. No required textbook; no exam; pass/fail credit only. (1 semester hour)

Texas Tech University
Guided Study
Division of Continuing Education
Box 42191
15th Street and Akron Avenue
Lubbock, Texas 79409-2191   (806) 742-2352

Description:

Created in 1923, Texas Tech University is a multipurpose state university which provides the opportunity for a liberal education for all students and for professional training at the undergraduate and graduate levels. The Division of Continuing Education recognizes continuing education as one of the university's major functions and offers programs for professional development, cultural personal enrichment, and nontraditional opportunities for degree-seeking students.

As part of the Division of Continuing Education, the Guided Study Program offers instruction by mail to all qualified students who are interested in academic, cultural, career, personal, and professional advancement, at both the high school and college levels.

Faculty:

Dr. Suzanne Logan, Director, Guided Study. There is a faculty of 122 members.

Academic Levels:
College
High School
Noncredit
Professional

Degree/Certificate Programs:

A maximum of 18 semester hours of credit toward a baccalaureate degree at Texas Tech may be completed through correspondence. Credits may also be applied toward associate degrees, diplomas, and certificates. Texas Tech students wishing to apply correspondence courses toward degree requirements must obtain approval of their academic deans prior to enrollment.

Admission Requirements:

Open enrollment. A student currently in high school must obtain written approval of his/her high school official to take a high school correspondence course. Enrollment in basic college correspondence courses is open to eligible senior-level high school students who must have written approval of their high school administrators.

Tuition:

College courses, $50 per semester hour; high school courses, $79 per ½ unit of credit; continuing education courses are $22 per CEU. There is a processing fee of $20 per course. Present members of the Armed Forces should contact their Education Officer for eligibility under DANTES. A course refund (less $10 for the course study guide) can be granted provided a written refund request is received within eight weeks of the date of enrollment. The portion of the course fee (75 percent, 50 percent, or 25 percent) to be refunded is determined by the date the study guide was mailed from the Independent Study Office and the date the refund request was received. No refund is made after eight weeks.

Enrollment Period:

Maximum completion time is nine months; the minimum time allowed is one month. One nine-month extension may be allowed upon payment of a $12 per month.

Equipment Requirements:

The cost of textbooks is not included in the tuition. Texts may be purchased locally or through the Texas Tech University Bookstore. Supplemental materials (slide sets, prints, and cassette tapes) usually require a deposit, a portion of which is refundable when the materials are returned in reusable condition to the Independent Study Office.

Credit and Grading:

The grading system for college courses is A, B, C, D, F; the minimum passing grade is D. Number grades are given for high school courses; the minimum passing grade is 70. Correspondence courses for which academic credit is awarded require proctored final examinations which comprise a substantial part of the final grade. Some courses also require other examinations. The proctor must be approved by Texas Tech. Credit is awarded in semester hour units.

Accreditations:

Southern Association of Colleges and Schools. Member of: National University Continuing Education Association.

COLLEGE COURSES

ACCOUNTING

Elementary Accounting I

Accounting for merchandise operations, proprietorships, negotiable instruments, specialized books of original entry, and the voucher system. (3 semester hours)

Elementary Accounting II

Second course in elementary accounting. Partnerships, corporations, cost accounting, assets, theory, principles of accounting, and interpretation of financial statements. (3 semester hours)

AGRICULTURAL ECONOMICS

Fundamentals of Agricultural Economics

Basic training in fundamental economic principles and their application to agricultural problems. (3 semester hours)

Principles of Marketing Agricultural Products

Introduction to the marketing of agricultural products emphasizing marketing costs, margins, and functions; and showing applications of economic principles to marketing problems. (3 semester hours)

Cooperatives in Agriculture

Organization and operation of agricultural cooperatives. (3 semester hours)

AGRICULTURAL SCIENCE

The Agriculture Industry

An overview of the agriculture with special topics including orientation, career guidance, and current trends. (1 semester hour)

AGRONOMY

Soil and Water Conservation

Factors affecting wind and water erosion; soil and water conservation practices; planning for optimum land use. (3 semester hours)

Soil Fertility Management

Nutrient availability as influenced by the properties of soils, use of fertilizers, and soil amendments; methods and time of application of fertilizer. (4 semester hours)

ANTHROPOLOGY

Cultural Anthropology

An introduction to the study of human culture and its variations in contemporary and recent historic peoples, both western and nonwestern. (3 semester hours)

BUSINESS LAW

Business Law

Nature and source of law, courts and procedure, contracts, Texas law of separate and community property, agency. (3 semester hours)

CURRICULUM AND INSTRUCTION

Computing and Information Technology

Use of computers as productivity tools, societal and ethical implications of computers, and applications of computers and related technology in society. (3 semester hours)

Introduction to Small Computers in Education

Designed for the student who is a beginner in the area of working with computers. Its purpose is to provide the student with a broad, general overview of what personal computers are, how they work, and what they can do. Terminology relating to personal computers and concepts involved in using personal computers also are covered. (3 semester hours)

ECONOMICS

Principles of Economics I (Micro)

Emphasis on theories of the firm, value and price determination, and functional distribution, with the application of these theories to the problems of particular firms, industries, and markets. (3 semester hours)

Principles of Economics II (Macro)

An introduction to modern economic society and theories of production and exchange. Emphasis upon monetary and fiscal policy and macroeconomics. (3 semester hours)

EDUCATIONAL PSYCHOLOGY

Individual Study/Control Theory and Reality Therapy

This course teaches the concepts of human relations from a control theory and reality theory perspective and how to apply the principles of reality therapy to take more effective control of your life. (3 semester hours)

Individual Study/Stress Management

Basic information about stress, its effects, and how to manage it are presented in this course. Experimental activities develop technical skills in coping with stress and burnout. Also productive coping mechanisms to attain excellence, success, and leadership are explored. (3 semester hours)

Seminar in Counseling/Reality Therapy and Control Theory

This self-contained course is designed to teach the concepts of control theory and the practice of reality therapy. The focus of the course is on your understanding your behavior from a control theory perspective and being able to apply the principles of reality therapy to take more effective control of your life. (3 semester hours)

Seminar in Counseling/Stress Management

Participants analyze and apply basic information about stress, its effects, and how it can be managed. Course activities require participants to apply their technical skills in order to cope with stress and burnout. By practicing producing coping mechanisms, participants will move toward their personal excellence, success, and leadership. (3 semester hours)

ENGINEERING

Professionalism and Ethics in Engineering

A course whose scope includes historical development, background and goals, moral reasoning and dilemmas, standards, law, safety and risk, case studies, the engineer's concern for safety, professionalism, professional responsibility and employer authority, rights of engineers, global awareness, codes of ethics, and fundamental responsibilities of engineers. (3 semester hours)

ENGLISH

Developmental Writing

Students are assigned to this course on the basis of testing and evaluation. Emphasizes the development of fluency and coherence in writing and increased capability in usage and grammar. (3 semester hours)

Essentials of College Rhetoric

Emphasis in the course is on grammar skills as they relate to writing and on rhetorical modes of exposition. (3 semester hours)

Advanced College Rhetoric

Focuses on writing from sources, research methods, and documentation. (3 semester hours)

Masterpieces of Literature

ENGL 2301. Representative works of Old and Middle English writers, Chaucer, Shakespeare, and Milton. (3 semester hours)

ENGL 2302. Six to eight masterpieces selected from the works of writers of the eighteenth, nineteenth and twentieth centuries. (3 semester hours)

Technical Writing

Introduction to the patterns of writing used in reports and letters for business, industry, and technology. (3 semester hours)

American Novel

Representative works of major American novelists. (3 semester hours)

Short Story

Short stories around the world. (3 semester hours)

Introduction to Literary Interpretation and Composition

A study of basic elements of grammatical usage, composition, and literary genres, with emphasis on fundamental knowledge and skills applicable to the analysis of literature and the process of composition. (3 semester hours)

FAMILY STUDIES

Courtship and Marriage

Designed to consider the role of interpersonal relationships of dating, courtship, and marriage. (3 semester hours)

FINANCE

Corporation Finance I

An introductory survey of corporation finance covering financial mathematics, capital budgeting, sources of funds, and financial analysis. Detailed analysis of the working capital decision. (3 semester hours)

Principles of Money, Banking, and Credit

A basic course, including consideration of monetary standards, organization and functioning of the commercial banking system and the Federal Reserve System, problems of money, prices, and credit control. Recent monetary and banking trends are emphasized. (3 semester hours)

Real Estate Fundamentals

Introduction to property law, finance, valuation, investment analysis and brokerage. Operations of the real estate market and the study of urban land use including urban growth, city structure, and land use planning. (3 semester hours)

Real Estate Finance

Mechanisms of real estate financing, sources of funds and financial institutions, governmental agencies. Financial instruments available to the investor, mortgage risk analysis, and loan principles. (3 semester hours)

Investments

Overview of various investment media and markets associated with them. Emphasis on fundamental and technical analysis, sources of information, and the efficient markets concept. (3 semester hours)

GEOGRAPHY

Regional Geography of the World

An introduction to the geography of world regions for students who have had no previous geography courses. (3 semester hours)

HEALTH, PHYSICAL EDUCATION, AND RECREATION

The Process of Recreation Programming

Study of the organization and planned use of recreation resources. Major emphasis will be on how to program recreation activities and experiences. (3 semester hours)

Managing Leisure Service Organizations

Application of contemporary techniques to the delivery of leisure services. Particular attention will be focused on the management of human resources. (3 semester hours)

HISTORY

Western Civilization I

Western Civilization from its dawn to the seventeenth century. Culture and the arts are stressed alongside politics. (3 semester hours)

Western Civilization II

The revolutionary transformations of European civilization in the seventeenth, eighteenth, and nineteenth centuries, world domination and the world wars, intellectual and cultural developments. (3 semester hours)

History of the United States to 1877

Most sections combine political, military, constitutional, and social history. Special sections, however, emphasize technology, agriculture, business, and family life. (3 semester hours)

History of the United States Since 1877

A continuation of the above course. (3 semester hours)

History of Texas

A survey of Texas history beginning with the Native American occupation and tracing the major social, political, and economic developments of the state into the modern era. (3 semester hours)

History of Sports and Recreation in the United States

Study of the development and role of sports and recreation in American social history with emphasis on organized amateur and professional sports. (3 semester hours)

The History of Baseball: A Mirror on America

Examines the history of the national pastime with an eye to how the sport has reflected and influenced American society since the late nineteenth century. (3 semester hours)

Modern Latin America

Survey of the principal events in Latin American history beginning with the independence movement and reaching into the contemporary scene. (3 semester hours)

HOTEL, RESTAURANT, AND INSTITUTIONAL MANAGEMENT

Hotel Operations

Principles and practices of managerial functions relating to the operation of hotel and motel facilities. (3 semester hours)

Introduction to Beverage Management

Principles and practices regarding the production, selection, storage, marketing, and serving of wine and spiritous beverages. Includes examination of wines and distilled spirits markets through out the world. (3 semester hours)

Hospitality Control I

Introduction to hospitality control devices needed to measure fiscal success. Includes computer applications in industry situation. (3 semester hours)

Hospitality Control II

Application of fiscal control devices in the hospitality industry. (3 semester hours)

Travel and Tourism

An analysis of the economic impact of travel and tourism in the hospitality industry, including demand for travel services and attraction development. (3 semester hours)

Beverage Control Management

Selection, storage, and service of beverages with emphasis on inventory control, sales promotion, and profits. (3 semester hours)

HUMAN DEVELOPMENT

Life Span Development

Introduction to the theories, processes, and enhancement of development for infants, young children, adolescents, and adults. (3 semester hours)

INFORMATION SYSTEMS AND QUANTITATIVE SCIENCES

Introduction to Business Statistics

Techniques of analysis of numerical data including measures of central tendency and dispersion, probability distributions, hypothesis testing, linear regression, and time series. (4 semester hours)

Introduction to Production and Operations Management

An overview of the production and operations function in organizations with examples of the application of computer and quantitative skills to management problems. Both design and operating problems are discussed. (3 semester hours)

MANAGEMENT

Managerial Communication

The application of oral and written communication principles to managerial situations; an overview, simulation, and analysis of the communication process in the business environment. (3 semester hours)

MARKETING

Introduction to Marketing

Marketing structures and agencies; motives and buying habits; types of middlemen, marketing institutions, and channels; current marketing practices; marketing of industrial and consumer goods. (3 semester hours)

MASS COMMUNICATIONS

Introduction to Mass Communications

A broad survey of communications in modern life with particular emphasis on print media, broadcasting, advertising, and public relations. (3 semester hours)

History of American Journalism

Study of the development of journalism in America from its European roots to the present and of its interrelation with society. (3 semester hours)

Principles of Public Relations

A study of the policies and procedures of creating and maintaining good will among organizations' various publics. Examines the many aspects of public relations as a staff and management function. (3 semester hours)

Introduction to Telecommunications

Basic instruction in the origin, history, development, regulation, and social responsibilities of broadcasting and cable communications. Examines new technology and telecommunication systems. (3 semester hours)

MATHEMATICS

Essential Mathematics

A remedial course for students with weak preparation in fundamental mathematics and geometry. (3 semester hours)

College Algebra

Inequalities; determinants; theory of equations; binomial theorem; progressions; mathematical induction. (3 semester hours)

Trigonometry

Trigonometric functions; radians; logarithms; solutions of triangles, identities; trigonometric equations; complex numbers; DeMoivre's Theorem. (3 semester hours)

Introductory Mathematical Analysis

MATH 1330. Set theory; inequalities; functions; matrices; linear programming; probability; elementary statistics; mathematics of finance. (3 semester hours)

MATH 1331. Differential, integral, and multivariable calculus. (3 semester hours)

Analytical Geometry

Fundamental concepts of analytical geometry. (3 semester hours)

Calculus I

Differentiation of algebraic functions, applications of the derivative, differentials, indefinite integrals, definite integrals. (3 semester hours)

Calculus II

Methods of integration, parametric equations, polar coordinates, hyperbolic functions, applications. (3 semester hours)

Calculus III

Partial differentiation; functions of several variables; multiple integrals. (3 semester hours)

Statistical Methods

Methods of analyzing data; statistical concepts and models; estimation; tests of significance; introduction to analysis of variance, linear regression, and correlation. (3 semester hours)

MUSIC

Songwriting

A beginning course for nonmusic majors. A practical approach to music theory through songwriting. Includes aural training, notation, textual setting, melodic writing, and chord assignment. (3 semester hours)

NUTRITION

Nutrition and Food

Science of nutrition and food as applied to everyday living. Designed to convey basic nutrition concepts as they apply to the individual students. (4 semester hours)

PHILOSOPHY

Beginning Philosophy

An introduction to philosophical thinkers, ideas, and methods. (3 semester hours)

POLITICAL SCIENCE

American Government Organization

Constitutions and organization of the governments of the United States, the states in general, and Texas in particular. (3 semester hours)

American Public Policy

The policy-making process in the governments of the United States, the states in general, and Texas in particular. (3 semester hours)

PSYCHOLOGY

General Psychology

Introduction to fundamental concepts in psychology. Emphasis on the physiological, social, and environmental determinants of behavior. (3 semester hours)

Child Psychology

A study of the developmental processes and environmental factors which shape the personality and affect the achievement of the child. (3 semester hours)

Mental Health

A study of the individual and social factors which contribute to the development of both healthy and unhealthy personalities. (3 semester hours)

Adolescent Psychology

A general review of approaches to the understanding of social behavior and development of the adolescent. Physical, mental, and emotional growth and adjustment are covered. (3 semester hours)

Introduction to Social Psychology

Study of individual experience and behavior in relation to social stimulus situations. Survey of experimental work and reports on current problems. (3 semester hours)

Personality

Principles of normal personality structure. (3 semester hours)

Psychology of Human Sexual Behavior

Study of human sexual behavior from a psychosocial viewpoint with emphasis on contemporary research methods and findings. (3 semester hours)

Abnormal Psychology

Personality deviations and maladjustments; emphasis on clinical descriptions of abnormal behavior, etiological factors, manifestations, interpretations, and treatments. (3 semester hours)

Drugs, Alcohol, and Behavior

Survey of psychological factors involved in drug use and an introduction to chemotherapy used in treatment of mental illness. (3 semester hours)

SOCIOLOGY

Introduction to Sociology

Human group behavior, influence on the individual, and relationships of individuals to each other as members of groups. (3 semester hours)

Current Social Problems

Problems in basic social institutions as marriage and the family, community, economy, government, education, health and welfare, recreation, etc. (3 semester hours)

HIGH SCHOOL COURSES

AGRICULTURE

General Agriculture

Course AG 1A. This course covers the agricultural industry and agricultural occupations with opportunities in agriculture; a study of farm animals including characteristics improvement, feeding, proper care, their products, and their health; farm management; marketing farm products. (½ unit)

Course AG 1B. This course is about life in rural America. It covers crop plants, their characteristics, improvement, and culture; weeds as crop plant enemies, their characteristics, and control; insects and diseases which attack crop plants, their classification and control; soils and other natural resources with methods of conservation. (½ unit)

ART

Beginning Drawing

This course is designed to develop your understanding of your visual environment and your representation of it on paper. Throughout the course, you will be introduced to the tools and techniques that artists use in 2D representation. You will develop a visual vocabulary and learn basic compositional principles. Drawing assignments will include studies in general drawing, contour drawing, basic form and value shading, perspective landscapes and seascapes, human figures, portraiture, and abstractions of nature in drawing. (½ unit)

BIOLOGY

Biology I

BIO 1A. This course explores the world of life: cells—the basic unit of life; genetics and heredity—the continuity of life; evolution—diversity of life; and life on earth (plants)—monerans, protists, and fungi. (½ unit)

BIO 1B. This course explores life on earth (animals); invertebrate animals; vertebrate animals; human biology; and ecological interactions. (½ unit)

BUSINESS COMMUNICATIONS

Business Communications

BCOM 1A. This course explores basic business communications skills, psychology of communication, review of grammar skills, sentence and paragraph formation. (½ unit)

BCOM 1B. Writing process, business letter format, types of written messages, speaking and listening, careers, job-searching and follow-up letters. (½ unit)

BUSINESS EDUCATION

Business Computer Programming

An introduction to computers, computer-related terminology, history and development of computers, use of the computer, communicating instructions to the computer, and problems and issues of computer use in society. Using BASIC computer language, students are introduced to problem-solving skills, algorithm development, and syntax. (½ unit)

Business Computer Application

An introductory course for the use of computers in the business world. The course covers basic system components, ways computers improve decision-making, applications software; and hands-on experience with word processing, database, and spreadsheets. Students must have access to a computer printer, word processing, software, database, and spreadsheet software. (½ unit)

Introduction to Business

IBUS 1A. The student should develop an appreciation and understanding of the American enterprise system; how business is organized; the need for well-trained workers; consumer rights and responsibilities and the rights and responsibilities of workers; investors, managers, and governments of the American economy. (½ unit)

IBUS 1B. The student will study the impact of computer technology on businesses, individuals, and the economy; the function of the financial services industry; how to balance a budget for a family; how to use credit wisely; the importance of a savings plan; and the nature and causes of economic risks and how insurance provides protection. (½ unit)

Record Keeping

RECK 1A. Basic clerical and computational skills for entry-level position: checking accounts, petty cash, budget records, and charge sales. Incorporates realistic business and personal use of manual and computer operations. (½ unit)

RECK 1B. Use of manual or computer operations for realistic business and personal record keeping problems: stock records, accounts payable, payroll, and general ledger accounts for small businesses. Acquire entry-level skills for bookkeeping and accounting. (½ unit)

Accounting

ACCT 1A. An introductory accounting course in which the student learns accounting as an information system and learns processing of financial data. (½ unit)

ACCT 1B. A continuation of introductory accounting exploring data processing applications, tools for management, and electronic information processes. (½ unit)

Business and Consumer Law

BLAW 1A. For this course, you will review the Constitution in relation to the legal system. You will learn the classification of crimes and torts and identify the regulations concerning contracts and the use of credit. You will identify situations which require professional assistance and learn how to utilize that assistance. By using analytical and critical thinking throughout the course, you will have the knowledge and skills to become a responsible citizen in business and personal relations. (½ unit)

BLAW 1B. This course helps you identify the different kinds of

working relationships; learn the responsibilities of being on one's own; become familiar with the various negotiable instruments; identify the types of business ownerships and what they entail; and plan for retirement. (½ unit)

Business Management and Ownership

BMO 1A. Includes facts, procedures, and concepts that will aid the student in becoming an effective member of the business community. Employment opportunities in the business world and business terms also are covered. (½ unit)

BMO 1B. A continuation of the above course. (½ unit)

ECONOMICS

Economics, Fundamentals of the Free Enterprise System and Its Benefits

A study of the American free enterprise system which is characterized by private ownership of the means of production and distribution of goods and services. Includes the role of free markets in the determination of prices and the allocation of the nation's resources. (½ unit)

ENGLISH

Correlated Language Arts I

CLA 9A. An integrated study of literature, language, writing, and reading skills. The combination of composition, grammar, vocabulary, and comprehension skills enhances the student's ability to understand the writing process. (½ unit)

CLA 9B. A continuation of *CLA 9A.* (½ unit)

Correlated Language Arts II

CLA 10A. An integrated study of language, writing, and reading skills. Helps the student to recognize major differences among poems, short stories, and plays. (½ unit)

CLA 10B. A continuation of *CLA 10A.* (½ unit)

Correlated Language Arts III

CLA 11A. An integrated study of literature from the colonial period through the late nineteenth century to improve the student's writing, language, and reading skills. Composition, grammar, vocabulary, and comprehension skills enhances the student's critical thinking skills. (½ unit)

CLA 11B. A continuation of *CLA 11A.* (½ unit)

Correlated Language Arts IV

CLA 12A. Course in world literature which combines and develops the student's language, literature, and composing skills. Emphasis is on basic language skills such as the fundamentals of grammar, basic organization of paragraphs, and basic analysis of literature. (½ unit)

CLA 12B. A continuation of *CLA 12A.* (½ unit)

English I

ENG 9A. An integrated study of language, grammar, and literature designed to help the student explore historical settings, literary techniques, and literary styles of many distinguished authors. (½ unit)

ENG 9B. An integrated study of grammar, rhetoric, and literature designed to enhance the student's reading and writing skills. The course also examines drama and discusses works of several eminent authors. (½ unit)

English II

ENG 10A. An integrated study of communication, lexicography, grammar, and literature designed to develop critical reading and writing skills. Introduces some major American writers of the late nineteenth and twentieth centuries. (½ unit)

ENG 10B. An integrated study of grammar, composition, syntax, and literature designed to increase student expertise and enjoyment in these areas. (½ unit)

English III

ENG 11A. A survey of American literature from America's beginnings to the twentieth century, with emphasis on clear expression and effective interpretation. Composition and grammar are included. (½ unit)

ENG 11B. American literature of the twentieth century studied by genres—short story, poetry, article and essay, biography, drama, and novel. Awareness of our language and its importance in the modern world for communication is increased. (½ unit)

English IV

ENG 12A. A study of British literature from 450 to 1780. The fundamentals of grammar and composition are also emphasized. (½ unit)

ENG 12B. A continuation of British literature from 1780 to today. Grammar and composition are explored in this course. (½ unit)

ENG 12A Honors. This survey course in British literature emphasizes the analysis of literature and the composing process. The fundamentals of grammar and mechanics also are emphasized in the composing process. To succeed in the course, the student must maintain a consistent study approach. (½ unit)

ENG 12B Honors. A continuation of studies in English literature and the fundamentals of grammar and mechanics, vocabulary, and theme writing. (½ unit)

FAMILY STUDIES

Advanced Child Development

Begins with the impact of parenting on the individual(s). Develops concepts related to prenatal and postnatal care, the development of children (including opportunities for making decisions), child care guidance techniques, career and job opportunities related to children, and special parenting techniques. (½ unit)

Individual and Family Life

Addresses the individual in the family and basic functions and roles of the family unit. Provides an opportunity to study the principles that affect family living, the responsibilities of adulthood, and career options and adjustments. (½ unit)

FRENCH

French Level I

FREN 1A. A beginning course in French. (½ unit)

FREN 1B. A continuation of the above course. (½ unit)

French Level II

FREN 2A. An intermediate course in French. (½ unit)

FREN 2B. A continuation of the above course. (½ unit)

GEOGRAPHY

World Geography Studies

GEO 1A. This course explores the nature of geography, physical setting of the earth, interaction of physical environments, and urban analysis. (½ unit)

GEO 1B. Continues the exploration of the nature of geography, emphasizing cultural geography including the economy and the customs of world regions. (½ unit)

GOVERNMENT

United States Government

A brief study of the American political heritage; modern political and economic systems; events leading to the writing of the Declaration of Independence and the Constitution; and informal amendments such as political parties, interest groups, and voting behavior. Legislative, executive, and judicial branches of the federal, state, and local government as well as civil rights are examined. (½ unit)

HEALTH

Health Education

Through decision making and problem solving, this course introduces wellness, personality, relationships, nutrition, fitness, human development, substance abuse, diseases, and environmental health. (½ unit)

Health Care Science

Course HCS 1A. This course introduces you to the different careers and skills needed to work in the medical field. Course content includes developing working relationships and patient relationships, legal and ethical issues, investigations of careers, and medical terminology. Entry level skills will be developed for safety and body mechanics, leadership, job seeking, and vital signs/CPR. (½ unit)

Course HCS 1B. The second course deals with human anatomy and physiology. Course content includes the different body systems, such as skeletal, muscular, cardiac, and endocrine. Basic information of the systems' functions in wellness as well as illness will be covered. (½ unit)

HISTORY

United States History

HIST 1A. American history from 1865 to the early twentieth century. (½ unit)

HIST 1B. American history from the early twentieth century to the present. (½ unit)

World History Studies

HIST 2A. This course covers world history from the prehistoric period to the seventeenth century. The development of western and eastern civilizations will be covered as well as the early civilizations in the Americas. (½ unit)

HIST 2B. The development of world civilization from early modern times to the present. (½ unit)

JOURNALISM

Journalism

Explores the essential elements of journalism from its history to its contemporary role through its basic features, journalistic writing, graphics, design and layout, and advertising. (½ unit)

LATIN

Latin Level I

LAT 1A. Reading and writing in Latin; learning Roman history and culture; understanding how Latin has influenced languages. (½ unit)

LAT 1B. A continuation of *LAT 1A.* (½ unit)

Latin Level II

LAT 2A. A continuation of *LAT 1B.* (½ unit)

LAT 2B. A continuation of *LAT 2A.* (½ unit)

LAW

Daily Life, Daily Law

This course is a look at the law as it affects the average person. You will learn how the legal system works as well as basic legal concepts. Topics covered include contracts, leases, warranties, marriage, divorce, child custody, child support, criminal law, rights of employees, sexual harassment, filing in small claims court, jury duty, and topics of special interest to minors. (½ unit)

MATHEMATICS

Pre-Algebra I

PALG 1A. Concepts and skills associated with understanding numbers and the place-value system; operations on numbers, factors and multiples, and fraction and decimal values. Continued study of skills and concepts associated with elementary algebra. Includes number operations, their properties and uses, decimals and fractions, and finding squares and square roots. (½ unit)

PALG 1B. A continuation of *PALG 1A.* (½ unit)

Algebra I

ALG 1A. This course will cover concepts and skills associated with integers, rational numbers, and their operations. Solving equations, inequalities, stated problems, manipulating exponential expressions, and techniques for factoring polynomials will be covered. (½ unit)

ALG 1B. This course will cover graphing of equations and inequalities, solving systems of equations; manipulating rational expressions, real numbers and radical expressions with emphasis on square root functions and quadratic equations. (½ unit)

Algebra II

ALG 2A. Linear equations and inequalities, polynomials, factoring, rational expressions, exponents, the quadratic formula, and complex numbers. (½ unit)

ALG 2B. Coordinate geometry, matrices, functions, systems progressions, and logarithmic and exponential functions. (½ unit)

Geometry I

GEOM 1A. Basics of geometry, including figures, measures, proofs, parallels, properties of congruences, and polygons. (½ unit)

GEOM 1B. A continuation of *GEOM 1A.* Similarity, circles, lines, areas, coordinate geometry, loci, inequalities, and solids also are included. (½ unit)

Analytic Geometry

Algebraic methods applied in the study of geometry. Graphing of lines, circles, ellipses, parabolas, and hyperbolas. Polar coordinates; parametric equations; algebraic curves; asymptotes. Knowledge of algebra and trigonometry is necessary. (½ unit)

Informal Geometry I

INFG 1A. Similarity, congruence, parallelism, and perpendicularity are topics you will examine. In addition, you will learn and apply measurement constructions, transformations, and properties of quadrilateral triangles and two- and three-dimensional figures. Create scale drawings of two- and three-dimensional figures as you learn the properties and essentials of plane geometry. (½ unit)

INFG 1B. A continuation of *INFG 1A.* (½ unit)

Trigonometry

Circular functions, basic identities, trigonometric equations, the law of sines and cosines. Common logarithms: characteristic and mantissa, using tables and interpolation, and computation. (½ unit)

Elementary Analysis

This course covers the real number system, analysis of relations and functions, polynomial functions, sequences and series, mathematical induction, and special functions. (½ unit)

Mathematics of Money

MOM 1A. With a "real world" emphasis, this course uses a problem-solving approach to work through such topics as earnings, deductions, budgets, investments, credit, mortgages, and secured loans. (½ unit)

MOM 1B. This course will help you learn about business finance. It focuses on the practical application of information concerning business revenue, costs, profits, controlling expenses, investments, maximizing profits, and financial trends. TAAS review included. (½ unit)

Computer Mathematics I

CMTH 1A. You will learn introductory programming using the BASIC language with applications in algebra, geometry, and consumer math. Skills will be developed using IF-THEN, FOR-next, GOTO, and sequential programming. (½ unit)

CMTH 1B. A continuation of the above course covering functions, subroutines, nested loops, and arrays with applications in algebra and geometry. (½ unit)

MUSIC

Music History and Literature

Works from major historical periods; composers; musical style; musical form; relationship of music to history. (½ unit)

Music Theory I

A study of basic pitch and rhythmic notation, scale structures, intervals, chord structure and movement, simple partwriting, and ear training. (½ unit)

NUTRITION

Food Science and Nutrition

This laboratory course emphasizes nutrition as it relates to dietary functions through the family life cycle, special dietary needs, and nutrient sources. Safety, sanitation, and nutrient retention in food preparation are addressed. It includes cultural influences on food patterns, management techniques, food preparation, and careers in food and nutrition. (½ unit)

PEER COUNSELING

Peer Counseling I: Project Self Discovery

This course enables you to take a long look at your inner world while seeing how you can help others. Designed as a "do-it-yourself kit," the course increases your knowledge of what people are like, introduces the basics of peer counseling, advances your general education, and improves your powers of self-understanding and self-expression. Course content emphasizes gaining self-confidence, self-acceptance, and self-discovery which includes identifying one's several "selves" and how they are combined to make up one's personality. (½ unit)

Peer Counseling II: Knowing Myself and Helping Others

This course focuses on helping students adjust emotionally while maturing physically. The author uses an effective approach by incorporating structured interaction with the student's peers. By stressing confidentiality and building the student's trust, the author encourages the student to be open about feelings and relations with others. (½ unit)

PHYSICAL EDUCATION

Bowling

Learning and practicing the basic mechanics of bowling such as stance, positions of the feet and ball, the approach, and the delivery. Scoring and understanding of the basic rules and etiquette of the game. A student must go to a bowling alley. (½ unit)

Dance I

Dance I is designed to acquaint you with the basic movements and techniques commonly used in all forms of dance. The course will lead you through beginning exercises and problem-solving activities to familiarize you with dance. Emphasis is placed on using proper and safe technique fitness-related material and student choreographics. You will be required to enroll in private lessons as a part of this course. (½ unit)

Dance II

Dance II increases the difficulty of dance techniques and introduces jazz styling. Again a strong emphasis is placed on using proper techniques, fitness, and student choreographics. Additional emphasis is given to nutrition for dancers. You will be required to enroll in private lessons as part of the course. (½ unit)

Foundations of Personal Fitness

This course will challenge you to develop your total fitness levels, including physical, mental, social, and emotional fitness, as you learn how to safely and effectively incorporate the five health-related components of fitness into your exercise program. (½ unit)

Golf

Understanding of how to apply the basic rules and principles governing golf and the ability to perform the following skills: the basic swing, pitching, chipping, putting, and playing out of the sand. Practice at a golf course is required. (½ unit)

Men's Artistic Gymnastics I

A study of the basic terminology and skills of men's basic gymnastics. Areas of study include tumbling, vault, low bar, and parallel bars. (½ unit)

Men's Artistic Gymnastics II

A study of the intermediate terminology and skills of men's gymnastics. Areas of study include floor exercises, rings, horizontal bar, and pommel horse. (½ unit)

Women's Artistic Gymnastics I

A study of the basic terminology and skills of women's gymnastics. Areas of study include tumbling, balance beam, low bar, and vault. (½ unit)

Women's Artistic Gymnastics II

A study of the intermediate terminology and skills of women's gymnastics. Areas of study include floor exercises, balance beam, uneven bars, and vault. (½ unit)

Racquetball

Understanding of rules, skills, and playing strategies. Practice on an organized team is recommended but not required. (½ unit)

Soccer

Rules, skills, and playing strategies. Practice on an organized team is recommended but not required. (½ unit)

Swimming I

(½ unit)

Swimming II

(½ unit)

Tennis

Basic skills are developed and basic rules for scoring match, terminology of the game, and basic singles and doubles strategies are learned. Team membership is not required but highly recommended. (½ unit)

Volleyball

This course is designed to teach the basic rules of the game and to develop playing skills. Participation in a volleyball league is required. (½ unit)

PHYSICAL SCIENCE

Introduction to Physical Science

INPS 1A. Fundamentals of physical science, including topics on matter and energy, motion, and electricity. (½ unit)

INPS 1B. A continuation of the above course. (½ unit)

Physical Science

PHSC 1A. The nature of science, importance of studying matter and energy, properties and measurement, forms and types of matter, the structure of matter, atoms and the periodic chart, physical changes, nuclear changes, motion, work, conservation of energy, and machines. (½ unit)

PHSC 1B. Electricity, magnetism, wave motion, sound waves, radiant energy, electromagnetic spectrum, electronics, aeronautics, rocket propulsion, technology, and engineering. (½ unit)

PHYSICS

Physics I

PHY 1A. Matter and energy, measurement, force, rectilinear motion, curvilinear motion, work, power, energy, thermal effects, change of state, kinetic theory of matter, heat and work, atomic structure, nuclear reactions, wave motion, and sound waves. (½ unit)

PHY 1B. The nature of light, reflection, refraction, diffraction and polarization, electrostatics, direct current circuits, heating and chemical effects, magnetic effects, electromagnetic induction; alternating current circuits, electronic devices, particle physics, and modern applications of physics. (½ unit)

PSYCHOLOGY

Psychology

After completing this course, you should have an understanding of the cycle of life, intellectual, physiological, and motivational characteristics, as well as the major theories of human behavior, abnormal behavior, and treatment. In addition, you will learn about social behavior, learning, thinking, and various states of consciousness. You will find this course helpful in understanding yourself and others as it takes you through lessons and activities that apply to your own life. (½ unit)

SOCIOLOGY

Sociology

This course examines people and their activities in social groups, emphasizing forces influencing individual behavior. (½ unit)

SPANISH

Spanish Level I

SPAN 1A. Begins the student's study of Spanish through listening, speaking, reading, writing, and learning about the culture while incorporating other essential elements for Spanish. (½ unit)

SPAN 1B. A continuation of the above course. (½ unit)

Spanish Level II

SPAN 2A. Continues the beginning student's study of Spanish through listening, speaking, reading, writing, and learning about the culture while incorporating other essential elements for Spanish. (½ unit)

SPAN 2B. A continuation of the above course. (½ unit)

NONCREDIT COURSES

BUSINESS

Business English

This basic, comprehensive course presents a thorough review of Standard English, including vocabulary, grammar, and composition. A variety of hands-on exercises help the student to use correct grammar and understand sentence structure as well as punctuate and capitalize correctly, write numbers correctly, and improve one's spelling ability. (2 CEUs)

Business Writing

The student can learn to write clearly, accurately, and fast; how to express valuable and complicated ideas in a way that pleases the reader and creates a pleasant, dignified image of you and the company; learn how to organize for the busy reader's needs, without fumbling over false starts and rewrites. These benefits apply equally to letters, reports, memos, and procedures—technical and nontechnical. (2 CEUs)

Entrepreneurship for Small Business: How to Write a Business Plan

This course explores the principles and practices of planning, starting, and operating a small-scale enterprise. You create your own actual business plan in preparation for securing financing. (3 CEUs)

CAREER EDUCATION

Projecting Yourself as a Winner

By working through the R.A.C.E. acronym—R, research; A, action plan; C, communication skills; and E, evaluation—you will develop new, personalized strategies and strengthen current skills. (1 CEU)

Re-entering the Workplace

This special noncredit course will help you learn about yourself, develop your skills, learn about jobs, determine your goals, conduct a job search, present yourself at your best, prepare for the interview, and start your new job. (2 CEUs)

EDUCATION

SAT and ACT Test Preparation

Improve your reading comprehension and analogy skills and build your vocabulary; prepare for ACT and SAT tests and learn college prep study skills and research skills. (3 CEUs)

ENGINEERING

Professionalism and Ethics in Engineering

The scope of this course in engineering ethics includes historical development, background and goals, moral reasoning and dilemmas, standards, law, safety and risk, case studies, the engineer's concern for safety, professionalism, professional responsibility and employer authority, rights of engineers, global awareness, codes of ethics, and fundamental responsibilities of engineers. (2, 4, or 6 CEUs) *Tuition:* $130, $245, or $360.

GENEALOGY

Genealogy

This course helps students find their ancestors. Lessons are arranged so students tackle a new phase of research with each lesson. Students learn how to search the home for genealogical facts, how and where to research, and how to write a family history. Differences between primary and secondary sources and how to document each also are discussed. (2.5 CEUs)

HOME INSPECTION

Inspecting Built-In Appliances

You will learn how to inspect and report procedures for major appliances attached to the structure such as dishwashers, compactors, ovens, and ranges. (1.5 CEUs) *Tuition:* $169 plus $20 processing fee.

Inspecting Plumbing Systems

This course presents information on how to check operation and identify leaks, corrosion, and other plumbing deficiencies. It includes: water heating systems, faucets, fixtures, commodes, lavatories, tubs, showers, drains, vents, and sewer systems. (1.5 CEUs) *Tuition:* $169 plus $20 processing fee.

Inspecting Electrical Systems

Inspection of different components such as gas, electrical, and fuel furnaces; heating and cooling distribution systems; refrigerated air conditioners; and heat pumps are covered in this course. (1.5 CEUs) *Tuition:* $169 plus $20 processing fee.

Inspecting Heating and Cooling Systems

Inspection of different components such as gas, electrical, and fuel furnaces; heating and cooling distribution systems; refrigerated air conditioners; and heat pumps are covered in this course. (1.5 CEUs) *Tuition:* $169 plus $20 processing fee.

Inspecting Structure and Site

You will learn how to inspect foundations and walls for cracks and water penetration and brick face for cracks. It also includes inspection of floor joints, wall framing, and roof support systems. Information on structural problems and landscape grading is presented. (1.5 CEUs) *Tuition:* $169 plus $20 processing fee.

PARALEGAL STUDIES

Introduction to the Legal Assistant Profession

This course presents a brief overview of the growing need for legal assistants, the birth and evolution of the profession, benefits and drawbacks of the profession, and what the future of legal assistants holds. (1 CEU) *Tuition:* $40.

Legal Terminology

During this course, you will study more than 500 legal terms used in the areas of criminal law, torts, contracts, personal property, bailments, agency, litigation, wills, estates, trust, real property, family law, negotiable instruments, and business organizations. This course provides a background for persons entering the legal field and/or in areas related to the legal field such as banking and insurance. (3 CEUs) *Tuition:* $120.

English for the Legal Assistant

You will review English grammar with emphasis on spelling, punctuation, capitalization, word usage, and sentence structure. (2 CEUs) *Tuition:* $80.

Introduction to the Law

This course introduces the American legal system including basic foundations of the law (both common and civil), the development and structure of the federal judicial system, various stages of litigation, and the U.S. Constitution as the source of rights and law. (1 CEU) *Tuition:* $40.

Civil Litigation

This course defines the basic concepts of civil litigation, with emphasis placed on federal civil litigation practice. (2 CEUs) *Tuition:* $80.

Writing for the Legal Assistant

This writing-intensive course stresses the fundamentals of clearly-written communications for the modern business world. Emphasis is on organizing and expressing ideas effectively in writing letters, memoranda, and reports. The use of clear, forceful English in written business communications is stressed. (2 CEUs) *Tuition:* $80.

Legal Research

This course provides you with a working knowledge of the major techniques of legal research and how to use a law library. During this class, you complete assigned problems in legal research and gain a basic knowledge of various legal research tools, including primary and secondary sources of law, judicial reports, and case findings. (2.5 CEUs) *Tuition:* $100.

Legal Writing

This course focuses on how to develop the logical and expressive skills necessary for effective legal writing. Through frequent writing assignments and examination of sample legal problems, you learn how to apply rules of law to fact situations and to construct effective legal arguments. (2 CEUs) *Tuition:* $80.

Corporate Law

This examination of various business entities includes partnerships, proprietorships, corporations, and unincorporated associations. Other topics include debt securities, directors' meetings, close corporations, and amendment of corporate bylaws. (2 CEUs) *Tuition:* $80.

Real Estate Law

This course presents the basic principles applicable to the use, enjoyment, and transfer of real property, including ownership, contracts, title, and transactions. (2 CEUs) *Tuition:* $80.

Introduction to Business Law

This course provides instruction and practice in handling both personal and business tasks. (2 CEUs) *Tuition:* $80.

Evidence

Important for trial preparation, this course helps you learn the critical skill of determining what evidence (witness testimony, physical evidence, photographs, in-court demonstration, etc.) is admissible in a court of law for the purpose of proving the case. You also learn why certain evidence may be objectionable. (2 CEUs) *Tuition:* $80.

Alternate Dispute Resolution

By reviewing appropriate federal and state ADR statues and regulations, you will gain a basic understanding of dispute resolution alternatives. Problem-solving exercises supplement your ADR knowledge for use within the litigation process. (2 CEUs) *Tuition:* $80.

Drafting of Legal Documents

This course includes instruction and practice in the drafting of pleadings, motions, orders, discovery, judgments, and other commonly used legal documents. (1 CEU) *Tuition:* $40.

Projecting Yourself as a Winner

By working through the R.A.C.E. acronym—R, research; A, action plan; C, communication skills; and E, evaluation—you will develop new, personalized strategies and strengthen current skills. (1 CEU) *Tuition:* $40.

Torts

This course provides instruction in the area of law that deals with private or civil wrongs or injuries other than the breach of contract. It concentrates on the elements of a tort, types of torts, damages and remedies, and workers' compensation laws. (2 CEUs) *Tuition:* $80.

Trial Preparation *Tuition:* You will learn the process which takes a lawsuit from inception to trial and recognize and perform the functions of a Legal Assistant throughout the process. (1 CEU) *Tuition:* $40.

REAL ESTATE

Real Estate Brokerage

This course covers the operational management of a real estate office. The student may take this course for credit with the Texas Real Estate Commission toward pre-licensing requirements, as a continuing education requirement to maintain a current Texas Real Estate License, or as credit toward obtaining a broker's license in the State of Texas. (2 CEUs)

WRITING

Creative Writing

This course presents the techniques of poetry and fiction while providing students practice in using the techniques to create original poems and short stories. Topics to be explored include poetic verse form, meter, characterization, and plot development. Practice in a variety of poetic and fictional genres also is included. (2 CEUs)

Creative Autobiography

This course will help you learn how your personal narratives can be presented in entertaining ways and with the kind of attention to detail that will make your experiences come alive both for your own enjoyment and for that of others. (2 CEUs)

Express Yourself in Poetry

While gaining a thorough grounding in the techniques used and the effects achieved by our best poets, you will write your own poems expressing your responses to life. Studies of precision in observation and of artistry in the use of language throughout the course have been designed to enhance your enjoyment of the poetry of others and to enrich the verse you write. Your instructor will evaluate and offer suggestions about the original poems you submit and indicate how publishers may view them according to prevailing critical taste. (2 CEUs)

Researching, Writing, and Publishing Local History

An overview of research techniques and sources of information for local history research. Provides information on how to write for publication and encourages the student to complete a research project and submit it to a publisher. (1.5 CEUs)

Letters from the People

By learning how to write effectively about matters that are important to you, this course will teach you how to communicate your point of view through letters. Learn how to assemble pertinent details needed to submit your letters for publication to affect opinion makers as well as the general public. (2 CEUs)

Writing and Publishing Stories, Books, and Articles

Precise, down-to-earth advice for composing your stories and articles. Editors can discover your works only if you know how to do the job of writing and marketing them well. In this course are ideas and examples as well as projects for you to submit to receive critical analyses of your fiction and/or nonfiction attempts. It is designed as an alternative to creative writing classes, workshops, or tutors so that you need not try to succeed by working and editing by yourself. (2 CEUs)

Upper Iowa University
External Degree Program
Directed Independent Study
605 Washington Street
P.O. Box 102
Fayette, Iowa 52142   (800) 553-4150

Description:
Located in northeast Iowa, Upper Iowa University is a private liberal arts institution founded in 1857. Upper Iowa University recognizes the need of adult students, lifelong learners, to study on their own time and at their own pace. In 1973, the university established one of the first and most successful external degree programs that offers an exciting and convenient opportunity for learning as an alternative to traditional classroom instruction. It addition to being designated with maximum convenience for learners, the External Degree Program allows credit for curriculum-related work experience, service schools, workshops, seminars, and other earlier learning. Today, students have been accepted from all 50 states and 43 foreign countries. Numerous companies and government agencies sponsor their employees in the program. Independent Study courses are prepared and conducted by regular members of the university faculty.

Faculty:
Kersten Shepard, Director. There is a faculty of 28 members.

Academic Levels:
College

Degree/Certificate Programs:
Normally, students have ten years after initial enrollment to complete their baccalaureate programs using requirements in effect at the time of enrollment. If the program is not completed within ten years, the requirements in effect at the time of next enrollment will be used to determine graduate requirements. At the present time, the following requirements exist: (1) a minimum of 120 semester hours, including the residency requirement (3 or 6 semester hours) approved as applying to the degree; (2) completion of a minimum of 30 semester hours from Upper Iowa, including 3 or 6 semester hours in residence; (3) a cumulative grade point average of no less than 2.0 and no less than 2.0 grade point in the major; (4) satisfactory completion of one of the designated majors (Management, Marketing, Public Administration); (5) completion of 24 of the last 30 semester hours from Upper Iowa University; (6) thirty-four (34) semester hours of course study completed in specific general education requirements.

Admission Requirements:
The minimal requirement for admission is graduation from an accepted public or private high school or comple-tion of a GED equivalent. Students transferring work from other colleges must have a 2.00 or "C" average for admission.

Tuition:
$135 per semester hour. $35 evaluation fee. A student must request withdrawal in writing. Refund of the tuition will be calculated by dividing the total number of lessons completed in the period of enrollment into the total number of lessons not submitted. An administrative fee will be charged to those students who withdraw without submitting any coursework.

Enrollment Period:
All requirements for each course, including examinations, must be completed within six months from enrollment. Two 3-month extensions may be granted upon payment of $15 per extension. A student may enroll in only one course initially, except with permission of the Provost. After successful completion of the first course, a student may register for two courses. A residency requirement is necessary for the granting of a degree.

Equipment Requirements:
The cost of textbooks and materials is not included in the tuition. Most of the courses include all required materials needed within the textbook and materials package available through the University Bookstore. Students designing supplementary readings in their courses may often find these books at their local libraries. Students should check with their local public libraries and interlibrary loan systems to obtain these books. If the books cannot be located from one of these sources, they may be available at Upper Iowa University's Library. If the books are available for circulation, they may be obtained by sending a written request to the Upper University Library.

Credit and Grading:
Each course has a final examination which must be proctored by a school administrator or clergyman; some courses have additional examinations which require proctors. A significant portion of the final grade is based upon examinations. The grading system is as follows: A, Excellent; B, Superior; C, Average; D, Passing; F, Failure; I, Incomplete; W, Withdrawal. D is the lowest passing grade; however, a 2.00 or "C" average is required both overall and in the major for graduation. Credit is awarded in semester hour units.

Accreditations:
North Central Association of Colleges and Schools.

COLLEGE COURSES

ART

Introduction to Art

An introduction to the visual arts through the study of the elements of art, the various art forms, and a chronological study of art history. (3 semester hours)

BIOLOGY

Environmental Biology

This course covers the basic areas of ecology, with emphasis on the effects of humankind on the biosphere in which we live and the interrelationship of all biological organisms. (3 semester hours)

BUSINESS ADMINISTRATION

Financial Accounting Survey

A survey of accounting practices, introducing the student to contemporary accounting statements and procedures with emphasis on the interpretation of data reflected in financial statements of a business organization. (3 semester hours)

Accounting Principles I

Accounting theory, recordkeeping, the accounting cycle, special journals, assets, liabilities, equity, business organization, capital, cash flow, introduction to cost accounting, analysis of cost-volume-profit and financial statements, capital budgeting, and payroll. (3 semester hours)

Accounting Principles II

A continuation of the above course. (3 semester hours)

Marketing Principles

This course surveys the role of marketing and its place in society, in profit and not-for-profit organizations. Emphasis is placed on consumer orientation, the marketing concept, product, price, distribution, and promotion. The course provides a basis of understanding for advanced marketing courses. (3 semester hours)

Management Principles

A look at modern management theory, including both functional and behavioral approaches to the administration of business enterprises. (3 semester hours)

Macroeconomic Principles and Microeconomic Principles

Fundamental concepts, principles, and analysis of national income (macroeconomics), value and distribution (microeconomics). (6 semester hours)

Management Information Systems

Procedures involved in the accumulation, processing, and dissemination of various types of information within an organization. Access to an IBM personal computer is required. (3 semester hours)

Business Ethics

This course examines philosophical questions of right and wrong in the special setting of the work environment. (3 semester hours)

Business Law I

An introduction to the nature and sources of law, and the methods by which laws are made; basic principles of contract law and property law as the foundations for business enterprise; tort law governing business relationships. (3 semester hours)

Business Law II

A survey of particular fields of law relevant to business operations; agency, partnerships, corporations; sales, commercial transactions, and bankruptcy; antitrust law; employment law; consumer protection. (3 semester hours)

Sales Management

This course provides an introduction to the recruitment, training, motivation, and management of a sales force. Included is an introduction to basic personal selling techniques. Emphasis is placed on sales as an integral element of the promotional mix. (3 semester hours)

Intermediate Financial Accounting I & II

Extension of theory and principles of general accounting with emphasis on analysis and interpretation of financial position and results of operations as reflected in the accounting reports of a business concern. (6 semester hours)

Federal Taxation I

Study of our present-day tax structure; theory and application of income tax law to individuals, partnerships, and corporations. (3 semester hours)

Federal Taxation II

A continuation of the above course, with emphasis on income tax law applicable to corporations, partnerships, and fiduciaries; and transfer (gift and estate) taxes. (3 semester hours)

Financial Management

An exploration of the instruments, policies, and institutions involved in financing the business firm; the administration of these funds; and the distribution of profits. (3 semester hours)

Consumer Behavior

This course provides a survey of research findings on consumer behavior drawn from marketing, economics, sociology, psychology, and anthropology. Emphasis is placed on implications of research to consumer satisfaction and on developing and understanding of the consumer decision-making process. (3 semester hours)

Human Resource Management

An overview of the policies and procedures in personnel administration in American business, including uses, sources, motivation, and maintenance of employees, with emphasis on the dynamics of social organization. (3 semester hours)

Supervision

A detailed examination of the fundamental concepts, principles, and dynamics of the supervisory process. (3 semester hours)

Advertising

This course examines advertising and its role in marketing. Included area a survey of the history of advertising, the media, and communication models, and an introduction to the creative side of advertising. Emphasis is placed on the formulation of objectives for advertising programs. (3 semester hours)

Small Business Management

A presentation of the organization and operation of small enterprises in services, retailing, wholesaling, and manufacturing for those aspiring to own, operate, and/or manage a small business or work for an organization serving small businesses. Topics covered include importance, status, problems, and requirements of small business. (3 semester hours)

Training and Development

This course involves the evaluation and study of trends in human resource training, education, and development activities within organizational settings. (3 semester hours)

Business Communication

Application of writing skills specifically for business. Includes annual reports, financial analysis, personal and formal letters, office memos, training, and informational documents. (3 semester hours)

International Business

Understanding of the global economy and an awareness of the political, historical, and social environment in which international business operates. (3 semester hours)

Marketing Management

This course focuses on strategy, concepts, and techniques involving the marketing function in organizations, with emphasis on marketing planning and decision making. (3 semester hours)

Compensation and Benefits Management

Fundamental concepts of compensation theory, government and union influences, job analysis and evaluation, building and maintaining compensation structure, comparable worth, performance and salaries. (3 semester hours)

Complex Organizations

An exploration of the structural and functional characteristics of formal organizations such as corporations, government agencies, schools, etc. Special attention will be given to such topics as: theories of management from Taylor to Theory Z; the relations between the internal structure of organizations and the different forms of social stratification throughout American society, i.e., class, racial, ethnic and gender stratification systems; and the new forms of management strategy in the global economy. (3 semester hours)

Personnel Selection and Evaluation

Policies, procedures, and problems in the selection of personnel, focusing on job analysis, validation, legal constraints, criteria, and application of specific techniques. (3 semester hours)

Labor Relations

A look at the basic principles of manpower use, wage structure, use of industrial psychology and collective bargaining, the union movement, human relations in industrial management, and modern labor laws and institutions. (3 semester hours)

Managerial Cost Accounting

A study of cost concepts and application related to the use of cost information by internal managers for purposes of planning, control, evaluation, and decision making. (3 semester hours)

Product Cost Accounting

A survey of the principles and practices of accounting for and accumulation of costs to manufacture products, with emphasis on job-order and process cost systems; methods of overhead cost distribution, standard cost systems, and departmentalization for cost control. (3 semester hours)

International Marketing

This course builds on topics from the Marketing Principles course, as applied to global situations. Emphasis is on the development of an appropriate marketing mix for international target markets. The importance of consumer orientation is stressed; international marketing research, consumer behavior, and cultural sensitivity are examined. (3 semester hours)

Auditing

An exploration of the concepts and procedures applicable to an audit of financial statements, with emphasis on procedures to substantiate amounts reported; along with the impact of internal control, quality of available evidence and statistical sampling on the determination of appropriate procedures. (3 semester hours)

Operations Management

A descriptive and analytical exploration of the process of managing the production of goods and services while maximizing customer satisfaction, minimizing costs, and optimizing resource utilization. (3 semester hours)

Advanced Financial Accounting

An extension of the theory and principles of financial accounting, with emphasis on FASB pronouncements applicable to accounting for business combinations, foreign operations, and partnerships. (3 semester hours)

Accounting for Not-For-Profit Organizations

An overview of the theory and application of FASB and other authoritative pronouncements related to accounting for governmental, fiduciary, and other not-for-profit organizations. (3 semester hours)

Contemporary Topics in Management

This course covers the most contemporary management issues. (3 semester hours)

Marketing Research

Demand analysis and consumer behavior; market analysis and segmentation; physical distribution; government regulation; industrial and international marketing. (3 semester hours)

Strategic Management

This is a course to introduce students to the critical business skills of managing strategic activities. A strategy reflects an organization's awareness of how, when, and where it should compete; against whom it should compete; and for what purposes it should compete. Strategic management is the set of decisions and actions that result in the formulation and implementation of plans designed to achieve an organization's objectives. (3 semester hours)

CHEMISTRY

General Physical Science

A survey course of astronomy, meteorology, geology, and chemistry/physics intended for students not majoring in the natural or physical sciences. (3 semester hours)

COMPUTER SCIENCE

Survey of Computer Concepts

An introduction to general computer concepts, along with the use of application software in the areas of spreadsheets, database management, and word processing. (3 semester hours)

ENGLISH

Basic Composition

A study and practice of expository writing, with narrative and descriptive compositions assigned regularly. Emphasis is on the development of sound understanding of rhetorical principles. (3 semester hours)

English Composition II

Further study and practice of expository writing, with emphasis on research technique, persuasion, and explanation. (3 semester hours)

Introduction to Literature

This course concentrates on the reading of selected works in fiction and poetry, and presents an introduction to literary analysis, interpretation, and evaluation. (3 semester hours)

HISTORY

American Civilization I

This course provides a broad overview of U.S. history, from the the earliest colonial settlements through the end of the Reconstruction period following the Civil War. Major themes examined are colonial society and life, the struggle for independence, adoption of the Constitution, the early national period, sectionalism, the Civil War, and Reconstruction. (3 semester hours)

American Civilization II

Provides a broad overview of U.S. history from the end of the Reconstruction period to the present. Major themes examined are industrialization, urbanization, protest and reform movements, emergence of the U.S. as a world power, the Great Depression, World War II, the Cold War, the Turbulent 1960s, and domestic and foreign problems of the 1970s and 1980s. (3 semester hours)

Recent America: The United States Since 1919

This course provides specialized study of the historical period examined in the second half of American Civilization II. Topics include the 1920s, the Great Depression, New Deal, World War II, Cold War, the civil rights movement, Vietnam, Watergate, stagflation, the 1980s, and contemporary American life. (3 semester hours)

American Economic History

A study of major landmarks in the growth and development of the American economy; the evolution of agriculture, industry, transportation and finance; the influence of government and international determinants. (3 semester hours)

MATHEMATICS

College Algebra

This course includes topics in algebraic operations, equations and inequalities, graphs and functions, polynomial functions, exponential and logarithmic functions, systems of equations and inequalities, matrices and determinants, sequence and series, and probability. (3 semester hours)

Quantitative Methods I

This course examines quantitative methods for treating problems arising in biological, management, and social sciences. Topics include review of sets, algebra, graphs and functions; systems of linear equations and matrices; linear programming; probability; derivations and integrals. (3 semester hours)

Elementary Statistics

An introduction to the simple problems of statistical inference. Descriptive statistics, probability distributions, estimation of parameters and level of significance, hypothesis testing, regression and correlation. (3 semester hours)

POLITICAL SCIENCE

U.S. Government

A survey of basic principles, institutions, and functions of American national government. The course is supplemented with U.S. Supreme Court holdings and with current examples of U.S. government at work. (3 semester hours)

State and Local Government

A survey of the basic principles, organization, and functions of government on the state, county, municipal, township, and district levels. (3 semester hours)

The Legislative Process

A general introduction to American representative assemblies, with primary attention to the U.S. Congress. Emphasis on the interplay of relationships with legislative bodies affecting the shaping of legislation. (3 semester hours)

Public Administration

A study of politics, administration, and bureaucratic policymaking at the local, state, and national levels with an emphasis on the relationships between government bureaucracies and the political system in the United States. (3 semester hours)

American Constitutional Law I

The role of the Judiciary and the U.S. Supreme Court in the American political system. A case approach to the development of U.S. constitutional law. Topics include the powers of the President and Congress, Federalism, the commerce clause, the taxing and spending power, and the contract clause. (3 semester hours)

American Constitutional Law II

Topics covered include civil liberties, equal opportunity and equal protection under the law for minorities, freedom of speech and religion, the right to privacy, and the rights of those accused of crimes. (3 semester hours)

Cases in Public Administration

A concentrated study in the techniques of public administration, including the public budgeting process, law enforcement administration, recreation administration, and the administration of other public services. (3 semester hours)

Public Budgeting Process

Budget planning, formulation, execution, and auditing; the sharing of power between the Executive and Legislative branches on taxing and spending; the agency role of advocacy in budget preparation; budgets as a reflection of public policy. (3 semester hours)

Administrative Law

The bureaucracy and the regulatory process; judicial review of administrative action; the Administrative Procedures Act of 1946; delegation, standing, exhaustion, sovereign immunity, rulemaking, tort liability, evidence, discretion, investigation, and enforcement. (3 semester hours)

PSYCHOLOGY

General Psychology

An introduction to the scientific study of behavior and mental processes, including major approaches and methodologies. The course samples a broad range of topics, including biological foundations, development, learning, cognition, personality, abnormal psychology, and social behavior. (3 semester hours)

Introduction to Human Services

A survey of the professions, programs, and agencies involved in the delivery of human services. (3 semester hours)

Substance Abuse

The effects of psychoactive drugs are studied in this course, as well as the origins of substance abuse, characteristics of substance abusers, and consequences for the individual, family, and society. Approaches to substance abuse treatment are discussed. (3 semester hours)

Abnormal Psychology

A survey of the major classifications of psychopathology, including conceptual approaches to the understanding of psychopathology, etiology, and treatment. (3 semester hours)

Research Methods

This course explores the development of skills essential to critical evaluation of behavioral research. The emphasis is on understanding the scientific method, research, methodologies, and statistical analysis. (3 semester hours)

Social Welfare Programs and Policies

An analysis of social policies in the United States, with emphasis on the dimensions of choice and alternative policies, along with assessment of contemporary social welfare issues, programs, and legislation. (3 semester hours)

Industrial Psychology

A study of the relationship between the individual worker and the work environment. Emphasis is on the exploration and application of the most influential theories. Topics include organizational dynamics, work motivation, job satisfaction, personnel selection and training, and work group influences. (3 semester hours)

Issue and Ethics in the Helping Professions

An analysis of issues and ethical problems involved in the helping professions and programs. (3 semester hours)

SOCIOLOGY

Social Problems

A critical investigation of selected social problems: their causes, development, and the alternative social policies that address these problems. Topics will include: substance abuse, the problems of family life, poverty and its relation to different forms of inequality. (3 semester hours)

Cultural and Racial Minorities

This course provides sociological perspectives for analysis of racial and ethnic minority groups, along with an examination of the development of American ethnic groups and the current position of ethnic and racial groups in the structure of modern America. (3 semester hours)

SPANISH

Advanced Beginning Spanish I

Introduction to the basic skills needed for communicating in Spanish, especially designed to develop communicative proficiency in Spanish. The focus of this course will be the development of listening comprehension skills and the emergence of rudimentary speech. (3 semester hours)

Utah, University of
Center for Independent Study
Division of Continuing Education
2180 Annex Building
Salt Lake City, Utah 84112   (801) 581-8801

Description:

Founded in 1850, two and one-half years after the arrival of the pioneers in the valley of the Great Salt Lake, the University of Utah has grown from the original handful of classes held in a private parlor to a vigorous and comprehensive institution of widely varied services requiring a 3,500 member teaching faculty for the 22,000 students on the 1,500 acre campus overlooking Salt Lake City. The Division of Continuing Education (DCE) is the University's major agency charged with providing service to the non-typical student, whether the contact with the University is on-campus or off-campus.

The Center for Independent Study celebrated its 75th year in 1992. In that year they served 3,166 students in 49 states and 21 foreign countries. Roughly 40 percent of the students are University of Utah undergraduates; the remaining 60% include traditional and nontraditional undergraduates, military personnel, secondary school teachers, and people interested in continuing education throughout

their lifetime. The student body ranges in age from 17 to 73. The The Independent Study program is best known for teacher recertification and endorsement and offers 23 educational studies courses.

Faculty:
Cynthia Grua, Director, Center for Independent Study.

Academic Levels:
College
Noncredit

Degree/Certificate Programs:
The University of Utah will accept up to a maximum of 45 quarter credit hours of correspondence study toward a baccalaureate degree.

Admission Requirements:
Courses are open to any individual with a working knowledge of English. High school students who have completed or nearly finished high school may enroll in a course during their final high school year. High school enrollment requires written approval of the student, a parent, and school principal. Some courses have required prerequisites. Military personnel may enroll through DANTES and should contact their Education Officer for details.

Tuition:
$45 per quarter credit hour plus $10 per course for manual or syllabus, payable at registration. Payment by VISA or MasterCard accepted. Refunds of course fees are calculated based on the date of registration; course manuals are not returnable. A $15 processing fee, $8 for each lesson submitted, and $15 for each exam taken are deducted before refunds are calculated. Students receive 100 percent refund (less processing fees) the first month. After 30 days, 3 percent of the original tuition total is also deducted for each calendar day. Following this schedule, no refunds are issued after 60 days.

Enrollment Period:
The maximum time allowed to complete a correspondence course is 1 year. One three-month extension may be permitted upon payment of a $30 extension fee.

Equipment Requirements:
The costs of textbooks and some required course syllabi are not included in tuition. These may be ordered from the University Book Store. Some courses require the use of an audiocassette or videocassette player; in those courses, a refundable deposit for the cassettes is required.

Credit and Grading:
Successful completion of all assignments and final examinations is required in credit courses; some courses have midterm tests. Final examinations must be supervised by an approved proctor, usually a local school official. Grading system is A, B, C, D, E, with D- as the minimum passing grade. Courses may be taken on a credit/noncredit option. Credit is awarded in quarter hour units.

Library Services:

Correspondence Study students may borrow books from the University of Utah Marriott Library. Periodicals are not circulated, but xerox copies are available upon request.

Accreditations:

Northwest Association of Schools and Colleges. Member of: National University Continuing Education Association.

COLLEGE COURSES

ACCOUNTING

Elementary Accounting

Course 221. Assumes the student has had no previous training in accounting or bookkeeping. The subject matter includes principles of double-entry bookkeeping; preparation and analysis of financial statements, liquid assets, receivables, inventories, and the sources of operating profiles. Upon completion of the course, the student should be able to keep a simple set of books and understand published financial statements and other financial information. (3 quarter hours)

Course 222. A continuation of Course 221. Considerable emphasis is placed on cash flows, inventory and financing activities. The sources of operating capacity—plant and equipment—are treated in detail. Liabilities such as contracts, notes and bonds are explained. The shareholders' equity and capital contributions of a corporation are discussed in detail. The student learns to understand the complexities of long term investments in corporate securities. (3 quarter hours)

ANTHROPOLOGY

Culture and the Human Experience

This course is designed to introduce students to the similarities and diversity of various groups of people worldwide. It will raise questions about how and why human populations have come to be what they are, stressing the importance of understanding a culture within its own context, not in the western context of right and wrong. In order to understand the human experience, this course will take the student through time and space, visiting African hunters and gatherers, South American horticulturists, Asian nomads, Indians of the American Southwest, and peasants of Europe and India. At the end of the journey, the student should begin to understand and appreciate the diversity of people of this planet. (5 quarter hours)

Human Origins: Evolution and Diversity

Physical anthropology looks for new information on the human organism. This course seeks answers to questions regarding biological legacy: Are we related to apes? Why do humans come in so many different shapes and colors? Will the human race become extinct due to current problems such as AIDS and pollution? Students of physical anthropology learn about the impact of the interrelationship of heredity, environment, and lifestyle on individuals, societies, and the planet. (5 quarter hours)

Archaeology of the Southwest

This study of prehistoric peoples of New Mexico, Arizona, parts of Colorado, and Utah begins with an introduction to contemporary Native American peoples of the region. The origins of prehistoric peoples, the beginnings and development of their characteristic cultures, and the later relationships within and beyond their culture area to the time of the Spanish conquest are reviewed. (4 quarter hours)

ART

Introduction to the Visual Arts

Designed to encourage the study and enjoyment of the visual arts, with emphasis upon awareness perception in painting, sculpture, and architecture. The student gains visual literacy and the course aims to establish some fundamental principles for critical judgments by the layman. No previous knowledge of art is required. (5 quarter hours)

Art Education in the Secondary Schools

This course focuses on planning an art program to meet specific needs and develop specific skills in creative problem solving, conceptualization, and studio. There is an emphasis on productive thinking, visual imagery, and aesthetic sensitivity. (3 quarter hours)

ART HISTORY

Introduction to the History of Art

Masterpieces of the Western world are presented in their cultural and historical settings. From elegant classical tradition to energetic and spontaneous modern art, each artistic movement is interpreted through its major paintings, sculptures, and works of architecture. Internationally known art experts and critics evaluate each work and help us understand why and how it was created. (4 quarter hours)

BIOLOGY

General Biology

Provides an introduction to the unifying concepts in biology including basic organization and life processes, genetics, development, physiology, behavior, evolution, and ecology. Human biology is covered to further students' knowledge of their bodies' structure, function, evolution, and ecology. This survey course will explore current research as well as the scientific knowledge gained over the past centuries. (5 quarter hours)

Human Ecology

A study of people and their relationship to the environment. The course approaches this topic from a broad biological base and is oriented toward the major problems facing modern society in its efforts to manage problems created by man-made ecosystems such as water and air pollution, radiation, health, population problems and food resources, and the effects produced by technological advancement. The student will learn how to evaluate society's actions in altering and adapting the environment. (3 quarter hours)

Human Physiology

An elementary course in human physiology which emphasizes concepts of function in terms of chemical and physical activity. The course covers the basics of cell function, muscle contraction, circulation, kidney function, respiration, the nervous system, digestion, metabolism, endocrinology, and reproduction. (5 quarter hours)

Human Genetics

The course is geared toward the nonscience-oriented as well as the science-oriented student. It covers the fundamentals of genetics via a study of human inheritance. The biological basis of man's inheritance, gene action, mutation, linkage, and probability will be some of the items discussed. Also covered are blood groups (e.g., ABO, Rh, MN), mutation, genetic engineering, sex determination, color blindness, and chromosomal abnormalities. New technologies are examined in relation to the study of gene products and gene location. (4 quarter hours)

CHEMISTRY

Organic Chemistry

The first quarter of a three-quarter sequence on the chemistry of organic molecules. Course content includes bonding, reaction theory, reaction mechanisms, stereochemistry, types of organic chemical reactions, and an introduction to spectroscopy. (4 quarter hours)

CIVIL ENGINEERING

Technical Engineering Drawing

A beginning course in engineering graphics. It focuses on standard topics such as lettering, instrumental and freehand drawing, geometric constructions, multiview projection, sectional views, dimensioning, and pictorial drawing. (2 quarter hours)

COMMUNICATIONS

The Editing Process

Concentrates on preparing written materials for publication. The course is strongly oriented toward newspaper production but involves activities that will help editors in any medium and help students become better critics of their own written work. Students complete workbook assignments that call for editing of style; trimming, condensing, and fitting copy to space requirements. The student will deal with problems of taste and ethics, libel, objectivity and accuracy; writing headlines; making up pages, and scaling and cropping pictures. Basic typography is included. (4 quarter hours)

Magazine Article Writing

This course focuses on writing and selling the feature article. It describes the magazine field and evaluates current magazine trends, particularly as they affect the writer. The course describes marketing of manuscripts from the viewpoint of the free-lance writer. The exercises teach the writer how to gather information through library research, interviews and observation, to organize facts to write purposefully and revise manuscripts. Emphasis is on developing an effective style. (4 quarter hours)

COMMUNICATION DISORDERS

Beginning Sign Language

Offers students basic communicative vocabulary in beginning sign language, the third most used language in the United States. Information on American Sign Language (ASL) and the deaf community will give the student a greater appreciation and understanding of this unique culture. Sign language involves finger spelling, signs, the body, and face. (3 quarter hours)

DRIVER EDUCATION

Introduction to Driver Education

A study of the content of the driver education curriculum and the proper sequence of the units taught in driver education. It is the basic course for certification required to teach in either public or private secondary schools or in commercial schools. (3 quarter hours)

Driver Education

This course outlines the procedure for management of driver education in the high schools and commercial schools. It deals with scheduling and placement within the curriculum, as well as acquisition of instructional resources, including automobiles required for the program. Special attention is devoted to budgeting, financing, and the role of the state. (3 quarter hours)

Driver Education Instructor Internship

This internship provides hands-on learning experiences for students in practice teaching situations. Internships may be taken with permission of the university instructor under the supervision of certified instructors in public school or commercial programs. Students living outside

of Utah should determine their state's certification requirements before registering. (3 to 10 quarter hours)

ECONOMICS

Economics as a Social Science

This course examines economics from both historical and theoretical perspectives. Students are exposed to a survey of issues focusing on institutional and structural change in economic growth as well as traditional micro- and macroeconomic analysis. Topics include the historical foundations of industrial capitalism, the development of economic institutions, supply and demand theory, models of firm competition, inflation, unemployment, the role of government policy (including the issue of debt), international trade and development and alternative approaches within economic theory. (5 quarter hours)

Principles of Economics (Microeconomics)

This course will introduce students to basic, microeconomic issues in markets that are fundamentally international. The first part of the course provides the student with some ideas of the graphic tools used in economics. Also, some concepts about what sort of issues economic analysis helps clarify will be presented with respect to consumer and firm behavior by introducing supply and demand analysis. The concepts of elasticity and input-output decision of the firm under perfect competition and monopoly will also be explored. The course's second part briefly introduces the methods to analyze international trade and how the human input is considered by the economist. (4 quarter hours)

Principles of Economics (Macroeconomics)

This course will provide the student with an understanding of macroeconomic issues. It will address the meaning of unemployment, inflation, economic growth, and the open-economy. (4 quarter hours)

U.S. Economic History

This course focuses on the causes and consequences of economic growth and development in the United States from the colonial period to the twentieth century. Sources of growth examined include resource development, land acquisition, industrial and agricultural development, technological change and labor force growth. The course also develops the negative side of American economic growth, including the exploitation of minorities, labor-management conflict, environmental degradation and other costs of growth and change. The overall objective is to develop an understanding of the influence of the past on the contemporary economy. (4 quarter hours)

Money and Banking

The areas of money, banking, and financial markets have as their common subject of study pieces of paper called financial assets. These assets include money, stocks, and bonds. Who creates them; why are they valuable; where are they traded; how do they affect the economy; how should they be controlled; the answers to these questions comprise the subject matter of this course. (4 quarter hours)

EDUCATION

Storytelling: The Use of Narrative in the Elementary School

Previews the value and principles of reading aloud and telling stories to audiences of all ages. The lessons provide not only theory but experiences in story selection, preparation, and presentation of reading/telling stories and poetry in elementary schools and related children's centers. (3 quarter hours)

Science in the Elementary School

This course is designed to provide teachers with the knowledge and skills necessary to teach science in the elementary classroom. The course describes a discovery-oriented approach to science teaching; it advocates having students do science rather than read about it. In a similar fashion the instruction in this class will be action-oriented. (3 quarter hours)

Social Studies in the Elementary School

This course provides a study of the social studies curriculum in the elementary school including content, method, and evaluation of social studies teaching. Lessons provide students with alternative ways of studying. Actual construction of materials and discussion of methods of teaching are an integral part of the course. Major areas of discussion include objectives for the social studies, social science disciplines, and the learning of social concepts, strategies of teaching, and instructional resources. (3 quarter hours)

Creative Teaching of Art in the Elementary School

This is an art course designed to help teachers, parents, recreational specialists, and others who work with children. It includes a study of creative educational practices in teaching art. Emphasis is placed on developing self expression and art experiences which lead to the appreciation and enjoyment of art in a child's life. Opportunity is provided for working with a variety of unique materials. (3 quarter hours)

Mathematics in the Elementary School

This course is a preservice course primarily for prospective teachers of mathematics in the elementary grades. The class focuses on conceptual understanding of mathematics through physical representations and models. (5 quarter hours)

Language Arts in the Elementary School

Covers methods in teaching the skills of writing, speaking, listening, and reading with suggestions for implementation by teachers in the elementary school. (4 quarter hours)

Content Area Reading in Secondary Schools

This course emphasizes the teaching of reading in middle and secondary schools. It is designed for content area teachers with little or no background in reading. Topics covered include: preparing students for reading assignments, reading flexibility, comprehension and study strategies, expository writing, and textbook evaluation. (3 quarter hours)

Diagnosis and Corrective Reading Strategies

This course is formulated for classroom teachers who want to learn to provide sound instruction and assessment for low-achieving readers. Although the focus of the course is on instruction and assessment in the regular classroom, remedial programs that might be implemented by reading specialists or clinicians are also presented. (4 quarter hours)

Kindergarten—Early Childhood Education

This course has multiple objectives including: 1. analysis of child development in relation to the particular age; 2. review of current research findings relevant to program development; 3. comparison of current trends in education for young children; 4. clarification of criteria in planning new programs for young children; 5. discussion of effective ways of working with children; 6. development of parent involvement. (3 quarter hours)

Reading in the Elementary School

The purpose of this course is to help prospective teachers develop a beginning understanding of theory and practice in reading instruction at the elementary school level. The focus of the course is on helping young students learn and develop their literacy skills—both reading and writing. Prospective teachers will read about and practice teaching strategies for integrating reading and writing into elementary classrooms. (4 quarter hours)

Children's Literature

Students in this course will be introduced to different genres of literature for young readers which promote language, moral, social, and cognitive development. Some of the authors who produce these works will be introduced. Students will develop selection and evaluation skills and will utilize literature by developing units and lessons as part of assignments that integrate literature into different content areas. (3 quarter hours)

Methods for Teaching

Recent educational literature on instructional methods, evaluation, classroom management and teacher effectiveness will be tied together with classroom activities. (3 quarter hours)

Principles of Graphic Communication

This course is designed for teachers who wish to visualize ideas through the use of various graphic production techniques. It covers preservation of pictures, lettering techniques, bulletin boards, posters and charts, design and composition of graphic materials, transparency production, slide production and microcomputer applications. Three lessons are dedicated to graphic production, spreadsheeting, and word processing. (4 quarter hours)

ENGLISH

Introduction to Creative Writing

This course assumes that the student has little or no background in creative writing. Students will learn the basic principles involved in developing ideas and in using words to create settings and moods, to draw believable characters, to write dialogue and to begin to create both poetry and fiction. (4 quarter hours)

Introduction to Shakespeare

This course is designed to introduce students to six Shakespearean plays and to the Shakespearean sonnets. Students will read *Romeo and Juliet, Macbeth, The Tempest, Antony and Cleopatra, King Lear* and *Hamlet*, as well as representative sonnets. (4 quarter hours)

Writing Fiction

This course is intended for the student who has already written some fiction and wants to concentrate more directly on either short stories or a novel. Students will examine some of the most important problems of writing fiction, will learn more ways to generate ideas, and will work on their own projects with guidance. (4 quarter hours)

FAMILY AND CONSUMER STUDIES

Psychology of Infancy and Childhood

The principle focus of this course is the interplay of biological factors, individual personality, social structure and the environmental forces that shape the growing child. Topics of contemporary social significance include the effects of divorce, single parenthood and parents' work and changing sexual attitudes and behavior. Home video option. (4 quarter hours)

Psychology of Adolescents

This course surveys recent psychological research concerning youth between childhood and adulthood. The course covers developmental, social, and clinical psychology as they pertain to the adolescent. A sample of topics includes intellectual, moral, and political development, social conformity, interpersonal attraction, sex roles and sexual identity, depression, anxiety and family relations. The emphasis is on understanding how psychological theories and principles apply to adolescence. (3 quarter hours)

FINANCE

Personal Finance

An introduction to the efficient management of family and personal finances. It will focus on budgeting; the use of consumer credit, its sources and costs. Students will study uses of savings plans, alternative mediums for liquid savings, using a commercial bank, and determining when to use various types of life insurance. Principles in the use of general insurance (health, auto, home protection), Social Security and planning for retirement, the economics of home ownership, income taxes and their minimization, the use of corporate bonds, common stocks, mutual funds, wills and estate planning are addressed. (4 quarter hours)

Business Finance

This basic course is designed to provide students with an understanding and appreciation of finance. The focus is through the eyes of the corporate treasurer whose function is to make certain that the firm has adequate funds to conduct its business. This involves a determination of financial needs, acquisition of the funds from various sources of capital, and the effective utilization of the financed assets. (4 quarter hours)

Risk and Insurance

This is an introductory course in the field of risk and insurance with the following objectives: 1. acquaint the student with all types of risk in business and personal life; 2. explain different techniques of risk control, especially loss prevention, self-insurance, and insurance whether private or social; 3. provide for basic understanding and use of different property, liability, life, and health insurance coverages; (4) introduce various types of insurance carriers, marketing systems, financial activities, and government regulations. (4 quarter hours)

Investment Principles and Practices

This is an introductory survey of investments. It presents the risk/reward trade-offs confronting the investor, the nature of the marketplace in which the investor's choices are focused, and the basic sources of information to make the choices. Attention is directed to the traditional approaches to investments, both technical and fundamental. An attempt is made to utilize all of these concepts to the benefit of both the casual and the professional investor. (4 quarter hours)

FOODS AND NUTRITION

Fundamentals of Nutrition

This course includes current topics in nutrition: protein, carbohydrate, lipids, digestion, absorption, maternal and infant nutrition, diet and chronic diseases, diet analysis and nutrition assessment. (3 quarter hours)

GEOGRAPHY

World Cultural Geography

A survey course designed to acquaint the student with basic data about the world's countries. Emphasizes differences in religion, language, race, history, social structure, and economic activities. The course is designed to help students understand the forces behind headlines of today. (5 quarter hours)

HEALTH EDUCATION

Healthy Lifestyles

This course provides information and activities which will lead to an understanding of and improvement in a person's total personal health status. It is a practical course. Students must be willing to get involved in actual behavior change throughout the course as well as contract for a personal health behavior change project. Topics covered in the text and lessons should aid students in exploring the areas of mental, physical, social, and spiritual health. (3 quarter hours)

Substance Use and Abuse

This course explores the current use of alcohol and drug use and abuse. The scope of the course includes psycho-social antecedents to drug abuse as well as psychological and physiological effects of commonly abused drugs. This course is designed as an introduction to incidences, effects, and dangers of substance use and abuse. Discussion covers populations at risk and ways to combat this problem. (3 quarter hours)

HISTORY

History of Civilization—Ancient to 1300 A.D.

The struggle of humanity to create a meaningful and fulfilling community life began in the river valleys of Egypt and Mesopotamia about 5,000 years ago. Building on those beginnings, the Hebrews, Greeks, Romans, Early Christians, and Germanic peoples developed cultural forms that coalesced in the High Middle Ages into that distinctively Western civilization from which our own world emerged. This course is a study of that development from about 3,000 B.C. to 1300 A.D. (5 quarter hours)

American Civilization

This course is a survey of United States history from the colonial period to the present with emphasis on political, economic, and social developments. Special attention is given to the founding of the United States as a nation, the adoption of the Constitution, national expansion, sectionalism and the Civil War, the Industrial Revolution, the emergence of the United States as a world power, current domestic and foreign relations, and the themes of race, class, and gender in American history. (5 quarter hours)

History of Utah

This course follows the unique political, economic, social, and cultural development of Utah from the earliest human occupation of the area to the 20th century. Emphasis is placed on the Mormon period, the struggle for statehood, Utah as the 45th state and non-Mormon contributions to the modern state. (5 quarter hours)

Ancient Greece

Provides a survey of ancient Greek history and civilization beginning with the Bronze Age cultures of Minoa and Mycenae, the rise of the polis and the Persian invasions, the Peloponnesian War and the collapse of the polis, the rise of Macedonia under Philip and Alexander, the conquests of Alexander and the establishment of the Hellenistic Kingdoms down to the Roman conquest of the East. All aspects of Greek culture and civilization will be examined. (5 quarter hours)

Ancient Rome

This course follows the history of Rome from the Bronze Age cultures of Italy and the rise of Rome in central Italy through the establishment of the Roman dominion of Italy, the Punic Wars and the creation of an empire, the collapse of the Republic in the Civil Wars and the founding of the Augustan Principate, the development of Imperial society and institutions, and the rise of Christianity up to the Barbarian invasions and the collapse of the western provinces of the Empire in the 5th century A.D. All aspects of Roman culture and civilization will be examined. (5 quarter hours)

LIBRARY SCIENCE

The Use of Books and Libraries

Designed to help prospective teachers, librarians, and beginning college students find their way in catalogs, encyclopedias, yearbooks, directories, book reviews, and to utilize information in research. (2 quarter hours)

Library Work with Children

This course is intended for teachers, librarians, and aides who are interested in children and the books they read. The course will consider reading guidance, children's interests and book choices, patterns of response to literature and ways to bring the child and book together. Issues in literature today will also be addressed. (5 quarter hours)

Reference Work

A study of the reference books found in most libraries. Challenges the student, teacher, or librarian to improve skills in locating materials by using general encyclopedias, dictionaries, handbooks, biographies, atlases, and indexes. Students are introduced to some of the outstanding books in the fields of science, history, literature, and education. (4 quarter hours)

Selection of Library Materials

Designed for teachers, librarians, and others interested in principles and standards of choosing materials for school, public, and special libraries. Emphasizes community analysis, evaluative criteria, review media, selection and collection policies, acquisition procedures, publishing and bookselling trades, collection maintenance, copyright, and intellectual freedom issues. (4 quarter hours)

Cataloging and Classification

An introductory course in the cataloging and classification of books for small public or school libraries; pamphlets and other commonly held nonbook materials are also covered. (4 quarter hours)

Management of the Library Media Program

This course covers the competencies which prepare an individual to effectively direct an instructional program which teaches students how to find, use, and analyze information and ideas and encourages both lifelong learning and reading for pleasure. The student is taught how to consult with other educators to support the curriculum and design learning strategies for the library media program. (3 quarter hours)

MARKETING

Principles of Marketing

Marketing is presented as part of an organic whole permitting the analysis of marketing problems in relation to social, psychological, political and economic forces which affect and are affected by the marketing process. This course is of value to both students of marketing and to those who wish to acquire an understanding of the basic function of business in the nation's economy. (4 quarter hours)

Introduction to Advertising

Provides students with a presentation of advertising as it is actually practiced—as a business, a marketing tool, a creative process, and as a hybrid discipline that employs elements of the various arts and sciences. Students will become acquainted with the operation of an advertising agency and with its interaction with external environment as well as the most current award-winning advertisements and campaigns. In addition to familiar advertising examples from large firms such as Pepsi and Coca-Cola, students will also be exposed to contemporary advertising cases from small companies and international firms. (4 quarter hours)

MATHEMATICS

Intermediate Algebra

A study of the basic operations of algebra, first degree equations in one, two, and three variables, quadratic equations in one and two variables, functions, graphs, radical equations, and imaginary numbers. (5 quarter hours)

College Algebra

Provides an introduction to the study of functions which parallels the development of the real numbers. Topics in the study of functions of a single variable include polynomials, rational functions and the transcendental functions, logarithm and exponential. Functions of several variables cover the first order (or linear) cases including linear inequalities and elementary matrix theory. Further topics include linear programming, progressions, mathematical induction, permutations and combinations. (5 quarter hours)

Plane Trigonometry

The study of trigonometry including graphing, triangles, sine and cosine functions, other circular functions, rotations and angles, trigonometric identities, laws of sines and cosines, vectors, complex numbers, polar coordinates, DeMoivre's identity. The purpose of the course is to combine plane geometry and algebraic methods into a foundation for solving problems in science and engineering. (5 quarter hours)

Elementary Statistics

Introduces students to the basic concepts of probability and statistics, emphasizing the practical applicability of these ideas in everyday decision making. Topics include describing data, finding data relationships, collecting useful data, understanding probability models and distributions, estimating population values from sample data, and testing hypotheses. (4 quarter hours)

Calculus

Course 111. The emphasis in this intuitive introduction to differential and integral calculus is on computation and interpretation. Some use is made of the elementary analytic geometry of circles, parabolas, ellipses, and hyperbolas. Topics include: coordinates, lines, functions and graphs, slope, derivative velocity and rates, derivatives of polynomials and rational functions, implicit differentiation, inverse functions, chain rule, differentials, continuity, related rates, second derivatives, curve plotting, maxima and minima, indefinite integral, applications, review of trigonometry, differentiation and integration of trigonometric functions, area, rectangular rule, trapezoidal rule, Riemann integral, numerical methods. (4 quarter hours)

Course 112. Calculation in the context of applications is emphasized in this continuation of the differential and integral calculus. Topics include: area, volume, arc length, surface area, average value, moments, center of mass, centroids and center of gravity, work, trigonometric functions, derivatives of trigonometric functions, logarithms and their derivatives, exponentials and their derivatives, integration formulas, integration methods for algebraic, exponential, logarithmic and trigonometric functions, improper integrals, numerical series, power series, L'Hôpital's rule. (4 quarter hours)

Course 113. The first year of calculus concludes with this course. Topics include: plane analytic geometry, polar coordinates, area in polar coordinates, vectors, parametric equations, space coordinates, scalar product, vector product, lines and planes, triple scalar product, cylinders, quadric surfaces, velocity, acceleration, tangent vectors, curvature, normal vector, vector calculus, functions of several variables, directional derivatives, tangent plane and normal line, maxima and minima, method of least squares, second derivative test, double integrals, applications, limits theorems, infinity, and areas. (4 quarter hours)

METEOROLOGY

Introduction to Meteorology

This basic course is for students who have minimal mathematical preparation and are nonscience majors. The chief aim of the course is to examine the forces behind the earth's weather in an attempt to better understand the global environment we live in, and to see how the science of meteorology strives to improve man's chances for survival. The whole realm of meteorological topics is considered, with special emphasis placed on such diverse subjects as atmospheric radiation, prediction of weather by computers, severe storms, frontal structure and activity, wave motion in the upper atmosphere, and environmental problems and air pollution. The course is designed to give students a broad introduction to the many disciplines involved in meteorology. (4 quarter hours)

MUSIC

Music for Elementary Teachers

A course in fundamentals oriented to the needs of the elementary teacher. The required text utilizes a branching program that allows the student to skip material with which he/she is familiar. Some recorded instruction and response allows the student to develop aural as well as intellectual music capacities. The course concentrates on the student's own knowledge of music fundamentals rather than on methods and techniques for teaching music. (2 quarter hours)

Continuing Education of Music: The Elements of Music

This beginning music theory course is intended for persons with no previous training in music. Begins with the notation of rhythm, meter, and pitch. The study proceeds with major and minor scales and key signatures. Other types of scales are also explored, such as the medieval modes and some twentieth-century forms. After these fundamentals are mastered, the course pursue intervals and a thorough understanding of chords and their construction. Students will also be introduced to a few basics in part-writing, and will conclude the work by becoming familiar with musical symbols, terminology, and vocabulary. (3 quarter hours)

Continuing Education of Music: Basic Concepts of Music

The goal of this course is to improve students' ability to listen to music. The first part of the course breaks music down into its individual component parts such as rhythm, melody, harmony, and form. Students examine how these component parts interact in texture, meaning and emotion, words, movement and style. Musical perception will be developed through active listening, increased ability to understand and apply musical boundaries, increased awareness of the interaction of music with its social, cultural, and historical contexts. The student may then apply all this to making personal musical choices from a new level with new awareness. (3 quarter hours)

Elementary Music Methods

Music itself is the instructional material of this program. Musical skills grow out of a teaching method centered on many kinds of meaningful experiences with music—singing, playing instruments, listening, moving—that interpret or recreate musical compositions, or provide for creative music-making by children. (3 quarter hours)

PHARMACOLOGY

Common Medicines

Students of all backgrounds are introduced to basic principles governing the proper use of common, over-the-counter medicines such as aspirin, cold remedies, and stomach medications and familiar prescription drugs such as antibiotics, stimulants, depressants and drugs that treat mental illness and herbal products. The potential benefits and risks of these medicines are emphasized. (3 quarter hours)

PHYSICS

Elementary Physics for Nonscientists

This is a basic course for students who have minimal mathematical preparation and are nonscience majors. The general aim is to arrive at a meaningful discussion of contemporary physics. Discussion covers classical topics such as motion and force, gravity, heat, light, and electricity lay the groundwork for the modern topics such as the quantum nature of matter and the structure of the atom and the nucleus. (5 quarter hours)

General Physics—Mechanics and Sound

The material covered will be mechanics and related subject matter. The laws of motion, static equilibrium, statistics, dynamics, conservation of momentum, conservation of energy, rotational motion and the laws of gravitation and planetary motion will all be studies. Fluids and introduction to thermal physics will also be included. This is a problem-solving course. (4 quarter hours)

General Physics—Heat, Electricity, and Magnetism

The content of this course is electricity and thermodynamics and related material. Electric charge, electrostatics, electric field, electric energy, electric circuits, electromagnetics, applied electricity, electromagnetic waves, thermal behavior of gases, the kinetic theory of gases and the Second Law of Thermodynamics, periodic motion and wave motion are also included in the problem-solving course. (4 quarter hours)

General Physics—Light and Modern Physics

The course covers optics and selected topics in modern physics. Geometrical optics, wave optics, applied optics, relativity, electrons, photons, atomic theory, atomic structure and nuclear physics, lasers, holography, color, condensed matter physics and elementary particle physics will be studied. This is a problem-solving course. (4 quarter hours)

Physics for Scientists and Engineers—Mechanics

This course is an introduction to systems of units, vectors, kinematics (the mathematical description of motion) and dynamics. Discussion includes Newton's laws of motion, energy and momentum, conservation, rotational kinematics and dynamics, rigid body equilibrium and gravitation. All of the basic mechanical quantities—velocity, acceleration, momentum, force, work energy and power—are introduced in this course. (4 quarter hours)

Physics for Scientists and Engineers—Electricity and Magnetism

An introduction to the basic phenomena of electricity, magnetism, and electromagnetism. Discussion includes electric charge and Coulomb's Law, the electric field, Gauss' Law, magnetic field, Ampere's Law, Faraday's Law, inductance, magnetic properties of matter. (4 quarter hours)

Physics for Scientists and Engineers—Waves, Optics, Light, and an Introduction to Modern Physics

This course includes discussion of oscillations, waves in elastic media, sound and electromagnetic waves, Maxwell's Equations, light and geometrical optics, interference, diffraction, light and quantum physics, fluid mechanics, temperature and expansion are all covered. (4 quarter hours)

POLITICAL SCIENCE

American National Government

This introductory course teaches the essential concepts students need to know to be an informed observer and participant in the American political system. The course addresses such subjects as "How was the American government developed? How does government make decisions? What rights and liberties does American government provide? What policies and programs does the government produce?" (5 quarter hours)

International Politics

Introduces students to global politics in a systematic fashion. In other words, we will study political systems, not individual countries or governments. It is designed to provide students with analytical skills to develop a conceptual understanding of international politics. (5 quarter hours)

The United States Constitution

Focus in this course is on the great issues which confront policy makers and the citizens in America today. Achievement of a good working acquaintance with the U.S. Constitution is an important course goal. (4 quarter hours)

The Africans

This course gives special attention to the thesis that contemporary Africa is the product of three major influences: an indigenous heritage, Western culture and Islamic culture. The coexistence of these three legacies helps to explain the diversity of African cultures and the people who are called African. (3 quarter hours)

PSYCHOLOGY

Psychology

This course offers students an up-to-date introduction to psychology. It covers topics ranging from biological bases of behavior to abnormality and social diversity. By emphasizing both fundamental principles and current developments, the course shows how the issues, methods, and applications of psychological research contribute to the body of knowledge that comprises this field. Students will get a broad base of knowledge about psychology, help them gain insight into important phenomena of their everyday lives, and allow them to see how psychology addresses issues that cross disciplines. (5 quarter hours)

Psychology of Infancy and Childhood

The principle focus of this course is the interplay of biological factors, individual personality, social structure and other environmental forces that shape the growing child. Topics of contemporary social significance include the effects of divorce, single parenthood and parents' work, changing sexual attitudes, and behavior among adolescents. Home video option. (4 quarter hours)

Psychology of Adolescents

This course surveys recent psychological research concerning youths between childhood and adulthood. The course covers developmental, social, and clinical psychology as they pertain to the adolescent. A sample of topics includes intellectual, moral, and political development; social conformity; interpersonal attraction; sex roles and sexual identity; depression; anxiety; and family relations. The emphasis is on understanding how psychological theories and principles apply to adolescence. (3 quarter hours)

Statistical Methods

This course covers the statistical treatment of data including graphical methods, the logic of hypothesis testing, measures of variability, the normal distribution and an introduction to correlation and statistical inference. (5 quarter hours)

Information Processing

The subject matter of this course involves cognitive psychology. In very simple terms, cognitive psychology is the scientific study of thinking. Therefore, like any other scientist, a cognitive psychologist observes the world by forming hypotheses, then designing and conducting experiments to test these hypotheses and then developing theories from the findings. What makes cognitive psychology unique is that it observes the mental world. You will find as you progress through the course that the mental world is not quite as tangible as the physical world, yet it is very fascinating to realize that mental events can be studies just as physical events can be studied. (4 quarter hours)

Survey of Clinical Psychology

An introduction to the types of problems seen and the various techniques used by clinicians. Emphasis will be placed on comparisons of all the different therapeutic techniques (e.g., cognitive, family, and behavior therapies). Comparison of different therapies will be on such dimensions as cost versus effectiveness and relevancy for different types of problems. Emphasis will also be placed on the varying roles of the clinician and on new trends in the fields. (4 quarter hours)

Abnormal Behavior

This course examines the fascinating range of abnormal behavior which the clinical psychologist encounters. Students will learn about diagnostic systems and treatment approaches and study various theories which have been developed to explain the origins of various clinical conditions. Students will also learn about mental retardation, problems which may affect the elderly, drug/alcohol abuse, and sexual disorders. (4 quarter hours)

Introduction to Social Psychology

A survey of research and theory on social behavior, covering a variety of issues related to interpersonal relationships and social interaction. Topics include affiliation; personal perception and impression formation; interpersonal attraction; attitude formation and change; conformity and social influence; helping; aggression; and sexual behavior. The course emphasizes current theoretical perspectives, and encourages students to apply them to their own day-to-day interactions. (4 quarter hours)

SOCIOLOGY

Introduction to Sociology

Designed to acquaint students with sociological approach to studying humans and their associations. The course is organized with two underlying objectives: 1. introduce students to the sociological perspective, the use of scientific method in studying human behavior, and the concepts that guide the thinking and research of sociologists; 2. describe what sociologists have discovered about how the social world is put together. This course attempts to explain and exemplify every major concept normally treated in an introductory course in sociology, to describe and explain the dominant theoretical positions in the field—and the debates associated with them. The course is divided into five sections, each concentrating on a particular aspect of our social world. (5 quarter hours)

Introduction to Social Statistics

This course is designed to provide an introduction to statistics to the most commonly used statistical methods found in the social science literature such as data description and presentation, measures of central tendency and variability, measures of association, estimation, and hypothesis testing. (5 quarter hours)

Introduction to Social Organization

This introductory social organization course provides a broad exposure to historical and contemporary theory and research in the area of social organization. This background sets a baseline for critical consideration of the theories and research results presented. The course then moves to the sociobiological perspective on social groupings. Students study interpersonal organization, societal organization, and world organization. Such units as the dyad, the family, bureaucracy, conflict groups, and the world economy will be considered. (3 quarter hours)

Introduction to Criminology

The objective of this course is to acquaint the student with fundamental terms, concepts, and theories in criminology and criminal justice. The orientation of this course is toward a comprehensive understanding of criminology and its relationship to sociology. Attention will be given to the development of sociological and criminological theory as a function of major philosophical movements. Topics to be covered include: concepts of law and criminology, theories of crime causation, crime typologies, and the operation of the criminal justice system. (4 quarter hours)

Juvenile Delinquency

This course is designed to acquaint the student with fundamental terms, concepts, theories, and treatment of modalities in juvenile delinquency. The orientation of this course is toward a comprehensive understanding of juvenile delinquency and its relationship to criminology. Attention will be given to the development of sociological and criminological theory as a function of sociological, psychological, and philosophical movements. Topics to be covered include the nature of delinquency, theories in delinquency, female delinquency, gang behavior, juvenile justice and constitutional law, and institutional care. (4 quarter hours)

The Criminal Justice System

The focus of this course is on the major issues confronting the criminal justice system. The course is also concerned with the future of criminal justice, including an emphasis on high-tech crime, computer crime, technology, international terrorism, and changes in individual rights in the face of burgeoning crime fighting technologies. (3 quarter hours)

SPECIAL EDUCATION

Human Exceptionality

This course is a general introduction to the characteristics of exceptional individuals and their education. Students with disabilities in the following areas will be addressed: intellectual differences (gifted and retarded), learning disabilities, emotional/behavior disorders, communication disorders, physical disabilities, hearing and visual impairments. Issues and trends, suggestions for teaching students with various disabilities, and the possible effects of a disabled student on the family will also be covered. (3 quarter hours)

WRITING

Introduction to College Writing II

This course is designed to acquaint students with the role of writing in college and in social, professional, political, and intellectual life. Students will become aware of the process of writing and how writers use language to persuade or move an audience. They will learn close reading and analysis skills to think critically about a subject and develop a sense of what is effective and appropriate writing in their major rhetorical setting, college. (4 quarter hours)

NONCREDIT COURSES

ACCOUNTING

Simplified Accounting for Managerial Control

This course is designed for small business owners, office managers, and anyone desiring simplified accounting/bookkeeping skills. Key subjects include understanding and reading balance sheets and income statements, accounts and setting up books. Specific descriptions will be given for all general ledger areas: assets, liabilities, owner equity, revenue, and expense. (Noncredit) *Tuition:* $105 plus $20 course manual.

LIBRARY SCIENCE

Church and Synagogue Librarianship

This course is an introduction to providing library services within a congregational setting for anyone interested in church/synagogue library work, especially the volunteer librarian. The focus is on assessing what you have, identifying a library's potential and handling the practical problems of room arrangement, staff, budget, selection and ordering resources, cataloging, circulation of library materials, helping others find the right resources, and promoting use of the library. (2 CEUs) *Tuition:* $105 plus $10 course manual.

MANAGEMENT

Effective Writing in Business

Designed to provide practical application in the art of writing effective business communications. Letters and memos will deal with such business activities as orders, inquiries, adjustments, applications for job, credits and collections, and selling by mail. A short, formal report will be included as the final assignment. (Noncredit) *Tuition:* $95 plus $10 course manual.

Utah State University
Independent Study Division
Life Span Learning Programs
UMC 5000
Logan, Utah 84322-5000   (801) 797-2137

Description:
  Utah State University was founded in 1888 as a land-grant institution. A rich curriculum is offered currently for technical, scientific, and professional training at both the undergraduate and graduate levels. Life Span Learning Programs include a Conference and Institute Division, a Class Division, and an Independent Study Division. The correspondence courses offered by the Independent Study Division are similar to campus resident courses in the content, amount, and quality of work required, as well as in the amount of credit allowed.

Faculty:
  Gary S. Poppleton, Director, Independent Study Division.

Academic Levels:
  College
  High School

Degree/Certificate Programs:
  A total of 45 quarter credits of correspondence study may be applied toward a baccalaureate degree, but none may apply toward a graduate degree. High school credit toward a diploma may be earned through Utah State University but the university does not grant high school diplomas.

Utah State University

COLLEGE COURSES

ACCOUNTING

Introduction to Financial Accounting

Introduction to the basic accounting cycle and financial state preparation. Application of basic accounting principles in determi financial position and income. (4 quarter credits)

Introduction to Managerial Accounting

Managerial uses of accounting information including planning geting), controlling, and decision making. Also includes sele financial accounting issues, statement of cash flow, and analysis interpretation of financial statements. (4 quarter credits)

Cost Accounting I

Accounting for planning and controlling business operations. Incl costing methods, cost control reporting, and budgeting. (4 qu credits)

ADULT EDUCATION

Foundations of Adult Education

This course reviews the historical and philosophical foundation adult and continuing education programs of many discipline emphasizes measurable factors in administration, curriculum program development and conducting and evaluating adult progr (3 quarter credits)

ANIMAL SCIENCE

Horse Production Practices

Breeding, feeding, care, and management of horses. (3 quarter cre

Animal Feeds and Feeding Practices

Feed composition and characteristics which influence animal pe mance. Digestion of feeds and nutrient utilization by animals. Em sis on diet formulation and feeding practices. (4 quarter credi

Principles of Animal Breeding

The role of genetic factors in influencing animal performance, application of selection principles and breeding systems to the provement of farm mammals. A computer simulated herd of beef or dairy cattle will provide experience in selection method quarter credits)

ANTHROPOLOGY

Introduction to Anthropology

An orientation to the basic areas of anthropology which inc primate antecedents of man, evolution of man, evolution of hu cultural and social life, and analysis of the nature and variabilit human kinship, economics, political, and religious institutions quarter credits)

Peoples and Cultures of the World

Intensive comparisons of the economic, political, kinship, and gious structures of representative societies from the major cul areas of the world. (5 quarter credits)

ART

Exploring Art

Aims to increase enjoyment of living through the sense of si Develops understanding of basic principles underlying the vis forms of art in everyday life. (3 quarter credits)

organization. This background sets a baseline for critical consideration of the theories and research results presented. The course then moves to the sociobiological perspective on social groupings. Students study interpersonal organization, societal organization, and world organization. Such units as the dyad, the family, bureaucracy, conflict groups, and the world economy will be considered. (3 quarter hours)

Introduction to Criminology

The objective of this course is to acquaint the student with fundamental terms, concepts, and theories in criminology and criminal justice. The orientation of this course is toward a comprehensive understanding of criminology and its relationship to sociology. Attention will be given to the development of sociological and criminological theory as a function of major philosophical movements. Topics to be covered include: concepts of law and criminology, theories of crime causation, crime typologies, and the operation of the criminal justice system. (4 quarter hours)

Juvenile Delinquency

This course is designed to acquaint the student with fundamental terms, concepts, theories, and treatment of modalities in juvenile delinquency. The orientation of this course is toward a comprehensive understanding of juvenile delinquency and its relationship to criminology. Attention will be given to the development of sociological and criminological theory as a function of sociological, psychological, and philosophical movements. Topics to be covered include the nature of delinquency, theories in delinquency, female delinquency, gang behavior, juvenile justice and constitutional law, and institutional care. (4 quarter hours)

The Criminal Justice System

The focus of this course is on the major issues confronting the criminal justice system. The course is also concerned with the future of criminal justice, including an emphasis on high-tech crime, computer crime, technology, international terrorism, and changes in individual rights in the face of burgeoning crime fighting technologies. (3 quarter hours)

SPECIAL EDUCATION

Human Exceptionality

This course is a general introduction to the characteristics of exceptional individuals and their education. Students with disabilities in the following areas will be addressed: intellectual differences (gifted and retarded), learning disabilities, emotional/behavior disorders, communication disorders, physical disabilities, hearing and visual impairments. Issues and trends, suggestions for teaching students with various disabilities, and the possible effects of a disabled student on the family will also be covered. (3 quarter hours)

WRITING

Introduction to College Writing II

This course is designed to acquaint students with the role of writing in college and in social, professional, political, and intellectual life. Students will become aware of the process of writing and how writers use language to persuade or move an audience. They will learn close reading and analysis skills to think critically about a subject and develop a sense of what is effective and appropriate writing in their major rhetorical setting, college. (4 quarter hours)

NONCREDIT COURSES

ACCOUNTING

Simplified Accounting for Managerial Control

This course is designed for small business owners, office managers, and anyone desiring simplified accounting/bookkeeping skills. Key subjects include understanding and reading balance sheets and income statements, accounts and setting up books. Specific descriptions will be given for all general ledger areas: assets, liabilities, owner equity, revenue, and expense. (Noncredit) *Tuition:* $105 plus $20 course manual.

LIBRARY SCIENCE

Church and Synagogue Librarianship

This course is an introduction to providing library services within a congregational setting for anyone interested in church/synagogue library work, especially the volunteer librarian. The focus is on assessing what you have, identifying a library's potential and handling the practical problems of room arrangement, staff, budget, selection and ordering resources, cataloging, circulation of library materials, helping others find the right resources, and promoting use of the library. (2 CEUs) *Tuition:* $105 plus $10 course manual.

MANAGEMENT

Effective Writing in Business

Designed to provide practical application in the art of writing effective business communications. Letters and memos will deal with such business activities as orders, inquiries, adjustments, applications for job, credits and collections, and selling by mail. A short, formal report will be included as the final assignment. (Noncredit) *Tuition:* $95 plus $10 course manual.

Utah State University
Independent Study Division
Life Span Learning Programs
UMC 5000
Logan, Utah 84322-5000   (801) 797-2137

Description:
 Utah State University was founded in 1888 as a land-grant institution. A rich curriculum is offered currently for technical, scientific, and professional training at both the undergraduate and graduate levels. Life Span Learning Programs include a Conference and Institute Division, a Class Division, and an Independent Study Division. The correspondence courses offered by the Independent Study Division are similar to campus resident courses in the content, amount, and quality of work required, as well as in the amount of credit allowed.

Faculty:
 Gary S. Poppleton, Director, Independent Study Division.

Academic Levels:
 College
 High School

Degree/Certificate Programs:
 A total of 45 quarter credits of correspondence study may be applied toward a baccalaureate degree, but none may apply toward a graduate degree. High school credit toward a diploma may be earned through Utah State University but the university does not grant high school diplomas.

Utah State University

Admission Requirements:

Admission to Utah State University is not required; an applicant must be 19 years of age or a high school graduate. Those under 19 who do not have a high school diploma or its equivalent must obtain the written permission of their high school principal.

Tuition:

College courses, $45 per quarter hour credit plus any audiovisual material fee (tapes, slides, videos; variable fee $10 to $20) payable at registration. Contact the Independent Study Division for high school tuition information. Prices are subject to change without notice and usually on an annual basis. A refund of registration fees (minus $15 handling fee and $5 per assignment handed in) will be made if requested within four weeks after the date of registration; within eight weeks of registration, 50 percent refund; no refund after eight weeks of registration. VA benefits for eligible veterans available for programs leading to a standard college degree.

Enrollment Period:

One year from registration date is allowed for completion of a course. The minimum time for completion is one month. An extension of six months may be granted upon payment of a $25 fee.

Equipment Requirements:

The cost of textbooks and supplies is not included in the tuition. Texts and supplies may be ordered from the U.S.U. Bookstore.

Credit and Grading:

To receive credit, the student must successfully complete all assignments and examinations in a course. Most examinations must be monitored by an approved proctor. All Independent Study courses yield grade points, except those taken on a pass/fail basis. Students must exercise the P-D-F option within three months from the date of registration or by the time they have submitted one-third of the assignments in the course/courses under consideration, whichever comes first. The grading system is A, B, C, D, F with plus and minus for grades A–D. Correspondence credits transferred-in are evaluated individually. Credit is awarded in quarter hour units.

Library Services:

Students are urged to establish a good working relationship with their local public library. If such facilities are not available, materials may be requested from the Distance Education Library Services of the Merrill Library on the campus.

Accreditations:

Northwest Association of Schools and Colleges. Member of: National University Continuing Education Association.

COLLEGE COURSES

ACCOUNTING

Introduction to Financial Accounting

Introduction to the basic accounting cycle and financial statement preparation. Application of basic accounting principles in determining financial position and income. (4 quarter credits)

Introduction to Managerial Accounting

Managerial uses of accounting information including planning (budgeting), controlling, and decision making. Also includes selected financial accounting issues, statement of cash flow, and analysis and interpretation of financial statements. (4 quarter credits)

Cost Accounting I

Accounting for planning and controlling business operations. Includes costing methods, cost control reporting, and budgeting. (4 quarter credits)

ADULT EDUCATION

Foundations of Adult Education

This course reviews the historical and philosophical foundations of adult and continuing education programs of many disciplines. It emphasizes measurable factors in administration, curriculum and program development and conducting and evaluating adult programs. (3 quarter credits)

ANIMAL SCIENCE

Horse Production Practices

Breeding, feeding, care, and management of horses. (3 quarter credits)

Animal Feeds and Feeding Practices

Feed composition and characteristics which influence animal performance. Digestion of feeds and nutrient utilization by animals. Emphasis on diet formulation and feeding practices. (4 quarter credits)

Principles of Animal Breeding

The role of genetic factors in influencing animal performance, the application of selection principles and breeding systems to the improvement of farm mammals. A computer simulated herd of either beef or dairy cattle will provide experience in selection methods. (3 quarter credits)

ANTHROPOLOGY

Introduction to Anthropology

An orientation to the basic areas of anthropology which include primate antecedents of man, evolution of man, evolution of human cultural and social life, and analysis of the nature and variability of human kinship, economics, political, and religious institutions. (5 quarter credits)

Peoples and Cultures of the World

Intensive comparisons of the economic, political, kinship, and religious structures of representative societies from the major culture areas of the world. (5 quarter credits)

ART

Exploring Art

Aims to increase enjoyment of living through the sense of sight. Develops understanding of basic principles underlying the visible forms of art in everyday life. (3 quarter credits)

BIOLOGY

Principles of Biology

An introduction to the fundamental principles and concepts of biology, including cellular structure and function reproduction, heredity, human biology, evolution and ecology, and organismal diversity. (4 quarter credits)

BUSINESS ADMINISTRATION

Introduction to Business

An investigation of the role of business in contemporary society, including an introduction to the general problems of business operations. (3 quarter credits)

Operations Research

Quantitative methods for resource allocation: liner programming, PERT/CPM, simulation, queing theory (waiting lines). (4 quarter credits)

Corporation Finance

How the corporation raises and manages its capital. A study of modern financial principles, methods, and institutions. Corporate organization, creation, and reorganization. (4 quarter credits)

Fundamentals of Marketing

Overview of the marketing function emphasizing concepts and terminology. Includes the basic marketing activities of product management, pricing, distribution, promotion, marketing research, and consumer behavior. (4 quarter credits)

Production Management

The field of production and operations management involves the planning, coordinating, and executing of all activities that create goods and services. Some of the specific techniques that are presented are forecasting, product and process design, material and inventory control, quality systems, scheduling, just-in-time systems and production planning. (4 quarter credits)

Consumer Behavior

This course is designed to acquaint the student with the forces which underlie the consumer buying process—the reasons why people buy. Included are discussions of consumer perception, attitudes, motivation, personality, learning, social class, culture, family influence, decision process, and applications from each area to marketing strategy. (4 quarter credits)

Retailing Management

The purpose of this course is to analyze that part of the marketing system which deals with the selling of goods and services to the final household consumer. The textbook attempts to synthesize and integrate into a systems framework the critical issues, processes, and techniques necessary to understand the managerial function as it relates to the field of retailing. (4 quarter credits)

BUSINESS EDUCATION

Managing Personal Finances

Provides information, reasoning tools, and experience to help the student develop decision making skills in the area of personal finance and financial planning. (3 quarter credits)

Office Systems Management

The major area of emphasis of this course is the introduction of current technology that affects office and information management. Specific topics covered include telecommunications and telephone systems, software application, copier and printer advancements, office re-cycling, LAN system security, facsimile features, power protection, and storage technology. (3 quarter credits)

CHEMISTRY

Introduction to Chemistry

A course designed primarily for students of nursing, liberal arts, and others whose major field does not require further chemistry. (5 quarter credits)

CIVIL ENGINEERING

Water Resources Engineering - Hydraulic

This course is designed to teach the student to apply fundamental principles and concepts to the solution of problems in open channel flow, hydraulic machinery, dynamic lift and drag, and potential flow. (3 quarter credits)

Applied Hydraulics

This course is designed primarily to serve non-engineering majors. It covers fluid statics and dynamics; flow in pipes and in open channels; flow measurement and pumps. (4 quarter credits)

Engineering Hydraulics

This course is designed to teach the student to apply fundamental principles and concepts to the solution of flow measurement, boundary layer, pipe flow, and open channel flow problems. (5 quarter credits)

COMMUNICATIVE DISORDERS

Hearing Science

Introduction to acoustics, the hearing mechanism, and the perception of sound. (3 quarter credits)

Listening Problems in the Classroom

Listening problems in the classroom; hearing, speech, room acoustic, and room amplification solutions; personnel role consideration. For elementary, secondary, and special education teachers and administrators, as well as audiologists and speech-language pathologists. (3 quarter credits)

Speech Science

Physiology and acoustics of speech perception and production. (3 quarter credits)

Listening and Speech Training for the Hearing Impaired

Basic considerations, programs, materials, and methods for providing listening and speech testing and training for children and adults with hearing impairments. (3 quarter credits)

Rehabilitative Audiology

Aural rehabilitative management of adults who are hearing impaired, including reduction of the barriers to communication that have resulted from hearing loss. (3 quarter credits)

Speech for the Hearing Impaired

Basic principles, evaluation procedures, and developmental strategies. (3 quarter credits)

Acoustics and Sound Systems in Schools

Acoustical problems of school classrooms increasing difficulty in listening and teaching in schools and materials, equipment, and methods for alleviating or compensating for such problems. (3 quarter credits)

ECONOMICS

Principles of Macroeconomics

A course for the general college student regardless of the field of specialization. Emphasis is on an understanding of principles and institutions that underlie the operations of the economic system. (5 quarter credits)

Principles of Microeconomics

A course for the general college student regardless of field of specialization. Emphasis is on economics of the market place with analysis of issues surrounding consumer behavior and typical business structures. (5 quarter credits)

Intermediate Microeconomic Theory

A course emphasizing the analysis of the behavior of consumers and business firms. Application of the theory of microeconomics will then be used in the solution of problems of the real world. (4 quarter credits)

ELEMENTARY EDUCATION

Teaching Reading

A beginning course in teaching reading. Considers the skills necessary in learning how to read: the methods and materials available in teaching reading in an elementary school. This course is divided into three areas: Reading Readiness; Primary Grade Reading Skills, and Intermediate Grade Reading Skills. (3 quarter credits)

ENGLISH

Elements of Grammar

An extensive review of elementary grammar with emphasis upon practical application. (3 quarter credits)

Great Literature of Britain

A study of representative masterpieces of British literature: Beowulf, Chaucer, Shakespeare, Swift, Dickens, Wordsworth, Conrad, etc. (3 quarter credits)

British Literature Survey to 1798

Critical study of representative writers and works of British literature from the Old English period through the 18th century, including Chaucer, Shakespeare, Spenser, Donne, Milton, Pope, and Swift. (5 quarter credits)

British Literature Survey from 1798

Critical study of representative writers and works of British literature from the Romantic, Victorian, and twentieth century, including Wordsworth, Coleridge, Byron, Shelley, Keats, Tennyson, Browning, Dickens, Conrad, Joyce, Eliot, Yeats, and Auden. (3 quarter credits)

Children's Literature

Prose and poetry through the elementary level. Must have access to children's library for reference books. (3 quarter credits)

FAMILY AND HUMAN DEVELOPMENT

Marriage and the American Family

This course has been designed to address many sensitive concerns that students, young and old alike, have about marital relationships and family life. It blends theory, research, and practice together within the framework of prevention. It includes social, economic, political, and historical context of family life. (3 quarter credits)

Human Growth and Development

An overview of development from conception to death and the dying process, emphasizing stages of physical and cognitive development as well as social, emotional, and personality development. (5 quarter credits)

Guidance of Children

Discipline problems and promises defined. Review of various guidance philosophies with emphasis on principles and teaching techniques. A practice set of guidelines for developing a personalized system of guidance. (3 quarter credits)

Child Abuse and Neglect: A Multidisciplinary Approach

This course is designed to provide a comprehensive overview of a significant social problem, child abuse and neglect. (3 quarter credits)

FISHERIES AND WILDLIFE

General Fishery Biology

This course will provide an introduction to the basic biology and ecology of fishes; their anatomy, respiration, nutrition, osmoregulation, and behavior are among the topics which will be presented—all with an ecological perspective. Students will also briefly study fish as a resource and the impact man can have upon this resource. (5 quarter credits)

FRENCH

Elementary French

LFR.101. A beginning course using the "natural approach." Work through the textbook with the instructor guiding step by step on audiocassette. (5 quarter credits)

LFR.102. Again, using the "natural approach," the instructor guides the student step by step on audiocassette. (5 quarter credits)

LFR.103. The "natural approach" continues. (5 quarter credits)

Intermediate French

LFR.201. An intermediate course. (4 quarter credits)

LFR.202. A continuation of the above course. (3 quarter credits)

LFR.203. A continuation of the above course. (3 quarter credits)

GEOGRAPHY

World Regional Geography

An introduction to the field of cultural geography. In the course, natural physical features of the world will be noted—mountains, oceans, rivers, etc.,—but the major emphasis will be upon mankind's utilization of the natural environment. (5 quarter credits)

Physical Geography

Geographic analysis of the distribution and processes concerned with elements of the natural environment (i.e., weather, climate, landforms, vegetation, soils, and water). (5 quarter credits)

Regional Geography: Anglo-America

A survey of general geography with emphasis upon the social and cultural viewpoint. The influence of geography of domestic and international problems; cultural, ethnic, and linguistic background; boundaries, population trends, national, economic, and governmental systems as they may reflect governmental problems. (3 quarter credits)

Regional Geography: Geography of Europe

A survey of general geography with viewpoint. The influence of geography of domestic and international problems; cultural, ethnic, and linguistic background; boundaries, population trends, national, economic, and governmental systems as they may reflect governmental problems. (3 quarter credits)

GEOLOGY

Introductory Geology

An introduction to minerals, rocks, and the processes that shape the earth including plate tectonics. The course also provides a review of geologic time and the physical history of the earth and life on earth. (5 quarter credits)

Historical Geology

Historical geology is an investigation of the physical and biological changes that have occurred over the past 4.6 billion years of our planet Earth's history as revealed by the geologic rock record. The course begins by learning how the basic geologic principles and concepts such as geologic time, plate tectonics, and rocks and fossils are used to interpret Earth's past and concludes with a chronological discussion of the history of Earth. (4 quarter credits)

HISTORY

Comparative Civilizations: Ancient and Medieval

A comparative survey of the major civilizations of the world in early times. Special attention will be given to political, religious, social, economic, artistic, and intellectual attainments of mankind to about A.D. 1500. (3 quarter credits)

Comparative Civilizations: Early Modern

A comparative survey of the major world civilizations during the period of transformation to European dominance, from about 1500 to 1900. (3 quarter credits)

Comparative Civilizations: Modern

A comparative survey of major world civilizations in the modern period. Special attention will be given to political, religious, social, economic, intellectual, and artistic achievements of man. (3 quarter credits)

American Civilization

The fundamentals of American history. (5 quarter credits)

The Civil War and Reconstruction

A course designed to examine the background and events leading up to the Civil War, the War, and the period of reconstruction. (3 quarter credits)

Recent America (1945–Present)

An in-depth examination of the critical issues of the dramatic post-World War II period. Among the key developments to be discussed are the Cold War, the Civil Rights Revolution, minority rights, the presidency, and social developments. (3 quarter credits)

INSTRUCTIONAL TECHNOLOGY

Use of Libraries and Learning Resources

Principle reference tools in each field are studies. Emphasis is placed upon reference materials for elementary, secondary, and public libraries. (3 quarter credits)

Undergraduate Research Creative Opportunity

Media production and utilization for teachers at the elementary/secondary grade level will be considered from the perspective of designing a technology of instruction. (3 quarter credits)

Developing Library Media Collections

Experience in reviewing, evaluating, and selecting instructional materials. Criteria for evaluation of all media. Use of standard evaluation and selection tools and reviewing publications, constraints, etc. (3 quarter credits)

LANDSCAPE ARCHITECTURE

Introduction to Landscape Architecture

This course endeavors to acquaint the student with the landscape in his or her environment, as a practical approach to the pleasure that comes from appreciation and understanding of subject. Emphasis is placed on design and arrangement of outdoor space as it relates to home living; however, public buildings and areas are discussed because of their interrelationship to each other and because all of these areas are the concern of the landscape architect. (3 quarter credits)

MANAGEMENT

Small Business Management

This program of instruction is designed to provide students with a practical overview of management principles and practices as they apply to the small business enterprise. (3 quarter credits)

Management and Organizations

Investigation and application of fundamental concepts of management and organization theory. (4 quarter credits)

Entrepreneurship of New Venture Management

Processes, methods, and steps involved in starting a new venture such as a small business. Emphasizes the planning, financing, conception, and management of new firms. (4 quarter credits)

MASS COMMUNICATIONS

Introduction to Mass Communications

Structures, functions, political, social and economic impacts of mass media: newspapers, books, magazines, radio, television, film, public relations, and advertising. (4 quarter credits)

MATHEMATICS

Basic Mathematics (Remedial)

Remedial arithmetic to help the student who has deficiencies in arithmetic gain a better understanding of the structure of arithmetic and to gain competence in the use of arithmetic to solve problems; to help the remedial mathematics student learn enough arithmetic so he/she can apply it to the solution of problems in his/her required general education courses such as physics, chemistry, and geology. (5 quarter credits)

Elements of Algebra (Remedial)

This course is designed to give those students with an inadequate preparation in beginning algebra the essentials of algebra. (5 quarter credits)

Intermediate Algebra

Covers the area between a first course in high school algebra and college algebra. (5 quarter credits)

College Algebra

Required for all higher work in mathematics, physics, chemistry, biological science, business, and engineering. (5 quarter credits)

Trigonometry and Algebra

A study of the trigonometric functions, trigonometric identities, solutions of triangles, solutions to trigonometric equations, complex numbers, laws of sines, cosines, and the compound angle formulas. (5 quarter credits)

MICROBIOLOGY

Elementary Microbiology

The biology, morphology, physiology, and significance of microorganisms; basic concepts governing growth and metabolism of microbes, the interaction between microbe and host, microorganisms and human diseases, and the microbiology of soils, water, and food. (4 quarter credits)

MUSIC

Enjoying Music

A nontechnical course designed to bring about a better understanding and enjoyment of music serving a wide range of musical styles and forms. The course is complete with taped listening exercises and examples. Cassette tapes are used in assignments. Students should have access to a cassette player. (3 quarter credits)

Fundamentals of Music

Musicians and laymen, at all levels of talent and perception, are fascinated by the sound of music through a systematic study of the basic characteristics of sound and the vocabulary of the musician. The purpose of this course is to familiarize the layman with the language of music and to suggest prerequisite skills for continued understanding, utilization, and enjoyment. (3 quarter credits)

NUTRITION

Nutrition for People

The relation of food to health; factors influencing nutritive requirements; problems applicable to individual interests. (3 quarter credits)

Human Nutrition

Latest nutrition concepts are presented for teachers and others interested in updating their basic understanding of nutrition. (3 quarter credits)

OCCUPATIONAL SAFETY AND HEALTH

Occupational Safety and Health Management

Management practices applied to loss prevention and control; survey of existing programs, laws, legislation, certification, professional ethics, and the various functions of the safety professional. (2 quarter credits)

OCEANOGRAPHY

Oceanography

Oceanography is a multidisciplinary subject that draws upon and integrates many fields of science. This course will combine information from geology, physics, chemistry, and biology to provide an overview of ocean processes. Included will be a discussion of man's interrelationship with the oceans historically and some of the social, economic, and political ramifications thereof. (4 quarter credits)

PHILOSOPHY

Introduction to Problems of Philosophy

Problem of reality, thought, and value in relation to the modern world. Both for students preparing for more advanced courses in philosophy and for those desiring an introduction to philosophical terminology and to ideas of philosophers ancient, medieval, and modern who have influenced present-day thought. (5 quarter credits)

Deductive Logic

Signs, symbols, and language in human behavior. Detection of common fallacies, ambiguity, vagueness. Structure of propositions; forms of valid inference; nature of deductive systems; recognition of formal fallacies. (5 quarter credits)

PHYSICAL EDUCATION

Dynamic Fitness

Designed to physically condition the body, incorporate a life-style of healthful living, and to understand the exercise physiology, of physical fitness and the essentials of a good dietary program. Special emphasis is on developing a good level of cardiovascular endurance, strength,

and flexibility, in that order. The understanding will result from study of the text and supplement. The application of the information is made concurrently in the student's health and fitness program. (3 quarter credits)

PHYSIOLOGY

Human Physiology

A survey of human physiology which deals with the functioning of the human body. It provides an understanding of various body functions and provides the student with a vocabulary which will permit him to understand better and appreciate the values of scientific investigation. (5 quarter credits)

PLANT SCIENCE

Introduction to Agricultural Plant Science

A survey course which includes a discussion of world crops, soil, water, agricultural chemicals, and structure and function of plants. (4 quarter credits)

Landscape Management in the Interior West

This course will present the information that enters into the decisions a landscape manager makes in conditions unique to the Interior West. Practical management concerns will be covered, such as pruning, weed control, fertilization, and irrigation. (3 quarter credits)

Fruit Production

Physiology, anatomy, propagation, sites, soils, climate, culture, irrigation, fertilizers, insect and disease control, harvesting, storage, marketing, economics. (4 quarter credits)

POLITICAL SCIENCE

United States Government and Politics

Designed to give a comprehensive knowledge of American governmental institutions. Special emphasis is on actual operation rather than a study of the forms of government. A general survey of the national system is included. (5 quarter credits)

PSYCHOLOGY

General Psychology

A survey course covering the basic areas of study in psychology. (5 quarter credits)

Human Development: General

A study of the human physical, cognitive, and developmental processes from birth to maturity. (3 to 5 quarter credits)

Career Exploration

This course is designed to enable students of all disciplines and levels of educational attainment to explore their career interests and potential. A number of the topics also directly apply to the development of general life-planning skills. (3 quarter credits)

Child Abuse and Neglect: A Multidisciplinary Approach

This course is designed to provide a comprehensive overview of a significant social problem, child abuse and neglect. (3 quarter credits)

Abnormal Psychology

A study of the abnormal behavior as seen from various perspectives in identification, classification, and treatment. (3 quarter credits)

PUBLIC HEALTH

Personal Health

A course in current health information for those persons who are now teaching or plan to teach health. Designed to be of value to students in their own personal lives as well. (2 quarter credits)

School Health Program for Elementary and Secondary Teachers

A course on the fundamentals of the elements of the school health program: health education, health services, and the school health environment. (3 quarter credits)

Introduction to Occupational Safety and Health

A study of health and safety problems encountered in industry and various occupations. (3 quarter credits)

Communicable Disease Control

Nature of the agents, mechanisms of transmission, control, and prevention of communicable diseases. (3 quarter credits)

Fundamentals of Epidemiology

Introduction to the study of the distribution and causes of communicable diseases in man and other animals. (3 quarter credits)

SOCIAL WORK

Introduction to Social Welfare

This course provides an overview of social policies and programs designed to promote the general welfare and ameliorate social problems. (3 quarter credits)

Child Abuse and Neglect: A Multidisciplinary Approach

This course is designed to provide a comprehensive overview of a significant social problem, child abuse and neglect. (3 quarter credits)

SOCIOLOGY

Introductory Sociology

This course is designed to provide the student with an understanding of fundamental sociological concepts and areas of investigation. Among the topics covered are personality development and social change. (5 quarter credits)

Population and Society

Emphasis is placed on population theories, factual information on population trends, sources of information on population, demographic processes and the role of these in society. (3 quarter credits)

Juvenile Delinquency

This course addresses the nature and cause of juvenile delinquency. While the course concentrates mainly on United States society, cross cultural comparisons with other nations are included. Among the topics covered are: the social construction of adolescence, the structure of the juvenile justice system, and the impact of family, mass media, and schools on delinquency. Special attention is focused on theories of delinquency and issues in the measurement of juvenile crime. (3 quarter credits)

Criminology

Introduction to the systematic study of crime. Part one of the course reviews the nature and extent of crime in the United States. Ecological and demographic tendencies of crime are discussed, especially the impact of such variables as age, gender, and race on U.S. crime rates. Part two of the course focuses on various psychological and sociological theories of crime, while part three reviews different types of crime (e.g., violent, property, and white collar crime) found in our society. (3 quarter credits)

SOIL SCIENCE

Soils, Water, and Environment: An Introduction

A survey of soils and water for food and fiber production, as sinks for wastes, and for recreational uses. Environmentally oriented. Pollution, natural resources, and energy needs are related to soil and water and to population pressures. (3 quarter credits)

General Soils

Review of the entire field of soil study, designed as a foundation course for all students of agriculture. (4 quarter credits)

SPANISH

Elementary Spanish

LSP.102. A beginning course open to students having had Spanish 101 or at least one, but not more than two, years of Spanish in high school. (5 quarter credits)

LSP.103. A beginning course open to students having completed Spanish 102 or at least one, but not more than three, years of Spanish in high school. (5 quarter credits)

Intermediate Spanish

LSP.201. An intermediate course open to students having completed Spanish 103 or at least two, but not more than three, years of Spanish in high school. (5 quarter credits)

LSP.202. An intermediate course open to students having completed Spanish 201 or at least three, but not more than four, years of Spanish in an integrated high school program. (5 quarter credits)

Advanced Grammar

LSP.304. The purpose and objective of this course is to provide an in-depth structural analysis of the various contrastive areas of English and Spanish with particular emphasis on those areas of Spanish which still present problems to the native speaker of English who has acquired a fair fluency in Spanish. (3 quarter credits)

LSP 305. A continuation of Course 304 to provide an in-depth structural analysis of the various contrastive areas of English and Spanish with particular emphasis on those areas of Spanish which still present problems to the native speaker of English who has acquired a fair fluency in Spanish. (3 quarter credits)

SPECIAL EDUCATION

Education of Exceptional Individuals

A survey of the characteristics of all types of exceptional children with emphasis on the educational and psychological implications on these conditions on the development of the child. (3 quarter credits)

STATISTICS

Business Statistics

Descriptive and inferential statistics, probability, sampling, estimation, tests of hypothesis, linear-regression and correlation, chi square, analysis of variance, time series, index numbers. (5 quarter credits)

Statistical Methods I

Introduction to statistical concepts, graphical techniques, probability distributions, estimation, and testing. (3 quarter credits)

HIGH SCHOOL COURSES

BIOLOGY

Biology and Me

This course is designed to acquaint the student with the planet on which we live. Subjects covered range from the least complicated structure, the atom, to the most complex organism, man. Major emphasis will be on the structure and function of organisms plus basic

Valdosta State College

biological processes. Representatives of major plant and animal groups will be studied. (1 unit)

ENGLISH

English Literature

A study of the periods of English literature, including an English novel and a Shakespeare play. (½ unit)

Exploring Literature

A beginning high school course with exposure in all literary types: novels, short stories, plays, poetry, etc. (½ unit)

Expository Writing

A high school course dealing with essay writing in preparation for college. (½ unit)

Journalism

A high school course dealing with the newspaper-style of writing. (½ unit)

Basic Composition

A study of basic sentence, paragraph, and short essay writing. (½ unit)

GEOGRAPHY

Geography

A high school course dealing with the effects of weather, landforms, resources, production, transportation, and people as a basis for understanding United States and world interdependence. (½ unit or 1 unit)

HISTORY

United States History

A high school course in American History beginning with the "Age of Exploration and Discovery" and continuing to the present. (½ unit or 1 unit)

World History

This is a survey course that will introduce the student to the development of early civilizations in the world, the growth and development of modern-nation states in Europe, the social and economic challenges that affected Western civilization, the religious forces of western man, the causes and results of European imperialism, and the study of the various cultures in the western world. (½ unit or 1 unit)

HOME ECONOMICS

Parenting

A course designed to explore the family unit. The course will cover premarital behavior, dating, marriage, career choices, raising a family, lifestyle choices, communications skills, child rearing, and home management skills. (½ unit)

Housing and Home Decorating

A course designed to help develop basic skills for making a home more beautiful and comfortable, and for learning how to spend housing dollars more wisely. Work will include house plan evaluation and drawing and use of colors and fabrics in interior design. (½ unit)

MATHEMATICS

Algebra

Given for those students who have had no algebra in high school. The completion of this course will substitute for a year of high school algebra. (1 unit)

SOCIAL SCIENCE

American Government

This course will be a study of government in the United States and a general view of democracy at work—the processes of government, how the system is organized, the ways in which this system is controlled, and the ways in which the government functions. (½ unit or 1 unit)

American Social Problems

This survey course is designed to acquaint students with several problems facing America. Emphasis will be given to crime and justice, violence, race, and variant sexuality. (½ unit or 1 unit)

Valdosta State College
Division of Public Services
Independent Study
Valdosta, Georgia 31601   (912) 247-3315

Description:
The Independent Study program of Valdosta State College is a service of The University System of Georgia Independent Study as offered by the Georgia Center for Continuing Education located at the University of Georgia in Athens, Georgia. For courses available, SEE **Georgia, University of.**

Accreditations:
Southern Association of Colleges and Schools.

Valley Forge Christian College
Charleston Road
Phoenixville, Pennsylvania 19460
          (215) 935-0450

Description:
Valley Forge Christian College was chartered under the name of Eastern Bible Institute on January 6, 1939 for the training of pastors, evangelists, missionaries, Christian education workers, and lay workers. It is now operated under the supervision of a Board of Regents representing the six districts of the Assemblies of God in the northeastern part of the United States and the Italian District of the Assemblies of God.

The college is located just southwest of Phoenixville on Charlestown Road astride the common boundary between Schuylkill and Charlestown Townships. The city of Phoenixville is located approximately 25 miles northwest of Philadelphia on Route 23. Historically, the area can be traced to William Penn and his immediate descendants. Not far from this site British and Colonial soldiers marched during the American Revolution. The college itself is located only a few miles from Valley Forge National Park, where General George Washington spent the winter of 1777–78.

The purpose of Valley Forge Christian College is to offer systematic training on the collegiate level to men and women for Christian service as either ministers or laypersons. College-level correspondence courses are available to persons who are not enrolled at the college. Some courses are offered in most of the main academic areas of the college's curriculum—Bible, Greek, theology, Church history, pastoral studies, missions, Christian education and psychology. Enrollment is approximately 600 with students from 30 different states and 5 foreign countries.

For courses available, contact the Director of Correspondence Study.

Faculty:
Donald Tucker, Director of Correspondence Study.

Academic Levels:
College

Degree/Certificate Programs:
Fifteen hours of credits earned by correspondence may be applied toward a degree program. Credits may be earned through Valley Forge Christian College or other accredited institution. Correspondence Study is not open to on-campus students.

Admission Requirements:
High school graduation if seeking degree credit. For application procedures, contact the Director of Correspondence Study.

Tuition:
Contact the college for current tuition information.

Enrollment Period:
Maximum time allowed to complete a course is one year.

Equipment Requirements:
There are additional charges for study guides and textbooks. Student must have access to cassette player for language courses.

Credit and Grading:
Credit is awarded in semester hour units. Grades are by letter system; GPA on 4-point scale. C is minimum passing grade.

Accreditations:
American Association of Bible Colleges.

Washington, University of
Distance Learning
5001 25th Avenue NE, GH-23
Seattle, Washington 98195   (800) 543-2350

Description:
The University of Washington's Distance Learning program began in 1912. It has grown steadily and currently enrolls over 2,000 students in 3,500 courses. Courses typically consist of study guides, assigned texts, assignments, examinations, and such supplementary materials as audiocassettes, videotapes, and computer disks. Certain noncredit courses required for university entrance are available. Independent study courses for college credit are similar to campus courses in content, quality, quantity of work required. Courses have the approval of the university department or school. Programs offered also include high school level as well as noncredit.

Faculty:
Dr. Muriel Dance, Head. There is a faculty of 65 members.

Academic Levels:
College
High School
Noncredit

Degree/Certificate Programs:
Up to 90 quarter credits of correspondence study may be applied toward an undergraduate degree (associate or bachelor) at UW; the last 45 credits must be earned in residence. Credits may also be applied toward certification in a professional program.

Admission Requirements:
Open enrollment; students currently in high school must have written written permission from the high school district.

Tuition:
$66 per quarter credit, and a $15 nonrefundable registration fee. Noncredit courses are treated as 3 credits for tuition payment. Prices are subject to change without notice and usually on an annual basis. Loans, grants, and discounts are not applicable to Independent Study. A full refund is allowed, minus a $15 withdrawal fee, if requested within 30 days of registration and materials are returned in good condition.

Enrollment Period:
The maximum time allowed to complete a course is one year with a six-month renewal option for a fee of $50. The minimum time allowed to complete a course is two months.

Equipment Requirements:
Study guides are supplied by the university, included in the tuition, but textbooks and other materials must be purchased by the student. Some courses require cassette tapes and players, records and players, and supplementary readings or lab kits, most of which must be supplied by the student; some may be rented from the school.

Credit and Grading:
Distance Learning is not a degree-granting program and therefore can not accept credits transferred-in; contact the University Admissions Office. Most examinations require approved proctors. The grading system is on a numeric scale 4.0–0.0. Grades are determined solely by each instructor. Credit is awarded in quarter hour units.

Library Services:
Students living within metropolitan Seattle have full library privileges at the University of Washington Library. Students living outside the Seattle area may request specific

library materials by mail through Resource Sharing, 253 Suzzallo Library FM-25, University of Washington Libraries, Seattle WA 98195-0001, or e-mail request to librss@u.washington.edu.

Accreditations:

Northwest Association of Schools and Colleges. Member of: National University Continuing Education Association.

COLLEGE COURSES

ACCOUNTING

Introduction to Accounting

Nature and social setting of accounting; uses of accounting information; introduction to basic accounting concepts, and some accounting techniques. (3 quarter hours)

Fundamentals of Financial Accounting

Principal procedures and concepts utilized in contemporary financial accounting and reporting. Preparation and interpretation of financial statements. (3 quarter hours)

AMERICAN INDIAN STUDIES

North American Indians: Pacific Northwest

Traditional societies of the Pacific Northwest from southern Alaska to northern California; significant areal features such as rank, totemic crests, guardian spirits, the potlatch, fishing, and foraging illustrated by comparisons and by selected ethnographic sketches. Examines the continuity between past and present. (5 quarter hours)

ANTHROPOLOGY

Introduction to Anthropology

Introduction to the subfields of archaeology, physical anthropology, and sociocultural anthropology through the examination of selected problems in human physical, cultural, and social evolution. (5 quarter hours)

Principles of Sociocultural Anthropology

Comparison of lifeways of various non-Western and Western peoples. Introduction to basic theories and methods used in the field. (5 quarter hours)

ASTRONOMY

Astronomy

Introduction to the universe, with emphasis on conceptual, as contrasted with mathematical, comprehension. Modern theories, observations, and ideas concerning nature and evolution of galaxies, quasars, stars, black holes, planets, and solar system. (5 quarter hours)

The Planets

For liberal arts and beginning science students. Survey of the planets of the solar system, with emphasis on recent space exploration of the planets and on the relationship of man and his earth to the other planets. (5 quarter hours)

ATMOSPHERIC SCIENCE

Weather

The earth's atmosphere with emphasis on weather observations and forecasting. Daily weather map discussions. Explanations of highs, lows, fronts, clouds, storms, jet streams, air pollution, and other features of the atmosphere. Physical processes involved in weather phenomena. (5 quarter hours)

BUSINESS

Basic Written Business Communications

Broad analytical approach to written communications as a management tool. Analysis of the psychology, semantics, planning, and principles of effective business writing. Practical application through messages that inform and persuade, grant and refuse; plus short business reports and applications for positions. (4 quarter hours)

The International Environment of Business

Prepares students to understand the most important aspects of the international political economy. Emphasis on the important relationships among nations and business and economic institutions that influence students' performances as managers, consumers, and citizens. (3 quarter hours)

Introduction to Law

Legal institutions and processes; law as a system of social thought and behavior and a frame of order within which rival claims are resolved and compromised; legal reasoning; law as a process of protecting and facilitating voluntary arrangements in a business society. (5 quarter hours)

CHEMISTRY

Introduction to General Chemistry

An introduction to chemistry with laboratory for students with little or no chemistry background. Atoms and molecules and their chemical changes, including the impact of chemistry on everyday life. (5 quarter hours)

General Chemistry

Course C140. For science, engineering, and other majors who plan to take a year or more of chemistry courses. Atomic nature of matter, nuclear chemistry, stoichiometry, periodic table, quantum concepts, chemical bonding, gas laws. (4 quarter hours)

Course C150. Introduction to inorganic chemistry, solids, solutions, acid-base, chemical equilibrium. (4 quarter hours)

COMMUNICATIONS

History and Development of Communication and Journalism

History and development of communication from prehistoric times; social and technical inventions; political and economic contexts. (5 quarter hours)

The Phenomena of Communicating

Types of communicating behaviors in progressively more complex situations, from individual cognition through interpersonal interactions to mass communicating. (5 quarter hours)

Legal Aspects of Communications

Regulations governing publication and broadcast in the mass media. (5 quarter hours)

ECONOMICS

Introduction to Microeconomics

Introduction to analysis of markets; consumer demand, production, exchange, the price system, resource allocation, government intervention. (5 quarter hours)

Introduction to Macroeconomics

Introduction to analysis of the aggregate economy; national income, inflation, business fluctuations, unemployment, monetary system, federal budget, international trade and finance. (5 quarter hours)

Intermediate Microeconomics

Choice decisions of individuals and firms; consequences of these decisions in product and factor markets. Consumption production and cost, exchange. (5 quarter hours)

EDUCATION

Basic Educational Statistics

Measures of central tendency and variability, point and interval estimation, linear correlation, hypothesis testing. (3 quarter hours)

Science Education: Elementary School Programs and Practices

Designed for classroom teachers with reference to the teaching and learning of science from kindergarten through grade six. Emphasis is placed on objectives, methods and materials as related to the concepts of processes of science. Students perform in-home experiments with assistance from instructor via e-mail. (3 quarter hours)

Workshop in Improvement of Curriculum: Using the Internet in Curriculum Development

In this course, educators will develop curriculum using the Internet as an investigational tool for classroom projects. (5 quarter hours)

ENGLISH

Reading Literature

Techniques and practice in reading and enjoying literature. Examines some of the best works in English and American literature and considers such features of literary meaning as imagery, characterization, narration, and patterning in sound and sense. Emphasis on literature as a source of pleasure and knowledge about human experience. (5 quarter hours)

Reading Fiction

Critical interpretation and meaning in fiction. Different examples of fiction representing a variety of types from the medieval to the modern periods. (5 quarter hours)

Children's Literature

An examination of books that form a part of the imaginative experience of children, as well as a part of a larger literary heritage, viewed in the light of their social, psychological, political, and moral implications. (5 quarter hours)

Shakespeare

A survey of Shakespeare's career as dramatist. Study of representative comedies, tragedies, romances, and history plays. (5 quarter hours)

Intermediate Expository Writing

Writing papers communicating information and opinion to develop accurate, competent, and effective expression. (5 quarter hours)

Beginning Verse Writing

Intensive study of the ways and means of making a poem. (5 quarter hours)

Beginning Short Story Writing

Introduction to the theory and practice of writing the short story. (5 quarter hours)

The Bible as Literature

Introduction to the development of the religious ideas and institutions of ancient Israel, with selected readings from the Old Testament and New Testament. Emphasis on reading the Bible with literary and historical understanding. (5 quarter hours)

Shakespeare to 1603

Shakespeare's career as dramatist before 1603 (including *Hamlet.* Study of history plays, comedies, and tragedies. (5 quarter hours)

Shakespeare after 1603

Shakespeare's career as dramatist after 1603. Study of comedies, tragedies, and romances. (5 quarter hours)

English Literature: The Late Renaissance

A period of skepticism for some, faith for others, but intellectual upheaval generally. Poems by John Donne and the "metaphysical" school; poems and plays by Ben Jonson and other late rivals to Shakespeare; prose by Sir Francis Bacon and other writers. (5 quarter hours)

Milton

Milton's early poems and the prose; *Paradise Lost, Paradise Regained,* and *Samson Agonistes,* with attention to the religious, intellectual, and literary contexts. (5 quarter hours)

English Novel: Early and Middle 19th Century

Studies in the novel in one of its classic phases. Authors include Austen, the Brontës, Dickens, Thackeray. (5 quarter hours)

The Modern Novel

The novel on both sides of the Atlantic in the first half of the 20th century. Includes such writers as Joyce, Waugh, Lawrence, Steinbeck, Hemingway, and Faulkner. (5 quarter hours)

American Literature: The Early Nation

Conflicting visions of the national destiny and the individual identity in the early years of America's nationhood. Works by Emerson, Thoreau, Hawthorne, Melville, and such other writers as Poe, Cooper, Irving, Whitman, Dickinson, and Douglass. (5 quarter hours)

American Literature: Later 19th Century

Literary responses to an America propelled forward by accelerating and complex forces. Works by Twain, James, and such other writers as Whitman, Dickinson, Adams, Wharton, Howells, Crane, Dreiser, DuBois, and Chopin. (5 quarter hours)

American Literature: The Early Modern Period

Literary responses to the disillusionment after World War I, experiments in form and in new ideas of a new period. Works by such writers as Anderson, Toomer, Cather, O'Neill, Frost, Pound, Eliot, Cummings, Hemingway, Fitzgerald, Faulkner, Stein, Hart Crane, Stevens, and Porter. (5 quarter hours)

American Literature: Contemporary America

Works by such writers as Ellison, Williams, O'Connor, Lowell, Barth, Rich, and Hawkes. (5 quarter hours)

Fantasy

Nonnaturalistic literature, selected folktales, fairy tales, fables, nonsense, ghost stories, horror stories, science fiction, and/or utopian literature—the supernatural and surreal, the grotesque, the fantastical. (5 quarter hours)

Advanced Expository Writing

Concentration on the development of prose style for experienced writers. (5 quarter hours)

Intermediate Seminar: Verse Writing

Intensive study of the ways and means of making a poem. Further development of fundamental skills. Emphasis on revision. (5 quarter hours)

Intermediate Seminar: Short Story Writing

Exploring and developing continuity in the elements of fiction writing. Methods of extending and sustaining plot, setting, character, point of view, and tone. (5 quarter hours)

Advanced Seminar: Verse Writing

Intensive study of ways and means of making a poem. (5 quarter hours)

Literature and Culture

Study of literature in its relation to culture. Focuses on literature as a cultural institution, directly related to the construction of individual identity and the dissemination and critique of values. (5 quarter hours)

ENVIRONMENTAL SCIENCE

Introduction to Environmental Studies

Natural history and human modifications of the natural world. Evolutionary biology, physical geography, toxicology, energy, economics, law, public policy. (5 quarter hours)

FRENCH

Elementary French

Course C101. Essentials of French grammar. Although all assignments and examinations are written, oral practice is provided through the use of tape recordings. (5 quarter hours)

Course C102. A continuation of *Course C101.* (5 quarter hours)

Course C103. A continuation of *Course C102.* (5 quarter hours)

GEOGRAPHY

World Regions

Spatial study of world regions, based on historical, cultural, political, economic, and other factors. An attempt to understand the underlying forces that have led to the formation of regions and regional patterns. (5 quarter hours)

Geography of Cities

Study of (1) systems of cities—their location, distribution, functions and competition, and (2) their internal structure—the location of activities within urban areas. Particular emphasis on current urban problems—sprawl, housing, segregation, economic growth, and metropolitan transportation. (5 quarter hours)

GERMAN

First-Year German

Course C101. For persons who have had no previous instruction in German. Acquisition of a fairly large vocabulary; grammar; practice in reading and writing. (5 quarter hours)

Course C102. A continuation of *Course C101.* (5 quarter hours)

Course C103. A continuation of *Course C102.* (5 quarter hours)

GERONTOLOGY

Biological Aspects of Aging

Introductory course on aspects of the biology of human aging and of functional changes associated with normal aging and with those illnesses that may be present in the elderly. Focus on the relationship between changes in physical function, environment, and quality of life. Includes theoretical perspective on aging as well as the aging process in specific physiological systems. Designed for upper-level undergraduate students with an interest in aging. (3 quarter hours)

Social and Cultural Aspects of Aging

From the perspective of various social science fields, the course examines the range and variation of relationships among age-linked attitudes and cultural values related to aging; the social and economic factors that influence the elderly in contemporary society; the effects of ethnic and sex differences in sociocultural aging. (3 quarter hours)

HISTORY

The Modern World

Political, economic, social, and intellectual history of modern Europe. (5 quarter hours)

The American People and Their Culture in the Modern Era: A History of the United States Since 1940

Through the study of documents, personal testimony, and other source materials, through written reports on historical problems, and through discussions, lectures, films, and audiovisual presentations, students are encouraged to examine evidence and to think "historically" about persons, events, and movements within the memory of their own generation and that immediately preceding theirs. (5 quarter hours)

Survey of the History of the United States

Supplies the knowledge of American history that any intelligent and educated American citizen should have. Objective is to make the student aware of his or her heritage of the past and more intelligently conscious of the present. (5 quarter hours)

History of Washington and the Pacific Northwest

Exploration and settlement; economic development, growth of government and social institutions; statehood. (5 quarter hours)

History of Modern Japan

Political, social, economic, and cultural development of Japan from the late Tokugawa period to the present with special emphasis on the cultural impact of the West. (5 quarter hours)

ITALIAN

Elementary Italian

Course C101. Basic study of Italian grammar and idiomatic usage of the language. All assignments and examinations are written, but oral practice is provided by the use of required tape recordings. (5 quarter hours)

Course C102. A continuation of *Course C101.* (5 quarter hours)

Course C103. A continuation of *Course C102.* (5 quarter hours)

LINGUISTICS

Fundamentals of Grammar

Introduction to basic grammatical concepts and terminology. Specifically intended for students planning to major in foreign languages or linguistics. (5 quarter hours)

Introduction to Linguistic Thought

Introduction to the scientific study of language, language and writing; phonological and grammatical analysis; language change; related disciplines. (5 quarter hours)

Language Development

First-language acquisition and use by children. Emphasis on theoretical issues and research techniques. (4 quarter hours)

MARKETING

Marketing Concepts

Analysis of tools, factors, and concepts used by management in planning, establishing policies, and solving marketing problems. Topics cover marketing concepts, consumer demand and behavior, location analysis, marketing functions, institutions, channels, prices, and public policy. (4 quarter hours)

Advertising

The management of the advertising function and its integration with other forms of promotion. Topics covered are planning the program; determining the most effective approach; evaluation of media and budget; advertising institutions; economic and social aspects. (4 quarter hours)

MATHEMATICS

Mathematics: A Practical Art

For students not planning to take additional mathematics courses. The exponential function; how it applies to a wide variety of phenomena. Elementary probability and statistics; their use in a variety of applications. (5 quarter hours)

Algebra with Applications

Use of graphs and algebraic functions found in business and economics. Algebraic and graphical manipulations to solve problems. Exponential and logarithmic functions; various applications to growth of money. (5 quarter hours)

Applications of Calculus to Business and Economics

Rate of change, tangent, derivative, accumulation, area, integral in specific contexts, particularly economics. Techniques of differentiation and integration. Application to problem solving. Optimization. (5 quarter hours)

Precalculus

Polynomial, rational, exponential, and trigonometric functions. (5 quarter hours)

Calculus with Analytic Geometry

Course C124. Differentiation, applications of derivative, integration. Calculus for natural science and engineering students. (5 quarter hours)

Course C125. Applications of integration, transcendental functions, methods of integration and improper integrals, introduction to first order ordinary differential equations. (5 quarter hours)

Course C126. Vectors and vector functions in space, functions of several variables and applications, multiple integrals. (5 quarter hours)

Mathematics for Elementary School Teachers

Development of the systems of whole numbers, integers, and rational numbers; measurement; basic geometric concepts; functions; elementary probability, and statistics. (3 quarter hours)

Elementary Linear Algebra

Systems of equations, vector spaces, matrices, linear transformations, characteristic vectors. (3 quarter hours)

Introduction to Differential Equations

Taylor series, first and second order ordinary differential equations. (3 quarter hours)

MUSIC

History of Jazz

Survey of the major periods and styles of jazz, New Orleans jazz to the avant-garde and popular jazz of today. Studies the main characteristics of each style. (3 quarter hours)

NUTRITION

Nutrition for Today

Basic and applied nutrition and food science. Identification and physiological roles of nutrients, nutritional requirements, problems with over- and under-nutrition and nutritional food-related diseases. Food additives, processing, safety, and their effects on overall nutrition. (3 quarter hours)

OCEANOGRAPHY

Survey of Oceanography

Origin and extent of the oceans; nature of the sea bottom; causes and effects of currents and tides; animal and plant life in the sea. (5 quarter hours)

PHILOSOPHY

Philosophical Issues in the Law

Analysis and critical assessment of various philosophical issues in law and legal reasoning. Material drawn from actual law cases, as well as writings by contemporary philosophers of law and lawyers. Topics include criminal responsibility, civil disobedience, abortion, reverse discrimination, enforcement of morals. (5 quarter hours)

Practical Reasoning

Introduction to logic emphasizing concepts and methods used for practical analysis of arguments in everyday contexts. Meaning, syllogism, logical diagrams, inductive and statistical inference, informal fallacies, argument structure, perhaps some beginning symbolic logic. A wide variety of examples, including logical puzzles are considered. (5 quarter hours)

Introduction to Logic

Elementary symbolic logic. The development, application, and theoretical properties of an artificial symbolic language designed to provide a clear representation of the logical structure of deductive arguments. (5 quarter hours)

POLITICAL SCIENCE

Introduction to Politics

Introduction to thinking about the political problems that affect our lives and shape the world around us. (5 quarter hours)

Introduction to Political Theory

Philosophical bases of politics and political activity. Provides an introduction to the study of politics by the reading of a few books in political philosophy. Organized around several key political concepts, such as liberty, equality, justice, authority, rights, and citizenship. (5 quarter hours)

Introduction to American Politics

Introduction to people, institutions, and politics in the American political system. Provides various ways of thinking about how significant problems, crises, and conflicts of American society are resolved politically. (5 quarter hours)

Introduction to International Relations

Analysis of the world community, its politics, and government. (5 quarter hours)

The Politics of Mass Communication in America

Role of mass audiences in politics from the standpoint of the communication strategies used to shape their political involvement. Topics include: social structure and political participation, political propaganda and persuasion, the political uses of public opinion, and the mass media and politics. (5 quarter hours)

American Foreign Policy

Constitutional framework; major factors in formulation and execution of policy; policies as modified by recent developments; the principal policy makers—President, Congress, political parties, pressure groups, and public opinion. (5 quarter hours)

Environmental Politics and Policy in the United States

Interrelations between technological and environmental change and policy formation. Consideration of political behavior related to these phenomena and the capacity of urban public organizations to predict change and to formulate policies that can take future states into account. (5 quarter hours)

PSYCHOLOGY

Psychology as a Social Science

Behavior from a social-science viewpoint. Emphasizes personality, individual differences, attitudes, and social behavior and influence. Includes related aspects of cognition, behavior disorders, states of awareness, motivation and emotion, learning, development, and research methods. (5 quarter hours)

Introduction to Personality and Individual Differences

Basic concepts and methods and background for more intensive study in the field of personality. (4 quarter hours)

Fundamentals of Psychological Research

Psychological research methodology and techniques. Topics include the logic of hypothesis testing, experimental design, research strategies and techniques, fundamentals of scientific writing, and ethical issues in psychological research. (4 quarter hours)

Elementary Psychological Statistics

Applied statistics in psychology. Describing data, probability theory, stating and testing hypothesis in psychology. Covers the more commonly used inference tests. (6 quarter hours)

Abnormal Psychology

An overview of major categories of psychopathology, including description and classification, theoretical models, and recent research on etiology and treatment. (5 quarter hours)

Developmental Psychology

Analysis of psychological development of the child in relation to biological, physical, and sociological antecedent conditions from infancy to adolescence. (5 quarter hours)

Introduction to Drugs and Behavior

Basic concepts of drug action emphasizing the behavioral consequences of the intake of a variety of drugs. (3 quarter hours)

Social Psychology

The effects of the social environment upon the formation of individual attitudes, values, and beliefs, and upon individual and group behavior. Discussion of major theoretical approaches and presentation of field and experimental research findings. (5 quarter hours)

Survey of Cognitive Psychology

Current theory and research in perception, attention, memory and learning, attitudes, thinking and decision making, and language. For the student who wishes a survey or intends additional work in any of the above content areas. (5 quarter hours)

Personality Development of the Child

Socialization theory and research, infant attachment and social relationships, development of aggressive and altruistic behaviors, sex-role development, moral development, parent and adult influences. Applied issues in social development and policy. (5 quarter hours)

RELIGIOUS STUDIES

Introduction to World Religions: Eastern Traditions

Introductory course in the history of religions, concentrating on religions that have developed in South Asia and East Asia. Primary attention to Hinduism and Buddhism. Other important Asian religions are discussed in relation to them, with emphasis on basic conceptual and symbolic structures. (5 quarter hours)

RUSSIAN

First-Year Russian

Introduction to Russian. Emphasis on oral communication with limited vocabulary. Basic grammatical features and some reading. (5 quarter hours)

SOCIOLOGY

Survey of Sociology

Human interaction, social institutions, social stratification, socialization, deviance, social control, social and cultural change. (5 quarter hours)

Introduction to the Sociology of Deviance

Examination of deviance, deviant behavior, and social control. Deviance as a social process; types of deviant behavior (e.g., suicide, mental illness, drug use, crime, "sexual deviance," delinquency); theories of deviance and deviant behavior; nature and social organization of societal reactions; and social and legal policy issues. (5 quarter hours)

Socialization

How social systems control the behavior of their constituent groups, and persons, through the socialization process, sanctions, power, allocation of status and rewards. (5 quarter hours)

The Family

The family as a social institution. Historical changes and societal variations in family patterns. Changes over the life cycle. Alternative family forms. (5 quarter hours)

Criminology

Survey of legal definitions, types of criminal behavior, trends and patterns, recidivism, characteristics of offenders, environmental influences, diagnostic methods, prediction, theories of crime and delinquency prevention, social policy. (5 quarter hours)

SPANISH

Elementary Spanish

Course C101. Recommended for those who wish to work primarily toward a reading knowledge of the language. (5 quarter hours)

Course C102. A continuation of *Course C101.* (5 quarter hours)

Course C103. A continuation of *Course C102.* (5 quarter hours)

Intermediate Spanish

Intensive practice in reading and writing. Functional review in grammar. All assignments and examinations are written, but oral practice is provided through purchase and use of tape recordings. (5 quarter hours)

STATISTICS

Basic Statistics

Objectives and pitfalls of statistical studies. Structure of data sets, histograms, means and standard deviations. Correlation and regression. Probability theory, the binomial and normal distributions. Interpretations of statistical estimates, confidence intervals, and significance tests. (5 quarter hours)

Basic Statistics with Applications

Objectives and pitfalls of statistical studies. Structure of data sets, histograms, means, and standard deviations. Correlation and regression. Probability, binomial and normal interpretation of estimates, confidence intervals, significance tests. Application to problems in the student's major field. (5 quarter hours)

Elements of Statistical Method

Elementary concepts of probability and sampling, the binomial and normal distributions. Basic concepts of hypothesis testing, estimation, and confidence intervals, t-tests and chi-square tests. Linear regression theory and the analysis of variance. (5 quarter hours)

Elementary Psychological Statistics

Applied statistics in psychology. Describing data, probability theory, stating and testing hypothesis in psychology. Covers the more commonly used inference tests. (6 quarter hours)

Basic Educational Statistics

Measures of central tendency and variability, point and interval estimation, linear correlation, hypothesis testing. (3 quarter hours)

TECHNICAL WRITING

Introduction to Technical Writing

Principles of organizing, developing, and writing technical information. Report forms and rhetorical patterns common to scientific and technical disciplines. Technical writing conventions such as headings, illustrations, style and tone. Numerous writing assignments required. (3 quarter hours)

Style in Scientific and Technical Writing

Grammatical structures and stylistic strategies within specific professional contexts. Achieving clarity and conciseness through word choice and placement, using a variety of sentence structures for appropriate emphasis, handling details, establishing effective tone. (3 quarter hours)

WOMEN'S STUDIES

Women and the Law

Focus on the status of women and the law; the legal status of single and married women, the rationale of protective legislation, and the effect of the legal changes such as the Civil Rights Act of 1964 and Equal Rights Amendments. Study of current cases on abortion, child care, tax laws, Social Security benefits, lesbianism, prostitution. (5 quarter hours)

WRITING

Intermediate Expository Writing

Writing papers communicating information and opinion to develop accurate, competent and effective expression. (5 quarter hours)

Beginning Verse Writing

Intensive study of the ways and means of making a poem. (5 quarter hours)

Beginning Short Story Writing

Introduction to the theory and practice of writing the short story. (5 quarter hours)

Advanced Expository Writing

Concentration on the development of prose style for experienced writers. (5 quarter hours)

Intermediate Seminar: Verse Writing

Intensive study of the ways and means of making a poem. Further development of fundamental skills. Emphasis on revision. (5 quarter hours)

Intermediate Seminary: Short Story Writing

Exploring and developing continuity in the elements of fiction writing. Methods of extending and sustaining plot, setting, character, point of view and tone. (5 quarter hours)

Advanced Seminar: Verse Writing

Intensive study of ways and means of making a poem. (5 quarter hours)

Basic Written Business Communications

Broad analytical approach to written communications as a management tool. Analysis of the psychology, semantics, planning, and principles of effective business writing. Practical application through messages that inform and persuade, grant and refuse; plus short business reports and applications for positions. (4 quarter hours)

NONCREDIT COURSES

COMPUTER SCIENCE

Developing a C Application

Students work one-on-one with the instructor to develop a C or C++ application which demonstrates their knowledge and skills in C programming. (4 CEUs) *Tuition:* $264.

MATHEMATICS

Intermediate Algebra

Similar to the third term of high school algebra. (Noncredit) *Tuition:* $186.

Washington State University
Extended Academic Programs
202/204 Van Doren Hall
Pullman, Washington 99164-5220
(800) 222-4978

Description:
Washington State University is a four-year land-grant institution with approximately 18,000 students. The correspondence program has been in existence for over fifty years and presently offers over 100 courses.

Faculty:
Ellen Krieger, Correspondence Course Administrator. Over 60 members of the regular WSU faculty teach correspondence study on a course-by-course basis.

Academic Levels:
College
Noncredit

Degree/Certificate Programs:
Up to 25 percent of the required credit hours for a degree program may be earned from correspondence study at WSU.

Admission Requirements:

Open enrollment. Acceptance for a correspondence course does not constitute admission to the University. Some courses have required prerequisites.

Tuition:

$90 per semester credit hour payable in full at time of registration. Prices are subject to change without notice. To drop a course and receive a refund, a student must submit a written request postmarked within thirty days of enrollment. No refunds will be approved after thirty days. A service charge of $15 plus $5 for each assignment submitted, will be subtracted from the amount of the refund. All course materials must be returned unused; otherwise, a fee will be assessed for the course syllabus. MasterCard and Visa accepted.

Enrollment Period:

Maximum time for completion of a correspondence course is one year. An extension of one year may be allowed upon payment of a $50 fee. The minimum time to complete a course is three months.

Equipment Requirements:

The cost of textbooks is not included in the tuition and may be ordered, separately from tuition payment, from the WSU Student's Book Corporation. Some courses require access to a tape cassette player and calculator, each furnished by the student. Some courses require student purchase of cassette tapes and/or slides.

Credit and Grading:

Final examinations require the supervision of an approved proctor. The grading system is A, B, C, D, F; minimum passing grade is D. Correspondence transfer credits from other institutions are accepted by WSU. Credit is awarded in semester hour units.

Library Services:

Students enrolled in independent study courses may use the WSU libraries upon presentation of course receipts. Otherwise, reference materials are most easily accessible through local libraries. Materials not available locally may be requested through Interlibrary Loan Services. To use this service, students should provide their social security number and their name to participating libraries.

Accreditations:

Northwest Association of Schools and Colleges. Member of: National University Continuing Education Association.

COLLEGE COURSES

ACCOUNTING

Introduction to Financial Accounting

The structure and interpretation of accounts and financial statements. (3 semester hours)

Introduction to Managerial Accounting

Introduction to managerial accounting; generation and use of accounting data for planning and controlling business operations. (3 semester hours)

Intermediate Accounting I

Theory underlying the determination of income, analysis, financial statements. (3 semester hours)

Intermediate Accounting II

Continuation of the above course. (3 semester hours)

ANTHROPOLOGY

Gender and Culture

Cross-cultural examination of the status and roles of women and men, the institution of marriage, and symbols of gender valuation. (3 semester hours)

Human Issues in International Development

Interdisciplinary analysis of complex interaction between tradition and modernity in Third World societies. (3 semester hours)

ARABIC

First Semester Arabic

Fundamentals of speaking, listening to, reading, and writing Arabic. Weekly tutoring sessions on the Pullman campus are required. (4 semester hours)

Second Semester Arabic

Continued development of basic skills. Weekly tutoring sessions on the Pullman campus are required. (4 semester hours)

Third Semester Arabic

Continuation of Arabic instruction. Weekly tutoring sessions on the Pullman campus are required. (4 semester hours)

Intermediate Arabic

Continuation of Arabic instruction. Weekly tutoring sessions on the Pullman campus are required. (4 semester hours)

ARCHITECTURE

The Built Environment

Planning and design of the built environment; products, interiors, structures; landscapes, cities; factors and process affecting environmental quality. (3 semester hours)

BIOLOGY

Direction in Biological Sciences

Understanding biology as a science and its effect on issues within society. (3 semester hours)

Biological Science Lab

Elements of structure and function of organisms. For nonmajor in biological sciences. (1 semester hour)

BUSINESS LAW

Law of Business Organizations

Law of partnerships, corporations, securities regulation, secured transactions and bankruptcy. (3 semester hours)

Law of Real Estate

Legal principles and precedents as they apply to the real estate environment. (3 semester hours)

CHILD, CONSUMER, AND FAMILY STUDIES

Family Systems: Understanding Family Interaction

Introduction to the study of the family processes; family generational, emotional, boundary, rule, and ritualistic systems. (3 semester hours)

Guidance in Early Childhood

Theories of child guidance; understanding of child behavior; strategies and techniques for effective group and individual guidance of young children. (3 semester hours)

Administration of Early Childhood Programs

Understanding aspects of child care program administration, organization, management, finance, programming, service delivery, evaluation, personnel and resource development. (3 semester hours)

COMMUNICATIONS

Mass Communications and Society

Mass media in contemporary society. (3 semester hours)

CRIMINAL JUSTICE

Introduction to the Administration of Criminal Justice

Agencies and process involved in the administration of criminal justice. (3 semester hours)

Introduction to the Juvenile Justice System

The social dimensions of juvenile delinquency, its nature, frequency, and distribution, with comparison and analysis of social control agencies. The role of law enforcement agencies, the courts, and community/individual programs of treatment will also be analyzed. (3 semester hours)

ECONOMICS

Fundamentals of Microeconomics

Theory and policy related to business competition, industrial organization, investment, and income distribution. (3 semester hours)

Fundamentals of Macroeconomics

Theory and policy related to unemployment, inflation, foreign trade, government spending, taxation, and banking. (3 semester hours)

Economics of Social Issues

Political economy of the U.S.; macroeconomic theory, unemployment and inflation, corporate power, distribution of wealth, pollution. (4 semester hours)

ENGLISH

Introductory Writing

Academic writing, critical thinking, reading, library skills. (3 semester hours)

Expository Writing

For students needing further development of writing skills before taking advanced writing courses; emphasizes research writing in the disciplines. (3 semester hours)

Advanced Writing

Writing argumentation and other forms of prose discourse. (3 semester hours)

Shakespeare

ENGL 305x. Shakespearean drama to 1600. (3 semester hours)

ENGL 306x. Shakespearean drama after 1600. (3 semester hours)

Women Writers

Women's artistic and intellectual contributions to prose, fiction, drama, and poetry. (3 semester hours)

The American Novel

Classic American novels in cultural perspective by such authors as Cooper, Hawthorne, Melville, Stowe, Twain, James, Jewett, Chopin, Crane, and Dreiser. (3 semester hours)

The Twentieth Century Novel

The novel in English in the literary and cultural context of the modern age. (3 semester hours)

English Romantic Literature

Major works by Blake, Wordsworth, Coleridge, Byron, Shelley, Keats, and others during Romantic literary revolt, especially 1798–1832. (3 semester hours)

Victorian Literature

Major works by Tennyson, Dickens, Browning, Swinburne, Wilde, and others in a dynamic age of change in Britain, 1832–1901. (3 semester hours)

FINANCE

Finance

Financial decision making, financial strategies investment in current and fixed assets, financial instruments, and capital markets. (3 semester hours)

Investments and Security Analysis

Investment objectives, security markets, market efficiency, and principles of security valuation. (3 semester hours)

FOOD SCIENCE AND NUTRITION

Nutrition for Living

Nutrition principles and applications to nutrient needs of all age levels; psychological, economic, and cultural implications of food. (3 semester hours)

Human Nutrition

Principles of human nutrition applicable to all ages of human development; impact of environment, economics, and culture on food and nutrition. (3 semester hours)

FRENCH

First Semester French

Fundamentals of speaking, reading, and writing. This course combines video, audio, and print to teach French in the context of French-speaking cultures. Students learn to associate what they hear with the familiar situations they see, while learning to understand and use authentic French from the French perspective. (4 semester hours)

Second Semester French

Continued development of basic skills in speaking, reading, and writing. (4 semester hours)

Third Semester French

Grammar review and further development of speaking, reading, and writing skills. (4 semester hours)

Intermediate French

Continued practice in spoken and written language; selected texts in a cultural context. (4 semester hours)

French for Travelers

French language skills presented for survival in a foreign travel setting. (1 semester hour)

French for the Professions

Communication in French for professional purposes: telephone and meeting role-plays, letter writing, television discussions of current events in the Francophone world. (3 semester hours)

GEOLOGY

Introduction to Geology

Introductory physical geology for nonscience majors; emphasis on western U.S. (3 or 4 semester hours)

Geology of the National Parks

Significant geologic features, processes, and geologic history of the national parks. (2 semester hours)

HINDI

First Semester Hindi

Fundamentals of speaking, listening to, reading, and writing Hindi. Weekly tutoring sessions on the Pullman campus are required. (4 semester hours)

Second Semester Hindi

Continued development of basic skills. Weekly tutoring sessions on the Pullman campus are required. (4 semester hours)

Third Semester Hindi

Continuation of Hindi instruction. Weekly tutoring sessions on the Pullman campus are required. (4 semester hours)

Fourth Semester Hindi

Continuation of Hindi instruction. Weekly tutoring sessions on the Pullman campus are required. (4 semester hours)

HISTORY

Modern Europe

War, revolution, industrialization, culture—18th to 20th centuries; imperialism, democracy, and totalitarianism. Europe's leaders Napoleon to Hitler; Post-WWII developments. (3 semester hours)

American History to 1877

Social, economic, cultural history of British mainland colonies/United States to 1877. (3 semester hours)

American History Since 1865

Social, economic, cultural history of United States, 1877 to present. (3 semester hours)

Civil War and Reconstruction

The Civil War as a problem in historical causation and social, political, and economic impact of the war. (3 semester hours)

Introduction to East Asian Culture

Civilizations of China and Japan. (3 semester hours)

History of Women in American Society

The roles of women—social, economic, political—in American history from colonial times to the present. (3 semester hours)

Pre-Modern History of East Asia

Geographical, socioeconomic, and intellectual influences upon the development of China, Japan, and Korea to the nineteenth century. (3 semester hours)

History of Women in the American West

The history of women in the American Northwest through women's literature, archives, and oral history. (3 semester hours)

United States, 1914–1941

America through World War I, cultural tensions of the 1920s, and the crises of the Depression and impending war. (3 semester hours)

United States, 1941–Present

International and domestic impact of World War II, era of Mc-Carthyism, American aspirations, tensions, and conflicts in the post-industrial era. (3 semester hours)

History of the Pacific Northwest

Emphasis on early white settlement, Indian difficulties, international rivalries, beginnings of government, and in the modern period, transportation, irrigation, hydroelectric and timber development, and urban growth. (3 semester hours)

HUMANITIES

World Civilizations I

Integrated study of social, political, and philosophical religious systems in early civilizations, with an introduction to distinctive art forms. (3 semester hours)

INSURANCE

Risk and Insurance

Types of risk and methods of protection; life, property and liability insurance, principles of risk management. (3 semester hours)

LANDSCAPE ARCHITECTURE

Professional Practice

Current office practices, design and construction management techniques; introduction to construction contract legal requirements within the practice of landscape architecture. (2 semester hours)

MANAGEMENT

Principles of Management and Organization

Principles of management and administration aimed at improving effectiveness of all types of organizations. (3 semester hours)

Organizational Behavior

Organizational behavior, motivation, leadership, communications, decision making, group dynamics. (3 semester hours)

Business Strategy and Policy

Overall management of the firm; top-level decision making and planning. (3 semester hours)

Personnel and Human Resource Management

Policy and practice in human resources utilization, selecting, training, motivating, evaluating, and compensating employees; labor relations; EEO legislation. (3 semester hours)

MARKETING

Marketing

Functions, methods, and middlemen used in marketing the principal types of goods; price policies, cost of marketing; government regulation. (3 semester hours)

Consumer Behavior

The investigation of social-psychological phenomena affecting consumer decision processes; learning theory and communication. (3 semester hours)

MATHEMATICS

Intermediate Algebra

Fundamental algebraic operations and concepts. (3 semester hours)

Precalculus Algebra

Functions and graphs, theory of equations, conic sections, logarithms, and exponentials. (3 semester hours)

Precalculus Trigonometry

Trigonometry, complex numbers, and discrete mathematics. (2 semester hours)

Calculus I

Differential and integral calculus of one variable with associated analytic geometry. (4 semester hours)

Calculus II

Techniques and applications of one-variable calculus; estimations, series, derivative of a vector function. (4 semester hours)

Introductory Linear Algebra

Elementary linear algebra with geometric applications. (2 semester hours)

Differential Equations

Linear differential equations and systems; series, numerical, and qualitative approaches; applications. (3 semester hours)

NURSING

Profession of Nursing

Theoretical/historical aspects of professional nursing; development of nursing roles, scopes of practice, problem solving, and ethical decision making. (2 semester hours)

PHILOSOPHY

Introduction to Philosophy

Nature and place of philosophy in human thought; problems and achievements. (3 semester hours)

Introduction to Ethics

Ethics through analysis of contemporary moral and social issues. (3 semester hours)

Philosophies and Religions of China and Japan

The philosophies and religions of China and Japan: their metaphysical, epistemological, ethical, social, and political positions and views of God and gods. (3 semester hours)

POLITICAL SCIENCE

American National Government

(3 semester hours)

Introduction to Comparative Politics

Nature of the state; fundamental problems of government and politics; ideological and institutional comparison of democracies and dictatorships. (3 semester hours)

State and Local Government

Institutions, processes and problems, with special reference to the state of Washington. (3 semester hours)

International Politics

Creation and operation of national, international, and supranational communities; major world problems since 1945. (3 semester hours)

American Public Policy

Institutions, processes, and substantive issues of American public policy and policy formulation. (3 semester hours)

Development of Marxist Thought

Marxist theory from the original writing of Marx and Engels to contemporary developments. (3 semester hours)

PSYCHOLOGY

Human Sexuality

Sexuality in personal development; personal, cultural, biological influences on sexual identification and behavior; fertility, reproduction, sexual functioning, sexuality and personality. (3 semester hours)

Introduction to Personality

Theories, concepts, methods, discoveries in psychology of personality. (3 semester hours)

Abnormal Psychology

Problems of abnormality from traditional and evolving points of view; types, therapies, outcomes, preventive techniques. (3 semester hours)

Principles of Development

Major theories of development; contribution of biological and environmental factors; relationship of these factors to child-rearing and social issues. (3 semester hours)

Psychological Disorders of Children

Intellectual and emotional disorders of children. (3 semester hours)

Motivation

Different motivational systems; analysis of environmental and biological factors influencing motivation, with emphasis on human motivation. (3 semester hours)

REAL ESTATE

Real Estate

Relationships between location and value; patterns of urban land use; legal, financial, and organizational framework of the real estate business. (2 or 3 semester hours)

Real Estate Administration

The case method of analyzing management policies, practices, and decision making in real estate firms. (3 semester hours)

SOCIOLOGY

Introduction to Sociology

Human society and social behavior; effects of groups, organizations, cultures, and institutions. (3 semester hours)

The Family

Family system and its interaction patterns; family life cycle from marriage through death: marital relations, divorce, sexuality, parenting crisis, abuse. (3 semester hours)

Criminology

Crime and society; nature, types, and extent of crime, theories of criminality; control of crime. (3 semester hours)

Sociology of Gender

Biological and social causes and effects of sex role socialization; male/female relationships including discriminatory practices, prostitution, and rape. (3 semester hours)

Corrections

History, facilities, processes, strategies for the correction and punishment of offenders, analysis of concepts of prevention and control of crime. (3 semester hours)

Sociology of Aging

Changes in behavior and social roles due to aging; economics and demographics of aging; social relations of the elderly; retirement and widowhood. (3 semester hours)

Theories of Deviance

Theoretical perspectives on deviant behavior; crime, juvenile delinquency, mental illness, suicide, alcohol and drug abuse, sexual deviance; social control. (3 semester hours)

SPANISH

First Semester Spanish

Fundamentals of speaking, reading, and writing. Audiotapes provide exposure to correct Spanish pronunciation, accent, and intonation, and a model for student imitation. (4 semester hours)

Second Semester Spanish

Continued development of basic skills in speaking, reading, and writing. Audiotapes provide exposure to correct Spanish pronunciation, accent, and intonation, and a model for student imitation. (4 semester hours)

SWEDISH

First Semester Swedish

Fundamentals of speaking, listening to, reading, and writing Swedish. Weekly tutoring sessions on the Pullman campus are required. (4 semester hours)

Second Semester Swedish

Continued development of basic skills. Weekly tutoring sessions on the Pullman campus are required. (4 semester hours)

Third Semester Swedish *Tuition:* Continuation of Swedish instruction. Weekly tutoring sessions on the Pullman campus are required. (4 semester hours)

THAI

First Semester Thai

Fundamentals of speaking, listening to, and writing Thai. Weekly tutoring sessions on the Pullman campus are required. (4 semester hours)

WOMEN'S STUDIES

History of Women in American Society

The roles of women—social, economic, political—in American history from colonial times to the present. (3 semester hours)

History of Women in the American West

The history of women in the American Northwest through women's literature, archives, and oral history. (3 semester hours)

Twentieth-Century American Women

(3 semester hours)

Women Writers

Women's artistic and intellectual contributions to prose, fiction, drama, and poetry. (3 semester hours)

ZOOLOGY

Evolution

For nonbiology majors. Basic principles of Darwinian evolution. (2 semester hours)

Principles of Conservation

Conservation of major natural resources through a biological approach; philosophical, economic, and political aspects of important conservation issues. (3 semester hours)

Weber State University
Independent Study
Continuing Education and Community Service
Ogden, Utah 84408-4005   (801) 626-6785

Description:

Weber State University takes pride in being recognized as a total or comprehensive college that provides programs for nearly 15,000 on campus students with varied interests and educational goals. Looking to go beyond the traditional college setting, Weber State University's Division of Continuing Education developed the independent study program. This program was designed specifically for people who can not attend regularly scheduled college courses.

Faculty:

Charles E. Schill, Program Administrator, Independent Study Program.

Academic Levels:
College
Noncredit

Degree/Certificate Programs:

Weber State University students may apply 45 credits of independent study toward a bachelor's degree.

Admission Requirements:

Anyone may enroll in an independent study course. These courses may be taken for college credit or noncredit. If the prospective student desires college credit, the college admission requirements must be fulfilled prior to completing the first course.

Tuition:

$50 per credit hour. A civilian overseas address will require an additional fee of $20 per course for airmail service. Visa and MasterCard accepted. Refund policy: a refund of 80 percent of the tuition will be made if withdrawal is within 30 days of enrollment, no lessons have been submitted, and no request for a grade has been made. Otherwise no refunds will be given. The request for a refund must be in writing and must be postmarked no later than 30 days after the enrollment date.

Enrollment Period:

Students may begin a course at any time during the year. The maximum time allowed to complete a course (including the final examination) is 12 months from the date of enrollment. A course may be extended up to six months for an extension fee of $10 per month per course.

Equipment Requirements:

Textbooks can be ordered by mail directly from the Independent Study Office. A course may include tapes, kits, or additional materials. These materials will be checked out to the student upon payment of a materials deposit. Upon return to the Independent Study Office, a refund will be made.

Credit and Grading:

If the student lives within 50 miles of the Weber State University campus, examinations must be taken at the WSU Testing Center located in the Stewart Library. If the student lives more than 50 miles away from WSU, examinations must be supervised by a qualified person. Approved examination supervisors are school principals, superintendents, guidance counselors, full-time school or public librarians, embassy officials, military education officers (for military personnel only), or hospital education directors. Teachers, employers, relatives, and close friends cannot be used as proctors. Grading system: letter grades are given (A, B, C, D, or E) only when the course is completed. Incompletes will be given at the instructor's discretion. Credit is awarded in quarter hours.

Accreditations:

Northwest Association of Schools and Colleges; Council of Accreditation of Teacher Education. Member of: National University Continuing Education Association.

COLLEGE COURSES

ACCOUNTING

Elementary Financial

Course 201. Introduction to the basic accounting cycle for service and merchandising companies, plus consideration of selected balance sheet topics. Check figures included. (3 quarter hours)

Course 202. A continuation of *Course 201* including discussion of remaining balance sheet topics, and consideration of basic principles of accounting for corporations and partnerships. (3 quarter hours)

Managerial Accounting

Analysis of cost behavior and the role of accounting information in the planning, controlling, and decision-making processes of a business enterprise. (3 quarter hours)

ANTHROPOLOGY

Introduction to Anthropology

Evolution and development of man and culture from pre-history to the present. (5 quarter hours)

BOTANY

Past, Present, and Future User of Plants

Survey of the world production and use of plants economically important to man as crops: lumber, fibers, sugars, grains, fruits, beverages, spices, drugs, pesticides, plant growth substances, etc. (4 quarter hours)

BUSINESS ADMINISTRATION

Introduction to Business

Relation of business person and firm to free enterprise economy and basic principles of major fields of business. (4 quarter hours)

CHEMISTRY

Introduction to Chemistry

The study of matter (substances) and the changes that matter undergoes. (5 quarter hours)

CHILD AND FAMILY STUDIES

Human Development

Fundamentals of growth and development relating to effective human relationships within the family and a study of behavior and cultural influences from infancy through adolescence. (5 quarter hours)

COMMUNICATIONS

Introduction to Mass Communication

The study of mass media communication from early development and the impact on society. The course considers newspapers, magazines, books, photography, film, radio, television, and multimedia. (3 quarter hours)

Mass Media and Society

A course which examines the non-legal, but ethical and social problems of mass media. The impact of television and the press, the management of the news, and the effects of the mass media on our quality of life will be discussed. (3 quarter hours)

CRIMINAL JUSTICE

Criminal Justice

This course covers the purpose, function, and history of law enforcement, courts, and corrections. (5 quarter hours)

ELECTRONIC ENGINEERING

Introduction to Digital Electronics

Introduction to the fundamentals of digital electronics. Number systems, boolean algebra, logic gates, flipflops, multiplexers, sequential and combinational circuits, and digital measuring devices. (4 quarter hours)

Digital Circuits Lab

Laboratory class to support the above course. Construct and analyze basic digital circuits. (1 quarter hour)

ENGLISH

Developmental Writing II

This course is designed for those who scored 16 or less on the ACT test, or those whose English placement test indicated a need for additional work to bring skills up to college-level writing. Subjects covered include the organization, development, editing, grammar, and usage of the English language. (3 quarter hours)

Vocabulary Building

Basic techniques for enlarging and improving vocabulary. (2 credit hours)

College Writing

Course EN111. Expressive, experiential, and expository writing. Principles of unity, coherence, development, organization, and style. (4 quarter hours)

Course EN112. Exposition, argumentation, persuasion, and documented research. (4 quarter hours)

Technical Writing

Basic principles of composition applicable to engineering, scientific and technical reports. (3 quarter hours)

Fiction Writing

Techniques of narration and description involving character in conflict. Basic, simplified approaches to the short story. (3 quarter hours)

Introduction to Fiction

A literature course designed to increase the student's appreciation of fiction. (3 quarter hours)

FINANCE

Personal Finance

Personal and family budgeting, installment buying, borrowing money, buying a home, and purchasing stocks and bonds. (4 quarter hours)

GEOGRAPHY

Physical Geography

The study of the physical elements of the environment; e.g., landforms, climate, natural vegetation, hydrology and soils, and their integrated patterns of world distribution. (5 quarter hours)

Introduction to Meteorology

Introduction course in the study of weather. Includes winds, storms, radiation, isolation, moisture, pressure, and temperature. (4 quarter hours)

GERONTOLOGY

Introduction to Gerontology

An introduction to the areas of biological, psychological, and sociological contributions to the field of gerontology, with an emphasis on personal awareness of myths, problems, and solutions relating to the older person in America. (5 quarter hours)

Introduction to Social Gerontology

A scientific study of social and psychological aging and the application of principles and strategies to facilitate adaptation to aging. The focus is on methods and systems for gathering data, demography of aging, social theoretical perspectives, psychological effects of aging, aging and the economy, and government and the politics of aging. (3 quarter hours)

Gerontological Development and Policy

National awareness, historical growth and policy development in response to gerontology in the United States will be covered. Specific examples will include social and health insurance, White House conferences, legislations, Administration on Aging, National Institute on Aging, scientific and applied groups, and the financing of programs. (3 quarter hours)

Ethnicity and the Aging Process

A study of the importance of ethnicity and social policy on the social functioning of older people. (3 quarter hours)

Societal Responses to Aging

A study of how aging, as a dimension of social organization, touches every live, every home, every community, and every relationship. (3 quarter hours)

Retirement: Adjustment/Planning

This course is designed to cover aspects of retirement relating to job change or discontinuance. The processes, events, social roles, and phases of life will be presented. (3 quarter hours)

HEALTH

Healthy Lifestyles

A self-appraisal of personal health with an emphasis on implementing reading research into the individual's lifestyle. The student will survey and activate preventive health measures in the areas of organic efficiency, mental/emotional health, stress management, American drug culture, sexuality and reproduction, chronic and degenerative disease, communicable disease, consumer health, environmental health, aging process, and death and dying. (2 quarter hours)

Introduction to Medical Science

Medical terminology roles and interrelationships in the health care team medical ethics and psychology of the patient. (3 quarter hours)

Medical Terminology

This course is designed to acquaint preprofessional students and personnel in health-related fields with medical terms of Greek and Latin origin and with common medical abbreviations and symbols. (3 quarter hours)

Biomedical Science Core

This core is a series of three five-credit courses which helps the student to understand how the basic principles of anatomy, chemistry, physics, and microbiology all interact to influence the functioning (physiology) of the human body, especially under clinical conditions. (5 quarter hours per course)

Functional Mechanism of Pathology for Paramedics

This is an independent study course open to students in the emergency care and rescue program. The course provides the prerequisite information necessary to successfully complete the paramedic program. (5 quarter hours)

Pathophysiology

This course introduces the student to the nature of common diseases and their effect on body systems. The student will learn to relate normal body functioning to the physiologic changes that occur as the result of illness, as well as the body's ability to compensate for the illness-related changes. This understanding of disease mechanisms will be applied to patient care. (4 quarter hours)

HISTORY

The History of World Societies

Course SS101. The history of the world civilizations from the beginning of recorded history up to the fifteenth century. Four major civilizations are discussed in the context of their social, cultural, political, economic, religious, scientific, intellectual, technological, and geographic factors. (4 quarter hours)

Course SS102. This course describes the history of world civilizations from approximately 1300 until 1871. It discusses the major world civilizations which existed during this period. Social, cultural, political, economic, religious, scientific, intellectual, technological, and geographic factors relating to these civilizations are also examined. (4 quarter hours)

Course SS103. The history of world civilization from 1871 to the present. (4 quarter hours)

American Civilization

A consideration of the historical, political, and economic growth of the United States from colonial beginning to the present. (5 quarter hours)

History of Africa

Africa from earliest times to the present. (5 quarter hours)

Diplomatic History of the United States

This course deals with how the United States has accomplished or failed to accomplish goals set by our founding fathers in the field of foreign relations. The student should emerge from this course with a better understanding of how the United States can cope with difficult subjects such as: "Salt II," hostages, and spy exchanges, as all of these topics have been handled and are handled through diplomatic negotiations. (5 quarter hours)

Far Western History

This course traces the settlement of the region from the Rocky Mountains to the Pacific Coast, and the influence of the Spanish in the Southwest. (3 quarter hours)

Utah History

This course deals with Utah's history over the past three centuries including study of the Indians, the fur trade, exploration, settlement by the Mormons, and twentieth-century development. (3 quarter hours)

Twentieth-Century Europe (1900 to Present)

A study of Europe from the First World War to the present. Emphasis on the new role of Europe. (5 quarter hours)

History of the Far East

Development of the Far East and its influence in the contemporary era. The nations of China, Japan, and Korea particularly are studied. (5 quarter hours)

History of the Middle East

The Middle East from the beginning to the present with emphasis upon the nineteenth and twentieth centuries. (5 quarter hours)

INTERIOR DESIGN

Design for Living

Elements and principles of design and color as they relate to functional home planning and individual and environmental goals. Analysis of the role of interior design fulfilling human needs. (4 quarter hours)

MANAGEMENT

Organizational Behavior and Management

An introductory course which explores the basic theories and concepts of management. The course emphasizes the behavioral aspects of management such as organizational design, employee motivation, organizational change and development, and organizational culture as well as organizational structure. (4 quarter hours)

MATHEMATICS

First Course in Algebra

A course concerning mathematical concepts of set, relations, functions, positive and negative numbers, rational expressions, linear equations and inequalities, and polynomial functions. (5 quarter hours)

Intermediate Algebra

This course studies exponents and radicals, exponentials and logarithms, polynomial and rational functions, and systems of equations. (5 quarter hours)

College Algebra

This course covers selected topics in algebra including inequalities, logarithms, theory of equations, matrices, determinants, and progressions. (5 quarter hours)

MUSIC

Introduction to Music

An introduction to music, its elements, language, and historical development. Students will develop critical awareness by becoming actively involved in the elements of music. (5 quarter hours)

Evolution of Jazz

A history of the evolution of jazz, important jazz musicians, and the various eras or changes in jazz since 1900. Audio tapes from each era enhance the course. (3 quarter hours)

Music Essentials: Piano

The course is designed to develop the knowledge and skills associated with reading, writing, and the ability to interpret the calligraphy (symbols) of music. The programmed approach allows the student to study the fundamentals of music at his/her own pace. (3 quarter hours)

PHILOSOPHY

Introduction to Philosophy

The course is designed to introduce the student to the problems and types of philosophy. (5 quarter hours)

PHYSICAL EDUCATION

Fitness for Life Concepts

Prescribe individualized programs for weight control, cardiovascular endurance, strength, and flexibility. Physical pre-test and post-test, midterm, and final. (2 quarter hours)

POLITICAL SCIENCE

American National Government

A course to help the student learn about the American system of government and to familiarize him/her with important political problems with which the American government is concerned. It is a course to help the student think clearly and dispassionately about government and politics, and to make judgments concerning political questions that are rational and based on the value of the American democratic tradition. (5 quarter hours)

Introduction to International Politics

Examines international relations by juxtaposing the traditional nation-state model (nationalism, sovereignty, realism, BOP) with the newer model of "complex interdependence" (mutual vulnerability to economic interdependence, nuclear war, and environmental dangers). (5 quarter hours)

Introduction to Public Administration

This course is designed to introduce the student to various elements of administration in the public sector including management techniques, budget processes, personnel policy, decision making, and organizational theory. The primary focus will be from the perspective of a first line supervisor. Motivational theory, informal organization, and personal career strategies will be emphasized. (5 quarter hours)

PSYCHOLOGY

Introduction to Psychology

An introductory course to the scientific study of human behavior. (5 quarter hours)

Psychology of Adjustment

Psychological foundations necessary for the understanding of both normal and abnormal adjustment patterns. Explores techniques for better adjustment. (3 quarter hours)

Interpersonal Relations and Communications

Analysis of communication as a conceptualization of interpersonal relationships and awareness of personal characteristics which either increase or impede accurate communication in interviewing or group interaction and appropriate use of psychological communication skills. (3 quarter hours)

Theories of Personality

A survey of the major theories of personality. (3 quarter hours)

Abnormal Psychology

A review of abnormal human behavior, its etiology, symptoms, and treatment. (5 quarter hours)

Advanced General Psychology

In-depth and comprehensive treatment of major areas and issues in psychology. A senior level overview and review course for graduating majors. (5 quarter hours)

Social Psychology

An empirically-based survey of the effects of social influence on the basic psychological processes of individuals: the individual in culture and society, the development of attitudes, and the impact of the group. (3 quarter hours)

SALES AND SERVICES TECHNOLOGY

Fundamental Selling Techniques

A retail, wholesale, and direct selling course. Emphasis on mastering and applying the fundamentals of selling. Preparation for and execution of sales demonstrations required. (4 quarter hours)

Retail Merchandising Methods

The study of the activities associated with the merchandising of products and services to the ultimate consumer, including types of retail institutions, store locations and layout, store design, pricing, selling, buying, and financial information. (4 quarter hours)

Distribution Principles

Examination of the distribution process of goods and services, the interrelationships of customer demands, production, pricing, promotion, and the movement of goods from producer to consumer. (5 quarter hours)

Visual Merchandising

Study of the visual approach to selling with emphasis on window display, interior display, counter and shadow box display, point-of-purchase display, and fixtures and materials used in visual merchandising. (3 quarter hours)

Introduction to Fashion Merchandising

A study of the fashion merchandising industry, including careers in design, manufacturing, wholesaling, promotion, and retailing, including well-known designers, manufactures promotion media, apparel and accessory retail institutions. (5 quarter hours)

Credit and Collection Methods

The study of specific credit and collection methods for retail, wholesale, and service industries, including cost of retail credit, credit investigation, methods of collecting bad accounts, securing new business through credit applications, and credit control (3 quarter hours)

Consumer Textiles

A study of fibers, yarns fabric structure, and finishes as they relate to buying wear, use, care, and household textiles. (4 quarter hours)

Buying Methods

The study of the retail buyer's duties, different buying organizations, and techniques and procedures of purchasing merchandise for resale. (4 quarter hours)

Advertising Methods

A study of advertising methods as they relate to local retail, wholesale, and service industries, including newspaper, magazine, radio, TV, mail, outdoor, and special promotion events. (5 quarter hours)

Customer Service Techniques

Provides practical "how to" instruction in techniques for improving customer relations and customer service for retail stores. Utilizes simulations, role plays, and individualized hands-on experiences with customer service. (4 quarter hours)

Principles of Supervision

Practical application of first-line supervisory skills, including choosing, organizing, training, and evaluating entry-level employees; making supervisory decisions; and solving first-line supervisory problems. (5 quarter hours)

Ethical Sales and Service

Principles, techniques, and analysis of ethics in sales and service professions. Utilizes group interaction and individualizes hands-on experiences. (3 quarter hours)

SOCIOLOGY

Introduction to Sociology

An introductory course of the systematic treatment of group life, social processes, and social control. (5 quarter hours)

Social Problems

The sociological analysis of deviant behavior in modern society. (5 quarter hours)

Western Carolina University
Cullowhee, North Carolina 28723

(704) 227-7211

Description:

The state university was founded in 1889 as a semi-public school. In 1905 it became a normal and industrial school and was designated a senior college in 1929. In 1972 Western Carolina University became a constituent institution of the University of North Carolina. WCU is a participant in a consortium of eight institutions within the University of North Carolina System offering college-level correspondence courses and other opportunities for individualized study at a distance from the university campuses. In the consortium arrangement, each institution originating a course provides instruction and awards academic credit, while responsibility for administration of the program lies with the office of Independent Studies at the University of North Carolina at Chapel Hill. SEE **North Carolina, University of - Chapel Hill.**

Faculty:

Pauline Christensen, Member of UNC Independent Studies Advisory Committee.

Accreditations:

Southern Association of Colleges and Schools.

Western Illinois University
Educational Broadcasting and Independent Study
1 University Circle
Macomb, Illinois 61455   (309) 298-2496

Description:

Western Illinois University was originally founded in 1899 as a normal school, and teacher education remains an important purpose of the institution. The university now includes the Colleges of: Education, Applied Sciences, Arts and Sciences, Business, Continuing Education, Fine Arts, Health, Physical Education and Recreation, School of Graduate Studies. The university also includes three divisions in Public Service, International Understanding, and Student Personnel Service.

The Independent Study Program was established in 1977 to meet the needs of students enrolled in an external degree program. Most courses offered are at the junior-senior level and duplicate as nearly as possible the content of courses offered in the regular WIU classroom setting. Courses are offered during all terms and are taught by WIU professors. Students must enroll by a specific date upon the announcement of the availability of courses for a given semester. WIU also participates in the Open Learning Fire Service Program, a project of the National Fire Academy to provide opportunities for fire service personnel to earn a degree or pursue professional growth by taking courses.

Faculty:

Dr. Joyce E. Nielsen, Director, Educational Broadcasting and Independent Study. There is a faculty of 75 members.

Academic Levels:

College

Degree/Certificate Programs:

High school graduation or GED. To register for graduate courses, the student must hold a baccalaureate degree from a regionally accredited institution.

Admission Requirements:

Enrollment in an Independent Study Program course does not constitute admission to a degree program at Western Illinois University. Enrollment of students from foreign countries is not encouraged due to postage costs and delays in communication.

Tuition:

$79.25 per semester hour for undergraduate students; $83.50 per semester hour for graduate students. Students receiving any form of financial assistance are advised to check with their Financial Aid Office to determine the extent of coverage available for Independent Study courses, including telecourses offered nationally. The Veterans Administration Regional Office (Illinois) reimburses veterans for a maximum of 5 semester hours of ISP coursework each semester.

Enrollment Period:

Students are enrolled for a course on a semester basis. Courses are announced in advance and enrollments will be closed when a class is filled. Students are encouraged to choose an alternate course when applying for enrollment. Enrollment is limited to two Independent Study courses per student. A student may withdraw from a course and receive full tuition credit or a refund during the first six weeks of the term. Written requests to withdraw must be sent to the Independent Study Program office.

Equipment Requirements:

The Independent Study Program office ships the study guide and book order form for each course via United Parcel Service. Books may then be ordered from the Western Illinois University bookstore. Students must bear the cost of textbooks, videotapes, audiotapes, telecourse fee, satellite transponder fee.

Credit and Grading:

Examinations must be proctored by an official in education. The exam is mailed directly to the educational institution where the proctor is employed and the proctor returns the completed exam to Independent Learning. Grading system: A, B, C, D, or F or Pass/Fail. Minimum passing grade is D; only grades of C or better count toward progress in meeting Board of Governors Bachelor of Arts degree requirements. Credit is awarded in semester hours.

Library Services:

Students in the western Illinois region have access to the WIU library. Distant students must rely on local libraries.

Accreditations:

North Central Association of Colleges and Schools. Member of: National University Continuing Education Association.

COLLEGE COURSES

AGRICULTURAL ECONOMICS
Marketing Grain and Livestock Products

Examine the trading of futures contracts as a basis hedge. Introductory material includes basic jargon, the use of hedging by agribusiness, and a pricing-strategy decision framework. A comparison of basis hedging and multiple hedging is considered in the context of business objectives, evaluation criteria, market risk, and profit potential. A video course. (3 semester hours)

Commodity Markets and Futures Trading

Study multiple hedging and speculation. An introduction to the institutions and jargon of the futures market is followed by the study of technical signals: bar chart, point-and-figure, moving averages, volume and open interest, momentum, HI/LO, %R, RSI, stochastics, and DMI. A video course. (3 semester hours)

Options on Futures

Explore the trading of options on futures contracts for hedging or speculative purposes. Familiarization with the jargon is followed by consideration of risk/return and effective-price profiles of option positions, hedging strategies for long and short cash positions, trading strategies, and an introduction to the Black pricing model. A video course. (1 semester hour)

Market Logic

The CBOT Market Profile (R) approach to market analysis was formulated by J. Peter Steidlmayer, developed by the Chicago Board of Trade, and can be used for day-trading and overnight positions. A video course. (2 semester hours)

ASTRONOMY

Astronomy

A study of major developments from the time of the Babylonians to the present. Requiring no prior knowledge of physics, the course emphasizes the Earth and our solar system. The last part of the course, however, is devoted to other stars and extragalactic astronomy, including clusters, superclusters of galaxies, quasars, and black holes. (3 semester hours)

BIOLOGY

Human Biology

Human genetics—including inheritance of chromosomes, sex determination, molecular genetics, mutations, and genetic engineering—is the focus of much scientific research. Study human evolution, behavior, ecology, and physiology in detail. (4 semester hours)

COMMUNICATION STUDIES

Broadcasting and Society

Divided into two parts, this course introduces you to the broadcast industry in America—its business practices, history, and regulation—and surveys the social impact of the broadcast media. Topics covered include broadcast journalism, violence on television, and the stereotyped portrayal of TV characters. (3 semester hours)

ECONOMICS

Managerial Economics

Focus on the application of economic principles that business firm managers use for making decisions. This course covers topics such as demand, revenue, production, costs, supply, pricing, and competition. You will learn how decisions affect profits and will study the tools and concepts necessary to maximize those profits. (3 semester hours)

Money, Banking, and Credit

Focuses on the monetary aspects of the U.S. economy, especially the role of depository financial institutions and the Federal Reserve System. Obtain an overview of the development the American banking system, the organizational aspects of commercial banks, the role of depository institutions and the Federal Reserve System in the creation of money, and the determinants of prices and output in the economy. (3 semester hours)

ENGLISH

Modern Drama

Survey some of the masterpieces of drama beginning with the plays of August Strindberg and Henrik Ibsen. The course traces various elements of theatre through the works of several established playwrights, including Oscar Wilde, Lady Gregory, John Synge, George Bernard Shaw, and Arthur Miller. In addition to reading several dramas, you have the opportunity to view and listen to a play. (3 semester hours)

Writing in the Humanities and Social Sciences

This course focuses on the humanistic fields—history, literature, sociology, education, religion, and art—but it is equally useful for those who want to write about the sciences, the business world, or current events from a humanistic perspective. (3 semester hours)

Topics in Literature: Personal Nonfiction—The Diary, Familiar Essay, and Autobiography

The diary, familiar essay, and autobiography are literary forms that reflect the writer's self directly, often with surprising insight and remarkable poignancy. You may select the six books you wish to read from a list of 32 titles by Jane Addams, Maya Angelou, Frederick Douglass, Loren Eiseley, Anne Frank, Thomas Merton, Anais Nin, Henry David Thoreau, and many other writers. (3 semester hours)

FINANCE

Risk Management and Insurance

The course also covers the operation of insurance companies and the role of insurance in an overall personal investment scheme. Some specific contracts to be analyzed include individual life, health, homeowners, and automobile policies. (3 semester hours)

FIRE SERVICE

Fire Protection Structure and Systems Design

Study the design principles involved in the protection of the structure from fire, the empirical tests and prediction procedures, control detection and suppression system design practices, and fundamentals of the hydraulic design of sprinkler and water spray systems with recent innovations. (3 semester hours)

Fire Dynamics

A study of fire propagation phenomenon in both fuel and air regulated phases. Variables in pre- and post-flashover fire development are discussed. The study of geometric, material, gaseous, fluid flow, and thermodynamic parameters enhances the course. (3 semester hours)

Analytic Approaches to Public Fire Protection

Designed to give a broad understanding of the characteristics of systems analysis and of its uses and limitations in fire protection and other problem areas. The course is illustrated with case studies and models using the systems approach to fire suppression and prevention. (3 semester hours)

Personnel Management for the Fire Service

Investigates personnel practices and management procedures, including collective bargaining, binding arbitration, applicable legislative procedures, and administrative and supervisory procedures. (3 semester hours)

Fire Prevention Organization and Management

Examine and evaluate the techniques, procedures, programs, and agencies involved with fire prevention. Consideration is given to related governmental inspection and education procedures. (3 semester hours)

Political and Legal Foundations of Fire Protection

Examine the legal limitations and responsibility and the liability of fire prevention organizations and personnel. This course also reviews judicial decisions. (3 semester hours)

Disaster and Fire Defense Planning

Covers the relationship of structural, climatic, and topographic variables to group fires, conflagrations, and natural disasters. The course includes concepts and principles of community risk assessment. (3 semester hours)

The Community and Fire Threat

Investigate the sociological, economic, and political characteristics of communities and their influence on the fire problem. It includes a review of the urban studies related to housing, structure abandonment, rent control, crime, false alarm and incendiary fire rates, and the fire problem. The roles of the fire department and fire prevention programs are examined, as are community and fire service role conflicts. (3 semester hours)

Managerial Issues in Hazardous Materials

Examine regulatory issues, hazard analysis, multi-agency contingency response resources, agency policies, procedures and implementation, public education and emergency information systems, health and safety, command post dynamics, strategic and tactical considerations, recovery and termination procedures, and program evaluation. (3 semester hours)

GEOGRAPHY

Climatology

This course focuses on the causes and distribution of climatic regions, with special emphasis on the application of climatology to our everyday lives. (3 semester hours)

Conservation and Management of Natural Resources

Examine such environmental problems as air and water quality, wildlife and soil conservation, waste and toxic substance management, and public lands management in their physical and regulatory contexts. The course emphasizes forest management and the preservation of biological diversity. A short history of the conservation movement in the United States is also presented. (3 semester hours)

GEOLOGY

Environmental Geology

An in-depth treatment of our relations with the physical environment. Study a range of topics—from the philosophical basis for the study of environmental geology to the geologic and human aspects of natural hazards such as flooding, landslides, earthquakes, and volcanoes. Other materials include water and human use; solid, liquid, and nuclear waste disposal; the geologic aspects of environmental health; mineral and energy resources; and environmental law. (3 semester hours)

HISTORY

American History to 1877

Survey the history of the United States through the Civil War and Reconstruction. How people lived and why they made the choices they did figure prominently in our story. Emphasis is on causes, meaning, insight into significant episodes, and relevance for the present. Where historians differ, alternative interpretations are presented. (3 semester hours)

American History Since 1877

Trace events from the end of the Reconstruction era to the present. Module I (1877–1900) includes the growth of industry during the Gilded Age, the politics of the era, protest efforts of wage earners and farmers, American overseas expansion, and the emergence of American cities. Module II (1900–1938) covers the evolution of the Progressive Movement, America's entry into and involvement in World War I, the paradoxical nature of the 1920s, and the New Deal response to the Great Depression. Module III (1938–present) highlights the historical developments of this era including America's deepening involvement in international affairs, beginning with World War II. (3 semester hours)

The American West

Follow the westward movement in U.S. history. Compare the "real West" with the West of legend and pop culture. Study the Indians as people, not merely as impediments to Anglo-American expansion. This course is less concerned with who went where and when than with the process of settling the West and its impact upon American culture. Differing interpretations of the "significance of the frontier" are considered. (3 semester hours)

Twentieth-Century Europe

Study the major historical themes in Europe from the pre-World War I period to the contemporary period. Both Western Europe (including Great Britain) and Eastern Europe (including the former Soviet Union) are covered in the course. Major topics include an overview of Europe before World War I, causes and consequences of World War I, the Russian Revolution, the search for stability in the 1920s, the great Depression, the rise of Fascism, the causes and consequences of World War II, postwar reconstruction and revival, the Cold War, detente, the movement toward European unity, and changes in Eastern Europe leading to the break-up of the Soviet satellite system and major reforms inside the former USSR. (3 semester hours)

American Law

The course examines the evolution of American law through four epochs: the colonial period, the early republic, post-Civil War years of urbanization and industrialization, and the twentieth century's reform eras. (3 semester hours)

Crime and Police

Survey the history of crime and police in the United States, France, Germany, Britain, and Ireland since the eighteenth century. Compare the different policing traditions of these countries and examines the development of crime in its social and cultural contexts. (3 semester hours)

Technology and Society

View technology as a process of continuity, integration, and accommodation rather that as a series of disconnected inventions and inventors. Investigate major technological innovations against the background of concurrent social and ideological influences and population movements. Consider the impact of various technologies upon past, present, and future societies. (3 semester hours)

The American Revolution and the New Nation

Covers the causes of the American Revolution, the nature of the War of Independence, the consequences of the conflict, and the issues of the Constitutional Convention of 1787. Emphasis is also given to the administrations of Washington and Adams. (3 semester hours)

HOME ECONOMICS

Introduction to Nutrition

Basic nutrition concepts and ways to apply your nutrition knowledge to everyday living. (3 semester hours)

Child Nutrition and Health

The development of food service and nutrition components in infant and preschool programs is covered. (3 semester hours)

Development of Mutual Resources: Parenting

Examine the principles and philosophies relevant to the process of parenting with emphasis on changing roles and responsibilities, child-rearing decisions, and diverse parenting perspectives. (3 semester hours)

INTERNATIONAL BUSINESS

International Business

Examine the ethical value systems of foreign markets and their impact on the business culture of U.S. corporations. (3 semester hours)

JOURNALISM

Reviewing and Criticism

Focusing on American film genres, you will review seven films (seen in theatres, on videotape, or on television. (3 semester hours)

MANAGEMENT

Management and Organizational Behavior

This comprehensive and integrated introduction to the principles of management emphasizes the management functions of planning, organizing, and control as well as such behavioral processes as communication, leadership, and motivation. (3 semester hours)

Human Resource Management

Examine the principles of personnel management as they relate to the function of personnel administration. Such topics as employee development, personnel recruitment, wage and salary administration, union-management relations, and performance evaluations are examined. (3 semester hours)

Operations Management

Focus on the supply side of both goods and service organizations. Gain an appreciation of the current problems and issues as well as the analytical tools used to resolve operational/production problems in the modern organization. Topics include quality control, inventory planning and control, scheduling and capacity planning, designing facilities, job design, and work measurement. (3 semester hours)

Managing in Organizations

Study the systems approach as a way of understanding and managing complex organizations. A central course theme is that organizational processes—rather than offices, groups, and functions—are the proper primary focus. The systems approach treats interdependence among process inputs as a given and recognizes this interdependence as a major source of organizational complexity. (3 semester hours)

MARKETING

Marketing Principles

Course objectives include developing ability in problem-solving concepts, using models in the marketing field, and evaluating decision-making techniques in marketing management and planning. From the study of the basic marketing mix elements through current marketing and social trends, this course enables you to realize your objectives. (3 semester hours)

Promotional Concepts

Gain insight into the importance of communication, advertising, and promotion to the life of a firm, business, or institution as a going concern. Learn to define, use, and apply the theories and concepts of advertising, promotion, professional selling, sales promotion, and direct marketing as well as to visualize how public relations and publicity relate to promotion. (3 semester hours)

Retailing Management

Gain an understanding of all facets of retailing management from a strategic perspective. Retailing career opportunities, store location and layout, organization, buying, selling, sales promotion, and control are examined. (3 semester hours)

MUSIC

Music in World Cultures

Survey the music in three world areas—India, Africa, and Latin America—with emphasis on the relationship between music and other aspects of culture, such as ethnic identity, religion, gender, and aesthetics. After a unit on the elements of music, the music of the regions is explored with guided listening activities, discussions of the cultural contexts of musical performance, and comparisons of the music of different areas (drawing on the music of other world areas covered in the text). (3 semester hours)

PHILOSOPHY

Moral Philosophy

A broad treatment of the central problems of moral philosophy, the course is organized around such major topics as the nature of morality, theories of value, varieties of egoism, theories of obligation, and views about rights and justice. Examine the contributions of classical philosophers such as Plato and Aristotle and the views of contemporary thinkers. The practical implications of various theories are explored. (3 semester hours)

POLITICAL SCIENCE

U.S. Foreign Policy

Since the end of World War II, the United States has been involved in cold wars, military conflicts, nuclear arms summits, and peace missions. Examine the decisions made to get us involved in these situations. This course focuses on the theoretical concepts involved in developing and implementing American foreign policies and explores the U.S. role in the major events in international relations from the latter stages of World War II to the present. (3 semester hours)

REAL ESTATE

Principles of Real Estate

This course stresses personal aspects, including information for decision making about home ownership, apartment rental, or selection of a condominium or mobile home. Real estate careers and those in brokerage, property management, appraising, investment counseling, and mortgage lending are introduced and reviewed. Other important course topics deal with the current status of land use controls and zoning, mortgages and financing, private property rights, and real estate contracts. (3 semester hours)

RECREATION ADMINISTRATION

Outdoor Recreation Perspectives

An introduction to outdoor recreational land uses, this course speaks to the outdoor enthusiast and conservationist as well as those planning a career in recreation leadership or park management. Topics include psychological, social, and economic factors of outdoor recreation in America; future leisure environments and equipment; the role of private enterprise; state and national outdoor facilities; and recreation carrying capacity, multiple use, and other administrative tools. (3 semester hours)

Leisure Service for the Elderly

Explores the theories and concepts of leisure and aging. This course is an introduction to the exciting and emerging field of gerontology as it relates to leisure. Study the meaning of leisure during the different stages of life, especially as a means of social integration and as a source of personal meaning for the elderly. Learn about the various leisure service settings available to senior citizens, the large number of leisure activities, and the future leisure environment and its effect on older persons. (3 semester hours)

SOCIOLOGY

Community

What holds a community together and enables it to function? Examine small towns, villages, neighborhoods, suburbs, and groups held together by religious, ethnic, tribal, and communal bonds. By comparing the characteristics of communities and what scholars say accounts for variations in community life, you will learn what circumstances create the communities and enable them to meet human needs. (3 semester hours)

Minority Peoples

Gain a fundamental understanding of the dynamics of majority/minority relations. Focus on those racial and ethnic groups of greatest national concern and interest in the United States plus certain groups that are subordinated in the social structure (e.g., women). Examine the role of white ethnic groups and immigration in the United States and race relations in other nations as well. (3 semester hours)

Sociology of Mental Health

Gain a sociologist's perspective of the history, causes, and treatment of mental illness in the United States. The course focuses on the nature and extent of the mental illness problem and its various manifestations, such as personality disorders, neuroses, psychoses, and sexual and personal adjustment disorders; treatment strategies and their limitations; the association of mental illness with age, sex, marital status, class, religion, and other sociological variables; and current issues and trends in rehabilitative policies and practices. (3 semester hours)

TOURISM

Tourism

Topics include components of the travel industry, modes of travel (air, train, ship, car, motorcoach), travel agents, reasons for tourist travel, travel destination area development, travel market research, and weather and health in travel. (3 semester hours)

Western Michigan University
Office of Self-Instructional Programs
Department of Continuing Education
Ellsworth Hall, Room B-102
Kalamazoo, Michigan 49008-5161
(616) 387-4195

Description:

The Office of Self-Instructional Programs offers correspondence courses as an alternative for students unable to attend campus classes. Developed by regular college faculty, these courses are comparable to classroom courses. Credit may be applied toward a degree at Western Michigan University or transferred elsewhere. There are currently over 2,300 students enrolled in 110 courses from 27 departments.

Faculty:

Geraldine A. Schma, Director, Self-Instructional Programs; Kay D. Fischoff, Assistant Director. There is a faculty of 72 members.

Academic Levels:

College

Degree/Certificate Programs:

No external degree is offered by Western Michigan University; however, students in the General University Studies Program may transfer up to 30 credit hours of correspondence study; all other university programs allow

15 semester hours. All courses are for undergraduate credit only and may be applied toward original teacher certification.

Admission Requirements:

No admission requirements for correspondence students enrolled through the Office of Self-Instructional Programs.

Tuition:

$118.25 per credit hour payable at registration. There is no additional fee for out-of-state residents. $25 for overseas postage. Prices are subject to change without notice and usually on an annual basis. Visa and MasterCard accepted. Tuition minus a $20 administration fee will be refunded if requested within 60 days following enrollment. All materials must be returned. Financial aid and academic scholarships are accepted at Self-Instructional Programs; however, the student must contact the Financial Aid Office for rules governing the student's situation. Veterans using the benefits under the Veterans' Readjustment Assistance Act should contact WMU's Office of Academic Records.

Enrollment Period:

The maximum time allowed to complete a course is one year. A three-month extension may be granted in reasonable cases upon payment of a $20 extension fee.

Equipment Requirements:

The cost of textbooks is not included in the tuition. Books may be purchased from the Western Michigan University Campus Bookstore, or purchased locally. Some courses require access to a cassette tape player, some require a calculator; both supplied by the student.

Credit and Grading:

Examinations are usually required if a course is being taken for credit. Examinations vary in form for each course; some examinations do not require a proctor. If required, the proctor is (usually a school official) approved by the Office of Self-Instructional Programs or at a Western Michigan Regional Center. Grading system is the 4.0 scale used in the undergraduate program at WMU. Letter grades or the credit/no credit option may be selected by the student upon registration. Credit is awarded in semester hour units.

Library Services:

A library card is issued to each student, allowing access for one year to all libraries on Western Michigan University's campus.

Accreditations:

North Central Association of Colleges and Schools. Member of: National University Continuing Education Association.

COLLEGE COURSES

ANTHROPOLOGY

Introduction to Archaeology

The science of archaeology is explored in terms of the methods and concepts used to discover and interpret past human behavior. Select portions of Old and New World prehistoric cultural sequences provide the frame of reference. (3 semester hours)

Topics in World Culture Areas: Indians and Eskimos

This course will survey Native American cultures, from the initial peopling of the New World by immigrants from Asia to the Age of Exploration and colonization of North America by Europeans. Emphasis will be placed on adaptive requirements of varying environments and the nature of human response to these conditions. (3 semester hours)

BIOLOGY

Environmental Biology

An introductory ecology course that will examine the relationships among living organisms and their environment. Emphasis will be placed not only on basic ecological principles but also on man and his environment. (3 semester hours)

Biological Science

A course in general biology intended primarily for students in elementary education. Especially emphasized will be those areas of biology that will be of special value in teaching science in the elementary classroom. "Laboratory-type" activities are incorporated generously to demonstrate biological concepts and to emphasize the importance of such activities in effective teaching. All necessary materials may be easily obtained and activities may be performed in any ordinary home or classroom setting. (4 semester hours)

Applied Botany

A course designed to inform students about good gardening practices and uses for both indoor and outdoor plants based on sound botanical information. Supportive material on soils, pesticides, light energy, horticulture, and landscape basics contributes to a thorough understanding for successfully growing and appreciating plants in everyday life. (4 semester hours)

Ecology

An introduction to the relationships of organisms to their environment and to one another. Interrelationships of individuals and the physical environment, dynamics of populations, and structure and function in the community and ecosystem are considered. The emphasis is on ecology as a science but environmental applications of ecological knowledge are also covered. (4 semester hours)

The Biology of Addictive Drugs

The study of modes of action and effects of psychoactive drugs, such as alcohol, marijuana, cocaine, amphetamines, heroin, methadone, LSD, PCP, and nicotine. (3 semester hours)

Biology of Aging

This course is designed to provide students with an understanding of the aging process. The emphasis will be placed on the anatomical, physiological, and molecular changes which occur in cells and organs with aging. Clinical applications are introduced where they provide additional insight into the aging process. (3 semester hours)

Medical Botany

From ancient folklore and witchcraft to modern pharmaceuticals, plants have always and still do play important roles in people's health. This course provides an opportunity to explore the modern as well as antiquated involvement of plants in human health and medicine. The therapeutic, toxic, and psychiatric properties of plants pertinent to the human body are emphasized. An attempt is made to compare natural and synthetic products and to look at local industries manufacturing medicines. (3 semester hours)

Plants of Southwestern Michigan

Vascular plants in this geographic region are studied in the field by habitat (community in which they live). Students are expected to visit different plant communities where they will observe, collect, and identify representative plants. Methods of plant identification, techniques of plant specimen preparation and pollination biology are also included. (3 semester hours)

Trees and Shrubs

A field course in the identification of trees and shrubs. Structural characteristics, habit of growth, geographical distribution and economic importance are examined. (3 semester hours)

BLACK AMERICAN STUDIES

Black Experience: From the African Beginnings to 1865

This course is designed to trace and analyze the history of the women/men of African blood in the Americas. The central theme of the class will be "survival" and "creativity development/" Some attention will be devoted to those settling in non-English speaking zones, the majority to Africans who settled in the United States. Starting with the West African, up to present day, the course will examine the origins of early man in Africa, the development of Sudanic Kingdoms, the rise of the coastal kingdoms, the arrival of Europeans, the origins of slave trade, white attitudes towards slavery, and the black economic situations faced by freed persons of color. Abolition, also the legal and economic position of persons of African descent before the Civil War, will be examined. (3 semester hours)

Black Experience: 1866–Present

This course will allow students to acquire a more educationally and historically sound approach to the Black Experience in the post bellum years. It allows adequate time to investigate the complexities of the African-American response to post Civil War changes and the coming of the twentieth century. (3 semester hours)

BUSINESS INFORMATION SYSTEMS

Introduction to Information Processing

Designed to meet business information needs, this course acquaints students with the computer as a tool. It emphasizes four major aspects: the computer as a machine, computer usage, information system, and the impact of computers. Access to any brand of computer is required. (3 semester hours)

Informational Writing

Development of the basic composition skills required of the competent writer in business and professions. Through continuing directed practice in writing, students develop competence in the organization and presentation of facts and information in writing. (3 semester hours)

Principles of Business Communication

This course focuses on written communication in modern organizations. Students will apply communication strategies in formulating objectives, structuring messages, and choosing appropriate communication channels to solve business problems. Assignments will center of writing appropriate to the business disciplines. (3 semester hours)

CHEMISTRY

History of Chemistry

This course traces the roots of chemistry from ancient technology through alchemy and medicine to the chemical revolution of Lavoisier and Dalton. It examines the nineteenth century basis of modern chemistry and the twentieth century clarification of the structural atom. (3 semester hours)

COMPUTER SCIENCE

Introduction to Computers

Provides the student with an introduction to the logic and structure of computing, some hands-on experience with BASIC programming language and familiarity with the range of computer applications in use today. In addition, it deals with some of the emerging ethical issues in the computer field. (3 semester hours)

CONSUMER RESOURCES AND TECHNOLOGY

Time Management

This course covers such topics as: importance of time; allocating your time; identifying and solving time wasters, characteristics and strategies of effective time managers; measuring effectiveness; dealing with interruptions; and supervisor wasting your time. (1 semester hour)

ECONOMICS

Contemporary Economic Problems

This course is designed to give students an overview of the field of economics. Macroeconomics and microeconomics are covered with emphasis on applications to current issues. A section on international economics is also included. (3 semester hours)

Principles of Microeconomics

An introduction to microeconomics, the study of the price system and resource allocation, problems of monopoly and the role of government in regulating and supplementing the price system. (3 semester hours)

Principles of Macroeconomics

This course is concerned with the economy as a whole. The subject matter deals, to a large extent, with the problems of inflation and unemployment, their impact upon the total output of a society and the distribution of this output. (3 semester hours)

Managerial Economics

This course is designed to illustrate how economic analysis can be applied to decision making. The focus is on economic analysis to decision making in the private business environment as well as in public and nonprofit organizations. (3 semester hours)

Labor Economics

An analysis of the nature and underlying causes of the problems facing the worker in modern economic society. Includes an examination of unions, collective bargaining, labor legislation, wages, unemployment and economic insecurity. This course combines both a theoretical and applied approach. (3 semester hours)

Money and Banking

This is a course dealing with the monetary policies and the institution of the financial sector of the economy. It will give the student a better understanding of the economic issues by explaining the theory and practices of monetary policy. (3 semester hours)

Intermediate Microeconmics

An examination of microeconomic theory, with emphasis on the theory of consumer behavior, the theory of the firm, and factory pricing. (3 semester hours)

EDUCATION

Personal Vocabulary Development

This course helps students increase efficiency in understanding the many and varied words encountered in daily reading. This ten-lesson course has two parts: (1) studying word meanings; (2) reading about words, language, and derivations. (2 semester hours)

Personal Reading Efficiency

This course teaches the student to assess reading rate, comprehension, and vocabulary. (2 semester hours)

Effective Reading for College Students

Designed to show the student how to make more effective use of text and reference books in academic subjects. Attention is given to chapter reading, vocabulary building, problem solving, concentration, note-taking and critical reading. (2 semester hours)

Critical and Creative Reading

This course teaches the student to assess reading weaknesses and then furnishes steps and drills to teach habitual improvement tactics. (2 semester hours)

ENGINEERING TECHNOLOGY

Introduction to Manufacturing

Industrial methods employed in current manufacturing processes. Analysis of hot and cold working processes, products, materials, case studies, management techniques, manufacturing productivity, performance testing, engineering design, and economic considerations. (3 semester hours)

ENGLISH

Thought and Writing

A writing course in which the student works closely with the instructor to develop a sense of language as a means for shaping and ordering experience and ideas and to develop imagination, thought, organization, and clarity in written work. (4 semester hours)

Film Interpretation

Studies in the motion picture as an art form. (4 semester hours)

News Writing

A course for persons interested in learning how to write journalistically. Students progress from writing simple leads to complex news stories and features. (4 semester hours)

Children's Literature

An exploration of the human and literary values in the best of children's books. Emphasis is on critical sensitivity and techniques necessary for interpreting and evaluating works representative of the major forms of children's literature—folktale and fantasy, fiction, and nonfiction, myth, and poetry. (4 semester hours)

Practical Writing

This upper-level basic writing course provides important and relevant concepts in English language usage and skills, and offers opportunities for the practice and use of these skills. It stresses the importance of effective communication to industry, science, business, or academic concentrations. (4 semester hours)

The English Bible as Literature

Study of selections from the Old and New Testaments and the Apocrypha. Some attention will be given to the influence of the English Bible on a few representative writers, musicians, and artists, but emphasis will be on the poetic, philosophical, and narrative elements of the Bible itself. (3 semester hours)

Feature and Article Writing

Study and practice in writing feature and magazine articles; attention to contemporary techniques and styles in documentary and personal reportage. (4 semester hours)

Studies in English: Writing for the Professional

This course provides techniques for improving writing by planning, organizing, and editing. Emphasis is on powerful writing that is clear, concise, and forceful. (1 semester hour)

GENERAL STUDIES

Introduction to the Non-Western World

This course is designed for students who will have only this brief survey to develop some understanding of the problems faced by the changing societies of Africa and Asia. The objective is to give the student an informed view of the relationship between the people of the United States and those peoples whose lives are influenced by such diverse factors as Islam, Buddhism, Hinduism, oil, international trade, commerce, industry, finance, population growth, poverty, malnutrition, and war. (4 semester hours)

Non-Western Societies in the Modern World: Sub-Saharan Africa

An analysis of the cultures of Sub-Saharan Africa and their transition from traditional to modern societies. A video enhanced course. (4 semester hours)

GEOGRAPHY

Human Geography

An introduction to those aspects of geography concerned with the efforts of humans to cope with the environment. Included are population and settlement forms, the utilization of resources, the impact of technology on human occupance of the earth, and the origin and dispersal of cultural elements among the various world realms. (3 semester hours)

Geography of Michigan

An introductory review of the location and importance of: (1) mineral wealth; (2) glaciation; (3) climate and weather; (4) vegetation and water; (5) Native Americans; (6) African Americans; (7) selected European ethnic groups; (8) population changes; (9) manufacturing; and (10) energy resources in Michigan. (3 semester hours)

HEALTH AND HUMAN SERVICES

Introduction to Employee Assistance Program: EAP Structure and Process in the Work Setting

This course will serve as the introductory and prerequisite for all courses in the major and minor. Content will focus on the organization of business and industry (both public and private); the organization of labor and labor unions; variations in labor-management relations across organizational types; discipline in union and non-union settings; grievances and arbitration; collective bargaining; historical overview of health and human services; laws/regulations regarding workers' compensation, EEO, health and safety; affirmative action; employee benefits and health financing; counseling and human services in the work place and EAP. (3 semester hours)

Pharmacology and Physiological Implications

This course provides opportunities to establish a basic understanding of drug classifications and how they influence the total person and their body physiology. The goal is to apply this knowledge to safe, effective use and to minimize adverse effects while enhancing the healing process. (3 semester hours)

Computers in Radiology: An Overview of Structure and Function

Overviews the role and structure of computers in radiology. Emphasis will be placed on common functional blocks throughout all of radiology, including picture archival, networks, teleradiology, and future developments. (1 semester hour)

HISTORY

American Culture

A study of significant concepts in American life focusing on the relationship of the individual to society as seen from the perspective of literature, the arts, and social and political theory. (3 semester hours)

American Minorities: The African American Experience 1866 to Present

A survey of the historical experiences of American ethnic groups such as Black Americans, Native Americans, and major European, Asian, and Hispanic communities. (3 semester hours)

Women in American History

Evolution of women's status within and outside the family and the participation of women in the major events of U.S. history. Influences of class, region, race, ethnicity, and religion on women's historical experience. (3 semester hours)

INDUSTRIAL ENGINEERING

Technical Communication

Focus will be on the objective presentation of practical, factual material relating to one's field. The primary aim is clear, concise writing, as demonstrated in assignments, designed to acquaint one with practical efforts in one's field of study. Assignments will cover logical organization of ideas in abstracts, descriptions of tools and procedures, graphic aids, letters, and interviews; major emphasis is on a researched formal report. (3 semester hours)

Report Preparation

Learning techniques and procedures for preparation of technical documents. Intensifying critical, analytical process of thinking, and executing writing and oral strategies for different situations. (3 semester hours)

Work Analysis

Methods engineering and measurement of human work systems. Techniques for operation analysis, work measurements, and work sampling. Predetermined basic motion-time systems and standard data development are introduced. (3 semester hours)

Operations Planning, and Control

Methods of controlling and coordinating production using production planning, scheduling, inventory control, and dispatching. (3 semester hours)

Quality Assurance and Control

Techniques of controlling quality in manufacturing systems. Topics include organization of quality, methods of measurement, and basic statistical tools. (3 semester hours)

MATHEMATICS

Computational Skills

A mastery-based course designed to sharpen computational skills involving whole numbers, fractions, decimals, percents, signed numbers, and simple geometric figures. (2 semester hours)

Introduction to Statistics

An introductory course in statistics for students possessing a limited mathematics background. Emphasis is on the use of statistical tools rather than theoretical development. Proper use and interpretation of methods is developed in the areas of medicine, biology, engineering, psychology, business and management. Calculator required. (4 semester hours)

MEDICAL TERMINOLOGY

Medical Terminology

This course is designed to acquaint students with medical terminology and professional acronyms. The course text uses a programmed learning approach. (1 semester hour)

OCCUPATIONAL THERAPY

Orientation to Occupational Therapy

This course provides the student with a broad overview of the profession and its core concepts. The course will also introduce the student to the professional vocabulary of occupational therapy and will include the history of the profession, current professional roles, and issues and trends in the field. (2 semester hours)

Growth, Development, and Aging

Involves study of the normal growth, development, and aging process throughout the life cycle. (3 semester hours)

Independent Study in Occupational Therapy: Psychiatric Conditions

Provides the student with an overview of psychiatric conditions. Topics include the nature and history of abnormality and the various neuroses and psychoses. Also covered are childhood disorders, disorders of the nervous system and the law and politics of abnormality. (3 semester hours)

PHILOSOPHY

Philosophy and Public Affairs

Case studies in the series draw examples from business, government, law, journalism, medicine, and scientific research. Altruism, confidentiality, privacy, public service vs. private interest, autonomy vs. paternalism, and loyalty are among the issues considered. The issues are discussed by panels of leaders in government, business, law, the media, and the military. A video enhanced course. (4 semester hours)

Mathematical Logic

The study of general methods of analyzing and validating deductive reasoning. Arguments expressed in everyday language are analyzed and translated into the symbolic notion of logic, and calculations are performed in this notation to check the validity of the arguments. The course includes a brief consideration of the application of logic to computers. (4 semester hours)

Ethical Issues in Health Care Institutions

Medical practice is very much a function of the organizational and institutional settings within which medical professionals work. Each of the five lessons in this course will focus on particular aspects of these organizational and institutional settings that raise ethical questions. Topics include: professional virtues; group decision-making; hospital ethics committees; allocation of medical resources; and research ethics. (2 semester hours)

Philosophical Topics: Medical Ethics

Addresses ethical questions raised by technological advances. Topics include: genetic screening, reproductive technology, distribution of scarce medical resources, organ donation and transplantation, the right to know, and workplace safety, the acquisition and dissemination of medical information, human and animal experimentation, and cost/benefit issues. (2 semester hours)

PHYSICAL EDUCATION

Learning Lab Activity: Beginning Bowling

This course develops an enjoyment of the game while learning the basic skills and requirements. (1 semester hour)

Learning Lab Activity: Beginning Golf

This course develops an enjoyment of the game. Skills are developed at your own pace by following step-by-step lessons. (1 semester hour)

Learning Lab Activity: Beginning Racquetball

Beginning Racquetball develops an enjoyment of the game while learning the basic skills and requirements. (1 semester hour)

Learning Lab Activity: Beginning Tennis

This course develops an enjoyment of the game. Skills are developed at your own pace by following step-by-step lessons. At the end of the lessons, the student will develop good forehand and backhand drives, and a good tennis serve. (1 semester hour)

Learning Lab Activity: Intermediate Bowling

Intermediate Bowling is designed to improve existing skills and teach new ones. You will become aware of faults and be assisted in correction/improvement of your game. Skill level will vary. (1 semester hour)

Learning Lab Activity: Intermediate Racquetball

This course is designed to guide you through improvement of your present racquetball play. Attained skill levels will vary with individual students. (1 semester hour)

Learning Lab Activity: Intermediate Tennis

Intermediate Tennis is designed to guide you through improvement of your present tennis play. Attained skill levels will vary. (1 semester hour)

POLITICAL SCIENCE

International Relations

A study of the nature of the international community and the forces which produce cooperation and conflict. Particular attention is given to analyzing power in terms of its acquisition and uses during both the cold war period and in the present post-Soviet era. (4 semester hours)

Political Topics: Practical Applications of Management Principles

Topics include selecting employees, training, orienting, supervising, evaluating performance, controlling expenses, preparing budgets and reports. (1 semester hour)

Asian Political Systems

The first part of this course consists of a systematic survey of the social, economic, and political characteristics of the area. Political culture, institutions and processes, including both traditional and modern forms, are examined. Major political problems, country differences, and various paths to modernization are analyzed. In the second part of the course, particular attention is given to the Chinese political system and its effort to modernize its economy and political system. (4 semester hours)

Russian and East European Politics

This survey of the dramatic changes encompassing Soviet, and now Russian, politics is divided into three sections. The first section presents an overview of the ideology, leading personalities, and traditional governmental and party structures of the Soviet Union. The second section focuses on the policies of reform and eventual collapse of the Soviet Union under Gorbachev. The third explores the new politics of the Commonwealth of Independent States and Russia as politics is reconstituted in the post-communist era. A brief overview of political developments in the former East European satellite states is also included. (4 semester hours)

PSYCHOLOGY

General Psychology

A cognitive and behavioral survey of major topics in psychology including development, perception, consciousness, learning and memory, motivation and emotion, mental ability and mental health. (3 semester hours)

Introduction to Human Behavior

An introduction to general psychology from the humanistic behaviorism point of view: the use of behavior to help people achieve their full potential. Emphasizes how the environment has a major influence on the way we are and how the environment can be changed so that we can become the kind of people we wish to be. (3 semester hours)

Child Psychology

An introduction to behavior principles in the analysis of complex behavior with an emphasis upon early childhood learning and the techniques for teaching the child at home and at school. Topics include mental retardation and behavioral assessment. (3 semester hours)

Abnormal Psychology

An introduction to the description, classification, and interpretation of human behavior labeled by society as "abnormal" with an emphasis on social variables and environmental conditions related to the acquisition and persistence of such behavior. (3 semester hours)

Organizational Psychology

A survey of business and industrial psychology, including such topics as understanding employee behavior, group behavior and leadership, personnel selection and placement, job design, worker motivation, job satisfaction, counseling and interviewing, and psychology of organization. (3 semester hours)

Advanced General Psychology

Designed to introduce nonmajors in psychology to modern behavior theory. Emphasis will be upon human behavior, both normal and abnormal, with a significant portion of the course devoted to the higher cognitive processes. (3 semester hours)

Topical Studies in Psychology: Brain, Mind, and Behavior

Designed to provide a comprehensive understanding of the human brain, the course presents current findings of a neuropsychological nature. (3 semester hours)

Topical Studies in Psychology: Industrial Psychology

Application of psychological principles to industry and other organizations. An examination of employee selection, job satisfaction, training, evaluation of performance, supervision, and working conditions. (3 semester hours)

Topical Studies in Psychology: The Mind

Recent neurological discoveries and cognitive theorizings are explored as explanations of everyday and unusual behaviors. Topics include aging, addiction, pain, healing, depression, language, thinking, and violence (with an emphasis upon murder). (3 semester hours)

RELIGION

Religions of the World

This course will interpret the overall message of four major religious traditions in order to examine the nature of religion. At the end of this study, one should have a deeper appreciation of the nature of religion, the diversity of religious traditions, and the fundamental religious character of human beings. (4 semester hours)

Religion in the Indian Tradition

This course draws materials primarily from the great religious traditions native to India, i.e., Brahmanism, Buddhism, Jainism, and Hinduism. Particular attention is paid to continuities of motif and practice that allow one to speak of "Indian Religion" as a unified phenomenon with a single history. Consideration is also given to such problems as the relationship between Indian religions and Indian culture and the relationship between Indian religious forms and the religious forms of other cultures. (4 semester hours)

SOCIAL WORK

Readings in Social Work: The Black Struggle for Justice

This course centers around the Civil Rights Movement from 1954 to 1965. (3 semester hours)

Readings in Social Work: The Black Struggle for Justice, 1965–Present

This course explores the ideals and strategies of such leaders as Dr. Martin Luther King, Jr. and Malcolm X. The struggle for justice in the streets and the legislative and political arenas are also covered. (3 semester hours)

SOCIOLOGY

American Society

An analysis of contemporary American society, including continuity and change in value systems, major institutions and their interrelationships and other aspects of social life. (3 semester hours)

Social Impacts of Science and Technology

Examines the social consequences of major scientific and technological changes. Since advances in scientific knowledge and technical innovations often challenge or disrupt existing social values and practices, much of the course explores social controversies with scientific or technical content. The course also considers the feasibility of assessing and controlling technology. (3 semester hours)

Computer Usage in the Social Sciences

Introduces the student to the logic and structure of computing and provides some exposure to the BASIC programming language. In addition, it focuses on application of computers in social science fields and some of the dominant ethical/social issues that have recently emerged. (3 semester hours)

Men and Women in Contemporary Society

An analysis of the changing roles of men and women over time, the social forces that define and change gender roles, and differing political perceptions of those changes. The course includes a look at a fictional world where gender differences as we know them do not exist. (3 semester hours)

Principles of Sociology

A survey of the discipline of sociology and its major fields of study. The biological, social and cultural factors underlying the development of human personality and the various forms and processes of group association are analyzed. (3 semester hours)

Modern Social Problems

The course aims to develop a theoretical framework for understanding selected social problems in American society in such areas as: intergroup conflict, race, poverty, juvenile delinquency and crime, population changes, and mass communication. Problems selected for emphasis may vary with the instructor. (3 semester hours)

Introduction to Criminal Justice

An overview of the criminal justice system as it currently operates in its three major components: police, courts, correction. A broad-based interdisciplinary perspective is employed to introduce the beginning student to the process of criminal justice in modern America.

Particular attention is placed on the discretionary authority of officials who are engaged in the decision making roles to process suspects from arrest to release. (3 semester hours)

Introduction to Social Psychology

An introduction to social psychological theory and research, covering the interaction of individuals and the relationships of individuals to groups. Includes such topics as social influence, attitudes, altruism, and aggression. (3 semester hours)

Modern Japanese Society

A study of the ongoing process of change in the major social institutions of Japan. Examines the characteristics of groups and individuals and their roles which have produced, and been affected by, contemporary Japanese Society. (3 semester hours)

Introduction to Social Gerontology

An exploration of the social, psychological, economic and physical aspects of aging. Consideration will be given to institutional programming for older people in America and other societies. (3 semester hours)

Criminology

An overview of the field of criminology. The areas considered range from the definitions, origins, and extent of crime and law, to causal theories of criminal behavior, to types of crime and victims. Particularly stressed is an analysis of the relationship between law and society and social structure to crime. (3 semester hours)

The American Healthcare System: Evolution and Prospects

This course will provide an integrated and interdisciplinary overview of how the health system evolved, its current status, and the nature of the forces that are bringing about change. (3 semester hours)

Organization of the Health Care System

This class will examine traditional and emerging ways in which health care is organized. A major concern will be the politics of health and the role of various interest groups (professional associations, unions, consumer groups) in the formation of health policy. Among the topics to be considered are the development of American medicine, the relationship of organizational structure to effectiveness in health organizations, the social control of health care organizations, and the growth of medical bureaucracy. (3 semester hours)

Juvenile Delinquency

A study of juvenile delinquency as a social problem. Extent, causative factors, methods of treatment and programs of prevention and control are covered. (3 semester hours)

Studies in Social Change: Social Institutions

An examination of art as a social institution, focusing on the structure, processes and change of ''art worlds,'' reviewing three theories of the role of art in society, and concluding with selected case studies in fine arts or popular culture. (3 semester hours)

VOCATIONAL EDUCATION

Curriculum Development in Career and Technical Education

Principles of analyzing, selecting, and arranging instructional materials for instruction purposes. (3 semester hours)

Teaching Methods for Career Technical Education

This course covers such topics as conducting discussions, brainstorming, buzz groups and question box techniques, guiding student study, directing student laboratory experiences, directing students in applying problem-solving techniques, employing the project method, introducing and summarizing a lesson, presenting an illustrated talk, demonstrating a manipulative skill, individualizing instruction and employing the team teaching method. (3 semester hours)

Principles of Career and Technical Education

Describing the scope and organization of vocational education and practical arts, determining legislative mandates, evaluating priorities, assessing needs, developing an active personal philosophy, identifying principles and practices. (3 semester hours)

Work-Site Based Education Programs

This is a study of duties and responsibilities of the teacher-coordinator. The organization and establishment of training programs, supervision of trainees on the job, development of individual training programs, establishing working relationships between school, business, and home, and participation in activities in the community, especially adapted to prospective coordinators. (3 semester hours)

Western Oregon State College
Monmouth, Oregon 97361   (503) 838-1220

Description:

Correspondence courses offered by Western Oregon State College are administered by the Office of Independent Study of the Oregon State System of Higher Education in Portland, Oregon. For courses available, SEE **Oregon State System of Higher Education.**

Accreditations:

Northwest Association of Schools and Colleges.

Western Washington University
Center for Distance Education and Independent Learning
University Extended Programs
Old Main 400
Bellingham, Washington 98225-9042
(360) 650-3650

Description:

The Independent Study Department was established in 1912 as a vehicle to help teachers increase their knowledge without having to come to the campus. Over the years it has evolved to include students who cannot fit a class into their on-campus schedule or who cannot come to the campus because of work or family commitments. Independent Study currently offers 60 correspondence courses in a variety of disciplines. Enrollment is approximately 1,200 students per year.

Faculty:

Janet Howard, Director. The faculty numbers 33. .

Academic Levels:

College

Degree/Certificate Programs:

Western Washington University allows up to 45 quarter hours of independent study credit toward the baccalaureate degree. Correspondence credits do not qualify for graduate credits.

Admission Requirements:

Student must be 18 years of age or a high school graduate. Some courses have required prerequisites. High school students wishing to take college courses must have permission of their high school counselors.

Tuition:

$56 per quarter hour credit plus nonrefundable $15 registration fee. Syllabus fee (nonrefundable) for each course ranges from $2 to $8. Contract courses are $75 per credit. A request for a refund must be made within thirty days of registration. If correspondence course assignments have been submitted, a variable service fee per assignment is deducted from the refund. Contract course refunds are determined by the number of conferences which have been held with the faculty advisor. Postage is paid by the student; a self-addressed, stamped envelope for returning corrected lessons must accompany each lesson assignment submitted. Foreign students must make arrangement ahead of time to pay postage for returning corrected assignments.

Enrollment Period:

A maximum of 1 year is allowed for completion of a course. One 6-month extension may be granted upon written request and payment of a $30 renewal fee. Only one extension is allowed. The minimum time for completion of a course is 7 weeks.

Equipment Requirements:

Textbooks must be purchased separately by the student and can be ordered by mail from the Student Co-Op Bookstore at Western Washington University or obtained locally.

Credit and Grading:

Examinations must be proctored by an education official, librarian, or a member of the clergy in student's community. Grading system is A, Superior; B, High; C, Average; D, Low Passing; F, Failure. Minimum passing grade is D. Pass/Fail grading is available on an optional basis. Credit is awarded in quarter hour units.

Library Services:

Western Washington University's Wilson Library provides a borrow-by-mail service for supplementary library materials. This service does not include textbooks.

Accreditations:

Northwest Association of Schools and Colleges; National Council for the Accreditation of Teacher Education.

COLLEGE COURSES

AMERICAN CULTURAL STUDIES

The Asian-American Experience

The history of Asians in the United States, the development of communities and the effects of the encounter between Asian cultures and the developing American cultural context. (3 quarter hours)

ANTHROPOLOGY

Introduction to Cultural Anthropology

The study of societies that contrast with Western civilization, leading to an acquaintance with the concept of culture and its importance to an understanding of human behavior. Emphasis will be placed upon understanding each culture from its own point of view rather than our own. (5 quarter hours)

Religion and Culture

Comparative study of religious thought, belief, and behavior; relationship of religious experience and institutions to other aspects of culture and society. (5 quarter hours)

Sex and Gender in Culture

Cross-cultural study of gender stereotypes, gender and language, gender and work roles, gender and religion. (4 quarter hours)

Peoples of Sub-Saharan Africa

Ethnographic survey of the peoples and cultures. Students will gain an overview of African geography and climate, plus an awareness of major events and cultures in African history. (5 quarter hours)

Joseph Campbell: Transformations of Myth Through Time

Explore primal mythologies, American Indian myths, the mythological and historical roots of the Exodus story in Egypt, and more. Noted author, scholar, teacher, and storyteller Joseph Campbell shows us how myth answers fundamental questions about our origins, our life, and our death. Student will view 14 videotapes in addition to assigned readings. (5 quarter hours)

Childhood and Culture

The process of socialization or enculturation viewed from a cross-cultural perspective. (4 quarter hours)

CANADIAN AMERICAN STUDIES

Introduction to Canadian Studies

A basic interdisciplinary course covering the major physical, historical, and sociopolitical aspects of Canada. (5 quarter hours)

EAST ASIAN STUDIES

The Cultures of East Asia: Political-Material Aspects

The political, economic, and social aspects of the evolution of civilization in China, Japan, Korea, and Mongolia from earliest times to the present. (5 quarter hours)

The Cultures of East Asia: Religio-Philosophic and Literary Aspects

The religions, secular, intellectual, and literary aspects of the cultures of China, Japan, Korea, and Mongolia; and the influence of these aspects of culture on political life from earliest times to the present. (5 quarter hours)

Traditional Chinese Medicine

Survey of traditional Chinese medicine from ancient times to the present, with reference to the social, political, philosophical, and religious context within which traditional Chinese medicine has been practiced. (4 quarter hours)

ECONOMICS

Introduction to Micro-Economics

An overview of the modern market economy as a system for dealing with the problems of scarcity. Operation and decision making of economic units; supply, demand, and resource allocation; analysis of various market and industry structures; shortages, controls. (4 quarter hours)

Introduction to Macro-Economics

An overview of the modern market economy as a system for dealing with the problem of scarcity. The analysis of relationships among such variables as national income, employment, inflations, and the quantity of money. The roles of government, expenditure, taxation, and monetary policy. (4 quarter hours)

EDUCATION

Foundations of Education

Differing views of human nature and leaning as they relate to educational aims, methods, and content. (4 quarter hours)

History of American Education

Historical development of formal education emphasizing the impact of cultural forces on evolution of the American system of public education. (4 quarter hours)

Introduction to Exceptional Children

An introduction to the special instructional needs of handicapped and gifted children. (3 quarter hours)

Elementary Classroom Management and Discipline

Development of teaching strategies designed to prevent and/or solve behavior problems; discussion of effective classroom management techniques; analysis of related child development and learning theory. (3 quarter hours)

School-Home-Community Relationships

Problems of communication and interaction among teachers, parents, and paraprofessionals, administrators, and community; conferencing, planning meetings, community survey. PR publications; use of mass media. (3 quarter hours)

Competencies for Continuing Education

Study of agencies and resources available to aid teachers and schools. Involves visits to community agencies. (3 quarter hours)

ENGLISH

Language and Exposition

A course in writing expository prose on topics drawn from personal experience or assigned reading. Practice in strategies for finding information, focusing on a topic, organizing a thesis, developing an idea, evaluating and revising preliminary drafts, summarizing written information; practice in writing the in-class essay. (4 quarter hours)

Expository Writing

An intermediate course in writing expository prose, with readings from various disciplines. (4 quarter hours)

Survey of American Literature

An overview of American literature and thought from 1620 to 1940. (5 quarter hours)

Women and Literature

This course offers an introduction to women writers in fiction. The reading list begins with a novel which partly represents the woman-as-victim tradition conventional in standard literary studies. From this basis, the reading list moves on to include a variety of more achieving women. All the works concern the social, work, and gender roles of women who are distinctly individual. (4 quarter hours)

Post-Colonial Literatures

Comparative study of the new literatures which have emerged since World War II in Africa, India, Middle East and/or West Indies. (4 quarter hours)

Introduction to Fiction Writing

An introductory course open to students who have not previously taken a college course in fiction writing. Study of appropriate models. (4 quarter hours)

Introduction to Poetry Writing

An introductory course in poetry writing. Study of appropriate models. (4 quarter hours)

Introduction to the Study of the English Language

Introduction to the structure, history, and use of the English language. Includes fundamentals of linguistic analysis (phonology, morphology, syntax, semantics, and pragmatics), historical development of English, developmental patterns of language acquisition, and regional and social language variation. (4 quarter hours)

Studies in National Literatures: The Literature of Ireland

Studies works of native Irish authors. Interactive e-mail version available. (4 quarter hours)

The Structure of English

Introduction of syntactic analysis and its application to texts. Topics include the structure of sentences, modification, complementation, and nominalization. Analysis of various types of written and spoken English to understand syntactic variation reflected in different dialects and styles. (4 quarter hours)

Cultural History of the English Language

Considers texts in Old, Middle, Modern, and present-day Englishes as reflective of cultural values, literary practice, and linguistic change. (4 quarter hours)

Topics in Language and Linguistics: Language and Gender

Examines the development of "difference" and "dominance" research theories in language and gender. Topics include defining sexist language and its impact on social perceptions of men and women, real and perceived cross-cultural differences between genders in conversation, and strengths and weaknesses of sociolinguistic methodologies in analyzing gender differences. (4 quarter hours)

Creative Writing: Poetry

Opportunity for disciplined expression in writing poetry. (4 quarter hours)

ENVIRONMENTAL STUDIES

Environmental Studies: A Scientific Approach

An introduction to environmental studies which stresses a scientific approach toward understanding the nature and scope of contemporary problems in man's environment. The course reflects application of physical, chemical, biological, and geologic principles to define ecological change, both natural and man-made. (3 quarter hours)

HISTORY

American History to 1865

From the European background to the end of the Civil War. (5 quarter hours)

American History Since 1865

From the end of the Civil War to the present. This course will begin with Reconstruction. (5 quarter hours)

Introduction to East Asian Civilization

The origins and evolution of the political, economic, and social aspects of East Asian civilization to the present. (5 quarter hours)

Black History in the Americas: The Slavery Era

Black life in the United States from first settlement to the Civil War era. Africans in bondage in America: African heritage of blacks in the Americas with emphasis on the United States. (5 quarter hours)

The Chinese Economy: From Stone Age to Mao's Age

Chinese economic and social history from earliest times to the present. (5 quarter hours)

Human Economic Action in an Unconstrained Market

A blend of economics and history, this course studies societies in which tax burdens are very low and in which the state does not manipulate the money supply or borrow significant sums to do its job. The inner logic of the market unconstrained by the complications and uncertainties caused by the economic interventions of the state will be examined. (4 quarter hours)

Human Economic Action in a Constrained Market

Study of societies in which the tax burden imposed by the state is so heavy, taxpayers may drastically change their behavior in the marketplace to avoid taxes. The state's manipulation of the money supply is significant. (4 quarter hours)

History of the Pacific Northwest

General history of the Pacific Northwest, state development, samples of local history, and state and local government. (4 quarter hours)

LIBERAL STUDIES

The Western Tradition I: The Ancient World

Interdisciplinary introduction to significant cultural themes from art, music, history, philosophy, and literature in the Western tradition. Concepts of man in Near Eastern and Mediterranean cultures: Mesopotamia, Egypt, Greece, Palestine, Rome. (5 quarter hours)

Myth and Folklore

An introduction to the study of myth and folklore and its cultural impact. (4 quarter hours)

LIBRARY SCIENCE

Introduction to Library Strategies

Introduces students to the nature of library research with emphasis upon strategies for carrying out inquiry, evaluating sources and incorporating the results into subsequent written assignments. (2 quarter hours)

LINGUISTICS

Sociolinguistics

Examines the relationship between society and language, concentrating on the following areas: address forms, variation theory, language use, sociolinguistics and education, multilingualism, language policy and language attitudes. (3 quarter hours)

MATHEMATICS

Intermediate Algebra

Pattern recognition and generalization, building mathematical models, and problem solving are emphasized. Supporting topics include: polynomials, linear and quadratic equations, inequalities, graphs, rational expressions, radicals and functions. (5 quarter hours)

Introduction to Mathematics

Introduction to the methods of thought and logic in mathematics. A cultural approach to mathematics which emphasizes practical problems of the type which can be solved with a hand-held calculator. (3 quarter hours)

Algebra with Applications to Business and Economics

Equations and inequalities, graphs and functions, exponential and logarithmic functions, mathematics of finance, systems of linear equations and matrices, systems of linear inequalities. (4 quarter hours)

Calculus with Applications to Business and Economics

Limits, rates of change, differentiation, graphing and optimization, integration, business applications, partial differentiation. (4 quarter hours)

Introduction to Statistics

This course deals with the nature of statistical reasoning, descriptive statistics, ideas of probability and measurement, sampling distributions, the binomial and normal distributions, confidence intervals, and the testing of statistical hypotheses. (3 quarter hours)

MUSIC

The Art of Listening to Music

Nontechnical basis for enjoyable listening to music; performance practices relating to symphony orchestras, instrumental ensembles, opera, choral groups, and solo performance. (3 quarter hours)

PSYCHOLOGY

Introduction to Psychology

Examination of basic psychological processes utilizing results of research investigations. (5 quarter hours)

Abnormal Psychology

Human behavior patterns culturally labeled as abnormalities, or as mental illness; their etiology, incidence, treatment, and social attitudes toward such patterns. Historical review of the concepts used to explain such behavior and of the research relating to the treatment of psychoses and neuroses. (5 quarter hours)

Developmental Psychology

Basic principles of development. Topics include behavior genetics, early experience, language, cognition, personality, and social development. (5 quarter hours)

SOCIOLOGY

Evolution of Society

Basic problems and concepts in the study of society; social change and organization; human behavior in the family, education, religion, cities, social class, race, age, sex and the structure of society; sociology as science and as response to human problems. (5 quarter hours)

Sociology of Deviant Behavior

A broad overview of concepts, issues, and research findings in the sociological study of deviant behavior; how deviance is defined, reacted to, and punished in American society. Emphasis on contemporary theoretical perspectives, along with current issues in deviance. (5 quarter hours)

Criminology

The study of adult crime, defined as violation of legal norms. The course focuses on problems of measurement and attempts to explain crime as a social phenomenon and a cultural product. It includes an indepth analysis of various forms and classes of crimes and their victims. (5 quarter hours)

Juvenile Delinquency

Historical origins of notion of childhood and creation of delinquency, extent and nature of deliquency in society, major theories and explanations of delinquent behavior, and review of society's reactions to delinquent behavior. (5 quarter hours)

Youth and Social Justice

Examines youth both as a distinct culture and as a dependent group within larger institutional structures of the family, economic system, educational system, and juvenile justice system. Contemporary issues of the '90s are featured: subservience within the family, physical and sexual abuse, segregated and low-investment schools, child poverty, and overly broad social control powers over adolescents. Looks at policy solutions to remedy youth inequalities. (5 quarter hours)

Advanced Topics in Family

Emphasis on current research in family sociology. Focuses on the changing roles in families today. (4 quarter hours)

VOCATIONAL EDUCATION

Occupational Analysis

The identification and use of information on occupational proficiency for teaching purposes. (3 quarter hours)

Technology Education: Safety Principles and Practices

Basic course in safety practices for technology education teachers in grades 1-12 and for vocational teachers who must meet state certification requirements. (2 quarter hours)

History and Philosophy of Vocational Education

Evolving issues, objectives, programs and legislation in vocational education. (3 quarter hours)

Community and Industrial Resources

A study of those resources available in the community and how they can be used to enhance the educational experience of students engaged in formal schooling. This course will fulfill a requirement for vocational industrial arts teacher certification. (1 quarter hour)

Wichita State University

Division of Continuing Education
1845 Fairmount
Wichita, Kansas 67208   (316) 689-3001

Description:
 Correspondence courses offered by Wichita State University are administered by Independent Study at the University of Kansas, Lawrence, Kansas. For courses available, SEE **Kansas, University of.**

Faculty:
 Dr. Jacqueline Snyder, Dean, Division of Academic Outreach.

Accreditations:
 North Central Association of Colleges and Schools.

Winston-Salem State University

Winston-Salem, North Carolina 27110
                              (919) 761-2070

Description:
 Winston-Salem State University is a state-supported institution for the preparation of teachers, principals, and

supervisors for all educational institutions, and for the training of nurses. The University is a participant in a consortium of eight institutions within the University of North Carolina offering college-level correspondence courses and other opportunities for individualized study at a distance from the university campuses. In the consortium arrangement, each institution originating a course provides instruction and awards academic credit, while responsibility for administration of the program lies with the office of Independent Studies at the University of North Carolina at Chapel Hill. See **North Carolina, University of - Chapel Hill.**

Faculty:
 Jerry Hickerson, Member of UNC Independent Studies Advisory Committee.

Accreditations:
 Southern Association of Colleges and Schools.

Wisconsin, University of - Extension

Independent Study
432 North Lake Street
Madison, Wisconsin 53706-1498
                              (608) 263-2055

Description:
 The University of Wisconsin has been offering Independent Study through correspondence since 1891 and enrolls over 12,500 participants a year. The program offers courses for university credit; courses for Continuing Education Units (CEUs), many at the professional level in engineering, business, and nursing; and high school courses. High school course offerings may vary from one semester to the next; interested students should check first with the Independent Study Office. Vocational courses are offered that have been developed by Wisconsin's vocational-technical schools.

Faculty:
 Sylvia N. Rose, Director of Independent Study; David L. Jensen, Registrar. Courses are written by the University of Wisconsin faculty. There are 400 faculty members and 100 subject specialists.

Academic Levels:
 College
 High School
 Noncredit
 Vocational

Degree/Certificate Programs:
 Although University of Wisconsin - Extension does not grant degrees, credit earned through the Independent Study program can be applied toward an associate or baccalaureate degree from the University. Degree candidates must meet a residency requirement, earning a specified number of credits on campus at the institution of their choice. Other than this, there is no specified limit on the number of

Independent Study credits accepted in transfer. Students should check with a resident adviser or a UW-Extension adviser to be sure the course chosen is appropriate to the student's degree objective. Wisconsin's correspondence program is used widely and nationally for transfer credits. Certificate and diploma programs are also available.

Admission Requirements:

Open enrollment. Students can enroll in any course so long as they meet the prerequisites as cited in the Independent Study catalog. No art course registrations (excluding art history) are accepted from overseas locations. Most courses for credit require high school graduation or consent of instructor.

Tuition:

$70 per semester credit plus a $30 service charge for each course registration. Fees for high school, noncredit, and professional courses vary. Course fees subject to change; contact Independent Study for current fees. A partial refund of the tuition fee will be issued only if the request to withdraw from a course is made during the first three months of enrollment and before one-half of the written assignments have been submitted. No grade is recorded if the withdrawal is made before taking the final examination. Textbook refunds (for texts purchased from the Extension Bookstore) will be granted only within three months from the time of enrollment, only when no assignments have been submitted, and only for a current edition or currently used books in new condition (not marked in anyway, including the writing of your name).

Enrollment Period:

Individuals may enroll at any time. The maximum time to complete a course is one year from the date of enrollment. Students may be granted an extension of six months to one year upon payment of a fee.

Equipment Requirements:

Study guide, textbooks, and cassette tapes (when used in the course), are packaged and sent to the student. The student pays for the cost of textbooks and cassettes in addition to tuition.

Credit and Grading:

Grading system is A, AB, B, BC, C, D, F; minimum passing grade is D. The Independent Study program recommends enrollment in only one course at a time; two at a time should be the maximum. Examinations are given under supervision and may be proctored by an educational official (or librarian, supervisor, or member of the clergy) in the student's community, approved by Extension. Credit is granted in semester hours.

Library Services:

Independent Study students should rely mainly on local libraries for their supplemental reading. The local library may request an interlibrary loan from the UW-Extension Library. No required course textbooks are available for loan. For certain courses, the student may borrow audiocassettes or other specified course materials from the

UW-Extension Library or the department offering the course for a rental fee.

Accreditations:

North Central Association of Colleges and Schools. Member of: National University Continuing Education Association.

COLLEGE COURSES

ACCOUNTING

Elementary Accounting I

Introduction to accounting concepts and procedures allied to proprietorship; the accounting cycle; valuation of current and fixed assets, liabilities, and proprietorship; presenting and interpreting financial data. (3 semester credits)

Elementary Accounting II

A continuation of *Elementary Accounting I*. An introduction to partnership and corporate accounting practices; formation and liquidation of partnership; division of partnership profit; reporting and recording long-term liabilities and stockholders' equity; introduction to cost accounting, budgeting, and special purpose statements. (3 semester credits)

Managerial Accounting

The analysis and interpretation of accounting data from the managerial viewpoint. Emphasis is on planning, control, and cost concepts relevant to decision making. (3 semester credits)

Intermediate Accounting I

Study of financial accounting. Intensive analysis of income and retained earnings statements; balance sheets and statements of change in financial position; concepts of present and future value; revenue recognition; income tax liability; cash investments and receivables; inventories; specific valuation problems; acquisition, depreciation, and disposal of fixed assets; and intangible assets. (3 semester credits)

Intermediate Accounting II

A continuation of *Intermediate Accounting I*. Intensive analysis of long-term investments; stockholders' equity; dilutive securities and earnings per share; pension costs; leases; accounting changes and error analysis; and financial reporting, analysis, and interpretation. (3 semester credits)

Cost Accounting I

Study of cost accumulation. Examines three basic cost accounting systems—product costing, job order costing, and standard costing—along with the cost of material, labor, and overhead appropriate to each system. Variable budgeting, special nonroutine problems, and capital budgeting also discussed. (3 semester credits)

Budgets and Budgetary Control

Theory and procedure of financial and operating budgets for management planning and controls. (3 semester credits)

Governmental Accounting

Concerned with the preparation and interpretation of financial reports prepared by and for governmental and nonprofit organizations, with focus on external financial reporting. Also discusses management accounting applicable to all nonprofit entities with emphasis on budgetary planning and the managerial uses of accounting data. (3 semester credits)

Advanced Cost Accounting

A continuation of the *Cost Accounting I*. Emphasis on interpretation of accounting information and quantitative techniques used in decision making and controlling organizational operations. Topics include cost allocation; capital budgeting; spoilage, waste, defective units; decentralization and transfer pricing; systems choice; inventory planning; cost accounting and linear programming; cost behavior and regression analysis; and accounting for payroll. (3 semester credits)

AFRICAN AMERICAN STUDIES

Introduction to Afro-American History

Surveys the Afro-American experience in the United States, beginning with the background of the transatlantic slave trade that carried millions of African people into bondage in the Western Hemisphere, including the North American mainland. The course sheds light on the unique aspects of the Afro-American experience through the colonial period, the American Revolution, the Civil War, and the postbellum years of emancipation in the nineteenth century. From this point, the focus turns to the political, economic, and cultural struggles of Afro-Americans against the barriers of institutionalized racism in twentieth-century America. Emphasis is given to the programs for racial betterment offered by major Afro-American leaders. (3 semester credits)

AGRICULTURAL ECONOMICS

Cooperation

A basic course in cooperative organization, development, principles, management, funding, and problems confronting cooperatives. The course is designed especially for teachers and for employees and leaders of cooperatives desiring a knowledge of the fundamentals of cooperation. (3 semester credits)

ANTHROPOLOGY

Introduction to Anthropology

General understanding of humans in relation to their cultures, their evolutionary development and diversity, their capacities for society and the development of these human societies including present societies. (3 semester credits)

ARABIC

First Semester Arabic

For students with no previous instruction in the language. Elements of reading, writing, and pronouncing Arabic, as well as essential facts about Arabic. (4 semester credits)

Second Semester Arabic

A continuation of *First Semester Arabic* beginning with a review. Emphasis is upon reading and writing with a final lesson on calligraphy. (4 semester credits)

ART

Creative Design

A basic course for high school, adult, and college students. Examines design as the language of all art. Units include the elements of line, plane, values, volume, space, color, and texture; the principles of contrast, balance, and unity; and design as a tool for visual communication. (3 semester credits)

ART HISTORY

History of Western Art: Prehistoric through Medieval

Study of the architecture, sculpture, and painting of the ancient civilizations bordering the eastern Mediterranean and the development of Western art. (3 semester credits)

History of Western Art: Renaissance to Contemporary

Study of the major periods in Western art, including the Renaissance, baroque, realism, impressionism, and the twentieth century. (3 semester credits)

ASTRONOMY

Survey of Astronomy

Introduces nonscience majors to astronomy and scientific theory and observation. (4 semester hours)

BEHAVIORAL DISABILITIES

The Exceptional Individual

This course provides a survey of the major categories of exceptional educational need focusing on etiology, treatment, functional levels, and social adjustment. (3 semester credits)

Caring for Children with Handicaps in Day Care, Preschool, and Family Day Care Homes

This course provides information on various handicaps and their behavioral consequences. Strategies are provided for teachers to use in dealing with the various handicaps they are most likely to encounter. (2 semester credits)

BOTANY

Survey of Botany

Principles of biology as illustrated by plants, including evolution, genetics, physiology, ecology, development, structure, and life cycles represented in the major plant groups. Also emphasizes the relationship between plants and humans. (3 semester credits)

BUSINESS LAW

Business Law

Law of contracts, agency, negotiable instruments, sales, partnerships, corporations, secured transactions, suretyship, accountant's legal liability, personal property, bailments, and documents of title, real estate, wills, trusts, and insurance. (3 semester credits)

CHEMISTRY

General Chemistry I

This and the following course are equivalent to a first-year chemistry course, except that the laboratory work is not included. Topics covered include fundamental concepts in chemistry, bonding, gas laws, periodic law, thermochemistry, equilibrium, oxidation-reduction reactions, acids and bases, colloids, properties of elements and their compounds, and others. (3 semester credits)

General Chemistry II

A continuation of General Chemistry I. (3 semester credits)

CHILD AND FAMILY STUDIES

Family Day Care

A course designed to teach family day-care providers what they need to know to create a psychologically and physically safe learning environment for children in their care. Topics include growth and development, health and safety, nutrition, child care, day care, and organization and record keeping for child care. (1 semester credit)

Early Childhood Education: The Assistant Child Care Teacher

This course covers basic child growth and development and involves working, under supervision, to set up and operate a developmentally oriented child-care classroom. (1 semester credit)

Early Childhood Education: The Child Care Teacher

Topics include self-assessment of skills in preparation for preschool teaching; discussion of requisite aptitudes, attitudes, and skills; preparing a developmental environment; schedules; materials selection; safe-place considerations; evaluation of environments, programs, materials, and teach-learning transactions. (3 semester credits)

Administration and Organization of Child Care and Early Childhood Education Programs

This course includes organization and administrative theory in application to early learning, child care, and child development service programs and systems; strategies in organizational development and issues and problems in management and supervision; and planning and policy development processes in designing systems to serve identifiable client interests and needs. (3 semester credits)

CLASSICAL STUDIES

Greek and Latin Origins of Medical Terms

Origins of the most frequently used terms of medicine and the sciences that contribute to it. Greek and Latin roots, prefixes and suffixes, and the methods of combining them. (3 semester credits)

Greek Drama in English

Plays of Aeschylus, Sophocles, Euripedes, and Aristophanes. (2 semester credits)

Classical Mythology

A study of the myths and legends of Greece and Rome, with emphasis on their sources and their importance in the history of Western artistic, psychological, and imaginative experience. (3 semester credits)

COMMUNICATIONS

Intercultural Communication

Analysis of the variables and communication behaviors involved in enhancing intercultural communication. A course aimed at promoting understanding. (3 semester hours)

COMPUTER SCIENCE

Fundamentals of FORTRAN Programming

This course is designed to introduce computer programming in FORTRAN. Although particularly suited to mathematical, scientific, and engineering problem solving, FORTRAN has useful application in many fields and is one of the most widely known and used programming languages. (2 semester credits)

CURRICULUM AND INSTRUCTION

School Curriculum Design

This course provides the opportunity for students to learn the essentials of curriculum development and to satisfy certification requirements where such a course is necessary. The course emphasizes K-12 curriculum design policies, procedures, and decision points. Specific attention is paid to the issues of scope, sequence, articulation, and materials selection, as well as an examination of those forces that affect curricular planning and implementation within the school community. (3 semester credits)

Health Information for Teachers

To acquaint the student with contemporary health information that is essential for optimal personal and community health. It acquaints the student with the structure and function of the school health program. (3 semester credits)

Children's Literature

This course discusses basic concepts in children's literature and presents a variety of views on such major issues as general book selection and evaluation of books for unbiased presentation of minority groups. As they complete written assignments, students will focus on practical approaches to choosing and using children's books in actual teaching situations. Course topics include theories for matching children and books; literary elements; illustrations; poetry; books on controversial topics; nonfiction; drama; and enhancing children's responses to literature through specific, planned activities. (3 semester credits)

DANISH

First Semester Danish

For those who have had no previous instruction in Danish. Pronunciation, grammatical structure, vocabulary building. (4 semester credits)

Second Semester Danish

This course is a continuation of *First Semester Danish*. (4 semester credits)

ECONOMICS

Introduction to Economics

A general course that presents basic principles and concepts needed to understand the economic environment. Emphasis is on economic problems relevant to everyday life and how individuals and facilities allocate limited resources among unlimited wants. Topics include the market system, macro- and microeconomic principles, national income analysis, business cycles and monetary policy, government spending and taxes, and international economics. (4 semester credits)

Principles of Macroeconomics

Includes a study of supply and demand, income determination and the multiplier, economic fluctuations, fiscal policy, money, banking, monetary policy, unemployment and inflation, and international trade and finance. (3 semester credits)

Principles of Microeconomics

Includes the study of supply, demand, and elasticity; household behavior; the firm in the long and short runs; competitive and monopoly markets; firm control and motivation; distribution of national income; wages, capital, and income distribution; and poverty. (3 semester credits)

Interpretation of Business and Economic Data

The nature of statistical data in business and economics; the use of tabular, graphical and numerical analysis; probability, estimation, and hypothesis testing; correlation and regression; index numbers; time series and forecasting; government policy; and international trade. (3 semester credits)

International Economics

A study of major aspects of international trade, finance and commercial policy under changing world conditions. Areas of concentration include various theories of international trade, effects of tariffs and quotas, exchange rate determination, balance of payments analysis and policy, international money systems, international economics institutions, and current problems. (3 semester credits)

International Business

A course for those who wish to learn about the practical aspects of international business. Information presented in this course should provide adequate knowledge to start and conduct an international business without being confused by the intricacies of international trade. (3 semester credits)

EDUCATIONAL POLICY STUDIES

Principles of Vocational, Technical, and Adult Education

A study of the philosophy, administration, and organization of vocational, technical, and adult education at the national, state, and local levels. (2 semester credits)

EDUCATIONAL PSYCHOLOGY

Human Abilities and Learning

The course considers how humans learn, with particular emphasis on learning in the school situation. Topics include intelligence, creativity, motivation, attitudes and values, evaluation, and conditioning. Emphasizes the ways people learn and how they can be helped to learn. (3 semester credits)

Child Development

Explores the social, physical, and cognitive development of children from birth to adolescence. An important component of the course is an introduction to the observational and experimental methods used to study children's development. (3 semester credits)

Human Development in Adolescence

This course presents an integrated overview of developmental processes and issues during the adolescent stage of life. Emphasis is upon the major physical, intellectual, and social changes occurring during adolescence. Vital contemporary issues regarding adolescents are also considered: love and sex, juvenile delinquency, moral development, self-concept, and establishing a meaning for one's life. (3 semester credits)

Educational Psychology of the Gifted, Talented, and Creative

An introduction to the education of the gifted, focusing on characteristics, program planning, identification, acceleration, grouping enrichment, curriculum models, creativity, cultural diversities, underachievement, handicapped gifted, parenting, and program evaluation. (3 semester credits)

Adult Development and Aging

Surveys several major contemporary theories of human development and aging. The current life span of Americans raises questions about qualitative changes in adulthood, stages of adult life, individual differences in rates and directions of development, the reversibility of certain developments, and the interplay of biological, environmental, and cultural factors. Topics include genetic influences, health care, intelligence and creativity across the life span, diversity of adult life styles, biological and physical aspects of development, cognitive changes with age, and work, leisure, and retirement. (3 semester credits)

Human Relations in the Educational Community

Examines human awareness and human rights in terms of self-concepts and sensitivity to others. The course emphasizes experiences that give insights into the effects of human relations on educational processes and goals. The focus is on development of teacher attitudes and examination of specific problems minority groups and women face in the educational community. (3 semester credits)

ENGINEERING

Critical Path Network Techniques

Application of CPM, PERT, and PDM techniques to the management of projects and programs. Includes use of the computer as a tool in CPM. Discusses and compares various methods for planning, scheduling, and controlling projects and project resources. (2 semester credits)

Statics

Force systems, moments, couples, resultants, rigid body equilibrium, frames and machines, truss analysis, friction, centroids, distributed loads, moment of inertia. Students must have access to a VHS videotape player. (3 semester credits)

Dynamics

Rectilinear motion, curvilinear motion, kinematics of plane motion, instantaneous center, relative velocity and acceleration, kinetics of particles, systems of particles and rigid bodies, conservation of energy, work-energy methods, impulse, momentum, impact. (3 semester credits)

Mechanics of Materials

Loads, stresses, strains, strain energy, Hooke's Law, temperature effects, torsion, shear, flexural stresses, beams, shear and moment diagrams, deflection (various approaches), statically indeterminate beams (various approaches), combined loading, columns. (3 semester credits)

Technical Writing I

Correspondence—Write letters, memos, and other short works; learn how to persuade; review grammar and conventions. (1 semester credit)

Technical Writing II

Report Writing—Plan and write short reports, including feasibility reports, proposals, progress reports, and instruction manuals; learn how to design reports to suit your audience and purpose and how to make important ideas stand out. (1 semester credit)

Technical Writing III

Formal Report—Plan and write a major report on a topic of your choice; learn to write for a varied audience, use visuals, and revise and edit your work. (1 semester credit)

Technical Writing I and II

This course is a combination of *Technical Writing I* and *Technical Writing II*. (2 semester credits)

Technical Writing I and III

This course is a combination of *Technical Writing I* and *Technical Writing III*. (2 semester credits)

Technical Writing II and III

This course is a combination of *Technical Writing II* and *Technical Writing III*. (2 semester credits)

Technical Writing

This course is a combination of the three courses *Technical Writing I, II, and III*. (3 semester credits)

Industrial Safety

Incorporates the major topics in safety that are common to industrial settings, including the many changes in the legal, management, technical, and human aspects of industrial safety that have occurred in the United States in the last decade. The aim of this course is to provide the current fundamental background knowledge and techniques needed to establish, maintain, and improve basic safety programs in industry, but it does not detail safety measures for any particular industry. (3 semester credits)

Economic Analysis for Engineers

This course focuses on the basic principles of investment analysis and the economic use of capital and presents methods for making engineering economy studies and selecting among various alternatives. These methods are applicable to decisions about engineering design, manufacturing process planning, and production control. (2 semester credits)

Introduction to Materials Science

An introductory course in materials science describing the relationship between internal structure and properties for engineering materials including metals, polymers, glasses, and ceramics. The course objective is to develop a systematic and fundamental approach to the understanding of materials behavior, both during fabrication of products and during service performance. (3 semester credits)

ENGLISH

Freshman English

Students will read and compose essays on controversial subjects. The course offers practice with constructing sound arguments and using secondary sources. The focus is on developing clear, well-organized, and objective essays. (3 semester credits)

Intermediate Composition

Zinsser's humorous commentary on writing as well as a series of contemporary essays will suggest ideas for writing strategies. Assignments focus on the kinds of essays required for most college courses. (3 semester credits)

Introduction to Creative Writing: The Short Story

Offers suggestions on such essentials of fiction writing as plot, characterization, point of view, and style. Students receive feedback on story ideas, stories, and revisions. (3 semester credits)

Creative Writing: Poetry

This course guides students through writing, revising, and publishing poetry. In addition to units on image, sound, line breaks, and other aspects of poetry, the course guide includes an appendix on how and where to publish poetry. Each assignment asks students to submit a poem and also to read and comment on contemporary poems included in the course anthology. (3 semester credits)

Introduction to Modern English and American Literature I: The Nineteenth Century

Introduces students to English and American works from the period between the publication of Blake's *Songs of Innocence* (1789) and the death of Queen Victoria (1901), a time which laid the foundation for modernism in art. Twelve audio programs developed with funds from the Annenberg/CPB Project add a new dimension to the study of literature by drawing on the expertise and enthusiasm of a nationwide faculty and the skill of professional actors and readers. (3 semester credits)

Introduction to Modern English and American Literature II: The Twentieth Century

Introduces students to English and American Poetry, fiction, and nonfiction of the twentieth century. Twelve audio programs developed with funds from the Annenberg/CPB Project enable students to hear professional readings of the literature as well as commentary by scholars and writers throughout the country. (3 semester credits)

Shakespearean Drama

Course U350-217. Explores Shakespeare's development as a dramatist in early comedies like *The Taming of the Shrew* and *Midsummer Night's Dream*, history plays like *Richard II* and *Henry IV*, and the tragedy of *Romeo and Juliet*. (3 semester credits)

Course U350-218. Explores the richness of six great Shakespearean tragedies (*Julius Caesar, Hamlet, Othello, King Lear, Macbeth,* and *Antony and Cleopatra,* two comedies (*Measure for Measure* and *The Winter's Tale*), and one romance (*The Tempest*). (3 semester credits)

The Courage to Write: Women Novelists of the Nineteenth Century

In this course, you will read and write about eight novels and hear them dramatized and discussed on award-winning audio programs. (3 semester credits)

African-American Studies—Introduction to Twentieth Century Afro-American Literature: The Fictional Vision

An examination of African American fiction from 1912 to 1984. Students will explore a history of racial injustice transformed into fiction of extraordinary power and importance for all readers. (3 semester credits)

American Indian Literature

Introduces the fiction, prose, and poetry of America's original inhabitants. Students will read works that explore our relationship to nature, the struggle between old traditions and new ways, American history, the family, spiritual values, and the roles of women. (3 semester credits)

Saul Bellow

Students will read three Bellow novels that reveal his probing yet often humorous presentation of the values and problems of contemporary culture. (1 semester credit)

Willa Cather

Three Cather novels demonstrate her remarkable versatility. Students will examine her portraits of the immigrant experience, the fear of aging, and the hunger for love and acceptance. (1 semester credit)

Doris Lessing

Three of Lessing's most influential novels introduce students to her keen insight into human nature, romantic relationships, and the quest for spiritual fulfillment. (1 semester credit)

Eudora Welty

This course offers a sampling of Welty, demonstrating her focus on the environment, characters, and life-styles of the American South. (1 semester credit)

Virginia Woolf

Woolf, considered one of the greatest twentieth-century writers, helped redefine the concept of the novel. Students will examine two of her experimental novels and her essay on fiction and feminism. (1 semester credit)

History of the English Language

A survey of the origins of the English language and its changes over the last 1,500 years. Students will explore English phonology, morphology, and syntax by focusing on linguistic change and the historical basis of modern English pronunciation, orthography, and dialects. (3 semester credits)

The Structure of English

Examination of the grammar and syntax of modern English, leading to a better understanding of the English language and of concepts necessary for basic linguistic research. (3 semester credits)

Ernest Hemingway

Two novels and a selection of short stories demonstrate the famous Hemingway Code as well as the dramatic action, objective tone, and psychological portraits associated with this famous author. (1 semester credit)

William Faulkner

A general introduction to Faulkner's life and work. Two novels and a collection of short fiction reveal some of the themes treated by this great Southern writer, such as the effect of history, the meaning of heroism, and the devastating results of racism. (1 semester credit)

The English Novel

Introduction to the literary giants of nineteenth-century England. The course guide emphasizes the universality of these novels and explores some of the major themes of nineteenth-century fiction. (3 semester credits)

The American Short Story

Students will read a wide variety of American stories, beginning with classics such as *Rip Van Winkle* and ending with contemporary experiments with short fiction. These readings will illustrate the diversity and power of this literary form. (3 semester credits)

Advanced Study in Creative Writing

Students will receive detailed criticism of either 30 pages of fiction or 30 pages of poetry. The course guide includes questions and answers about fiction and poetry, interviews with two authors, a glossary, and general suggestions about submitting work for publication. (3 semester credits)

FINANCE

Principles of Finance

Introductory course in corporation finance. Examines the financial objectives of firms, the context within which firms pursue their objectives, and the use of tools, techniques, and models of finance to make successful decisions. Topics include financial ratio analysis, forecasting, planning and control; credit policy, cash management, and short-term financing; capital budgeting; dividend policy and variation; and lease financing, warrants, and convertibles. (3 semester credits)

Investments

Concerned with the efficient management of investments to provide adequate return on unconsumed income. Provides a working knowledge of available investment alternatives, the operation of the markets for securities in the United States, and how to find information on particular investment opportunities. Focuses on the investment environment, three approaches to investment in common stocks, essential aspects of managing a portfolio of securities, fixed income securities, and alternative investment opportunities. (3 semester credits)

Consumer Education and Personal Finance

Emphasis on the development of effective money management techniques through understanding the economy and business community and consumer resources and sources of consumer information and protection. Topics include goal setting and financial planning, insurance, borrowing and credit, taxes, housing, and investments. (3 semester credits)

Financial Management

Examines theories underlying financial decision-making models and their application to decision making under uncertainty. Emphasis on cash flows and their certainty. Topics include risk and valuations, capital budgeting, long-term financing, financial structure, and dividend policy and internal financing. (3 semester credits)

FORESTRY

Introduction to Forestry

Introduction to forest biology, forest management for multiple uses, and forest products. Addresses both biological and political components of forestry. (2 semester credits)

FRENCH

First Semester French

Provides the fundamentals of French and a good working knowledge of basic French vocabulary and grammar. The course also introduces the student to French culture. A cassette, which is coordinated with the textbook, provides the opportunity for oral practice. The cassette is included at no additional cost when the textbook is purchased. (4 semester credits)

Second Semester French

A continuation of *First Semester French.* (4 semester credits)

Third Semester French

A course designed to give students a solid background in French at the intermediate level and to help them develop their skills in reading, writing, and understanding French. It includes a thorough grammar review, readings on current topics and on everyday life in France, and active use of essential grammatical structures, vocabulary, and idioms. (3 or 4 semester credits)

Fourth Semester French

A continuation of *Third Semester French.* Includes a grammar review, readings on everyday life and active use of essential grammatical structures, vocabulary, and idioms. Reading selections also include short texts by notable French authors. (3 or 4 semester credits)

Business French

Course U400-219. Presents the basic vocabulary and forms used in business in France along with general information about the economic life of the country. Vocabulary is introduced in reading passages and examples of letters and forms. Each lesson contains a reading passage, a French-English vocabulary, study questions based on the reading, a vocabulary exercise, grammar review exercises, and composition questions. (2 semester credits)

Course U400-313. An overview of the French economy as well as many important aspects of business in France (banking, types of businesses, insurance, stock market, postal and financial services, transports, investments). The course provides instruction in the vocabulary and structures needed to read and write for communication in this specialized field and offers thorough training in commercial French correspondence. (3 semester credits)

Introduction to French Literature, Seventeenth- and Eighteenth-Century Authors

An introductory study of the literature of France's "classical" period and the Age of Enlightenment, with a brief introduction to that of the Middle Ages and the Renaissance. Literary works—primarily plays, poetry, and essays—are examined within their historical context, and the student is introduced to the fundamentals of literary criticism. (3 semester credits)

Introduction to French Literature, Nineteenth-Century Authors

An introduction to the principal authors of nineteenth-century France through the examination of representative poems, novels, plays, and other writings. The student is introduced to the basic techniques of literary criticism as a means of appreciating the works studied. (3 semester credits)

Intermediate Composition

A systematic review of grammar covered in earlier courses with sufficient exercises to review all points. Also includes the study of French vocabulary and expressions to be used in short compositions designed to develop students' ability to express themselves in written French. (3 semester credits)

Advanced Composition

This course is designed to give the student experience in writing essays in French on a variety of topics of interest. It includes short French reading passages that serve as the nucleus for each lesson and provide vocabulary, expressions, grammar patterns, and stylistic models for the written work. (2 semester credits)

Panorama de la civilisation fran*caaise

A general survey of French history from prehistoric times to the Constitution of 1958. Emphasis is given to French rulers such as Clovis, Charlemagne, Louis XIV, and Napoleon. Traditional themes such as political events, constitutional developments, economic change, religious conflicts, and intellectual history are included. (3 semester credits)

André Malraux

Revolution, China, Communism, East versus West, immortality through art—these and other topics are treated in the works of Malraux. (1 semester credit)

Maupassant

A brief discussion of Guy de Maupassant's life as reflected in his writing, followed by a comprehensive analysis of three of his best-known stories—*Boule de Suif, Une Partie de campagne*, and *Le Horla*—each representing a different dimension of his work. (1 semester credit)

Camus

The student follows the evolution of Camus's humanistic thought from the casual indifference of some early fictional characters to shared commitment and social responsibility for others. (1 semester credit)

Simone de Beauvoir

Introduces Simone de Beauvoir as philosopher, novelist, essayist, feminist, humanist, and autobiographer. (1 semester credit)

Colette

Examines Colette's life, her literary reputation, and her skill as a writer, with emphasis emphasis on her attitudes toward feminism. (1 semester credit)

Zola

A brief discussion of the life, works, and theories of Émile Zola, followed by a comprehensive analysis of Zola's major novel *Germinal*, emphasizing themes as well as techniques and featuring detailed analyses of several key passages. (1 semester credit)

Diderot

An introduction to Diderot's *Jacques the Fatalist and His Master* and the literary scene in France prior to the French Revolution. (1 semester credit)

Flaubert

An introduction to the life of Gustave Flaubert and a stylistic and structural analysis of *Madame Bovary*. (1 semester credit)

Sartre

An introduction to the life of Jean-Paul Sartre—philosopher, novelist, dramatist, critic, journalist, and political commentator—through a study of his first novel, *La Nausée*. The study includes references to existentialism, the philosophy with which Sartre's name has been inseparably linked. (1 semester credit)

GEOGRAPHY

Global Physical Environments

Examines the physical environment in terms of atmospheric (climate and weather), geomorphic (landforms and erosion), biotic (vegetation), and edaphic (soil) subsystems. The course strives to increase the student's understanding of the diverse environments present on earth and the visual landscape encountered in everyday living. Extensive map study helps the student explore areas both exotic and familiar. (3 semester credits)

Environmental Conservation

Discusses problems arising from human use of earth resources in an ecosystem context. The course addresses the interaction of people with technology, with the use of resources, and with the use of energy. Also discussed in depth are pollution as a symptom of our environmental malaise and our exponentially expanding population, consumption, and technology on a finite planet. (3 semester credits)

GEOLOGY

General Geology

The study of the earth, its materials, structure, processes, and history. The student will learn distinguishing characteristics of common rocks and minerals; movements of viscous and solid portions of the earth and the effects of such movements; work of agents of erosion such as moving water, wind, glacial ice; and interactions of internal and external earth forces. This course emphasizes gaining familiarity with geologic and topographic maps. (3 semester credits)

GERMAN

First Semester German

Pronunciation, grammatical structure, and vocabulary building for those with no previous instruction in German. (4 semester credits)

Second Semester German

Study of grammatical structures of a more complex nature and development of reading ability. Emphasis on vocabulary and idioms in texts of literary and cultural merit. (4 semester credits)

Third Semester German

Reviews grammar and continues the development of reading ability. Works of increasing difficulty are read with close attention to vocabulary, idioms, and difficulties of grammatical and sentence structure. (4 semester credits)

Fourth Semester German

Continues to develop reading ability. Students read works of recognized literary merit. (3 or 4 semester credits)

Introduction to German Literature I

Short stories by masters of the German *Novelle* with emphasis on literary matters as language difficulty diminishes. (3 semester credits)

Introduction to German Literature II

A continuation of *Introduction to German Literature I*. (3 semester credits)

Intermediate Composition, First Semester

To develop and improve skill in writing German. Thorough grammar review with extensive exercises and controlled composition. (3 semester credits)

Intermediate Composition, Second Semester

Continuation of *Intermediate Composition First Semester* with greater emphasis on free composition. (3 semester credits)

The Classical Period

Selected works of Lessing, Goethe, and Schiller, with stress primarily upon literary matters. (3 semester credits)

Thomas Mann

The works selected for this course are only a sample of the multifaceted oeuvre of this meticulous and complex Nobel laureate. (1 semester credit)

Günter Grass

Günter Grass is one of Germany's most popular and politically involved contemporary writers. To a considerable degree his work represents an effort to come to grips with the recent German past using innovative, sometimes startling techniques. (1 semester credit)

Goethe's *Faust*

This course covers both parts of the drama with a view toward a careful interpretation of the main themes. (3 semester credits)

Applied German Philology

Designed for teachers and students of German who wish to learn about the history of the German language. The course includes a study of etymology and an explanation and discussion of many linguistic phenomena encountered in New High German phonology, morphology, and syntax. (3 semester credits)

GREEK

Elementary Greek

Course U428-103. The first semester introductory course in Classical Greek. Introduction to Greek grammar and syntax and practice in reading short passages from ancient authors. The basic essentials of Greek grammar are covered including all declensions of the noun and all tenses of the verb. (4 semester credits)

Course U428-104. A second semester course in Classical Greek. Introduces the irregular verbs and reviews the uses of the subjunctive and optative moods. The primary emphasis is on reading longer passages from classical authors with close attention to the syntactic structures used. The second half of this course is devoted entirely to a careful reading of Plato's *Crito*. (4 semester credits)

Plato

Introduction to Plato's *Crito*. For the intermediate student who has studied Greek but who has not read Plato before. (2 semester credits)

Xenophon and the New Testament

An introduction to Greek prose of two periods: a book of the *Anabasis* of Xenophon and the *Gospel According to St. Luke.* (3 semester credits)

Homer - *The Iliad*

Introduction to the poetry of Homer and the life of the Homeric age. (3 semester credits)

HEALTH EDUCATION

Introduction to Mental Health and Stress Management

This course is designed to familiarize you with everyday stressors. The course introduces a variety of intervention techniques used to combat stress and discusses ways to reduce stressful behaviors in your daily life and at work. (3 semester credits)

HEBREW AND SEMITIC STUDIES

First Semester Hebrew - Biblical

Designed for students interested in biblical Hebrew only and who have had little or no previous instruction in the language. The course provides a working knowledge of grammar and an acquaintance with the essential vocabulary used most frequently in biblical Hebrew. The student obtains an elementary knowledge of reading, writing, and pronunciation. (4 semester credits)

Second Semester Hebrew - Biblical

Of particular interest to theological and other students whose main interest is Biblical Hebrew. Review of grammar covered in First Semester Hebrew - Biblical and readings of selections from the Book of *Genesis*. (3 semester credits)

First Semester Hebrew - Modern

For those who have had little or no previous instruction in the language. Emphasis on modern standard usage and spoken Hebrew. The student obtains a basic working knowledge of Hebrew grammar and conversation and an acquaintance with the essential vocabulary used most frequently in Hebrew today. (4 semester credits)

Second Semester Hebrew - Modern

Review of grammar studied in the above course; reading of continuous text throughout the course; beginnings of Hebrew composition. (2 semester credits)

Biblical Texts: Readings from the Book of Esther

Of particular interest to divinity students and Bible teachers. Study aids include vocabularies, explanatory notes, exercises, and grammatical information. (2 semester credits)

Modern Hebrew Conversation, Intermediate Level

For students who have completed second semester Hebrew. Passages are selected from current modern Hebrew prose writings. (3 semester credits)

Biblical Texts: Readings from Exodus and Leviticus

Of particular interest to theological and other students whose main interest is Biblical Hebrew. Reading selections from Exodus and Leviticus. (3 semester credits)

Biblical Texts: Readings from Joshua

Selections from the Book of Joshua with comprehensive word lists, explanatory notes, exercises based on the text under study, and cumulative vocabularies. (3 semester credits)

Jewish Cultural History I

Survey of Jewish intellectual history from biblical times through the golden age in Spain, including the Aprocrypha, Josephus, Philo, Oral Law, Talmud, and Midrash. (4 semester credits) of unusual interest. (3 semester credits)

Jewish Cultural History II

Continuation of the preceding course from medieval times to the present. The course discusses a variety of cultural and religious responses; Kabbalah; Hasidism; Jewish cultural life in Europe, the United States, and Israel; Yiddish and modern Hebrew literature. (4 semester credits)

First Semester Yiddish

For those who have little or no previous systematic instruction in the language. Emphasis is on standard usage and spoken Yiddish. The student obtains a basic working knowledge of Yiddish grammar and conversation and an acquaintance with the essential vocabulary used most frequently in Yiddish today. (4 semester credits)

Second Semester Yiddish

A continuation of *First Semester Yiddish.* (4 semester credits)

HISTORY

American History, 1492−1865: The Origin and Growth of the United States

A general survey of American history from the era of exploration to the close of the Civil War. The thirteen units of study are well balanced between political history and social and economic developments. From colonial and revolutionary origins in the first four units, the next nine carry national development through the shaping of the new nation, territorial expansion, the rise and transformation of political parties, the age of reform, the diverging economies and societies of North and South, the crises of the 1850s, and the Civil War. (4 semester credits)

American History, 1865 to the Present: The Origin and Growth of the United States

This general survey of American experience from Reconstruction of the South after the Civil War through 1990 examines major changes in America's role in international affairs, political developments, social change especially in the status of blacks and women, and the transformation of the national economy. The course is designed to illustrate patterns of continuity and discontinuity over the past 125 years. (4 semester credits)

Western Civilization: The Stone Age to 1715

This course presents a broad overview of Near Eastern and European human development from the earliest records of human existence until the eighteenth century. Students examine the roots of modern institutions and issues and to learn about many aspects of life during this very long span of human history. (3 semester credits)

Western Civilization from 1715 to the Present

This course surveys the history of Western civilization from 1715 to the present, a period of rapid change in political, social, economic, intellectual, and cultural life. (3 semester credits)

Ancient History: The Ancient Near East and Greece

A survey of the social, political, and cultural development of the ancient Near East and Greece. A detailed view of the cultures of Mesopotamia, Egypt, and Greece from the beginnings of civilization to the Hellenistic partitions of the empire of Alexander the Great, with emphasis on the social and political institutions of each area. Includes a brief survey of the ancient cultures of Asia Minor and Palestine. (3 semester credits)

Ancient History: Roman Republic and Empire

An introductory survey of the social, political, and cultural development of the Roman world from prehistory to the sixth century A.D. Emphasis is on the Roman Revolution, the Roman Principate, and imperial society and culture. (3 semester credits)

English History, England to 1688

A general survey of the social and political history of England from the Roman invasion of 55 B.C. to the Glorious Revolution at the close of the seventeenth century. Special emphasis is given to the everyday lives of ordinary men and women as well as to the more traditional themes such as political events, constitutional developments, economic change, and religious conflict. (3 semester credits)

British History, 1688 to the Present

A general survey of economic, social, and political developments in Britain from the later seventeenth century to the advent of Margaret Thatcher. Special attention is paid to the Industrial Revolution, the growth of democracy, the rise and decline of the British Empire, and the consequences of Britain's active participation in two World Wars. (3 semester credits)

Independent Reading

Students who would like to read on a selected topic in the areas of ancient, medieval, women's, American, or Wisconsin History can arrange to do so by addressing a special request to the Department of History for a study plan, indicating specific topic of interest. (1, 2, or 3 semester credits)

History of Wisconsin

Surveys Wisconsin's past and focuses on the social history of its diverse peoples. Beginning with the era prior to European exploration

and continuing through the 1980s, this course traces the experiences of Indians and missionaries, fur traders and farmers, white immigrants and African Americans, business titans and socialists, and men and women of differing social classes and backgrounds. Notable figures—including Black Hawk, Robert M. LaFollette, and Joseph McCarthy—are highlighted, as are significant events such as the Civil War and the two world wars. Other topics round out this overview, among them the volatile world of politics, economic development in the Dairy State, pioneering conservation efforts by Aldo Leopold and others, and battles over civil rights in the 1960s and treaty rights in the 1980s. (3 semester credits)

U.S. Women's History

This survey course introduces students to major developments in women's lives from the seventeenth through the twentieth centuries. Emphasis is on cultural attitudes toward women and on ordinary women's experiences of and impact on work, family, and politics, with attention given to differences by race, class, and ethnicity. (4 semester credits)

Women in European History: From the Eighteenth Century to the Present

A survey of women in European history from the eighteenth century to the present, this course examines ideals and gender ideologies as well as women's varied experiences. Some of the topics explored include women and work, the ideal of domesticity, the "New Woman," women and war, and women's liberation. This course concentrates on both individuals and groups of women, considering the ordinary as well as the extraordinary, to help students understand the full story of European women from Ireland to Russia during the past three centuries. (3 semester credits)

History of Soviet Russia

Deals with the political, economic, social, and diplomatic history of the U.S.S.R. from its revolutionary origins to the present. The course examines the changes which have occurred in the Soviet Union in the past half century and which have propelled that country from being one of the most backward in Europe to its current position of world importance. Among the topics discussed are the revolutions of 1917 and the ensuing civil war; the struggle for power after Lenin's death; the Stalin era and its impact on life in the U.S.S.R.; the devastating effects of World War II and the subsequent cold war; and changes after Stalin's death. (3 or 4 semester credits)

Independent Reading

Students who would like to read on a selected topic in the areas of ancient, medieval, women's, American, or Wisconsin history can arrange to do so by addressing a special request to the history department for a study plan indicating a specific topic of interest. (1 to 3 semester credits)

ITALIAN

First Semester Italian

This course presents the fundamentals of Italian pronunciation, vocabulary (including idiomatic expressions), grammatical principles, and introduces the student to Italian culture. (4 semester credits)

Second Semester Italian

A continuation of *First Semester Italian*. (4 semester credits)

JOURNALISM

News Writing

A basic university course in journalism. Principles and practice in news and feature story writing for print media, essentially the newspaper. Limited coverage of other news channels including broadcast media. (3 semester credits)

Public Relations

Introduction to fundamental principles and practice of public relations in industry, business, education, social welfare, and government. (3 semester credits)

Writing Feature Articles

This course focuses on the principles and practice of writing feature articles for magazines and newspapers. Presents broad concepts which underlie all informative writing, whether by staff or free-lance persons. (3 or 4 semester credits)

LATIN

Elementary Latin

Course U524-103. Designed primarily for those beginning the study of Latin, it includes sufficient foundation work to enable students to read Caesar. Emphasizes reading ability. (4 semester credits)

Course U524-104. A continuation of the preceding course. Selections from Aulus Gellius, Nepos, Caesar, Phaedrus, Justin, and Sallust, with attention to historical background, exercises in grammar, composition, and scansion. (4 semester credits)

Cicero's *Orations*

Six orations of Cicero. Drill in finished translation that reproduces the literary style of the author. Simple reports on syntax, style, and history. (4 semester credits)

Vergil

Four books of the *Aeneid*, with stress upon finished translation in good English. A study of prosody, word derivation, rhetorical figures, mythology, and the literary style of the author. (4 semester credits)

General Survey

Course U524-301. Selections from authors of the Roman Republic, including Ennius, Plautus, Terence, Catullus, Lucretius, Sallust, Vergil, and Horace, illustrating the social, political, and intellectual life of the nation. (3 semester credits)

Course U524-302. Selections from authors of the Roman Empire, including Livy, the elegists, the Senecas, minor historians, Petronius, Lucan and other epic poets, the Plinii, Quintilian, Martial, Tacitus, and Juvenal. (3 semester credits)

Intermediate Latin Composition

To train the student to write Latin, gain a knowledge of the Latin point of view, appreciate Latin syntax and idioms. Vocabulary building is emphasized. (2 semester credits)

Advanced Latin Composition

A continuation of the above course. (2 semester credits)

Horace - Satires and Epistles

The selections represent varied subjects, some of which are developed through informal reports. The aim is to enjoy the form and to discover both the poet and Republican Rome. (3 semester credits)

LINGUISTICS

Introduction to Linguistics

This introductory course covers the basic techniques of analysis at three levels of speech: sounds, word formation, and syntax. (3 semester credits)

LITERATURE IN TRANSLATION

Camus

The student follows the evolution of Camus's humanistic thought from the casual indifference of some early fictional characters to shared commitment and social responsibility for others. (1 semester credit)

Simone de Beauvoir

An introduction to Simone de Beauvoir as philosopher, novelist, essayist, feminist, humanist, and autobiographer. (1 semester credit)

Colette

Examines Colette's life, her literary reputation, and her skill as a writer, with emphasis on her attitudes toward feminism. (1 semester credit)

Zola

A brief discussion of the life, works, and theories of Émile Zola, followed by a comprehensive analysis of Zola's major novel *Germinal*, emphasizing themes as well as techniques and featuring detailed analyses of several key passages. (1 semester credit)

Diderot

An introduction to Diderot's *Jacques the Fatalist and His Master* and the literary scene in France prior to the French Revolution. (1 semester credit)

Flaubert

An introduction to the life of Gustave Flaubert and to a stylistic and structural analysis of *Madame Bovary.* (1 semester credit)

Maupassant

A brief discussion of Guy de Maupassant's life, as reflected in his writing, followed by a comprehensive analysis of three of his best-known stories—*Boule de Suif, Une Partie de campagne*, and *Le Horla*—each representing a different dimension of his work. (1 semester credit)

Sartre

This course introduces the student to the life of Jean Paul Sartre—philosopher, novelist, dramatist, critic, journalist, and political commentator—through a study of his first novel, *Nausea*. This study includes references to existentialism, the philosophy with which Sartre's name has been inseparably linked. (1 semester credit)

André Malraux

Revolution, China, Communism, East versus West, immortality through art—these and other topics are treated in the works of Malraux. (1 semester credit)

Thomas Mann

The works selected for this course are only a sample of the multifaceted oeuvre of this meticulous and complex Nobel laureate. (1 semester credit)

Günter Grass

Günter Grass is one of Germany's most popular and politically involved contemporary writers. To a considerable degree his work represents an effort to come to grips with the recent German past using innovative, sometimes startling, techniques. (1 semester credit)

The Tales of Hans Christian Andersen

Covers a selection of Andersen's tales, exposing the student to Andersen's humor and his questioning of the opinions, ideas, and values of his readers. It shows why Andersen's works have survived him and continue to be read all over the world. (3 semester credits)

Miguel de Unamuno

This course deals with Unamuno's personal philosophy and literary theories as they are developed in three of his major novels. (1 semester credit)

MANAGEMENT

Introduction to the American Business Enterprise

Surveys the economic, social, legal, and political dimensions of business; examines the primary functions performed within a business; introduces management issues affecting business organization. (3 semester credits)

Microcomputer Applications

A course recommended for learning how to use the microcomputer. Emphasis is placed on using the IBM PC with the most popular kinds of computer software such as spreadsheets, database management, and graphics. (3 semester credits)

Introduction to Management Information Systems

Provides future managers with a basic knowledge of information systems and computers. Includes the study of information system concepts, the use of information systems for operational and management decision making, the impact of information systems on organization and management, end user programming and application development, and experience in the use of productivity packages. At the end of the course, the student should be able to use productivity software for personal, course-related, or managerial tasks; design an information system and the selection of hardware and software for a business; and communicate with computer programmers and systems analysts. Students must have access to a computer with the following software: word processing, database, and spreadsheet. (3 semester credits)

Organization and Management

Introductory course in the principles of management. Emphasis is on the primary duties of a manager—planning, decision making, organizing, controlling, leadership, motivation, communication—and the alternatives available to carry these concepts into action. (3 semester credits)

Production Concepts

Examines modern concepts and models for producing goods or services and for planning, organizing, and controlling the production process. (3 semester credits)

Compensation Management

Provides an overview of current compensation practices in the United States. Specifically, the course explores the interrelationship between an organization's reward system and its various internal and external influences, presents relevant compensation techniques and the issues surrounding their use, discusses the theoretical concepts underlying current pay practices, and covers the issues involved in administering a compensation program. Students will practice the evaluation, pay range development, and will research a contemporary compensation topic. (3 semester credits)

Retailing

Successful retail management. Emphasizes analytical and research methods applicable to the problems of retail management. (3 semester credits)

Personnel Management

A comprehensive study of the effective management of the human resource component of an organization including concern for the productivity of employees, legal provisions impacting on them, and the quality of work life they experience. Academic or theoretical portions of the course are accompanied by practical applications. Topics include planning, job design, recruitment, placement, performance appraisal, compensation, training and development, career

planning, health and safety, equal employment opportunity, and unionization. (3 semester credits)

Gender Issues in Management

Vital contemporary issues such as women's roles in the workplace, power and tokenism, sexual harassment, networking, and stress and time management are discussed. The course provides a comprehensive, interdisciplinary treatment of gender-related issues and their impact on management and incorporates experiences unique to women of color. Sex-role stereotypes and socialization processes that have affected both females and males are examined in detail. (3 semester credits)

Organizational Behavior

Theories and applications of behavioral science in organizations. Emphasis is on individual and small group behavior, job attitudes, individual decision making, group formation and development, social influence, group decision making and problem solving, intergroup relations, leadership in organizations, organizational change and behavior. (3 semester credits)

Business Communications

Instruction in and application of the principles and practices of communication used in business and the professions. This includes the writing of short and long reports, letters, and memos as well as the sending and receiving of oral and nonverbal messages. A video presentation is required. Basic language skills are emphasized. (3 semester credits)

Managing the Small Business

This course is intended to aid both the student and practitioner in overcoming a lack of organization and planning and to provide a comprehensive understanding of how a business works. Students will have the opportunity to apply and integrate knowledge gained in other business courses. Practitioners also will have an opportunity to analyze their own businesses in a way that can help them improve overall operations. (3 semester credits)

Labor-Management Relations

Labor-management relations theory and application. Emphasizes labor organization, structure, management, and methods; collective bargaining, grievance arbitration, contract administration, and sources and areas of potential labor-management disputes and their resolutions. (3 semester credits)

Purchasing and Materials Management

Examines the principles of and the contributions materials procurement and materials management make to the successful operation of an organization whether profit, nonprofit, charitable, or governmental. Topics include procedures, computerization, flow of information, function, specification, quality, quantity, inspection, supplies selection, price, forward buying, foreign purchasing, and legal aspects. (3 semester credits)

Administrative Policy

A study of the planning administration of an organization from the top management point of view. Course includes policy development, implementation, control, and integration of the technical, social, economic, political, and functional activities of an organization. (3 semester credits)

MARKETING

Principles of Marketing

Introductory course that examines the marketing concept and its functions; the necessity of research before action in marketing; segmenting markets and developing positions; options available in each part of the marketing mix of product, place, price, and promotion; how marketing programs are written and controlled; how to evaluate marketing efforts; and how to apply marketing knowledge to one's life and work. (3 semester credits)

Marketing in Service Organizations

The course offers a reconsideration of traditional marketing topics in the context of a variety of service organizations. Emphasis is placed on how product-oriented marketing activities need to be adjusted or even reinvented to accommodate ''nonproducts.'' (3 semester credits)

MATHEMATICS

Intermediate Algebra

Gives the equivalent of intermediate mathematical competence. A modular course. (4 semester credits)

College Algebra

Gives the equivalent of advanced mathematical competence—algebra. A modular course. Functions and graphs; linear functions; arithmetic and geometric sequences; polynomial, composite, and inverse functions; exponential and logarithmic functions and equations; complex numbers and roots of equations; the algebra of polynomials and zeros of real polynomials; systems of linear equations; matrix methods and solution by determinants. An audio tape accompanies each assignment. (3 semester credits)

Trigonometry

Gives the equivalent of advanced mathematical competence—trigonometry. Starts with a discussion of some relevant concepts from algebra and geometry, then uses right triangles to develop the trigonometric functions of an acute angle. (2 semester credits)

Algebra and Trigonometry

Covers the material of *Colllege Algebra* and *Trigonometry*. (5 semester credits)

Theory of Arithmetic

Set theory, logic, patterns and sequences, different bases, word problems, prime factorizations, exponents, decimals and real numbers, probability. (2 semester credits)

Real Numbers and Informal Geometry

Geometric constructions of rational and algebraic numbers; angles, polygons, and other figures; tesselations; applications of similarity; area; volume. (2 semester credits)

Calculus and Related Topics

A calculus course primarily for prebusiness students. (5 semester credits)

Calculus and Analytic Geometry I

A modular course consisting of courses Differentiation, Applications of Differentiation, Basic Integration, Applications of Integration, and Transcendental Functions (*see* descriptions under Noncredit section below). (5 semester credits)

Calculus and Analytic Geometry II

A modular course consisting of courses Integration Techniques, Infinite Series, Plane Curves, Polar Coordinates and Vectors, and Vector Functions (*see* descriptions under Noncredit section below). (5 semester credits)

Calculus and Analytic Geometry III

A modular course consisting of courses Partial Differentiation, Multiple Integrals, Vector Analysis, First Order Differential Equations, and Second Order Differential Equations (*see* descriptions under Noncredit section below). (5 semester credits)

Mathematics for Computer Science

A modular course consisting of courses Sets and Sequences, Matrices and Graphs, and Functions and Order Structures (*see* descriptions under Noncredit section below). (3 semester credits)

Brief Introduction to Differential Equations

A modular course consisting of courses First Order Differential Equations and Second Order Differential Equations (*see* descriptions under Noncredit section below). (2 semester credits)

Techniques of Differential Equations

A modular course consisting of courses Series Solutions of Differential Equations, Laplace Transforms and Numerical Methods, and Stability and Boundary Value Problems (*see* descriptions under Noncredit section below). (3 semester credits)

Advanced Calculus I

Topological properties of Euclidean space; fundamental notions of limits, continuity, differentiation, and integration for functions of one r more variables; convergence and uniform convergence of infinite series and improper integrals; Fourier series. (3 semester credits)

Advanced Calculus II

Transformations; differentials; chain rules; inverse and implicit function theorems; transformation of multiple integrals; differential forms; theorems of Green, Gauss, and Stokes. (3 semester credits)

Modern Algebra I

Groups, normal subgroups, and factor groups; Cayley's Theorem; rings; ideals; homomorphisms; integral domain; fields; polynomial rings; field extensions; zeros of polynomials. (3 semester credits)

Complex Analysis

Elementary functions of a complex variable; conformal mapping; complex integrals; the calculus of residues. (3 semester credits)

METEOROLOGY

Weather and Climate

Designed to familiarize the student with various weather systems, particularly those affecting the United States and to explain the atmospheric processes that produce them. The course is descriptive, with considerable emphasis on fundamental concepts involved in cloud formation, pressure systems and fronts, jet streams, severe storms, rainmaking, and forecasting. (2 semester credits)

MUSIC

Appreciation and History of Music

Course U660-101. The purposes of this course are to increase your enjoyment of music by proceeding gradually from simple to more advanced levels, and to expand your horizons by developing new tastes. The intent is to arouse in the student an interest and curiosity in music, while imparting a knowledge of composers and their works and the periods of history in which they lived, that will help one respond to this musical heritage. This course begins with the nineteenth-century Romantic period and then turns to the eighteenth-century classical period as well as covering the materials of music. (2 semester credits)

Course U660-102. A continuation of the above course beginning with a consideration of the Middle Ages and Renaissance, and proceeds to the main currents in baroque music. The course concludes with the music of the twentieth century and a special look at the American scene. (2 semester credits)

Basic Concepts of Music

This course is designed to teach basic skills and understanding of music concepts to help students become ''empowered listeners'' who are able to make informed choices about what they will listen to and so have a greater enjoyment of music. Each of the twelve units is accompanied by a half-hour audio program on cassette, and "core repertory" tapes present other music works that provide examples of concepts throughout the course. Topics of study include rhythm, melody, harmony, form, style, meaning and emotion, and making choices to become an empowered listener. (3 semester credits)

NORWEGIAN

Beginning Norwegian I

For those with no previous instruction in the language. Also recommended for students who can speak the language but have never learned to read it or to analyze its grammatical structure. (4 semester credits)

Beginning Norwegian II

A continuation of *Beginning Norwegian I*. (4 semester credits)

NUTRITION

Nutrition Today

Nutrition and its relationship to humans and their biological, social, and physical environment; current issues and concerns that affect the nutritional status of individuals and various population groups. (3 semester credits)

PHILOSOPHY

Introduction to Philosophy

An introduction to some of the basic problems of philosophy considered to be of great importance to leading thinkers from ancient Greece to the present. (4 semester credits)

Elementary Logic

This course helps the student develop an ability to symbolize and appraise various forms of reasoning. This symbolization and appraisal are carried out with the help of elementary mathematical techniques. The course is an introduction to symbolic logic. (4 semester credits)

Introduction to Ethics

Beginning with a discussion of some varieties of relativism, which contends that moral preference is merely a matter of taste and sentiment, we consider various theories of what makes an action right, and of what makes an agent praiseworthy. Also considered is the criteria by which competing ethical theories may be rationally appraised, and touch on the connections between religion and morality. (4 semester credits)

Ethics in Business

Examining the difference between legal and moral issues from a philosophic perspective, the course uses actual cases to motivate interest in this timely subject. Twelve audiotapes developed with funds from the Annenberg/CPB Project add discussions and dramatic vignettes on real-life applications of philosophic principles. (4 semester credits)

Introduction to the Philosophy of Religion

(4 semester credits)

PHYSICS

General Physics I

Equivalent to the traditional, non-calculus-based, first semester physics course, with the exception of the laboratory work, which is not offered. Subject matter includes mechanics, heat, wave motion, and sound. (3 semester credits)

General Physics II

A continuation of *General Physics I*. Subject matter includes electricity and magnetism, light and optics, and atomic physics. (3 semester credits)

POLITICAL SCIENCE

American National Government

An introductory course in political science dealing with the federal governmental system and its relationship to state and local governments in a post-industrial nation. Subject matter includes the constitutional basis, structure, and democratic political processes of government at the national level; policy making; civil rights and liberties; and some of the problems facing our contemporary world. (3 semester credits)

Dilemmas of War and Peace

A multimedia, multidisciplinary course designed by a team of nationally recognized experts. Bringing together materials from a wide variety of individual fields of study, it provides students with a balanced and comprehensive introduction to war, peace, and world-order studies. The course offers a survey of the history of war and peace, analyzes the causes of war and conditions of peace, reviews a variety of suggested solutions to the war problem, and provides a context for students to understand the current world situation and prospects for world peace. It also addresses the contemporary and future problems of ecological security. (3 semester credits)

Public Personnel Administration

An introduction to and overview of public personnel management. The emphasis is on state and local governments, where more than 80 percent of government employees in America work. Actual practices in governments are explored. (3 semester credits)

PORTUGUESE

First Semester Portuguese

Offers practical reading knowledge of Portuguese, including short stories by Brazilian authors. Training in translation and elementary composition. Emphasis is on Brazilian Portuguese; pronunciation is that of Rio de Janeiro. (4 semester credits)

Second Semester Portuguese

A continuation of *First Semester Portuguese*. Emphasis is on reading. Exercises in grammatical principles, translation, and composition. (4 semester credits)

PSYCHOLOGY

Introduction to Psychology

Behavior including its biological basis, development, motivation, learning, emotion, personality, language, and social behavior. (3 semester credits)

Abnormal Psychology

Addresses psychological disorders (following the American Psychiatric Association's *Diagnostic and Statistical Manual IV*) and other problems of adjustment that frequently come to clinical attention. Emphasis on characteristics, diagnostic criteria, research on etiology, and approaches to treatment. (3 semester credits)

Introduction to Social Psychology

Basic psychological factors in social behavior, including social perception, attitudes, prejudice, discrimination, attraction, social influence, modeling, prosocial behavior, aggression, sexual behavior, social exchange and group behavior. (3 semester credits)

Child Psychology

Psychological development of the child to early adolescence. Learning principles, motor, language, cognitive, emotional, and social development of the child. (3 semester credits)

RUSSIAN

First Semester Russian

Introduction to basic Russian vocabulary and grammar and experience in reading, writing, and speaking in Russian. The course is intended for students with no previous instruction in Russian. (4 semester credits)

Second Semester Russian

A continuation of *First Semester Russian,* this course increases the student's knowledge of basic Russian and further develops reading and writing ability. (4 semester credits)

Third Semester Russian

This course rounds out the student's knowledge of basic Russian grammar and offers more advanced reading in several of the arts and sciences. The coursework includes exercises in grammar, translating, and original composition. (4 semester credits)

Fourth Semester Russian

A continuation of *Third Semester Russian*, helping students to develop good techniques for translating and vocabulary building and provides practice in original Russian composition. (4 semester credits)

SOCIAL WORK

Social Welfare: Programs, Practice, and the Profession

Presents perspectives on social work practice and a general framework appropriate for individuals, families, groups, organizations, and communities. Adapts basic social work skills and traditional approaches to enhance successful social work practice with client groups of various ethnic origins and social classes. (3 semester credits)

Social Problems of Aging and Old Age

Growth of the aged population; a comparative view of the role of old people in various societies; factors that account for the changed position of the aged in our society; problems of the aged and proposed solutions. (3 semester credits)

Child Welfare Services

Provides general and specific information about child welfare—how it works and why it is important rather than the how-to in child welfare. Course content includes the social, economic, and historical background of the principal problems in child welfare. (3 semester credits)

SOCIOLOGY

Marriage and Family

Looks at definitions and varieties of families, explores the life cycle, and considers some of the problems facing the contemporary family. Twelve audiotapes developed through the Annenberg/CPB Project add new dimensions to the discussion of the American family. (3 semester credits)

Sociological Foundations

Examines a broad range of human social relationships and social structures and the many forces—historical, cultural, and environmental—that shape them. (3 semester credits)

Social Problems

Personal and social maladjustments, problems of poverty, physical and mental deficiencies, delinquency, family disorganization, and racial and cultural minorities. (3 semester credits)

Racial and Cultural Minorities

Examines the interaction of social and cultural groups in America: processes leading to group contact, characteristics, and contributions of ethnic groups in the United States; sources of prejudice mechanisms and problems of group adjustment; contemporary status or principal minority groups; and proposals for reduction of intergroup tensions. (3 semester credits)

SPANISH

First Semester College Spanish

Teaches the fundamentals of Spanish, providing basic vocabulary, grammar and pronunciation, training in translation and elementary composition, and practical reading knowledge. Also introduces the student to Hispanic culture. (4 semester credits)

Second Semester College Spanish

Begins with a review of *First Semester Spanish* and continues to develop skills in reading, writing, and understanding Spanish. Also continues introducing the student to Spanish culture. (4 semester credits)

Third Semester Spanish

Provides a solid background at the intermediate level by further developing the student's skills in reading, writing, translating, and understanding Spanish. Includes a thorough grammar review; a study of key vocabulary, idioms, and constructions; and the reading of short stories. (4 semester credits)

Fourth Semester Spanish

A continuation of *Third Semester Spanish*. Grammar review; key vocabulary, idioms, and constructions; reading, writing, and translating. Includes the reading of a short novel that is organized much like a collection of short stories. (4 semester credits)

Elementary Survey of Spanish Literature, from the Twelfth to the Eighteenth Centuries

An introduction to the principal works, authors, and currents of Spanish literature from its beginnings in the Middle Ages through the eighteenth century, with emphasis on the *siglo de oro,* or Golden Age (sixteenth and seventeenth centuries). The readings—poetry, narrative prose, theater—consist chiefly of selections from the masterpieces rather than complete works. Includes brief introductions to the historical contexts in which the works were created. (3 semester credits)

Elementary Survey of Spanish Literature, Nineteenth and Twentieth Centuries

An introduction to the principle works, authors, and movements of Spanish literature of the nineteenth and twentieth centuries: Romanticism, *costumbrismo*, Realism and Naturalism, *modernismo* and the "Generation of 1898," early twentieth-century avant-garde movements, post-Civil War currents. Includes a brief introduction to fundamentals of literary criticism, plus relevant information about the historical contexts surrounding the works read. (3 semester credits)

Intermediate Composition

A third-year-level language course which reviews the fundamentals of Spanish grammar and emphasizes original composition. Develops students' usage of natural, everyday vocabulary and ability to express themselves in correct, idiomatic written Spanish. (3 semester credits)

Modern Spanish Readings

Novels short stories, essays, plays, and poetry by Spanish writers of the twentieth century. Emphasis on literary interpretation and appreciation, with some translations of key passages required. Introductions place authors in their historical and artistic contexts. (3 semester credits)

Advanced Composition

A comprehensive advanced grammar and composition course. Designed to give students (especially high school teachers) experience in expository writing in Spanish on a variety of interesting topics and high-level language mastery. Short reading passages by major contemporary Hispanic authors serve as expressions, grammar patterns, and stylistic models for the written work and as an in-depth language review. Two optional review units are included. (3 semester credits)

Miguel de Unamuno

Miguel de Unamuno, one of Spain's most celebrated essayists and novelists, has written prose works of extraordinary philosophical and esthetic interest. This course deals with Unamuno's personal philosophy and literary theories as they are developed in three of his major novels. (1 semester credit)

STATISTICS

Principles of Statistics

Introduces students with limited mathematical background to the key concepts of experimentation, inference from data sets, and decision making. Examines the main issues and methods of modern statistics and illustrates them by examples from the world around us. Stresses the importance of knowing the field in which statistical research is being done so that improper application of the raw data can be avoided. (3 semester credits)

SWEDISH

First Semester Swedish

For those who have not had previous instruction in Swedish. The course corresponds to the first semester of Swedish at the university level. Three cassette tapes are part of the required material. (4 semester credits)

Second Semester Swedish

This course is a continuation of *First Semester Swedish*. (4 semester credits)

WOMEN'S STUDIES

Women, Social Institutions, and Social Change

Investigates and analyzes women's position in contemporary U.S. society. Emphasizes the diversity of women's experiences, especially in regard to race and class, as well as similarities among women. The first part of the course explains the "gender systems" theoretical framework and illustrates how our understanding of the word *women* reflects basic patterns of social interaction. The second part examines the family and the economy—the two fundamental institutions in U.S. society that shape women's lives. The third part focuses on the feminist movement's efforts to change the prevailing American gender system. (3 semester credits)

Women and Their Bodies in Health and Disease (Elementary Level)

This course is offered for natural science credit and covers basic facts about the structure and functioning of the female body. Particular attention will be paid to adjustments the body makes during normal physiological events (menstruation, sexual and reproductive activity, menopause, exercise) and during disease processes. The effects of various drugs and environmental factors are described. The relationships between women, as both patients and practitioners, and the health care system are discussed. (3 semester credits)

HIGH SCHOOL COURSES

ART

Basic Drawing

Basic drawing exercises that deepen perception and concentration promote rapid development of drawing skills. Exercises from the text are based on research suggesting the right hemisphere of the brain facilitates drawing activity. Includes the fundamentals of line, space, proportion, and shading. (½ unit)

Art and Culture

A study of art within the everyday experience of people of all times and cultures. This course considers how to look at art, how to talk and write about art, and how to related the art form to the life of the artist. (½ unit)

Creative Design

Examines design as the language of all art. Units include the elements of line, plane, value, space, volume, color, and texture; the principles of contrast, balance, and unity; design as a tool for visual communication. (½ unit)

BIOLOGY

General Biology I

The first half of a survey course in general biology. Topics include investigating the life sciences; the importance of the cell; the chemicals of life; life, cells, and sex; plant reproduction; reproduction of life; chromosomes and heredity; and sex, genes, and chromosomes. (½ unit)

General Biology II

A continuation of General Biology I. The course deals with basic nutrition; digestion; transport systems in plants and animals; respiration, excretion, and locomotion; nervous systems of animals; chemical and behavioral controls; the changing forms of life; and life in its environment. (½ unit)

BUSINESS

General Business

Deals with today's business and economic worlds—how they function and how to use their services. Studies money management, banking, credit, savings and investments, and insurance. (½ unit)

Basic Bookkeeping for Business I

Equivalent to the first semester of high school bookkeeping, this course presents fundamental principles of bookkeeping and the accounting cycle with added emphasis on bookkeeping for the small business. (½ unit)

Basic Bookkeeping for Business II

A continuation of *Basic Bookkeeping for Business I*. Equivalent to the second semester of high school bookkeeping. Expands on principles taught in the above course and introduces work on data processing, payrolls, special journals, taxes and depreciation, and accruals. (½ unit)

Stocks, Bonds, and the Beginning Investor

Explains basic investment information including the importance of financial planning and the different types of investments; the advantages and risks of stocks and bonds and how and where they are bought and sold; how to evaluate financial yield; how to read market quotations in newspapers; and how to develop a personal financial plan. (½ unit)

ECONOMICS

Contemporary Economics

A general economics course designed to acquaint you with how the economy of the United States operates, to help him/her relate what is learned about economics in daily life, and to apply principles learned in the course to current economic issues communicated in the media. Topics include: introduction to economics; the role of the consumer; buying and saving; supply and demand; business organization; monopoly power; economics of the labor market; macroeconomics and the monetary system; government spending and taxes; the level of economic activity and the business cycle; stabilization policy; inflation; international trade and development; and alternative economics systems and political economy. (½ unit)

ENGLISH

Attack on Grammar

For high school students who wish to improve their writing skills by beginning at the most basic level: the grammar of the sentence. The course corresponds to one semester of ninth-, tenth-, eleventh-, or twelfth-grade English and may be taken at any time. (½ unit)

First Year High School English

Course H10. Parallels the kind of work usually given in the first semester of high school English. The aim of this course is to give students knowledge of basic paragraph structure, the ability to understand what they read, and experience in writing clear prose. (½ unit)

Course H11. Parallels the kind of work usually given in the second semester of ninth-grade English. Although it follows the above course, it is not dependent upon the first semester course; thus, anyone desiring a course based primarily on literature may enroll. Through the literature, the student studies composition. (½ unit)

Second Year High School English

Course H20. The assignments in this course focus on understanding literature and learning to write about it effectively. Study questions are provided to assist the student with reading the literature. The reading for the course is a novel and a play. (½ unit)

Course H21. Emphasizes composition and literature. The composition section of the course emphasizes the importance of organization through outlining and of revising the original draft. The reading for the course includes a novel, a play, and a few selections of poetry. (½ unit)

American Literature

Course H30. Parallels the kind of work usually given in the first semester of third- or fourth-year high school English. The course covers selections in American literature from colonial times through the nineteenth century. Both poetry and prose selections are studied. Each assignment includes background information about the life and times of the author being studies as well as selections from the author's works. (½ unit)

Course H31. This course deals essentially with literature (both prose and poetry) of the twentieth century. It may be taken as a sequel to the above course or independently. Each lesson includes background information about the life and times of authors studied, selections from their works, and written assignments. The course not only covers some of the major twentieth-century American authors, but offers a sampling of contemporary figures. (½ unit)

FRENCH

First Semester High School French

This course deals with the essentials of reading, writing, and speaking, with an emphasis on the practical. Vocabulary, idiomatic expressions, and grammatical principles of written and spoken French are presented by means of model conversations about everyday, real-life situations and are used actively by the student. (½ unit)

Second Semester High School French

Students are given the opportunity to develop their skills in reading, writing, and understanding French. (½ unit)

Third Semester High School French

This course is designed to give students a solid background in French at the intermediate level and to help them develop their skills in reading, writing, and understanding French. (½ unit)

Fourth Semester High School French

A continuation of *Third Semester High School French.* (½ unit)

Fifth Semester High School French

This course is designed for students who have completed two years of high school French. It focuses primarily on reading and writing French and includes a thorough grammar review. (½ unit)

Sixth Semester High School French

A continuation of *Fifth Semester High School French.* (½ unit)

Seventh Semester High School French

Designed for students who have completed three years of high school French. The course includes readings on current topics and everyday life in France, a thorough grammar review, active use of essential grammatical structures, vocabulary and idioms, and reading selections from notable French authors. (½ unit)

Eighth Semester High School French

A continuation of *Seventh Semester High School French.* (½ unit)

Introduction to French Literature, Seventeenth- and Eighteenth-Century Authors

This is an introductory study of the literature of France's "classical" period and the Age of Enlightenment, with a brief introduction to that of the Middle Ages and the Renaissance. Literary works—primarily plays, poetry, and essays—are examined within their historical context, and the student is introduced to the fundamentals of literary criticism. (1 unit)

Introduction to French Literature, Nineteenth-Century Authors

This course is an introduction to the principal authors of nineteenth-century France through the examination of representative poems, novels, plays, and other writings. The student is introduced to the basic techniques of literary criticism as a means of appreciating the works studied. (1 unit)

Intermediate Composition: A Workbook in Creative Writing

This course emphasizes writing creatively in French. The student refines grammatical knowledge, enlarges active vocabulary, and concentrates on sound French sentence patterns. (1 unit)

GEOGRAPHY

Physical Geography I

The purpose of this course is to introduce physical landscapes and to learn why places look the way they do. The course stresses the connected nature of plants, animals, soils, and landforms in the landscape. Topics covered include: the distribution of heat, pressure, wind, and precipitation and how these features unite to form world climatic patterns; the distribution of water around the world; and the factors that influence the distribution of plants and animals. It also outlines the biological regions of the world. (½ unit)

Physical Geography II

This is the second semester of a beginning physical geography course. The purpose of the course is to introduce physical landscapes and to explain why places look the way they do. The course stresses the connected nature of plants, animals, soils, and landforms in the landscape. This course emphasizes soils and landforms and discusses the following topics: internal forces of plate tectonics; volcanism; folding and faulting, which build up the landscape; the external forces of weathering, mass wasting, water and wind erosion, and glaciation, which wear down the landscape; and the distinctive landscapes that are created when these geomorphological agents work together. (½ unit)

GERMAN

First Semester High School German

This course deals with the fundamentals of German grammar, syntax, and pronunciation. (½ unit)

Second Semester High School German

This course is a continuation of *First Semester High School German* and further develops the study of the fundamentals of German. (½ unit)

Third Semester High School German

This course develops skill in reading German texts of moderate difficulty and emphasizes acquisition of vocabulary and familiarity with common idioms. (½ unit)

Fourth Semester High School German

This course is a continuation of *Third Semester High School German* and further develops reading skill and acquisition of vocabulary. (½ unit)

Fifth Semester High School German

The objectives of this course are to further expand vocabulary and to provide additional practice in reading German prose of moderate but increasing difficulty. (½ unit)

Sixth Semester High School German

A continuation of *Fifth Semester High School German.* (½ unit)

Introduction to German Literature I

Short stories by masters of the German Novelle with emphasis on literary matters as language difficulty diminishes. (1 unit)

Introduction to German Literature II

A continuation of Introduction to German Literature I, with readings expanded to include drama as well as prose. (1 unit)

Intermediate Composition, First Semester

A systematic review of grammar, intended for students wishing to acquire greater facility in expressing themselves in German. (1 unit)

HEALTH

Personal and Family Health

This course is designed to help you discover ways to promote your own health and that of your family. The course stresses maternal and child care, since the foundation for a healthy adult life begins before birth and is dependent upon a healthy childhood. Other key topics include mental and physical health, substance abuse, AIDS, and other sexually transmitted diseases, and first aid. (½ unit)

HISTORY

History of the United States to 1877

This course begins with the age of discovery and the rivalry of European powers for domination of the New World. The course traces the development of the United States as a democratic nation and the evolution of an American life-style. The course is built on a chronological framework and stresses critical thinking rather than factual content. It aims to develop the student's self-confidence in dealing with historical materials along with an understanding and appreciation of the American heritage. (½ unit)

History of the United States - 1877 to Present

The course explores the history of the United States from 1877, the end of Reconstruction, to the present. It stresses the historical background of current social and economic problems as well as political events, thus providing opportunities for students to develop their own positions on controversial issues. The emphasis is on development of skills in critical thinking, weighing of evidence, thoughtful analysis in dealing with such topics as the quest for social justice, labor-management relations, the role of the United States in world affairs. (½ unit)

LATIN

First Semester High School Latin

The course deals with the essentials of reading and writing, with some attention given to pronunciation. (½ unit)

Second Semester High School Latin

Continues and enlarges upon the fundamentals of Latin grammar and vocabulary begun in First Semester High School Latin. (½ unit)

Third Semester High School Latin

New vocabulary and points of grammar (including the subjunctive) advance the students' understanding of Latin. (½ unit)

Fourth Semester High School Latin

This course offers the student the opportunity to read Latin authors of prose and poetry, including Caesar, Pliny, Ovid, and Vergil. (½ unit)

MATHEMATICS

First Semester Algebra

Numbers, sets, and operations; linear equations and problem solving; polynomials; factoring. (½ unit)

Second Semester Algebra

Fractions and fractional equations; linear inequalities; functions, relations, and graphs; systems of linear equations; problem solving; irrational numbers and radical expressions; variation; quadratic functions and equations. (½ unit)

Geometry I

The first semester of a modern one-year course in elementary geometry. Points, lines, and planes; angles and triangles; congruences; direct and indirect proof; geometric inequalities; perpendicular lines and planes; parallel lines and planes; quadrilaterals. (½ unit)

Geometry II

The second semester of a modern one-year course in elementary geometry. Areas; Pythagorean theorem; similarity and proportion; introductory coordinate geometry; circles, spheres, secants, tangents; characterization theorems, concurrence, constructions; circumference and area of a circle; arc length and areas of sectors; volumes of prisms, pyramids, cylinders, cones, and spheres. (½ unit)

Advanced Algebra I

Topics include a review of first-year algebra, operations with rational numbers and polynomials, linear equations and inequalities, sets, problem solving, factoring, operations with algebraic fractions, integral and rational exponents. (½ unit)

Advanced Algebra II

A continuation of Advanced Algebra I. Topics include operations with radical expressions; definition and operations with complex numbers; quadratic equations and inequalities; radical equations; systems of linear equations and inequalities; problem solving; 2-by-2 determinants; relations, functions, and graphs; linear and polynomial functions; composite and inverse functions; and exponential functions. (½ unit)

College Algebra

Gives the equivalent of advanced mathematical competence—algebra. An audiotape accompanies each assignment. (½ unit)

Trigonometry

Gives the equivalent of advanced mathematical competence—trigonometry. Starts with a discussion of some relevant concepts from algebra and geometry, then uses right triangles to develop the trigonometric functions of an acute angle. Contains many applications in photography, architecture, biology, archaeology, astronomy, physics, engineering, and music, with much attention to the relationship between math and the real world. (½ unit)

METEOROLOGY

Weather and Climate

This is a descriptive course with emphasis on fundamental concepts related to cloud formation, pressure systems and fronts, jet streams, severe storms, rainmaking, and forecasting. It discusses the various weather systems affecting the United States and the atmospheric processes producing them. (1 unit)

MUSIC

Beginning Music Theory I

This course is an introduction to the written and aural aspects of music theory, especially designed to proceed developmentally and sequentially to carefully study beginning music theory. The written assignments cover properties and notations of sounds; enharmonics; interval study of major and minor seconds, thirds, sixths, and sevenths; perfect, augmented, and diminished intervals; the tritone; major scales; natural, relative, and parallel minor scales; and triads. The aural assignments on the audiotapes develop skills to aurally recognize major and minor seconds, thirds, sixths, and sevenths; perfect, augmented, and diminished fourths, fifths, and octaves; major scales, natural, harmonic, and melodic minor scales; duple and triple meter; and tempi. (1 unit)

Beginning Music Theory II

The written assignments consider simple, duple, triple, quadruple, and compound meters; syncopation; the hemiola; phrases; various cadences; anacrusis in melodic patterns; conjunct and disjunct motion; melodic sequence; triads and their inversions; triads and chords in succession; circle of fifths; nonharmonic tones; seventh chords; harmonizing melodies; harmonizations using I, ii, ii7, IV, V, V7 chords. The aural assignments on the tape recordings develop skills to aurally recognize meters, rhythmic patterns, the anacrusis, various cadences, major and minor triads, and chords in a series of progressions. (1 unit)

POLISH

Reading Polish I

This course offers practice in writing the language and teaches Polish pronunciation and basic conversation. (1 unit)

Reading Polish II

This course is a continuation of *Reading Polish I* and gives additional practice in reading, writing, and translating Polish. (1 unit)

POLITICAL SCIENCE

American Government Today

A basic course in local, state, and national government showing how the government works and what it does. Much of the emphasis is on how government affects the lives of individuals. Students will be given an introduction to government structure, taxes, voting, and their basic rights as American citizens. (½ unit)

RUSSIAN

First Semester High School Russian

The course offers an elementary foundation in reading, writing, and pronunciation. (½ unit)

Second Semester High School Russian

The basic grammar and vocabulary begun in *First Semester High School Russian* are continued and enlarged upon in this course. Additional emphasis is placed on translating idiomatically from Russian into English and English into Russian. (½ unit)

Third Semester High School Russian

New points of grammar and idiomatic expressions, fresh vocabulary, and familiar forms combine to round out students' understanding of the language and their ability to express themselves in the Russian language. (½ unit)

Fourth Semester High School Russian

Upon completion of this course, the student will have studied all of the basic Russian grammar and should be prepared to continue with advanced Russian reading and writing. (½ unit)

Fifth Semester High School Russian

This course reviews basic Russian grammar, builds vocabulary, and gives the student practice in reading, translating, and writing original compositions in Russian. (½ unit)

Sixth Semester High School Russian

A continuation of Fifth Semester High School Russian, with similar course work. In addition, the student will do more advanced reading and writing on several of the arts and sciences. (½ unit)

Seventh Semester High School Russian

Designed to increase the ability to comprehend, read, and write in Russian. Practice making accurate translations into English is provided. (½ unit)

Eighth Semester High School Russian

A continuation of Seventh Semester High School Russian. (½ unit)

Russian for Reading Knowledge

Recommended for high school seniors who want to learn a language in less than one year. The course covers basic Russian grammar and vocabulary and teaches the student to read and translate in both the humanities and sciences. (2 units)

Beginning Conversation and Composition in Russian

Gives practice in Russian composition, conversation, and pronunciation. Student must have access to a cassette tape recorder. (1 unit)

SOCIAL STUDIES

Quest for Equality: A Look at the American Women's Movement

The student will review the major feminist issues and their origins in the American quest for equal opportunity for all, through the nineteenth-century women's movement, to contemporary feminism. The Study Guide provides the framework for understanding such matters as legal rights, economic status, political status, education, marriage, and male/female relationships. The essays and memoirs of such notables as Abigail Adams, Susan B. Anthony, Lucy Stone, Elizabeth Cady Stanton, Margaret Sanger, Virginia Woolf, Sheila Tobias, Myra and David Sadker, and Betty Friedan illustrate the issues. (½ unit)

SPANISH

First Semester High School Spanish

Teaches the fundamentals of Spanish, providing basic vocabulary, grammar and pronunciation, training in translation and elementary composition, and practical reading knowledge. Also introduces the student to Hispanic culture. (½ unit)

Second Semester High School Spanish

A continuation of the preceding course. (½ unit)

Third Semester High School Spanish

Begins with a review of first and second semester high school Spanish and continues to develop skills in reading, writing, and understanding Spanish. (½ unit)

Fourth Semester High School Spanish

A continuation of the preceding course. (½ unit)

Fifth Semester High School Spanish

Provides a solid background at the intermediate level by further developing the student's skills in reading, writing, translating, and understanding Spanish. Includes a thorough grammar review; a study of key vocabulary words, idioms, and constructions; and the reading of short stories. (½ unit)

Sixth Semester High School Spanish

A continuation of the preceding course. (½ unit)

Seventh Semester High School Spanish

A continuation of Sixth Semester High School Spanish and designed for students who have completed three years of high school Spanish. The course continues to provide a solid background at the intermediate level by completing the thorough grammar review begun in Fifth Semester High School Spanish. (½ unit)

Eighth Semester High School Spanish

A continuation of Seventh Semester High School Spanish and completion of the fourth year of high school Spanish. This course is entirely devoted to the reading of a short novel that is organized much like a collection of short stories. (½ unit)

Elementary Survey of Spanish Literature

An introduction to the literary movements, principal writers, and representative works of the nineteenth and twentieth centuries. (1 unit)

STUDY SKILLS

Power Reading

Offers practical instruction designed to help increase reading speed, comprehension, and retention. The course guide outlines skills and techniques, including word analysis, prereading and pacing, skimming and scanning, memorization and note taking, drawing conclusions, reading for bias, and the five-step SARME method of journal and text analysis. (½ unit)

NONCREDIT COURSES

AGRICULTURAL ECONOMICS

Cooperatives

A basic course in cooperative organization, development, principles, management, financing, and operations. The course is designed especially for students, employees, and leaders of cooperatives desiring a general overview of cooperative enterprises. (6.6 CEUs) *Tuition:* $65.

ART

Basic Drawing

Basic drawing exercises that deepen perception and concentration promote rapid development of drawing skills. Exercises from the text are based on research suggesting the right hemisphere of the brain facilitates drawing activity. Includes the fundamentals of line, space, proportion, and shading. (6 CEUs) *Tuition:* $68.

Self-Directed Painting or Drawing

Designed for the part-time artist or anyone seriously interested in aquiring further experience in an artistic medium already familiar to them. Under the guidance of an experienced faculty member, and based on previously completed work, The student plans a direction for improvement of special areas such as drawing skills, color, painting techniques, composition, portrait, landscape. (3 CEUs) *Tuition:* $55.

ART HISTORY

Art and Culture

A study of art within the everyday experience of peoples of all times and cultures. This course considers how to look at art, how to talk and write about art, and how to related the art form to the life of the artist. (6 CEUs) *Tuition:* $68.

ASTRONOMY

The Solar System

An overview and historical background of astronomy, including electromagnetic radiation, astronomical observation, the earth, the moon, the other planets and their moons and rings, solar system debris, and the sun. (10 CEUs) *Tuition:* $140.

Stars and Galaxies

Surveying nearby stars, analyzing starlight, binary stars, relativity, stellar energy generation and evolution, late stages of evolution (red giants, white dwarfs, supernovas, pulsars, black holes), the Milky Way, and other galaxies, quasars, the expanding universe, and the big bang. (10 CEUs) *Tuition:* $140.

BOTANY

EcoSploring

An introduction to forest ecology using student-identified outdoor laboratories. Seven ecological principles are explored through reading, observation, and simple measurements in real forest settings. Principles are: introduction to the ecosystem, the environment, energy flow, nutrient cycling, ecosystem change, relationships between organisms, humans in the ecosystem. (Course must be done while leaves are on trees.) (4.8 CEUs) *Tuition:* $30.

BUSINESS

Basic Bookkeeping for Business I

Presents basic principles and procedures for accounting common to all businesses. Explains how business transactions are recorded and how records are used to make financial reports. Correct interpretation of these reports provides the information needed for successful operation of the business. Emphasis is given to bookkeeping for small businesses. (8 CEUs) *Tuition:* $60.

Basic Bookkeeping for Business II

An expanded and in-depth study of principles learned in the above course. (8 CEUs) *Tuition:* $60.

Elementary Accounting I

(14 CEUs) *Tuition:* $75.

Elementary Accounting II

A continuation of the above course. (14 CEUs) *Tuition:* $75.

Managerial Accounting

(14 CEUs) *Tuition:* $100.

Intermediate Accounting I

(14 CEUs) *Tuition:* $100.

Intermediate Accounting II

(14 CEUs) *Tuition:* $100.

Cost Accounting I

(14 CEUs) *Tuition:* $100.

Budgets and Budgetary Control

(14 CEUs) *Tuition:* $100.

Governmental Accounting

(14 CEUs) *Tuition:* $100.

Advanced Cost Accounting

(14 CEUs) *Tuition:* $100.

Stocks, Bonds, and the Beginning Investor

Six half-hour taped discussions explore what successful investment is all about and different types of investments, as: money market funds, stocks, bonds, treasury notes; how they are bought and sold; their advantages and risks; returns on investments; and the importance of your financial planning. Explains Wall Street's unfamiliar terms and how to read the financial pages. (6 CEUs) *Tuition:* $60.

Principles of Finance

(14 CEUs) *Tuition:* $75.

Investments

(14 CEUs) *Tuition:* $75.

Consumer Education and Personal Finance

(14 CEUs) *Tuition:* $75.

Managerial Finance

(14 CEUs) *Tuition:* $75.

Business Law

Law of contracts, agency, negotiable instruments, sales, partnerships, corporations, secured transactions, suretyship, accountant's legal liability, personal property, bailments and documents of title, real estate, wills, trusts, and insurance. (14 CEUs) *Tuition:* $75.

Introduction to the American Business Enterprise

(14 CEUs) *Tuition:* $75.

Microcomputer Applications

(14 CEUs) *Tuition:* $75.

Introduction to Management Information Systems

(14 CEUs) *Tuition:* $75.

Organization and Management

(14 CEUs) *Tuition:* $75.

Production Concepts

(14 CEUs) *Tuition:* $75.

Compensation Management

(14 CEUs) *Tuition:* $75.

Retailing

(14 CEUs) *Tuition:* $75.

Personnel Management

(14 CEUs) *Tuition:* $75.

Gender Issues in Management

(14 CEUs) *Tuition:* $75.

Organizational Behavior

(14 CEUs) *Tuition:* $75.

Business Communications

(14 CEUs) *Tuition:* $75.

Managing the Small Business

(14 CEUs) *Tuition:* $75.

Labor-Management Relations

(14 CEUs) *Tuition:* $75.

Purchasing and Materials Management

(14 CEUs) *Tuition:* $75.

International Business

(14 CEUs) *Tuition:* $75.

Administrative Policy

(14 CEUs) *Tuition:* $75.

Introduction to Service Management

Management development course designed to provide awareness and understanding of the techniques need and responsibilities important to the job of service supervisor, technical supervisor, or manager. Emphasis is on management practices, supervision, planning or service operations and budgeting of revenue and expenses for service activities. (4 CEUs) *Tuition:* $75.

Leadership and Supervision in Service Management

Helps service managers develop the leadership and supervisory skills needed to function effectively as people managers in the 1990s. Included are assignments on the supervisory responsibilities of the service manager, the transitions that new managers make, how to communicate more effectively, how to control performance through appraisal, how to build an effective team, motivation, and training. (5 or 7 CEUs) *Tuition:* $75.

Manufacturing Systems—Material and Capacity Requirement Planning

Identifies the functions of material requirements planning (MRP) and capacity requirements planning (CRP) with emphasis placed on the respective roles each of these applications play within the structure of a formalized manufacturing system. Required inputs and outputs of each application are presented as are the mechanics essential to the successful operation of MRP and CRP. (12 CEUs) *Tuition:* $75.

Management-Minded Supervision

For new, experienced, or potential supervisors. Course provides insight and understanding of the nature of supervision and the supervisor's responsibilities including motivating; communicating; training and organizing work; delegation; problem solving and decision making; and improving productivity. (14 CEUs) *Tuition:* $65.

Principles of Marketing

(14 CEUs) *Tuition:* $75.

Marketing in Service Organizations

(14 CEUs) *Tuition:* $75.

C.P.M. Review: A Correspondence Study Course for the C.P.M. Examination

Designed for individuals preparing to take the Certified Purchasing Manager's Examination. Emphasis is on providing specific subject matter information for passing the examination. The course is made up of four separate modules that can be obtained individually for $50 each. Two certification points will be awarded for successful completion of each module. (12 CEUs) *Tuition:* $175.

Dust Control Services

Helps people most directly involved in dust control services to better understand their services, their customers, their products, and their selling practices. (14 CEUs) *Tuition:* $50.

Deciding Whether to Start Your Own Business

A service-oriented course will guide those with a potential business idea through the process one needs to go through when deciding whether or not one is emotionally, professionally, and financially prepared to start a business. Students develop a plan that explores and includes one's goals and objectives, personal characteristics, knowledge, and background; a brief market analysis and identification of financial needs; and the legal structure of the prospective business. (6 CEUs) *Tuition:* $60.

Apparel Rental Services

Designed to develop your understanding of the scope of marketing in an apparel rental setting. Discover the threats and opportunities that affect rental services and then develop marketing strategies to address those factors. Strategy lessons cover issues such as choosing target customers, providing services, setting prices, creating efficient distribution, and promoting the company. (14 CEUs) *Tuition:* $50.

Managing Information and Records for Small Business

Designed for the individual currently involved with or planning to develop a systematic record-keeping system for a small business. The course focuses on why records are needed, how to create record-keeping systems, management of records, accounting systems for the small business, and microcomputers for records management. (5 CEUs) *Tuition:* $60.

COMPUTER SCIENCE

Introduction to AutoLISP Programming

Explains how to customize AutoCAD, turning the general purpose design package into an even more powerful tool for your particular needs. Designed for experienced users of AutoCAD, the course does not require prior knowledge of programming. (4 CEUs) *Tuition:* $275.

Advanced AutoLISP Programming

Designed for experienced users of AutoCAD, this course requires that you know AutoLISP programming through looping and branching functions. When you have completed the course, you will be able to delve into the AutoCAD objects for a variety of applications. (5 CEUs) *Tuition:* $275.

DISASTER MANAGEMENT

Aim and Scope of Disaster Management

A basic DMC course that defines the scope and objectives of the field of disaster management, looks at concepts and terms, differentiates between natural disaster assistance and refugee operations, examines tools and methods, and looks at some technology appropriate to the field. **This course and the following courses are available in Spanish language versions.** (2 CEUs) *Tuition:* $60.

Principles of Management

This course provides an overview of management from a disaster and emergency standpoint looking at issues such as program planning, decision making, information management, program supervision, monitoring and control, personnel, and leadership. It also examines issues such as motivation, group dynamics, managing work groups, structure and organization, and criteria for addressing a program. (3.5 CEUs) *Tuition:* $70.

Natural Hazards: Causes and Effects

This course examines in detail the physical characteristics, geographic distribution, impact, response, and mitigation of natural hazards such as earthquakes, tsunamis, volcanoes, tropical cyclones, floods, drought, desertification, and deforestation. (3 CEUs) *Tuition:* $70.

Disaster Preparedness

A look at the prerequisites for preparedness planning, action plans and procedures, training issues and models, preparedness roles and responsibilities, public awareness and warnings, as well as providing preparedness action plans and checklists. (2.5 CEUs) *Tuition:* $60.

Damage and Needs Assessment

An examination of common approaches to disaster assessment and looks at assessment teams, survey methods, tools, and techniques. The course covers procedures for handling emergency supplies and services, housing, agriculture, lifelines, and droughts and famines, including the establishment of surveillance systems after a disaster. (3 CEUs) *Tuition:* $70.

Disaster Response

A look at disaster response planning, roles and responsibilities, initial emergency operations, emergency operations by sector, emergency operations support and management, plus recovery and rehabilitation. (3 CEUs) *Tuition:* $70.

Environmental Health Management after Natural Disaster

A look at the effects of natural disasters on environmental health. It examines factors to consider for effective management, looks at pre-disaster health measures, measures to be taken during the disaster and in the aftermath, and rehabilitation measures. (2 CEUs) *Tuition:* $60.

Health Services Organization in the Event of Disaster

A look at the organization of first-level care at the disaster site, rural healthy services for disaster situations, the implementation of a disaster plan in a health care facility, and methods of updating and evaluating hospital disaster management plans. (2 CEUs) *Tuition:* $60.

Emergency Health Management After Natural Disasters

An overview of the effects of disaster on health and an examination of the issues in disaster preparedness, coordination of national relief activities, the management of mass casualties, and epidemiologic surveillance and disease control. Topics such as food and nutrition, temporary settlements, communications and transport, management of health relief supplies, management of international relief assistance, and the re-establishment of normal programs are also covered. (2.5 CEUs) *Tuition:* $65.

Epidemiologic Surveillance After Natural Disaster

An overview of risk factors for communicable diseases after disasters, a look at post-disaster potential for communicable disease epidemics, and an examination of methods for setting up systems for the surveillance of communicable and selected noncommunicable diseases. The operational aspects of the control of communicable diseases after disasters are also covered. (2 CEUs) *Tuition:* $60.

Emergency Vector Control After Natural Disaster

A look at three broad areas: disaster preparedness, control measures for specific vectors, general control actions. The course examines issues such as contingency plans, vector- and rodent-related diseases, program management, pesticides and pesticide application, surveillance, and evaluation. (2.5 CEUs) *Tuition:* $65.

ECONOMICS

Introduction to Economics

(16 CEUs) *Tuition:* $115.

Principles of Macroeconomics

(14 CEUs) *Tuition:* $75.

Principles of Microeconomics

(14 CEUs) *Tuition:* $75.

Interpretation of Business and Economic Data

(14 CEUs) *Tuition:* $75.

International Economics

(14 CEUs) *Tuition:* $75.

International Business

(14 CEUs) *Tuition:* $75.

EDUCATION

Introduction to Child Care in a Family Day Care Setting

Designed for family day care providers. Topics include normal child growth and development, child-provider relationships, health and safety, nutrition, and caring for a child. (2.4 CEUs) *Tuition:* $16.

Family Day Care as a Profession

Designed for family day care providers. Topics include introduction to family day care, family day care as a profession, and child care in the wider community. (2.4 CEUs) *Tuition:* $16.

ENGINEERING

Solid Waste Landfills

Presents, in depth, the design, plan, operation, closure, and longer-term care of landfills. Topics include gas movement, leachate control and treatment, site evaluation, and hazardous and special waste disposal. (2 CEUs) *Tuition:* $100.

Solid Waste Recycling

Opportunities for recycling and the steps necessary to develop a successful recycling program are presented in this course. Topics include recycling approaches, alternative technologies for recycling, marketing recycled materials, planning a community recycling program, implementing a mandatory recycling program, developing a recycling center, and operating a commercial recycling service. (2 CEUs) *Tuition:* $100.

Waste Composting

Modern approaches to the composting of waste materials are presented in this course. Topics include scientific principles of waste composting, composting of municipal solid waste and yard waste, developing a composting project, operating a successful facility, and markets for compost. (2 CEUs) *Tuition:* $100.

Waste to Energy

Modern approaches to converting waste materials to energy are presented in this course. Topics include energy production and marketing, air quality protection, residuals management, siting, contractual agreements and financing, and system start-up and operation. (2 CEUs) *Tuition:* $100

Collecting and Transporting Recyclables and Solid Waste

Describes the principles and methods of developing an effective and efficient system for collecting recyclables and solid wastes to meet the increasing pressure on haulers and municipalities to handle more materials in more ways without increasing costs. This self-study course consists of ten self-graded assignments and two university-graded exams. (2 CEUs) *Tuition:* $100.

Concrete Structures

Reinforced concrete design emphasizing a practical approach based on the current 1983 ACI Code. Includes most aspects of the design of beams and columns except the torsion problem for beams and biaxial bending for columns. One-way slabs are also included. (14.4 CEUs) *Tuition:* $295.

Photogrammetry

Basics in aerial photogrammetry with emphasis on computational aspects, the photographic process, image distortions, vertical photographs, scale, relief displacement, tilted photographs and rectification, stereoscopic viewing, stereoscopic parallax, heights of objects from relief displacement and parallax, stereoscopic plotting instruments, introductory photo interpretation, and remote sensing. (14.4 CEUs) *Tuition:* $240.

Basic Engineering Refresher

Designed to help prepare you for the FE (Fundamentals of Engineering) examination, the first of two examinations leading to registration as a professional engineer. All states use this exam. The lessons review concepts in mathematics, economics, thermodynamics, power, and refrigeration, fluids and hydraulics, chemistry, electricity, materials, mechanics of materials, statics, and dynamics. (10 CEUs) *Tuition:* $240.

An Introduction to Value Analysis and Value Engineering for Architects, Engineers, and Builders

Applies value analysis to construction projects. Tools and techniques of value analysis are presented as well as its role within an organization. (15 CEUs) *Tuition:* $750.

Storm and Sanitary Sewer Design

Covers the basic topics essential to good sewer design including administration, investigation, methods of determining storm water and sanitary sewage quantities, sewer hydraulics, system design, materials, and structural requirements for underground construction. (10 CEUs) *Tuition:* $200.

An Introduction to Value Analysis and Engineering for Industries, Services, and Governmental Agencies

Value analysis is applied to manufactured products. Value analysis is a system devised and developed to eliminate unnecessary costs. Tools and techniques of value analysis are presented as well as its role within an organization. (15 CEUs) *Tuition:* $750.

Operations Decisions in a Production Enterprise

The course provides practical experience in making management decisions at a production company and begins when you receive your own simulated company. As the head of your company, you make all decisions related to production, research and development, transportation, investment, and marketing. (10 CEUs) *Tuition:* $240.

ENGLISH

Attack on Grammar

A course for students of all ages and professions who wish to improve their writing skills by beginning at the most basic level—the grammar of the sentence. (4 CEUs) *Tuition:* $55.

Effective Business English

A course designed for those who wish to polish their skills in writing the most common types of business correspondence: letters, memos, summaries, and reports. (4 CEUs) *Tuition:* $55.

Advanced Creative Writer's Workshop

The heart of this course is response: an instructor's thoughtful, professional comments on one's novel, poetry, short stories, or other creative work in progress. The student may submit for critique a total of 30 pages of prose or 30 pages of poetry, either new or revised material. (9 CEUs) *Tuition:* $65.

Vocabulary Building

Students can expand their working vocabulary by examining prefixes, suffixes, and roots as well as idioms, sources of new words, and easily confused words. (4 CEUs) *Tuition:* $55.

Fundamentals of Manuscript Editing

An introduction to the process of editing that covers problems from initial preparation of copy to correcting proof. The course is designed to be useful to anyone who needs to know the standard procedures and objectives of editing, including clarity, correctness, and consistency of style. Writers, high school teachers, and administrators responsible for publications, those who seek employment as editors, and anyone preparing for civil service examinations in editing will be guided by experienced instructors through the fundamentals of copy preparation and editing. The course emphasizes manuscript editing rather than production and design. (4 CEUs) *Tuition:* $55.

Writing the Nonfiction Book

A course that guides and encourages writers through all phases of producing nonfiction books: getting ideas, researching and planning, writing, and marketing. (13 CEUs) *Tuition:* $95.

Introduction to Composition

Students will explore the fundamentals of composition by reading and composing essays on controversial subjects. The course offers practice with constructing sound arguments and using secondary sources. (9 CEUs) *Tuition:* $65.

Intermediate Composition

Recommended to those interested in improving their writing skills. Students will use model essays to suggest strategies for various types of essay writing and will have the opportunity to select their own topics. (9 CEUs) *Tuition:* $65.

Creative Writing: The Short Story

Students will explore the essentials of fiction writing and receive feedback on their work. (9 CEUs) *Tuition:* $65.

Creative Writing: Poetry

This course guides students through writing, revising, and publishing poetry. (9 CEUs) *Tuition:* $65.

Introduction to Modern English and American Literature I: The Nineteenth Century

The course guide includes a poetry anthology (Blake, Wordsworth, Keats, Whitman, Dickinson, Browning) and a glossary of literary forms. (12 CEUs) *Tuition:* $65.

Introduction to Modern English and American Literature II: The Twentieth Century

(12 CEUs) *Tuition:* $65.

The Courage to Write: Women Novelists of the Nineteenth Century

(12 CEUs) *Tuition:* $48.

FRENCH

French for Reading Knowledge: Beginning Level

This course gives students a reading knowldege of French. It covers essential French grammar and structure and teaches students to read and and translate various texts in the humanities and sciences. It is especially useful for students preparing for the French graduate-level reading knowledge requirement. (10 CEUs) *Tuition:* $48.

French for Reading Knowledge: Intermediate Level

This is an intermediate translation course for those students who have already acquired the basics of French grammar, sentence structure, tenses, and idioms. Emphasis is upon reading various texts in the sciences and humanities to prepare students for graduate-level reading knowledge examinations or for personal enrichment. (15 CEUs) *Tuition:* $50.

Directed Reading and Translation Course

This is an individualized course designed to give the student experience in reading and translating French texts of special interest to him/her. The texts may be selected by the student with the help of the instructor, in various fields of interest such as literature, the sciences, or law. This course also provides help for individuals who, in their field of specialization, have to read French material for their research or professional development. (10 CEUs) *Tuition:* $60.

French Review

An intensive review of French to help you brush up on your reading, writing, and comprehension skills, as well as to enhance your knowledge of the French language and culture. (10 CEUs) *Tuition:* $55.

Business French

This course is especially useful for individuals who need to expand their knowledge of French economy and business for professional or personal enrichment. (20 CEUs) *Tuition:* $70.

GENEALOGY

Introduction to Genealogical Research

Provides a solid research background in the sources and techniques used in tracing ones's family tree. Consists of a series of lessons combining readings from the texts, additional introductory material, and a series of study recommendations. The student will be expected to take three research trips (one to a country courthouse, one to a public or research library, and another to a church/cemetery) and submit a brief written report on each. The student will also be required to produce a substantial example of his or her genealogical research using the sources and techniques covered in the lessons. (10 CEUs) *Tuition:* $40.

GERMAN

A Foundation Course in Reading German

For those with no previous instruction in German who wish to gain quickly a reading knowledge of the language. Much of the grammar is ignored, but complex constructions are stressed. Especially useful to graduate students preparing for the German requirement for the Ph.D. degree. (10 CEUs) *Tuition:* $48.

Business German

This course is designed to familiarize students with the form and specialized vocabulary of business letters used in export and import. (6 CEUs) *Tuition:* $45.

HORSE SCIENCE

Elementary Horse Science

This course is designed to provide background information for persons interested in the equine field. The material will be of help to the future horse owner as well as to the person having considerable experience with horses. It covers topics such as horse selection, health, feeding, blemishes, unsoundness, breeding, and management, and gives instruction on equitation and the choice of riding equipment. (6 CEUs) *Tuition:* $40.

ITALIAN

Italian for Reading Knowledge

Intended for students with no previous training in Italian who wish to acquire rapidly a thorough reading knowledge of the language. May also serve as a rapid review of Italian grammar and verbs, for reading purposes. Readings are primarily in the form of thought-provoking quotations from Italian writers in various fields. Especially useful for graduate-level reading knowledge examination. (10 CEUs) *Tuition:* $60.

JOURNALISM

Writing for Fun and Profit

A practical course for beginning writers which explores 12 specific article fields. (9.6 CEUs) *Tuition:* $85.

Power Reading

Offers practical instruction designed to help increase reading speed, comprehension, and retention. (5 CEUs) *Tuition:* $65.

Writing Your Life Stories

Designed to help the student recall the stories of his/her life and write about them. (10 CEUs) *Tuition:* $80.

MATHEMATICS

Numbers and Basic Operations

Rational number operations; sums, products, and quotients of monomials and polynomials. (3.8 CEUs) *Tuition:* $34.

Factoring, Fractions, and Exponents

Basic product-factoring identities, operations with algebraic fractions, integral and rational exponents. (3.8 CEUs) *Tuition:* $34.

Linear Equations and Inequalities

First-degree equations and inequalities in one variable, fractional equations, problem-solving using equations and inequalities. (3.8 CEUs) *Tuition:* $34.

Radicals, Complex Numbers, and Quadratics

Operations with radical expressions, operations with complex numbers, solution of quadratic equations and inequalities in one variable, radical equations. (3.8 CEUs) *Tuition:* $34.

Graphs and Systems of Equations

Plane graphs, solutions of linear systems by addition and substitution, dependent and inconsistent systems, systems of linear inequalities, verbal problems. (3.8 CEUs) *Tuition:* $34.

Functions

Functions and graphs, linear functions, mathematical induction, infinite arithmetic, and geometric sequences. (3.8 CEUs) *Tuition:* $34.

Sets and Sequences

Logic, sets, sequences, algorithms and pseudocode, integer division. (4.8 CEUs) *Tuition:* $42.

Matrices and Graphs

Matrices, relations, partitions, computer representation of digraphs. (4.8 CEUs) *Tuition:* $42.

Functions and Order Structures

Functions, partially ordered sets, trees. (4.8 CEUs) *Tuition:* $42.

Differentiation

Analytic geometry, functions, differentiation, chain rule. (4.8 CEUs) *Tuition:* $42.

Applications of Differentiation

Limits and continuity, increments, Newton's method, mean value theorem, curve tracing, maximum and minimum problems, related rates. (4.8 CEUs) *Tuition:* $42.

Basic Integration

Antidifferentiation, definite integrals, the fundamentals theorem, approximate integration. (4.8 CEUs) *Tuition:* $42.

Applications of Integration

Area, distance, volumes, arc length, surfaces of revolution, averages, moments and centroids, work. (4.8 CEUs) *Tuition:* $42.

Transcendental Functions

Trigonometric and inverse trigonometric functions, logarithmic and exponential functions, indeterminate forms and l'Hôpital's rule. (4.8 CEUs) *Tuition:* $42.

Integration Techniques

Trigonometric integrals, trigonometric substitutions, rational functions, integration by parts, special substitutions, improper integrals. (4.8 CEUs) *Tuition:* $42.

Infinite Series

Sequences and limits, infinite series, tests for convergence, absolute and conditional convergence, power series, Taylor's theorem. (4.8 CEUs) *Tuition:* $42.

Plane Curves

Curve plotting, loci, conic sections, hyperbolic functions. (4.8 CEUs) *Tuition:* $42.

Polar Coordinates and Vectors

Polar coordinates, polar curves and areas, vectors and parametric equations, space coordinates and vectors. (4.8 CEUs) *Tuition:* $42.

Vector Functions

Products of vectors, lines and planes, surfaces, vector functions, tangential vectors, curvature and normal vectors. (4.8 CEUs) *Tuition:* $42.

Partial Differentiation

Partial derivatives, tangents and normals, directional derivatives, the chain rule, maxima and minima, derivatives of integrals. (4.8 CEUs) *Tuition:* $42.

Multiple Integrals

Double and triple integrals, with applications. (4.8 CEUs) *Tuition:* $42.

Vector Analysis

Differentiation of products of vectors, polar coordinates, exact differentials and line integrals, vector fields, Green's theorem, review of complex numbers. (4.8 CEUs) *Tuition:* $42.

First Order Differential Equations

Linear equations, separable equations, exact equations and integrating factors, homogeneous equations, applications. (4.8 CEUs) *Tuition:* $42.

Second Order Differential Equations

Second order linear differential equations: homogeneous equations, linear independence, reduction of order, equations with constant coefficients, nonhomogeneous equations, undetermined coefficients, variation of parameters, applications. (4.8 CEUs) *Tuition:* $42.

Series Solutions of Differential Equations

First and second order differential equations, power series, series solutions at ordinary points, Euler equations, regular singular points, and Bessel's equation. (4.8 CEUs) *Tuition:* $42.

Linear Equations and Laplace Transforms

Higher order linear equations, nonhomogeneous problems, Laplace transforms, discontinuous forcing functions, the convolution, systems of differential equations, and autonomous systems. (4.8 CEUs) *Tuition:* $42.

Introduction to Partial Differential Equations

Separation of variables, Fourier series, sine and cosine series, the heat equation, the wave equation and Laplace's equation, eigenvalues and eigenfunctions, and Sturm-Liouville problems. (4.8 CEUs) *Tuition:* $42.

Geometry I

The first semester of a one-year course in elementary geometry. Points, lines, and planes; angles and triangles; congruences; direct and indirect proofs; geometric inequalities; perpendicular lines and planes; parallel lines and planes; quadrilaterals. (10 CEUs) *Tuition:* $50.

Geometry II

The second semester of geometry continuing the above course. Similarity and proportion; Pythagorean Theorem; circles and spheres; areas and volumes; constructions and loci. (10 CEUs) *Tuition:* $50.

Review of College Algebra

Basic manipulations, exponential and logarithmic functions, systems of linear equations and inequalities, polynomial equations, complex numbers, and sequences. (4 CEUs) *Tuition:* $45.

Review of Trigonometry

Definitions, graphs, and properties of the circular (trigonometric) functions; identities; inverse functions; trigonometric equations and inequalities; applications to geometry, complex numbers, periodic phenomena, and vectors. (4 CEUs) *Tuition:* $45.

Review of Basic Calculus

Functions and limits; derivatives through the chain rule and applications to curve-tracing and max-min problems; definite and indefinite integrals and applications to areas, volumes, moments, and averages. (6 CEUs) *Tuition:* $55.

Review of Intermediate Calculus

Calculus of transcendental functions; advanced integration techniques; improper integrals; indeterminant forms; infinite sequences and series. (6 CEUs) *Tuition:* $55.

Review of Vector Calculus

Three-dimensional vector space; vector algebra; scalar and vector products and applications; velocity and acceleration; line and surface integrals; divergence and curl; Green's theorem, divergence theorem, and Stokes's theorem. (6 CEUs) *Tuition:* $55.

NURSING

Personal and Family Health

This course is designed to help you discover ways to promote your own health and that of your family. The course stresses maternal and child care, since the foundation for a healthy adult life begins before birth and is dependent upon a healthy childhood. Other key topics include mental and physical health, substance abuse, AIDS and other sexually transmitted diseases, and first aid. (4.8 CEUs) *Tuition:* $55.

Adult Patient Assessment: Subjective and Objective Data Base

For nurses who are not familiar with the components of the history and physical examination, this course offers and introduction. The learner is guided through the process of physical assessment. The subjective data base (Health History) and the objective data base (Physical Assessment) are included. (4 CEUs) *Tuition:* $60.

Interpersonal Relations - Utilizing the Basics: Effective and Therapeutic Communications in Nursing

This audiocassette course has been specifically designed to help nurses augment their ability to utilize effective communications as part of a therapeutic relationship. The course assists nurses in evaluating effective communications, and in providing information and emotional support to others. The problem-solving process and crisis intervention are presented, with theories and techniques to facilitate communications. (3 CEUs) *Tuition:* $60.

Writing for Nursing Publications

This course will guide nurses through the writing process—from becoming aware of publishing opportunities to developing a topic and understanding the procedure for submitting an article to a nursing publication. Nurses will learn to identify what editors look for, and how to avoid problems and pitfalls relating to copyrights. (4 CEUs) *Tuition:* $60.

PHYSICS

Fundamentals of Mechanics

Vectors and their use, static equilibrium, uniformly accelerated motion, Newton's laws. (5 CEUs) *Tuition:* $48.

Mechanics beyond Newton's Law

Work and energy; linear momentum; motion in a circle; rotational work, energy, and momentum; mechanical properties of matter. (5 CEUs) *Tuition:* $48.

Heat and Sound

Gases and kinetic theory; thermal properties of matter; thermodynamics; vibration and waves; sound. (5 CEUs) *Tuition:* $48.

An Introduction to Electricity and Magnetism

Electric forces and fields; electric potential; direct-current circuits; magnetism; electromagnetic induction. (5 CEUs) *Tuition:* $48.

Alternating Currents, Electromagnetic Waves, and Light

Alternating currents; electromagnetic waves; the properties of light; optical devices; interference and diffraction. (5 CEUs) *Tuition:* $48.

Modern Physics

Three revolutionary concepts: energy levels and spectra, the atomic nucleus, and the physics of the very large and the very small. (5 CEUs) *Tuition:* $48.

POLISH

Reading Polish I

An introductory reading course that gives practice in writing and teaches Polish pronunciation and basic conversation. (16 CEUs) *Tuition:* $60.

Reading Polish II

A continuation of the above course. (16 CEUs) *Tuition:* $60.

Directed Reading and Translating in Polish

An individualized course in which students read and translate Polish materials that are of particular interest to them. (16 CEUs) *Tuition:* $60.

RUSSIAN

Russian for Reading Knowledge

A reading course designed for anyone wanting to learn Russian in a very short time. Covers basic Russian grammar and teaches the student to read and translate in both the humanities and the sciences. The course is also recommended for students who have had some Russian but need to review. (26.4 CEUs) *Tuition:* $90.

Directed Reading and Translating in Russian

An individualized course in which students read and translate Russian materials that are of particular interest to them. The readings may be selected by the student or by the instructor. (20 CEUs) *Tuition:* $80.

Beginning Conversation and Composition in Russian

Gives practice in Russian composition, conversation, and pronunciation. The student must have access to a cassette tape recorder. (10 CEUs) *Tuition:* $60.

SPANISH

Spanish for Reading Knowledge

Designed to provide a reading knowledge of Spanish for those with little or no previous instruction in the language. Basic points of grammar and intensive training in reading are presented. (8 CEUs) *Tuition:* $40.

VOCATIONAL COURSES

AGRICULTURE

Dairy Production and Management

A course in dairy production and management designed for the farmer actively involved in a diary operation, for persons employed or interested in employment on a dairy farm, and for those who will be working with dairy farms in other capacities. (4 semester credits) *Tuition:* $184.40.

DENTAL ASSISTING

Dental Assisting I

Designed to provide the basic knowledge needed to work as a dental assistant. The course consists of basic theory, history, and terminology and focuses on fundamental skills such as caring for equipment, following common dental procedures, and assisting with four-handed dentistry. It is designed to stand alone as a basic course of instruction or to provide the basis for continued work for the dental assistant who wishes to complete the second course in the sequence, *Dental Assisting II*, in preparation for the Dental Assisting National Board certification examination (DANE). (3 semester credits) *Tuition:* $138.30.

Dental Assisting II

The second in a two-course sequence designed to prepare dental assistants for the Dental Assisting National Board certification examination (DANE). The course includes radiology, dental specialties, and office management. Students learn problem solving and decision

making, workload management, safety and sanitation rules, and professional communication. (3 semester credits) *Tuition:* $138.30

ECONOMICS

Economics

A basic course intended to give students an understanding of the American economic system. Fundamental principles that guide economic decisions and action, and their impact, are presented. (3 semester credits) *Tuition:* $138.30.

FOOD SERVICE

Food Beverage and Controls

Principles of cost controls, menu development, and merchandising techniques as they relate to sales and profit. Consideration is given to examples of food service accountability in conjunction with financial statements. (3 semester credits) *Tuition:* $138.30.

INTERIOR DESIGN

Fundamentals of Interior Design

The course is a survey of the various periods in decorative arts, including the characteristics, design motifs, and identifying features of styles from antiquity, the Middle Ages, the Italian Renaissance, the Hispanic periods, the French periods, the English periods, the American periods, and miscellaneous styles. (3 semester credits) *Tuition:* $138.30.

Textiles

This course provides basic information on the selection, use, and care of textile fabrics. All fibers, natural and synthetic, are studied. The most recent technology in construction, finishes, and color application is emphasized. Fabrics for consumer use, such as wearing apparel and household furnishings, are discussed. (3 semester credits) *Tuition:* $138.30.

MATERIALS MANAGEMENT

Industrial Purchasing I: Fundamentals of Purchasing

This course is helpful to students who intend to pursue a career in a purchasing department of a modern business and for those persons already employed in a purchasing department who wish to upgrade their knowledge. It is an introduction to the technique of buying from the right source, at the right time, with the right quantity and quality. (3 semester credits) *Tuition:* $138.30.

WRITING

Writing Fundamentals

An in-depth review of the essential tools for writing: basic grammar, sentence structure, punctuation, and paragraph development. (3 semester credits) *Tuition:* $138.30.

Written Communications

A writing course designed to prepare students to function in the working world. Emphasizes the development of writing style. (3 semester credits) *Tuition:* $138.30.

Oral/Interpersonal Communication

Emphasizes positive interpersonal communication. Focus is on analyzing the communication process, sending and interpreting nonverbal messages, listening, overcoming communication obstacles, communication in the organization, working with small groups, and preparing and delivering a formal presentation. (3 semester credits) *Tuition:* $138.30.

Technical Reporting

Teaches the preparation of oral and written technical reports. Types of reports include progress and process reports, proposals, technical letters and memos, technical research reports, and case studies. (3 semester credits) *Tuition:* $138.30.

Wisconsin, University of - Green Bay

Extended Degree Program
ES 109
2420 Nicolet Drive
Green Bay, Wisconsin 54301 (414) 465-2423

Description:
Four University of Wisconsin System institutions offer Extended Degree Programs to the residents of Wisconsin. These programs provide alternatives to the busy adult whose lifestyle or circumstances prevent his/her attending regularly scheduled, traditional on-campus courses. University of Wisconsin - Extension Independent Study courses may apply to the Extended Degree Programs, with approval of the appropriate institution. *See also* Wisconsin, University of - Platteville; Wisconsin, University of - River Falls; and Wisconsin, University of - Superior.

Academic Levels:
College

Degree/Certificate Programs:
Baccalaureate.

Accreditations:
North Central Association of Colleges and Colleges.

COLLEGE COURSES

GENERAL STUDIES

General Studies Degree Program

The General Studies Degree at the University of Wisconsin - Green Bay is a Bachelor of Arts Degree with a major in General Studies and an individualized career-related area of emphasis. This combination of studies equips the student with liberal arts skills that can contribute to the ability to manage people, information, and products. For additional information, write or call Extended Degree Program at the above address or telephone number.

Wisconsin, University of - Madison

Department of Engineering Professional Development
432 North Lake Street
Madison, Wisconsin 53706-1498
(608) 262-9787

Description:
The Professional Development Degree in Engineering is a unique advanced degree available from UW-Madison. This flexible continuing education program is designed to meet the individual goals of practicing engineers and scientists and to incorporate faculty guidance and counseling.

Academic Levels:
Professional

Degree/Certificate Programs:
Graduate.

Admission Requirements:
A bachelor's degree in engineering or a related science is necessary to qualify.

Accreditations:
North Central Association of Colleges and Schools.

PROFESSIONAL COURSES

ENGINEERING

Professional Development Degree

Independent Study correspondence courses from the University of Wisconsin - Extension as well as on-campus courses, institutes, short courses, and telecommunications courses from accredited universities fulfill the degree requirements. Appropriate continuing education courses may be as applicable as undergraduate and graduate credit courses. For complete information about the program, write to the Department of Engineering Professional Development at the above address.

Wisconsin, University of - Platteville

Extended Degree Program
510 Pioneer Tower
Platteville, Wisconsin 53818   (608) 342-1468

Description:
Four University of Wisconsin System institutions offer Extended Degree Programs to the residents of Wisconsin. These programs provide alternatives to the busy adult whose lifestyle or circumstances prevent his/her attending regularly scheduled, traditional on-campus courses. University of Wisconsin - Extension Independent Study courses may apply to the Extended Degree Programs, with approval of the appropriate institution. *See also* Wisconsin, University of - Green Bay, Wisconsin, University of - River Falls; and Wisconsin, University of - Superior.

Academic Levels:
College

Degree/Certificate Programs:
Baccalaureate.

Accreditations:
North Central Association of Colleges and Schools.

COLLEGE COURSES

BUSINESS

Business Administration Degree

The Business Administration Degree is a Bachelor of Science Degree. Credit can be granted for business and business-related experience.

Credit also transfer from Wisconsin technical colleges, and from American Council on Education-evaluated military education and occupations specialties, and corporate and professional training programs. For additional information, write or call Extended Degree Program at the above address or telephone number.

Wisconsin, University of - River Falls
Extended Degree Program
College of Agriculture
River Falls, Wisconsin 54022 (715) 425-3239

Description:
Four University of Wisconsin System institutions offer Extended Degree Programs to the residents of Wisconsin. These programs provide alternatives to the busy adult whose lifestyle or circumstances prevent his/her attending regularly scheduled, traditional on-campus courses. University of Wisconsin - Extension Independent Study courses may apply to the Extended Degree Programs, with approval of the appropriate institution. *See also* Wisconsin, University of - Green Bay, Wisconsin, University of - Platteville, and Wisconsin, University of - Superior.

Academic Levels:
College

Degree/Certificate Programs:
Baccalaureate.

Accreditations:
North Central Association of Colleges and Schools.

COLLEGE COURSES

AGRICULTURE
Broad Area Studies in Agriculture
The Broad Area Studies in Agriculture is a Bachelor of Science Degree offered by UW-River Falls. The program offers technical, scientific, and management features in the following areas: agricultural business and economics; agricultural engineering and education; marketing; animal science; conservation; earth sciences; land management and land use planning; farm management; soil, food, or plant sciences. For additional information, write or call Extended Degree Program at the above address or telephone number.

Wisconsin, University of - Superior
Extended Degree Program
237 Old Main
Superior, Wisconsin 54880   (715) 394-8487

Description:
Four University of Wisconsin System institutions offer Extended Degree Programs to the residents of Wisconsin. These programs provide alternatives to the busy adult whose lifestyle or circumstances prevent his/her attending regularly scheduled, traditional on-campus courses. University of Wisconsin - Extension Independent Study courses may apply to the Extended Degree Programs, with approval

of the appropriate institution. *See also* Wisconsin, University of - Green Bay, Wisconsin, University of - Platteville, and Wisconsin, University of - River Falls.

Academic Levels:
College

Degree/Certificate Programs:
Baccalaureate.

Accreditations:
North Central Association of Colleges and Schools.

COLLEGE COURSES

GENERAL STUDIES
Individualized Major
The individualized Major is a bachelor's degree that lets students combine at least three academic areas in the existing university curriculum to design a unique major that reflects their backgrounds, prior academic experience, personal preferences, and that takes the job market into consideration. It is intended for students whose educational objectives can not be met through an existing academic program. For additional information, write or call Extended Degree Program at the above address or telephone number.

Wyoming, University of
Office of Correspondence Study
School of Extended Studies and Public Service
P.O. Box 3294, University Station
Laramie, Wyoming 82071-3294
(307) 766-5632

Description:
Correspondence study was founded at the University of Wyoming in 1893. Through its School of Extended Studies and Public Service, the university offers courses through the Office of Correspondence Study. There are over 2,300 enrollments per year at the college, high school, and noncredit levels. The toll-free telephone number is (800) 4488-7801, ext. 4; the FAX number is (307 766-3445.

Faculty:
Michael Cassity, Coordinator, Office of Correspondence Study; Jeannie Peacock, Office Manager. There are also 10 subject specialists and 10 public school instructors.

Academic Levels:
College
High School
Noncredit

Degree/Certificate Programs:
At the University of Wyoming, up to 24 semester hours of credit toward a baccalaureate degree may be earned by correspondence study. No graduate credit is offered.

Admission Requirements:

Open enrollment. Students at the University of Wyoming must obtain permission to enroll in correspondence study for credit.

Tuition:

$76 per semester hour, payable at enrollment, for student without a baccalaureate degree; $117 per semester hour if student has a baccalaureate degree. An additional correspondence study fee of $15 per course is charged. Overseas airmail fee is $20 (optional). HIgh school courses are $76 per one-half unit (one semester) plus a registration fee of $15 per course. Prices are subject to change without notice and usually on an annual basis. Refund policy: 60 percent if student withdraws within one month of the date of enrollment; 40 percent if student withdraws within two months of the date of enrollment; 20 percent if student withdraws within three months of the date of enrollment; no refund if more than three months have elapsed since date of enrollment.

Enrollment Period:

The enrollment period for a correspondence course is nine months from the date of registration. Only one extension of one year is permitted with a $25 extension fee. Minimum time for completion of a course is six weeks.

Equipment Requirements:

Course fees do not include costs of textbooks and workbooks. Texts may be purchased from the University Bookstore or rented from the Correspondence Study rental library. All books purchased from the University Bookstore will be re-purchased if still used in the correspondence course. Some courses require audiovisual materials which are supplied by the school for a refundable deposit.

Credit and Grading:

Examinations must be supervised by an approved proctor. In most courses, all examinations must be passed in order to pass the course. Grading system: A through F; D is the minimum passing grade (C in some cases). Satisfactory/Unsatisfactory (S/U) available on request. In general, correspondence credit earned from accredited universities with correspondence programs is accepted. Credit is awarded in semester hour units.

Accreditations:

North Central Association of Colleges and Schools. Member of: National University Continuing Education Association.

COLLEGE COURSES

ACCOUNTING

Principles of Accounting I

An examination of the fundamental concepts and procedures employed by reporting entities in the communication of financial information in accordance with generally accepted accounting principles to outside interested parties. (3 semester hours)

Principles of Accounting II

A continuation of the above course involving financial statement preparation and analysis, corporations, partnerships, international accounting, cost accounting and budgeting. (3 semester hours)

AGRICULTURAL ECONOMICS

Agriculture Economics I

An Introduction to basic macroeconomic principles and reasoning with special emphasis upon agriculture and the place of agriculture in the general economy. (3 semester hours)

Economics of World Food and Agriculture

Study of the economic, social, technical, and institutional problems of world agricultural development, with special emphasis on outlook for world food production. (3 semester hours)

AMERICAN INDIAN STUDIES

History of North American Indians

A study of American Indian history through 500 years and across the continent. Consideration is given to Indian political, social, and economic continuity and change. The main focus centers of how Indian peoples experienced and responded to times of dramatic change. (3 semester hours)

ANIMAL SCIENCE

Feeds and Feeding

Nutrient classification and use, feed value, ration formulation and feeding domestic animals. (4 semester hours)

Animal Nutrition

Digestion and metabolism of nutrients, nutrient requirements, feed composition, ration formulation and feeding various classes of farm animals. (5 semester hours)

ANTHROPOLOGY

Introduction to Physical Anthropology

Basic concepts relating to the origin, evolution and biological nature of the human species. (3 semester hours)

Introduction to Cultural Anthropology

This course introduces the student to foreign, especially non-Western, cultures through anthropological concepts. (3 semester hours)

ART

Art: History and Criticism

An introduction to the major arts of the world from prehistory to early twentieth century, with emphasis on painting, sculpture and architecture of Western civilization. (3 semester hours)

BIOCHEMISTRY

Introductory Comparative Biochemistry

The first portion of the course includes a short unit on organic chemistry; followed by a discussion of the biochemistry of carbohydrates, proteins, lipids, and nucleic acids. (4 semester hours)

BUSINESS ADMINISTRATION

Introduction to Business

A broad overview of business and an insight into business organization and operation. Consideration is given to identifying and establishing interrelationship among significant business activities—management, accounting, statistics, production, personnel, marketing, and finance. (3 semester hours)

Legal Environment of Business

Provides a broad overview of business-related legal topics. Students will be familiarized with the legal framework, constitutional law, administrative law, contracts, torts, employment law, consumer law, international law, social responsibility, and business ethics. (3 semester hours)

COMPUTER SCIENCE

Computer Information Systems

An introduction to computers and information processing, computer systems and hardware, computer software, information processing systems, information systems and information resource management. Word processing, a database language, and an electronic spreadsheet program are used in "hands-on" exercises. (3 semester hours)

CROP SCIENCE

Weed Science and Technology

Management and physiological principles involved in control of economically important farm and range weeds. (4 semester hours)

Current Topics in Seeded Forages: Production and Utilization

Description, adaptation, establishment, management, diseases, insects, weeds, economics, and utilization of forage crops. Videotapes are utilized in this course. (2 semester hours)

ECONOMICS

Principles of Macroeconomics

How economic society is organized and uses scarce resources to provide for its material wants. National income analysis; business cycles, the banking system; monetary and fiscal policy. Inflation and unemployment. (3 semester hours)

Principles of Microeconomics

Value and price theory; monopoly and public policy; markets for productive goods and services; labor economics; alternative forms of economic organization and international trade. (3 semester hours)

Intermediate Macroeconomics

National income aggregates and accounting; equilibrium analysis of output, employment, and the price level; general equilibrium analysis; introduction to economic dynamics. (3 semester hours)

Intermediate Microeconomics

Contemporary theory of demand, production, cost, and supply; theory of the firm; market price under monopoly, monopolistic competition, oligopoly; theory of factor prices. (3 semester hours)

EDUCATION

Teaching Reading and Study Strategies in the Content Areas

This course is designed to provide students majoring in secondary education programs with a knowledge of reading factors as they relate to various disciplines. The content of the course includes estimating students' reading ability, techniques for vocabulary development, questioning strategies, and developing reading-related study skills. (2 semester hours)

EDUCATIONAL ADMINISTRATION

Teacher and Elementary School Administration

Provides the elementary teacher with information relative to teacher-administrator relationships. Topics stressed include discipline, legal status of teachers, evaluation, and general knowledge of administra-

tion. Simulation materials are used to create typical classroom situations. (2 semester hours)

Teacher and Secondary School Administration

Designed to inform the secondary teacher of the modern educational practices in school administration and management and to stress the teacher's responsibilities and relationships in the total school operation. (2 semester hours)

EDUCATIONAL FOUNDATIONS

Educational Tests and Measurements

Designed to provide competency in the construction of teacher-made tests, the selection and use of standardized tests, the use of other evaluative devices, and the application of elementary statistics to education measurements. (3 semester hours)

Issues in Contemporary Education

This course is developed to acquaint the student with factors involved in issues in current American education. (2 semester hours)

ENGLISH

English Composition I

A composition course with emphasis on expository writing and close, analytical writing. (3 semester hours)

Introduction to Literature

Introduction to literary study including poetry, fiction, drama, and nonliterary works. (3 semester hours)

Critical Reading and Writing

Practice and guidance in writing expository essays. (3 semester hours)

American Literature II

A survey of major figures and literary movements from Whitman to Faulkner. (3 semester hours)

Regional U.S. Literature: The West

Major themes and writers in Western American literature: the frontiersman, Indian, trails, mining, cattlemen, settlers, etc. (3 semester hours)

FRENCH

First Year French I

Fundamentals of grammar, composition, conversation, and reading. (4 semester hours)

First Year French II

Fundamentals of grammar, composition, conversation, and reading. (4 semester hours)

Second Year French I

Reading simple novels, short stories, and dramas; grammar review; conversation. (4 semester hours)

GEOGRAPHY

Conservation of Natural Resources

Geographical analysis of the conservation of natural and human resources and the political, social, and ethical ramifications of our environmental policy. (3 semester hours)

GEOLOGY

Introduction to Geology

A one-semester survey of geology which introduces the student to the earth's physical make-up and history. (2 semester hours)

GERMAN

Second Year German I

Reading simple novels, short stories, and dramas, grammar review; conversation. (4 semester hours)

HEALTH EDUCATION

Personal and Community Health

To acquaint students with the field of health education and to develop knowledge and understanding about personal and community health; and to acquaint the physical education major with his/her future role in health education. (3 semester hours)

Standard First Aid and Personal Safety

Study of accident prevention, examination procedures, and first aid care for victims of accidents or sudden illness before medical assistance is available. New Red Cross content is presented. CPR is presented. (2 semester hours)

HISTORY

Western Civilization I

A basic survey of western European civilization from the decline of the Roman Empire to 1700. (3 semester hours)

Western Civilization II

A broad survey of European history in the Western tradition from 1700 to the present. (3 semester hours)

United States History I

A survey of United States history 1607–1865. (3 semester hours)

United States History II

A survey of United States history from Reconstruction to the recent past. (3 semester hours)

History of Wyoming

A study of Wyoming from its beginning to the present. (2 semester hours)

History of North American Indians

A study of American Indian history through 500 years and across the continent. Consideration is given to Indian political, social, and economic continuity and change. The main focus centers on how Indian peoples experienced and responded to times of dramatic change. (3 semester hours)

History of Mexico

An intensive course in Mexican development with emphasis on the twentieth century. The Mexican Revolution of 1910 forms the focus of the course, showing how this nation transformed itself into a modern nation state. Topics explored before and after the Revolution include diplomatic relations with the United States, incorporation of the Indian into the mainstream and the growth of the mestizo class, church-state relations, uses of land and other natural resources, the role of the military, and the growth of Mexican nationalism. (3 semester hours)

The Social History of American Women

This course will explore the everyday life experiences of American women from the seventeenth century to the present with a focus on the complex influence of gender, race, and class in shaping these experiences. The course will then turn to an analysis of the ways in which women's dissatisfaction with their position in society formed the basis for the development of American feminism and led to the formation of an organized women's movement. (3 semester hours)

HOME ECONOMICS

Nutrition

Relationship of food to maintenance of health and importance to the individual and society. (2 semester hours)

Personal Finance

To acquaint students with personal budgeting and financial matters and relate those activities to the financial institutions involved. (3 semester hours)

Foundations of Marriage

Focus on relationship development and factors affecting marital satisfaction and stability. (3 semester hours)

HUMAN COMMUNICATION

Introduction to Human Communication

Introduction of theories and research investigated by social and behavioral scientists on the process of communication. Orients beginning students of communication by focusing on concepts and issues central to human communication. (3 semester hours)

LIBRARY SCIENCE

Literature for Children

A survey course, the purpose of which is to prepare prospective elementary teachers and library/media generalists to provide knowledgeable service in the use of print and nonprint materials in the area of literature for children. This course includes study of evaluative criteria, wide reading, viewing and listening as well as discussion of literature for children. (3 semester hours)

Library/Media Materials for the Teenager

Designed for prospective library/media specialists and for those junior and senior high school teachers who wish to strengthen their backgrounds in the utilization of a wide, balanced collection of books, periodicals, films, records, tapes and other similar resources in working with teenagers. The course involves reading books and consideration of nonbook media that speak to the modern teenager. (3 semester hours)

Selection of Instructional Materials

A study of principles and practices in the selection of print and nonprint materials for utilization in school and public libraries. Emphasis will be given to the evaluation of materials in light of community needs and principles of intellectual freedom. (3 semester hours)

Administration of the School Library/Media Center

Deals with finance, housing, personnel, collection, records and services of the school library. Instruction in the use of the library and publicity or educational interpretation concerning the library are also discussed. (3 semester hours)

MASS MEDIA

Introduction to Mass Media

An overview of mass media, newspapers, magazines, books, radio, television, and films, and a study of their historical development with emphasis on understanding the techniques of expression and impact on American culture. A survey of the content of mass media; consideration of contemporary problems and trends. (3 semester hours)

MATHEMATICS

Theory of Arithmetic I

This course is designed primarily for prospective elementary teachers.

It presents a fairly rigorous treatment of the basic operations of arithmetic including whole numbers, integers, rational numbers and real numbers. Logic and problem solving are an integral part of the course. (3 semester hours)

Theory of Arithmetic II

A continuation of the above course. Among the topics covered are geometry, probability, statistics, and algebraic concepts. (3 semester hours)

College Algebra

Emphasizes those aspects of algebra that are important in the study of calculus: notation of algebra, exponents, factoring, functions, graphing, inequalities, theory of equations, conics and logarithms. (3 semester hours)

College Trigonometry

This course emphasizes those aspects of trigonometry important in the study of calculus. Topics include: angle measurement, trigonometry functions, graphing, laws of sines and cosines, identities, equations, polar equations, complex numbers, DeMoivre's theorem. (3 semester hours)

Algebra and Trigonometry

This course covers the content of the courses *College Algebra* and *College Trigonometry* (see above). It is designed for the student with considerable prior exposure to trigonometry. (5 semester hours)

Calculus I

Calculus with emphasis on physical science applications. Topics covered are plane analytic geometry, differentiation, applications of the derivative, differential equations, integration, and applications. (4 semester hours)

Calculus II

A continuation of the above course. Topics include elementary functions, derivatives, integrals, analytic geometry, infinite series, and applications. (4 semester hours)

Calculus III

A continuation of Calculus I and II. Topics covered are vectors and solid analytic geometry, partial differentiation, multiple integration, differential equations. (4 semester hours)

Elementary Linear Algebra

Linear equations and matrices, vector spaces, linear transformations, determinants, orthogonality, eigenvalues and eigenvectors. (3 semester hours)

Differential Equations I

Topics include solution of ordinary differential equations, integral transforms. Emphasis placed upon construction of mathematical models arising in physical science. (3 semester hours)

Business Calculus I

Topics include review of functions, their graphs and their algebra; derivatives and their applications, techniques of differentiation; the calculus for the exponential and logarithmic functions with applications to business; integration and applications; the trigonometric functions and their calculus; differential equations and applications. (4 semester hours)

MUSIC

Introduction to Music

A course in music appreciation designed for the student who has had little or no musical training. Emphasis is on developing listening skills. (3 semester hours)

United States Ethnic Music

A survey of American folk music, Indian music, work music and other music indigenous to various ethnic groups. (2 semester hours)

NURSING

Medical Terminology

This course will introduce the student to medical terminology. It includes word structure of medical-surgical terms, body parts and organs, body systems, and commonly used medical abbreviations. (1 semester hour)

Developmental Influences on Health

This survey course provides the opportunity for students to explore the interaction between development and health. Human development of physiological, psychological, cognitive, sociocultural lines of defense are discussed across the life span. Selected theories associated with development over the life span and implications for nursing are identified. This course provides a foundation for more in-depth consideration of developmental factors related to health maintenance. (3 semester hours)

The Family as Client

Family concepts and theories will be applied through the nursing process to the assessment and care of the family unit as client. Contemporary concepts and theories about the family will be explored. (2 semester hours)

PHYSICAL EDUCATION

Foundations of Coaching

Coaching means having knowledge and skill in coaching theory, teaching methodology, administration and management, psychology, sociology, exercise physiology, and perhaps other areas. The major purpose of this course is to provide prospective coaches with current information about scientific foundations of coaching. The content of this course is required for application of the Athletic Coaching Permit in the State of Wyoming. (3 semester hours)

POLITICAL SCIENCE

American and Wyoming Government

Fundamental introductory course which meets the requirements of the Wyoming statutes providing instruction in the provisions and principles of the constitutions of the United States and Wyoming. (3 semester hours)

PSYCHOLOGY

General Psychology

A basic introductory course covering a general survey of psychology through lecture notes, audio tapes, and assigned readings. Topics treated include the development of behavior, the physiological mechanisms of behavior, perception, motivation and emotion, learning, intelligence, individuality and personality, and mental health. (4 semester hours)

Child Psychology

The development and behavior of children from conception to adolescence with emphasis on the major roles played by maturation and learning. The purpose of the course is to acquaint the student with the area of child study in terms of research findings, and theories of child development. (3 semester hours)

Cognitive Psychology

This course deals with those higher mental processes that are primarily unique to human beings from both a theoretical and a research orientation. Emphasis is placed upon the interrelationships between the various cognitive processes, and upon the continuity of those processes with perceptual and noncognitive activities. It is concerned with how information is processed and remembered. (3 semester hours)

The Adolescent

This course emphasizes a descriptive view of adolescent development. Consideration is given to physical and physiological growth; intellectual, cognitive, academic, and vocational development; changes in attitudes, interests, and activities; and development of interpersonal relationships. (3 semester hours)

Understanding Exceptional Children

This course deals with those higher mental processes that are primarily unique to human beings from both a theoretical and a research orientation. Emphasis is placed upon the interrelationships between the various cognitive processes, and upon the continuity of those processes with perceptual and noncognitive activities. It is concerned with how information is processed and remembered. (3 semester hours)

Abnormal Psychology

This course provides a general overview of abnormal behavior with emphasis on types, etiology, and treatment methods. (3 semester hours)

Alcoholism

Patterns of alcohol use and theories of abuse and addiction will be presented along with current knowledge on incidence, health effects, economic costs, and trends in treatment. Issues range from the pharmacology of ethanol to societal concerns with problem drinking. (3 semester hours)

Theories of Personality

This is an extensive study of the major theoretical approaches to the explanation of personality as well as the historical trends that culminated in the theories. (3 semester hours)

RANGE MANAGEMENT

Principles of Range Management

Basic principles of range management as they apply to various regions and vegetative types. The relationship of range management practices to livestock production, wildlife management, forestry, hydrology, and other land uses. (3 semester hours)

SOCIOLOGY

Introductory Sociology

An introductory course providing both a survey of the discipline and a foundation for other sociology courses. Major areas of interest—ranging from small groups and families to bureaucracies and movements are explored. Significant concepts and theories are introduced, along with the tools of social research. Though much attention is given to contemporary American society, comparative and historical material is included. (3 semester hours)

Social Problems and Issues

Explores various approaches to defining and identifying social problems and applies basic sociological concepts and methods to the analysis of social problems and issues. (3 semester hours)

SPANISH

First Year Spanish I

Fundamentals of grammar, composition, conversation, and reading. (4 semester hours)

First Year Spanish II

Fundamentals of grammar, composition, conversation, and reading. (4 semester hours)

STATISTICS

Fundamentals of Statistics

The goal of this course is to present the central ideas and applications of statistical inference. Topics include probability, probability models, inferences for means, variances and parameters of discreet distributions. (3 semester hours)

THEATRE

Introduction to Theatre

Study of selected major periods in theatre history, utilizing a selected play from each period as the basis for the study of the development of theatre as an art form from the Golden Age of Greece through the late 19th century. (3 semester hours)

HIGH SCHOOL COURSES

ACCOUNTING

Bookkeeping I

The first semester concentrates on the fundamentals of bookkeeping, journalizing procedures, preparation of a work sheet and simple formal statements, purchasing and sales of merchandise, and recording of cash receipts and payments. In the second semester the student will practice all work of a bookkeeping period. (1 unit)

ART

Introduction to Art

Fundamentals and principles of two-dimensional art for the beginning artist. These principles include basic form, line, color, texture, balance, composition, and perspective. (½ unit)

BUSINESS

Business Mathematics

Students will learn fundamental operations with whole numbers, fractions, decimals and percents through a personal-use application to business problems, thereby providing them with a competency applicable to everyday living. (½ unit)

Business Law

The study of business law will promote a better understanding of legal terms and the rights and responsibilities of citizens under law. This course will also classify the utilization of professional assistance in legal situations which require such assistance. (½ unit)

ENGLISH

Grammar

Emphasizes those aspects of grammar in which high school students often err. Also beneficial to refresh basic skills in grammar for daily communication. (½ unit)

American Literature

Interpretation and appreciation of American literature and its relationship to the times and culture of the United States. (½ unit)

English Literature

Deals with English literature and its relationship to the times and culture of England. (½ unit)

Composition

Structural aspects of composition, clarity of self-expression, grammar, language usage. (½ unit)

HOME ECONOMICS

Interpersonal Relationships

Personal development as an individual and as a member of the family. Learn to communicate clearly, to resolve conflict in a positive manner, and to make realistic, informed choices in order to achieve satisfying adult lives. (½ unit)

Food for Everyday Life

The course concentrates on the kinds and amounts of foods essential to health and on the reasons for using these various foods in the daily diet. The course deals also with planning meals, kitchen design, and how to be a good consumer in the selection, storage, and preservation of food. (½ unit)

Consumer Living

Designed to help people make wise decisions in managing home, personal income, insurance, and savings. Purchases of clothing, home furnishings, and equipment are also covered. (½ unit)

MATHEMATICS

General Mathematics

A one-semester course designed for the student who is deficient in the fundamentals of arithmetic. Some applications to career situations and problems of interest to consumers will be included. (½ unit)

Algebra I

The first year of college preparatory algebra for the beginning student. The fundamentals of algebra including the language and terminology of modern algebra are covered. (1 unit)

Algebra II

The fundamentals of college preparatory algebra. It is the first and second semesters of a second course in algebra. (1 unit)

SCIENCE

Biology

The first half of a one-year survey of general biology. Designed to familiarize the student with the basic principles and living systems. This course has a video component requiring a refundable deposit of $110. (½ unit)

An Introduction to Forestry

The objectives and concepts of forestry, forest protection, silviculture, forest mensuration, and utilization of forest resources, forest conservation, wildlife management, range management, forest recreation, and opportunities in forestry. (½ unit)

SOCIAL STUDIES

World History

This is the first half of a one-year course in world history. It covers the development of civilizations from prehistoric times through the Middle Ages. (½ unit)

History of the United States

This course is a survey of United States history from the period of exploration through contemporary events. A two-semester course, it satisfies the graduation requirement for United States history for most states. (1 unit)

United States Government

Current political issues and recent occurrences in government circles will be better understood with a background knowledge as supplied by this study of the federal government. (½ unit)

Social Problems

Examines current social issues and problems. Problems studied include crime, the environment and terrorism. (½ unit)

Introduction to Psychology

Provides an in-depth introduction to the basic concepts of psychology. The course content includes: perception; learning; growth and development; biology and behavior; personality; and social aspects of behavior. (½ unit)

SPANISH

First Year Spanish

Acquire common Spanish vocabulary, comprehend easy reading matter, and compose elementary sentences in Spanish. Student's understanding of spoken language and ability to speak Spanish are cultivated through the use of tapes. A two-semester course. The student must purchase audiocassettes at a cost of $30 each semester. (1 unit)

NONCREDIT COURSES

EDUCATION

The School Board

For the new, the experienced, and the prospective school board member. Covers the roles, functions, and responsibilities of the local school board member. The fee for this course includes the textbook. (4 CEUs) *Tuition:* $134.

HANDWRITING ANALYSIS

Handwriting Analysis

An introduction to the science of handwriting analysis. Better understand yourself and others through an examination of personality characteristics as seen through writing. (4 CEUs) *Tuition:* $134.

Section 2
Proprietary Schools

American Academy of Nutrition

3408 Sausalito
Corona del Mar, California 92625

(800) 290-4226

Description:

Founded in 1985 under the approval and authorization of the California State Department of Education, the Academy is a small school specializing in quality education offered on a very personal basis. The Academy offers a diploma program which educates the graduate in the field of human nutrition and nutrition counseling. It is a basic yet comprehensive nutritional science course using the most up-to-date books and materials available. The course is primarily for people who are (1) concerned about their own health and (2) the professional in the health care field. The Academy also offers an Associate in Science degree program. Individual course offerings are available for enrollment by either a degree or non-degree student.

Faculty:

Peter Berwick, President/Administrator; Annemaria Ballin, Education Director; Bruce B. Miller, Director of Nutrition Research; Sandy Berwick, Director of Student Services.

Academic Levels:

College
Vocational

Degree/Certificate Programs:

Diploma

Admission Requirements:

Students must have a high school education or the equivalent and must be, in the opinion of the faculty, capable of successfully completing the course.

Tuition:

Comprehensive Nutrition Program $1,485 including all materials. The Associate of Science degree in Applied Nutrition is $1,285 per segment of a six-segment program. Individual course enrollment $290 includes the course study guide. Refund policy: within five days of enrollment, full refund except for registration fee; remaining refund policy is based upon amount of course completed (no work completed, 100 percent refund; 10 percent of work completed, 90 percent refund; 11 to 25 percent of course completed, 75 percent refund; 26 to 50 percent of course completed, 50 percent refund; no refund if over 50 percent of the course has been completed.

Enrollment Period:

The maximum time to complete each segment of the degree program is fifteen months. An extension of time may be obtained upon payment of a small administrative fee.

Equipment Requirements:

All books and materials are included in the tuition for the Comprehensive course. Books and videos are purchased separately for individual course enrollments.

Credit and Grading:

Grading scale: Letter grades are used. Minimum passing grade is C- (70). Questions on examinations are multiple choice and essay; there are independent study projects required as well. Degree students must have examinations proctored by an approved official (school principal, college testing officer, notary public, military education officer, etc.)

Accreditations:

Distance Education and Learning Council; California State Department of Education.

COLLEGE COURSES

NUTRITION

Associate of Science Degree Program

A student must complete 60 credit hours of study. The sequence of study is set forth for Segments A through D. Student must complete each segment of courses in each segment before progressing to the next segment. General electives and nutrition electives complete the course credit requirements for the program. Students may transfer credits from other accredited institutions, subject to faculty approval. (60 credits)

VOCATIONAL COURSES

BUSINESS

Business Mathematics

Review of basic mathematics for business; bank records; merchandising; payroll; finance; real estate; accounting; annuities and investments; case studies. (3 credits)

Managing a Small Business

Small business and self-employment; how to get started; finding and screening employees; marketing products and services; accounting, financial, inventory matters; special topics; case studies; examination

ENGLISH

English: Reading Enhancement

Develop reading skills to improve comprehension, motivation, concentration, organization, and vocabulary; techniques for more effective studying, reviewing, memory development and exam taking; parts of speech and sentence structure; discerning the author's perspective and bias; how to read literature, math, graphs, and maps. (3 credits)

MARKETING

Direct Marketing (Selling) Skills

Creative selling techniques; evaluating your buyer; planning a successful presentation; skills for finalizing the sale; successfully managing a sales force; selling in the future. (3 credits)

NUTRITION

Comprehensive Nutrition Program

This course is intended for health and nutrition professionals who wish to increase their knowledge and credibility. It is also well suited for those who find themselves helping family and friends on an informal basis with their nutrition questions. This is a non-degree program. The courses included are: Understanding Nutrition I, Understanding Nutrition II, Nutrition Counseling Skills, Anatomy and Physiology, Vegetarian Nutrition, and Environmental Challenges and Solutions. See course descriptions below. Graduates receive a diploma. (Noncredit)

Understanding Nutrition I

A foundation on the principles of nutrition; comprehensive study of the nutrient elements; in-depth examination of carbohydrates, fats and proteins; the role of vitamins, minerals and body fluids; digestion, metabolism and weight management; alternative nutrition practices; recognizing and evaluating differing points fo view; examination and critique of current nutrition trends; case studies. (3 credits)

Understanding Nutrition II

Nutrients and physical activity; life cycle nutrition; nutrition for the elderly; risk factors for chronic diseases; consumer concerns about food safety; environmental consciousness; alternative nutrition practices; how to recognize and evaluate opposing nutritional viewpoints; examination and critique of current nutrition trends; case studies. (3 credits)

Child Development

Foundations of child development; conception, prenatal, and birth; heredity; infant social and emotional development; growth and maturation; the developing child—learning, language, social processes; sexuality, morality, and self-control; the ''special needs'' child. (3 credits)

Nutrition Counseling Skills

The psychology of nutrition counseling; evaluating and understanding the client's attitude; how to illustrate the importance of good nutrition principles; interpreting the counseling session; how to identify and express your feelings toward the client; identifying inappropriate eating behaviors; recognizing dietary misconceptions; interpreting the results of nutrition research; making diet recommendations; applying appropriate strategies to specific problems; evaluating progress and spotting potential failure; utilizing proper counseling techniques; how to use client data forms in counseling; case studies. (3 credits)

Eating Disorders and Weight Management

Causes and physical effects of anorexia and bulimia; nutritional complications of eating disorders; profile of individuals with an eating disorder; approaches to treating eating disorders; recovering from an eating disorder; emotional and physical factors related to obesity; medical conditions related to obesity; practice counseling session and case studies. (3 credits)

Public Speaking

The process of public speaking; selecting a topics and purpose; supporting ideas; organizing and delivering a speech; informative and persuasive speaking; special speaking occasions; speaking in small groups and conferences; listening effectively; responding to questions and comments; preparing and evaluating speeches. (3 credits)

Environmental Challenges and Solutions

Scope and severity of environmentally triggered illnesses; a comprehensive view of the little-known effects that common pesticides and toxic chemicals have on our health; an in-depth picture of chemical sensitivities and how to recognize them; proper chemical questionnaires; understanding environmental illness; how to stay well in a polluted environment; the use and effects of pesticides in our food supply and what to do about it; designing a lifestyle that will protect children from common household toxic chemicals; alternative to unsafe cleaning supplies; case studies. (3 credits)

Women's Special Health Concerns

Dieting and fat during childbearing years; the importance of carbohydrates and minerals; foods to eat in the home and when dining out; managing menopause without estrogen; exercise, nutrition, and menopause; combining therapies to manage menopause; case studies; examination and critique of current nutrition trends. (3 credits)

Vegetarian Nutrition

Planning a vegetarian life-style; risks of a non-vegetarian diet; supplementation for vegetarians; understanding the scientific basics; how to create balanced vegetarian menus; special protein needs and how to meet them; case studies in vegetarianism; examination and critique of current vegetarian nutrition trends. (3 credits)

Human Biology

An introduction to human biology; the principles of chemistry; chromosomes, cells and genes; nutrition and digestion; function of the circulatory, nervous, endocrine, urinary and immune systems; reproduction, development and aging; principles of heredity; environmental issues; case studies. (3 credits)

General Chemistry

Application of chemistry to nutrition; matter, measurements, and calculations; atoms and molecules; electronic and nuclear characteristics; forces between particles; nutrition-related chemical reactions; the states of matter; acids, bases, and salts. (3 credits)

Pregnancy, Pediatric and Adolescent Nutrition

Preconception nutrition; planning a proper diet for pregnancy and lactation; nutrition for infancy through adolescence; vitamin and mineral supplementation; the nutrition connection to learning and behavior; attention deficit disorder; examination and critique of current nutrition trends; diet plans for children with special needs; case studies. (3 credits)

Sports Nutrition

The principles of fitness, motivation and conditioning; nutrition for the athlete; stress management; preventing accidents; stretching, posture, and aerobics; vitamin and mineral supplementation for fitness; high and low intensity exercise; cross-training; walking for weight control; case studies. (3 credits)

Community Nutrition

The role of nutrition in public health; educational foundation for nutrition entrepreneurs; the art and science of policy making; planning and managing public nutrition programs; understanding and influencing consumer behavior; food assistance programs; nutrition assessment of all age groups; case studies; community learning activities. (3 credits)

Organic and Biochemistry

Nutrition/food applications of organic and biochemistry; molecular formulas of organic compounds; physical properties of compounds; characteristics of enzymes; function of cofactors; description of biochemical pathways. (3 credits)

Healthy Aging

The role of nutrition in health aging; the aging process; mental consequences of aging; influencing the aging process; evaluation of different points of view to a health way of aging; case studies. (3 credits)

Anatomy and Physiology

The relation between structure and function in the body; identifying all of the body's systems; the role of the immune system; chemical and mechanical steps in the breakdown of food and nutrients; the relation of saturated fats in the diet to cancer, stroke, and heart disease; understanding the nervous system; consequences of vitamin and mineral deficiency; regulation of fluid input; potential of environmental damage to an embryo; oxygen, nutrients, and energy; case studies. (3 credits)

PSYCHOLOGY

Psychology

The brain, biology, and behavior; sensation and reality; memory, intelligence and creativity; conditions and learning; motivation and emotion; health, stress, and coping; abnormal psychology; gender, sexuality, social behavior and human relations. (3 credits)

American College of Prehospital Medicine
365 Canal Street
Suite 2300
New Orleans, Louisiana 70130

(504) 561-6543

Description:

The college was founded in 1991 to provide educational opportunities leading to the granting of undergraduate degrees for emergency medical services professions. It also provides special programs such as short courses, workshops, conferences, and seminars to enhance the knowledge of those serving in the emergency medical services field. The college also offers short, self-study curricula which may be granted continuing education credits for EMS personnel and specialized community programs which may address, but need not be limited to, first aid, cardiopulmonary resuscitation, infant and child care, wellness, and prudent heart living.

Faculty:

Richard A. Clinchy, III, Chairman of the Board and Chief Executive Officer.

Academic Levels:
College
Professional

Degree/Certificate Programs:

Associate, Bachelor. The Associate of Science in Emergency Medical Services degree and the Associate of Science in Hazardous Materials Technology degree each require the completion of 70 semester hours of prescribed courses of which 30 semester hours may be accepted in transfer. The Bachelor of Science in Emergency Medical Services requires the completion of 130 semester hours of prescribed courses of which 80 semester hours may be accepted in transfer. Individual courses may also be pursued by qualified students.

Admission Requirements:

Open to all students age 18 or over, possessing proof of high school graduation or GED and certified as an emergency medical services professional at a level not lower than Emergency Medical Technician-Basic. Registered nurses with an involvement in emergency medical services, are eligible for admission to any of the degree programs offered by the college.

Tuition:

Associate of Science in Emergency Medical Services $4,150 (includes $150 registration fee); Associate of Science in Hazardous Materials Technology $4,850 (includes $150 registration fee); Bachelor of Science in Emergency Medical Services $6,850 (includes $150 registration fee). Tuition may be financed with the college.

Enrollment Period:

Studies may begin at any time. However, the curriculum is set up on a prescribed schedule of courses which are to be taken each semester. A semester for these purposes is a six-month period of time and does not begin or end on any particular fixed date during the year.

Equipment Requirements:

For students enrolled after December 1. 1994, other than incidental clerical supplies, the tuition paid includes all study guides, textbooks, workbooks, and ancillary audiovisual materials the student will need to complete the courses.

Credit and Grading:

Grades of A, B, C, D, or F will be assigned. Examinations must be proctored. Credit is awarded in semester hour units.

Library Services:

Students may borrow books or periodicals from the college library for a period not to exceed thirty days. Approximately 90 days following receipt of a student's first tuition payment, the college will initiate a subscriptions to *Annals of Emergency Medicine* and *Emergency.*

Accreditations:

Distance Education and Training Council.

COLLEGE COURSES

EMERGENCY MEDICAL SERVICES
Associate of Science in Emergency Medical Services

Required courses include English Composition I and II; Contemporary North American Literature; Essential Business Mathematics; Psychology: The Behavior of People; Sociology: Human Social Behavior; When It's Your Turn to Speak—Public Speaking; Computers in EMS and Fire Services; Basic Anatomy and Physiology; EMS Law; Streetsense; Practical EMS Problems and Solutions. Elective courses may be selected from: Electrocardiography; EMS Dispatch; Pediatric Emergencies; Environmental Emergencies; Trauma Management; Dive Medicine; Hazardous Materials Injuries. Credit may be granted for current level of EMS certification, other EMS/fire education, and previous collegiate education. Up to 30 semester hours may be accepted in transfer. (70 semester hours)

Associate of Science in Hazardous Materials Technology

Required courses include English Composition I and II; Basic Anatomy and Physiology; Hazardous Materials Chemistry; Hazardous Materials Regulations I; Hazard Communication Standards; Hazardous Materials Emergency Response; Hazardous Materials Injuries; Hazardous Materials Health Effects; Hazardous Materials and the Environment. Elective courses may be selected from: Electrocardiography; EMS Dispatch; Pediatric Emergencies; Environmental Emergencies; Trauma Management; Dive Medicine; Hazardous Materials Injuries. Credit may be granted for current level of EMS certification, other EMS/fire education, and previous collegiate education. Up to 30 semester hours may be accepted in transfer. (70 semester hours)

Bachelor of Science in Emergency Medical Services

Required courses include: English Composition I and II; Contemporary North American Literature; Essential Business Mathematics; Psychology: The Behavior of People; Sociology: Human Social Behavior; When It's Your Turn to Speak—Public Speaking; Computers in EMS and the Fire Services; EMS Law; Streetsense; Advanced

Anatomy and Physiology; Medical Emergencies Management; Pharmacology; EMS Management; Statistics in Health Care Research; Report Writing; Research Project. Elective courses may be selected from: Electrocardiography; EMS Dispatch; Pediatric Emergencies; Environmental Emergencies; Trauma Management; Dive Medicine; Hazardous Materials Injuries. Credit may be granted for current level of EMS certification, other EMS/fire education, and previous collegiate education. Up to 80 semester hours may be accepted in transfer. (130 semester hours)

American Military University
9104-P Manassas Drive
Manassas, Virginia 22111   (703) 330-5398

Description:

The university was founded in 1991 and offers correspondence courses leading to the Master of Arts in Military Studies. Contact the university for further information. The university's Internet worldwide web site address is: http://www.netscan.com/amunet.

Accreditations:

Distance Education and Training Council.

Art Instruction Schools
500 South Fourth Street
Minneapolis, Minnesota 55415 (612) 339-8721

Description:

Art Instruction Schools is a wholly-owned subsidiary of the Bureau of Engraving, Inc. It and has been offering art courses by correspondence since 1914. For each lesson, students must submit artwork that demonstrates proficiency in the techniques and concepts presented in the lesson.

Faculty:

Thomas R. Stuart, President.

Academic Levels:

Noncredit

Degree/Certificate Programs:

Recommendations for college credit are listed in *The National Guide to Educational Credit for Training Programs* published by the American Council on Education/Oryx Press.

Tuition:

Contact the school for current tuition and fees.

Enrollment Period:

Students may enroll at any time.

Credit and Grading:

Students applying for college credit are required to take proctored, objective art examinations. In Fundamentals of Art, an examination may be taken after Lessons 14 or 22 (at which time a student may apply for credit for the portion completed) or upon completion of the entire Fundamentals of Art program. Similarly, in Specialized Art, students may

take an examination after Lesson 17 or upon completion of the course. Students are also required, as part of the examination, to submit a portfolio which is evaluated by a faculty committee and is part of the final grade.

Accreditations:

Distance Education and Training Council.

NONCREDIT COURSES

ART

Fundamentals of Art

Part 1. Basic Drawing and Design I. The objectives of this part of the course are to introduce students to drawing, design principles, and color concepts. Fundamental techniques of drawing to achieve accurate proportions, form, foreshortening, and textures; fundamentals of representational, abstract and nonobjective designs; application of color principles through planning, mixing, and use.

Part 2. Basic Drawing and Design II. This part of the course has the objective of enabling students to use a variety of art media and techniques creatively. Drawing and rendering animals; perspective, including one-point to multiple-point, and spacing, shadows, reflections, and plane projections; history and techniques of lettering; identification of lettering styles; lettering tools; pen and brush lettering and creative lettering; still life art, including positive and negative shapes, sight-size drawing, lighting, backgrounds, enlarging and reducing; pictorial composition.

Part 3. Figure Drawing and Studio Techniques. The objective of this part of the course is to provide students with an understanding of human anatomy that will enable them to draw the nude and draped figure. Figure drawing, including proportions, skeleton, and muscles; action and expressions; foreshortening and distortion; head, hand, and foot studies; drawing the draped figure—with an introduction to fashion illustration; studio techniques, including art studios, care and use of tools and materials, tricks of the trade, the airbrush, mounting photographs and artwork, matting, preparation of keylines (mechanicals or paste-ups), and instructional aids such as the use of a grid.

Specialized Art

Part 1. Design, Composition, and Reproduction. The objective of this part of the course is to provide an understanding of advanced problems in design, reproduction, and composition. Commercial printing processes (letterpress and offset lithography), reproduction of art screens, applying tone to line art, color reproduction, silk screening; advanced design problems, processes, techniques, and commercial applications; advanced study of composition, underlying picture patterns, rendering styles, analysis of shapes, values, and color in picture arranging.

Part 2. Painting Techniques. The objective of this part of the course is to provide an understanding of various painting techniques and media. Value and color problems in transparent and opaque media; their application to fine art and advertising art.

Part 3. Cartooning. This part of the course has the objective of providing an understanding of cartooning as a creative and expressive art, including the history of cartooning styles and techniques. Study of cartooning using ink, acrylics, Zip-A-Tone shading sheets, colored papers, felt cloth, and other media on illustration boards, texture sheets, acetate, and other surfaces doing dry brush renderings, creating collages, and using other techniques.

Part 4. Art in Advertising. The objective of this part of the course is to provide an understanding of the functions and responsibilities of an art director and an advertising agency; to provide an awareness of the creative process for an advertisement by analyzing client's needs, researching, and choosing visuals, layout tools and techniques; to develop an understanding of cartoons as part of the advertising message and to experiment with the styles and techniques involved in preparing advertising cartoons. Construction of an advertising campaign; service and institutional advertisements; psychology of advertising; functions and responsibilities of the art director; functions of the advertising agency; tools and techniques used in advertising art studios and agencies.

Part 5. Advanced Drawing and Painting. The objectives of this part of the course are to enable students to select subjects, compose, use perspective, and apply color theory to drawing from nature and painting portraits. Composition as it relates to landscape space, aerial perspective, drawing and painting portraits, review of head anatomy and form; placement, background considerations, color mixing, and painting methods.

Part 6. Advanced Illustration. The objectives of this part of the course are to familiarize students with the tools and techniques used by professional illustrators and to provide students with an understanding of the problems of creating artwork for book, fashion, editorial, and advertising illustrations. Developing illustrating skills and advanced rendering techniques for illustrating skills and advanced rendering techniques for book, fashion, editorial, and advertising illustration.

Breastfeeding Support Consultants
228 Park Lane
Chalfont, Pennsylvania 18914 (215) 82201281

Description:
Lactation consultant and breastfeeding counselor courses are offered by correspondence as well as optional combination and distance study-resident training. Contact the school for further information.

Accreditations:
Distance Education and Training Council.

California College for Health Sciences
Correspondence Division
222 West 24th Street
National City, California 91950
(619) 477-4800

Description:
Formerly known as the California College for Respiratory Therapy, the college offers both resident and correspondence programs. The school was initially founded in 1975 as a resident program to prepare credentialed respiratory technicians for work in the San Diego healthcare community. In 1978, the college took its first step into the nontraditional realm of higher education by designing a unique correspondence program. The correspondence method is designed for experienced respiratory therapy technicians working in the field, whereas the resident method is designed for entry level students needing a more guided and tutored form of instruction.

The purpose and educational objectives of the correspondence programs are to increase the competency level of respiratory therapy employees and to provide a mechanism for non-credentialed technicians and therapists to become certification-eligible and registry-eligible by the National Board for Respiratory Care (NBRC). This learning process is accomplished without the student having to attend a structured, campus-based AMA-accredited respiratory therapy program.

The college offers both undergraduate and graduate programs to those wishing to enter or advance in the health and human services industries. Associate degree programs provide a solid foundation in the areas of respiratory care and medical transcription. The Bachelor of Science and Master of Science programs for healthcare professionals offer further opportunity for career advancement. The college also offers child care professional training and continuing education courses in nursing and respiratory care.

Faculty:
Kenneth B. Scheiderman, President; Dale K. Bean, Education Director. There is a faculty of 18.

Academic Levels:
College
Professional

Degree/Certificate Programs:
Certificate of Completion for documentation to the NBRC. Certification-eligible respiratory technician; registry-eligible respiratory therapist.

Admission Requirements:
High school graduate or equivalent. Other requirements depending upon program followed. Contact the college for detailed information.

Tuition:
Tuition varies depending on course/program. Contact the college for current tuition and fees. Three special financing plans are available for deferred payments plus finance charges. Refund policy: Full, if within five calendar days of signing enrollment agreement. After five days and prior to receipt of first completed examination, full refund except application fee and enrollment fee. After starting course, pro rata policy (percentage of units completed). Scholarships may be available through the American Respiratory Therapy Foundation or student's place of employment.

Enrollment Period:
Maximum time varies by program (6 to 18 months). Interruption of training: Student may request extension of 6 months with payment of an extension fee. No classroom attendance requirements.

Equipment Requirements:
Basic instructional modules are included in the tuition costs. Textbooks are not included in the tuition and must be purchased by the student (available from the School).

Credit and Grading:
Transfer credits from other institutions may be in English, humanities, and science only and must be from

accredited programs and college level. To earn the therapist level certificate, the student must take or transfer-in at least 3 semester hours each of course work in anatomy/physiology, biology, chemistry, physics, mathematics, and microbiology. Progress in the program will be monitored by grades earned in unit examinations provided with each module. Graduation requirements are successful completion of all unit examinations with C average; grade of 75 percent or more on final (proctored) examination; pass an evaluation of clinical skills.

Accreditations:

Distance Education and Training Council; American Medical Association. Licensed by the State of California, Department of Education, Office of Private Postsecondary Education.

COLLEGE COURSES

BIOLOGY

Introduction to Biology

A course in selected biological principles and concepts. Major areas of study include cell structure and function, physical and chemical properties in living matter, energy transfer, genetics and development, evolution and ecology. (3 semester hours)

Human Anatomy and Physiology

A separate course in human anatomy and physiology. This course is also available within the Respiratory Therapy Technician Program. Covers basic anatomy and physiology of the major human systems. (4 semester hours)

Introduction to Medical Microbiology

Fundamentals of human medical microbiology. Introduces the viruses, bacteria, fungi, protozoans, worms and other groups which are of major medical significance. The course presents the characteristics and habits of each microbial group, followed by a system-by-system survey of important organisms and their effects on the human body. (3 semester hours)

CHEMISTRY

Introduction to Chemistry

Fundamentals of inorganic, organic, and biochemistry. Includes atomic theory, measurement, properties and structure of matter, chemical bonding, chemical calculations, ions and solutions, acid-base theory and physiological chemistry. (3 semester hours)

ENGLISH

English Essentials

A basic review of English skills including grammar, punctuation, spelling and rules of composition and writing. (3 semester hours)

Effective Communication Through Technical Writing

An introduction to writing and other professional communications. Topics include research, organization, style and presentation techniques of various modes of communication. (3 semester hours)

MATHEMATICS

Algebra Essentials

An introductory and review course in the mathematical skills and concepts necessary for algebra. A first course in college algebra including algebraic equations, exponents, polynomials and sets. (3 semester hours)

PHYSICS

Physics for the Health Sciences

Fundamentals of mechanics and heat including force, inertia, levers, weights, fluids and gas behavior, the kinetic theory of matter, pressures and temperature. (3 semester hours)

SOCIOLOGY

Dealing With Death and Dying

A course for the health professional presenting the personal, social and professional aspects of the dying patient. Major areas of study include social and cultural aspects of death, the role of the various helping professions, the dying child, ethical issues, suicide, funeral practices, and the process of grief and bereavement. (3 semester hours)

Theory and Practice in the Human Services

A survey of social structure theory and its implications for health professionals and institutions. Topics of study include an introduction to the helping professions, patient advocacy, counseling, rehabilitation, consulting, management and supervision. (3 semester hours)

PROFESSIONAL COURSES

RESPIRATORY THERAPY

Respiratory Therapy Technician Program

Anatomy and Physiology. A modular course, including cells, tissue, skin, skeletal system, and the muscular, digestive, nervous, endocrine, circulatory and renal systems. (4 credits)

Respiratory Anatomy and Physiology. Topics include the structures of the respiratory system and their functions, gross anatomy of the lungs, ventilation, respiration, and control of ventilation. (2 credits)

Math and Physics of the Respiratory System. A general overview of mathematical formulae, physical concepts, the gas laws, humidity deficit and air flow patterns. (1 credit)

Infection Control and Sterilization Techniques. A general discussion of microbiology, including a classification of bacteria, identification of organisms, other micro-organisms, bacterial growth patterns, nosocomial infection, sterilization techniques, and isolation procedures. (1 credit)

Cardiopulmonary Resuscitation. CPR is discussed regarding the decision to resuscitate, types of death, codes necessitating CPR, the ABC's, hazards, equipment and drugs. (1 credit)

Pharmacology. A discussion of drug names, administration, the "drug receptor" concept, biotransformation of drugs, routes of administration, calculating dosages, a review of the autonomic nervous system, bronchodilation, drugs used in respiratory therapy and non-respiratory therapy drugs. (1 credit)

Acid-Base Balance and Oxygen Transport. Topics include blood gases, oxygen transport, hypoxia/hypoxemia, carbon dioxide transport and acid-base balance. (1 credit)

Pulmonary Function. Pulmonary function is discussed regarding the purpose of the testing, lung volumes and capacities, spirometry, method of testing, abnormal tests, vital capacity, flow rates and specialized testing. (1 credit)

Pulmonary Diseases. A summary of diseases, including the common cold, COPD, asthma, bronchiectasis, pneumonia, tuberculosis, cancer, fungus infections, pneumoconiosis, cystic fibrosis, ARDS, pulmonary embols and neurological disorders. (1 credit)

Oxygen and Gas Therapy. Topics included are the physical properties of gases, carbogen, helium, gas storage, regulatory agencies, cylinder safety systems, gas regulators, gas flowmeters, oxygen blenders, reasons for oxygen delivery, precautions and hazards, oxygen delivery equipment, oxygen analyzers and environmental oxygen. (2 credits)

Aerosol and Humidity Therapy. This lesson discusses humidity, the purposes of humidity/aerosol, clinical applications, humidifiers, aerosols, nebulizers and guidelines for therapy. (2 credits)

Chest Physiotherapy and Rehabilitation. A discussion of postural drainage and concomitant techniques, conventional segmental bronchial drainage positions and rehabilitation. (2 credits)

IPPB Therapy. IPPB is discussed regarding the goals, indications, complications, contraindications, effectiveness and techniques of therapy. In addition, an equipment review is given along with a discussion of adjunctive equipment and incentive spirometry. (2 credits)

Airway Management. Aspects of airway management included are obstruction of the airway, intubation, tracheostomy, other emergency procedures, endotracheal tube maintenance, infection control, and suction technique. (1 credit)

Mechanical Ventilation. Topics included are the indications for mechanical ventilation, types of ventilators, ventilator characteristics, expiratory phase controls, ventilation techniques, IMV, effects and complications of mechanical ventilation, instituting and maintaining mechanical ventilation, weaning procedures, circuit change, troubleshooting and pediatric and neonatal ventilation. (3 credits)

Neonatal and Pediatric Respiratory Therapy. Topics include fetal anatomy and physiology, labor and delivery, the infant and high risk infant, cardiac and pulmonary disease in the infant, resuscitation, ventilation, newer ventilation techniques, diseases of children and psychological considerations. (1 credit)

Clinical Evaluation. (20 credits)

Respiratory Therapist Program

Patient Assessment and EKG Interpretation. An introduction to patient assessment, including history, physical, general systems observation, chest roentgenography, sputum examination, infant assessment and invasive cardiac monitoring. In addition, a section on EKG interpretation includes cardiac anatomy and physiology, normal EKG rhythms and arrhythmia interpretation guidelines. (1 credit)

Cardiopulmonary Resuscitation. A course in basic life support, including the physiology of CPR, risk factors from heart disease, providing CPR, recognizing and removing airway obstruction, resuscitation of the small child and infant, introduction to the cardiac electrical conduction system, review of EKG therapy, defibrillation, drug therapy in CPR and manual resuscitation bags. (1 credit)

Oxygen and Gas Therapy. A module containing the indications for oxygen therapy, types of hypoxia, causes of hypoxemia, the effects of hypoxia/hypoxemia, hazards and precautions to oxygen therapy, oxygen delivery systems, assessing the effectiveness of oxygen therapy and carbon dioxide, helium and hyperbaric therapy. (2 credits)

Advanced Pharmacology. A summary of respiratory pharmacology, including the anatomy of a prescription, mucolytic agents, bronchospasm, common respiratory drugs, and aerosol delivery. (2 credits)

Humidity and Aerosol Therapy. A module containing a summary of mucociliary clearance, principles of humidification, humidification devices, aerosol therapy, factors affecting particle deposition, types of nebulizers and hazards of aerosol therapy. (1 credit)

Advanced Infection Control and Sterilization Techniques. This module covers such topics as basic groups of micro-organisms, bacterial identification, pneumonia producing pathogens, control of bacteria,

nosocomial infections, respiratory equipment surveillance programs, sterilization techniques, and isolation procedures. (2 credits)

Chest Physiotherapy and Rehabilitation. A discussion that includes postural drainage, manual techniques, assessing the effectiveness and need for CPT, contraindications for CPT, rehabilitation and home care programs. (1 credit)

IPPB and Incentive Devices. A discussion of the indications, contraindications, hazards of and alternatives to IPPB, operation of the Bird Mark 7, monitoring the treatment, a typical procedure for administration, incentive devices-SMI and a typical procedure for administration of an incentive device. (2 credits)

Acid-Base Balance and Oxygen Transport. Topics include body acids and bases, ventilation/perfusion abnormalities, quantitative assessment of deadspace ventilation, oxygenation, pulmonary artery blood gases, the shunt equation and technical errors in blood gas monitoring. (1 credit)

Pulmonary Function. Discussion includes spirometers, blood gas analyzers, exercise testing, flexible fiberoptic bronchoscopy, preoperative patient evaluation, technical errors, tests of pulmonary mechanics and calculation of bedside spirometry. (1 credit)

Airway Management. This module contains topics such as airway obstruction, oral and nasal pharyngeal airways, endotracheal intubation, securing the endotracheal tube, the tracheostomy, hazards of intubation and tracheostomy, endotracheal tube cuffs, special purpose artificial airways and tracheal suctioning. (2 credits)

Continuous Mechanical Ventilation. Topics include review of normal pulmonary physiology, effects of positive airway pressure on normal physiology, indications for and initiation of mechanical ventilation, patient and ventilator monitoring, adjusting the ventilator, complications of mechanical ventilation, weaning, IMV, and adult CPAP. (5 credits)

Respiratory Diseases. A review of respiratory diseases, including chronic obstructive pulmonary disease, chronic restrictive pulmonary disease, infectious pulmonary disease, pulmonary embolus disease and pulmonary pathology due to trauma. (1 credit)

Neonatal and Pediatric Respiratory Therapy. Topics include fetal anatomy and physiology, labor and delivery, the infant and high risk infant, cardiac and pulmonary disease in the infant, resuscitation, ventilation, newer ventilation techniques, diseases of children and psychological considerations. (1 credit)

Respiratory Therapy Management & Supervision. Topics in this module include introduction to management and supervision, management planning, organization of human resources, basic approach to management problems, human resources, employee relations, job descriptions, budget and in-service education. (1 credit)

Respiratory Therapist Clinical Evaluation. (22 credits).

Cambridge Academy
1111 SW 17th Street
Ocala, Florida 34474   (800) 252-3777

Description:

Cambridge Academy was founded in 1978 and offers home study high school education leading to a high school diploma. The program supplies a background in mathematical and communication skills, an understanding and appreciation of our social heritage, and knowledge to participate in society, as well as fundamental understanding of general science and biology. The curriculum consists of courses in three areas: college preparatory, general education, and basic education.

Faculty:
Tanzee Nahas, Director; Ray Silver, Superintendent.

Academic Levels:
High School

Degree/Certificate Programs:
Diploma.

Admission Requirements:
Student must be past the mandatory public school attendance age in his/her state. Completion of eighth grade and be 16 year of age (or have parent sign for student if under the compulsory school age in the state of residence.

Tuition:
$459 per grade level plus a $25 nonrefundable registration fee. Monthly payment plans available; in-house financing with interest fee payments. Some courses may require additional fees and/or deposits.

Enrollment Period:
Maximum time to complete a self-paced grade-level is twelve months. Time period may be extended at the option of the academy, upon the student's written request.

Equipment Requirements:
Cost of books are added to the student's account.

Credit and Grading:
Grading System: A, B, C, D, F. Minimum passing grade is D (60 percent). Transfer credits are accepted if from other accredited secondary institutions.

Accreditations:
Distance Education and Training Council.

HIGH SCHOOL COURSES

BUSINESS

Business Law

Emphasizes the importance of business law in everyday life and provides practical guidelines for becoming effective citizens and consumers.

Personal Typing

A practical course. Typewriter required.

Computer Awareness

An introduction to the new age of computers: what they do and how they work (does not require a computer).

Accounting I

Basic principles which include the combination journal, fiscal reports, payroll and data processing (beginning). Provides job-entry level skills required for an accountant in a small business or records clerk in a large business.

Accounting (Advanced)

Expands concepts and principles covered in Accounting I and introduces information needed for a more thorough understanding of accounting.

ENGLISH

Development Reading, Level I

Basic level reading comprehension building, using short, short stories. Includes vocabulary, tips for reading aloud, and a focus on main ideas.

Reasons in Writing

A composition course which explores many forms of writing. Usually required for college composition courses.

Vocabulary for the College Bound

Analyze word derivatives and learn impressive and striking words. Improve your word power. A great help for even those who do not have college plans.

English Literature

Surveys the British greats: *Beowulf, Macbeth*, the Romantics, and more.

Language Exercises

Elementary practice in grammar, punctuation, and general English mechanics.

Increasing Your Word Power

A course that exposes you to vocabulary through context studies.

Short Story Classics

A creative writing and literature course; builds fiction writing skills while featuring a selection of famous short stories.

Composition and Enjoying Literature I

A beginning composition and literature course that increases writing and literary skills.

Composition and Enjoying Literature II

An integrated course designed to enhance writing skills and to provide students with confidence in literary analysis.

Composition III

Designed and integrated to work as a companion course with literature. Students will practice multiple types of composition styles.

Enjoying Literature III

Selections from all over. Reading of acclaimed short stories and *The Pearl*, a short novel which questions the morals and values of people.

Reading Comprehension I

A beginning course designed to increase basic reading skills.

Reading Comprehension II

An intermediate course designed to increase basic reading skills.

Reading Comprehension III

Designed to increase basic comprehension skills.

Elements of Writing, Third Course

This integrated course focuses on developing effective writing skills. Students are required to read one novel each semester, and may choose from four selections.

Grammar/Composition I

A composition course to help improve your grammar skills and strengthen your writing skills. Learn how to "Show-not-Tell" and use strong similes, metaphors, and verbs.

MATHEMATICS

Geometry I, II

Geometric relationships and proofs. Integrates geometry with arithmetic, algebra, and trigonometry. Geometry I and II constitutes a full treatment of geometry as a system of measurement and logic.

Personal Finance

Instruction for everyday life skills. Practice in check writing, installment buying, figuring materials for home repair projects, and more.

Elementary Algebra I

A full-year Algebra course required for entrance into most colleges. Covers topics from simple equations through simple geometry and trigonometry.

Algebra II / Trigonometry

A follow-up course to Elementary Algebra. Required for entrance into most colleges.

Math Applications I

A course designed to teach you how to solve word problems.

Math Applications II

A follow-up course to Math Applications I. Learn to master the steps and find the missing pieces to solve more complex math problems.

Math Applications III in the Workplace.

A course designed to solve word problems in actual vocational settings.

Basic Math

A simple course designed to develop the basic skills necessary for Pre-Algebra.

A simple course designed to develop and refine the skills needed for most vocations.

SCIENCE

Chemistry

Investigate characteristics and changes in matter. Discover atoms, molecules, and basic elements and compounds they create.

Earth Science

A study of the earth and other bodies in space. Includes experiments that can be done with equipment in your own home.

General Science

An easy-to-understand study of life, health, earth, and physical science with many thorough and enjoyable student exercises.

Physics (Advanced)

The mechanics of solids and fluids, heat wave phenomena, electricity, and magnetism.

Everyday Biology/Everyday Physiology

Presents a study of life, which includes plants, animals, and genetics for everyday living. Counts as two courses.

Modern Biology

The study of the life. Prepares the student for more complex study of life forms.

Earth Science and Physics Workshop

An introductory study of the earth, solar system, and stars. A beginner's approach to physics, through the study of sound and light. Includes simple exercises and fun projects.

Biology and Chemistry Workshop

An introductory study of biology—examining the life cycles of plants and animals. An introduction to chemistry—focusing on the properties of metals and other elements. Included are several safe experiments.

Technology in Your World

An interesting look at the progression of technology and how it affects us today. Many opportunities to design, invent, or be innovative.

SOCIAL STUDIES

American Government

Emphasizes and encourages citizen participation. Discusses the U.S. Constitution, political parties, the justice system, the economic system, and federal, state, and local government.

Consumer Economics

Designed to develop your skills as a consumer. Informs about credit, checking accounts, budgeting, energy conservation, and taxes.

Early American History

Prehistory to 1898. Traces major events: founding of the English colonies, American Revolution, writing of the Constitution, westward expansion, Civil War, and industrial expansion.

Justice: Civil and Criminal

A realistic interpretation of the American legal system: legal and Constitutional rights, consumer law, contractual obligations, and more.

Map Skills

Learn more about the world through the use of maps.

Psychology for You

An investigation into human nature. Understanding yourself, your relationships with others, and the society in which you live.

World History and You

A basic level course which tells the simple version of mankind's story from prehistory to the present.

Global Studies (Advanced)

A college prep course that surveys the history of the world's cultures from prehistory to the present.

Contemporary American History

1898 to the present. Traces major events of the twentieth century: the World Wars, the Great Depression, Vietnam, and current issues.

SPANISH

Spanish I

A video-based course. Learn Spanish through the lives and countries of the people you will meet. Build your vocabulary and understanding as you learn to communicate and begin to read, speak, and write in another language.

Spanish II

A video-based course. Prepares the student for extensive reading, writing, and conversing.

STUDY SKILLS

A Student's Guide to Personal Success

A course that focuses on basic and practical information, designed to improve and build good communication skills. Topics include: following directions, reading newspapers, using the library, travel and transportation, using a computer, and developing self-esteem.

Citizens' High School
188 College Drive
Orange Park, Florida 32073 (904) 276-1700

Description:

Citizens' High School (CHS) was founded in 1981 and offers a complete high school diploma curriculum. The educational objective of CHS is to give the student a solid foundation in the conventional academic areas: e.g., English, civics, science, and mathematics. Later in his/her studies, the student has the opportunity to pursue vocational or more advanced academic courses. All courses are available individually or as part of a high school curriculum. Graduation comes after a student has earned sixteen credits.

Faculty:

Larry S. Lark, President; Onna L. East, Education Director. The instructional staff includes six faculty, six subject specialists, and six counselors.

Academic Levels:

High School
Noncredit
Vocational

Degree/Certificate Programs:

Diploma. A minimum of school year (4 credits) must be completed from Citizens' High School.

Admission Requirements:

Any person who has a working knowledge of the English language may enroll. Students under the compulsory school attendance age of their state must submit an exemption certificate from their local school authorities.

Tuition:

Individual course prices are varied; payment plans are available. Tuition for 1 year, $475; 2 year, $690; 3 year, $810; 4 year, $930.

Enrollment Period:

The maximum time to complete an independent course is one year. To

Equipment Requirements:

The tuition covers textbooks, study guides, cassettes, examinations. Some courses require that the student have access to a cassette player.

Credit and Grading:

Examinations are open book. Grading system: A, 90–100; B, 80–89; C, 70–79; D, 65–69; F, 64 and below; minimum passing grade is 65. Credit is granted in units.

Library Services:

The school serves as a reference source and encourages student to write with questions.

Accreditations:

Distance Education and Training Council.

HIGH SCHOOL COURSES

ACCOUNTING

Accounting I

This course presents the complete accounting cycle for three major types of businesses: proprietorships, partnerships, and corporations. The double-entry method of accounting is learned and realistic problems and applications are used to help students apply what they learn. Utilizing a real-world situation, students are given the opportunity to apply all of these principles at the end of the course by completing a simulated activity. This simulation includes one month's transactions for a merchandising business that is organized as a partnership. In addition to the daily transactions, students will complete the end-of-period statements such as the balance sheet and income statement. (1 unit)

Accounting II

This is a continuation of the principles and theory learned in the beginning course with an emphasis on corporate accounting and specialized activities. Through a realistic simulation, students will demonstrate the accounting principles necessary for maintaining a set of books for a corporation that sells microwave ovens and cookware. (1 unit)

AUTOMOTIVE TECHNOLOGY

Automotive Electrical Systems

This course describes the basic principles, construction, and operation of electrical systems to help troubleshoot, repair, and maintain automotive electrical components such as electronic ignitions, current regulators, and zener diodes. (1 unit)

BUSINESS

Introduction to Business

The purpose of this course is to present the student with a solid foundation about what business is, how it operates, and how it is managed. The course offers a practical and interesting presentation of the factors that affect our nation's economy. In addition, topics and concepts needed to help students deal with and become part of the contemporary business world are included. (1 unit)

Computer Literacy

Assuming the student has no previous computer knowledge or experience, this course presents concepts in an easy-to-understand manner. Students will learn about the impact of computers on society, the development of information processing, how information systems are created, and what computers will mean for the future. (1 unit)

Skills for the Electronic World

This course presents such topics as understanding the work ethic, office politics, goal setting, time management, written and oral communications, listening skills, telephone etiquette, etc. This course will provide students with skills needed for survival, promotion, and success in today's competitive, complex business office. (1 unit)

Keyboarding/Typewriting I

This beginning course covers the development of basic skills and the mastery of fundamental applications (such as business letters and tables). The successful student will type 30–35 words per minute upon completion of this course. (1 unit)

Keyboarding/Typewriting II

This intermediate level course is a continuation of the introductory course and includes applications of more sophisticated business documents, such as special types of letters, tables, forms, and reports. The successful student will type 40–45 words per minute upon completion of this course. (1 unit)

Keyboarding/Typewriting III

This advanced course continues the study of formatting and typing all types of business documents, but in a realistic, office-style simulated approach. Further skill development and production activities are included so that the successful student will type 60 words per minute upon completion. (1 unit)

Clerical Office Procedure

This course includes six projects that provide students with basic training and practice in such job-related duties as preparing monthly statements, keeping accounts receivable records, preparing daily and periodic summary sheets, computing sales taxes and markups, filling out sales slips, preparing payroll records, recording in a sales journal, writing checks and deposit slips, and recording cash receipts and cash payments. (1 unit)

Business Filing

This is a concise, practical approach to the filing rules using alphabetic, subject, numeric, and geographic methods. The rules taught are endorsed by the Association of Records Managers and Administrators. (1 unit)

Business Records Control

This course is an in-depth study of filing systems, which refines the student's ability to handle documents in an alphabetical, subject, numerical, or geographical system. Information is provided on modern records control systems such as micrographics and optical data disk storage. (1 unit)

Calculating Machines

This course will help students develop competency in using the 10-key touch method on calculators while, at the same time, increase their ability to solve common business problems. The 10-key pad is also utilized on many computer terminals, word processors, and microcomputers, thus making it an increasingly important skill. Students will have to provide a 10-key electronic display or printing calculator with a full-size keyboard (as opposed to a pocket calculator). (1 unit)

Payroll Procedures

This course presents an authentic, write-it-once accounting system to provide experience in preparing payroll records using a pegboard. (1 unit)

Introduction to Word Processing

This modern course introduces students to the basic concepts of word processing and prepares them to succeed in today's electronic office. Such topics as the document cycle, and planning, implementing, and controlling a system are included. Career opportunities in word processing are presented. (1 unit)

Civil Service Office Skills

An ideal pre-employment course that contains information basic to most office positions. The course covers a broad spectrum of job skills and information, reinforces terminology for specialized fields, and reviews essential office skills and procedures. (1 unit)

Administrative Office Procedures

This comprehensive course presents what the office is now and what—because of revolutionary technological developments—it is fast becoming. Students completing this course will later be able to adapt positively to the inevitable changes in the workplace. The four parts of the course focus on: (1) working with others, (2) basic office skills, (3) critical office procedures and understandings, and (4) key technological developments. Critical topics such as telecommunications, workstation management, and administrative support functions are included. (1 unit)

General Office Simulation

This course is designed to help students make the transition from textbook assignments to the duties required in a business office. The goal of the course is to teach students to make decisions independently. Students will utilize skills learned in all other business courses to complete the tasks and activities. (1 unit)

BUILDING TRADES

Estimating for the Building Trades

This course includes a complete set of sample house plans to provide on-the-job training for estimating building costs, from excavation to finish hardware. Topics included are print reading, specification, framing, electrical, plumbing, and HVAC. (1 unit)

Electrical Construction Wiring

In this course electrical theory and wiring procedures are covered with hands-on activities and numerous detailed illustrations. Contents include: print reading, grounding, wiring, flexible, rigid, and thin-walled conduit, circuits, and multi-family dwellings. (1 unit)

Industrial and Commercial Wiring

This course covers the special requirements for industrial and commercial wiring. How to install and service electrical equipment of all types from motors to swimming pool fixtures to lighting for display cases are included. (1 unit)

Plumbing - Installation and Design

An introduction to plumbing theory and proven ''how-to'' techniques for installing appliances and piping fixtures. Design and installation of a complete residential plumbing system is thoroughly detailed. Contents include: joining, installing, and supporting pipe; waste, vent, and storm water piping; testing and inspecting; plumbing a house; safety on the job. (1 unit)

CAREER DEVELOPMENT

Getting a Job

This capstone course offers students an organized approach to finding and securing the jobs they want. Students will learn how to develop an effective resume and cover letter, how to present themselves in an interview, and how to leave a job with excellent references. (1 unit)

CARPENTRY

Fundamentals of Carpentry I: Tools, Materials, and Practices

This introduction to carpentry provides a guide through carpentry basics. Included are building materials, insulation, new energy-saving materials, rigging, scaffolding, ladders, modular construction, metal framing, safety and OSHA regulations. (1 unit)

Fundamentals of Carpentry II: Practical Construction

This course covers practical techniques for on-the-job residential construction, from laying out building lines to finishing interiors. Clearly illustrated, step-by-step sequences make complex subjects such as roof framing clear and understandable. The course covers regional differences in construction methods, form work, and alternative solutions to common carpentry problems. (1 unit)

CIVICS

Civics

This course covers what American democracy means in terms of the rights and responsibilities of citizens. The up-to-date discussions help students relate important concepts to everyday life and develop the attitudes that lead to responsible action in society. (1 unit)

ECONOMICS

General Economics

This subject gives the student the basic principles of economics and how they relate to the individual as well as government and business. The student is encouraged to think for him/herself about the major economic problems of the day. (1 unit)

Basic Economics

This course explains basic economics and how it affects the student's everyday life. Through practical application of economic concepts and skills the student will learn: how to read a bar graph and tables, write a check, figure compound interest, read the for W-2 wage and tax statement, plan a personal budget, read a stock market report, read a unit pricing label, read the want ads. (1 unit)

ENGLISH

Basic Communication Skills and Letter Writing

Part I of this course covers topics such as capitalization, subject and verb agreement, punctuation, and the correct usage of troublesome words. Part II teaches the principles of writing as well as the approaches for writing various types of communications. The typewriter is utilized in the completion of most activities which are realistic business documents. (1 unit)

English 2600

This course reinforces and further develops the concepts covered in English 2200. (1 unit)

English 3200

Simple, compound, and complex sentence structure are covered; as well as subordination and other methods to achieve sentence variety. (1 unit)

Basic Literature

Reading in the content areas: literature, social studies, and science motivates students to become intellectually and emotionally involved in what they read. (1 unit)

Literature I

The short story, the essay, the play, the lyric poem, and the personal narrative are the types of literature defined. Other literature skills covered are plot and character, point of view, setting, mood, tone, and theme. Activities in word attack skills and reading skills help the student better understand what has been read. (1 unit)

Literature II

Literature skills introduced in Literature I are further developed. Additional word attack skills are stressed as well as composition skills. (1 unit)

Advanced Business Communication

This course gives the student an opportunity to refine the essential skills of punctuation, grammar, and spelling in a realistic format. All activities are presented within actual business documents that the student must correct. (1 unit)

GEOGRAPHY

U.S. Geography

Our United States, well-illustrated with maps and photographs, provides a brief look at the history, geography, natural resources, main industries and major points of interest in the 50 states, District of Columbia, and U.S. territories. (1 unit)

HISTORY

American History

This course offers a complete chronological history of our political, social, and economic development. It includes all the basic concepts and challenging questions and exercises. Also covered is the U.S. in the mid-80s to encourage new thoughts of the United States today. Students learn about the problems involved in: meeting the needs of every American citizen; making our cities safe and beautiful; protecting our environment; meeting energy needs; improving education and medical care; developing foreign policy; working for peace in the world. (1 unit)

INDUSTRIAL TRADES

Sheet Metal Shop Practice

This course includes hands-on projects that show how to punch, drill, rivet, fold edges, make seams, turn burrs, raise, notch, crimp, bend, groove, solder, and cut. Also clearly described are plastic components used in air conditioning, heating, and sheet metal trades. Simplified triangulation and radial line development are covered. (1 unit)

Machine Shop Operations and Setups

This basic course introduces conventional machine and hand tool operations. It describes and explains steel, alloys, heat-treating, machineability, numerical controls, EDM, ECM, USM, magnetic pulse forming, and electrolyte grinding. Strong emphasis on shop safety is provided. (1 unit)

Welding Fundamentals

This course is for learning safety and care of equipment while being guided through proper set-up procedures. Welding exercises are provided to help develop basic skills and techniques and minimize materials waste. Topics include these types of joints: FCAW, SMAW, GTAW, GMAW, TIG, MIG, PAW, and RW. (1 unit)

Low Pressure Boilers

This course is an introduction to stationary engineering. Topics include: boiler and fittings; feed water, steam, and combustion accessories; draft control; water treatment; boiler operation; boiler room safety. (1 unit)

Metallurgy

This course covers clearly and concisely information about the terms, principles, and manufacturing processes. Contents include: producing ferrous and nonferrous metals; shaping and forming metals; physical metallurgy; mechanical properties; material testing; heat and surface treatment; steel classifications. (1 unit)

Metallurgy Theory and Practice

Course material covers metallurgy theory and principles as they apply to industrial processes, such as: cold forming, molding, casting, welding, and machining. Also included are designing, selecting, heat-treating, and processing of ferrous and nonferrous metals and alloys. (1 unit)

Fundamentals of Electricity

This course covers the basics of electricity, electronics, controls, and computers. An understanding of the relationship between electrical and electronic principles and their application in modern industrial components is presented. Contents include: circuits, magnetism, regulators, generators and motors, controls, measuring instruments, and computers. (1 unit)

Electricity and Electronics - Basic

This practical course helps build job skills quickly with hands-on presentation of electricity and electronics in everyday use. Nearly 70

"Interesting Things to Do" provide practical experience. Among the major subjects are producing electricity, basic safety, electrical circuits, everyday applications, communications electronics, and soldering. (1 unit)

Nuclear Power in Industry

This course covers the applications of nuclear materials in industry, schools, medicine, and research. Also discussed are conditions under which nuclear matter might be hazardous. Techniques for measuring radiation and protecting the environment are specified. (1 unit)

MATHEMATICS

Basic Math

This course begins with the basics: addition, subtraction, multiplication, division of whole numbers, fractions, and decimals. Percentages and measurements are also discussed. (1 unit)

General Mathematics

This course sets a firm foundation in operations, solving equations, working with negative numbers, decimals and fractions, plane geometry, percent and probability, and line graphing. (1 unit)

Vocational Math

This course reviews the essentials of decimals, fractions, equivalents, percents, and weights and measures. These basics are then applied to practical business problems such as checking accounts, interest computation, discounts, and commercial loans. (1 unit)

Algebra I

Algebra is taught by repetition and constant review in the much publicized John Saxon presentation. Skills from previous chapters are regularly demanded on later tests for reinforcement. (1 unit)

Algebra II

This course offers a review of the topics of Algebra I as more advanced concepts are interwoven. The goal is a total assimilation of the fundamentals of algebra. (1 unit)

Geometry

This course not only offers a complete course in geometry, but practical applications that make geometry relevant. There are numerous examples of the concepts and skills of geometry. Also included are computer, calculator, career, and consumer applications. (1 unit)

SCIENCE

Basic Science

The principles of electromagnetism, atomic physics, cell and organism biology, human sense organs, meteorology and astronomy (including space travel) are presented in a clear, basic overview. (1 unit)

Biology

This course is supported by a very detailed, up-to-date textbook covering everything from botany to ecology. (1 unit)

Chemistry

The comprehensive content includes theoretical as well as descriptive chemistry. Concepts are covered individually and relationship to everyday life is demonstrated. (1 unit)

Physics

Everyday phenomena are used to teach fundamental concepts. (1 unit)

SPANISH

Spanish I

A practical introduction to Spanish. (1 unit)

Cleveland Institute of Electronics
1776 East 17th Street
Cleveland, Ohio 44114   (216) 781-9400

Description:
Cleveland Institute of Electronics was founded in 1934 to answer the need for a high quality, professional electronics program to train radio station personnel. Its founder soon recognized a need for a way that technicians could learn electronics in their spare time, and the home study aspect of electronics training was introduced. New courses were added, including several which offered preparation for taking the government-administered FCC License examination. The selection of CIE courses now goes far beyond the communications field and includes beginner as well as advanced programs that meet the specialized needs of many electronics-related industries. Today, CIE is the world's largest independent home study school specializing exclusively in electronics career training. The Institute offers 13 different electronics programs to an active student body of 10,000. It also offers special programs to industry.

Faculty:
John R. Drinko, President; Dan Hadorn, Education Director; Chris Pakiz, Treasurer. The instructional staff includes a faculty of six plus three counselors.

Academic Levels:
College
Vocational

Degree/Certificate Programs:
Diploma, Certificate, Associate Degree (Associate of Applied Science Degree in Electronics Engineering Technology).

Admission Requirements:
For the AAS Program, high school graduation or equivalent (GED). A limited number of non-high school graduates may be accepted providing the student has previous experience in electronics or demonstrates skills or ability to complete the program successfully. For other programs, open admission.

Tuition:
Costs vary depending upon program taken, and range from $1,495 to $5,995 including individual equipment necessary for the course and supplied by CIE. Pro rata refund plan.

Enrollment Period:
For general programs, individual completion times are listed in the CIE catalogue and are designed to provide ample time to complete all lessons. They include periods to take care of review, vacations, emergencies. This is based on the assumption that a student will devote an average of twelve hours per week to the course. A 3-month extension is available for an amount equal to the down payment of the installment payment plan. The usual maximum time is five years; minimum is eighteen months.

Cleveland Institute of Electronics

Equipment Requirements:

Supplied by CIE and included in the tuition. In addition, CIE operates a bookstore for all students and graduates, offering a wide variety of educational reference books, study aids, electronics tools and equipment, plus other items useful to the electronics student or professional. All items available through mail order.

Credit and Grading:

Numerical system (percentage): 93–100, A; 85–92, B; 78–84, C; 70–77, D. Passing grade is 70 percent except for the AAS degree program which requires the student to maintain a 78 percent cumulative average for the term and for the entire program. All examinations are open book except the final examination which must be proctored. A failing grade in an examination means that the examination must be retaken. Five failing grades in succession will result in academic dismissal. CIE accepts credits transferred-in from other institutions for the AAS program only. Selected CIE courses include materials to prepare the student for the Federal Communications Commission Radiotelephone Operator License.

Library Services:

The Institute bookstore has a lending policy which requires a deposit. Instructors often provide photo copies to the students. There is a toll-free number for student service and/or instructional help. The bimonthly newspaper, *The Electron,* lists jobs available.

Accreditations:

Distance Education and Training Council; Ohio State Board of School and College Registration.

COLLEGE COURSES

ELECTRONICS ENGINEERING TECHNOLOGY

Associate Degree Program

A CIE student can pursue an Associate Degree Program, with full laboratory support, without attending a single class. The program is designed for the electronics student who wants to prepare for service as a senior technician or engineering assistant. The graduate will be prepared to work independently or as a team member with electrical and electronics engineering groups in manufacturing, design, research, development, and use of electronic equipment and equipment and components. The Associate in Applied Science Degree in Electronics Engineering Technology is equivalent to a residential, two-year college level program to prepare persons for work in the field of electronics. The Associate Degree is awarded when the student satisfactorily completes all of the required reports, lessons, and supervised examinations. The Associate Degree program includes 254 lessons and 397 experiments using Microprocessor Training Laboratory, Personal Training Laboratory and CIE Multimeter, Digital Security Control Device, and CIE Oscilloscope. 254 lessons. There are 3 supervised examinations and 5 technical papers required. The completion time allowed is a maximum of eight terms of study of six months each. (106 credit hours)

VOCATIONAL COURSES

AUTOMOTIVE ELECTRONICS

Automotive Electronics

This course provides a solid core of electronics principles and practical applications plus specialized training in automotive controls and systems based on microprocessor technology. The concentration of lessons in digital and microprocessor technology will allow graduates to cope with constant changes in the field of automotive electronics. This is a laboratory-intensive course and the lessons illustrate how physical quantities are changed to electrical signals by various automotive sensors, and how electronic, digital, and microprocessor systems process the signals; and how the processed signals are converted back to physical action by control actuators to make the vehicle respond properly. 100 lessons. A completion time of 24 months is allowed. (23 credit hours)

BROADCAST ENGINEERING

Broadcast Engineering

This course is designed to provide the specialized training needed for a career as a broadcast engineer or technician. The program includes important electronics theories and principles, as well as special emphasis on AM and FM radio, TV, film equipment, and FM stereo. 95 lessons. A completion time of 24 months is allowed. (20 credit hours)

COMPUTER SCIENCE

Computer Operation and Programming

This course is intended for students who have not had prior electronics training or experience and intend to work in the field of computer electronics. The course contains lessons that provide a solid core of electronic principles and practical applications plus specialized training in digital and microprocessor technology necessary to troubleshoot and maintain a computer system. In addition, basic programming techniques in assembly language, DOS, BASIC, and C-Language are taught to students so they can write simple programs. The training provided in this course will enable graduates to analyze, install, troubleshoot, and maintain the various types of electronic components, equipment and systems used in business, manufacturing, and servicing industry. The concentration of lessons in digital and microtechnology plus the programming skills will allow graduates to deal with computer hardware. 161 lessons. A completion time of 42 months is allowed. (53 credits)

ELECTRONICS ENGINEERING TECHNOLOGY

Electronics Engineering

This course is an advanced-level course designed for technicians and engineers who want a deeper understanding of electronic circuits, computers, and advanced mathematics. Prerequisites are a high school diploma or equivalent with at least one year of algebra or geometry; or the completion of any CIE course or equivalent, an in-depth working experience in the field of electronics, or the permission of CIE's Director of Instruction. 110 lessons. A completion time of 30 months is allowed. (70 credit hours)

Electronics Engineering Technology

This course prepares the student to become highly-skilled specialists in electronics problem diagnosis and troubleshooting. Students graduate as electronics technician specialists fully qualified to work in electronics systems research, development, planning, and production. This is a laboratory-intensive course that contains all the lessons and equipment described for *Electronics Technology with Digital Laboratory* plus experiments using CIE's Personal Training Laboratory with CIE Multimeter, CIE Oscilloscope, and Digital Security Control Device. 216 lessons. A completion time of 48 months is allowed. (91 credit hours)

Industrial Electronics

This course is designed to provide students with the ability to read and understand many different types of schematics and operational manuals. Students graduate with the occupational skills necessary to troubleshoot, maintain, and repair a wide array of industrial electronic equipment, including robotics, regulated power supplies, digital switching units and more. This course provides a well-rounded electronics education, but because it does not contain laboratory work, it is best suited for those students who already have some previous education or practical experience in electronics. A completion time of 18 months is allowed. 78 lessons. (23 credit hours)

ELECTRONICS TECHNOLOGY

Electronics Technology

This course provides a well rounded electronics education, including occupational skills needed to understand, analyze, install, troubleshoot, and maintain the various types of electronics equipment used in business, manufacturing, and service industries. There are 80 lessons with a completion time of eighteen months allowed. (24 credit hours)

Electronics Technology with Laboratory

This course is designed to prepare a person with no electronics experience to be an employable electronics technician in 24 months or less. There are 93 lessons and 201 laboratory experiments using CIE's Personal Training Laboratory with CIE's Analog Multimeter. A completion time of 24 months is allowed. (33 credit hours)

Electronics Technology with Digital Laboratory

This course is a beginning-level course that expands on the lessons from *Electronics Technology with Laboratory* to include digital logic and systems training. Students graduate prepared for jobs in instrumentation, digital troubleshooting, and industrial plant maintenance. This is a labortory-intensive course. 134 lessons. A completion time of 36 months is allowed. (44 credit hours)

Electronics Technology and Advanced Troubleshooting I and II

This program is designed for the individual who intends to service consumer electronics equipment such as televisions and stereos. It is designed to guide the student through analog and digital electronics with emphasis on electronics servicing and troubleshooting. There are 118 lessons and 245 lab experiments using CIE's Personal Training Laboratory with CIE Multimeter, CIE Oscilloscope, Color TV, and Color Bar Generator. 118 lessons. A completion time of 36 months is allowed. (38 credit hours)

Electronics Technology with Digital and Microprocessor Laboratories

Provides a well-rounded education in electronics with laboratory support throughout. The program includes the MTL-1 microprocessor training lab which covers both 8-bit and 16-bit microprocessors. There are 155 lessons with 259 lab experiments using CIE's Personal Training Laboratory with Multimeter, CIE Oscilloscope, Digital Security Control Device, and Microprocessor Training Laboratory. 155 lessons. A completion time of 42 months is allowed. (53 credit hours)

Electronic Communications

This course is designed to provide students with the occupational skills necessary to maintain and repair electronic communication systems of all types. Students graduate with the technical training required for

U.S. government licensing in areas such as two-way mobile radio, satellite communications, air and railroad traffic control, and are qualified for positions at radio and TV broadcasting stations and microwave relay stations. Some prior electronics experience is recommended for this course. 84 lessons. A completion time of 24 months is allowed. (17 credit hours)

Ecols International Tourism Institute
674 North St. Clair Street
Suite 1950
Chicago, Illinois 60611   (800) 342-2733

Description:
   The institute was founded in 1962 and offers diploma courses in airline, travel, hospitality, computer, and home-based travel training. Contact the institute for further information.

Accreditations:
   Distance Education and Training Council.

English Language Institute of America, Inc.
925 Oak Street
Scranton, Pennsylvania 18515 (717) 941-3406

Description:
   Known as The English Language Institute of America since 1964, the Institute was founded in 1942 as The Better Speech Institute of America, Inc. and has been in continuous operation since then. The Institute offers only one course, "Practical English and the Command of Words," which offers the opportunity to improve one's mastery of the English language. Approximately 12,000 students enroll in the Institute's course annually. The Institute is a subsidiary of International Correspondence Schools (ICS).

Faculty:
   Gary Keisling, President; James Lytle, Vice President of Education; Connie Dempsey, Education Director.

Academic Levels:
   Noncredit

Degree/Certificate Programs:
   Certificate of Completion.

Admission Requirements:
   Open enrollment to any individual who, after examining sample materials, feels that he/she can work effectively in a self-directed learning situation using the course materials.

Tuition:
   Contact ICS for current tuition.

Enrollment Period:
   The course is sent to the student in four quarters over a six-month period. On an average, a student spends 50-100 study hours during the six months.

Equipment Requirements:
All materials included in the tuition payment.

Credit and Grading:
Quarterly self-administered and self-checked pre-tests and post-tests. Final examination is a self-administered, open-book test that is graded by the Institute. The minimum passing grade is 65 percent.

Accreditations:
Distance Education and Training Council.

NONCREDIT COURSES

ENGLISH LANGUAGE SKILLS

Practical English and the Command of Words

The English Language Institute, in offering this course, recognizes that effective communication is a demand of contemporary business life, and that the prerequisite of effective communication is a mastery of its basic tool: language. The acquisition of knowledge, the exchange of ideas and information, the very process of thinking, are based on language. By expanding one's vocabulary and by improving one's language skills, a person can improve his/her processes of mental perception, clarity of thought, and precision of verbal expression. The mastery of this basic tool of communication may be to a large measure instrumental in determining a person's economic and social position in life. The overriding objective of the course, then, is to provide the means for an individual to improve his/her mastery of the English language. The course's specific objectives are the development of accurate perception of ideas; precise thinking; fluent, confident speech; clear, easy-to-read writing; and greater personal effectiveness. The objectives are achieved through the attention given to all phases of language and effective communication: vocabulary development, pronunciation, enunciation, voice, diction, grammar, spelling, punctuation, usage, and writing.

Futures in Education, Inc.
1450 Frazee Road
San Diego, California 92108   (619) 297-5311

Description:
The mission of Futures in Education, Inc. is to offer a secondary education program which considers the student as a holistic learner and matches student needs with a wide variety of learning resources in a caring environment. This innovative program offers an alternative to families seeking individualized instruction. Futures High Schools are located at the following three locations:

2204 El Camino Real, Oceanside, CA 92054; 26440 La Alameda, Suite 350, Mission Viejo, CA 92691; 1450 Frazee Road, Suite 301, San Diego, CA 92108. Address inquiries to either of these locations or the corporate office as listed above for this entry.

Faculty:
Dr. Karen Bishop, President.

Academic Levels:
High School

Degree/Certificate Programs:
Diploma. The diploma is awarded upon completion of required and elective courses totaling 220 credits.

Admission Requirements:
Registration is continuous and students may enroll at any time during the year.

Tuition:
Enrollment fee $100; registration fee $50; tuition for two semesters $4,000. Monthly payment plan available.

Credit and Grading:
Credit is awarded upon demonstrated mastery of course objectives.

Accreditations:
Western Association of Schools and Colleges.

HIGH SCHOOL COURSES

ART
Art
Introduction to Art

Crafts

COMPUTER SCIENCE
Computer Science
Keyboarding

Computer Programming

Word Processing

ENGLISH
Composition
Writing Lab

Vocabulary

Library Science

Creative Writing

Introduction to the Newspaper

ENGLISH LITERATURE
Literature
Literature A/B

American Literature and Composition

Short Story

World Mythology and Composition

Shakespeare and Composition

Modern Novel

Children's Literature and Composition

FAMILY LIFE
Family Life
Child Development

Preschool Experience

MATHEMATICS
Mathematics
Basic Math

Consumer Math

Pre-algebra

Algebra I

Geometry

Algebra II

PERSONAL DEVELOPMENT
Personal Development
Decision Making

Human Behavior

Health

Physical Education

READING
Reading
Reading Improvement

Advanced Reading

Individual Reading

SCIENCE
Science
General Science

Life Science

Physical Science

Earth Science

SOCIAL SCIENCE
Social Science
Volunteer Work

World History

Geography/Culture

United States History

American Government

The Legal System

Economics

Grantham College of Engineering
34641 Grantham College Road

P.O. Box 5700

Slidell, Louisiana 70469-5700 (504) 649-4191

Description:

Grantham College of Engineering, established in 1951, is a specialized institution teaching electronics and supporting subjects. The Bachelor of Science in Engineering Technology (B.S.E.T.) Program has been developed for adults who are employed in electronics and allied fields. The objective of this program is to upgrade such mature workers to higher-level, better-paying positions. Grantham programs are entirely by correspondence. The curriculum is a non-laboratory program based on the presumption that the student either already has or will obtain (on his/her own) proficiency in the operation of test equipment, hand tools, etc. Its main objective is to provide college-level correspondence instruction in electronics engineering technology and supporting subjects.

Formerly located in Los Angeles, California, the college moved to Slidell, Louisiana in 1990.

Faculty:

Donald J. Grantham, President; Juan A. Henriquez, Education Director; Philip L. Grantham, Director of Student Services. There is a faculty of 3 plus an adjunct faculty of 4 members.

Academic Levels:

College

Degree/Certificate Programs:

Associate of Science in Engineering Technology; Bachelor of Science in Engineering Technology. The program consists of four phases. The Associate Degree program requires completion of the first three phases. The Bachelor Degree Program requires completion of the Associate program plus the fourth phase. Credit is allowed for work experience (12 semester hour credits) and 21 additional "transfer-in" credit hours as follows: English, 6; History or Social Science, 6; Biology, Psychology, or Life Science, 3; Chemistry, 3; and Electives, 6. These may be earned by correspondence.

Admission Requirements:

To enroll in the Grantham electronics degree program, the applicant must be at least 18 years of age and should be a high school graduate or have equivalent educational attainment. This is only advisory; it is not meant to preclude the enrollment of any adult who, in the college's opinion, is likely to benefit from the program, but with the requirement that the student be terminated if not able to complete the first 16 lessons satisfactorily.

Tuition:

B.S.E.T. programs $2,100 per semester; B.S.C.S. program $2,400 per semester. Prices include $150 registration fee. All books, lesson guides, software, hardware, grading services, instructional assistance, and the awarding fo degrees is included. Additional fees apply to residents of foreign countries for airmail postage. Deferred payment plans available. Pro-rata refund for withdrawal.

Enrollment Period:

Each phase takes from 12 to 24 months to complete. Maximum time permitted for completion of each phase is 24 months for each of four phases; no minimum time requirements. Time extensions allowed.

Equipment Requirements:

No tools required. All required study materials supplied at no additional charge to tuition. Overseas students must pay postage for returned lessons and materials. Personal computer required in computer-major program and must be supplied by the student.

Credit and Grading:

Even though numerical grades are given on individual tests and review examinations, a letter grade is given for each phase as a whole. Letter grades used are: A, 97–100; B, 85–92; C, 77–84; D, 70–76. Minimum passing grade is D (70). The final examination for each phase must be proctored.

Accreditations:

Distance Education and Learning Council.

COLLEGE COURSES

ELECTRONICS TECHNOLOGY

Electronics B.S.E.T. Degree Program

Phase E-1. Consists of the following courses: Electricity with Technical Mathematics (8 semester credit hours); Electronic Devices and Circuits (5 semester credit hours); Electronic Communication Principles and Systems (3 semester credit hours); Antennas, Transmission Lines, and Microwaves (2 semester credit hours); Topics in Precalculus and Problem Solving (2 semester credit hours).

Phase E-2. Consists of the following courses: Intermediate Technical Mathematics, Part I (2 semester credit hours); Introduction to Computer Technology (3 semester credit hours); Intermediate Technical Mathematics, Part II (3 semester credit hours); Principles of Economics (3 semester credit hours); BASIC Programming and Applications (3 semester credit hours); Microprocessor Systems Engineering (4 semester credit hours); Advanced Electronic Communications Systems (3 semester credit hours).

Phase E-3. Consists of the following courses: Calculus with Differential Equations (5 semester credit hours); Concepts in Mechanics (3 semester credit hours); Technical Report and Proposal Writing (2 semester credit hours); Analog Integrated Circuits (3 semester credit hours); Physics: Sound, Heat, Electromagnetics, and Optics (3 semester credit hours); Advanced Microprocessors (3 semester credit hours).

Phase E-4. Special Topics in Mathematics (2 semester credit hours); Circuit Analysis (2 semester credit hours); Solid-State Circuit Analysis and Design (4 semester credit hours); Design, Patents, and Product Liability (3 semester credit hours); Systems and Signal Theory (6 semester credit hours); Control Systems (5 semester credit hours).

COMPUTER TECHNOLOGY

Computer B.S.E.T. Degree Program

Phase C-1. Consists of the following courses: Electricity with Technical Mathematics (8 semester credit hours); Introduction to Information Technology (3 semester credit hours); Electronic Devices and Circuits (5 semester credit hours); Introduction to Microcomputer Applications (3 semester credit hours); Topics in Precalculus and Problem Solving (2 semester credit hours).

Phase C-2. Consists of the following courses: Intermediate Technical Mathematics, Part I (2 semester credit hours); Introduction to Computer Technology (3 semester credit hours); Intermediate Technical Mathematics, Part II (3 semester credit hours); Principles of Economics (3 semester credit hours); BASIC Programming and Applications (3 semester credit hours); Microprocessor Systems Engineering (4 semester credit hours); Programming with Pascal (3 semester credit hours).

Phase C-3. Consists of the following courses: Calculus with Differen-

tial Equations (5 semester credit hours); Concepts in Mechanics (3 semester credit hours); Technical Report and Proposal Writing (2 semester credit hours); Introduction to Engineering Graphics and CADD (3 semester credit hours); Physics: Sound, Heat, Electromagnetics, and Optics (3 semester credit hours); Advanced Microprocessors (3 semester credit hours).

Phase C-4. Consists of the following courses: Special Topics in Mathematics (2 semester credit hours); Circuit Analysis (2 semester credit hours); Solid-State Circuit Analysis and Design (4 semester credit hours); Design, Patents, and Product Liability (3 semester credit hours); Computer Operating Systems (4 semester credit hours); Engineering Approach to Digital Design (4 semester credit hours); Industrial Robots (3 semester credit hours).

Hemphill Schools
2562 East Colorado Boulevard
Pasadena, California 91107   (818) 568-8148

Description:

Hemphill Schools has been instructing by the correspondence study method since 1920. Spanish language courses are offered in art, sewing, photography, radio-TV repair, electricity, air conditioning, computer programming, video repair, refrigeration, accounting, English (ESL), automotive electronics/electricity, diesel mechanics, and automotive mechanics.

Faculty:

Yolanda Jimenez-Agheli, Vice President.

Academic Levels:

Vocational

Degree/Certificate Programs:

Diploma.

Admission Requirements:

Must know how to read and write in Spanish. Only for the Accounting course must the student have completed at least the 8th grade.

Tuition:

Varies with each course; contact the school for specific information.

Enrollment Period:

A maximum of 2 years allowed per course. A course may be interrupted for no more than 3 months.

Equipment Requirements:

Some course materials such as tools and kits supplied by the School. School will advise the student as to those materials which must be purchased at time of enrollment.

Credit and Grading:

The minimum passing grade is 70 percent.

Accreditations:

Distance Education and Training Council.

VOCATIONAL COURSES

VOCATIONAL EDUCATION

Technical Training for Spanish-Speaking Students

The Hemphill Schools offers the following technical courses in the Spanish language: Accounting; Air Conditioning, Electricity, and Refrigeration; Artistic Drawing; Auto Mechanics; Diesel Mechanics; English Language for the Spanish Speaking; Radio, Electronics, and Television.

Hospitality Training Center
220 North Main Street
Hudson, Ohio 44236   (216) 653-9151

Description:

The Hospitality Training Center (formerly Motel Managers School) was founded in 1961 in Carey, Ohio by Robert W. McIntosh and Charles W. Heck. The purpose of the school was to train individuals to become motel managers. In 1963 Duane R. Hills acquired a franchise from the founders for northeast Ohio, Pennsylvania, and New York and established an office in Hudson. In 1967 Mr. Hills purchased the parent company Modern Schools, Inc. and formed Modern Schools International, Inc. The name was changed to Motel Managers School in 1985 to better reflect the specific nature of the business. The current name was adopted recently.

A home study course in airline and travel career training is offered as well as a combination home study-resident training program in motel management. An additional training site is located at the Aurora Inn, Routes 306 and 82, Aurora, Ohio 44202.

Faculty:
Duane R. Hills, President.

Academic Levels:
Vocational

Degree/Certificate Programs:
Diploma.

Admission Requirements:
Criteria for enrollment includes the following: must have the ability to benefit from the training program; high school graduation or equivalent; must be willing to relocate to acquire a position; personal and telephone interview; ability to communicate; must be a mature adult between 21–65 years of age; two character references; no previous felonies.

Tuition:
Contact the school for current tuition and fees.

Enrollment Period:
The maximum time to complete the course is two years. The minimum time is six months.

Credit and Grading:
All tests are personally graded with written response to errors plus a general itemized comment on the final page of the test. A "corrected" copy is attached and the student receives a percentage grade. Minimum passing grade in 75 percent.

Library Services:
Upon request from the student, additional reading material will be recommended by the Director of Education.

Job Placement Assistance:
The Center provides each student with 100 professionally printed resumes and upon completion of the program 12 monthly issues of the Center's *Job Opportunity Bulletin* which lists job opportunities all over the country.

Accreditations:
Distance Education and Training Council.

VOCATIONAL COURSES

MOTEL MANAGEMENT

Motel Management Training Program

This program covers all aspects of motel management and has home study and resident training components.

TRAVEL INDUSTRY

Airline/Travel Career Training Program

This program is a home study course.

Hypnosis Motivation Institute
18607 Ventura Boulevard
Suite 310
Tarzana, California 91356   (800) 6000-HMI

Description:

The Hypnosis Motivation Institute, founded in 1967, is a nonprofit organization and consists of a resident college and a correspondence division. The resident school admits approximately 30 students per month and current enrollments are over 300 students. Home study students in hypnosis/hypnotherapy currently number 500.

Faculty:
Dr. John G. Kappas, President; George Kappas, Director.

Academic Levels:
Vocational

Degree/Certificate Programs:
Certificate.

Admission Requirements:
Students must be at least 18 years of age with high school diploma or equivalent; Wonderlic Scholastic Level Exam and Taylor-Johnson Temperament Analysis Profile.

Tuition:
$495 per Volume; Each Volume contains six 2-hour VHS lessons. Three-, six-, and nine-volume discounts. Enrollment fee $95 per Volume. Materials only $95 per 2-hour lesson. Any 2-hour VHS lesson can be purchased individually.

Enrollment Period:
18 months for home study course.

Credit and Grading:
Open book examinations. Grading system: A, 100%–90%; B, 89%–80%; C, 79%–70%; F, 69% and below. Minimum passing grade is C.

Library Services:
Visiting students can attend resident classes and view an extensive video library on various subjects within the field of hypnosis/hypnotherapy.

Accreditations:
Distance Education and Training Council.

VOCATIONAL COURSES

HYPNOTHERAPY

Foundations in Hypnotherapy

HMI's Foundations of Hypnotherapy course represents the nucleus of all of HMI's philosophy and is the required first step in HMI training for students seeking HMI educational awards and Union certification. Regardless of the students' background or previous training, the Foundations course is the most important as well as the most fun and exciting of all of HMI's training. The Foundations course is full of demonstrations and practical assignments. The principal goals of the course are the "Emotional and Physical Suggestibility and Sexuality" concepts, created by Dr. John Kappas. Greatly responsible for HMI's success and reputation, these written and oral exams provide the hypnotist with a behavioral profile that enables them to organize their linguistic pattern to perfectly match the suggestibility of the subject. The use of the "E & P" suggestibility profile renders virtually everyone hypnotizable. Another tenet of HMI philosophy established in the course is the "Message Unit Theory of Hypnosis," providing students with a precise understanding of exactly what hypnosis is, how it is created, and the difference between inductions that organize vs. disorganize the inhibitory process. The Foundations course is equally dedicated to understanding these vital theoretical concepts and the practical skills of testing suggestibility, interpreting the results, and hypnotizing the subject according to his or her suggestibility pattern.

Volume 1. *Class 1:* Introduction; History of Hypnosis; Message Unit Theory; Definition of Hypnosis; Induction Demonstration; Emotional and Physical Suggestibility; Practicum and Assignment #1. *Class 2:* Message Unit Theory; Environmental Hypnosis; Hypersuggestibility; Scale of Imagination; Emotional and Physical Suggestibility; Maternal/Paternal Inductions; Pre-Induction Speech; Written Suggestibility Tests; Demonstration: Inferred Arm Raising Test; Practicum and Assignment #2. *Class 3:* Various Hypnotic Inductions; Demonstration: Auto-Dual Induction; Demonstration: Eye Fascination; Hypersuggestibility and De-hypnotizing; Deepening Techniques; Emotional and Physical Sexuality; Post-Suggestion to Re-Hypnosis; Practicum and Assignment #3. *Class 4:* Message Unit Theory; Three Stages of Somnambulism; Demonstration: Literal vs. Inferred Suggestion; Practicum and Assignment #4. *Class 5:* First Consultation; Goal of First Session; Demonstration: Consultation; Dynamics of the First Session; Hypnotic Territory; Post-Suggestion to Re-Hypnosis; Hypersuggestibility; Foundations for Therapy; Professional Practice of Hypnotherapy; Practicum and Assignment #5. *Class 6:* Emotional and Physical Sexuality; Stages of Development; Incongruent Behavior; Defense Mechanisms; Left/Right Brain Theory; Attraction of Opposites; Ethnic Influences; Differences in E & P Priorities; Practicum and Assignment #6.

Volume 2. *Vol. 2–1*, Hypnotic Modalities; *Vol. 2–2*, NLP, Part 1; *Vol. 2–3*, NLP, Part 2; *Vol. 2–4*, Ericksonian Hypnosis; *Vol. 2–5*, Kappasinian Hypnosis; *Vol. 2–6*, Clinical Case Presentation.

Volume 3. *Vol. 3–1*, Hypnotic Regression; *Vol. 3–2*, Dream Therapy; *Vol. 3–3*, Hypno-Diagnostic Tools, A; *Vol. 3–4*, Hypno-Diagnostic Tools, B; *Vol. 3–5*, Hypnodrama; *Vol. 3–6*, Clinical Case Presentation.

Volume 4. *Vol. 4–1*, Child Hypnosis; *Vol. 4–3*, Medical Hypnosis; *Vol. 4–4*, Fears and Phobias; *Vol. 4–5*, Defense Mechanisms; *Vol. 4–6*, Clinical Case Presentation.

Volume 5. *Vol. 5–1*, Emotional and Physical Sexuality, Part 1; *Vol. 5–2*, Emotional and Physical Sexuality, Part 2; *Vol. 5–3*, Systems Theory; *Vol. 5–4*, Adult Children of Dysfunctional Families; *Vol. 5–5*, Sexual Dysfunction; Vol. 5–6, Clinical Case Presentation.

Volume 6. *Vol. 6–1*, Low Blood Sugar; *Vol. 6–2*, Eating Disorders; *Vol. 6–3*, Substance Abuse; *Vol. 6–4*, Crisis Intervention; *Vol. 6–5*, Counseling and Interviewing; *Vol. 6–6*, Clinical Case Presentation.

Volume 7. *Vol. 7–1*, Law and Ethics; *Vol. 7–2*, Advertising and Promotion; *Vol. 7–3*, First Consultation; *Vol. 7–4*, Habit Control; *Vol. 7–5*, General Self-Improvement; *Vol. 7–6*, Clinical Case Presentation.

Volume 8. *Vols. 8–1, 8–2, 8–3*, Mental Bank Seminar; *Vol. 8–4*, Mental Bank Review; *Vol. 8–5*, Clinical Case Presentation; *Vol. 8–6*, Clinical Case Presentation.

Volume 9. *Vols. 9–1 to 9–6*, Handwriting Analysis.

ICS Center for Degree Studies
925 Oak Street
Scranton, Pennsylvania 18515 (717) 342-7701

Description:
The ICS Center for Degree Studies, founded in 1975, is a nontraditional proprietary institution offering postsecondary education in business and technology by correspondence instruction. It is one of the largest of any type to offer Associate Degrees and it is the first independent study school to be granted accreditation by the Middle States Association of Colleges and Schools. The Center for Degree Studies provides specialized credentialed education designed to fulfill practical needs—career, job advancement, self-improvement—to all qualified adults who seek it.

The International Correspondence Schools is a division of the National Education Corporation (NEC), a world leader in the field of human resources development. It has worldwide operations in vocational and industrial training, educational publishing, and home health care services. SEE **International Correspondence Schools** for additional information.

The courses listed below have been evaluated for college credit by the Program on Noncollegiate Sponsored Instruction for Adult Learning and Educational Credentials of the American Council on Education. The college credit recommended for these courses can be found in *The National Guide to Educational Credit for Training Programs* published by the American Council on Education/Oryx Press.

Faculty:
Gary E. Keisling, President; James Lytle, Vice President of Education; Connie Dempsey, Education Director.

Academic Levels:
College

Degree/Certificate Programs:
Associate is Specialized Business (Accounting, Applied Computer Science, Business Management [Management, Finance, Marketing], Hospitality Management. Associate in Specialized Technology (Civil Engineering, Electrical Engineering, Electronics Technology, Industrial Engineering, Mechanical Engineering).

Admission Requirements:
High school graduation or a state-approved GED Equivalency Certificate. Some courses have prerequisites.

Tuition:
$689 to $1,389 per semester depending on equipment provided with the semester.

Enrollment Period:
A maximum of six years will be permitted for completion of the four-semester degree program. Students taking less than a four-semester program will be permitted a maximum of eighteen months for the completion of each full semester, or a pro rated period of time for advanced standing.

Equipment Requirements:
All materials for successful completion of a course are included in the tuition charges.

Credit and Grading:
The Center for Degree Studies uses a number-letter system of grading, with number grades being assigned to examinations and letter grades to completed courses. The letter grade for each course is found by counting the average of the lesson examination grades as two-thirds of the course grade and the proctored examination grade as one-third. Letter grades are converted to quality points for the purpose of computing the Quality Point Average for each semester and the Cumulative Quality Point Average for more than one semester. Quality points range from 4.0 for an A grade to 0 for an I grade. A, 90–100 percent, Excellent, 4.0 quality point equivalent; B, 81–91 percent, Good, 3.0 quality point equivalent; C, 75–80 percent, Average, 2.0 quality point equivalent; D, 70–74 percent, Passing, 1.0 quality point equivalent; I, Below 70, Incomplete, 0 quality point equivalent. Final examinations are given for each semester, and must be supervised by a proctor selected by CDS. Advanced standing may, on approval by the Director of the Center, be granted to those applicants who have completed comparable work with a passing grade from accredited institutions, as evidenced by an official college transcript or evidence of CLEP certification, or who have life/work experience. All applicants accepted with advanced standing must complete a minimum of 25 percent of the total credit hours with the ICS Center for Degree Studies to be eligible for the Center's degree.

Candidates for the Associate in Specialized Technology degree are required to attend a two-week (eleven-day) resident laboratory training session at Lafayette College in Easton, Pennsylvania, or a college to be designated by the Center. Resident laboratory training is not required for Mechanical Drafting and Design Technology. This requirement will be fulfilled in the summer months during or following the fourth semester.

Accreditations:
Distance Education and Training Council; Middle States Association of Colleges and Schools.

COLLEGE COURSES

ACCOUNTING

Accounting I

This course includes a review of the nature of accounting; financial reports, including the balance sheet and income statement; recording transactions, the trial balance, journal entries and posting; adjustments, and cash versus accrual method of accounting; the work sheet, the accounting cycle; accounts and procedures for a merchandising business, special journals, payroll accounting. (3 credits)

Accounting II

Topics covered include: an explanation of cash, accounts receivable, notes receivable, investments, and inventory. Also, the nature of fixed assets, accounting for current and long-term liabilities. Particular emphasis is placed on partnership accounting and corporate ownership and management. A comprehensive case study dealing with the entire accounting cycle for a merchandising firm operating as a corporation is included. (3 credits)

Cost Accounting

Cost accounting concepts and the interpretation of reports. Development of timekeeping and payroll procedures. The setting of overhead rates. Accounting for scrap, spoiled, and defective goods. Accounting for by-products, development of cost analyses, process cost accounting, job-order cost accounting, standard costs. (3 credits)

Federal Taxation

This course provides a practical study of government income tax regulations, including a history of federal income tax and tax-saving principles, and instruction on completing individual and partnership returns. It also covers income tax regulations as applied to corporations, including income and expense, capital gains and losses, and payment of Social Security. (3 credits)

Intermediate Accounting I

A comprehensive study of contemporary accounting theory, concepts, and procedures and their application to financial reporting. Intermediate problems pertaining to cash, receivables, inventories, plant and equipment, and investments in securities. (3 credits)

Intermediate Accounting II

A continuation of Intermediate Accounting I. Intermediate problems pertaining to current and long-term liabilities, stockholders' equity, pensions, and income taxes; financial statement analysis, price-level accounting, and fund and cash flow reporting. (3 credits)

Managerial Accounting

A study of advanced accounting concepts, including partnerships, installment sales; consignments, home office and branch, business combinations, and fund accounting. (3 credits)

BUSINESS

Introduction to Business

A study of business and its functions, including finance, production, marketing, and administration. This functional study is developed around a framework involving goal setting, organizational design, and decision making. (3 credits)

Business Communication

Study of parts of speech, proper usage, punctuation and capitalization, vocabulary building, and sentence structure. How to prepare a speech, conversational speech, conferences, public speaking, and parliamentary procedure. Mechanics of letter style and advanced writing techniques. Scope of report writing, examples of body, paragraph system. A project is included. (3 credits)

Business Law I

An introduction to the study of law, its nature and administration. The law of contracts, bankruptcy, and commercial paper. (3 credits)

Business Law II

A study of agency, partnerships, real property, and corporations, concluding with an introduction to trade regulations. (3 credits)

Business Statistics

Course content includes presentation of data, frequency distributions, averages, dispersion and skewness, index numbers, time series analysis, correlation and forecasting, introduction to the theory of probability and statistical inference. (3 credits)

Communications

The course covers relationship of words, phrases, and clauses; rule for capitalization, abbreviations, and punctuation; effective speech; principles of good letter writing; scope of report writing; component parts of reports; gathering and arranging facts and data; rough draft; rewriting; examples of introduction and body; headings; summarizing conclusion; checklist; synopsis; typing details. (3 credits)

Composition and Rhetoric

Practice in expository writing and the application of rhetorical principles. Wide variety of reading to stimulate good writing and skill in composition. (3 credits)

Structured Systems Analysis

Introduces an overview of the system development life cycle. Emphasis on current system documentation through the use of both classical and structured tools (techniques fo describing process flows, data flows, file design, input and output designs, and program specifications). Emphasis will be placed on information gathering and reporting activities, on the analysis phase, and the interaction of the various participants in the systems process. (3 credits)

Systems Design

A study of the system development methodology and the role played by the systems analyst in developing business applications. Hierarchy charts, IPO, decision tables, and structured English are among the tools discussed and applied. (3 credits)

BUSINESS DATA PROCESSING

Introduction to Computer Concepts

A nontechnical course in modern business data processing—what it is and what it can do. An introduction to the field for those who want the techniques of electronic data processing. This course includes consideration of the systems investigation, defining scope and purpose. (3 credits)

COMPUTER SCIENCE

Computer Science I - Computer Applications and Operations

Elementary programming and hardware concepts and terminology, data representation, flowcharting and elementary BASIC programming concepts. Lecture materials emphasize microcomputers. (3 credits)

Computer Science II - BASIC Programming Fundamentals

Comparing and branching; selecting alternative paths; translating two-directional flowcharts into linear programs, using multiple comparisons; subtotaling; internal subroutines; multiple control breaks; defining a table; loading and printing numeric arrays; searching a table; maintaining a data file; alphabetic and numeric sequencing; coding sorts; merging files; formatting lines, columns, and references; producing graphics; reverses and output; using pexels; creating graphs. (3 credits)

Computer Science III - Computer and FORTRAN Fundamentals

Basic industrial computer systems; computer fundamentals; digital and analog systems; software and programming; computer-aided control systems; interfacing principles. FORTRAN IV programming; fundamental FORTRAN IV concepts; writing simple FORTRAN programs; statement functions; use of magnetic tapes and disks; review of function and subroutine subprograms. (3 credits)

Introduction to Programming

Overview of program creation; information organization; programming concepts; program design; program instructions; overview of major programming languages; the program development cycle; programming project—design and code programs in pseudocode. (3 credits)

Programming in BASIC

This course will offer the student a thorough foundation in the BASIC programming language. Topics covered include writing BASIC statements, control breaks, data storage, sequential tape files, and color, sound, and graphics. (3 credits)

Programming in C

Introduction to the general-purpose programming language C and its increasing use in developing various types of software on microcomputers and minicomputers. An emphasis is placed on the language's economy of expression, its use of function and command libraries, modern control flow and data structures, and C's rich set of operators. (3 credits)

COBOL Programming

Overview of the language; COBOL programming theory; index file creation and maintenance; relative files; sequential files; report writing. This course utilizes an educational version of a COBOL compiler. (4 credits)

Advanced COBOL Programming Techniques

Top-down design and structured programming techniques including string processing, procedures, searching, sorting, introduction to data structures, and table processing. (4 credits)

The Microcomputer and Its Applications

Hardware and software; word processing; database management; spreadsheets; telecommunications; setting up the computer; an overview of BASIC and DOS. This course utilizes computer-based training diskettes. (3 credits)

Business Computer Systems and Applications

Evolution of computers in business; organization and storage of business data; an effective inventory system; database concepts;

manual accounting systems versus computerized systems; spreadsheets; evaluating online accounting; market research; mail merge; integrated marketing packages; word processing; desktop publishing; electronic mail; evaluating business solutions. (3 credits)

Directed Project

Application of technology to a real business problem. Student has a choice of one of a number of projects to undertake. The project will include system analysis, design, programming, and installation of an automated and manual solution. (3 credits)

Advanced Business Applications

In this course the student will employ CBT disks to further explore the capabilities of word processing, spreadsheets, database management, and telecommunications. (3 credits)

ECONOMICS

Economics I

This course defines the economizing problem, develops it, and explores its future implications. The course emphasizes economic growth. Macro and micro economic concepts are examined in terms of a discussion of three fundamental economic questions: (1) what is to be produced? (2) where is it to be produced? and 3) how is it to be produced? (3 credits)

Economics II

This course continues the study of macro and micro economic concepts. Emphasis is placed upon the economics of inequality and poverty. The material is organized to answer two fundamental questions: (1) to whom shall resources be distributed? (2) when will the ''poverty amidst plenty'' problem be resolved? (3 credits)

ENGINEERING TECHNOLOGY

AC and DC Motors and Controls

Principles of generator and motor operation; ratings and efficiency; principles of induction motors and synchronous motors; performance and speed control; single-phase motors; principles of motor control systems; motor-circuit protective devices; solid-state drive systems; SCRs as AC to DC converters; installation and maintenance of drive systems. (2 credits)

Application of Industrial Electronics

Color TV system; basic industrial electronic systems application; voltage and frequency controllers; nondestructive test equipment; resistance welding equipment; dielectric and induction heating; cranes, and materials handling; advanced troubleshooting; analysis of systems; test equipment applications; safe troubleshooting practices; troubleshooting industrial systems. (3 credits)

Basic Industrial Computer Systems

Computer fundamentals; digital and analog systems; software and programming; computer-aided control systems; interfacing principles. (1 credit)

Basic Surveying I

Covers basic principles of tapes and accessories; electronic measurements; leveling; use of transit and theodolite; adjustment of instruments; angle measurement; triangulation; trigonometric leveling; balancing traverse; error of closure; computation of area by latitudes and departures. (3 credits)

Basic Surveying II

Tangents and horizontal curves; grades and vertical curves; compound and reverse curves; transition curves; superelevation; field layout of simple, compound, and spiral curves; vertical parabolic curves; elevations on vertical curves; metric system of measurements; conversion of international and other metric units to English units, and vice versa; use of conversion factors; conversion tables. (3 credits)

Circuits and Components Testing

Reactive circuits; resistance; capacitance and inductance; reactance and impedence; resonant circuits; applications of resonant circuits. D-C principles experiments; A-C principles and components experiments; electrical measurements and instruments experiments; electronic and instruments experiments; reactive circuits experiments; electronic components experiments; basic electronic circuits experiments. (4 credits)

Computer-Aided Drafting and Design

Fundamentals, applicaitons, and equipment associated with CADD; CADD concepts and components; basic CADD commands and functions; constructing CADD engineering drawings; editing and facilitation; generation of color; 3-D modeling; graphics partial programming; CAD/CAM; industrial applications; manufacturers equipment. (1 credit)

Computer-Aided Manufacturing

Basic robotic manufacturing principles; fundamentals of robotics, programming; applicaitons; robot components; control systems; sensors; robot programming and languages; artificial intelligence; applications engineering; processing operations; assembly and inspection; implementing robotics; safety, training, maintenance, and quality; future applications; computer numerical control (CC) and its role in a manufacturing environment; fundamentals of CC; comparison to numerical control; machine tool measuring systems; components; programs and programming; machine tools used in industry; personnel and training requirements; preventive maintenance and servicing; current and future applications. (2 credits)

Concrete

Production of concrete; proportioning of concrete mixes; tests for concrete; field methods in concrete construction. (2 credits)

Earthwork

Surveys for determining grade; cross-sectioning; earthwork computations; formation of embankments; shrinkage and swell; subsidence; moving cut to fill; mass diagrams. (1 credit)

Electrical/Electronic Fundamentals and Measurements

Transformer fundamentals; electrical measurements and instruments; checking simple circuits; troubleshooting with basic meters; how a voltmeter works; how an ammeter works; A-C measuring instruments; miscellaneous electrical measuring instruments. Electrical measurements and instruments; electronic quantities and testing principles; multipurpose test instruments; bridge-type instruments; oscilloscopes; component testers; digital test equipment. (3 credits)

Electrical Installation Practices

Review of sizing conduit, conductors, and boxes; review of circuits; testing circuits; running cable; cutting openings; mounting and grounding boxes; preparing cable and installing cable in boxes; wiring commonly used devices; plugs and receptacles; line and extension cords; split-wired and switched receptacles; switch circuits; dimmers; wiring and mounting lampholders and lighting fixtures; use of nipples and hickeys; wiring appliance circuits; wiring doorbell circuits and electric space heaters; conduit bending; raceways; busways; industrial power distribution systems; definitions and explanation of code. (2 credits)

Electrical Machines

Principles and characteristics of DC and AC machines, electrical connections; ratings; performance and speed control; thermal overload protection; types of drive systems; efficiency of DC and AC machines and transformers. (4 credits)

Electronic Circuits

Electronic systems; electronic devices and amplification; audio and R-F circuits; oscillators, feedback and waveform generators; electronic power supply systems; industrial receivers, transmitters, and video systems; servo and control systems; pulse and logic circuits; programmable controllers and microprocessor. Troubleshooting electronic equipment and systems; logical troubleshooting methods; instrument selection; measuring techniques; interpreting data and results; use of manufacturers' instructions; test instruments maintenance. (3 credits)

Electronic Instrumentation and Control

Automatic testing of electronic devices; electronic instrumentation and control: physical properties and their measurement Part 1; physical properties and their measurement Part 2; measuring instruments and signal processing; transducers; introduction to control systems; controllers; control system methods; data logging, transmission, and display; control applications, maintenance and troubleshooting. Industrial electronic circuit applications: interfacing process variables; motor control and servo systems; numeric control systems; programmable controllers; industrial robots. (3 credits)

Engineering Economy

Cash flow; time value of money; investment methods; use of interest tables; engineering valuation; canons of ethics for engineers. (1 credit)

Engineering Materials

Composition and properties of metals, ceramics, concrete, glass, graphite, plastics, and wood. (2 credits)

Engineering Mechanics

Scope of engineering mechanics; collinear and concurrent forces; center of gravity of bodies; freebody diagrams; characteristics of friction; bodies on level and inclined surfaces; kinematics; translation and rotation; kinetics; force-mass-acceleration method; collision of two bodies. (3 credits)

Fluid Mechanics

Properties of materials; intensity of pressure; flow of liquids through pipes; Bernoulli's theorem; resultant forces due to liquid pressure; center of pressure; Chezy-Darcy formula; Hazen-Williams formula; Reynolds number; flow of water in open channels; rate of discharge through wires. (3 credits)

Fundamentals of Electricity

D-C principles: nature of electricity; preventive maintenance; electric cells and batteries; electrical components and Ohm's Law; basic circuit arrangements; electrical language and hardware; magnetism and electromagnetism; D-C generators. A-C principles and components: alternators; transformers; inductance and capacitance; A-C circuits; rectification and electronic devices; electric energy distribution; types of electric circuits. (3 credits)

Fundamentals of Electronics

Electrical components; resistive, capacitive, and inductive components; basic semiconductor components; semiconductor switching devices; special semiconductor devices; rectifiers and electron tubes; switching and connection devices; basic electronic circuits; logic circuits; gating and counting circuits; pulse digital circuits. (3 credits)

Geodetic Surveying

Horizontal and vertical control surveys; monuments and markers; triangulation surveys; state plane coordinate systems; methods of projection; construction and maintenance surveys; subdivision of city blocks into lots. (3 credits)

Highway Construction and Design I

This course covers soil studies; subgrades and drainage; location surveys; selection of route; establishing grade lines; traffic studies; signs; volume and speed studies; safety appurtenances. (3 credits)

Highway Construction and Design II

The course covers maintenance of untreated surfaces; stabilized soil-bound surfaces; rigid concrete pavements; flexible bituminous pavements; design of pipe culverts. (2 credits)

Industrial Systems

Characteristics and applications of storage batteries; lighting control systems; principles of motor control systems; control components; protective devices; solid-state motor drive systems; definition and classification of telemetering systems; transmission data signals; computations in telemetering; telemetering for automatic control; electric power systems control. (2 credits)

Introduction to Microprocessors

Introduction to computers; introduction to microprocessor applications; microprocessor basics. (2 credits)

Kinematics

Linkages; quick-return mechanisms; kinematics of link mechanisms; spur gearing, worm, and worm gears; gear cutting; use of gear trains; compound gearing; ratchet mechanisms; types and uses of CAMs; fundamentals of CAM motion; CAM profiles. (4 credits)

Land Surveying

Determination of true meridian; latitudes and longitudes; rectangular system of dividing land; subdivision of townships and sections; identifying and restoring corners; correction of defects in original surveys; legal descriptions. (3 credits)

Linear and Digital Integrated Circuits

Linear and digital integrated circuits; linear and digital circuit principles; integrated circuit techniques; linear integrated circuits; digital integrated circuits; integrated circuit logic systems; troubleshooting linear and digital IC systems; pulse circuits experiments; logic circuits experiments; linear and digital integrated circuits experiments. (3 credits)

Manufacturing Processes

Cutting tools; machine tools; powder metallurgy; hot and cold working of materials; stamping, drawing and forming; heat treatment; welding techniques; special forming techniques; electrical and chemical machining; tension, compression, torsion, impact and hardness testing of materials; nondestructive testing techniques; use of vernier calipers, micrometers, gages, gage blocks, and sine bars; basic numerical control; numerical control programming. (4 credits)

Mechanical Design I

Stress analysis; work, energy, and power; beam deflections; design stress; normal and tangential acceleration; moment diagrams; friction; lubrication systems; strength of materials; ball and roller bearings; calculations of bearing loads. (3 credits)

Mechanical Design II

Shaft design and seals; fasteners; couplings; welding and weld designs; belting; change drives; hoists and conveyors; ropes; brakes; clutches; power screws; gears; cams; flywheels; springs; seals and sealants; cylinders, heads, and plates; fluid power; fluid torque convertors; governors; professional registration. (3 credits)

Mechanical Drawing

Drawing equipment; lettering; eight drawing plates; geometrical drawing problems; projections of simple solids; foreshortened views in projection; common conventions; lifting and test cover; hanger assembly. (1 credit)

Mechanics of Materials

The course includes simple stresses; fixed and moving loads on beams; reactions at beam support; continuous beams; points on inflection; shear and bending moment diagrams; moment of inertia and section modulus; theory of column design; radius of gyration. (2 credits)

Microprocessor Applications

Working with an uncomplicated microprocessor, the MC 6802, Part 1; microprocessor programming principles, Part 1; working with an uncomplicated microprocessor, the MC 6802, Part 2; microprocessor programming principles, part 2; interfacing through serial and parallel ports; troubleshooting microprocessor equipment, Part 2; other families of microprocessors; microprocessor experiments. (3 credits)

Operational Analysis

Part 1: Operation analysis procedures; procedure for effecting operation improvements; selection of process and tooling. *Part 2*: Working conditions; plant layout and material handling; motion study. (2 credits)

Planning and Control

Nature of production control; demand forecasting. Economic order quantity; critical-path method; quality costs and their control inspection function; vendor relation; manufacturing planning for quality; quality improvement; fundamentals of materials control; acquisition of materials; storage of materials; control of materials during manufacture; paper-work control; systems approach to materials control. (3 credits)

Plant Facilities

Plant layout; definition; scope, importance, advantages, and nature of layout projects; effect of storage, services, and materials handling on plant layout; collection and analysis of data necessary for the development and presentation of layouts; industrial layout; growth planning; manufacturing plant layouts; industrial layout; warehouse design; types of warehouses; use of computer; design factors; alternatives and implementation; materials handling; introduction; sealing equipment; trucks; conveyors; pneumatic systems; bulk handling systems and components; grab attachments; long distance transportation; auxiliary equipment; specialized components. (2 credits)

Productivity Engineering

The productivity cycle; measurement, evaluation, planning and improvement; definitions of productivity; factors affecting productivity; productivity engineering and management; productivity measurement at a national level; the need for productivity measurement; the total productivity model; computations in the application of the total productivity model; productivity management using the model; implementing the model; productivity improvement techniques; materials-based, employee-based, product-based, task-based; setting up productivity improvement programs. (2 semester hours)

Pulse and Logic Circuits

Pulse circuits: pulse techniques; pulse generators; waveshaping circuits; timing and synchronization; pulse circuit applications; troubleshooting pulse circuits. Logic circuits: logic circuit fundamentals; introduction to number systems; logic devices and diagrams; logic families; applications of logic circuits; troubleshooting logic circuits. (3 credits)

Reinforced Concrete Design

The course covers design and analysis of rectangular beams, T-beams, double-reinforced beams. (2 credits)

Resident Laboratory Training

The two-week eleven-day session includes the use of various measuring instruments for performing a series of comprehensive experiments. The experiments are designed to provide familiarization with instrumentation, equipment, preparation of data, and laboratory reporting techniques. (3 credits)

Statistical Quality Control

Part 1. Objectives of statistical quality control; some representative applications; some fundamental statistical concepts; why the control chart works; examples of a process in control; examples of processes out of control.

Part 2. Directions for simple X and R charts; the selection of rational subgroups; different adaptations of the control chart for variables.

Part 3. Some fundamentals of the theory of probability; the control chart for fraction defective; the control chart for defects; some aspects of the relationship between control charts and certain other statistical techniques.

Part 4. Some aspects of specifications and tolerances; some fundamental concepts in acceptance sampling; dodge-roming type systems for acceptance sampling by attributes.

Part 5. Some other types of systems for acceptance by attributes; acceptance sampling by variables; some aspects of life testing and reliability; some cost aspects of quality decision. (3 credits for completion of Parts 1 through 5)

Structural Steel Design

The course covers selection of rolled steel shapes for beams and column; allowable unit stresses; design of connections; eccentric loading; design of column base plates. (3 credits)

Technical Materials

Use of metrics; fundamental laws of chemistry; metallic and nonmetallic elements; organic chemistry; unit operations; composition and properties of materials. (3 credits)

Technical Science

Use of metrics; nature of heat; expansion of gases; carnot's cycle, fundamental laws of chemistry; metallic and nonmetallic elements; organic chemistry, unit operations. Mathematical modeling and problem solving is used extensively. (2 credits)

Technical Writing

This course is designed to help students improve writing skills in preparation for technical professions. Specialized training is offered in writing of proposals, reports, instructions, letters, abstracts, resumes, etc. (3 credits)

Technology Orientation

This course traces the development of engineering and engineering technology. It focuses on contributions from primitive times to the twentieth century. In addition to engineering technology, the student is introduced to topics in technical mathematics including the use of a scientific calculator. (1 credit)

Time Study

Part 1. Responsibilities of labor and management in time studies; stop watches and equipment; procedure in taking the study; rating operator performance; setting the standards. (2 credits)

Tool Design I

Single-point, multiple-point, and rotary tools; control of tool wear and failure; types of work-holding devices; power presses; shearing and die-cutting; design of piercing, blanking, and compound dies; bending, forming, and extrusion dies; forging dies. (3 credits)

Tool Design II

Principles of gaging; types and applications of inspection gages; tools for soldering, brazing, and mechanical joining processes; general considerations in tool design; safety; tool materials; heat-treating; fits and tolerances. (3 credits)

Topographic Drawing and Surveying

The course includes use of drafting instruments; azimuths and bearings of lines; topographic symbols and contours; plotting cross sections and profiles; city and village maps; determination of distance by stadia; stadia surveys for locating topography; plane-table surveying; topographic maps; methods of control. (5 credits)

ENGLISH

Introduction to Literature

Reading and analysis of the main genres of literature; poetry, fiction, and drama. Themes and forms of literature are demonstrated and explained. (3 credits)

FINANCE

Principles of Finance

Includes a review of the history of money, monetary systems, and credit. Also covered is the role of finance in various forms of business organizations, capital budgeting, sources of funds, marketing securities, capital structure, foreign expansion, and reorganization of a business firm. (3 credits)

Securities and Investments

This course discusses the basic principles underlying investment decisions. It includes a comprehensive study of securities and markets, fundamental and technical analysis, and portfolio selection. (3 credits)

Personal Financial Management

A study of the fundamental concepts and importance of personal financial management. The course involves the management and financing of fundamental assets including how to protect against events that might make good asset and liability management useless. (3 credits)

HISTORY

Man in the Twentieth Century

An analysis of major events and influences in this century, interpreting the decline of European hegemony, the rise of the new world powers, and the emergence of the Third World. (3 credits)

HOSPITALITY INDUSTRY

Introduction to the Hospitality Industry

This introductory course to the hotel restaurant business covers its origins and history, its organization, job opportunities in the front and back office, and in restaurant and banquet services. (3 credits)

Hospitality Law and Insurance

This course is an introduction to the study of the law, its nature, and administration. It covers the law of contractors, bankruptcy, and commercial paper. The law is discussed as it applies to the hospitality industry, as are the legal responsibilities of hotel personnel and of guests, and basic insurance principles and needs in the hospitality industry. (3 credits)

Hospitality Marketing and Advertising

The purpose of this course is to describe the techniques of advertising, the function of advertising in the marketing area, and the role of advertising in the marketplace. It explores marketing and advertising applications specific to the hospitality areas. (3 credits)

Hospitality Purchasing and Storage

This course covers the types of buyers and their functions, and it evaluates the performance of buyers. It also covers the purchasing process, discussing how to prepare and check specifications and where to purchase. The section on storage discusses efficient layout for receiving, how to evaluate merchandise, storage areas for food and nonfood items, and the use and maintenance of storage areas. (3 credits)

The Tourism Process

This course begins by tracing tourism through the ages and discussing travel before modern times. Next, it provides some insight into the purpose and scope of present day travel and the composition and size of the tourism industry. It identifies major tourist markets, methods of selecting target markets, as well as jobs in the tourist industry. The course concludes with an explanation of the business relationships between hospitality facilities and travel agencies. (3 credits)

Basics of the Catering Business

After answering the most commonly asked questions about catering, the first part of the course deals with fees and types of catering events. Then it covers the basics of starting and operating your own catering business. Finally, the course deals with the caterer's kitchen, and coping with a less than ideal kitchen. (3 credits)

Nutrition and Menu Planning

Good nutrition is instrumental to maintaining healthy body organs and a healthy digestive process. The digestive process is explained in detail. The text then identifies the essential nutrient groups and their sources. The course concludes with a discussion of ways to provide healthy daily menus. (3 credits)

Quantity Food Production

The primary concerns of this course are supervisory and management principles and procedures that maximize efficiency in quantity food production. The course is divided into two sections, the first dealing with the management concerns related to facilities, tools and equipment, menus and recipes, purchasing and storage, and sanitation and safety. The second section covers the actual preparation and service of a wide range of foods. (3 credits)

Beverage Operations

This course covers the profitability of alcoholic beverages, legal control of alcohol, the types of wine and wine service, and the types of malt beverages and distilled spirits. Also covered are the purchase, storage, and control of alcoholic beverages for a profitable operation. (3 credits)

Hospitality Accounting

This course reviews the nature of accounting and financial reports. It covers the balance sheet, income statement, transaction recording, the trial balance, journal entries, posting, adjustments, and the cash method versus the accrual method of accounting. The work sheet, the accounting cycle, accounts and procedures for merchandising business, special journals, and payroll accounting are also covered, as are the specifics of accounting for the hospitality business. (3 credits)

Hospitality Engineering Systems

This course introduces the engineering and maintenance department and explains its function. It provides a basic grounding in electrical, plumbing, heating, refrigeration and ventilation systems. It covers the housekeeping department and its functions and training methods. It closes with a discussion of sanitation as related to food and water handling to control bacteria, yeasts, molds, viruses, parasites, insects, and rodents. (3 credits)

MANAGEMENT

Personnel Management

A study of the role of the personnel department in the selection, orientation, and training of employees. Among the topics covered are the procedures used in the formulation of personnel policies, employee evaluation programs, and wage and salary administration. The effect of unionism on personnel management is also reviewed. (3 credits)

Principles of Management

Presents ideas on leadership, the basic management functions of planning, organizing, controlling, motivating, and coordinating. Also, this course covers employee behavior, morale, complaints and grievances, training and communication. Emphasis is on the importance of management in business enterprise. (3 credits)

Production Management

An introduction to the production function, including factors affecting plant layout, nature and purpose of production planning, factors in material control, purchasing techniques, materials inspection, analysis of customers' complaints, and occupational safety. (3 credits)

Supervisory Management

Management functions supervisors must perform. Theory and applications relating to the theme: the essence of supervisory management is working with and through people. Applies the concepts of planning, organizing, leading, and controlling to specific supervisory situations. Also discusses Management Information Systems. (3 credits)

Management Information Systems

The design, development, use, evaluation and improvement of information management systems. Emphasis on the concept of an integrated system, designed to produce decision-aiding information for all levels of management. A survey of existing MIS tools and software is included. (3 credits)

MARKETING

Marketing Research

The nature and scope of marketing research, including marketing research procedures, are described. Also covered in detail are the topics of sampling and sampling methods, primary and secondary data sources, questionnaire scales, data analysis, and development of summary statistics. (3 credits)

Advertising Principles

The purpose of this course is to describe, at a very basic level, the techniques of advertising, the function of advertising, advertising in the marketing area, and the role of advertising in the marketplace.

Principles of Marketing

This course introduces the meaning of marketing and product management. Emphasis is placed on the behavioral science approach to marketing, the tools of marketing, and managing the marketing function. (3 credits)

MATHEMATICS

Analytic Geometry and Calculus

Rectangular coordinates; graphs of linear equations; conic sections; exponential, logarithmic, and trigonometric functions; continuity; limits; derivatives and their applications, including derivatives of implicit functions, parametric equations, and trigonometric, exponential, hyperbolic, and logarithmic functions; integrals and their applications; methods of integration; polar coordinates. (4 credits)

Applied Math

After covering the use of the metric system this course introduces the

student to the practical application of calculus to electronics. Topics to be covered range from graphic differentiation to partial derivatives to the application of double integrals to electrical circuits. (3 credits)

Math for Business and Finance

A review of percentages, discounts, interest, present worth, sinking funds, and installment buying. Includes pricing, depreciation, investments, and insurance. The use of symbols and their application, equations and formulas. Importance of statistics - table and chart construction. (3 credits)

Technical Mathematics I

Use of formulas; algebraic operations; solution of linear equations; use of determinants; quadratic equations; use of exponents; operations with imaginary numbers; use of logarithms. (2 credits)

Technical Mathematics II

In this course the student is introduced to practical geometry and plane trigonometry. In practical geometry, topics discussed range from lines to polygons to solids. In plane trigonometry the topics discussed range from angles to trigonometric functions to trigonometric identities. (2 credits)

PUBLIC RELATIONS

Public Relations

This course deals with the evolution of public relations, including the organization and responsibility of a public relations department and the importance of communications research. Special emphasis is placed on dealing with the press, government, community, employees, and customers. The course concludes with the techniques of good public relations writing. (3 credits)

RETAILING

Retail Management

The purpose of this course is to present an analysis on the basics of retailing, management of a successful retail business, and merchandising principles. (3 credits)

SALES MANAGEMENT

Sales Management

An analytic look at the field of sales management including organization of the sales force and the relations of the sales organization to other internal departments and the external community. Also covered in this course are the product and the market place. (3 credits)

PHYSICAL SCIENCE

Physical Science

This course discusses the various principles that define and govern the physical universe as we know it. The disciplines introduced include: chemistry, physics, and earth and space sciences. (3 credits)

PHYSICS

Physics

The topics covered in this course are heat, electricity, light and sound. The nature and properties of each are presented, The areas discussed range from circuits to optical instruments to infrasonics and ultrasonics. (3 credits)

PSYCHOLOGY

Human Behavior

The main thrust of this course is to show the interaction of the three disciplines that comprise the behavioral sciences—anthropology, sociology, and psychology. The course emphasizes the study of human behavior in its cultural, social, and organizational relationships. (3 credits)

Industrial Psychology

Application of psychology to industrial organizations; psychology of attitudes; morale and group processes; supervisory leadership; measuring proficiency; selection and placement; psychological tests; design of jobs and man-machine systems; training in organizations; motivation at work; fatigue; accidents and their prevention; psychological factors in labor turnover; counseling, interviewing, and job contracts; organizations psychology. (3 credits)

SAFETY

Industrial Safety

Overview of the need for safety awareness in the industrial workplace; specific procedures for handling various materials; operating different kinds of machinery; performing job tasks safely; how the human body is constructed and how it works; which parts of the human body are most frequently injured and how to protect them; survey of the regulations designed to improve industrial safety. (2 credits)

ICS Learning Systems
925 Oak Street
Scranton, Pennsylvania 18515 (717) 342-7701

Description:

ICS Learning Systems International Correspondence Schools) was founded in 1891 and was the first proprietary correspondence school in the United States. ICS has enrolled over nine million students since that time. Enrollments for 1994 totaled 249,273. ICS now occupies a modern 120,000 square foot facility in Scranton, Pennsylvania. Course offerings range from high school to college level.

ICS pioneered the use of Dial-a-Question, a toll-free telephone service used by students for educational assistance. One of the Home Study Divisions of National Education Corporation, ICS includes the ICS Center for Degree Studies among its offerings (SEE **ICS Center for Degree Studies**). Formed in 1975, the Center is authorized by the Pennsylvania Department of Education to award the Associate in Specialized Technology degree and the Associate in Specialized Business degree. For information regarding high school courses, See **ICS - Newport/Pacific High School**.

Faculty:

Gary Keisling, President; James Lytle, Vice President for Education; Connie Dempsey, Education Director.

Academic Levels:
College
High School
Vocational

Degree/Certificate Programs:
Diploma, Certificate, Associate Degree.

Admission Requirements:

Minimum age is 17. Depending upon the program of instruction desired, requirements can range from eighth grade to high school graduation or GED equivalency. Applicants enrolled in secondary schools must submit releases from school administrators. Applicants under 18 years of age must provide guarantor's signature. Guarantor not required if applicant is a member of the Armed Services.

Tuition:

Varies considerably, depending upon the course. Down payment and monthly payment plans are available. Some courses approved for VA benefits. Pro rata refund policy.

Enrollment Period:

Depending upon the program, the maximum time allowed could range from 2 to 6 years. Allowances are made for breaks in the instructional program through study time extensions.

Equipment Requirements:

All materials for successful completion are included in tuition charges.

Credit and Grading:

The grading system is numeric and the minimum passing grade is 70 percent. The honor system is used for a majority of the tests. Transfer-in credit granted upon faculty approval.

Accreditations:

Distant Education and Training Council; licensed by the Pennsylvania Department of Education, Board of Private Correspondence Schools.

VOCATIONAL COURSES

AIR CONDITIONING AND REFRIGERATION
Air Conditioning/Refrigeration Course

This course includes instructional units covering the following topics: Introduction to Refrigeration; Refrigeration Systems; Refrigeration Servicing; Cooling and Heating; Air Conditioning Systems.

ART
Art

This course includes study units covering: Line Drawing; Tone Drawing; Composing the Picture; Watercolor Painting; Animal Art and Pastels; Drawing Buildings: Interiors and Exteriors; Magic Art Oil Painting; Realistic Portraits; More About Oil Painting; Drawing Standing Figures; Figures in Motion and Repose.

AUTOMOTIVE TECHNOLOGY
Auto Mechanics

This course includes instructional units which cover the following topics: Shop Practices and Basic Automobile Systems; Automobile Exhaust and Electrical Systems; Automobile Ignition Systems and Engine Tune-Up; Automobile Power Trains; Automobile Brakes and Steering Systems; Automobile Engine Overhaul.

Diesel Mechanics

The instructional units for this course cover the following topics:

Diesel Engine Fundamentals; Systems of the Diesel Engine; Diesel Engine Operation; Developing Skills for Troubleshooting and Repair; Maintenance and Overhaul.

BUSINESS

Bookkeeping

Study units cover banking, payroll, inventory, how to keep a journal, make a ledger, prepare a balance sheet, and other aspects of bookkeeping.

CATERING/GOURMET COOKING

Catering/Gourmet Cooking

This course includes study units covering: The Big Business of Catering and Gourmet Foods; Starting Your Catering Business; The Caterer's Kitchen; The Caterer's Equipment; Basic Techniques of Cuisine and Service; Seafood; Vegetables; Meat and Poultry; Desserts and Pastry; A Caterer's Guide to Dining Etiquette; Six Thousand Dishes of Classic Cuisine; Ethnic Cuisines and Customs; Getting Down to Business.

COMPUTER SCIENCE

Computer Programming

This study units for this course cover the following topics: The Magic of Computers; An "Inside" View; The System and the Software; Program Design—The Game Plan; Putting Your Microcomputer to Work; A Lesson in BASIC Programming; Computer Logic—The Limits of Computer "Intelligence"; Control Breaks—Taking Intermediate Totals; Tables and Arrays—Lists of Similar Data; Merging—Functions; Advanced Printing and Graphics Techniques.

DAY CARE MANAGEMENT

Child Day Care

This course includes study units covering the following topics: Child Care Today: An Urgent Need; Child Growth and Development; How to Start Your Child Care Facility—Basic Steps; Licensing, Accreditation, and Certification; The Facility; Equipment; Staff; Planning and Implementing for the Environment; Health, Safety, and Nutrition; Guidance; Working with Parents; Financing and Budget.

ELECTRICITY

Electrician

This course includes instructional units covering the following topics: Basic Knowledge for the Electrician; Basics of Wiring; Electrical Principles, Lamps, and Multitester; Circuits, Schematics, and Measurements; Motors and Motor Control; Heating and Lighting Practice; Applications and Estimating.

ELECTRONICS

Basic Electronics

Offers training needed for an entry-level job in the industrial and communication areas of electronics (assembler, inspector, customer representative, technician, apprentice). Fundamentals of electricity, use of formulas, schematics, diagrams, electronic devices, circuits and their applications, use of electronic test and measuring instruments.

FASHION MERCHANDISING

Fashion Merchandising

This course includes study units covering the following topics: The Field of Fashion; Line and Design in Fashion; Color in Fashion; Point-of-Sale Merchandising; Creation of Fashion Apparel; Merchandising Fashion Accessories; Merchandising Home Furnishings; Advertising and Publicity in Fashion Merchandising; Fashion Writing for Sales Promotion; Visual Merchandising; Fabrics in Fashion; Fashion Buying; Fashion Direction and Coordination.

HOSPITALITY INDUSTRY

Hotel/Restaurant Management Course

This course includes instructional units covering the following topics: The Hospitality Industry; Front Office Operations; Marketing Hospitality Services; Fundamentals of Foods; Quantity Food Production; Law for the Hospitality Industry.

INTERIOR DECORATING

Interior Decorating

This course includes study units covering the following topics: Meeting Your Decorating Client; Floor Treatments; All About Walls; Windows: Plain and Dressed; Designing with Furniture; Identifying Furniture Styles and Periods; How to Use Color in Interior Decorating; Lighting for Illumination and Special Effects; Fabrics in Interior Design; Accessories from A to Z; The Elements and Principles of Design; Low-Cost Decorating; Decorating from Building Plans.

PARALEGAL STUDIES

Legal Secretary

This course includes study units covering the following topics: The Nature of the Legal Profession; Legal Structure; Legal Research; Legal Terminology and Phraseology; Client Interviews: Communication Skills and Procedures; Public Resources and How to Use Them; Drafting Legal Documents I—Form, Content, and Style; Drafting Legal Documents II: Form, Content, and Style; Drafting Legal Documents III: Form, Content, and Style; Drafting Legal Documents IV: Form, Content, and Style; Discovery Techniques—Part I; Discovery Techniques—Part II; How to Prepare Clients and Witnesses for Hearings and Trials; How to Process a Civil Action; Managing the Legal Office.

PHYSICAL FITNESS

Fitness and Nutrition

This course includes study units covering the following topics: The Fitness Field: Broadening Horizons; Exercise and How It Affects The Body; Muscles in Motion; How to Design a Sports Conditioning Program; Exercise Testing and Evaluation; The Fitness Leader in Class; Movement Repertoire for a Fitness Class; Skills for Promoting Lifestyle Change; Injury Prevention and First-Aid Treatment; Nutrition for Optimal Performance; Management Skills for the Fitness Field.

SMALL BUSINESS MANAGEMENT

Computer-Assisted Small Business Management

This course includes study units covering the following topics: How to Succeed in Business; Essentials of Business Enterprise; Personnel Management; Budgeting for Your Business; Principles of Marketing, Part 1; Principles of Marketing, Part 2; Accounting, Part 1; Accounting Part 2; Payroll Accounting; Introduction to Business Finance.

SURVEYING AND MAPPING

Surveying and Mapping

This course includes 4 instruction units and covers the following topics: Technical Mathematics; Elementary Surveying; Drawing for the Surveyor; Land and City Surveying.

TELEVISION REPAIR

TV and VCR Repair Course

This course includes study units and covers the following topics: Introduction to TV Troubleshooting; TV Technology; Understanding Schematics and Circuit Diagrams; Television Tools and Test Instruments; The Television Signal; The Television Receiver; TV Tuners; From the Tuner Through the Video Amplifier; TV Receiver Circuits; Horizontal Deflection System; Color Transmission; Colorimetry; The Color Television Receiver; Introduction to VCR Troubleshooting; VCR Troubleshooting.

VETERINARY ASSISTANT

Veterinary Assistant

Covers anatomy, nutrition, breeding, general care; how to read x-rays, assist in surgery, anesthesia, and more.

ICS Newport/Pacific High School
925 Oak Street
Scranton, Pennsylvania 18515 (717) 342-7701

Description:

The Newport/Pacific High School is a division of the International Correspondence Schools (ICS)—National Education Corporation. It offers a complete high school diploma course. ICS also offers other vocational and avocational courses featuring uniquely designed educational materials and student educational services. For details regarding admission requirements, enrollment procedures, and other pertinent data, SEE **International Correspondence Schools.** There are three programs available, each requiring the completion of 21 units of credit. Required subjects are listed for each of three available programs in the following paragraphs. Elective subjects are listed below under subject headings.

The Adult Program contains minimum basic requirements for practical living and offers the widest possible choice of elective courses. Required subjects include Politics and People; Literature I; U.S. History; Fitness; Consumer Math; Systems of the Body; English; Civics; General Science; Word Power; General Math I; World History; Human Relations; General Math II; Writing for Success; and Nutrition. Five units of elective subjects are also required.

The Vocational Program offers vocational instruction along with the required subjects which are the same as for the Adult Program above. Five units of elective vocational subjects are required.

The Academic Program is designed for persons planning to attend college. The required subjects are Politics and People; Literature I; U.S. History; Fitness; Algebra I; General Science; English; Civics; Biology; Literature II; Geometry; World History; Human Relations; Algebra II; Writing for Success; Inorganic Chemistry. Five additional units of credit from elective subjects are required.

Accreditations:

Distance Education and Training Council.

ART

Introduction to Art

(1 unit)

AUTOMOTIVE TECHNOLOGY

Automotive Body Rebuilding

(2 units)

Automobile Refinishing

(1 unit)

Basic Automobile Systems

(1 unit)

Automobile Electrical Systems and Tune-up

(2 units)

Automobile Engine Overhaul

(1 unit)

Customizing Vans, Trucks, and Autos

(1 unit)

Diesel Engine Fundamentals

(2 units)

Truck and Tractor Components

(2 units)

Introduction to Motorcycle Repair

(1 unit)

BUILDING TRADES

Basic Architecture

(1 unit)

Basic Carpentry

(2 units)

Basic Masonry

(1 unit)

Basic Plumbing

(1 unit)

Blueprint Reading

(1 unit)

Introduction to Drafting

(1 unit)

BUSINESS EDUCATION

Accounting (Basic Bookkeeping)

1 (unit)

Business Law I

(1 unit)

Business Law II

(1 unit)

Modern Business Management

(2 units)

Office Secretary I

(1 unit)

Office Secretary II

(1 unit)

Public Relations

(1 unit)

Sales Management

(1 unit)

Salesmanship

(1 unit)

Stenoscript

(1 unit)

Typing

Typewriter is required. (1 unit)

COMPUTER SCIENCE

Introduction to Computer

No computer required. (1 unit)

Introduction to Computer Programming

No computer required. (2 units)

CONSERVATION

Fish and Land Management

(1 unit)

Forestry

(1 unit)

Wildlife Management

(1 unit)

Conservation Management

(1 unit)

ELECTRICITY

Electrical Safety and Equipment

(1 unit)

Electrical Practices

(1 unit)

Tools for Electric Wiring

(1 unit)

ENGLISH

Business Communications

(1 unit)

Everyday Writing

(1 unit)

Literature III

(1 unit)

Literature IV

(1 unit)

Reading Improvement

(2 units)

FASHION MERCHANDISING

Introduction to Fashion Merchandising

(1 unit)

GUN REPAIR

Introduction to Gun Repair

(1 unit)

INTERIOR DECORATING

Introduction to Interior Decorating

(1 unit)

LAW ENFORCEMENT

Law Enforcement: Patrol Procedures

(1 unit)

Law Enforcement: Criminal Investigation

(1 unit)

MATHEMATICS

Applied Business Math

(1 unit)

Calculus: Function and Use

(1 unit)

Trigonometry and Analytical Geometry

(1 unit)

MEDICAL/DENTAL OFFICE MANAGEMENT

Introduction to Medical/Dental Office Management

(1 unit)

PRACTICAL LIVING

Introduction to Food Catering

(1 unit)

Nutritional Foods

(1 unit)

Your Personal Image

(1 unit)

SCIENCE

Behavioral Science

(1 unit)

Physical Science

(1 unit)

SOCIAL STUDIES

World Geography

(1 unit)

TRAVEL INDUSTRY

Introduction to Travel Agent

(1 unit)

VETERINARY ASSISTING

Introduction to Animal Sciences

(1 unit)

IMC - International Management Centres
Castle Street
Buckingham, England MK18 1BP
44-280-817222

Description:
IMC-International Management Centres was founded in 1964. Courses are offered in general management and all major fields of professional management. Contact the organization for course descriptions and current tuition and fees.

Faculty:
Dr. Gordon Wills, Principal.

Accreditations:
Distance Education and Training Council.

Institute of Physical Therapy
1690 U.S. 1 South
Suite 1
St. Augustine, Florida 32086   (904) 826-0084

Description:
The institute was founded in 1966 by Stanley V. Paris. It offers continuing education seminars on a nationwide basis. The Advanced Master of Science in Physical Therapy program, restructured in 1991, was begun in response to the need for advance education in clinical physical therapy specialty areas, such as orthopaedics, manual therapy, sports therapy, geriatrics, and neurology. The institute currently enrolls over 300 students nationwide.

Faculty:
Dr. Stanley V. Paris, President; Patricia King Baker, Education Director. There is a faculty of 33 members.

Academic Levels:
Graduate
Noncredit

Degree/Certificate Programs:
Degree, Certificate, Diploma.

Admission Requirements:
Applicants must be licensed physical therapists with a minimum of a bachelor's degree in physical therapy. Minimum GRE scores of 900 must be submitted prior to matriculation. A maximum of 12 transfer credits may be transferred into the program (with the approval of the graduate program director and provided the course were completed with a B or better grade and taken no more than two years prior to admission).

Tuition:
Varies per course. Overall cost of program is $13,000. Student loans available to qualified students through TFC Financial Services, Faculty Development Scholarship, and Flagler Scholarship Program. Pro rata refund policy with

DETC conformance. Home study manuals, videos, and reference articles are included in tuition fee.

Enrollment Period:
The maximum time to complete the program is five years. Absence extending for more than one year may be excused by the program director. A continuing student fee of $50 per year is required. A student who has not taken a course within a two-year period must re-apply for admission.

Equipment Requirements:
Home study manuals, videos, and reference articles are included in tuition fee.

Credit and Grading:
A, B, C, and F letter grades are used as well as Pass and Fail. Overall grade point average of B or better is required for graduation.

Library Services:
The institute has an on campus library consisting of over 2,000 books, 5,000 articles, periodicals, audio- and video-tapes.

Accreditations:
Distance Education and Training Council.

International Aviation and Travel Academy
300 West Arbrook Boulevard
Arlington, Texas 76014-3199   (800) 678-0700

Description:
The International Aviation and Travel Academy was established in 1971 as Braniff Education Systems and was purchased by KDW Schools, Inc. in 1986. At IATA, training makes the difference. With state-of-the-art equipment, experienced staff, and a broad range curriculum, the academy provides industry employers with high caliber personnel. Graduates have been recruited by over 300 companies. An Airline/Travel Industry and Golden Passport home study courses are offered.

Faculty:
Kenneth D. Woods, President; Stanley W. Larson, Education Director; Ron Clary, Director of Training.

Academic Levels:
Vocational

Degree/Certificate Programs:
Diploma.

Admission Requirements:
Student must be a U.S. citizen or a permanent resident alien; at least 17 years of age; high school completion or equivalent. Travel and Tourism applicants: Industry criteria are such that an obvious physical or mental disability, overweight, condition, drug addiction, chronic medical problem or felony arrest record could hamper employment possibilities in public contact positions.

Tuition:
Contact the academy for current tuition and fees.

Credit and Grading:
Numerical grades are used. Minimum passing grade is 70.

Accreditations:
Distance Education and Training Council.

VOCATIONAL COURSES

TRAVEL INDUSTRY

Airline/Travel Industry

The 14 lessons cover the fundamental skills necessary to make professional travel arrangements. Learning resources are provided to assist students in their studies, including nationwide access by telephone to instructors with years of industry experience.

Careers in the Travel Industry. A wide-ranging discussion of career opportunities in the travel industry with job descriptions of the many different positions available.

Professional Development and Career Planning. A unit designed to guide in the development of a professional attitude consistent with the travel industry. Activities and exercises on interviewing skills, resume preparation, and job search skills are presented.

Airport Related Operations. An explanation of the cooperative roles of government, community, business, and airlines in the development and operation of a typical major airport.

The Lodging Industry. An overview of hotels, motels, resorts, and executive conference centers in the travel industry with an emphasis on job skills and tasks of the travel agent. An introduction to travel marketing concepts and face-to-face retail and commercial selling strategies for travel agencies.

Travel Agency Operations/Sales Marketing. A comprehensive study of the duties and functions of today's travel agency with an emphasis on job skills and tasks of the travel agent. An introduction to travel marketing concepts and face-to-face retail and commercial selling strategies for travel agencies.

Rail/Bus/Rent-A-Car/Cruises. An overview of the role of railroads, bus lines, and rental car companies in the travel business. A study of the cruise as a travel product, a look at the major cruise operators, ship descriptions, and practice in obtaining schedule and fare information from cruise brochures.

Customer Service Skills/Telephone Sales Techniques. Instruction on the use of proven customer service techniques to increase sales and retain customers. A study of the fundamental techniques used by the travel industry in marketing and selling travel products by telephone.

Selling Domestic and International Travel. Instruction on the techniques for selling domestic travel destinations, including Hawaii, Florida, California, and North American ski resorts. Instruction on the techniques for selling international travel destinations including Mexico, Europe, and the Caribbean.

U.S. Travel Geography/Airlines of North America. A practical study of the geography of the United States and North America with an emphasis on major travel destinations, airports, and city code designators. A study of the development of the airline industry in North America from its beginning, through deregulation, and into the future.

World Travel Geography/International Airlines. A practical study of the geography of the world with an emphasis on major travel destinations, airports, and city code designators. A look at the major

international airlines, their route structures, equipment, and identifying codes.

How to Use the Official Airline Guides and Travel Planners. Detailed explanation and practical exercises on the use of the North American and World Wide Editions of the Official Airline Guides. Detailed explanation and practical exercises related to the formats and use of the Official Airline Guide Travel Planners and Hotel/Motel Guides.

Domestic and International Tariff Skills. An introduction to the use of the domestic airline tariff to determine fares, routings, and rules. An introduction to the use of the international tariffs to construct fares, routings, and the roles for international ticketing.

Ticket Writing/Travel Industry Automation. An introduction to airline and travel agent tickets with hands-on practice problems on basic ticketing procedures. An introduction to the basic operation of computerized reservations systems. Instruction on the fundamentals of the agent set, basic entry formats, and keyboard functions.

Basic SABRE Computer Skills/Travel Project/Review. Introduction and basic instruction on the procedures and computer entries necessary to access and use the American Airlines SABRE computerized reservation system; practical operational exposure to Apollo, WorldSpan, SystemOne reservations systems; and a state-of-the art Computerized Typing Lab. Comprehensive case-study review and exam over entire course.

Golden Passport Series

This program consists of eight lessons designed to teach individuals the basic elements of the travel and tourism industry. The lessons are specifically designed to be interesting and informative.

Introduction to the Travel Industry. Introduction to travel and the possibilities of the world of travel.

Airlines. Airline codes, worldwide route systems, and airline equipment are presented.

Cruises. Learn selling techniques and terms used in booking individuals and groups.

Hotel, Rental Cars, and the Travel Planner. Explore facets of the hospitality and accommodation industry from booking hotels, reserving cars, and skillfully planning itineraries.

Geography. Contains maps and photos to help learn interesting facts and details about the world's most desirable destinations.

Official Airline Guides and Tariff. Practical exercise in the use of both the North American and European Airline Guides as well as instruction in computing airline fares.

Group Tour Development. Various facets of group tour development are explored.

Travel Agency Ownership. Learn what motivates people to travel and how to turn needs into a business for yourself.

International School of Information Management
P.O. Box 470640
Aurora, Colorado 80047   (800) 441-ISIM

Description:
The school (ISIM) was founded in 1987 and offers programs leading to the Master of Science in Information Management and Master of Science of Business Administration. The mission of the school is to provide working

adults with flexible opportunities to study business and information management, and to acquire the skills and knowledge they need to succeed in a rapidly changing world. ISIM courses are application-oriented to better prepare students for the demands of today's workplace. Special emphasis is placed on the leadership functions of decision making, team building, and communication in dealing with the people, environment, proces,a nd project aspects of an enterprise. Students work individually and in teams to complete assignments and master the course content. To participate in ISIMnet's learning community, students must have access to a computer with a communications capability.

Instruction is delivered through ISIMnet, an educational computer conferencing environment. Students use a personal computer to connect to ISIMnet three or four times a week, at their own convenience. Students interact with one another and with their instructors online by posting and receiving messages on ISIMnet, their virtual classroom. ISIMnet also provides electronic mail for private messages.

Faculty:
Mary Adams, Vice President.

Academic Levels:
Graduate

Degree/Certificate Programs:
Master of Business Administration (MBA) and Master of Science (MS) degrees plus a variety of corporate training courses. Each degree program requires the completion of 50 units of credit.

Admission Requirements:
Applicants must submit the following documents: application for admission; evidence of bachelor's degree from an accredited or state-approved college or university, or an equivalent certified degree from a recognized foreign college or university; official transcripts of all previous college study; resume of employment and professional accomplishments; three letters of recommendation (one preferably from current employer); a goals statement reflecting academic, professional, and personal goals that the applicant hopes to achieve by completion of ISIM's program. Student must have functional familiarity with word processing or text editing and online communications technology.

Tuition:
$250 per unit (subject to change). Total tuition costs for the 50-unit MBA or MS program are $12,500. A study guide for each course is included in the tuition fee. Payment plans are available.

Enrollment Period:
Enrollment can be accomplished at any time.

Equipment Requirements:
Books, software, materials, and online charges are the responsibility of the student.

Credit and Grading:
Letter grades of A, B, or U (unsatisfactory) are assigned. Academic credit is granted on the basis of courses passed.

Library Services:
The Internet provides access to databases and academic library collections around the world. ISIM provides information about accessing the Internet.

Accreditations:
Distance Education and Training Council.

GRADUATE COURSES

BUSINESS ADMINISTRATION

Master of Business Administration Program

Courses required include Management; Accounting; Quantitative Analysis; Finance; Marketing Management; Managerial Economics; Strategic Planning; Strategies for Change; Emerging Technologies; Capstone Project. Electives may be chosen from the following courses: Data Communications; Systems Design; Telecommunications Policy; Telephony; Customers, Markets, and Technology in Technology-Intensive Organizations; Information Systems Policy; Planning for Information Networks; Technology and the Global Environment. (50 credits)

INFORMATION MANAGEMENT

Master of Science in Information Management Program

This program consists of 50-units of six 5-unit core courses, three 5-unit electives, and a 5-unit project. Courses required include: Management of Information Systems; Information Systems Strategic Planning; Technology Ethics and Social Responsibility; Telecommunications; Emerging Technologies; Capstone Project. Electives may be chosen from the following courses: Data Communications; Systems Design; Telecommunications Policy; Telephony; Customers, Markets, and Technology in Technology-Intensive Organizations; Information Systems Policy; Planning for Information Networks; Technology and the Global Environment. (50 credits)

Keystone National High School
515 Market Street
P.O. Box 616
Bloomsburg, Pennsylvania 17815

(717) 784-5220

Description:
The school was founded in 1978 and offers correspondence courses leading to a high school diploma. Both college and career prep options are available. Contact the school for further information and for current tuition and fees.

Accreditations:
Distance Education and Training Council.

The Laural School
2538 North 8th Street
P.O. Box 5338
Phoenix, Arizona 85010   (602) 994-3460

Description:

The Laural School was founded in 1978 and offers the following programs: Dental Assistant Course, Medical Assistant Course, Dental Receptionist/Secretary Course, Medical Receptionist/Secretary Course, Business Secretary Course, Medical Secretary Course, Legal Secretary Course, plus new special Bookkeeping and Accounting Courses. These latter courses are especially unique because they include cassettes and "Learning Windows" to make them easy and enjoyable.

Faculty:

Laura Fabricant, President; Greg Fabricant, Educational Director. There is a faculty of 7 plus subject specialists and counselors.

Academic Levels:

Vocational

Degree/Certificate Programs:

Diploma.

Admission Requirements:

Open enrollment for adults; minors with parental consent.

Tuition:

Basic Bookkeeping Course, $489; Bookkeeping and Accounting Course, $689; Dental Assistant Course, $589; Medical Assistant Course, $589; Medical Secretary Course, $589; Business Secretary Course, $569; Medical Secretary Course, $569; Legal Secretary Course, $729. Deferred payment plans available. Pro rata refund plan.

Enrollment Period:

The maximum time allowed to complete course is two years or length of payment plan. Extensions granted.

Equipment Requirements:

All required equipment provided by the School, included in tuition payment. Cassette player for the bookkeeping and accounting courses offered at an additional fee.

Credit and Grading:

Examinations by honor system. Grading system: A, 95–100; B, 85–94; C, 75–84, D, 70–74; below 70, failure. Minimum passing grade is D, 70 percent.

Accreditations:

Distance Education and Training Council.

VOCATIONAL COURSES

DENTAL ASSISTING

Dental Assistant Course

In this course, the student learns both "front and back" office skills, some of which include the following: the profession of dentistry; dental-medical terminology; dental law; human relations; reception procedures and telephone techniques; administrative planning; the appointment book; record keeping; typing and correspondence; financial records; systems of the body; diet and nutrition; the use and care of office equipment; drugs, first aid, and emergency care; radiographic or x-ray techniques, and chairside assisting.

MEDICAL ASSISTANT

Medical Assistant Course

This course includes the following: present and past history of medicine; human relations; reception procedures; medical emergencies; the appointment book; administrative planning; medical and financial records; business office; medical law; the use and care of office equipment; basic medical knowledge; the medical assistant in the examining room; laboratory tests; radiology/x-rays; typing and correspondence; medical terminology and vocabulary.

SECRETARIAL SCIENCE

Legal Secretary Course

This course covers the following topics: the law office and you; legal filing and other office procedures; telephone and reception procedures; wills and codicils; vocabulary, foreign sounding terms and words and their meanings; collection procedures, time sheets, lawyers fees, and statement preparation; real estate; deeds and mortgages; typing; practice and typing actual forms; shorthand or rapid writing; how to get and keep the job you always wanted.

Medical Secretary Course

This course covers the following topics: the practice of medicine today; preparation of medical and office forms; administration of the business office; people and personnel; professional and business records; reception procedures; medical terminology and vocabulary; medical law; the appointment book; typing and correspondence; shorthand or rapid writing; how to prepare for an interview.

Business Secretary Course

This course covers the skills which will prepare the student for a career as a business secretary: your place in the general business office today; filing and records management; secretarial duties and responsibilities; copying machines, calculators and other office machines; duties and responsibilities of a receptionist; the mailing department; administrative duties; supplies and basic office information; typing; correspondence and preparation of business forms; shorthand or rapid writing; getting your job and keeping it.

Basic Bookkeeping Course

25 lessons. Includes cassettes and "Learning Windows."

Bookkeeping and Accounting Course

52 lessons. Includes cassettes and "Learning Windows."

Learning and Evaluation Center
515 Market Street
P.O. Box 616
Bloomsburg, Pennsylvania 17815-0616
          (800) 255-4937

Description:

Learning and Evaluation Center was established in 1974 as a service to junior and senior high schools for students in need of a "summer school alternative." On the recommendation of a school official, failed students can be referred to the Learning and Evaluation Center for correspondence credit make-up work in all general subjects, fifth through twelfth grades. Each subject extension contains thirty hours of make-up materials with a six-week deadline for completion. Although enrollment is at its peak during the summer months, the Center provides make-up service year-round.

Faculty:

Isaiah L. McCloskey, President; Lisa Hagemeyer, Director of Student Services; Mimi Beyer, Educational Specialist. There a faculty of 6 members.

Academic Levels:

High School

Degree/Certificate Programs:

Credit make-up.

Admission Requirements:

Students must have taken subject and failed for regular school year and must be referred by high school official.

Tuition:

$75 per subject extension; reinforcement courses are $95.

Enrollment Period:

The maximum time to complete a course is six weeks; minimum time is three weeks.

Equipment Requirements:

All materials are included in the per extension course fee.

Credit and Grading:

Examinations are open book. All work is hand-evaluated by certified classroom instructors. After evaluation, a pass/fail report is issued promptly to the referring school official. Student must complete a course within the six-week deadline; failure to meet due date without requesting an extension results in disqualification. A competency level of 75 percent must be met. Complete refund (less postage and handling) is given if student decides not to perform contract. Student must inform Center within ten days after enrolling.

Accreditations:

Distance Education and Training Council.

HIGH SCHOOL COURSES

BIOLOGY

Biology 10 through 12

A study of the book, *The Chemicals of Life,* by Isaac Asimov. The book is required reading. Comprehensive assignments (including vocabulary) follow each chapter.

ENGLISH

English 5

Grammar and usage sections include parts of speech, abbreviations, verb tenses, direct objects, contractions, adjective and adverb comparisons, kinds of sentences, subjects and verbs, and comma rules. Vocabulary study covers synonyms, antonyms, and homonyms. Students also learn about types and parts of books. Exercises provide practice in all areas.

English 6

Grammar and usage sections include parts of speech, principal parts and tenses of verbs, pronoun antecedents, double negatives, using prepositions as adjectives and adverbs, kinds of sentences, and subjects and verbs. Composition section covers paragraphing, outlining, and introduction to writing letters. Exercises provide practice in all areas.

English 7

Grammar dealing with the parts of speech and differentiation of the speech parts, spelling exercises, forming plurals of nouns, forming principal parts of verbs, using verbs correctly, usage exercises. Comprehensive assignments covering basic skills in all of the above.

English 8

Grammar and usage sections include parts of speech, parts of a sentence, kinds of sentences, principal parts of verbs, troublesome verbs, capitalization and punctuation rules (with direct quotations). Vocabulary study deals with affixes, root words, and context clues. Assignments and exercises provide practice in all areas.

English 9

Grammar and usage sections include identifying parts of speech; spelling exercises; capitalization exercises; comma exercises; quotations; writing skills exercises. Comprehensive assignments covering all of the above.

English 10

Grammar and usage areas include review of eight parts of speech, parts of a sentence, kinds of sentences, sentence patterns, capitalization and punctuation rules, parts of verbs, and subject and verb agreement. Vocabulary study involves affixes and foreign roots, synonyms, antonyms, and homonyms. Literature study includes figurative language (idioms, similes, metaphors), structured poetry, outlining, newspaper study, and library study. Comprehensive assignments follow each area.

English 11

Grammar, review of eight parts of speech; vocabulary; sentence fragments; word ending sounds; structure agreement; spelling. Literature: *The Diamond Necklace, The Tell-Tale Heart, The Old Man at the Bridge,* and *The Man and the Snake* (all with comprehensive assignments).

English 12

Grammar—a review of eight parts of speech, modifiers, sentences, and paragraphs; writing good letters; data sheet; letter of application; reference letters; purchase order blanks; job application blanks; letter of thanks. Literature: *An Occurrence at Owl Creek Bridge, The Lottery,* and *The Monkey's Paw.* All with comprehensive assignments.

HEALTH

Health 9 through 12

A study of the book, *The Human Body,* by Isaac Asimov. Covers the general construction of the human body, function of body systems and organs, and terminology as applied to such functions. The book is required reading. Each unit contains comprehensive assignments including vocabulary.

HISTORY

American History and Government 10 through 12

A study of the book, *A Short History of the Civil War,* by Bruce Catton. Deals with the War, its causes and effects, with emphasis on the changes in government created by the War. The book is required reading with comprehensive written assignments.

MATHEMATICS

Mathematics (General) 5

An overall review of general mathematics including the following principles for whole numbers, fractions, and decimals; place value, rounding, and the four basic operations. Also covers the basic manipulation of fractions. Each lesson is accompanied by an assignment. Comprehensive review ends the extension.

Mathematics (General) 6

An overall review of general mathematics including the following principles for whole numbers, fractions, and decimals; place value, rounding, and the four basic operations. Also covers the basic manipulation of fractions and understanding percentages of numbers. Each lesson is accompanied by an assignment. Comprehensive review ends the extension.

Mathematics (General) 7

A step-by-step review of general mathematics, applying the four basic operations on numbers to whole numbers, fractions, and decimals, plus the application of percents. Theory along with ample number of example problems. Each lesson is accompanied by an assignment.

Mathematics (General) 8

An overall view of general mathematics including each of the following: addition and subtraction of whole numbers, addition and subtraction of fractions, addition and subtraction of decimals; simple percentage, and ratio proportion. Each lesson is accompanied by an assignment.

Mathematics (General) 9

A concise review of general mathematics divided into six areas of study: introduction of numbers, addition, subtraction, multiplication, division, and percentage. Each lesson is preceded by a general discussion dealing with relevant theory followed by a series of example problems. Comprehensive assignments follow each lesson.

Mathematics (General) 10

A carefully designed review of general mathematics, applying decimals, plus the application of percents. Denominate numbers are also reviewed along with the measurement of area and volume. Each lesson is accompanied by an assignment.

Mathematics (General) 11 and 12

A comprehensive review of general mathematics covering the same topics as Mathematics (General) 10, but with a greater level of difficulty in the assignments. Additional consumer topics are included such as calculating gross earnings, payroll deductions, and net earnings. Each lesson is accompanied by example problems and assignments.

Algebra I (9 through 12)

A review of math skills and fundamental properties of algebra. Some topics include basic terminology, working with whole numbers, fractions and decimals, properties of signed numbers, manipulation of monomials and square roots, using formulas, order of operation. Each lesson contains an ample number of example problems and assignments.

Algebra II (10 through 12)

A review of important algebraic properties and skills. Some topics include basic terminology, properties of signed numbers, manipulation of algebraic expressions, solutions of linear equations, and solving with the quadratic formula. Each lesson contains an ample number of example problems and assignments.

POLITICAL SCIENCE

Problems of Democracy/Economics 10 through 12

All material is based on the book, *The Big Change: America Transforms Itself - 1900–1950,* written by Frederick Lewis Allen. Divided into three parts of equal length. Explores the social changes in America from the turn of the century to 1950. Describes living conditions of Americans and how people in the first half of the twentieth century were affected by the changes in politics, business, industry, and philosophy. The book is required reading with comprehensive assignments following each section.

SCIENCE

Biology 10 through 12

A study of the book *The Chemicals of Life* by Isaac Asimov. The book is required reading. Comprehensive assignments (including vocabulary) follow each chapter.

Science (General) 7 and 8

A study of the book, *The Web of Life,* by John H. Storer. The book is concerned with how man relates to other living things on planet earth. The book is required reading. Comprehensive assignments (including vocabulary) follow each chapter.

Physical Science (General) 9 through 12

A study of the book, *Geology Made Simple,* by William H. Matthews, III. Various readings are assigned within the book with comprehensive assignments following each reading. Vocabulary is an integral part of each assignment.

SOCIAL STUDIES

American Cultures 7 and 8

Deals with the causes and effects of the American Revolution. A study of Bruce Bliven's book *The American Revolution* with emphasis on social conditions, government, and economics of the period. The book is required reading with comprehensive written assignments.

World Cultures 7 and 8

A study of Ancient Egypt with emphasis on geography and the earliest establishment of government, economics, and religion. Elizabeth Payne's book, *The Pharaohs of Ancient Egypt* is required reading with comprehensive written assignments.

Geography (U.S.) Junior High - 7 through 9

A study of United States physical geography and its physical position to the world. Covers the 50 states in terms of locations, climates, capitals, postal abbreviations, populations, sizes, shapes, and industries. Landforms, bodies of water, and geographical vocabulary are also studied. Map reading, particularly road maps, is included. Comprehensive assignments follow each segment ending with a review.

Social Studies (Civics) 9 through 12

A basic study of the *Constitution of the United States of America.* Five separate study segments divided into six to eight hours of study per segment. Emphasis is on interpretation of the Constitution. Comprehensive assignments follow each study segment.

World Cultures 10 through 12

The Russian Revolution reviews the sweeping changes in Russia in the early part of this century. Robert Goldston, the author, starts with a brief review of pre-revolution history, then weaves through the political maneuvering caused by the unrest of the proletariat and the final seizure of power by the Bolsheviks. The book is required reading and each chapter is followed by comprehensive assignments.

Lifetime Career Schools
101 Harrison Street
Archbald, Pennsylvania 18403 (717) 876-6340

Description:

Founded in 1944, Lifetime Career Schools offers home study courses in the following subject areas: Modern Landscaping, Flower Arranging and Floristry, Modern Dressmaking, and Doll Hospital School. All programs are general in nature and are based on theory and practice for those seeking entry-level vocational skills. Courses in bookkeeping and secretarial science are also offered. Lifetime Career Schools was formerly located in Los Angeles.

Faculty:

Michael J. Zadarosni, President.

Academic Levels:

Vocational

Degree/Certificate Programs:

Certificate.

Admission Requirements:

Student must be 18 years of age or have parental permission. Ability to read and comprehend English at the tenth grade level.

Tuition:

Contact the school for current course/program tuition and costs. Installment payment plan with down payment available. Full refund within thirty days. Pro rata refund plan available prior to completion of one-half of the lessons in a program.

Enrollment Period:

Maximum time to complete a course is two years.

Equipment Requirements:

The school supplies additional texts, training kits, and some necessary tools and patterns. The student must supply flowers for the Floristry course, sewing machine for the Modern Dressmaking Course, and whatever special tools the student desires.

Credit and Grading:

Honor system for examinations. Letter grades: 95–100 percent, A; 90–94 percent, A-; 85–89 percent, B; 80–84 percent, B-; 75–79 percent, C. Minimum passing grade is C.

Accreditations:

Distance Education and Training Council.

VOCATIONAL COURSES

DOLLS

Doll Hospital School

This course was established after a long period of research and covers not only doll repair, but doll making, doll designing, doll clothing manufacture, and doll collecting. The course is comprised of 20 sets of lessons, each set containing 5 lessons. Subjects covered include: the wonderful world of dolls; getting started; your workshop; rag dolls; embroidered faces for rag dolls; doll types; preparing dolls for restoration; shaping and mending parts; what to charge; the boneyard parts system; paints and painting; eyes and their ways; more about eyes; advertising your doll hospital; customer relations; eyelashes; the care of doll hair; wigs and wig making; where to obtain supplies; stocking the hospital; single-loop restringing; double-loop restringing; attaching ceramic heads, arms and legs to bodies of cloth and kid; antique bodies of cloth and kid; licenses and permits; attaching plastic parts to modern cloth bodies; soft plastic doll bodies; types of doll heads; methods of mounting doll heads; legal responsibilities; the betsy wetsy doll; tiny tears doll; how to weave a human hair wig; making apple dolls; the shop sign; repairing plastic parts; making repairs that last; walking dolls (Sweet Sue, Saucy Walker, Ideal's Posie); more about walking dolls; Alexander walking doll "Cissy"; the ballerina doll; Cisette and Alexanderkins dolls; major surgery; china, porcelain and bisque: the fundamentals of ceramics; cementing of china parts; restoring parts and sections; specialized repairs on china dolls and figurines; the magic of making ceramic repairs inconspicuous; character dolls; artistic considerations in doll designing; corn husk dolls; design of wire armature dolls; construction of armature dolls; dolls of wood; design and carving of wood dolls; human figure proportions and their adaptation to doll design; glass dome pictorial design; glass dome pictorial pieces; dolls of wax; dollmaking by paper strip modeling; papier-mache dolls; casting parts from bits of paper; how to use rubber molds for reproducing parts; production painting with airbrush; ceramic reproductions; dolls made from self-hardening and oven-hardening clays; true ceramic dolls; more on ceramics; sock dolls; the dressing of dolls; commercial doll-clothes patterns; miscellaneous patterns; stuffed animal patterns; fabric selection for doll clothing; the "lay-on" method of doll clothes design; the "pin-on" method of doll clothes design; how to adapt patterns for varied effects and styles; doll shoes; doll hats; clothing accessories; period and historical costuming; costuming dolls of all nations; dolls through the ages; antique dolls - their identification and valuation; identification marks; portrait dolls; collecting for fun and profit; paper dolls; mechanical dolls; marionettes; doll houses and furniture; production doll making; starting a mail order business; exhibiting dolls; magazines and booklets on dolls; doll books.

DRESSMAKING

Modern Dressmaking

This course includes coverage of the following topics: your sewing machine; dressmaking vocabulary; sewing machine operation; sewing supplies; fabric construction; fabrics and fabric terms; pattern selection; fabric shopping; interfacings, interlinings, linings, underlinings; notions for shortcut sewing; pattern adjustment; fabric preparation; layout, cutting, and marking; stitching and seam construction; seams and seam finishes; shortcut garment construction; pressing techniques; hand sewing; zippers; darts and tucks; button selection; types of buttonholes; bound buttonholes; stain removal and fabric care; gathering and shirring; pleats; plackets; garment fitting; pockets; patch pocket applications; bias and bias binding; ruffles; facings; collars; casings; sleeves; cuffs and sleeve finishes; women's pants; waistbands; fasteners; hems; lining a garment; working with special fabrics; delicate fabrics; fake fabrics; special cutting layouts; decorative trimmings; belts; mending, repairing, recycling; maternity clothes and infants' wear; sewing for children; sewing for men and boys; construction techniques - menswear; tailoring; traditional tailoring methods; contemporary tailoring methods; alterations and remodeling; sewing machine attachments; applique and machine embroidery; patchwork and quilting; actionwear and outerwear; home accessories; window treatments; curtains and draperies; slipcovers.

FLORISTRY

Flower Arranging and Floristry

The major subjects covered in this course are: tools used in floral work; corsage construction materials; structure and function of flowers and foliage; harvesting and care of flowers; chemical preservatives; corsage foliage; common florist flowers; wiring for corsage designs; ribbon and bows; corsage orchids; assembling the corsage; fantasy flowers; styling the corsage; equipment for arranging flowers; selection of materials; potted plants; constructing the arrangement; floral designing, color; table arrangements; modern foliage plants; dried flowers; artificial flowers; special occasions; church decorating; hobby gardens and money-making specialties; winning ribbons and judging; weddings; the profitable business of funeral arrangements; your business and how to run it.

LANDSCAPING

Modern Landscaping

This course covers the following subjects: planning the small home grounds; the entrance development; planning the livable garden; geometric gardens; planning the garden work center; plant classification; design of shrub borders; principles of plant selection; planning of foundation plantings; designs of flower borders; principles of design; tree planting locations; how plants live and grow; planting lists; plant identification; plant diseases and their control; cultivation of plants; effect of topography on design; surveying in its relationship to landscape planning; grafting and budding; lawns; sprinkler systems; how to build modern garden features; temperature control; soil; simple method of learning landscape drafting; soil improvement; surveying in its relationship to landscape planning; how to make drawings that secure landscape jobs; how to build walks, roads, and pavements; water features; design and planting of public grounds; growing of plants; pruning ornamentals; transplanting techniques; tree surgery; entering the landscape profession; how to estimate job costs; advertising your business; your professional library.

McGraw-Hill Continuing Education Center
National Radio Institute
4401 Connecticut Avenue, NW
Washington, District of Columbia 20008
(202) 244-1600

Description:
National Radio Institute (NRI) has been offering at-home technical and professional training for more than 78 years. Since 1914, NRI has enrolled over a million and a half people from across the nation and around the world. NRI is part of the McGraw-Hill Continuing Education Center, the home study arm of McGraw-Hill, Inc. As one of the nation's largest publishers and a world leader in education and information resources, McGraw-Hill's vast experience adds to the effectiveness of the NRI at-home training programs, providing the student with the most up-to-date technology and information available.

Faculty:
Harold B. Reeb, General Manager; E. Dwight Lipin, Industrial Sales Manager. The instructional staff includes 12 faculty, 13 subject specialists, 18 student service specialists, and 104 other staff members.

Academic Levels:
Vocational

Degree/Certificate Programs:
Diploma.

Admission Requirements:
Open enrollment; students must be 18 years of age or older unless enrollment application is accompanied by a letter from the parent or guardian requesting acceptance.

Tuition:
Contact the school for current tuition and fees. All courses offer convenient time-payment plants. All career courses are VA approved and also eligible for vocational rehabilitation assistance. Refund policy complies fully with the guidelines of the Distance Education and Training Council.

Enrollment Period:
A maximum time of 36 months is allowed for completion of most courses; there is no minimum time. Students are encouraged to submit lessons each month on a regular basis. Factory-located residence training is available, but not required, as follows: one week at York Institute, York, Pennsylvania, for students in the Master Course in Air Conditioning, Refrigeration, and Heating; one week at Tecumseh Service Center, Grafton, Wisconsin, for students in Small Engine Repair.

Equipment Requirements:
Training aids and study materials are provided by the Center and are included in the tuition. Student must supply general household hand tools.

Credit and Grading:
Examinations are multiple choice; selected hands-on projects in many courses hand-graded by instructors. Student must have a C average to graduate.

Library Services:
The school makes available to its students a wide range of supplementary materials such as files of electronic equipment manufacturers, service information, and schematic diagrams.

Job Placement Assistance:
At the student's request, the Center will forward transcripts and a letter of recommendation to prospective employers.

Accreditations:
Distance Education and Training Council.

VOCATIONAL COURSES

AIR CONDITIONING, REFRIGERATION, AND HEATING

Basic Course in Air Conditioning and Refrigeration

This course introduces the industry and prepares the student to perform practically any service or repair job on residential air conditioners, dehumidifiers, refrigerators, freezers, or temperature control units.

McGraw-Hill Continuing Education Center

There are 30 lessons covering the basics of residential cooling and refrigeration plus training in automotive air conditioning and heating.

Master Course in Air Conditioning, Refrigeration, and Heating

This course is an entry-level course consisting of 51 lessons, and eight hand-on training kits. This course prepares students for full- or part-time employment as HVAC technicians. All of the lessons and equipment included with the Basic Course are supplied plus: twenty-one additional lesson texts including training in heating systems, transport refrigeration, and commercial air conditioning, plus six lessons in solar heating and heat pumps. Also included for practical experience is a high-performance vacuum pump, a tool essential for purging HVAC systems. The Master Course also includes, at not extra tuition, an optional week of residence training at the York Institute (not required for graduation).

APPLIANCE SERVICING

Basic Professional Appliance Servicing

The course includes 30 lessons covering the most popular high-volume appliances: introduction to electricity; incandescent and fluorescent lamps; your service shop; fundamentals of heat-producing appliances; servicing heat-producing appliances; how electric motors work; servicing electric motors; small motor appliances; servicing cordless appliances; vacuum cleaners and floor polishers; sewing machines; electrical wiring fundamentals; the electrical service entrance and panel box; electrical fixtures and switches; basic appliance electronics; mixers, blenders, and food processors; garbage disposals and trash compactors; automatic clothes washers; servicing automatic washers; clothes dryer; commercial washers and dryers; automatic dishwashers; business practices; electric water heaters, electric ranges; gas appliances.

Master Course in Professional Appliance Servicing

This course contains all 30 lessons given in the preceding course plus 12 additional lessons covering large appliances, and 6 bonus lessons addressing solar technology: garage door openers; microwave ovens; energy conservation; refrigeration components; home freezers; troubleshooting refrigerators and freezers; room air conditioners; servicing air conditioning and heat pumps; solar heating; attic ventilation; and more.

AUTOMOTIVE TECHNOLOGY

Master Course in Automotive Servicing

This course consists of 51 lessons and four training kits, and prepares students for entry-level positions as automotive mechanics and technicians. All aspects of automotive operations and service are covered in the lessons which include topics such as: engine construction and operation; servicing engine lubricating and cooling systems; engine fuel and exhaust systems; automotive brakes and antilock braking systems; tires and tire service; automotive electricity and electronics; servicing starter motors; servicing charging systems; automotive carburetors; gasoline fuel injection systems; superchargers; turbochargers; detonation control systems; automotive emission control systems; diesel engine fuel injection systems; engine trouble diagnosis; engine tune-up and test instruments; engine cylinder blocks; heads, crankshafts, and bearing; rear suspensions and shock absorbers; front suspension systems; two- and four-wheel steering systems; operation and servicing of clutches; servicing automotive heaters and air conditioners; GM, Chrysler, and Ford transmissions; construction, operation, and servicing of differentials and transaxles; and more. Hands-on training kits feature servicing tools plus the student's choice of an automotive oscilloscope or the OTC Monitor 2000 Electronic Diagnostic Tester.

BOOKKEEPING

Contemporary Bookkeeping and Accounting

The 32-lesson course covers the basic principles needed to keep the books for a small business, then goes further to train students in the use of a personal computer to speed up the accounting process and produce accurate financial statements and reports. The course prepares students to start their own home-based businesses, advance on the job, or keep the books for their own existing businesses. Lessons include: becoming a home-based entrepreneur; business and the balance sheet, preparing a balance sheet; preparing an income statement; your business and the law; the business plan; understanding cash flow; accounting for inventory; accounting for plant and equipment; keeping payroll and income taxes; managing accounts receivable with your computer; managing accounts payable with your computer; budgeting and forecasting with your computer; and more. Also included are 7 kits, featuring and IBM compatible AT computer system. General ledger and spreadsheet software, and assorted materials for hands-on practice.

BUILDING TRADES

Building Construction

This course consists of 70 lessons and 11 hands-on projects covering fundamental, practical homebuilding. This course covers all elements of the building sequence, from lot selection to construction terminology and energy efficiency. Lessons include such topics as: selecting the site; working drawings and specification; building materials; foundations and excavations; floor framing; joists; subflooring; framing exterior walls; roofs and rafters; wall sheathing and insulation; ventilating and finishing the roof; laying brick; chimneys and fireplaces; horizontal and vertical sidings; windows, doors, and stairways; interior trim; wallboard; operative hardware; calculating heat loss; heating systems and fuels; central systems; air conditioning; plumbing; working with electricity; surface coatings; site finishing; estimating for profit; getting down to business; and more. The course features a central training project in which the student builds a scale-model of the NRI American Dream Home, a design commissioned for NRI.

Home Inspection

This course prepares students to inspect homes prior to real estate transactions, remodeling, or renovation. The course consists of 32 lessons covering topics ranging from construction specifications to electrical systems, plumbing, heating, security, landscaping, and the inspection process itself. In addition, the course features six hands-on training kits, including an IBM AT compatible computer and home inspection software the student can use to compile and generate quality inspection reports.

BUSINESS

Desktop Publishing and Design

This is an entry-level course that prepares the student to set-up and run a home-based business in desktop publishing. The course includes lessons and hands-on training kits covering basic publication design principles as well as computer methods in desktop publishing.

Word Processing

This course shows students how to prepare business, academic, legal, and medical documents, and how to market word processing and database management services.

COMPUTER PROGRAMMING

Computer Programming

This course covers computer programming beginning with QBASIC, then continuing with C, Visual Basic, and Windows programming. Included in the course are nine training kits and 42 lessons.

Programming in C++ with Windows

This course consists of 50 lessons and eight training kits. An IBM compatible 486sx-based computer system is included in the course for hands-on training. The following software is also included: MS-DOS, QBASIC, Borland C++, and Microsoft Windows. The course is structured in four basic sections. The first presents the fundamentals of computer literacy, explaining the essentials of hardware, software, and how computers operate. The second section presents an introduction to the C programming language. The third section stresses techniques for software design and object-oriented programming using C++ as the programming language. The final section teaches the student how to write applications for the Windows environment.

DRAFTING

Computer-Aided Drafting

This course gives students the hand-on skills and equipment needed for an entry-level position as a drafter. The course includes an IBM 486 compatible computer complete with professional CAD software.

ELECTRONIC MUSIC

Electronic Music Technology

This course includes 40 lessons and 10 training kits. Lessons include basic electronic lessons plus: introduction to the computer; using computers to make music; periodic waves and time constants; sound theory; generating audio waveforms; filtering and wave shaping; distortion and special effects; electronic musical instruments; sampling and waveform duplication; musical theory and notation; analog synthesizers; digital synthesizers; the MIDI Interface and MIDI Standards; sequencers; composing with the computer; electronic troubleshooting; recording sound; mixers and multitrack recording; maintaining and repairing electronic instruments; and more.

ELECTRONICS

Basic Electronics with Lab

This is a fundamental course in elementary electronic theory, and contains 24 lessons, one reference text, and seven hands-on training kits. This course is intended for those who need to learn basic electronics in order to help them with their primary careers. Lessons include: introducing you to electronics; current, voltage, and resistance; series circuits; parallel circuits; how resistors are used; how coils are used; how coils and capacitors are used together; how diodes work; how transistors work; how transistors are used; integrated circuits; power supplies for electronic equipment; how amplifiers work; how oscillators work; modulation and demodulation; superheterodyne receivers; introduction to computers; basic computer arithmetic; digital logic circuits; flip-flops, registers, and counters; microprocessors and microcomputers; and more. Equipment featured in the course for hands-on training includes the NRI Discovery Lab, and a 25 MHz oscilloscope.

Cellular Telephone Installation, and Servicing

This an entry-level course specializing in the installation, troubleshooting, and repair of cellular phone systems, skills developed from a solid conventional phone servicing foundation also provided in the course. Includes all of the basic electronics lessons plus: modulation and superheterodyne receivers; basic telephone systems; telephone circuits; smart telephones; cordless, mobile, and cellular telephones; telephone data handling equipment; telephone system troubleshooting and repair; cellular phone station equipment; and more.

Industrial Electronics and Robotics

This course consists of 56 lessons and 10 training kits that prepare the student for careers servicing and operating complex industrial robotic equipment. Lessons include the basic electronics lessons plus: how microcomputers work; microprocessors; advanced 16- and 32-bit microprocessors; microcomputer memories; data conversion systems; pulse waveform generators; operational amplifiers; instrumentation; automatic control and feedback systems; motors, generators, and motor controls; software and programming; digital troubleshooting equipment; the logical approach to microcomputer repair; lasers and optoelectronics; robotics; robot power sources; robot programming; industrial sensors; speech synthesis; robot applications; introduction to programmable logic controllers; PLC organization and operation; PLC programming; installing and maintaining programmable controllers; and more.

Microcomputers and Microprocessors

This course consists of 45 lessons and 12 hands-on training kits and is designed to prepare students for jobs as entry-level computer service technicians, or to start part-time or full-time computer servicing businesses of their own. The course features hand-on training with an 80486sx-based computer system and diagnostic hardware and software.

Digital Electronics Servicing

This entry-level course covers the theory, operation, and servicing of digital circuitry, and equipment. The 40 lessons and 11 kits concentrate on teaching students how to use the DMM oscilloscope and logic probe provided to perform tests and measurements required to service and repair different types of digital equipment.

Electronic Circuit Design

This course is directed at the serious, career-minded individual seeking training in the design and application of electronic circuits. The course consists of 44 lessons, six electronic design laboratory kits, and a 25 MHz oscilloscope. The emphasis is on providing training for engineering technicians involved in lab work, research, and high-tech electronic design in contrast to the service/repair orientation of other NRI courses.

PC Applications Specialist

This is an entry-level course that prepares students to provide computer services for clients. The course includes background information about microcomputer hardware, software, and popular computer applications. There are 32 lessons and six hands-on training kits, including an IBM 486sx compatible computer and Microsoft Works software.

PC Troubleshooter

This is an entry-level course preparing students to install computers and provide such maintenance and repair services such as diagnosing system failures, replacing damaged chips, retrieving lost data, and troubleshooting faulty disk drives and circuit boards.

Professional Electrician Course

This course consists of 40 lessons and 10 hands-on training kits and prepares individuals for entry-level career positions as construction, maintenance, industrial, or utility electricians.

Security Electronics

This is an entry-level course consisting of 40 lessons and 10 kits. Lessons include the basic electronics courses plus: principles of security; intrusion detection devices; perimeter protection systems;

area protection systems; alarm and signaling systems; automobile protection systems; personnel identification systems; wireless security systems; environmental reporting and control; closed-circuit television systems; fire and smoke detection; central station reporting systems; field engineering and troubleshooting; and more.

ENGINE REPAIR

Small Engine Repair

This course includes 45 lessons covering the theory of operation, servicing, troubleshooting, and repair of various types of small engines and small-engine-powered equipment including lawn mowers, chain saws, mopeds, outboard motors, and snowmobiles.

GUNSMITHING

Gunsmithing

The course consists of 50 lessons and six hands-on training kits covering all phases of the gunsmithing trade: firearm safety, repair, restoration, finishing, ammunition, and customizing plus selling, trading, and importing guns.

LOCKSMITHING

Locksmithing and Security Systems

This course includes lessons covering locksmithing and security systems. It includes basic preparation for installing, maintaining, and repairing these systems.

PARALEGAL STUDIES

Legal Assistant Program

This course consists of 30 lessons and nine hands-on training kits, including an IBM PC/AT compatible computer and specially developed legal applications software similar to that used extensively in the paralegal profession. Lessons include: walking a case through the system: a step-by-step approach; contract law; intentional torts; criminal law; criminal procedure; researching the law; interviewing clients and witnesses; citing the law; Shepardizing cases; corporations and partnerships; consumer protection; bankruptcy law; the discovery process; wills and estates; constitutional law; pre-trial motions; real estate law; family law; trial preparation; the Uniform Commercial Code; a paralegal business; legal ethics for legal assistants; computer-assisted legal writing; computer-assisted legal research systems; and more.

TELECOMMUNICATIONS

Telecommunications Technology

Fifty-four lessons support the total of 13 training kits with discussions of theory, equipment, and applications in each important area of telecommunications. The course answers the increasing demand for entry-level training in the installation, troubleshooting, and repair of telecommunications equipment. Major training kits include the NRI Discovery lab, a digital multimeter, and IBM PC/AT compatible computer system, 2400 baud fax modem, diagnostic breakout board, and communications software.

Radio Communications

This is an entry-level course for service and maintenance work related to the two-way radio communications field (mobile, marine, aircraft, cellular). The course consists of 49 lessons and 10 training kits.

TRAVEL INDUSTRY

Travel Career Training

The course consists of 42 lessons covering such topics as: domestic travel markets; the airline industry; international travel; airport layout and codes; flight selection and the Official Airline Guide; connections and the OAG; computer reservations systems; airline fares; airline tickets; hotel reservations; rental cars; customer relations; cruises; rail travel; tours, charters, and group travel; client records; selling travel; conference and meeting planning; learning to use your microcomputer; determining flight availability; how to start your own agency; and more.

VIDEO/AUDIO SERVICING

Master Course in Video/Audio Servicing with Specialized TV, VCR, and Audio System Training

This course includes 64 lessons and 10 training kits. Lessons includes the basic electronics lessons plus: electronic troubleshooting; audio amplifiers; audio amplifiers; audio systems equipment; compact disc players and digital audio; electronic tuning; video/audio signal processing; color signal processing; TV power supplies and remote controls; stereo television; cable television; videocassette recorders; VCR control systems; repairing VCRs; camcorders; test equipment; and more. The training kits feature a color TV, VCR, and audio rack system including CD player and AM/FM stereo cassette.

Master Course in Video/Audio Servicing with Specialized VCR Training

This course has the same 64 lessons as the above course but has a hi-fi/stereo VCR as the featured training kit in place of the color TV and audio kits.

WRITING

Fiction Writing

Students enrolled in this course acquire skills and develop talents for creating short stories and novels. Lessons include such topics as: becoming a writer; strategies for success; putting fiction on paper; writing for today's market; mastering the tools for good writing; creating images with words; characterization—whose story is it:; setting, situation, and theme; conflict and viewpoint; description and narrative; images, scenes, and dialogue; unity and motivation; plotting; action; conflict resolution; fiction techniques; beginnings, middles, and endings; writing the short story; keeping your reader's attention; devices for adding suspense; business records for writers; creating on your computer; short story workshop; writing the novel; revising your novel; marketing your novel; and more.

Nonfiction Writing

This course consists of 32 lessons, eight personally graded writing projects, and various home projects and reading assignments. This course is specifically designed to teach writing and marketing techniques for creating publishable manuscripts. Students learn how to write essays, feature articles, and nonfiction books.

Microcomputer Technology Center
14904 Jefferson Davis Highway, Suite 411
Woodbridge, Virginia 22191   (800) 448-2077

Description:

Microcomputer Technology Center was founded in 1989 and offers a course in computer operations and programming (EduTech). Contact the school for a course description and current tuition and fees.

Faculty:

Marcellina Hawkes, Chief Executive Officer.

Accreditations:
Distance Education and Training Council.

Modern Schools of America, Inc.
2538 North 8th Street
P.O. Box 5338
Phoenix, Arizona 85010   (602) 990-8346

Description:
Founded in 1946, Modern Schools of America offers correspondence instruction in gun repair. There are two courses, the Basic Gun Repair Course and the Master Course in Gunsmithing. The latter course is a continuation of the first course. There have been over 50,000 students enrolled since the school began.

Faculty:
Laura Fabricant, President; Gail King, Educational Director.

Academic Levels:
Vocational

Degree/Certificate Programs:
Certificate.

Admission Requirements:
Open enrollment. Students must have signature of approval from parent or guardian if under the age of 18. Students need manual dexterity.

Tuition:
$695 for the Basic Gun Repair Course (31 lessons); $985 for the Master Course in Gunsmithing (65 lessons). Deferred payment plan available. VISA and MasterCard accepted. Pro rata refund plan.

Enrollment Period:
There are no time limits for completion of the courses.

Equipment Requirements:
Equipment and supplies are generally included in the tuition; check with the school for specifics.

Credit and Grading:
The grading system is: A, 95-100 percent; B, 85-94 percent; C, 75-84; percent; D, 70-74 percent. Minimum passing grade is 70 percent.

Accreditations:
Distance Education and Training Council.

VOCATIONAL COURSES

GUN REPAIR

Basic Gun Repair Course

Lesson 1. Gunology; .38 Smith & Wesson Chief Special; Safety. Lesson 2. Where and How To Begin; .45 Colt M-1911; glossary of terms. Lesson 3. That First Project - 1; .38 Smith & Wesson Military and Police; gun laws and gun repairmen. Lesson 4. Completing Your First Project - 2; Ruger Bearcat; sources of supply. Lesson 5. Basics of Stock Finishing; Ruger Automatic; Your workshop.

Lesson 6. How to Get Professional Stock Finishing Results; Charter revolver; bookkeeping - legal and financial. Lesson 7. Fitting custom recoil pads, Colt single action revolver; buying and selling firearms. Lesson 8. Butt plates, swivels and more about pads; Hi-Standard Sentinel revolver; gun laws and legislation. Lesson 9. Checkering fundamentals; Daisy; your federal firearms records; Lesson 10: Checkering extras and carving (including how to make a checkering cradle); Crosman 760, public relations and advertising.

Lesson 11. Setting up your own shop; Remington M-550; firearm service records; 12. Setting up your workbench—a most important place; Remington M-572; gunpowder and ballistics. Lesson 13. Your guide to hand tools; Remington M-66; history and development. Lesson 14. Your guide to measuring tools; Remington M-514; National Rifle Association. Lesson 15. How to choose the right power tools for you; Marlin M-39A; Beretta 92F.

Lesson 16. More about power tools and their use; Remington M-580-581-582; building your library. Lesson 17. How to choose your lathe; Savage M-88; how to read precision instruments. Lesson 18. How to use (adjust) your lathe; Savage Savage .22/410 combination; open and peep sights. Lesson 19. Step-by-step soldering; Winchester M-200 series; telescope sight mounting. Lesson 20. Step-by-step welding; Marlin M-49 and 99 series; butt stock alterations, recoil pads, and refinishing stocks.

Lesson 21. All about sights; Winchester M-94; bluing equipment, tools, polishing, cleaning and failures. Lesson 22. All about sights; Savage M-99; advising your customers on selecting shotguns, rifles and pistols. Lesson 23. Keep it clean - a most important lesson; Remington M-700; handloading. Lesson 24. Cleaning supplies, equipment, and lubricants; Remington M-740-742; pricing your work. Lesson 25. Basic Repair Methods, Part 1; Remington M-760; actions.

Lesson 26. Basic Repair Methods, Part 2; Remington M-788; blowups and cartridge nomenclature. Lesson 27. Basic barrel repair; Browning Hi-power; SAAMI; unsafe arms and ammo combinations; Lesson 28. Barrel rebuilding; Winchester M-88; hard to find tools. Lesson 29. Learn antique restoration for fun and profit, Part 1; Marlin M-336; Public Relations - how to write a news release. Lesson 30. Antique Restoration in Depth, Part 2; Mauser M-98; tables of measurements.

Lesson 31. The finer art of polishing and jeweling, Part 1; Ithaca M-37; Luger automatic. Lesson 32. The finer art of polishing and jeweling, Part 2. Remington M-11; Winchester M-61. Lesson 33. Learn custom finishing and plating; Winchester M-12; Winchester M-62A; Lesson 34. All about bluing; Remington M-1100; J.C. Higgins M-30.22. Lesson 35. Choosing inletted stock; Remington M-870; Remington M-141. Lesson 36. Fitting and shaping the inletted stock; Winchester M-1400; Remington M-8 and 81.

Lesson 37. A personal thing—customizing; Winchester M-1200; Winchester M-05-07-1-. Lesson 38. More customizing and sporterizing too; Stevens M-311; Remington M-721-722. Lesson 39. Welcome additions—accessorizing; Mossberg M-500; Remington M-31. Lesson 40. Time to decide—full- or part-time; Stevens M-94; Winchester M-97.

GUNSMITHING

Master Course in Gunsmithing

Lesson 41. Business Administration: how to set up a part time shop - full time shop. Methods of getting started on shoestring financing; pitfalls and how to avoid them. Legal requirements. Lesson 42. Headspacing: why it is important, how each type is measured, breech pressure. Lesson 43. Shotgun Chambers: nomenclature, how measured, corrections, long-forcing cones for pattern improvements, lapping, headspacing, etc. Lesson 44. Shotgun Bores: types of barrels, inspection, cutting, down barrels, straightening patterns. Lesson 45. Shotgun Chokes: cleaning, lapping, types of built-in chokes, custom choking, choke device installation (Poly-Choke, Cutts Compensator, Lyman).

Lesson 46. Shotgun Ribs: how to repair, how to reinstall ribs that are loose, how to install Poly-Fether Air ribs. Lesson 47. Installing Rifle Barrels: Rim fire, chambering, headspacing, breeching. Standard replacements and custom barrels. Lesson 48. Installing Shotgun Barrels: break open single barrels, bolt action shotgun barrels; double barrel break open barrels, pump and semiautomatic barrels. Lesson 49. Installing Handgun Barrels: how to remove revolver barrels, install replacements, clearance, breeching, coning. Installing semi-auto handgun barrels. Lesson 50. Installing Center Fire Rifle Barrels: subcontracting, contoured, threaded and rough chambered, barrel blands, pre-timed, pre-contoured, and pre-chambered barrels.

Lesson 51. Private Brand Names and Serial Numbers: how to recognize private brand name guns, cross references, data, Serial numbers/dates of various models. Lesson 52. The Money Maker: common malfunctions: tricks of the trade in quick inspection to pin point the problem, quick corrections. General servicing techniques. Lesson 53. Servicing and Building Muzzle Loaders: Cleaning, restoration, building kits for pleasure and profit, etc. Lesson 54. Accurizing the Colt .45 Automatic: the M1911A1, heliar welding, inserting strips into receiver, installation of trigger stops, Micro-sights, BoMar sights. Lesson 55. U.S. M-1 Carbine (military and commercial): trigger group disassembly and reassembly, malfunctions and corrections, sporterizing, accurizing, gas piston maintenance.

Lesson 56. Noble Shotguns: Interchangeable parts - where to obtain them; exploded drawings; gun instructions; drawings released by Noble during its existence. Lesson 57. Crosman M-130 Pistol: one of the most successful single shot pneumatic pistols ever designed. Special tools required, check valve inspection and maintenance, pump setting adjustments, complete factory service information. Lesson 58. Crosman M-140 Rifle: malfunctions, customizing the M140 and M1400, proving trigger pull, lubrication, safety removal and repair. Lesson 59. Savage M-110 Rifle (CF): headspacing, breech bolt, sear, variations of models, barrels, ejectors, letters designating variations, basic disassembly, malfunctions and corrections, factory gunsmith service bulletins. Lesson 60. Remington M-11/48 (Mohawk-48) Semi-Auto Shotgun: popularity both in production and public acceptance; variations, modifications, design improvement, failures, exploded side views, complete factory service information.

Lesson 61. Browning .22 LR Semi-Auto Rifle (RF): unique features, bottom ejection, hammerless design, new models, complete Browning guns servicing instructions, malfunctions and corrections, proper maintenance. Lesson 62. Remington Model 552 Semi-Auto Rifle (RF): Complete factory instructions, variations, field service manuals, disassembly and reassembly, checklist of failures and corrections. Lesson 63. Baretta Semi-Auto Shotgun: variations, Magnum, trigger guard assembly, removal and repairs, AL2 and AL1 complete repair instructions. Lesson 64. Springfield M-1903 Rifle: history, Model 1901, experimental, Krag, modifications, Springfield Arsenal, Rock Island Arsenal, complete government field manual, malfunctions and corrections, customizing, assembly and disassembly, Models 1903. Lesson 65. Colt Frame Models "E" and "I" Revolver. Sequence for inspection and repair, basic tools, tolerances, complete breakdown and cutaway illustrations.

National College of Appraisal and Property Management
3597 Parkway Lane
Suite 100
Norcross, Georgia 30092   (800) 362-7070

Description:
The college (NCAPM), founded in 1987, is a division of Professional Career Development Inc. It offers courses in real estate appraisal and property management. Contact the college for further information regarding course availability and tuition/fees.

Accreditations:
Distance Education and Training Council.

National Tax Training School
4 Melnick Drive
P.O. Box 382
Monsey, New York 10952   (914) 352-3634

Description:
Founded in 1952, the National Tax Training School now enrolls from 2,000 to 2,500 students annually. It offers both a basic and an advanced course in Federal Taxes, as well as guidance on how to start, develop, and operate one's own tax practice in home or office. Graduates of these courses are offered postgraduate services, including a Revision Service to keep abreast of all changes in tax laws, rules, and regulations; also, a Consultation and Advisory Service with the School. These services extend five years after graduation. In addition, there is a Life Time Placement Assistance service, free of charge.

Faculty:
Ben D. Eisenberg, President; William Moller, Educational Director. There is a faculty of 4 members.

Academic Levels:
Vocational

Degree/Certificate Programs:
Certificate.

Admission Requirements:
Open enrollment.

Tuition:
Basic course $274.75 when paid in advance; Higher course $239.75. Costs subject to change. Contact the school for current tuition.

Enrollment Period:
Although many students complete the course in three months, the school allows up to one year for completion without extra charge. Extension beyond one year includes an extension fee for each six months.

Equipment Requirements:
Training materials included with tuition.

Credit and Grading:
Examination on the honor system. Grading is A through D; minimum passing grade: C.

Accreditations:
Distance Education and Training Council.

VOCATIONAL COURSES

FEDERAL INCOME TAXES

Federal Income Tax Course (Basic)

The topics covered in this course include: history/general principles; personal exemptions; tax computation; items excluded from gross income; items included in gross income; gain or loss on the sale or exchange of property; basis for determining gain or loss; gains and losses on the sale or exchange of capital assets; business deductions; other allowable deductions; depreciation and depletion; business and casualty losses; bad debts; self-employment tax; declaration of estimated tax; sale of taxpayer's residence; miscellaneous provisions; payroll taxes (business taxes)/income withholding; social security and F.U.T. taxes.

Higher Course in Federal Taxation

This course is divided into two sections. Section I covers the following topics: individuals' taxes; gross income inclusions; gross income exclusions; sales and exchanges; tax-free exchanges; basis; capital gains and losses; business deductions; non-business deductions; personal deductions; income averaging; minimum and maximum tax; inventories; installment sales; depreciation and depreciation recapture; depletion; bad debts; and losses. Section II includes the following subjects: the net operating loss; partnerships; estates and trusts; corporations; specially taxed corporations; capital changes; securities, stock options, and restricted stock; pension and profit-sharing plans; foreign income and foreign taxpayers; withholding and estimated tax; social security and self-employment tax; audits and refunds; and estate and gift taxes.

National Training, Inc.
188 College Drive
P.O. Box 1899
Orange Park, Florida 32067-1899
(904) 272-4000

Description:
Established in 1978, National Training is a proprietary postsecondary vocational education school designed to serve individuals desiring skill training. The methods employed in implementing this goal are a combination home study and resident training. National Training is also engaged in industrial training and retraining through refresher courses tailored to individual corporate needs. Courses are offered in tractor-trailer driving and heavy equipment operation. The school trains approximately 4,000 men and women per year. National Training offers its courses to individuals with no (or limited) experience in this field. The first course includes instruction to enable the student to become either an independent trucker or a company driver. A second course provides the information necessary to drive diesel semi tractor-trailers, to perform routine inspections and preventive maintenance on trucks, to develop the proper road driver skills, to prepare for the Department of Transportation (D.O.T.) written examination and equipment road test, and to operate one's own trucking business. A third course provides training for heavy equipment operators and small earth moving contractors. Depending upon which program is chosen, the courses consist of 48-77 home study lessons and 2-3 weeks of resident training at the school's training grounds in Green Grove Springs, Florida.

Faculty:
Frank J. Lark, President; Larry S. Lark, Education Director.

Academic Levels:
Vocational

Degree/Certificate Programs:
Certificate.

Admission Requirements:
A high school diploma is preferred; applicants with an eighth-grade education may be accepted. A general aptitude test is required of every applicant regardless of level of formal education. Applicants must be 20½ years of age or older to enroll and must be 21 or older when they attend resident training. An applicant must possess a valid motor vehicle operator's license and have an acceptable driving record when reporting for resident training. A student residing in the state of Florida must secure a Florida Chauffer's Driver License prior to attending the resident portion. An applicant must pass the Department of Transportation (D.O.T.) physical examination.

Tuition:
Costs subject to change without notice. Contact the school for possible changes. Commercial Drivers License Preparation Program $2,795 (home study portion $1,000, resident portion $1,795). CDL Prepared Independent Truckers Course $3,595 (home study portion $2,500, resident portion $1,095. It is the student's responsibility to secure and pay for food and housing during the Resident Training portion. Installment payment plan available. Refund policy in accordance with Distance Education and Training Council guidelines.

Enrollment Period:
A student must complete at least five lessons per month of the home study portion (there are 48-77 lessons altogether). The maximum time allowed for completion of the course is one year. The average time for completion is six and one-half months. The required resident portion is three weeks (150 hours), but may be extended at no extra cost if the school feels the student requires more time. The resident portion consists of classroom, field training observation, and the actual operation of vehicles.

Equipment Requirements:
All training materials and equipment are supplied by the school and are included in the tuition.

Credit and Grading:

All home study lessons must be completed with a minimum grade of 75 percent. Resident training is graded as follows: Excellent, 95 to 100 percent; Good, 90 to 94 percent; Average, 80 to 89 percent; Below Average, 75 to 79 percent; Failure, Below 75 percent.

Job Placement Assistance:

Inquiries from potential employers concerning graduates are placed on the school bulletin board.

Accreditations:

Distance Education and Training Council. Licensed by the Florida State Board of Independent Postsecondary Vocation, Technical, Trade and Business Schools.

VOCATIONAL COURSES

TRUCK DRIVING

Independent Trucker's Course - Home Study Training

This home study portion of the course consists of 77 lessons covering the following: Introduction and familiarization with terms used in the trucking industry; History of motor trucks; Expansion of the industry; The role of trucks in wartime; Trucking today; Driver qualifications; The driver's eyesight; Perception and distance; Physical disabilities; Driving and drinking; The use of drugs; Driver reaction.

D.O.T. definitions; Truck talk; D.O.T. driver qualifications; D.O.T. driving regulations; D.O.T. emergency equipment requirements; D.O.T. prohibited practices; Driver's knowledge of emergency equipment; Hours of service; The driver's daily log.

Maintenance regulations; Introduction to preventive maintenance; The driver's role in preventive maintenance; Checks you must make; Know the "why" of preventive maintenance; The Diesel engine; The lubricating system; Maintenance of equipment; Effect of temperatures on engine starting.

General driving instructions; Instruments; Cummins diesel; Diesel accessories; Fuel system; Cooling system; Detroit diesel; Transmissions—driving precautions; Shifting the Roadranger transmissions; Shifting the Spicer.

Correct road practice; Electrical systems; Propellor shafts and axles; Air brakes; Parking brakes and wheels; Steering gear and and front end alignment; Springs; Cab.

Owner/operators vs. salaried drivers; Various kinds of hauls; Costs and profits; Driver responsibilities; Equipment; Taxes, licensing and permits; Logging, certification and safety.

Driving tips; The mover; Driver on the road; Growth of a trucking company; Financial success.

Shop tools; Importance of fasteners; Fasteners; Adhesives, sealants, specialty and plastic fasteners; Belts; Chains; Engines (how they work); Basic engine; Gasoline fuel system; L-P gas fuel system; diesel fuel system; Intake and exhaust systems; Governing systems; Test equipment, diagnosis, and engine tune-up; Fuels; Lubricants; Coolants.

Independent Trucker's Course - Resident Training

The Resident Training is completed at the School training grounds. It consists of the following: Orientation; Introduction to various units; Interstate Commerce Commission and U.S. Department of Transportation regulations; Operator forms (bill of lading, placards, etc.); Accident prevention and reporting; D.O.T. regulations, documents, forms and permits; Refrigeration theory and film; Proper loading and unloading; Tie-down procedures; Various kinds of hauls; Load and cargo analysis; Field training on obstacle and training course (bob tail, straight back, forward drive, alley dock, straight back drop, serpentine, etc.); Instruments; Transmission and brake systems; Preventive maintenance; Defensive driving; Coupling and uncoupling trailers; Pre-trip inspection; Daily log review and testing; Resident training quizzes and tests; Safety films; Independent trucking contracts and leases; Keeping records; Costs and profits; Road driving on city, county, state and federal highways.

Commercial Drivers License Preparation Program

The home study portion of this program consists of 48 lessons. The resident training portion consists of three weeks (150 clock hours).

The home study lessons cover the following topics: Introduction and familiarization with terms used in the trucking industry; History of motor trucks; Expansion of the industry; The role of trucks in wartime; Trucking today; Driver qualifications; The driver's eyesight; Perception and distance; Physical disabilities; Driving and drinking; The use of drugs; Driver reaction.

D.O.T. definitions; Truck talk; D.O.T. driver qualifications; D.O.T. driving regulations; D.O.T. emergency equipment requirements; D.O.T. prohibited practices; Driver's knowledge of emergency equipment; Hours of service; The driver's daily log.

Maintenance regulations; Introduction to preventive maintenance; The driver's role in preventive maintenance; Checks you must make; Know the "why" of preventive maintenance; The Diesel engine; The lubricating system; Maintenance of equipment; Effect of temperatures on engine starting.

General driving instructions; Instruments; Cummins diesel; Diesel accessories; Fuel system; Cooling system; Detroit diesel; Transmissions—driving precautions; Shifting the Roadranger transmissions; Shifting the Spicer.

Correct road practice; Electrical systems; Propellor shafts and axles; Air brakes; Parking brakes and wheels; Steering gear and and front end alignment; Springs; Cab.

Resident training is completed at the school's training grounds and consists of classroom, driving range, and "over-the-road" instruction with school equipment. The student is taught driver techniques, defensive driving, Department of Transportation regulations, log book procedures, and other related subjects. The student also participates in practice driving on a specially prepared driving range on the training grounds and operates tractors with trailers on local area highways and city streets over selected routes. The student will drive in the daytime, dusk, and/or night.

NRI Schools
4401 Connecticut Avenue, N.W.
Washington, D.C. 20008   (202) 244-1600

Description:

In 1968, the National Radio Institute (NRI) was acquired by McGraw-Hill, Inc. Courses from NRI are offered by the McGraw-Hill Continuing Education Center at the same address as above. For detailed course descriptions, SEE **McGraw-Hill Continuing Education Center.**

The Paralegal Institute

TPI Schools
Center for Career Studies
3602 West Thomas Road, Suite 9
Phoenix, Arizona 85019   (602) 272-1855

Description:

The Paralegal Institute, founded in 1975, provides home study training to those interested in careers as lawyers' assistants. The training consists of theories, information, and skills required by the legal assistant in various specialized areas of legal practice. Variously called lawyers' assistants, legal assistants, paralegal, lay assistants, and investigators, these persons have received specialized training in the field of law-related matters, and perform tasks and render services under the direct supervision of a licensed attorney.

Faculty:

John W. Morrison, President; Richard F. Yanko, Director of Education; Pauline V. Garcia, Director of Student Support.

Academic Levels:
Vocational

Degree/Certificate Programs:
Diploma; Associate degree.

Admission Requirements:

High school diploma or certificate of equivalency. Individual exceptions may be made for life experience which indicates an equivalent competence.

Tuition:

Tuition fees range from $750 to $3,200. A required down payment of $50 12 to 34 monthly installments, depending on program. Pro rata refund plan available. MasterCard and VISA accepted.

Enrollment Period:

Maximum time allowed to complete a course is two years.

Equipment Requirements:

All materials required including textbooks are paid for in the tuition.

Credit and Grading:

The grading system: A, 98–100; B, 94–97; C, 88–93; D, 75–87. Minimum passing grade is 75%.

Accreditations:
Distance Education and Training Council.

VOCATIONAL COURSES

ACCOUNTING

Bookkeeping and Accounting Program

Includes the following sequence of courses: Module A, Introduction and the Accounting Cycle; Module B, Special Journals and Payroll; Module C: Merchandise Accounting, Notes, and Bad Debts; Module D: Assets, Partnerships, and Corporations; Module E: Special Conditions, Analysis, and Computers.

COMPUTER SCIENCE

Personal Computer Specialist Program

Includes the following sequence of courses: Module A, A Brief Introduction to Computers (11.25 credit hours); Module B, The Details of Hardware (6.75 credit hours); Module C: Applications Software Packages (11.25 credit hours); Module D, Information Systems (9 credit hours); Module E,Human Aspects of Computer Use (6.75 credit hours).

MEDICAL TRANSCRIPTION

Medical Transcription

Includes the following sequence of courses: Module I, Introduction; Module II, Medical Terminology; Module III, Advanced Terminology; Module IV, Fundamentals of Medical Transcription; Module V, Advanced Medical Transcription.

PARALEGAL STUDIES

Introduction to the American Legal System

A complete overview of the American legal system including basic legal concepts, court structure, criminal justice system, legal ethics, legal research, and major areas of substantive law such as torts, contracts, real property, and wills and probate. (5 credits)

Legal Research

This course is designed to teach the fundamentals of legal research. The student will learn the research tools and techniques necessary to find the actual law, but also how to use the various secondary materials which assist in the research process. Some of the topics covered are: case reporters, digests, codes, annotated codes, annotated reporters, citators, looseleaf services, legal encyclopedias, treatises, and computerized research services. (10 credits)

Litigation and Trial Practice

This paraprofessional specialty will help the student play a prominent role in trial practice. The course will give a broad knowledge of litigation practice, law and procedure. Special emphasis is made on the role of the lawyer and those responsibilities that may be delegated to the legal assistant. Attention is also given to preparation of process, investigation, discovery and trial preparation. (10 credits)

Criminal Law and Procedure

This course is designed to give an understanding of both the law and procedural aspects of criminal justice and to prepare for a career in criminal justice. (10 credits)

Business Organizations

When is a partnership better than a corporation? What procedure is followed in setting up a corporation? What must be included in the articles of corporation? How are corporate minutes drafted? These questions are important to most businesses in any community and a student's knowledge in this specialty will provide assistance to lawyers in answering them for their clients. (9 credits)

Real Property

Real estate law is one of the most lucrative aspects of the legal profession. There is a great demand for real estate specialists not only in law firms but also in banks, title companies, real estate brokerages, and many other aspects of business. This area of the law has unlimited opportunities for paralegals who are interested in becoming involved in this dynamic and important aspect of life. (11 credits)

Trusts, Wills and Estate Administration

This area of specialty is for legal assistants working with attorneys whose practice consists of some (or all) probate. This unit of study introduces the legal assistant to the essential requirements of wills, trusts, types of estate and estate taxes. It takes the student by a step-by-step process through all procedures involved in both formal and informal probate. Special emphasis is placed on the roles of various participants in the administration of a probate matter—the lawyer, the personal representative of the estate, the court, and the legal assistant. A review of the responsibilities that can be delegated to the legal assistant is included. Attention is given to training legal assistants in how to execute many of the probate forms necessary from the commencement through the completion of the probate procedure. (10 credits)

Bankruptcy

An important aspect of most law practices is bankruptcy law; it is a highly specialized area of practice which involves a great deal of work, especially suited for the paralegal. (9 credits)

Administrative Law and Process

The course covers delegation of authority to agencies, legislation oversight, judicial review, disclosure of information, the administrative process, procedural due process, formal adjudications, rules and rulemaking, obtaining judicial review, and more. (7 credits)

Associate Degree in Paralegal Studies

This program is composed of sixty semester hours which includes fourteen semester hours of general education credits. The program consists of four semesters. The student may select any four specialties and has a maximum time of nine months to complete each semester. Examinations must be proctored. Contact the Institute for complete details.

Peoples College of Independent Studies

A Division of Southeastern Academy, Inc.
233 Academy Drive
P.O. Box 421768
Kissimmee, Florida 34742-1768

(407) 847-4444

Description:

The Peoples College of Independent Studies, a division of Southeastern Academy, Inc., is a nonsectarian, coeducational, private institution founded in 1985. It offers specialized associate degree programs in travel and tourism management, personal computer programming, electronics technology with personal computer servicing and industrial controls or communications specializations; non-degree programs in communication electronics with microprocessor technology, computer servicing and electronics technology, industrial electronics and microprocessor technology, personal computer programming, business computing, and an avocational program in powerboat handling and seamanship.

Faculty:

D. L. Peoples, President; Terry W. Murphy, Education Director; Leonette Miles, Supervisor of Admissions. There is a faculty of 11 members.

Academic Levels:
Vocational

Degree/Certificate Programs:
Associate Degree; Diploma.

Admission Requirements:
High school graduation or equivalent. Transcript of high school grades required. Must attain 18 years of age by the completion of the resident portion of training. Applicants must be in good health, have good eyesight and hearing.

Tuition:
Contact the school for current tuition and fees. Monthly payments plans available for all programs. Refund policy of the Distance Education and Training Council applies to all courses and programs.

Equipment Requirements:
All required books and equipment are included in the tuition fee.

Accreditations:
Distance Education and Training Council; Florida State Board of Independent Post-Secondary Vocational, Technical, Trade, and Business Schools.

VOCATIONAL COURSES

COMPUTER SCIENCE

Personal Computing

This program provides a thorough background in basic personal computer operations with emphasis on the three most commonly used computer applications: word processing, spreadsheet, and database management. An introduction to the BASIC computer programming language is also included. There are four courses: Microcomputers and MS/DOS; Word Processor; Spreadsheet; and Introduction to BASIC.

Business Computing

This program will teach the basic skills needed to create computer programs for business applications. Focus is on the programming languages most commonly used in business: BASIC, COBOL, and C. There are 13 courses covering: Data Processing and BASIC; Mathematics for Computers; Principles of Programming; Data Concepts; Database Management; Accounting I; Systems Analysis and Design; Advanced BASIC; Accounting II; COBOL I; C Language 1; COBOL II; C Language 2.

Computer Programming

This program teaches the basic skills needed to create computer programs for business applications. Focus is on the programming languages most commonly used in business: BASIC, COBOL, and C.

Specialized Associate Degree in Computer Programming

This in-depth program is a complete home study program for those wishing to enter the field of business computer programming. There are 20 courses covering: Data Processing and BASIC; English; Mathematics for Business; Principles of Programming; Accounting I; Mathematics for Computers; Data Concepts; Psychology in Business; Systems Analysis and Design; Communication in Business; Accounting II; COBOL I; C Language 1; Control Language Applications; Database Applications; RPG III: Structured Programming; RPG III: Reports; COBOL II; RPG III: File Updating; RPG III: Interactive Processing.

ELECTRONICS TECHNOLOGY

Electronics and Microprocessor Technology

This program will teach the basics of modern electronics. There are nine course including 40 subject units covering: DC Electronics; AC Electronics; Semiconductors and Amplifiers; Advanced Electronic Circuits; Digital Fundamentals; Advanced Digital Circuits; Microcomputer Fundamentals; Advanced Microcomputers; Software, Programming, and Applications.

Industrial Electronics and Microcomputer Technology

This program teaches how to service and maintain electronic circuits, microprocessor controls, and other equipment used in industrial electronics applications. There are ten courses covering 45 subject units: DC Electronics; AC Electronics; Semiconductors and Amplifiers; Advanced Electronic Circuits; Digital Fundamentals; Advanced Digital Circuits; Microcomputer Fundamentals; Advanced Microcomputers; Software, Programming and Applications; Industrial Controls.

Computer Servicing and Electronics Technology

This program is designed to give the student the knowledge and skills necessary to enter the field of electronics technology and microcomputer service and repair. Ten courses include 45 subject units: DC Electronics; AC Electronics; Semiconductors and Amplifiers; Advanced Electronic Circuits; Digital Fundamentals; Advanced Digital Circuits; Microcomputer Fundamentals; Advanced Microcomputers; Software, Programming and Applications; Personal Computer Servicing.

Specialized Associate Degree in Electronics Technology

This comprehensive program gives the student the opportunity to earn a college associate degree at home, according to his/her own schedule. The fifteen courses include 55 subject units: DC Electronics; AC Electronics; Semiconductors and Amplifiers; Advanced Electronic Circuits; Mathematics for Business; Digital Fundamentals; Advanced Digital Circuits; Communications in Business; English; Microcomputer Fundamentals; Advanced Microcomputers; Psychology in Business; Software, Programming and Applications; Industrial Controls; Personal Computer Servicing.

Professional Career Development Institute

6065 Roswell Road
Suite 3118
Atlanta, Georgia 30328   (770) 729-8400

Description:

The institute (PCDI) was founded in 1987. It offers courses in paralegal, bookkeeping and accounting, animal care, interior decorating, VCR repair, travel, gunsmithing, personal computer, hotel and restaurant management, medical and dental office assisting, home inspection, personal computer repair, fitness and nutrition, auto mechanics, medical transcriptionist, conservation, floral design, legal transcriptionist, electrician, and tax preparation.

Tuition:

Tuition varies from $489 to $989. Contact the institute for course availability and current tuition/fees.

Accreditations:

Distance Education and Training Council.

Richard M. Milburn High School

14416 Jefferson Davis Highway
Suite 12
Woodbridge, Virginia 22191   (703) 494-0147

Description:

The school was founded in 1975 and offers courses in full four-year high school diploma program. Also offered are Spanish, Saudi-Arabic, and German Headstart courses. Contact the school for further information.

Accreditations:

Distance Education and Training Council.

SCI - National Institute for Paralegal Arts and Sciences

164 West Royal Palm Road
Boca Raton, Florida 33432   (800) 669-2555

Description:

The institute was founded in 1976. It offers a program leading to the Paralegal Specialized Associate Degree as well as paralegal specialty courses and a paralegal diploma program. Contact the institute for further information.

Accreditations:

Distance Education and Training Council.

Southeastern Academy

233 Academy Drive
P.O. Box 421768
Kissimmee, Florida 34742-1768
                                   (407) 847-4444

Description:

Southeastern Academy is a nonsectarian, coeducational, private institution specializing in career training for the travel industry. Southeastern Academy trains for entry level positions within the airline, travel agent, hotel, tour, and car rental industries. It offers both an extension home study/ resident and a full resident program. Southeastern Academy is located on a modern 31-acre self-contained campus in Kissimmee, Florida. It offers full dormitory and cafeteria services to students. Southeastern Academy was chartered on August 2, 1974.

Faculty:

David L. Peoples, President. There is a faculty of 22.

Academic Levels:

Vocational

Degree/Certificate Programs:

Diploma.

Admission Requirements:

High school graduation or equivalent. Transcript of high school grades required. Must attain 18 years of age by the completion of the resident portion of training. Applicants must be in good health, have good eyesight and hearing, and have a stated or demonstrated interest to succeed in a travel career.

Tuition:

Contact the school for current tuition and fees. The costs for travel, student housing, and meal plans are not included in tuition. Financial aid plans available. Refund policy of the Distance Education and Training Council applies to all programs.

Enrollment Period:

Resident portions of the home study/resident program is of an eight-week durations. The resident portion is required for graduation.

Equipment Requirements:

All required books and equipment are included in the tuition fee.

Credit and Grading:

Graduation is dependent upon the satisfactory completion of both the Home Study and Resident portions. A grade of 70 percent must be maintained in the Home Study portion, which must be completed within a specified time. In the Resident portion, a grade average of 70 percent in each core curriculum course and combined average of 70 percent in the professional business course. The student must attain the required typing speed of 25 words per minute. Minimum passing grade: 70 percent on home study material; 70 percent on resident material.

Library Services:

A reference library facility is available during the resident phase.

Accreditations:

Distance Education and Training Council; Florida State Board of Independent Post-Secondary Vocational, Technical, Trade, and Business Schools.

VOCATIONAL COURSES

TRAVEL INDUSTRY

Airline/Travel Industry Program

This program is a combination home study/eight-week resident program designed to qualify students to enter any part of the vast travel industry, including airlines, hotels, travel agencies, resorts, car rental agencies, cruise lines, and tour operators. The overall educational objective is to teach students the specific technical and professional skills required for public-contact employment in the airline and travel industries. The 10-lesson home study segment includes the following subject areas: The Travel Industry; Travel Markets; Flight Selection; Connecting Flight Selection; Travel Planner/Client Records; Computer Reservation Systems; Fares; Ticketing; Tours and Cruises; Hotel/Car Rental Procedures. The eight-week resident training segment has the major emphasis on the use of American Airlines SABRE computerized reservations system and its application in both the airline and travel agency environments. The classroom instruction is particularly important for teaching interpersonal skills such as Professional Development, Customer Awareness, and Communication Skills. Students

who successfully complete the program will be able to demonstrate competencies in the following subject areas: Airline Ticketing; Travel Agency Functions; Travel Markets; Hotel/Car Rental Procedures; Professional Development/Customer Awareness Skills; and Communications and Typewriting.

Stenotype Institute of Jacksonville, Inc.
500 Ninth Avenue North
Jacksonville Beach, Florida 32250
(904) 246-7466

Description:

The Stenotype Institute of Jacksonville had its origin in 1940 as a resident school. In the mid-1950s the home study court reporting course was added and both programs continue today. Dictation is taught to the home study student by the use of cassette tapes.

Faculty:

Thyra D. Ellis, President; Mary W. Dryden, Education Director. There is a faculty of 6 members.

Academic Levels:

Vocational

Degree/Certificate Programs:

Diploma.

Admission Requirements:

High school diploma. The equivalent of a high school diploma will require that a student take and pass a Stenotype Institute entrance examination. Previous training in commercial subjects is not necessary.

Tuition:

$4,500. Full cost payable in 45 monthly installments of $100 each. Payment plan available. Approved for Veterans Benefits. Pro rata refund policy.

Enrollment Period:

The time required to complete the Court Reporting course depends entirely upon the ability and industry of the individual student. Certification depends upon proficiency alone, not upon the time spent in the school. The average time needed to complete the Home Study Court Reporting Course is 60 months.

Equipment Requirements:

The student must furnish the following equipment which is not included in the tuition payments, but can be purchased through the school: stenotype machine in case (manual); stenotype machine in case (electric); luxury carrying case; tripod; reporter pads (50 pads to a case). Shipping charges will be added to the cost of the equipment or materials.

Credit and Grading:

Examinations are proctored. Academic courses are graded on a percentage basis. A grade of 100 percent is perfect; any grade under 80 percent is unacceptable as credit toward graduation. If a student fails to earn a grade of at

674

least 80 percent in an academic course, he/she may repeat the course one time. The student must satisfactorily complete the Court Procedures course with a grade of B or above.

Job Placement Assistance:

There is no additional cost to any student, graduate, or alumnus for placement service. It is both national and local. While employment is not guaranteed, the Institute will help the student in finding placement where possible.

Accreditations:

Distance Education and Training Council; Career College Association.

VOCATIONAL COURSES

STENOTYPING

Notereading

All theory principles learned. Student transcribes each theory lesson from actual notes written on that theory lesson. Student also transcribes notes of court reporting students during this section of the notereading phase. Emphasis is placed on fast and accurate transcription. The following is applicable only to students who choose to take a position as an official notereader transcriber for court reporters instead of continuing with Machine Shorthand and Advanced Court Reporting. Transcription of notes of reporters from actual Civil, Circuit, and Criminal cases; from conventions, conferences, board meetings, and all types of hearings. Student learns how to proof own work swiftly. Transcripts compared with notes for accuracy.

Machine Shorthand Theory

Basic principles of writing on the stenotype machine, leading to more difficult abbreviations and vocabulary. Emphasis on accuracy and knowledge of stenotype keyboard and combinations. Dictation drills.

Machine Shorthand Beginning Speed

Continued drills on more difficult vocabulary, with emphasis on both accuracy and speed. Official speed tests 80 wpm through 120 wpm.

Advanced Court Reporting

Machine Shorthand Beginning Speed. Continued drills on more difficult vocabulary, with emphasis on both accuracy and speed. Official speed tests through 140 wpm.

Machine Shorthand Intermediate Speed. Longer dictation periods, using difficult literary material. Dictation of Jury Charges, Judges' Opinions, and simple two-voice testimony. Official tests through 160 wpm.

Machine Shorthand High Speeds. Very difficult legal, literary, and medical dictation. More difficult Jury Charge and Judges' Opinion dictation. Four-voice testimony.

Transcription

Transcription I. Transcription from own notes.

Transcription II. Transcription from own notes.

Transcription III. Transcription from own notes and from dictated court and convention notes.

English

Study of English grammar; the rules of punctuation, capitalization, and writing of numbers; spelling; vocabulary enrichment; and special emphasis on homonyms and other commonly confused words.

Legal Terminology and Law

Includes the study of courts and legal systems in the United States; general legal terminology; procedures and legal terms involved in civil and criminal litigation; and terminology associated with such other areas as probate, real property, contracts, negotiable instruments, and domestic relations.

Medical Terminology

Includes the study of general medical terms (including roots, prefixes, and suffixes) and the terminology of the various body systems, together with an overview of anatomy and physiology to assist in an understanding of these terms.

Court Procedures *Tuition:* Students "report" simulated court scenes which include four or more voices. Students must dictate two hours from their own notes as a court reporter dictates for a typist.

Trans World Travel Academy
Suite 214
11495 Natural Bridge Road
St. Louis, Missouri 63044-9842
(800) 942-7467

Description:

The Trans World Travel Academy (TWTA) was founded in 1978 as an operating department of Trans World Airlines, Inc. At that time the academy operation concentrated on a home study/residency program called *The Basics of Selling Travel.* In addition to continuing this successful program, the academy began a flight attendant training division in 1984. Today the academy offers both home study courses as well as computerized reservations sales training, aircraft mechanics school, and corporate and customized training programs. The educational objective is to provide quality travel industry training and to provide the travel industry with highly skilled individuals for entry level positions. The Trans World Travel Academy is owned and operated by Trans World Airlines.

Faculty:

Michael L. Kelly, Staff Vice President; Frank A. Bugler, Director.

Academic Levels:
Vocational

Degree/Certificate Programs:
Certificate.

Admission Requirements:

Only individuals 18 years of age are considered; must have a high school diploma or equivalent.

Tuition:

Contact the Academy for current tuition and fees. Credit cards accepted. Pay-as-you-go payment plan available. Refund policy is in accordance with the guidelines of the Distance Education and Training Council.

Enrollment Period:

Students may enroll at any time. Residency training for The Basics of Selling Travel is held at TWTA's headquarters in St. Louis, Missouri; for The Basics of Becoming a Flight Attendant at TWA's Charles A. Lindbergh Training Center in St. Louis, Missouri.

Equipment Requirements:

All texts and materials included in tuition. Housing and meals for two-day residency seminar for The Basics of Becoming a Flight Attendant are paid by the student.

Credit and Grading:

While most students scores are higher, the minimum accepted grade on any exercise, quiz, or examination is an 80% correct score. Students must maintain an overall average score of 80% or better and must submit lessons in a timely manner. Numerical percentages are maintained as part of the students academic record.

Library Services:

Students may use the TWTA on-site library when completing the residency portion of the courses.

Accreditations:

Distance Education and Training Council.

VOCATIONAL COURSES

TRAVEL INDUSTRY

The Basics of Selling Travel

Home Study Program. The home study portion of this course covers the following topics: travel professionals; destination geography; Western Hemisphere destinations; domestic air travel; Eastern Hemisphere destination; international travel; selling travel; railroads and car rentals; cruises; hotels; tours; sales service and follow-up; communications; travel agency business procedures; domestic air fares; ticketing; international air fares; geography and codes review; future of travel industry.

Optional Residency Program. Two weeks (80 hours) of classroom computer training at TWTA's St. Louis campus; displaying and interpreting flight availability; booking itineraries including air/car/hotel; creating passenger name records (PNRs); modifying reservations; making special service requests; accessing and interpreting fare displays; applying fare construction itineraries; utilizing telephone sales techniques; career preparation and interview techniques. The residency classes are scheduled throughout the year. Resident training must be completed no later than ninety days following home study completion or one year following enrollment.

The Basics of Becoming a Flight Attendant

Home Study Program. The highlights of this course are: introduction to the flight attendant job; travel geography—United States destinations; world travel—international destinations, climate; time zones, airline timetables, ticketing; types of aircraft and galley equipment; in-flight services; flight attendant duties and responsibilities; flight attendant health and safety; flight attendant lifestyle—managing international travel; the flight attendant image—putting it all together.

Residency Seminar. The Home Study program must be completed before enrolling. Students will participate in group discussions and hands-on activities. Includes a mock meal service in an aircraft cabin trainer, practice interviews, and a tour of the Flight Attendant and Pilot training facility. Students attending the two-day seminar are given the option of providing their own housing or selecting reduced rate hotel accommodations located near the TWA Charles A. Lindbergh Training Center in St. Louis, Missouri. Meal costs are extra.

Travel Lab
Wilma Boyd Career Schools, Inc.
One Chatham Center
Pittsburgh, Pennsylvania 15219

(800) 245-6673

Description:

The Boyd School - Travel Lab was founded in 1968. It offers a home study airline/travel program with the same objectives as the full resident program. The home study program also includes an optional four-week resident portion in Pittsburgh. A branch campus is located at Concourse Tower II, Suite 200, 2090 Palm Beach Lakes Boulevard, West Palm Beach, FL 33409.

Approximately 1,500 students are enrolled annually in the home study program. The Boyd School is a division of Millcraft Industries.

Faculty:

Ruth Delach, President; Elizabeth McKinney, Executive Vice President; Nancy Waite Kist, Educational Director. Travel Lab has a faculty of 25 and 3 counselors.

Academic Levels:

Vocational

Degree/Certificate Programs:

Certificate.

Admission Requirements:

High School graduation or GED equivalency. An applicant must attain 18 years of age by the completion of the home study program. Applicants under 18 who are still in high school must obtain written approval of their high school guidance counselor or principal.

Tuition:

$200 registration fee; home study tuition $1,995, 4-week resident tuition $1,000, 2-week accelerated $600. Installment plan available. Pro rata refund plan. The student is responsible for food and housing while in Pittsburgh for the resident portion.

Enrollment Period:

A maximum of twenty months is allowed to complete the home study course. Interruption of training may be granted upon written request. The optional resident portion is for four weeks at the Travel Lab headquarters in Pittsburgh.

Equipment Requirements:

All materials and equipment needed for both the home study and resident portions are supplied by the School and are included in the tuition payments.

Credit and Grading:

The grading system is A, Excellent (94–100 percent); B, Good (86–93 percent); C, Average (77–85 percent); D, Below Average (70–76 percent); F, Failing (Below 70 percent). A grade of 70 percent or more is required on the final examination. Home Study examinations are open book; Resident Program examinations are proctored.

Job Placement Assistance:
Available only after satisfactory completion of resident portion of training.

Accreditations:
Distance Education and Training Council; Independent Colleges and Schools.

VOCATIONAL COURSES

TRAVEL INDUSTRY

Travel Lab Program

Home Study. The home study portion of this program consists of 10 textbooks and 26 lesson assignments. The program includes the following topics: Book 1 - Introduction to Travel. Packet 1 - Travel Terminology. Book 2 - Domestic Travel. Packet 2 - Domestic Itineraries. Book 3 - International Travel. Packet 3 - International Itineraries. Book 4 - The Airlines. Packet 4 - The Business Traveler. Book 5 - Car Rentals, Cruises, Hotels, and Tours. Packet 5 - The Travel Planner. Book 6 - Air Fares. Book 6 II - Ticketing. Packet 6 - International Air Fares and Ticketing. Book 7 - The Travel Agency. Packet 7 - The Meeting Planner. Book 8 - Selling Travel. Packet 8 - Keyboarding. Book 9 - The Computer. Packet 9 - Professional Image. Book 10 - Career Development. Packet 10 - The Job Hunt.

Resident. The optional resident training program is designed to enlarge and refine the knowledge and skills acquired through the home study lessons. The students gain practical training and experience through "hands-on" practice at the school's simulated airline and travel industries facilities. This program includes: computerized reservation systems; ticketing procedures; travel information and travel agency procedures; introduction to personal computers; airport procedures; travel communication; professional development.

Truck Marketing Institute
1090 Eugenia Place
Carpinteria, California 93013-2011
(805) 684-4558

Description:
The Truck Marketing Institute began in 1964 and has provided industry-wide training programs for the motor truck manufacturers to develop professionalism in truck selling. Its "Precision Truck Selling" (PTS) courses provide a medium for strengthening or expanding a truck sales force. The courses are suited for new truck personnel as well as for updating truck specialists. Each year over 3,500 truck dealer, fleet, and component supplier students are enrolled. Most students are from the United States and Canada, but TMI has overseas students as well.

Faculty:
Robert J. Godfrey, President; Mark E. Godfrey, Education Director. There is a faculty of two and one subject specialist.

Academic Levels:
Vocational

Degree/Certificate Programs:
Certificate.

Admission Requirements:
High school graduation or GED and sponsorship by employer; basic skills in mathematics and English.

Tuition:
Contact the school for current tuition and fees. Payment with enrollment or on a 30-day invoice. Refund policy of the Distance Education and Learning Council applies to all enrollments. No refund after 50 percent of the course has been completed.

Enrollment Period:
The maximum time allowed to complete a course is one year. Average time to complete: PTS I, 10 weeks; PTS II, 36 weeks; PTS III, 42 weeks; PTS IV, 39 weeks.

Equipment Requirements:
Textbooks and tests included in tuition; no other materials required.

Credit and Grading:
Examinations are open book home study tests. Grading is by percentage. The minimum passing grade is 75 percent.

Accreditations:
Distance Education and Learning Council.

VOCATIONAL COURSES

TRUCK SELLING

Precision Truck Selling: Light Duty Models

Course I of the PTS Series. It comprises five lessons, each calling for a study time of between one and two hours, including test preparation. Subjects covered in the lessons are as follows: Lesson 1. Getting to know trucks: types, terms, weights, ratings. Lesson 2. Body, engine, option codes. Trim and paint codes. Curb and model weights. Lesson 3. Weight distribution—simplified; chassis components. Gross weight ratings. Lesson 4. Fundamentals of performance for light trucks and recreational vehicles. Lesson 5. More about RVs; trailer towing; off-road applications. Diesel power. Optional equipment.

Precision Truck Selling: Light/Medium Duty Trucks

Course II of the PTS Series. There are ten lessons, averaging three to four hours of time for study and completion of the Achievement Test. Subjects included are as follows: Lesson 1. Introduction to market and models. Truck types and terms; current truck line models. Lesson 2. Gross weight rating systems—GVWR and GAWR; fundamentals of truck weight distribution. Lesson 3. Weight distribution by truck types; distributions of abnormal loads. Gross Axle Weight Ratings; the how and why of GAWR. Lesson 4. Load-carrying components: frame, front and rear axles; component designs, strength and ratings. Lesson 5. Load-carrying components: tires and wheels. More insights into GAWR. Lesson 6. Load-carrying components: springs, shock absorbers, hydraulic brake systems; FMVSS-121 air brakes. Lesson 7. Fundamentals of truck performance: work, torque, horsepower, engine ratings. Lesson 8. Applied truck performance: power available versus power demands; performance prediction procedures. Lesson 9A. Driveline fundamentals: transmission functions; mid-speed performance determinations. Lesson 9B. Choosing the driveline: transmission and axle combinations; selecting axle ratios. Lesson 10A. Basics of diesels for medium-duty trucks; electrical systems. Lesson 10B. Emission controls; noise abatement; safety, size and weight regulations: options, accessories, special equipment; course summary.

Precision Truck Selling: Heavy-Duty Diesels

Course III of the PTS Series. The subject coverage in the lessons is as follows: Lesson 1. Economics of heavy trucks; productivity and cost relationships; introduction to the metric system. Lesson 2. Heavy truck model types and terms; maximum loading within size and weight limits. Lesson 3. Truck weight distribution; planning for optimum payload capacity. Lesson 4. Tractor-trailer weight distribution; procedures to achieve maximum load capacity. Lesson 5. Heavy-duty truck chassis components: frame, springs, axles, wheels, tires; GAWR rating system. Lesson 6. Basics of torque and power; performance prediction procedures; reserve power and gradeability; performance in customary and metric units (S.I.). Lesson 7. Choosing the drivetrain: engine torque and power characteristics; shift pattern charts. Lesson 8. Determining gradeability and performance at low speeds and off the road; traction ability and limitations. Lesson 9. Vehicle speed control: FMVSS-121 air brake systems; engine brakes; transmission and driveline retarders. Lesson 10. The support systems: electrical, cooling, intake, exhaust; emissions and noise control; power take-offs; truck safety; driver environment; course summary.

Precision Truck Selling: Mid-Range Diesels

Course IV of the PTS Series. Students can expect to devote from four to five hours for each of the ten lessons in the course. Subject coverage in the lessons is as follows: Lesson 1. Truck weight ratings and market classes. Mid-range diesel chassis and cab types. Reasons for dieselization. Lesson 2. Operating costs; economic advantages of diesel engines. Basic truck dimensions. Lesson 3. Understanding diesel engines: torque and power; technical advantages of diesels; interpreting specifications. Lesson 4. Mid-range diesel performance: axle ratios; geared speed; performance at road speeds; energy saving devices. Lesson 5. Performance in low- and mid-speed ranges; transmissions and rear axles for mid-range diesel trucks. Lesson 6. Selecting the best driveline combination; shift pattern charts; clutch and propellor shaft; PTOs. Lesson 7. Weight distribution for trucks and tractors. Lesson 8. Loads, ratings and load-carrying components: frame; suspensions; wheels and tires. Lesson 9. Brakes and safety: brake systems—power assisted hydraulic, full-air; parking brakes; CG height. Lesson 10A. Support systems: cooling, electrical and fuel; diesel fuel concerns. Noise control. Truck productivity. Lesson 10B. "The Metric Connection." Treatment of major procedures in metrics: torque and power; axle ratios; geared speeds; performance; weight distributions; dimensions.

Westlawn Institute of Marine Technology
733 Summer Street
Stamford, Connecticut 06901   (203) 359-0500

Description:

The Westlawn Institute of Marine Technology (formerly Westlawn School of Yacht Design) was founded in 1930. It was acquired by the National Marine Manufacturers Association in 1968 and is now conducted as a not-for-profit school, operating as a service to the boating industry. The School has a cooperative program with the New York Institute of Technology, leading to a Bachelor of Science degree in Mechanical Engineering with a major in small craft design.

Faculty:
Norman Nudelman, Education Director.

Academic Levels:
College
Vocational

Degree/Certificate Programs:
Bachelor, Diploma. In cooperation with the New York Institute of Technology, 36 credits from Westlawn may be transferred toward NYIT's required 138 credits for the Bachelor of Science in Mechanical Engineering degree.

Admission Requirements:
Two years of high school mathematics. For credit toward NYIT's bachelor degree program, the student must have a high school diploma or its equivalent, and must take the Scholastic Aptitude Tests (SAT) in English and Mathematics.

Tuition:
Contact the school for current tuition and fees. A pro rata refund plan is available. Veterans benefits available.

Enrollment Period:
The maximum time allowed to complete the course is 4 years. An extension for good cause may be arranged.

Equipment Requirements:
Textbooks are supplied by the school and are included in the tuition. Technical tools such as drafting equipment and mathematical instruments must be supplied by the student and are not included in the tuition; average cost to student approximately $450.

Credit and Grading:
There are 37 separate lesson assignments which must be completed with a grade of 75 percent or better. A lesson with a grade less than 75 percent can be resubmitted. There are 23 question papers, 10 review papers, and 4 examinations. The final examination requires the complete design of three boats. The examinations are open book.

Job Placement Assistance:
Available.

Accreditations:
Distance Education and Training Council.

VOCATIONAL COURSES

YACHT DESIGN

Yacht Design Home Study Course

The course covers construction in wood, fiberglass and aluminum. Types of craft include high-speed boats, sailing yachts and multihulls. Some of the subjects covered include: scope of boat designing; basic laws of flotation; how boats are propelled; basic hull types; necessary mathematics; expression of problems in formula style; use of decimals; cubes, squares and roots; curve sheets and graphs; drafting instruments and their use; lay-out of sheets and determination of scales; preliminary specification; typical complete design and set of specifications; shading and lettering.

Displacement by Simpson's Rule; obtaining center of buoyancy; displacement by waterline method; vertical center of buoyancy; block, prismatic, fineness and other coefficients; calculations for wetted surface; center of gravity determination; theory of a set of lines;

importance of resistance; wave-making and eddy-making resistances; lay-out of ideal form for minimum resistance; preparing and analyzing curves of areas; metacentric analysis of sailing vessel lines; Rayner and Colin Archer theories; parasitic resistances; speed-length ratios; theory of stability; metacentric height; moments of inertia; calculating BM and GM; trapezoidal rule; GZ arms; GZ table; curve of righting arms; Blom's method; longitudinal stability; stabilizing devices; calculations for change of trim; foot-pounds; moment to trim one inch; tons per inch immersion; effect of ballasting; statical and dynamic stability; heeling; squatting; the meaning of a set of lines; waterlines; sections; buttocks; diagonals; V-bottom vs. round; layout of lines sheets; station spacing for Simpson's rule; sheer lines; section shapes; designed waterline; use of various lines in fairing; preparing offset tables; examples of hull lines of boats of different types; conical development of plywood hulls.

Boat building materials; weights and uses; wood planking; plywood; fiberglass construction; aluminum construction; formulas for scantings; typical construction drawings; longitudinal construction; stopwaters; screw fastenings; use of nails; rivets and bolts; fastening materials; drawing of profiles; eye-balance; determination of freeboard; stacks, masts and rigging as they apply to appearance; locating ports and windows; inboard construction profiles; examples of profiles; rails and bulwarks; layout of cabins; salons-staterooms-galleys-toilets; engine rooms; headroom; placement of doors; basic requirements of a successful cabin.

Gasoline engines; diesel engines; formula for determination of power; fuel consumption; determination of maximum useful rotative speeds; outboard motors; inboard-outboard drives; installation problems; spreading thrust; reduction gears and V-drives; engine testing; theory of propellors; computing the speed of a boat; speed charts; determination of correct diameter and pitch; Keith and Crouch methods; the rudder in theory; rudder areas; rudder posts; blade thickness; steering efficiency.

Theory of sails; interaction between sails; sloops-cutters-yawls; ketches-schooners-catboats; sail proportioning; Marconi and gaff rigs; masts and spars; standing and running rigging; calculating sail area; relationship of centers; lateral plane determination; CLP; center of effort; special hull shapes for sailing efficiency; auxiliary engines; rigging and spar sizes; multihulls-catamarans and trimarans.

Stepless speed boats; hydroplanes; aspect ratio; plane angles; location of steps; skidding; reducing skin friction; dihedral angles; special steering gears; installation of racing engines; special problems of high speed.

Deck machinery; fire-fighting equipment; boat plumbing; bilge plumbing; proper pipe sizes; hydrostatic test for tanks; fire prevention regulations; tank fillers, vents, strainers; exhaust pipe problems; heating; electric systems and generation plants; lighting requirements; voltages; electric shore systems; electrolysis protection; lightning protection; deck fittings; anchor and boat handling gear; specifications.

World College
Lake Shores Plaza
5193 Shore Drive
Suite 113
Virginia Beach, Virginia 23455-2500
(804) 464-4600

Description:
World College was conceived in 1982 to provide a high quality, independent study, bachelor-level education in electronics technology at an affordable cost. The baccalaureate degree program offers students academic preparation for careers in electronics, telecommunications, electrical power, and computer and control systems. Some of the general education courses are offered through the Independent Study Program of Ohio University. These may be substituted by a general education elective of equal credit at the discretion of World College.

Faculty:
John Randall Drinko, President.

Academic Levels:
College

Degree/Certificate Programs:
The Bachelor of Electronic Engineering degree requires the successful completion of 139 semester hours. The minimum residency for the bachelor's degree is one fourth of the total credit hours required for graduation or one semester in upper level courses for transfer students, whichever is greater.

Admission Requirements:
A new freshman student is a student who has never attended another college and is pursuing a baccalaureate degree. Applicant must be a high school graduate or possess a recognized equivalent. $250 enrollment fee.

Tuition:
$2,000 per year (semester). Tuition is payable by VISA, MasterCard, or Discover. Pro rata refund policy as per DETC guidelines.

Enrollment Period:
Student may begin study at anytime. The semester begins upon enrollment and extends for one year. Eight semesters are required for the completion of degree requirements.

Equipment Requirements:
Lab equipment, assignment books, study guides, and all materials needed to complete the program are included with tuition, except for a personal computer system and required textbooks and study guides for courses completed through Ohio University. These latter items must be purchased by the student.

Credit and Grading:
Letter grades A, B, C, D, and F are used. Minimum passing grade is D. Examinations must be proctored at the World College office or at another college, university, or high school. Credit is awarded in semester hour units.

Accreditations:
Distance Education and Training Council.

COLLEGE COURSES

COMPUTER ENGINEERING TECHNOLOGY

Digital Electronics I

Covers numbering systems, logic gates, truth tables, and general coverage of digital devices such as: flip-flops, counters, adders, multiplexers, and demultiplexers. (4 credits, including 1 lab)

Digital Electronics II

In-depth analysis of digital devices used in microcomputers with emphasis on coutners, shift registers, decoders, and A/D and D/A converters. (4 credits, including 1 lab)

Advanced Digital Laboratory

Covers serial and parallel shift registers, arithmetic logic units, timing and logic controls, three bus architecture, tri-state logic, control lines, circuitry, and ROM and RAM memory. (1 credit)

Microprocessor Theory and Applications

Covers the operation and architecture of a microprocessor, programming in machine and assembly language and interfacing techniques and devices. This course utilizes the CIE designed Microprocessor Training Laboratory. (4 credits, including 1 lab)

Computer-Aided Circuit Design and Drafting

Based on Micro-Cap software, covers drawing circuits and the editing of these circuits, AC analysis using frequency response curves, DC analysis using varying inputs and transistor curve tracing. (2 credits)

C-Language Programming

Covers a systematic and structured approach to problem solving with emphasis on flowcharting and pseudo-coding. (3 credits)

Digital Data Communications

Covers the concepts and principles of digital communication with emphasis on modems, bulletin boards, and local area networks. (3 credits)

Computer Applications in Business

Covers various software with emphasis on database management and spreadsheet applicaitons.

ELECTRONICS ENGINEERING TECHNOLOGY

Electric Circuits I

Covers fundamental principles of DC circuits including Ohm's law, Kirchoff's laws, series and parallel circuits and equivalent circuits. (4 credits, including 1 lab)

Electric Circuits II

Covers fundamental principles of AC circuits with emphasis on steady state AC circuits, along with relationships of frequency and impedance being analyzed and resonance studied. (4 credits, including 1 lab)

Solid State Electronic Devices

Covers theory and principles of operation of solid state devices including diodes, transistors, and FETs. (4 credits, including 1 lab)

Electronic Circuits I

Covers unregulated and regulated power supplies and different configurations of amplifiers. (4 credits, including 1 lab)

Electronic Circuits II

Covers operational amplifiers and other analog circuits and subsystems commonly found in the field of industrial controls and communications. (4 credits, including 1 lab)

Electronic Circuit Troubleshooting

Covers measurement techniques and usage of electronic test equipment in troubleshooting. Includes troubleshooting steps and methods and their application to electronic circuits. (3 credits)

Symptoms in Electronic Circuits

Covers system analysis and symptom diagnosis in electronic circuits. (3 credits)

Network Analysis I

Covers duality, superposition, Thevenin's and Norton's theorems, Ohm's and Kirchoff's laws applied to AC circuits with emphasis on a nonlinear analysis of electronic circuits with active devices. (4 credits, including 1 lab)

Solid State Circuit Design

An in-depth analysis and design of complex solid state circuits. (4 credits, including 1 lab)

Network Analysis II

Covers resonant circuits, Nodal method of analysis, mesh analysis, usage of determinants in solving linear systems of equations, two-port linear network analysis and matrix theory and its applicaitons in electronic circuits. (4 credits, including 1 lab)

Electrical Power and Machines

Covers principles of power generation with emphasis on DC motors and generators, three phase circuits, and single phase and three phase induction motors. (4 credits)

Electronic Communications I

Covers the AM and FM receiving and transmitting with emphasis on modulation methods.

Electronic Communications II

Covers transmission lines, antennas, digital transmission and multiplexing, and microwave and satellite communication. (4 credits)

Control Systems I

Covers industrial controls with emphasis on position, force, motion, fluid and temperature transducers, and signal transmission and conditioners. (3 credits)

Control Systems II

Covers system concepts with emphasis on analog and digital controllers, power interfaces, Laplace transforms, and system response. (3 credits)

Control Systems I Laboratory

A labortory course supporting the theory course Control Systems I through the use of experiments and computer simulation. (2 credits, including 2 lab)

Control Systems II Laboratory

A laboratory course supporting the theory course Control Systems II through the use of experiments and computer simulation. (2 credits, including 2 lab)

Senior Design Project

Students are to design and implement an individual project. The proposal will be approved and monitored through periodic reports by the faculty, and the final result will include a detailed technical description, schematics, parts list, costs, test results, technical report, software and audio or video presentation of the project. (3 credits, including 1 lab)

HUMANITIES

Ethics: Concepts and Problems

Covers classic and/or modern philosophical views of human values, ideals, and morality. Provides survey of some problems, concepts, and results of ethics including selected philosophers of past and present. (3 credits)

MATHEMATICS

Topics in Technical Mathematics

Covers fractions, decimals, signed numbers, powers and radicals, formula evaluation and rearrangement, proportion, and reading graphs. (1 credit)

Algebra and Trigonometry I

Covers solving equations and inequalities, functions and their graphs, trigonometry of the right triangle and trigonometric functions of every angle. (3 credits)

Algebra and Trigonometry II

Covers systems of equations, complex numbers, quadratic and equations of higher order, trigonometric functions, and trigonometric identities and equations. (3 credits)

Technical Calculus I

Covers analytic geometry, limits, derivatives, simple integration, indefinite integrals with emphasis on applications of derivatives and integrals. (3 credits)

Technical Calculus II

Covers definite integral, derivatives of transcendental functions, integrals of transcendental functions, infinite series, Maclaurin series, Taylor series, L'Hospital's Rule, Fourier series, and introduces differential equations. (3 credits)

PHYSICS

Technical Physics

Covers Newton's Laws of Physics as applied to linear, circular, and periodic motion, concepts of magnetic and electrostatic fields plus magnetic circuit theory, photoelectric effect with emphasis on light sensitive and light emitting devices. (3 credits)

Finite Mathematics

Covers elementary probability and development of statistical concepts. (3 credits)

PSYCHOLOGY

General Psychology

Covers topics in experimental and clinical psychology including physiological bases of behavior, sensation, perception, learning, memory, human development, social processes, personality, and abnormal behavior. (3 credits)

Psychology of Adjustment

Covers dynamics, development, and problems of human adjustment. (3 credits)

SOCIAL SCIENCE

Principles of Microeconomics

Covers basic theory and economic analysis of prices, markets, production, wages, interest, rent, and profits. (3 credits)

Principles of Macroeconomics

Covers the nature of managerial concepts, managerial functions, and organizations structure with emphasis on current issues. (3 credits)

Quantitative Business Statistics

Covers sampling plans, point and interval estimation, classical decision theory, contingency table analysis, simple regression, correlation analysis and nonparametric statistics. (3 credits)

Marketing Principles

Covers principles of marketing management with emphasis on practices and problems of a marketing manager. (3 credits)

Financial Accounting

Covers the principles of the accounting process and external financial reporting. (3 credits).

TECHNICAL WRITING

Technical Writing I

Covers the development of effective writing style with emphasis on report writing for business and industry. (3 credits)

Technical Writing II

In-depth coverage of various communication tasks including preparation for oral presentations and standard approach to document writing. At the end of the course, students submit a 12-page research paper. (4 credits)

Section 3
Private, Nonprofit, and Governmental Institutions

American Health Information Management Association
Independent Division
Suite 1400
919 North Michigan Avenue
Chicago, Illinois 60601   (312) 787-2672

Description:

Recording of medical record information is not new. Many historians date it back to 25,000 B.C. when medical men painted murals of ancient surgical techniques on cave walls. Over the centuries increasing knowledge has expanded health care services and generated a growing volume of medical data that must be preserved. Today, sophisticated information-keeping systems and medical advances mean that a technician's studies encompass many disciplines, among which are: biological science, medical terminology, medical record science, legal aspects, and data processing.

Founded in 1928, the American Health Information Management Association (AHIMA) is the national organization of professional medical record administrators and technicians. Major goals of the association are to promote quality education programs for the medical record profession and to recruit qualified individuals into the field. The association also strives to improve medical record standards, supervises a professional registry, administers the accreditation process, and interprets the profession to other medically related groups and to the general public.

In 1962, the first home study course—the "Correspondence Course for Medical Record Personnel" was initiated. In 1979, a new home study program, the "Independent Study Program in Medical Record Technology" was introduced. It consists of 17 modules of study. The objective of the program is to provide both an educational opportunity for qualified individuals unable to attend approved academic programs for medical record technicians, and to improve patient care through increased knowledge of medical record practice and procedures.

Academic Levels:

Vocational

Degree/Certificate Programs:

Certificate. With 30 semester hours of academic credit, the student may sit for the accreditation examination.

Admission Requirements:

High School graduation or its equivalent (GED); minimum typing speed of 45 words per minute. Requirements for enrollment may not be waived.

Tuition:

Contact AHIMA for current tuition/fees. Partial refunds for withdrawal available, depending upon current status. Tuition may be paid in monthly installments. Many medical facilities provide tuition reimbursement for employees. Students are urged to check with their work supervisors.

Enrollment Period:

The Essentials of an Accredited Educational Program for the Medical Record Technician, established by the American Medical Record Association in collaboration with the American Medical Association, were used to develop the Independent Study Program in Medical Record Technology. The program consists of 17 modules; each module is a self-contained unit of study, taken in numerical sequence. The first 16 modules consist of 96 lessons; the 17th module is directed clinical practice in which learning experiences are reinforced through supervised practice. The enrollment period is 36 months; some students may complete the Program in less time. One 6-month extension may be allowed for a $75 extension fee.

Equipment Requirements:

The cost of required textbooks is not included in the tuition cost; the student must have access to a standard cassette tape recorder and a typewriter. The school supplies tape cassettes, microscope, slides, and course materials.

Credit and Grading:

A proctored examination is required for each of the first 16 modules after successful completion of the lessons in that module. Students are responsible for obtaining proctors. A minimum grade of 70 percent is required on examinations. If a student fails to pass the original examination, one (only) alternate examination may be taken. A, 90–100; B, 80–89; C, 70–79.

AMRA Credentialing: Medical Record Technology graduates who have a minimum of 30 semester hours (or 45 quarter hours) of academic credit in prescribed areas from accredited postsecondary institutions are eligible to write the national qualifying examination for medical record technicians. Passing the examination entitles an individual to use the initials A.R.T. (Accredited Record Technician) after his/her name. Students are encouraged to obtain these additional requirements prior to enrollment, or concurrently with enrollment in the Medical Record Technology program. College credit for courses may be awarded by colleges and universities based on the recommendations for credit established by the American Council on Education and listed in *The National Guide to Educational Credit for Training Programs* published by the American Council on Education/Oryx Press.

Library Services:

The Foundation of Record Education Resource Center provides library services to individuals all over the world.

Job Placement Assistance:

Resume referral service is available to members of AHIMA.

Accreditations:

Distance Education and Training Council.

VOCATIONAL COURSES

MEDICAL RECORD TECHNOLOGY
Orientation to the Health Care Field

Overview of the health care delivery system, including health care facilities and services, practitioners, organizations and consumers, content and purposes of the medical records, and a description of American Medical Record Association history and organization. (Module 1).

Medical Record Content and Format

Major topics covered in the course are purpose of health records and regulations governing content of health records in various health care settings. (Module 2).

Medical Terminology

This module consists of sixteen lessons. The first lesson introduces word elements used to form medical terms. Ten lessons present medical terms pertaining to various body systems; three lessons contain medical terms related to oncology, systemic diseases, and special types of therapies; the last lesson presents terminology relating to anesthesiology, pharmacology, and medicine in general. (Module 3).

Medical Transcription

Processing and medical reports on patient history, physicals, radiology, operations, pathology, discharge summaries, and autopsies. (Module 4).

Numbering and Filing Systems; Indexes; Registers

Covers acceptable practices in maintaining health records, including types of supplies and equipment used and the common indexes and registers and the methods used to compile them. In addition, students complete the following practical assignments: organizing a terminal digit file; preparing papers justifying a new and/or existing numbering and filing system for a hospital health information service; practicing alphabetical and phonetical filing, completing an accession register, and thorough Tumor Registry and Cancer Program coverage. (Module 5).

Legal Aspects of Health Information

An overview of the U.S. legal system; concepts of confidentiality, patient's rights, consents, and authorization for treatments; the health record as a legal document, release of health information; methods of retention and destruction of health records. (Module 6).

Introduction to Computers in Health Care

A study of the basic components of computers and their application to health care. (Module 7)

Health Statistics

Statistical concepts and procedures used in preparation of statistical reports including various methods of presenting data such as the use of histograms, pictograms, bar graphs, and pie diagrams. Basic data processing concepts. (Module 8).

Medical Staff

The organization and function of the medical staff in the hospital and other types of health care facilities. (Module 9).

Basic Pathology of Disease Process

The study of the causes, effects, and treatment of various diseases and conditions. The 24 lessons cover diseases of all body systems and other special categories of diseases. (Module 10).

Nomenclature and Classification Systems

Major topics covered in the course are IDC-9-CM coding principles and practice; diagnosis-related groups and case-mix classification; other selected nomenclature and classification systems; and ambulatory coding. (Module 11).

Federal Health Programs

Provides an overview of the Department of Health and Human Services, as well as the five major federal health program: Medicare and Medicaid, Professional Standards Review Organizations, Health Maintenance Organizations, End-Stage Renal Disease Programs, and Health Systems Agencies. (Module 12).

Quality Assurance

Major topics covered in the course are quality assurance perspective; quality assessment; utilization management; and risk management. (Module 13).

Trends in Health Care Delivery

Covers major issues affecting the health care delivery system; education, certification, and/or licensure, and the probable future of medical record practitioners and other members of the health care team; acute care, ambulatory care, preventive medicine, mental health services, long-term care, and comprehensive health programs; the patient's right to privacy and access to health records; and the effect of federal and state legislation on the health care delivery system. (Module 14).

Supervisory Principles and Practices

Covers fundamental leadership principles and techniques for good management; also provides information on job descriptions, policies and procedures, work schedules, budgets, and employee on-the-job training. (Module 15)

Planning for Health Information Services

This course covers planning techniques in designing the physical layout and work-flow patterns of a department, including the department's organization, major functions, staffing requirements, recruitment sources, and kinds of intradepartmental communications. Some attention is also given to health care practitioner's role of providing consultation services to other health care facilities. (Module 16)

Directed Clinical Practice

Major topics covered in the course are health record maintenance, processing, and services. Methods of instruction include practical experience under supervision and monitored examination. (Module 17). Directed Clinical Practice (DCP) is guided experience in applying medical record knowledge and skills to actual medical record practice. The experience is performed in one or more health care facilities (e.g., general hospital, nursing home, ambulatory care center) under the direction of an RRA or ART supervisor. A general hospital usually can provide all experiences, whereas other facilities may not. Although practice in more than one facility is not required, the more different facilities visited the broader is the experience that is gained. The student selects and makes arrangements for the Directed Clinical Practice site(s). If employed in a health care facility, it may be used for DCP; however, previous work experience is not counted toward DCP Module completion. (Module 17).

American Institute for Chartered Property Casualty Underwriters/Insurance Institute of America
720 Providence Road
P.O. Box 3016
Malvern, Pennsylvania 19355-0716
(215) 644-2100

Description:

The American Institute for Chartered Property Casualty Underwriters, Insurance Institute of America are companion educational organizations directly supported by the property-liability insurance industry to help meet its personnel development and professional education needs.

The American Institute for Chartered Property Casualty Underwriters is responsible for administering the Chartered Property Casualty Underwriter (CPCU) Program. The Insurance Institute offers programs in General Insurance, Insurance Adjusting, Management Studies, Risk Management, and Underwriting. Boards of Trustees made up of representatives of all segments of the property-liability insurance community—mutual and stock companies, agency and brokerage firms, and educators—govern the Institutes. In addition to formal classes publicly offered on campuses or privately conducted at insurance companies, independent study programs are offered that primarily benefit those individuals who, because of distance and time factors, choose to study at their own pace.

Academic Levels:
Professional

Degree/Certificate Programs:
Certificate.

Tuition:
Contact the Institutes at the above address/telephone number for enrollment procedure and current cost information.

Equipment Requirements:
The Institutes supply all students with current topical outlines which list the assigned textbooks and their publishers, the weekly readings, illustrative questions applicable to each topic, and suggested effective study methods.

Credit and Grading:
The Institute's national examinations, made up of a series of essay questions, test a candidate's ability to master a body of knowledge and to communicate it clearly to others. Program examinations are three hours in length and must be proctored.

Accreditations:
Courses have been evaluated by the Program on Noncollegiate Sponsored Instruction of The Center for Adult Learning and Educational Credentials, of the American Council on Education. College/university credit recommendations are listed in *The National Guide to Educational Credit for Training Programs* published by the American Council on Education/Oryx Press.

PROFESSIONAL COURSES

INSURANCE

Accredited Adviser in Insurance Program

Principles of Insurance Production. This course gives the student technical knowledge of insurance products required to meet needs of individuals for personal insurance. The first eight assignments are concerned with an introduction to insurance, insurance sales, exposure identification, legal liability, and personal lines insurance. The remaining portion introduces commercial insurance sales, packages, property insurance, and commercial general liability insurance. Specific topics include principles of insurance, insurance law, the sales process, personal insurance coverage, the risk management process with emphasis on exposure identification, and an introduction to commercial insurance.

Multiple-Lines Insurance Production. This course is designed to give the student technical knowledge of commercial insurance products to meet the needs of clients for commercial insurance. The entire course is concerned with major commercial lines insurance coverages. Specific topics include the major commercial insurance products, package policies, account development, and insurance sales and coverage.

Agency Operations and Sales Management. This course has the objective of providing the student with knowledge of agency operations and sales management in the insurance business. Specific topics covered include managerial operations affecting the sale of insurance, personal production planning, automation, ethics, and specific producer topics such as competition, time management, creating a sales proposal, how to sell the underwriter, and the subjects of suspecting, prospecting, and approaching the prospect.

Associate in Automation Management

Essentials of Automation. Major topics covered in the course are central processing units; input and output devices; storage; large computer systems; microcomputers; communications; management information systems; programming languages; word processors; data managers; spreadsheets; graphics; social concerns and issues.

Automation in Insurance. Major topics covered in the course are automation of insurance information; objectives of company automations; underwriting and claims; marketing; life and health insurance; company automation; agency information management; interface procedures and problems; rate making; and statistical services.

Managing Automated Activities. Major topics covered in the course are the management process; office automation; planning automation projects; project management techniques; system design; purchasing, installation, and conversion of hardware and software; managing system growth, trends, and small group study, independent study, and additional preparation based on prescribed texts and study guide. Credit is contingent on passing a nationally administered three-hour essay examination.

Associate In Insurance Accounting Finance Program

Statutory Accounting for Property and Liability Insurers. This course seeks to provide the student with an understanding of state statutory accounting requirements for property liability insurers. Through detailed study of the NAIC Annual Statement for Fire and Casualty Insurance Companies, this course develops the principles of statutory accounting, contrasts them with generally accepted accounting principles, and facilitates the actual preparation of the Annual Statement and other required reports. Specific topics covered include aspects of statutory accounting requirements, including introduction to insurance accounting and finance, annual statement reporting, assets, liabilities and policyholders surplus, estimated liabilities for losses and loss adjustment expenses, earned and unearned premiums (other liabilities, capital, and surplus), insurance company revenues and expenses, written premiums, losses and loss expenses, expenses, investment income; other income, reinsurance accounting, GAAP (other financial reporting requirements).

Insurance Information Systems. The course provides the student with an understanding of fundamental needs, tools, and controls required for development and management of insurance information systems. This course analyzes the recording, processing, and reporting of accounting information for insurance companies. It considers statistical, managerial, and financial reporting requirements and explores the application of computers in insurance. Specific topics covered include aspects of information management systems, computers and insurance, overview of insurance information systems, data flows and data storage, cycles (premium, loss, reserve, reinsurance, treasury investment, payroll, and nonpayroll expenditure), budgeting and plan-

687

ning, management reporting, statistical reporting, data integrity, system controls, auditing.

Insurance Company Finance. The course seeks to provide the student with an understanding of basic financial management principles as applied to property and liability insurers as well as understanding of the financial environment in which these companies operate. With an overall emphasis on financial institutions and the larger financial environment, this course presents principles of finance from an insurance company perspective. It includes cash management, capital structure, taxation, financial planning, investment management, and financial markets and instruments. Specific topics covered include elements of finance in insurance, including financial systems, financial management, cash management, capital structure, insurance company income, taxation, financial planning, economic environment, financial markets, money markets, capital markets, investment policy, financial analysis of insurance companies.

Associate in Claims Program

Principles of Insurance and Property Loss Adjusting. The objective of this course is to provide the student with knowledge of selected basic principles of insurance and understanding of property loss adjustment fundamentals. Content covered includes selected principles of insurance, key definitions, insurance contract analysis (including study of the various limitations on amounts of recovery under insurance contracts), fundamental procedures of property loss adjusting, investigation and reports to insurers, and estimation of building losses.

The Claims Person and the Public. This course will enable the student to understand human relation problems, communication challenges, and legal rights between insured and insurer involved in the claims handling process.

Principles of Insurance and Liability Claims Adjusting. The course provides the student with knowledge of basic liability claims adjusting procedures and the human behavioral response, associated with adjusting. Knowledge of functional areas affecting company operations. The course content includes functions of the claims department, coverage, liability, claims investigation, negotiation, settlement, rehabilitation, organization of insurers, rate making, financial structure, and insurance regulation.

Property Insurance Adjusting. This course provides the student with an understanding of concepts relevant to adjustment of property losses. The content covered includes apportionment of losses, insurable interest, estimating and adjusting losses (building, personal property, and merchandise), salvage, and business interruption.

Liability Insurance Adjusting. This course provides the student with an understanding of legal concepts relevant to adjustment of more complex liability claims. The content covered includes casualty claims practices, contract law, torts, medical aspects of damages, claims, evaluation, negotiations, settlement, automobile liability, product liability, professional liability, and workers compensation.

Associate in Management Program

The Process of Management. The objective of this course is to provide the student with knowledge of management concepts and managerial problem solving. The course covers major functions in the management process, organization, motivation, planning and control, and managerial analytical tools.

Management and Human Resources. This course seeks to provide the student with knowledge and understanding of human behavior in organizations. The content covered includes organizational behavior, work groups, individual behavior, two-person work relationship, leadership, group behavior and organizational change.

Managerial Decision Making. Content covered includes a systematic framework for evaluation of decisions, sources of inaccuracy and error in decision making, the individual human decision-making process, the organizational decision-making process, and the role of computers in that process.

Management in a Changing World. This course provides the student with knowledge of management decision making in a complex and changing world. The course content includes organization development, organizational systems strategic planning, systems approach to organizational development, team development, performance appraisals, and stress management.

Associate in Marine Management

Ocean Marine Insurance. Major topics covered in the course are: hull exposures, insurance, and underwriting; marine liability exposures, protection, and indemnity insurance; other marine liability insurance; cargo exposures, insurance, and underwriting; adjustment of total average, particular average, and general average.

Inland Marine Insurance. Major topics covered in the course are: inland marine property classes in the *Nationwide Marine Definition,* including transit and motor truck cargo, contractor's equipment, bailees and bailors, builder's risk and installation floaters, difference in conditions, instrumentalities of transportation and communication, dealers, miscellaneous commercial floaters, personal articles, and outboard motors.

Associate in Loss Control Management Program

Hazard Identification and Analysis. This course seeks to provide the student with an understanding of the loss control management process, consisting of identifying and analyzing hazards, and developing alternative loss control measures. The content covered includes in-depth analysis of principles relating to the identification and control of workplace hazards with emphasis on property, accidental, and health hazards.

Loss Control Applications and Management. The course provides the student with an understanding of loss control management processes, including selection of effective and economical controls to minimize hazards or losses resulting from hazards, implementing these controls and monitoring the results. The content covered includes application of principles taught in the course described above to designing integrated loss control programs for specific hazards associated with products, workers' compensation, crime, transport and cargo, general liability, and property losses. Special attention is given to problem solving and decision making techniques. Case studies are used.

Accident Prevention. Major topics covered in the course are: causes and costs of industrial accidents; safeguards against hazards in industrial settings; principles and practices for formulating recommendations to control hazards.

Property Protection. Major topics covered in the course are: fire safety, including hazards of materials and particular occupancies; building design and indoor storage; principles of fire safety; fire detection/signaling/suppression; loss control for pressure vessels, boilers, and machinery; property conservation; security management; transportation loss control; and catastrophic loss control.

Industrial and Environmental Hygiene. Major topics covered are: fundamental concepts of industrial hygiene and environmental protection; workplace hazards arising from biological, physical, ergonomic, and chemical stresses; hazards to the environment from various pollutants; measures for controlling industrial and environmental hygiene hazards.

Associate in Premium Auditing Program

Principles of Premium Auditing. This course provides the student with an understanding of the premium audit function in insurance and of the process that serves as a framework for premium audits. The content of this course defines the premium auditing function, establishes its relationship to other insurance company operations, and systematically develops the principles and procedures of insurance premium auditing. The specific topics covered include the nature of premium auditing, insurance company operations, underwriting, insurance law, planning premium audits, review of insured's operations, the insured's employees, evaluation of accounting systems, design of audit programs, auditing EDP accounting systems, verification and analysis, the auditor's report, communication in the premium audit.

Premium Auditing Applications. This course seeks to provide the student with an understanding of how premium auditing principles are used to determine premiums for specific lines of insurance. Specific topics covered include insurance rates and premiums, workers' compensation insurance, workers' compensation premium determination, classification of workers' compensation insurance of maritime workers, general liability: (coverages and premium bases, classification and audit procedures) commercial auto premium determination, truckers premium determination, garage policy premium determination, premium determination of commercial property insurance, other applications and premium auditing careers.

Associate in Research and Planning Program

Business Research Methods. This course seeks to provide the student with an understanding of methods of effective business research as they relate to property and liability insure. The content of this course discusses the elements of logical analysis and the use of research methods such as measurement, sampling, secondary research, surveys, qualitative techniques, and statistical analysis. This course provides an overview of the research process and the evaluation and reporting of results. The specific topics covered include the nature of business research, scientific thinking, logical arguments, the research process, research design, measurement, sampling, secondary data sources and survey instrument design, scaling and data collection, experimentation, simulation, and qualitative, research techniques, elements of analysis, statistical analysis and research reports.

Strategic Planning for Insurers. The objective of this course is to provide the student with an understanding of the methods of strategic planning as they relate to property and liability insurance. The content of this course explores the processes and factors involved in choosing policy directions for insurance firms, including strategic planning, scanning the business, regulatory, and social environments, competitive analysis, forecasting, resource assessment, market strategy, product strategy, systems development, and human resource planning. Specific topics covered include aspects of planning, including corporations and social change, introduction to strategic planning, strategic decision situations, strategic plans, scanning the environment, the business and regulatory environment, forecasting and corporate models, economic forecasting, assessing strengths and weaknesses, competitive positioning and market strategy, product planning and development, systems development, human resource planning.

Associate in Risk Management Program

Structure of Risk Management Process. This course provides the student with an understanding of exposure identification and evaluation in risk management decision making and of the financial management foundation for choosing risk management alternatives. Knowledge of business organization objectives and general management principles. The course content covered includes procedures for identifying and analyzing property, income, liability, and personal loss exposures; characteristics of risk control and risk financing techniques; guidelines for selecting appropriate risk management techniques; and, the contribution of proper risk management to an organization's profits and productivity.

Essentials of Risk Control. The course content covered includes guidelines for selecting risk management techniques, appropriate employment and administration of risk control techniques, and coordination of the total risk management effort.

Essentials of Risk Financing. The objective of this course is to provide the student with knowledge of risk functioning techniques leading to minimization of financial consequences of losses and claims. Content covered includes risk financing techniques; financing property, liability, and personal losses; accounting and tax aspects of accidental losses, risk retention, pricing, selection of insurers, and allocating costs.

Associate in Underwriting Program

Principles of Property Liability and Underwriting. This course includes underwriting function and decision-making process with special attention to coverage analysis, loss control, reinsurance for underwriters, numerical tools, pricing, information/financial analysis, decision making and monitoring, and communications. Case studies are used.

Personal Lines Underwriting. The content covered includes nature of personal lines insurance; understanding automobile, residential, farm, ranch, personal inland marine, pleasure boat, and personal liability insurance; electronic data processing and account underwriting. Case studies are used.

Commercial Liability Underwriting. This course is designed to enable the student to identify, describe, and evaluate factors to consider in underwriting commercial liability insurance. Content covered includes legal foundations of liability; underwriting the commercial enterprise (commercial auto liability, general liability, product liability, workers' compensation); medical, professional, and special liability insurance; surety bonds, and account underwriting. Case studies are used.

Commercial Property and Multiple-Lines Underwriting. Content covered includes applications of the underwriting process to commercial property and multiple-lines risks, with emphasis on analyzing frequency and severity of fire and other perils, construction, occupancy hazards and controls, indirect loss exposures, marine risks, crime insurance, and package policies.

Chartered Property Casualty Underwriter Program

The goals of the ten CPCU courses listed below are to enable students to (1) describe the broad range of risk management techniques; (2) analyze systematically all types of insurance contracts; (3) describe the coverage provided by approximately 50 property-liability insurance contracts and important types of life and health policy provisions; (4) apply this loss control and loss financing technical knowledge in managing their own loss exposures and those of others; (5) explain the organizational structure and functional roles of the various segments of the insurance industry; (6) describe how insurance fits into and is affected by the economic, legal, financial, and social environment that surrounds it; and (7) understand the nature of professionalism and act within that framework. Students who satisfactorily complete all ten national examinations and meet ethical and experience requirements are awarded the Chartered Property Casualty Underwriter professional designation.

Accounting and Finance. This course seeks to develop an understanding of the basic principles of accounting and finance, and the accounting and finance practices of insurance companies. The course covers accounting fundamentals, valuation of balance sheet accounts, income statements, analysis of financial statements, and financial management. Analyzes in detail insurance company accounting and financial management and the relationship between financial analysis and insurance company solvency.

1. Commercial Property Risk Management and Insurance and 2. Commercial Liability Risk Management and Insurance. Course 1 provides a detailed understanding of commercial property loss exposures and insurance coverages, along with some noninsurance alternatives. Course 2 provides a detailed understanding of commercial liability loss exposures, along with the insurance and noninsurance techniques available to deal with them.

Economics. Emphasis is placed on the fundamental concepts of micro and macro economics. Subjects covered include product pricing, national income accounting, monetary and fiscal policy, inflation, unemployment, and the international economy.

Insurance Company Operations. Examines insurance marketing, underwriting, reinsurance, rate making, claims adjusting, loss control activities, and other functions and activities. With respect to each, current status and development are explored, and the impact of regulation and other social/environmental factors is considered.

Insurance Issues and Professional Ethics. This course discusses a wide range of current issues relating to property and liability insurance, including price discrimination and regulation, changes in tort law, captive and government insurers, international insurance. Concludes with an examination of professionalism and ethics, including rules, guidelines, and disciplinary procedures.

The Legal Environment of Insurance. This course is based on general business law, particularly the areas of and agency law, and emphasizes the application of business law to insurance situations. It also deals with the rapidly growing areas of administrative and consumer law.

Management. Topics include the historical development of management, basic management functions, behavioral processes, environmental influences, management information systems, and the decision making process.

Personal Risk Management and Insurance. The first half of the course describes the nature of the various personal loss exposures and the effect that our changing society has on them. Also covers homeowners insurance contracts, automobile coverages, and life insurance. Second half of the course covers health insurance, retirement planning, investments, and business insurance and estate planning. Course concludes with a detailed case analysis.

Principles of Risk Management and Insurance. This course covers risk management concepts; measurement and treatment of loss exposures; insurance and society; related legal concepts such as indemnity, insurable interests, and tort law: fundamentals of insurance contracts.

The goals of the five CPCU courses listed below are to enable students to (1) understand major property and liability insurance contracts and the functions insurers perform in providing insurance protection, (2) apply principles of economics, law, finance, and accounting to property-liability insurance as an economic and social institution, and (3) develop the professional attitudes and communication skills needed to channel their knowledge and energy to best serve the insurance public. Students who satisfactorily complete all five national examinations and meet ethical and experience requirements are awarded the Chartered Property Casualty Underwriter professional designation.

Analysis of Insurance Functions. This course analyzes the formation and organization of insurers, insurance marketing, risk selection, reinsurance, rate making and reserves, loss prevention, the preparation and scope of insurers' financial statements, and claim management. Course also covers human motivation and professional ethics. Students have the option of pursuing an in-depth study of one of three specialty areas of insurance—adjusting, risk management, or underwriting.

Economics, Government, and Business. The course covers national income accounting; price determination; income distribution; monetary and fiscal policy; the theory and practice of international trade; public finance; the economics of the firm under competition, oligopoly, and monopoly. Course also treats government regulation of business, particularly of insurance, in an era of growing social responsibility. Antitrust regulation and the control of competition receive special attention, as does the protection of consumers.

Insurance and Business Law. The treatment of contract law is followed by several topics on the distinctive features of insurance policies as contracts. The principles of agency and tort law are illustrated extensively with examples and special situations from an insurance setting. This course also covers the law of bailments, commercial paper, corporations, partnerships, real property, and sales.

Management, Accounting, and Finance. Topics in management are structured around five basic management functions: planning, organizing, directing, leading, and controlling. The accounting topics cover accounting terms and concepts, and their application in managerial decisions and in the interpretation of financial statements. The topics devoted to corporate finance are designed to teach the objectives of financial management and the available methods of obtaining and using financial resources to maximize the profits of a firm.

Program in General Insurance

Property and Liability Insurance Principles. Content covered includes the concept of risk, insurance, risk management, insurance contracts, types of insurers, marketing, loss, claim, loss control, underwriting, reinsurance, pricing, and insurance regulations.

Personal Insurance. Content covered includes property insurance (including fire, indirect losses and business interruption, burglary and theft, boiler and machinery), ocean and inland marine insurance, and personal and business coverages.

Commercial Insurance. Content covered includes casualty insurance (including liability risks, general liability, workers' compensation, automobile and aviation insurance), bonding, and life, health, and social insurance.

American Institute for Paralegal Studies
1 Lethbridge Place, Suite 23
P.O. Box 835
Mahwah, New Jersey 07430   (908) 529-4448

Description:
    The American Institute for Paralegal Studies, Inc., is an educational institution offering paralegal training courses throughout the United States primarily on campuses of colleges and universities. The program is geared to the adult working student and is taught over a period of nine months. Correspondence courses are also offered in selected topics as described below.

Academic Levels:
    Vocational

Degree/Certificate Programs:
    Certificate.

Admission Requirements:
    Students may enroll at any time of the year.

Tuition:
    Contact the American Institute for Paralegal Studies for enrollment procedure and current cost information.

Accreditations:

The courses described below have been evaluated by the Program on Noncollegiate Sponsored Instruction, The Center for Adult Learning and Educational Credentials of the American Council on Education. College/university credit recommendations are listed in *The National Guide to Educational Credit for Training Programs* published by the American Council on Education/Oryx Press.

VOCATIONAL COURSES

PARALEGAL STUDIES

Estates and Trusts

This course is intended for those who have complete Course B-304, a resident course offered at various colleges and universities. The course further develops the basic understanding of estate planning and administration of decedents estates. Topics covered include: accumulation of assets, filing an inventory and payment of debts, federal estate taxes, gift taxes, state taxes, formal accounting, and distribution of assets.

Legal Research and Writing II

This course seeks to review and utilize legal materials available for research purposes. This course is intended for those who have already completed *Course B-205, Legal Analysis and Writing* offered in a resident course at various colleges and university campuses). The course is an independent analysis of and concentrated practice in the use of the tools of legal research.

Personal and Injury Litigation - Torts II

The purpose of this course is to attain a thorough understanding of personal injury litigations and pleadings that pertain to pre-trial and post-trial activities. The course is for students who have already had a course in basic civil law. It examines all aspects of personal injury law. Some of the areas reviewed are the theoretical aspects of negligence, breach, mental and emotional damage, concepts of due care, causation, malpractice, and defenses to causes of action.

Real Estate

This course is further study all forms of ownership and a review basic principles in the sale and exchange of all real estate. The course is recommended for those who have completed a course on real estate transfer and ownership. The course will substantially review all forms of ownership in and from present to future interests, processes of closing and settlement, agreement of sale, modification and adjustment of contracts, recordation, title abstraction, mortgages, and leasing. The course also covers surveys and recording.

American School
850 East 58th Street
Chicago, Illinois 60637   (312) 947-3300

Description:

One of the oldest and largest of all correspondence institutions, the American School from its beginning was chartered as a nonprofit institution; it has no owners or stockholders, but is controlled by a Board of Trustees. The American School was started in Boston in 1897 by R.T. Miller, Jr. and a group of selected graduates and faculty members from the Massachusetts Institute of Technology and Harvard University. The original purpose, quoting from the School's Charter, was "...to bring much-needed training to America's wage earners."

Since 1897, the American School has been giving a "second chance" to many who otherwise might never have been able to finish high school. During the intervening years, over 2,000,000 men and women have enrolled in all of the various courses offered. Approximately 30,000 students throughout the world are currently enrolled in its various programs. from the high school program; approximately 20,000 students throughout

Faculty:

William M. Hunding, President; Mary E. McKeown, Vice President and High School Principal. There is a faculty of 140.

Academic Levels:

High School

Degree/Certificate Programs:

Diploma. Two programs are offered: (1) High School Program, which includes a General High School Course and (2) College Preparatory Course. Each requires 16 units for graduation. American School also cooperates with over 4,500 public and parochial schools to provide make-up credits to serve the home-bound student or those who have to travel extensively, and to provide high-interest subjects for the potential drop-out.

Admission Requirements:

Completion of 8th grade; not now in high school or has permission of public school authority. Overseas students encouraged.

Tuition:

One year of high school, $379; two years, $579; three years, $779; four years, $979. Individual subjects prices from $44 to $154. Rebate available if paid in full. Monthly payment plan available. Twelve scholarships available annually to highest ranking graduates for continuing their education at the college level. Refund policy based upon amount of course completed.

Enrollment Period:

Self-paced; up to four years.

Equipment Requirements:

The tuition covers registration, instruction, all text material, consulting privilege, and postage on all material sent to the student. Tapes for languages and shorthand courses extra.

Credit and Grading:

Grading system: A, 93–100; B, 85–92; C, 76–84; D, 65–75; F, Below 65. Passing grade is 65 percent. Honor system for examinations. The Carnegie unit system is used for awarding credit.

Accreditations:

Distance Education and Training Council; North Central Association of Colleges and Schools as a Special Function

School. Recognized as a nonpublic school by the Illinois Office of Education.

HIGH SCHOOL COURSES

ACCOUNTING

Fundamentals of Accounting

Starting a bookkeeping system; posting the opening entry; debits and credits; journalizing transactions; posting; six-column sheet; income statement and balance sheet; closing the ledger; special journals and subsidiary ledgers; recording purchases on account; cash payment; sale of merchandise on account; cash receipts; the general journal; bank deposits and reconciliation of bank statements; work sheet with adjustments; financial reports; adjusting and closing entries; payroll records; depreciation; bad debts and accounts receivable; the use of the cash register; adapting bookkeeping methods to the business; sales taxes and other sales and purchases transactions; notes and interest; accrued expenses. (1 unit)

ART

Art - How to Draw

Elementary pencil technique, shading, proportions of face and figure, basic shapes, texture and shape, composition, basic lines, line drawing. (½ unit)

AUTOMOTIVE TECHNOLOGY

Automotive Repair

Introduces students to the technical design and repair of the major automotive systems. It stresses understanding various designs in use and how they function, using the proper tools and safety precautions, common problems and troubleshooting. (1 unit)

Automotive, Know Your Car

Automotive servicing; hand tools; automotive engines; fuel systems; ignition systems; electrical systems, the chassis; preventive maintenance. (½ unit)

BIOLOGY

Biology

Introduces the study of living things, both plants and animals. Beginning with a look at the chemical, cellular, and genetic basis of life, the course focuses on the major groupings of plants and animals, ending with a study of human biology. For each unit there are activities for students to do. For a nominal fee students may receive a laboratory kit and manual to perform and report experiments in conjunction with the examinations submitted. (1 unit)

BUILDING TRADES

Blueprint Reading I, Building Trades

Introduction to working drawings; elevation and plan views; symbols; conventions; terminology; scaling and dimensioning; architect's scale; dimensioning standards; structural details; sections, full size details, framing plans; survey and plot plans; property lines, topographic maps, locations, grading, and landscape plans; regional variations; foundations, chimneys, wall and roof framing; four 18'x 26' blueprints or working drawings for a house. (½ unit)

Blueprint Reading II, Building Trades

Dimensional and three-dimensional drawings, shape descriptions, drawing to scale. Study of symbols for basic materials on working drawings. Study of a brick-veneer residence, together with plans. Specifications are dealt with in detail with set of complete specifica-tions. A study is made of commercial buildings—store and apartment. Light frame construction is dealt with, also plank and beam con-struction, cement masonry, and framing with steel. Modules are described. Two complete sets of prints are included, one on a frame residence and one on a branch bank. An entire chapter is devoted to metrics as it applies to building. The appendix covers working stresses for wood structural members, stair layout and glossary. (½ unit)

BUSINESS

General Business

Meeting economic needs and wants; how business serves the econ-omy; measuring with metric; moving toward your career; consumer rights and responsibilities; practical money management; using bank-ing services; meeting needs and wants with credit; insuring against economic risks; saving and investing; moving ideas; goods and people; government in the economy; starting your career. (1 unit)

Personality Development for Work

This is a half-credit course designed to help students learn how to relate successfully to other people on the job and to aid them in deciding what type of job will best fit their personality. Assignments deal with understanding yourself, improving self-esteem, personal appearance and health, standards of conduct, developing a positive attitude, motivation, coping with conflict, discrimination, communi-cating, getting a job and advancing in your career. (½ unit)

Business Law

This course emphasizes the application of law to the individual in his roles as citizen, consumer, and employee. It covers such topics as consumers' rights, contractual agreements, rights of buyer and seller, types and forms of commercial paper (drafts, bills of exchange, etc.), employment contracts, insurance, personal and real property, wills, partnerships, corporate organization, and government regulation of business. The course aims at actively involving the student in the solution of concrete problems. (1 unit)

CARPENTRY

Carpentry I

Carpentry as a trade; accident prevention; tools; construction lumber; wood products; insulation; hardware, rough and finish; adhesives; concrete; and blueprint reading. (1 unit)

CAREER PLANNING

Planning Your Career

This course is designed to help students as they make decisions about their career now and in the years to come. It starts with helping students think about how their interests, abilities, values and personal-ity relate to choosing a job and ends with practical advice on how to get one. Along the way topics such as on-the-job training, financial aid for going to college or vocational school, where to go to find out about particular careers are covered. (1 unit)

CHEMISTRY

Chemistry (Non-lab)

This course introduces students to the basic concepts and principles of chemistry by means of understanding current chemistry-related and technological issues our society faces. Fore example, the law of conservation of matter and the balancing of chemical equations are studied in relationship to the issue of conserving chemical resources. The topics studied include supplying our water needs, conserving chemical resources, petroleum, food, nuclear chemistry, air, our bodily health, nitrogen products and chemical energy. (1 unit)

CHILDHOOD EDUCATION

Child Care

The care and guidance of children from infancy through eleven years of age. Areas of study include guidance for the parents in how to raise a child, equipment and clothing for the infant, medical and nursing care, food and dietary needs of the baby, daily care, and growth and development of the infant. The various stages of development of older children are discussed and problems and general characteristics for each age group are given. (1 unit)

CIVICS

Social Civics

Social Civics is the study of how our government is organized and run at the national, state and local levels. Beginning with a study of the origins of government, this course covers topics such as our federal constitution, our electoral system, political parties, and government policy and involvement with business, labor, education, and other areas of our national life. (1 unit)

COMPUTER LITERACY

Computer Literacy

This course is designed for students who have little or no experience in using a computer. The aim of the course is to give students a general overview of how computers operate and what they can and cannot do. While students are not required to use an actual computer in this subject, they are required to complete pencil-and-paper simulations of computer tasks and to complete a checklist for evaluating the best configuration of personal computer hardware and software to meet their current needs. (½ unit)

CONSUMER ECONOMICS

Consumer Economics

Practical knowledge of marketing, advertising, buying, selling, standards, trades, and labeling. This subject deals not only with those subjects but teaches how to use your bank, how to budget, what you should know about insurance, social security, prices, etc. (1 unit)

DRAFTING

Basic Drafting

Drafting—a universal language; drafting in industry; technical sketching; using drafting instruments; lettering on drawings; line symbols in drafting; geometric figures and constructions; laying out a drawing; auxiliary views; production drawings; dimensioning a drawing; making pictorial drawings; technical illustration; electrical and electronics drawings; pattern drawings; making graphs and charts; architectural drafting; methods for making prints; common fastening devices. (1 unit)

ECOLOGY

Ecology

This is a basic course on understanding our environment and its problems. Part of the course is the study of ecology—the study of how living things interact with each other and their physical environment. The course also examines the most pressing environmental problems of our day—our need for food and water and energy, the problems of the urban environment and over-population. (1 unit)

ELECTRICITY

Fundamentals of Electricity

The atom; static electricity; dynamic electricity; Ohm's law and its applications; electrical circuits; series, parallel, and series-parallel circuits; advanced circuit types; magnetism; electromagnetism; simple electrical generators; primarily cells; secondary cells; direct current; the direct current armature; direct current field structure; alternating current principles; inductance in AC circuits; capacitance in AC circuits; electric motors; speed characteristics of DC motors; AC motors; transformers; autotransformers; regulators; power rectifiers; DC and AC meters; electron tubes; electron tube circuits; solid state devices; solid state circuits; automatic control circuits; computer technology; electrical/electronic safety. (1 unit)

ENGLISH

American Literature

A survey of American literature from colonial times to the present. A study is made of the short story, novel, essay, biography, magazines, poetry, and drama. Examples from the best are given, together with historical accounts of the periods and sketches of leading writers. (1 unit)

World Literature

The student reads a selection of fiction, drama, poetry, and nonfiction prose from English and American literature as well as writings from other countries. Emphasis is placed on the literature and culture of different parts of the world and of different periods of time. (1 unit)

English I: Composition and Grammar

This, the first of one-half unit courses in Composition and Grammar, stresses a positive interest in language and encourages the student to enjoy words and to see what a powerful tool language is. In the sections on Grammar the student learns what patterns constitute a good English sentence by studying models of good writing. However, the most important part of the course is the training the student gets in writing - how to gather material and to put material together in a coherent way. (½ unit)

English II: Composition and Grammar

This course builds on the student's knowledge of words, grammar, and writing acquired in English I. The student develops communication skills through writing themes, business letters, and composing short speeches. The speeches may be submitted to the School on tapes if the student so desires. (½ unit)

English III: Composition and Grammar

This course stresses writing. Students learn to write using vivid language and various sentence patterns. Students expand their familiarity with the use of library resources and are introduced to the documented research paper. (½ unit)

English IV: Composition and Grammar

This course offers the student additional study of word use, sentence structure, and the writing of longer compositions. Further study of punctuation and use of the library are also included. (½ unit)

Business English

The course stresses the writing of effective business communications. Students learn how to write request, transmittal, confirmation, and follow-up letters and memos, human relations letters, letters to customers and prospective customers, and administrative and public relations communications. There are special units on employment letters and business reports. (1 unit)

Elementary English (Remedial)

Elementary English introduces the student to some of the fundamental points of grammar and sentence structure and also explains the correct usage of some common but troublesome words. The subject helps to prepare the student for work in regular first year English.

English Literature

A survey of English Literature from Anglo-Saxon times to the present. Selections include short stories, poems, plays, and non-fiction prose. The last examination covers an outstanding English novel. The course gives the student an introduction to the major English writers and their works. (1 unit)

Introduction to Literature (Remedial)

This course covers the main types of imaginative writing: short stories, poetry, and plays. The student is introduced to the basic literary forms and is given a background of myths, legends, and fables which he/she will need in reading more advanced literature. Longfellow, Kipling, London, and Shakespeare are among the authors included.

Literature I

Using a wide choice of poems, short stories, plays, and nonfiction prose, Literature I introduces the student to some excellent writing and also helps him/her to become familiar with basic literary terms and critical standards. By presenting literary devices and showing how they are used, the study guide and textbook lead the student to an understanding of the structure and meaning of selected literary works. (½ unit)

Literature II

This course expands on the question of how literary works are constructed. As in Literature I, the student studies English and American works as well as selections, both old and new, from other countries. (½ unit)

Practical English

Planned for the person who wishes a working knowledge of everyday English; word selection; sentence usage; and paragraph construction. Correctness in writing is stressed as well as development of correct spoken English. (1 unit)

Understanding English 1

This course gives the student practice in writing effectively and correctly. The student studies parts of speech, sentence structure, spelling, capitalization, punctuation, and grammar. Practice in writing effective sentences and paragraphs is emphasized in this course. (1 unit)

Understanding English 2

This course continues the work begun in Understanding English 1 with emphasis on word usage, vocabulary, paragraph development, composition, and letter writing. Effectiveness and correctness in writing are stressed. (1 unit)

FRENCH

French I

The purpose of this course is to teach students to understand, speak, read, and write simple French and to lay the foundation for a more thorough mastery of the French language. It includes the study of the present and past tenses of regular and irregular verbs, pronouns, adjectives, idiomatic expressions, and sentence structure. (1 unit)

French II

Expands on the grammatical principles and vocabulary students learned in French I. It emphasizes correct usage in context and thinking "in French" through the use of visuals and dialogue formats. (1 unit)

GARDENING

How to Garden

This subject is intended for the homeowner or apartment dweller who wants basic information on how to select, grow, and care for plants. Topics covered include the effects of water, soil, and nutrients on the plant; how to plant outdoor and house plants; choosing trees and shrubs; maintaining a lawn; choosing the right plant for growing conditions; and controlling garden pests. (1 unit)

GEOGRAPHY

World Geography

This course gives students basic knowledge about the major geographic regions of the world. It covers the location, terrain, rivers, mountains, and seaports of a region and how these things influence people's lives. How people are distributed over the earth, and how they make their living from the earth, and how they in turn affect the earth are discussed. (1 unit)

HEALTH

Physiology and Health

This course approaches health education from the perspective of wellness. This means that it aims to provide the basis for wise decisions and choices that promote our total physical, mental, and social well-being. The topics are very wide-ranging from personal health and fitness to family and social health, from a discussion of how our bodily systems function to safety and first aid. Important topics of current concern such as drug abuse and illegal drugs and sexually transmitted diseases are also covered. (1 unit)

HISTORY

United States History

Starting with Columbus' discovery of the New World and the European settlers who followed, this course traces the history of the United States down to the present. It includes sections with special emphasis on the efforts to expand democratic ideals in the areas of politics, economics, and individual rights. (1 unit)

World History

This course in world history focuses on developments in western Europe from the earliest times to the present, but it also includes a section on civilizations in Asia, Africa, and America. (1 unit)

HOME ECONOMICS

Clothing

This course is about how to make the most of your looks and how to get the most for your clothing dollar. It is also about the basic steps in making your own clothes. Students learn about the basic principles of color and design and how to apply these in choosing clothes which flatter their figure, the cloth-making process and fabric selection, planning their wardrobe, taking proper care of their clothing, how to use a pattern, how a sewing machine operates, and how to do simple handstitches. For the last exam in the course, students submit a completed sewing project from a kit provided. Access to a sewing machine is recommended, but not required. (1 unit)

Food Study

This course discusses nutrition in relation to your diet, giving specific advice on what is a good diet, how to sort out false nutritional claims from valid ones, and the needs of special groups such as children, athletes, the elderly, and pregnant women. It also provides detailed information about such subjects as cholesterol and its relation to diseases, the safety of our food supply and the government's guidelines for a high-carbohydrate, low-fat diet. The study guide contains a supplementary section on the basic rules for cooking various types of foods and a section on basic cooking equipment as well as an appendix list of cookbooks. (1 unit)

HOME LIVING

Home Planning and Decorating

This course is concerned with making decisions in selecting and furnishing a home. topics covered include the principles of design, housing and furniture styles, judging the soundness of the basic structure of a house, making a floor plan, and conserving and using energy efficiently. (1 unit)

Home Repair and Maintenance

Tools that can be kept at home; building materials; structural parts of the house; exterior walls, roof and floor coverings; doors and windows; interior walls and ceilings; cabinets; concrete; masonry; fireplace and landscape maintenance; paints and decorating; repairing and refurbishing furniture; upholstery; potable water; waste disposal and central cleaning systems; heating; home cooling; insulation and home energy saving. (1 unit)

JOURNALISM

Journalism

Becoming acquainted with reporting; writing the news lead; writing the complete story; writing the general story types; writing the simple story types; writing the complex story types; writing the special story types; editing the news. (1 unit)

MARKETING

Marketing, In Action

Distribution and sales promotion,; economic setting of distribution; responsibilities of distribution; channels of distribution; markets are people; marketing strategy; determining consumer demand; influencing consumer buying decisions; sales promotion and advertising; advertising moves forward; scope of advertising; purposes of sales promotion and advertising; headlines and illustrations; magic of color; trademarks; brand names and slogans; periodical media; mass media; television and radio; direct-mail media; sales-promotion campaigns; direct-mail marketing. (1 unit)

MATHEMATICS

Algebra I

Course covers symbols and sets; variables and open sentences; axioms, equations, and problem solving; the negative numbers; inequalities, and problem solving; working with polynomials; special products and factoring; working with fractions; graphs; sentences in two variables; the real numbers; functions and variation; quadratic equations and inequalities. (1 unit)

Algebra II and Trigonometry

Fundamental operations; factoring; fractions; linear equations in one unknown; linear systems; square root; exponents; radicals; functions and graphs; quadratics; irrational equations; imaginary and complex numbers; graphs of quadratics in two variables; systems solvable by quadratics; binomial theorem; logarithms; trigonometry; ration, proportion, and variation; progressions. (1 unit)

Applied Business Mathematics

Personal cash and bank records; everyday buying problems; special buying problems; personal finance; income from commissions; borrowing money; savings, life insurance, investments; home expenditures; travel and transportation; taxes; problems of a small business; agriculture and petroleum industries; numeration systems and probability. (1 unit)

Essential Mathematics I

Reading and writing numbers; addition; subtraction; multiplication; division; factoring; cancellation; fractions; decimals; percentage; denominate numbers. (½ unit)

Essential Mathematics II

Introduction to geometry; lines; angles; polygons; squares; rectangles; parallelograms; triangles; trapezoids; circles; sum of angles; names of triangles; right triangles; ratios and proportions; graphs; metric system; solid figures; volumes of solids. (½ unit)

Geometry

Fundamental ideas and terms; fundamental definitions, assumptions, and theorems; use of fundamental facts and ideas in proof; proof and application of theorems about triangles and parallel lines; polygons; quadrilaterals; circles; measurement of angles in circles; indirect proof and inequalities; locus; construction and design; ratio and proportion; similar polygons; numerical trigonometry and other means of indirect measurement; areas; regular polygons and circles. (1 unit)

PHOTOGRAPHY

Photography

Introduces students to both the technical and artistic aspects of taking photographs. On the technical side, students learn about such things as operating a camera, selecting film and what happens in a darkroom. On the artistic side, students learn about vocabulary for discussing photographs, elements of composition, and a brief overview of the history of photography. Students are required to submit examples of their work and therefore must have access to a camera. (½ unit)

PHYSICS

Physics (Non-lab)

Introduction to physics, motion, force, and conservation laws, vibration and waves, heat and energy, electricity and electromagnetic radiation, optics and light, atoms and matter. Students are introduced to the theoretical and practical sides of physics and learn to work problems dealing with each of the concepts taught. (1 unit)

PSYCHOLOGY

Psychology for Life Today

In this course students study factors which affect behavior such as habits, attitudes, emotions, and personality, and how they are developed. It also includes discussions of how we learn, how to plan our life's work and how to get along with others. (1 unit)

READING

Reading Skills

This subject is intended for the student who needs to review basic reading skills. Topics include word analysis and meaning; word origins, prefixes and suffixes; context; understanding book parts; main ideas; author's purpose; looking things up; functional reading.

RETAILING

Retail Merchandising

The course is a comprehensive survey of retailing and the distribution of goods to consumers through retail stores. All phases of the field are thoroughly explored—financing, buying, pricing, display, stock control, data processing, store organization, advertising, and government regulation. The student receives an extensive background in the marketing process itself as well as in the role of retailing in that process. (1 unit)

SALESMANSHIP

Fundamentals of Selling

The selling job; patterns of distribution; the salesperson's knowledge and skills; determining customer demands; product knowledge; the company and its policies; physical and mental characteristics; language and arithmetic skills; steps in the sale; plus selling; aids to personal selling; sales promotion; mass selling through written communication; telephone, radio, television, and other group presentations; legal relations and ethics; regulation of selling practices; ethics in selling; progress in selling; sales management. (1 unit)

SCIENCE

Earth Science

This subject explores the planet we live on through use of geology, meteorology, and oceanography; investigates the movements of land, air, and water; how mountains are formed; what happens below the surface of the earth; and the earth's relationship to the sun, moon and space. (1 unit)

General Science

This is a basic introduction to the sciences covering the physical sciences (physics, chemistry), the living world (biology, ecology), the planet earth (geology, oceanography, meteorology) and space and beyond (astronomy and various aspects of the study of the universe). Science activities, biographies of scientists and reading lists are included in each chapter. (1 unit)

Oceanography

In this course, the student is introduced to oceanography, a science which is involved with many other sciences. The course centers around the geology, biology, physics, and chemistry of the ocean. An assignment on the history of oceanography shows that the early explorers were in fact the first oceanographers. The scientific instruments and techniques of today's oceanographers are discussed in another assignment. Included in the section on the future and economic importance of the ocean's resources is a discussion of the hazards of pollution and some possible solution to pollution problems. (1 unit)

SECRETARIAL SCIENCE

Medical Secretary

Personality; appointments; public relations; patients' histories; medical office bookkeeping; keeping financial records; insurance in medical practice; completing forms accurately; correspondence; the art of filing; clinical office procedures; medical practice; working with a specialist; office management; professional miscellany; handy knowledge; the medical secretary in a hospital; preparation of manuscripts; the doctor and the law; rights, duties, and pitfalls; the dental secretary; medical terminology. (1 unit)

Secretarial Practice

This course focuses on the needs of the modern office worker. It stresses communication and interpersonal skills, including proper handling of the telephone; the processing of information, and the managing of records in modern business organizations; common business documents and procedures; and efficient time and task management. (1 unit)

Shorthand (Forkner)

A practical system of shorthand which combines the easily written longhand letters of the alphabet and selected simplified symbols. This system is designed for speeds up to 120 words a minute; it is relatively simple, can be learned quite readily, and is ideal for personal use. This system of shorthand is available as a high school elective. (1 unit)

Shorthand (Gregg)

This course provides a student with a foundation in Gregg Shorthand. Practice in writing shorthand as well as transcribing it is acquired. Through the use of records the student learns to take dictation. (1 unit)

Typewriting

Learning the keyboard; lower case characters; speed and control; figures, symbols, upper case characters; typing for personal use; business letters; typing for control; reconstruction of basic skills; personal typing problems; tabulation; manuscript, special office problems; building skills in business letter production; tabulation and statistical copy; sustained production; supplementary typing problems in the office. (1 unit)

SOCIOLOGY

Sociology

This course investigates the process of socialization—how individuals learn to become part of the groups around them such as the family, community and nation. It also discusses various types of social organization and institutions, how cultural and social change comes about, and some of the major studies of group behavior done by sociologists. (1 unit)

SPANISH

Spanish I

This course is designed to teach the student the basics of Spanish. It emphasizes grammar and vocabulary, including the present, simple past, and imperfect verb tenses, pronouns, adjectives, and word order. Students are also introduced to various idiomatic forms and expressions. (1 unit)

Spanish II

This course begins with a short review of Spanish I and then continues with the study of grammar and composition begun in the first year of the course. In this second year of study, however, greater stress is placed on the student's reading and writing the language for increased proficiency. (1 unit)

SPEECH

How to Talk More Effectively

The course includes many facets of public speaking: speaking effectively; widening one's interest; developing poise, personality, and voice; speaking correctly; organization and preparation; presiding at meetings; persuasion; humor; the ABCs of speaking; use of microphones; selling; town meeting techniques; interviews; conference and sales meetings; informative talks; telephoning; and practicing. (½ unit)

Army Institute for Professional Development
United States Army Training Support Center
Student Services Division
Fort Eustis, Virginia 23604-5168

(804) 878-4774

Description:

The Army Institute for Professional Development (IPD) was founded in 1976. The Army Correspondence Course Program (ACCP) is the formal, nonresident extension of the United States Army Training and Doctrine Command service schools' curricula which are centrally administered by the IPD. Enrollment is restricted to Active and Reserve component military personnel, federal civil service personnel, ROTC cadets, and allied military students. An average annual enrollment exceeds 300,000 students, 93 percent of whom are active duty and reserve component soldiers. Eligible applicants should contact their base Education Officer for further information or contact the Student Services Division at the above address.

Faculty:
Ned C. Motter, Director.

Accreditations:
Distance Education and Training Council. Selected courses are recommended for postsecondary credit by the American Council on Education's Office on Educational Credit and Credentials. SEE *The Guide to the Evaluation of Educational Experiences in the Armed Forces*, published by the American Council on Education/Oryx Press.

Berean College
1445 Boonville Avenue
Springfield, Missouri 65804   (417) 862-2781

Description:
Founded as Berean School of the Bible in 1948, the institution serves the distance education needs of the Assemblies of God. The name was changed to Berean College and the college degree program was added in 1985. Both degree and nondegree studies are available. Berean College provides (1) ministerial credential preparation required by the districts of the Assemblies of God, (2) the opportunity for pastors to implement intensive Bible study in their local churches, (3) the opportunity for systematic study of the Bible for individuals who could not attend a residential college, and (5) the nontraditional educational requirements of individual students of the residential colleges. Courses have been developed in Spanish to serve the Hispanic population of the Assemblies of God in the United States. The parent institution is the General Council of the Assemblies of God.

Currently more than 500 students are taking degree courses in addition to over 20,000 non-degree course enrollments each year.

Faculty:
Dr. Zenas J. Bicket; President; Dr. Joseph Nicholson, Education Director; Russell Wisehart, Dean of Instruction; Steve Kersting, Registrar; Dilla Dawson, Director of Promotions and Production. There is a faculty of six plus five subject specialists.

Academic Levels:
College
Noncredit

Degree/Certificate Programs:
Certificate; Diploma.

Admission Requirements:
High school diploma or equivalency for degree level courses plus over the age of 21; special permission must be granted by the Board of Administration if the student is under 20 years of age; open enrollment for non-college level courses.

Tuition:
College level courses are $69 per credit hour; graduate level $129 per credit; $20 per course for institute level. A discount is given to ministerial candidates in the ministerial training program. Refund policy: prior to the completion of one unit of study and before the student submits materials for grading, a 90 percent refund will be given (the college will be entitled to the enrollment fee plus 10 percent of the tuition); after the student has submitted the first unit examination, or has completed up to 25 percent of the course, whichever comes first, a 75 percent refund will be given (the college will be entitled to the enrollment fee plus 25 percent of the tuition); after completion of 25 percent but prior to the completion of 50 percent of the course, the enrollment fee plus 50 percent of the tuition will be refunded by the college; if the student completes more than 50 percent of the course, the college is entitled to retain the enrollment fee plus full tuition.

Enrollment Period:
Students may enroll at any time. The maximum time to complete a course is one year.

Equipment Requirements:
For noncredit courses, all texts, study guides, etc. are ordered with the course and are included in the total price for the course. College-level study materials are priced separately from the tuition and must be purchased by the student.

Credit and Grading:
Examinations must be proctored for students in the degree program; open book examinations for nondegree courses; closed-book-unproctored for ministerial students. Letter grades are given. Minimum passing grade for college-level courses is D; for nondegree courses, C. Credits for transfer are accepted from schools accredited by regional accrediting agencies, American Association of Bible Colleges, and the Distance Education and Training Council. Credit is awarded in semester hour units.

Library Services:
Students are encouraged to use local libraries.

Job Placement Assistance:
Limited counseling on ministerial assignments with the Assemblies of God is available.

Accreditations:
Distance Education and Training Council.

Berean College

COLLEGE COURSES

ANTHROPOLOGY

Cultural Anthropology

A survey of the cultural and social aspects of man. The application of Biblical concepts to the study of anthropology is given major attention. (3 semester hours)

BIBLE

Old Testament Survey

A Study of the work of God in relation to man, as portrayed in the Old Testament. The course includes all the events from man's creation to the New Testament account of his redemption. Special emphasis is placed on the historical and prophetic contexts of the events and on the development of the nation of Israel. Significant individuals in Old Testament history are given particular attention. (3 semester hours)

New Testament Survey

A panoramic view of New Testament messages, doctrines, personalities, and problems of interpretation. This course encourages the student to mature spiritually as the scriptural principles discussed are put into practice in relationships with God, with others, and with oneself. (3 semester hours)

Pentateuch

A study of the origin of the earth and mankind as presented in the first five books of the Old Testament. The history of the nation of Israel is traced from its beginnings until the time of the entrance into the Promised Land. The course includes in-depth study of creation theories, the Flood, and the concept of holiness as presented in Leviticus. (3 semester hours)

Historical Books

An interpretive survey of the historical books of the Old Testament, from Joshua through Esther. The material covers approximately 1,000 years from the entrance of Israel into the Promised Land until its return after the Exile. The background, structure, and content of each book are examined. (3 semester hours)

Hebrew I

A study of the semitic language of the ancient Hebrews. Fundamentals of Hebrew are stressed, with attention given to the use of these skills in translation. The study of Hebrew will greatly increase one's ability to minister God's Word from the Old Testament. Audiocassettes are a part of this course. (3 semester hours)

Greek I

An introduction to the fundamentals and grammar of the Greek New Testament. The course includes a study of certain verb, noun, pronoun, and adjective forms. The student will also learn to apply the knowledge to the translation of selected portions of Scripture. Eight cassette tapes are a part of the course. (3 semester hours)

Greek II

A continuation of the study of basic elements in the grammar of the Greek New Testament. Certain verb, noun, pronoun, and adjective forms are studied in greater detail than in Greek I. The elements of syntax and grammar that are essential to translation and exegesis are emphasized. Audiocassette tapes accompany the course. (3 semester hours)

Genesis

A tracing of the thread of God's plan of redemption from its beginning promise in Eden to the formation of God's chosen people through whom the plan would be realized. (2 semester hours)

Major Prophets

A study of the lives of Isaiah, Jeremiah, and Ezekiel and of the divine message God asked each to proclaim. The course stresses the importance and meaning of each message and burden for the Church today. (3 semester hours)

Minor Prophets

A study of the minor prophets in the light of their times and ours, the doctrines they preached, and the meanings and fulfillment of their prophecies. This course covers 12 books of the Old Testament which are probably the most neglected in preaching, teaching, and devotional study. (2 semester hours)

Gospel of John

An examination of the life, character, and ministry of Jesus Christ. The course includes not only the historical context but also the divine perspective presented by John the evangelist. (2 semester hours)

Acts

A study of the continuing ministry of the risen Christ by the Holy Spirit through the Church, as described in the Book of Acts. The course deals with the birth of the Church, the spread of the gospel, and the victories provided by Christ through the Spirit. (2 semester hours)

Romans

A practical study of Paul's letters to the Romans. The course deals with the background of the book and its relation to the rest of the Pauline writings. Special attention is given to the terms "flesh," "Spirit," and "law," in the epistle. (2 semester hours)

Galatians and Romans

An interpretive study of Paul's letters to the Galatians and Romans, with investigation of background material, key theological issues, and matters pertaining to the life, character, and ministry of Paul. Application of the teachings of these books to contemporary problems is emphasized. (3 semester hours)

First Corinthians

An exegetical-expository approach to First Corinthians. The course places emphasis on how Paul handled the difficult problems he confronted in the church at Corinth. Special in-depth study of stewardship is accomplished through supplemental reading. (3 semester hours)

Hebrews

An analytical and topical approach to the rich Christological truths taught in the epistle to the Hebrews. The course also provides insight into Old Testament forms of worship and their prophetic aspects. Stress is placed on Christ as the fulfillment of the Old Covenant. (2 semester hours)

Apologetics

An examination of two basic themes: faith and knowing. The course provides an explanation of the relationship between the two themes and answers several basic questions. (3 semester hours)

Hermeneutics

The science and art of Biblical interpretation, or a study of what God has said to man in sacred Scripture. The course includes the principles for discovering the meaning of a document (science) and the qualifications and preparation of the interpreter (art). (3 semester hours)

COUNSELING

Principles of Counseling

An application of general counseling principles to pastoral counseling.

The course emphasizes characteristics of people counseled, techniques of counseling, and the various forms of counseling. A strong Biblical emphasis underlies the study. (2 semester hours)

EDUCATION

Principles of Teaching

A study of the basic principles of effective teaching based on the Christian philosophy of education. The course includes characteristics and needs of various age-level students, ways in which Christian teachers can meet these needs, the fundamental responsibilities of the teacher, modern educational methods, and steps in preparing, presenting, and evaluating a lesson. (3 semester hours)

ENGLISH

Basic English

A basic study of the fundamentals of English grammar. The study of nouns, adjectives, phrases, and clauses is designed to increase the student's capacity to understand written English. (3 semester hours)

English Composition

An analytical and synthetic study of the skills necessary to write in standard English at the college level. Traditional writing forms are examined to provide the student with logical methods of development and illustration. The goal of the course is more effective written communication. (3 semester hours)

Principles of Journalism

A practical study of writing as an extension of Christian ministry. The course gives theory and applied experiences in news writing, feature writing, and the composition of headlines. Guidance is also provided for the publication of church bulletins or newspapers. (2 semester hours)

INTERPERSONAL RELATIONS

Interpersonal Relations—Human Relations

A study of one's relationships with God, oneself, and others, based on the Biblical concept of *agape* love. The agape concept is examined thoroughly and applied to every kind of human relationship. (3 semester hours)

MUSIC

Introduction to Church Music

A study of the use of music in church services, in evangelism, and in cross-cultural ministry around the world. The course emphasizes the important role music can play as an adjunct to Christian education, and as an effective tool in the spread of the gospel. (2 semester hours)

PHILOSOPHY

Logic

A study of the rules of straight thinking. The course makes such rules explicit by identifying and analyzing arguments of various kinds. Many of the applications concern contemporary life and ministry. (3 semester hours)

PSYCHOLOGY

Introduction to Psychology

An interpretive study of psychology, including intrinsic values, motivational response techniques, peer relationships, and other psychological concepts as they apply to Christian life and service. The course deals with such topics as coping with personal problems and the effect of personality problems on human relationships. Supplementary taped materials are available for the course. (3 semester hours)

Educational Psychology

An application of psychological principles to the design and guidance of educational experiences. The course provides the tools needed to make the teaching-learning process a more effective and rewarding part of Christian ministry. Topics covered include student and environmental factors which affect the learning process, educational design principles, and the role of the Holy Spirit in Christian educational theory. (3 semester hours)

RELIGIOUS STUDIES

World Religions

A survey of eight major non-Biblical religions of the world: Islam, Zoroastrianism, Hinduism, Buddhism, Sikhism, Confucianism, and Shintoism, with Jainism also receiving minor consideration. The course concludes with a survey of Judaism and Christianity and a comparison with all world religions. (3 semester hours)

SCIENCE

General Physical Science

A survey of the fundamentals of science with particular emphasis on those areas of physical science which affect day-to-day life. (3 semester hours)

SOCIOLOGY

Introduction to Sociology

A general survey of the nature and scope of sociology. The central focus of the course is mutual dependency as a basic human characteristic—man as a social being. (3 semester hours)

SPEECH

Public Speaking

The values and fundamentals of effective speech in Christian ministry. The course deals with speech and the speaker, resources available to the speaker, the speaker and the audience, and intercultural aspects of speech. (2 semester hours)

THEOLOGY/HISTORY

The Holy Spirit

A Biblical examination of the person, work, gifts, and ministry of the Holy Spirit. (3 semester hours)

Christology

A comprehensive study of what the Scriptures say about Jesus Christ. The course introduces the student to Old Testament typology and to the prophecies concerning Christ's present and future work. Controversial historical and contemporary views of Jesus are examined in relation to the Bible portrayal. (2 semester hours)

Soteriology

A study of the doctrine of salvation—the work of Christ in bringing lost man into fellowship with God. The course includes the doctrines of repentance, faith conversion, regeneration, justification, adoption, sanctification, and prayer in the life of a Christian. Included in the study are an analysis of Biblical passages relating to salvation and an evaluation of historical and contemporary views of salvation. (2 semester hours)

Theology and Angelology

A systematic study of the Biblical doctrines of God and angels. Two main themes are covered: personal divine involvement and personal angelic involvement in human activity. (2 semester hours)

Doctrines of Man and Sin

A study of the teachings of Scripture concerning man and sin. The course corrects some of the false ideas about the origin of man and his nature. Personal application of truth to the lives of students and persons to whom they will minister is a specific focus of the study. (2 semester hours)

Eschatology

A study of Biblical teaching concerning last things and the final outcome of the present order. Topics treated include the second coming of Christ, the tribulation, and the nature of predictive prophecy. A number of current eschatological systems are analyzed. (2 semester hours)

Old Testament Biblical Theology

A developmental study of the major Old Testament doctrines. The course includes what the Old Testament teaches about God, creation, man, sin, the Messiah, revelation, inspiration, angels, Satan, the various testaments and covenants, judgment, and life after death. This advanced course would be preceded by introductory courses in systematic theology and the Old Testament. (3 semester hours)

Church History

A study of the trends of social, cultural, and political developments as they relate to present-day civilization and the role of the Church. The course stresses the fact that Jesus Christ is the focal point of God's intervention in human affairs. Supplementary audio tapes are available to accompany the study. (2 semester hours)

THEOLOGY/MINISTRIES

Principles of Preaching

An introduction to the spiritual and practical techniques of sermon preparation and delivery. These techniques are applied by directed experience to sermon preparation and delivery in actual ministry. Attention is given to sermon types and to the organization, content, logical structure, functional elements, and spiritual principles of a sermon. (3 semester hours)

Teaching in the Church

A survey of the skills needed to teach creatively. The course reviews various concepts of revelation and draws teaching principles from the ways in which God speaks to people through His Word. (3 semester hours)

Strategy for Church Growth

A study of the principles that underlie the growth of the church. The course will assist the student in identifying reasons for growth or lack of growth in a local church. Procedures for making a diagnostic study of a local church are included. (3 semester hours)

Evangelism Today

A study of the Biblical principles and modern techniques of effective evangelism, with an emphasis on how God is working through His people today. Methods of personal and mass evangelism point out ways all Christians in a local church can work together to evangelize their areas of life and service. (3 semester hours)

Pastor Church, and Law

A comprehensive study of American church law—for ministers, church administration, and ministerial students. The course addresses contemporary legal questions with accurate, up-to-date answers. (2 semester hours)

Introduction to Missions - Missions Orientation

A review of the concepts and principles of missions. The course introduces lay persons to the work of the professional missionary so the two can work side by side in the work of spiritual outreach. (2 semester hours)

Pastoral Theology

A comprehensive treatment of the practical aspects of pastoral ministry. Subjects covered include the pastor as a divinely called servant, as as Spirit-filled leader, a preacher, a teacher, a counselor, an administrator, and as a spouse and parent. The contributions of 20 experienced ministers form the foundation for this study. (3 semester hours)

Leadership Principles for Christian Education

A study of the theoretical principles of leadership and administrative roles and practical applications of those principles in the local church situation. Both secular and Christian ideas of leadership are examined and related to Christian education. (3 semester hours)

NONCREDIT COURSES

BIBLE

Bible Survey

An examination of the books of the Old and New Testaments in the context of the history, geography, and culture of Bible times. The course includes the main events, characters, and teachings of each book and shows how they relate to God's plan of salvation. (Noncredit)

Old Testament Studies

A comprehensive analysis of Hebrew canon. The course acquaints the student with key facts in each book of the Old Testament. The student will gain spiritual enrichment and a foundation for understanding Old Testament history, poetry, and prophecy. (Noncredit)

Old Testament Survey

A Study of the work of God in relation to man, as portrayed in the Old Testament. The course includes all the events from man's creation to the New Testament account of his redemption. Special emphasis is placed on the historical and prophetic contexts of the events and on the development of the nation of Israel. Significant individuals in Old Testament history are given particular attention. (Noncredit)

New Testament Survey

A panoramic view of New Testament messages, doctrines, personalities, and problems of interpretation. This course encourages the student to mature spiritually as the scriptural principles discussed are put into practice in relationships with God, with others, and with oneself. (Noncredit)

Life of Christ

A chronological study of the life of Christ from the parallel accounts of the four Gospels. The life and ministry of Jesus are divided into generally accepted periods. The course is informative, inspirational, and practical in its application. (Noncredit)

Pauline Epistles

A detailed study of Paul's epistles written either to churches or to individuals. The treatment of each epistle includes background information, occasion, place and date of writing, and an exposition of the contents of the letter. A study of the Pauline epistles is basic to understanding God's plan for the Church and for individual Christian living. (Noncredit)

Hebrews and General Epistles

An exposition of the Book of Hebrews, with an emphasis on the contrasts between the Old and New Covenants. The general epistles of James, Peter, John, and Jude are also studied. As an introduction to the writers and their messages, the course will enrich the life of the student who masters the practical truths of these books. (Noncredit)

First Corinthians

An exegetical-expository approach to First Corinthians. The course places emphasis on how Paul handled the difficult problems he confronted in the church at Corinth. Special in-depth study of stewardship is accomplished through supplemental reading. (Noncredit)

Studies in Revelation

An expository study of the Book of Revelation. The course emphasizes the unifying message of the book: the final triumph of Christ and the Church. Traditional interpretations of the symbolism and prophetic truths of Revelation are presented. (Noncredit)

Bible History and Geography

A survey of Bible lands geography and history. The survey of history moves from the journeys of Abraham and Israel through the rise and fall of nations and empires to the spread of the gospel as recorded in the New Testament. A concluding section brings the student a contemporary update on archaeology. (Noncredit)

Survey of Bible Customs

An introduction to Bible backgrounds and everyday life in Bible times. The course emphasizes the cultural (oriental) and time settings of the Bible to aid in the interpretation of passages which are difficult for 20th-century readers. (Noncredit)

Acts

A study of the continuing ministry of the risen Christ by the Holy Spirit through the Church, as described in the Book of Acts. (Noncredit)

Romans

A practical study of Paul's letters to the Romans. The course deals with the background of the book and its relation to the rest of the Pauline writings. (Noncredit)

CHRISTIAN EDUCATION

Knowing Your Bible

A study of the background of the Bible directed toward making the teaching of the Bible in the local church more effective. Principles of study and interpretation that facilitate the study of the Bible are given special attention. (Noncredit)

Understanding Our Doctrine

An overview of the important doctrines of the Bible. The terms and concepts relating to important scriptural teachings are studied. (Noncredit)

Mastering the Methods

An analysis of the elements which constitute an effective teaching/learning experience. The course explores the basic philosophy of Christian education, the practices of teaching, and the steps involved in lesson preparation, presentation, and evaluation. (Noncredit)

Your Sunday School at Work

A survey of the purposes, organization, and curriculum of a Sunday school. The course emphasizes the importance of a strong Sunday school program in church growth and individual spiritual maturation. (Noncredit)

Age Level Handbooks

A study of the specialized needs and training of the various age levels of the Sunday school. Each handbook is written by a specialist from the national Sunday School Department and offers insight into understanding the specific age level. (Noncredit)

COUNSELING

Principles of Counseling

A study of the basic concepts and techniques of counseling, including the effective use of Scripture in counseling. Attention is given to special areas of counseling: young people, the emotionally and mentally ill, and those with marriage problems. (Noncredit)

Child Guidance

A study of the basic concepts of parent-child relationships and the stages of child development. The course discusses Christian guidelines for effective childrearing by parents and all who work with children. (Noncredit)

EDUCATION

Home and School Discipline

A study of child discipline for parents, teachers, and all persons concerned with the Christian training of children. Illustration and actual case studies apply the course content to home and school situations. (Noncredit)

JOURNALISM

Principles for Christian Writers

A study of the fundamentals of writing for Christian publications. This course covers all aspects of Christian writing, including types of articles, research, style, necessary records and filing, and submitting material for publication. The student is aided in analyzing the writings of others and is required to write a general variety of article types. (Noncredit)

MUSIC

The Director of Church Music

A survey of the various types of music programs useful in the church. The course emphasizes the importance of evangelical, God-honoring, Spirit-directed music. Although the course is intended primarily for the choir director or church music director, even those with little or no formal musical training will benefit from the study. (Noncredit)

The Director of Church Instrumental Music

A study of the use of instrumental music in the church. The course reviews Biblical patterns established by Old Testament instrumentalists and gives suggestions on coping with practical problems faced by church musicians today. Although the course does include some material that presumes the student has at least minimal skills in music fundamentals, the study is directed primarily to persons without extensive training in music who are interested in developing instrumental programs in the church. (Noncredit)

THEOLOGY/HISTORY

The Holy Spirit

A Biblical examination of the person, work, gifts, and ministry of the Holy Spirit. (Noncredit)

History of the Church

A survey of the great movements, revivals, and conflicts that have marked the Church from its earliest days to the 20th-century Pentecostal revival. The course emphasizes the fact that no one can properly appreciate or understand the great variety in the Christian church today without a knowledge of the vast sweep of church history preceding it. (Noncredit)

History of the Assemblies of God

A study of the origin and development of the Assemblies of God. The study examines the forces which brought the Fellowship of ministers and churches together and how the spirit and effectiveness of the Pentecostal revival must be retained. (Noncredit)

How to Study the Bible

An introduction to the various methods and tools for meaningful Bible study. The practical application of the methods and tools is illustrated. (Noncredit)

THEOLOGY/MINISTRIES

Principles for Christian Teaching

A practical study of the principles essential to effective Christian teaching. The course examines the teaching situation, teaching for meaningful responses, and the significance of the teacher to the total experience of Christian learning. (Noncredit)

Principles of Christian Education

A survey study of the theory and practice of church administration. The principles recommended are scriptural and can be applied to both large and small churches. The practical insights can be used in planning in every department of the church. (Noncredit)

Church Education Administration

A study of the Biblical objectives of Christian education and the responsibilities of the church, pastor, and church education staff. (Noncredit)

Youth Ministry

A study of principles on which youth ministry should be based. This course, designed for youth ministers and others who work with youth, emphasizes that ministry is something done with youth rather than to or for youth. (Noncredit)

Pastoral Theology I

A study of the pastor's duties and opportunities in counseling and in conducting weddings, baptismal services, funerals, and dedication ceremonies. The course offers a wide choice of suggested materials so that proper selections can be made for specific occasions. (Noncredit)

Homiletics

An examination of the selection and interpretation of sermon texts, gathering and arranging materials, and the basic elements of sermon construction. Special attention is given to expository sermons. The course is designed for the beginning preacher or the person who occasionally delivers a gospel message. (Noncredit)

Pastor, Church, and Law

A comprehensive study of American church law—for ministers, church administration, and ministerial students. The course addresses contemporary legal questions with accurate, up-to-date answers. (Noncredit)

Parliamentary Law

An examination of the basic principles of parliamentary procedure. (Noncredit)

Missionary Principles

A study of the apostle Paul's methods for establishing self-supporting, self-governing, and self-propagating national churches. (Noncredit)

History of Missions

A panoramic view of missions from Pentecost to the present. The course is built on the philosophy that every committed Christian should have a working knowledge of the Christian world mission. (Noncredit)

Pastoral Theology II

A comprehensive treatment of the practical aspects of pastoral ministry. Subjects covered include the pastor as a divinely called servant, as as Spirit-filled leader, a preacher, a teacher, a counselor, an administrator, and as a spouse and parent. The contributions of 20 experienced ministers form the foundation for this study. (Noncredit)

Leadership Principles for Christian Education

A study of the theoretical principles of leadership and administrative roles and practical applications of those principles in the local church situation. Both secular and Christian ideas of leadership are examined and related to Christian education. (Noncredit)

Assemblies of God Polity

An examination of the constitution and bylaws of The General Council and district councils of the Assemblies of God. Emphasis is placed on relationships between ministers, local churches, district councils, and The General Council. A portion of the course is devoted to the "Statement of Fundamental Truths," the 16 official doctrinal statements of the Assemblies of God. (Noncredit)

Doctrines of the Bible

A systematic presentation of the major teachings of the Bible. The course outlines the principal doctrines of Scripture and provides a basic introduction for subsequent in-depth studies of specific doctrines. (Noncredit)

Pentecostal Truth

A systematic historical study of the Holy Spirit. The various aspects of the person, work, and ministry of the Holy Spirit are studied in the light of the Scriptures and in doctrinal developments throughout the history of the Church. (Noncredit)

Dispensational Studies

A survey of God's plan for the ages. The millennial age is presented as the "confluence" of all previous covenants and dispensations. The unifying thread of the study is God's great plan and purpose of redemption throughout all of His dealings with man. (Noncredit)

Heaven

A systematic study of what the Bible teaches about the kingdom of heaven, man's inheritance in heaven, the new heavens, and the new Jerusalem. The course discusses the destiny of the believer after death. (Noncredit)

Prophetic Light

A scriptural foundation for the main themes of prophecy. The course surveys the great prophetic events which the prophets saw by revelation under the anointing and inspiration of the Holy Spirit. Definitions of prophetic words and terms as well as principles for right interpretation are included. (Noncredit)

Gifts of the Spirit

A scriptural and practical study of the nature and value of the gifts of the Holy Spirit. The course deals with questions and difficulties that sometimes arise and provides practical instruction concerning the operation of the gifts. (Noncredit)

The Pentecostal Experience—Doctrine of Glossolalia

A Biblically based study of the phenomenon and meaning of glossolalia. Answers are given to the various objections to and misunderstandings of the Pentecostal experience. (Noncredit)

The Believer's Security

A detailed study of the Bible teachings concerning the security of the believer. The course examines the doctrine of salvation, the importance of works of faith by the believer, and the possibility of one who has believed finally falling away. (Noncredit)

Catholic Home Study Institute
781 Catoctin Ridge
Paeonian Springs, Virginia 2222129
(800) 258-CHSI

Description:
The Catholic Home Study Institute offers adults the opportunity for postsecondary education in the Catholic Faith by correspondence. The Catholic Church first provided home study lessons in the 1920s as a follow-up to missionary visits by priests traveling through the South. Later, these lessons were taken over by the Knights of Columbus and became their famous introductory course on the Catholic Faith, a home study course that has been responsible for thousands of conversions. The Catholic Home Study Institute was established by the Catholic Church in 1983 under the leadership of Bishop Thomas Welsh; the Church granted it Pontifical approval.

Faculty:
Bishop Thomas J. Welsh; Marianne E. Mount, Executive Director.

Academic Levels:
College
Noncredit

Degree/Certificate Programs:
Certificate. Any course can be taken for noncredit. Courses have been evaluated for college/university credit by the Program on Noncollegiate Sponsored Instruction of the American Council on Education. The recommendations for credit are listed in *The National Guide to Educational Credit for Training Programs* published by the American Council on Education/Oryx Press. The Institute also offers adults the opportunity to earn the Pontifical Diploma for successfully completing 15 correspondence courses based on a designated curriculum. Other requirements will include a comprehensive examination and a letter of recommendation by an appropriate ecclesiastical authority such as one's pastor or religious superior. For further information on the Pontifical Diploma, please write to the Institute.

Admission Requirements:
High school graduation or equivalent.

Tuition:
Tuition subject to change. Contact the Institute for current rates. Payment plan of 50 percent down and two monthly installments.

Enrollment Period:
The maximum time to complete a course is one year. After one year, three-month extensions up to one additional year may be granted upon payment of a small fee for each extension.

Equipment Requirements:
All textbooks and materials are supplied by the school.

Credit and Grading:
Transfer credits are accepted only from another Pontifical Institute for the purpose of earning a Pontifical Diploma. Grading system: A, 90–100; B plus, 87–89; B, 80–86; C plus, 77–79; C, 70–76; D, 65–69. Minimum passing grade is 65. Examinations for college credit must be proctored; noncredit courses use closed book examinations and honor system. Credit is awarded in semester hour units.

Library Services:
Additional help is available by mail or telephone (at student's expense) from staff theologians.

Accreditations:
Distance Education and Training Council.

COLLEGE COURSES

RELIGIOUS EDUCATION
Catechesis of the High School Student
Identifies the characteristics of youth, the "whole person" approach to catechetics; defines "real assent" and lists principle teaching tools, emphasizes lesson planning, the place of imagination, memory, intellect and will along with effective and proven teaching techniques. Explains appropriate and established means of motivation. (3 semester hours)

RELIGIOUS STUDIES
Christian Spirituality in the Catholic Tradition
Introduction to the origin and development of Christian asceticism, identifying the early and subsequent spiritual schools and their leaders. Following chapters trace the emergence of western monasticism with emphasis on Augustine and Benedict. Continues the development of spirituality through the subsequent centuries up until modern times. (3 semester hours)

God, Man and the Universe
Introduction to doctrinal theology. Examines the fundamental teachings of the Catholic Church as contained in the First Article of the Apostles Creed—God the Creator, original sin and the fall of man. Thirteen lessons include an introduction to revelation, the relationship between Scripture and Tradition, the Trinity, Providence, the angels, satan, and evolution. (3 semester hours)

Introduction to Sacred Scripture
Introduces basic scriptural concepts: inspiration, inerrancy, and canonicity. Traces the origin of the Bible, the transmission of the text; explains the different versions of the Biblical texts, the major pertinent documents of the Church dealing with Scripture. Discusses the scope of hermeneutics, the presuppositions affecting interpretation, textural criticism, the contribution of archaeology and geography. Explains and critiques methods of redaction and exegesis. (3 semester hours)

Jesus Christ, Mary and the Grace of God
Introduction to doctrinal theology. Examines the fundamental teachings of the Catholic Church as contained in the Second Article of the Apostles Creed—Jesus Christ, Mary and divine grace. Sixteen lessons include Jesus Christ in Scripture, the Church's teaching on the Person and work of Jesus Christ, the hypostatic union, heresies, the role of Mary, the doctrine of grace, and the virtues and gifts of the Holy Spirit. (3 semester hours)

Nature of Christian Spirituality

Introduces a study of Christian holiness, examines the relevant instruments employed by the Holy Spirit in inviting and leading the Christian to a more intimate union with God: grace, revelation, the meaning and relationship of old and new covenants, the significance of the cross of redemption. Develops understanding of agape and the Church. Reviews the theology of St. Thomas concerning God's love and sanctifying grace. Explores the roles of Son and Spirit in the spiritual life of the human person. Integrates the charismatic and the hierarchical aspects of ecclesial life. Concludes with an exposition of the place of the Sacraments in the growth of holy community with emphasis on the primacy and centrality of the Eucharist. (3 semester hours)

The Philosophy of Communism

Traces the evolution of society that preceded the emergence of radical socialism; shows Marx as its logical leader; explains "dialectical materialism" and covers the range of Marxist concepts and principles dealing with materialism, the human person, the state, private ownership, religion; gives Marxist prophecy concerning the present world; discusses the proletarian revolution, the communist future; and explains the effect of communism on the Church. (3 semester hours)

Theology of the Sacraments: Part One

Introduction in nine lessons to sacramental theology, to liturgy and to the theological/historical development of the Sacraments of Eucharist and Penance. (3 semester hours)

Theology of the Sacraments: Part Two

Introduction to theology of the Sacraments of Baptism, Confirmation, Holy Orders, Matrimony and Anointing of the Sick. Twelve lessons include scriptural sources, Church traditions, councils and New Code of Canon Law regarding these Sacraments, as well as lessons on sacramentals, indulgences and fast and abstinence. (3 semester hours)

The Ten Commandments Today, Part A

Introduction to moral theology, its terms and concepts. Provides detailed application of concepts to first five commandments of the Decalogue seen from the point of view of Scripture and Church teaching. Ten lessons introduce moral theology, moral responsibility, conscience, objective moral principles, and the first five commandments. (3 semester hours)

The Ten Commandments Today, Part B

A continuation of the study of basic moral theological principles, the last five commandments of the Decalogue. Thirteen lessons complete this two-part presentation of basic moral theology. (3 semester hours)

Christian Spirituality in the Catholic Tradition

Introduction to the origin and development of Christian asceticism, identifying the early and subsequent spiritual schools and their leaders. Following chapters trace the emergence of western monasticism with emphasis on Augustine and Benedict. Continues the development of spirituality through the subsequent centuries up until modern times. (3 semester hours)

NONCREDIT COURSES

RELIGIOUS STUDIES

Ancient Church History

Introduction to the Church's first 1,000 years of history. Fifteen lessons begin with the establishment of the Church from the time of Christ, her early organization, the persecutions, well known saints of the early Church, Church councils and controversies, the Golden Age

of the Fathers, St. Augustine, Byzantium and the barbarians, Islam, and the end of the ancient world. (Noncredit)

Certified Medical Representatives Institute, Inc.

4316 Brambleton Avenue, SW
Roanoke, Virginia 24018   (703) 989-4596

Faculty:

The Certified Medical Representatives Program was established by the Institute to provide and administer a complete educational and professional development program designed primarily for the needs of medical representatives employed in the United States and Canada. The curriculum has been designed in a broad manner in order to enforce and complement the sales-training programs offered by pharmaceutical companies. Courses and examinations have been developed under the supervision of educators in various universities throughout the United States.

Academic Levels:
Professional

Degree/Certificate Programs:
Certificate.

Tuition:
Contact the Institute for current cost information and enrollment procedure.

Credit and Grading:
Upon successful completion of required scientific subjects and other elective courses which are closely related to his/her professional responsibilities, the medical representative is awarded the C.M.R. designation by the Institute. The C.M.R. award certifies the professional competency of the representative in pertinent areas of knowledge and signifies a certified career representative.

Accreditations:
The Institute's courses have been evaluated by the Program on Noncollegiate Sponsored Instruction, The Center for Adult Learning and Educational Credentials of the American Council on Education. Recommendations for college/university credit are listed with the course in *The National Guide to Educational Credit for Training Programs* published by the American Council on Education/Oryx Press.

PROFESSIONAL COURSES

MEDICAL REPRESENTATIVE DEVELOPMENT

Behavioral Pathology and Treatment

The course provides introduction to psychotherapy, psychoanalytic theory and modern psychotherapy, an overview of behavior disorders which includes pharmacology and neurotransmitter activity. The course also covers a list of behavioral disorders which includes some of the following: anxiety disorders, affective (mood) disorders, psychotic disorders, organic mental disorders, and impulse control disorders. Methodology includes self-study with text, audiotape, and pre- and post-tests, progress checks, and final examination.

Cardiovascular System

Topics of this course include functions and components of the cardiovascular system, circulation, lymphatic system, cardiovascular system disorders, and related pharmacology. Methodology includes self-study with text, audiotape, pre- and post-tests, progress checks, and final examination.

Digestive System

This course covers the structure and function of the digestive system, the physiology of digestion and absorption, disorders of the system and the pharmacology of drugs related to digestive system disorders. Methodology includes self-study with text, audiotape, pre- and post-test, progress checks, and final examination.

Endocrine System

The course covers the anatomy and physiology of the endocrine system and its components; disorders of the system; and pharmacology related to the endocrine system. Methodology includes self-study with text, audiotape, pre- and post-tests, progress checks, and final examination.

Healthcare Community

Topics covered include current issues that affect the relationships between professional groups; the education and development of physicians; types of physicians; a description of the roles of nurses, physician assistants, pharmacists, dentists, and other healthcare professionals. Also covered is the role of professional associates in the healthcare community; an overview of healthcare funding and private health insurances; a discussion of government programs such as Medicare and Medicaid recent developments in healthcare delivery; demographics and attitudes of patients and a description of hospitals and long-term care facilities. Methodology includes self-study with text, audiotape, pre- and post-tests, progress checks, and final examination.

Human Body, Pathology and Treatment

This course covers objectives and concerns of the health profession, basic body chemistry, body cells, tissues and defenses, body systems, and treatment approaches. Methodology includes self-study with text, audiotape, pre- and post-tests, progress checks, and final examination.

Immune System

The course covers production and function of the cells of the immune system, structure and function of antibodies, humoral and cell medicated immunity, immune response, hypersensitivity, autoimmunity, immunodeficiency disorders including acquired immune deficiency syndrome, pharmacology of drugs relevant to immune system disorders and the production of immunity and transplant immunology. Methodology includes self-study with text, audiotape, pre- and post-tests, progress checks, and final examination.

Integumentary System

The topics in this course are the anatomy and physiology of the integumentary system, pharmacology of drugs related to skin disorders, disorders of the integumentary system including etiology, symptoms, and treatments. Methodology includes self-study with text, audiotape, pre- and post-tests, progress checks, and final examination.

Introduction to Pharmacology

The course covers basic principles of drug actions and interactions; therapeutic classes of drugs—anti-inflammatory drugs, cardiovascular drugs, and antineoplastic drugs and drug administration. Methodology includes self-study with text, audiotape, pre- and post-tests, progress checks, and final examination.

Musculoskeletal System

This course covers the anatomy and physiology of the musculoskeletal system, disorders of the system and pharmacology related to the system. Methodology includes self-study with text, audiotape, pre- and post-tests, progress checks, and final examination.

Nervous System

Topics in this course include the anatomy and physiology of the nervous system and its component parts, common disorders of the nervous system, and related pharmacology. Methodology includes self-study with text, audiotape, pre- and post-tests, progress checks, and final examination.

Pharmaceutical and Medical Research

This course covers types of research and research institutions, governmental regulation, clinical trials, research design, methodology and analysis including scientific methodology, data collection and statistical analysis, cost analysis and ethical constraints. Methodology includes self-study with text, audiotape, pre- and post-tests, progress checks, and final examination.

Pharmaceutical Industry

The text consists of three chapters, an audiotape, glossary, chart of important professional organizations for pharmacists and pharmaceutical companies. Progress checks are interspersed throughout the course. Course covers contributions of early drug wholesalers to the pharmaceutical industry in America; factors that contributed to the increasing costs of drug research and development, as well as the high cost of drug research and development in affecting the pharmaceutical industry. Methodology includes self-study with text, audiotape, pre- and post-tests, progress checks, and final examination.

Reproductive Systems

This course covers the anatomy and physiology of the male and female reproductive systems, disorders of the reproductive systems, and methods of diagnosis and pharmacology relevant to the reproductive systems. Methodology includes self-study with text, audiotape, pre- and post-tests, progress checks, and final examination.

Respiratory System

This course covers structure and functions of the respiratory system, mechanics of breathing, gas exchange, disorders of the system and the pharmacology relating to anti-inflammatory agents, central nervous system drugs, autonomic system drugs, expectorants and bronchodilators in relation to these disorders. Methodology includes self-study with text, audiotape, pre- and post-tests, progress checks, and final examination.

Sensor Organs

Topics includes are the receptor functions, vision, hearing and equilibrium, taste, smell; disorders and pharmacology related to disorders of the sensory organs. Methodology includes self-study with text, audiotape, pre- and post-tests, progress checks, and final examination.

Trends and Issues in Healthcare

This course covers a description of how public support for the medical establishment influenced its growth during the 1960s and 1970s. Tends in healthcare are analyzed. A discussion/overview of the changing healthcare delivery system; the medical malpractice crisis; society's response to epidemic and catastrophic diseases; healthcare on the uninsured; transplants and allocations or organs; foregoing or terminating life-sustaining treatments; abortions; Medicare and Medicaid programs and the percentage of each healthcare dollar that goes toward physician fees and hospital costs. Methodology includes self-study with text, audiotape, pre- and post-tests, progress checks, and final examination.

Urinary System

Topics included in this course are urinary system anatomy, with strong emphasis on the kidney; physiology or urine formation; disorders of the urinary system; diagnostic procedures; and pharmacology relevant to urinary system disorders. Methodology includes self-study with text, audiotape, pre- and post-tests, progress checks, and final examination.

Christopher Academy
510 Hillcrest Avenue
Westfield, New Jersey 07090   (201) 233-7447

Description:

The Christopher Academy, in conjunction with the Saint Nicholas Montessori College, England and Ireland, provides training in the Montessori Method. This training course consists of the philosophy and theories of Dr. Montessori, as well as how to present the Montessori curriculum and materials to children from 2½ to 5 years of age.

The course is delivered by experts in the Montessori Method of education. The initial phase of this training is accomplished through a 9–24-month correspondence program involving reading materials, assignments and examinations. The workshop section of 60 hours (10 days) is presented in an actual Montessori classroom so the student teachers can see the full advantage of the Montessori curriculum.

Academic Levels:
Professional

Degree/Certificate Programs:
Certificate.

Tuition:
Contact the Academy for enrollment particulars and cost information.

Accreditations:

The course described below has been evaluated by the Program on Noncollegiate Sponsored Instruction, The Center for Adult Learning and Educational Credentials of the American Council on Education. The recommendation for university/college credit is listed with the course in *The National Guide to Educational Credit for Training Programs* published by the American Council on Education/Oryx Press.

PROFESSIONAL COURSES

MONTESSORI METHOD

St. Nicholas Montessori Training Course I

Upon completion of this program, the teacher will be able to discuss the Montessori philosophy of education, and the growth and development of a child from birth to five years of age; to develop a Montessori curriculum with appropriate stress on all physical, emotional, and educational needs for a child from 2½ to 5 years old; to demonstrate skills in the use of Montessori apparatus and activities. This course provides its student teachers with the qualifications to teach in a Montessori school or classroom. It emphasizes the Montessori theory and philosophy as well as instruction in the use of Montessori apparatus.

College for Financial Planning
4695 South Monaco Street
Denver, Colorado 80237   (303) 220-1200

Description:

The College for Financial Planning, founded in 1972, is a nonprofit educational institution offering a curriculum to prepare individuals for testing by the International Board of Standards and Practices for Certified Financial Planners, Inc. (IBCFP). The Certified Financial Planner (CFP) Professional Education Program consists of six separate parts, each of which is followed by a corresponding national IBCFP test. It is designed for self-study, utilizing unique study materials that include textbooks and study guides specially prepared by the academic staff of the College. Classroom instruction also is available through the College's adjunct faculty and affiliate colleges and universities, as well as through select corporations. Individuals who complete the CFP Program learn to recognize existing and potential client problems and to recommend solutions over a broad range of financial circumstances.

Academic Levels:
Professional

Degree/Certificate Programs:
Certificate.

Tuition:
Contact the College for enrollment procedure and current cost information.

Credit and Grading:

To qualify for certification by the IBCFP, an individual must fulfill certain requirements, including submission of a transcript indicating completion of a financial planning education program that has been registered with the IBCFP and successful completion of the six-part national IBCFP certification examination series. Proctored examinations are required.

Accreditations:

The courses described below have been evaluated by the Program on Noncollegiate Sponsored Instruction, The Center for Adult Learning and Educational Credentials of the American Council on Education. Credit recommendations are listed in the *National Guide to Educational Credit for Training Programs* published by the American Council on Education/Oryx Press.

PROFESSIONAL COURSES

FINANCIAL PLANNING

Financial Paraplanner Program

This course covers the financial planning process, the time value of money, principles of risk management, life insurance, health insurance, property and liability insurance, investment principles, equity investments, fixed income investments, mutual funds, income tax planning, pension and profit-sharing plans, other retirement plans, principles of estate planning, and estate transfer and planning or estate taxes. Methodology involves periodic proctored examinations at various collegiate institutions.

Tax Preparer I: Individual Tax Returns

This course covers basic filing considerations, accounting considerations, installment sales, taxpayer employer identification number, changing accounting methods, nonbusiness incomes, adjustments to income, itemized deductions, qualified residence interest after 1987, interest allocation rules, charitable contributions, business income and expenses, like-kind exchanges, farming considerations, income tax payments and credits; individual income tax computations, amended returns, claims for refund and tax deficiencies and penalties, running a tax preparation practice, and standards for tax practice.

Tax Preparer II: Partnerships, Corporations, and Fiduciary Returns

The course covers computation of partnership taxable income (allocation of income and losses, partnership distributions, partnership-partner transactions, and terminations); at-risk and passive activities rules; computation of corporate tax, dividends-paid deduction, dividend distributions, and dividends received by corporate stockholders; corporate alternative minimum tax, collapsible corporations, personal holding companies, and accumulated earnings tax; estate and trust personal exemptions, distributable net income, and distributions to beneficiaries; computation of S corporation taxable income and pass-throughs to shareholders; S stock; worksheet—S corporation shareholder's basis for indebtedness from the S corporation; summary of tax treatment of S corporation distributions to shareholders; election under code section 1368(e)(3)to distribute accumulated earnings and profits in priority order; partnership and corporate formations and liquidations; corporate liquidations and the "General Utilities" rule; simple trusts; complex trusts and estates; and grantor trusts.

Fundamentals of Financial Planning (CFP I)

This course covers the financial planning process, regulation of financial planners, insurance, investments and financial institutions, individual income tax principles, retirement and estate planning concepts, the time value of money, monetary policy and the business cycle, client data gathering, the construction of personal financial statements, budgeting, and debt management.

Insurance Planning (CFP II)

This course gives students an understanding of risk management and risk analysis including interpreting the insurance contract; coverages provided by property and liability insurance; the areas of life and health insurance; group and social insurance; the organization and internal functions of private insurers; and to enable the student to demonstrate an understanding of processes associated with the determination of insurance needs and purchase of insurance products.

Investment Planning (CFP III)

This course covers the investment environment, security markets, regulation, and sources of information; risk/return and tools for analysis; modern portfolio theory; valuation of debt and preferred stock; government securities; valuation of common stock; security selection, options, and convertible securities; futures; physical assets and gold; real estate; investment companies; and the economic environment and portfolio construction.

Tax Planning and Management (CFP IV)

The objectives of this course are to provide the student with an understanding of the fundamentals of individual income tax; considerations in selecting a business form; tax planning for the acquisition and disposition of property; tax advantaged investments; tax planning alternatives; tax traps; and personal tax management processes.

Retirement Planning and Employee Benefits (CFP V)

This course provides the student with an understanding of personal retirement planning, qualified retirement plans; government-sponsored retirement planning, qualified retirement plans; government-sponsored retirement plans, and employee benefits involving group life and medical insurance and related programs, and nonqualified deferred compensation.

Estate Planning (CFP VI)

The objective of this course is to introduce the student to the fundamentals of an estate plan, including federal estate and gift taxation as well as specific exclusion and valuation techniques that reduce the size of the gross estate; to enable the student to provide specific estate planning recommendations.

Credit Union National Association
Certified Credit Union Executive Program
P.O. Box 431
Madison, Wisconsin 53701   (608) 231-4055

Description:

The Certified Credit Union Executive (CCUE) Program is sponsored by the Credit Union National Association (CUNA). CUNA is the national trade association for 22,000 credit unions in the United States. The CCUE Program is primarily an independent study program developed by an advisory committee of credit union executives and educators. In some localities, CCUE courses are also offered by colleges in a conventional classroom format. The CCUE program was initiated in 1975 and is a professional development program for credit union personnel.

To participate in the CCUE program, a candidate must be actively engaged in the credit union industry and must complete a curriculum of ten independent study courses designed to broaden knowledge and enhance management skills. Successful completion of all ten courses qualifies a candidate for CCUE designation.

Course completion is validated by national examinations prepared by college and university professors, and administered under strict control in colleges and universities in the candidates' home areas. The program is designed primarily for self-study, and participants desiring professional assistance may contact the CCUE Coordinator at the Credit Union National Association.

Academic Levels:
Vocational

Degree/Certificate Programs:
Certificate

Credit Union National Association

Admission Requirements:

Enrollment is restricted to those individuals actively engaged in the credit union industry as employees or volunteers.

Tuition:

Fees vary, depending upon the course. Contact the Coordinator, Certified Credit Union Executive Program at the above address for current fees.

Enrollment Period:

Courses include from 10 to 15 self-paced lessons.

Equipment Requirements:

Student pays the cost of textbooks which are selected by college and university faculty members. Study guides which accompany the textbooks are prepared by faculty members. Review guides are available for examination preparation.

Credit and Grading:

Examinations are proctored and are administered by college and university professors in local areas throughout the United States.

Accreditations:

Recommendations for credit at the lower division baccalaureate level have been determined by the Program on Noncollegiate Sponsored Instruction, The Center for Adult Learning and Educational Credentials of the American Council on Education. Their recommendations for credit are listed in *The National Guide to Educational Credit for Training Programs* published by the American Council on Education/Oryx Press.

VOCATIONAL COURSES

CREDIT UNION MANAGEMENT

Accounting I

Course emphasis is on those areas of financial accounting relevant to external reporting by credit unions. Topical areas include: accounting principles, basic accounting cycle and financial statements, analysis of revenue and expense; analysis of asset, liability and equity accounts, preparation of financial statements, and present value concepts.

Accounting II

Course emphasis is on the preparation and use of reports for management decision making. Topical areas include: management accounting, cost behavior, cost flows and capital budgeting, financial statement analysis, measuring performance, planning and control, budgeting, standard costing, internal control, audits, and cost allocations.

Business Law

Course provides a study of business law and a working knowledge of legal terminology. Topics include social forces and legal rights; contracts, including nature, offer and acceptance, capacity, mutuality and consideration, legality, form and interpretation, transfer of rights, and discharge; agency; commercial paper, including nature, negotiability and transfer, rights of parties, notes and drafts, bankruptcy, and management of corporation.

Credit and Collections

This course covers various aspects of credit. Topics include nature and role of credit; types of consumer credit, and their management and investigation; basis of credit decision; decision and salesmanship in consumer credit; numerical scoring systems, collection policies, practices, and systems; and business and government credit functions, and control of credit operations.

Credit Union Accounting

Major topics covered in the course are accounting principles, recording transactions, preparing financial statements, accounting systems, internal control procedures and reconciliations, accounting for loans and investments, fixed assets and depreciation, the basic accounting cycle and financial statements, analysis of revenue and expense, analysis of asset, liability and equity accounts, preparation of cash flow statements, and present value concepts.

Data Processing

Major topics covered in the course include an overview of computer functions, hardware, software, systems, and how they are integrated in business and credit, and credit union settings.

Economics

Topics covered include basic economic concepts and national income; pricing, supply, and demand; incomes and living standards; business organization; labor and industrial relations and the economic role of government; national income, savings, investment, and consumption; income determination, business cycles, and forecasting; prices and money, the banking system, and monetary policy; fiscal policy and price determination; pricing and the productive factors, wages, interest, and profits; international trade and finance; and economic problems and alternate economic systems.

Economics and the Monetary System

Major topics covered in the course are basic macroeconomics concepts and theories such as supply and demand, inflation, GNP, and elasticity, and the classic and Keynesian approaches. Upon such a foundation, the course covers issues in money and banking such as money's functions, types of financial institutions, the structure and operations of the Federal Reserve Systems, open market and money-market operations, the money supply and its impact on prices and employment, monetary and fiscal policies, and the national debt and international trade.

Financial Counseling

Course provides instruction and material that enable the counselor to meet the demands of the credit union members. Topics include family resource management and consumer decision making; consumer credit; family budget components; social security, life insurance, and annuities; savings and investments; estate planning, wills, and trusts; consumer education; types and techniques of counseling; and evaluation and ethics.

Financial Management I

Major topics covered in the course are an introduction to finance and the financial services industry. The course continues by reviewing the creation of money and credit and analyzing the factors that affect the supply and cost of credit. The course's major emphases, however, are cash and investments, interest rates, forecasting and budgeting, risks, capitalization, and ricing member services.

Introduction to Credit Unions

The course covers credit union origins and introduction into North America; depression and credit union development; new leadership, World War II, post-war expansion; credit union as a legal entity; development and functioning of board of directors; motive power for a credit union; ethics in the credit union; and credit union relationships and professionalism. Methodology involves self-study utilizing a study guide, recommended texts, and a review guide for examination preparation.

Management

This course presents the principles of sound management. Topics include motivation, organizing, human factors in organizing, decision making, planning, leadership and directing, controlling, and management and development.

Marketing

This course covers the facts and principles of marketing. Topics include the marketing concept and structure; market information and buyer behavior; consumer and intermediate customers' buying behavior; product, packaging, and branding decisions; consumer and industrial goods; product planning and time-place utility; channels of distribution; promotion; pricing; strategy and integrating the market program; and controlling marketing programs and the cost-value to society.

Money and Banking

Major topics covered in the course are the nature and structure of financial institutions, money and its functions, the history and creation of money, the Federal Reserve System, open market operations, changing interest rates, the money supply and its impact on prices and employment, money-market operations, the national debt and the economy, and international economies.

Personnel Administration

Course topics include systems and procedures, office layout, records management, information media, supervisory skills, staff development, salary administration, job evaluation, labor relations, performance appraisal and training methods, benefit programs, and management's responsibility and dealing with people.

Risk Management and Insurance

This course covers concepts and principles needed to produce and operate a program of risk measurement and control. Topics include the concept of risk; the risk management function; identification, measurement, and control of risk; important concepts of insurance; property and liability risk exposures and insurance; personal risk exposure and the uses of life and health insurance; the institution and selection of insurance organizations; risk management in credit unions; selection and application of noninsurance tools; and selection and application of various types of insurance.

Defense Security Institute

Department of Defense
c/o Registrar
Defense General Supply Center
Richmond, Virginia 23297-5091

(804) 275-3861

Description:

The U.S. Department of Defense Security Institute (DoDSI) is an activity established by the Secretary of Defense. The Institute is under the management oversight, policy direction, and technical guidance of the Deputy Under Secretary of Defense (Policy). The Institute serves as the Department of Defense focal point for promoting activities supporting DoD security programs in education and training, research and development, and career development. The Institute presents correspondence courses relating

to the Department of Defense Security Programs. These courses are designed for U.S. Government personnel, plus selected employees and representatives of U.S. industry.

Four operating departments manage and provide the education, training, and special publications and products for DoDSI. The Educational Programs Department primarily produces or coordinates production of the DoDSI recurring and special publications and products and produces or supports development of correspondence courses. The Industrial Security Department primarily produces and conducts courses and special training in the DoD Industrial Security program, the Key Assets Protection Program, and in automated information systems security. The Personnel Security Investigations Department produces and conducts courses and special training in the DoD personnel security investigations. The Security Management Department produces and conducts courses and special training in the DoD information security program, personnel security program, and in general security requirements and management.

Academic Levels:
Professional

Degree/Certificate Programs:

In order to receive a course diploma, students must demonstrate mastery of course content through formal examination, formally evaluated criterion exercises, the completion of graded written exercises, faculty observation and evaluation, and graded homework assignments or some combination thereof. For most courses, students who do no meet minimum academic or performance standards are given a certificate or letter of attendance in lieu of a course diploma. In all courses, the faculty identify the marginal student early on in the course. All students are assigned to faculty advisors, and when students develop academic or performance problems, their advisors work with them in free time to improve their mastery of the required knowledge or skills.

Admission Requirements:

Enrollment is restricted to federal government personnel, plus selected employees and representatives of U.S. industry.

Accreditations:

The correspondence courses have been evaluated by the Program on Noncollegiate Sponsored Instruction, The Center for Adult Learning and Educational Credentials of the American Council on Education. Credit recommendations are listed in *The National Guide to Educational Credit for Training Programs* published by the American Council on Education/Oryx Press.

PROFESSIONAL COURSES

DEFENSE SECURITY

Personnel Security Adjudications

This course covers introduction to the personnel security program; employing activities' initial responsibilities; personnel security investigations; central adjudication; adjudicative issues; and continuous evaluation. Lessons deal with the history, foundation, and scope of the personnel security program; the responsibilities and methods of the various agencies involved in the personnel security program; the investigations used in the personnel security program with explanation of their uses, elements, and idiosyncrasies; the adjudicator's responsibilities; and the adjudication policy guidelines.

Structures of Industrial Security

The course covers Defense Investigative Service structure and functions. Defense Industrial Security Program structure and functions, processing of government clearances, facility security administration, principles and criteria of physical security, and basic concepts of automated data processing.

Diamond Council of America
9140 Ward Parkway
Kansas City, Missouri 64114 (816) 444-3500

Description:
The Diamond Council of America was founded in 1944. It offers correspondence courses in Diamontology and Gemology leading to certificates of Certified Diamontologist and Guild Gemologist offered to members of the Diamond Council of America and their employees.

Faculty:
Jerry Fogel, Executive Director.

Academic Levels:
Vocational

Degree/Certificate Programs:
Certificate.

Admission Requirements:
Enrollment restricted to employees of members of the Diamond Council of America.

Tuition:
Contact the school for current tuition and fees.

Enrollment Period:
No time restriction, although courses are usually completed within 12 months.

Accreditations:
Distance Education and Training Council.

VOCATIONAL COURSES

DIAMONTOLOGY

Diamontology

This course leads to a certificate of Certified Diamontologist.

GEMOLOGY

Gemology

This course leads to a certificate of Guild Gemologist.

Educational Institute of the American Hotel and Motel Association
1407 South Harrison Road
P.O. Box 1240
East Lansing, Michigan 48826-1240
(517) 353-5500

Description:
The Educational Institute is a nonprofit educational foundation offering twenty-nine courses covering every area of hospitality operations. Internationally recognized certificates are awarded for completion of each course. Currently, over 2,000 students are enrolled in the Institute's correspondence program which has served individuals from over eighty countries.

The Institute, located on the campus of Michigan State University, was founded in 1952 and has become the world's largest educational resource center for the hospitality field. The courses are designed to improve skills and attitudes while preparing for advancement within a hospitality career. All materials are continually reviewed by leaders in the industry and academia to ensure that they reflect the latest thinking and technology.

Students may take individual courses or concentrate on a specific area of hotel/motel operations by earning a Certificate of Specialization in Rooms Division Management, Food and Beverage Management, Marketing and Sales Management; Accounting and Financial Management, or Engineering and Facility Management. These certificates each require the completion of five designated courses. Students may also complete an eight-course Hospitality Operations Program or twelve-course Hospitality Management Diploma.

Faculty:
E. Ray Swan, President; Karen Kayne, Registrar. Teaching staff includes a faculty of 6 members, 7 subject specialists, and a support staff of 70.

Academic Levels:
Vocational

Degree/Certificate Programs:
Diploma, Certificate, Certificate of Specialization.

Admission Requirements:
Open enrollment.

Tuition:
Individual course: U.S. and Canada, $175; other countries, $225; Certificate of Specialization: $750; Diploma, $1,740; Hospitality Operations Program, $1,190. Discounts are available for multiple-course enrollment. Time payment plans are offered for students enrolling for three or more courses at once. Hotel corporations often reimburse employees for tuition. Refund policy available, subject to length of time after enrollment.

Enrollment Period:

The maximum time allowed for completion of single course is four months; there is no minimum time requirement. Interrupted training allowed with specified re-enrollment fee. Seminars and Group Study Programs available.

Equipment Requirements:

Textbooks and student certification manuals are included in the tuition.

Credit and Grading:

Forty percent of the final grade is based on grades received on four progress tests, and sixty percent on the final examination. A minimum passing grade of ninety percent or better receives a certificate "with honors." Certificates are awarded for passing grades of 69 percent and above. Examinations must be proctored. The Educational Institute does not accept transfer credits but offers a challenge examination option which allows students to obtain course credit without completing the coursework. Students may also challenge any of the Institute's programs.

Accreditations:

Distance Education and Training Council. Licensed by the Michigan Department of Education. Member of: Council on Hotel, Restaurant, and Institutional Education (CHRIE).

VOCATIONAL COURSES

HOTEL AND MOTEL CAREER TRAINING

Introduction to the Hospitality Industry

Covers both the lodging and food service industries and offers special insights from successful industry professionals to help you better plan your career goals.

Hospitality Today

Introduces the student to the organization and structure of hotels, restaurants, and clubs from a management perspective. Explains franchising and management contracts, business ethics, human resources, marketing, career opportunities, and more.

Organization and Administration

Takes a people-oriented approach and stresses the importance of communications and interpersonal relations.

Food and Beverage Management

How to profitably manage a food and beverage operation, including techniques for planning, implementing, and evaluating.

Basic Sanitation

Covers all the basics of food service and hotel/motel sanitation, and includes the managerial side of sanitation concerns.

Hospitality Supervision

Includes the latest know-how on increasing productivity, labor cost control, communication, motivation, time management, accommodating change, and resolving conflict.

Financial Accounting for the Hospitality Industry I

How to apply basic accounting terminology, rules, procedures, and concepts to everyday business situations.

Facilities Management

A comprehensive overview of hotel engineering systems to help you make informed management decisions. Shows non-engineers how to interpret important data from the physical plant sector. Learn about energy, water, communication systems, food service equipment, laundries, groundskeeping, solid waste removal, and more.

Tourism and the Hospitality Industry

How to market your property and community as a tourist destination and respond to the needs of domestic and international travelers.

Front Office Procedures

Includes computer applications throughout every phase of the guest cycle. Shows how front office activities and functions affect other departments and stresses how to manage the front office to ensure that the property's goals are met.

Housekeeping Management

Provides a thorough overview, from the big picture of maintaining a quality staff, planning and organizing to the technical details of cleaning each area of the hotel. Covers the new pressures and demands facing housekeeping executives and shows how you can make a difference in determining whether or not guests return to your property.

Food and Beverage Service

How to plan for and successfully manage the different types of food and beverage operations that might be found in a lodging property, including coffee shops, gourmet dining rooms, room service, banquets, lounges, and entertainment/show rooms.

Hospitality Industry Training

How to develop, conduct, and evaluate one-on-one and group training that will reduce turnover, improve employees' job performance, and help your organization attain its goals.

Hospitality Human Resources Management

How to recruit and retain high-caliber employees in tomorrow's shrinking labor pool. The technical and legal challenges of hospitality human resources management. Apply the specifics on recruiting competent people, dealing with unions, and offering benefits programs.

Financial Accounting for the Hospitality Industry II

This course helps the student to understand departmental accounting and readies him/her for accounting responsibilities at the supervisor and managerial levels.

Marketing of Hospitality Services

This course shows to use proven marketing techniques to improve business at the property; spells out how to develop, implement, and evaluate a marketing plan; and helps to understand how to identify and reach the customers wanted by using marketing techniques specific to hospitality services.

Hospitality Energy and Water Management

This course gives the background, knowledge, and expertise necessary to conserve water, avoid water problems, and organize an energy savings program in both lodging and food service operations. Provides operating tips that will enable the student to make immediate cost-saving changes.

Hotel/Motel Security Management

Discusses security issues and concerns that affect the property on a daily basis.

Hospitality Law

This course gives an understanding of potential legal problems and how important legal considerations can affect your operation.

Resort Management

How to take advantage of the skyrocketing demand for "mini-vacations" and the latest in health club/spa facility management. Includes the concierge function and computer systems.

Hospitality Purchasing Management

This course offers the knowledge needed for buying major commodities and non-food supplies, and how to manage food purchasing.

Bar and Beverage Management

Details of profitably managing a bar and beverage establishment, including control systems, hiring and training, and responsible alcohol service. Includes essential information of a wide range of beverage products.

Managerial Accounting for the Hospitality Industry

How to identify costs, develop realistic budgets, forecast, and plan cash flow. Incorporates the latest revision to the uniform system of accounts and features case studies of actual properties.

Food and Beverage Controls

How to take charge of the complexities of controlling food, beverages, labor, and sales income.

Hospitality Industry Computer Systems

How to improve the property's efficiency while serving the guest better.

Hotel/Motel Sales Promotion

Discusses new ways to sell rooms and food and beverage services to business travelers, leisure travelers, travel agents, and meeting planners. Industry pros give tips on sales programs that worked for them and suggest how to play up the unique features of the property.

Convention Management and Service

How to address meeting planners' needs and concerns confidently, creatively, and effectively.

Hospitality Industry Engineering Systems

This course offers ways to cut costs and still provide for guest satisfaction and comfort, high employee productivity, and peak efficiency in all major systems and equipment. Helps you communicate effectively with contractors and vendors.

Emergency Management Institute
Home Study Program
16825 South Seton Avenue
Emmitsburg, Maryland 21727 (301) 447-1172

Description:

The mission of the Emergency Management Institute is to serve as a national focal point for the development and delivery of emergency management technical training and professional education. The purpose is to enhance the mitigation, preparedness, response, and recovery capabilities of federal, state, and local government emergency managers and others in the public and private sectors who have responsibility for serving the public in time of disaster or emergency. That responsibility spans the entire spectrum of emergencies from natural disasters to technological calamities to national security crises. Emergency Management Institute and the National Fire Academy delivers these programs at the National Emergency Training Center in Emmitsburg, Maryland.

The Emergency Management Institute is located on a 107-acre campus (formerly St. Joseph's College). Just south of the Pennsylvania border, the campus is 70 miles northwest of Baltimore and 75 miles north of Washington, D.C.

Faculty:

Laura Buchbinder, Superintendent; Steve Sharro, Deputy Superintendent; Gary L. Chase, Home Study Program Administrator.

Academic Levels:

Vocational

Degree/Certificate Programs:

Certificate.

Admission Requirements:

All courses are open to the general public. Group enrollment as well as individual enrollment is available for all courses.

Tuition:

There is no charge for enrollment.

Enrollment Period:

The maximum time for completion of a course is one year.

Equipment Requirements:

Course materials may be obtained through either your local or state Office of Emergency Management or by writing to the Administrative Office of the Home Study Program.

Credit and Grading:

Each course includes a final examination and those who score 75 percent or better are issued a certificate of completion. One semester hour of college credit may be obtained for each course; contact the EMI Home Study Program for details.

Library Services:

The Learning Resource Center (LRC) provides current information and resources on emergency management and related subjects. It houses a collection of over 40,000 books, periodicals, and research documents, as well as audiovisual materials such as films, videotapes, slide/tape programs, and microfiche. Although library materials do not circulate off-campus, the staff does make available photocopies of various journal articles and research papers for individuals requesting specific information. The LRC provides limited reference and referral services in response to telephone and mail requests.

Accreditations:

Distance Education and Training Council.

VOCATIONAL COURSES

EMERGENCY MANAGEMENT

Emergency Program Manager: An Orientation to the Position

Designed primarily for emergency program managers, this home study course provides an introduction to Comprehensive Emergency Management (CEM) and the Integrated Emergency Management System (IEMS). Included is an in-depth look at the four phases of comprehensive emergency management: mitigation, preparedness, response, and recovery. Text includes illustration, diagrams, and figures. In most units, there also appear "Things to Do" boxes which provide worksheets, exercises, and future tasks. Approximately 8–12 hours are required for completion.

Emergency Management, USA

This course contains information about natural and technological hazards and the threat of nuclear attack. Participants are led through the development of personal emergency preparedness plans and are encouraged to become involved in the local emergency preparedness network. Approximately 10–12 hours of study are required for completion. Text is accompanied by illustrations, maps, charts, and diagrams. A final examination is included in the back of the text.

Radiological Emergency Management

The subject course includes information on a variety of radiological emergencies including: radiological emergency management; nuclear attack; nuclear power plant accidents; radiological transportation accidents. Approximately 8–12 hours are required for completion.

Preparedness Planning for a Nuclear Crisis: A Citizen's Guide to Civil Defense and Self-Protection

The subject course includes information on the following: the effects of nuclear weapons; evacuation and sheltering; preparation and stocking of fallout shelters; development of emergency plans to improve the chance of survival for individuals and families. Approximately 10–14 hours are required for completion.

Hazardous Materials: A Citizen's Orientation

The subject course includes information on the following: hazardous materials and human health; hazardous materials regulations; identifying hazardous materials; preparing for hazardous materials incidents; hazardous materials in the home. Approximately 10–14 hours are required for completion.

Extension Course Institute
United States Air Force
Gunter Annex
Maxwell Air Force Base, Alabama 36118
(205) 416-4252

Description:

The Extension Course Institute was founded in 1950 to offer United States Air Force career development and specialized, professional military education courses. Through the years, ECI has continually strived to meet Air Force needs by providing extension education to airmen and airwomen (and members of other services) throughout the world. This continuous pattern of growth at ECI has demanded the integration of various technologies to keep abreast of current methods of extension education. In support of the growing enrollment, ECI has adopted automation to keep pace with the ever increasing demand for current course materials. New enrollments average over 35,000 per month.

Description:

Enrollment is restricted to active duty, National Guard, or Reserve members of the U.S. military services (retired military personnel are not eligible); Civil Air Patrol senior member officers or cadets who have achieved the General Billy Mitchell Award or higher; Civil Service employees of the U.S. Government; Air Force Reserve, National Officers' Training Corps (AFROTC) students (eligible to enroll in job related specialized and career development courses only); civilians of international countries employed by a Department of Defense agency; international military officers eligible for Foreign Military Sales training programs as specified in Department of the Air Force Regulation 53–8 (may request enrollment in USAF professional military education courses); Air Force contractor employees in accordance with AFR 5–55 (job related career development courses and specialized courses only); and Red Cross Volunteers donating their services to the Air Force on an extended basis (when the course requested pertains to training needs, career development courses, and specialized courses only). Eligible applicants should contact their base Education Officer for further information or contact ECI at the above address.

Faculty:
Colonel Jerry L. Sailors, Commandant.

Accreditations:

Distance Education and Training Council. Selected courses are recommended for postsecondary credit by the American Council on Education's Office on Educational Credit and Credentials. SEE *The Guide to the Evaluation of Educational Experiences in the Armed Forces* published by the American Council on Education/Oryx Press.

Gemological Institute of America
1660 Stewart Street
Santa Monica, California 90404
(800) 421-7250

Description:

In 1930, jeweler Robert M. Shipley conducted a course in the classification and evaluation of gemstones at the University of Southern California Extension. He had just returned from Europe where he had been introduced to the practical applications of gemology for jewelers. That combination of the scientific world of gemology and the commercial world of jewelry was not very well known in the United States. It was Shipley who made it so. Persuaded by his friends, he wrote a home study course on the subject. That was the beginning of the Gemological Institute of America. The next ten years saw the completion of the correspondence program, the addition of research and testing laboratories, and the development of a resident program of study.

GIA is now a nonprofit corporation; its Board is chosen from the country's leading business professionals, research scientists, and members of the jewelry industry. Today the Gemological Institute of America is the largest scientific and educational facility in the field. From Shipley's first home study course, it has grown into an organization staffed by a faculty of experts in mineralogy, the jewelry arts, education, marketing, and other aspects of gemology. Santa Monica, California is the location of GIA's main campus, Research Laboratory, and a GIA Gem Trade Laboratory. The Eastern Division in New York City includes classrooms, offices, and two GIA Gem Trade Laboratories. The New York City campus is at 580 Fifth Avenue, New York, NY 10036; telephone (212) 944-5900.

Faculty:

William E. Boyajian, President; J. F. Ellis, Vice President of Operations; Dennis Foltz, Vice President of Education; Kathryn Kimmel, Vice President of Marketing and Public Relations; Courtney A. Walker, Vice President and Chief Financial Officer. There is a faculty of 48 members.

Academic Levels:

Vocational

Degree/Certificate Programs:

Certificate; Diploma.

Admission Requirements:

Students younger than seventeen must have the permission of a parent, guardian, or school counselor. Otherwise, there are no requirements. Overseas students welcomed.

Tuition:

The tuition for any of the courses can be paid in installments plus a finance charge. For tuition, see individual course descriptions below. Tuition for foreign students is slightly higher; contact the Institute for particulars. Some courses, when taken in groups, cost less in total than if taken individually, as follows: Gemologist Program (Diamonds, Diamond Grading, Colored Stones, Gem Identification, and Colored Stone Grading) $2,795; Diamonds Program (Diamonds and Diamond Grading) $1,095; Colored Stones Program (Colored Stones, Gem Identification, and Colored Stone Grading) $1,895; Graduate Jewelry Sales Program (Diamonds, Colored Stones, Jewelry Display, Counter Sketching, Fine Jewelry Sales, Advanced Fine Jewelry Sales, and Gold and Precious Metals) $2,495. If a student chooses to disenroll, GIA will give a refund of the amount paid in excess of the registration fee, and pro rate the cost of the training received. GIA courses are approved by the Veterans Administration. Prices are subject to change without notice. Contact the institute for current costs.

Enrollment Period:

No time limit restrictions. Inactive students may resume their studies at any time.

Equipment Requirements:

Texts and necessary references are provided as part of each course. The Diamond Course and the Gem Identification Course require that students have access to instruments such as a 10X loupe (or microscope) and a pair of diamond tweezers (for the Diamond Course) and the following for the Gem Identification Course: refractometer, polariscope, 10X loupe, specific gravity liquids, dichroscope, polarizing filter, tweezers. Other instruments not required but very useful are: binocular microscope, ultraviolet light (longwave and shortwave), thermal reaction tester, spectroscope, immersion cell, emerald filter. All of these instruments are available from Gems Instruments Corporation.

Credit and Grading:

Examinations are administered under the proctorship of a licensed teacher or a librarian. A final examination (also proctored) is taken upon completion of the three gem courses. Students may also take their examinations at GIA's offices in either New York or Santa Monica. A passing grade is required on every lesson before a student may take the examination for the course. Minimum passing grade: 75 percent for written examinations; 100 percent (pass/fail) for the 20-Stone examination.

Library Services:

GIA's Library has one of the largest, most comprehensive collections of books and periodicals on gems and jewelry in the world. Containing more than 14,000 volumes and subscribing to more than 125 professional journals, it is constantly acquiring new, rare, out-of-print, and historically important publications. It also has a collection of audio and video tapes. Santa Monica students use the library for research. Home Study students, New York City residence students, and graduates have access to the services of the Santa Monica library by phone or letter. There is a smaller library facility on the New York campus.

Job Placement Assistance:

GIA maintains a listing of job openings.

Accreditations:

Distance Education and Training Council.

VOCATIONAL COURSES

GEMOLOGY

Diamonds

This consists of 22 fast-paced assignments. Some have questionnaires that the student sends to the instructor, while others have self-testing quizzes that allow you to quickly measure your understanding of the material. Topics covered include the four Cs of diamond value; explaining quality, beauty, and value to customers; talking about weight with customers; using color to sell diamonds; cut in buying and selling diamonds; simulants and synthetics; the international diamond market; cutting styles; finding and evaluating suppliers; how your competitors price their goods; selling the myth and romance of diamonds; security procedures for sales personnel; store image, advertising, and jewelry. *Tuition:* $595; $757 with audiotape option.

Diamond Grading

This course continues diamond education by focusing on the vital skill of diamond grading. Each grading factor is discussed at length, and you get to grade actual diamonds with stones furnished by GIA. In addition to the written assignments, there are four practical work lessons in which you grade at least seven diamonds. *Tuition:* $695; $857 with audiotape option.

Colored Stones

This course provides a wealth of practical knowledge for use every day in selling more successfully. Emphasis is placed on the sales potential of colored stones as well as ethical representation and disclosure. Course topics include: quality and value factors; characteristics that make gems beautiful and unique; factors that influence gemstone color; the nature and origins of gems, synthetics, imitations, and organic materials; enhancements; jewelry metals; jewelry as a fashion accessory; faceted cut styles; the care and cleaning of gems; gems and jewelry marketing and sales. Individual gems covered include cultured pearls, turquoise, lapis lazuli, opal, peridot, jade, quartz, chalcedony, garnet, zircon, spinel, topaz, tourmaline, chrysoberyl, emerald, aquamarine, ruby, sapphire, alexandrite, amethyst, citrine, tanzanite, coral, and ivory. There are 40 written assignments. *Tuition:* $695; $980 with audiotape option.

Gem Identification

This course includes the following topics: making critical observations; basic and advanced magnification techniques; testing procedures; measuring refractive index; polariscope testing; spectrum analysis; detecting pleochroism; determining specific gravity; separating diamonds from simulants; detecting enhancements and imitations; observing and interpreting fluorescence; auxiliary tests; putting gem identification skills to work in the store. The course consists of 6 written assignments plus practice work. *Tuition:* $895.

Colored Stone Grading

This course complements the product knowledge and testing skills taught in the Colored Stones and Gem Identification courses. Topics include: characteristics of gemstones; quality factors; light and color; human color vision; describing color accurately; causes of color in gemstones; grading color (with grade charts); clarity characteristics; examining stones for clarity; assigning a clarity grade; cutting styles; grading proportions and finish; size and weight; recutting; market value and price; creating an effective grading environment; buying and selling colored stones; displaying colored stones; appraising. *Tuition:* $595.

Counter Sketching

This new course is especially designed for those with little or no sketching talent. Easy-to-follow diagrams and handy reference cards walk you through each of six sketching projects. Topics include: tools, tips, and good techniques to get you quickly into the flow of things; how to sketch gems alone and in rings; how to sketch metals and finishing styles; how to sketch existing pieces; what colors to use for over 50 popular gems; popular mountings and settings; how to use sketches to close sales; how to avoid jewelry problems at take-in; what parts go into jewelry; how to purchase parts and stones for inventory; how to figure markup; how rings are assembled; what to be careful of with stones; how to start, hire for, and manage a customized jewelry service. Video included. *Tuition:* $495.

Gold and Precious Metals

Topics include: karatage of gold; fineness of silver and platinum; working properties; physical characteristics; communicating technical terminology; luster and reflectivity; trends in consumer behavior; add-on sales; understanding market prices; prospecting; mining and refining; availability; new technologies; how to guard against underkarating; sales and promotion techniques; quality marking and karat stamping; assaying; how plating is done; care and cleaning; fashion trends. *Tuition:* $295; $395 with audiotape option.

Pearl and Bead Stringing

Topics include: why custom strung jewelry is popular; what you should know about pearls; a fascinating look at bead types, shapes, and sizes; how to suggest the right style; how to deal with special requests or problems; how to use the past to sell the present; how not to string; what to watch out for; how to choose the right clasps and decorative parts; how to work with threads and wires; handy tools to have; how to use tricks of the trade; how to buy wisely; how to deal with the unusual; how to start a service; in store or at home; how other did it. Video included. *Tuition:* $495.

Pearls

This course gives the student the product information needed to build customer interest in cultured pearls. Course topics include: the history and romance of pearls; how pearls form; the history and science of pearl culturing; judging and explaining factors which influence beauty and value; the cultured pearl industry from oyster cage to sales counter; freshwater pearls; separating imitations from natural and cultured pearls; buying and appraising; displaying, advertising, promoting, and selling cultured pearls. The course consists of 16 written assignments and 3 grading projects. *Tuition:* $695.

Jewelry Display

This course provides training for owners, managers, jewelry display designers, and salespeople. Course topics include: developing and communicating your image; using different types of displays; basic rules for good display design; creating a viewing area (including modifying windows designed for other types of merchandise); lighting techniques for effect and economy; developing color schemes; making and obtaining display accessories and props; making pads and panels; using signs to inform and inspire; managing and maintaining displays; planning and setting up different types of displays; developing a designer's eye; creating theme windows. There are 16 written assignments. *Tuition:* $395.

Fine Jewelry Sales

This course covers the following topics: the characteristics of a successful salesperson; analyzing and improving your sales approach; important steps in selling; what motivates people to buy jewelry; turning lookers into buyers; demonstrating merchandise; choosing the right blend of hard facts and romance; turning objections into selling points; closing sales confidently; special sales problems; the modern jewelry store; jewelry departments and how they interact; diamonds; gold jewelry; colored stones; cultured pearls; special orders and custom jewelry; appraisals and repairs; safeguards and insurance; style and fashion in jewelry sales. *Tuition:* $225; $265 with audiotape option.

Insurance Replacement Appraisal

Topics include: ways of determining the value of a piece of jewelry; what it takes to prepare and write insurance appraisals; ethical dilemmas; how insurance companies manage the replacement process; meeting the criteria for a good appraisal; appropriate methodology; how insurance works; the underwriting process; basic methods of determining value; creating accurate word-pictures of the jewelry you are appraising; step-by-step process of assembling an appraisal; electronic and photographic record-keeping; updating an appraisal; key tools for appraising. *Tuition:* $450.

Gemologist Program

Includes the following courses: Diamonds, Diamond Grading, Colored

Stones, Gem Identification, and Colored Stone Grading. *Tuition:* $2,795; $3,404 with audiotape option.

Diamonds Program

Includes the Diamonds and Diamond Grading courses. *Tuition:* $1,095; $1,418 with audiotape option.

Colored Stones Program

This course includes the Colored Stones, Gem Identification, and Colored Stone Grading courses, studied in that sequence. Video included. *Tuition:* $1,895; $2,180 with audiotape option.

Graduate Jewelry Sales Program

This course includes Diamonds, Colored Stones, Jewelry Display, Counter Sketching, Fine Jewelry Sales, Advanced Fine Jewelry Sales, and Gold and Precious Metals. *Tuition:* $2,495; $2,995 with audiotape option.

Graduate School, USDA
Correspondence Program
Room 1114, South Agriculture Building
14th and Independence Avenue, S.W.
Washington, District of Columbia 20250
(202) 720-7123

Description:

The Graduate School of the United States Department of Agriculture is a private, nonprofit educational institution and receives no appropriated funds. It serves adults who have left full-time schooling and who want to continue to learn and cope throughout life. Its objective is to provide a dynamic continuing education program to help individuals improve their job performance, further their careers, and enrich their lives; to help organizations increase their efficiency, effectiveness, and productivity. The Graduate School does not grant degrees and has never sought that authority or accreditation. It features classroom instruction day and evening, special courses, seminars, workshops, consulting services, and correspondence study.

The school was established in 1921 by the Secretary of Agriculture. Since that time the school has helped more than one million people with their continuing education objectives. The school is open to all adults regardless of their place of employment or education background.

The U.S. Office of Personnel Management accepts Graduate School credits for examination and qualification purposes on the same basis as those from accredited schools. Some Graduate School courses have been designated as receiving college credit recommendations by the American Council on Education's Program on Noncollegiate Sponsored Instruction. These recommendations are listed in *The National Guide to Educational Credit for Training Programs* published by the American Council on Education/Oryx Press. The Program on Noncollegiate Sponsored Instruction "evaluates and makes credit recommendations for formal educational programs and courses sponsored by noncollegiate organizations who are nondegree-granting and who offer courses to their employees, members, or customers. The credit recommendations are intended to guide colleges and universities as they consider awarding credit to persons who have successfully completed noncollegiate-sponsored instruction."

Faculty:

Norma L. Harwood, Director, Correspondence Study Programs; Trumella Fullard, Program Specialist; Brenda Stewart-Walker, Program Assistant; Sister Grace Leslie, Staff Aide. Correspondence Study has a faculty of 50 members.

Academic Levels:
College
Noncredit

Degree/Certificate Programs:
Certificate of Accomplishment.

Admission Requirements:
Open enrollment for any course unless that individual course requires prerequisites. Overseas students welcomed.

Tuition:
Contact the school for current tuition and fees. Tuition is payable upon registration and includes specific charges for tuition, services, textbooks (if needed), and supplies. VISA, MasterCard, Diners Club accepted. Scholarship assistance available on a need basis; contact the school. Refund requests should be submitted in writing. If a student withdraws within 30 days of the official registration date, has submitted no lessons, and returns all books and materials in new condition, a full refund is given. A pro rata refund schedule based upon the number of CEUs for which the student has registered will be applied for withdrawal within 90 days of enrollment. There are no refunds after 90 days of enrollment.

Enrollment Period:
The maximum time for completion of a course is one year. If all assignments are not completed within this period, the course enrollment will expire. If requested before the expiration date, an additional year of time can be granted for a fee.

Equipment Requirements:
All necessary materials other than ordinary writing supplies are provided with registration. These include textbooks and references, course guides (lessons) and supplements, and any special paper or other supplies.

Credit and Grading:
Credit is awarded in semester hour units (converted from the quarter hour system January 1992). Examinations are proctored. Credits or CEUs for each course follow individual description below. Grading system: A, Excellent (90 to 100 percent); B, Good (80 to 89 percent); C, Fair (70 to 79 percent); D, Passing (60 to 69 percent); F, Failure (below 60); I, Incomplete; W, Official Withdrawal. Those who wish to assure the transfer of credits from the Graduate School to a degree-granting institution should obtain approval in advance from an official at that degree-granting

institution. Recommended credits for correspondence courses successfully completed at the Graduate School, USDA are listed in *The National Guide to Educational Credit for Training Programs* published by the American Council on Education/Oryx Press.

COLLEGE COURSES

ACCOUNTING

Principles of Accounting I

This course covers accounting principles and practices, including the accounting cycle, financial statements, accounting for merchandise and cash transactions, procedures for periodic reporting, accounts receivable and accounts payable, deferrals and accruals, and payables. (2 semester hours)

Principles of Accounting II

The course covers receivables, inventories, plant assets, notes payable, partnerships, corporations, and long-term debt. (2 semester hours)

Principles of Accounting III

This course covers statement of changes in financial position; financial statement analysis; accounting for decentralized operations and manufacturing operations; job order cost accounting; process cost accounting; standard cost accounting; profit reporting for management analysis; differential analysis; and accounting for individuals and nonprofit organizations.

REA Borrower Accounting (Electric)

Designed especially for employees of REA electric utility borrowers and others interested in their accounting procedures. The following topics are covered in the course: accounts and accounting records used through construction accounting procedure; methods of opening, maintaining, and closing books; financial and statistical reports and their analysis; technical aspects of REA electric-borrower accounting; continuing property records; budgeting; requesting, accounting for, and repaying REA loan funds. (1 semester hour) *Tuition:* $258.

REA Borrower Accounting (Telecommunications)

Designed for employers of REA telephone borrowers and others interested in telephone accounting procedures. The following topics are covered in the course: recommended books of account and basic accounting systems applicable to the telephone industry; accounting to be performed during the periods of organization, initial construction, and operations; requesting and accounting for REA and rural telephone bank loan funds; recommended plant accounting procedures including construction and retirement work order accounting. Successful completion of the course enables the student to understand accounting systems applicable to the telephone industry in general and to maintain accounting records and accounting procedures applicable to telephone utilities financed by loans approved by REA and/or the Rural Telephone Bank. (1 semester hour)

Cost Accounting I

This course covers job order cost accounting, inventory valuation procedures, and labor costs. (1 semester hour)

Cost Accounting II

This course covers process cost systems, production reports, average cost of work in process, by-product costing, joint costing; and allocation of common costs. (1 semester hour)

Cost Accounting III

Course covers planning and control involving use of cost data, budgeting manufacturing and non-manufacturing costs, standard costs, direct costing, breakeven analysis, capital expenditure analysis, and computerized cost accounting in a nonprofit service center. (1 semester hour)

Federal Government Accounting I

The course provides study and application of basic principles and practices of accounting in federal agencies. Concepts and methods of fund control systems. Practice with basic records—obligation control, cash disbursement, object class, general ledgers, and cost ledgers. Accounting for funding, processes-appropriation, apportionment, allotment, obligation, disbursement, and reimbursement. Transfer appropriation, accounts-consolidated, and working fund advances. (2 semester hours)

Federal Government Accounting II

This course covers property accounting, working capital funds, financial statements for federal government activities, budget execution reports and reports on obligations, transfer of obligating authority to field offices, and statement of financial condition for Treasury Department. (2 semester hours)

Internal Auditing I

This course covers professional standards and ethics, staff/line conflict relative to audits, preliminary surveys, elements that should be present for presentation of deficiency findings, use of computers for audits, and fraud prevention. (3 semester hours)

Internal Auditing II

Course covers legal requirements imposed on boards of directors relative to internal audits, coordination of internal and external audits, counseling of management based on the findings of the audit, and modern and updated audit procedures involving the use of computers and modeling. (3 semester hours)

Evaluating and Reporting on Internal Control Systems

This course covers the scope and background of internal controls, OBM guidelines, vulnerability assessments, documenting, evaluating, and reporting on cycles and related controls, and problem-solving methodologies. (1 semester hour)

COMPUTER SCIENCE

Introduction to Information Systems Technology

This course provides an overview of electronic digital computer data processing, with special emphasis on the history and evaluation of data processing, data representation, arithmetic, equipment, applications software, systems development cycle, and modes of processing. (2 semester hours)

Introduction to Computer Programming

This course covers the development of algorithms for computer programs, program development and debugging, flowcharts and decision tables, pseudocode, introduction to BASIC, introduction to FORTRAN, introduction to COBOL, system documentation and logical design, physical system design, and feasibility analysis and system implementation. (3 semester hours)

EDITING

Introduction to the Editing Process

Course covers editing techniques and processes, marking up copy for typesetting and determining format, composition (typesetting), and preparing front and rear matter. (3 semester hours)

Advanced Practice in Editing

Course covers copy editing, substantive editing, writing, and editing for specialized audiences, and publications management. (3 semester hours)

Proofreading

Course covers proofreading and proofmarks, measuring types and space, alternate marking systems, production process, procedures, tasks, queries and questions, and special proofreading problems. (3 semester hours)

Intermediate Editing Principles and Practices

The course covers copy editing, graphic design, copyright, and stylistic errors. (3 semester hours)

Printing, Layout, and Design

The course covers planning, printing, production, print media and the printing process, composition, book binding, typography and design, photographs, layout, copy editing, and design. (3 semester hours)

Thesaurus Building

Course covers interrelationships among terms, structure (alphabetical versus hierarchical display), and sources of thesauri. (1 semester hour)

Editing Technical Manuscripts

Course covers technical definitions, author-editor relationships, illustrations, procedures writing, international audiences, and review of camera-ready material. (3 semester hours)

Basic Indexing

Course covers index editing, index preparation, computers and indexing, and indexing as a business. (3 semester hours)

Applied Indexing

Covers letter-by-letter indexing; indexing style and format differences; time and cost estimates; merging index; hierarchical indexing; and comprehensive in-depth indexing. (3 semester hours)

Publishing Management

The course covers management practices of government and private publishing entities, including selection of supervisory staff, writers, and editors; government regulations on printing; copyright laws; Freedom of Information Act and Privacy Act; clearance and review procedures for policies, quality, and content; fitting and evaluating materials for various audiences; problems of distribution; reader surveys; economics of publishing; and a brief review of management principles. (3 semester hours)

Special Topics in Editing

This course covers abstracting, casting tables, editing with electronic equipment, indexing, and preparing charts. (1 semester hour)

ENGINEERING

Basic Electricity

Course covers fundamental concepts and safety; DC circuits; AC circuits; inductance and capacitance; electromagnetism; electrical instruction; and motors and transformers. (2 semester hours)

Basic Electronics

The course covers electronic principles, diodes, transistors and electric tubes, tuned circuits, detectors, amplifiers (audio, RF, power, IF), oscillators, receivers and transmitters, and transmission lines and antennas. (3 semester hours)

Solid State Fundamentals

This course covers PC boards, diodes, diode circuits, and testing of diodes, power supplies, other diodes (i.e., EDs and pressure sensors), transistors, transistor circuits, and transistor testing, SCRs and Triacs, integrated circuits, and introduction to fiber optics. (2 semester hours)

Electric Transmission and Distribution

The course covers theory; transmission terminal facilities; transmission lines; mechanical design; primary and secondary distribution systems; capacitors, transformers, and system protection; planning and load characteristics; and auxiliary equipment. (2 semester hours)

Electrical Wiring

The course covers wiring of single- and multiple-family dwellings; services for commercial and industrial establishments; and specialized and hazardous locations. Specifics include conductor sizing, grounding, panel sizing, cable types, and blueprint reading. (2 semester hours)

Hydraulics I

The course covers applicable units and their conversions: force, weight, mass, pressure, heat, and area; measuring devices such as parameters, manometers, and plezometers; Pascal and Archimedes laws; resolution of forces; moments, the hydrostatic pressure diagram; static loads on structures; and the stability of dams. (2 semester hours)

Hydrology I

This course covers elementary meteorology and statistics; measurements and interpretation of streamflow, precipitation, and other basic data; hydrologic cycles; physics of soil moisture; infiltration theory; and rainfall runoff relations. (3 semester hours)

Hydrology II

The course covers hydrographs and their uses; relationships between runoff, rainfall, and storm derivation; features and functions of reservoirs; and calculation of sediment load in a stream. (3 semester hours)

Strength of Materials

This course covers the basics of strength of materials including stress and deformation; engineering materials, and riveted joints; thin-walled pressure vessels and welded joints; torsion; centroids and moments of inertia; shear and moment in beams; stresses, design, and deflection of beams; statically indeterminate beams; combined stresses; columns; and impact loading and strain energy. (3 semester hours)

Fiber Optic Communications

This course covers optics and light wave fundamentals, optical fibers, integrated optics, light sources and detectors, light couplers and detectors, modulation, noise and detection, and system design. (2 semester hours)

Engineering Mechanics I (Statics)

This course covers basic principles, coplanar parallel and concurrent force systems, coplanar and noncoplanar nonconcurrent force systems, friction, center of gravity, centroids, and related aspects. (2 semester hours)

Engineering Mechanics II (Dynamics)

This course covers basic problems involving rectilinear motion, kinetic forces on rigid bodies, forces on bodies traveling along any path, rotational motion, forces perpendicular to the plane of motion, and forces of impulse and momentum. (2 semester hours)

ENGINEERING MANAGEMENT

Stormwater Management

The course covers the drainage basin, legal aspects of drainage, drainage planning, analysis of rainfall, engineering methodologies, floodplain management, and water quality. (3 semester hours)

ENGLISH

Better Letters

The course covers communication skills, rules for letter writing, measuring readability, and analyzing letters. (1 semester hour)

Writing for Government and Business

This course covers correct grammatical usage, rules of punctuation, spelling, and writing communications that readers can comprehend. (1 semester hour)

Introduction to Speechwriting

This course covers locating speech material, developing and supporting various types of speeches, maintaining audience attention through delivery, and audience analysis. (2 semester hours)

Report Writing

The course covers sentence structure, effective word usage and correct grammar, preparing reports for specific audiences, and composing long and short reports. (1 semester hour)

Effective Writing for Professionals

The course covers outlines and their use in writing, using grammatical reference sources, spelling and punctuation rules, writing for specific audiences, and appropriate use of active and passive audiences. (1 semester hour)

LIBRARY SCIENCE

Basic Reference Services and Reference Tools

This course covers the functions of a reference service; reference role of library technicians; characteristics of reference materials; analysis of questions; types of sources—dictionaries, encyclopedias, indexes and abstracts, bibliographies, U.S. government documents, geographical information sources, and nonprint media reference sources. (1 semester hour)

Introduction to Library Techniques

Course covers the role of the library technician, different types of library resources, basic library organization, and basic library services. (2 semester hours)

Descriptive Cataloging

The course provides an overview of cataloging functions in libraries; catalogs, cataloging cards and authority files, technical reading of a book, introduction to AACR2, access points and forms of entry, elements of bibliographic description: title, statement of responsibility, edition, publication place, date, publisher, physical description, and descriptive cataloging aids. (2 semester hours)

Library Media Services

This course covers administration, selection, evaluation, processing, and organization and maintenance of nonprint materials. (2 semester hours)

Subject Cataloging and Classification

The course covers general concepts of subject cataloging and classification of monographs, specific classification schemes, which include DDC, LCC, Cutter Expansive, Brown's, Colon Classification, SuDoc, Guelph, book numbers, LC and Sears Subject Headings lists, coordinate indexing, PRECIS, and MARC and bilbiographic networks. (2 semester hours)

The Use of Archives and Manuscripts

The course covers the history and types of archives, techniques for describing and using archives, archival resources in federal, state, local history, genealogy and church, university, and private institution archives, reference and finding aids, and special archives—maps, audiovisual materials, and machine-readable files. (3 semester hours)

Introduction to Bibliographies

The course covers the history of bibliographic systems in the United States, types of bibliographies, library resources used for identifying books, periodicals, newspapers, and nonprint materials, format and design of reports and bibliographies, and bibliographic citation procedures and styles. (2 semester hours)

MANAGEMENT

Modern Program Manager

This course covers strategic management, environmental analysis, preparation of budgets, designing program structures, the team concept, management by objectives, project planning, and evaluation. (1 semester hour)

Information and Records Management

This course covers the history and role of IRM, records inventory and disposition schedules, six basic file types, file maintenance and filing equipment, effective subject filing, correspondence management, directives, mail and copier management, forms management, maintenance of inactive records, and impact and importance of technologies. (2 semester hours)

MATHEMATICS

Calculus I

This course covers include variables, functions, limits, continuity, derivatives, maxima and minima, mean value theorem, and approximation methods for finding roots. (3 semester hours)

Calculus II

The course covers simple integration; the definite integral; approximation methods of integration and integration of trigonometric functions. (3 semester hours)

College Math

This course covers determinants, powers and roots, vectors, algebraic equations and fractions, scientific notations, analytic geometry, graphs, functions, trigonometry, and basic electric circuits. (3 semester hours)

METEOROLOGY

Dynamic Meteorology I

This course covers fundamental concepts, thermodynamics, thermodynamics of water vapor, hydrostatic equilibrium and geopotential, and stability. (3 semester hours)

Dynamic Meteorology II

This course covers vector analysis; equations of motion; horizontal motion; variations of wind, pressure, and thermal fields in the vertical; mechanism of pressure change; and weather prediction. (3 semester hours)

PARALEGAL STUDIES

Introduction to Law for Paralegals

This course covers constitutional law, criminal law, contracts law, tort law, wills and trusts law, real estate law, consumer protection law, skills of case analysis, and components of an opinion. (2 semester hours)

Business Law I

The course covers aspects of law essential to conduct of modern business; contracts, bailments, sales, and warranties. (2 semester hours)

Business Law II

The course covers aspects of law essential to conduct of modern business agency, partnerships, corporations, corporate stock and shareholders, personal and real property, leases, and estates and trusts. (2 semester hours)

Criminal Law

This course covers legal aspects of criminal law: elements of specific crimes, common defenses, and the proof necessary to convict persons of crimes. (2 semester hours)

Family Law

This course covers the legal aspects of divorce, annulment, separation, adoption, legitimization, alimony and child support, as well as related tax consequences of divorce and separation. (2 semester hours)

Legal Literature

Course covers statutory materials, court cases, administrative law materials, various secondary sources, uses of the computer in legal research, and updating materials. (2 semester hours)

Legal Research

This course covers statutory materials, court cases, administrative law materials, various secondary sources, use of the compute in legal research, updating materials, and writing memoranda and briefs. (2 semester hours)

Legal Writing I

The course covers leases, employment contracts, wills, case briefs, and interoffice memoranda. (2 semester hours)

Legal Writing II

Course covers pretrial writing in the form of a memorandum and pleadings; a trial brief; legal correspondence of various types; and legislative drafting. (2 semester hours)

Tort Law

This course covers duty owed, proximate cause, defenses, negligence, vicatious liability, product liability, strict liability, and defamation. (3 semester hours)

Constitutional Law

The course covers source and scope of judicial power; federal power to regulate interstate commerce; federal taxing and spending power; the state's exercise of police power; equal protection; racial discrimination, state action, economic, social discrimination; due process; the individual's right to privacy; freedom of speech, press, and religion; standing, mootness, and ripeness; political questions; and advisory opinions. (2 semester hours)

Wills, Trusts, and Estate Administration

This course covers client interview; tax considerations, intestacy, distribution by operation of law, elements of a will, trusts, complex wills, execution and other formalities, revocations, codicils and other means of changing a will, will substitutes, and probate. (2 semester hours)

Administrative Law and Procedure

This course covers principles and practice of administrative law in the federal field; provisions of Administrative Procedure Act dealing with formal and informal rulemaking and adjudication; notice, hearing, evidence, findings, and control by the courts, with a discussion of pertinent and applicable principles of constitutional law. (2 semester hours)

FOIA and the Privacy Act

The course covers the Freedom of Information Act: legislative history, publication, requirements, procedures and processing requests, ex-

emptions, and fees; and the Privacy Act: definitions, limitations of disclosure, access to records, publication requirements, exemptions and new systems reports. (2 semester hours)

Litigation

The course covers the process of civil litigation for paralegals; factual investigation of the client's case; preparation of pleadings and pretrial motions that are necessary to commence and defend a lawsuit; discovery devices available for obtaining relevant information from opposing and third parties and what to do with that information in preparing for a trial; and, finally, post-trial proceedings and settlement documents. (2 semester hours)

Real Estate Transactions

This course covers property rights and interests; legal aspects of real estate transactions and settlement; and drafting of a real estate sales contract and settlement documents. (2 semester hours)

PERSONNEL ADMINISTRATION

Federal Personnel Procedures

The course covers the background of federal personnel system, using the federal personnel manual, processing personnel actions, position classification, staffing and placement, affirmative employment, adverse actions, grievance and appeals, retirement, reductions in force, training, labor-management relations, and benefits and leave. (2 semester hours)

PHYSICS

General Physics I

The course covers kinematics, dynamics, gravitation, equilibrium, energy, fluids, temperature, kinetic theory, heat, thermodynamics, waves, and sound. (3 semester hours)

General Physics II

This course is a continuation of General Physics I and includes the introduction of electric field, magnetism, circuits, light and electromagnetic waves, relativity, quantum theory and quantum mechanics, atoms, radioactivity, and nuclear energy. (3 semester hours)

STATISTICS

Elements of Statistics

Major topics covered in the course are empirical frequency distributions, measures of central tendency, measures of variation, probability, sampling distributions estimation, tests of significance, regression and correlation, and nonparametric methods. (3 semester hours)

Advanced Agricultural Statistics

This course covers normal distribution, binomial distribution, student distribution, hypothesis testing and confidence intervals, regression, correlation, chi-square tests, analysis of variance, multiple regression, and sample surveys. (3 semester hours)

Sample Survey Methods

The course covers the principles of sample design, biases and nonsampling errors, simple random sampling, stratified simple random sampling, duster sampling, stratified cluster sampling, multistage sampling, double sampling, systematic sampling, sampling frames, and multiframe sampling. (4 semester hours)

SUPERVISION

Modern Supervisory Practice

This course covers planning, communications, decision making, problem solving, human behavior, and supervision. (2 semester hours)

Success-Oriented Supervision

The course covers leadership styles, motivation, problem solving, decision making, interviewing, and personnel functions. (2 semester hours)

Griggs University
12501 Old Columbia Pike
P.O. Box 4437
Silver Spring, Maryland 20914-4437
(301) 680-6570

Description:

Griggs University was founded in 1990 as a division of Home Study International. It offers programs leading to the Associate of Arts degree in personal ministries, Bachelor of Arts degree in religion, Bachelor of Arts degree in theological studies, adult education, and independent study. Contact the university for enrollment, tuition, and other requirements. For courses applicable to the degree programs, SEE **Home Study International.**

Faculty:

Dr. Joseph E. Gurubatham, President.

Accreditations:

Distance Education and Training Council.

Hadley School for the Blind
700 Elm Street
Winnetka, Illinois 60093   (312) 446-8111

Description:

The Hadley School is the world's only correspondence school for blind students. It was founded by William A. Hadley, himself blind, in 1920. All courses are offered to blind students throughout the world, tuition free. Hadley offers over 100 brailled and/or recorded courses and makes college-level courses available to blind students through cooperation with the Universities of Indiana, Loyola, California, and Wisconsin. Hadley's teaching staff, including the international offices, totals 82 (26 legally blind and 56 sighted). Hadley maintains eight overseas offices, furnishes (by request) a recorded anthology of articles taken from current periodicals and produces the *Hadley Focus* six times a year. Hadley School is supported entirely by gifts, grants, and bequests from foundations, corporations, service groups, and individuals. Toll-free telephone number outside Illinois: 1-800-323-4238.

Faculty:

Dr. Robert J. Winn, President; Steven Wilder, Director of Student Services. There is a faculty of 26.

Academic Levels:

High School
Noncredit

Degree/Certificate Programs:

Certificate; High School Diploma.

Admission Requirements:

Enrollees must be legally blind. There are no age or other admission requirements.

Tuition:

All Hadley courses are offered tuition free to blind students throughout the world.

Enrollment Period:

No minimum or maximum time requirements to complete a course. Students may enroll at any time during the year, but may not take more than three courses at any one time.

Equipment Requirements:

Braille and/or cassettes furnished. Students must have their own braillers, cassette players, and typewriters, depending upon their own needs.

Credit and Grading:

Graduation from the Hadley High School Program requires the completion of 16 Carnegie units. Credit is given for all high school courses previously completed. Programs available for both High School Diploma and the Equivalency GED Examination. The Hadley School College program cooperates with various universities to offer courses through their correspondence divisions. Hadley does not offer a college degree; most universities will accept approximately 32 credit hours by correspondence. Course examinations are submitted by students to Hadley professional staff for correction, grading, and return. No proctored examinations. Grading system: A, Excellent; B, Above Average; C, Average; D, Below Average but Passing; NG, No Grade; NC, No Credit (Final).

Job Placement Assistance:

Counseling and guidance provided by all faculty and student service staff members for job placement and other assistance whenever possible.

Accreditations:

Distance Education and Training Council; North Central Association of Colleges and Schools as a special function school; National Accreditation Council for the Visually Impaired.

HIGH SCHOOL COURSES

BIBLE

New Testament Survey

A complete and concise survey of the writings of the New Testament, including the Gospels, Acts, the Epistles, and the Book of the Revelation of St. John. (½ unit)

Old Testament Law and History

A survey of the historical writings of the Old Testament from Genesis through Esther. (½ unit)

Old Testament Poetry and Prophecy

A survey of the poetical and prophetical writings of the Old Testament from Job to Malachi. (½ unit)

Your Bible

This course examines the origin of scripture texts, preservation of manuscripts, development of translations and formation of the canons of both Old and New Testaments. (½ unit)

BRAILLE

Braille Placement

A placement test for the student who has had previous experience with Grade One Braille. Lesson reports must be submitted in written or recorded form. Upon successful completion of the required material, the student is enrolled in English Braille II, the study of Grade Two Braille. (Noncredit)

Braille Writing

A comprehensive course for the student who reads Grade Two Braille and wishes to master correct braille writing skills. Braille reports are required. Students must have access to braille writing materials (slate and stylus or braille-writer). (½ unit)

English Braille I

First steps in braille reading. This course will enable the student to read letter-by-letter braille as well as the numbers and punctuation marks. Lesson reports must be submitted in written or recorded form. (½ unit)

English Braille II

This course takes over where English Braille I stops. The student will learn to read all the abbreviations of Grade Two Braille, and the world of literature will be at his/her fingertips. Lesson reports must be submitted in written or recorded form. Prerequisite: English Braille I, Relevant Braille, or Braille Placement. (½ unit)

English Braille Reading Review

A collection of short stories to sharpen braille reading skills. This course will provide an excellent review of all Grade Two Braille symbols. Reports must be submitted in written or recorded form. Prerequisite: Grade Two Braille skills. (½ unit)

Essentials of Nemeth

The Nemeth Code is the braille code for the special signs and symbols used in mathematical and scientific materials. This course will teach how to read the Nemeth Code. The student must master the code before he/she can take courses in the mathematical or scientific areas. Prerequisite: Good Grade Two Braille skills. (½ unit)

Grade Three Braille

A special system of highly contracted braille for note taking and speed in writing. Prerequisite: Competency in Grade Two Braille. (½ unit)

Rapid Braille Reading

This course utilizes the latest techniques of rapid reading as taught to the sighted so that higher braille reading speeds can be achieved. Prerequisite: Good Grade Two Braille reading ability. (Noncredit)

Relevant Braille

This is a course in reading and writing Grade One Braille. It is intended for the person who wishes to do his major reading by recordings, and wants the additional advantage of reading and writing personal notes, recipes, addresses, telephone numbers, etc. Success in these skills can form the basis for the later study of Grade Two Braille. (Noncredit)

BUSINESS

Business English

A comprehensive review of grammar, spelling, punctuation, proper capitalization and the use of figures in business letters. Also included are exercises in deductive logic and lists of troublesome words. Typed reports required. Prerequisite: Business English Profile. (½ unit)

Business English Profile

A placement test to determine course entry in the Business English Curriculum. (Noncredit)

Business Law

A study of the concepts and rules of human relations to provide the theory behind the language of the law, the courts and how they work. Areas covered include: agency, personal property, sales, legal instruments, ownership, insurance, credit and collections, government regulation of business, guaranty and suretyship. (1 unit)

Business Letter Writing

A course in the mechanics and techniques of effective business correspondence. Topics include: format, style, letters of acknowledgment, mail ordering, letters of application, etc. Typed reports required. Prerequisite: Business English Profile or Elements of Expression. (½ unit)

Computer Science

A course in the concepts of data processing intended to provide some of the theory behind new accounts, automated inventory control, and payroll processing - along with the development of step-by-step procedures for these and other business applications. Techniques for problem solving, flow-charting, compiling, testing and documentation are presented. Upon completion of the course, the student will be in a position to evaluate his interest in pursuing further training in business data processing or computer programming. (1 unit)

Economics

This course is an introduction to the study of Economics. Topics include: supply and demand, buying and selling, consuming and producing, labor and full employment, credit, the free enterprise system, government and general welfare, the welfare budget, deficit spending, procedures for measuring economic health and techniques for budgeting and planning for personal economic security. (1 unit)

Financing in the American Economy

A comprehensive study in the world of finance and economics. Topics covered include consumers and their role with government and business, the corporation, financing, capital and equity stock, banking and the federal reserve system, methods of financing an institution, lending institutions and economic functions of government. Prerequisite: Introduction to Business Management. (1 unit)

Introduction to Business Management

An overview of the world of business which covers marketing, management, finance, and personnel. Topics covered include written and oral communication, marketing, advertising, purchasing, budgeting, accounting, data processing, and labor-management relations. Prerequisite: 3 years high school. (½ unit)

Managing People

The focus of this course is on the psychological principles of handling problems with people and major areas of personnel management. The text covers employee motivation, communication, delegation of authority, decision making, promotions and salaries. Prerequisite: Introduction to Business Management. (1 unit)

Principles of Marketing

This course covers all phases of marketing. Topics include: market research, packaging, distribution, promotion, sales, wholesale vs. retail, and trademarks. The text deals with the intricacies of marketing in a changing business environment. Prerequisite: Introduction to Business Management. (1 unit)

CLASSICAL AND BIBLICAL LANGUAGES

Classical Greek

A survey of Greek grammar and literature of the ancient Hellenic period. Prerequisite: 3 years of high school. (1 unit)

Classical Hebrew

A comprehensive introduction to Biblical Hebrew. Prerequisite: 3 years of high school. (1 unit)

Latin

I. An introduction to the Latin language and to the study of ancient Roman civilization. The relationship of English to Latin is stressed. (1 unit)

II. A continuation of Latin I. The material provides vivid glimpses of Roman life. Prerequisite: Latin I. (1 unit)

III. Selected readings from the Roman classics. Prerequisite: Latin II. (1 unit)

New Testament Greek

An introductory grammatical survey of New Testament Greek. Prerequisite: 3 years of high school. (1 unit)

COMMUNICATIONS SKILLS

Basic Typing

I. A typing course for the student who wishes to gain keyboard knowledge, personal and business letter writing, and general typing skills. (½ unit)

II. This is a continuation of Basic Typing I. Topics include: skill building, symbol learning, horizontal-vertical centering, timed tests, and manuscript writing. Prerequisite: Typing keyboard knowledge or Basic Typing 1. (½ unit)

College Typewriting

Carefully planned lessons and special projects provide structured practice material and procedures that have been classroom tested and proved effective. (½ unit)

Effective Listening

A course designed to show the importance of developing effective listening skills. The student will learn how to improve these skills, how to take notes, how to get the important points from a lecture, and how to be a good listener in both business and personal situations. Chapters on sound environment, noise pollution, and leisure listening are included. (½ unit)

Speech

Practical, helpful lessons in voice development, effective oral communication, and persuasive speech. (½ unit)

DEAF-BLIND STUDIES

Independent Living Without Sight and Hearing

A practical course for deaf-blind adults. Topics include: adjustment, communication methods, voice recreation, travel, education, employment, available services, etc. Enrollments are also accepted from blind persons with normal hearing, sighted persons, or anyone who has an interest in the deaf-blind. (Noncredit)

ENGLISH

A Stepladder to English Grammar

A self-paced, multilevel approach to learning the fundamentals of English grammar. Prerequisite: English Profile. (Noncredit)

Advanced Composition

This course is for the student who has a mastery of grammar, syntax, and general composition techniques. It covers most types of writing, but stresses the need for creativity as well as method. Prerequisite: Writing Placement.

Beginners' English

In this course, the student is introduced to basic sentence structure in a clear, concise way. It lays the groundwork for further pursuit of grammar at a higher level. Excellent for the student whose native tongue is not English. (Noncredit)

Creative Writing

A course recommended for aspiring writers. It presumes a mastery of grammar, punctuation and spelling. This course concentrates entirely upon techniques and content. It will allow the student to try fiction and non-fiction writing. Typed reports required. (½ unit)

Early America

For a description of this course, which carries ½ unit of English and ½ unit of Social Science, *SEE* **Social Science.**

Elements of Composition

An introduction to methods and techniques of writing smooth, unified, and effective sentences and paragraphs. Near the end of the course, the student submits one complete essay. Prerequisite: Writing Placement. (½ unit)

Elements of Expression

This course covers good sentence-building, sentence variety, verbs, modifiers, punctuation, paragraphs, etc. Prerequisite: English Profile. (½ unit)

English Grammar Review

A thorough review of word forms, punctuation, and sentence structure. Everything the student needs to know about English grammar. Prerequisite: English Profile. (½ unit)

English Literature to 1900

An historical survey of English Literature from its beginnings to 1900. Selections from representative works are offered. (1 unit)

English Profile

A preview examination for correct and effective use of English. Composed of five parts: spelling, capitalization and punctuation, grammar, recognition of parts of speech, and usage. This course is a placement test for A Stepladder to English Grammar, Elements of Expression, and English Grammar Review. (Noncredit)

Essentials in Spelling

I and II. The aim of this program is perfection in spelling. Training in spelling is combined with practice in writing sentences. This course is ideal for high school students. (½ unit)

Modern American Literature

A survey and guide to twentieth century trends in the literature of the United States. The approach is both analytical and critical. (½ unit)

Modern English Literature

A survey and guide to twentieth century English literature. (½ unit)

Verse Writing

I. This course offers detailed instruction on composing poems artistically for the modern reader and a study of traditional verse structure. Prerequisite: submission of two original poems. (½ unit)

II. Presents a complete treatment of all traditional verse forms. Topics include rhyme, meter, imagery, symbolism, and figures of speech. Abundant practice is offered in constructing poetic composition. Prerequisite: Verse Writing I. (½ unit)

Writing Placements

Placement tests are designed to reveal the student's knowledge of punctuation and the more sophisticated aspects of grammar and sentence structure so that he can be enrolled in one of three courses: Elements of Composition, Advanced Composition, or Creative Writing. Reports must be submitted in braille or printed form. (Noncredit)

GENERAL EDUCATION DEVELOPMENT TEST (GED)

GED Test Preparatory Program

I. A series of five diagnostic tests will determine which skills are strong or in need of improvement. Available in braille or on cassette. (Noncredit)

II. Six lessons designed to help the student increase his reading speed and comprehension, and to interpret reading materials in social studies, natural sciences, and literature. Available in braille or on cassette. (Noncredit)

III. This course tests the student's knowledge of English grammar, spelling, punctuation, and usage. Available in braille or on cassette. (Noncredit)

IV. A review of the fundamentals of mathematics, with an introduction to algebra and geometry. Available in braille only. (Noncredit)

V. A brief survey of the basic parts of the Constitution, emphasizing the branches of government. Available in braille or on cassette. (Noncredit)

INTERNATIONAL LANGUAGES

English Through French, I - IV

1 Braille volume per level and a variable number of cassettes depending upon the needs of the individual student. (1 unit per level)

English Through Italian, I - IV

1 Braille volume per level and a variable number of cassettes depending upon the needs of the individual student. (1 unit per level)

English Through Portuguese, I - IV

1 Braille volume per level and a variable number of cassettes depending upon the needs of the individual student. (1 unit per level)

English Through Spanish, I - IV

1 Braille volume per level and a variable number of cassettes depending upon the needs of the individual student. (1 unit per level)

English Conversation, I - IV

Conversations in the English language designed to meet the needs of the individual student. Prerequisite: A working knowledge of the English language. (1 unit per level)

Spanish Braille

Prerequisite: Fluency in the Spanish language. (½ unit)

Spanish-American Literature

I. Lectures in Spanish on colonization, independence, and literary movements to 1910. (1 unit)

II. A continuation of the preceding course. Deals with the contemporary period from 1910 to the present.

Spanish Literature

I. Lectures in Spanish covering major literary movements—drama, poetry, and prose from 1140 to 1700. Prerequisite: Fluency in the Spanish language. (1 unit)

II. A continuation of the preceding course. Covers the years 1701 to the present. (1 unit)

MATHEMATICS

Abacus

I. Instruction in the everyday use of the abacus for business and personal needs. (½ unit)

II. A continuation of the preceding course. This course covers all aspects of fractions, percentages, and square roots. (½ unit)

Applied Mathematics

A study of the basic concepts and structures of mathematics, intended to develop proficiency in addition, subtraction, multiplication, division, fractions, decimals, percentages, etc. Prerequisite: Knowledge of the Nemeth Braille Code for Mathematics or completion of Lessons 1–5, Essentials of Nemeth. (1 unit)

Doing It the Metric Way

This course covers the basic units of measurement used in the metric system. The meter, liter, gram, and kilogram are discussed. The Celsius System and Derived Metric Units are described in detail. The historical development of the Metric System and the prospects for its future growth in the United States are highlighted. Prerequisite: A background in basic mathematics. (½ unit)

General Mathematics

Beginning with a review of fractions, decimals, and percentages, this course covers ratio and proportion, profit and loss, interest and taxation, work and distance problems, geometric figures, symbolic arithmetic and a basic introduction to algebra and geometry. Prerequisite: knowledge of Nemeth Code for Mathematics or completion of Lessons 1–5, Essentials of Nemeth. (1 unit)

MODERN LANGUAGES

English I Through French

An introduction to conversational English for French-speaking people. Prerequisite: Grade One French Braille. (1 unit)

English II Through French

A continuation of English I Through French, and introduction to English Braille Grade Two. Prerequisite: English I Through French. (1 unit)

Esperanto One

With a basic vocabulary of approximately 800 words, this course has a conversational approach from the first lesson on. The text is easy and excellent for beginners. It also offers a quick and practical review for those with some experience in the language who want to further develop their conversational abilities. Prerequisite: Grade Two Braille reading skills. (1 unit)

French

I. An introduction to the pronunciation and grammar of the French language. Readings in French deal with the literature, life, history, and culture of the French. Prerequisite: Grade Two Braille reading skills. (1 unit)

II. A sequel to French I, with similar features. Selections from the works of well-known French authors are included. (1 unit)

III. An introduction to French Literature. This course includes a review of grammar and punctuation, with practical exercises. Prerequisite: French II. (1 unit)

IV. A reading course in French Literature. Prerequisite: French III. (1 unit)

French Braille Abrege

II. An introduction to contracted French Braille. Prerequisite: 2 years of French and English Braille Grade Two reading skills. (½ unit)

III. A continuation of the preceding course. Upon completion of this course, the student will be able to read publications produced in French Braille. (½ unit)

German

This course is based on a conversational textbook widely used in schools, colleges, and universities. The course is particularly applicable to students and tourists, and especially valuable for people of German descent. The course contains, in addition to many practical exercises and a functional vocabulary in the textbook, a selection of German orchestral music and songs, courtesy of the German Consulate in Chicago. (1 unit)

Italian

I. This course has a conversational approach from its very beginning. It is useful for beginners, vacationers, or for those who wish to use it in their schoolwork. (1 unit)

II. This course follows the same methodology as the preceding course. (1 unit)

Modern Hebrew

A grammatical study of Hebrew as it is used today. Prerequisite: 3 years of high school. (1 unit)

Spanish

I. Basic conversational Spanish through exercises in pronunciation, grammar, and reading. (1 unit)

II. A sequel to Spanish I, with similar features. (1 unit)

III. A reading course which introduces the student to the culture and civilization of Spain. Prerequisite: Spanish II. (1 unit)

IV. A study based on contemporary Spanish braille magazines. The student has the opportunity to increase his vocabulary and write compositions in Spanish. Prerequisite: Spanish III. (1 unit)

MUSIC

Braille Music Notation

Instruction in reading the Braille Music Notation Code, which is based on the Literary Braille Code. Piano is emphasized, but there are lessons for voice, strings, and organ. Some formal music training is essential. The course is in braille, but students are asked to submit their lessons on cassette. Prerequisite: Accuracy in reading and writing Grade Two Braille. Student must submit a brailled account of his music background and interest. (½ unit)

Music Appreciation

An introduction to the history, terminology, and theory of music. (½ unit)

RADIO COMMUNICATION

Amateur Radio

I. This course includes elementary theory and regulations to prepare for Exam Element 2 for the Novice Class FCC license. Study and practice materials for the Morse Code (3 code tapes and oscillator) are provided after the first lesson is satisfactorily completed. Prerequisite for students using braille version of test: A knowledge of the Nemeth Braille Code for Mathematics or completion of Lessons 1–5, Essentials of Nemeth. (Noncredit)

II. This course includes general theory and regulations to prepare for Exam Element 3 for the General Class FCC license. Prerequisite: Amateur Radio I or a Novice Class License. (1 unit upon completion Amateur Radio I and II)

III. This course will include intermediate theory and regulations to prepare for Exam Element 4A for the Advanced Class FCC license. Prerequisite: Amateur Radio II or a General Class license.

REHABILITATION FOR THE VISUALLY HANDICAPPED

Career Planning

Provides guidelines for the visually handicapped person who is seeking a secure and satisfying place in the world of work. Topics include the labor market, choice of an occupation, self-evaluation, community resources, how to secure a job, and retirement plans. (½ unit)

First Aid Without Fear

This course contains first aid information designed specifically for the blind. (½ unit)

Foods

Evaluates and describes kitchen equipment, appliances, and procedures with emphasis on aspects specific to the blind. Later chapters concern the basic food groups, all categories of baking, and use of the home freezer. (½ unit)

General Home Making

Deals with scheduling household duties, cleaning the home, budgeting, entertaining, child care, safety, sewing, and personal grooming. (½ unit)

Home Repairs

Information and up-to-date resources on home repairs. Topics include tool selection, painting, electrical and plumbing repairs, etc. (½ unit)

Introduction to Rehabilitation

Practical guidance for the blind adult. This course covers the history and availability of braille, the experience and effects of blindness, the meaning and methods of rehabilitation, and opportunities for mobility, employment and recreation. (1 unit)

Laundry

Discusses the washing and drying of common fibers, fabrics, and finishes and explains the action of soaps, detergents, water softeners, and other products used in laundering. (Noncredit)

You, Your Eyes, and Your Diabetes

Facts about diabetes written in clear, concise language for the visually-impaired diabetic. This course concentrates on the diabetic who has recently experienced visual complications, and helps him/her to understand and deal with his/her problem.

SCIENCE

General Science

This course covers many interesting areas in the field of general science, including weather, properties of matter, basic astronomy, sound, heat, light, etc. (1 unit)

Personal Health and Hygiene

A course designed to help the student achieve and maintain well-being of mind and body. Topics include nutrition, exercise, fatigue, skin care, dental care, mental health, etc. (½ unit)

The Human Eye

An informative course on the biology of the eye, eye disease, accident prevention, and treatment. This course is particularly useful to teachers and paramedical professionals who deal with newly-blinded patients. Both sighted and blind students may apply for enrollment. (½ unit)

SOCIAL SCIENCE

Bicentennial History for Americans

A course designed to focus attention on the crucial years of 1760–1790. Topics include: The Colonial Wars, Declaration of Independence, Yorktown, New Governments, Making a Constitution, Meaning of the Constitution. (½ unit)

Canadian History

The story of Canada from the Viking explorations to the present day. This course will insure the Canadian student a deeper appreciation of his country's history and will give other students a better understanding of Canada. (½ unit)

Citizenship

Here are the necessary facts about the functions and structures of the federal government for the person preparing to become an American citizen. For the citizen, this course provides the opportunity to rediscover the meaning of being an American. (½ unit)

Early America

This course covers literature dealing with the first two and a half centuries of our nation's history. Topics include exploring and settling of America, the development of an American society, the American Revolution, framing the Constitution, and the Westward movement. (½ unit)

Personal Psychology

An introduction to the principles of psychology with emphasis on a practical understanding of human behavior. Topics include heredity, environment, motivation, persuasion, emotions, mental health, job satisfaction and techniques of learning. (1 unit)

Rights and Responsibilities

A study detailing the Bill of Rights. In this course, through the study of actual court cases, the student will learn one's rights as a citizen; why one has these rights; where one's rights originated; and how these rights are interpreted, enforced, and protected. (½ unit)

World History

I. A study of the ancient and medieval worlds with emphasis on Europe and Asia. The Renaissance and the exploration of the Western Hemisphere are treated in depth. The course ends with a discussion of the Protestant Reformation. (1 unit)

II. A study of the political, economic, and social developments of the modern world from 1750 to the present. Prerequisite: World History I. (1 unit)

VOCATIONAL TRAINING FOR THE VISUALLY HANDICAPPED

Introduction to Medical Transcription

Instruction for the student who wishes to work in a hospital setting. The student studies office procedures, etymology, and medical vocabulary. Prerequisite: Profile Test for Medical Transcription. (½ unit)

Medical Transcription

A course for the potential expert in medical transcription. The skills to be learned include transcribing complex medical reports from actual recordings dictated by doctors, covering a variety of medical situations. Prerequisite: Introduction to Medical Transcription. (½ unit)

Profile Test for Medical Transcription

A cassette tape profile test to be transcribed into both Grade Two Braille and typewritten form. Successful completion of this assignment will enable the student to be enrolled in Introduction to Medical Transcription. (Noncredit)

Selling Techniques

A current treatment of the selling process. Topics include practical ways to develop a winning telephone technique, how to make your voice your selling asset, ways to improve sales, how to overcome sales objections, and much more. (½ unit)

Health Insurance Association of America

Insurance Education Program
1015 Connecticut Avenue, N.W.
Suite 211
Washington, D.C. 20036-3998 (202) 223-7780

Description:

The Health Insurance Association of America (HIAA) is a voluntary trade association whose membership consists of approximately 340 insurance companies which are responsible for about 85 percent of the United States and 90 percent of the Canadian health insurance business written by insurance companies. The general purpose of the Association is to promote the development of voluntary health insurance for the provision of sound protection against loss of income and financial burden resulting from sickness or injury.

The Association has sponsored a formal educational program since 1958 that currently consists of a two-part individual health insurance course and a three-part life/health insurance course. These courses are designed to give the student comprehensive knowledge and understanding of the technical as well as the socioeconomic aspects of the group life/health and individual health insurance business.

Tuition:

Contact the Health Insurance Association for enrollment procedures and current cost information.

Equipment Requirements:

HIAA provides self-study materials that candidates can use to prepare for examinations. Guides for Course Leaders are available for Group Life/Health Parts A and B.

Credit and Grading:

Achievement in these course is assessed through a comprehensive examination for each course part. Students' principal method of preparation for final examinations is through independent study. Examinations must be supervised.

Accreditations:

Courses have been evaluated by the Program on Noncollegiate Sponsored Instruction, The Center for Adult Learning and Educational Credentials of the American Council on Education. Recommendations for credit are listed in *The National Guide to Educational Credit for Training Programs* published by the American Council on Education/Oryx Press.

PROFESSIONAL COURSES

HEALTH INSURANCE

Group Life/Health Insurance: Parts A, B, and C

This course in three parts requires approximately 150 hours to complete. The course aims to furnish students with a comprehensive knowledge of the technical and socioeconomic aspects (Parts A and B) as well as the advanced and specialty areas (Part C) of the group life and health insurance business.

Part A: Covers development of group health insurance, analysis of coverages, marketing, underwriting, pricing and rate making.

Part B: The contract, issue and administration, claims, financial analysis of group operations, regulations, and taxation, industry organizations.

Part C: Design and funding of group life and health insurance for traditional insurance coverages, retired employee, flexible benefits, rehabilitation, automobile, homeowners and legal programs; health care cost containment approaches, thorough introduction to data processing and its function in group insurance. Instructor-directed or self-instructional with supervised examinations.

Individual Health Insurance: Parts A and B

This course requires approximately 100 hours to complete, including test preparation and testing time. The course aims to enable students to have an in-depth understanding of individual health insurance and of the social and economic responsibilities of the industry.

Part A: History and development of health insurance; types of coverage; contracts; marketing; and understanding.

Part B: Claims; premiums and rates; regulation and taxation; government program (U.S. and foreign); cost, delivery, and financing of health care.

Home Study International
12501 Old Columbia Pike
Silver Spring, Maryland 20904

(301) 680-6570

Description:

Formerly known as Home Study Institute, Home Study International (HSI) was established in 1909, enrolling 130 students that first year. It has an enrollment of over 2,000 students, maintains six overseas branches, and provides correspondence education for kindergarten, elementary, secondary, and college levels. Although designed to serve the needs of the Seventh-day Adventist school system, it has always welcomed anyone who wished to study, whether for self-improvement or for upgrading in education. Griggs University, a division of Home Study International, offers programs leading to the associate and baccalaureate degrees.

Faculty:

Dr. Joseph E. Gurubatham, President; Dr. Alayne Thorpe, Education Director.

Academic Levels:
College
High School
Elementary

Noncredit

Degree/Certificate Programs:

Home Study International does not grant the baccalaureate degree, but its courses may be used as transfer credits to many colleges which do grant degrees. Griggs University, a division of Home Study International, was founded in 1990 and grants the Associate of Arts degree in personal ministries, Bachelor of Arts degree in religion, Bachelor of Arts degree in theological studies, adult education, and independent study. HSI courses may be used as transfer credits. HSI awards a High School Diploma and certificates of promotion for each elementary grade level.

Admission Requirements:

For elementary school, a formal application is required; also a report card (or copy) of previous year; a written statement from the previous principal regarding grade placement; if this is the first time in school, the student must take an evaluation examination. For high school, written permission from the school the student is presently attending is required. Eighth-grade students may enroll for high school courses with written permission from present school official. For college courses, graduation from high school or equivalency certificate is required; high school seniors may enroll for college courses with written permission from present school official. At the discretion of Home Study International, students over 21 may be permitted to take college courses without a high school diploma.

Tuition:

Preschool course $75; kindergarten course $195; grades 1–6 $265; junior high school $110 per course—five to six courses possible—plus $30 enrollment fee; high school $270 per unit (two-semester course) with $60 enrollment fee; college $35 per semester hour with $60 enrollment fee. Monthly payment plan available. Refund policy: cancellations must be submitted in writing. For a full refund, cancellation must be made within 5 business days after midnight of the date of the postmark of the application. After five days, if no tests or lessons have been graded, a percentage of the tuition will be retained. If a student withdraws after a number of lessons/exams have been graded, HSI will retain a fee plus a percentage of the tuition, based on how much of the course has been completed.

Enrollment Period:

Courses are geared so that each lesson/submission takes about one week (of a regular school-time course) to complete.

Equipment Requirements:

Costs of textbooks are extra and are paid for by the student. Texts may be purchased from Home Study Institute.

Credit and Grading:

Midterm and final examinations must be supervised by a school official or a responsible adult who is not a member of student's family; weekly lesson assignments are open book. There are periodic examinations, depending upon the number of lessons in the course. For most courses, the semester (final) exam counts approximately 50 percent of the final grade; midterm exams count for 25 percent, and lessons for 25 percent. Grading system: A, B, C, D, F. Minimum passing grade is D-. The pass/fail option is not available.

Accreditations:

Distance Education and Training Council. Member of: National University Continuing Education Association; International Council for Distance Education.

COLLEGE COURSES

BIOLOGY

The Human Body in Health and Disease

A survey of the structure, function, health, and diseases of the human body. Emphasis is placed on the understanding of the physiologic mechanisms that maintain each body system. A general foundation in the vocabulary of anatomy and physiology is a primary part of the course. Normal body structure and function are used as the basis to present information on human health and disease principles. (4 semester hours)

A Scientific Study of Creation

A study of the evidences supporting a Creative origin of the earth. The approach is scientific rather than Biblical. (2 semester hours)

BUSINESS

Principles of Accounting I

An introduction to accounting, books of original entry, statements of condition and operation, and controlling accounts. Practice set work and elementary work related to income tax. (3 semester hours)

Principles of Accounting II

A study of statements, worksheets, and periodic adjustments for proprietorship, partnership, and corporate forms of business organizations. (3 semester hours)

Introduction to Business

This course introduces the student to what really goes on in the business world. Topics include industry, finance, accounting, marketing, economics, management, etc. (3 semester hours)

Typing

A skill-building course for the development of speed and accuracy. An introduction to typing letters, reports, tables, and forms. (4 semester hours)

Principles of Marketing

This course provides the student with an introduction to marketing management. It is based upon applying the marketing system to the analysis, planning, implementation, and control of marketing situations. It is founded upon the marketing concept and the process of market segmentation. (3 semester hours)

COMMUNICATIONS

Introduction to Oral Communication

A study of the theory, basic levels, and forms of communication. Instruction in the processes of oral expression with practice in interpersonal, nonverbal, small group, and public speech exercises. (3 semester hours)

EDUCATION

Philosophy of Adventist Education

A course in the philosophy of education with particular emphasis on the principles of Seventh-day Adventist education. (3 semester hours)

Health Education

A practical and theoretical study of health education in elementary and secondary schools. Students examine all aspects of contemporary school health practice and all common health problems of school children. Practical experience in health education is gained by evaluation of a health education program. (3 semester hours)

Teaching Social Studies

A practical course that approaches social studies teaching from a management perspective, with emphasis on involvement in the kind of learning activities teachers will use in the classroom. (3 semester hours)

The Teaching of Reading

A course describing in detail workable methods for teaching reading as a basic skill. (2 semester hours)

Mathematics in the Elementary School

The theories of learning and mental development related to teaching mathematics; how skills in basic arithmetic operations and numbers concepts are taught at the elementary level; and the individualized laboratory approach. Includes practical suggestions for the Christian teacher and an introduction to resources for continued learning. (3 semester hours)

Evaluation in Teaching

This course examines the relationship between teaching, learning, and evaluation; the use of instructional objectives; how to choose and use standardized tests; how to construct and use classroom tests to measure specific learning outcomes; and how to award fair marks. (3 semester hours)

Fundamentals of Curriculum Development

Emphasis is placed on design, development, and upgrading of curriculum for the elementary and secondary schools. Includes a focus on the conceptual framework of our society that often forces change in curriculum. (3 semester hours)

ENGLISH

Composition

This course is designed to advance writing skills for college and professional pursuits by bringing observation, thoughtfulness, organization, sense of audience, and sense of self to bear on student writing. (3 semester hours)

Research and Literature

A study of poetry, short stories, drama, and the process of writing a research paper. (3 semester hours)

American Literature: Beginnings to 1860

A survey of American literature from colonial times to the Civil War. (3 semester hours)

American Literature: 1860 to Present

A survey of American literature from the Civil War to the present day. (3 semester hours)

American Literature

A survey of American literature from the Puritans to the 20th century. (4 semester hours)

English Literature

Provides students with exposure to the canonical works of the English literary tradition. Introduces students to the major literary genre and the historical periods that produced them. (4 semester hours)

English Literature: Beginnings to Renaissance

A comprehensive survey of the leading English authors, from old English times to 1800, in the context of their literary and historical times. Special emphasis is placed on literary analysis and interpretation, with regular composition assignments. (3 semester hours)

English Literature: Renaissance to Present

A comprehensive survey of English literature from 1800 to the present with emphasis on literary analysis and interpretation. (3 semester hours)

Charles Dickens and Mark Twain

Students will read major works of each author, placing their artistic development into historical context, investigating the role of each author as a representative, critic, and reformer of his own society, and analyzing the way each author uses humor as social commentary. (3 semester hours)

FRENCH

French I

An introduction to written and spoken French through a study of basic vocabulary and grammar; listening and speaking skills developed with cassette tapes and notes on phonetics; and information about the French culture. (4 semester hours)

GEOGRAPHY

Cultural Geography

A regional and cultural study of various countries, with emphasis on the interrelationships of the social and physical aspects of these areas. The principal features of climate topography, resources, and industry are portrayed through factual and cartographic studies. (4 semester hours)

GREEK

Elementary Greek I

A study of the elements of the language of the New Testament; a good working vocabulary and carefully selected readings provided. (4 semester hours)

Elementary Greek II

A continuing study of the elements of the language of the New Testament; a good working vocabulary and carefully selected readings provided. (4 semester hours)

Intermediate Greek I

The aim of this intermediate course in Greek is to provide a fair working knowledge of the New Testament in the original language. (3 semester hours)

Intermediate Greek II

This course continues to refine the student's working knowledge of the New Testament in the original language. (3 semester hours)

HEALTH

Health Principles

A study of physiology, including the principles governing community and personal health and the methods of applying these principles to successful daily living. (2 semester hours)

Nutrition

A course designed not only to provide an introduction to the relationship between nutrition and good health, but to explore the basic medical and chemical aspects of nutrition. (3 semester hours)

HISTORY

History of World Civilization I

The development of civilization from antiquity to the mid-17th century with emphasis on the political, economic, and other cultural institutions as they affected the development of man. (3 semester hours)

History of World Civilization II

The development of civilization from the mid-17th century to the present with emphasis on the political, economic, and other cultural institutions as they affected the development of man. (3 semester hours)

American Civilization I

The political, social, constitutional, and cultural development of the United States from its earliest beginnings to the Civil War. (3 semester hours)

American Civilization II

The political, social, constitutional, and cultural development of the United States from the Civil War to the present. (3 semester hours)

American Government

An introduction to the forms, functions, and processes of the American national government. this course also explores the development of political ideologies and influence groups. (3 semester hours) semester hours)

Early Christian Church

The significant trends and events in the development of Christianity from the time of Christ to the Reformation, including a study of the church in relation to the Roman Empire, the influence of the church fathers, Christological controversies, the rise of the papacy, and medieval society. (3 semester hours)

Modern Christian Church

The church from pre-Reformation to the present time, its development in Europe and in America. A study of the main branches of Protestantism and their relation to the State, the Catholic Counter Reformation, and the Evangelical movement. (3 semester hours)

MATHEMATICS

College Algebra

An advanced study of linear, quadratic, and simultaneous equations; laws of exponents; graphs; progressions; variations; the binomial theorem; and logarithms. (3 semester hours)

Probability and Statistics

Introduces the student to common elementary descriptive and inferential statistical concepts and procedures used in research and business. It is designed for individuals who have basic arithmetic skills and knowledge of fundamental research methodologies. Emphasis is placed on practical applicaitons rather than theoretical explanation. (4 semester hours)

MUSIC APPRECIATION

Music Appreciation

The student is introduced to music history and composition. The course also helps the student develop a sensitive ear. (3 semester hours)

PSYCHOLOGY

Introduction to Psychology

The basic principles and concepts in psychology, including the principles of motivation, learning, and perception. Designed to introduce college students to history, development, and present scope of psychology with additional emphasis on non-Western psychological approaches. (3 semester hours)

Organization and Work

Focuses on describing, understanding, and explaining behavior in organizations. The issues of controlling, managing, and influencing behavior in the work environment are addressed. (3 semester hours)

Psychology of Learning

A survey of fundamental psychological principles and theories related to the problems and methods of learning and teaching, and to the understanding and development of the individual learner. (3 semester hours)

Independent Study in Psychology

Provides an opportunity to work in collaboration with an instructor on a research project in psychology. It is a means to understanding and conducting research using the appropriate methods and presenting that research in a viable manner. (1 to 3 semester hours)

RELIGION

Bible Survey

A book-by-book study of both the Old and New Testaments designed to provide a foundation for other religion courses for those students who have not had secondary Bible. (4 semester hours)

Jesus and the Gospels

A comprehensive study of the life and teachings of Jesus as unfolded in the four gospels with analytical attention to the gospel writers and their writing in an attempt to reveal the impact of His self-revelation on that age and ours. (3 semester hours)

Principles of Christian Faith

An intensive topical study of the Bible truths that form the foundation and structure of Christian belief as understood by Seventh-day Adventists. (3 semester hours)

Adventist History

An investigation of Seventh-day Adventist church history with a preliminary review of backgrounds and foundations of the Advent message from apostolic times. Concentration on the church's beginnings in America, the 1844 experience, history, organization, and development of the Seventh-day Adventist denomination in America and in the world with special attention being given to the writings of the prophets, particularly Ellen G. White. (3 semester hours)

World Religions

A general course dealing with world religions and contemporary expressions of faith; the distinctions between cult, sect, and denomination; and the place of dialogue and mission in a religiously pluralistic world. (3 semester hours)

Prophecies of Daniel

A verse-by-verse examination of one of the most important prophetic books in the Bible; one whose messages are vital to those living in the last days. (2 semester hours)

The Book of Revelation

A study of the last book of the Bible, and the most important prophecies in the New Testament. Particular study is given to those prophecies that focus on the return of Christ. (2 semester hours)

Old Testament Prophets - Early

A study of the writings of the "early" Old Testament prophets arranged in chronological order. (3 semester hours)

Old Testament Prophets - Later

A study of the writings of the "later" Old Testament prophets arranged in chronological order. (3 semester hours)

Christian Ethics and Modern Society

Designed to aid students in applying the principles of Christianity to the ethical issues of modern society. (3 semester hours)

Acts and the Epistles

A detailed examination of the exciting stories of the first-generation Christians as they struggled to spread their faith. Students will study Acts and all of the epistles of Paul (3 semester hours)

Science and Christian Belief

A thorough and detailed examination of the harmony between science and the Bible. This course helps the student see the complementary relationships between the Word of God and natural law. (1 semester hour)

Prophetic Guidance

A study of one of the principal means by which God communicates with people. The work of His prophets in Old Testament times is explained. The tests and functions of a true prophet are examined. The works and life of Ellen G. White and God's influence on His remnant church through her are stressed. (2 semester hours)

SOCIOLOGY

General Sociology

A general introduction to the basic forms of human association and interaction dealing with the social processes, institutions, culture, and personality development. (3 semester hours)

SPANISH

Spanish I

A study of simple spoken and written Spanish with a small amount of practice in writing and speaking. Cassette tapes build accurate pronunciation and provide listening exercises. (4 semester hours)

Spanish II

The reading, grammar, and composition needed for a better knowledge of the language. Continued practice with spoken Spanish. (4 semester hours)

THEOLOGY

Principles of Bible Instruction

Seeks to help the student develop the necessary skills and expertise that are vital for success in Bible instruction. The course strives to be neither too preachy nor too academic while catering to the academic needs and emphasizing the need for a close encounter with God. (3 semester hours)

Church Leadership and Management

This course addresses the four-dimensional role of the pastor—person, administrator, church leader, and priest. (3 semester hours)

Personal Evangelism

A study of the dynamics of personal evangelism, with primary emphasis on instruction rather than exhortation. A clear biblical perspective on the priesthood of all believers; practical counsel for leading someone to Christ; a strategy for visitation; a Bible study methodology; and techniques in getting decisions. (3 semester hours)

Practicum in Ministry

Specialized training program for theological studies majors. (2 to 3 semester hours)

HIGH SCHOOL COURSES

BUSINESS

Bookkeeping and Accounting

A career-oriented approach to basic accounting principles featuring an integration of manual and automated accounting systems. The student learns how to organize financial records. (1 unit)

Typing

A skill-building course for the development of speed and accuracy. An introduction to typing letters, reports, tables, and forms. (1 unit)

Word Processing

A skill-building course that introduces the student to word processing in general and WordPerfect in particular. Students will refine skills learned in typing while developing formatting skills and learning the fundamentals of desktop publishing. (1 unit)

ENGLISH

English I

An introduction to literary forms and the devices that produce quality writing; a study of the structure of words and sentences; and practice in writing sentences, paragraphs, and short compositions. (1 unit)

English II

Personal experiences, interests, and opinions serve as a springboard to writing. Polishes skills taught in English I. Literary models provide stimulating examples of paragraph unity and development of word choice. (1 unit)

American Literature

A study of the leading American authors from colonial days to the present with attention to their lives, the times in which they lived, and the changes in literary ideology that affected their work. Students learn major literary techniques and genres. Practice in composition is provided and the ability to analyze literary works is stressed. (1 unit)

English Literature

A study of the major English writers in the context of historical time periods. Trends and ideologies are emphasized and the sociological influence of prominent writers is discussed. Composition practice is included, chiefly in the framework of the analysis of literary works. (1 unit)

Structure of Writing

A thorough study of English grammar and usage provides a basis for honing writing skills. Assignments in keeping a journal and expository and descriptive writing are included. (½ unit)

Adventist Literature

Concepts of good literature are studied through examples from the works of Seventh-day Adventist writers, past and present. Included are the essays, character sketches, poetry, short stories, and hymn lyrics. A large part of the course is devoted to the study of Ellen White's book *The Desire of Ages*. (½ unit)

FRENCH

French I

An introduction to written and spoken French through a study of basic vocabulary and grammar; listening and speaking skills developed with cassette tapes and notes on phonetics; and information about the French culture. (1 unit)

French II

More practice in spoken French with an increased emphasis on reading, grammar, and composition. (1 unit)

HEALTH

Health

While studying physiology and anatomy, the student becomes aware of the components of good health and the importance of physical fitness. The student explores how the relationship between mind and body affects health. Topics include natural remedies, the effects of tobacco and drugs, first aid, Christian sexual conduct. (½ unit)

HISTORY

World History

A careful and thought-provoking overview of world history from ancient times to the twentieth century. The student will study the great issues, inventions, figures, and ideas which made the past and shaped the present. (1 unit)

American History

An in-depth examination of the founding and development of the United States. Students will follow the growth of America from a handful of colonies to one of the world's most powerful nations. A study of colonial times, the organization of the nation, and its history to the present. (1 unit)

American Government

A comprehensive survey of the operation of federal, state, county, and city governments: statute making, diplomacy, labor policies, public finance, etc. Emphasis is placed on the work of the government in promoting the interests of the people and in addressing itself to current topics. (1 unit)

HOME ECONOMICS

Clothing Construction

The student learns sewing techniques and expands his/her wardrobe by preparing the attractive garments assigned. An observer/supervisor who knows how to sew well is required. Topics include: selection and alteration of patterns, techniques for repairing and laundering garments, principles of dress and grooming. (½ unit)

Foods

This course provides a basic knowledge of the fundamentals of nutrition and meal planning. Topics include: the healthful preparation of food, benefits of a vegetarian diet, managing the food budget, preparing well-balanced meals, setting an attractive table. (½ unit)

Home Planning

Students learn the "hows and wherefores" of home buying and owning. Topics include: choosing the type and location of a new home, financing, furnishing the rooms, interior decorating. (½ unit)

MATHEMATICS

Consumer Math

The fundamental math skills and how to use them in solving practical consumer problems. Budgeting your money, income and property taxes, investing in stocks and bonds, finding interest rates, sales tax and commissions, choosing your credit union or savings account. (1 unit)

Algebra I

Topics covered include integral equations, factoring, fractions, simultaneous equations, quadratic equations, the theory of exponents, graphs. (1 unit)

Algebra II

This course carries the advanced student further into the field of mathematics as he begins to apply skills taught in Algebra I and Geometry. This course cannot be divided into semesters. (1 unit)

Geometry

The student is introduced to the principal concepts of geometry and is armed for all courses in higher mathematics. (1 unit)

RELIGION

Bible I - Breakthrough With God

Through the study of the book of Genesis and the Gospel of Matthew the young Christian discovers God's plan for the human family as originally conceived and as it was demonstrated in the life of Jesus Christ. Bible principles for guidance in daily living are brought into focus. Creation, the Flood, the patriarchs, origin and history of the Bible, Jesus, repentance and belief, baptism, prayer, and the Sabbath. (1 unit)

Bible II - Breakthrough with God's Church

Traces the history of the church from Old Testament times and the early Christian believers on down to today, revealing how God's overall plan and purpose have been carried out in the affairs of nations. The last section helps the student to develop Christian standards in music and social relationships. (1 unit)

Bible III - Breakthrough with God's Word

The steps in becoming a follower of Christ and the dynamics of Christian growth and living are studied in the writings of Paul and others. The Bible becomes and indispensable companion and guidebook in the student's search for truth. (1 unit)

Bible IV - Breakthrough with God's World

Counsel for maturing to adulthood. Specific topics studied are self-realization, choosing a vocation, entering post-secondary education, witnessing, handling financial matters, marriage, physical fitness, and relating to the community. (1 unit)

SCIENCE

Biology

An introductory course that surveys the structure, function, classification, and interrelationships of living organisms. The first semester includes the chemical and hereditary nature of life and a survey of microbes and multicellular plants. The second semester covers the vertebrates and man, and ends with the ecological relationships of living things. (1 unit)

Chemistry

Designed to meet various curriculum requirements, this is an introductory course covering chemical theory and descriptive chemistry, with emphasis on the structure and periodicity of the elements. Reinforced with simple lab experiments. Topics include: chemical energetics, measurement, structure of atoms, bonding, stoichiometry, gases, ionization, hydrocarbons, oxidation, and reduction. (1 unit)

SPANISH

Spanish I

A study of elementary Spanish. Practice in speaking and writing is an integral part of the course. Cassette tapes help to develop accurate pronunciation and provide listening exercises. Topics covered include: verb conjugation, counting, nouns and pronouns, sentence patterns, vocabulary, and spelling skills. (1 unit)

Spanish II

This course develops and refines skills taught in elementary Spanish and concentrates on the reading, grammar, and composition needed for a better knowledge of the language. (1 unit)

NONCREDIT COURSES

ADULT EDUCATION

The Work of the Bible Instructor

The study of the call and the work of the Bible instructor emphasizing methods of giving and correlating Bible studies. Suggestions for meeting common objections and a helpful analysis of the relation of the Bible instructor to other workers in the field are included. (Noncredit)

Literature Evangelism

A practical study of techniques for approaching clients, delivering the canvass, and closing sales for gospel literature. Purpose, attitude, commitment, and personal preparation are emphasized. (Noncredit)

ELEMENTARY COURSES

ELEMENTARY SCHOOL

Kindergarten

The Kindergarten course includes the following topics: Character Development; Bible; Health Science; Social Studies; Handwriting; Language; Reading; Mathematics.

Grade One

Courses are available in the following subjects: Art and Music; Bible; Health Science and Social Studies; Language; Reading; Mathematics; Spelling; Handwriting.

Grade Two

Courses for this grade level include: Art and Music; Bible; Health Science and Social Studies; Language; Reading; Mathematics; Spelling; Handwriting.

Grade Three

Courses are available as follows: Art, Music, and Physical Education; Bible; Health Science and Social Studies; Language; Reading; Mathematics; Spelling; Handwriting.

Grade Four

Courses for this grade level include: Art, Music, and Physical Education; Bible; Health Science and Social Studies; Language; Reading; Mathematics; Spelling; Handwriting.

Grade Five

Available for this grade level are: Art, Music, and Physical Education; Bible; Health Science and Social Studies; Language; Reading; Mathematics; Spelling; Handwriting.

Grade Six

The following courses are offered for this grade level: Art, Music, and Physical Education; Bible; Health Science and Social Studies; Language; Reading; Mathematics; Spelling; Handwriting.

Junior High School

Seventh Grade. Courses available at this grade level are: Bible; English; Mathematics; Social Studies; Science and Health; Elementary Typing.

Eighth Grade The following courses are offered for this grade level: Bible; English; Mathematics; Science and Health; United States History; Elementary Typing.

ICI University
6300 North Beltline Road
Irving, Texas 75063   (800) 444-0424

Description:
ICI University was founded as International Correspondence Institute in 1967 by the Division of Foreign Missions of the Assemblies of God. In 1972 ICI moved to Brussels, Belgium to facilitate its international purpose: to provide courses and academic programs suited to independent study instruction.

Faculty:
Dr. George M. Flattery, President; J. Warren Flattery, Education Director; Dr. Robert A. Love, University Relations; Dr. Carl B. Gibbs, Dean of Bible and Theology. There is a faculty of 18 plus 84 subject specialists.

Academic Levels:
College
Noncredit

Degree/Certificate Programs:
Bachelor of Arts, 128 credit hours; Advanced Diploma, 96 credit hours; Associate of Arts, 64 credit hours; Advanced Certificate, 14 to 17 credit hours. In the degree program, majors in Bible, Theology, Missions, Religious Education, Church Administration, and Church Ministries are offered. A student who already possesses a Bachelor of Arts degree may study for a second one with ICI for which a minimum of 32 additional credit hours are required.

Admission Requirements:
Open admission except for the degree program. For a degree, the student must submit a certificate or diploma indicating completion of secondary level (high school), or by earning a grade of at least "C" in ten degree program subjects.

Tuition:
$69 per credit for United States students. In other nations, tuition is set by the ICI National or Regional Director. There is a program application fee, a final examination fee, and postage per course. Contact ICI for scholarship assistance and for refund policy information.

Enrollment Period:
One year is allowed to complete a given subject. A time extension may be granted upon application and payment of an additional fee. Most subjects can be finished within three months with regular study at the rate of 8 to 12 hours per week. Group study in resident school classes is encouraged.

Equipment Requirements:
Textbooks for the degree program courses may be purchased from ICI, or if they are available, through local bookstores. Study guides and student packets designed for each course must be purchased from ICI through the national offices. Costs for these materials are included in the course price (excluding postage).

Credit and Grading:
Final examinations are administered by an official ICI examiner. Grading scale: 90-100 percent (Excellent); 80-89 percent (Above Average); 70-79 percent (Average); 60-69 percent (Below Average); 59 percent or less (Unacceptable). An average of 70 percent in all ICI course work attempted is required for graduation. The minimum passing grade is 60 percent.

Library Services:
Many ICI National Directors provide library services either personally or through relationships with libraries or resident schools.

Accreditations:
Distance Education and Training Council. Member of: Association of European Correspondence Schools; International Council for Distance Education; National University Continuing Education Association.

COLLEGE COURSES

BIBLE

New Testament Survey
Knowledge, change, action: these terms reflect the objectives of Dr. Jesse Moon for the course. A panoramic view unifies the messages of the various doctrines, personalities, and problems. (3 credits)

Old Testament Survey
The work of God in relation to man begins in the Old Testament. All the events from man's creation up to the point of his redemption occur in this larger portion of the Bible. These events are dissected into their historical and prophetic contexts. Along with the progression of the nation of Israel, individuals who made significant contributions to this progress are thoroughly discussed. (3 credits)

Galatians and Romans
From its earliest days the Christian church has raised questions concerning the relationship between law and grace. These questions are examined in the light of Paul's letters. In addition to the interpretive study of these letters, other interesting details concerning the life and ministry of the apostle Paul are presented. (3 credits)

Gospel of John
The life, character, and ministry of Jesus Christ are examined, not only in their historical context but also from the divine perspective presented by John the Evangelist. (2 credits)

Genesis
An interpretive study of Genesis. The thread of God's plan of redemption is traced from its beginning promise in Eden to the formation of God's chosen people through whom it would be realized. (2 credits)

Acts
Deals with the continuing ministry of the resurrected Christ in the world through the Holy Spirit. (3 credits)

Hermeneutics
Hermeneutical principles and rules. (3 credits)

Corinthians

An in-depth study of the Corinthian letters. An overview of 2 Corinthians is included in this course. (3 credits)

Themes from the Major Prophets

A study of Isaiah, Jeremiah, and Ezekiel. (3 credits)

The Minor Prophets

The twelve books of the minor prophets; course covers their contributions as seen in the light of their times and ours, the doctrines they preached, the meanings and fulfillments of their prophecies. (2 credits)

Pentateuch

Traces the origin of both the earth and mankind in general. Included in the course are studies on the creation theories, the Flood, and the concept of holiness in the Book of Leviticus. (3 credits)

Old Testament Historical Books

An interpretive survey of the historical books of the Old Testament, from Joshua through Esther. It covers about 1000 years from the entrance of the nation of Israel into the Promised Land until its return after the Exile. The background, structure, and content of each book is examined. (3 credits)

Hebrews

Analytical and topical studies to bring out the Christological truths in the epistle to the Hebrews. (2 credits)

Greek I

This course is an introduction to the fundamentals and grammar of the Greek New Testament. Includes a study of certain verb, noun, pronoun, and adjective forms. In addition, the student learns to apply his knowledge to the translation of selected portions of scripture. Audiocassette tapes accompany this course. (4 credits)

Greek II

Continues the study in basic elements of the grammar of the Greek New Testament. Presented are certain verb, noun, pronoun, and adjective forms on a more detailed level than in *Greek I*. Emphasized are those elements of syntax, and concepts of grammar that are essential to translation and exegesis. (4 credits)

Hebrew I

This course is a study in the Semitic language of the ancient Hebrews. Basic fundamentals of Hebrew are stressed with attention given to these skills in translation. (4 credits)

Hebrew II

This course is a continuation of *Hebrew I* with study of Hebrew vocabulary, grammar, and syntax. It enables the student to read, understand, and translate the easier passages of narrative prose in the Hebrew Bible. Audiocassettes accompany this course. (4 credits)

CHRISTIAN MINISTRIES

The Bible and the Church

The student investigates the nature and authority of the scriptures. Also considered are the biblical basis for the church, its Old Testament antecedents, its beginning, nature, and purpose. (2 credits)

God and Angels

A study of the biblical doctrines of God and angels. Presents a broad biblical view of the subject to help the student understand better the nature of God and angels. (2 credits)

The Life of Christ

This course is a study of the life of Christ from the viewpoint of the synoptic Gospels—Matthew, Mark, and Luke. (2 credits)

The Corinthian Letters

This course covers the study of 1 and 2 Corinthians and gives the student a view of life in the city of Corinth and the problems which these epistles were written to correct. The course provides a deeper insight into the apostle's character and ministry. (2 credits)

Themes from the Major Prophets

A study of Isaiah, Jeremiah, and Ezekiel. (3 credits)

A Study in the Book of Hebrews

Analytical and topical studies to develop the main themes in the epistle to the Hebrews. (2 credits)

Daniel and Revelation

A study of biblical prophecy which concerns events of the end-time. The course covers passages of other Old and New Testament books, in addition to Daniel and Revelation, when such passages help promote a better understanding of biblical prophecy. The second coming of Jesus Christ is the central theme of the course. (2 credits)

Paul's Letters to Pastors

A basic study of the epistles of 1 and 2 Timothy and Titus that describe God's strategy for a healthy church. (2 credits)

Evangelism Today

Examines the biblical principles and modern techniques of effective evangelism. (2 credits)

The Church's Educational Task

Examines what the Bible has to say about such concepts as teaching, training, and religious instruction. In general, the course discusses the church's role and responsibility to train and instruct its members and families in the Word of God. (2 credits)

The Work of the Pastor

Focuses on the pastor's call to and preparation for Christian ministry. Examines the relationships that are vital to successful ministry, and reviews the pastor's primary responsibilities. (2 credits)

The Worship of God

This course is designed to give a clear understanding of Christian worship as it is directed by the Holy Spirit. Presents biblical models of worship as guidelines for both individual and corporate worship. (2 credits)

The Bible and Missions

A biblical study about the missionary task of the church. Focuses on world evangelism and discipleship. (2 credits)

CHRISTIAN SERVICE

A Study of Bible Doctrines

An introductory and systematic study of basic Bible doctrines. Major topics include the nature of God, the acts of God, the activities and limitations of angels, the Creation, the fall of man, God's redemptive plan, the origin of Scriptures, the church, and God's ultimate plan for mankind. (1 credit)

A Study of Salvation

Concerns the doctrine of salvation. It presents salvation as both the will and work of God which rests upon the atoning work of Christ. The biblical teaching on election and foreordination is examined as background for consideration of the respective roles of God and man in salvation. Included in this study are the biblical teachings of repentance, faith, conversion, regeneration, justification, adoption, sanctification, and glorification. (1 credit)

A Study of the Holy Spirit

An introductory course on attributes of the Holy Spirit and His activities in the world from Creation to the present. (1 credit)

A Survey of the New Testament

Emphasizes the historical setting, characteristics, and teachings of the books of the New Testament. (1 credit)

A Survey of the Old Testament

An introduction to the Old Testament. Emphasizes the history of God's people, paying special attention to God's mighty acts and the prophetic words He gave concerning those acts. It deals with the sequence and meaning of the experiences of God's people. (1 credit)

Studies in Hermeneutics

This course interacts with the student on methods of carefully organized Bible study. The student learns effective techniques for general study and then applies them to the Bible by means of study questions. (1 credit)

Studies in Christian Maturity

Introduces the subject of the Christian's growth. Gives attention to the role of Christian service in the believer's growth and leads the student to interact constantly with the Word of God. (1 credit)

Studies in Church Ministry

A practical study of the church and the men and women who make it a reality. The course pays special attention to the church's redemptive ministry and the need for the believer to participate actively in this ministry. (1 credit)

A Study of Spiritual Gifts

Gives attention to three different groups of spiritual gifts: (1) gifts of ministry, (2) other ministry gifts, and (3) gifts of the Spirit. (1 credit)

A Study of Christian Ethics

Deals with the sources or problems, methods of problem solving, and ways of finding solutions from a Christian perspective. Major universal problems are presented, such as problems in social and family relationships, problems of the single person, problems related to human sexuality, and problems related to suffering and death. The course gives biblical solutions for all of these problem areas, and it develops principles which provide a solid foundation for the Christian to find solutions for problems—his or those of others. (1 credit)

Studies in Prayer and Worship

Emphasizes the priority of God's glory and God's kingdom over man's needs and wants. Prayer and worship as they relate to Christian service are particularly emphasized. (1 credit)

Studies in Starting New Churches

Stresses the importance of establishing new churches as a means of evangelization Gives guidelines to that any local church can be involved in planting churches. (1 credit)

A Study of Preaching and Teaching

A basic study of two Bible methods of communicating God's Word. The student is guided in the understanding and mastery of practical ways to prepare and present lessons and sermons from Scripture. (1 credit)

A Study of Christian Leadership

A course that presents the biblical foundations of leadership. Introduces the student to the theory and practice of leadership and guides him in the application of both biblical and theoretical principles. (1 credit)

Studies in Christian Stewardship

A study of what the Bible says about stewardship. (1 credit)

Studies in Christian Education

A study of the biblical basis for the nurturing ministry and the practical application of teaching in the church today. Gives emphasis to the needs of the pupils in various stages of human development and to the various opportunities for Christian nurturing through the ministry of local church programs, sharing groups, and the Christian home. (1 credit)

Studies in Personal Evangelism

A practical course on the important ministry of soul winning. (1 credit)

A Study of Christian Character

Involves a practical study of Galatians 5 and related Scriptures. Emphasizes the development of Christian qualities and their outworking in the Christian's relationships and service. Also emphasizes biblical definitions and examples in describing the nine dimensions of spiritual fruit and makes practical applications that relate these characteristics to the individual Christian life. (1 credit)

CHURCH MINISTRIES

A Strategy for Church Growth

Designed to acquaint the student with the importance of the Great Commission in relation to world evangelization. Identification of the principles that underlie the growth of the church. (3 credits)

Introduction to Missions

Two mission themes, international and biblical, are treated throughout this course. (2 credits)

Principles of Preaching

An introduction to the spiritual and practical techniques of sermon preparation and delivery. Attention is given to the sermon's parts, classification, organization, content, logical principles, functional elements, and spiritual principles. (3 credits)

Introduction to Christian Education

An overview of the function and the place of Christian education in the local church today. The course summarizes the biblical, theological, historical, and philosophical foundations, as well as the basic objectives of Christian education. It also examines the materials and methods for Christian teaching, and it surveys various educational agencies in the church, the process of administering a Christian education program, the development of effective leadership in the church, and the specific roles of the pastor and the director of Christian education. (3 credits)

Pastoral Ministries

An examination of the minister, his preparation, his relationships, and his primary ministerial responsibilities. (3 credits)

Church Business

An introductory study of many of the principles, procedures, and techniques used in today's business world as they apply to the local church and its leadership. (3 credits)

Expository Preaching

A practical course in the methodology of preaching, emphasizing the step-by-step process of constructing expository sermons. (3 credits)

Teaching in the Church

Develops skills needed to understand the problems and possibilities associated with teaching others to teach creatively. (3 credits)

Christian Counseling: Agape Therapy

A paraprofessional approach to Christian counseling. (3 credits)

Worship: A Biblical Survey

A biblical survey of worship based on the theme "Worship in Spirit and Truth." The study searches the biblical text from Genesis to Revelation, reviewing and interpreting those Scriptures which provide insights for worship in the Spirit. (2 credits)

Christian Education Leadership

this course increases the student's knowledge of the theoretical aspects of leadership and of administrative roles. It also presents practical applications in the local church situation. Examines both the secular and Christian ideas of leadership and relates them to Christian education. Other leadership needs and principles for the church are also covered. (3 credits)

Introduction to Church Music

The course deals specifically with music in church services, in evangelism, in cross-cultural ministry, and as an adjunct to Christian education. (2 credits)

Pastoral Counseling

This course is primarily concerned with teaching the student about the people he counsels, the techniques of counseling, and the various forms of counseling. Using a strong biblical emphasis, this course considers the student to be a counselor-in-training. (2 credits)

Agape and Human Relations

Based upon a biblical model, this course focuses on practical applications for individuals in all of their relationships: with God, with others, and with themselves. (3 credits)

GENERAL STUDIES

Introductory English

A fundamental course in the beginnings of grammatical English. Among the topics discussed are nouns, adjectives, phrases and clauses. This course is an introduction to English grammar. (3 credits)

English Composition

An analytical and synthetic study of the skills necessary to perform an efficient level of college writing. Fundamental skills are defined and applied through usage, with traditional writing forms examined to provide the student with logical methods of development and illustration. (3 credits)

Basic English

Includes letter writing, sentence patterns, grammar fundamentals, punctuation, and mechanics. (2 credits)

Writing Better English

This course shows how an author's point of view and choice of language determine style. Covers grammar fundamentals not discussed in *Basic English* and looks at the forms an English sentence may take. Shows how varying forms can add interest to writing. The course demonstrates how to organize sentences into effective paragraphs and use them to narrate, describe, explain, or persuade; also discusses some useful, special topics such as outlining, research, report, and summary writing. (2 credits)

Fundamentals of Music

A study of the value and function of music as an avenue of human expression and ministry within the church. Covers basic concepts of melody, musical scale systems, major and minor tonality, rhythm, and harmony, along with the system of musical notation. Suggestions are given for the development of a music program in the church. (2 credits)

People and Their Beliefs

A survey of ten of the prominent living religions of the world: Animism of the Third World, religions of India (Hinduism and Sikhism), of East Asia (Taoism, Confucianism, Buddhism, Shintoism), and of the Middle East (Judaism, Christianity, and Islam). (2 credits)

Guidelines for Leadership

This course provides students with a contemporary theology of Christian leadership. It discusses leadership theory, presents servanthood leadership as a model for Christian leaders, discusses biblical principles of leadership and describes the major functions of leadership. (2 credits)

The Church: Pentecost to the Reformation

An introductory study of Christianity from its birth to the beginnings of the Reformation. The course provides an introduction to history as a discipline and emphasizes the importance of history in relation to Christian faith. Deals with the apostolic church, the early church fathers, the ecumenical councils, the emergence of medieval theology and church practice, and the beginning of the Renaissance in Europe. The course content includes a consideration of major Christian theologians, the relationship of the church and state, and the rise of monasticism and missions. (2 credits)

Introduction to Psychology

An interpretive study of psychology designed to enhance understanding of intrinsic values, motivational response techniques, and peer relationships as they apply to all aspects of Christian life and service. (3 credits)

How to Speak in Public

Designed to increase the student's awareness of the importance of speech in all areas of life and human cultures. Main emphasis is on the values of Christian ministry through speech. (3 credits)

General Physical Science

The fundamentals of science with particular emphasis on areas of physical science which affect the student from day to day. (3 credits)

Sociology

A general survey course about the nature and scope of sociology, including its basic methods and concepts. (3 credits)

World Religions

This course furnishes a survey of eight of the nine major nonbiblical religions of the world: Islam, Zoroastriansim, Hinduism, Buddhism, Sikhism, Confucianism, and Shintoism, with Jainism receiving minor consideration. The final unit presents a survey of Judaism and Christianity and concludes with a comparison of all world religions. (3 credits)

Principles of Teaching

The first unit deals primarily with the characteristics and needs of students at different ages and how Christian teachers can meet these needs. The second unit looks into the fundamental responsibilities of the teacher and how to fulfill them. The third unit provides practical help in the use of modern educational methods, while the last unit presents the steps in preparing, presenting, and evaluating the lesson. (3 credits)

Logic

A study of the rules of straight thinking. This course makes such rules explicit by identifying and analyzing arguments of various kinds.

Many of the applications concern contemporary Christian life and ministry. (3 credits)

Educational Psychology

Deals with the application of psychological knowledge to the design and guidance of educational experiences. A Christian perspective is maintained and the role of the Holy Spirit is emphasized. Wherever possible, applications of psychological principles to Christian education are described. Prerequisite: a course in Introductory Psychology. (3 credits)

Cross-Cultural Communication

This course addresses: how communication and culture relate, how to reach people where they are, how different people think and express ideas across cultures and subcultures, and how the thoughts and expressions of people affect their behavior. (2 credits)

Principles of Journalism

This course is designed to help the student to develop the ability to write as an extension of Christian ministry. Application of the principles of journalistic writing. (2 credits)

Church History I

Compares the trends of social, cultural, and political development as they relate to present-day civilization and the role of the church. (3 credits)

THEOLOGY

The Bible and the Church

This course is a basic study of bibliology and ecclesiology. The student investigates the nature and authority of the Scriptures. The second half of the course considers the biblical basis for the church, its Old Testament antecedents, its beginning, nature, and purpose. (3 credits)

Theology Proper and Angelology

A systematic study of the biblical doctrines of God and angels. (2 credits)

Pneumatology

The person, work, gifts, and ministry of the Holy Spirit are examined in this biblical study. (3 credits)

Christology

An introduction to Old Testament typology as well as to the prophecies concerning His present and future work. Presents controversial historical and contemporary views of Jesus and relates them to the Word of God. (2 credits)

Soteriology

A study of the doctrines of salvation—the work of Christ in bringing lost man into fellowship with God. This study includes the doctrines of repentance, faith, conversion, regeneration, justification, adoption, sanctification, and prayer in the life of a Christian. (2 credits)

Anthropology and Hamartiology

Discusses the teachings of Scripture and seeks to correct false ideas with regard to man and sin. The course is structured in such a way that the materials will be applicable to the student personally and to his/her ministry. (2 credits)

Eschatology

A study in the doctrine of Eschatology or the area of biblical teaching dealing with the final outcome of the present order. Addresses the teachings of "end times" and gives the biblical picture of the events and their importance in relation to contemporary Christian life. The second coming of Christ, tribulation, and the value of predictive prophecy are among the topics discussed. (2 credits)

Old Testament Biblical Theology

This course traces the development of major Old Testament doctrines. It deals with what the Old Testament teaches about God, creation, man, sin, the Messiah, revelation, inspiration, angels, Satan, the various testaments and covenants, judgment, and life after death. It provides a wealth of material for preaching and teaching from the Old Testament. (3 credits)

Apologetics

Faith and knowing are the two consistent themes of this course. The relationship between them is examined and explained. (3 credits)

Insurance Data Management Association
85 John Street
New York, New York 10038 (212) 669-0496

Description:

The Insurance Data Management Association (IDMA) is a nonprofit professional association dedicated to increasing the level of professionalism among insurance data managers. Fifty-three insurance organizations are represented by nearly five hundred individual members nationwide. In addition to a seven-course curriculum, successful completion of which leads to designation as a Certified Data Manager (CDM), the Association sponsors technical seminars, conducts meetings and forums for pertinent topics, and produces an analysis package for special state data reports.

The IDMA curriculum incorporates courses from the American Institute for Property and Liability Underwriters as well as IDMA-designed courses. Curriculum activities are coordinated by the Education Committee and advised by an Academic Advisory Committee. Courses are designed to facilitate self-study and performance is tested in examinations administered twice yearly.

Academic Levels:
Professional

Degree/Certificate Programs:
Certificate.

Tuition:
Contact the Director of the Association for enrollment procedure and cost information.

Enrollment Period:
A student can begin with any one of the courses in the sequence.

Accreditations:
The courses have been evaluated by the Program on Noncollegiate Sponsored Instruction, The Center for Adult Learning and Educational Credentials of the American Council on Education. College/university credit recommendations are listed in *The National Guide To Educational Credit for Training Program* published by the American Council on Education/Oryx Press.

PROFESSIONAL COURSES

INSURANCE DATA MANAGEMENT

Data Administration

This course includes the definition and benefits of data administration; standards, policies, and procedures for data use; data organization; data administration, management, and quality considerations; principles and use of data dictionary; data dictionary and directory systems-design, meta-entities, input and output; implementation (developer's and user's viewpoint); and distributed database environment and auditing.

Insurance Accounting and Data Quality

Major topics include: accounting and data management functions; products of accounting and the system involved; overview and very detailed exploration of data quality issues; quality control from set up to maintenance to emergency/contingency responses; statistical examinations; and state mandated statistical data monitoring system.

Insurance Collection and Statistical Reporting

Major topics include: descriptions and history of insurance information systems; descriptions of automation techniques and results; standards and guidelines; cycles; objectives and specific departmental needs within the company; statistical reporting to agents; specific characteristics of agent reporting; responding to special state data requests; and rate-making data and systems.

John Tracy Clinic

806 West Adams Boulevard
Los Angeles, California 90007 (800) 522-4582

Description:

The John Tracy Clinic School was established in 1942 to serve preschool (0–6) deaf children and their parents. The focus is on parent education. The School works with children but parent involvement is a necessary part of the Program. The Correspondence Division was begun in 1943 with a preschool course. A course for parents of deaf-blind children was added in 1974, and a course for parents of hearing-impaired babies was added in 1980. All three courses are available in English and Spanish. There are no resident requirements.

Faculty:
Dr. Sandra Meyer, Director.

Academic Levels:
Noncredit

Degree/Certificate Programs:
Certificate of Completion.

Admission Requirements:
Must be a parent of a preschool (0–6) deaf or deaf-blind child; worldwide service.

Tuition:
All services of the John Tracy Clinic are free to parents of preschool deaf and deaf-blind children. Professional persons or organizations pay a fee. Contact the Clinic for additional information.

Enrollment Period:
As long as the parents report on a regular basis, the enrollment is active. If enrollment is interrupted, a family may re-enroll as long as the child is six years of age or under.

Equipment Requirements:
No special equipment is needed.

Credit and Grading:
None.

Accreditations:
Distance Education and Training Council.

NONCREDIT COURSES

DEAF/BLIND CHILDREN (TRAINING FOR PARENTS)

Correspondence Course for Parents of Young Deaf Children - Part A, Deaf Babies

The course is free of cost to parents of hearing-impaired babies from birth to 2 years of age. Available in English or Spanish.

Correspondence Course for Parents of Preschool Deaf Children

The course is free of cost to parents of hearing-impaired children ages 2 through 6 years of age. Available in English or Spanish.

Correspondence Learning Program for Parents of Preschool Deaf-Blind Children

The course is free of cost to parents of hearing and visually impaired children of any age. Available in English and Spanish.

Marine Corps Institute

United States Marine Corps
Marine Barracks
8th and I Streets, S.E.
Washington, D.C. 20390   (202) 433-2632

Description:

The Marine Corps Institute, an official training activity of the United States Marine Corps, prepares and administers correspondence courses designed to increase the general military and technical proficiency of Marines. It also develops testing and instructional materials in all essential subjects. Use of the correspondence courses is restricted to members of the Armed Forces or civilian employees of the Armed Forces. The Institute was founded in 1920 by General J. Lejeune. There have been over 5 million enrollments since being founded; the current enrollment exceeds 300,000 per year. The completion rate exceeds 92 percent for all Marine Corps enrollments. Courses are offered in Marine Corps technical skills and professional military education.

Faculty:
Lt. Col. James S. Sfayer, USMC, Deputy Director. The instructional staff includes 174 members; 50 subject specialists.

Academic Levels:
Vocational
Professional

Degree/Certificate Programs:
Certificate.

Admission Requirements:
Courses are available only to members of the Armed Forces, NROTC, or civilian members of the Department of Defense. The student must be recommended by his/her commanding officer.

Tuition:
No tuition.

Enrollment Period:
The maximum time allowed to complete a course is 1 year; 2 years for professional military education programs. One 6-month extension may be permitted.

Equipment Requirements:
The Institute supplies textbooks, study guides, maps, tables, etc. as required.

Credit and Grading:
Minimum passing grade is 65 percent on final examination for the Specialized Skill Training (SST) program (may be repeated once); 75 percent on final examination for Professional Military Education (PME) program (may be repeated once). Examinations for enlisted personnel courses (SST) must be proctored; Professional Military Education program course examinations are open book.

Library Services:
Complete materials for all courses are located at 19 Marine Corps base libraries.

Accreditations:
Distance Education and Training Council.

Massachusetts Department of Education
Bureau of Student, Community, and Adult Services
Correspondence Instruction
1385 Hancock Street
Quincy, Massachusetts 02169 (617) 770-7582

Description:
The Commonwealth of Massachusetts, Department of Education, through the Bureau of Student, Community, and Adult Services, offers high school credit and noncredit courses in various fields. The high school credit courses are, in most cases, suitable for young people and adults. Many high school graduates enroll in courses just for refresher and a sprinkling of college graduates also take the high school courses. The noncredit courses may sometimes be used as credit courses at the discretion of the guidance counselors of the particular schools. Many of these courses are designated

as noncredit because they are not courses that are usually offered in high schools.

Faculty:
Ellen H. Maddocks, Director of Correspondence Instruction; Rosalie A. Buchiacho, Registrar. There is a faculty of 35.

Academic Levels:
High School

Degree/Certificate Programs:
Certificates are issued without charge to students who complete a high school credit course with a passing or better mark. If the student wishes to transfer credit (high school units) to his/her local high school, a processing fee of $1 per transcript is charged.

Admission Requirements:
Open enrollment. Students may enroll in correspondence courses at any time of the year. To obtain credit for a course, high school students must have the written consent of their school principal or guidance counselor. This consent assures the Bureau and the student that the credit will be accepted by the school upon the successful completion of the course.

Tuition:
Tuition varies per course. Out-of-state tuition is higher than for Massachusetts residents. Contact the Massachusetts Department of Education for current registration fee, tuition, and cost of textbooks. Refund policy: there are no cash refunds. By acts of the Massachusetts State Legislature, the following legal residents of Massachusetts may enroll without charge (except for the registration fee for each course plus costs of texts) upon presentation of acceptable proof of eligibility for free instruction: (1) Veterans of World Wars I, II, Korean, or Vietnam conflict; (2) members of the Armed Forces who are both residents of Massachusetts and currently stationed in Massachusetts; (3) legally blind persons; (4) senior citizens (65 years of age or over); (5) patients in state, country, or federal hospitals in Massachusetts; (6) inmates of correctional institutions in Massachusetts. Veterans may submit copy of military discharge papers and evidence of residence if applying for the first time. Senior citizens must submit proof of age and evidence of residence if applying for the first time. Inmates must have their applications signed by the appropriate education officer.

Enrollment Period:
Students are allowed up to two years to complete a course. Under unusual circumstances, a time extension beyond the two-year limit may be allowed at the discretion of the supervisor in charge of student services. Request for an extension must be made in writing before the two-year limit has expired. No time extensions will be allowed if none of the lessons has been sent in at the time of the request. There is a fee for any time extension granted.

Equipment Requirements:

Cost of books and materials must be borne by the student and may be purchased from the Bureau.

Credit and Grading:

Examinations must be proctored by any public or private school official provided the student makes arrangements in advance. Letter grades are used: A (90–100 percent), Superior; B (80–89 percent), Above Average; C (70–79 percent), Average; D (60–69 percent), Low Passing; F (below 60 percent), Failure; INC, Incomplete (work may be resubmitted). The final grade for a course gives equal weight to the lesson average and the examination grade. Both must be passing or better to successfully complete the course. A re-examination fee will be charged where applicable. Credit is awarded in Carnegie units (1 unit is equal to the work completed in class sessions of at least 40 minutes on 180 school days).

Accreditations:

Member of: National University Continuing Education Association.

HIGH SCHOOL COURSES

ART

Basic Drawing Techniques

A "must" course for the beginner in art. The student will learn the necessary information about the basic structure of objects, perspectives, light and shade, local color, and composition. At the same time, the student learns how to interpret one's surroundings (indoors and outdoors) and ideas into concrete drawings. (½ unit)

Interior Design

Part 1. This course in Interior Design is planned to help the student develop understanding and confidence in making wise choices— economically as well as for reasons of beauty. It will cover the principles of good design essential to a beautiful home. Color coordination, window and wall treatments, furniture arrangements are only a few of the topics covered. (½ unit)

Part 2. A continuation of Part 1. (½ unit)

AUTOMOTIVE TECHNOLOGY

Automotive Engines

The theory of operation and the construction, maintenance, and repair of automobile engines are explained in terms understandable to the beginner. The lessons discuss in detail shop practice; fundamentals of the automobile, engine operation, measurements and types; engine construction; the electrical, fuel, lubrication, and cooling systems; troubleshooting, engine and electrical system service. The course meets the standards set by the automotive industry and the American Vocational Association. (½ unit)

Automotive Chassis

The lessons in this course include servicing the fuel, lubrication, and cooling systems; drive lines; rear axles, and differentials; springs, and suspension, servicing the steering system, and brakes; tires; and body frame. Uses same text as the above course. (½ unit)

BUSINESS

Bookkeeping

Part 1. An introductory course provides not only facts about business but the record-keeping practice needed by operators of small shops or retail stores and by clerical employees who work with financial information. The teaching approach is practical rather than theoretical. Simple balance sheets and profit and loss statements are taught first to give an understanding of the end-result of record-keeping. Emphasis is then given to recording the most common transactions and tracing them through to the final statements. (½ unit)

Part 2. A continuation of the above course. (½ unit)

Typewriting

Part 1. Basic typewriting skills for personal or vocational use are taught effectively by correspondence. The touch system is used throughout the course. Basic letter styles, manuscript and correspondence procedures and the typing of business forms are included. (¼ unit)

Part 2. A continuation of the above course. (¼ unit)

Applied Business Law

Part 1. A study of legal rules applying to business situations and transactions. As a way of introduction, the course offers a comprehensive review of law in general as it relates to society and its members, including a discussion of the fundamentals of civil and criminal law and an examination of the court system. This is followed by materials on contracts, bailments, sales, debtors, and creditors, commercial paper, employment, agency, insurance, property, and business organization. The student learns about business law through the reading of textual materials and by reflecting upon hypothetical as well as actual problems. (½ unit) 2).

Part 2. A continuation of the above course. (½ unit)

Small Business Management

This is a practical how-to-do-it course for the young adult just starting out in business, the senior citizen starting a new career, or anyone engaged in business on his/her own. The topics covered include marketing channels; pricing policies; serving customers; salesmanship; advertising and sales promotion, purchasing policies and procedures, stock control; financing a business; financial problems; insurance; credit and collection; budgeting; human relationships; selection, training, and promotion of employees; selecting a location; securing a building and equipment; office operations; government regulations; taxation. (½ unit)

ENGLISH

English for Everyone

Part 1. This basic English course promotes proper verbal expression by teaching all the components of the sentence. Each lesson focuses on a different part of speech and adds punctuation, grammar, and spelling tips. (½ unit)

Part 2. This part adds to basic concepts of Part 1, but also asks the student to use these skills in writing a series of compositions, starting with a brief paragraph and leading to a book report and a final paper. (½ unit)

English IX

Part 1. Short stories, poetry, essays, and sketches, biographies, and personal recollections, three plays (one by Chekhov, one by Robert Sherwood about Abe Lincoln, and Shakespeare's *Romeo and Juliet),* and finally Dickens' novel, *Great Expectations,* make up the reading for this diversified course in English. The student is a self-teacher in the Language Skills section which uses a programmed text for guidance. The writing of compositions, some work on summarizing, and a review of grammar are stressed to give a clearer idea of how to express oneself well. A novel of the student's own choice is read and interpreted. (½ unit)

Part 2. A continuation of the above course. (½ unit)

English X

Part 1. In this course the student will consider aspects of modern day problems as interpreted by basic language skills and strengthened by advanced skills for variety and enrichment. By following clear direction to plan compositions, and how to write social and business letters correctly, the student will learn to express his/her own ideas. A variety of reading is presented by novels such as *Silas Marner, The Bridge of San Luis Rey,* and a book of the student's choice. Interesting classical selections, short stories, poetry, and essays point out the overlapping problems of the past and present. Political ideas of today are emphasized by an in-depth study of *Julius Caesar.* (½ unit)

Part 2. A continuation of the above course. (½ unit)

English XI - College Preparatory

Part 1. The concern in this course is with the most important writers of our country from colonial days to the present. The student is taught what to look for in a literary work and how to judge the quality of what is read. Among the writers studied are Thoreau, Emerson, Hawthorne, Harte, Whitman, Twain, Stephen Crane (with special emphasis on *The Red Badge of Courage),* several black writers, Willa Cather, Hemingway, Faulkner, Steinbeck, Benet, Frost, Sandburg, and others. The language skills portion of the course emphasizes practice in English and composition. (½ unit)

Part 2. A continuation of the above course. (½ unit)

English XI - General

Part 1. The literature text for the course, *Adventures for Americans,* contains short stories, poems, plays, and essays by some of America's best writers, past and present. *English 3200* is a programmed grammar text which allows the student to work through problem areas of grammar on his/her own. (½ unit)

Part 2. Included in this second part are units on newspapers, advertisments, and how to separate fact form opinion. The student will choose from one of three modern plays *(Death of a Salesman, The Miracle Worker,* or *Inherit the Wind)* for independent reading, as well as a novel, short stories, or a selection of poems. (½ unit)

English XII - College Preparatory

Part 1. This survey of literature introduces representative British writers from Anglo-Saxon times to our own. The history of drama, the arts as aids in interpreting literature, literary terms and techniques, the recognition of recurring dynamic changes in taste, the relationships between political and literary history will help the student understand his/her literary heritage. Great works and great names are studied intensively. Shakespeare's *Macbeth* is explored in detail. Language skills receive constant attention; composition practice is included in each lesson. Spelling is discussed in terms of a phonetic alphabet. (½ unit)

Part 2. A continuation of the above course. (½ unit)

English XII - General

Part 1. This course uses the text *Who We Are,* a volume that explores a culturally rich and vital mixture of people - the young, the old, and men and women of every race and religion. The unit on The Young explores the experience of growing up in America, and looks at the problems of the elderly. The Men and Women unit studies the relationships between the sexes, both in the past and present. (½ unit)

Part 2. This part uses the text *What We Believe,* a book meant to give students as complete an idea as possible of what Americans believe, both about themselves and about their country. It begins with an examination of our personal values, then explores the myths and dreams on which our country was built. The final section on Fantasy and Imagination explores some of the private hopes and fears - the dreams and visions—of the American mind. The student will also read a novel, consider the mechanics of choosing and applying for a job, and review the structure of our language in the sections on grammar. (½ unit)

Improving Your Reading Skills

Part 1. This course is designed for people who have already learned to read. It will challenge the student of any age to improve his/her ability to think as he/she reads. The course offers an original simplified, individual plan for one who is baffled by the need of working more quickly through the vast mass of printed matter confronting him, such as applications for licenses, directions, advertising, news items, questionnaires, contracts and agreements, as well as reading for his/her own enjoyment. (½ unit)

Part 2. A continuation of the above course. (½ unit)

FRENCH

French I

Part 1. An introduction to French as it is presently written and spoken. This is a basic course for beginners featuring various reading, writing, and conversational exercises allowing the student to learn French in an interesting and practical manner. Basic vocabulary, fundamentals of French grammar, frequently used verbs, and useful idiomatic expressions are learned in this course. (½ unit)

Part 2. A continuation of the above course. (½ unit)

French II

Part 1. This course, a logical continuation of French I, builds upon the knowledge acquired in the basic course. In addition to more advanced grammatical and conversational exercises, reading selections from well-known French authors are included and discussed through question-answer type exercises. (½ unit)

Part 2. A continuation of the above course. (½ unit)

LATIN

Latin I

Part 1. Text and Study Guide used together provide, in easy stages, thorough training in the grammar of the most widely used language in all the world's history. The main objective is to teach Latin in the most economical and effective way. Latin is taught as an aid to effective English, and Roman life and culture are interpreted in terms of their significance to modern society. The course is geared to college entrance requirements, but the translation exercises are interesting to adults. (½ unit)

Part 2. A continuation of the above course. (½ unit)

Latin II

Part 1. Life in a Roman family, selections from the great historian Livy, the story of the golden fleece, some of Pliny's letters, samples of Latin literature just for fun, and selected passages from the seven books of Caesar's *Gallic Wars* are the main substance of the course. The emphasis is on comprehension of what is read and further vocabulary with some review grammar. (½ unit)

Part 2. A continuation of the above course. (½ unit)

MATHEMATICS

Business Mathematics

Part 1. The basic operations are first reviewed through a study of problems faced by every individual in daily life. Considerable attention is devoted to personal finance, borrowing money, housing expenditure, transportation, taxes, problems of a small business, retail buying and selling practices, the use of mathematics by the wholesaler and manufacturer, business ownership, everyday measurements, and civil service problems. (½ unit)

Part 2. A continuation of the above course. (½ unit)

General Mathematics

Part 1. This part covers not only the four fundamental operations on whole numbers, but also fractions, decimals, ratio and proportion, percents, income/earnings for taxes and banking; credit cards, loans (for home, auto, insurance and life and health). (½ unit)

Part 2. A continuation of Part 1 including savings and investments, business operations and accounting; expressions and equations; reciprocals and general equations; graphic points, equations, pairs and slopes, and a lesson on sines and cosines. (½ unit)

Elementary Algebra

Part 1. Using "modern" language and methods, this course is the standard approach to college level mathematics. The course is not rigorous but does cover topics from the language of algebra through quadratic functions and equations. (½ unit)

Part 2. A continuation of the above course. (½ unit)

Intermediate Algebra

Part 1. This course is a continuation of Elementary Algebra. It covers operations, properties of real numbers, equations, polynomials, fractions, irrational numbers and quadratic equations and functions. Also included are logarithms, series, permutations and trigonometry. The text is clearly written with several model problems and answers to odd-numbered exercises. The motif and language are modern and readable. (½ unit)

Part 2. A continuation of the above course. (½ unit)

Geometry

Part 1. The course begins with basic definitions and goes on to study angles and perpendicular lines, triangles and polygons, the use of the Pythagorean Theorem, circles, constructions, measuring plane and solid figures and on into coordinate geometry. (½ unit)

Part 2. A continuation of the above course. (½ unit)

SCIENCE

General Biology

Part 1. A solid non-laboratory course in the science of living things. This part considers, among other topics, the chemical basis of life, the cell - its structure, nutrition, growth and reproduction; heredity and genes, bacteria and diseases; and structure, function and reproduction in flowering plants. (½ unit)

Part 2. Includes the following: worms, insects, fish, reptiles, birds, mammals, the human framework and bodily functions; and an introduction to ecology, environmental changes and conservation. (½ unit)

Modern Health

Part 1. Covers the importance of diet to well-being; what we know about alcohol and smoking; the problems of drug use and abuse; understanding mental illness; the relationship between physical health and emotional stability; and growing opportunities in health careers. (½ unit)

Part 2. A continuation of the above course. (½ unit)

Chemistry

Part 1. This course is designed for both the student who needs a sound preparation for further study and those who seek simply to better understand the complex world around them. A comprehensive coverage of classical chemistry, from atomic structure to radioactivity, is supplemented by enrichment lessons on household chemistry, the environment, and the ever-current problems of drugs. A non-laboratory course which provides thorough training for college entrance. (½ unit)

Part 2. A continuation of the above course. (½ unit)

SOCIAL SCIENCE

American History - College Preparatory

Part 1. The course shows why men acted the way they did and how the past has shaped the present, and gives insight into the complexities of America today. Coverage and discussion beginning with early colonization and ending with the Vietnam War. (½ unit)

Part 2. A continuation of the above course. (½ unit)

American History - General

Part 1. This course gives an overview of the nation's growth and development. The impact of technology is stressed, not only for its effect on our country's growth but also its influence on our relations with other nations. This part covers prehistory through 1898. (½ unit)

Part 2. A continuation of the above course. Covers the period from 1898 to the present.

World History

Part 1. This course gives a comprehensive overview of global history and features in-depth studies of famous individuals and their impact on society. The student is encouraged to think for him/herself, to interpret historical events in the light of history as it is being made today, and in particular, the student is encouraged to see the importance of technological and scientific advances and their impact on the growth of civilization. This part covers the rise of the West and the age of Europe. (½ unit)

Part 2. A continuation of the above course. This part continues the story of mankind, with empires beyond Europe and the modern world. (½ unit)

Problems of Democracy

Part 1. This course covers the working of our democratic system of government. (½ unit)

Part 2. A continuation of the above course. (½ unit)

General Psychology

Part 1. Topics covered include heredity and environment, human development, learning and conditioning, memory, the beginnings of thinking and language, solving problems and thinking creatively, motivation, emotion, and sensory experience. (½ unit)

Part 2. This part continues with perception, altered states of consciousness, biological foundations of behavior, mental testing, personality, abnormal behavior, psychotherapy, judging societies, and the individual in society. (½ unit)

Consumer Economics

This course is a dynamic treatment of the forces and influences which shape our daily living. The emphasis is on how our economic system operates and the relationship between business enterprise and individual decision-making. Includes practical consumer problems such as those faced by individuals and families in managing income, buying and spending wisely, using credit, using advertising and information aids, choosing insurance policies, investing and owning or renting a home. (½ unit)

SPANISH

Spanish I

Part 1. This basic course in Spanish is based on sound linguistic analysis. The program uses deductive methods to develop comprehension necessary for reading and writing skills. All the important points of Spanish grammar are introduced and mastered at a continually controlled pace. Sequential study is emphasized. (½ unit)

Part 2. A continuation of Part 1. (½ unit)

NONCREDIT COURSES

CIVIL SERVICE AND LICENSE PREPARATION

Basic Civil Service Training

This course provides an intensive pre-employment review of the knowledge and basic skills in English and arithmetic necessary for Civil Service positions such as junior and senior clerk typist. The major topics are English grammar, including punctuation, capitalization, vocabulary, and spelling, as well as arithmetic. The mathematics included in the course involves the four operations on whole numbers, decimals, and fractions, percents, business applications, and ratio/proportion. There is also a section on general business training which covers correspondence, filing, communications and office machines. In addition to the above, there is a section on aptitude and skill which encompasses most of the requirements for clerical and office work. (Noncredit)

Building Custodians' Preparation

This course provides technical information needed to prepare for the Massachusetts state civil service examination for junior building custodian. Topics discussed include cleaning methods, care and maintenance of oil burners, the operation of electrical generators and motors, electrical wiring, fire prevention, the care of floors and lavatories, etc. (Noncredit)

ENGINEERING

Basic Television

Part 1. This course explains the theory of the home television receiver and is illustrated in technical but simple terms. Individual parts of the receiver are studied separately. The FM sound track is studied, and one assignment on servicing, plus two assignments on the color systems and receivers. (Noncredit)

Part 2. A continuation of the above course. (Noncredit)

Basic Electronics

Part 1. Starting with electrons and the atom, the course progresses to d-c circuits, magnetism, a-c circuits, vacuum tubes, and transistors. The fundamental principles taught are applied in areas of communications electronics (especially radio and television), industrial electronics, and the computer. Basic principles are explained first, followed by typical applications and common troubles. (Noncredit)

Part 2. A continuation of the above course. (Noncredit)

Transistors

Part 1. After studying transistors and diodes, the emphasis is on transistor circuits in action. The common emitter, common collector and common base circuit are all studied both by DC and graphical analysis—also, the effect of temperature on these circuits. Oscillators and power supplied are also covered. (Noncredit)

Part 2. A continuation of the above course. (Noncredit)

ENGLISH

Vocabulary Building

This course has been designed to increase one's vocabulary in order to express oneself more forcefully and effectively. It also covers how language has evolved and why we employ some of the words and expressions which have come to us from many sources. (Noncredit)

GENERAL EDUCATION DEVELOPMENT TEST (GED) PREPARATORY PROGRAM

High School Equivalency Preparation

Fifteen short lessons take the student through the basics and on the road to certification. A battery of five tests are taken. A review course in English grammar and usage, basic math, and reading comprehension is offered. Certificates are not issued for the completion of this course; the student is prepared to take the GED high school equivalency tests. (Noncredit)

MATHEMATICS

Everyday Review of Mathematics

This course is a refresher for those far removed from their formal schooling days. It is intended as a review and brush up for algebra and other more advanced courses. It covers the four fundamental operations on the whole numbers, fractions and decimals; also percents, ratio and proportion, consumer and business applications. (Noncredit)

The Metric System

This is an elementary course in the metric system of measurement. It is designed to give students with little or no background in metrics a basic understanding of the history, characteristics, and uses of the metric system. The text materials, questions, and activities of the course will stress everyday consumer concerns which will result from the increased use of metric notation by American business and industry. (Noncredit)

SOCIAL SCIENCE

Practical Politics

Actual incidents are described in the story of the people, the procedures, and the pressures of the legislative process at the state level. (Noncredit)

Law and the Legal System

Part 1. An introduction to law, legal institutions, and basic principles of the American legal system. The systems of courts in the United States are explained. The functions of judge and jury are examined. Various judicial remedies are identified. The student is introduced to fundamental principles, rules, and features of the American legal system such as due process, the distinction between criminal and civil law, the obligation of courts to follow precedent, statues of limitations, immunities from legal action, the distinction between equity and common law. (Noncredit)

Part 2. A study of civil as well as criminal procedures with special attention to constitutional guarantees. Other topics include: legislation in the United States, the functions of administrative agencies, negligence and torts. The student learns about law through the reading of textual materials and through the case study method. (Noncredit)

Preparation for Naturalization

This course is designed primarily to help immigrants prepare for the naturalization examination, but it is also very informative for anyone wishing to pursue a short, clear and concise course in United States history through the implementation of the Constitution and fundamental principles of American government. (Noncredit)

Napoleon Hill Foundation
1440 Paddock Drive
Northbrook, Illinois 60062   (708) 998-0408

Description:

The Napoleon Hill Foundation was established in 1962 to foster, perpetuate, and disseminate throughout the world the lifetime research, writings, and teaching of Napoleon Hill. The Foundation is a nonprofit, charitable, educational organization dedicated to disseminating the works of Dr. Hill to social service agencies, educators, business and industry, prison inmates, minority groups, and all individuals interested in the principles of success and personal achievement.

Faculty:

W. Clement Stone, President; Dr. Jack Early, Education Director; Michael J. Ritt, Jr., Executive Director.

Academic Levels:

Noncredit

Degree/Certificate Programs:

Certificate.

Admission Requirements:

Students must be able to read and write.

Tuition:

Contact the Foundation for current tuition/fees. VISA and MasterCard accepted.

Enrollment Period:

The maximum time to complete the course is 18 months; minimum time is 3 months.

Equipment Requirements:

Course material is included in the tuition. Refund policy follows the standard guidelines of the Distance Education and Training Council.

Credit and Grading:

Examinations are open book and are included with each lesson. Grading system: A, B, C, D with plus and minus. Minimum passing grade is C-.

Accreditations:

Distance Education and Training Council.

NONCREDIT COURSES

GUIDANCE

Positive Mental Attitude (PMA) Science of Success Course

This course includes 17 individual lessons, each covering one of the success principles as follows: Definiteness of Purpose; The Master Mind Principle; Applied Faith; Going the Extra Mile; Pleasing Personality; Personal Initiative; A Positive Mental Attitude; Inspired Feeling (Enthusiasm); Self-Discipline; Accurate Thinking; Controlled Attention; Teamwork; Learn from Adversity and Defeat; Creative Vision (Imagination); Maintenance of Sound Health; Budgeting Time and Money; Cosmic Habit Force (The Law Which Fixes All Habits).

National Center for Logistics Management
819 Meetinghouse Road
Cinnaminson, New Jersey 08077
(609) 786-9112

Description:

The National Center for Logistics Management opened its doors as an educational institution in 1923. It provides specialized education to students interested in pursuing a career in the field of transportation and logistical management. The home study student is provided with experience that best emulates the kinds of situations and activities that occur within the transportation industry.

Faculty:

College

Academic Levels:

Certificate.

Tuition:

Contact the center for current tuition/fees and enrollment requirements.

Credit and Grading:

The course has been evaluated by the Program on Noncollegiate Sponsored Instruction of the Center for Adult Learning and Educational Credentials, American Council on Education, Washington, D.C. College credit recommended for the successful completion of the course is listed in *The National Guide to Educational Credit for Training Programs* published by the American Council on Education/Oryx Press.

COLLEGE COURSES

TRANSPORTATION

Business Logistics Management

This course of 130 hours covers the distribution systems, order entry, materials handling, storage systems, public and private warehousing, distribution center analysis, price and service selection, information retrieval, customer service, techniques of negotiation, and rate structure versus cost of service. (3 semester hours)

Export/Import Transportation and Documentation

This course of 300 hours provides students with proper techniques in foreign commerce through a proper understanding of the basic tools and terminology, the techniques of import-export, and the requirements of governmental agencies and the method of identifying and entering export markets. This course will thoroughly cover the terms of sale, banking and financial documents, marine insurance, and commercial invoices. (6 semester hours)

Industrial Traffic Manager

This course is designed for managers and persons aspiring to advance in transportation, marketing, or materials management with industrial companies or carriers. It provides and extensive overview of transportation and its relationship to the corporate structure. (3 semester hours)

Interstate Commerce Law and Practice

This course of 300 hours teaches that although the transportation industry has been deregulated, no substantive changes have taken place in the law that have lessened its power of enforcement. It defines what parties are subject to the act and the extent to which the Interstate Commerce Commission has jurisdiction over transportation. (3 semester hours)

Loss and Damage I and II

This 300-hour course provides specialized treatment of an important traffic function. It covers the principles of claims and proper procedures to be applied by shippers and carriers in loss, damage, or overcharge situations. The basic laws of carrier liability are explained and illustrated by leading cases. (3 semester hours)

Transportation Law and Regulatory Reform

This 130-hour course provides students with an understanding of the federal transportation regulatory system through knowledge of the Constitution, the Interstate Commerce Commission, and the Administrative Procedure Act. (3 semester hours)

Transportation Pricing, Theory and Practice I and II

Pricing Theory I: This course teaches fundamental procedures of traffic management from the viewpoint of on-the-job requirements in the field. It provides training and practice in freight classification; tariff interpretation and selection; rate checking techniques; zip code pricing; contracts and negotiations; routing; and other elements of everyday incidences in the transportation department. *Pricing Theory II:* this course is concerned with more advanced aspects of traffic management techniques of rate construction and tariff compilation. Freight rate relationships are studied by use of the tariff publications that express them. Terminal facilities and switching; demurrage and storage; reconsignment and diversion; transit; and embargoes are similarly treated in this course. Both Pricing Theory I and II require 300 hours. (3 semester hours)

Warehousing

This course of 130 hours is designed to familiarize the student with the role of the warehousing function and the economy and its relationship to the transportation function. Details are provided in warehousing operations; inventory control; ''Just-In-Time''; layout; and the proper uses of storage and handling equipment; packaging; labor and productivity cost controls; and the options of using either a private or public warehouse facility. (1 semester hour)

National Safety Council
Safety Training Institute
Home Study Programs
1121 Spring Lake Drive
Itasca, Illinois 60143-3201   (708) 285-1121

Description:
   Founded in 1913, the National Safety Council is a nongovernmental, not-for-profit public service organization. The Council, through its Safety Training Institute, provides home study programs for supervisors in safety supervision and human relations. The programs are designed to assist first-line supervisors in developing positive safety attitudes among their employees, and to help supervisors fulfill their responsibilities for accident prevention. Toll-free telephone number from outside Illinois: 1-800-621-7619.

Faculty:
   Gary P. Fisher, Director.

Academic Levels:
   Noncredit

Degree/Certificate Programs:
   Certificate.

Admission Requirements:
   Open Enrollment.

Tuition:
   Members of National Safety Council are eligible for discounted rates. Contact the Safety Training Institute for current tuition and fees. Often the supervisor's company will pay for the course. Refund plan is available for those students enrolled on their own (that is, not enrolled by their companies).

Enrollment Period:
   The course must be completed within a twelve-month period.

Equipment Requirements:
   All materials needed for the course, including textbooks, are paid for by the tuition.

Credit and Grading:
   The minimum passing grade is 70 percent. The student is tested at the end of each lesson in the course.

Accreditations:
   Distance Education and Training Council.

NONCREDIT COURSES

SAFETY EDUCATION

Supervising for Safety

Teaches supervisors the fundamentals of accident control and better production without injury and waste. The course is divided into the following 12 units: Safety and the Supervisor; Know Your Accident Problems; Human Relations; Maintaining Interest in Safety; Instructing for Safety; Industrial Hygiene; Personal Protective Equipment; Industrial Housekeeping; Material Handling and Storage; Guarding Machines and Mechanisms; Hand and Portable Power Tools; Fire Protection.

Supervisor's Guide to Human Relations

This course is designed primarily, but not exclusively, for supervisors who have completed the basic course, Supervising for Safety. The course concentrates on a step-by-step procedure for developing and managing people. It also focuses on solving actual job problems. This course is divided into the following ten units: Responsibilities of the Supervisor; Leadership, Discipline, and the Supervisor; Directing the Work Force; Dissatisfaction - Its Causes and Correction; Personality Factors in Safety; Good Safety Attitudes and How to Develop Them; Motivation for Safe Behavior on the Job; Influence of Tension and Stress in Failures to Perform Work Safely; Communications in Safety; Fitness to Lead—Applying the Principles.

Protecting Workers' Lives

This course is designed to help today's workers learn the basics of safety and health. It teaches a person what he/she can do to prevent accidents both on and off the job. The course is divided into the following 12 units: Introduction; The OSHAct; Safety and Health Standards/Safety and Health Committees; Hazard Recognitions, and Safety Hazards, Part 1; Safety Hazards, Part 2, Occupational Health;

Health Hazards, Part 1; Health Hazards, Part 2; Fire Prevention; Eliminating Hazards; Workplace Inspections and Evaluating Safety and Health Programs; Collective Bargaining and Off-the-Job Safety and Health.

National Sheriffs' Association
1450 Duke Street
Alexandria, Virginia 22314-3490
(703) 836-7827

Description:
The National Sheriffs' Association is a nonprofit professional service organization dedicated to enhancing the professional capabilities of criminal justice agencies and personnel in the United States and to promoting effective law enforcement and correctional services at the county and local level. The association provides meaningful training programs on an ongoing basis. Hundreds of training projects to improve the professional knowledge and skills of criminal justice personnel at all levels have used instructional materials prepared by the association.

The Jail Officer's Training Program is designed to fulfill basic training needs of jail officers through a course of independent study by correspondence. It has also been designed to serve as an in-depth basic training program.

Academic Levels:
Noncredit

Degree/Certificate Programs:
Certificate.

Admission Requirements:
Open to members of the profession.

Tuition:
Contact the National Sheriffs' Association for current tuition/fees.

Enrollment Period:
The course must be completed within six months.

COLLEGE COURSES

ADULT DETENTION
Jail Officers' Training Program

The course examines the elements impacting on the adult detention environment. Included are the historical perspectives, legal ramifications, and the role and responsibilities of the detention personnel. Special sections of the course cover the following topics: basic issues—the American jail, legal rights and responsibilities within the corrections environment, litigation procedure, written communications, role concepts, attitudes, and interpersonal communication, dealing with stress; security—basic jail security principles, books and admissions, classification of inmates, disciplinary procedures contraband control, key and tool control, patrol procedures in the jail, escort of inmates, hostage incidents in the jail, release procedures; special procedures—sick call, recreation and visiting, diabetic and epileptic inmates, medical problems confronting women inmates, drug withdrawal in the jail, alcohol abuse emergencies in the jail, psychological disorders (psychopathic and neurotic personalities), homosexual be-

havior in the jail, and suicide prevention; and supervision—supervising inmates (principles and skills), personal supervision situations in housing and general areas, special supervision problems in the jail, supervision of inmates in dining areas, and the supervision of minimum security inmates.

New England School of Banking
P.O. Box 431

Description:
The New England School of Banking offers a program in banking education for junior and middle management bankers. The Commercial Banking Major was established in 1957. The Trust Major was added in 1967. The school is sponsored by the six New England state bankers' associations. The goal of the school is to provide bankers with the knowledge needed to assume greater responsibility, an understanding of the complexity of the industry, and an awareness of banking's role in today's society.

Faculty:
The school faculty is drawn from both the academic and banking communities.

Academic Levels:
Professional

Degree/Certificate Programs:
Certificate.

Tuition:
Contact the Executive Director of the School for enrollment procedure and current cost information.

Enrollment Period:
Each major is a two-year summer program (one-week resident session each year) at Williams College, Williamstown, Massachusetts, plus 110 hours of independent study. The majors are designed to increase students' knowledge of the technical and managerial aspects of their own specialists and to introduce them to other commercial and trust banking subjects. Lectures, case studies, role playing, workshops, and computer simulations are used.

Credit and Grading:
The program has been evaluated by the Program on Noncollegiate Sponsored Instruction, The Center for Adult Learning and Educational Credentials of the American Council on Education. College/university credit recommendations are listed in *The National Guide To Educational Credit for Training Programs* published by the American Council on Education/Oryx Press.

PROFESSIONAL COURSES

BANKING
Commercial Banking Major

The purpose of this course is to expand students' knowledge of the technical and managerial aspects of their own specialties and to introduce them to other commercial banking subjects in a rapidly changing banking environment. The course covers the history of banking, American financial system, management of bank assets and liabilities analysis of financial statements, bank investments, lending and loan administration, sales management and marketing, financial instruments and markets, and related bank management topics such as communications and personnel. In the bank simulation game during the summer resident training, students work in groups to make decisions and determine policy in the operation of a commercial bank. In addition to on-campus instruction, students are assigned case problems to be completed between the two resident sessions for evaluation by an instructor.

Trust Banking Major

The purpose of this course is to increase students' knowledge of the technical and managerial aspects of their own specialties and to introduce them to other trust banking subjects in a rapidly changing banking environment. The course covers trust investments, fiduciary tax, fiduciary law, and trust department operations. The methods of instruction include workshops, seminars, and group discussions during the summer resident training. In addition to on-campus study, students are assigned case problems to be completed between the two resident sessions for evaluation by an instructor.

NHRAW Home Study Institute
1389 Dublin Road
P.O. Box 16790
Columbus, Ohio 43216   (614) 488-1835

Description:

The Northamerican Heating, Refrigeration, and Airconditioning Wholesalers Association (NHRAW) began offering correspondence training in heating and airconditioning in 1962. The NHRAW Home Study Institute was established in 1969 as a not-for-profit service to the industry. It now operates as a division within the Association. The school has its own reference library. Mass enrollment from the public at large is not the objective of the Institute. Rather, its whole effort is directed toward practical, highly-personalized assistance to a limited number of industry students, newcomers as well as those already experienced in airconditioning. The enrollment each year consists of approximately 1,400 individuals, more than 95 percent of whom are on-the-job employees of wholesaling and contracting companies in the industry.

Faculty:
James H. Healy, Director.

Academic Levels:
Vocational

Degree/Certificate Programs:
Diploma.

Admission Requirements:
It is preferred that an applicant be employed by a heating/airconditioning firm. Ninety-five percent of the students are so employed. Non-industry persons should contact NHAW direct for consultation. Applicants should be from North America.

Tuition:
Contact the school for current tuition and fees. Discounted fees available for NHAW members, associates, and sponsored non-members.

Enrollment Period:
Students may enroll at any time.

Equipment Requirements:
All text materials are supplied by the school.

Credit and Grading:
Numerical percentage grading system; 70 percent is the minimum passing grade. Examinations on the honor system.

Accreditations:
Distance Education and Training Council; Ohio State Board of School and College Registration.

VOCATIONAL COURSES

AIR CONDITIONING, REFRIGERATION, AND HEATING

Fundamentals of Heating

Provides an overview of heating concepts and basic system components. Discusses for the beginner or the non-technical employee, comfort principles, house construction and factors affecting heat loss, humidification, common service complaints, and identification of system components.

Fundamentals of Cooling

Provides an overview of cooling concepts and operating principles. Tailored for the new employee (or someone new to cooling), there are many veteran installers, salesmen, and office staff personnel who could benefit from an organized study of house construction and factors affecting heat gain, unit operation and common service problems.

Basics of Total Comfort Conditioning

This is a combination of the two preceding courses (Fundamentals of Heating and Fundamentals of Cooling).

Heating and Cooling System Design

Covers the calculation of heat loss/heat gain and size air distribution system.

Modern Hydronic Heating

All major hydronic equipment and specialties are explained. Lessons show how to calculate heat loss, size piping systems and select pumps for all popular systems used in both residential and light commercial buildings. Nine different design problems are completely detailed, including one on the design of a light factory. There are also lessons on planning and installing systems, plus one on servicing, including a comprehensive troubleshooting guide.

Heating and Cooling Controls

All lessons concentrated on just one subject - electric powered controls. Instructional material explains how each control works and what it does in the system. Rules for tracing control diagrams are established; servicing and circuit checkout procedures are detailed. Both 24 volt and millivolt circuits, gas, oil and airconditioning controls are analyzed.

Servicing Comfort Cooling Systems

Planned to help any person interested in installing, troubleshooting, or repairing airconditioning systems. A valuable prerequisite to attendance at a factory school. Instructional material includes lessons on basic electricity, cooling controls, installation of add-on cooling, piping, refrigerant components, plus testing and servicing air cooled air conditioners.

Basic Electricity

Developed specifically as a first step toward the detailed study of heating and cooling controls. Covers electrical fundamentals, AC and DC circuit analysis, magnetism, how current is generated, and transformers. Essential information for those who have never had in-depth formal instruction in electricity, or who wish to advance in control technology.

Basic Office Math

Provides introductory instruction in how to compute earnings, payroll, simple productivity, discounts, interest, margins, markdowns, inventory turnover and profit analysis. An introduction to basic operating statement and balance sheet complete the program.

Managing a Contracting Business

Provides instruction on building an accounting system using the dual allocation system based on UDAP (Universal Dealer Accounting Program). Explains measuring and applying overhead using the dual allocation method, determining profit and expense variations by department, calculating return on investment, analyzing financial statements, budgeting and cash flow forecasting.

Professional Selling

Course details how to find customers, make an effective sales presentation, deal with objections, close a sale and manage time efficiently.

Counter Service and Sales

Objective is to provide an overview of the non-technical duties and basic responsibilities of a heating/cooling/refrigeration (wholesale) counter sales clerk.

Fundamentals of Solar Heating

Provides an overview for the experienced HVAC technician in basic component functions, equipment selection guidelines, control modes, installation and servicing hints for solar space heating and domestic water heating. (Solar cooling not covered).

North Dakota Division of Independent Study

North Dakota Department of Public Instruction
Box 5036 State University Station
Fargo, North Dakota 58105-5036

(701) 237-7182

Description:
Founded in 1935, the Division of Independent Study provides high school courses for credit or personal enrichment, and offers a complete high school curriculum. It issues high school diplomas upon completion of certain required courses. High school credits by examination or by life experience are available through the Division. There are approximately 5,000 course enrollments per year.

Faculty:
Robert R. Stone, Jr., State Director, Division of Independent Study. There is a faculty of 12 plus 2 administrators and 6 support personnel.

Academic Levels:
High School

Degree/Certificate Programs:
Diploma. It is possible to take the entire program for a high school diploma. Transfer-in credits are accepted from other correspondence schools.

Admission Requirements:
Open admission. Applications from students presently enrolled in a high school, or those of compulsory school age, must have the application signed by the local school administrator.

Tuition:
$50 per ½ unit credit plus $5 handling fee; $15 study guide fee. Remittance must accompany the application. A processing fee of $10 plus $7 for each lesson or test evaluated is retained on all requests for refunds; no refunds will be made after two weeks from date of enrollment. Scholarships based on need are available from the Division through the T.W. Thordarson Scholarship Fund.

Enrollment Period:
A maximum of one year is allowed to complete a course. An extension of one year may be granted for good reason and payment of an extension fee.

Equipment Requirements:
The cost of textbooks and materials is not included in the tuition. Most courses require the purchase of student worksheets.

Credit and Grading:
Examinations must be proctored by an approved supervisor. The grading system is as follows: A, 94–100 percent; B, 87–93 percent; C, 80–86 percent; D, 70–79 percent; F, 0–69. The minimum passing grade is D, 70 percent. Credits are awarded in standard ½ units (per semester course).

Library Services:
A book library is available to students who do not have access to a library.

Accreditations:
North Central Association of Colleges and Schools. Member of: National University Continuing Education Association.

HIGH SCHOOL COURSES

AGRICULTURE

General Agriculture

Covers all phases of farming including livestock, crop production, marketing and conservation. (½ credit)

Livestock Production

Of interest to the livestock producer and students interested in livestock production. All types of livestock farming. (½ credit)

Feeding Farm Animals

Introductory course with emphasis on nutrients and feedstuffs. For students and livestock producers who have studied elementary agriculture or who have had experience with livestock husbandry. (½ credit)

Farm Management

A course to assist students interested in a career related to agriculture. Especially adapted to farmers wishing to update their farm management practices. (½ credit)

Farm Power and Machinery

This course covers the fundamentals of selection, function and use of tractors and farm machinery. Specifics of repair and adjustment are not covered in this course. (½ credit)

ART

Calligraphy

Students will gain an appreciation of handsome lettering and the ability to create their own attractive work. Experience in basic letter proportions and spacing serves as a foundation for understanding the historical development of lettering styles. Lettering examples, instructional diagrams, and page design will be an important part of each lesson. (½ credit)

Fashion Design

Designed to develop taste and judgment in personal clothing choices and to develop skill in presenting design ideas. No previous art training required. (½ credit)

Interior Design

A study of design principles for creating a comfortable and attractive home. No previous art training required. (½ credit)

Beginning Painting

Develops skill and sensitivity in working with color, line and shape. Tempera paint, crayon, and collage are used in learning principles of composition and color. (½ credit)

Art Craft

Macramé, block printing, and other projects are introduced. Appreciation of good design qualities and understanding of color relationships is emphasized. (½ credit)

Basic Drawing

The student is encouraged to grow in artistic skill and enjoyment through an understanding of form and design. Develops abilities in working with charcoal, pencil, pen and ink. (½ credit)

Lettering and Poster Design

A practical course in making signs and posters. Emphasizes lettering and layout design. Calligraphy is included. (½ credit)

Knowing About Art

A course in art appreciation. (½ credit)

RELIGIOUS STUDIES

The Old Testament as History and Literature

Any version of the Bible may be used. (½ credit)

The New Testament as History and Literature

Any version of the Bible may be used. (½ credit)

BUSINESS EDUCATION

Elementary Typewriting

First semester. Designed for personal use typing as well as for students interested in a business-related career. Students must have access to a typewriter. (½ credit)

Second semester. Concentrates on improving speed and accuracy in typing. Business letters, tables, forms and manuscript type problems. Student must have access to a typewriter. (½ credit)

Office Procedures

Student must know how to type and have access to a typewriter. Designed to prepare students for a wide range of entry-level office jobs and to provide an understanding of human relations. (½ credit)

Elementary Shorthand

First semester. Designed for students interested in a secretarial career. (½ credit)

Second semester. Concentrates on improving dictation and transcription skills. (½ credit)

Accounting

First semester. A study of basic accounting principles and concepts needed for career or personal-use recordkeeping. (½ credit)

Second semester. More advanced procedures related to accounting are presented. (½ credit)

General Business

First semester. Stresses money management, consumer rights and responsibilities, check-writing procedures, credit practices and trends in business. (½ credit)

Second semester. A study of saving and investing money, insurance, transportation, taxes, and the world of work. (½ credit)

Business Law

Practical application of everyday business and commercial problems including legal terms. (½ credit)

Business Mathematics

This course is designed to develop competencies in mathematics for business and personal finance use. Everyday mathematical problems relating to salaries, fringe benefits, banking, home ownership, credit cards, taxes, travel and recreation, are presented. (½ credit)

COMPUTER SCIENCE

Introduction to Computers and Programming

First Semester. A simple hand-on approach to learning about computers. The student starts working with the computer in lesson 1. The student writes simple programs in BASIC as well as learning about existing software. Vocabulary is stressed. The student should have access to a microcomputer from the Apple II family. (½ credit)

Second Semester. This course is a continuation of the First Semester course described above. (½ credit)

ENGLISH

Developmental English

For students who have had difficulty mastering the fundamentals of English grammar and usage, the course concentrates on basic skills involving recognition and use of verbs, nouns, adjectives and adverbs; spelling; punctuation; vocabulary; and construction of simple, compound and complex sentences. (½ credit)

Journalism

This course is designed for students who wish to explore the nature of newspaper work. It gives information about and practice in writing news stories, editorials, interviews, feature stories and sport stories. Students are introduced to the essentials of copywriting, proofreading, writing headlines, and the laying out of pages. It emphasizes the goal of writing simply, forcefully, and accurately. (½ credit)

Freshman Literature

Conflict, theme, character, plot and setting are explained and combined to aid a student in understanding a short story, poetry, drama *(Antigone)*, and mythology *(The Odyssey)*, A book report is required. (½ credit)

Freshman Language and Composition

The course covers traditional grammar and its use; a step-by-step writing process with assignments relating to everyday life; and related skills such as spelling, vocabulary, and library use. (½ credit)

Sophomore Literature

Arranged partly by major type—short story, poetry, drama, novel and partly by theme—lessons provide readable selections by significant world writers to help students become more aware of the forms of literature and of the writer's relevant themes. (½ credit)

Sophomore Language and Composition

The course covers basic skills in using verbs, pronouns, adjectives and adverbs; techniques in constructing effective sentences; and practice in composing descriptive, narrative, and expository paragraphs. (½ credit)

Junior Language and Composition

This course enables students to comfortably and competently deal with all aspects of writing. Progressing from basic spelling and grammar skills, the student will advance to the organization, prewriting, revision, and completion of essays, articles, reports, and stories. (½ credit)

Senior Language and Composition

As well as working with the essay form and using it in their required research paper, students study ways to improve writing style, vocabulary, and usage. They also explore propaganda devices and semantics. (½ credit)

Business English

Covers the basic English skills and business writing in letters, memos and reports, telegrams, form messages, and news releases. (½ credit)

American Literature

Through a thematic and chronological study of such writers as Stephen Crane, Mark Twain, and Ray Bradbury, the student will discover how historical events and cultural heritage unique to America have influenced our literary ideas. (½ credit)

English Literature

Using a chronological approach from Anglo-Saxon to modern times, the course explores not only a rich variety of British literature but also the historical and cultural changes that influenced the writers. As students read the selections, they will discover the grace of Elizabethan, Romantic, and Victorian poetry; the charm and perceptiveness of British prose; and the power of English drama. (½ unit)

World Literature

As the student studies literature concerning the nature and character of man, he becomes acquainted with stories, plays, and poetry of many countries through several centuries. (½ credit)

Creative Writing

Attention is given to the student's ability to organize and revise his/her expression of original ideas and interpretations. The course is designed for juniors, seniors and adults interested in demonstrating independent thinking, writing and self-criticism. (½ credit)

The Novel

Most of the novels deal with problems of young people in their search for identity and maturity. Other concerns addressed are the struggle for freedom, defects in society, and the corruption of power. (½ credit)

FRENCH

First Year French

First semester. Acquaints students with French language, culture, and history. No previous knowledge of French is required. Course is based on simplified grammar and vocabulary, with stress upon the spoken language. (½ credit)

Second semester. A continuation of the above course. (½ credit)

Second Year French

First semester. Develops the student's ability to read, write, and speak French. (½ credit)

Second semester. A continuation of the above course. (½ credit)

GERMAN

First Year German

First semester. Through an easy-to-understand approach, students are introduced to the German language, history, customs, and songs. Students learn how to read, write, and carry on simple conversations in German. (½ credit)

Second semester. A continuation of the above course. (½ credit)

Second Year German

First semester. (½ credit)

Second semester. (½ credit)

HOME ECONOMICS

Personal Management for Independent Living

This course is designed to prepare the student for the experiences and responsibilities that independence will bring. A wide variety of topics is covered including wardrobe planning, money managing, meal planning, job hunting, and housing. The student will work on personal problems or plans to be used long after the course is completed. (½ credit)

Family Relations

Concerned with the individual and family in today's society. Topics include understanding oneself, friends and family; dating, courtship and marriage; parenthood, old age and death. (½ credit)

Creative Cooking

Topics include eating for fitness, buying and preparing appetizing foods, using a microwave oven, entertaining with foods, etc. Preparation of recipes is optional. (½ credit)

Etiquette

Students are made aware of accepted behavior for varied occasions and situations which they will encounter in life. (½ credit)

Home Management

Explores the skills necessary to purchase, furnish, and maintain a home. Practical solutions to common problems in home management. (½ credit)

Dollars and Sense

Students develop skills for the use of personal and family resources. Topics include money management, consumer responsibilities, and preparation for a job interview. (½ credit)

Everyday Nursing

Daily health habits, as well as home care for minor illnesses, are discussed. Emergency first aid procedures are thoroughly covered. (½ credit)

Child Development

Discusses the growth and development of children from conception to age six. Special emphasis is given to prenatal development and the importance of health care during pregnancy. (½ credit)

INDUSTRIAL ARTS

Basic Electricity

A practical course in electricity with a minimum of equipment required. (½ credit)

Home Wiring

A practical course for the farmer or homeowner who wishes to learn the fundamentals of wiring buildings. (½ credit)

Small Engines

Exploded views of small engine components give the student a basic understanding of the systems that make up a small engine. Will provide understanding of small engines used on many labor-saving devices and recreational vehicles.

Automotive Engines

Covers the basic principles of operation of the internal combustion engine used in modern automobiles. The course deals with computer technology, electronics, and emission control used in modern automobile engines. (½ credit)

Automotive Chassis

Course explains the principles of all automobile components except the engine. It deals with the operation of the running gear, the control system, and the power train of the modern automobile. (½ credit)

Aviation

Covers the history and theory of flight, the structure of the aircraft (the engine and instruments), flight technique, navigation, meteorology, and air traffic control. (½ credit)

Mechanical Drawing

Teaches the fundamentals of mechanical drawing, including lettering, simple drawing principles, and correct way of reading drawings. (½ credit)

Arc Welding

Teaches the fundamentals and techniques of arc welding with stick electrodes. The course deals with the selection and classification of electrodes and their use. (½ credit)

Welding Processes

Examines the variety of current welding methods which is creating an increasing need for specialists in the field. (½ credit)

LATIN

First Year Latin

First semester. A richer vocabulary will result as the student becomes aware of the English words which are derived from Latin. Glimpses of Roman life and the influences on present day civilization are studied. Grammar is introduced as needed. (½ credit)

Second semester. Emphasis on increasing vocabulary. Grammar drill is continued. (½ credit)

Second Year Latin

First semester. There is a continuation of vocabulary building through the study of word roots showing a wide variety of meanings. (½ credit)

Second semester. Drill on vocabulary building and grammar will continue. (½ credit)

MATHEMATICS

Consumer Mathematics

First semester. Focuses on the basic mathematical skills required for wise consumer decisions. Topics include personal banking, consumer credit, car ownership and travel. (½ credit)

Second semester. Concerns solving consumer financial problems such as home ownership, taxes, insurance, investments and budgeting. (½ unit)

General Mathematics

First semester. Emphasis on basic mathematical skills and problem solving in consumer and career applications. The practical side of mathematics will be studied. (½ credit)

Second semester. Introduction to the basic mathematical skills in algebra, geometry, and statistics. (½ credit)

Algebra

First semester. Includes study of positive and negative numbers, equations, inequalities, polynomials, factoring, and problem solving. (½ credit)

Second semester. Emphasis on using the properties of real numbers. Linear equations, graphing, radicals, and quadratic equations are introduced. Develops mathematical skills and concepts for more advanced mathematics. (½ credit)

Geometry

First semester. Concentrates on the basic terms of geometry giving their meaning and notation. Measurement, angles, congruent triangles, parallels and polygons are studied. (½ credit)

Second semester. This is a continuation of the above course. More advanced theorem proofs. A study of similarity, loci, area, volume, circles, and spheres. (½ credit)

Advanced Algebra with Trigonometry

First semester. The emphasis is on expanding the student's understanding of mathematical concepts and developing proficiency with mathematical skills. Topics included are linear and quadratic equations and inequalities, relations, functions, radicals, imaginary and complex numbers, and systems of equations and conics. (½ credit)

Second semester. Stresses polynomial functions, exponential and logarithmic functions, probability, statistics and trigonometric functions and identities. (½ credit)

Trigonometry

A preparatory subject for college engineering and mathematics courses. Studies the concepts of trigonometric functions and their graphs, trigonometric equations, logarithms of trigonometric functions and special identity formulas. (½ credit)

Precalculus

First semester. This course is designed to prepare college-bound students for a first course in calculus. The format of the course provides a transition between high school and college mathematics courses. This course covers intermediate algebra, trigonometry, and vectors. (½ credit)

Second semester. Completion of one semester of precalculus. (½ credit)

MUSIC

Fundamentals of Music

With the lesson material and the lesson work all contained in the student worksheets. The student studies key signatures and scales, rhythms, intervals, chords, and types and forms of music. (½ credit)

Music Appreciation

Lessons discuss various aspects of music from classical to blues to twentieth-century compositions. (½ unit)

NORWEGIAN

First Year Norwegian

First semester. Pronunciation is stressed through the use of phonetic language and recordings. The full year course should enable a student to use correctly the fundamentals of the language in speaking, reading, and writing. (½ credit)

Second semester. A continuation of the above course. (½ credit)

PHOTOGRAPHY

Photography

Designed exclusively for the amateur 35mm photographer who wants to improve the quality and consistency of each color picture. Student must have a manual 35mm camera. Developing is not included. (½ unit)

PHYSICAL EDUCATION

Individual and Team Sports

Emphasis is placed on the value of individual sports as a lifetime activity and on creating a better understanding of the rules and basic principles of five major team sports. Individual sports covered are archery, golf, tennis, bowling, and skiing. Team sports studied are football, baseball, hockey, basketball, and soccer. (½ credit)

Alcohol, Tobacco, and Drugs

Stresses the making of intelligent decisions concerning alcohol, tobacco, and drugs as well as becoming aware of programs available to those who need help. (¼ credit)

First Aid, Nutrition, and Exercise Plans

Emphasis is placed on basic first-aid, proper nutrition, and the RCAF exercise plan. Creates an awareness and interest in the benefits of physical fitness. (¼ credit)

Modern Health

A practical study of physiology, hygiene, health and safety practices. (½ credit)

RUSSIAN

First Year Russian

First semester. Recommended for all students interested in the language with or without previous knowledge of Russian. Course is based on simplified grammar and vocabulary, stresses the spoken language. (½ credit)

Second semester. A continuation of the above course. (½ credit)

SCIENCE

Biology

First semester. A study of photosynthesis, cell reproduction, heredity, microbiology, multicellular plants, and invertebrates. (½ credit)

Second semester. A study of vertebrates, human biology, and ecological relationships, populations, and human environmental problems. (½ credit)

Chemistry

First semester. Involves the study of matter, the structure of the atom and compounds, the classification of the elements, naming inorganic compounds, writing and balancing chemical equations as well as conducting some basic chemistry experiments. (½ credit)

Second semester. Involves the study of gases, liquids, solids, solutions, coloids, water, acids, bases and ionic equations; oxidation-reduction equations, reaction rates and equilibria, organic and nuclear chemistry, as well as conducting some basic chemistry experiments. (½ credit)

Ornithology

A study of birds including migration patterns, food habits, nesting practices and usefulness to man. (½ credit)

Physical Science

First semester. A study of the metric system, atoms, molecules, nuclear reactions, metals, fossils, fuels, water and environmental problems, and organic compounds, including plastics and synthetic fibers. (½ credit)

Second semester. A study of forces, motion, work, energy, sound, color, heat, light, magnetism, and electricity and electronic theory. (½ credit)

Physics

First semester. Introduces students to the fundamental physics including motion, force, vectors, phases of matter, heat, and waves. (½ credit)

Second semester. Students study light, electricity, magnetism, electronics, and nuclear reactions. It includes some basic physics experiments. (½ credit)

Wildlife Management

Understanding the importance of our role in preserving native wildlife. Includes sections on hunting, fishing, trapping, habitat and production. (½ credit)

Entomology

The study of insect life, showing insects' relationships to human welfare. (½ credit)

Conservation of Natural Resources

Students learn how to wisely use our country's air, water, soil, wildlife, landscape, vegetation, and minerals. (½ credit)

SOCIAL STUDIES

International Relations

International Relations presents the viewpoints of the five principals in the present international system: the Soviet, the American, the Chinese communist, the Third World, and a United States ally. This approach allows the student to look at the world from each point of view. (½ credit)

North Dakota History

A study of North Dakota's history from its geological development to the present. The course emphasizes Indian history, the arrival of the railroad, early settlement, the agrarian revolt, the Nonpartisan League, the Great Depression, and post-World War II North Dakota. (½ credit)

American Government

An examination of our federal government with emphasis on the three branches of the system. The course also includes discussion of citizen rights, political party participation, the voting process and financing the government. (½ credit)

Comparative Government

Concentrates on the three major types of political systems with emphasis on teaching the student to learn and think independently about each. (½ credit)

Minorities in America

Details the problems, achievements, and history of U.S. minority groups through the study of three major ethnic groups: the Native Americans, the Afro-Americans, and the Mexican Americans. (½ credit)

Local History

This course connects history with the student's life and community. The community is the classroom wherein a student completes such activities as making a rubbing of a tombstone in a local cemetery, studying the architecture of a local building, interviewing a senior citizen, and tracing his/her family tree. Adaptable to each locality. (½ credit)

North Dakota Government

Covers the formation, structure and operation of the state government. Discusses the three branches of state government and examines county, city, township and special governments as well. (½ credit)

Problems of Democracy

First semester. Human problems requiring decisions and explanations are approached from the standpoint of psychology, sociology, and economics. (½ credit)

Second semester. Key concepts of political behavior are studied at the national, state, and local levels of government. The roles of the President, Congress, Supreme Court, and Federal bureaucrats are presented, as well as that of the nature and function of the state and local decision makers. (½ credit)

Psychology

The course covers basic psychological concepts and vocabulary and allows students to apply psychology to their own lives. Topics covered include human development and behavior, learning perception and emotion, psychological disorders, and social behavior. (½ credit)

Sociology

Introduces the student to the study of people and their life in groups. The student learns to analyze institutions, social problems, and human behavior in a value free manner. (½ credit)

Economics

Basic economic theory is applied on a practical level. Case studies emphasize the economic decisions faced by individuals and nations. (½ credit)

U.S. History

First semester. A study of our nation's history beginning with the pre-colonial period and progressing through the nineteenth century. Emphasis is given to the Revolutionary period and the Civil War. (½ credit)

Second semester. A study of our nation's history from 1900 to present. Emphasis is placed on World Wars I and II as well as the Great Depression. (½ credit)

World Geography

First semester. This course creates an awareness and appreciation of natural surroundings. Includes map work, basic geographic terms, and an introduction to cultural geography. (½ credit)

Second semester. Emphasis is on physical geography and world political divisions. (½ credit)

World History

First semester. A multidisciplinary approach to Asian, African, and American history from pre-history through 1900; Europe to 1300. (½ credit)

Second semester. A multidisciplinary approach to Asian, African, and American history from 1900-1980s. Europe from 1300-1980s. (½ credit)

Project Self-Discovery

The course is designed to help students examine the many ''selves'' which make up their personalities. It aids students in learning to like, respect, and feel comfortable with themselves. (½ credit)

SPANISH

First Year Spanish

First semester. Develops the student's ability to understand, speak, read and write Spanish to the point of effective communication. Pronunciation and phrasing are aided by the use of recordings. (½ credit)

Second semester. A continuation of the above course. (½ credit)

Second Year Spanish

First semester. (½ credit)

Second semester. A continuation of the above course. (½ credit)

Seminary Extension Independent Study Institute
Suite 500
901 Commerce Street
Nashville, Tennessee 37203-3631
(615) 242-2453

Description:

The Seminary Extension Independent Study Institute was established in 1951 as the extension arm of the six theological seminaries of the Southern Baptist Convention. It presently enrolls over 2,000 students by correspondence. Correspondence students live in the 50 states and 20 foreign countries. Extension centers are located throughout the country. The goal of Seminary Extension is to bring continuing theological education within reach of every minister, regardless of age, geographical location, or level of formal educational background. Although Seminary Extension does not grant degrees, many of the courses offered are at the college level and may be accepted by some degree-granting institutions as transfer credits.

Faculty:
Dr. Doran C. McCarty, Executive Director.

Academic Levels:
College
Noncredit

Degree/Certificate Programs:
Certificate, Diploma. The Certificate programs of the Basic Curriculum Series are designed for pastors and lay preachers who prefer easy-to-read materials; although dealing with adult concepts, each course is written on a simplified reading level. A study guide is the only textbook; no written tests are required. Two Certificates are awarded

students who complete prescribed courses of study in the Basic Curriculum Series: the Certificate of Merit for any ten courses; the Distinguished Citation Certificate for an additional ten courses. The Diploma programs of the College-Level Curriculum Series are ideally suited for pastors who have completed at least the high school diploma but have been unable to attend a seminary, and for those others who are interested in academically oriented study. Seminary graduates will find these to be helpful as refresher courses. Most of these courses are based on a standard college or seminary textbook, supplemented by a study guide. Four diploma programs are available in the College-Level Series: Pastoral Ministries, Educational Ministries, Biblical Studies, and the Advanced Diploma. Any student desiring to transfer Seminary Extension credit for college-level courses is encouraged to clear his plans with the institution of his choice before enrolling with Seminary Extension.

Admission Requirements:

Students must be 16 years of age or older. If college credit is desired, student must have high school diploma or equivalent.

Tuition:

Basic courses $32 per course plus $8 for postage on an individual course basis; regular diploma-level courses $36 per course plus $8 postage fee; A.C.E. diploma-level course $39 plus $8 postage fee. Prices subject to change each June.

Enrollment Period:

The maximum time allowed to complete a course is one year with time extensions available. There is no minimum time; interrupted training is permitted.

Equipment Requirements:

The Basic Curriculum Series uses cassette tapes; the student must have access to a cassette player. Textbooks must be purchased by the student for individual courses in the college-level program. Students outside the United States should check with the school regarding postage costs. Spanish language textbooks for courses New Testament Theology, History of Christianity, and Dynamics of Teaching may be ordered directly from the Baptist Book Store, 960 Chelsea Street, El Paso, Texas 79903 (Telephone: 915/778-9191).

Credit and Grading:

Seminary Extension will accept in transfer up to eight courses similar to subjects offered and germane to the program (i.e., religion, Bible, theology). Examinations for college-level courses must be proctored. Basic curriculum courses (high-school level) are graded on a satisfactory/unsatisfactory basis. College-level courses are graded on an A, B, C, and F basis. Minimum passing grade is C (70). Some courses listed below have been evaluated for baccalaureate-level credit by the American Council on Education's Office on Educational Credit and Credentials, Program on Noncollegiate Sponsored Instruction. For recommended credit, refer to *The National Guide to Educa-*

tional Credit for Training Programs published by the American Council on Education/Oryx Press.

Library Services:

All six Southern Baptist Seminaries make their library books and tapes available by mail to all Seminary Extension students for a small service fee.

Accreditations:

Distance Education and Training Council. Member of: National University Continuing Education Association.

COLLEGE COURSES

BIBLE

How to Understand the Bible

An introduction to the nature and purpose of the Bible and how to understand it.

Biblical Backgrounds

A systematic study of the historical geography and archaeology of Bible lands and peoples.

Old Testament Survey, Part I

A general introduction to the study of the Old Testament, plus a historical survey of Hebrew history through David.

Old Testament Survey, Part II

A historical survey of Hebrew history from King Solomon through the fall of Jerusalem, plus a study of the prophets through Ezekiel.

Old Testament Survey, Part III

A study of the Old Testament books not included in Parts I and II, including the Exile and return, the later minor prophets, and the worship, wisdom, and apocalyptic literature.

Exodus

A study of the book of Exodus.

Job

A study of the book of Job.

Studies in Psalms

A study of the types of Psalms and their setting in worship.

Studies in Isaiah

A study of various sections of the book of Isaiah.

Jeremiah

A study of the prophet Jeremiah.

Hosea

A study of the book of Hosea.

The Post-Exilic Prophets

A study of the prophets after the period of Judah's exile, with major attention to the message of Malachi.

New Testament Survey: Background and Introduction

A study of the interbiblical period and the first century setting.

New Testament Survey: The Gospels

A survey of the life, ministry, and teachings of Jesus.

New Testament Survey: The Early Church

A historical-exegetical survey of the expansion of Christianity from Pentecost to Patmos (Acts through Revelation).

A Study of Matthew's Gospel

An overview of the Gospel of Matthew, focusing on the purpose of the Gospel, the major events in the life of Jesus, and the teachings of this Gospel on faith, salvation, and the Christian life. One unit of four lessons discusses Jesus' Sermon on the Mount in Matthew 5–7.

Mark

A study of Mark's Gospel.

Luke

A study of Luke's Gospel

John

A study of John's Gospel.

Acts

A study of the book of Acts.

Romans

A study of the books of Romans.

First Corinthians

A study of Paul's first letter to the church at Corinth.

Ephesians and Philippians

A study of Paul's letters to the Ephesian and Philippian Christians.

Colossians and Philemon

A study of Paul's letters to the Colossians and Philemon.

Hebrews

A study of the epistle to the Hebrews.

General Epistles

A study of the epistles of 1 and 2 Peter, James, and Jude.

Revelation

A study of the book of Revelation.

PASTORAL MINISTRIES

Formation for Ministry

A study of the meaning of ministry, some spiritual, personal, and professional requirements for ministry, and ways in which ministry may be expressed.

The Pastor as a Person

A study of the life and ministry of a pastor in today's world.

Pastoral Care

A study of the role of the pastor as "shepherd of the flock." General principles of effective pastoral care are studied.

Pastoral Ministries

A study of the life and work of the pastor in relation to the church's mission, with attention to the fulfilling of varied pastoral functions.

Public Worship

A study of the nature and purpose of worship. The art of building worship services for the local church today is stressed.

Evangelism

A study of the biblical basis of evangelism, a church program of evangelism, and personal witnessing.

Contemporary Christian Preaching

A study of the role of preaching and the preacher, the scope and purpose of the sermon, and how to organize and deliver a sermon.

Pastoral Leadership in a Small Church

A study of the unique dynamics of the small church, including suitable styles and methods of pastoral leadership.

Pastoral Care with the Terminally Ill

This performance-based course helps ministers grow in their ability to provide Christian counsel and support to terminally ill persons.

Educational Ministry in the Church

An overview of educational work within a Southern Baptist church from the standpoint of administration.

Childhood Education in the Church

A study of the developing nature and needs of children (infancy through age eleven), how they learn, what the church teaches, and how the church teaches through age-group workers.

Dynamics of Teaching

A study of principles and methods of teaching youth and adults.

Teaching the Bible to Adults

This performance-based course stresses an improved understanding of the Bible, adults, and teaching techniques as steps toward more effective Bible teaching.

Fundamentals of Music

An introduction to the basic skills in reading, understanding, and directing music.

Leading a Music Ministry in a Smaller Church

A study of ways to design and conduct an effective music ministry in a smaller church, especially under the leadership of the part-time director or a lay volunteer.

Christian Hymnody

A survey of the origins, structure, style and content of Christian hymnody.

Southern Baptist Polity

A study of how Southern Baptists relate to each other through their churches, associations, state conventions, and national convention.

Developing Leaders for Ministry

A study of leadership and ways to discover, enlist, train, and guide volunteer leaders in the church.

Women in the Church

A study of various views about women, with special consideration of: (1) biblical teachings about women, (2) the significance of women as followers of Christ, (3) the place women have occupied and should occupy in Southern Baptist churches.

How to Plant a Church

This course outlines practical steps in beginning and developing a new congregation. Emphasis is on experience more than lecture. The student works through those steps in a real or simulated situation.

Church Growth

An introduction to church growth principles and strategies as related to a church's sense of purpose.

THEOLOGY

Systematic Theology

A survey of Christian doctrines, with emphasis upon revelation, God, creation of man, the person and work of Jesus Christ, the church, the Christian life, and the Christian hope. A Spanish-language version of this course is also available.

New Testament Theology

A thematic study of the teachings of the New Testament.

History of Christianity

A study of the history of Christianity.

History of Christian Thought

A survey of historical theology through the English Reformation, with chief attention given to historical documents. An amplified guide treats material from the Baptist perspective.

Southern Baptist Heritage

An overview of Baptist history, with emphasis on Southern Baptists, and a review of important Baptist doctrines.

Survey of Baptist Missions

A study of the biblical basis of missions, the history of Christian missions, and how Baptists have worked together to confront the challenge of world evangelization.

Introduction to Christians Ethics

A study of the ethical principles of the Bible and Christian responsibility in contemporary society.

Christian Stewardship

A study of the biblical teachings on stewardship, including a consideration of the purpose and promise of stewardship, with application to the totality of human life. Special attention is given to tithing as one expression of stewardship.

NONCREDIT COURSES

BIBLE

Understanding the Bible

An introduction to Bible study, including a study of the meaning of biblical inspiration, the nature of the Bible, principles of interpretation, the general structure of the Bible, and methods and resources for Bible study. (Also available in Spanish).

The Life of Christ

A survey of the life and teachings of Christ. (Also available in Spanish).

Great Men of the Bible

A biographical and expository study of selected biblical characters.

Great Doctrines of the Bible

A study of ten major biblical doctrines.

Great Passages of the Bible

An expository study of ten of the most outstanding Bible passages, with suggested sermon ideas. Cassette program available.

The Holy Spirit

A study of the person and work of the Holy Spirit. Biblical teachings are related to daily experiences.

Overview of the Old Testament, Part 1

Covers the books of Genesis through Esther.

Overview of the Old Testament, Part 2

Covers the books of Job through Malachi.

Overview of the New Testament, Part 1

Covers the books of Matthew through Ephesians.

Overview of the New Testament, Part 2

Covers the books of Philippians through Revelation.

ECCLESIOLOGY

Planning Church Work

A study of the importance of planning the work of a church, how community characteristics and resources should influence planning, principles and methods of planning, and examples of how planning can be done on specific church projects.

Evangelism in Action

A study of what it means to be a Christian and how a pastor, guided and empowered by the Holy Spirit, can improve his personal witness and the evangelism ministry of his church.

How Churches Teach People

A study of why, what, and how churches teach people, with emphasis on the pastor as teacher, the teaching function of the members, and the educational program, particularly the Sunday School. Each age group, preschool through adult, is considered.

How Southern Baptists Work Together

A survey of basic Baptist distinctives and polity, including the local church, the association, the state convention, and the Southern Baptist Convention. Denominational agencies are presented as servants of the churches. Cassette program available.

ENGLISH

Remedial English

English 2200 (7th grade level); *English 2600* (9th grade level); *English 3200* (11th grade level). English grammar learned or reviewed easily. Programmed instruction method used so that student discovers immediately whether his responses are correct. No registration fee; if the student wants his/her work checked, the Seminary Extension Independent Study Institute will grade the assignments for a fee of $15; add $2 per course for postage and handling in the U.S.; other countries will be billed for actual cost of postage. *Tuition:* English 2200, $16; English 2600, $18; English 3200, $19.

PASTORAL MINISTRIES

The Work of a Pastor

An introductory study, including helps in planning a worship service, preparing a sermon, conducting the ordinances, counseling persons in trouble, enlisting and training lay workers, and other functions as a pastor. (Also available in Spanish).

How to Prepare and Deliver a Sermon

A survey of steps in preparing and delivering a sermon. (Also available in Spanish).

The Pastor as Leader

A study of the leadership role of the pastor.

The Pastor as Counselor

A study of the ministry of the pastor in counseling persons experiencing personal crises.

The Bivocational Minister

A study of the bivocational minister's role and work, including his call and contribution, biblical and historical roots, and his tasks, skills, and relationships.

Family Life Today

A study of the family from a Christian perspective, with attention to biblical and contemporary patterns of family life. Christian teachings are applied to such issues as family communication, conflict, finances, divorce, sexuality, and worship in the home. Cassette program available.

The Minister's Wife

A study of the special needs and concerns of persons married to pastors or other church or denominational staff members. Areas of discussion include: self-identity, interpersonal relationships, marriage and family, church relationships, personal careers, community and world relationships, and personal growth and development.

United States Coast Guard Institute
P.O. Substation 18
Oklahoma City, Oklahoma 73169-6999
(405) 680-4262

Description:
The Coast Guard Institute was founded in 1928 to give Coast Guard military and technical training courses. The mission of the Institute includes developing and administering rating courses, specialty courses, servicewide examinations for enlisted personnel, selection examinations for warrant officers and license examinations for merchant vessel personnel. The Institute maintains about 120 courses. The average student load is 50,000 students with 18,000 course completions per year. The Institute also prepares and processes over 9,000 enlisted advancement examinations and over 1,800 warrant officer selection examinations per year. During each year over 7,000 candidates are examined for Merchant Marine licenses.

Enrollment is restricted to active duty and reserve members of the United States Armed Forces, Coast Guard Auxiliarists, retired Coast Guard personnel, civilian employees of the Coast Guard, and other specified personnel. Eligible applicants should contact their base Education Officer or the USCGI at the above address.

Faculty:
Cdr. Roland Isnor, Commanding Officer. The instructional staff consists of 11 faculty (officers), 46 subject specialists, 5 educational specialists, and 5 writer-editors.

Academic Levels:
College
Vocational
Professional

Admission Requirements:
Any active duty Coast Guard personnel, Coast Guard Reservist, Coast Guard Auxiliarist, Coast Guard civilian employee, Coast Guard retired person, and any member of the United States Armed Forces.

Tuition:
No tuition.

Enrollment Period:
Maximum time allowed to complete a course is 24 months; student will be disenrolled if course is not completed in this time.

Equipment Requirements:
All pamphlets, textbooks, and special kits when applicable are furnished by the Institute.

Credit and Grading:
Examinations must be proctored; the grading system is percentage of items correct. Minimum passing grade is 80 percent, with the exception of navigation courses which require 90 percent.

Library Services:
Library facilities are available on larger stations. Manuals, directives, and instructions are available in personnel offices of smaller stations.

Accreditations:
Distance Education and Training Council. Selected courses are recommended for postsecondary credit by the American Council on Education's Program on Noncollegiate Sponsored Instruction, Office on Educational Credit and Credentials. These recommendations are listed in *The Guide to the Evaluation of Educational Experiences in the Armed Services,* published by the American Council on Education/Oryx Press.

United States Postal Service
Office of the Registrar
William F. Bolger Management Academy
10000 Kentsdale Drive
Potomac, Maryland 20858-4320
(301) 983-7000

Description:
Postal training and development programs are controlled by the Department of Training and Development, a department within the Human Resources Group located at the U.S. Postal Service Headquarters in Washington, D.C. This department ensures that all postal training and development programs support the performance requirements and career development objectives of the 80,000 employee organization. Courses are offered at the William F. Bolger Management Academy, the Technical Training Center, and Postal Employee Development Centers at major post offices. The William F. Bolger Management Academy was established in 1968 as the Training and Development Institute to provide training experiences to the 800,000 Postal Services employees. The training and development activities include career development opportunities for Postal Service managers, supervisors, and craft employees to aid in personal and organizational development.

The William F. Bolger Management Academy delivers correspondence programs to postal managers, supervisors, and other employees to develop and prepare themselves for entry into more formal training in the craft, maintenance, and supervisory areas. Students applying for credit must pass a proctored final examination.

Academic Levels:
Vocational

Degree/Certificate Programs:
Certificate.

United States Postal Service

Enrollment is restricted to employees of the United States Postal Service.

VOCATIONAL COURSES

ACCIDENT INVESTIGATION

Vehicle Accident Investigation

This course covers data collecting, interviewing, calculations, highway and human factors, road and tire evidence, vehicular evidence, forms, analysis of accidents.

COMMUNICATIONS

Report Writing for Postal Managers

Provides an understanding of the mechanics of report writing. Review of grammar; spelling; word mechanics; usage; editing and proofreading; planning, preparation, and evaluation of written reports.

CUSTOMER SERVICE

Customer Service Representative

Provides an overview of knowledge, skills, and techniques of effective salesmanship/sales management, and enables students to design customized user service. Covers the role of the customer service representative, product knowledge and customized service programs; sales processes, including precall planning and use of visual sales aids; time and territory management; customer relations and psychology of selling.

DIESEL MECHANICS

Basic Diesel Mechanics, Module I - Basic Diesel Maintenance

This course provides a foundation in the principles of diesel engines, electrical systems, and transmissions. Includes basic diesel principles; engine structure; fuel, air intake, exhaust, lubricating, cooling electrical, and transmission systems; clutches.

Basic Diesel Mechanics, Module II - Mack-Diesel Maintenance

The course includes topics related to the Mack-diesel engine, including engine structure, fuel, air intake, exhaust, lubricating, cooling, and electrical systems; engine operation; engine testing and run-in; troubleshooting and failure analysis; shop manual organization.

ELECTRONICS

Basic Electricity

Covers the fundamental principles of electricity, including the behavior of AC and DC electrical circuits; use of formulas and equations essential to an understanding of electricity; fundamentals of magnetism, resistance, inductance, and capacitance.

Introduction to Basic Mathematics and Electricity

This course is a refresher in basic arithmetic operations such as addition, subtraction, multiplication, and division. Positive and negative numbers, fractions, square roots, powers of ten. Also includes an introduction to electrical units and prefixes, elementary algebraic equations, formulas, rectangular coordinates, trigonometric relations, and vectors.

Power Transistors

Designed to develop awareness of thermal, frequency, and size problems associated with power transistors. Considers compromises that enable both low and high frequency power transistors to operate at high temperatures and currents. Includes regulator circuits and overload protection.

Transistors and Transistor Applications

Develops a theoretical understanding of transistors and their use in common electronic circuits. An in-depth study of solid-state theory, transistor amplifiers, load line analysis, equivalent circuit analysis, feedback, tuned circuits, multivibrators, and modulation.

Digital Electronics

Introduces the principles of digital electronics. Basics of numbering systems, including methods of conversions between systems; various coding schemes; circuit introduction to Boolean algebra; elements of digital electronics.

MAINTENANCE ADMINISTRATION

Administration of Maintenance Programs—Module I

This course provides an understanding of the principles of managing a maintenance organization. An introduction to the management elements of planning, organizing, controlling, and directing. Also covers staffing, scheduling, human interaction, motivation, safety, and communications.

PNEUMATICS AND HYDRAULICS

Basic Pneumatics and Hydraulics

Develops a basic theoretical understanding of hydraulic and pneumatic systems. Covers in logical sequence the fundamentals of hydraulics and pneumatics and the operation of fluid power components. Topics include physics of fluids, basic systems and circuit diagrams, control and measurement of flow, component equipment functions.

SECRETARIAL SCIENCE

Secretary to the Postal Executive

Provides an overview of the principles of management and business communications. Includes principles and applications of effective communication, with emphasis on making the secretary an effective office manager.

Index

AMERICAN INDIAN STUDIES
Arizona, University of 23
Minnesota, University of 269
Washington, University of 558
Wyoming, University of 616
AMERICAN STUDIES
Indiana University 191
Iowa, University of 210
Kansas, University of 224
Minnesota, University of 269
Pennsylvania State University 413
ANATOMY
Arizona, University of 23
ANIMAL SCIENCE
Arizona, University of 23
Brigham Young University 59
Colorado State University 116
Kentucky, University of 231
Missouri, University of 303
Oklahoma State University 393
Utah State University 550
Wyoming, University of 616
ANTHROPOLOGY
Alaska, University of - Fairbanks 14
Arizona, University of 23
Arkansas, University of 35
Ball State University 47
Bemidji State University 53
Berean College 698
Brigham Young University 59
California, University of 79
Colorado, University of 111
Columbia International University 120
Concordia University 123
Creighton University 125
Florida, University of 151
Georgia, University of 164
Goddard College 171
Idaho, University of 174
Illinois, University of 182, 187
Indiana University 191
Iowa, University of 210
Kansas, University of 224
Louisiana State University 244
Minnesota, University of 270
Mississippi Valley State University 301
Missouri, University of 303, 312
Nevada, University of - Reno 339
New Mexico, University of 345
North Carolina, University of 348
North Dakota, University of 356
Northern Iowa, University of 363
Ohio University 372
Oklahoma State University 393
Oklahoma, University of 382
Oregon State System of Higher Education 407
Pennsylvania State University 413
Southern Mississippi, University of 490
Tennessee, University of 511
Texas Tech University 527
Texas, University of - at Austin 519
Utah State University 550

Utah, University of 542
Washington State University 564
Washington, University of 558
Weber State University 569
Western Michigan University 577
Western Washington University 584
Wisconsin, University of - Extension 589
Wyoming, University of 616
ANTIQUES AND COLLECTIBLES
Pennsylvania State University - College of Agricultural Sciences 424
APOLOGETICS
Columbia International University 119
APPLIANCE SERVICING
McGraw-Hill Continuing Education Center 664
ARABIC
Washington State University 564
Wisconsin, University of - Extension 589
ARCHITECTURAL ENGINEERING
Pennsylvania State University 422
ARCHITECTURE
Minnesota, University of 270
Washington State University 564
ART
American School 692
Arizona, University of 30
Art Instruction Schools 628
Brigham Young University 59, 69
California, University of 79
Eastern Washington University 135
Florida, University of 155
Futures in Education, Inc. 640
Georgia, University of 164
ICS Learning Systems 652
ICS Newport/Pacific High School 654
Idaho, University of 179
Indiana State University 188
Indiana University 202
Iowa, University of 211
Louisiana State University 250
Massachusetts Department of Education 740
Minnesota, University of 270
Mississippi, University of 292
Missouri, University of 312
Nebraska, University of - Lincoln 325, 329
North Carolina, University of 348
North Dakota Division of Independent Study 749
Oklahoma State University 393
Oklahoma, University of 382, 389, 391
Oregon State System of Higher Education 407
Pennsylvania State University 422
Sam Houston State University 443
South Dakota, University of 462
Southern Illinois University at Carbondale 487

Tennessee, University of 515
Texas Tech University 530
Upper Iowa University 537
Utah State University 550
Utah, University of 542
Wisconsin, University of - Extension 589, 602, 606
Wyoming, University of 616, 620
ART EDUCATION
South Dakota, University of 460
Texas, University of - at Austin 519
ART HISTORY
Brigham Young University 59
California, University of 80
Kansas, University of 224
Pennsylvania State University 413
Texas, University of - at Austin 520
Utah, University of 542
Wisconsin, University of - Extension 589, 606
ASIAN STUDIES
Michigan, University of 266
ASTRONOMY
Alabama, University of 6
Arizona, University of 23
Ball State University 47
California, University of 80
Central Arkansas, University of 94
Florida, University of 151
Idaho, University of 174
Indiana University 191
Kentucky, University of 231
Louisiana State University 244
Minnesota, University of 270
Missouri, University of 304
New Mexico, University of 345
North Carolina, University of 348
Northern State University 368
Oklahoma State University 393
Oklahoma, University of 382
Pennsylvania State University 413
South Carolina, University of 452
South Dakota, University of 460
Texas, University of - at Austin 520
Washington, University of 558
Western Illinois University 574
Wisconsin, University of - Extension 589, 606
ATMOSPHERIC SCIENCE
Arizona, University of 23
Missouri, University of 304
Oregon State System of Higher Education 407
Washington, University of 558
AUTOMOBILE REPAIR
Arizona, University of 30
AUTOMOTIVE ELECTRONICS
Cleveland Institute of Electronics 638
AUTOMOTIVE TECHNOLOGY
American School 692
Citizens' High School 634
ICS Learning Systems 652

LITERATURE IN TRANSLATION
Wisconsin, University of - Extension 597

LOCKSMITHING
McGraw-Hill Continuing Education Center 666

LOGIC
Southern Illinois University at Carbondale 488

MAINTENANCE ADMINISTRATION
United States Postal Service 758

MANAGEMENT
Alabama, University of 9
Arkansas, University of 38
Ball State University 49
California, University of 85
Central Arkansas, University of 95
Central Michigan University 102
Chadron State College 105
Eastern Kentucky University 131
Eastern Michigan University 134
Florida, University of 153, 158
Georgia, University of 167
Governors State University 173
Graduate School, USDA 719
ICS Center for Degree Studies 651
Kentucky, University of 234
Louisiana State University 247
Minnesota, University of 281
Missouri, University of 308
Nebraska, University of - Lincoln 327
Nevada, University of - Reno 341
North Dakota, University of 358
Northern Iowa, University of 365
Ohio University 377
Oklahoma State University 396
Oklahoma, University of 386
Oral Roberts University 405
Pennsylvania State University 418
Sam Houston State University 445
Southern Illinois University at Carbondale 488
Southern Mississippi, University of 491
Texas Tech University 529
Utah State University 553
Utah, University of 549
Washington State University 566
Weber State University 571
Western Illinois University 576
Wisconsin, University of - Extension 598

MANAGEMENT COMMUNICATIONS
Brigham Young University 65

MANAGEMENT INFORMATION SYSTEMS
Pennsylvania State University 419

MANAGERIAL ECONOMICS
Brigham Young University 65

MARINE SCIENCE
South Carolina, University of 454

MARKETING
Alaska, University of - Fairbanks 16
American Academy of Nutrition 625
American School 695
Arizona, University of 25
California, University of 85
Central Michigan University 102
Chadron State College 105
Eastern Kentucky University 131
Florida, University of 154
Georgia, University of 167
ICS Center for Degree Studies 651
Kentucky, University of 234
Louisiana State University 247
Minnesota, University of 281
Mississippi State University 298
Mississippi, University of 294
Missouri, University of 309
Nebraska, University of - Lincoln 328
Northern Iowa, University of 365
Northwood University 371
Ohio University 377
Oklahoma State University 396
Oklahoma, University of 386
Oral Roberts University 405
Pennsylvania State University 419
Sam Houston State University 445
Southern Mississippi, University of 491
Texas Tech University 529
Utah, University of 546
Washington State University 566
Washington, University of 560
Western Illinois University 576
Wisconsin, University of - Extension 598

MARKETING EDUCATION
Eastern Washington University 136

MASS COMMUNICATIONS
Alabama, University of 9
Iowa, University of 216
Texas Tech University 529
Utah State University 553

MASS MEDIA
Brigham Young University 72
Florida, University of 154
Goddard College 171
Murray State University 324
Wyoming, University of 618

MATERIALS MANAGEMENT
Gannon University 162
Wisconsin, University of - Extension 613

MATHEMATICS
Adams State College 4
Alabama, University of 9, 12
Alaska, University of - Fairbanks 16
American School 695
Arizona State University 33
Arizona, University of 25, 29
Arkansas State University 44
Arkansas, University of 38, 41
Auburn University 46

Brigham Young University 65, 72, 77
California College for Health Sciences 630
California, University of 85, 89
Cambridge Academy 632
Central Arkansas, University of 95
Central Michigan University 102
Chadron State College 105
Citizens' High School 637
City University 108
Colorado, University of 113
Concordia University 124
Creighton University 125
East Texas State University 128
Eastern Kentucky University 131
Eastern Michigan University 134
Eastern Washington University 136
Florida, University of 154, 156, 159
Futures in Education, Inc. 641
Georgia, University of 167
Graduate School, USDA 719
Hadley School for the Blind 724
Home Study International 729, 731
ICS Center for Degree Studies 651
ICS Newport/Pacific High School 655
Idaho, University of 177, 180
Illinois, University of 185, 187
Indiana State University 189
Indiana University 200, 206, 208
Iowa, University of 216
Kansas, University of 227
Kentucky, University of 234, 237
Kirkwood Community College 240
Learning and Evaluation Center 661
Louisiana State University 247, 251, 253
Mary Hardin-Baylor, University of 256
Marywood College 261
Massachusetts Department of Education 741, 743
Michigan, University of 266
Minnesota, University of 281, 287-288
Minot State University 290
Mississippi State University 298, 300
Mississippi Valley State University 302
Mississippi, University of 294
Missouri, University of 309, 315
Murray State University 324
Nebraska, University of - Lincoln 328, 333, 337
Nevada, University of - Reno 341, 343-344
New Mexico, University of 346
North Carolina, University of 352, 355
North Dakota Division of Independent Study 751
North Dakota, University of 358
Northern Colorado, University of 361
Northern Iowa, University of 365
Northern State University 368
Northwood University 371
Ohio University 378
Oklahoma State University 396, 399